Critical Qualitative Research
R E A D E R

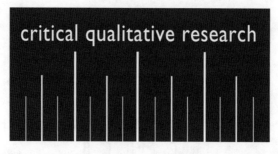

critical qualitative research

CRITICAL ISSUES FOR LEARNING AND TEACHING

Shirley R. Steinberg and Gaile S. Cannella
Series Editors

Vol. 2

The Critical Qualitative Research series
is part of the Peter Lang Education list.
Every volume is peer reviewed and meets
the highest quality standards for content and production.

PETER LANG
New York • Washington, D.C./Baltimore • Bern
Frankfurt • Berlin • Brussels • Vienna • Oxford

Critical Qualitative Research
READER

EDITED BY
Shirley R. Steinberg and
Gaile S. Cannella

PETER LANG
New York • Washington, D.C./Baltimore • Bern
Frankfurt • Berlin • Brussels • Vienna • Oxford

Library of Congress Cataloging-in-Publication Data

Critical qualitative research reader / edited by
Shirley R. Steinberg, Gaile Sloan Cannella.
p. cm. — (Critical qualitative research; v. 2)
Includes bibliographical references.
1. Qualitative research. 2. Social sciences—Research.
3. Education—Research.
I. Steinberg, Shirley R. II. Cannella, Gaile Sloan.
H62.C697427   001.4'2—dc23   2012002737
ISBN 978-1-4331-1233-1 (hardcover)
ISBN 978-1-4331-0688-0 (paperback)
ISBN 978-1-4539-0558-6 (e-book)
ISSN 1947-5993

Bibliographic information published by **Die Deutsche Nationalbibliothek**.
Die Deutsche Nationalbibliothek lists this publication in the "Deutsche
Nationalbibliografie"; detailed bibliographic data is available
on the Internet at http://dnb.d-nb.de/.

Cover art provided by Eelco B. Buitenhuis
Cover image: Painting "Research into the Unknown"
Amersfoort, Netherlands

The paper in this book meets the guidelines for permanence and durability
of the Committee on Production Guidelines for Book Longevity
of the Council of Library Resources.

© 2012 Peter Lang Publishing, Inc., New York
29 Broadway, 18th floor, New York, NY 10006
www.peterlang.com

Printed in the United States of America

Contents

Preface: What's Critical About Qualitative Research?.. ix
Shirley R. Steinberg

PART ONE: ON RESEARCH

1 Critical Advocacy Research: An Approach Whose Time Has Come............................ 2
Carolyn M. Shields

2 Critical Pedagogy and Qualitative Research: Moving to the Bricolage........................ 14
Joe L. Kincheloe, Peter McLaren and Shirley R. Steinberg

3 The Conceptual Context of Knowledge.. 33
Donald Easton-Brooks

4 Basic Concepts in Critical Methodological Theory:
Action, Structure and System within a Communicative Pragmatics Framework 43
Phil Francis Carspecken

5 The Critical Power of Place 67
Margaret Somerville

6 Methodology Is Movement Is Methodology 82
Mirka Koro-Ljungberg

7 All That Jazz: Doing and Writing CQR in a Material World.............................. 91
P. L. Thomas and Renita Schmidt

8 Deploying Qualitative Methods for Critical Social Purposes 104
Gaile S. Cannella and Yvonna S. Lincoln

PART TWO: ON INTERPRETATION

9 Interpretive Approaches to Multi-Level, Multi-Method, Multi-Theoretic Research 116
Kenneth Tobin

10 A Hitherto Concealed Experience That Transcends Thinking from the Position of Subjectivity........ 129
David W. Jardine

11 Circulating Critical Research: Reflections on Performance and Moving Inquiry into Action 153
Madeline Fox and Michelle Fine

12　The Critical Aesthetic: Living a Critical Ethnography of the Everyday.............................166
　　Andrew Hickey

13　Critical Cultural Studies Research: Bricolage in Action 182
　　Shirley R. Steinberg

PART THREE: ON THE POLITICAL

14　Maintaining a Vibrant Synergy among Theory, Qualitative Research, and Social Activism
　　in This Ever-Changing Age of Globalization 200
　　Pepi Leistyna

15　Enlightening the Stranger Within: (Re)viewing Critical Research from/on/in the Centre 221
　　Jon Austin

16　Avoiding the Missionary (Dis)position: Research Relations and (Re)presentation 235
　　Mairi McDermott and Athena Madan

17　Who Will Be Heard? Qualitative Research and Legal Decisions about Facilitated Communication.....246
　　Missy Morton

18　Governing Young Children's Learning through Educational Reform:
　　A Poststructural Analysis of Discourses of Best Practice, Standards, and Quality 257
　　Marianne N. Bloch and Ko Eun Kim

19　Asking Critical Questions of Philanthropy and Its Impact on U.S. Educational Policy:
　　Tracking the Money in School Reform 276
　　Kathleen deMarrais

PART FOUR: ON THE MARGINALIZED

20　Writing Diasporic Indigeneity Through Critical Research and Social Method....................296
　　George J. Sefa Dei and Marlon Simmons

21　Choosing Agency in the Midst of Vulnerability: Using Critical Disability
　　Theory to Examine a Disaster Narrative 307
　　Elizabeth McAdams Ducy, Laura M. Stough, and M. Carolyn Clark

22　Excluded Narratives, Anti-racism and Historical Representation: Methodological Implications........318
　　Timothy J. Stanley

23　Researching the Discursive Function of Silence: A Reconsideration of the
　　Normative Communication Patterns in the Talk of Children with Autism Labels....................329
　　Jessica Nina Lester

24　Indigenous Knowledges in Education: Complexities, Dangers, and Profound Benefits 341
　　Joe L. Kincheloe and Shirley R. Steinberg

PART FIVE: ON PEDAGOGY AND TEACHING

25　Teachers as Critical Researchers: An Empowering Model for Urban Education....................364
　　Ernest Morrell

26　Listening in the Liminal: The In-between Spaces of Teaching Youth About Career and Adulthood 379
　　Amanda Benjamin

27　Action Research for Critical Classroom and Community Change 390
　　Greg S. Goodman, Walter Ullrich and Pedro Nava

28　Technical Assistance as Inquiry: Using Activity Theory Methods to Engage
　　Equity in Educational Practice Communities 408
　　Elizabeth B. Kozleski and Alfredo J. Artiles

29　Teaching in England: December 2010...420
　　Victoria Perselli

30 A Critical Approach to the Teaching and Learning of Critical Social Science at the College Level 429
    Claudia Sanchez and JoAnn Danelo Barbour
31 One School's Approach to Enhancing Parental Well-being:
    A Collaborative Research Practitioner Model. 441
    Marcelle Cacciattolo, Joanne Richmond and Denise Barr
32 Democracy, Freedom and the School Bell 455
    Frances Helyar

PART SIX: ON DOING CQR

33 Towards a Rhizomatic Methodology: How Queer! 468
    Mark Vicars
34 In Search of Critical Knowledge: Tracing Inheritance in the Landscape of Incarceration 479
    Carolina Muñoz Proto
35 Tradition, Authority and the Doing of Research: Perspectives from the Middle East 491
    Ramzi Nasser and Radhika Viruru
36 Psychiatric Survivors, Psychiatric Treatments, and Societal Prejudice:
    An Inquiry into the Experience of a Marginal Group 500
    Michael O'Loughlin and Marilyn Charles
37 Positive Education: The Use of Self-Study Research Methodology
    to Assess Its Place in Higher Education Settings 512
    Jeanne Carroll, Marcelle Cacciattolo, and Tarquam McKenna
38 Collective Narrative Analysis and the Understandings of Young People 524
    Farhat Shahzad
39 Exploring Possibilities for Critical Relational De/Colonising Methodologies in
    Early Childhood Education Contexts in Aotearoa 536
    Jenny Ritchie and Cheryl Rau
40 Writing as Critical Literacy Engagement: Outliers and the Recursive
    Nature of Critical Qualitative Research 548
    Jeff Park
41 Foucauldian Scientificity: Qualitative Methodology-21 555
    Patti Lather

About the Contributors 567
Index 579

What's Critical About Qualitative Research?

Shirley R. Steinberg

Actually, everything is critical in qualitative research. Critical in the sense that it is essential; critical in the sense that it issues scrutiny; and, critical in the sense of stemming from critical theory, a philosophy which situates itself smack dab in the middle of power and politics.

We've been through the *Qual-Quant Wars* of the late 20th century, we've written *ad nauseam* about the oppression of positivism, empiricism, and scientism. As qualitative researchers we have been defensively disseminating our research, as scholars, teachers, and graduate supervisors, we have protected our students and metaphorically (or maybe not) jumped across tables attempting to be noticed, to be respected, and to be taken seriously.

And now, in the second decade of a new millennium, we are standing on top of our chipped, laminated classroom tables and declaring not only that we are qualitative and damn proud of it, we are critical. We are critical in the sense that what we research matters, we believe that research is a social theoretical act, and that it must be headlined by a socially just and equitable praxis. We believe that research must be contextual and is tentative in its surroundings. This reader is a credo to the belief that most research exists in a complicated web of power, neo-liberalism, patriarchy, Western linear thinking, and elitism. The *Critical Qualitative Research Reader* is our attempt to situate a humanistic research paradigm, which cannot be separated from the political.

The contributors to this reader are part of a growing community of researchers who dare to push against the egocentrism of Western research. It is with great pleasure that we invite researchers from all disciplines to consider the possibilities offered by criticalizing our qualitative work.

* * *

Chapter two was previsouly published as: Kincheloe, J. L., McLaren, P. & Steinberg, S. R. (2011). Critical Pedagogy and Qualitative Research: Moving to the Bricolage. In Denzin, N. and Lincoln, Y. (eds.) *Sage Handbook of Qualitative Research* 4th Ed. Thousand Oaks: SAGE.

Chapter eight was previsously published as: Cannella, G.S. & Lincoln, Y.S. (2009). Deploying qualitative methods for critical social purposes. In Denzin, N.K. & Giardina, M. D., (eds.) *Qualitative inquiry and social justice: Toward a politics of hope*. Walnut Creek, CA: Left Coast Press.

Chapter thirteen was previously published as: Steinberg S. R. (2006). Critical Cultural Studies Research: Bricolage in Action. In Tobin, K. and Kincheloe, J. (eds.) Doing Educational Research: A Handbook. Rotterdam: Sense Publishers.

Chapter twenty-four was previously published as: Kincheloe, J. L, & Steinberg, S. R. (2008). Indigenous Knowledges in Education: Complexities, Dangers, and Profound Benefits. In Denzin, N., Lincoln, Y. and Smith, L. (eds) *Handbook of Critical and Indigenous Methodologies*. Thousand Oaks, CA: SAGE.

Chapter thirty-two was previously published as: Helyar, F. (2006). Democracy, Freedom, and the School Bell. In Tobin, K. and Kincheloe, J. (eds.) *Doing Educational Research: A Handbook*. Rotterdam: Sense Publishers.

Chapter forty-one was previously published as: Lather, P. (2009). Foucauldian Scientificity: Qualitative Methodology-21. In Lather, P. *Engaging Science Policy: From the Side of the Messy*. New York: Peter Lang Publishing.

PART ONE

On Research

CHAPTER ONE

Critical Advocacy Research:
An Approach Whose Time Has Come

Carolyn M. Shields

I n the current educational research climate dominated by quasi-experimental scientific studies and sophisticated statistical analyses, randomized controlled trials and replicable analyses have become the new "gold standard" (Hargreaves, 2003). Nevertheless, not everyone is enamored with the currency; Lather (2004) wrote that "the movement towards "evidence-based policy and practice" oversimplifies complex problems and is being used to warrant governmental incursion into legislating scientific method." She continued, "It calls for critical readings of current policy and direct engagement in policy forums—putting critical theory to work" (p. 759). Despite considerable confusion about "what constitutes credible research and how to interpret it for practical purposes" (Manzo, 2004, p. 16), there often seems to be little room for qualitative research studies, let alone those called for by Lather, studies firmly grounded in critical ontologies, epistemologies, and methodologies.

In 1998, Maxine Greene asserted that we live in a "society of unfulfilled promises"—one in which a gap in school performance between majority and minoritized youth is indicative and reflective of disparities in opportunities for our country's citizens. Further, and even more distressing to many, is the fact that, despite America's claims to be the best and most powerful democracy in the world, there are still huge disparities in health care, income, insurance coverage, high school and university graduation rates, incarceration rates and so forth. Education has not fulfilled its mandate to be the "great equalizer." Moreover, the situation is not solely confined to the United States, but is repeated in most developed countries worldwide.

As we consider the appropriate role of educational leaders and researchers in these contexts of wealth and disparity, we note considerable frustration with repeated attempts to implement educational reform and considerable discouragement on the part of many with apparent minimally successful results. Research that fails to take account of this reality holds little promise for redressing wrongs and making a difference in social, cultural, political, or economic outcomes of individuals or societies. Hence, the need for critical research—research that is both rigorous and activist, that has the potential to inform both policy and practice and, at the same time, to empower both researcher and participants alike—to be taken seriously is long overdue. In fact, the potential of critical research has barely been tapped, in that many scholars from critical perspectives tend to produce eloquent conceptual writing and de-emphasize needed empirical studies.

Purpose

This chapter has two purposes: first, to clarify the term "critical advocacy research," including reflection on some appropriate standards of rigor and quality; and, second, to consider the ability of such research both to empower its participants and to influence the social fabric of the nation. From the outset, therefore, it is apparent that critical research is openly ideological and hence (as all doctoral students are taught) must have a clear thread of argumentation running through the research problem, the purpose, theoretical lens, methodology, analysis, interpretations, and conclusions. The ideological position must no longer be "the clandestinely ideological research conducted by quantitative and more traditional qualitative researchers that helped legitimate societal inequality" identified by Lather (1986). Given today's polarized and politicized climate of accountability and conservatism, it is not surprising to note that taking such an openly ideological position is still not, however, generally accepted by all members of the research community.

For that reason, conceptual and methodological clarity and explicitness of research perspective must enable research designs to withstand the inevitable charges of bias and lack of rigor. In critical advocacy-oriented research, the researcher must both carefully reflect on the role of critical epistemologies in grounding research that is intended to highlight inequities in our current systems and also be willing to advocate meaningful change. At the same time, given the unabashed intent to use the outcomes of critical research for advocacy, the researcher must take special care to construct and conduct research that is rigorous, trustworthy, and authentic. Clearly, the researcher must distinguish between identifying one's ideology up front as a basis for identifying the parameters of the investigation and shaping the findings to conform with one's predetermined ontological biases. For that reason, careful attention must also be paid to the development of some well-designed standards of conduct and excellence.

Critical Advocacy Research

In this chapter, then, I argue, with Bourdieu (1977), Said (1994), and others, that most researchers enjoy a social location of power and privilege, one that requires that we take a stance as public intellectuals. I assert that critical research which begins with questions of inequity and disparity holds the most promise for promoting policies and practices that can lead to economic, ecological, and human justice, and a sustainable global future. Hence, in this chapter, I will elucidate theoretically and demonstrate through examples from practice how it is possible to conduct critical research that is rigorous and ethical, and that, at the same time, has as its goal both empowerment and significant change. The time has come for critical advocacy research to come into its own.

Clarifying the Term

Critical research begins with the premise that research's role is not to describe the world as it is, but also to demonstrate what needs to be changed. Although initially influenced by Marxist thinkers and arguments and assumptions arising from a group of scholars known as the Frankfurt School, critical research has expanded to embrace various theoretical perspectives focused on elucidating inequity (queer theory, critical race theory, critical poverty theory, critical feminism, post-colonialism, and so forth). As Foster (1986) clarified a quarter of a century ago, critical researchers "do not presume to give a positivist and unilateral definition of history and society" but instead, probe "foundational assumptions that are normally taken for granted" (p. 71). Primarily, critical researchers "examine sources of social domination and repression, but with the caveat that since we ultimately make our worlds, we can ultimately change them" (p. 71). Or as Lather (1992) describes it, critical inquiry "takes into account how our lives are mediated by systems of inequity such as classism, racism, and sexism" (p. 87).

Critical researchers, steeped in evidence of social and structural inequities that include and privilege some groups and members of society to the exclusion and marginalization of others, are often so passionate about redressing these inequities that they begin with the assumption that their views are widely understood and generally shared. Yet, they must begin by recognizing that due to the very multiple perspectives they claim to value, not everyone sees the world in the same way. Some people, for example, have myopically lived their lives oblivious to the inequities around them. Indeed, the myth of the American dream, with its stories of people who have overcome adversity, worked hard, and pulled themselves up by their own bootstraps, have seemed so convincing that many people have failed to recognize the inherent error of that storyline. Thus, we commonly encounter school principals and superintendents who have never considered that a "no tolerance" policy may adversely target some elements of the population; that differential minority immigrant status (Ogbu, 1992) may be associated with disparate and conflicting attitudes and assumptions about education. Some educators have never reflected on the hegemonic roots of the educational norms, policies, curriculum, or accountability procedures they implement, support and perpetuate, or on the ways in which they often continue to perpetuate inequitable student outcomes.

For that reason, critical educators must not take awareness of the "unfulfilled promises" and social inequity for granted. Several years ago, for example, a young colleague and I were making a presentation at a prominent national conference. Early in the presentation, when my colleague made reference to Maxine Greene's notion of "a society of unfulfilled promises," she was amazed to be interrupted by a senior faculty member (coming from a different tradition), who asked, "What do you mean by unfulfilled promises?" Obviously our starting assumption was neither universally understood nor shared. More recently I experienced more dramatic evidence of the need to be explicit about our starting point and our goals. I had asked my doctoral students to read several articles that drew on Foucault's (1980) use of the panopticon to develop such concepts as surveillance, discipline, a regime of truth, and performativity.[1] Much to my surprise, when I read what had been intended as a critical reflection on these articles, one student, reading with an unquestioning positivist lens, had assumed their discussions to be normative descriptions rather than critical analyses.

Thus, to avoid obvious misunderstanding, the critical researcher must carefully delineate the problem to be researched, clarify his or her epistemological assumptions, and ensure both data and analyses are presented explicitly. Anderson, for example, in his critique of the ISLLC standards, had stated, "I will in this article explore the standards as a disciplinary practice and as ideology, using a critical approach to discourse analysis developed by Fairclough (1992)" (2001, p. 202). He went on to state, "My analysis is also informed by an approach to discourse analysis developed by Foucault (1984), who emphasizes that dominant discourses are determined by power struggles." My point is not to criticize Anderson's strong and compelling analysis of the standards as "disciplinary practice," but to demonstrate how easily the very basis of the argument being made by critical researchers can be misconstrued. Hence, the student (who arguably missed many textual cues) believed that the dominant discourse, arising from the power struggle, was now an irrefutable norm and that disciplinary practice was to be taken at face value as the way "discipline" should be enacted in a school.

Once a critical researcher has developed a clear line of argument from the problem prompting a particular investigation, his or her epistemological location, and the selected critical, theoretical framework, it may be useful to take an abductive reasoning (see Evers & Wu, 2006) approach to the analysis, investigating alternative explanations for one's findings, before concluding systemic inequity. Evers and Wu pose the question: "How is it possible to approach data in a theoretically sensitive way so that patterns are able to emerge unforced without the antecedent theory functioning either as a preconception that imposes an interpretation on the data or as a set of hypotheses that the data may confirm of [*sic*] disconfirm?" (p. 517). How do critical researchers avoid "confirmation bias"—seeing "in the case only whatever is brought to it in the prior theory" (Evers & Wu, 2006, p. 522) or "the tendency to emphasize evidence that supports a hypothesis and ignore evidence to the contrary" (Littell, 2008, p. 1300). Could Anderson usefully have offered alternative possible explanations of the standards before concluding that the accompanying teacher test exemplified a continued negative and hegemonic influence of a power elite on education.

Because critical researchers still struggle to swim upstream in a positivistic current of quasi-experimental design and interpretation, it is important to work to ensure that research data are carefully embedded in a reasonable "inferential network" about socially just education, the presence of an uneven playing field, and the need for a more equitable and more inclusive approach to education. The key here is "reasonable" because critical researchers must avoid the trap of treating the data and inferential network in a positivistic way, as though it represents the only possible interpretation or valid perspective. Hence, despite our conviction that our lens, focused on "unfulfilled promises," provides the necessary perspective on the inequities inherent in a given phenomenon, we must avoid falling into the trap of denying that other legitimate perspectives also exist. Evers and Wu (2006) argue that in abductive reasoning, "the justification of a generalisation relies on the fact that it explains the observed empirical data and no other alternative hypothesis offers a better explanation of what has been observed" (p. 513); in other words, it uses "inference to the best explanation" (p. 528). The critical researcher may accept this challenge, recognizing that it must be taken up in a way that holds true to their critical perspective—in other words, avoiding the positivist and unitary explanation earlier rejected by Foster, but also rejecting a relativism that assumes the equal validity of each alternative interpretation.

Thus, Tooms (2007) can justifiably argue that "*the Right Kind of Queer* is an educational leader who lives and works within a double bind of 'don't-ask-don't tell' politics that reproduces heteronormative power through their efforts to fit as a leader" (p. 36); she can further argue that "this particular kind of leader is an overachiever and workaholic who lives with a different, lesser, set of Civil Rights" (p. 36). At the same time, she will not (and does not) negate the possibility that others will disagree with this conclusion, arguing instead that their sexual orientation is not necessarily a "civil right."

My point here is that critical researchers will gain credibility as they do not fall into the same error made by those they critique—that of ridiculing or rejecting out of hand differing interpretations, whether based on differing ideologies or on erroneous factual grounds. As Foster urged in 1986, "critical theory has three tasks: understanding, critique, and education" (p. 72); hence the need to raise consciousness, to develop understanding, to urge reflection, and to advocate redress—but at the same time to avoid (insofar as possible) further polarizing an already emotionally and ideologically charged research landscape.

Justifying Interpretations

It is interesting that, although in the early days of qualitative research, scholars such as Guba, Lincoln, and Marshall were urging a break from trustworthiness standards that were derivative of quantitative research, the early standards for qualitative research, all of which were derivative of qualitative standards, still dominate the fields of qualitative and critical research. In 1985, Marshall asked researchers to consider whether the quest for trustworthiness (emphasizing credibility, transferability, dependability, and neutrality) "sacrifices something valuable" (p. 356). She argued that, among other reasons, "researchers choose qualitative methodology…for research that cannot be done experimentally for practical or ethical reasons" (p. 356). A similar argument can be made today: researchers choose critical advocacy research for studies that cannot be done experimentally and that require an ethical advocacy stance to address injustice and/or inequity. Hence, similar questions must be asked: what are we sacrificing by continuing to focus on outdated derivative standards? Marshall (1985) wrote that the radical critique requires us to examine how the "education system functions in the interests of more powerful social classes" and hence, that it maintains the "myths of meritocracy and democracy" (p. 361), while it continues to marginalize and disadvantage some students and to advantage and privilege others. She argued that we need "research designed to capture the words of the underclass, the hidden structured connections among organizations, the informal policies or the unanticipated outcomes of policies on particular populations" (p. 367). This research, she argued 25 years ago, must "explore its unique goodness—its ability to explore multiple and competing perspectives and ideologies, to identify under-represented voices, to challenge commonly accepted 'truths'." It must therefore be judged by different standards, those she called "goodness standards"—standards that can be undermined by an excessive emphasis on the typical "trustworthiness criteria."

A year later, Lincoln and Guba (1986) also emphasized the derivative nature of commonly accepted trustworthiness criteria, the criteria that, as Huberman and Miles (1983) argued, test research "in context." To move beyond this paradigm, Lincoln and Guba developed and urged the adoption of "unique criteria of authenticity"—fairness, ontological authentication (raising consciousness), educative authentication (increasing understanding of constructions rooted in different value systems), catalytic authentication (getting theory into action), and finally, tactical authentication (ensuring empowering action).

Only a few years later, Lather (1992) wrote about how the proliferation and legitimacy of paradigms with such competing goals as prediction, understanding, emancipation, or deconstruction had contributed to a "transdisciplinary disarray regarding standards and canons" (p. 89). She, too, focused on the emergence of critical inquiry as a means of emphasizing meaning-making in the human sciences. More recently, Schwandt (2007) argued that although "the very act of generating evidence or identifying something as evidence is itself an interpretation" and that "every interpretation is made in some context or background of beliefs, practices, or traditions," it does not mean that every interpretation is the subjective, personal view of the interpreter (p. 11). In fact, he argues, "interpretation is not simply an individual cognitive act but a social and political practice" (p. 12). Moreover, he acknowledges that this view stands in "sharp contrast to what is, more or less, a standard epistemological account of establishing the objectivity and truthfulness of claims that we make about the world" (p. 12).

It is clear that although the "orthodox consensus about what it means to do science has been displaced" (Lather, 1992, p. 89)—and indeed, has been displaced for more than a quarter of a century—normative views related to the need for objectivity and trustworthiness die hard. Nevertheless, there are other, clearly articulated and equally valid standards of interpretation that one can use for critical advocacy research. The necessity, it seems to me, is to ensure that one selects standards appropriate to the intent and design of the research and then makes those standards explicit.

Moral Courage: Taking an Advocacy Approach

Before I continue, I need to clarify my use of the terms advocacy and activist—for I use them here relatively interchangeably. Both imply taking a stance on behalf of a person or a position in which one believes. Both imply moral action and, hence, the need for the researcher to take a courageous stance. Neither implies that the educational researcher must take up a banner and march in a protest rally, demonstrating for the urgency of a particular position (although one may do so on occasion). Despite the fact that *activist* has connotations that may suggest a more public stance, I am persuaded that both activism and advocacy are marks of the public intellectual who takes a reasoned, moral, and public stance based on the information and understanding one has.

Thus, in 2006, when Oakes and Rogers argued that Dewey was on the right track when he decried the "absence of a robust public sphere" and called for "'public intelligence' to confront the cultural norms and politics of privilege that sustain structures of inequity both in and out of school" (p. 16), they were supporting a position of both advocacy and activism. Given our levels of higher education and our positions of public trust with respect to society's children and youth, educational leaders and educational researchers occupy a position of relative power and privilege in today's society. Hence, we are in a strong position to exercise roles as activists and public intellectuals and to advocate for the kind of dialogue that might constitute a more robust public sphere. Said (1994) argued that those who occupy a position as public intellectuals must play a role that "has an edge to it"—a role that

> cannot be played without a sense of being someone whose place it is publically to raise embarrassing questions, to confront orthodoxy and dogma (rather than to produce them), to be someone who cannot easily be co-opted by governments or corporations, and whose raison d'être is to represent all those people and issues that are routinely forgotten or swept under the rug. The intellectual does so on the basis of universal principles: that all human beings are entitled to expect decent standards of behavior concerning freedom and justice from worldly powers or nations, and that deliberate or inadvertent violations of these standards need to be testified and fought against courageously. (p. 9)

Similarly, Bourdieu (1977) stated that "the primary contribution of social scientists to society is to illuminate the mechanisms of domination and to show how these mechanisms reproduce social inequities, thus making the social sciences inherently critical" (p. 29). And yet in the current context of public scrutiny and high levels of public accountability, many educational leaders feel deskilled and silenced, reluctant to take on a role they perceive to be increasingly bureaucratized. Many researchers fear that if they do not conform to the current "gold standard," they will neither be successful in grant applications or in tenure bids. There seems to be a fear of speaking out, of engaging constituents in broader debate about how to overcome the persistent inequities in school and society, or of advocating action or policy that might polarize rather than unite powerful stakeholders. Instead of confronting orthodoxy and dogmas, as urged by Said, we are more likely to be co-opted by them.

Nevertheless, as Baker (in Oakes & Rogers, 2006) stated: "We are going to have to learn to think in radical terms" if we want to make a difference. To promote "enlightened understanding" (Bode, 2001) and participation of the general public in dialogue and debate about conflicting ideologies; to present alternative and relevant interpretations, strategies, and solutions, educational researchers will need to take a more active role in informing, empowering, and legitimizing public participation. Critical research provides the basis for such advocacy.

Moreover, critical researchers must be clear that taking a stand as an advocate does not imply biased, distorted, or sloppy research, but can (and must) be associated with rigor and relevance. It does imply that those with power and privilege should work on the side of those without. In other words, for the critical researcher, taking an advocacy position is, in many ways, a moral imperative.

Illustrating a Critical Advocacy Approach

Let me give an example from my own research. Some years ago, I conducted a number of studies in schools on a portion of the Navajo reservation in the United States. My quest was to determine why, despite being extraordinarily well equipped and having a rich array of material resources, Navajo students in these schools continued to be less successful than their non-Navajo peers and to experience even less success if they enrolled in post-secondary programs at local or regional colleges or universities. I surveyed both students and parents and found no statistically significant differences in the family lives (parental education, books in the home, income levels) of students who were successful and those who were not. I interviewed students and parents and found that the Navajo parents were as interested in, and supportive of, their children's education as non-Navajo parents. I interviewed teachers and school administrators and found little difference in their teaching philosophies, in their postgraduate training, or in their linguistic ability. In short, from a relatively objective (modernist, or positivistic perspective), the continued lesser school achievement of Navajo children seemed to be mysterious and unexplainable. It must, one might have argued, simply be due to different levels of motivation and interest on the part of the children themselves.

However, my research did not stop with these preliminary investigations. I subsequently conducted a series of critical investigations, in which I took as my starting point a post-colonial, domination perspective (Ashcroft, Griffiths, & Tiffin, 2002; Gandhi, 1998; Prasad, 2003). In these critical studies, I was careful not to speak *for* the Navajo, but to talk *with* them and to share ways in which I and my colleagues as White educators were not only complicit in the current minoritized and dominated state of American Indian students, but to consider ways in which we could begin to address implicit racism and hegemonic power (see, for example, Shields & Lopez, 1993; Shields & Seltzer, 1997; Shields, 1993, 2002). Through this critical lens, I recognized that the Navajo students, although in the numerical majority, were still minoritized in that they were studying a dominantly White, middle-class curriculum, primarily taught by educators steeped in the dominant culture. Moreover, for the most part, their education followed the domination perspective of Cummins (1986) instead of an empowerment perspective, in that the instruction was mostly transmissive, the community played no viable role in the education of its children, the Navajo language and culture were largely ignored in the schools, and evaluation and assessment were for the purpose of legitimation and not advocacy. Using a critical lens that began with Foster's (1986) recognition of the need to challenge taken-for-granted assumptions that perpetuate "sources of social domination and repression" (p. 71), I began a new series of interviews with parents, teachers, and school principals. And, as a result, in an early publication (Shields & Lopez, 1993) I examined the planning effort of a small Navajo school attempting to effect changes to improve student learning. I concluded that planners would have to pay more attention to the creation of a shared vision and asked a number of questions about how to overcome a "dysfunctional culture."

When I asked teachers what would help the students achieve more academic success, the blunt response of one teacher, "better parents!", was reiterated in various ways. Another stated:

> The Navajo students who are doing the very best in school are going to come from those families who have probably not taught them the language, but have insisted that they get a good education and prepare to go to college.

Teachers told me that parents were duplicitous in that they said they supported education but kept their adolescents home to help with transportation or look after younger children—especially if a family member needed to be taken to the doctor. My critical lens immediately required I challenge the assumption undergirding the statement, recognizing that here, two valid, valuable, and competing values were coming into conflict. Parents did value education, but in the remote and isolated expanse of the Navajo reservation, families living in traditional hogans out in the semi-desert valley had no public means of transportation and no nearby neighbors or child-care facilities to expedite the medical appointment. Hence, having older children help with the medical appointment was not a rejection of the value of schooling, but a strong validation of the importance of family.

When parents were asked about incorporating Navajo language and culture into the curriculum, numerous hegemonic statements were made. Some made such illogical comments about the Navajo as "We live in a society of English. They chose to come here and so they need to learn to speak English" or "We are an English country," "English is the language of the United States and English is an international language!" or "Indian peoples in this area live in America and should be required to learn English." Others said that culture "should be taught at home, if the parents want it." Others believed that schools should focus on helping students "who struggle with English" to become better able to use the language in which they must function and not "force them to learn a language of limited use."

Subsequent analysis of these and other data showed a very different picture of some possible reasons for the apparent lack of academic success. Educators clearly were operating from deficit perspectives, pathologizing the Navajo students, and seeking as much to "fix" or to "cure" them as to educate them (Shields, Bishop, & Mazawi, 2005). Some parents also believed that the Navajo should have long ago been better assimilated into the White, English-speaking, dominant culture and that if they had chosen to resist, their failure should be attributed to this resistance.

From this critical perspective, it is absolutely inappropriate to simply report the perspectives of stakeholders; instead they must be understood and explicated through a critical lens, using as starting points notions of colonization (Prasad, 2003; Said, 1994), hegemony, or domination. The findings demonstrate that pathologizing—a mode of colonization used to govern, regulate, manage, marginalize, or minoritize students primarily through hegemonic discourses—is operating in these schools. Thus, regardless of how hard working the students, how supportive the parents, how dedicated some teachers, the dominant discourses position the students as inferior. Educators in general do not expect them to succeed and certainly do not hold them to the same high expectations as their non-Navajo peers.

Such discourses serve to disempower; they give the clear message that school is not for the likes of—in this case—the Navajo, who are not represented in the curriculum or in the assignments and activities of the textbooks. Clearly a science project in which students are asked to record and analyze the family's use of electricity by reading the meter is an impossibility for students living in a traditional hogan, far from any source of electricity except the battery of their car or truck. Similarly, being asked to create a piñata to celebrate the Mexican festival of Cinco de Mayo would not only have little meaning, but be almost impossible when there is only one general store within 50 miles and it does not carry papier-mâché. Moreover, asking the students to make models of hogans, shade houses, and to bake fry bread for one week of the year (as I have seen on several occasions) in order to celebrate Native American week seems more than slightly incongruous in a community in which 98% of the students are Navajo, and hence, in which Navajo culture should figure prominently all year round.

Using a less critical research lens is likely to lead to the essentializing of the Navajo students, the exoticizing of their lifestyle, and perhaps to the conclusion that to be successful in school, they must abandon their traditional lifestyle. Nevertheless, during my series of critical ethnographic studies (as reported elsewhere; see for example, Shields, 1999; Shields & Seltzer, 1997), I have found students have been able to boot up the school computers, connect to the Internet to seek information for an assignment, travel in a rented limousine formally dressed in long gowns or tuxedos for the prom one day, and dress in ornate costumes covered with tinkling brass decorations or feathers to energetically perform an intricate jingle dance or hoop dance the next day. They do not need to give up their traditional language, culture, or traditions in order to be successful in school; indeed, as Cummins (1986) argues, education must be additive rather than subtractive, for it is immoral and unconscionable to ask students to renounce what is important at home to succeed at school.

Let me be clear: for critical advocacy-oriented research, the analysis is only the beginning. Given that very few (some would argue 10–20) people read any given peer-reviewed scholarly article, publishing an analysis that argues for the elimination of deficit thinking and the adoption of a more empowering and additive curriculum is unlikely to have any positive effect or to bring about any significant change. Moreover, even having a brief follow-up discussion with the school principal or making a formal presentation to the school board (as I did) will effect little if any change.

What I now firmly believe, advocate, and argue as an essential component of critical advocacy-oriented research is for the researcher to engage the stakeholders on an ongoing basis with the findings and implications of a critical research study, to emphasize the authenticity criteria described earlier, to ensure that people's understandings are indeed changed, and that such new comprehension leads to action that is tactical and strategic (in this case, towards a more empowering approach to educating the Navajo).

Ten years after my critical studies of Navajo schooling, I wonder what might have occurred had I specifically advocated for educational discourses that depathologized the students, not just holding one meeting in which I stated that the change was necessary, but modeling it, demonstrating instances of deficit thinking, and providing alternatives. What if I had then (as I try to now) taken Lincoln and

Guba's (1986) authenticity criteria more seriously? Could I have facilitated new discourses focused not on deficits, but on agency, community, social justice, deep democracy, and academic excellence? I wonder how I might have worked with the board and the school administrators to help them reposition members from both the dominant and the minoritized groups—providing an impetus for the full inclusion of all community members, and perhaps offering training for elders who (because of their own experiences with residential schools) were unfamiliar with ways in which parents could be productively involved in their children's schooling (and by this I do not mean finding ways to encourage more parents to come into the school on hegemonic White, middle-class terms).

I did try to exemplify *fairness*, trying to provide evidence of differing educator and stakeholder perspectives. It could also be said that *ontological authenticity*—"improvement in the individual's (and group's) conscious experiencing of the world" (Lincoln & Guba, 1986, p. 22—was achieved—at least for members of the school board who considered my findings. Nevertheless, how could I have helped parents and teachers with differing perspectives to hear and understand each other; what dialogic fora could I have initiated and facilitated? Doing so might also have helped me fulfill the *educative authenticity* criteria, helping participants not only to hear each other's perspectives but to increase their understanding of the "whys of various expressed constructions" (p. 23), at the same time enhancing their understanding of "the groups they represent" (p. 23). Hence, school board members might have better understood, and then decided to address, some of the underlying racism and deficit assumptions of the teachers they had hired. *Catalytic authenticity* is sometimes known as "feedback-action validity" (p. 23). Hence helping participants to not only hear and understand the data, but to decide on, and implement action strategies to redress wrongs is the next step. Finally, *tactical authenticity* would ensure that the selected action was an appropriate response to the findings. Helping school board members and the superintendent to respond in educative ways to the parents who believed that the Navajo had chosen to go to America, and hence should learn English, might be a positive tactical example. Ignoring the inappropriateness and incorrectness of parental perceptions, and instead canceling all Navajo instruction would not be an appropriate tactical response.

I recall, almost 20 years ago now, asking my university department advisor how much time I should spend in the field doing research. His unequivocal answer was "as little as possible, because your job is to get tenure." My answer today would be quite different; to an inquiring young researcher who might ask that question, I would respond, "As long as it takes to make a difference." In other words, conducting critical, advocacy-oriented research requires a commitment of the researcher to support and advocate for those whose voices are not always clearly heard. It implies a commitment to work to influence policies and practices that perpetuate marginalization and exclusion rather than integration and membership in school communities. It is a commitment never addressed when I was a graduate student and one that was (and still is) often rejected out of hand by other researchers and scholars whose path to tenure and respectability is more traditional.

Yet, despite my strong conviction that educational research that is worth doing has an activist edge, it is appropriate to issue a caution. Because it is more difficult to fund research that does not meet the current "gold standard," and because taking an advocacy stance often brings the researcher into conflict with people who hold the power—legislators, school district administrators, university tenure committees—it is not without risks. Thus, it is incumbent on each researcher selecting the critical, advocacy path to reflect on the advice I received two decades ago, to calculate the risks, and to make an informed decision.

Summary

A critical, advocacy-oriented approach to research requires both a clearly articulated epistemological stance up front and a courageous and-long term engagement and follow-through. Critical research, as with all other kinds of research, *is* in some way promotional (Schwandt, 2007). It promotes a particular question, gives prominence to certain values, ideologies, and methodologies—but that recognition does not inherently distort or negate it. Indeed, the challenge is to conduct research with as much independence, credibility, rigor, and discipline as possible, but then, once one has drawn some conclusions, to take on the role of activist and ensure that the findings are not only understood but, where appropriate, acted upon.

This is quite different from taking an activist or advocacy position up front and selecting respondents, cases, or variables *in order to prove a point*. Hence, I am not advocating what Bob Stake (2008) has described as "sneaky undeclared advocacy of programs or practices" but a reasoned advocacy based on solid findings and interpretations. Thus the foundation for any advocacy is not the desire of a sponsor or the impassioned beliefs of a researcher, but research that has been both designed and conducted with as much detail, care, and accuracy as possible.

Identifying the theoretical framework at the outset assists the reader to develop both an understanding of the research but also of its parameters. But this is not "sneaky undeclared advocacy"—indeed it is not advocacy at all. If, for example, in a given study, a researcher discovers that, in a particular school, refugee students are impeded from engagement in learning because the teacher repeatedly makes derogatory comments about their lack of previous schooling experiences and communicates an expectation they will fail, action is called for—action I call activism, not based on a predetermined position, but on the outcome of the research study itself and my moral imperative as a public intellectual. To do otherwise would be unethical and immoral. If a critical investigation results in contradictory or inconclusive findings, it may not be possible or ethical to advocate action; instead, ensuring that all perspectives are clearly explicated and examined is warranted. But if we have conducted careful and accurate investigation that permits us to identify potential problems that must be addressed, challenges to overcome, behaviors that impede the success of some children, or inappropriate outcomes of certain policies, then it is incumbent on us to act.

Indeed, it seems to me that taking a stand, engaging with the school district and its educational leaders about the detrimental impact of deficit thinking and hegemonic programming on Navajo students is the most credible way to conduct authentic inquiry and ethical research. This is particularly true when one is conducting studies focused on people who have been typically underrepresented, silenced, or marginalized by the mainstream culture, but who are striving for agency, authentic voice, and empowerment.

Eisenhart (2006), in a discussion of the gold standard of quasi-experimental design, commented that "experimental research on causal effects isolates variables...and investigates their relationship to other variables...." She went on to say:

> This procedure will work if the variables being measured do not change over time, are not variably influenced by circumstances and are not affected by human intention or desire....The problem is that in education and other social practices all else is not equal, and little if anything remains constant. (pp. 699–700)

As I have attempted to illustrate here, one cannot control for attitudes, assumptions, hegemonic use of power, or deficit assumptions. One cannot easily control for competing and conflicting cultural variables such as those I described earlier.

The important issues for educational researchers revolve around ways to create educational opportunities and learning environments that offer equitable access and outcomes to all students. We must name power and privilege where we find it and challenge its inappropriate uses when we identify them. These deep-seated, politicized ideologies are clearly affected by, and affect, human intention and desire. They must be identified, surfaced, and challenged if more researchers, educators, and members of the general public are to work, with Maxine Greene, to ensure that ours becomes a society of fulfilled promises.

Educators and educational researchers must turn the mantra that "all are created equal" into practice so that all members of our global society can experience equitable access, opportunities, and outcomes. We are not simply literary critics, scholars of the classics looking for a new angle for a dissertation, or historians looking for a new story. I am persuaded that for *educational* researchers to be responsible is to use our power, privilege, and position in the field to promote justice and enlightenment and not just advance my career or add to the archives. We must be able, when all is said and done, to ask of ourselves, "Has our research done anything to level the playing field, to overcome disparity, to promote a more mutually beneficial democratic society?" It is my hope that we will find the necessary courage to be able to answer in the affirmative.

Note

1. They included Anderson's (2001) critical analysis of the ISLLC standards, Perryman's (2009) analysis of an OfSTED inspection in England, and Tooms's (2007) examination of the challenges facing closeted LGBTQ administrators.

References

Anderson, G. L. (2001). Disciplining leaders: A critical discourse analysis of the ISLLC national examination and performance standards in educational administration. *International Journal of Leadership in Education, 4*(3), 199–216.

Ashcroft, B., Griffiths, G., & Tiffin, H. (Eds.). (2002). *The empire writes back: Theory and practice in post-colonial literatures* (2nd ed.). London, England: Routledge.

Bode, B. H. (2001). Reorientation in education. In S. J. Goodlad (Ed.), *The last best hope: A democracy reader* (pp. 92–100). San Francisco, CA: Jossey-Bass.

Bourdieu, P. (with Passeron, J. C.). (1977). *Reproduction in education, society and culture*. London, England: Sage.

Cummins, J. (1986). Empowering minority students: A framework for intervention. In N. M. Hidalgo, C. L. McDowell, & E. V. Siddle (Eds.), *Facing racism in education* (Reprint Series No. 21). Cambridge, MA: Harvard Educational Review. (First published in *Harvard Educational Review, 56*(1), 1986, 18–36.)

Eisenhart, M. (2006). Qualitative science in experimental time. *International Journal of Qualitative Studies in Education, 19*(6), 697–707.

Evers, C. W., & Wu, E. H. (2006). On generalising from single case studies: Epistemological reflections. *Journal of Philosophy of Education, 40*(4), 511–526.

Foster, W. (1986). *Paradigms and promises: New approaches to educational administration*. Buffalo, NY: Prometheus.

Foucault, M. (1980). *Power/knowledge: Selected interviews and other writings 1972–77*. New York, NY: Pantheon Books.

Foucault, M. (1984). The order of discourse. In M. Shapiro (Ed.). *Language and politics*. Oxford, England: Blackwell.

Gandhi, L. (1998). *Postcolonial theory: A critical introduction*. New York, NY: Columbia University Press.

Greene, M. (1998). Introduction: Teaching for social justice. In W. Ayers, J. A. Hunt, & T. Quinn (Eds.), *Teaching for social justice* (pp. xxvii–xlvi). New York, NY: Teachers College Press.

Hargreaves, D. (2003). *Education epidemic: Transforming secondary schools through innovation networks*. London, England: Demos.

Huberman, A. M., & Miles, M. (1983). Drawing valid meaning from qualitative data: Some techniques of data reduction and display. *Quality and Quantity, 17,* 281–339.

Lather, P. (1986). Research as praxis. *Harvard Educational Review, 56*(3), 257–277.

Lather, P. (1992). Critical frames in educational research: Feminist and post-structural perspectives. *Theory into Practice, 31*(2), 87–99.

Lather, P. (2004). Scientific research in education: A critical perspective. *British Educational Research Journal, 30*(6), 759–772.

Lincoln, Y. S., & Guba, E.g. (1986). But is it rigorous? Trustworthiness and authenticity in naturalistic evaluation. In D. D. Williams (Ed.), *Naturalistic evaluation*. San Francisco, CA: Jossey-Bass.

Littell, J. H. (2008). Evidence-based or biased? The quality of published reviews of evidence-based practices. *Children and Youth Services Review, 30,* 1299–1317.

Manzo, K. K. (2004). Leading commercial series don't satisfy "Gold Standard". *Education Week, 24*(3), 16–17.

Marshall, C. (1985). Appropriate criteria of trustworthiness and goodness for qualitative research on educational organizations. *Quality and Quantity, 19,* 353–373.

Oakes, J., & Rogers, J. (2006). *Learning power: Organizing for education and justice*. New York, NY: Teachers College Press.

Ogbu, J. U. (1992). Understanding cultural diversity and learning. *Educational Researcher, 21*(8), 5–14; 24.

Perryman, J. (2009). Inspection and the fabrication of professional and performative processes. *Journal of Education Policy, 245*(5), 611–631.

Prasad, A. (2003). *Postcolonial theory and organizational analysis: A critical engagement*. New York, NY: Palgrave Macmillan.

Said, E. W. (1994). Representations of the intellectual. In E. W. Said (Ed.), *Representations of the intellectual: The 1993 Reith lectures* (pp. 3–17). London, England: Random House.

Schwandt, T. A. (2007). Judging interpretations. In S. Mathison (Ed.), Enduring issues in evaluation [Special issue]. *New Directions for Evaluation, 114*, 11–25.

Shields, C. M. (1993). A planning paradox: One school's effort to restructure to meet the needs of a Native American student body. *Educational Planning, 6(3)*, 48–61.

Shields, C. M. (1999). Learning from students about representation, identity, and community. *Educational Administration Quarterly, 35*(1), 106–129.

Shields, C. M. (2002). *Understanding the challenges, exploring the opportunities, and developing new understandings: Examining the effects of the past four years* (Unpublished report completed for San Juan School District).

Shields, C. M., Bishop, R., & Mazawi, A. E. (2005). *Pathologizing practices: The impact of deficit thinking on education.* New York, NY: Peter Lang.

Shields, C. M., & Lopez, C. G. (1993). What I want for my children is what I want for all children: Planning to serve the needs of minority students. *Planning and Changing, 24*(1/2), 69–85.

Shields, C. M., & Seltzer, P. (1997). Complexities and paradoxes of community: Toward a more useful conceptualization of community. *Educational Administration Quarterly, 33*(4), 413–439.

Stake, R. (2008, March). The price of playing a superhero: Why researchers should eschew advocacy and concentrate on inquiry. In *Inquiry and advocacy: Reconsidering the distinction for a postmodern era still committed to scientific research.* Symposium conducted at the annual meeting of the American Educational Research Association, Chicago, IL.

Tooms, A. (2007, April). *"Is that a wedding ring?" A look at the panopticons of identity politics lived by gay school administrators serving homophobic communities.* Paper presented at the annual meeting of the American Educational Research Association, Chicago, IL.

CHAPTER TWO

Critical Pedagogy and Qualitative Research: Moving to the Bricolage

Joe L. Kincheloe, Peter McLaren and Shirley R. Steinberg

Criticality and Research

Over the past 35 years of our involvement in critical theory, critical pedagogy, and critical research, we have been asked to explain how critical theory relates to pedagogy. We find that question difficult to answer because (1) there are many critical theories; (2) the critical tradition is always changing and evolving; and (3) critical theory attempts to avoid too much specificity, as there is room for disagreement among critical theorists. To lay out a set of fixed characteristics of the position is contrary to the desire of such theorists to avoid the production of blueprints of sociopolitical and epistemological beliefs. Given these disclaimers, we will now attempt to provide one idiosyncratic "take" on the nature of critical theory and critical research in the second decade of the 21st century. Please note that this is our subjective analysis and that there are many brilliant critical theorists who disagree with our pronouncements. We tender a description of an ever-evolving criticality, a reconceptualized critical theory that was critiqued and overhauled by the "postdiscourses" of the last quarter of the 20th century and has been further extended in the 21st century (Collins, 1995; Giroux, 1997; Kellner, 1995; Kincheloe, 2008b; McLaren & Kincheloe, 2007; Roman & Eyre, 1997; Ryoo & McLaren, 2010; Steinberg & Kincheloe, 1998; Tobin, 2009; Weil & Kincheloe, 2004).

A reconceptualized critical theory questions the assumption that societies such as Australia, Canada, Great Britain, New Zealand, and the United States, along with the nations in the European Union, are unproblematically democratic and free (Steinberg, 2010). Over the 20th century, especially after the early 1960s, individuals in these societies were acculturated to feel comfortable in relations of domination and subordination rather than equality and independence. Given the social and technological changes of the last half of the century, which led to new forms of information production and access, critical theorists argued that questions of self-direction and democratic egalitarianism should be reassessed. Researchers informed by the postdiscourses (e.g., postmodernism, critical feminism, poststructuralism) came to understand that individuals' view of themselves and the world were even more influenced by social and historical forces than previously believed. Given the changing social and informational conditions of late-20th century and early-21st century, media-saturated Western culture (Steinberg, 2004a, 2004b), critical theorists have needed new ways of researching and analyzing the construction of individuals (Agger, 1992; Flossner & Otto, 1998; Giroux, 2010; Hammer & Kellner, 2009; Hinchey, 2009; Kincheloe, 2007; Leistyna, Woodrum, & Sherblom, 1996; Quail, Razzano, & Skalli, 2004; Skalli, 2004; Steinberg, 2007, 2009; Wesson & Weaver, 2001).

Partisan Research in a "Neutral" Academic Culture

In the space available here, it is impossible to do justice to all of the critical traditions that have drawn inspiration from Karl Marx; Immanuel Kant; Georg Wilhelm Friedrich Hegel; Max Weber; the Frankfurt School theorists; Continental social theorists such as Jean Baudrillard, Michel Foucault, Jürgen Habermas, and Jacques Derrida; Latin American thinkers such as Paulo Freire; French feminists such as Luce Irigaray, Julia Kristeva, and Hélène Cixous; or Russian socio-sociolinguists such as Mikhail Bakhtin and Lev Vygotsky—most of whom regularly find their way into the reference lists of contemporary critical researchers. Today, there are criticalist schools in many fields, and even a superficial discussion of the most prominent of these schools would demand much more space than we have available (Chapman, 2010; Flecha, Gomez, & Puigvert, 2003). The fact that numerous books have been written about the often-virulent disagreements among members of the Frankfurt School only heightens our concern with the "packaging" of the different criticalist schools. Critical theory should not be treated as a universal grammar of revolutionary thought objectified and reduced to discrete formulaic pronouncements or strategies. Obviously, in presenting our version of a reconceptualized critical theory or an evolving criticality, we have defined the critical tradition broadly for the purpose of generating understanding; as we asserted earlier, this will trouble many critical researchers. In this move, we decided to focus on the underlying commonality among critical schools of thought at the cost of focusing on differences. This is always risky business in terms of suggesting a false unity or consensus where none exists, but such concerns are unavoidable in a survey chapter such as this. We are defining a criticalist as a researcher, teacher, or theorist who attempts to use her or his work as a form of social or cultural criticism and who accepts certain basic assumptions:

- All thought is fundamentally mediated by power relations that are social and historically constituted;

- Facts can never be isolated from the domain of values or removed from some form of ideological inscription;

- The relationship between concept and object and between signifier and signified is never stable or fixed and is often mediated by the social relations of capitalist production and consumption;

- Language is central to the formation of subjectivity (conscious and unconscious awareness);

- Certain groups in any society and particular societies are privileged over others and, although the reasons for this privileging may vary widely, the oppression that characterizes contemporary societies is most forcefully reproduced when subordinates accept their social status as natural, necessary, or inevitable;

- Oppression has many faces, and focusing on only one at the expense of others (e.g., class oppression versus racism) often elides the interconnections among them; and finally

- Mainstream research practices are generally, although most often unwittingly, implicated in the reproduction of systems of class, race, and gender oppression (De Lissovoy & McLaren, 2003; Gresson, 2006; Kincheloe & Steinberg, 1997; Rodriguez and Villaverde, 2000; Steinberg, 2009; Villaverde, 2007; Watts, 2008, 2009a).

In today's climate of blurred disciplinary genres, it is not uncommon to find literary theorists doing anthropology and anthropologists writing about literary theory, political scientists trying their hand at ethno-ethnomethodological analysis, or philosophers doing Lacanian film criticism. All of these inter- and cross-disciplinary moves are examples of what has been referred to as bricolage—a key innovation, we argue, in an evolving criticality. We will explore this dynamic in relation to critical research later in this chapter. We offer this observation about blurred genres, not as an excuse to be wantonly eclectic in our treatment of the critical tradition but to make the point that any attempts to delineate critical theory as discrete schools of analysis will fail to capture the evolving hybridity endemic to contemporary critical analysis (Denzin, 1994; Denzin & Lincoln, 2000; Kincheloe, 2001a, 2008b; Kincheloe & Berry, 2004; Steinberg, 2008, 2010, 2011). Critical research can be understood best in the context of the empowerment of individuals. Inquiry that aspires to the name "critical" must be connected to an attempt to confront the injustice of a particular society or public sphere within the society. Research becomes a transformative endeavor unembarrassed by the label "political" and unafraid to consummate a relationship with emancipatory consciousness. Whereas traditional researchers cling to the guardrail of neutrality, critical researchers frequently announce their partisanship in the struggle for a better world (Chapman, 2010; Grinberg, 2003; Horn, 2004; Kincheloe, 2001b, 2008b).

Critical Pedagogy Informing Social Research

The work of Brazilian educator Paulo Freire is instructive in relation to constructing research that contributes to the struggle for a better world. The research of the authors of this chapter has been influenced profoundly by the work of Freire (1970, 1972, 1978, 1985). Concerned with human suffering and the pedagogical and knowledge work that helped expose the genesis of it, Freire modeled critical theoretical research throughout his career. In his writings about research, Freire maintained that there were no traditionally defined objects of his research—he insisted on involving the people he studied as partners in the research process. He immersed himself in their ways of thinking and modes of perception, encouraging them to begin thinking about their own thinking. Everyone involved in Freire's critical research, not just the researcher, joined in the process of investigation, examination, criticism, and reinvestigation—all participants and researchers learned to see more critically, think at a more critical level, and to recognize the forces that subtly shape their lives. Critiquing traditional methods of research in schools, Freire took a critical pedagogical approach to research that serves to highlight its difference from traditional research (Kirylo, 2011; Mayo, 2009; Tobin & Llena, 2010).

After exploring the community around the school and engaging in conversations with community members, Freire constructed generative themes designed to tap into issues that were important to various students in his class. As data on these issues were brought into the class, Freire became a problem poser. In this capacity, Freire used the knowledge he and his students had produced around the generative themes to construct questions. The questions he constructed were designed to teach the lesson that no curriculum or knowledge in general was beyond examination. We need to ask questions of all knowledge, Freire argued, because all data are shaped by the context and by the individuals that produced them. Knowledge, contrary to the pronouncements of many educational leaders, does not transcend culture or history.

In the context of reading the word and the world and problem-posing existing knowledge, critical educators reconceptualize the notion of literacy. Myles Horton spoke of the way he read books with students in order "to give testimony to the students about what it means to read a text" (Horton &

Freire, 1990). Reading is not an easy endeavor, Horton continued, for to be a good reader is to view reading as a form of research. Reading becomes a mode of finding something, and finding something, he concluded, brings a joy that is directly connected to the acts of creation and re-creation. One finds in this reading that the word and world process typically goes beyond the given, the common sense of everyday life. Critical pedagogical research must have a mandate to represent a form of reading that understood not only the words on the page but the unstated dominant ideologies hidden between the sentences as well.

Going beyond is central to Freirean problem posing. Such a position contends that the school curriculum should in part be shaped by problems that face teachers and students in their effort to live just and ethical lives (Kincheloe, 2004). Such a curriculum promotes students as researchers (Steinberg & Kincheloe, 1998) who engage in critical analysis of the forces that shape the world. Such critical analysis engenders a healthy and creative skepticism on the part of students. It moves them to problem pose and to be suspicious of neutrality claims in textbooks; it induces them to look askance at, for example, oil companies' claims in their TV commercials that they are and have always been environmentally friendly organizations. Students and teachers who are problem posers reject the traditional student request to the teacher: "just give us the facts, the truth, and we'll give it back to you." On the contrary, critical students and teachers ask in the spirit of Freire and Horton: "Please support us in our explorations of the world."

By promoting problem posing and student research, teachers do not relinquish their authority in the classroom. Over the last couple of decades, several teachers and students have misunderstood the subtlety of the nature of teacher authority in a critical pedagogy. In the last years of his life, Freire was very concerned with this issue and its misinterpretation by those operating in his name. Teachers, he told us, cannot deny their position of authority in such a classroom. It is the teacher, not the students, who evaluates student work, who is responsible for the health, safety, and learning of students. To deny the role of authority the teacher occupies is insincere at best, dishonest at worst. Critical teachers, therefore, must admit that they are in a position of authority and then demonstrate that authority in their actions in support of students. One of the actions involves the ability to conduct research and produce knowledge. The authority of the critical teacher is dialectical; as teachers relinquish the authority of truth providers, they assume the mature authority of facilitators of student inquiry and problem posing. In relation to such teacher authority, students gain their freedom—they gain the ability to become self-directed human beings capable of producing their own knowledge (Kirylo, 2011; Siry & Lang, 2010).

Freire's own work was rooted in both liberation theology and a dialectical materialist epistemology (Au, 2007), both of which were indebted to Marx's own writings and various Marxist theorists. Standard judgments against Marxism as economistic, productivist, and deterministic betray an egregious and scattershot understanding of Marxist epistemology, his critique of political economy, and Marx's dialectical method of analyzing the development of capitalism and capitalist society. We assert that the insights of Marx and those working within the broad parameters of the Marxist tradition are foundational for any critical research (Lund & Carr, 2008); Marxism is a powerful theoretical approach to explaining, for instance, the origins of racism and the reasons for its resiliency (McLaren, 2002). Many on the left today talk about class as if it is one of many oppressions, often describing it as "classism." But class is not an "ism." It is true that class intersects with race, and gender, and other antagonisms. And while clearly those relations of oppression can reinforce and compound each other, they are grounded in the material relations shaped by capitalism and the economic exploitation that is the motor force of any capitalist society (Dale & Hyslop-Margison, 2010; Macrine, McLaren, & Hill, 2009).

To seriously put an end to racism, and shatter the hegemony of race, racial formations, the racial state, and so on, we need to understand class as an objective process that interacts upon multiple groups and sectors in various historically specific ways. When conjoined with an insightful class analysis, the concept of race and the workings of racism can be more fully understood and racism more forcefully contested and as a result more powerful transformative practices can be mobilized. Class and race are viewed here as co-constitutive and must be understood as dialectically interrelated (McLaren & Jarramillo, 2010).

Teachers as Researchers

In the conservative educational order of mainstream schooling, knowledge is something that is produced far away from the school by experts in an exalted domain. This must change if a critical reform of schooling is to exist. Teachers must have more voice and more respect in the culture of education. Teachers must join the culture of researchers if a new level of educational rigor and quality is ever to be achieved. In such a democratized culture, critical teachers are scholars who understand the power implications of various educational reforms. In this context, they appreciate the benefits of research, especially as they relate to understanding the forces shaping education that fall outside their immediate experience and perception. As these insights are constructed, teachers begin to understand what they know from experience. With this in mind they gain heightened awareness of how they can contribute to the research on education. Indeed, they realize that they have access to understandings that go far beyond what the expert researchers have produced. In the critical school culture, teachers are viewed as learners—not as functionaries who follow top-down orders without question. Teachers are seen as researchers and knowledge workers who reflect on their professional needs and current understandings. They are aware of the complexity of the educational process and how schooling cannot be understood outside of the social, historical, philosophical, cultural, economic, political, and psychological contexts that shape it. Scholar teachers understand that curriculum development responsive to student needs is not possible when it fails to account for these contexts.

Critical teacher/researchers explore and attempt to interpret the learning processes that take place in their classrooms. "What are its psychological, sociological, and ideological effects?" they ask. Thus, critical scholar teachers research their own professional practice. With empowered scholar teachers prowling the schools, things begin to change. The oppressive culture created in our schools by top-down content standards, for example, is challenged. In-service staff development no longer takes the form of "this is what the expert researchers found—now go implement it." Such staff development in the critical culture of schooling gives way to teachers who analyze and contemplate the power of each other's ideas. Thus, the new critical culture of school takes on the form of a "think tank that teaches students," a learning community. School administrators are amazed by what can happen when they support learning activities for both students and teachers. Principals and curriculum developers watch as teachers develop projects that encourage collaboration and shared research. There is an alternative, advocates of critical pedagogy argue, to top-down standards with their deskilling of teachers and the dumbing-down of students (Jardine, 1998; Kincheloe, 2003a, 2003b, 2003c; Macedo, 2006).

Promoting teachers as researchers is a fundamental way of cleaning up the damage of deskilled models of teaching that infantilize teachers by giving them scripts to read to their students. Deskilling of teachers and the stupidification (Macedo, 2006) of the curriculum take place when teachers are seen as receivers, rather than producers of knowledge. A vibrant professional culture depends on a group of practitioners who have the freedom to continuously reinvent themselves via their research and knowledge production. Teachers engaged in critical practice find it difficult to allow top-down content standards and their poisonous effects to go unchallenged. Such teachers cannot abide the deskilling and reduction in professional status that accompany these top-down reforms. Advocates of critical pedagogy understand that teacher empowerment does not occur just because we wish it to do so. Instead, it takes place when teachers develop the knowledge-work skills, the power literacy, and the pedagogical abilities befitting the calling of teaching. Teacher research is a central dimension of a critical pedagogy (Porfilio & Carr, 2010).

Teachers as Researchers of Their Students

A central aspect of critical teacher research involves studying students, so they can be better understood and taught. Freire argued that all teachers need to engage in a constant dialogue with students, a dialogue that questions existing knowledge and problematizes the traditional power relations that have served to marginalize specific groups and individuals. In these research dialogues with students, critical teachers listen carefully to what students have to say about their communities and the problems that confront them. Teachers help students frame these problems in a larger social, cultural, and political context in order to solve them.

In this context, Freire argued that teachers uncover materials and generative themes based on their emerging knowledge of students and their sociocultural backgrounds (Mayo, 2009; Souto-Manning, 2009). Teachers come to understand the ways students perceive themselves and their interrelationships with other people and their social reality. This information is essential to the critical pedagogical act, as it helps teachers understand how they make sense of schooling and their lived worlds. With these understandings in mind, critical teachers come to know what and how students make meaning. This enables teachers to construct pedagogies that engage the impassioned spirit of students in ways that move them to learn what they do not know and to identify what they want to know (A. Freire, 2000; Freire & Faundez, 1989; Janesick, 2010; Kincheloe, 2008b; Steinberg & Kincheloe, 1998; Tobin, in press).

It is not an exaggeration to say that before critical pedagogical research can work, teachers must understand what is happening in the minds of their students. Advocates of various forms of critical teaching recognize the importance of understanding the social construction of student consciousness, focusing on motives, values, and emotions. Operating within this critical context, the teacher-researcher studies students as living texts to be deciphered. The teacher-researcher approaches them with an active imagination and a willingness to view students as socially constructed beings. When critical teachers have approached research on students from this perspective, they have uncovered some interesting information. In a British action research project, for example, teachers used student diaries, interviews, dialogues, and shadowing (following students as they pursue their daily routines at school) to uncover a student preoccupation with what was labeled a second-order curriculum. This curriculum involved matters of student dress, conformance to school rules, strategies of coping with boredom and failure, and methods of assuming their respective roles in the school pecking order. Teacher-researchers found that much of this second-order curriculum worked to contradict the stated aims of the school to respect the individuality of students, to encourage sophisticated thinking, and to engender positive self-images. Students often perceived that the daily lessons of teachers (the intentional curriculum) were based on a set of assumptions quite different from those guiding out-ofclass teacher interactions with students. Teachers consistently misread the anger and hostility resulting from such inconsistency. Only in an action research context that values the perceptions of students could such student emotions be understood and addressed (Hooley, 2009; Kincheloe, 2001a; Sikes, 2008; Steinberg, 2000, 2009; Vicars, 2008).

By using IQ tests and developmental theories derived from research on students from dominant cultural backgrounds, schools not only reflect social stratification but also extend it. This is an example of school as an institution designed for social benefit actually exerting hurtful influences. Teachers involved in the harmful processes most often do not intentionally hurt students; they are merely following the dictates of their superiors and the rules of the system. Countless good teachers work every day to subvert the negative effects of the system but need help from like-minded colleagues and organizations. Critical pedagogical research works to provide such assistance to teachers who want to mitigate the effects of power on their students. Here schools as political institutions merge with critical pedagogy's concern with creating a social and educational vision to help teachers direct their own professional practice. Anytime teachers develop a pedagogy, they are concurrently constructing a political vision. The two acts are inseparable (Kincheloe, 2008b; Wright & Lather, 2006).

Unfortunately, those who develop noncritical pedagogical research can be unconscious of the political inscriptions embedded within them. A district supervisor who writes a curriculum in social studies, for example, that demands the simple transference of a body of established facts about the great men and great events of American history is also teaching a political lesson that upholds the status quo (Keesing-Styles, 2003; McLaren & Farahmandpur, 2003, 2006). There is no room for teacher-researchers in such a curriculum to explore alternate sources, to compare diverse historical interpretations, or to do research of their own and produce knowledge that may conflict with prevailing interpretations. Such acts of democratic citizenship may be viewed as subversive and anti-American by the supervisor and the district education office. Indeed, such personnel may be under pressure from the state department of education to construct a history curriculum that is inflexible, based on the status quo, unques tioning in its approach, "fact-based," and teacher-centered. Dominant power operates in numerous and often hidden ways (Nocella, Best, & McLaren, 2010; Watts, 2006, 2009a, 2009b).

Traditional researchers see their task as the description, interpretation, or reanimation of a slice of reality; critical pedagogical researchers often regard their work as a first step toward forms of political action that can redress the injustices found in the field site or constructed in the very act of research itself. Horkheimer (1972) puts it succinctly when he argues that critical theory and research are never satisfied with merely increasing knowledge (see also Agger, 1998; Britzman, 1991; Giroux, 1983, 1988, 1997; Kincheloe, 2003c, 2008a, 2008b; Kincheloe & Steinberg, 1993; Quantz, 1992; Shor, 1996; Villaverde & Kincheloe, 1998; Wexler, 2008). Research in the critical tradition takes the form of self-conscious criticism—self-conscious in the sense that researchers try to become aware of the ideological imperatives and epistemological presuppositions that inform their research as well as their own subjective, intersubjective, and normative reference claims. Critical pedagogical researchers enter into an investigation with their assumptions on the table, so no one is confused concerning the epistemological and political baggage they bring with them to the research site.

On detailed analysis, critical researchers may change these assumptions. Stimulus for change may come from the critical researchers' recognition that such assumptions are not leading to emancipatory actions. The source of this emancipatory action involves the researchers' ability to expose the contradictions of the world of appearances accepted by the dominant culture as natural and inviolable (Giroux, 1983, 1988, 1997; Kincheloe, 2008b; McLaren, 1992, 1997; San Juan, 1992; Zizek, 1990). Such appearances may, critical researchers contend, conceal social relationships of inequality, injustice, and exploitation. If we view the violence we find in classrooms not as random or isolated incidents created by aberrant individuals willfully stepping out of line in accordance with a particular form of social pathology, but as possible narratives of transgression and resistance, then this could indicate that the "political unconscious" lurking beneath the surface of everyday classroom life is not unrelated to practices of race, class, and gender oppression but rather intimately connected to them. By applying a critical pedagogical lens within research, we create an empowering qualitative research, which expands, contracts, grows, and questions itself within the theory and practice examined.

The Bricolage

It is with our understanding of critical theory and our commitment to critical social research and critical pedagogy that we identify the bricolage as an emancipatory research construct. Ideologically grounded, the bricolage reflects an evolving criticality in research. Norman K. Denzin and Yvonna S. Lincoln (2000) use the term in the spirit of Claude Lévi-Strauss (1968 and his lengthy discussion of it in *The Savage Mind*). The French word bricoleur describes a handyman or handywoman who makes use of the tools available to complete a task (Harper, 1987; Steinberg, 2011). Bricolage implies the fictive and imaginative elements of the presentation of all formal research. The bricolage can be described as the process of getting down to the nuts and bolts of multidisciplinary research. Research knowledges such as ethnography, textual analysis, semiotics, hermeneutics, psychoanalysis, phenomenology, historiography, discourse analysis combined with philosophical analysis, literary analysis, aesthetic criticism, and theatrical and dramatic ways of observing and making meaning constitute the methodological bricolage. In this way, bricoleurs move beyond the blinders of particular disciplines and peer through a conceptual window to a new world of research and knowledge production (Denzin, 2003; Kincheloe & Berry, 2004; Steinberg, 2011).

Bricolage, in a contemporary sense, is understood to involve the process of employing these methodological processes as they are needed in the unfolding context of the research situation. While this interdisciplinary feature is central to any notion of the bricolage, critical qualitative researchers must go beyond this dynamic. Pushing to a new conceptual terrain, such an eclectic process raises numerous issues that researchers must deal with to maintain theoretical coherence and epistemological innovation. Such multidisciplinarity demands a new level of research self-consciousness and awareness of the numerous contexts in which any researcher is operating. As one labors to expose the various structures that covertly shape our own and other scholars' research narratives, the bricolage highlights the relationship between a researcher's ways of seeing and the social location of his or her personal history. Appreciating research as a power-driven act, the critical researcher-as-bricoleur abandons the quest for some naive concept of realism, focusing instead on the clarification of his or her position in the web of reality and the social locations of other researchers and the ways they shape the production and interpretation of knowledge.

In this context, bricoleurs move into the domain of complexity. The bricolage exists out of respect for the complexity of the lived world and the complications of power. Indeed, it is grounded on an epistemology of complexity. One dimension of this complexity can be illustrated by the relationship between research and the domain of social theory. All observations of the world are shaped either consciously or unconsciously by social theory—such theory provides the framework that highlights or erases what might be observed. Theory in a modernist empiricist mode is a way of understanding that operates without variation in every context. Because theory is a cultural and linguistic artifact, its interpretation of the object of its observation is inseparable from the historical dynamics that have shaped it (Austin & Hickey, 2008). The task of the bricoleur is to attack this complexity, uncovering the invisible artifacts of power and culture and documenting the nature of their influence not only on their own works, but on scholarship in general. In this process, bricoleurs act on the concept that theory is not an explanation of nature—it is more an explanation of our relation to nature.

In its hard labors in the domain of complexity, the bricoleur views research methods actively rather than passively, meaning that we actively construct our research methods from the tools at hand rather than passively receiving the "correct," universally applicable methodologies. Avoiding modes of reasoning that come from certified processes of logical analysis, bricoleurs also steer clear of preexisting guidelines and checklists developed outside the specific demands of the inquiry at hand. In its embrace of complexity, the bricolage constructs a far more active role for humans both in shaping reality and in creating the research processes and narratives that represent it. Such an active agency rejects deterministic views of social reality that assume the effects of particular social, political, economic, and educational processes. At the same time and in the same conceptual context, this belief in active human agency refuses standardized modes of knowledge production (Bresler & Ardichvili, 2002; Kincheloe & Berry, 2004; McLeod, 2000; Selfe & Selfe, 1994; Steinberg, 2010, 2011; Wright, 2003a).

Some of the best work in the study of social complexity is now taking place in the qualitative inquiry of numerous fields including sociology, cultural studies, anthropology, literary studies, marketing, geography, media studies, nursing, informatics, library studies, women's studies, various ethnic studies, education, and nursing. Denzin and Lincoln (2000) are acutely aware of these dynamics and refer to them in the context of their delineation of the bricolage. Yvonna Lincoln (2001), in her response to Joe

L. Kincheloe's development of the bricolage, maintains that the most important border work between disciplines is taking place in feminism and race-ethnic studies.

In many ways, there is a form of instrumental reason, of rational irrationality, in the use of passive, external, monological research methods. In the active bricolage, we bring our understanding of the research context together with our previous experience with research methods. Using these knowledges, we tinker in the Lévi-Straussian sense with our research methods in field-based and interpretive contexts (Steinberg, in press). This tinkering is a high-level cognitive process involving construction and reconstruction, contextual diagnosis, negotiation, and readjustment. Researchers' interaction with the objects of their inquiries, bricoleurs understand, are always complicated, mercurial, unpredictable, and, of course, complex. Such conditions negate the practice of planning research strategies in advance. In lieu of such rationalization of the process, bricoleurs enter into the research act as methodological negotiators. Always respecting the demands of the task at hand, the bricolage, as conceptualized here, resists its placement in concrete as it promotes its elasticity. In light of Lincoln's (2001) discussion of two types of bricoleurs, (1) those who are committed to research eclecticism, allowing circumstance to shape methods employed, and (2) those who want to engage in the genealogy/ archeology of the disciplines with some grander purpose in mind, critical researchers are better informed as to the power of the bricolage. Our purpose entails both of Lincoln's articulations of the role of the bricoleur (Steinberg & Kincheloe, 2011).

Research method in the bricolage is a concept that receives more respect than in more rationalistic articulations of the term. The rationalistic articulation of method subverts the deconstruction of wide varieties of unanalyzed assumptions embedded in passive methods. Bricoleurs, in their appreciation of the complexity of the research process, view research method as involving far more than procedure. In this mode of analysis, bricoleurs come to understand research method as also a technology of justification, meaning a way of defending what we assert we know and the process by which we know it. Thus, the education of critical researchers demands that everyone take a step back from the process of learning research methods. Such a step back allows us a conceptual distance that produces a critical consciousness. Such a consciousness refuses the passive acceptance of externally imposed research methods that tacitly certify modes justifying knowledges that are decontextualized, reductionistic, and inscribed by dominant modes of power (Denzin & Lincoln, 2000; Foster, 1997; Kincheloe & Berry, 2004; McLeod, 2000).

In its critical concern for just social change, the bricolage seeks insight from the margins of Western societies and the knowledge and ways of knowing of non-Western peoples. Such insight helps bricoleurs reshape and sophisticate social theory, research methods, and interpretive strategies, as they discern new topics to be researched. This confrontation with difference so basic to the concept of the bricolage enables researchers to produce new forms of knowledge that inform policy decisions and political action in general. In gaining this insight from the margins, bricoleurs display once again the blurred boundary between the hermeneutical search for understanding and the critical concern with social change for social justice (Jardine, 2006a). Kincheloe has taken seriously Peter McLaren's (2001) important concern—offered in his response to Kincheloe's (2001a) first delineation of his conception of the bricolage— that merely focusing on the production of meanings may not lead to "resisting and transforming the existing conditions of exploitation" (McLaren, 2001, p. 702). In response, Kincheloe maintained that in the critical hermeneutical dimension of the bricolage, the act of understanding power and its effects is merely one part—albeit an inseparable part—of counterhegemonic action. Not only are the two orientations not in conflict, they are synergistic (DeVault, 1996; Lutz, Jones, & Kendall, 1997; Soto, 2000; Steinberg, 2001, 2007; Tobin, 2010).

To contribute to social transformation, bricoleurs seek to better understand both the forces of domination that affect the lives of individuals from race, class, gender, sexual, ethnic, and religious backgrounds outside of dominant culture(s) and the worldviews of such diverse peoples. In this context, bricoleurs attempt to remove knowledge production and its benefits from the control of elite groups.

Such control consistently operates to reinforce elite privilege while pushing marginalized groups farther away from the center of dominant power. Rejecting this normalized state of affairs, bricoleurs commit their knowledge work to helping address the ideological and informational needs of marginalized groups and individuals. As detectives of subjugated insight, bricoleurs eagerly learn from labor struggles, women's marginalization, the "double consciousness" of the racially oppressed, and insurrections against colonialism (Kincheloe & Steinberg, 1993; Kincheloe, Steinberg, & Hinchey, 1999; Kincheloe & Berry, 2004). In this way, the bricolage hopes to contribute to an evolving criticality.

The bricolage is dedicated to a form of rigor that is conversant with numerous modes of meaning making and knowledge production—modes that originate in diverse social locations. These alternative modes of reasoning and researching always consider the relationships, the resonances, and the disjunctions between formal and rationalistic modes of Western epistemology and ontology and different cultural, philosophical, paradigmatic, and subjugated expressions. In these latter expressions, bricoleurs often uncover ways of accessing a concept without resorting to a conventional validated set of prespecified procedures that provide the distance of objectivity (Thayer-Bacon, 2003). This notion of distance fails to take into account the rigor of the hermeneutical understanding of the way meaning is preinscribed in the act of being in the world, the research process, and objects of research. This absence of hermeneutical awareness undermines the researcher's quest for a thick description and contributes to the production of reduced understandings of the complexity of social life (Jardine, 2006b; Selfe & Selfe, 1994).

The multiple perspectives delivered by the concept of difference provide bricoleurs with many benefits. Confrontation with difference helps us to see anew, to move toward the light of epiphany. A basic dimension of an evolving criticality involves a comfort with the existence of alternative ways of analyzing and producing knowledge. This is why it's so important for a historian, for example, to develop an understanding of phenomenology and hermeneutics. It is why it is so important for a social researcher from a metropolitan center to understand forms of indigenous knowledge, urban knowledge, and youth knowledge production (Darder, 2010; Dei, 2011; Grande, 2006; Hooley, 2009; Porfilio & Carr, 2010). The incongruities between such cultural modes of inquiry are quite valuable, for within the tensions of difference rest insights into multiple dimensions of the research act. Such insights move us to new levels of understanding of the subjects, purposes, and nature of inquiry (Gadamer, 1989; Mayers, 2001; Semali & Kincheloe, 1999; Watts, 2009a, 2009b; Willinsky, 2001; Kincheloe & Steinberg, 2008; Kincheloe & Berry, 2004).

Difference in the bricolage pushes us into the hermeneutic circle as we are induced to deal with parts in their diversity in relation to the whole. Difference may involve culture, class, language, discipline, epistemology, cosmology, ad infinitum. Bricoleurs use one dimension of these multiple diversities to explore others, to generate questions previously unimagined. As we examine these multiple perspectives, we attend to which ones are validated and which ones have been dismissed. Studying such differences, we begin to understand how dominant power operates to exclude and certify particular forms of knowledge production and why. In the criticality of the bricolage, this focus on power and difference always leads us to an awareness of the multiple dimensions of the social. Freire (1970) referred to this as the need for perceiving social structures and social systems that undermine equal access to resources and power. As bricoleurs answer such questions, we gain new appreciations of the way power tacitly shapes what we know and how we come to know it.

Ontologically Speaking

A central dimension of the bricolage that holds profound implications for critical research is the notion of a critical ontology (Kincheloe, 2003a). As bricoleurs prepare to explore that which is not readily apparent to the ethnographic eye, that realm of complexity in knowledge production that insists on initiating a conversation about what it is that qualitative researchers are observing and interpreting in the world, this clarification of a complex ontology is needed. This conversation is especially important because it has not generally taken place. Bricoleurs maintain that this object of inquiry is ontologically complex in that it cannot be described as an encapsulated entity. In this more open view, the object of inquiry is always a part of many contexts and processes; it is culturally inscribed and historically situated. The complex view of the object of inquiry accounts for the historical efforts to interpret its meaning in the world and how such efforts continue to define its social, cultural, political, psychological, and educational effects.

In the domain of the qualitative research process, for example, this ontological complexity undermines traditional notions of triangulation. Because of its in-process (processual) nature, interresearcher reliability becomes far more difficult to achieve. Process-sensitive scholars watch the world flow by like a river in which the exact contents of the water are never the same. Because all observers view an object of inquiry from their own vantage points in the web of reality, no portrait of a social phenomenon is ever exactly the same as another. Because all physical, social, cultural, psychological, and educational dynamics are connected in a larger fabric, researchers will produce different descriptions of an object of inquiry depending on what part of the fabric they have focused on—what part of the river they have seen. The more unaware observers are of this type of complexity, the more reductionistic the knowledge they produce about it. Bricoleurs attempt to understand this fabric and the processes that shape it in as thick a way as possible (Kincheloe & Berry, 2004).

The design and methods used to analyze this social fabric cannot be separated from the way reality is construed. Thus, ontology and epistemology are linked inextricably in ways that shape the task of the researcher. The bricoleur must understand these features in the pursuit of rigor. A deep interdisciplinarity is justified by an understanding of the complexity of the object of inquiry and the demands such complications place on the research act. As parts of complex systems and intricate processes, objects of inquiry are far too mercurial to be viewed by a single way of seeing or as a snapshot of a particular phenomenon at a specific moment in time.

A deep interdisciplinarity seeks to modify the disciplines and the view of research brought to the negotiating table constructed by the bricolage (Jardine, 1992). Everyone leaves the table informed by the dialogue in a way that idiosyncratically influences the research methods they subsequently employ. The point of the interaction is not standardized agreement as to some reductionistic notion of "the proper interdisciplinary research method" but awareness of the diverse tools in the researcher's toolbox. The form such deep interdisciplinarity may take is shaped by the object of inquiry in question. Thus, in the bricolage, the context in which research takes place always affects the nature of the deep interdisciplinarity employed. In the spirit of the dialectic of disciplinarity, the ways these context-driven articulations of interdisciplinarity are constructed must be examined in light of the power literacy previously mentioned (Friedman, 1998; Kincheloe & Berry, 2004; Lemke, 1998; Pryse, 1998; Quintero & Rummel, 2003).

In social research, the relationship between individuals and their contexts is a central dynamic to be investigated. This relationship is a key ontological and epistemological concern of the bricolage; it is a connection that shapes the identities of human beings and the nature of the complex social fabric. Bricoleurs use multiple methods to analyze the multidimensionality of this type of connection. The ways bricoleurs engage in this process of putting together the pieces of the relationship may provide a different interpretation of its meaning and effects. Recognizing the complex ontological importance of relationships alters the basic foundations of the research act and knowledge production process. Thin reductionistic descriptions of isolated things-inthemselves are no longer sufficient in critical research (Foster, 1997; Wright, 2003b).

The bricolage is dealing with a double ontology of complexity: first, the complexity of objects of inquiry and their being-inthe-world; second, the nature of the social construction of human subjectivity, the production of human "being." Such understandings open a new era of social research where the process of becoming human agents is appreciated with a new level of sophistication. The complex feedback loop between an unstable social structure and the individual can be charted in a way that grants human beings insight into the means by which power operates and the democratic process is subverted. In this complex ontological view, bricoleurs understand that social structures do not determine individual subjectivity but constrain it in remarkably intricate ways. The bricolage is acutely interested in developing and employing a variety of strategies to help specify these ways subjectivity is shaped.

The recognitions that emerge from such a multiperspectival process get analysts beyond the determinism of reductionistic notions of macrosocial structures. The intent of a usable social or educational research is subverted in this reductionistic context, as human agency is erased by the "laws" of society. Structures do not simply "exist" as objective entities whose influence can be predicted or "not exist" with no influence over the cosmos of human affairs. Here fractals enter the stage with their loosely structured characteristics of irregular shape—fractal structures. While not determining human behavior, for example, fractal structures possess sufficient order to affect other systems and entities within their environment. Such structures are never stable or universally present in some uniform manifestation (Slee, 2011; Varenne, 1996). The more we study such dynamics, the more diversity of expression we find. Taking this ontological and epistemological diversity into account, bricoleurs understand there are numerous dimensions to the bricolage (Denzin & Lincoln, 2000). As with all aspects of the bricolage, no description is fixed and final, and all features of the bricolage come with an elastic clause.

Employing a "Method" Within Bricolage: Ethnography as an Example

As critical researchers attempt to get behind the curtain, to move beyond assimilated experience, to expose the way ideology constrains the desire for self-direction, and to confront the way power reproduces itself in the construction of human consciousness, they employ a plethora of research methodologies (Hyslop-Margison, 2009). We are looking at the degree to which research moves those it studies to understand the world and the way it is shaped in order for them to transform it. Noncritical researchers who operate within an empiricist framework will perhaps find catalytic validity to be a strange concept. Research that possesses catalytic validity displays the reality-altering impact of the inquiry process and directs this impact so that those under study will gain self-understanding and self-direction.

Theory that falls under the rubric of postcolonialism (see McLaren, 1999; Semali & Kincheloe, 1999; Wright 2003a, 2003b) involves important debates over the knowing subject and object of analysis. Such works have initiated important new modes of analysis, especially in relation to questions of imperialism, colonialism, and neocolonialism. Recent attempts by critical researchers to move beyond the objectifying and imperialist gaze associated with the Western anthropological tradition (which fixes the image of the so-called informant from the colonizing perspective of the knowing subject), although laudatory and well-intentioned, are not without their shortcomings (Bourdieu & Wacquaat, 1992). As Fuchs (1993) has so presciently observed, serious limitations plague recent efforts to develop a more reflective approach to ethnographic writing. The challenge here can be summarized in the following questions: How does the knowing subject come to know the Other? How can researchers respect the perspective of the Other and invite the Other to speak (Ashcroft, Griffiths, & Tiffin, 1995; Brock-Utne, 1996; Goldie, 1995; Gresson, 2006; Macedo, 2006; Myrsiades & Myrsiades, 1998; Pieterse & Parekh, 1995; Prakash & Esteva, 2008; Scheurich & Young, 1997; Semali & Kincheloe, 1999; Steinberg, 2009; Viergever, 1999)?

Although recent confessional modes of ethnographic writing, for example, attempt to treat so-called informants as "participants" in an attempt to avoid the objectification of the Other (usually referring to the relationship between Western anthropologists and non-Western culture), there is a risk that uncovering colonial and postcolonial structures of domination may, in fact, unintentionally validate and consolidate such structures as well as reassert liberal values through a type of covert ethnocentrism. Fuchs (1993) warns that the attempt to subject researchers to the same approach to which other societies are subjected could lead to an "'othering' of one's own world" (p. 108). Such an attempt often fails to question existing ethnographic methodologies and therefore unwittingly extends their validity and applicability while further objectifying the world of the researcher. Foucault's approach to this dilemma is to "detach" social theory from the epistemology of his own culture by criticizing the traditional philosophy of reflection. However, Foucault falls into the trap of ontologizing his own methodological argumentation and erasing the notion of prior understanding that is linked to the idea of an "inside" view (Fuchs, 1993). Louis Dumont fares somewhat better by arguing that cultural texts need to be viewed simultaneously from the inside and from the outside.

However, in trying to affirm a "reciprocal interpretation of various societies among themselves" (Fuchs, 1993, p. 113) through identifying both transindividual structures of consciousness and trans-subjective social structures, Dumont aspires to a universal framework for the comparative analysis of societies. Whereas Foucault and Dumont attempt to "transcend the categorical foundations of their own world" (Fuchs, 1993, p. 118) by refusing to include themselves in the process of objectification, Pierre Bourdieu integrates himself as a social actor into the social field under analysis. Bourdieu achieves such integration by "epistemologizing the ethnological content of his own presuppositions" (Fuchs, 1993, p. 121). But the self-objectification of the observer (anthropologist) is not unproblematic. Fuchs (1993) notes, after Bourdieu, that the chief difficulty is "forgetting the difference between the theoretical and the practical relationship with the world and … imposing on the object the theoretical relationship one maintains with it" (p. 120). Bourdieu's approach to research does not fully escape becoming, to a certain extent, a "confirmation of objectivism," but at least there is an earnest attempt by the researcher to reflect on the preconditions of his or her own self-understanding—an attempt to engage in an "ethnography of ethnographers" (p. 122). As an example, critical ethnography, in a bricolage context, often intersects—to varying degrees—with the concerns of postcolonialist researchers, but the degree to which it fully addresses issues of exploitation and the social relations of capitalist exploitation remains questionable. Critical ethnography shares the conviction articulated by Marc Manganaro (1990):

> No anthropology is apolitical, removed from ideology and hence from the capacity to be affected by or, as crucially, to effect social formations. The question ought not to be if an anthropological text is political, but rather, what kind of sociopolitical affiliations are tied to particular anthropological texts. (p. 35)

This critical ethnographic writing faces the challenge of moving beyond simply the reanimation of local experience, an uncritical celebration of cultural difference (including figural differentiations within the ethnographer's own culture), and the employment of a framework that espouses universal values and a global role for interpretivist anthropology (Silverman, 1990). Criticalism can help qualitative researchers challenge dominant Western research practices that are underwritten by a foundational epistemology and a claim to universally valid knowledge at the expense of local, subjugated knowledges (Peters, 1993). The issue is to challenge the presuppositions that inform the normalizing judgments one makes as a researcher.

Although critical ethnography (Hickey & Austin, 2009) allows, in a way conventional ethnography does not, for the relationship of liberation and history, and although its hermeneutic task is to call into question the social and cultural conditioning of human activity and the prevailing sociopolitical structures, we do not claim that this is enough to restructure the social system. But it is certainly, in our view, a necessary beginning (Trueba & McLaren, 2000). Clough (1998) argues that "realist narrativity has allowed empirical social science to be the platform and horizon of social criticism" (p. 135). Ethnography needs to be analyzed critically not only in terms of its field methods but also as reading and writing practices. Data collection must give way to "rereadings of representations in every form" (p. 137). In the narrative construction of its authority as empirical science, ethnography needs to face the unconscious processes on which it justifies its canonical formulations, processes that often involve the disavowal of oedipal or authorial desire and the reduction of differences to binary oppositions. Within these processes of binary reduction, the male ethnographer is most often privileged as the guardian of "the factual representation of empirical positivities" (Clough, 1998).

Critical research traditions have arrived at the point where they recognize that claims to truth are always discursively situated and implicated in relations of power. We do not suggest that because we cannot know truth absolutely, truth can simply be equated with an effect of power. We say this because truth involves regulative rules that must be met for some statements to be more meaningful than others. Otherwise, truth becomes meaningless and, if that is the case, liberatory praxis has no purpose other than to win for the sake of winning. As Phil Carspecken (1993, 1999) remarks, every time we act, in every instance of our behavior, we presuppose some normative or universal relation to truth. Truth is internally related to meaning in a pragmatic way through normative referenced claims, intersubjective referenced claims, subjective referenced claims, and the way we deictically ground or anchor meaning in our daily lives. Carspecken explains that researchers are able to articulate the normative evaluative claims of others when they begin to see them in the same way as their participants by living inside the cultural and discursive positionalities that inform such claims.

While a researcher can use, as in this example, critical ethnography (Willis, 1977, 2000) as a focus within a project, she or he, as a bricoleur (Steinberg, 2011) employs the additional use of narrative (Janesick, 2010; Park, 2005), hermeneutic interpretation (Jardine, 2006a), phenomenological reading (Kincheloe, 2008b), content analysis (Steinberg, 2008), historiography (Kincheloe, 2008b), autoethnography (Kress, 2010), social media analysis (Cucinelli, 2010; Kress, 2008; Kress & Silva, 2009), anthropology (Marcus & Fischer, 1986), quantitative analysis (Hyslop-Margison & Naseem, 2007), and so on; and the bricoleur creates a polysemic read and multiple ways of both approaching and using research. The bricolage, with its multiple lenses allows necessary fluidity and goes beyond a traditional triangulated approach for verification. The lenses expand the research and prevent a normalized methodology from creating a scientistic approach to the research. Bricolage becomes a failsafe way in which to ensure that the multiple reads create new dialogues and discourse and open possibilities. It also precludes the notion of using research as authority.

Clearly, no research methodology or tradition can be done in isolation; the employment of the bricolage transcends unilateral commitments to a singular type of research. In the face of a wide variety of different knowledges and ways of seeing the universe, human beings' confidence in what they think they know collapses. In a counter colonial move, bricoleurs raise questions about any knowledges and ways of knowing that claim universal status. In this context, bricoleurs make use of this suspicion of universalism in combination with global knowledges to understand how they have been positioned in the world. Almost all of us from Western backgrounds or nonWestern colonized backgrounds have been implicated in some way in the web of universalism (Scatamburlo D'Annibale & McLaren, 2009). The inevitable conflicts that arise from this implication do not have to be resolved immediately by bricoleurs. At the base of these conflicts rests the future of global culture as well as the future of multicultural research and pedagogy. Recognizing that these are generative issues that engage us in a productive process of analyzing self and world is in itself a powerful recognition. The value of both this recognition and the process of working through the complicated conceptual problems are treasured by bricoleurs. Indeed, bricoleurs avoid any notion of finality in the resolution of such dilemmas. Comfortable with the ambiguity, bricoleurs as critical researchers work to alleviate human suffering and injustice even though they possess no final blueprint alerting them as to how oppression takes place (Kincheloe & Berry, 2004; Steinberg, 2011).

Toward a Critical Research

Within the context of multiple critical theories and multiple critical pedagogies, a critical research bricolage serves to create an equitable research field and disallows a proclamation to correctness, validity, truth, and the tacit axis of Western power through traditional research. Employing a rigorous and tentative context with the notions presented through Marxist examinations of power, critical theory's location and indictment of power blocs vis-à-vis traditional noncritical research methodologies, a critical pedagogical notion of emancipatory research can be located within a research bricolage (Fiske, 1993; Roth & Tobin, 2010). Without proclaiming a canonical and singular method, the critical bricolage allows the researcher to become participant and the participant to become researcher. By eschewing positivist approaches to both qualitative and quantitative research (Cannella & Steinberg, 2011; Kincheloe & Tobin, 2009) and refusing to cocoon research within the pod of unimethodological approaches, we believe critical theory and critical pedagogy continues to challenge regularly employed and obsessive approaches to research.

References

Agger, B. (1992). *The discourse of domination: From the Frankfurt School to postmodernism.* Evanston, IL: Northwestern University Press.

Agger, B. (1998). *Critical social theories: An introduction.* Boulder, CO: Westview.

Ashcroft, B., Griffiths, G., & Tiffin, H. (Eds.). (1995). *The post-colonial studies reader.* New York: Routledge.

Au, W. (2007). Epistemology of the oppressed: The dialectics of Paulo Freire's theory of knowledge. *Journal for Critical Education Policy Studies, 5*(2). Available at http://www.jceps.com/index.php?pageI D=article&articleID=100

Austin, J., & Hickey, A. (2008). Critical pedagogical practice through cultural studies. *International Journal of the Humanities, 6*(1), 133–140. Available at http://eprints.usq.edu.au/4490/

Bourdieu, P., & Wacquaat, L. (1992). *An invitation to reflexive sociology.* Chicago: University of Chicago Press.

Bresler, L., & Ardichvili, A. (Eds.). (2002). *Research in international education: Experience, theory, and practice.* New York: Peter Lang.

Britzman, D. (1991). *Practice makes practice: A critical study of learning to teach.* Albany: SUNY Press.

Brock-Utne, B. (1996). Reliability and validity in qualitative research within Africa. *International Review of Education, 42,* 605–621.

Cannella, G., & Steinberg, S. (2011). *Critical qualitative research: A reader.* New York: Peter Lang.

Carspecken, P. F. (1993). *Power, truth, and method: Outline for a critical methodology.* Unpublished manuscript, Indiana University.

Carspecken, P. F. (1999). *Four scenes for posing the question of meaning and other essays in critical philosophy and critical methodology.* New York: Peter Lang.

Chapman, D. E. (Ed.). (2010). *Examining social theory: Crossing borders/ reflecting back.* New York: Peter Lang.

Clough, P. T. (1998). *The end(s) of ethnography: From realism to social criticism* (2nd ed.). New York: Peter Lang.

Collins, J. (1995). *Architectures of excess: Cultural life in the information age.* New York: Routledge.

Cucinelli, G. (2010). *Digital youth praxis and social justice.* Unpublished doctoral dissertation, McGill University, Montréal, Québec, Canada.

Dale, J., & Hyslop-Margison, E. J. (2010). *Paulo Freire: Teaching for freedom and transformation.* Dordrecht, the Netherlands: Springer.

Darder, A. (2010). Schooling bodies: Critical pedagogy and urban youth [Foreword]. In Steinberg, S. R. (Ed.), *19 urban questions: Teaching in the city* (pp. xiii–xxiii). New York: Peter Lang.

Dei, G. (Ed.). (2011). *Indigenous philosophies and critical education.* New York: Peter Lang.

De Lissovoy, N., & McLaren, P. (2003). Educational "accountability" and the violence of capital: A Marxian reading. *Journal of Education Policy, 18,* 131–143.

Denzin, N. K. (1994). The art and politics of interpretation. In N. K. Denzin & Y. S. Lincoln (Eds.), *Handbook of qualitative research.* Thousand Oaks, CA: Sage.

Denzin, N. K. (2003*). Performative ethnography: Critical pedagogy and the politics of culture.* Thousand Oaks, CA: Sage.

Denzin, N. K., & Lincoln, Y. S. (2000). Introduction: The discipline and practice of qualitative research. In N. K. Denzin & Y. S. Lincoln (Eds.), *Handbook of qualitative research* (2nd ed.). Thousand Oaks, CA: Sage.

DeVault, M. (1996). Talking back to sociology: Distinctive contributions of feminist methodology. *Annual Review of Sociology, 22,* 29–50.

Fiske, J. (1993). *Power works, power plays.* New York: Verso. Flecha, R., Gomez, J., & Puigvert, L. (Eds.). (2003). *Contemporary sociological theory.* New York: Peter Lang.

Flossner, G., & Otto, H. (Eds.). (1998). *Towards more democracy in social services: Models of culture and welfare.* New York: Aldine.

Foster, R. (1997). Addressing epistemologic and practical issues in multimethod research: A procedure for conceptual triangulation. *Advances in Nursing Education, 20*(2), 1–12.

Freire, A. M. A. (2000). Foreword. In P. McLaren, *Che Guevara, Paulo Freire, and the pedagogy of revolution.* Lanham, MD: Rowman & Littlefield.

Freire, P. (1970). *Pedagogy of the oppressed.* New York: Herder and Herder.

Freire, P. (1972). *Research methods.* Paper presented at a seminar on Studies in Adult Education, Dar es Salaam, Tanzania.

Freire, P. (1978). *Education for critical consciousness.* New York: Seabury.

Freire, P. (1985). *The politics of education: Culture, power, and liberation.* South Hadley, MA: Bergin & Garvey.

Freire, P., & Faundez, A. (1989). *Learning to question: A pedagogy of liberation.* London: Continuum.

Friedman, S. (1998). (Inter)disciplinarity and the question of the women's studies Ph.D. *Feminist Studies, 24*(2), 301–326.

Fuchs, M. (1993). The reversal of the ethnological perspective: Attempts at objectifying one's own cultural horizon: Dumont, Foucault, Bourdieu? *Thesis Eleven, 34*(1), 104–125.

Gadamer, H.-G. (1989). *Truth and method* (2nd rev. ed., J. Weinsheimer & D. G. Marshall, Eds. & Trans.). New York: Crossroad.

Giroux, H. (1983). *Theory and resistance in education: A pedagogy for the opposition.* South Hadley, MA: Bergin & Garvey.

Giroux, H. (1988). Critical theory and the politics of culture and voice: Rethinking the discourse of educational research. In R. Sherman & R. Webb (Eds.), *Qualitative research in education: Focus and methods.* New York: Falmer.

Giroux, H. (1997). *Pedagogy and the politics of hope: Theory, culture, and schooling.* Boulder, CO: Westview.

Giroux, H. (2010). *Zombie politics and the age of casino capitalism.* New York: Peter Lang.

Goldie, T. (1995). The representation of the indigenous. In B. Ashcroft, G. Griffiths, & H. Tiffin (Eds.), *The post-colonial studies reader.* New York: Routledge.

Grande, S. (2004). *Red pedagogy: Native American social and political thought.* Lanham, MD: Rowman & Littlefield.

Gresson, A. D., III. (2006). Doing critical research in mainstream disciplines: Reflections on a study of Black female individuation. In K. Tobin & J. Kincheloe (Eds.), *Doing educational research.* Rotterdam, the Netherlands: Sense Publishers.

Grinberg, J. (2003). "Only the facts?" In D. Weil & J. L. Kincheloe (Eds.), *Critical thinking: An encyclopedia.* Westport, CT: Greenwood.

Hammer, R., & Kellner, D. (2009). *Media/cultural studies: Critical approaches.* New York: Peter Lang.

Harper, D. (1987). *Working knowledge: Skill and community in a small shop.* Chicago: University of Chicago Press.

Hickey, A., & Austin, J. (2009). Working visually in community identity ethnography. *International Journal of the Humanities, 7*(4), 1–14. Available at http://eprints.usq.edu.au/5800/

Hinchey, P. (2009). *Finding freedom in the classroom: A practical introduction to critical theory.* New York: Peter Lang.

Hooley, N. (2009). *Narrative life: Democratic curriculum and indigenous learning.* Dordrecht, the Netherlands: Springer.

Horkheimer, M. (1972). *Critical theory.* New York: Seabury.

Horn, R. (2004). *Standards.* New York: Peter Lang.

Horton, M., & Freire, P. (1990). *We make the road by walking: Conversations on education and social change.* Philadelphia: Temple University Press.

Hyslop-Margison, E. J. (2009). Scientific paradigms and falsification: Kuhn, Popper and problems in education research. *Educational Policy, 20*(10), 1–17.

Hyslop-Margison, E. J., & Naseem, A. (2007). *Scientism and education: Empirical research as neo-liberal ideology.* Dordrecht, the Netherlands: Springer.

Janesick, V. (2010). *Oral history for the qualitative researcher: Choreographing the story.* New York: Guilford.

Jardine, D. (1992). The fecundity of the individual case: Considerations of the pedagogic heart of interpretive work. *British Journal of Philosophy of Education. 26*(1), 51–61.

Jardine, D. (1998). *To dwell with a boundless heart: Essays in curriculum theory, hermeneutics, and the ecological imagination.* New York: Peter Lang.

Jardine, D. (2006a). On hermeneutics: "What happens to us over and above our wanting and doing." In K. Tobin & J. L. Kincheloe (Eds.), *Doing educational research* (pp. 269–288). Rotterdam, the Netherlands: Sense Publishers.

Jardine, D. (2006b). *Piaget and education.* New York: Peter Lang.

Keesing-Styles, L. (2003). The relationship between critical pedagogy and assessment in teacher education. *Radical Pedagogy, 5*(1). Available at http://radicalpedagogy.icaap.org/content/issue5_1/03_ keesing-styles.html

Kellner, D. (1995). *Media culture: Cultural studies, identity, and politics between the modern and the postmodern.* New York: Routledge.

Kincheloe, J. L. (1998). Critical research in science education. In B. Fraser & K. Tobin (Eds.), *International handbook of science education* (Pt. 2). Boston: Kluwer.

Kincheloe, J. L. (2001a). Describing the bricolage: Conceptualizing a new rigour in qualitative research. *Qualitative Inquiry, 7*(6), 679–692.

Kincheloe, J. (2001b). *Getting beyond the facts: Teaching social studies/ social sciences in the twenty-first century* (2nd ed.). New York: Peter Lang.

Kincheloe, J. (2003a). Critical ontology: Visions of selfhood and curriculum. *JCT: Journal of Curriculum Theorizing, 19*(1), 47–64.

Kincheloe, J. L. (2003b). Into the great wide open: Introducing critical thinking. In D. Weil & J. Kincheloe (Eds.), *Critical thinking: An encyclopedia.* Santa Barbara, CA: ABC-CLIO.

Kincheloe, J. L. (2003c). *Teachers as researchers: Qualitative paths to empowerment* (2nd ed.). London: Falmer.

Kincheloe, J. L. (2004). Iran and American miseducation: Coverups, distortions, and omissions. In J. Kincheloe & S. Steinberg (Eds.), *The miseducation of the West: Constructing Islam.* Westport, CT: Greenwood.

Kincheloe, J. L. (2007). *Teachers as researchers: Qualitative paths to empowerment.* London: Falmer.

Kincheloe, J. L. (2008a). *Critical pedagogy primer* (2nd ed.). New York: Peter Lang.

Kincheloe, J. L. (2008b). *Knowledge and critical pedagogy.* Dordrecht, the Netherlands: Springer.

Kincheloe, J. L., & Berry, K. (2004). *Rigour and complexity in educational research: Conceptualizing the bricolage.* London: Open University Press.

Kincheloe, J. L., & Steinberg, S. R. (1993). A tentative description of post-formal thinking: The critical confrontation with cognitive theory. *Harvard Educational Review, 63,* 296–320.

Kincheloe, J. L., & Steinberg, S. R. (1997). *Changing multiculturalism: New times, new curriculum.* London: Open University Press.

Kincheloe, J. L., & Steinberg, S. R. (2008). Indigenous knowledges in education: Complexities, dangers, and profound benefits. In N. K. Denzin, Y. S. Lincoln, & L. T. Smith, (Eds.), *Handbook of critical and indigenous methodologies.* Thousand Oaks, CA: Sage Publishing.

Kincheloe, J. L., Steinberg, S. R., & Hinchey, P. (Eds.). (1999). *The postformal reader: Cognition and education.* New York: Falmer.

Kincheloe, J. L., & Tobin, K. (2009). The much exaggerated death of positivism. *Cultural Studies of Science Education, 4,* 513–528. Kirylo, J. (2011). *Paulo Freire: The man from Recife.* New York: Peter Lang.

Kress, T. (2010). Tilting the machine: A critique of one teacher's attempts at using art forms to create postformal, democratic learning environments. *The Journal of Educational Controversy, 5*(1).

Kress, T. (2011). Singing a different tune: An auto/ethnographic journey into and out of the land of educational technology. In K. Tobin & A. Shady (Eds.), *Transforming urban education: Collaborating to produce success in science, mathematics and technology education.* Rotterdam, the Netherlands: Sense Publishers.

Kress, T., & Silva, K. (2009). Using digital video for professional development and leadership: Understanding and initiating teacher learning communities. In I. Gibson et al. (Eds.), *Proceedings of Society for Information Technology & Teacher Education International Conference 2009* (pp. 2841–2847). Chesapeake, VA: Association for the Advancement of Computing in Education (AACE).

Leistyna, P., Woodrum, A., & Sherblom, S. (1996). *Breaking free: The transformative power of critical pedagogy.* Cambridge, MA: Harvard Educational Review.

Lemke, J. L. (1998). Analyzing verbal data: Principles, methods, and problems. In B. Fraser & K. Tobin (Eds.), *International handbook of science education* (Pt. 2). Boston: Kluwer.

Lévi-Strauss, C. (1968). *The savage mind.* Chicago: University of Chicago Press.

Lincoln, Y. (2001). An emerging new bricoleur: Promises and possibilities—a reaction to Joe Kincheloe's "Describing the bricoleur." *Qualitative Inquiry, 7*(6), 693–696.

Lund, D., & Carr, P. (Eds.). (2008). *Doing democracy: Striving for political literacy and social justice.* New York: Peter Lang.

Lutz, K., Jones, K. D., & Kendall, J. (1997). Expanding the praxis debate: Contributions to clinical inquiry. *Advances in Nursing Science, 20*(2), 23–31.

Macedo, D. (2006). *Literacies of power: What Americans are not allowed to know* (2nd ed.). Boulder, CO: Westview.

Macrine, S., Hill, D., & McLaren, P. (Eds.). (2009). *Critical pedagogy: Theory and praxis.* London: Routledge.

Macrine, S., McLaren, P., & Hill, D. (Eds.). (2009). *Revolutionizing pedagogy: Educating for social justice within and beyond global neo-liberalism.* London: Palgrave Macmillan.

Manganaro, M. (1990). Textual play, power, and cultural critique: An orientation to modernist anthropology. In M. Manganaro (Ed.), *Modernist anthropology: From fieldwork to text.* Princeton, NJ: Princeton University Press.

Marcus, G. E., & Fischer, M. M. J. (1986). *Anthropology as cultural critique: An experimental moment in the human sciences.* Chicago: University of Chicago Press.

Mayo, P. (2009). *Liberating praxis: Paulo Freire's legacy for radical education and politics.* Rotterdam, the Netherlands: Sense Publishing.

McLaren, P. (1992). Collisions with otherness: "Traveling" theory, postcolonial criticism, and the politics of ethnographic practice—the mission of the wounded ethnographer. *International Journal of Qualitative Studies in Education, 5,* 77–92.

McLaren, P. (1997). *Revolutionary multiculturalism: Pedagogies of dissent for the new millennium.* New York: Routledge. McLaren, P. (1999). *Schooling as a ritual performance: Toward a political economy of educational symbols and gestures* (3rd ed.). Boulder, CO: Rowman & Littlefield.

McLaren, P. (2001). Bricklayers and bricoleurs: A Marxist addendum. *Qualitative Inquiry, 7*(6), 700–705.

McLaren, P. (2002). Marxist revolutionary praxis: A curriculum of transgression. *Journal of Curriculum Inquiry Into Curriculum and Instruction, 3*(3), 36–41.

McLaren, P. (2003a). Critical pedagogy in the age of neoliberal globalization: Notes from history's underside. *Democracy and Nature, 9*(1), 65–90.

McLaren, P. (2003b). The dialectics of terrorism: A Marxist response to September 11: Part Two. Unveiling the past, evading the present. *Cultural Studies/Critical Methodologies, 3*(1), 103–132.

McLaren, P. (2009). E. San Juan, Jr.: The return of the transformative intellectual. *Left Curve, 33,* 118–121.

McLaren, P., & Farahmandpur, R. (2003). Critical pedagogy at ground zero: Renewing the educational left after 9–11. In D. Gabbard & K. Saltman (Eds.), *Education as enforcement: The militarization and corporatization of schools.* New York: Routledge.

McLaren, P., & Farahmandpur, R. (2006). Who will educate the educators? Critical pedagogy in the age of globalization. In A. Dirlik (Ed.), *Pedagogies of the global: Knowledge in the human interest* (pp. 19–58). Boulder, CO: Paradigm.

McLaren, P., & Jaramillo, N. (2010). Not neo-Marxist, not post-Marxist, not Marxian, not autonomist Marxism: Reflections on a revolutionary (Marxist) critical pedagogy. *Cultural Studies <=> Critical Methodologies, 10*(3), 251–262.

McLaren, P., & Kincheloe, J. L. (2007). *Critical pedagogy: Where are we now?* New York: Peter Lang.

McLeod, J. (2000, June). *Qualitative research as bricolage.* Paper presented at the annual conference of the Society for Psychotherapy Research, Chicago.

Myrsiades, K., & Myrsiades, L. (Eds.). (1998). *Race-ing representation: Voice, history, and sexuality.* Lanham, MD: Rowman & Littlefield.

Nocella, A. J., II, Best, S., & McLaren, P. (2010). *Academic repression: Reflections from the academic industrial complex.* Oakland, CA: AK Press.

Park, J. (2005). *Writing at the edge: Narrative and writing process theory.* New York: Peter Lang.

Peters, M. (1993). *Against Finkielkraut's la défaite de la pensés culture, post-modernism and education.* Unpublished manuscript, University of Glasgow, Scotland.

Pieterse, J., & Parekh, B. (1995). Shifting imaginaries: Decolonization, internal decolonization, postcoloniality. In J. Pieterse & B. Parekh (Eds.), *The decolonization of imagination: Culture, knowledge, and power.* Atlantic Highlands, NJ: Zed.

Porfilio, B., & Carr, P. (Eds.). (2010). *Youth culture, education, and resistance: Subverting the commercial ordering of life.* Rotterdam, the Netherlands: Sense Publishing.

Prakash, M., & Esteva, G. (2008). *Escaping education: Living as learning within grassroots cultures.* New York: Peter Lang.

Pryse, M. (1998). Critical interdisciplinarity, women's studies, and cross-cultural insight. *National Women's Studies Association Journal, 10*(1), 1–11.

Quail, C. B., Razzano, K. A., & Skalli, L. H. (2004). *Tell me more: Rethinking daytime talk shows.* New York: Peter Lang.

Quantz, R. A. (1992). On critical ethnography (with some postmodern considerations). In M. D. LeCompte, W. L. Millroy, & J. Preissle (Eds.), *The handbook of qualitative research in education.* New York: Academic Press.

Quintero, E., & Rummel, M. K. (2003). *Becoming a teacher in the new society: Bringing communities and classrooms together.* New York: Peter Lang.

Rodriguez, N. M., & Villaverde, L. (2000). *Dismantling White privilege.* New York: Peter Lang.

Roman, L., & Eyre, L. (Eds.). (1997). *Dangerous territories: Struggles for difference and equality in education.* New York: Routledge.

Roth, W.-M., & Tobin, K. (2010). Solidarity and conflict: Prosody as a transactional resource in intraand intercultural communication involving power differences. *Cultural Studies of Science Education, 5*(4), 807–847.

Ryoo, J. J., & McLaren, P. (2010). Aloha for sale: A class analysis of Hawaii. In D. E. Chapman (Ed.), *Examining social theory: Crossing borders/reflecting back* (pp. 3–18). New York: Peter Lang.

San Juan, E., Jr. (1992). *Articulations of power in ethnic and racial studies in the United States.* Atlantic Highlands, NJ: Humanities Press.

Scatamburlo-D'Annibale, V., & McLaren, P. (2009). The reign of capital: A pedagogy and praxis of class struggle. In M. Apple, W. Au, & L. Armando Gandin (Eds.), *The Routledge international handbook of critical education* (pp. 96–109). New York and London: Routledge.

Scheurich, J. J., & Young, M. (1997). Coloring epistemologies: Are our research epistemologies racially biased? *Educational Researcher, 26*(4), 4–16.

Selfe, C. L., & Selfe, R. J., Jr. (1994). The politics of the interface: Power and its exercise in electronic contact zones. *College Composition and Communication, 45*(4), 480–504.

Semali, L., & Kincheloe, J. L. (1999). *What is indigenous knowledge? Voices from the academy.* New York: Falmer.

Shor, I. (1996). *When students have power: Negotiating authority in a critical pedagogy.* Chicago: University of Chicago Press.

Sikes, P. (2008). Researching research cultures: The case of new universities. In P. Sikes & A. Potts (Eds.), *Researching education from the inside: Investigations from within.* Abingdon, UK: Routledge.

Silverman, E. K. (1990). Clifford Geertz: Towards a more "thick" understanding? In C. Tilley (Ed.), *Reading material culture.* Cambridge, MA: Blackwell.

Siry C. A., & Lang, D. E. (2010). Creating participatory discourse for teaching and research in early childhood science. *Journal of Science Teacher Education, 21,* 149–160.

Skalli, L. (2004). Loving Muslim women with a vengeance: The West, women, and fundamentalism. In J. L. Kincheloe & S. R. Steinberg (Eds.), *The miseducation of the West: Constructing Islam.* Westport, CT: Greenwood.

Slee, R. (2011). *The irregular school: Schooling and inclusive education.* London: Routledge. Soto, L. (Ed.). (2000). *The politics of early childhood education.* New York: Peter Lang.

Souto-Manning, M. (2009). *Freire, teaching, and learning: Culture circles across contexts.* New York: Peter Lang.

Steinberg, S. R. (2000). The nature of genius. In J. L. Kincheloe, S. R. Steinberg, & D. J. Tippins (Eds.), *The stigma of genius: Einstein, consciousness, and education.* New York: Peter Lang.

Steinberg, S. R. (Ed.). (2001). *Multi/intercultural conversations.* New York: Peter Lang.

Steinberg, S. R. (2004a). Desert minstrels: Hollywood's curriculum of Arabs and Muslims. In J. L. Kincheloe & S. R. Steinberg (Eds.), *The miseducation of the West: Constructing Islam.* Westport, CT: Greenwood.

Steinberg, S. R. (2004b). Kinderculture: The cultural studies of childhood. In N. Denzin (Ed.), *Cultural studies: A research volume.* Greenwich, CT: JAI.

Steinberg, S. R. (2007). Cutting class in a dangerous era: A critical pedagogy of class awareness. In J. Kincheloe & S. Steinberg (Eds.), *Cutting class: Socioeconomic status and education.* Lanham, MD: Rowman & Littlefield.

Steinberg, S. R. (2008). Reading media critically. In D. Macedo & S. Steinberg (Eds.), *Media literacy: A reader.* New York: Peter Lang.

Steinberg, S. R. (2009). *Diversity and multiculturalism: A reader.* New York: Peter Lang.

Steinberg, S. R. (2010). Power, emancipation, and complexity: Employing critical theory. *Journal of Power and Education, 2*(2), 140–151.

Steinberg, S. R. (2011). Critical cultural studies research: Bricolage in action. In K. Tobin & J. Kincheloe (Eds.), *Doing educational research* (2nd ed.). Rotterdam, the Netherlands: Sense Publishing.

Steinberg, S. R. (in press). *The Bricolage.* New York: Peter Lang.

Steinberg, S. R., & Kincheloe, J. L. (Eds.). (1998). *Students as researchers: Creating classrooms that matter.* London: Taylor & Francis.

Steinberg, S. R., & Kincheloe, J. L. (2011). Employing the bricolage as critical research in science education. In B. J. Fraser, K. Tobin, & C. J. McRobbie (Eds.), *The international handbook of research in science education* (2nd ed.). Dordrecht, the Netherlands: Springer.

Thayer-Bacon, B. (2003). *Relational "(e)pistemologies."* New York: Peter Lang.

Tobin, K. (2009). Repetition, difference and rising up with research in education. In K. Ercikan & W.-M. Roth (Eds.), *Generalizing from educational research* (pp. 149–172). New York: Routledge.

Tobin, K. (2010). Global reproduction and transformation of science education. *Cultural Studies of Science Education, 5.*

Tobin, K., & Llena, R. (2010). Producing and maintaining culturally adaptive teaching and learning of science in urban schools. In C. Murphy & K. Scantlebury (Eds.), *Coteaching in international contexts: Research and practice* (pp. 79–104). Dordrecht, the Netherlands: Springer.

Trueba, E. T., & McLaren, P. (2000). Critical ethnography for the study of immigrants. In E. T. Trueba & L. I. Bartolomé (Eds.), *Immigrant voices: In search of educational equity.* Lanham, MD: Rowman & Littlefield.

Varenne, H. (with McDermott, R. P.). (1996). Culture, development, disability. In R. Jessor, A. Colby, & R. Shweder (Eds.), *Ethnography and human development.* Chicago: University of Chicago Press.

Vicars, M. (2008). Is it all about me? How Queer! In P. Sikes & A. Potts (Eds.), *Researching education from the inside: Investigations from within.* Abingdon, UK: Routledge.

Viergever, M. (1999). Indigenous knowledge: An interpretation of views from indigenous peoples. In L. Semali & J. L. Kincheloe (Eds.), *What is indigenous knowledge? Voices from the academy.* Bristol, PA: Falmer.

Villaverde, L. (2007). *Feminist theories and education primer.* New York: Peter Lang.

Villaverde, L., & Kincheloe, J. L. (1998). Engaging students as researchers: Researching and teaching Thanksgiving in the elementary classroom. In S. R. Steinberg & J. L. Kincheloe (Eds.), *Students as researchers: Creating classrooms that matter.* London: Falmer.

Watts, M. (2006). Disproportionate sacrifices: Ricoeur's theories of justice and the widening participation agenda for higher education in the UK. *Journal of Philosophy of Education, 40*(3), 301–312.

Watts, M. (2008). Narrative research, narrative capital, narrative capability. In J. Satterthwaite, M. Watts, & H. Piper (Eds.), *Talking truth, confronting power: Discourse, power, resistance* (Vol. 6). Stoke on Trent, UK: Trentham Books.

Watts, M. (2009a). Higher education and hyperreality. In P. Smeyers & M. Depaepe (Eds.), *Educational research: Educationalisation of social problems.* Dordrecht, the Netherlands: Springer.

Watts, M. (2009b). Sen and the art of motorcycle maintenance: Adaptive preferences and higher education in England. *Studies in Philosophy and Education, 28*(5), 425–436.

Weil, D., & Kincheloe, J. (Eds.). (2004). *Critical thinking and learning: An encyclopedia for parents and teachers.* Westport, CT: Greenwood.

Wesson, L., & Weaver, J. (2001). Administration-educational standards: Using the lens of postmodern thinking to examine the role of the school administrator. In J. Kincheloe & D. Weil (Eds.), *Standards and schooling in the United States: An encyclopedia* (3 vols.). Santa Barbara, CA: ABC-CLIO.

Wexler, P. (2008). *Social theory in education.* New York: Peter Lang. Willinsky, J. (2001). Raising the standards for democratic education: Research and evaluation as public knowledge. In J. Kincheloe & D. Weil (Eds.), *Standards and schooling in the United States: An encyclopedia* (3 vols.). Santa Barbara, CA: ABC-CLIO.

Willis, P. E. (1977). *Learning to labour: How working class kids get working class jobs.* Farnborough, UK: Saxon House.

Willis, P. (2000). *The ethnographic imagination.* Cambridge, UK: Polity.

Wright, H. K. (2003a). An introduction to the history, methods, politics and selected traditions of qualitative research in education [Editorial]. *Tennessee Education, 32*(2), 5–7.

Wright, H. K. (Ed.). (2003b). Qualitative research in education. *Tennessee Education, 32*(2).

Wright, H. K., & Lather, P. (Eds.). (2006). Paradigm proliferation in educational research. *International Journal of Qualitative Studies in Education, 19*(1).

Zizek, S. (1990). Beyond discourse analysis. In E. Laclau, (Ed.), *New reflections on the revolution of our time.* London: Verso.

CHAPTER THREE

The Conceptual Context of Knowledge

Donald Easton-Brooks

The goal of research is to explore questions or hypotheses in order to gain a clearer understanding of a situation or a relationship between variables. In essence, the goal of research is to gain knowledge. In the hard sciences (e.g., biology, chemistry, physics) this epistemology is a simpler construct. In these fields, there are concrete disciplinary-based laws that serve as absolutes for which knowledge is both explored and gathered. For instance, when measuring some effect of gravity, the physicist pulls from Newton's law of gravity, which suggests that things will fall (Newton, 1989). So, no matter what object is dropped, without restrictions, the object will fall. No matter how you measure gravity, the object will always fall, 100% of the time. In social science research, often the field examines human response, actions, or attitudes. While the field does not have absolute knowledge in which research is based, it does have the law of human response. This law suggests that people will react or respond. Further, the law of human response is more complex than the law of gravity. When measuring gravity, if you repeatedly drop an object at just the right time, angle, speed, and weight, that object will fall in the exact same place within less than 1% margin of error. On the other hand, when measuring human response, if a question is repeatedly asked at just the right time of day, and with just the right tone, we cannot confirm that we will get the exact same response nearly 100% of the time. We can, however, speculate that responses given will be based on some human experience and knowledge.

What further complicates the law of human response is that knowledge is very relevant and is based on cultural and historical experiences. For instance, if a researcher was to ask a group of people to respond to the impact of current educational policy on academic outcomes, we can hypothesize that the responses given are based on knowledge that reflects a cultural or historical experience with educational systems. Hunter (1991) proposed the following:

> All human experience has context. There are always preconditions and prior circumstances—there is always a history. And invariably, the larger context is a complex reality that defies simple explanation.

Yet to even attempt to understand a facet of social life without at least partially reconstructing both the instructional and historical settings within which it is rooted would be folly. Our understanding would be flawed from the outset. (p. 3)

History is essential in understanding an individual's perception or knowledge of social phenomenon. However, within history, there are cultural influences. Some (Freire, 1976; Ogbu, 2000) argue that it is the cultural interpretation of history that makes human perception or knowledge complex. However, they are not complex simply for this reason. The complexity of knowledge lies in the confirmation given to perceptions of historical and cultural events. Within historical and cultural events, there is often more than one approach to events such as conflicts, discoveries, wars, relationships, etc. Most often, the differences in these perceptions are reflective of a dominant culture and a non-dominant culture's view of the same events. Given the power associated with dominant cultures (e.g., wealth, control of resources), acceptable knowledge often reflects their interpretation of history.

These interpretations reflect a "grand narrative" or a "master narrative" (Klages, 1997), which generates a biased set of knowledge or framework for which the system functions. This knowledge not only influences the functionality of a society, it influences the economic, political, religious, and educational function of a society as well. When presented in this fashion, the point of view of the majority overpowers the point of view of many minority, oppressed, and underclass communities. In turn, the knowledge developed from these narratives creates categorical labels such as *order* vs. *disorder*; *right* vs. *wrong*; *civilized* vs. *non-civilized*. By developing these dichotomous categories, it helps those in the majority feel a sense of achieved stability. In Derrida's idea of "totality" (Payne, 1998), this achieved stability gives the majority in a society a sense of having a unified system. However, Derrida would argue that because of the nature of totality, this stability is ever changing. Nevertheless, this system is homogenous and does not include the beliefs or the mini-narratives of its subcultures (e.g., minorities, underclass, or oppressed groups). In turn, the system is filled with flaws and systematic errors. In particular, by rejecting or not accepting the mini-narratives of its minority communities, this system knowingly or unknowingly "dehumanizes" (Freire, 1976) this sector of its community. A way to combat these flaws in this system is to pay attention to the historical errors committed by not including mini-narratives as part of the systematic decision-making process.

This chapter will deconstruct the concept of knowledge in order to understand the point to which the information we have and gather influences the way we collectively perceive knowledge. In order to deconstruct the concept of knowledge, it is important to first explore historical thoughts about the concept or meaning of knowledge. After deconstructing knowledge, this chapter will present a reconstruction of knowledge by exploring the relevancy of individual and collective knowledge. Finally, the chapter will explore the value of collective knowledge by taking into account the value of cultural experiences when developing theoretical frameworks associated with cultural context of knowledge.

Deconstructing the Concept of Knowledge

We use the construct knowledge to suggest that we have or someone has some information. However, knowledge is not truly valuable unless it is shared or expressed. But how does one come to a point of knowing information, and how do we know if the information presented is reliable? These questions have plagued the minds of epistemologists for centuries. The earliest dialogs on the nature of knowledge focused on determining true or absolute knowledge. The thought was that by determining true absolute knowledge, one could easily distinguish the difference between true versus false knowledge. In theory, this approach accords more readily with the approach of the hard sciences (e.g., developing theoretical frameworks based on true absolute knowledge). However, in the field of social science, this static approach to knowledge is limiting, because knowledge can be viewed as a relative interpretation of human experiences.

This idea of true knowledge and relative knowledge has been an epistemological approach stemming back to Plato and Aristotle. Plato saw change as chaotic and questioned how we can know anything if the world is in constant motion. While developing the Academy, a school for mathematics and philosophy, Plato questioned the notion of change as a construct of knowledge and of relative knowledge. He viewed individuals as naturally selfish and only interested in their own survival and well-being. Therefore, he concluded that most people did not know really what they claimed to know, and he pushed for more rigorous examination of absolute truth. In Plato's view, true knowledge is universal and political leaders and philosopher kings should determine this *form* or *idea* of knowledge. He believed that these leaders were qualified rulers on matters of knowledge and morality. Plato's approach suggests that the grand narratives of a selected group of people were essential in determining true knowledge for all people.

Aristotle, a pupil of Plato, had an opposing view of knowledge. His exploration of knowledge stemmed from the question presented by other Greek philosophers, *how could one be certain of knowledge?* While agreeing with Plato that knowledge should reflect universal principles, Aristotle disagreed that knowledge should be defined by political leaders. He viewed knowledge as fundamentally empirical. He felt that knowledge could be observed and categorized and that the evidence gathered from this technique was an interpretation of the relative certainty that the observation represented relative knowledge. He believed that relative knowledge was indeed an absolute knowledge. When resolving questions, Aristotle introduced inductive reasoning as a strategy for empirically understanding knowledge by 1) considering previous knowledge of the subject, 2) gathering general consensus of opinions on the subject, and 3) studying topics related to the subject. This approach called for the examination of many possible examples to arrive at an underlying principle. These principles represented certain and uncertain knowledge. Certain knowledge was constructs that clearly defined a concept (e.g., addition, subtraction, law of gravity), while uncertain knowledge related to the probability of results (i.e., law of human response).

The competing epistemological approaches of Plato and Aristotle have a great impact on the position on knowledge taken by researchers today. However, the approaches of these scholars were more apparent in the presentation of *rationalism* and *empiricism* in the scientific revolution of the 17th century. Both approaches were concerned with the foundation of knowledge. Although Aristotle emphasized logical and empirical methods of obtaining knowledge, rationalism followed his thought that knowledge is reflective of human experience. As Descartes contests, "I think, therefore I am."

On the other hand, empiricism follows the principles of Plato that knowledge is independent of human experience and thus representative of an absolute universal truth. It is evident why this approach has relevance in the hard sciences. When manipulating concrete objects, or as Plato would propose *matter*, certain universal principles are relevant in resolving a problem. Empiricists argue that universal principles are also relevant when assessing human response. These theorists view the knowledge gained from sensory organs as universal knowledge. For instance, the knowledge perceived by touch transforms into knowledge about what objects feel like. The knowledge perceived by vision translates into knowledge of what things taste like. The approach suggested in this theory is that there is no prior existence of knowledge before a person experiences a new situation. For instance, once something is heard, it is new knowledge. This approach suggests that once knowledge is gained it can be used to define similar experiences.

Here is another point on which Plato and Aristotle differ. Plato suggests that knowledge represents an *idea* or a *form*. For instance, when an object is heard, that object takes on an absolute form (e.g., a bell). In essence, any proposed knowledge either truly corresponds to an external definition of that knowledge or represents some other knowledge. On the other hand, if the two different sounds arrive in different contexts, Aristotle would propose that the sounds have likeness (e.g., bellness).

Could it be that both of these truths exist? From Plato's argument, in particular, there are some definable elements. Let's assume the sound is a bell. We can define this sensory-perceived knowledge as the ringing of a bell. This is an absolute truth. So, if we were to hear the bell again, we can understand the sound as a ringing of a bell. From the view of Aristotle, the sound is relative, and could possibly have a likeness of a bell. However, human condition (e.g., experience) can help define or further categorize the bell. For instance, if one has experienced other bells, that person may suggest the bell being heard is a specific type of bell—a bell made of a certain material that gives a unique sound. Additionally, given that the same bell is heard twice, the sound may project a different tone depending on where a person hears the bell. Finally, given the ability of the person to recognize different tones, the bell may sound different. While indeed, the absoluteness of the argument is that the sound is a bell, the sound the bell makes is relative to the experience of the individual hearing the bell and shapes how the individual defines the bell.

This approach represents *pragmatic epistemology*, which suggests that two competing approaches can exist to explain a phenomenon, even if the approaches may seem contradictory. Pragmatism proposes that knowledge consists of models that attempt to represent a situation in order to collectively answer an existing question. In this approach, the assumption is that no one model can represent all information relative to solving a question. Basically, a question, both simple and complex, is complex. To answer a question with only one model increases the probability that the answer to the question is incorrect. This approach concludes static outcomes, which suggest that the results related to the question represent the model or do not represent the model.

There are other approaches that take on the same elements as pragmatism: *constructivism*, *positivism*, *conventionalism*, and *radical empiricism*. These epistemologies do not propose absolute answers to a question. Rather, these approaches assume that a question is resolved by exploring all possible influences. These approaches are not intent on looking for absolute truth, but on discovering knowledge that is gathered from the exploration of multiple models and empirical data.

Some forms of pragmatism take the approach of *fallibilism*. This epistemology proposes that all approaches and existing knowledge have purpose in explaining a phenomenon or situation. Furthermore, philosophers of this approach also argue that it is possible that all knowledge related to a phenomenon or situation can be in error. For instance, for centuries the common belief was that the world was flat and if a ship sailed too far, it could fall off the face of the earth. Upon further exploration, it was found that this knowledge was in error. The major doctrine of fallibilism argues that absolute certainty about knowledge is impossible. This approach is often confused with skepticism, which proposes the abandonment or suspension of prior knowledge when investigating new knowledge. Fallibilism accepts that prior knowledge and judgments are relative to justify and logically conclude perceived knowledge.

The fallibilism approach also suggests that prior knowledge can be revised by further empirical observations and that perceived knowledge should not be accepted as the final truth, even if knowledge is related to foundational practices (i.e., rules of logic and mathematics). For instance, as presented earlier in this chapter, the understanding of the law of gravity offers that if dropped, things will fall. After further exploration, Albert Einstein's (1920) general theory of relativity reshaped physicists' and astronomers' thoughts about gravity by suggesting that space, time, light, motion, and energy play a significant role in understanding the function of gravity. Based on this work, physicists' and astronomers' exploration of the nature of the universe has suggested that things do not simply fall, but are pulled to the center of the earth. More so, scientists' understanding of the earth's gravitational relationship with the moon and the gravitational relationship between rings around Saturn and the planet shows that a planet's gravitational pull is more complex than objects simply falling to the ground.

Unlike the approaches of Plato and empiricism, the latter epistemological approaches, pragmatism and fallibilism, propose that knowledge is never absolute and recognize that knowledge is only relevant to what we understand about that construct at the present time. Further, the approaches suggest that in order to develop a working or collective knowledge of a construct, it is important that all possible angles to a question are explored and that empirical approaches are taken to better understand the construct being examined. Whether examining approaches associated with the hard sciences or with human response, the relevancy of these approaches is that to gather knowledge about a construct, it is essential that researchers examine various influences on that construct.

Reconstructing the Concept of Collective Knowledge

The epistemological approaches presented above demonstrate how one gets to knowledge. However, the approaches do not suggest how one comes to know if the information s/he has represents knowledge. As proposed, knowledge is more valuable when it can be expressed and shared with others. However, a common dilemma associated with expressed or shared knowledge is that knowledge presented is not always mutually or collectively understood or agreed upon. The complexity of this dilemma lies in the frame of reference in which individuals present and perceive the information. For instance, Nebraska is one of the top corn-producing states in the U.S. The state is so known for its production of corn that the mascot of the University of Nebraska is a corn husker. Based on the state's reputation for producing a high volume of corn, one may suggest that the best corn is grown in Nebraska. However, can we collectively agree that this assumption is true?

Further, information or knowledge can be perceived as valuable based on if the person presenting the information is perceived to have a level of significance. For instance, there are a number of self-help books designed to assist individuals overcome some issue that may be negatively affecting their lives. Given the authors' experience with a situation or possession of an advanced degree in the area on which they have written, it is often easy to trust the information or knowledge is reliable. However, can we collectively agree that what is experienced by one person or presented by an "expert" in the field will help everyone dealing with the issue presented in the self-help book?

Although there is valuable information that helps us make decisions about a situation, sometimes this same information is not relevant to others, and vice versa. If we experience similar experiences as others, the frame of reference in which we experience the situation may be different. An example of this is the experience people have with the civil rights movement. While many saw the movement as a way to promote equal rights among African Americans, others felt that it was not about equality but about equitability. The Civil Rights Act (1964) that followed the movement permitted many ethnic minorities to access opportunities that were not before made available. However, in many African American communities this act also came at a cost. The biggest cost was school busing. Even though busing came about eight years after the Civil Rights Act, and some would say was influenced by the Coleman Report (1966), the issues associated with public schools for African Americans has bothered politicians and African American leaders since the end of slavery (Bennett, 1988; Du Bois, 1902; Washington, 1896; Watkins, 2001; Woodson, 1933). Given the documented poor school conditions in many African American schools, African American students were bused to schools more "suitable for learning." Often these schools were in predominantly European American communities. This action eventually had a negative influence on the connection between African American communities and community schools.

Before the Civil Rights Act, many in the African American community felt that equality was not possible, mainly because of the inequality in wealth and economic opportunities between minorities and non-minorities. Therefore, some in the community felt more strongly about developing a community of equitable opportunities. The point of equitable opportunities was that the community would not necessarily be equal to European American communities, but the community would be provided the same opportunities for success as European American communities. There were those in the community who felt busing was not the answer to bettering their community. They felt that providing the same books, libraries, and school conditions as the European American community would provide their children with similar opportunities as European American children.

The complexity of this issue, as with any other situation in which a group of people is influenced by the approach or knowledge of others, is getting people to collectively buy into the same truth about a situation or about knowledge of a situation. While one person or a group can have information about an experience, the information is only relevant to that individual or group. In the example of an effect of the Civil Rights Act on schooling, those who constructed the Act were politicians and African American leaders. However, what was not considered were the mini-narratives of those who were optimally affected by the Act (e.g., the community, parents, and school teachers). As presented by fallibilism, in order to gather knowledge about a situation, it is important to explore all angles associated with a situation.

A way of exploring the different angles of a situation to come up with a more collective understanding of it is through interaction and negotiation. Sociologist Rick Stephens (1987) proposes that knowledge is discovered through the *construction of reality*. In this procedure, an individual goes through a series of processes to come to the conclusion of collective reality or collective knowledge. First, an individual simply experiences a new situation or event. In this process, the individual makes sense of the new experience by pulling from similar experience(s) (i.e., knowledge) s/he has had that is closely associated with this new situation. In turn, the person develops an *individual definition* about the newly experienced situation. Therefore, the knowledge about the situation, the bias, is relative to that person's experience of the situation.

To come closer to constructing collective knowledge, the individual must confirm if this relative knowledge from the newly experienced situation is actually meaningful or valid. Marx suggests that our basic purpose is to reproduce ourselves. This process occurs mentally, physically, spiritually, socially, and emotionally. But for this reproduction to come about, we need others. For instance, we cannot reproduce physically, meaning producing a baby, without the assistance of others. While we do not need their physical contact, we do need a physical part of the opposite sex to reproduce. Further, we cannot be social without interacting with others. Without others, we live in isolation. In Stephens's (1987) approach, before an individual can accept that the knowledge from the newly experienced situation is true knowledge, the individual must negotiate with others to determine whether his/her individual knowledge is valid. This does not suggest the individual must agree with others' knowledge about the same situation, but this process helps them confirm or reject his/her individual definition of the situation experienced.

Through this process, the individual is able to estimate a collective definition or collective knowledge about the newly experienced situation. The process proposes that allowing others to influence our perception of an experience helps us develop collective knowledge. The process is not to make one change his or her individual knowledge about the situation. The process is to assist the individual in developing a more accurate understanding of the newly experienced situation. Therefore the individual is then able to *internalize* this experience and utilize this experience as a frame of reference when experiencing similar situations. This process of collective knowledge does not propose that there is a true absolute knowledge. Instead it proposes that knowledge is relative and subject to change as experiences change or different variables (e.g., mood, people, gender, race, culture, etc.) are added to the situation. Further, the process follows a Vygotskian (1978) approach to knowledge, which suggests that new knowledge is built upon existing knowledge. Therefore this process may cause a reshaping of knowledge, thus making knowledge relative and changeable.

More so, as we negotiate with others about our ideas of a new situation, we often limit our interactions to those who have similar values or beliefs (e.g., religion, politics, etc.) to us. Rarely do we practice fallibilism, making sure all angles are explored before knowledge resembles some level of truth. It seems that we place more value in those who share our truth about the world and the way it functions than in those who do not necessarily share our same truth. For instance, when experiences associated with race arise, we tend to negotiate our experiences about that situation with someone of the same race or with someone who shares our value about race and race relations. This situation also holds true when it comes to experiences with gender, religion, politics, etc.

The downfall of this type of negotiation is that it can contribute to false knowledge about an experience. When living in a culture in which a class system exists or a culture in which majority culture and minority cultures do not share the same belief about similar experiences, this type of negotiation can cause divides and mistruths between different groups. In this instance, the truth of the majority culture tends to have more weight than minority cultures. Therefore, often the narratives associated with the experience of majority culture (grand narratives) overshadow the narratives of the same experience of minority cultures (mini-narratives). This tends to occur when two cultures have a strong belief about historical experiences within a culture that over time has not been resolved. The result is that a strong belief about the other culture is felt (e.g., black people are angry or hate white people; or white males are racist and sexist).

Cultural Conceptual Context of Knowledge

It is difficult to suggest examining the cultural conceptual context of knowledge without examining the relationship between dominant and non-dominant cultures. But before this examination, it is important to conceptualize culture as presented in this chapter. Culture is the reflection of a lifestyle that people have adopted. Therefore culture is representative of how we elect to live and how we go about our own lives. We can have various cultures (e.g., ethnic-culture, gender-culture, religious-culture, etc.). These cultures can interlock or inter-connect (Collins, 2003) and reform to create different cultures. For instance, U.S. African Americans comprise over 16 different subcultures. These cultures are influenced by more factors, such as language (Afro-Cubans, Louisiana-Creole, etc.), region (west coast, northeast, southern, etc.), and a combination of both.

In a sense, culture, cultural understanding, and cultural context of knowledge can present a complex challenge to those studying impacts of systems on cultural groups. As proposed by Stephens (1987), when we connect with a new experience, we enter a situation with an intentional or unintentional frame of reference. In many cases, this frame of reference is based on our own understanding of another culture formulated on our conscious or subconscious view of our own culture. Therefore, before we take on the action of negotiating to further understand another culture, initially we view another culture through the values we have about our own culture. This process makes it easy to form biases about a culture that is different from our own.

What gives cultural bias power is when a majority of the people in a community or society believes the bias about a culture to be true. As biases manifest in a community, it is difficult to eliminate them, even to the point that those whom the biases are directed at believe them to be true. Freire (2003) suggests this phenomenon happens because oppressed groups often take on the views and beliefs of their oppressors because they have no other role model. He suggests that the oppressed tend to function in the mode of pleasing their oppressor in order to find a level of comfort in the society. Goffman (1959), in *The Presentation of Self in Everyday Life*, suggests that we function in this way to save face and to reduce feeling embarrassed or uncomfortable in a social setting or society. Freire further suggests that for the oppressed to recover from or get out of this dehumanizing state, oppressed groups must revolt and create or push for a system that is more humanizing (i.e., "conscientização", p. 17).

Collins's (2003) work on black feminist thought proposes that humanization can occur as black women take ownership of how they are viewed by outsiders. Mainly, given that cultural interpretations occur as a result of the values we have about our own culture, it is easy to develop pessimistic thoughts about a different cultural group. If the actions of a group are different from our culture, it is easy to label another culture as *disorderly*, *wrong*, or *non-civilized*. Collins explains that to eliminate these biases, knowledge is essential in empowering oppressed communities. For these communities to reach a level of empowerment, their knowledge must help them change the paradigm by which they are viewed.

To change the paradigm, the community must change the consciousness of its individuals and socially transform political and economic institutions so that social change is possible. The importance of this change is based on a paradigm by which the oppressed community is analyzed. Collins explains that the concepts, paradigms, and epistemologies used to analyze the community should not be based on the conceptual lens of the dominant culture. For the oppressed community to be seen as valuable, the community must develop and analyze itself using its own concepts, paradigms, and epistemologies.

Collins further suggests that for the oppressed community to reconceptualize these terms, two empowering efforts must take place. First, the community has to foster a fundamental paradigmatic shift, which embraces the culturally relevant interlocking factors of oppression. By understanding how these interlocking factors work together to form oppression, the community would better understand how to promote effective and empowering change. The second empowering effort the oppressed community must make is to debate the epistemological theories related to its community. By debating these theories, the community can better assess what is true and valid about itself. For instance, Easton-Brooks and Davis (2007) found that the financial status among African Americans is based on those factors that influence historical African Americans' financial status (e.g., debt, ability to obtain wealth, history of poverty, and available assets), rather than the traditionally used variable socio-economic status (SES). By reconceptualizing the financial influence on the academic outcomes of African American students, the researchers found that the concept of wealth was more reflective of a cultural relevant paradigm for explaining academic outcomes among African Americans than the traditionally used SES variable.

These two approaches are important, because they empower the oppressed community to reconceptualize concepts, paradigms, and epistemologies from within the community. Collins explains that this gives an oppressed community value and control over how they want to be viewed. This reflects Freire's (2003) thoughts of the powerlessness of oppressed communities. He explained that oppressed communities see themselves as an inferior reflection of dominant culture. Both Freire and Collins suggest that this paradigm is what keeps oppressed communities oppressed. Freire proposes that for an oppressed community to revolt against its oppressor, it must discard the values directly and indirectly placed on it by that oppressor. Collins advocates that through reconceptualizing, dominant cultures' values are replaced with values that are culturally relevant.

As oppressed communities reconceptualize factors that support oppression, Collins proposes a new paradigm. She suggests that these communities should analyze oppressive factors as a collective unit of oppression, rather than individual components of oppression. For instance, race, class, and gender should not be examined as individual factors that influence oppression, but should be examined as one overarching structure of oppression. Individual factors associated with oppression should not be viewed as stand-alone variables (Collins, 2003). The main reason for this type of assessment is the idea that there is not just one factor that promotes oppression; there are a number of interacting systems that promote oppression (e.g., financial status, education, politics, etc.).

This approach shows that by examining oppressive factors as an interlocking system, the community would be better able to deconstruct how oppression affects the community, come to a realization of what actually happens in the community, and debate which factors keep the community from progressing. Once it deconstructs concepts, paradigms, and epistemologies that promote oppression, the community uses these intersecting factors to reconstruct or reconceptualize concepts, paradigms, and epistemologies that are relevant to it.

Informally, cultural groups do go through this process at some level. However, factors such as the overpowering voice of dominant culture, the desire to save face (to be comfortable), limited resources, or the lack of a platform from which to express cultural biases, mean many cultural groups deal with their frustration at society at large from within. In this process, cultural groups are developing cultural collective knowledge that is relevant to the group's survival. Therefore these mini-narratives rarely extend outside of cultural boundaries. This process focuses the dominant culture to use their frame of reference (i.e., knowledge) to explain the experiences of other cultural groups. The complexity of this issue is that when dominant culture attempts to assess minority cultures using the lens of the dominant culture, the results, more times than not, are inaccurate.

Conclusion

Durkheim (2000) suggested that the historical lessons of education should serve to prevent us from repeating the errors that have been committed in the development of educational pedagogy. By learning from historical errors, education should lend itself to the underclass, the working class, and oppressed communities. However, historically, this has not been the case. From the early Greek and Roman eras, to the Middle Ages, and to the Renaissance era, educational pedagogies have been influenced by the dominant culture's economic, religious, and/or class status (Durkheim, 2000). These influences did not necessarily include the values of a cultural responsive approach to education.

The errors of not including the mini-narratives of diverse communities in the pedagogy are evident in U.S. educational history. In the early 1630s, the Puritans, whose educational foundations are the bases of U.S. pedagogy, created an educational structure based on Christianity (Kizer, 2003). During this time, to be educated in a school setting, one needed to conform to the Puritan church's approach to education. This approach suggested that the voice of knowledge was based on a mono-cultural approach, which excluded external possession of knowledge. Freire (1976) describes this approach as "banking education" (p. 100), in which an educational system does not account for cultural influence in determining knowledge. During the era of Puritan education, if one was unsuccessful in this academic structure, it was not the fault of the school; it was the fault of the individual.

While more of the northern and middle colonies' schools centered on Puritan educational pedagogy, the foundation of southern states was "knowledge is power" (Cheek, 2003). In this approach, many believed that this power was a privilege of whites. This mindset led many southern states to pass laws against educating slaves.

This sustained cultural prominence has continued throughout U.S. educational history. From the 1830 Indian Relocation Act, the 1848 Treaty of Guadalupe Hidalgo, and the 1865 end of legalized slavery, the education of U.S. ethnic minorities had been affected by war, the lack of economic opportunity, and ethnic-cultural survival. In addition, these historical events produced an educational system that did not look to reflect the cultural diversity of the U.S. population; instead, it worked to "Americanize" ethnic minorities. This Americanization, through education, was not meant to enhance the knowledge of ethnic minorities, but rather to equip them with skills, because during this time U.S. ethnic minorities were seen as "impossible to cultivate" (Woodson, 1933, p. 2). Therefore, training programs were developed to provide ethnic minorities with a "skill," similar to the approach most states take to modern-day prisoners.

Indeed, we must learn from the errors of our history. As we continue to examine knowledge about issues affecting our schools, communities, etc., we must explore all angles impacting the situation we are exploring, even if this means examining the hard questions about our own perceptions. Further, as we set out to find some level of truth for resolving the situation, we must consider mini-narratives, even if it means engaging in interactions that we may not agree with or that may cause us discomfort. While truth is only relevant to our experiences or how we negotiate our experiences, it is essential that we approach our research from a multidimensional framework that causes us to deconstruct and reconstruct the meaning of what we are exploring, so our research findings closely match a level of information that proposes close connection with collective knowledge.

References

Bennett, L. (1988). *Before the Mayflower*. New York, NY: Penguin Books.

Cheek, K. (2003). *Education in the Southern colonies*. Retrieved January 20, 2003, from http://www.nd.edu/~rbarger/www7/soucolon.html

Civil Rights Act, 42 U.S.C. § 1971 (1964).

Coleman, J., et al. (1966). *Equality of educational opportunity*. Washington, DC: U.S. Government Printing Office.

Collins, P. H. (2003). *Black feminist thought: Knowledge, consciousness, and the politics of empowerment*. New York, NY: Routledge.

Du Bois, W. E. B. (1902, September). Of the training of black men. *The Atlantic Monthly, 90,* 1–14.

Durkheim, E. (2000). *The nature of education*. In B. A. U. Levinson et al. (Eds.), *Schooling the symbolic animal: Social and cultural dimensions of education* (pp. 57–61). Lanham, MD: Rowman & Littlefield.

Easton-Brooks, D., & Davis, A. (2007). Wealth, traditional socioeconomic indicators, and the achievement debt. *The Journal of Negro Education, 76*(4), 530–542.

Einstein, A. (1920). *Relativity: The theory of relativity*. New York, NY: Henry Holt.

Freire, P. (1976). *Education, the practice of freedom* (M. B. Ramos, Trans.). London, England: Writers and Readers.

Freire, P. (2003). *Pedagogy of the oppressed* (30th anniversary ed.). New York, NY: Continuum.

Goffman, E. (1959). *The presentation of self in everyday life*. New York, NY: Anchor Books.

Hunter, J. D. (1991). *Culture wars: The struggle to define America*. New York, NY: Basic Books.

Kizer, K. (2003). *Puritans*. Retrieved January 20, 2003, from http://www.nd.edu/~rbarger/www7/puritans.html

Klages, M. (1997). *Postmodernism*. Retrieved February 7, 2001, from http://www.colorado.edu/English/ENGL2012Klages/pomo.html

Newton, I. (1989). *The preliminary manuscripts for Isaac Newton's 1687 Principia, 1684–1686*. Cambridge, England: Cambridge University Press.

Ogbu, J. (2000). Understanding cultural diversity and learning. In B. A. U. Levinson et al. (Eds.), *Schooling the symbolic animal: Social and cultural dimensions of education* (pp. 190–206). Lanham, MD: Rowman & Littlefield.

Payne, M. (Ed.). (1998). *A dictionary of cultural and critical theory*. Malden, MA: Blackwell.

Stephens, R. (1987). *Introduction to Sociology, SOC 101*. Greenville College, Greenville, IL.

Vygotsky, L.S. (1978). *Mind in society: Development of higher psychological process*. Cambridge, MA: Harvard University Press.

Washington, B. T. (1896, September). The awakening of the Negro. *The Atlantic Monthly, 78,* 12–22.

Watkins, W. H. (2001). *The white architects of black education: Ideology and power in America (1985–1954)*. New York, NY: Teachers College Press.

Woodson, C. G. (1933). *The mis-education of the Negro*. Trenton, NJ: Africa World Press.

CHAPTER FOUR

Basic Concepts in Critical Methodological Theory: Action, Structure and System within a Communicative Pragmatics Framework

Phil Francis Carspecken

The purpose of this chapter is to provide a succinct summary of key concepts pertinent to critical qualitative research, framed within the philosophical and social-theoretical framework of critical pragmatics. Critical qualitative research has origins in the critical pedagogic work of Paulo Freire (2000) and the now-classic critical ethnography of Paul Willis (1977). Its theoretical features were expanded upon during the 1980s by educational theorists like Michael Apple (1979, 1986), Henry Giroux (1983) and Peter McLaren (1999). A well-known and frequently cited discussion and summary of this methodological practice by Joe Kincheloe and Peter McLaren has appeared in various editions of *The Landscape of Qualitative Research* (2008).

My own work in critical qualitative research has emphasized highly specific articulations of methodologically useful concepts from the philosophy of communicative pragmatics (for example, Carspecken 1996, 2003). Teaching critical qualitative research in a two-semester sequence for many years at Indiana University, I have refined, deepened and expanded the communicative pragmatics frameworks in ways rather far ahead of my publications. In this chapter I give an overview of some of the key concepts and theories I teach and how they relate to each other within a methodological model I present as Figure 1 below. I apologize to readers in advance for producing a fairly dry summary of the concepts with no real examples of the sort of creative and many times exciting work that can be done with them and that has been done many times by students at Indiana University. The methodological theory is fairly tight and rigorous so that the forest is often difficult to see as a whole given the many trees. Dry though it may be, this chapter gives an accurate though truncated introduction to key critical-methodological ideas that can well serve fieldwork and data analysis.

Critical qualitative research has from the start been concerned with the interconnection of knowing and doing, theory and practice. In the case of Freire, research and pedagogy were combined so that knowledge generation, consciousness raising and mobilization for social change all merged together. Participatory action research (PAR), originated by Orlando Fals-Borda, likewise worked out ways to combine research with social activism, putting an emphasis on community (rather than researcher) leadership and egalitarian relationships (Fals-Borda & Rahman, 1991). Critical ethnographies modeled on Willis's classic study, *Learning to Labor* (1977), usually sought to describe oppressive social processes in terms of the implicit knowledge embedded in the practices of students within and outside schools, without directly working with the participants or directly engaging in efforts to contribute to social change other than publishing their results. Despite the differences in practice, critical pedagogy, participatory action research and critical ethnography share the need for a theory and epistemology that capture internal connections between knowledge, action, power, human identity and other basic concepts.

Freire's term "conscientization" addresses the internal connection between epistemology and social theory in ways that distinguish the critical theory of knowledge from all forms of empiricism, including positivism. We have a marked departure from empiricism and positivism as soon as we understand that social-scientific knowledge is not only *about* social phenomena but is itself a feature of social phenomena. A sound theory of knowledge has to drop representational theories, in which knowledge is always *about* something that is not itself knowledge. Knowledge must be understood ontologically and socially. It is simultaneously about social reality as well as a form of self-knowing and a feature of social reality and human identity. Moreover, as a feature of social phenomena as well as self-knowledge, knowledge will more often than not be distorted, that is, have ideological forms that function to reproduce relations of power which not only disadvantage subordinated groups, but also constrain and deform self-understandings so as to limit opportunities for people to meet needs for dignity, respect and full self-development.

Social-scientific knowledge uses empiricist methodologies in its dominant forms—the forms that are produced by researchers who receive the largest grants and who also work in the private sector to help design management and organizational structures as well as inform marketing strategies and rank and sort young people through testing practices in line with class divisions. It is distorted knowledge with social functions. But knowledge in popular culture also has systemic distortions serving social functions. Critical research is well served by distinguishing itself from mainstream social-scientific research through rigorously formulating its theory of knowledge and rigorously critiquing empiricist, positivist and non-critical interpretivist/phenomenological methodologies. This is a central goal for critical qualitative research. In addition, critical qualitative research aims to understand itself as a practice that works with people to raise critical consciousness rather than merely describe social reality. A critical qualitative research project will typically be a project in conscientization. It will work with people to make implicit forms of knowing-how into explicit and criticizable forms of discursive knowledge. It will contribute to social change directly and thus not only by informing policy decisions.

The process of coming to understand distortions in dominating forms of both social-scientific knowledge and popular knowledge has to make use of epistemological principles that totally escape the empiricist and positivist frameworks. Knowledge is rooted in actions rather than perceptions. Knowledge production involves consciousness raising and the articulation of implicit know-how into explicit forms of knowing-that. This understanding of knowledge was articulated by both Marx and Dewey long ago, but within a limited philosophical framework: instrumental pragmatism (see Xie & Carspecken, 2008, for an elaborated discussion of Hegel, Marx, Dewey and contemporary communicative pragmatics). Communicative pragmatics is distinguished from instrumental pragmatics through the insight that knowing how to act communicatively has structures of implicit knowledge that supervene over knowing how to act instrumentally.

Conscientization works at the level of knowing-how, the implicit knowledge humans learn when socialized within cultures so that they can enter into social relationships, communicate with others in their culture, take on and maintain identities and coordinate their activities with other people in relation to the physical world so as to meet basic material needs. In the process of conscientization, knowing-how is moved into explicit forms of discursive knowledge so that implicit assumptions, conceptual categories, beliefs and norms embedded within socially constructed practices can be communicatively examined and critiqued.

This process of consciousness raising, moving implicit knowledge into explicit and criticizable forms, requires changes in identity attachments because forms of acting and interacting within social formations are tied to existential needs for having validated identities. Consciousness raising means expanding and changing self-understandings in ways that initially can feel existentially threatening to people who must drop deep-seated patterns of maintaining identity security. But at the same time, the change in identity-securing knowledge brings freedom and liberation with it because distortions in the socially constructed implicit knowledge that is embedded within and maintains social practices are usually anchored to fixed forms of human identity: fixed forms of being a valid man, woman, person of color, person of a particular social class.

What sort of theory of knowledge, then, can capture these subtle connections between knowing, acting, being a person, social practices and reflection or consciousness raising? As already indicated, in the critical qualitative methodological theory I summarize here, the movement from instrumental forms of philosophical pragmatism that we find in both Marx and Dewey to communicative pragmatism is regarded as greatly important and useful. Habermas's theory of communicative action (1984, 1987) and Brandom's work on "explicitization" (Brandom, 1998) are the key developments in moving from instrumental to communicative pragmatism. The kind of knowledge that is framed with the orientation of changing something tangible (something objective, objectified or objectivated) differs from and in fact is subordinated in relation to the kind of knowledge that is framed with the orientation of reaching a mutual understanding with other subjects.

The basic concepts reviewed in this chapter include an overall model relating action conditions, actors' awareness of conditions, the meaning of actions, the consequences of actions and systems that link consequences back to new action conditions. This model can be used for virtually any research design in social and psychological research. It is very helpful when formulating research questions and then making decisions about sampling and methods. The article also gives overviews of theories of meaning, structure, power and human identity.

An Overall Methodological Model

The several complex components of this methodological theory can be represented in a single graphic on the next page.

A brief written description of the figure would go like this: studies in the human sciences will have "object domains," things to do their research on and about, that in some way will come back to the items depicted in the above figure. Social phenomena can be understood as coordinated human actions, conditions related to action and action coordination, how much and what type of awareness actors have of the conditions within which they act, how awareness works in contexts of power and differential volitional strength in relation to actions, the meaning of actions (meaningful actions, communicative actions), the consequences of actions (including human experiences) and the relation of consequences to new conditions of action in the constitution of a social system. Usually a research design will focus on relations between only some of the components above or, in the case of a descriptive ethnography, will focus on a single component (like meaning). Even psychological research can be related to this diagram because in critical theory we make use of a theory of thinking and all forms of self-monitored subjective states that involves the internalization of communicative action and other forms of social relationships.

In a classical sort of critical ethnography, like Willis's *Learning to Labor* (1977), action conditions include class position (conceptualized as external to volition of actors and objective), race and gender identity commitments and themes in the culture (conceptualized as internal to volition of actors), tacit to low levels of awareness of action conditions, meanings that especially thematize identity claiming and identity maintenance through the pragmatics of routine interactions (having a laugh, bantering, fighting, etc. for Willis's participants) with action consequences that reproduce cultural milieu (the cultural domain of action conditions) and eventually reproduce class structure (the movement from school into working class jobs in the case of Willis's participants). Willis's study, *Learning to Labor*, can be regarded as the inaugural study for critical ethnography and critical qualitative research; and every component of Figure 1 is discussed and related to the other components in Willis's book. Many other kinds of social research only focus on some of the components of the above diagram, but what is focused on can always be understood in terms of the larger contexts in which it is involved.

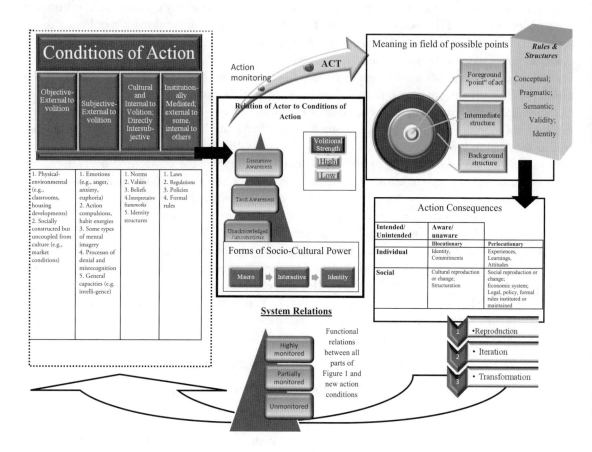

Figure One: General Features of Critical Methodology

Basic Social-Theoretical Concepts and Their Methodological Significance

In this section I will cover basic principles of critical social theory as I teach it and write about it. Most of these principles and concepts are directly represented in Figure 1 but some are implicit to what may be seen in that figure. I will organize the discussion in this order: a) communicatively coordinated action and culture, b) communicative structures and meaning, c) human identity, d) cultural structures, e) types of cultural structure, f) action conditions, g) power, h) theory of systems.

A. Communicatively Coordinated Action and Culture

Human society is based on a principle that we do not find anywhere else in nature: communication. Although there are animal species that have developed communicative systems and coordinate actions between members through intersubjectivity, human beings have enormously more sophisticated languages and are able not only to communicate about various things for various reasons but are able to communicate about how they are communicating. Human societies involve forms of coordinated action that are non-causal in nature and that can be changed by humans themselves through discussions, in principle. Power relations and ideologies, discussed later in this article, block the in-principle *possible* avenues through which people together collectively determine the social institutions, laws, division of labor and so on in communicatively rational ways. Because relations between human beings are not causally determined, freedom and self-determination and collective will formation that addresses the interests of *all* people are potentialities. Communicatively rational relations, as opposed to causal relations, give the critical researcher a standard with which to find many various forms of power that curtail the potentiality for personal and collective freedom.

Coordinated actions are based at bottom on shared norms, values, assumptions and beliefs which are instantiated, negotiated and argued over in daily interactions with other people. Everyday negotiations about norms, values and beliefs usually take place at surface levels of culture with more deep-seated beliefs and norms only implicitly or tacitly understood by cultural members, such that they are not recognized or challenged as often as are components of the surface structure. This layered feature of culture will be examined a bit later in this essay. Human social actions are coordinated also through power relations, markets and formal laws, but to understand these forms of coordination we must first understand communicatively coordinated action. Without communicatively coordinated social action there would be no markets, no laws, no formal rules, no ideologies, no organized police forces and penal institutions. That is why it is so important to have a deep understanding of communicatively coordinated action and its structures.

Communicatively coordinated action is based on relations between subjects rather than relations between objects (and rather than relations between a subject and an object), and hence coordinated social action cannot be studied or explained in the same ways that coordinated events in physical nature can be studied and explained. Human subjects hold each other accountable and responsible for what they do. When people disagree with each other they are expected to give reasons for their disagreements and listen to counter-reasons. Much of this takes place at surface levels of cultural milieu, which contains deeper layers of assumptions and beliefs that are not commonly questioned or even noticed. Simple disagreements and disputes in everyday life are resolved continuously through communicative practices. Each time they happen participants necessarily assume that they are fundamentally free to agree or disagree with each other and to act in diverse ways, such that they are responsible for the actions they do take on. Hence a fundamental way in which actions are coordinated socially is through shared norms, values and beliefs that are maintained through basic everyday communicative practices. Norms, values and beliefs are inherently criticizable. Agreements on them require reasons, in principle. In reality many everyday norms and values are rationally discussed and critiqued by people, but this often takes place on the surface of a deep structure of more fundamental norms and beliefs. And these deep-seated norms and beliefs often escape the discursive awareness of actors such that they can be and usually are distorted, ideological but not understood in this way by the people who live and act through them.

The term "culture" can be understood as the historically cumulative deposit of knowledge, beliefs, values, norms and identity structures of a human group. Within culture we have both objectivated forms of knowledge and objectified cultural products but also a vast amount of knowledge that remains implicit in the form of knowing-how to act and interact. Culture is important not only because it is the milieu through which people communicate with each other but because it is the milieu through which people make sense of their situations generally, monitor and explain their own actions (including non-communicative ones) and form and maintain their personal identities. Culture is also the means by which societies store knowledge and beliefs in documents, and transmit the results of historically developing learning processes to the next generation.

B. Communicative Structures and Meaning

The basic communicative situation is one in which there are two or more people who share access to the objective situation they are in, who also share understandings of cultural norms and who each have subjective states and intentions that only they themselves have access to. One unique feature of the critical qualitative research methodology outlined in this article is its specific theory of communicative processes and structures. Figure 2 provides a graphic representation of the basic communicative situation as theorized in Habermas's theory of communicative action and as similarly discussed by philosophers like Donald Davidson (see Davidson, 2001).

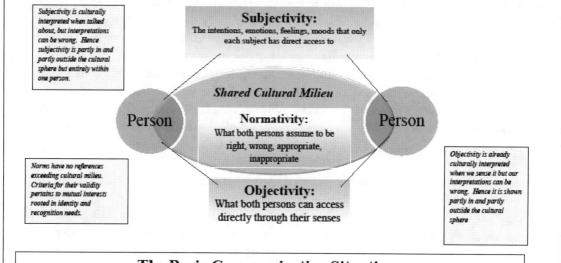

Figure Two

The three distinctive domains of the basic communicative situation—objectivity, subjectivity and normativity—are related to three types of validity claims that feature in each and every imaginable communicative act. Meaning is constituted by a cluster of validity claims that fall into three types: objective, subjective and normative. To understand meaning is to understand this cluster of validity claims. Even non-linguistic acts of meaning involve these three types of validity claim. For example, imagine that you and I are attending a talk together and the speaker says that the theory of evolution must be wrong because if it were right then we human beings would be nothing more than "advanced monkeys." In the United States there are people who give such talks because they oppose the theory of evolution for religious reasons. Let's imagine that you and I are at such a talk, and after the speaker makes this statement you look at me and I raise my eyebrows and make a facial expression that means "This is a silly, ridiculous statement." You nod your head in agreement. My meaning did not use language but to understand it you would have to grasp a cluster of validity claims falling into each category of the normative, the objective and the subjective. Subjective claims I am making may include a feeling like disgust I am having that anyone could make a statement like this. It is subjective because it is a *feeling* I am having. As *my* feeling it is not something you have access to in the way that I do and hence it is subjective because subjective states are states that only one person has direct access to.

Objective claims carried by my raised eyebrows include many things, but one of them would be the implication that there is objective evidence for the theory of evolution. All people in principle could have the same sort of access to this sort of evidence, like fossil and genetic evidence supporting evolutionary theory. Objective claims concern facts and events that can be accessed by all people in the same ways. Normatively I implicitly claim that it is appropriate for me to act in this way towards you at this time. There are many more subjective, objective and normative claims involved in my act, and to understand the meaning of my act you and anyone who observes the act would have to grasp these claims, some of which are more implicit than others, to understand my intended meaning. To be more accurate here, when people understand meaning from the acts of others they understand several possible clusters of validity claims falling into a field that we can call the "meaning field." We are not sure which cluster of claims the actor would endorse or intended with her act, but the range of possible meanings is bounded. Meaning is always constituted by a cluster of validity claims that fall into these three categories. Notice also that my act of winking at you in this context would convey a claim related to the kind of person I am. This will be called the "identity claim" and further explained later in the article. The identity claim is a fourth claim carried by meaningful acts. Below we will also examine value claims in distinction from normative claims.

When a meaningful act is addressed from one person to another it can be understood or misunderstood. If it is misunderstood, one or more of the claims made by the actor would be misunderstood. For example, you might misunderstand my raising of the eyes to mean that I *approve* of what the person said. Different cultures assign different meanings to eyebrow raising and even within one culture eyebrow raising can mean different things depending upon context and past relationships between people. If a meaningful act is understood by another in the way that the actor intended it to be understood, then the receiver of the act can still disagree with any of the validity claims carried by the act. You might understand my act much as I intended it to be understood, but think there is no objective evidence supporting evolutionary theory. Or you might understand my act as I intended it to be understood, but think it was inappropriate for me to communicate to you like this in this situation. Perhaps you would think that I am *pretending* to feel disgusted, to make a good impression on you, when I really feel something else. You might think that my claim to be sincere in communicating this to you (another subjective claim, being sincere) is not true and that I am really trying to trick you in some way. All validity claims are *criticizable*. This is a hugely important point, something fundamental to critical theory. Below is a summary of the validity claims carried as clusters by all meaningful actions, both linguistic and non-linguistic:

Subjective claims and assumptions pertain to experiences that only one person can directly access. All communicative acts carry some subjective claims and assumptions. Subjective claims and assumptions can be made explicit with words and expressions like "I *feel* such and such," "you/he/they *feel* such and such," "I/you/she *intend* such and such."

Objective claims pertain to features of the physical world that all humans have access to. Objective claims and assumptions can be made explicit with words and expressions like "There is/was/will be such and such a state of observable affairs," "When x, y, z occur then a, b, c result," with the references structured by multiple access and located in spatial/temporal relations.

Norms about what is right, wrong, appropriate, inappropriate, and so on also are claimed and assumed in all communicative acts. Normative claims can be made explicit with statements using words like "should," "should not," "duty," "obligation," "prohibition," "right," "wrong," "responsibility" and others.

Values are also *often* carried in communicative actions as claims or assumptions. Values can be made explicit with words like "good," "bad," "important," "beautiful," "desirable," "significant," and so on. Value claims are arguably not *always* a feature of communicative acts, whereas norms, objective claims and subjective claims are. Remember that normative claims are claims about what is right, wrong, appropriate, and so on. Every act of communication will include normative claims because at the very minimum there must be a claim that the communication being made, at the time and within the context it is being made, is appropriate. Every action of communication also must use language or other signs (gestures, facial expressions, etc.) which only carry meaning because they are normed—there is a range of correct ways to use language and other signs and a range of incorrect uses. But value claims, claims about what is good, bad, beautiful, valuable, and so on, are not absolutely required by communication. They are so frequently parts of communicative actions, and they tell us much about a culture, and therefore they are presented here and explained here. But they are not as fundamental as normative, subjective and objective claims.

Those four categories cover all the basic types of rational claim and assumption that are carried in communicative acts, though I will add the "identity claim" a bit later on in this section. The first three categories are ones that we will *always* find in all communicative acts. The fourth claim, value claims, are *usually* found in communicative acts. Again, we owe this insight to Jürgen Habermas (1984, 1987; but see also Davidson, 2001). Claims and assumptions fall into these four categories, but in addition we have "beliefs" and "theories" or "implicit theories" carried by many communicative acts. If a parent tells a teacher that she should strictly discipline the parent's child at school, because otherwise the child will become "spoiled" or even a criminal later in life, then a whole theory of human development is claimed. Unraveling all the assumptions and specific validity claims within this theory would be arduous, and much of it would not be fully thought out by the parent—it would be an implicit theory with unfilled spaces. There are many implicit theories carried by meaningful actions that a researcher will want to make explicit and carefully examine.

Now it is time to take a look at another feature of the internal connection between validity claims and meaning. Validity claims carried by meaningful acts are claimed or assumed at different levels; they have different locations on a continuum from highly foregrounded to deeply backgrounded. To introduce this idea consider the following hypothetical meaningful act. Let's say that a friend has come to our house in order to work on a co-authored paper with us, but she looks very ill to us so we ask her to please lie down. We say, "Please lie down!" Notice that if she does lie down, then this was not caused: she agreed to lie down for reasons that she could supply if asked. And notice that if she objects it will be due to a validity claim issue, disagreeing with one of the claims that constitute the meaning of our act. She could say, "Oh no, I don't feel as bad as I look" (our assumption of a subject state she has is objected to); or "It is not appropriate for you to ask me to lie down, I am female and you are male" (our assumption that the request we made is normatively appropriate is objected to); or she might say, "But there is no place to lie down!" (our assumption that there is an objective situation that would facilitate her lying down is objected to). Notice also that if we had said, "Lie down or you will be punished" or "Lie down; I am a professor and you are a graduate student so you must obey my commands," then in these cases power is added to the situation. She is not caused to lie down, but she may agree to lie down only to avoid negative sanctions rather than because she really agrees with the validity claims carried by our request.

Now, our meaningful act, "Please lie down!", which was made because our friend looks ill, carries validity claims at different levels. The foreground is what we would call the main point of the act, the meaning intended by the actor (if the hearer misunderstands, it is because she misunderstands intended meaning; she has the intention wrong). A cluster of validity claims constitute the point of our act: "I want you to lie down" (subjective), "I care about you" (subjective), "You *look* ill" (objective because of "look"), "You are feeling ill" (subjective but although put in the foreground it is really just off the foreground; *looking* ill is more in the foreground).

There is an intermediate level of validity claims that are presupposed for the foregrounded claims to be intelligible. One way to get at the intermediate level (and also deeper levels) is to imagine objections to claims in the foreground, and then the responses that the original actor would give to defend those foregrounded claims. Hence the following claims go into the intermediate area of our "validity horizon" (Carspecken, 1996) as we call this sort of reconstruction: "If a person looks ill, she is probably feeling ill" (relation between objective and subjective states: a relational claim), "I am a good friend/caring person" (identity claim), "If feeling ill, lying down will result in feeling better" (relational claim of subjective-objective-subjective), "We have enough time for you to lie down" (objective).

There are two more levels of claim we can articulate for this hypothetical act. They, along with the ones already articulated as foregrounded and intermediate, are included in Figure 3: an example of a validity horizon. Notice that backgrounded claims will usually involve generalized principles, implicit theories, worldview assumptions and other things that characterize an entire culture or an entire dis-

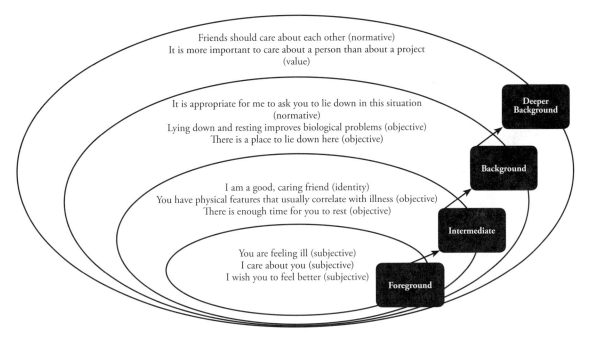

The Validity Horizon: Meaning is constituted by criticizable validity claims that can be representing on a continuum from foregrounded to backgrounded. As claims recede from the foreground they are more likely to become assumptions that are taken for granted and implicitly grasped. But they can always be articulated explicitly with reasons for and against them. There are four main types of claim or assumption with all acts of meaning: objective, subjective, normative and identity. Value claims may also be involved.

Figure Three: The Validity Horizon

course, one of several, that can be found within an entire culture. A single meaningful act will implicate backgrounded assumptions and beliefs, but a researcher will often not be able to understand such things until she has spent much time with the people she studies. She will have to understand many diverse acts carrying similar backgrounds to gain some confidence in bringing out those backgrounded assumptions. A single foreground can be supported in principle by diverse, more backgrounded assumptions and claims, but when we get to know our participants and their culture well, we are able to find the specific backgrounded beliefs implicitly held by our participants. Figure 3 provides a graphic representation of the validity horizon of the meaningful act used as an example.

Notice that another kind of claim is included in this graphic—the identity claim, which has been mentioned a few times already but not explained. Meaningful acts cannot avoid having relevance to the kind of person the actor claims to be, and the qualitative researcher can learn much from reconstructing the range and types of identity claims routinely made by the people in her study. Identity claims are carried by all meaningful acts but at different levels of foregrounding or backgrounding. In this case the identity claim seems to be at an intermediate level because it is not the main point of the act but is strongly implied by the act just the same. During a job interview the applicant will probably often foreground identity claims because she will be very aware that things she says and the ways that she says them will convey an impression to the interviewers of what kind of person she is. In conversations with close friends identity claims will often be very backgrounded and nearly unnoticed. The nature of this identity claim will be discussed next.

C. Human Identity

The study of human identity is quite popular in many forms of qualitative social research, but once again we find more precision and theoretical guidance with critical social theory. One of the criticizable claims that accompany meaningful acts is the identity claim. In critical qualitative research a theory of identity claims is used that originates in the philosophy of George Herbert Mead (1934) and has received further refinement and elaboration by Habermas (especially 1987, Ch. 5). Habermas does not discuss human identity as a *claim* that is criticizable like the other claims, but that is nevertheless how it should be construed, as something that accompanies actions and perhaps does not really exist aside from being claimed in action and thought. A popular point made in much social science literature today is that the human self is neither unified nor essential but rather fragmented and constructed. If we understand the self as a process involving claims—existential claims—that manifest in different ways and in different domains but always in relation to an audience of some kind (concrete, abstract, specific, or general audiences), then this idea of a non-essential and potentially fragmented self takes on more precision. Let's examine this theory of the self next.

Identity claims can be examined on both a vertical temporal axis and a horizontal one. Vertically, human beings claim identities that are the products of their life histories, in the form of a self-narrative or autobiography. The same person can and will tell somewhat different stories about her life depending on when the self-narrative is told and to whom and how much of it is actually told. Implicitly, people generally take everyday life events up into *implicit* ongoing stories about themselves. It might be more accurate to say that people integrate life experience in relation to implicit possibilities for articulating life stories, either partially or comprehensively if some project calls for a full story. Integration of experience does not conform to a single story line but rather to implicit structures from which a range of discursive narratives can be expressed. Wilhelm Dilthey was an early thinker who noted that the life story or autobiography serves the function of synthesis for fully lived experiences, taking the notions of unity and synthesis from Kant's arguments about the unity of perceptional experience via the transcendental "I" (Dilthey, 1991). This is an important insight, but fully discursive life stories do not seem to be the structures of synthesis; rather, people synthesize, unify life experiences with implicit structures giving a range of possible narratives. That is one reason for inconsistency in identity claims; when they are articulated as life stories the stories will be different from time to time and audience to audience. Furthermore, people rarely articulate comprehensive life stories—this happens when someone writes an autobiography, or attempts to tell their full story to an intimate friend, or maintains a diary, but in other circumstances people only provide partial life stories when needed. Humans expect each other to be able to give self-narratives as a way to identify themselves (explain who they are) and also as a way to justify horizontal identity claims discussed below. Narrative research and life-history research have become popular methods in qualitative research. Cultures supply a variety of narrative forms for producing one's self-narratives, inclusive of typical character forms and plots. These are influenced, in contemporary societies, by movies, novels and now Internet-posted self-stories using Facebook and other programs.

Horizontally, identity claims are performed with every meaningful act. Every act claims an identity for the actor in rough terms of what kind of person she is. A certain way of saying something, for example, can indicate whether the person identifies with a geographic area or whether the person claims to be of the well-educated class in her society, or whether the person claims to be a leader who should be taken seriously or a reasonable and flexible person, and many other things. A single performed identity claim can be unpacked to reveal always a combination of many categories (age, gender, class, race, etc.) and qualities (confident, competent, humble, deferential, etc.). A qualitative researcher can work out and articulate these "horizontal" identity claims as well as the cultural structures upon which they depend. There are many structures within all cultures that provide "material" from which identities can be determined, claimed, constructed and evaluated, both in the vertical and horizontal sense. There are culturally shared ideas about what makes a good person, a bad person, a smart person, a dull person, etc.; about how women should or can be, how men should or can be, older people, younger people, people of a certain region or social class, of a certain geographical region, a certain political or religious persuasion, and many other things. Identity claims are made and understood through cultural structures that actors understand holistically; each identity claim is also a claim about what kind of person that actor is *not* and therefore an entire structure delimiting possible ways to be a person has to be understood to understand a singular identity claim. These claims are performed and thus understood implicitly. They are features of the pragmatic commitments people make to each other during interactions. For example, if during an interaction someone tells us, "I will finish the report for you by tomorrow morning," this will be said along with a performed identity claim, performed through the gestures and tone of voice used and other paralinguistic features of the act that would include "I am a trustworthy person." And hence one of the objections that might be made to the many claims carried by this speech act could be "Why should I trust you?" A common way a person can back up a challenged identity claim is to provide a partial life story: "I have produced reports overnight many times for many different people and never once failed to have one done by morning." Finally, consider the case of an explicit, discursively made horizontal identity claim like "I'm competent, trustworthy, reliable and pleasant mannered" (something that might be said in a job interview). The full horizontal identity claim still resides within the pragmatics and performance of the act but in a case like this with semantic reinforcement. The words used could be used ironically to convey an opposite identity claim, which means that identity claims made as part of meaningful acts are fundamentally performative and implicit.

In summary, humans claim their identities performatively at some level of backgrounding and foregrounding with every meaningful act, and claim them differently in different contexts, with different people and so on. In addition, humans have possible self-narratives on hand through which they integrate their life experiences. All humans, unless damaged or suffering from a mental illness, can give a story about themselves and sometimes, in some situations, this is what is expected. Just as cultures supply structures through which identities are performed as claims horizontally in meaningful acts, cultures supply narrative forms for self-stories with different characters (hero, victim, etc.) in different standardized plots. The actual telling of a self-narrative will creatively make use of standardized cultural narrative forms but can use these forms in innovative ways.

On the "me"

These features of human identity pertain to the "me" structure of the self. The "me" is our sense of *what kind of person* we are, and it requires taking the position of others in relation to ourselves. Human beings internalize the culturally generated perspectives of others when acquiring communicative competencies, and this internalization also gives us a sense of what kind of person we ourselves are. Once internalized, these "other" positions are used by people to monitor themselves as they act. Humans desire and even need to maintain stable, respected social identities, stable and valid "me" constructions, and much of their action can be understood in terms of this particularly human desire and need. In addition, when people criticize each other for violating norms or otherwise behaving inappropriately, such criticisms operate upon the identity need. People will sometimes agree that they have acted badly, apologize and change their activities because they wish to be a *better sort of person* in their own judgment. Thus the "me" and the specific domain of human needs associated with it (needs for recognition from others, for respect, for dignity) is a big feature of all social life.

People monitor their own action, and acquire as well as maintain the "me" part of their identities, by taking the position of other subjects in relation to themselves. Three more concepts help us to understand this. One is that of the "significant other." Adults often have certain specific people in their lives whose opinion of them matters a lot—a lot more than the opinions of other people. Significant others can be parents, close friends, spouses, inspiring professors or teachers. Another concept is one we also get from George Herbert Mead: "generalized other." A "generalized other" position is an abstraction learned and internalized by children when growing up and acquired by adults when they move into new cultures or subcultures. Children initially begin to develop a "me" only through significant others—usually their parents. But as they grow they learn to adopt the position of an entire group towards themselves—how does the neighborhood view certain actions and things, how do the kids at school view certain things? All of us internalize generalized other positions and monitor our own actions from those positions. Yet another concept is that of the "reference group." Because there are diverse generalized other positions that we all internalize, sociologists can specify some of them as "reference groups." The kids at school might be one reference group for a student, but the people in a neighborhood in which she lives another. Some generalized other positions, however, cannot be identified to actual groups. We internalize generalized other positions from movies and television, literature and other sources.

On the "I"

Here is where the concept of "I" becomes important. We humans respond to our own "me" formations in that we can and do judge ourselves, we change our actions in light of our self-judgments, we take responsibility for what we do and what we don't do, and we can tell our life stories critically, neutrally, or approvingly, as if we are more than what is represented in these stories. As Habermas nicely expresses it, humans "are both the authors and critics of their self-narratives." To be an author, critic, responsible subject, self-judge and so on is to have an "I." What we are, as human beings, is not fully captured by the "me." We all claim slightly different "me" identities in different social contexts, and as we move through the years of life, our social identity can change, sometimes even dramatically. Yet something within us, so to speak, seems to transcend these changes, and something about each of us transcends our "me" constructions in order to monitor them, self-judge them, be responsible for them and so on. Finally, our own actions can surprise us. We are a *source* of action, but the actions that come forth are not strictly programmed by a social identity. They can be spontaneous, surprising, new. All of this calls for the concept of the "I."

On the one hand, the "I" is the source of our uniqueness as individuals. We use the word "I" to refer to the source of our actions and to the potentiality that is there in all of us for new types of action. We all have potentiality and uniqueness that is not fully represented in a "me." As we move through life we explore this potentiality we have, which is unknown to us. We "realize" our potentialities if we are fortunate through a life process of learning and development. This aspect of the "I" is connected to the human process of *self-realization*, which individuates us, brings forth our accomplishments and achievements in work and social life.

On the other hand, the "I" responds to our own actions and "me" formations, taking responsibility for them. It takes the position of a *generalized other* to monitor and judge the self. In this way the "I" is also a "we." It is the moral-practical agent who is able to act on generalized rules. This moral aspect of the "I" is in one sense the opposite of individuation. It is from a "we" position that it acts so that it will prescribe rules of action to itself that it expects *any* person to follow in the same situation. When acting primarily from this position we do the "right thing" no matter how we are feeling or desiring or fearing at the time, and no matter what particular attributes we have in our usual "me" claims. This "I" is the principle of *autonomy* in the human self. It also develops over time because we have to learn to act autonomously according to generalized moral principles and rules as we mature. Instead of "self-realization," the development of greater moral consciousness and autonomy (which, remember, means acting more from a "we" position than an individuated position) is called *self-determination*. Autonomy and self-determination are possibilities only because human identity is structured socially and requires the "we" position.

Relevance to Qualitative Research

This theory of the self is very important for critical qualitative research for a number of reasons. First, cultures differ in terms of the material they provide for human identity formations, so discovering and articulating the range of possible ways to be a person in a culture is an excellent and deep way to get a handle on it, understand it and critique it. For example, in some cultures and subcultures there are only a few ways in which one can be an appropriate man or woman; in other cultures and subcultures there are more ways for bringing gender into one's identity. In fact, cultures have different *structures* (see section below) that humans draw upon to make their identity claims. As discussed already, understanding the identity structures afforded by a culture will tell us about power relations in that culture.

Secondly, a good deal of routine social action can be understood if we understand the identity concerns of the actors. Maintaining a valid social identity is extremely important for most people, and they will act routinely to maintain a valid sense of themselves. The more a qualitative researcher can understand the identity concerns of her participants, the more she will understand many other things about the culture; what values, norms and beliefs are available and in play. The same cultural components that are important to human identities feature in other aspects of culture like the beliefs it makes available about nature, about what a good life is, about religion, about the relation between individuals and groups and much more.

Thirdly, cultures differ in terms of how much self-realization and self-determination (autonomous moral action) they facilitate for their members. Some cultures are very closed in terms of what are considered acceptable forms of self-expression for people of specific social statuses (restricting self-realization), and this would usually be related to the extent to which this culture encourages or discourages reflection in challenging norms and beliefs (restricting self-determination). The way these restrictions work in cultures and ideologies is by tying certain norms and beliefs to restricted ways of being a valid person, such that challenging the norm or belief is automatically to become, in some way, a "bad person" in the eyes of other cultural members.

Hence certain kinds of *power* can only be understood by understanding this theory of self. For example, in a strictly patriarchal culture which holds that women are inferior to men and should not be allowed to do certain things as a result—like go to school—the self-realization needs of women will be blocked. The range of "me" formations available to women will be limited. Females who naturally experience desires to become scholars or excel in sports or have an active political life will find these impulses for self-realization blocked. And if such cultures make it normatively "bad" to question these beliefs about women, then they will usually have "me" labels for women that do question and challenge patriarchal beliefs and norms which are negative. Words like "bitch" are used in English-speaking nations in this way. They designate a negative form of being a woman. If women themselves internalize the generalized other positions from which these judgments come, then they will experience oppression. They will have desires and needs to self-realize in ways that would give them a negative "me" in the culture, and if they themselves believe in the negative "me" categories, then they are likely to repress those desires and needs to their detriment.

Freedom is experienced or denied at many levels; economic and political opportunities will be either freeing or oppressive or somewhere between, but opportunities for self-realization and autonomy also will either be limited and oppressive or freeing as well. This level of freedom is subtle because it is connected directly to human identity formation and identity needs, which in turn require an internalized "we" position. When a "we" position is not really "we" but actually a position that privileges one group over others, then freedom is blocked at a subtle but truly important level. For example, in a patriarchal society, women are socialized into taking a "we" position from which they are expected to agree that females should subordinate themselves to males in various ways, and not to do so means one is a bad person, a bad female. But that "we" position is not really a true "we" position—one that represents collective interests equally. Only reflection and critique can reveal "we" positions that are really privileging some groups over others. More will be said about power and freedom in a section below.

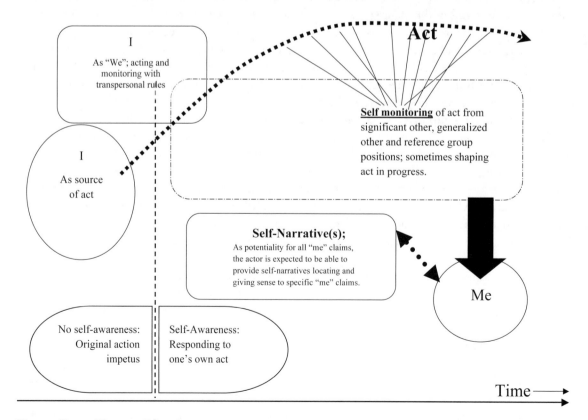

Figure Four: Human Identity

D. Cultural Structures

What Is Structure?

Validity claims, beliefs, assumptions, identity claims and more are drawn upon by actors from their culture holistically, as forms of structure. Cultures have components and themes that are structured in various ways. Cultural structures can be found and reconstructed by researchers. "Structure" in this sense comes from structuralism and should not be confused with "class structure," "occupational structure" and so on. In this critical methodological theory we distinguish "structure" from "system." Systems are dynamic processes located in space and time such that processes in one part of a system will have effects on processes in other parts of the same system. Economics, for example, studies systems of activity in this sense, and later in this article we will examine other types of social systems.

But structures do not exist in space and time. Structures are features of meanings and cultures. One part of a structure *implicates* other parts of the same structure all at once so that to understand a single part one has to understand the entire structure. The grammar of a language is a good example of structure in this sense—and in fact structuralism originated with the work of a linguist, Ferdinand Saussure (2009). The insight was picked up in other fields like mathematics and cognitive psychology and then in cultural anthropology with the work of Lévi-Strauss. Today we think of structure from a post-structuralist position in that we regard structures as constantly changing, claimed with every meaningful act in potentially new ways and forms. "Structuration" is a term invented by Anthony Giddens to describe the link between structure and real human activities that do take place in time and space (see Giddens, 1979). Structures change, even with every act in at least slight ways, and thus involve a process and must be understood in terms of process. Structures exist, argues Giddens, "virtually"—outside time and space. With every meaningful act, structures are "instantiated" and grasped by actors holistically. We can say that structures are *claimed*, not just instantiated, because the conceptual and moral relations they implicate all at once can in principle be made explicit and critiqued. Structures as a whole are criticizable. In addition, Giddens's notion of virtual existence and structure can be combined with Bourdieu's well-cited theory of the habitus (Bourdieu, 1977) and Carspecken's work on action impeti (Carspecken, 1999). But there is no room in this short article to elaborate on those connections here. Stable structures simply involve processes in which the same structural forms appear over and over in routine social actions, giving rise to a reproductive process. Changing structures involve something other than reproduction—processes of change that may be directional or not, and often related to other kinds of change like economic change and globalization.

Types of Cultural Structure

First of all, there are layers in culture—surface cultural themes, beliefs, categories and so on that most people are readily aware of, and layers of deeper structure that begin to escape the awareness of cultural members the deeper we go. The deeper layers of structure are *implicated* by the more surface layers in ways that correspond to the levels we identified for validity horizons. This article has already presented enough material to understand the basic idea here. Validity claims at the surface levels of a meaningful act implicate more deep-seated assumptions. These assumptions in turn implicate yet more deep-seated assumptions and beliefs, sometimes along with images and metaphors that are deeply taken for granted by cultural members and very often unnoticed. In a culture that assumes the world is flat, many surface validity claims will be made that implicate this deeper assumption, and if no one in the culture ever questioned that assumption, it will just operate as a deep structure in the beliefs of this culture. Structures are ways in which reasons for acting implicate more reasons and other reasons. Some such implicated reasons will be within the conscious awareness of cultural members. Others will be tacitly grasped by members, and yet others will escape their awareness entirely.

Inferential relations that connect actions to reasons for the actions to other reasons (reasons for reasons) and so on vary by type. Anthropologists have studied myths, legends, architectural practices, kinship systems, beliefs and various practices from various cultures to reveal implicated structures underlying them (see Lévi-Strauss, 1983; Bourdieu, 1977). Some cultures, usually those of fairly simple societies lacking much institutional differentiation and lacking complexity in the division of labor, display remarkable consistencies in the structures implicated across many of their diverse practices, rituals and myths. Here is an example, a structure reconstructed by an anthropologist for the Murngin culture (see Seung, 1982, p. 24):

pure, sacred	male	superior	fertilizing (rains)	bad season
impure, profane	female	inferior	fertilized (land)	good season

The above cultural structure for the Murngin permeated many domains of life of the people. It is a common structural form found in cultures and societies that do not have a complex division of labor and are not undergoing processes of rapid change. This kind of structure is based on binary oppositions and homology. For example, male is in opposition to female, which means that to understand cultural assumptions about the attributes common to women, feminine ways of acting and talking, motherhood, mother parenting styles, and so on, one has to understand how female is not male in this culture. The category of female is dependent on its culturally specific opposition to male and its place in a set of horizontal categories that are also in binary oppositions. In Willis's classic critical ethnography, *Learning to Labor*, we find a structure of the same form but with different contents:

The Lads	Masculine	Street knowledge	Non-conformity	Own time	Violence to lads	Real world	The "now"	The laugh of the lads
Others (girls, conformist boys, Indian minority students)	Feminine	School Knowledge	Conformity	Time controlled by teachers and bosses	Knowledge to teachers	School world	The future	The command of teachers and bosses

This structure was implicated continuously by many diverse kinds of meaningful actions exhibited by these boys in daily life inside and outside of school. Jokes and bantering frequently contrasted, implicitly, being masculine with being feminine. Making fun of teachers, or other members of the lads or those boys in school who studied hard often worked through making them seem feminine rather than masculine. Non-verbal actions like destroying school property, playing practical jokes on teachers and conformist students, disrupting lectures, refusing to do school assignments, fighting and threatening to fight, stealing and drinking and smoking all also instantiated this same structure.

Willis spent much time talking to these boys in small groups, asking them to explain why they did what they did, which is the way most qualitative researchers would pursue the same goal—discovering and reconstructing structures within which culturally specific categories and themes take their sense. If you asked a lad why he tormented or at least teased a conformist student, the boy would respond with something like "Because he's a poof." "Poof" is a slang word meaning a feminine male, a male who does not manifest the masculine qualities of defying authority, willing to fight physically, refusing to follow official rules, not believing what teachers say about the values that should be endorsed for a good life and so on. Thus reasons for actions could always be provided by the lads, and key words and expressions like "poof" and "having a laugh" were used to make these reasons explicit. A semantic lexical structure was found in this way: culturally specific uses of words and expressions that are associated with the underlying category structure.

Notice that structures are *ways* in which validity claims are made and linked. The words and the underlying categories in the structure of Willis's lads generally fuse objective, subjective and normative categories through the logic of binary opposition and homology. A "poof" for the lads, for example, is a male (objective category) who is willing to conform with teachers and formal rules (a general subjective orientation), who is inferior to other types of males (evaluation) because females are inferior to males in general (evaluation), and whose identity should be avoided (normative). A single term in a semantic lexical structure fuses normative, objective, subjective and identity claims, but the critical qualitative researcher can separate and articulate the clusters of claim, as in the validity horizon explained above.

There are other types of structure that can be discovered within cultures. Some are logical-hierarchical, some are heavily constituted by metaphors (see Spradley, 1979 and 1980, for detailed instructions on how to discover some such structures, particularly those with lexical representations and practices). There are also specifically conceptual structures that have different forms dependent on the degree to which reflection and negation have gone into their constitution, a topic that can only be adequately explained in a chapter-length paper. Unfortunately I have no room to write any more about cultural structure here.

F. Action Conditions

The social theory of Anthony Giddens is helpful for understanding the concepts of action conditions and action consequences (see Giddens, 1979, 1984). Giddens was inspired by some formulations made by Marx, to the effect that human beings make their own history but do so within conditions that they did not choose. That is, humans act freely in fundamental respects but always within complex circumstances involving social, political and historical factors. We act with and often for reasons, which relates to our essential freedom as human subjects, but we are often within unfree circumstances, conditions. Moreover, we are never fully aware of all of the conditions of relevance to our actions, and our freedom is also limited by this factor: the forms and levels of our awareness. Awareness of life circumstances, social and political positioning, is additionally often distorted through ideologies.

Expanding upon Giddens, it is possible to distinguish between types of action conditions. Some conditions of action are external to our volition in the sense that they are not directly constituted communicatively and intersubjectively, so that changing one's position on them with reasons does not change the conditions themselves. For example, if we have to make economic decisions during a time of rampant inflation, then inflation is a condition that confronts us externally, and although our beliefs *about* inflation can be changed communicatively, through reasoning, inflation itself cannot be changed in this way. The same is true of subjective states we experience: if we experience a strong state of fear then this state is not something we can change directly with reasons, though our thoughts *about* the fear can be changed with reasoning. However, there are always many conditions of action that are purely cultural and that immediately change if reasons we consider change our endorsement or rejection of them. These include norms, values, beliefs and identity structures. This kind of condition I call "internal to volition" because as soon as our rational position on them changes, the conditions themselves change. The other kinds of condition I call "external to volition" because they are factual in nature and do not change directly when our reasoning about them changes. Hence we have four main categories of action condition:

Objective-external: physical conditions that may be important, like whether or not there are needed supplies in a classroom, how crowded a room is, how much money the actor has access to, and many other things; and socially constructed conditions like job markets, consumer markets, whether or not a person has a university degree and so on.

Subjective-external: these are subjective states that the actor as well as other people are experiencing at the time of action, like feeling very anxious, attracted to another person, irritated by another person, anger, euphoria and so on.

Cultural-internal: conditions that an actor can in principle engage directly in communicative ways such as norms, values, beliefs and identity concerns.

Institutionally-mediated: these are conditions that are communicatively and rationally determined but only by one group of people (law makers, policy makers, etc.). Once they are formulated and put into practice they affect all people as external to volition—only an institutionally formal process, to which different groups have different degrees and levels of access, can change them.

Let's be sure we understand the difference between external and internal to volition, in the way I am using these expressions. Given the *same* physical environment, socially constructed market situation, or subjective feeling, different actors will have to cope with the identified conditions, but they can act *differently* because of their beliefs, values, endorsed norms and identity concerns. If feeling very anxious, for example, some actors will hide their anxious feelings from others while other actors will talk about feeling nervous with those around them; and this will be due to different identity concerns they have or different norms they endorse. Given the same physical environment, economic situation, career opportunity structure, etc., different people will again act differently because they do not hold to the same values, beliefs, etc. The four categories of action conditions are presented in the chart below:

Conditions of Action			
Objective; external to volition	Subjective; external to volition	Cultural and internal to volition; directly intersubjective	Institutionally mediated; internal to some, external to others
1. Physical-environmental (e.g., classrooms, housing developments) 2. Socially constructed but uncoupled from culture (e.g., market conditions)	1. Emotions (e.g., anger, anxiety, euphoria) 2. Action compulsions, habit energies 3. Some types of mental imagery 4. Processes of denial and mis-recognition 5. General capacities (e.g., intelligence)	1. Norms 2. Values 3. Beliefs 4. Interpretative frameworks 5. Identity structures	1. Laws 2. Regulations 3. Policies 4. Formal rules

Below are examples of conditions of action and levels of awareness that actors had of them, in my study of Croxteth, Liverpool (1991). In this study it was found that community members had very different ideas about schooling, politics and life in general from those held by volunteer teachers:

Conditions of Action Internal to Volition	Degree of Articulation/Level of Awareness
Age relations in Croxteth, with expectations that younger people unquestioningly accept the authority of older people	Not articulated for community volunteers and teachers; uncontested and not in discursive formulation. [Yet tacitly implicated in objections to "progressivism" and in "schooling for discipline and control".]

Reified knowledge; beliefs in traditional curriculum, and importance of examinations	Not articulated for most community activists and teachers; uncontested and not in discursive formulation. Where articulated and contested by a minority of teachers, no alternative articulated.
Schooling for employability belief (the main reason for schooling is so that students can get good jobs later on in life)	Not articulated and uncontested for both groups. No clear alternatives.
Schooling for discipline and control as a philosophy of school (suggesting formal and authoritative teacher-pupil relationships)	Under-articulated (almost tacit) for community volunteers; contested by teachers. Alternative partially formulated.
Progressivism as a philosophy of schooling (suggesting informal teacher-pupil relationships)	Discursive and contested. Held by many teachers, opposed by many community activists.
Patriarchal beliefs	Not articulated by community initially, eventually under-articulated by women from the community. Under-articulated by male teachers. Highly articulated and critically by some female teachers
Community Power Ideology	Discursive and contested. Held by teachers; opposed by many community activists.
The Social Wage Ideology	Discursive and contested. Held by many community activists and opposed by those in favor of community power.
Relation of examinations to job market	Within the discursive awareness of all participants but "as a fact of nature" for most, a matter of critique for only some.
Social class	Within the discursive awareness of all participants, a matter of critique for all.
Time constraints on teaching and political activities	A matter of constant complaint by most teachers
Existing textbooks and other educational infrastructure (state of the buildings, size of the buildings, condition of the classrooms)	Experienced more as a resource than as a constraint
Educational law: school resources distribution	Discursive and contested.
Educational law: examination policies	Discursive, taken for granted by community, affirmed by some teachers and contested by a few teachers.

G. Power

In our hypothetical example of wishing to have a friend lie down that I introduced much earlier in this article, we have seen that we could push her to *cause* her to lie down or we could achieve a communicative agreement with her so that she willingly lies down. In between these two extremes are cases in which power may be used to have our friend lie down. If our friend refused to lie down for reasons, instead of debating these reasons with her we could use power. We could threaten her in some way. We could tell her that if she doesn't lie down, we will use karate on her to beat her up. If she complies to avoid being harmed in this way, she is using her freedom of choice, and her action is not caused by our threat, but she is also not agreeing with the validity claims of our original request. This is use of power on our part.

Power can be understood in terms of the relation an actor has to conditions of action. Conditions of action can be thought of as resources and constraints on acting. Having lots of money is a condition of action that is a resource, but having very little money is a condition of action that is a constraint. Similarly, feeling angry when one wishes to make a favorable impression on a person who values calm and restrained expression is a constraint, but feeling angry when one wishes to frighten a person for some reason is a resource. These kinds of conditions convey forms of power when they primarily constrain an actor rather than resource her. The examples were from the external-objective and external-subjective categories. Cultural conditions of action are different because in principle they can be changed directly through the giving and taking of reasons. A person can immediately stop following a norm after hearing convincing reasons to do so, or thinking of convincing reasons to do so. A person cannot, by contrast, directly change conditions of action that pertain to the physical environment or to the marketplace or even those conditions that pertain to emotional states and habit patterns through communicative processes. And thus different forms of power are associated with cultural conditions of action. Power that works through culture will correspond to what is called ideology. The fourth category of condition of action, institutionally mediated conditions like laws and formalized rules, is directly communicative for some groups in society—the law makers, policy makers and so on—but not for many of those who must follow such laws, policies, formal rules and so on. Institutionally mediated conditions of action are forms of power that vary according to how much access people have to the decision-making processes that put such conditions into place. Political power is the name for this category.

To work out a typology of socio-cultural forms of power we can first consider the case of coercion. Coercive power is power that works by threatening people with negative sanctions if they do not comply with a command or law or formal rule. Use of a weapon, use of psychological coercion, use of economic power to deprive a person of things she needs unless she complies with what is asked of her, all of these are examples of coercion. There are also many cases of institutionally legitimated coercion in all human societies, where one person may not agree to the reasons behind a command or law but where most of society does agree that she and everyone else in her situation ought to comply. Police forces, penal laws and the like are examples of institutionally legitimated coercion.

But there are other forms of power that are more subtle than coercion. On the macro level, in many societies some classes of people control material resources to a far greater extent than other classes of people. They have more power as a result, and this power is called economic power. In some societies, some groups of people are favored by laws while other people are disadvantaged by them. For example, in the nation of South Africa for many decades the apartheid system legally discriminated against black people and favored white people. In the United States before its civil war, laws made it possible for slavery to exist, and a slave had no rights and was considered the property of a slave owner, by law. In many societies for many centuries, laws favored men and restricted women. Political power, like economic power, is conceptualized at the macro level.

Culture and ideology of wide distribution also often constrain some groups of people while favoring others, and when we examine this from the level of a culture as a whole, it is a macro level form of power that we call "cultural power." The ideology of patriarchy is an example. Beliefs that men are superior to women, that women should defer to men, that husbands should rule the family and so on permeate patriarchal societies to affect many social interactions. Ideologies are structures of belief that are widely accepted by a society or a group of people within a society but that in principle could be critiqued if their basic assumptions were made explicit and opened to debate. Ideologies carry power when they *internally* block the ability of people affected by them to openly and freely criticize their principles and assumptions. For example, peasants living during medieval periods of history were exploited by landowners and the aristocracy. But peasants were taught that their place in society was supposed to be what it is, because it was mandated by heaven or dictated by God. They were taught that it would be wrong to challenge this belief, and thus only a very bad sort of person (a negative form of "me") would challenge it. The consequence was that many peasants accepted their exploited position as being their rightful place in the cosmos. This is power working through ideology, because the very idea of making the assumptions of a belief system explicit so that reasons could be given for and against them was prohibited by a norm tied to identity structures. Only a "bad person" would do such a thing, and people need to feel they are valid persons. Of course, many times ideologies, cultural power, is combined with political and economic power so that those who do not buy into a legitimating system of belief will usually still be politically and economically oppressed by a dominant group.

The qualitative social researcher will usually want to understand how forms of power work specifically within actual interactions they observe and possibly take part in. Here is where we see macro forms of power directly *instantiated* in micro forms of action and interaction. Many of these forms of power seem legitimate to the people who are affected by them. Many might seem legitimate only because they work as surface structures implicating deep cultural structures that are not recognized by cultural members but that are in principle criticizable. Interactive forms of power take various main forms, like normative (based on cultural norms pertaining to status differences), charm/charismatic (based on the personality of a leader who can win loyalty from subordinates), contractual (either via written formal contracts between people or interactively established agreements to subordinate one's self to another's authority in return for concrete goods or favors).

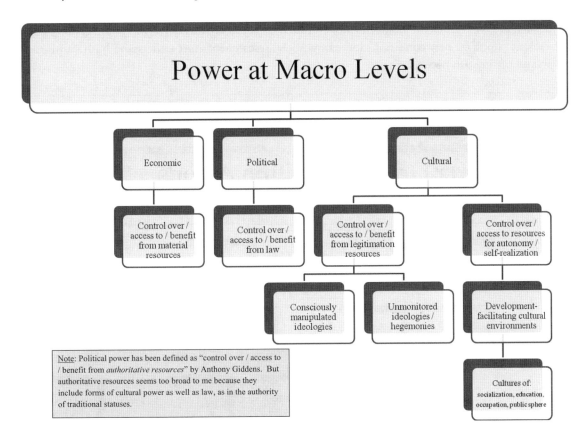

Figure Five: Power at Macro Levels

In summary, the critical theory of society enables us to understand what distinguishes human social organization and social processes from physical processes in nature by understanding communicative action and how it presupposes a free subject who can agree or disagree with another subject, for reasons. This in turn enables us to understand cultural and ideological forms of power that will be found in all human societies because these forms of power work by blocking actors from recognizing implicit assumptions, claims and beliefs they actually subscribe to in their daily activities and even thoughts, and also from criticizing such assumptions and beliefs when they are recognized. Again, the most common way that ideological power blocks criticizability is through tying and fixing forms of identity to certain norms and beliefs, such that to question the beliefs is to be a bad sort of person, according to the culture. Political and economic power, on the other hand, work as constraints on action from the outside. They cannot be changed directly through reasoning and critique. They can only be changed through institutional processes which formulate laws and put laws into place, through social movements and revolutions.

H: Theory of Systems

All actions have multiple consequences. Some of the consequences are intended and some are not. Some of the consequences are within the awareness of the actor and some are not. Human societies must have stable relations between the aggregate consequences of many actions made by many people and the conditions of action that give rise to those very consequences. This relation between large numbers of action consequences and action conditions is called the social system. In the critical theoretical framework described here, an important distinction is made between culture (which, remember, has structure) and social system. Because social actions require culture and have meaning, in that actors will be able to give reasons for what they do, and because social actions will always have consequences that include effects on new conditions for acting, social researchers must understand both culture and system and distinguish between them.

Note: Micro-level forms of power as manifested in power and authority claims within interactions are represented here. Most of these forms instantiate macro-level forms of power, and assumptions, beliefs, ideologies and worldview structures supporting micro-level power claims are implicated with each instantiation but often exceed actor's awareness.

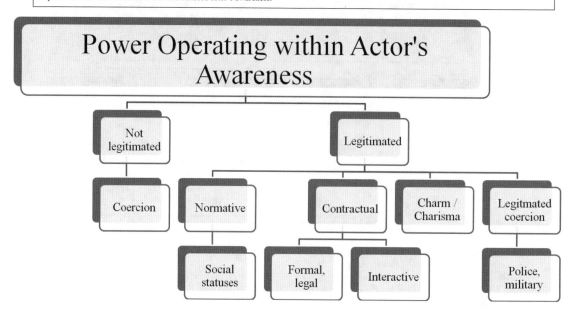

Figure Six: Power Operating within Actor's Awareness

Relations between action consequences and action conditions take many diverse forms. In modern societies the economic sphere of action has "uncoupled," as Habermas calls it (1987, Ch. 6), from the cultural and even political spheres of society as a whole. The economic system relates action consequences to new action conditions through market relations. Prices for products change continuously as the result of aggregate patterns of buying as well as the decisions of producers on what kinds of and how many products to produce. This system of action has detached to a large extent from culture because actors in market situations act in largely individualized ways, calculating which economic decisions will best meet their interests. Collectively decided norms, values and morals are removed from the situation to a considerable degree. The aggregate consequences of large amounts of buying and selling activities through markets have functions relating to trends in the economic subsystem. Economic trends include expansions and contractions of the economy as well as periods of stability. This complex system is related to other complex systems of action like education, and it results in changes to culture as well. For the individuals acting economically, the aggregate action consequences that result are not intended, only the individually experienced consequences are intended. However, governments can study economic patterns and then pass laws with the intention of regulating the economic system.

Other kinds of relations between action conditions and action consequences involve the cultural domain directly. For example, when teachers teach students, the consequences of their teaching activities have many functions for the social system. Knowledge produced by past generations is transmitted, and the division of labor in society is reproduced for the next generation by teaching special forms of knowledge to diverse groups of students who will work in different fields in their adult lives. These are intended action consequences within a system.

But there are many unintended action consequences associated with the education systems of any society which have functions for systems as well. For example, many teachers unconsciously interact with boys differently than they do with girls. Boy and girl students receive different "messages" implicitly in this way about what roles they should take on in society. By acting on these implicit messages, boys and girls will either reproduce traditional gender roles or, if a culture is going through a period of change, take on new and non-traditional gender roles. Because role behavior has connections with the division of labor in households as well as in the paid-economic sphere, the implicit messages taught by teachers have functions for the social system as a whole. The hidden curriculum in schools subtly socializes children differently based on class, race and gender, in a way that has functions for the division of labor and distribution of wealth in society as a whole.

Summary and Conclusions

Critical qualitative research is exciting, political, meaningful, and mind-expanding when actually practiced. Both fieldwork experiences and data analysis are richly meaningful and transformative. This chapter no doubt seems rather dry by contrast. The methodological theory supporting critical social research has been developed in quite rigorous and detailed ways. Learning it, especially when it is presented in a condensed overview like this one, has its dry moments, for sure. It is like learning a language in many ways. A language is beautiful when spoken and used to express discoveries and insights. But learning the grammar and phonetics of a new language has its tedious moments. The critical qualitative researcher takes a set of basic concepts and their relations into the field and uses them creatively so that every new study is like a new work of art. Moreover the art in this case is something collective, shared with others—one's participants—and involves changes in action, consciousness and, we always hope, society. My apologies to readers who have found this piece lacking in excitement and inspiration. Believe me, doing critical social research is one of the most meaningful things one can experience. For readers who are new to critical social research I suggest making use of Figure 1, in particular, when planning an initial study, and then going right into the field and coming back to reading methodological theory during nights and weekends when your study is actually in process. Learning the concepts and theory I have overviewed here happens most profoundly by actually trying to apply it.

References

Apple, M. (1979). *Ideology and curriculum*. London: Routledge & Kegan Paul.

Apple, M. (1986). *Teachers and texts*. London: Routledge & Kegan Paul.

Bourdieu, P. (1977). *Outline of a theory of practice*. Cambridge: Cambridge University Press.

Brandom, R. (1998). *Making it explicit*. Cambridge, MA: Harvard University Press.

Brandom, R. (2001). *Articulating reasons*. Cambridge, MA: Harvard University Press.

Carspecken, P. F. (1991). *Community schooling and the nature of power: The battle for Croxteth Comprehensive*. London: Routledge.

Carspecken, P. F. (1996). *Critical ethnography in educational research: A theoretical and practical guide*. New York: Routledge.

Carspecken, P. F. (1999). *Four scenes for posing the question of meaning, and other explorations in critical philosophy and critical methodology*. New York: Peter Lang.

Carspecken, P. F. (2003). Ocularcentrism, phonocentrism and the counter-enlightenment problematic: Clarifying contested terrain in our schools of education. *Teachers College Record, 105*(6), 978–1047.

Davidson, D. (2001). *Subjective, objective, intersubjective*. Oxford: Oxford University Press.

Dilthey, W. (1991). *Selected works: Vol. 1. Introduction to the human sciences*. Princeton: Princeton University Press.

Fals-Borda, O., & Rahman, M. A. (1991). *Action and knowledge: Breaking the monopoly with participatory action research*. New York: Apex Press.

Freire, P. (2000). *Pedagogy of the oppressed*. London: Continuum.

Giddens, A. (1979). *Central problems in social theory*. Berkeley: University of California Press.

Giddens, A. (1984). *The constitution of society*. Cambridge, England: Polity Press.

Giroux, H. (1983). *Theory and resistance in education*. London: Heinemann.

Habermas, J. (1984). *The theory of communicative action* (Vol. 1). Boston: Beacon Press.

Habermas, J. (1987). *The theory of communicative action* (Vol. 2). Boston: Beacon Press.

Kincheloe, J., & McLaren, P. (2008). Rethinking critical theory and qualitative research. In N. K. Denzin & Y. S. Lincoln (Eds.), *The landscape of qualitative research* (3rd ed., pp. 403–456). Thousand Oaks, CA: Sage.

Lévi-Strauss, C. (1983). *Structural anthropology* (Vol. 2). Chicago: University of Chicago Press.

McLaren, P. (1999). *Schooling as a ritual performance*. New York: Rowman & Littlefield.

Mead, G. H. (1934). *Mind, self and society*. Chicago: University of Chicago Press.

Saussure, F. (2009). *Course in general linguistics*. Books LLC

Schutz, A. (1972). *The phenomenology of the social world*. London: Heinemann.

Seung, T. K. (1982). *Structualism and hermeneutics*. New York: Columbia University Press.

Spradley, J. (1979). *The ethnographic interview*. New York: Harcourt, Brace, Jovanovich.

Spradley, J. (1980). *Participant observation*. Austin, TX: Holt, Rinehart and Winston.

Willis, P. (1977). *Learning to labor: How working class kids get working class jobs*. London: Gower.

Xie, X., & Carspecken, P. F. (2008). *Philosophy, learning and the mathematics curriculum: Dialectical materialism and pragmatism related to Chinese and U.S. mathematics curriculum*. Rotterdam: Sense.

CHAPTER FIVE

The Critical Power of Place

Margaret Somerville

I've always had an uneasy relationship with water. My earliest memories of water are growing up by the side of Belfast Lough in Ireland. Here, I skimmed stones across the Lough with my brothers, shivered as I learned to swim, chased gulls and watched the big ships glide down from the harbour, on their way to other places. On the surface the water seemed safe and inviting. It sparkled on summer days. As children we splashed through the waves, the water raced over our toes, washing stones as shiny as a seal's back. I remember the sea at night with lights in the distance; the other side, across the water. As a child, I dreamed of rowing to the other side to see what was there. But on dull, winter days when the mist settled over the Lough we imagined the water as deep, mysterious and frightening. Ships were shadows in the fog, and their foghorns were familiar sounds of winter. They were going somewhere into the world beyond. (May Lecky, 2008).

I begin this chapter with a place story. This particular story was told by a participant in a collective biography workshop[1] designed to share the possibilities of collective biography as a methodology (Haug, 1987) for researching people's deep attachments to their local places. Participants were invited to tell a story about their earliest memories of water using an adaptation of Haug's collective biography. In collective biography memory work, the storyteller remembers the sensory qualities of sound, smell, movement, feelings associated with a particular memory in order to evoke its embodied quality.

One possible approach we have identified is to concentrate on a particular situation, rather than on life in its entirety. Once we have begun to rediscover a given situation—its smells, sounds, emotions, thoughts, attitudes—the situation itself draws us back into the past, freeing us for a time from notions of our present superiority over our past selves; it allows us to become once again the child—a stranger—whom we once were. (Haug et al., 1999, p. 47)

Frigga Haug developed this method in relation to the feminist project of reconceptualising the body through deconstructing the effects of discourses of the body and changing the stories we tell.

Through the process of responding and working on each other's stories in the group, the individual stories together become a collective process of tranformative memory work. In our workshop we adapted the process to memory work about place with a focus on water places. As each participant told a story, others listened in silence, and each story elicited more stories in a process of collective remembering. The stories ranged from people's earliest memories of being swished and sung to in the bath as a baby, to playing in flooded backyards when the irrigation waters were released from the river; from the mists of the Belfast Lough to a suburban backyard swimming pool in western Sydney. Place was a powerful signifer for everyone in the workshop.

Everyone has embodied place memories, and place storytelling is a generative meeting point for these individually held memories. In telling a story about a place memory, we are telling about something that is both inside and outside of our selves. It is not like telling our internally scripted life story because the focus is on the outside world and a single memory, thus escaping from the confines of an individualised psychological framework. And yet, a place story is not separate from us; it resides in our bodies and cannot be objectified or entirely externalised; it connects what is outside of us and what is inside. A place memory recalls the past but it lives on in us, so it links the past and the present. Each person tells the specific embodied place story that is uniquely theirs and yet each story elicits a proliferation of place memories from everyone else. Through this dynamic process the storytelling becomes collective. Place stories connect—to other worlds and other places—and yet they are deeply local and embodied, participating in the materiality of specific local places. There is nothing else quite like "the stones washed as shiny as a seal's back" as a memory of a water place, but we can all participate in the sensory qualities it evokes and these in turn call up more of our own stories. Place stories participate in the real and the symbolic. We know the mists in winter over the Belfast Lough, the shadowy ships and the fog horns are real, and yet in this story they become sensory phenomena that evoke flights of the imagination to elsewhere.

The participants found the storytelling workshop an engaging and moving experience. They said they felt connected to others in the workshop through the storytelling, temporarily moving out of the alienating experience of the conference to share deeper meanings through their place stories. Place, according to Gieryn (2000) is thus remarkable because it is "an unwindable spiral of material form and interpretative understandings or experiences" (p. 471). It is this critical power of place that I want to explore in this chapter.

Place as a Conceptual Framework

In the above I have illustrated how a focus on place enables a form of collective storytelling that evokes embodied place stories from a group of research participants. Here I want to establish what it means to employ place as a conceptual framework, as a lens through which to view the world. If we think, for example, of using the concept of "environment", rather than place, we would come up with an entirely different set of stories and assumptions. The concept of environment derives from the scientific method and is embedded in the discourses and discursive practices of the natural sciences. The discourse of the scientific method assumes a separation between subject and object, between the researcher and the object of the research, evident through the practices of generalisability, validity and replicability in scientific experimentation.

If we asked qualitative research participants to tell a story about the environment, it is likely that the story would be about something outside of, and unrelated to, their sense of self, a story about a place that is somehow emptied of human inhabitation. We know, on the other hand, that all places on our planet are impacted by human interactions with the environment. A story about place necessarily involves our sense of self because, as Gruenewald (2003b, p. 621) points out, places shape our identities as much as our interactions shape our places: "As occupants of particular places with particular attributes, our identity and our possibilities are shaped."

Even in the small story at the beginning of this chapter, it is evident that place as a concept bridges the local and global, the material and symbolic, the individual and the collective. It is also a powerful bridge between different forms of knowledge such as scientific and everyday knowledge, knowledge within different disciplines and between indigenous and non-indigenous knowledges. In my very early place work with Aboriginal people in the town where I lived (Cohen & Somerville, 1990; Somerville, 1990), I learned the concept of place as a way to communicate meaningfully across our two different knowledge systems and experiences of the world. For my friend and local indigenous elder Patsy Cohen, who initiated our collaborative research, place was the structuring principle for our work together. She wanted to research the place where she had been removed from her family as a child, and we went there with all of the people who had connections with that place. I saw an empty barren paddock. They read a place peopled with stories and lives that reached back into a timeless past prior to white settlement.

Through this collaborative research I learned about place as a structuring principle of knowledge. I learned that we construct places through the stories we tell, and that different stories meet, collide, and converge in this space of cultural contact. I also learned the absence of my own embodiment in the places of this landscape in listening to simple embodied stories like the one about the dry grass:

I've seen 'em too go and get that—
you might see a lot of grass up against a tree
a tree or a fence
very soft grass
and they'd go and get that
and it'd blow like the wind you know
they'd go and get this
and they'd stuff it into bags
and they'd make bed ticks out of them
they used this a lot, dry grass
that catches up on the netting fences
they used that as a bed tick
it was just as soft as a bed to sleep on
it's very warm in winter
because it warms up and keeps the heat
that is what a lot of them done
this is about what I know.
(Bill Lovelock, *Body/Landscape Journals*, Somerville, 1999, p. 12)

This question of how I can be embodied in the landscapes of these stories was something I took up later in bodywork. The concept of place has continually enabled my learning as a middle-class, white, settler woman from my Aboriginal partner researchers about how I can be embodied in this landscape, and it has enabled us to find a meeting place for our different meanings and experiences. In this sense any concept of place includes the sense of learning, of place-making work, and is a possible site of (post) colonial negotiations.

In two seminal papers published in 2003, David Gruenewald linked the concept of place to education. In making this connection he articulated the parallel objectives of "decolonisation" and "re-inhabitation" as essential characteristics of a critical place-conscious education. He defined decolonisation as the process of identifying and deconstructing the stories and practices through which people and places are exploited and destroyed, and re-inhabitation as the process of "identifying, affirming, conserving, and creating those forms of cultural knowledge that nurture and protect people and ecosystems" (Gruenewald, 2003a, p. 9). In exploring decolonisation and inhabitation through empirical research, I have identified three intertwined elements that constitute an "enabling pedagogy of place" (Somerville, 2010). These elements of *story*, *body*, and *contact zone* offer a methodological framework for researching and analysing how we learn place and form community.

Story: Our Relationship to Place is Constituted in Stories and Other Representations

This element focuses on the constitutive power of language as story. I expand the usual understanding of story to embrace other representations such as visual art, performance and poetry, as well as the stories of scientists, policy makers, agriculturalists and so on. Each discipline and artistic modality has its own forms and genres of place stories that can be elicited and read as constitutive place practices. The element of story links with the analytical strategy of storylines (Davies, 2000; Sondergaard, 2002) that allows us to deconstruct how stories function to shape places: "A storyline is a condensed version of a naturalised and conventional cultural narrative, one that is often used as the explanatory framework of one's own and others' practices and sequences of action" (Sondergaard, 2002, p. 191). Davies (2000) notes that "stories we observe, hear, read, both lived and imaginary, form a stock of imaginary storylines through which life choices can be made" (p. 81). According to Gruenewald (2003b), for example, dominant storylines of place "deny our connection to earthly phenomena,…[and] construct places as objects or sites on a map to be economically exploited" (p. 624). Alternative storylines are often suppressed and invisible but when sought out enable other possibilities for learning and inhabiting place.

Body: Place Learning is Necessarily Embodied and Local

This element is related to a necessary focus on materiality, on the body, and on body/place relations. The mind/body binary is regarded as primary and foundational in Western thought and other dualities such as culture/nature, male/female, objectivity/subjectivity follow. In each of these instances one side of the binary is privileged over the other and in many strands of place research, the subject/object binary (i.e., the separation of the human subject from the environment) is regarded as the problematic basis on which environmental exploitation is founded. The paradigm wars expressed in the subjectivity/objectivity debates are an example of the power of the scientific paradigm that continues to reinstate the binary opposition and the privileging of objectivity over subjectivity. In *Volatile Bodies*, feminist philosopher Liz Grosz proposed to interrogate philosophy by "putting the body at the centre of our notion of subjectivity" (Grosz, 1994, p. 5). The element of *body* in place-based research takes up this idea to put the body at the centre of our thinking about place, leading to a focus on body/place connections. The element of body refers not only to the human body but to non-human bodies and to the materiality of places. This thinking leads to a different ontology of self-becoming-other in the relationship between humans and the natural world (Somerville, 2007).

Contact Zone: Place is a Contact Zone of Cultural Contestation

This element focuses on the characteristic of specific local places as sites for the intersection of multiple and contested stories. This characteristic of place has been theorised as "the contact zone" (Pratt, 1992, 1999) and is especially significant in the relationship between indigenous, and other subjugated knowledges, and Western academic thought. In contact zone theorising, as opposed to understanding the meeting point as assimilation or hybridity (third space), it is important to hold multiple different stories in productive tension. Carter maintains that the main function of the in-between space of the contact zone is to preserve difference, even to the point of suspending meaning (Carter, 1992). The contact zone is an important element when considering the multiplicity of different stories about a place such as scientific stories, oral histories of place, popular responses to place, immigrant experiences of place and so on. It is in the in-between space of excitement and struggle of the contact zone (Somerville & Perkins, 2003) that contradictory "stories and histories of connection, exploitation and care continue to converge within public and personal spheres", opening up possibilities for cultural transformation "when individuals find the words and images that enable people to re-imagine familiar country" (Sinclair, 2001, p. 57).

A Methodology of Postmodern Emergence

The conceptual framework of place and the three theoretical principles of place pedagogy outlined above converge in a methodological framework I have described as a postmodern emergent methodology (Somerville, 2007). The articulation of this methodology came from many years of my own place research but also from attempting to understand the conditions of the emergence of new knowledge from a large number of research students. The qualities of postmodern emergence were, and continue to be, most apparent in the students that I have supervised whose research of necessity moves outside the boundaries of the conventions of academic knowledge production. I had noticed that for each student who was embarking on an alternative form, there was only the diverse productions of others before them but not any way to theorise a more general approach to understanding that form of knowledge generation. Postmodern emergence came from my attempt at this theorising.

A postmodern emergent methodology extends Richardson's "Writing: A Method of Inquiry" (Richardson, 1994), in which the act of representing ("writing up") research is reframed as an integral part of the knowledge making that occurs in the research process. In this influential article Richardson claims writing as data collection, analysis and representation. She explored her commitment to writing-as-a-method-of-inquiry through writing her research in a range of genres including "drama, responsive readings, narrative poetry, pagan ritual, lyric poetry, prose poems and autobiography" (Richardson, 1997, p. 3). Each time a piece of research was represented in these ways, new insights emerged. The aim of these transgressive forms was to open up and disrupt taken-for-granted ways of interpreting the world. For Richardson, this writing as research necessarily opened herself to radical transformations, making spaces for existential doubts and uncertainties. Even more subversive, I was inspired by the disrupted forms of representation offered by Trinh Minh-Ha with stories, quotes and images from her films juxtaposed intertextually in forms that denied easy and conventional meanings. Trinh worked with the pause, and with silence, in attempting to articulate the unsayable: "The heart of the matter is always somewhere else than where it is supposed to be. To allow it to emerge, people approach it indirectly by postponing until it matures, by letting it come when it is ready to come" (Trinh, 1992, p. 1). Trinh's focus, unlike Richardson's, is not on the content of the creative product but on the space between the creation and the theorising that generates new thought.

An Ontology of Postmodern Emergence

For me, and for my students researching in this space, an ontology of a postmodern emergent methodology focuses on the undoing of self; the space of unknowing; the absences, silences and disjunctures of the liminal space with no narrative; the relational of any coming into being; and the messy, unfolding, open-ended and irrational nature of becoming-other-to-oneself through research engagement. Such an ontology needs to incorporate elements of our past self-history (ontogeny), who we imagine ourselves to be, and our embodied relationship with others. It also includes our participation as bodies in the "flesh of the world" (Merleau-Ponty, 1962), a reciprocal relationship with objects and landscapes, weather, rocks and trees, sand, mud and water, animals and plants, an ontology founded in the bodies of things. In this ontology, bodies of things are dynamic, existing in relation to each other, and it is in the dynamic of this relationship that subjectivities are formed and transformed. And within this there is the relationship with inanimate objects and technologies that we can intentionally manipulate—stone, wood and clay, pencils, crayons, brushes and paints, computers, words and paper, cloth, thread and scissors—among the myriad other things that we humans have chosen to use in the process of becoming-other to ourselves.

An Epistemology of Postmodern Emergence

In developing an epistemology of postmodern emergence, I draw on Grosz's critique of causation in *Becomings* (1999) where she profoundly challenges the empiricist model of the enchained determinism of cause and effect. According to Grosz, the time of becoming is expressed in the work of Darwin, Nietzsche, Bergson and Deleuze in concepts of chance, randomness and open-endedness: "The endless unfolding of the new, restless transformation, upheaval, redirection and digression, which ensures the impossibility of the same even through the modes of repetition that each of these thinkers sees as central to the surprise and unpredictability of difference" (Grosz, 1999, p. 5). It is through these "modes of repetition", which I refer to as the iterative processes of representation and reflection, that the new emerges. There is a moment of stasis or pause where something is produced, a form of representation. An epistemology of postmodern emergence, then, requires a new theory of representation. This new theory of representation embraces multiple modes of expression, such as stories, song, dance and paintings, as well as interviews, academic prose and other forms of writing. The focus is on the creation of meaning from the relationship between the parts. These multiple creations are "naïve" in the sense that although they may be subject to the erasure of deconstruction, they are produced and valued in and of the moment, a pause in an iterative process of representation, engagement and reflexivity.

These naïve forms are the means by which we display and engage with the ongoing products of our research. A tape-recorded interview, for example, can be regarded as such a pause, a relational artefact of the interaction between researcher and researched, a recorded oral performance. This recorded oral performance retains its own integrity in the pause but it can be transcribed and reinterpreted at any time by its inclusion in an assemblage of other representations. Digital technologies have made all this more possible and may even be integral to this new theory of representation. These forms enable us and our participants to engage with the research and to perform it for others outside the research act. Meaning is dynamic and constituted intertextually between the various elements of the performance or representation. In looking back over my research there is a proliferation of representations in journal notes, interviews and transcripts, new and old photographs, paintings, drawings, storytellings and maps. These are dismantled and reassembled to create new productions from the research, each time working between the logics and poetics of the research, between the images and the rational meanings that are assigned to them.

In an epistemology of postmodern emergent methodologies, the focus is on making meaning from working the space in between. It is not about producing a more authentic version of reality, of writing up qualitative research as fiction, or producing artworks to represent the outcomes of the research. These forms are essential in the processes of our research but each of these artefacts is only a pause in an iterative process of representation and reflection. According to Paul Carter, what he calls "creative research" has a different object: "It explores the irreducible heterogeneity of cultural identity, the always unfinished process of making and remaking ourselves through our symbolic forms" (Carter, 2004, p. 13). In moving towards an epistemology of postmodern emergent methodologies, I propose a move from deconstruction to creation and conditional representation. It opens up a space for a different sort of writing that enables the articulation of ideas or understandings that are not yet there. This writing enacts the process of these concepts coming into being.

Methods for Place Research

In this section I describe some key research methods that I have developed within the context of the conceptual, theoretical and methodological frameworks described above. I provide examples from recently published collaborative research (Somerville & Perkins, 2010) and offer ideas about how these different methods have contributed to the place research. In each of the sections I begin with an extract of the relevant place writing and then elaborate on the general and specific aspects of the method concerned.

Body/Place Journal Writing

As the sun appears over the shadow of the headland it lights white-trunked paperbarks and white spoon-bills sleeping on long black legs on the little sand island. In the broad curve of the estuary even the sea sounds round. Rosellas chatter in casuarinas, butcher birds water-chime their musical notes and a huge osprey, with fluffy feet and brown wings tinged with white, lands on the island. Five black cormorants take over from the white spoonbills who now dip long beaks into shallow water. High above, white seed-fluff clouds drift across the palest blue sky, reflected in the new deep green of the river. The sun, now bright and strong, warms my back and draws out patterns of ripples and bird prints on the smooth skin of the sand island. On the edge, the curves made by water and tide are sculpted into body hollows in the rosy golden light. All are cradled in the big belly of the river with its ever-changing shapes of sand and water. (Somerville & Perkins, 2010, p. 33)

The method that I have come to call body/place journal writing was developed in response to ill-ness and bodily pain from an excess of abstract rational thought in academic work that separated me from the materiality of my world. I had noticed that in the Aboriginal stories I had recorded that the body was always already present in a way that did not happen in my Western academic language. The first process in my own body/place learning was to work with a massage practitioner who believed that massage—the touch of skin on skin by another—could surface awareness of body-in-place embedded in bodily tissue (Carmont, 1996). This tissue awareness surfaced in images spoken during the mas-sage—rock, mountain, ledge, water—to be later recalled and written down. I then started to respond with this body/place writing as an immediate sensory response to the landscapes of my research, a dif-ferent version of fieldwork journal writing based on the sensory experience of the body-in-place at any particular moment.

Much of Grosz's theorising, especially in relation to Lacanian psychoanalysis and French feminist philosophies, was central to this reconceptualisation of body/place connections. Lacan, following on from Freud, offered a possible way of theorising the emergence of the embodied subject into language in the "mirror stage", the point at which binary oppositions are created (Lacan, 1977). Focussing on this moment of becoming, the French feminists (see, for example, Cixous, Kristeva, Irigaray) variously take this up as a generative space for writing, and theorising, the body. My own approach was to take it up in relation to body/place connections as a way to write myself into the landscapes of my research in an immediate present.

The body/place journal writing above is taken from a chapter of *Singing the Coast* (Somerville & Perkins, 2010) based on collaborative research with Gumbaynggirr people on the mid north coast of New South Wales about their local places. I use the metaphor of singing country to invite readers to participate actively in renewing our relationship to settled coastal landscapes through listening to, and telling their stories. In Chapter 2, "Crying-songs", I create a dramatic performance of the iterative tell-ing of a massacre and rebirth story. The piece of writing was extracted from my journal and the purpose of including it is to emplace and embody the story but also my connection to it as listener. In this way the reader has some access to the place of this story, to a sense of its past history and contemporary present through the immediate sensory response juxtaposed with the transcript quotes from recorded stories as in the collective indigenous voice of oral place storytelling.

Oral Place Storytelling

Just along the beach
beautiful blue beach in there
mullet come just in the mouth
of the Lake
was a terrible lot of them
mostly big sea mullet

along the beach for pipis and things
we ate lilly pillies
wild cherries, raspberries
five corners, they're nice
and just along the beach
you get them little white berries
we used to eat those,
geebungs, another one
rolypolies, gooseberries
you're never short of things
to eat.
(Chapter 4, "Eating Place", p. 87)

Oral place storytelling as a method evolved from my earliest place work with Patsy Cohen and involves recording people's activities and oral storytelling in places using photography and audio recording. I have coined the term oral place story to distinguish this method from oral history, which has a chronological structure and is essentially about recapturing the past, often as an adjunct to written documents that are seen as superior primary source material in historical research. In my research with Patsy Cohen, as I described above, we organised a day where everyone who had been connected to the Ingelba Reserve, where Patsy had spent the first five years of her life, met and we recorded the place stories as they walked around the landscape reading the signs of their life there. Each living place or home was identified by the lichen-covered hearthstones embedded in the earth, recalling memories of the tin shacks that housed generations of families. Pieces of crockery, sulky wheels, exotic plants, and all of the other artefacts of their life there evoked stories of how they lived in that place. Lunch by the river elicited more stories of fishing, of the spirit creatures that live in the river, and these then merged into other *goonge* (ghost) stories of the min min lights, spirit presences and signs from the spirit world.

In the example quoted at the beginning of this section from Chapter 4, "Eating Place", I recreated the oral performance of arrival with several of the elders at the lake where they lived and caught most of their food. The most commonly told stories in all of this work were about eating from their local places and the intimate knowledge of place that comes from this practice. Beginning with the stories themselves, it became apparent, through clustering them at different levels of chapter and within each chapter, that the stories clustered fell into groups according to the ecologies of food places. Yarrawarra people lived on prawns, crabs, and fish from the estuary; turtles, swamp hens, eels from the swamp; pipis, gugumbals, and abalone from the beach and rockpools; mullet, tailor, mackerel, whiting, jewfish, bream, trevally from the sea; kangaroo, possum, and porcupine from the surrounding bushlands; and turtles, eels and cobra from the river. In between all of these places people ate native fruits such as lilli pillis, wild cherries, nyum nyums and pigface as they walked on their tracks through the dunes and coastal heathlands. The chapter is then organised according to the structure of "thinking through country", the categories of local food ecologies that emerged from the stories of eating place.

The stories were incorporated into the chapters in different ways according to the nature of the story oral performance. Some, as in the quote above, are told as storytelling events, and while they may be told by individuals, they are shared or collective cultural stories. These stories are included as scanned lines, without being assigned an individual identity. In this sense they produce a pause, creating white space in the midst of black print, slowing down the proliferation of interpretation and leaving the story its own space. This white space also signals silence, for the words that aren't said, and for the many speakers who own and tell these stories. They are used in the text of this chapter to mark section breaks between different food ecologies, to move from one place to another, a kind of walking, in-between space. Other stories are separated out from the text by line breaks and indentations and assigned to an individual speaker. These are also regarded as storytelling events, but they have less of a collective quality and can take up their place in an intertextual narrative account where the juxtaposition of different forms of writing and different sequences of stories form the meaning of the whole. Still others are incorporated in quote marks into the narrative account that loosely holds the stories together, forming part of the narrative structure but not in themselves performances. These stories give a sense of the multiplicity of conversations, the exchange between researchers and research partners through which meanings about place are created.

Deep Mapping

> Baga Baga Nyambaga
> that's where he fell over
> when he was speared
> his knee was like that
> and his body
> well the roads go over his body
> and his head on an angle like this,
> so the road goes right over the middle of him.
> The roads change the structure of it
> but they don't change the meaning
> of the place
> it may not exist the way it did
> when it was first thought
> but it's always gonna be
> in the memory of the people.
> (Chapter 6, "A Language of Landscape", p. 176)

In this story southern Gumbaynggirr elder Ken Walker talks about the place where the Nyamba man was speared and fell, making the shape of the bend in the Nambucca River which gave Nambucca its name. The story embodies the sense of the relationship between body and landscape embedded in the creation stories, but also of the ongoing relationship that is impacted by modern development but which is not destroyed by it. The meaning of the place is held in the memory of the people and transmitted through stories.

Deep mapping maps these cultural processes. It is a further development of the oral place story method in which oral stories about place are recorded and at the same time marked on a map of the landscape. In the deep mapping process, a road map of country is used to mark the places on the map where the story events happened. The story is digitally recorded and transcribed and key story excerpts and places names are identified. The roads and towns are then removed from the map using Photoshop software and the place names and story text are inserted, in symbolic reversal of the processes of colonisation. These maps are then used for further research and storytelling, and as community-owned resources for cultural teaching. The stories produced in this way can be story events of everyday life, of past histories and memories, and of dreaming or creation stories. These can be the same places, with creation stories, histories and stories of everyday life occurring simultaneously in place in layers over deep time. We use the descriptor "deep" to indicate this layering over time with dreaming stories of the deep past continuing to exist in the present and each visible in a palimpsest of layers.

An example of this palimpsest of stories made evident through deep mapping is the recording of a walking story which followed the route that people travelled when they walked from Bowraville Mission to Stuart Island in the Nambucca River. After we had recorded the 10 kilometre walking story it became clear that this walking trail followed the route of one of the ancestral dreaming stories, the story of Birrugan's last battle, that we had recently mapped back onto country. The story had been recorded by a linguist some 60 years ago and preserved in library archives. A group of Gumbaynggirr people brought the language home in these recordings, which were then connected back to country through storytelling and mapping. The arrival point of the walking trail, in particular, overlapped with both historic and contemporary stories of Girr Girr, now known as Stuart Island, an important place both traditionally and historically for Gumbaynggirr people. Stuart Island is now a golf course and, energised through the processes of deep mapping, local Gumbaynggirr people became politically active to have pipes inserted into the causeway leading to the island to allow salt and fresh waters to move freely and protect the health of the river.

> Yeah well, it just goes to show you that you had a history that was a wonderful history, you had a great history. There's not only white history that you've been taught about, they thought that was the only history that existed, but really you've got to go back and find your own traditions and your own stories that you know are irreplaceable and they go back a long time before, before anybody else's stories, because, you know, we're probably one of the oldest people on this planet. (Ken Walker, p. 164)

Art as a Method of Enquiry

In a later project about water in the drylands of the Murray-Darling Basin, I worked collaboratively with Chrissiejoy Marshall to develop an emergent arts-based method to research alternative stories and practices of water. Chrissiejoy Marshall is a Yuwalaraay speaker who grew up in the drylands of western New South Wales with a deep knowledge of Noongahburrah (water people) culture. Although she was researching the development of a training package in conflict resolution, in order to make any knowledge claims at all she had to think through Country. The necessity to engage with the development of an alternative methodology that sits between Western knowledge traditions and her Aboriginal knowledge of Country meant that she was particularly reflexively aware of this process.

The methodology, evolved directly from her relationship to her birth country, was developed in visual, oral and written forms. She produced a painting and an accompanying oral story that structured and informed each cluster of meanings, or chapters, based on her knowledge frameworks of Country. The paintings allowed her to explore different meanings than were possible in the English language. In addition, by moving between the paintings, the oral storytelling, and the writing, Marshall was able to generate new knowledge from the space in between these different forms of meaning. This paralleled my own articulation of a methodology of postmodern emergence, and the combination of these approaches produced an open and evolving methodology for place research that enabled partner researchers to represent their place stories in a variety of creative forms.

In the project Aboriginal artists were employed as partner researchers to express their meanings of water and water places through storytelling and artworks. One of these artists was Badger Bates, a Paakantji artist and cultural knowledge holder from Wilcannia on the Darling River in western NSW. His lino prints, made by carving lino with the marks and stories of the landscape, continue the process he learned from his grandmother of carving emu eggs. The translation of mark making and story telling into lino prints is a means of making visible alternative cultural meanings of water. These meanings are not immediately evident, nor are they meant to be. They embody pedagogical processes of teaching and learning through which non-indigenous peoples can begin to become knowledgeable in these alternative stories. In the lino print that Badger made of *Iron Pole Bend, Darling River, Wilcannia*, for example, the connections between places of intense intimate attachment and the vast networks of other story places is made evident.

The story text that goes with this lino print is minimal but contains a great deal of codified information that is further made visible in the work.

> The Iron Pole Bend on the Darling River is where Granny used to sit down to fish and she saw the water dog or Ngatyi there. We lived near this bend in a tin hut when I was a kid. In the print you can see the dead fish in the dried-up Lake Wytucka on the left hand side, this hasn't had water in it for a long time. The two Ngatyi are in the river with fish, mussels and shrimps. In the sky you can see Bytucka the moon, the Seven Sisters, and the emu in the Milky Way.

We are looking down on the landscape in this print, at a place where different waterways come together. We know from the title and the text that the place is marked by a sign of the colonisation of the river, the iron pole, but the iron pole itself does not appear in the work. It is only a place marker for another set of stories. The print is structured around the Ngatyi, or rainbow serpents, who play a central part in the great creation stories, particularly in relation to water. Badger says the Ngatyi are his signature symbol. In this print the Ngatyi are almost indiscernible, immersed deep in the radiating lines of force that represent the energy of the waters. From their mouths the flow of waters bursts forth; their bodies create the shape of the rivers. The waters of the river are alive with the river's creatures—cod, catfish, shrimp, yabby, and mussels.

The story text tells the viewer that the image is replete with stories that incorporate the contemporary with the distant past. It is a story of the everyday—of the place where Badger's granny caught fish for their daily food, near where Badger grew up in a tin hut on the banks of the Darling River. It is a place where Granny, and later Badger himself, saw the "water dog", the spirit creature of the waterways that signals the presence of a special place. It tells us about the current environmental state of Lake Wyntucka, which has been dry for a long time, so the fish are represented in skeletal form. Around the edges of the water we can see the mythical creatures whose travels and storylines make connections with other places. The Kangaroo leaps under the symbol the special creation place, Koonenberry Mountain; the Goanna is walking from its story place, and the Brolga flies in from far away. We know they are spirit creatures because we can see their internal structures.

At the top of the print, in a hybrid combination of a bird's-eye view and a more typical Western vertical view where the sky is at the top, we can see the moon, and the emu in the Milky Way. The position of the black shape of the emu within the stars of the Milky Way tells people about the cycles of feasting and ceremony. Earth country, water country and sky country are interconnected in this print that opens the intimate attachments of the everyday and home to the rhythms of water, earth, moon and stars.

The deep time and knowledge of story places is represented as a time that exists beyond personal or intergenerational memory. It is also, importantly, a time that is connected to the present in cyclical rather than linear time. Space, and the way the artwork delineates the spaces and places of these stories, is conceived differently. The frame of the print does not foreclose meanings within its square boundaries because the meanings are both allusive and elusive. It points always to connections elsewhere in the flow of the waters and the storylines. The waters flow in from somewhere else and travel to elsewhere. The mythical creatures travel into the frame of the print but are not bounded by it. The meanings of the storylines are *elusive* too, in the sense that no-one can know all the layers and complexity of any story, or know all of the stories.

This is just one example of over a hundred artworks and stories that were produced during the three years of the project. In addition, non-indigenous researchers undertook research through body/place journal writing and photographs, which added to the body of data in this project. Conversations between the research team were recorded at a number of different locations throughout the system of waterways and these conversations were used to structure the series of exhibitions of artworks and stories throughout the project.

Art Exhibitions as Public Pedagogy

In each of the three years of this project about water in the drylands we developed an exhibition of the artworks and stories created during the year. We worked collaboratively to develop the exhibition, recording our ideas-in-progress as we went and creating catalogues to make our evolving ideas visible. After the project was finished we were invited to exhibit the best of the artworks from the exhibitions and we decided to conduct a small study to explore the meanings and effects of the exhibition as a public pedagogy of place. To do this we recorded and analysed the events that were organised around the opening of the exhibitions. These events comprised a Welcome to Country address, the talk that as lead researcher I have at the opening to contextualise the exhibition in terms of the research project, and the cross-cultural conversation generated by the artists at the Artists' Talk. I have written about the analysis of the three events in terms of how educational research can be transmitted to a larger audience through the notion of art as public pedagogy of place (Somerville, in press). Here I will focus on the conversations generated within the Artists' Talk.

In this instance the exhibition took place in Albury, a regional city on the Murray River, in the city gallery. Albury is close to the major irrigation areas of the Murray River, where local people have powerful vested interests in the removal of water for irrigation, and there is also a growing tourist market around the arts, fine dining, and the place. The building is an historic colonial building, and the art exhibition is in a large open white space on the second floor. Yorta Yorta artist Treahna Hamm and Paakantji artist Badger Bates organised the space and structured the process of the Artists' Talk session on the Saturday morning after the opening the night before. There was a large audience with a noticeable presence of Aboriginal participants. The artists arranged the chairs in concentric circles around the perimeter of the gallery, reshaping the square space into a circle. In the centre of the circle a white painted plinth displayed Treahna's woven turtles. Her Murray cod made from chicken wire and woven thread, filled with items of rubbish commonly found in the fish, was suspended above the plinth. The artists sat in the circle on a colonial antique chaise longue, and the artworks on the square white walls were a still backdrop to the dynamic space of people and conversation. The artists introduced themselves and their work, communicating their openness and inclusion, doing the translation and emotional work of the contact zone.

Early in the conversation the artists opened the floor to questions and comments. An older white woman spoke about her attachment to the land as a long-time landowner in the area. She said she tells stories to the grandkids about the land and the river so they too will learn its intergenerational stories. Later she said how her grandchildren ask her why she tells the same story over and over and she tells them it is because she does not want them to forget. "People need to know their stories, know their history," she says. She went on to talk about how she spoke against the weirs that block the flow of waters at a public meeting, but when she did the meeting ended. Later in the conversation she said that she would take up Treahna's metaphor of the river as a body, with the kidneys being the system of flows that cleans out the water, and the weirs the blood clots that stop this flow. She felt that this would give her a more powerful language to communicate her ideas to such a public audience.

Badger welcomed this woman's comments and concerns, and they were taken up throughout the conversational exchanges that followed. This is just one example of the depth of audience engagement and learning offered in this session. The artists reinforced all of the audience stories, questions and responses and the conversation flowed from the space of the exhibition with its artworks and stories to larger questions of caring for the environment, to climate change, to the fate of the earth, and to the relationship of all this to global indigenous knowledges of place. The final conversation was about the importance of cultural flows, the idea that there is a parallel relationship between flows of water and flows of indigenous cultural knowledge about water. Badger places this idea back into the circle of the contact zone and says that everyone has a cultural connection to the rivers, and cultural flows are everyone's responsibility. In this way the space the artists created inside the circle allowed ideas, feelings, thoughts, the inchoate, and the not-yet-thought to reside in there where they are mediated by the safety of mutual concerns about place and waterways.

Participatory Community Place-making

In participatory community place-making, I discuss the further application of some of the above methods to the development of transformative research with disadvantaged communities. The method of participatory community place-making was developed as a two-day workshop in which participants learn elementary research skills and design a small project in individual place research on the first day and in collective place research on the second. I had previously constructed a training program to teach Aboriginal community participants to record oral place stories as a capacity-building responsibility of researchers working with marginalised and disadvantaged communities. This three-day workshop conducted over six months was compressed to a one-day workshop which covered understanding research and research ethics, interviewing and transcribing skills, and the development of representations of research such as posters and small iBooks using iPhoto software. Each participant designed a small individual project and was given feedback within the group. The second day was based on collective place story research as described in the beginning of this chapter and was conducted as a collective place storytelling exercise to model the method, followed by the design of a series of such workshops around the themes that arose from the storytelling.

This method was delivered as a participatory community place-making activity at the Neighbourhood House in the remote community of Orbost in far eastern Victoria. Previously a logging and agricultural area, the community is undergoing change as "treechangers" move in from the city and the rural industries experience a decline. Twelve people participated in both days of the workshop and designed individual and collective projects around their chosen theme of "the old time dance". Individual projects produced a community-based ripple effect with each of the participants designing a small individual project to collect memory stories about the old time dance. A lively oral place storytelling workshop related to the theme generated at least six further themes for more storytelling over the next six weeks prior to the event of the recreation of the old time dance. These included such themes as the making of the frock; memories of the dance music; ballroom-dancing lessons; boy meets girl; the after-dance suppers, and so on. Beneath all this was a sense that the old time dance performed many functions in community building and cohesion in this place and that some of these functions could be recaptured by bringing people together for this participatory community place-making research.

Conclusion

In this chapter I have begun with a single place story generated within a collective biography workshop about water to illustrate the multiple possibilities of place storytelling in research. From this I have extrapolated the potential of place as a conceptual framework for connecting the local and global, the real and the symbolic, the individual and the collective, and our inner sense of ourselves with the external world. I have used this embodied and emplaced example as a platform to propose a framework of place as a way to create conversations between positivist and postpositivist disciplines, and to build a bridge between Western and indigenous knowledges. I use examples from my early collaborative research with Australian indigenous communities to illustrate this in practical, grounded terms.

From this I make the link to learning and the development of a theoretical framework of pedagogies of place as a way to link the concept of place to education. In this I propose three essential intertwined elements summarised as story, body, and contact zone for a postcolonial place pedagogy. This conceptual and theoretical framework leads into the evolution of a methodology of postmodern emergence from my own place research, and the research of the many doctoral students for whom a radical alternative stance was not a choice but a necessity. An ontology of postmodern emergence acknowledges the messy, unfolding, open-ended nature of becoming-other-to-oneself in the production of new knowledge. An epistemology of postmodern emergence is a creative alternative to endless deconstruction and proposes a new understanding of representation in the generation of knowledge through research as a pause in an iterative process of reflection and representation where each of the artefacts of the research (recorded oral stories, transcripts, writing, etc.) can be (re)assembled to generate new meanings.

A number of methods have been articulated within these conceptual, theoretical and methodological frameworks including body/place journal writing, oral place storytelling, deep mapping, artmaking as method, and community participatory placemaking. Each of these methods embodies the critical power of place to invert the binaries through which much of our research is constructed and, in particular, to generate knowledge from between the binary forms rather than on one side or the other. Body/place writing interrogates the separation of bodies from places but also instates a body-place connection into the scene of writing as inquiry. Oral place storytelling reclaims the power of the oral by presenting oral stories as significant in the structuring of knowledge through representing the oral in the written form in ways that challenge conventional narrative structures of written language. Oral place stories make place a central structuring feature rather than time, as oral history does, thus making the time of the past present in a contemporary sense to disrupt such binaries as traditional and non-traditional understandings of indigenous cultural stories.

Deep mapping disrupts taken-for-granted knowledge of maps and map making and uses a powerful form of visual representation to present contemporary knowledge of deep time which continues to exist and to be celebrated in the present. The application of art as method of inquiry further extends Richardson's writing as a method of inquiry to enable the expression of meanings that are not available in words but which can then be translated into words through inhabiting the space between visual and verbal representations and meanings.

In writing of art as public pedagogy and participatory community research, I have shown how these methods have been extended to broader community settings, the first to explore whether the exhibition of artworks and stories produced through research can function as a public pedagogy and the second to build capacity for participatory place research with disadvantaged communities, who so often have little control over the ways they are represented and researched. This process enables community members to decide for themselves what they will research and how they will represent the knowledge they produce for and with their communities.

Acknowledgements

In this chapter I have drawn on my own work published elsewhere, as indicated in the reference list, to provide examples of the theoretical ideas in practice. I would like to acknowledge the editorial assistance of Sue Collins.

Note

1. The workshop was conducted with colleagues from the Space Place and Body research group at the AARE Annual Conference as part of a symposium *Methodologies for Sustainable Places* (Somerville, de Carteret, & Devos, 2008).

References

Carmont, C. (1996). *Tissue talk* (Unpublished PhD thesis). University of New England, Armidale, NSW, Australia.

Carter, P. (1992). *Living in a new country: History, travelling and language.* London, England: Faber & Faber.

Carter, P. (2004). *Material thinking: The theory and practice of creative research.* Carlton, VIC, Australia: Melbourne University Publishing.

Cohen, P., & Somerville, M. (1990). *Ingelba and the five black matriarchs.* St. Leonards, NSW, Australia: Allen & Unwin.

Davies, B. (2000). *A body of writing: 1990–1999.* Walnut Creek, C.A.: AltaMira Press.

Gieryn, T. F. (2000). A space for place in sociology. *Annual Review of Sociology, 26,* 463–496.

Grosz, E. A. (1994). *Volatile bodies: Toward a corporeal feminism.* St. Leonards, NSW, Australia: Allen & Unwin.

Grosz, E. A. (1999). *Becomings: Explorations in time, memory, and futures.* Ithaca, NY: Cornell University Press.

Gruenewald, D. A. (2003a). The best of both worlds: A critical pedagogy of place. *Educational Researcher, 32*(4), 3–12.

Gruenewald, D. A. (2003b). Foundations of place: A multidisciplinary framework for place-conscious education. *American Educational Research Journal, 40*(3), 619–654.

Haug, F. (1999). *Female sexualisation: A collective work of memory* (Verso Classics ed.; E. Carter, Trans.). London, England: Verso.

Lacan, J. (1977). *Ecrits: A selection.* London, England: Tavistock.

Merleau-Ponty, M. (1962). *Phenomenology of perception.* New York, NY: Humanities Press.

Pratt, M. L. (1992). *Imperial writing and transculturalism.* London, England: Routledge.

Pratt, M. L. (1999). Geographies of identity and difference. In D. Massey et al. (Eds.), *Human geography today* (pp. 151–167). Cambridge, England: Polity Press.

Richardson, L. (1994). Writing: A method of inquiry. In N. K. Denzin & Y. S. Lincoln (Eds.), *Handbook of qualitative research.* Thousand Oaks, CA: Sage.

Richardson, L. (1997). *Fields of play: Constructing an academic life.* New Brunswick, NJ: Rutgers University Press.

Sinclair, P. (2001). *The Murray: A river and its people.* Melbourne, VIC, Australia: Melbourne University Press.

Somerville, M. (1990). *Ingelba and the five black matriarchs.* St. Leonards, NSW, Australia: Allen & Unwin.

Somerville, M. (1999). *Body/landscape journals.* Melbourne, VIC, Australia: Spinifex Press.

Somerville, M. (2007). Postmodern emergence. *Qualitative Studies in Education, 20*(2), 225–243.

Somerville, M. (2010). A place pedagogy for "global contemporaneity". *Educational Philosophy and Theory, 43*(2), 326–344.

Somerville, M. (in press). Art, community and knowledge flows. In T. Fenwick & L. Farrell (Eds.), *Knowledge mobilisation and educational research: Politics, languages and responsibilities.* London, England: Routledge.

Somerville, M., de Carteret, P., & Devos, A. (2008, December). A collective biography of place. In *Methodologies for sustainable places.* Symposium conducted at the AARE Annual Conference, Brisbane, QLD, Australia.

Somerville, M., & Perkins, T. (2003). Border work in the contact zone: Thinking indigenous/non-indigenous collaboration spatially. *International Journal of Intercultural Studies, 24*(3), 253–266.

Somerville, M., & Perkins, T. (2010). *Singing the coast.* Canberra, ACT, Australia: Aboriginal Studies Press.

Sondergaard, D. M. (2002). Poststructural approaches to empirical analysis. *Qualitative Studies in Education, 15*(2), 187–204.

Trinh, T. Minh-Ha. (1992). *Framer, framed.* New York, NY: Routledge.

CHAPTER SIX

Methodology Is Movement Is Methodology

Mirka Koro-Ljungberg

I n this chapter I contemplate ideas in regard to methodological movement in research designs that can support diverse epistemological and methodological goals and transformative efforts associated with critical qualitative research. Many of the ideas presented have been influenced by indigenous perspectives, situated knowledges and Massumi's (2002) conceptualizations of movement. As Battiste (2008) put it, "there is no singular author of indigenous knowledge and no singular method for understanding its totality" (p. 500). Thus, it is my purpose to share what could be gained by conceptualizing methodology through movement. More specifically, I propose that methodological movement follows different theoretical and practical paths depending on changing sociopolitical, spiritual, and relational circumstances; therefore, both opening up and closing down ways to know and conceptualize knowledge.

When methodology is conceptualized in flux and continuously changing, researchers face many possibilities and challenges that accompany methodological flexibility, levels of comfortableness and familiarity with epistemological and methodological diversity, and puzzlement associated with unorthodox and often personal conceptualizations of research (see Bloom & Sawin, 2009). Most importantly, methodological movement occupies conceptual and theoretical spaces in which openness to difference, otherness, and complex "eventhood" of present and future methodological happenings serve as impetus for methodological decision making. Thus, methodological and theoretical assemblage put forward later in this chapter, including illustrations and exemplars, are inaccurately describing the phenomenon, yet necessary for dialogue to occur (see Spivak, 1997).

Furthermore, static, theoretically and methodologically singular research approaches might appear insufficient in studies that aim to reconceptualize and relocate complex social and institutional structures of oppression and exclusion (see, e.g., Adams & Jones, 2008; Weis & Fine, 2004). Methodological stability, linearity, and singularity might not accommodate diverse and possibly overlapping theoretical perspectives, multiple standpoints, or crossing lines of inquiry suggested and used by many critical qualitative researchers and participant communities. From a perspective of colonized, misrepresented, or silenced, the singularity of knowledge can indicate domination, undesirable impositions, and disempowering control of Western thought.

Massumi (2002) also questioned the linearity and predictability in science. He proposed that "when a surprise arrives, the scientist is already looking back. Her story of accumulated knowledge, the availability of techniques and methodologies, and the corroborating company of her peers places her immediately in a posture of confidence. The surprise has been converted into an anticipation of recognition…proper scientific activity starts from a preconversion of surprise into cognitive confidence" (p. 233). Similarly, it is not uncommon among researchers to turn surprises encountered during research processes into anticipation of methodological recognition, validity, and scientific conformability. According to Massumi (2002), "from the movement a newness irrupts, procedures already ready-at-hand clamp down for the knowing capture" (p. 236). To work against Massumi's notion of anticipated science and loss of surprises, I propose that linear designs for critical qualitative research can benefit from reconceptualization and separation from well-circulated methodological grand narratives and narrowly defined textbook approaches that tend to simplify research design choices and processes. Instead, in the context of critical qualitative research, I advocate for simultaneous and fluid uses of multiple theories, epistemologies, and research approaches that can highlight, for example, different cultural and political aspects of oppression or injustice. Cheek (2010) asked scholars to consider what conducting research for social justice means and how intentions can be translated to methodological actions—how do scholars follow through with their promises about inequity, and how do these promises carry out methodologically? Also how are research projects operationalized from the outset, and who is in charge and who decides what to study? Cheek also questioned whether research focusing on action would actually translate knowledge about findings to improved social justice. I will approach this chapter by being inspired by Massumi's (2002) conceptualizations of movement and Cheek's (2010) call to closely investigate how intentions to promote social justice could be translated to methodological action.

Shifting from Predetermined and Stable Research Plans Toward Methodological Movement

Various qualitative researchers (e.g., Bogdan & Biklen, 2006; Luttrell, 2010; Silverman & Marvasti, 2008) provide effective and well-written comprehensive summaries and abbreviated descriptions of how to design studies, collect, and analyze data. However, I worry that some qualitative research plans and decision-making processes might be portrayed as rational and simplified acts that are easily replicable and reproducible. Even though an increasing number of authors have argued for epistemological situatedness to highlight methodological complexities—for example, by placing methodological decision making in the context of theoretical frameworks (see, e.g., Creswell, 2007; Guba, 1990; Koro-Ljungberg, Yendol-Hoppey, Smith, & Hayes., 2009; Lather, 2008)—methodological movement conceptualized simultaneously in both horizontal and vertical spaces has not gained sufficient attention. Those studies well grounded in theories and epistemologies might still fail to accommodate and take into account methodological morphidity, therefore not leaving sufficient room for methodological modifications. This possible lack of methodological flexibility and adjustment can limit access and availability of situated knowledges, and it can create epistemological supremacy by promoting a particular—and superior—version of truth and knowledge. On the contrary, from the perspective of methodological movement and fluidity, research approaches can be perceived as temporary, flexible, and open-ended paths that enable engagement with participants, collaborative communities, nature, and environment in different levels (i.e., knowledge production, emotions, embodiment, and spirituality).

Albeit methodological implications of more fluid and deterritorializing paths toward inquiry in general deserve more attention than diverse practices associated with anticolonizing, such research has been used and documented by various scholars. It is not uncommon that indigenous researchers advocate and highlight the role of spirituality (Grande, 2008; Meyer, 2008), healing (Dillard, 2008; Meyer, 2008), and embodiment and bodily experiences (Meyer, 2008; Saavedra & Nymark, 2008) in knowledge production. For example, according to Meyer (2008), Hawaiian epistemology spirituality synergizes with one's courage, enabling fearless questioning and searching for deeper meanings, whereas the body represents the central space for knowledge: "Our body holds truth, our body invigorates knowing, our body helps us become who we are" (p. 223).

Others such as Kincheloe and Steinberg (2008) have indicated that knowledge is multidimensional and complex. They argued for a transformative science approach that "synthesizes ways of knowing, expressed by the metonymies of hand, brain, and heart" (p. 152). Yanchar, Gantt, and Clay (2005), in turn, characterized critical methodology as ongoing radical reflection and revision of existing methods. Yanchar et al. proposed that critical methodology resonates with ad hoc violations, counter narratives, tacit knowledge, and historically unorthodox research practices that are essential to science. Furthermore, they explained that critical methodology consists of contextual and evolving theory of inquiry including creative processes of theory formation and problem solving, methods that are evolving and occurring simultaneously with critical examination of basic research assumptions and theorizing, and philosophical frameworks that are changeable and open to critique. Denzin and Lincoln (2008) also illustrated various layers of epistemologies and disruptive methodological complexity when they outlined the methodology of borderland epistemology as ethical, critical, performative, healing, transformative, decolonizing, and participatory. Borderland epistemology builds on commitments to dialogue and cultural autonomy without relying on or advocating for one single paradigm or interpretive strategy.

Even though the existing literature and documented examples of critical methodology can provide helpful instances, they mostly operate at the ideological level, providing less methodological details and suggestions for how described ideologies can be translated to methodological action or how research design could be modified to accommodate proposed ideological shifts. Similar to Adams and Jones (2008), I would like to see more (methodological) movement that can transform static nouns to verbs and actions. In movement discourses, nouns turn into acts of knowing, inquiring, healing, interacting, interpreting, sensing, empowering and transforming, and so on. Next, I will provide examples of how methodological movement could be put to work during critical qualitative research processes and how knowing, which in this approach is placed at the shifting and temporary center folding of a research inquiry, can be envisioned.

Mapping Methodological Movement

It is possible that methodological flexibility conceptualized as a form of movement can assist researchers to stimulate transformation and promote elimination of oppression and injustice, because movement can enable researchers to accommodate continually changing complexities of social life, social and natural circumstances, structures, interactions, and so on, in their research. Rather than claiming to describe, explain, or interpret cultural or social phenomena, it could be fruitful to utilize tracings, arts, maps, cultural systems, spatial illustrations, multivoiced narratives, and other types of diverse images of shifting theories, methodologies, narratives, and cultures. This methodological move away from authoritarian and researcher-centered knowing acknowledges that all descriptions and representations of theories, data, research designs, and interpretations are already compromised, limited, and overlapping, and therefore always insufficient and partially escaping.

More specifically, methodological movement can create and follow different paths, depending on epistemological goals, theories, physical locations of researchers and participants, unknowns and mysteries, among others. The path of research design is also partially guided by limits set by various sociopolitical circumstances and elements including theoretical, geographical, and discursive categories and linguistic labels. As a result of these diverse and situated circumstances and positionings, none of the methodological paths created during qualitative research processes can be identical to one another or completely duplicated by other researchers. Rather, methodological movement passes through different, in-between spaces of knowing, researching, living, interacting, interpreting, and spaces of loss and uncertainty that might be difficult to prepare for, anticipate, or document. For example, multiple theories or simultaneous uses of various theoretical perspectives might be needed to address current sociopolitical phenomena under the study. To study Western capitalist societies and the predicament of women within them, both Marxist and feminist analysis might be needed; or, researchers' interpretative and analytical work might need to include simultaneous and/or hybrid analysis approaches combining elements from methods traditionally described as narrative analysis, grounded theory, discourse analysis, political analysis, and visual analysis. Alternatively, researchers could use completely undocumented and/or evolving ways to work with different information/data sources in order to highlight equally important, but conceptually and ideologically different, aspects of data.

From the methodological movement perspective, different aspects of the research process, that is, framework, sample, methods, or forms of representation, are not stable or singular tasks or closed entities with predetermined positions. Instead, various research tasks and frameworks can function as prohibitors or facilitators along the path of methodological movement. Methods, approaches, and information/data are overlapping and contextually bounded, thus creating different impacts on the movement each time they interact with other aspects of research design. Knowledge is intensified by theories and actions. Theories, actions, transformations, and healing form their distinct yet connected intersections with knowing. Intensity and speed of methodological movement is being shaped by different in-between spaces of theories and experiences, that is, a combination of theoretical perspectives, epistemologies, existing literature, interactions with participants and communities, and interpretive and analytical work and social structures, creativity, and spirituality. For example, when researchers' and participants' roles change, the path of methodological movement shifts, and speed and intensity of movement are being altered.

Additionally, it is important to note that it is not my intention to describe any particular types of interactions, theories, or body experiences suitable for critical qualitative research, because this move would characterize these entities and processes as stable and fixed. Rather, the possibilities and limits set by a researcher, participants, and sociopolitical structures always shape, reshape, and undo how knowledge is constructed, valued, and implemented and what experiences, theories, and policies are encountered when moving through research processes. In other words, knowing is not a result of methods but an intensifying fold and unanticipated source of energy along methodological paths. However, knowing does not imply a source of energy with known and predetermined direction. Instead, in critical qualitative research, knowing as a fold and source of energy always carries an aspect of uncertainty, undirectionality, and anticipation when accounting for mysteries and unknowns in social lives.

Conceptual Residue and Deviating Examples Associated with Methodological Movement

In the following table (Table 1), I illustrate conceptual residue of methodological transformations when moving from predetermined and stable research plans toward methodology as movement as methodology. I borrow some of the concepts from Massumi (2002), who proposed that to understand lived experiences they need to be topologically described using concepts such as continuous variation, intensive movement, transpositionality, event, durational space, modulation, and biogram. When transferring some of Massumi's concepts to the context of qualitative methodology, I am aware that my examples come with terrible powers. MacLure (2010) and Massumi (2002) referred to the example as a single instance that nevertheless stands for other instances and cases alike. Examples activate details, and every detail is essential to the example's success: "Every example harbors terrible powers of deviation and digression" (Massumi, 2002, p. 18).

	Predetermined and stable research plans	Research plans that enable methodological movement
Knowing	Singular knowledge	Variations in knowledge
Researcher/participant roles	Subjectivity (e.g., described through subjectivity statement, participant description)	Transpositionality
Focus of analytical work	Meanings, understandings, critique among others	Events in different conceptual spaces
Relation to time	Sequence	Durational space
Planning and description of the research plan	Following textbook recommendations, step-by-step, fixed plans	Open-endedness and retrospective process description

Table 1. Conceptual residue of methodological transformations

Variations in Knowledge and Transpositionality

"An object subsumes a multiplicity that evolves situationally. Every object is an evolving differential: a snow balling, open-ended variation on itself" (Massumi, 2002, p. 216). Methodological movement can travel through overlapping, simultaneous, or bypassing knowledges and variations of self. Knowing is not singular but possible, continuously reconceptualized and restructured. Knowledge encounters its variations. Massumi (2002) proposed that "when a body is in motion, it does not coincide with itself. It coincides with its own transition; its own variation. The range of variations it can be implicated in is not present in any given movement, much less in any position it passes through" (p. 4). More specifically, in the context of research inquiry, knowing (i.e., epistemological purpose, desire to know, and possibilities for knowledge) adds intensity and speed to the methodological movement (see Figure 1). In this case, knowing does not refer to Western tradition; rather, knowing is viewed as relational (see Kincheloe & Steinberg, 2008). In relational (e)pistemology, as described by Thayer-Bacon (2003), knowing extends beyond correspondence theories of truth and reality and cannot be separated from the subject, and fallibility must be compensated through plurality.

Dillard (2006) also highlighted variations in knowledge when she drew from Black feminist thought, feminist psychology, and spirituality while conceptualizing endarkened feminist epistemology. She proposed that from an endarkened, feminist perspective self-definitions form one's participation and responsibility, and research is a purposeful, intellectual, and spiritual pursuit. Through concrete experiences meanings are formed and individuals do not exist outside their communities, power relations, or historical contexts: "To know something is to have a living relationship with it, influencing and being influenced by it, responding to and being responsible for it" (Dillard, 2006, p. 20). Furthermore, Dillard (2006) argued that different perspectives have merit, value, and standing because they exist.

I view Saavedra and Nymark's (2008) research as another example of variations in knowledge and transpositionality. Saavedra and Nymark depicted *Mestizaje* as a "metodologia" in which multiple epistemologies such as queer, feminism, postmodernism, and postcolonialism interact and influence researchers' positions, perspectives, and inquiries. Similarly, Anzaldúa (2003) proposed that *La Mestiza* researcher has to move from convergent thinking, analytical reasoning, rationality, and single goals toward a more whole perspective that includes, rather than excludes, because the future depends on the mixing of two or more cultures and creating new consciousness. Anzaldúa also described transpositionality through multidimensional unity: "I am an act of kneading, of uniting, and joining that not only has produced both a creature of darkness and a creature of light, but also a creature that questions the definitions of light and dark and gives them new meanings" (p. 182).

"Eventhood" of Methodology

Rather than being fixated by meanings or understandings that can be possessed, critical qualitative researchers could alternatively shift attention to the "eventhood" and happenings along the path of the research process as encouraged by Schostak and Schostak (2008). Eventhood of methodology conceptualizes research designs through material practices, narrative pragmatics, and situational ethics. Research and interactive events happen and "readings of data" can be later used to listen for these occurred events. Schostak and Schostak also proposed that researchers' focus could be directed to the play of doubt and suspension of belief, the almost nothing that means so much, the schizophrenic and the paranoid, the in-betweens and the contested spaces, the repetitions and rhythms, and the intertextuality among others.

The eventhood of research could be mapped and traced through diverse relational, epistemological, and methodological landmarks. Massumi (2002) wrote that "landmarks stand out, singularly. Most of us would be capable of pasting them together into a visual map. But to do that, you have to *stop* and think about it. It takes effort—an effort that interferes with the actual movement of orientation" (p. 180). For example, methodological reflections and documentation (i.e., note taking) will stop the actual process of doing and engaging in interactions and analysis, possibly also changing the direction of future movement. These delays and demobilizations create spaces, gaps, and unknowns between different methodological spaces, which also cannot be explained or rationalized later. According to Massumi (2002), "to get a static, measurable, accurately positioned, visual form, you have to stop the movement. This capsizes the relation between movement and position. Now position arises out of movement. Static form is extracted from dynamic space, as a quantitative limitation of it" (p. 183).

Utilization of Durational Space

Methodological movement becomes difficult to carry out and implement in research designs that combine multiple approaches, theories, and interactions sequentially or that rely on time/timing as one main methodological coordinate. In other words, sequential uses of qualitative research approaches or practices preciously lack movement because each unit, method, and approach can be separated out and described individually and in its totality. In comparison, during methodological movement, time loses its orderly effect because it becomes impossible to separate out and distinguish it from spatial, emotional, intuitive and other considerations. Time multiplies, and its multiplying effects impact movement. In other words, approaches, interactions, methods, and knowings happen simultaneously and reactionally, and semantic chains become inseparable. Once time and singularity are perceived as problematic and interrupted, the existing models of research design become insufficient and less useful to address complex sociopolitical problems, especially in this context associated with oppression and injustice.

Aquaspace, a laboratory for cutting-edge multimedia work that utilizes divergent art practices in alternative environments, illustrates one example of fluid and durational space. This laboratory adapts itself to spaces in different cities or cyberspace. For example, one multimedia group show, "Dis solve", consisted of three exhibitions in varied locations: the tourist district, the commercial district, and the residential district. The exhibitions addressed the specific histories of their location, while simultaneously engaging in the three branches of metaphysics—cosmology, ontology, and reality. Each location specifically addressed and playfully questioned ideas and concepts of space, territories, and boundaries along with the possibilities of deterritorialization (see Drain, n.d.). Another example of possible methodological movement that creates unexpected methodological speed in unexpected spaces is "Critical Mass", an intensive mass event in which bikers share a bike ride home The movement of "bike-body" creates intensifying and rhizomatic power that carries its own productive intensity; it transforms the fabric of roads by slowing and speeding up the city and its people alongside and through its movements. The transitional connection with the city is "potentially transfiguring for a moment in that it rubs up against the social and economic codes inflected in and structured by the very materiality of the city. These actions are powerful participatory events that are equally transitional, evocative, and constructive" (Hester, 2006, para. 3).

Open-endedness and Retrospective Description of Research Process

Massumi (2002) proposed that position is secondary to movement and derived from it—position is movement residue. When one situates Massumi's proposition in a research context, methodological movement, rather than the stability, of theoretical, subjective, or experiential positions of the researcher and participants becomes emphasized. It can become impossible to concisely describe the beginning or ending positions because movement itself might not have identifiable beginnings or endings. Massumi also exemplified that when movement takes place it can never be situated in any point; rather, it is passing across all points: "The points or positions [along movement] really appear retrospectively, working backward from the movement's end" (Massumi, 2002, p. 6). Methodological movement and its paths and positions can only be described upon arrival, once research has stopped and interactions with participants have been discontinued. However, at "the point of arrival", or temporary discontinuation, researchers are no longer describing the movement itself, but the outcomes, reactions, or implications of research. Massumi explained that only after we stop running are we able to look back and see what set us to run. He argued that participation precedes recognition. More specifically, "the separately recognizable, speakable identities of the objects and subjects involved in the unfolding event come into definition only retrospectively" (p. 231). Furthermore, Massumi explicated that an ongoing event is always accompanied by an uncertain outcome; the contextual identity of the event is still open for amendment. Uncertainty of outcomes calls for researchers to give up their safe spaces as described by Burdick and Sandlin (2010), who referred to a methodology of discomfort that "decouples authorial power from research and opens channels for democratic and social imagination by abstracting the researcher herself from the safe place of the known and the accepted" (p. 354).

Furthermore, I propose that methodological movement does not imply unplanning or promote ad hoc research approaches but careful, detailed planning, and use of various methodological textbooks can be very helpful during planning processes. Research plans and designs serve as preliminary drafts and temporary maps guiding inquiries. These plans and maps are expected to change, shift, and alter during methodological movement and research processes. According to Schostak and Schostak (2008), radical research is not a mechanical replication of textbook approaches, rather it is situated within irresolvable tension between worldviews. Radicalness of research is about "constructing the cooperation necessary to engage with change, to keep up with the productions of differences and, thus, to be creative about developing ever-inclusive communities" (Schostak & Schostak, 2008, p. 9).

Back to Intensifying Folds of Knowing

Methodological movement multiplies approach, method, position, theory, and experience among others, and through this multiplication researchers are able to put forward more complex representations of lived experiences and sociopolitical conditions that produce existing discourses and practices. According to Massumi (2002), movement "enables a continuous, complexifying, cross-referencing of variations to each other—an indexing of aspects of unfolding experience to its own products and of its products to their ever-changing, unperceived field of emergence" (p. 156). Similar to Cannella and Manuelito (2008), who argued for anticolonial social science that facilitates transparent public conversations about research processes during which no issue is off limits, I consider that methodological movement can bring to the forefront at once various overlapping and complex methodological, theoretical, personal, and ethical issues that researchers face when conducting research, but that they have not had methodological space to talk about. Methodological movement can also take advantage of the "epistemic advantage of the oppressed" (see Narayan, 2003). From this perspective, researchers, collaborators and those oppressed can operate within two sets of practices (one of the colonizers and one of the colonized) that can lead to critical insights because each perspective provides a critique of the other, creating a greater conceptual space (Narayan, 2003). Finally, thinking about research design as a form of movement enables researchers to move to a space "that opens an outside perspective on the self-other, subject-object axis" (Massumi, 2002, p. 51), which, in turn, might be needed when studying complex sociopolitical conditions.

Anticolonial social science discourses raise important methodological questions such as what happens to knowledge, methodologies, and research approaches when borders, identifiers, and origins become blurred, transitioned, penetrable, or unidentifiable. These conceptualizations of methodology as movement might not be able to penetrate through all layers of oppression and injustice or satisfactorily answer policy calls for increased effectiveness and scientificism. Similarly, uncertainties linked with movement and controversies associated with alternative ways to conceptualize linear research processes can limit the applicability of presented ideas. Cannella and Lincoln (2009) were concerned that critical qualitative researchers are caught in a paradox when trying to deconstruct power relations at the same time they are creating and recreating power in their current research projects. As indicated by Cannella and Lincoln, some possible reasons for why critical perspectives might not be empowering can include the isolated environment of academy, disqualification of critical qualitative research by the conservatives, and the sociopolitical impact of hypercapitalism. The authors suggested that researchers should find out if there are unexpected locations and specific circumstances in which qualitative research has been successful to work against injustice. How else could critical qualitative researchers work against these oppressive academic structures that prescribe the type of work they can do? Would it be helpful if scholars, policy makers, and representatives of institutional review boards and funding agencies were more connected to human communities across races, locations, nations, and disciplines? According to Cannella and Lincoln (2009), "research conceptualizations, purposes, and practices would be grounded in critical ethical challenges to social (therefore science) systems, support for egalitarian struggle, and revolutionary ethical awareness and activism from within the context of community. Research would be relational (often as related to community) and grounded within critique of systems, egalitarian struggle, and revolutionary ethics" (p. 68).

To conclude, a methodological approach to critical qualitative research that is fluid, complex, and instable cannot be copied, reproduced, externally evaluated by "experts", or traced to the original. Instead, from this perspective, every research project needs to create its own movement, intensity, and speed that are reflected upon and problematized while being generated or lived through. Massumi (2002) proposed that no model (research or methodological) can claim the final reflection or correspondence to reality. It is not about reflection, either; rather "it is about *participation*. Differential participation" (p. 205). Methodological movement can generate productive and stimulating effects when researchers participate, not only orchestrate, in research and when researchers use methodological decisions to advocate for change and when more intimate relationships between theory and practice are used. Methodological movement might also multiply knowledges, cross-reference variations emerging as a powerful alternative to colonizing and researcher-driven methodologies. Rather than using methodology to look back and anticipate the recognition of existing knowledge, it can be revitalizing and emancipatory to allow critical qualitative research to surprise us.

References

Adams, T., & Jones, S. (2008). Autoethnography is queer. In N. Denzin, Y. Lincoln, & L. Tuhiwai Smith (Eds.), *Handbook of critical and indigenous methodologies* (pp. 373–390). Los Angeles, CA: Sage.

Anzaldúa, G. (2003). La conciencia de la mestiza: Towards a new consciousness. In C. McCann & S.-K. Kim (Eds.), *Feminist theory reader: Local and global perspectives* (pp. 179–187). New York, NY: Routledge.

Battiste, M. (2008). Research ethics for protecting indigenous knowledge and heritage. In N. Denzin, Y. Lincoln, & L. Tuhiwai Smith (Eds.), *Handbook of critical and indigenous methodologies* (pp. 497–509). Los Angeles, CA: Sage.

Bloom, L., & Sawin, P. (2009). Ethical responsibilities in feminist research: Challenging ourselves to do activist research with women in poverty. *International Journal of Qualitative Studies in Education, 22*(3), 333–351.

Bogdan, R., & Biklen, S. (2006). *Qualitative research for education: An introduction to theories and methods* (5th ed.). Boston, MA: Pearson.

Burdick, J., & Sandlin, J. (2010). Inquiry as answerability: Toward a methodology of discomfort in researching critical public pedagogies. *Qualitative Inquiry, 16*(5), 349–360.

Cannella, G., & Lincoln, Y. (2009). Deploying qualitative methods for critical social purposes. In N. Denzin & M. Giardina (Eds.), *Qualitative inquiry and social justice* (pp. 53–72). Walnut Creek, CA: Left Coast Press.

Cannella, G., & Manuelito, K. (2008). Feminism from unthought locations: Indigenous worldviews, marginalized feminisms, and revisioning an anticolonical social science. In N. Denzin, Y. Lincoln, & L. Tuhiwai Smith (Eds.), *Handbook of critical and indigenous methodologies* (pp. 45–59). Los Angeles, CA: Sage.

Cheek, J. (2010). Human rights, social justice, and qualitative research: Questions and hesitations about what we say about what we do. In N. Denzin & M. Giardina (Eds.), *Qualitative inquiry and human rights* (pp. 100–111). Walnut Creek, CA: Left Coast Press.

Creswell, J. (2007). *Qualitative inquiry & research design: Choosing among five approaches* (2nd ed.). Thousand Oaks, CA: Sage.

Denzin, N., & Lincoln, Y. (2008). Introduction: Critical methodologies and indigenous inquiry. In N. Denzin, Y. Lincoln, & L. Tuhiwai Smith (Eds.), *Handbook of critical and indigenous methodologies* (pp. 1–20). Los Angeles, CA: Sage.

Dillard, C. (2006). *On spiritual strivings: Transforming an African American woman's academic life.* Albany: State University of New York Press.

Dillard, C. (2008). When the ground is black, the ground is fertile: Exploring endarkened feminist epistemology and healing methodologies in the spirit. In N. Denzin, Y. Lincoln, & L. Tuhiwai Smith (Eds.), *Handbook of critical and indigenous methodologies* (pp. 277–292). Los Angeles, CA: Sage.

Drain. (n.d.) About aquaspace. Retrieved from www.drainmag.com/AQUASPACE/about.htm

Grande, S. (2008). Red pedagogy: The un-methodology. In N. Denzin, Y. Lincoln, & L. Tuhiwai Smith (Eds.), *Handbook of critical and indigenous methodologies* (pp. 233–254). Los Angeles, CA: Sage.

Guba, E. (1990). *The paradigm dialog.* Newbury Park, CA: Sage.

Hester, B. (2006). *Between actions: Working through Tom Nicholson's practice from the multiple middle.* Retrieved July 7, 2010, from www.drainmag.com/ContentDeterritorialization/Essay/Hester.html

Kincheloe, J., & Steinberg, S. (2008). Indigenous knowledges in education: Complexities, dangers, and profound benefits. In N. Denzin, Y. Lincoln, & L. Tuhiwai Smith (Eds.), *Handbook of critical and indigenous methodologies* (pp. 135–156). Los Angeles, CA: Sage.

Koro-Ljungberg, M., Yendol-Hoppey, D., Smith, J. J., & Hayes, S. B. (2009). (E)pistemological awareness, instantiation of methods, and uninformed methodological ambiguity in qualitative research projects. *Educational Researcher, 38*(9), 687–699.

Lather, P. (2008). Getting lost: Critiquing across difference as methodological practice. In K. Gallagher (Ed.), *The methodological dilemma: Creative, critical, and collaborative approaches to qualitative research* (pp. 219–231). Abingdon, England: Routledge.

Luttrell, W. (Ed.). (2010). *Qualitative educational research.* New York, NY: Routledge.

MacLure, M. (2010, May). *The "terrible powers" of the example.* Presentation at the 6th International Congress of Qualitative Inquiry, Urbana, IL.

Massumi, B. (2002). *Parables for the virtual.* Durham, NC: Duke University Press.

Meyer, M. A. (2008). Indigenous and authentic: Hawaiian epistemology and the triangulation of meaning. In N. Denzin, Y. Lincoln, & L. Tuhiwai Smith (Eds.), *Handbook of critical and indigenous methodologies* (pp. 217–232). Los Angeles, CA: Sage.

Narayan, U. (2003). The project of feminist epistemology: Perspectives from a nonwestern feminist. In C. McCann & S.-K. Kim (Eds.), *Feminist theory reader: Local and global perspectives* (pp. 308–317). New York, NY: Routledge.

Saavedra, C., & Nymark, E. (2008). Borderland-*mestizaje* feminism: The new tribalism. In N. Denzin, Y. Lincoln, & L. Tuhiwai Smith (Eds.), *Handbook of critical and indigenous methodologies* (pp. 255–276). Los Angeles, CA: Sage.

Schostak, J., & Schostak, J. (2008). *Radical research: Designing, developing and writing research to make a difference.* London, England: Routledge.

Silverman, D., & Marvasti, A. (2008). *Doing qualitative research.* Thousand Oaks, CA: Sage.

Spivak, G. (1997). Translator's preface (G. Spivak, Trans.). In J. Derrida (Ed.), *Of Grammatology* (Corrected edition, pp. ix–lxxxvii). Baltimore, MD: Johns Hopkins University Press.

Thayer-Bacon, B. (2003). *Relational "(e)pistemologies".* New York, NY: Peter Lang.

Weis, L., & Fine, M. (2004). *Working method: Research and social justice.* New York, NY: Routledge.

Yanchar, S., Gantt, E., & Clay, S. (2005). On the nature of a critical methodology. *Theory & Psychology, 15*(1), 27–50.

CHAPTER SEVEN

All That Jazz: Doing and Writing CQR in a Material World

P. L. Thomas and Renita Schmidt

Michael built a bridge…Michael tore it down / If I stand and holler…will I stand alone?" sings the speaker in the last lines of "Kohoutek" from the Athens, Georgia, alternative rock band R.E.M. These lyrics speak beyond the narrative of the song to the lives and work of critical educators, critical scholars, and critical researchers, who spend those lives and careers building and tearing down bridges—and ultimately feeling as if when we stand to "holler," we often find ourselves alone.

If and when critical educators rise above the normative forces that seek to silence us, those same forces often do have the power to isolate. It is those norms of teaching, scholarship, and research that we are confronting here as we consider doing and writing CQR in a material world. Our discussion is guided by two metaphors—jazz and the material world.

While researching a scholarly book project on comic books and graphic novels, Paul came across this comment: "Comic books and jazz are often described as being the two uniquely original American art forms" (Rhoades, 2008, p. 3). Marginalized text (comic books) and marginalized music (jazz) share the patterns of oppression found in the power of *norms*. Being unlike the norms for text and music, comics and jazz had to push against, work within, and ultimately rise above (and reshape, ironically) those norms in order to survive.

In this chapter, Nita examines her own journey toward *doing* CQR, and Paul considers the relationship between jazz (and other art forms such as quilting) and composing scholarly texts in order to confront the irony of scholarly writing norms silencing CQR. Throughout, Nita and Paul discuss the neoliberal norms that characterize the material world (made popular in Madonna's "Material Girl") and thus prevent, silence, and marginalize CQR.

Doing CQR in the Material World (Renita Schmidt)

Jazz—spontaneous music that relies on improvisation to mirror the individuality so important to the genre. Individuality that discourages replication, seems unrehearsed, but is dependent upon talent, skill, finesse, and craft. To define jazz is to oppress it as an art form.

CQR—critical qualitative research that relies on improvisation to mirror the individuality of the researcher and participants. CQR challenges us to consider researcher perspective, a topic that is too often silenced. To define CQR is to oppress it as a research form.

Growing up in the 1960s in a working-class family shaped my thinking about who and what I could be as a professional. Becoming a college professor was not on my radar; in fact, when I was a child I did not know a woman who was a researcher or educator at an institution of higher learning. My father was not college educated, but my parents always assumed that I would attend college, for my mother had gone to college and was the first in her family to do so. Mother was a "dietician at Mayo Clinic" (as she proudly tells everyone who will listen)—a professional, working woman. For me as a child, that simply meant I was the only one I knew whose mother worked outside of the home.

Today I also realize that Mom made more money than Dad, but this was never discussed in my home while I was growing up. It was an oppressive silence that kept my home a patriarchal one in theory and practice. If we didn't talk about money, then my father could still be seen as the breadwinner and my mother could maintain her dream of giving her children more than she had as a child. Today, family members joke about our "strong women" and the historical evidence of an upbringing that was much more matriarchal than patriarchal in reality. We joke but do not reflect on the oppression inherent in silencing talk about who was "bringing home the bacon." We poke fun at being strong in Garrison Keillor's land of Lake Wobegon, "where the women are strong, the men are good looking, and the children are above average." But tension bubbled below the jocularity. Are women supposed to be strong?

So I was raised by strong women but in the age when women lived under patriarchy willingly. Women's voices in my family were silenced, women's lives were distorted; my upbringing did not lead to the belief that I could be "anything I wanted to be" as I entered adulthood. I entered college thinking I should major in music. Music was what I was good at. But it was traditional, classical piano lessons and definitely not the jazz we speak of here! That same patriarchal culture of my home would never have considered jazz as an alternative to the music I was privileged to study. I play several instruments, sing, and sight read very well. But improvise? Never. I struggle to play "Happy Birthday" without music. My "training" was traditional. Classical. Elitest.

My parents (my mother in particular) saw her work as a necessity but really a sacrifice of her own life accomplishments—her dream was the assurance that her children would have more than she had as a child. She didn't work to fulfill her own needs or personal desires. She needed money for her children's college educations—a means to better us as individuals and citizens. So I studied classical piano and then learned to play the organ to fulfill her hopes that I would some day become a parish worker in a church—an organist and music director for the rest of my life. It was my mother's very traditional dream—not my own. Matriarchy is also oppressive.

I escaped to teaching. For teaching was a safe option that would provide me with a "regular job"— an important criterion for a productive life in the family in which I was reared.

Teaching did seem a natural choice for me. I was good at school. Reading was something that was easy and pleasurable to me, and I even saw test taking as a break from the routine (although I loved routine, too) and looked forward to several days of extra reading time when I completed a test before time was up. I once told my third-grade teacher that my finger was broken and I could not write. (I was balking at workbook pages and comprehension questions, however, and not really writing itself. We did not "write" in my elementary school.) She allowed me to sit in the back of the room for three days reading quietly before she called my mother and discovered it was a lie. Reading was (and still is) my love. It was not "doing" school.

As a teacher of elementary-aged children, it was enjoyable for me to help children unlock reading pleasure by finding books they enjoyed. Nothing was more satisfying than finding an author or series that a child grabbed on to voraciously, and then talking with them about those books when they finished reading. This sated me completely as a novice teacher.

I was good at teaching, and I wanted to continue to grow as a teacher and study ways to become a better teacher. The other teachers in my school did not want to discuss this. There was not time for this in our busy days. I needed to continue my own studies, but teaching did not provide me with that opportunity.

Could I enter a doctoral program and continue to study ways to be a better teacher when two of my children were in college and the third was in high school? Only because my husband made enough money to financially support the family. Was I a strong enough woman?

Part of my doctoral studies involved my creation as a teacher researcher. As an elementary teacher, I believed my doctoral work would involve studying statistical research based on positivist forms of thinking. I was raised in the Midwestern United States where the Iowa Tests of Basic Skills had reigned supreme throughout my school life. My doctoral mentors, however, introduced me to qualitative research and the opportunity to improve my own practice and that of other teachers by asking researchable questions. Qualitative research opened a new world to me as an interpreter of my own teaching practices. The first study I did was a critical look at my own practices with Accelerated Reader (AR)—a computerized reading program. My critical look at AR confused my former colleagues and made them ask me, "Who are you becoming in that doctoral program?" They did not understand this as research. It was liberal, academic madness.

My studies also coincided with the election of George W. Bush and the enactment of No Child Left Behind, Bush's first change/reform initiative as president. Based on the work of the National Reading Panel, NCLB created new limitations on what would count as "research," especially in the field of reading/literacy. The National Reading Panel had been commissioned by NICHD (The National Institute of Child Health and Human Development) in 1997 to study all research related to reading instruction to make suggestions that would help schools and teachers reach the needs of every learner. Hundreds of thousands of research studies and articles were available for dissemination. It was an impossible task, and one of the panel's first decisions was to limit the research that was reviewed. The National Reading Panel (2002) developed and adopted "a set of rigorous research methodological standards" (p. 4) to identify a final set of experimental and quasi-experimental research studies for detailed analysis. Five main reading topics (phonemic awareness, phonics, fluency, comprehension, and vocabulary) were determined and studied.

Not one qualitative study was deemed worthy of dissemination by the panel.

President Bush also followed the panel guidelines closely as he worked to enact No Child Left Behind. His first No Child Left Behind summary included these statements in shaded boxes:

- We have a genuine national crisis. More and more, we are divided into two nations. One that reads, and one that doesn't. One that dreams, and one that doesn't.

- Too many of our children cannot read. Reading is the building block, and it must be the foundation, for education reform.

- The federal government must be wise enough to give states and school districts more authority and freedom. And it must be strong enough to require proven performance in return.

My initial critical analysis of this document was immediate and simple. The strength of the nation was dependent upon reading? If you couldn't read, you couldn't dream? The implications inherent in this discourse disturbed me. Who were these people who couldn't read? My brother had trouble learning to read but I was quite certain he had dreams. These ideas reflect core neoliberal values: success in education promotes economic growth, reading (the Reading Success Equation) is the backbone of that growth, creation of a shared sense of community or feeling of "one for all and all for one" when it comes to progress (Edmondson, 2004).

I attempted to visit the U.S. Department of Education website and found that their settings automatically "transformed" the address I had typed (www.ed.gov) into nclb.gov. The entire department was overtaken by the work of NCLB. The patriotic red, white, and blue of the page surprised me. The boy's head superimposed on a book that was colored with red and white stripes and blue stars as a patriotic icon shocked me. The warlike "Take Action" heading was troublesome, but the most disturbing portion of the page was this section:

> It's a new era in education and we want you, as parents and community members, to be part of the transformation. Here on the official *No Child Left Behind* website you can find answers to your questions about the new education law signed by President Bush on January 8, 2002.

Saying "we want you, as parents and community members, to be part of the transformation" reminded me of Uncle Sam's pleas from my own childhood in the 50s and 60s—good citizens unite! What I could not understand was why teachers were not included in an invitation for a new era in education. As a teacher, I felt left out, ignored. This was offensive to me as a member of the teaching profession, but also the beginning of my own realization of the power and oppression of teachers in my own country, a place I was taught to love by a father who was a World War II veteran. Boundaries were blurry, and I began to wonder about truth.

I suppose I should be thankful for President Bush's first initiative. It opened up my inquisitiveness about CQR, and created purpose for my work as a researcher. I began to explore critical pedagogy with a newfound sense of purpose and urgency. I wondered what others would say about this website and knew that my own critical discourse analysis of the website text would be interesting. I set out to write the documentation I needed for the Institutional Review Board at my university. They had a few questions, and ultimately decided that my work was exempt. They did not consider my work "real" research.

At the time, I was glad. I could begin my study and not worry about an informed consent document for my participants. When this work was presented at a national conference, I was asked to describe my participants. My work was marginalized by the fact that I knew my participants or had a connection with them by the very fact that I had to personally ask them to look at a webpage in order to discuss the feelings they had in reading the page. My peers were confused. The critique of the content on the webpage was considered thorough and worthy, but the webpage had no distinct author and was available as a public document for all to see. The research could not be considered adequate because of my "problems" with participants.

So I accepted a position at a small university that I saw as a "teaching college." I would be expected to publish, but teaching was supposed to be my top priority. That pleased me.

This was a nationally accredited program working within the boundaries of National Council for Accreditation of Teacher Education (NCATE). Our conceptual framework states that we create teachers as scholars and leaders, and we are required to print that conceptual framework on every syllabus for our teacher education courses. While I do not agree with the "requirement" made upon us by NCATE—to write a conceptual framework document that guides our program and then forcing us to print it in a variety of places—I *do* find many of the ideas within the framework to be important ones which I espouse, hope for, and expect in the production of knowledge for all people in my profession.

The problem becomes more one of asking the right questions when it comes to the production of knowledge and our epistemologies of what it means to be a teacher. Society at large (many teachers included) does not believe teachers need to be scholars or leaders. It is a teacher's responsibility to pour the knowledge into students without teaching them to ask why, who says so, or what else instead? That belief must be challenged, but placing our ideas on a syllabus is not enough.

My research today meshes with my beliefs about teachers as scholars and leaders and how they make decisions about what they will teach in their classrooms. I suppose this is where my work has truly turned the corner towards becoming critical—it is my hope that the research I do today will transform teachers into believing they are scholars and leaders. Freire (1999) encouraged us to teach students to read the world and not just the word as a way of learning through what he calls "conscientização" or "learning to perceive social, political, and economic contradictions and to take action against the oppressive elements of reality" (p. 17). Teachers have to first see themselves as scholars and leaders if we want students to truly consider how to make our world a better place in which to live. School has to encourage transformative thinking and learning within the production of knowledge, and schools that use standardized, cookie-cutter materials for all children will not be places where this occurs.

Unfortunately, transformation is not understood as a viable way of "doing school." My sister-in-law (a physician) sometimes inquires about my work, and one day when I complained to her about teachers using only textbooks in the classroom she said, "What should schools use if not textbooks?"

Her words speak to the broad assumptions and stereotypes that people carry about what it is we *do* in school. Teachers fill students up with knowledge in standardized ways so they will "leave no child left behind" and ensure everyone of success in school. That kind of traditional thinking predominates schools across the U.S. As Paul and I argue in this chapter, when students learn only in this way, there is no possibility for producing problem solvers and thinkers for the 21st century. The future holds exciting possibilities for how we might learn, communicate, and access knowledge. CQR can help us accomplish that.

In my brief experience (less than 10 years) with "doing" CQR, I have had trouble garnering permission for doing anything "critical" with school districts in my region. When I was an elementary teacher in rural Iowa public schools, I was interested in helping my students have good conversations with books (Atwell, 1998; Peterson & Eeds, 2007). I had never heard of critical literacy, and no one I studied with until I worked on my doctorate mentioned it as a possibility for my work with teachers and children. Today I wonder whether if I had learned about CQR when I was an elementary teacher I ever would have left the classroom, so now I work to help teachers have critical conversations about race, class, gender, and sexuality with their students as a way to think about what is happening in the world economically, socially, and politically. It is my hope that this will lead to transformation in the ways people think about justice and equity in the world.

We are at war in the Middle East. Knowledge about "why" is sketchy and unclear for too many people in the world—Americans especially. Some believe George W. Bush's ideas that Saddam Hussein was responsible for 9/11 and was gathering weapons of mass destruction to begin a war on us—it was right to declare war first. Others believe that the current war in Afghanistan is Barack Obama's war—a war for oil and control of the region. In thinking about how ideas about this era are thought of today and how they will be reported in the future, it seems important to consider how knowledge about this period was produced and how is/will it be perpetuated over time. Isn't it rational that teachers could shape the transformation of how we think about history? Isn't that the beginning of building citizens for the 21st century?

In school settings, history is often the study of wars. A critical pedagogue asks learners to consider whose voices are heard in that telling and whose voices are not heard. There is always an effort to ask why something happened, and not just an emphasis on how it happened. How does that emphasis shape the work done by critical qualitative researchers?

When many military men and women from our state began to be deployed to Afghanistan for service, I wondered what children in our schools knew and understood about the country and why we were there at war. One of the graduate students at our university who studied young adult literature with Paul was interested in beginning literature discussions with her students. She agreed to work with me on a project with her fifth graders, reading *The Breadwinner* by Deborah Ellis and other books about children living in conflict.

During that work, we discovered misunderstandings, confusions, and tensions that created new spaces for learning through talk and multiple sign systems. In *The Breadwinner* after Parvana's father is taken away by the Taliban, Parvana disguises herself as a boy and begins to work in the market as an interpreter and trader. When a Taliban soldier approaches Parvana and asks her to translate a letter from a family member, he begins to cry. Many of the students were confused by the behavior of this soldier they thought was evil. As one child said, "I thought the Taliban were bad. How can he be crying?" Bryce's picture (below) is an example of that confusion.

Bryce's drawing identifies the importance for making time in school to have epistemological discussions about identities. Bryce sees the Taliban in a binary way—all bad and never good—and he cannot understand why this soldier is crying over a letter. The Talib soldier is drawn very large, and Bryce has framed him with a cloud-like formation above his head and lines running down the sides of the cloud that separate him from the rest of the picture. Perhaps Bryce feels the soldier does not want anyone to see him crying, and that he may feel uncomfortable being seen in public demonstrating emotion over a sentimental letter. The soldier's gun is prominently displayed across his chest, very much like one of the soldier images we included in the text set. The soldier is also wearing what looks like the turbans often worn by Afghani men. Bryce depicts Parvana (the protagonist) as a very small figure sitting on a rug in the marketplace. In fact, in this illustration Bryce does not name her Parvana, but simply tags her as the "Letter Reader." Because of the size and perspective, we know that the soldier is the most important figure in Bryce's illustration. His confusion over whether or not a Taliban soldier can be both good and bad is obvious. Although Bryce is confused about what is good and what is evil, his background knowledge seemed to be increasing thanks to available access to the images and materials in the text set we used in the study.

As one child told me, "I didn't know there was a place called Afghanistan until we read these books." And yet this research was not sanctioned or desired as research by the school district. Permission was granted by the principal, but the district deemed it "not helpful." Merriam's (2009) ideas about critical inquiry come to mind: "In critical inquiry the goal is to critique and challenge, to transform and empower" (p. 10).

There were no final quantifiable answers in this CQR. Transformation appeared in other ways. Oppression is very much alive in the NCLB school world in which we live.

Writing CQR—All that Jazz? (P. L. Thomas)

I finally settled on jazz.

But it could have just as easily been comic books, collage, or quilting (and quilting was very hard to ignore). I chose jazz because—like comic books, collage, and quilting—it represents the qualities that concern me here as I write about the walls and closed doors that inhibit expression, the ways in which we write about CQR. As Adrienne Rich (2001) warns: What is "rendered unspeakable, [is] thus unthinkable" (p. 150). And despite the critical commitments of educators, scholars, researchers, we often "render unspeakable" critical messages because we ironically maintain traditional paradigms for the texts of our research even as our research and scholarship confront the hegemony of tradition.

(And I cringe every time I say or write "hegemony" because as a privileged term among the educated elite, it is a paradoxical word labeling the exact condition it creates when placed into text.)

Jazz began as confrontation and suffered marginalization for that confrontation, along with its other deviations from normalized standards of music—collaboration, improvisation, synthesis. And of course, the attacks on the form always failed to acknowledge social context: Is it possible jazz was marginalized because it sprang from oppressed people, people discounted as deficient when measured against the ruling class?

Growing up in Oklahoma City, Ralph Ellison (2003) learned a great deal about jazz—and indirectly, art, creativity, living, and life. About the jazz musicians he encountered as a youth, he wrote:

> Their driving motivation was neither money nor fame, but the will to achieve the most eloquent expression of idea-emotions through the technical mastery of their instruments…and the give and take, the subtle rhythmical shaping and blending of idea, tone and imagination demanded of group improvisation. (p. 229)

Jazz musicians of Ellison's childhood, then, stood outside both the norms of music, of capitalist society, and of mechanistic assumptions driving modern humans: "But they lived [life] fully, and when they expressed their attitude toward the world it was with a fluid style that reduced the chaos of living to form" (p. 229).

Ellison (2003) also wrote about Charlie Parker, Bird, who personified the improvisational nature of jazz as a confrontation of musical norms and as a confrontation of *entertainer*. Parker, like T. S. Eliot, Ellison argued, pursued "the artful juxtaposition of earlier styles" (p. 259). And the power of jazz to form and reform the norms of music and entertainment was also a critical commentary on the broader culture:

> In the United States, where each of us is a member of some minority group and where political power and entertainment alike are derived from viewing and manipulating the human predicament of others, the maintenance of dignity is never a simple matter, even for those with higher credentials. (p. 260)

The careers of Parker and Ellison offer for our discussion here the delicate and complex interplay of both message and medium as they wrestled within and against the hegemonies of culture and the market. Parker (like Louis Armstrong) and Ellison suffered the oppression of the dominant culture, racism, as well as the rejection of their own race because when the medium that once was marginalized is allowed *in*, that normalizing tarnishes the medium for those still seeking the *change*.

And this is the great paradox of critical pedagogy, CQR, and the writing of that research. As critical educators, researchers, scholars, and writers, we are always working to get *in*, but destined always to fight against whatever *in* is—both in the messages of our work and the mediums and conventions within which we choose to express those messages.

To write critically must be a confrontation equal to *being* critical, to *doing* CQR.

But the structures that exist in the world of academia and the paradigms of scholarship and research remain recalcitrant to critical research and scholarship and nearly deaf and blind to *writing* critically. And here is my story.

During the past year or two, a pattern has emerged when I submit work for publication in peer-reviewed scholarly journals. I tend to choose publications that are themselves critical, although I also target progressive and even traditional publications because I believe speaking *only* in critical contexts is failing the central tenet of critical confrontation. Part of my scholarship agenda is to take progressives by the shoulders and shake them out of their slumber, to raise my voice to traditionalists…just because there is some catharsis in screaming ("If I stand and holler…will I stand alone?").

Yet, I am rarely surprised or disturbed when mainstream academic journals and other publications reject my scholarship and my op-ed submissions. I assume the message simply doesn't fit within the paradigms of their world views: *You can trash schools and teachers, but please don't bash the good ol' USA. And please don't remind us of the disproportionate percentage of children living in poverty…in the good ol' USA….*

What has begun to trouble me—what has led me to this section of our chapter—is that on several recent occasions, I have had an eerily similar experience with multiple critical publications. Peer reviewers reject my work (and even characterize the pieces as shoddy), but the editors ask me to revise and resubmit because the editors believe I have the right message, just some issues we need to address with the medium, my writing style.

I have begun to consider my scholarly work something akin to jazz, hoping that it is recursive and hoping that readers *feel* as if it is improvised. I write scholarly pieces and even books guided by the style of Kurt Vonnegut's novels and essays, driven by the same urge to communicate that fuels my poetry.

Part of my call to be *critical* is a recognition that thought, teaching, learning, and being fully human are all *not* linear acts or states of being. To cobble together prose that projects a mechanical and artificial linearity is thus distorting critical scholarship and critical research.

It is dishonest.

Dishonest in the same way that ascribing blame to schools for the achievement gap while suggesting that schools exist in a social vacuum. Dishonest in the same way that the Obama administration directly states that teacher quality is the greatest contributor to student success while ignoring the mountains of evidence that the greatest influence is student affluence or poverty.

Giroux (2010) identifies the failure of public discourse from pundits and politicians, both of whom prosper in the so-called marketplace of ideas by "wrapping themselves in the populist creed of speaking for everyday Americans" (para. 1). The bankrupt arguments hidden beneath pandering to simplistic faith in rugged individualism exist in wider political discourse and in the more narrow debates about education. While Giroux focuses on the content of these neoliberal claims, I have experienced equally silencing dynamics within the traditional, the progressive, and the critical mechanisms of scholarship, dynamics that marginalize not only *what* is expressed but also *how* we communicate within and outside our field of education.

While critical scholars are accurate when we point our fingers at the oppressive influence of norms, we must be even more vigilant about *ourselves*. The mechanisms that guide how we submit, review, and publish CQR are themselves ripe for critical confrontations. Let's look at those mechanisms and then end this section by calling for a critical redefinition of scholarly writing.

One gatekeeping mechanism is how we present calls for articles, chapters, or books. Most calls address themes, content, and topics, but the only ways in which those calls address *how* the pieces are written tend toward the most mechanical aspects of preparing a manuscript—word count, margins, fonts, citation requirements. The very mechanical nature of calls for submissions reinforce expectations of traditional types of text for academic and scholarly publication.

Qualitative and critical approaches and perspectives have been seeking equal voices and credibility for decades against the norms of quantitative and traditional approaches and perspectives. To be seen as *rigorous* (a norm itself that oppresses and silences), critical publications have embraced peer review. But as I have experienced, the power of peer review to increase sophistication and quality of the voices of critical perspectives and scholarship also can serve to marginalize or omit. When the peers conducting the reviews are themselves trapped within paradigms of what constitutes scholarly discourse, the texts accepted and thus published maintain a status quo and also perpetuate that status quo since potential scholars embrace published text as a template for what to submit.

This dynamic, of course, is working within the normative paradigms of tenure and promotion. Critical educators and scholars who seek a voice within academia seek that voice within a mechanism that requires them to conduct research and scholarship, to submit that work for publication, and to be published. How are critical educators and researchers who are marginalized by their newness to behave *bravely*, to confront not only the norms of ideas and ideology but also the norms of expression?

As well, editors stand as powerful influences on the nature of text; in my experience, I have been fortunate to experience editors who have had the courage to rise *critically* above the limitations of *normal*, of scholarly writing. But even when those editors have intervened, I have had to argue for and explain myself, including writing openings to accepted pieces that explain my work is purposeful—not shoddy or careless. It is as if a jazz musician has to preface each piece with a brief classical piece, proving she or he is competent.

One of my commitments as a critical scholar is to submit and publish op-ed pieces in local, state, and national media. I feel compelled to introduce a critical voice into the notably *uncritical* popular discourse. My experiences in the popular discourse parallel the patterns I have detailed above with norms of expression blocking my entry into scholarly publications—even scholarly publications that are critical.

In the popular media, responses to my op-ed work often include charges that I am not being objective. Since I participate in the online commentary of my published pieces, I try to clarify that I do not claim to be objective; further, I attempt to explain that objectivity is not the barometer for rigor or *truth* that most people assume, both inside and outside academia.

The great problem that I face is not the unwillingness to hear that I experience in popular discourse—often that door is a predictable one (mischaracterize my message and then attack that mischaracterization)—but that the power of norms, particularly related to expression, raises its hand within academia as often as outside academia.

Nash (2004) opens his *Liberating Scholarly Writing: The Power of Personal Narrative* with "I." His argument is about the nature of scholarly writing, and his opening personal narrative confronts the writing his students have offered him over his career as a teacher: "I remember almost nothing of what I've read" (p. 1). I have been teaching for almost 30 years now, and I agree, adding that the ideas and language of students is almost universally lifeless, passionless.

And that lifelessness, that *lack of passion*, parallels most scholarly writing, regardless of the messages. Nash (2004) offers his argument for scholarly personal narrative (SPN) within his concern for student and academic writing and within his own self-described postmodern perspective "because [he is] convinced that radical introspection and storytelling in scholarly writing have both particular (offering value for the storyteller) and universalizable (offering value for others) possibilities for professionals" (p. 3). Yet, Nash recognizes standard arguments for traditional approaches to writing scholarship and academic text—concerns about rigor, reliability, validity, and perceptions of "touchy-feely" and "anti-intellectual" works (p. 4).

However, Nash (2004) contends, as do I, that different views of scholarly and academic texts "redefine the idea of 'rigor,'" as well as challenge narrow perception of validity and reliability (p. 5). The philosophical lens, the methodology of our research, the evidence and conclusions of our research and scholarship, and the medium of expressing that research and scholarship can and should be critical reexaminations of the assumptions that drive practice and even worldviews:

> Thus, whenever I refer to the "real world" in my work, I do not mean the scientific world. My real world is not the world that can be empirically tested, measured, interviewed, weighed, or taxonomized, even though I am the first to admit that this story of the world can be of great value to scholars and researchers. Instead, I am speaking of the real world that each of us narrativizes, the storied world that each of us inhabits. (Nash, p. 8)

While I build much of my scholarly writing life on the essential arguments offered by Nash (2004), I must note that I move beyond his postmodern claims and his concern for students (without discounting either) and toward a critical perspective aimed at scholars and researchers. Along with conducting and promoting CQR, we must reconsider how we write about that research, including the following areas:

Audience. I agree with Nash (2004): "I, for one, would be proud to be called a 'public intellectual'" (p. 8). But I also recognize that scholars and academics who write for multiple audiences—lay and professional—simultaneously tend to be discounted by both. The goal of critical scholars who write, however, should be to write to all potential audiences in order to tear down the walls that oppress *as well as* to challenge any reader's perception of what should count as quality writing. When we categorize one level of language for a lay audience, we are being condescending and oppressive to that audience and we are trivializing the exact message we hope to share. And when we reserve another level of language for our scholarly peers, we are being insular as well as further corrupting our philosophical commitments and our messages.

Collaboration. Scholarly writing is traditionally treated as an act in isolation—either through the solitary work of a single researcher who assumes an objective stance (isolating even her/himself from the act of expression) or through the assigning of text and ideas to individual researchers, scholars, and writers (consider the weight of "first author," "second author," and the like). Critical scholars should embrace through their writing that *all expression is collaborative* and synthesis. At the very least, meaning through text requires the reader, the writer, and the text (Rosenblatt, 1995). But, beyond the basic essential nature of discourse, the writing of CQR should confront and explore the collaborative nature of producing text through multiple authors as well as through peer response to text as that text is being drafted, discovered, and completed. To embrace collaboration is to reject the reductive nature of ownership of words and ideas.

Citation. Once we admit that collaboration is as central to human expression as subjectivity (and with that embrace both as positive, not negative, aspects of being fully human), we are then necessarily confronting documentation and citation norms. To cite the sources of ideas we are weaving into our synthesis of ideas is an act of empowerment for those sources, ourselves, and our readers; thus, I am not here rejecting citation of sources. However, I am challenging the use of citation, documentation, and style sheets when they silence anyone, when those norms close the doors of discourse.[1] As I noted above, I struggled with the jazz metaphor because the quilting metaphor calls to me as a vivid metaphor for the work of critical educators, scholars, and researchers as we gather pieces from a wide variety of sources in order to sew together something new and vibrant. For writers of CQR, we should be vigilant to seek ways of creating text that honors the sources of our journey while also valuing the integrity of the text and the possibilities that lie beyond the mechanics of formatting text.

Narrative. The central thrust of Nash (2004) is the power of narrative, specifically personal narrative. When I ask students to submit writing in courses, I always suggest that they open any piece with a story, something real that engages the reader and helps that reader care about the focus of the piece. Traditional academic and scholarly writing is expository, third person, and mechanical ("In the following paragraphs, this paper will…" as well as engaging subheads such as Methodology and Conclusions). CQR should be written as an argument against those norms.

Voice. While traditional research is couched in a disembodied "objective" persona, CQR should bring the people involved in the research and scholarship forward, moving beyond merely allowing first person to infuse text with the voice and voices involved in the stories. Voice includes more than person—diction, sentence formation and variety, paragraph formation and variety, and ultimately how text expresses the unique qualities of all involved in producing that text.

Craft. As I noted above, citation style sheets can work against the aims of critical educators. For example, APA style guidelines discourage first person and figurative language, suggesting that figurative language, for example, can obscure meaning. I, however, believe that writers of CQR can practice craft in the writing of research as an avenue to enhance and expand meaning. Another aspect of craft, building on *how* we form our messages, includes expanding the variety and type of sources (and here our reconsideration of citation guidelines, voice, and craft overlap) we incorporate into our scholarly and academic writing, our quilting of words and ideas.

In both message and medium, then, I see the critical researcher embodying in their doing and writing of CQR, guided by Freire (1998): "If education cannot do everything, there is something fundamental that it can do. In other words, if education is not the key to social transformation, neither is it simply meant to reproduce the dominant ideology" (p. 110).

This Is Our Story…No, *This* Is Our Story—CQR as Admission of Context

In our material world, there is no context—every *thing* and every *person* is an island. Facts and truth are also decontextualized, and simple to identify. The material world both embraces and is defined by the narrowest assumptions of "scientific." Quantifying confirms that which is quantified. Our material world lives by the motto "numbers don't lie"; it is driven by a blind faith in the rugged individual pulling him/herself up by the bootstrap.

But there is always a different story, or actually, other stories.

Margaret Atwood's *The Handmaid's Tale* is essentially a narrative of the *layers* of meaning and truth associated with any person or any person's story. Readers follow Offred (June) as she tells her story, but she continually backtracks, starts over, recounts, and recants: "This is reconstruction. All of it is a reconstruction....I made that up. It didn't happen that way. Here is what happened....It didn't happen that way either....All I can hope for is reconstruction" (pp. 134, 261, 263).

Once the primary narrative ends, Atwood includes Historical Notes—a technique that often baffles readers who fail to read further, thinking the last section isn't part of the story. However, in this last chapter, "Historical Notes on *The Handmaid's Tale*," much is revealed. Readers learn that the story of Offred (June) has been discovered as cassette recordings she left behind after her apparent escape. That the narrative is built from recordings instead of a written recreation complicates the narrative.

Then, readers learn through the scholar presenting at a symposium in the last section that the text read is also a manipulated transcript of those tapes: Scholars, as researchers do, having found the tapes, made decisions about their order and fashioned a transcript:

> As all historians know, the past is a great darkness, and filled with echoes. Voices may reach us from it; but what they say to us is imbued with the obscurity of the matrix out of which they come; and, try as we may, we cannot always decipher them precisely in the clearer light of our own day. (p. 311)

Thus, more *scholarly* complexity is added to the text of Offred's (June's) narrative.

The Handmaid's Tale reveals itself as metanarrative about the nature of telling and retelling, about the layers of truth and reality that exists with any person or life, and about the nature of scholarship. The last section stands as parody of academia and scholarship: The audience sitting quietly while the scholar talks about the reconstruction of Offred's (June's) life—and that reconstruction is for the scholar and the other academics.

Whose story is this? And what is true, real, fact?

As researchers, scholars, academics, and educators, we stand facing the walls of traditional conventions of research, scholarship, and discourse. As critical researchers, scholars, academics, and educators, we have an obligation to push beyond those walls, both in doing and writing CQR. The material world is not as simple as our cultural mythologies suggest, and the norms that drive how we do and express our worlds prove themselves to be *one* of the stories, not the only story, not the best story, not the right story.

As with Offred (June), the goal is not capturing that one, seemingly true narrative; the goal is the doing and then the writing, bringing the multitude of voices to the arena of ideas where, like jazz musicians, we can each and together create something new and valuable.

The goal is the pursuit, both lived and shared in joy, laughter, and humor—and not in the bitter seriousness of objective scholarship:

> Humor: the divine flash that reveals the world in its moral ambiguity and man in his profound incompetence to judge others; humor: the intoxicating relativity of human things; the strange pleasure that comes of the certainty that there is no certainty. (Kundera, 1995, pp.32–33)

Note

1.   As a side note, I was contacted by a graduate student recently who had two points deducted from her final essay because the professor claimed the use of a font other than Times New Roman was in violation of APA guidelines.

References

Atwell, N. (1998). *In the middle: New understanding about writing, reading, and learning* (2nd ed.). Portsmouth, NH: Heinemann.

Atwood, M. (1998). *The handmaid's tale.* New York: Anchor. (Original work published 1985).

Edmondson, J. (2004). Reading policies: Ideologies and strategies for political engagement. *The Reading Teacher, 57*(5), 418–428.

Ellison, R. (2003). *The collected essays of Ralph Ellison* (J. F. Callahan, Ed.). New York, NY: Modern Library.

Freire, P. (1998). *Pedagogy of freedom: Ethics, democracy, and civic courage* (P. Clarke, Trans.). Lanham, MD: Rowman & Littlefield.

Freire, P. (1999). *Pedagogy of the oppressed.* New York, NY: Continuum.

Giroux, H. A. (2010, July 12). The disappearing intellectual in the age of economic Darwinism. *truthout.* Retrieved July 19, 2010, from http://www.truth-out.org/the-disappearing-intellectual-age-economic-darwinism61287

Kundera, M. (1995). *Testaments betrayed: An essay in nine parts* (L. Asher, Trans.). New York, NY: Harper Perennial.

Merriam, S. B. (2009). *Qualitative research: A guide to design and implementation.* San Francisco, CA: Jossey-Bass.

Nash, R. J. (2004). *Liberating scholarly writing: The power of personal narrative.* New York: Teachers College Press.

National Reading Panel. (2002). *Teaching children to read: An evidence-based assessment of the scientific research literature on reading and its implications for reading instruction* (Report of the National Reading Panel). Washington, DC: NICHD.

Peterson, R., & Eeds, M. (2007). *Grand conversations: Literature groups in action.* Portsmouth, NH: Heinemann.

Rhoades, S. (2008). *A complete history of American comic books.* New York, NY: Peter Lang.

Rich, A. (2001). *Arts of the possible: Essays and conversations.* New York, NY: W. W. Norton.

Rosenblatt, L. M. (1995). *Literature as exploration* (5th ed.). New York, NY: Modern Language Association of America.

CHAPTER EIGHT

Deploying Qualitative Methods for Critical Social Purposes

Gaile S. Cannella and Yvonna S. Lincoln

Twenty years ago, in her *Harvard Educational Review* article, Elizabeth Ellsworth (1989) questioned the assumption that critical perspectives or critical research were either empowering or transformative. She argued that critical theory was embedded within patriarchal forms of reason, Enlightenment logic, and male domination, such that the attempted adoption of a critical lens can easily create the illusion of justice while actually reinscribing old forms of power.

Beyond Ellsworth's criticisms, it is also clear now that critical inquiry cannot be described utilizing traditional research language like models, predetermined linear methods, or any forms of unquestioned methodologies (Richardson, 2000). Indeed, even several of the foundational terms of critical theory—divided consciousness, false consciousness—imply a singular truth to which adherents must pledge allegiance, lest they be charged with failing to see or own this singular truth. Further, some critical perspectives would challenge the notion of a singular truth while remaining concerned about power and oppression. Although many contemporary researchers claim to use critical qualitative research methods (and we are among those), these inquiry practices often do not transform, or even appear to challenge the dominant or mainstream constructions.

Our intent here is to explore why much of the critical/critical theorist work that has been done has not always resulted in any form of increased social justice. We echo Ellsworth's question: Why does this not feel empowering? Our own questions, however, go further, and we explore the issues of how we filter research through a critical lens? How do we deploy qualitative methods (which are by and large far less linear than conventional experimental and quantitative methods) for critical historical, social justice and policy purposes? How can we be more explicit about critical methodologies, and make both our methodologies and our analyses clearer and more accessible to a larger set of publics? How do we construct an environment that values a critical perspective? Is it possible to construct critical research that does not simultaneously create new forms of oppressive power for itself, or for its practitioners? What does a critical perspective mean for research issues and questions, for frames that construct data collection and analyses, and forms of interpretation and re-presentation? How do we effect a wider dissemination of critical studies such that we prompt a broader civic debate around our analyses?

The Criticism Inherent in Critical Perspectives

One of the major, but unexplored, issues surrounding critical perspectives is what, precisely, is meant by them. Thus, we are offering a preliminary definition of how we are using the term "critical perspectives." By critical perspectives, we mean any research that recognizes power—that seeks in its analyses to plumb the archaeology of taken-for-granted perspectives to understand how unjust and oppressive social conditions came to be reified as historical "givens." These taken-for-granted perspectives might include, for example, unequal educational opportunity, racism, the acceptance of an inevitability of poverty, the relegation of women to second-class political and economic status, the systematic devaluation of homemaking and childrearing as productive economic activity, romanticized views of children and childhood that actually create forms of oppression for those who are younger (Cannella, 1997), and the like. The foundational questions to critical work are: Who/what is helped/privileged/legitimated? Who/what is harmed/oppressed/ disqualified? In addition to poststructural analyses and postmodern challenges to the domination of grand narratives, the range of feminist perspectives, queer theory and its critique of forms of normalization, as well as anti-colonialist assessments of empire, are included in our broad definition. Such research, in addition to searching out the historical origins of socially and politically reified social arrangements, also seeks to understand how victims of such social arrangements come to accept and even collaborate in maintaining oppressive aspects of the system.

Further, critical perspectives seek to illuminate the hidden structures of power deployed in the construction and maintenance of its own power, and the disempowerment of others (e.g. groups, knowledges, ways of being, perspectives). Frequently, these power structures (whether hidden or obvious) are/can be tied to late capitalism and more currently, neoliberalism and its counterpart, invasive hyper-capitalism. Neoliberalism, with its political roots in globalization and the discourse of "free" markets (however inequitably these markets actually function), serves as an economic backdrop to the redistribution of wealth in the guise of liberal political theory. The real power of neoliberalism has been to create corporate states and individuals who are more powerful and more wealthy than many nations, but further, to facilitate corporate power (Said, 1979) that is not restricted by national boundaries, and, finally, to concentrate wealth in an ever-smaller set of hands. As capital has been created, so has more extensive and dire impoverishment, both at home and abroad.

Critical perspectives also inquire deeply into the usages of language and the circulation of discourses which are used to shape all of social life, from advertising to decisions regarding the candidate for whom we should vote. Primarily, however, critical researchers are interested in the "language games" which maintain power relations, which appear to prevent transformative action, and which insistently shape a dulled, misled, and/or false public consciousness. Language gives form to ideologies and prompts action, and consequently, is deeply complicit in power relations and class struggles.

Next, critical perspectives are profoundly engaged with issues of race, gender and socioeconomic level, as major shapers as well as components of historically reified structures of oppression. Often, a given scholar's focus will be on one of the three, but increasingly, consciousness of how various forms of oppression and privilege intersect (Collins, 2000), results in a focus on the interactive nature, and institutionalization, of power, oppression, and injustice. An example would be the hybrid condition of injustice suffered by individuals based on race, economic status, or class, and the particular political destitution of women. More recently, scholars have also been deconstructing whiteness, the invisible advantage assumed because of it, and the oppressions suffered by the intersecting of societal power structures based on gender, sexual orientation, and economic status.

Finally, along with race, class, and gender, indigenous scholars virtually always approach relations between themselves and imperialist forms of power from the perspective of colonialism, neocolonialism, and postcolonialism. Relations shaped by conquest and occupation inevitably demand critical interrogation, for the lasting vestiges of cultural, linguistic, and spiritual destruction alter forever the cultural landscape of an indigenous people (Spivak, 1999).

So Why Are Critical Perspectives Not Empowering?

One might well ask, since critical perspectives are profoundly engaged with powerful issues of our time, why is it that so little critical research becomes a part of civic debate? Why does so little important work make it to the editorial pages of newspapers, or into venues routinely perused by intellectuals and engaged citizens, such as the *Atlantic Monthly* or *Harper's*, but is instead aimed at the even smaller audiences captured by such publications as *Daedalus* or *Tikkun?* Certainly, the lack of wider public discussion surrounding such research is one reason why most of such work has not yet resulted in any measurable increase in social justice, nor has it had any real visible transformative effect on social policy or education.

Critical perspectives have already acknowledged the role of the research "construct" in the generation and perpetuation of power for particular groups, especially knowledge and cultural workers such as academics (Knorr-Cetina & Mulkay, 1983; Greenwood & Levin, 2000). Indeed, knowledge production, traditionally the province of the scholarly profession, has finally seen its flowering in the information age and the information society. However, even when we recognize this research/power complicity, we must still, as academic knowledge generators and producers, conduct research, both because of the influence that it holds within dominant discourses and, more selfishly, because that is what we are hired to do in certain kinds of institutions. Critically-inclined academics, however, continue to struggle with how to rethink our fields in ways that generate critically oriented questions and methods, even while addressing issues such as voice, representation, and the avoidance of new forms of oppressive power. Although qualitative methods and alternative paradigm inquiry offer possibilities for the generation of epistemologies and methodologies that insist upon the examination of themselves, even qualitative inquiry creates power for, and all too frequently, a focus on the researcher herself. Thus, we are caught in the paradox of attempting to investigate and deconstruct power relations, even while we are ourselves engaged in a project which creates and re-creates power accruing primarily to us.

We believe that three issues can be identified that contribute to the continued marginalization of critical theorizing and critical pedagogy. One issue is endogenous to critical theories themselves, while two others are exogenous, but each of the issues can be addressed by the community of critical knowledge workers. First, we discuss things that academics do to keep their work from being read by broader audiences. These practices are both tied to training and to the insulated environment that is the academy. Second, we believe that there are political forces, particularly on the political right, that have a large stake in quelling serious critiques of schooling practices, critical research, and critical researchers (Horowitz, 2006). Conservative forces within and external to the academy mount rigorous efforts at systemic and systematic disqualification of critical qualitative research and those who produce it, the most serious effort thus far having been to "capture" federal resources sufficiently to deny funding to qualitative and critical researchers, while mandating that "what works" is primarily or solely randomized experiments (Mosteller & Boruch, 2002; National Research Council, 2002). Third, we believe the effects of neoliberal and hyper-capitalism have created additional social problems (e.g., increasing poverty of some segments of Western society, demands for goods and services which outstrip the global ability to produce or deliver them, unquestioned nationalisms) which in turn have led to a de-emphasis on certain forms of academic knowledge production. We would like to deal with each of those in turn.

'Repressive Myths', Difficult Language, and Writing Complexities

When Ellsworth (1989) speaks of "repressive myths" associated with critical theorizing and critical pedagogy, she refers to forms of language which "operate at a high level of abstraction" (p. 300), the overall effect of which is to reinscribe certain forms of oppression within the classroom. In part, this occurs because

> …when educational researchers advocating critical pedagogy fail to provide a clear statement of their political agendas, the effect is to hide the fact that as critical pedagogues, they are in fact seeking to appropriate public resources (classrooms, school supplies, teacher/professor salaries, academic requirements and degree) to further various "progressive political agendas that they believe to be for the public good—and therefore deserving of public resources…." As a result, the critical education "movement" has failed to develop a clear articulation for its existence, its goals, priorities, risks, or potentials. (p. 301)

Some of the foregoing criticism has since been answered by the critical community, but some critical theorizing remains connected to patriarchy and rationalist abstraction. Ellsworth found, in her media course, that concepts borrowed from the critical pedagogy literature were singularly unhelpful in uncovering the experiences of racism and other "isms" brought to her classroom, and recognized that she and her students needed to move away from the regulating aspects of rationalism, which "operate[s] in ways that set up as its opposite an irrational Other,"[1] as it "has become a vehicle for regulating conflict and the power to speak" (p. 301), silencing some voices and marginalizing others.

Rationalistic argumentation, however, is not the only issue the critical educationists face. The issue of abstraction, of difficult languages and "complicated writing styles", make the work of many critical researchers appear less transparent than it might be, and appears to create a smaller audience than the ideas warrant. At times, we have been guilty of the same charge, so we abstain from adopting some sort of literary high ground here. Indeed, at times, the material we undertake to deconstruct and de-mystify demands a complex political and philosophical treatment, circling as it does around abstruse social and democratic theory. Nevertheless, as Lather (1996) makes clear, language itself possesses a "politics", wherein "Clear speech is part of a discursive system, a network of power that has material *effects*" and thus, "Sometimes we need a density that fits the thought being expressed" (p. 3). Additionally, St. Pierre (2000) reminds us that the "burden of intelligibility" lies with the reader/receiver as well as with the writer/constructor. She asks the question: "How does one learn to hear and 'understand' a statement made within a different structure of intelligibility?" (p. 25). We would argue, however, that Lather's analysis regarding the deskilling effects of "clear and concise plain prose" and its relationship to a pervasive anti-intellectualism in American society, while true, does not mitigate the necessity of making our theories and arguments more accessible to a broader set of audiences in order to further public scrutiny and debate about these ideas.

Consequently, while we strongly hold to the premise that sound theorizing is both academically necessary and epistemologically moral, and that there indeed might be some "violence of clarity," a kind of "non-innocence" in plain prose, it is also clear that many who would like to understand the foundational elements of what is being argued either cannot, or will not, struggle with our terminologies and languages. The requirement that thinking differently necessitates speaking differently becomes a barrier. Rather than being the rational argument makers, we are unfortunately cast in the mold of being Ellsworth's "irrational Other." Thus, in part, the problem of critical pedagogues and theorists is partially one of our own making and partially one of difficult circumstance. When dominant understandings are so thoroughly embedded within truth orientations, critical language and abstract terminologies sometimes ensure that ideas will not be received by a patient audience that has learned to expect answers to generalizable solutions.

There are, however, greater reasons why so little critical qualitative research makes it into the public realm of debate. One of these reasons is linked to the backlashes against feminisms and other traditionally marginalized knowledges. As Patricia Hill Collins (2000) explains in her discussion of Black feminist thought, as critical work and resistance become evident related to intersecting oppressions, new forms of power are generated to silence/ignore the traditionally oppressed, and to reinscribe/reinstate power for those who have been traditionally privileged.

Reinscribing Oppressive Forms of Knowledge: Attacking Diversity and Discrediting Critique

As we and others have written, the civil rights successes of the 1960s resulted in new possibilities for academia and the acceptance of the voices and knowledges of those who have been traditionally marginalized. In academia, women and gender studies, ethnic studies, and diverse research philosophies and methodologies emerged and gained credibility. Yet, there were those who were not happy with these gains across society in general and in academia specifically. For example, as women made gains in the workplace and elsewhere, actions were taken to resubjugate them/us (Faludi, 1991). As women made gains in traditional domains of academia, there was/is a backlash against their leadership styles, their research topics, their publication outlets, and so on.

In society in general, a movement was specifically designed and funded to (re)inscribe a monocultural conservative agenda in the media, the judiciary, and in academia. Foundations and think tanks were created that funded a range of broad-based societal activities including particular forms of literature used to discredit feminisms, qualitative research methods, and constructs like affirmative action and multiculturalism. Most are familiar with these activities by now because of the past seven years of a U.S. government administration that has been entirely supported by this monocultural agenda. However, most (even academics) do not notice the ways that this activity has entirely transformed the expectations for intellectual engagement; for example, when an academic discussion is conducted via the media, most listeners are not aware that three out of four panel members are employed by "right of center" foundations or think tanks.

An Example of Narrowed Scholarship: Privileging Evidence-Based Research

Specific academic activities have ranged from publications designed to discredit feminist, critical, postmodern, and postcolonial voices, to funding for students whose purposes would be to build careers using the narrowed academic agenda, to the redeployment of public grant funding privileging monocultural practices (Lincoln & Cannella, 2004). Contemporarily, a major example is the discourse of evidence-based research infused throughout government agencies and invading academic fields like medicine, education, and business within nation states and globally. Constructs like controlled experiments, replicability, efficiency, validity, and generalizability are again imposed as superior, more sophisticated, and representing quality (Cannella & Miller, 2008). All the language is present, from designs that use 'randomized experiments,' to quantitative orientations like 'correlational,' 'disciplined,' and 'rigorous,'—reference terms used as legitimation like 'medicine' and 'technology' as academic fields of power, the degrading of the field of education, calls for what our 'children deserve,'—to actions that would redeploy 'funding.' This discourse is not simply found in academic journals, but it is used in testimony of academics before Congress as illustrated in the words of Jeffrey Pfeffer in March 2007: "Organizations... ought to base policies NOT on casual benchmarking, on ideology or belief... but instead should implement evidence-based management." He goes on to promote notions like high performance culture, gold standard, and "what we know" (Evidence-Based Management, 2007).

Critiques have come from a range of perspectives. Two articles in different fields demonstrate this further. In the *Journal of Management Studies*, Morrell (2007) uses Russian Formalism to illustrate the ways that the evidence-based systematic review technique is used to defamiliarize the conventional notion of systematic and the ways that the term transparency is reinvented to reinforce assumptions and values within the evidence-based discourse. Further, credibility is generated by invoking a powerful discipline like medicine, as well as calls for thoroughness and rigor, while referring to practices like narrative as older or obsolete. The discourse methods privilege a perspective in which critique of the evidence-based construct is not permitted. In *Social Theory & Health* (2008), Wall uses feminist post-structural analyses to demonstrate how the discourse of evidence-based research positions and labels nurses as subjects of humanist individualism who are blamed for rejecting research and interpreted as 'laggards,' yet are excluded from the very game that would control them. Further, feminine and nursing ways of knowing, like esthetics, personal, and ethical knowledges are excluded. As Wall states: "What passes for objective research is a search for what elites want knowledge about" (p. 49). And, in contemporary times, those elites want knowledge to be about efficiency, measurement, objectives/outcomes/benchmarks, profiteering, and corporate capitalism. Other critiques of evidence-based research call attention to a lip service that is paid to qualitative methods while practices are put forward that would exclude its possibilities (Freshwater & Rolfe, 2004), the ways that postmodern (or other such) critiques reveal the choices, subjectivities, and genres through which particular authors/researchers choose to function (Eaglestone, 2001), and the limits of evidence-based perspectives even in the legitimating 'power' field of medicine (e.g., the interplay between observation and theory even in critical realist work, the subjectivity even within 'randomized trials,' the denial of individual patient circumstances and variations, the limitation of patient rights within the assumptions of evidence-based research) (Cohen, Stavri, & Hersh, 2004).

Critiques and deconstructions have occurred, yet evidence-based research discourses are alive, expanding, and most likely invading locations that would surprise us all. Recently a Google search resulted in 35,500,000 sites, with over 14,000,000 of those devoted to the U.S. government and evidence-based research/practice. Examples of the actual funded entities related to the sites abound, like the U.S. Department of Health & Human Services, Agency for Healthcare Research and Quality, *Evidence-based Practice Centers*. In October 2007, a third wave of 14 centers in the U.S. and Canada were funded to "review all relevant scientific literature on clinical, behavioral, and organization and financing topics to produce evidence reports and technology assessments." Funded centers include the ECRI Institute, RTI International, Minnesota and Oregon Evidence-Based Practice Centers, and the Blue Cross and Blue Shield Association, as well as U.S. and Canadian universities like Duke, Johns Hopkins, and Vanderbilt (Canadian examples include the Universities of Alberta and Ottawa).

In the U.S., the Council for Excellence in Government (2008) has created alliances like the *Coalition for Evidence-Based Policy* with corporate partners like the Annenberg, Bill and Melinda Gates, Ford, and William T. Grant Foundations as well as Geico, Goldman Sachs, Google, Johnson & Johnson, and Microsoft, just to name a few. The coalitions mission is to "promote government policymaking based on rigorous evidence." Conducting activities like the April 2008 workshop "How to Read Findings to Distinguish Evidence-Based Programs from Everything Else" and deploy funds like $10,000,000 to a HHS evidence-based home visitation program, the coalition claims (through an independent evaluation conducted by the William T. Grant Foundation) to have been "instrumental in transforming a theoretical advocacy of evidence-based policy among certain (federal) agencies into an operational reality."

One could go on and on with examples, but here we would rather note that the discourse is invasive, often hidden from the public eye (and even the gaze of many politicians) through legislation embedded within hundreds of pages of text. The discourse (and its agents) literally restructures public agencies and redeploys research funds to support itself. Further, it creates ties with, and gives a greater voice to, the financially elite of society. The obvious next step, in addition to the controlling and discrediting of a range of people, perspectives, and ways of being, is to further produce and support the discourse through neoliberal, hyper-capitalist, free-market profiteering that commodifies and industrializes everything; this 'next step' is much less of a 'next step' than corresponding insidious function. Examples of this also abound, like the corporation *Evidence Based Research, Inc. (EBR)* with headquarters located in Vienna, VA. Organized in two divisions, Millitary Studies and Decision Systems, the company sells its ability to address problems all around the globe, ranging "from creating systems to measuring political and economic reform... to designing improved systems for decision making... (to) improving the ability of coalition forces to provide disaster relief and peacekeeping services." (2008). Does anyone hear (read) further construction of the 'military industrial complex' using evidence-based discourses here? But there are also many other examples that we can find familiar in our own fields—like the selling of school 'turnaround specialist' programs for 'evidence-based failing' schools (read evidence and failing as industry-created test scores, by the way). And, again, we could go on and on.

Challenges to postpositivist science (or critical realism) are certainly *prohibited* (excluded), while the *ritual* of experimental science is certainly reinscribed. Critical perspectives (and critical research) are certainly silenced. Further, the discourse on evidence-based research creates an elite group who become so because of their willingness to accept and use the discourse—those who would invoke validity, generalizability, replicability, and intervention are given the *right to speak and act*. The notion of evidence is used to reinforce the reinscribed *appeal to reason*, the will to truth that creates the claim to reason versus folly, labeling those who would be discredited as half truths, without intellect, as relativist or nonsensical. Evidence-based research further constructs, and is constructed by, a range of *disciplinary technologies* that are broad based from appeals to surviving illness (for everyone, as in medicine) to publishing in "upper tier" journals (as representing quality and intellectual sophistication), to specific area technologies like evidence-based research that would raise achievement test scores. This discourse can literally erase critical and qualitative research methods, as well as critical voices of those who have been traditionally placed in the margins (whether as people of color, women, children/students, nurses, patients, or anyone who would challenge positivist 'evidence-based' science).

Perhaps the main, and interconnected, reason for the almost invisibility of critical qualitative research in attempts to transform inequitable societal conditions is the corporatization of knowledge. As illustrated in our discussion of the ways that the discourse of evidence-based knowledge is used to redeploy resources and control fields of understanding, a neoliberal hyper-capitalism has invaded all aspects of scholarship, values that influence decision making, and administration While this invasion is certainly monocultural and masculinist, it certainly goes beyond the imposition of these particular ideologies because of the importance played by resources and finances in societies dominated by capitalism. A major example in the corporatization of knowledge is the construction of the contemporary corporate university.

Corporatization of Knowledge

While colleges and universities have always been more closely connected to capitalism and the business community than many of us would like, recent discourse practices that have supported decreases in percentages of public taxes designated for higher education have resulted in an increased openness to neoliberal capitalism as a means of survival. As a fundamentalist hyper-capitalism has invaded (and, we would add, has been strategically infused into) all of society (in the U.S. and probably globally), so too has higher education been transformed. Even historically cultural knowledge is now being commodified, patented, labeled as 'wonderfully entrepreneurial, and sold for a profit. Further, a hypercapitalist perspective has been/is being used to interpret all of life, whether to explain human action as self-benefiting, knowledge as valuable because of market possibilities, or 'saving' the environment as a profitable venture (Cannella & Miller, 2008), and again, we could go on and on.

This corporate fundamentalism is probably the most profound influence on higher education today. University presidents are hired to function like CEO's; deans are employed as fund raisers; faculty 'stars' are recruited with large salaries that increase pay inequities in their fields; yet, the general faculty workforce is becoming increasingly female, temporary, and low paid. This larger group of faculty has little voice in the governance of the institution.

In 1969, over 96 percent of academic faculty were in tenure-track appointments. Currently, less than 40 percent of faculty members are in tenure-track appointments (Washburn, 2005). Even if the newly constituted workforce is talented and informed, it is not protected by freedoms of scholarship that would counter CEO administrators or customers that are not satisfied. The reconstituted workforce is expected to go easy on customers and teach whatever content is predetermined (by those with power—whether financial, legislative, or administrative). Research 'superstars' are employed with tenure for exorbitant amounts of money and often named to 'chaired' positions funded by wealthy donors; less than 50 percent of the remaining faculty are employed in tenured or tenure-track positions. The workforce has become one in which faculty votes concerning academic issues can potentially be carried by low-paid academic workers who have no choice but to be controlled by the administrators who hire them. Salaries are increasingly inequitable across the range of individuals employed to teach, with the larger group of temporary, low-paid workers being women. Inequity and corporatized power abound.

If this corporatization of the workforce continues as retirements occur of those who are tenured, the voices of faculty who have actually been the determiners of both research and curricular content will be silenced. Examples of this academic erasure can be easily found generally, but especially in colleges/schools that do not have alumni donors who can be used to 'leverage' (in business terminology) power. Overall, attempts by administrators to require program faculty to determine curricular benchmarks (another business term) and to prove the quality of research, while on the surface appearing justifiable, actually fosters a perspective that assumes faculty incompetence and need for regulation. Some administrators have even imposed curricular content on entire universities without faculty governance by creating required courses for all students (like freshman courses literally constructed and imposed on all programs by university presidents). Faculty of public institutions of higher education have been forced by administrators to accept partnerships with private charter school corporations, to offer graduate programs strictly designed to generate revenue, and to offer online courses and programs using social content that is not appropriate for learning at a distance, just to name a few.

Those who are rewarded as faculty appear to be those who 'buy into' the corporate entrepreneurial function. Short- or long-term profit is privileged over education gains. Professors are commodities to be traded, as the institution gives up those who are less likely to generate money for those who are proven grant writers or 'inventors' whose work can be patented and sold for great profits (Andrews, 2006; Mohanty, 2004). Professors are expected to be entrepreneurs by constructing courses, workshops, conferences, and academic programs that generate profits, as well as obtaining grants. Further, as with capitalism in general, this entrepreneurial perspective demonstrates a remasculinizing of academia (Baez, 2008) in that the privileging of competition and the call for training a particular type of worker is also focused on the fields that have not accepted notions of hyper-capitalism, entrenprenurialism, and competition. For example, teacher education (a traditionally female gendered field) is blamed for all the problems in education (although those problems are constructed from a neoliberal, market perspective); yet, business schools are not held responsible for the fate of the U.S. economy (Saltman, 2007).

This context privileges knowledge that can be converted into profit—either as a direct commodity for financial gain, as the knowledge that is preferred by an outside donor, or as the knowledge that would attain grants redeployed for positivist and masculinist purposes like evidence-based research knowledge. Fields that do not result in a profit or that would actually challenge the free-market perspective are certainly placed in the margin, if not entirely erased. Critical forms of research and knowledges certainly fall into this category.

Can We Create Critical Transformations?

We believe that qualitative methods can be used for critical social purposes. However, academics will most likely need to be strategic and persistent in this endeavor.

(1) First, knowledge of what's happening in society is necessary to understand the discourses that dominate; many of us have not been aware of the agendas and actions that surround us, and further, have not engaged in informed critique. In "Meetings Across the Paradigmatic Divide," Moss (2007) uses the work of Mouffe (2000) that focuses on agonistic pluralism to suggest that we construct an

agonistic politics that searches for common ground, continually fosters engagement with diverse paradigms, and values pluralism in democracy.

(2) Second, researchers will need to determine if there are, in unexpected locations, specific investigations/circumstances in which qualitative methods have been successful in addressing critical social purposes. Since research would no longer accept the objectivity of positivist science, research would no longer be appropriately located in the "objective," protected ivory tower. Research conceptualizations, practices, and researchers themselves would be inextricably interconnected to human communities (e.g., locally, academically, nationally, racially). Therefore, in addition to research purposes, researchers would serve as informed reflexive community members, as well as scholars who conduct research as informed by human community relations. Rather than statistical technicians, scholars could be expected to spend time exploring the range of interconnected societal structures that impact individuals and communities.

(3) Third, a *revolutionary* critical social sciences (e.g. feminisms, postcolonial perspectives) will need to be strategically placed at the center of academic research discussions, conceptualizations, and practices. Successful strategies will necessitate networking, collaborative planning, and persistent support for each other (Mohanty, 2004). Research conceptualizations, purposes, and practices would be grounded in critical ethical challenges to social (therefore science) systems, supports for egalitarian struggle, and revolutionary ethical awareness and activism from within the context of community. Directly stated, research would be relational (often as related to community) and grounded within a critique of systems, egalitarian struggle, and revolutionary ethics.

Revolutionary critical inquiry could ask questions (and take actions) similar to the following that challenge social (and therefore science) systems:

How are particular groups represented in discourse practices and social systems?

What knowledges are silenced, made invisible, or literally erased?

What are examples of oppressions (and/or new exclusions) that are being made to sound equitable through various discourses?

How do elite groups define values, constructs, and rhetoric in ways that maintain matrices of power?

Research that supported egalitarian struggles for social justice would ask questions like:

How are particular discourses infused into the public imaginary (e.g., media, parenting, medicine)?

How are power relations constructed and managed through?

Perhaps the most important for us as researchers is the development of a nonviolent revolutionary ethical consciousness. As researchers who are concerned about equity and regulation, we would ask how we construct research practices that facilitate our becoming aware of societal issues, rhetoric, and practices that would continue forms of marginalization or that would construct new forms of inequity and oppression.

(4) Finally, critical work is likely not possible without the construction of alliances within/between academia and the public that would place at the forefront concern for equity and justice. Scholarship in higher education must actively work to counter corporatization of knowledge from within by challenging controlling, narrow discourses of accountability, quality, and excellence. Further, to inquire into the regulatory and equity issues that are most important to a range of communities, both inside

and outside of academia, and to construct new ways to share those inquiries, we must be involved with them. Networks, collaborations, and strategic forms of dissemination are necessary that address foundationally issues like: enlarging the public's understanding of the research imaginary; generating unthought discursive spaces; and public critique of the ways that groups are privileged and silenced by various forms of research, science, and academic practice.

Note

1. For an interesting note on this same topic, see the brief discussion of rationalism and a-rationalism, in Lincoln (1985).

References

Andrews, J. G. (2006, May/June). How we can resist corporatization. Academe, Retrieved May 27, 2006, http://www.aaup. org/publications/Academe/2006/06mjandrtabl.htm

Baez, B. (2008, March). *Men in crisis? Race, gender, and the remasculinization of higher education.* Paper presented at the American Educational Research Association Meeting. New York, NY.

Cannella, G. S. (1997). *Deconstructing early childhood education: Social justice and revolution.* New York, NY: Peter Lang.

Cannella, G. S., & Miller, L. (2008). Constructing corporatist science: Reconstituting the soul of American higher education. *Cultural Studies-Critical Methodologies, 8*(1), 24–38.

Cohen, A. M., Stavri, P. Z., & Hersh, W. R. (2004). Criticisms of evidence-based medicine. *Evidence-based Cardiovascular Medicine,* 8, 197–198.

Collins, P. H. (2000). *Black feminist thought: Knowledge, consciousness, and the politics of empowerment.* New York, NY: Routledge.

Council for Excellence in Government. (2008). *Coalition for Evidence-Based Policy.* Retrieved May 8, 2008, http://www.excelgov.org/index.php?keyword=a432fbc34d71c7

Eaglestone, R. (2001). *Postmodernism and Holocaust denial.* Duxford: Icon Books.

Ellsworth, E. (1989). Why doesn't this feel empowering? Working through the repressive myths of critical pedagogy. *Harvard Educational Review, 59*(3), 297–324.

Evidence-Based Management. (2007). Jeffry Pheffer testifies to congress about evidence-based practices. Retrieved April 28, 2007, http://www.evidence-basedmanagement.com/research_practice/commentary/pfeffer_congressional_testimony

Evidence Based Research, Inc. (2008). Retrieved May 5, 2008, http://www.ebrinc.com/html/about_organization.html

Faludi, S. (1991). *Backlash: The undeclared war against American women.* New York, NY: Anchor Books, Doubleday.

Freshwater, D., & Rolfe, G. (2004). *Deconstructing evidence-based practice.* Abbingdon: Routledge.

Greenwood, D. J., & Levin, M. (2000). Reconstructing the relationships between universities and society through action research. In N. K. Denzin & Y. S. Lincoln (Eds.), *Handbook of qualitative research* (2nd ed., pp. 85–106). Thousand Oaks, CA: Sage.

Horowitz, D. (2006). *The professors: The 101 most dangerous academics in America.* Washington, DC: Regnery Publishing.

Knorr-Cetina, K., & Mulkay, M. (Eds.). (1983). *Science observed: Perspectives on the social study of science.* London: Sage.

Lather, P. (1996). Troubling clarity: The politics of accessible language. *Harvard Educational Review, 66*(3), Retrieved 5/6/08, from http://www.edreview.org/harvard/1996/fa96/f96lath.htm

Lincoln, Y. S. (1985). Epilogue: Dictionaries for languages not yet spoken. In Y. S. Lincoln, (Ed.), *Organizational theory and inquiry: The paradigm revolution.* (pp. 221–228). Thousand Oaks, CA: Sage.

Lincoln, Y. S. & Cannella, G. S. (2004). Qualitative research, power, and the radical right. *Qualitative Inquiry, 10*(2), 175–201.

Mohanty, C.T. (2004). *Feminism without borders: Decolonizing theory, practicing solidarity.* Durham, NC: Duke University Press.

Morrell, K. (2007). The narrative of "evidenced based" management: A polemic. *Journal of Management Studies, 45* (3), 614–635.

Moss, P. (2007). Meetings across the paradigmatic divide. *Educational Philosophy and Theory, 39*(3), 239–245.

Mosteller, F., & Boruch, R. (2002). *Evidence matters: Randomized trials in education research.* Washington, DC: Brookings Institution Press.

Mouffe, C. (2000). *The democratic paradox.* London: Verso.

National Research Council. (2002). *Scientific research in education* (Committee on Scientific Principles for Education Research, R. Shavelson & L. Town (Eds.), Center for Education, Division of Behavioral and social Sciences and Education). Washington, DC: National Academy Press.

Richardson, L. (2000). Writing: A method of inquiry. In N. K. Denzin & Y. S. Lincoln (Eds.), *Handbook of Qualitative Research* (2nd ed., pp. 923–948). Thousand Oaks, CA: Sage.

Said, E. (1979). *Orientalism.* New York, NY: Vintage Books.

Saltman, (2007). *Capitalizing on disaster: Breaking and taking public schools.* Boulder, CO: Paradigm Publishers.

Spivak, G. C. (1999). *A critique of postcolonial reason: Toward a history of the vanishing present.* Cambridge, MA: Harvard University Press.

St. Pierre, E. A. (2000). The call for intelligibility in postmodern educational research. *Educational Researcher, 29*(5), 25–28.

U.S. Department of Health and Human Services. (2008), Evidence-based practice centers. Agency for Healthcare Research and Quality. Retrieved May 8, 2008 http://www.ahcpr.gov/clinic/epc/

Wall, S. (2008). A critique of evidence-based practice in nursing: Challenging the assumptions. *Social Theory & Health, 6,* 37–53.

Washburn, J. (2005). *University Inc: The corporate corruption of higher education.* New York, NY: Basic Books.

PART TWO

On Interpretation

Interpretive Approaches to Multi-Level, Multi-Method, Multi-Theoretic Research

Kenneth Tobin

In this chapter I lay out a multi-theoretic methodology and associated methods for research on teaching and learning. Sociocultural theory is presented as an affordance for undertaking research that has the goals of transforming individual and collective practices while explicating, refining, and expanding theory. The examples I use are situated in ongoing research in an urban high school in the Bronx of New York City, in a class taught by Reynaldo Llena, who was an environmental chemist in the Philippines before becoming a science teacher in the United States. At New York High we collaborated on research in science classes in which Llena was a teacher-researcher. Several students from his classes also participated as co-researchers. Having the teacher and some students involved as researchers opened up possibilities to learn from the research while transforming enacted curricula in a variety of ways.

I examine a number of areas that have emerged as central in my program of research, which began in the early 1970s and continues to this day. The key topics I address include cogenerative dialogue, authenticity, event-focused inquiry, use of narrative, microanalysis, emotions, difference as a resource, beyond dichotomies, and prospects for educational research.

Cogenerative Dialogue

A common form of cogenerative dialogue (i.e., cogen) involves a small group consisting of different types of people who have a "shared" experience. For example, each week Llena and three students from his class might meet with me, a university researcher, for about 45 minutes to an hour. At least in the beginning, the teacher selects student participants based on their differences from one another. Later, any of the participants can suggest and invite others to join cogen. Usually cogen is video recorded, the saved file becoming a data resource for analysis. Frequently, there is no formal chairperson and issues that focus on dialogue arise from a lesson taught some time earlier in the day. It is customary for cogen to be scheduled during lunchtime and for lunch to be provided for participants.

In cogen, successive speakers listen attentively to what is said and add to an ongoing dialogue in ways that sustain focus. Almost always the focus is on the improvement of some aspects of the teaching and learning environment. Accordingly, all participants contribute orally about the quality of the learning environment, what factors detract from learning, and what might be done to improve participation and learning. Frequently, artifacts are brought to cogen to focus the dialogue and/or to analyze. The amount of talk and turns at talk are shared equally among participants, and efforts are made to include everybody's contributions and reach consensus on issues that emerge. It is not necessary for everybody to agree on the outcomes. What is essential is for all participants to support what is decided and respect the rights of participants to retain their differences. The process is hermeneutic in that all proffered ideas are thoughtfully considered in relation to an established focus, and efforts are made to ascertain the extent to which those ideas are viable.

We record and save digital files containing the video and audio records of what happened in cogen and then analyze what happened using a variety of methods to examine verbal and non-verbal interactions. The approaches we adopt transcend dichotomies such as those represented by the labels qualitative and quantitative research. Analyses afford comparisons of the enacted culture in cogen and science classes. Changes in both fields can be co-related and discussed in depth during cogen, affording further changes in both fields. Gradually, we considered cogen to be a transformative methodology, its continuous change being evident in analyses of what happens in cogen and other fields in which cogen participants are active, mediating their identities and those of peers with whom they interact (Tobin, 2009).

Differences are considered as resources for cogen and reaching agreed-to outcomes that benefit the collective. If cogen is structured around difference and equitable participation, all of those who participate will speak, be heard by co-participants, work hard to understand the perspectives of all others and show respect for them, and change their own standpoints, afforded by their interactions with others. In making these claims we emphasize that actions can take many forms, most of which are not explicitly oral (i.e., they involve "inner speech") and enact non-verbal conduct. While listening to others contributing to dialogue, a person obviously interacts socially in a variety of ways about which s/he is aware and many more about which s/he is unaware. For example, radical listening might involve raising questions (but not speaking them overtly) about the meanings of terms and the implications of suggested actions. At the same time, listening to and making sense of others' oral contributions will be associated with the emergence of emotions that aggregate over time as emotional energy, which can be communicated with others in facial expressions, eye movements, head and body movements, gestures, etc. Radical listening involves opening up to learning from others; that is, being receptive to learning by being in the field and to co-participation with others. Emmanuel Lévinas (1999) theorized passivity in terms of the acquisition of knowledge by being in the world with others, and being receptive to learning from them. What is learned is not under the control of the actor—hence passivity is an apt term. I consider passivity as dialectically related to agency (Roth, 2007). Accordingly, as participants interact in cogen, culture is enacted continuously by all of them; that is, culture is produced agentically and created passively in a dynamic flux.[1]

The use of cogen as a methodology for classroom research provides insights into participants' cultures, similarities and differences both contributing to the cultural flux. Because of structures, such as the selection of participants and rules they endeavor to follow, interactions will likely converge to a mutual focus as culture is enacted. Accordingly, the analyses of cogen are generative, providing pathways that can be co-explored in other fields within classes and/or schools and other institutions.

Authenticity

Among the ethical standpoints that apply to the conduct of research in the social sciences are those related to beneficence. Is it possible to undertake research with others such that all participants in the research benefit from their involvement? To the extent possible we enact research with the goal that individuals and collectives that participate in studies benefit as a result of their participation. Accordingly, in the design of a study it is important to plan to test for beneficence. In the case of the researchers, who plan and seek permission to conduct research, the ways in which they benefit often are hidden. They should benefit by learning from research, authoring publications and presentations, and gaining symbolic capital from their status as "researcher." But how do others involved in research benefit? Although we encourage the teacher and students to be co-researchers, their doing so benefits our learning and the quality of publications—i.e., we are likely to benefit more than them, even if they are co-authors (Tobin, Seiler, & Walls, 1999). Accordingly, to more explicitly address beneficence, we adapted the authenticity criteria described by Ebon Guba and Yvonna Lincoln (1989) to align with our research methodology (see Tobin, 2006).

Ontological authenticity requires all participants to change their ontologies as they participate in research. Evidence of such changes includes differences in the stories participants tell about what is happening, changes in what they notice occurring as curricula are enacted, and shifts in their priorities for what should happen in class. Given this criterion, it is most important that researchers do not possess an agenda they seek to prove through the conduct of a study. For example, researchers with a history of studying gender differences in science classes should not begin with an expectation of gender differences and conclude with the same standpoint. At the very least, beginning assertions should be nuanced by the research. Studies should be designed to show progressive subjectivity of selected participants, including the principal investigators, but also other participants as well. This goal can be afforded by designing research to allow all participants to learn about one another's experiences and the stories they tell about them.

Educative authenticity concerns participants from different stakeholder groups understanding their own standpoints and how they relate to those from other stakeholder groups (e.g., students understanding the standpoints of teachers and vice versa). This goal is hermeneutic, and radical listening can afford all participants understanding the standpoints of others, not just in terms of what they mean but also in terms of each suggestion's potential to improve the quality of social life should it be adopted by the collective. This goal embraces the value that difference is a resource for improving the quality of social life. It is important to know that this goal is not coercive—to change the standpoints of others. Instead, educative authenticity embraces a value that individuals and groups have the right to be different and conduct social life according to different standpoints. A caveat is that while valuing difference, the collective should build solidarity and agree on principles that afford the attainment of shared motives. That is, through dialogue a collection of participants should arrive at consensus regarding issues at hand even though particular individuals might continue to hold standpoints that differ from collectively negotiated next steps.

Catalytic authenticity recognizes the importance of institutions changing, not just individuals within them. The goal of catalytic authenticity focuses on forms of conduct that can improve institutions like science education within the school or school district, civil conduct within the school and/or classroom, and collaborative approaches to building positive school spirit among all students and teachers, etc. Accordingly, efforts should be made to disseminate what is learned from a study to include individuals and collectives throughout an institution (e.g., students, teachers, school leaders). From the point of view of the research design, methods should be used to assess the extent to which positive institutional changes occurred that were attributable to the conduct of research.

Tactical authenticity recognizes that not all individuals are appropriately placed in social space to benefit from research in which they are involved. Procedures should be enacted to ensure that the rights of individuals go beyond merely the right to participate. The goal should be for all to benefit from being involved in research in ways that match those benefits experienced by others who may be better placed socially to benefit from the research. For example, once we have learned in a study that groups of individuals habitually come late to school and do not participate actively in science, it is imperative that researchers enact activities to enhance participation of habitual latecomers. Similarly, during a particular study, tactical authenticity would necessitate that researchers go beyond describing achievement gaps between males and females and endeavor to eliminate such gaps.

One example of an intervention planned to address tactical authenticity concerned individuals identified as disruptive. During cogen Llena proposed that participants enact a buddy system in which cogen participants would select from any of Llena's science classes students (i.e., buddies) who could benefit from assistance to improve their learning. Cogen participants volunteered to be mentors for peers whose conduct was regarded as limiting their own learning and in some cases as disruptive to the learning of others. Llena adjusted ways in which students were assessed such that mentors received extra credit for improvements when buddies arrived at school each day and on time; came to class regularly, on time, and ready to work; did not disrupt the teacher or others in the class; interacted with others in a civil manner; and had a record of their homework, did it, and submitted it for assessment. Teachers and students regarded the buddy system as a resounding success, disseminated it throughout the school, and continued to adopt it for the time in which we undertook research in the school (i.e., for more than four years).

Event-focused Inquiry

We adopted William Sewell Jr.'s theories of culture, i.e., dialectically interrelated practices and schema, experienced as patterns that have thin coherence and interrelated contradictions (Sewell, 2005). We also embraced Jonathan Turner's idea that social life is lived simultaneously at the macro, meso, and micro levels (Turner, 2002). Accordingly, at any one of those levels culture is experienced as patterns and contradictions. We saw promise in the idea that events could be defined in terms of contradictions that arose as culture was enacted. If the research lens was focused at the meso level during an interpretive study, then events could be defined in terms of what happened either side of a selected contradiction. Sewell described this approach as event-focused, where an event might be macro, such as the French Revolution. In science education an example of a macro-level event is the No Child Left Behind (2001) legislation in the United States. Since most of our classroom research originates at the meso level and then extends to the micro and macro levels, we began to ponder many ways in which contradictions unfold in social life. A common occurrence is for the flow of culture to be breached by an interaction, experienced as a contradiction. Pierre Bourdieu (1992) noted that habitus reveals itself in its breakdown. Similarly, Anne Swidler noted that culture is invisible during settled times and visible in unsettled times (Swidler, 1986). Accordingly, event-focused research at the meso level might involve the identification of breaches in cultural enactment and ruptures of cultural equilibria. Sewell highlighted the importance of structures being transformed during an event, and the event itself being a catalyst for collective and individual change.

We consider culture to be enacted in fields, which are structured and unbounded—analogous to gravitational and magnetic fields (Tobin, 2010). Fields can be defined by activity, which involves a dialectical relationship between individual and collective. Activity is collective and oriented toward motives, which are also collective (Roth & Lee, 2007). While participating in activity, individuals act in pursuit of their own goals as they contribute to the collective attaining its motives (i.e., there is a division of labor whereby individuals enact complementary roles). Contradictions can arise when an individual's goals are inconsistent with a collective's motives, often because the individual is disinterested or resistant. Alternative individual and collective goals can also be present and take priority over official motives. In such cases an individual's agency might take her/him in a different direction as s/he pursues different goals. For example, in our research in urban science education it was frequently the case that students did not value motives which oriented toward science education. Instead, students were highly motivated to earn the respect of all participants in the field. Accordingly, most students' actions were aligned with earning respect. When this occurred, those concerned were considered to enact culture in a different field of activity. Since fields are unbounded, it is easy for actors to participate in multiple fields while they are in a particular geographic space, such as a classroom. Also, it is easy to switch action back and forth between fields. When this happens, researchers might observe switches as contradictions, which could be considered as events to be studied.

Use of Narrative

We consider event selection as analogous to using a zoom lens. As we zoom in on the micro level, we select from video files and other resources significant and complete episodes for analyses, which usually begin at the meso level with the telling of a vignette. After creating a suitable narrative, we identify contradictions and capture and save the complete event. We often request teacher and student researchers to identify and select vignettes from a lesson or cogen. To afford this practice we use software such as StudioCode and QuickTime to edit digitized files of a recent lesson. For logistical reasons we suggest that video vignettes are relatively short, in the vicinity of 2 to 3 minutes of class time. Sometimes vignettes will be much shorter, and on rare occasions they might be as long as 10 to 12 minutes. We request that the person selecting a vignette provides a description of what happened and why the vignette was selected. Narratives, like all stories, are not descriptions of everything that happens. Rather they represent what happened that was considered most important and show how what happened interconnects central characters and events. Once we have a vignette we endeavor to obtain narratives from different participants in the research. This goal reflects our valuing of polyphonia and polysemia. We expect different stakeholders to describe what happened in different ways and identify different events as salient. When we interpret the data resources, it is important to retain different perspectives, ensuring that in addition to reporting patterns of coherence we also report and learn from contradictions (i.e., perspectives that differ from the patterns).

After selecting vignettes and associated events, the first analytical move is holistic—to obtain the stories associated with the vignettes and events. Following the collection of stories we use ethnographic methods in interpretive studies at the meso level. These studies seek to answer two questions that are initially broad—What is happening in this vignette or event? And why is it happening? The theoretical frameworks underpinning the search for answers to these questions include phenomenology and hermeneutics. In finding answers we go beyond our personal analyses of video and audio files to include the perspectives of other participants involved in the vignette or event or who were present in the activity from which the vignette was extracted. Conversations about vignettes and events are video recorded and become data resources for the research. Sometimes individuals analyze what happened in vignettes and events when they are alone, and at other times they work with a group of co-participants, such as during cogen.

In the preceding paragraphs I used the term analysis to apply to the activity of individuals reviewing a vignette or event to make sense of it. I note that in some cases when a video file is reviewed a holistic reflexive process is involved as narratives are constructed. On other occasions, micro-analytic techniques are used as a video file is sped up or slowed down, often using frame-by-frame analysis to assist in figuring out what happened and why it happened. That is, on some occasions the interpretive process is holistic and involves narrative and in other cases the process is more analytical and empirical in nature. From a perspective that rejects binaries, it seems more acceptable to regard interpretation as holistic, including both narrative and analytical methods, each presupposing the existence of the other.

An angry interaction

Llena selected the first vignette for analysis from a science lesson on the conversion of units. The vignette involved an altercation he had with one of his students whom we refer to as Kelly. The context for the altercation includes an English Language Learner (ELL) teacher whom we call Ms. Fereny. Even though 80% of the students in the class had an Individualized Education Program (IEP), a special education specialist was not assigned to the class to assist Llena. Instead, the school administration assigned an ELL teacher, presumably because there was a shortage of special education teachers available at that time. The chief problem with the ELL teacher was that her native language was French whereas the native language of most students in the class was Spanish. Accordingly, the students did not regard her as helpful or necessary. Due to illness, Llena was absent from school for two days prior to the lesson he selected for analysis. In Llena's absence, Fereny taught the class, and despite her best efforts she confused many students about how to convert from one unit system to another (e.g., from cm to mm). Furthermore, Fereny administered an achievement test on the work she taught and most students did not perform well. The students were frustrated with Fereny's inability to teach science and Llena's frequent absence from class.

As Llena taught the class following his absence, many students spoke to one another as he taught. A constant noisy buzz and inattention from students were frustrating and distracting to Llena, who called on Kelly to answer a question even though she did not have her hand raised. In actual fact, Kelly was offering to help the person next to her and had just asked her whether or not this student understood how to convert units from one system to another. Kelly realized that Llena had selected her because she was inattentive and considered his practice to be unfair and disrespectful because she was helping one of her peers. Accordingly, Kelly raised her voice as she inquired why Llena was picking on her. An increase in the intensity and pitch of her voice reflected annoyance and indignation at Llena's lack of respect for her. Kelly's utterance also served as a challenge to Llena's authority as a teacher. Immediately he responded by telling her to "stop rubbish." Llena's reaction to Kelly's initial outburst added to the insult. Accordingly, Kelly once again raised her voice as she made a case to the class that Llena was unreasonable. The emotional climate was heating up as successive speakers injected anger into their turns at talk.

As an example of the way in which we have used narrative in our research, I provide an example in the textbox to depict a contradiction that arose in a science class taught by Llena. The narrative provides some of the background context needed to make sense of an altercation that occurred, an event identified by Llena as a resource from which we could learn.

Conversation and Prosody Analyses

After undertaking meso-level analyses of selected events we used several methodologies for microanalyses—including analyses of conversation, proxemics, prosody, facial expression, and gaze (Harrigan, Rosenthal, & Scherer, 2005). In the selection of events within vignettes, we used "the possibility to transform" as a criterion. An event was considered for selection if it involved a contradiction, as previously explained, or if it was noteworthy in regard to our theoretical framework—an exemplar or nonexemplar. Having decided that part of a vignette was noteworthy, we carefully examined the video using frame-by-frame inspection to ascertain beginning and closing interactions for the event. The process was subjective, reflecting our sense of what was important and taking a pragmatic stance that events should be neither too short nor too long. At the micro level, events tend to vary in duration from about 12 to 30 seconds.

Having selected an event, we replay it several times to get a sense of what happened and then, using thick description to capture the most salient characteristics, we describe what happens as a story.

What happens next depends partly on the length of the event being micro-analyzed. Our preference is to dissect an event into segments, each less than 10 seconds in duration. This allows us to coordinate the analysis of video and audio using QuickTime, StudioCode, and Praat (http://www.fon.hum.uva.nl/praat/). The reason for selecting segments of less than 10 seconds in duration is that Praat will produce prosodic measurements and show distributions of data for such segments. For each <10s segment we adapt conventions of Paul ten Have to create a transcription to afford analyses of the text we intend to use in the analysis, and we measure relevant time intervals, fundamental frequencies, and intensities (Have, 2010). The transcript routinely includes measurements for characteristics such as intonation, frequency contours and changes of syllables and words, variations in loudness/intensity, cadence, gestures, body movements and orientations, facial expressions, and gaze (Roth & Tobin, 2010). When it is relevant to do so, we analyze the higher frequency spectrums for utterances, inspect formants, and obtain and analyze a spectral slice for singularities of interest (e.g., when emotions peak; Tobin, 2010).

As an illustration of the methods we typically employ in microanalyses, I include in Table 1 the transcription conventions used in a recent chapter and in Table 2 data that provide deeper insights than can be obtained from ethnography alone (Tobin & Llena, 2007).

Convention	Description
(0.4)	time in seconds of a pause between utterances indicated as a numeral
((Students felt …))	comments from us are provided to provide context
=	no pause between successive turns
[	start of overlapping speech
{2.4}	time in seconds for preceding utterance
\ 12.1 µWm⁻²\	the power of an utterance in the air measured in watts per square meter i.e., μWm^{-2}
ha:	lengthening of preceding phoneme by approx one tenth of a second for each :

Table 1. Transcription conventions

Llena continued to teach how to change a quantity with units in centiliters to milliliters. As he spoke about the task he was doing, he also uttered comments that reflected what had happened earlier in his clash with Kelly. It was as if the incident with Kelly afforded the creation of emotionally laced comments. Llena stated, "I can't believe this ah girl doing this ah." This comment was followed by student laughter and Kelly also called out, "Although." Llena continued, "I don't believe." As he uttered the first syllable of "don't" a female student laughed for 0.6s. As her laugh concluded, Llena focused his talk on the conversion of units, noting, "Very many ((student laughter occurred)). I dunno ((student laughter occurred)) How big a unit? ((student laughter occurred)) A milliliter?" After a pause of 0.4s, a sixth instance of student laughter occurred, lasting for 0.4s. In less than the 10s it took for this event to unfold there were six instances of individual and collective laughter. It is possible that this laughter, some of which was intentional and some of which seemed like an involuntary response to others laughing at the unusual nature of what was unfolding, contributed to sustaining a shared mood of playfulness that was an affordance for Kelly's response to being called a "rude student." The sixth instance of laughter, from a female sitting next to Kelly, may have acted as a resonant structure for Llena's next utterance (turn 01 in Table 2). Although the laugh had only power in the air of 2.3 µwm⁻² and duration of 0.4s, it sounded shrill, and its separation from Llena's previous utterance made it seem even more pronounced. Furthermore, the student who laughed was the leader of the buddy group of which Kelly was a part.

This short segment provides a good example of an interaction chain created in resonance with the structure of Kelly "speaking back" to Llena. Within the same short segment, Llena continued to speak agentically as he taught about conversion of units. The result was a mixture of talk that was both created unconsciously and produced purposively. That is, the interaction chain is an example of the passivity|agency[2] relationship. Similarly, the six instances of laughter probably were created and produced with and without intention.

The following transcription is based on an event that occurred directly after the sixth laugh finished. This event, which consisted of 9 turns, provides examples of conversation and prosody analyses.

Turn	Speaker	Text
01	Llena	you're such a rude student.
02	Kelly	oooo. you have every nerve to call me a rude student when you have twenty million hands in the air {5.3} \12.9 µwm^{-2}\
03	Llena	excuse me. [That's what you're doing {1.9} \30.5 µwm^{-2}\
04	Kelly	[just say you
05	Kelly	come on. I won't say I'm sorry. I won't take your class.
06	Llena	=temp, temp, temper ((Kelly overlaps this turn of talk with indecipherable words))
07	Llena	temp, temp, temper. that's what you are doing. temp, temp, temper.
08	Kelly	exactly ((class giggles))
09	Llena	((mimics)) she said exactly. temp, temp, temper ((prolonged class laughter))

Table 2. Transcription of an event involving an altercation between teacher and student

The duration of the event was approximately 25s. The power of sound in the air was 25 µwm^{-2}, well above the average for Llena, Kelly, or the class. Llena and Kelly both uttered words and phrases that exceeded their average power in the air. For Kelly the most notable was: "Oooo. You have every nerve to call me a rude student when you have twenty million hands in the air (5.3s, 12.9 µwm^{-2})." This utterance was relatively lengthy and above the class average power in the air for utterances (9.4 µwm^{-2}, which included the teacher's talk). The relatively high power in the air of words and phrases is evidence that the verbal exchange was heating up.

Kelly's utterance of exactly (0.6s, 9.6 µwm^{-2}) was followed by Llena's sarcastic remark, "She said exactly. Temp. Temp. Temper" (2.0s, 9.9 µwm^{-2}). Kelly and Llena uttered the two syllables of exactly with similar duration, 0.2s (eggs) and 0.4s (sactly). Llena injected more energy into the first syllable, using intonation to provide a sarcastic lilt. The word exactly followed the phrase "she said" (0.3s, 7.4 µwm^{-2}). The power in the air of "she" (0.2s, 1.5 µwm^{-2}) was far less than "said" (0.1s, 21.7 µwm^{-2}). Llena began his utterance relatively softly, inserted more power into "said," and then mimicked "exactly." Llena's taunting of Kelly during the interactions may have been intended to show he was in control and unafraid of Kelly's verbal tantrum. Prosody, facial expressions, body orientation, and upper body movements conveyed the idea that Llena was taunting. It was as if he dared Kelly to "bring it on. Give me your best shot."

A great deal of data can be obtained using applications such as Praat. It is important to be consistent in what is included in different charts and tables and ensure that only data used in the analyses and interpretations are included in reports. For example, the prosody analysis undertaken for the study used as an illustration in this paper was very comprehensive and included intensive analyses of the relationships between energy-frequency relationships for different emotions. Although these relationships were interesting, they have not as yet been included in any of the papers we have written. Accordingly, we do not report them even though the data are available.

Research on Emotions

Our research has studied the production of emotions as culture is enacted in urban science classes. We have employed frameworks that derive from the work of Emile Durkheim (1912/1995) and Randall Collins (2004), who examined interaction ritual chains in relation to participants collaborating to produce success. An integral part of this work involved emotions and the extent to which they were shared within a collaborative group. Using Collins' framework we examined science classes through lenses that noted the extent to which there was mutual focus, synchrony, entrainment, shared mood, collective effervescence, and solidarity. We used the ethnographic and micro-analytic methods described earlier in the chapter to search for patterns and associated contradictions at the meso and micro levels. As is the practice in event-focused analysis, contradictions were frequently used to define events that were subsequently analyzed in more detail.

One of the key features of Collins' theory is that emotions are valenced and have magnitude. For example, Turner (2007) proposed a theory and supporting empirical evidence for one positively (i.e., happiness) and three negatively valenced primary emotions (i.e., fear, sadness, and anger). At a micro level, emotions are produced continuously, and positive emotional energy (EE) can build up when chains of happiness-related emotions are produced. Similarly, negative EE can build up when chains of emotions such as anger, fear, and sadness occur. Durkheim noted that events are imbued with EE. Accordingly, if an event produced positive EE then even thinking or speaking about the event can rekindle positive EE. Similarly, thinking and/or speaking about an event in which there was a buildup of negative EE can catalyze EE having similar valence and magnitude, as can getting involved in a similar event at a later time. According to Collins' theory, as EE builds up there is a shared mood that can erupt into collective effervescence such as laughter, clapping, cheering, and booing. The laughter described in the earlier example involving Llena and Kelly might have been associated with surplus positive EE as students became amused at the unusual nature of the altercation between a student and her teacher.

As emotions emerge and structure the present, they are constituted in history and anticipate the future. At a given moment the emotions produced contribute to and are structured by an emotional climate (EC) that is a complex aggregation of the emotions that unfold in the field (distributed across a collective). The emotions associated with events studied at the micro level might not sum to represent EC nor would they determine EC, which is experienced at meso and macro levels and is mediated by longer time scales and multiple fields. In our research we used a rating procedure to obtain measures of EC for a class and groups of participants within a class. In terms of method, we discussed emotions with students and the significance of their nature, valence, and strength. We then asked the teacher and students to rate EC using the following scale: (5) strongly positive, (4) positive, (3) neutral, (2) negative, and (1) strongly negative. We started the process with the instruction "When the buzzer sounds please use the scale to rate the emotional climate for the previous 3 minutes." The participants used audience response software to record their perceptions of emotional climate. When a computer-generated buzzer sounded, each participant pressed the appropriate numeral on the keypad of his/her clicker. Ratings were then transmitted automatically via Bluetooth to a computer where they were saved in a spreadsheet. Each clicker was electronically linked to a student and provided us with a set of EC readings that could be analyzed for individuals, collections of individuals organized according to social categories (e.g., gender, ethnicity, language), and the class as a whole. Descriptive and inferential statistics were then used as part of the analysis of EC. For example, in a recent study we used the class average EC for each 3–minute episode to analyze digital video with StudioCode, coding each interval according to its average EC and then creating separate movies containing the episodes categorized as low, medium, and high EC (Tobin, Ritchie, Hudson, Oakley, & Mergard, in press). These movies were then analyzed using multiple methods so that we could identify important differences in teacher and student roles in classes that differed in terms of EC. For example, a feature of teaching we described as nagging characterized highly negative EC segments. The teacher used loud, high-pitched speech to gain the attention of students and/or to scold them for misbehavior. When we showed the teacher and students printed offprints from the video (i.e., photographic images), participants, including students and the teacher, associated the teacher's stance, body orientation, head angle, and facial expression with nagging and described those aspects of his role as unpleasant. Prosodic analyses supported the oral comments from participants and, interestingly, when any of the research group, including the teacher, students, and university researchers, listened to the audio from the composite video we realized that just listening to the composite tape was a catalyst for the creation of high levels of negative EE.

During the lesson on the conversion of units, prior to Llena and Kelly having the altercation, the variation in EC ranged from 3 (neutral) to 2 (negative) as Llena taught continuously from the chalkboard and then to 4 when he asked students to copy some material into their notebooks. Freed from the necessity of having to listen quietly and follow as the teacher taught from the board, the students broke out into a buzz of chatter and laughter as they interacted freely. The chart of EC and time for the 10 3–minute segments is provided in Figure 1 below.

Emotions can be measured in the moment through the coordination of (a) video stream and frame-by-frame analysis and (b) conversation and prosody analysis. For each video segment to be analyzed, we undertook multiple passes to get a sense of the emotions produced by each participant observed in the segment (i.e., captured by the camera). Audio contributions were also analyzed holistically in relation to what was observed visually. Slow-motion and frame-by-frame analyses were used to examine body movement and orientation; hand/arm movement, orientation, and gestures; facial expressions; head orientation and movement; and eye gaze. With the advent of facial emotion recognition software (Sebe et al., 2006), sophisticated analyses of frontal faces from video files can be undertaken to obtain measures of the emotions for each frame in a video clip (Figure 2).

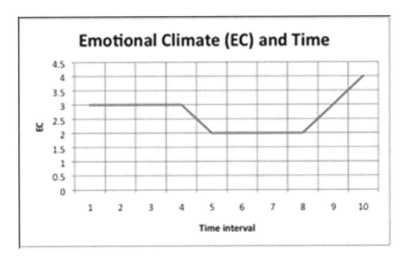

Figure 1. EC measures during the lead up to the altercation between Llena and Kelly.

The possibilities now exist to relate "in the moment" emotions measured at the micro level from facial expressions to emotions measured in other ways, including from prosody and cardio-physiological hardware such as finger pulse oximeters (Rainville, Bechara, Naqvi,& Damasio, 2006).

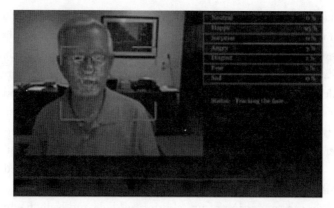

Figure 2. Facial emotion software can provide a profile of "in the moment" emotions.

The Centrality of Difference

One of the key tenets of our research is to avoid the privileging of our own voices and viewing difference in terms of deficits. We adhere to an approach that we describe as polyphonic and polysemic. Using such labels is neither necessary nor sufficient for a non-deficit approach to be enacted. Like positivism (Kincheloe & Tobin, 2009), deficit referents can be pervasive and unconsciously applied during all phases of research. Accordingly, it is imperative to examine all claims and the evidence associated with them from the standpoint of whether or not they embrace deficit perspectives. If claims are framed in terms of deficits, it is important that they are reframed to align with espoused (non-deficit) perspectives. All claims should be supported with evidence and juxtaposed with contradictions—that is, claims should be nuanced by their associated contradictions, which are expected components of social life. These are methodological consequences of our acceptance of Sewell's position on culture; enacted as practices and schemas, experienced as patterns having thin coherence and associated contradictions.

In the context of this paper, it is important to examine the aggregation of claims across levels. For example, how do we synthesize what is learned at the micro level with what is learned from studies undertaken at the meso level? Just as claims arising from research within any one level should be nuanced, so too should claims across levels. That is, our expectation is that when aggregating data across levels, the patterns we observe will have thin coherence and an explicit association with contradictions. Similarly, what is learned from prosody analysis would complement what is learned from an analysis of facial emotions, but not in a way that implies thick coherence. Instead, we expect and would search for nuances to enrich the interpretation. The search for contradictions is not regarded as explaining away errors but instead is considered a means to identify the fine structure of high-quality research—a way of explicating and adding to theory through the conduct of research that is multi-level, multi-method, and multi-theoretic.

Beyond Dichotomies

I have endeavored to move beyond a dichotomous way of looking at research and criteria for judging quality. I do not see the sense in describing research in terms of the data resources used in a study. It makes no sense to me to label research as quantitative because numbers are used, statistics are involved, or quantitative measurements are included. Analogously, it makes no sense to describe research as qualitative when qualitative data resources and associated methods are used to support claims. Instead, it makes much more sense to me to think of research in terms of the logics used in arriving at conclusions and the manner in which conclusions are framed and nuanced. As Fred Erickson noted in his classic chapter on interpretive research (Erickson, 1986), if it is possible to count in a study, then do so. Also, if quantitative data are involved, and it makes sense to use statistical methods to analyze them, then go ahead and use statistical methods. Throughout this chapter, I have been conscious of the value of using multiple theories to frame research of the sort that I have been doing since the 1970s. In our search for relevant research in other fields, we have used a multiplicity of methods, types of data, and theoretical frameworks. Rather than taking a stance that the research was beyond the zones of applicability for our work, we sought to adapt it with the goal of pushing boundaries of possibility. We are aware that we want to do more than examine quantitative data descriptively and we accept the challenge of learning new ways to analyze data and explore distributions associated with multivariate measures obtained at the micro level. Just as Bose Einstein statistics were applied to a new range of problems in physics and latent trait models were used in educational measurement, we are aware of the necessity to search for more appropriate ways to identify patterns and contradictions in the data distributions we obtain in our research. As Sewell commented in his book on the logics of history, studies that employ quantitative data and those that use qualitative data probably have more in common than they have differences when it comes to the logics underlying their studies. To emphasize differences without acknowledging the value of sameness is another example of creating a binary that often leads to oversimplified stance taking.

Prospects for Educational Research

For many years now we have developed approaches to the analysis and interpretation of qualitative data resources based on our regard of difference as a resource for learning. This standpoint led directly to polysemia and a methodological preference for polyphonia.

In writing this chapter I have been tormented by the thought that readers might regard my approach as primarily empiricist. At times I have felt a strong pull toward producing a chapter that focused on interpretive research grounded primarily in participant observation and the use of ethnographic methods within frameworks that are primarily hermeneutic, phenomenological, and transformative. I have consciously resisted this force because with today's technology we can vastly improve the quality of research on the science of teaching and learning. To refer to it in this way is more than a semantic move and is not a shift toward scientism. Instead, I embrace a conscious decision to examine social life in ways that cohere with our life experiences—i.e., as a multilectic experience[3]of macro, meso, and micro fields. In so doing it was beneficial to adopt multi-theoretic and multi-method approaches. Given a multilectic stance that rejects dichotomies, the chapter has unfolded in ways that shine light on what I consider to be emergent and dynamic priorities.

I have encountered opposition from colleagues who have been allies during the past decade as I have pushed on the boundaries of multi-level research. They experience enough challenge in doing their work in a theoretical domain that includes theoretical work at the macro and meso levels of social life. They view my move into the micro and then to the ultra micro/neural levels as an unnecessary threat—that using ultra micro and neural-level data will lead to biological determinism and perhaps even worse. Although there may be good reasons for pessimism, my personal stance is to use advanced technologies that allow us to probe human activity across the spheres of social life. If we undertake research in a polyphonic way that is informed by the voices of scholars and participants in numerous fields, there is a possibility for rich amalgams to form, from which new forms of education might emerge. As I look along the road ahead I can see enormous promise in terms of many new technologies that can be used as tools for making sense of human interaction. As we begin to incorporate these tools into our practices as researchers, we will necessarily invoke new theories and listen to new voices, as we understand what is happening and why it is happening in exciting new ways that have implications for the structuring and restructuring of education. However, a glance in the rear-view mirror provides a reminder of the necessity to learn from our colleagues who have labored throughout the 20th century and beyond to show the pitfalls of scientism and the positivistic standpoints that supported oversimplified research, not only in the sciences, but also in the social sciences. The strident moves in the past two decades toward solitary ways of knowing and doing (e.g., insisting on the use of randomization and experimental designs in educational research) are cause for concern. It is to be hoped that multi-level, multi-method, and multi-theoretical designs will forge new pathways in education and flourish in the decade ahead.

Notes

1. We use the terms created and produced respectively to distinguish culture through passivity and agency (which are dialectically interrelated).
2. The Sheffer stroke (|) denotes a dialectical relationship between agency and passivity; each presupposing the existence of the other.
3. I prefer this term when more than two constructs are regarded as being parts of a whole in which each construct is recursively related to and presupposes the other. Gene Fellner first used this term in a colloquium and I use it here in much the way he used it there.

References

Bourdieu, P. (1992). The practice of reflexive sociology (The Paris workshop). In P. Bourdieu & L.J.D. Wacquant, *An invitation to reflexive sociology* (pp. 216–260). Chicago, IL: University of Chicago Press.

Collins, R. (2004). *Interaction ritual chains*. Princeton, NJ: Princeton University Press.

Durkheim, E. (1995). *The elementary forms of religious life* (K.E. Fields, Trans.). New York, NY: Free Press. (Original work published 1912)

Erickson, F. (1986). Qualitative research on teaching. In M. C. Wittrock (Ed.), *Handbook of research on teaching* (3rd ed., pp. 119–161). New York, NY: Macmillan.

Guba, E., & Lincoln, Y. S. (1989). *Fourth generation evaluation*. Newbury Park, CA: Sage.

Harrigan, J., Rosenthal, R., & Scherer, K. R. (Eds.). (2005). *The new handbook of methods in nonverbal behavior research*. Oxford, England: Oxford University Press.

Have, P. ten (2007). *Doing conversation analysis: A practical guide* (2nd ed.). London, England: Sage.

Kincheloe, J.L., & Tobin, K. (2009). The much exaggerated death of positivism. *Cultural Studies of Science Education, 4*, 513–528.

Lévinas, E. (1999). *Alterity & transcendence* (M. B. Smith, Trans.). New York, NY: Columbia University Press.

No Child Left Behind Act of 2001, Public Law No. 107–110, 115. Stat. 1425 (2002).

Rainville, P., Bechara, A., Naqvi, N., & Damasio, A. R. (2006). Basic emotions are associated with distinct patterns of cardio-respiratory activity. *International Journal of Psychophysiology, 61*, 5–18.

Roth, W.-M. (2007). Theorizing passivity. *Cultural Studies of Science Education, 2*, 1–8.

Roth, W.-M., & Lee, Y. J. (2007). "Vygotsky's neglected legacy": Cultural-historical activity theory. *Review of Educational Research, 77*, 186–232.

Roth, W.-M., & Tobin, K. (2010). Solidarity and conflict: Prosody as a transactional resource in intra- and intercultural communication involving power differences. *Cultural Studies of Science Education*. doi:10.1007/s11422–009–9203–8

Sebe, N., Lew, M. S., Sun, Y., Cohen, I., Gevers, T., & Huang, T. S. (2006). Authentic facial expression analysis. *Image and Vision Computing, 25*, 1856–1863. doi:10.1016/j.imavis.2005.12.021

Sewell, W. H., Jr. (2005). *Logics of history: Social theory and social transformation*. Chicago, IL: University of Chicago Press.

Swidler, A. (1986). Culture in action: Symbols and strategies. *American Sociological Review, 51*, 273–286.

Tobin, K. (2006). Qualitative research in classrooms: Pushing the boundaries of theory and methodology. In K. Tobin & J. L. Kincheloe (Eds), *Doing educational research: A handbook* (pp. 15–59). Rotterdam, NL: Sense.

Tobin, K. (2009). Research priorities for transforming urban science education. In W.-M. Roth & K. Tobin (Eds.), *World of science education: North America* (pp. 439–459). Rotterdam, NL: Sense.

Tobin, K. (2010). La colaboración para transformar y reproducir la didáctica de la sciencias. *Enseñanza de lasCiencias, 28*, 301–313.

Tobin K., & Llena R. (in press). Restructuring a dysfunctional special education and ELL's science classroom using cogenerative dialogues. In K. Tobin & A. A. Shady (Eds), *Transforming urban education: Collaborating to produce success in science, mathematics and technology education*. Rotterdam, NL: Sense.

Tobin, K., Ritchie, S. R., Hudson, P., Oakley, J., & Mergard, V. (in press). Relationships between emotional climate and the fluency of classroom interactions. *Learning Environments Research*.

Tobin, K., Seiler, G., & Walls, E. (1999). Reproduction of social class in the teaching and learning of science in urban high schools. *Research in Science Education, 29*, 171–187.

Turner, J. H. (2002). *Face to face: Toward a sociological theory of interpersonal behavior*. Stanford, CA: Stanford University Press.

Turner, J. H. (2007). *Human emotions: A sociological theory*. New York, NY: Routledge.

CHAPTER TEN

A Hitherto Concealed Experience That Transcends Thinking from the Position of Subjectivity

David W. Jardine

Preamble

Now the question arises as to how we can legitimate this hermeneutical conditionedness of our being in the face of modern science. We will certainly not accomplish this legitimation by making prescriptions for science and recommending that it toe the line—quite aside from the fact that such pronouncements always have something comical about them. Science will not do us this favor. It will continue along its own path with an inner necessity beyond its control and it will produce more and more breathtaking knowledge and controlling power. It can be no other way. (Gadamer, 1977, p. 10)

If the application of science were simply the problem of how, with the help of science, we might do everything we can do, then it is certainly not such application that we need as humans who are responsible for the future. For science as such will never prevent us from doing anything we are able to do. The future of humanity, however, demands that we do not simply do everything we can. (pp. 196–197).

The hermeneutic phenomenon is basically not a problem of method at all. It is not concerned primarily with amassing verified knowledge, such as would satisfy the methodological ideal of science—yet it, too, is concerned with knowledge and with truth. But what kind of knowledge and what kind of truth? (Gadamer, 1989, p. xxii)

I

There is something of Immanuel Kant's 1784 Enlightenment declaration in the character of hermeneutics: *"Sapere Aude!*: 'Have courage to use your own understanding!'—that is the motto of the Enlightenment" (1983, p. 41). Hermeneutics, too, is about growing up, and becoming experienced and knowledgeable in and about the world, and learning to take responsibility for the way you make through that life and that world. But, as Gadamer asks, what kind of knowledge and what kind of truth, if not amassing verified knowledge? What kind of knowledge and what kind of truth, if we ceased being wrapped up in increasingly breathtaking controlling power?

Hermeneutics is interested in our "hermeneutic conditionedness," that is, in the convivial lives we live, the life everything in the world lives, full of all its multifariousness, casualness, ambiguity, interdependency, and doubt. It resists the grandiose exaggerations and simplifications that often pass as knowledge, and resists, too, the in-the-end unfounded belief that we can definitively secure ourselves against our interdependent *being* in the world. We can, of course, do what is needed, make ourselves safe within the limits of time and space, and it is often precisely right to do so. However, despite all of its real and feigned controlling power, modern science and its breathtaking accomplishments, along with political assurances and their regimes of surveillance and terror alerts, along with the numbness of ill-founded opinion, still leave us in a finite world with finite lives, still, each of us, responsible for the future in which it may not be right to do everything we can do simply because it is possible to do so. We're left still having to understand what is going on and what do to in this difficult convivial world of ours that inhabits us as much as we inhabit it.

Hermeneutics is thus also about raising ourselves up out of thoughtlessness and the stifling confines of an unexamined life and learning to experience and understand what we can of this interdependent being *without* putting ourselves in the place of Kant's judge, who *demands* that life simply follow orders (as goes the implicit image of constructivism; see Jardine, 2005). Learning to experience and understand this interdependent being doesn't involve a conservative maintenance of the traditions that, in part, shape everyday life at its most routine and thoughtless, but something more difficult. It involves seeking out those moments when traditions are opened up by the arrival of the young, the new, "the fecundity of the individual case" (Gadamer, 1989, p. 38), and are called to account by such arrivals. This, hermeneutics suggests, is where the convivial *life* of *living* traditions and *living* disciplines of knowledge *lives*. In these moments, what might have passed for a finished, secured and self-enclosed identity (of ourselves and of the things we experience) can, even momentarily, "waver and tremble" (Caputo, 1987, p. 7) and, in such movement, start to show forth and remake its flourishing interdependencies and worldliness, and revive, perhaps, its "hospitality for what is to come [*avenir*]" (Derrida & Ferraris, 2001, p. 31).

Hannah Arendt (1969) encapsulates the situation that is of deep hermeneutic interest in education:

> We are always educating for a world that is or is becoming out of joint, for this is the basic human situation, in which the world is created by mortal hands to serve mortals for a limited time as home. Because the world is made by mortals it wears out; and because it continuously changes its inhabitants it runs the risk of becoming as mortal as they. To preserve the world against the mortality of its creators and inhabitants it must be constantly set right anew. The problem is simply to educate in such a way that a setting-right remains actually possible, even though it can, of course, never be assured. Our hope always hangs on the new which every generation brings; but precisely because we can base our hope only on this, we destroy everything if we so try to control the new that we, the old, can dictate how it will look. Exactly for the sake of what is new and revolutionary in every child, education must be conservative; it must preserve this newness and introduce it as a new thing into the old world. (pp. 192–193)

In the midst of these realities, overcoming immaturity, hermeneutically conceived, is not had through "the repudiation of childhood" that Susan Bordo (1987, p. 98) locates at the heart of the Cartesian project (and which likely underwrites Immanuel Kant's Enlightenment call for "maturity"—oddly enough, the source of Jean Piaget's genetic epistemology; see Jardine, 2005). In understanding the convivial world and our hermeneutic conditionedness in it, always at the heart of such conditions are the multifarious, delicate and difficult relationships between the old and the young, the new and the established, the revolutionary and the conservative, traditions and their transformations. At its heart, hermeneutics is interested in these moments of setting right anew, cultivating, caring for and becoming experienced in this possibility, although it can, of course, never be assured. This is why Hans-Georg

Gadamer (1977), in describing hermeneutics, easily links up "the new, the different, [and] the true," (p. 51) and why it is to this that our attention must turn to understand what hermeneutics offers. Also, this describes in short order why there is something deeply pedagogical about hermeneutics and its understanding of our convivial knowledge of the world. The young and the old, the established and the new, the student and the teacher, are already present in how the convivial life of that world is lived. How we might approach that living that occurs between the old and the young, without the old simply reprimanding the young for its immaturity, hints at how hermeneutics hints at a pedagogy left in peace.

Even failing such hospitality—even under conditions of threat and retrenchment, when possibilities of setting right are shut down, when the new and the different becomes suspicious—ancestral traces of the traditions that have foreclosed around us can be *understood*, not just suffered. The binding threads can sometimes be loosened, made visible, utterable, and thus *possibly* made more forgiving and susceptible to transformation. And as cannot be denied, sometimes such moments can be met with increased violence, vigilance and closure. There is no universal hope here (here is one spot where hermeneutics steps out of line with Immanuel Kant's Enlightenment motto), simple plan or path, no ensuring methodology, and there is certainly nothing inevitable about becoming experienced in the ways of the world and what such experience might bring. Coming to understand these matters as a matter of profound delicacy and contingency, always in need of being revived and renewed, is at the heart of hermeneutic work, and key, here, is the presumption, now a bit more distantly akin to the Enlightenment call, that understanding our suffering just might help ameliorate it. It might help us flourish. It is here, again, that hermeneutics bears a kinship to the contingent hopes of pedagogy. Its fragile hope lies in the good of becoming experienced in the ways of the world and becoming someone in the process.

There are, of course, many other shadows to such Enlightenment-like hopes and promises. I've worked with teachers who, once they begin to be able to experience the tightly bound threads that wind around the hallways and classrooms of their own schools, their own students, their own practices—all of which so often silently passes as "the real world," or "just the way things are"—find these experiences unbearable. Some find themselves sometimes looked at askance and with suspicion when they try to articulate that which heretofore had gone without saying, as if articulation of this life living under the surface is itself some sort of threat to the feigned calmness of "the real world" of schooling. My own depression, distraction, hopelessness, and pain attest, as well, to the weight that experience sometimes brings, even with its sometimes joyous promise. Nevertheless, and (to accord Derrida his due; see Gadamer & Derrida, 1989) with the presumption of goodwill,

> the hermeneutic imagination works from a commitment to generativity and rejuvenation and to the question of how we can go on together in the midst of constraints and difficulties that constantly threaten to foreclose on the future. The aim of interpretation, it could be said, is not just another interpretation but human freedom, which finds its light, identity and dignity in those few brief moments when one's lived burdens can be shown to have their source in too limited a view of things. (Smith, 1999, p. 29)

Hermeneutics is, therefore, about becoming educated, becoming experienced, and this freedom of which David Smith speaks is not had through cutting ourselves off from this difficult, convivial life, and becoming some autonomous fantasy-self, some abstract "I am" (see Jardine, 2008a) but finding ways to open up and understand that very life, my very life, with all its lived entanglements that I knowingly or unknowingly inhabit:

> Some wishes cannot succeed; some victories cannot be won; some loneliness is incorrigible. But there is relief and freedom in knowing what is real; these givens [what Gadamer calls our "hermeneutic conditionedness"] come to us out of the perennial reality of the world, like the terrain we live on. One does not care for this ground to make it a different place, or to make it perfect, but to make it inhabitable and to make it better. To flee from its realities is only to arrive at them unprepared. (Berry, 1983, p. 92)

There is thus a pedagogy to hermeneutics, the cultivation and work it requires, and freedom it portends, and it is not for the faint of heart. This is not the freedom of an abstract, autonomous, worldless, self-determining individuality, but frail, vulnerable, *human* freedom.

Hermeneutics wants to ground understanding back into an experiential conviviality of the world, the very life-world seemingly fragmented and rebuilt under logico-mathematical surveillance by the Cartesian threats and doubts. It wants to understand the world's dependent co-arising out from under the shadow of threat. This is part of the phenomenological origins of contemporary hermeneutics, that it includes a desire to undo our forgetfulness of our interdependent being, and to let things be (see Heidegger, 1962) what they convivially *are*, fully "contaminated," unrendered and unpurged by the demand for clarity and distinctness.

This is why, in educational research, hermeneutic work always includes efforts, again and again, and in the circumstances of the topic being discussed, to break the spell of those threats and doubts, to open up anew to their worldly interrelatedness the remnants of fragmentation and isolation found scattered in the world. In the world of education, such shards are found everywhere—in schools, in curriculum guides, in assessment procedures, in institutional structures and the fetishes of method and surveillance, in the worries of student-teachers who've been schooled for years, in the ancestral legacies of current educational presumptions, and so on. This is a difficult hermeneutic truth, that the fragmentation, security regimes and surveillance that come under threat becomes codified in the very images and ideas, hopes and desires that students and teachers bear with them into such settings. They become codified in such a way that they are experienced simply as "the way things are." Requisite of such ordinariness, it seems, is a profound sort of amnesia, where we can no longer quite remember how things became like this, or why, or whether anything was ever any different. Thus, hermeneutics, in part, involves a cultivation of memory (see Jardine, 2006). This is one thread of the kind of truth it seeks (more on this below).

Even knowledge itself bears these scars in the fragmented bits and pieces often found in curriculum guides and their requisite schooled assessment procedures. Attempts, in hermeneutics, at interrupting this codification and opening it up, attempts to revive the threads of interdependence and co-inhabitation, therefore, are often experienced as themselves the *source of threat* rather than as attempts to ameliorate threat and its codified consequences by referring back to the life heretofore cast in a zone of deep shadow.

Under threat, things, so to speak, contract, and their rich, difficult relatedness is foregone and forgotten (as if these connections were "revocable and provisional"; Gray, 2001, pp. 35–36), in favor of the simplified, the efficient, the universally standardizable and manageable, the certain, the clear, the tried and true. Left in peace, things can flourish, and their convivial conditionedness can become admitted, experienced and understood. Left in peace, we can allow ourselves to experience this truth: "We are *always already everywhere inhabited* by the Other in the context of the full reality" (Smith, 2006, p. xxiv). Glimpsed, here, is that, *even under threat*, everything and everyone, every image and every idea we encounter in this full reality is abundantly and irrevocably inhabited, always, already and everywhere. Convivial connections and relationships are everywhere and start to slowly become experienceable and understandable once the "hardened identity" (Huntington, 2003, p. 266) induced by doubt and demands for secured clarity and distinctness is cracked. Even the retractions and hardening that threat induces no longer bespeak just "the way things are" but hint allegorically at old and familiar war stories. This, too, is part of the co-inhabited lives we have lived, this story of entrenchment and protection and security, these descriptions of high schools as "the trenches," and the one about the old, battle-scarred teacher who is always ready to tell fresh-faced and newly arriving teachers of their inevitable fate, and that she, too, was once hopeful and full of enthusiasm.

Hermeneutics can begin to open up a way for students and teachers to experience the abundant flourishing of relatedness that is afoot in the world, for good or ill. But—and this point needs constant reiteration—pursuing these explorations also can make it more difficult, more painful, to witness the flattening and deadening of such matters in far too many school settings.

Once the world becomes interpretable and its mutual co-inhabitations and interdependencies become visible and experienceable, one can, ironically, begin to feel more isolated.

II

Given its interest in our interdependent conditionedness, hermeneutics cannot begin by attempting to secure an independent, unconditioned, purified, self-identical subjectivity as a platform for launching inquiry into this world and our lives in it. Hans-Georg Gadamer (1989, p. 276) bluntly states, "subjectivity is a distorting mirror" in the endeavor to inquire into the convivial, multifarious, co-inhabited lives we actually live. The image of subjectivity that we have inherited (even into the project of education, where conviviality is key) comes, in part, as a consequence of the Cartesian project of threatening the convivial world with doubt and purging it of anything not clear and distinct. This purging has two correlates: I am purged of my being someone and become an abstract, self-identical, "I am" who wields the methods of logico-mathematical knowledge; and the world becomes subjected to this self-purged subject's demand that the world itself be purged of anything not clear and distinct. The convivial world thus becomes the world only insofar as it is rendered beyond doubt, that is, only insofar as it is, so to speak, "logico-mathematizable" (the core idea of which is the principle of identity, A=A). And, as the wielding of state-based standardized examinations proves, such purging has become the developmental goal of education itself, to produce "subjects" (students) who, *only* when subjected to objectively standardized assessment procedures (themselves purged of the convivial knowledge and ways of the living disciplines whose knowledge is supposedly being tested) can then be judged to be or not to be "educated."

Up against this long and convoluted inheritance, Gadamer states that "the idea that self-consciousness possesses the unquestioned primacy that modern thinking has accorded it may now quite justifiably be doubted" (Gadamer, 2007, p. 272), thus pushing aside the longstanding, presumed starting point for inquiry within the self-clarified security-perimeters of the "I am." Such a starting point—the platform of the controlling power of modern science—belies and occludes the lived realities of the always already everywhere, of conviviality, of mutually inhabited and inhabiting co-existence. This is not a matter of suggesting that modern science "toe the line" (Gadamer, 1977, p. 10) in these matters. Modern science, in light of the Cartesian inheritance, is quite clear that this is *precisely* where it begins. Hermeneutics is not interested in arguing *this* point, that perhaps modern science should do something else. It is not anti-science. There is not a so-called paradigm war here over the same ground. What hermeneutics is interested in unmasking is how the *dominance* of this way of thinking has occluded and cast into deep shadow our convivial lives and the knowledge and truth of those lives—the very convivial world that modern science cannot know, given its demands to purge this very world of what it deems its convivial contaminations.

"A substance is that which requires nothing except itself in order to exist" (Descartes, 1637/1955, p. 255). Regarding this founding presumption, Gadamer (1989) states, "the concept of substance [and its formal-logical consort, the principle of pure, uncontaminated identity, A=A] is...inadequate for historical being and knowledge. [There is a] radical challenge to thought implicit in this inadequacy" (p. 242). It is this radical challenge—setting down the threat-induced fixations with subjectivity, self-consciousness and substance—that is posed by Gadamer's understanding of the hermeneutic enterprise: "I have retained the term 'hermeneutics'...not in the sense of a methodology but as a theory of the real experience that thinking is" (Gadamer, 1989, p. xxxvi) once it gives up the threat-contraction mechanism of Cartesian substance/identity as inadequate to the matters at hand.

What is at stake in hermeneutics is "a hitherto concealed experience that transcends thinking from the position of subjectivity" (Gadamer, 1989, p. 100). And it is this experience—hermeneutic experience—that forms the core prospect of a pedagogy left in peace.

III

Where do we find this experience? At first blush, it seems that it might be rare and rarified, but in fact, it is quite ordinary. It is something commonly recognizable, but not commonly recognized for what it *is*.

To recover something of this experience and help us recognize what kind of knowledge and what kind of truth it portends, *Truth and Method* (Gadamer, 1989) begins with a discussion of *aesthetic experience*, and how our understanding of what this experience *is* has been de-potentiated, in fact *falsified*, under the shadow of Cartesianism. Gadamer believes that aesthetic experience offers a clue to the experience of the conviviality of the world, although this character of aesthetics has been hidden from view because of the dominance and pervasiveness of modern science and its understanding of knowledge and truth.

Key to Gadamer's long and often convoluted exploration (1989, pp. 42–100) is an interest in an immediate phenomenological reality: in our everyday experience of the world, simple things sometimes strike us, catch our fancy, address us, speak to us, call for a response, elicit or provoke something in us, ask something of us, hit us, bowl us over, stop us in our tracks, make us catch our breath. "Over and above our wanting and doing," things sometimes "*happen to us*" (Gadamer, 1989, p. xxviii, emphasis added) and call us to account:

> The word for perception or sensation in Greek was *aesthesis*, which means at root a breathing in or taking in of the world, the gasp, "aha," the "uh" of the breath in wonder, shock, amazement, and aesthetic response. (Hillman, 2006, p. 36)

Rich and memorable events and experiences happen to us, catch our attention and ask things of us. As such, the venture of coming to understand such things is characterizable as "more a passion than an action" (Gadamer, 1989, p. 366)—we often experience ourselves drawn out of ourselves and into the charm of unsecured things, drawn into thinking, questioning, admiring, exploring, participating, far beyond the limits of methodological self-security, far beyond, often, the limits where we had heretofore comfortably come to rest. These interruptions of subjectivity can be large or small, profound and life-changing, or simply quizzical turns of attention. Aesthetic experience is thus the experience of being drawn out of our subjectivity, summoned, one might say, out of any foreclosed or "hardened" (Huntington, 2003, p. 266) identity, and into a teeming world of relations that lives "over and above our wanting and doing."

We don't experience the thing summoning us thus as simply an object sitting in front of us from which we are indifferently gleaning data. The thing experienced thus is, so to speak, experienced as witnessing us, *facing us*:

> Things speak; they show the shape they are in. They announce themselves, bear witness to their presence: "Look, here we are." They regard us beyond how we may regard them, our perspectives, what we intend with them, and how we dispose of them. (Hillman, 2006, p. 33)

The object of aesthetic experience is experienced as *addressing us*. *We* are caught in *its* regard and not just vice versa. Every teacher understands this experience, that one's students are not just there in front of us, but are thinking about us as much as we are thinking about them. And the book we are reading or the mathematical equation we are pondering sometimes tells us something about ourselves and our thinking as much as we are attempting to tell each other about it. Sometimes we can experience a student's geometric musings as holding an insight we need to catch up to, and sometimes we're not fleet enough, and the track trails away beyond our ken. All this, again, is phenomenologically and pedagogically commonplace.

The object, thus aesthetic experienced, "would not deserve the interest we take in it if it did not have something to teach us that we could not know by ourselves" (Gadamer, 1989, p. xxxv). *It* has something to teach *us* because it speaks out of a cluster of occluded, perhaps unnoticed, relations and dependencies we are already living within, that are *already at work* "before you know it," that is, before the deliberate deployment of methods aimed at controlling and managing its arrival. This sense of binding threads of obligation, commitment, implication, responsibility, and so on, is how the convivial world is experienced. We *belong to it* "beyond our wanting and doing," and aesthetic experiences make the living character and limits of such belonging experienceble, thinkable, utterable, and perhaps transformable. They make experiencable, thinkable, utterable and perhaps transformable who we understand this "we" and what we understand this "belonging" to be, and how we may have unwittingly limited or falsely presumed things about this "we" and this "belonging."

What is *striking* in such experiences is the realization that these convivial co-inhabitations have already always and everywhere been going on and that I have already always and everywhere been living in their midst, however unaware I may have been of their formative and constitutive effects (Gadamer calls this phenomenon "historically effected consciousness"; 1989, pp. 341–380). Again, this is why self-consciousness is not an adequate starting point for understanding such experiences. Such experiences are often accompanied by a weird, almost embarrassing bemusement, even humiliation, regarding that unawareness: "*Where have I been?*" (Jardine, 2008b, p. 161).

In another context, Gadamer (2007) beautifully alludes to Rilke's poem "On the Archaic Torso of Apollo" (see Palmer, 2007, p. 124) when he describes this same experience in light of the work of art:

> The intimacy with which the work of art touches us is at the same time, in enigmatic fashion, a shattering and demolishing of the familiar. It is not only the impact of "This means you!" ["*Das bist du!*"] that is disclosed in a joyous and frightening shock; it also says to us: "You must change your life!" (p. 131)

Aesthetic experience, writ large or small, is thus a reverse of the movement of the inward contraction necessitated by the "requires nothing but itself" logic of substance. Once you become practiced in allowing such experiences to "expand to their full breadth of illuminative meaning" (Norris-Clarke, 1976, p. 188), something very disorienting begins to occur:

> *Every word* breaks forth as if from a center and is related to a whole, through which alone it is a word. *Every word* causes the whole of the language to which it belongs to resonate and the whole world that underlies it to appear. (Gadamer, 1989, p. 458, emphasis added)

This is a central characteristic of this concealed experience of thinking exemplified, but not limited to, aesthetic experience. To be a word, a thing, a person, entails this outward movement, a "responding [to] and summoning [of]" (p. 458) multiple and multifarious worlds. Gadamer characterizes this ecstatic outwards movement—a "dimension of multiplication" (p. 458)—as an *ontological* matter that "breaks open the *being* of the object" (p. 362). It breaks open not only *what* we understand something to be, but *how* we understand it, and our understanding of it, to *exist*. The ontology of the thing and the ontology of the one experiencing that thing undergo a shift away from the logic of substance, where a thing or a self is what it is independently of anything else. The thing experienced and the one undergoing such an experience are both released from the seeming security of self-containment out into convivial, difficult and multifarious worlds, and we can begin to understand and experience the world and ourselves as such, as multiple, as making and being made, as unfinished and full of co-inhabitations that go far beyond my experience of them. In "enigmatic fashion," the once-familiar, routine, ordinary and taken-for-granted becomes strange, and full of forgotten relations who have something to say to be about who I thought I was and who I might be becoming.

"A substance is that which requires nothing except itself in order to exist" (Descartes, 1637/1955, p. 255) will not do, here. On the contrary, hermeneutically understood, "only in the multifariousness of voices does [any word, any thing, any "self"] exist" (Gadamer, 1989, p. 284), even though we live, for the most part, in sleepy unawares of this ontological condition and the experiences that invoke, invite and betray it.

There is, of course, an ecological echo here to this image of breaking forth wherein each seemingly isolated thing in reality *is* its constitutive ecological surroundings. Things *are* all of their convivial re-lations. We can *draw* boundaries around such matters, and such drawing is commonplace and often vitally necessary. But we can't *give* such matters a boundary (Wittgenstein, 1968, p. 33). Even though, in the day-to-dayness of things, we can identify this tree, that bird, and so on, this familiarity and or-dinariness can block our ability to experience and understand that somehow, that Pine Grosbeak at the feeder *is* these Rocky Mountain foothill surroundings, as it also somehow *is* the breath I intake when it suddenly appears, wakes me up and whispers, in a small and fleeting way, that I must change my life if I am to understand this ecological, pedagogical and hermeneutic complicity and conditionedness. The sort of knowledge and sort of experience requisite of such a challenging ontological insight is tellingly characterized by Gadamer (1989) in a way that itself has ecological echoes. It is "knowing one's way around" (p. 260).

IV

This is the radical challenge that comes from letting go of the ontology of substance. Any word, any thing, any "self" requires *everything else* in order to exist. Differently put, any word, thing or self only properly *is* in the whole world. Experienced or understood out of relation to the whole, a word, thing or self is no longer understandable as *what it is*, but only *as rendered* by our wanting and doing. And even as thus rendered, our rendering is *itself* part of this whole. It is one of the things we can do, sometimes to breathtaking effect. If we forget this, and project the (again, often warrantable and necessary and understandable) *outcome* of our isolating rendering as the reality of the world, we commit a grave error, mistaking our wilful drawing of boundaries for an ontological reality that antedates the convivial life in which such drawing occurs as a sometimes-warranted way to proceed.

This inversion is what hermeneutics wishes to critique in its critique of science's dominance and forgetfulness. It is not that it should "toe the line" and do something different within the domain of its doings, but that it, in its dominating power, has occluded *its own living origins*. The convivial life-world, that very world which hides under the will to dominate and control, is the world *within which* domi-nating and controlling are often vital and worthwhile ways to proceed *and not the other way around*. The world under threat does not capture "the way the world really is" but describes, rather, one of the things that we, *in* this convivial, ongoingly negotiated and multifarious world, can and sometimes must do, often with breathtaking results. The clarity and distinctness of threat-induced and hardened identi-ties (A=A) that result "does not change in the least the fact that these are human formations, essentially related to human actualities and potentialities and thus belong to…the life-world" (Husserl, 1970, p. 130). By reversing this situation and claiming objectivity for itself and subjectivity for all others, logico-mathematical knowledge erases from memory its own living basis, the very basis that makes it a *living* discipline. Once we take the *results* of threat to be the "reality" that was there all along, hidden under-neath what then becomes understood as the convivial "surface" (underneath, one might say, the "veil" of conviviality), everyday life becomes imagined to be a sort of opinion-filled, perspective-filled, "these are my experiences"-filled, post-hoc, revocable and provisional, subjective froth with no knowledge or truth value attached.

It is thus not the objective sciences' *understanding of the world* that is at issue for hermeneutics. It is the objective sciences' *understanding of themselves* that has gone amiss, especially within the confines of schooling. For example, the life of mathematics as a living, convivial, traditional and contemporary, debatable and settled, set of practices, forms of evidence, ways of speaking and arguing, ways of demonstrating and debating, is replaced with the amassed and to-be-memorized information demanded by standardized examinations. Teachers start "teaching to the test" by teaching, not the practice of mathematics, for example, but only its rote and repeatable rules and their efficient application. One loses track of the living fields out of which such rules emerge and within which such rules might find the proper measure of their application. Students and teacher alike thus get cut off from the very life-world of that living discipline as something actually practicable in the world.

This systematic and deliberate erasure, in schools, of the convivial experiences of the living practice of a living discipline of, say, mathematics, and instead teaching to the test that requires only filled-in blanks on standardized examinations that can be marked by a machine, even fails at its own goal. Even though many teachers protest that, with high-stakes examinations coming, there is no time for the "frills" of convivial exploration, such seeming "frills" prove to be vital to those teachers' professed interests, the interests of their students, and the well-being of the living disciplines of knowledge that are entrusted to them in schools. In a study of 12,800 students from 26 elementary and secondary schools, those who worked in classrooms that engaged mathematics as a living discipline saw a statistically significant increase in their performances on standardized provincial examinations, as high as 1.5 standard deviations in some classes. Those who were in classrooms that maintained the status quo and continued to "teach to the test" saw no statistically significant change in such measures of student performance (Friesen, 2010).

V

"The sciences are self-sufficient and alone guarantee their own reflection" (Piaget, 1965, p. 225). This captures in quick turn the dilemma hermeneutics faces when attempting to step outside of the logic of self-enclosure, and how hermeneutics must constantly have an ear cocked to how this logic has become deeply encoded in the convivial world and our attempts to understand it. The promise to be self-sufficient and self-guaranteeing that comes from threat-based enclosure in fact occludes its own ability to understand itself and its origins in the convivial world.

Even that most obvious and commonplace of things, "experience," is entangled in these shadows and dropped threads. This is why, in *Truth and Method*, a great deal of attention is given to the difference between the two German terms for "experience": *Erlebnis* (Gadamer, 1989, pp. 60–80) and *Erfahrung* (pp. 346–361). *Erlebnis* is etymologically linked to the intimacies of one's personal and inner life (*Leben*, to live). *Erfahrung* contains the roots both of a journey (*Fahren*) and of ancestry (*Vorfahren*, those who have journeyed [*Fahren*] before [*Vor-*]). Hermeneutically understood, therefore, in these aesthetic moments, we are drawn out of ourselves, our constructions, our methods and our "our"-centeredness, and invited into something of a worldly sojourn, an *experience* (*Erfahrung*) that does not issue from "myself."

Of course, there is something of *Erlebnis* in such moments of being drawn out of ourselves—"This means you!" (Gadamer, 2007, p. 131); "from it no one can be exempt" (1989, p. 356), it is "not something anyone can be spared" (p. 356) or undergo on someone else's behalf (see Arthos, 2000). Moreover,

everything that is experienced is experienced by oneself, and thus contains an unmistakable and irreplaceable relation to the whole of this one life. Its meaning remains fused with the whole movement of life and constantly accompanies it. One is never finished with it. (Gadamer, 1989, p. 67)

And this is because, as with my students and them with theirs, I am never finished with living the life *in which* a particular experience has occurred and in which it is constantly being re-sorted, re-evaluated, remembered, forgotten, highlighted or ignored. However, *what* I am summoned to experience (*Erfahrung*) transcends the limits of my experience (*Erlebenis*) and is not available in a simple reflection upon an inner inventory of my perspectives, beliefs or opinions. "The whole of this one life" is not lived inside a "cabinet of consciousness" (Heidegger, 1962, p. 89) and interacting with the world only within the limits of my own wanting and doing. This is why hermeneutics does not remain within the confines of phenomenology and its interest in reflecting on the immanent confines of what is *given* in lived-experiences (*Erlebnisse*). My convivial life in and through the world is not laid out in front of me as a given, open to simple self-conscious reflection, nor is it laid out as something whose shape and future is wholly within the purview of my wanting and doing. My life and my experiences are experienced not as a given, but as "a task that is never entirely finished" (Gadamer, 1989, p. 301), and, despite its lived intimacy as my life and no one else's, it is experienced as a task which is akin to Bronwen Wallace's (1987, pp. 47–48) wonderful insight about anthropological artifacts: "The shards of pottery, carefully labeled and carried up through layered villages flesh out more hands than the two that made them." That pottery shard itself carries this convivial ontology with it, fleshing out villages and hands, summoning worlds, breaking forth "as if from a center" (Gadamer, 1989, p. 458, emphasis added), and *Erfahrung*, "experience," bears a kinship here to this convivial ontology. It is something undergone in the world, with others, and within the not-at-all revocable and provisional limits of that multifarious co-inhabitation. My own life, in all its lived, experiential immediacy (summoned by the term *Erlebnisse*) fleshes out more lives and is full of more "experiences" (*Erfahrung*) than this confine of "myself."

Differently put, and just like this pottery shard, *I am* only in the whole of the world which I will not outlive or outrun. Unlike this pottery shard, I also must learn to *live with this insight* and suffer it. This whole, convivial world does not belong to me as my conscious and cabineted possession. I belong to it. This is the great movement of part and whole that Gadamer explores far beyond the confines of textual interpretation. It is important to note that it also hints at how this hitherto concealed experience is full of a penumbra of *mortality* that is at the heart of the pedagogical prospect of setting things right anew. "What has to [be] learn[ed]…is not this or that particular thing, but insight into the limitations of humanity. This experience is the experience of human finitude. The truly experienced person is one who has taken this to heart" (Gadamer, 1989, p. 357). I can only speculate that perhaps it is *this insight* that is most deeply concealed and most deeply and silently serves as the hidden impetus for our often frantic and often accelerating efforts to secure ourselves against the conviviality of the world and ourselves within it. To the extent that our very impermanence and mortality itself is experienced as a threat against which we can secure ourselves, we find ourselves in "a state of permanent war" (Wood, 2006, p. 16), and the convivial world, and our insight into its mortal life and our mortal lives within it, becomes once again occluded.

VI

This sort of knowledge and truth that hermeneutics seeks—one might call it "becoming *worldly*"—bodes not just for the displacement and decentering of self-consciousness but also for its humiliation. What comes along with cultivating this hermeneutic experience of the convivial world is the inevitable insight: "*The center is everywhere.* Each and every thing becomes the center of all things. This is the absolute uniqueness of things, their reality" (Nishitani, 1982, p. 146):

> *Kai enthautha*, "even there," at the stove, in that ordinary place where every thing and every condition, each deed and thought is intimate and commonplace, that is, familiar, "even there," in the sphere of the familiar, *einai theous*, "the gods themselves are present." (Heidegger, 1977b, p. 234)

"Something awakens our interest—that is really what comes first!" (Gadamer, 2001, p. 50). "Something is going on, (*im Spiele ist*), something is happening (*sich abspielt*)" (Gadamer, 1989, p. 104; we can see in the German terms here the reason for Gadamer's [1989, p. 101 ff.] exploration of "play" [Spiel] as providing a clue to the ontology of such matters). Something is *always already everywhere* going on, something has *always already everywhere* happened and this happenstance of the aesthetic experience of such already-realities always arrives too late for a consciousness bent on asserting its dominance over such matters.

This is the *aesthesis*, the intake of breath—the "hale" in its suggestion of wholeness—when something happens that hits home and calls for our attention. "Understanding begins...when something addresses us. This is the first condition of hermeneutics" (Gadamer, 1989, p. 299), and in such address, we experience ourselves as *called upon* to make something of the world(s) that thus open up and surround the life we thought we knew. This is the breaking of the hubris of self-consciousness that imagines itself to be first and foundational. This is the "hitherto concealed experience" (Gadamer, 1989, p. 100), often cast in a zone of deep shadow (Illich, 1992, p. 19).

When we are struck and drawn out into the convivial world, what we encounter no longer

> has the character of an object that stands over and against us. We are no longer able to approach this like an object of knowledge, grasping, measuring and controlling. Rather than meeting us in our world, it is much more a world into which we ourselves are drawn. [It] possesses its own worldliness and, thus, the center of its own Being so long as it is not placed into the object-world of producing and marketing. The Being of this thing cannot be accessed by objectively measuring and estimating; rather, the totality of a lived context has entered into and is present in the thing. And we belong to it as well. Our orientation to it is always something like our orientation to an inheritance that this thing belongs to, be it from a stranger's life or from our own. (Gadamer, 1994, pp. 191–192)

This hermeneutic insight into the convivial interdependence of things weighs a bit heavy at first, but it does portend a pedagogy left in peace that is simple, pleasurable and intellectually venturous and immediate.

Pursuing such a pedagogy has a strange but familiar effect. An inheritance—wherein everything we encounter (the hesitations of commas, this hypotenuse, that characterization of democracy in Social Studies, in fact, *every single curriculum mandate*) has within it the totality of multiple lived contexts—is never experienced as just indifferently lying there but has been, deliberately or otherwise, *handed to us* as something we are always already everywhere multifariously and variously *in the midst of*. We find *ourselves* living there, multifariously and variously, here, and there, aware or unawares. It is never an object we are dealing with but always an entrustment, and our already always everywhere "interest" (Latin, from *inter* ["in the middle of"] *esse* ["things"]) in such matters is what teachers wish to cultivate in their students and in themselves. It is as if we are being handed back ourselves in being handed such matters. Finding these threads of interest is finding the hermeneutic experience at the heart of pedagogy.

VII

> The knowledge, skills, and attitudes listed in the curriculum guides are not fixed and final and given and meant simply to be delivered. Rather, such matters are, by their very nature, susceptible to a future (new questions, concerns, evidence, applications, transformations, additions, re-interpretations, explorations, occlusions, discoveries, happenstances and so on) that is *still arriving*. *That* is what it means to call mathematics or poetry or biology or writing a *living* discipline. It doesn't simply mean that there are lots of old books, old ancestors, and fixed cannons of wisdom that students must simply accept as given and finished and final. It means that this still-arriving, yet-to-be-decided future will have something to say about what we have understood these old books, these canons, these wisdoms and ancestors to mean [more strongly put, what we have understood them to *be*]. In such a light [each moment of convivial work] *adds itself* to that ongoing, living conversation. In understanding a contour of, for example, the

living discipline of mathematics, we take part in something which abounds beyond the bounds of our own efforts and, in such partaking, we keep such matters open to question, susceptible to the future. That, we suggest, is what good teachers spontaneously do—they keep the world(s) open to the arrival of the young, and they teach the young the ways of such worlds. And, to spin this again, we learn from the young what might become of this world, because they always bring with them the questions that we could have not asked without their arrival. Simple, in its own way. To experience such abundance—to experience, paradoxically, how a curriculum topic goes beyond my experience of it—is an experience of its truth. (Jardine, Clifford, & Friesen, 2006, pp. 211–212)

Those very mundane topics listed so dully in the curriculum guide thus undergo an "increase in being" Gadamer (1989, p. 40) if we treat them properly. If we treat them properly, as living features of a convivial world, nothing is quite yet what it will be. Those topics undergo such an increase because they "are not" yet fully themselves because they *are* open to a future that has yet to arrive where they will be taken up anew, beyond our wanting and doing. "A" is thus never quite equal to itself. This defines their *living* character. Thus, even though, to use Jean Piaget's term, we find that our living shapes itself into plateaus of equilibrium or, to use Hans-Georg Gadamer's terms, that the Spiels of our living transform themselves, with our work and attention, into "structures" and "works" (see below), this transformation is not into something impervious and self-identical. These structures and works and plateaus remain vulnerable and susceptible, they remain interpretable. Treating them as if they are not, trying to harden them so that they become invulnerable to the threat of becoming, changes their nature.

So, "even there, in that ordinary place," in my Elementary School Curriculum Inquiry class a few years ago now, something familiar and commonplace comes up, a structure that has seemingly lost its Spiel. Many of the students had practicum placements in classrooms where, routinely, every morning, day after day, children and teachers gathered to "do calendar." Many of my students complained that this had become a time of rote repetition, of a rather mind-numbing slowness. A sense of heavy familiarity surrounded these classroom practices.

An envelope with the names of the days of the week, another with the names of the months of the year, another with the numbers 1 through 31, plastic slots where the words "Yesterday was…" "Today is…" and "Tomorrow will be…" were carefully printed out, and where, each day, the names of the days of the week could be re-slotted. Each morning, yesterday's yesterday-name gets put back in the day-names envelope, and yesterday's today-name gets moved to the "Yesterday was…" slot. Yesterday's tomorrow-name gets moved into the "Today is…" slot and a new name is fished out of the name envelope to fill the now-vacant "Tomorrow will be…" slot. Often the numbers of the days already past that month are read through in unison, and the next number is found and clipped on to the display. And, as for the numbers 1–31, during October, they were printed on orange pumpkins in an effort to liven up things a bit with Halloween approaching, and everyone in my class, now coming up to mid-January, already knew that there were numbers on red hearts coming in February, and 31 neatly numbered green construction paper Christmas trees were already stored away till next December.

And, of course, each day, a Popsicle stick was put in a cup marked "ones" tacked to the wall underneath the calendar. And each day, the number of sticks was counted. And every 10 days, these "ones" were bundled up with an elastic band and put in another cup marked "tens," and those bundles themselves were re-counted on each arrival of a new bundle.

As one practicum student said, "My kids 'get it' already. They're bored. Enough!" Things had deadened, flattened out, and this morning ritual had become full of hardened, mindless repetitions. Everyone in my class knew about the (admittedly limited and unspectacular) value of learning the days of the week, learning about past, present and future tenses, about place value, and so on and on. But this time was no longer a convivial morning gathering and settling, no longer educative or informative, no longer interesting. As the old Latin etymology indicates, teachers and students alike no longer experienced this as being in the middle (*inter*) of something (*esse*) to which we variegatedly belong. Nothing, it seems, is going on. Little is happening. Despite the joyous perseverance with which this classroom routine may have begun at the beginning of the school year, it now "speaks out of a story which was once full of enthusiasm, but now shows itself incapable of a surprise ending. [We have] heard enough" (Smith, 1999, p. 135).

So the question came up: "Should we do calendar in our classrooms?"

"Young people [my students, and those students in their practicum and future classrooms] want to know if, under the cool and calm of efficient teaching and excellent time-on-task ratios, life itself has a chance, or whether the surface is all there is" (Smith, 1999, p. 139). We began a discussion in our curriculum class about whether the surface is all there is in these days of the week, and this odd parade of names that circle by our students, and us, over and over again. Why do we repeat these over and over again? Is there life here, or just routine thoughtlessness and memorization, stuff students simply "need to know"? Is there some experience to be had here, some memory to be revived, some story to be told, here, under the hardened, flattened, familiar surface?

> A teacher who remembers well teaches curriculum as a story, not just as a collection of trivia which seems to have no connection with anything but itself and which must be remembered in an unhealthy way, that is, crammed, to pass an exam. (Smith, 1999, p. 135).

Despite the immediacy of the arrival aesthetic experiences and their draw, at first, when we come upon something heretofore unexamined and unconsidered, some cultivation is often necessary, some work is needed to prepare ourselves, to break up the hard ground, to invite arrival. It often takes whiling and gathering and returning—work and persistence—to become able to experience being addressed. We all, after all, have been well schooled out of such matters and such practice. As we slowly began our curriculum class discussion, variously and multifariously, different students knew something of these days and their names, had thought or heard of it once, or had never heard of it before and thought it was just a bunch of names, and on and on. Laptops opened. Brief searches. Scrawls on whiteboards.

"Look at this!" and a few students gather around a screen, one search leads to another, one thread gets caught in the weave of another.

Things, slowly, started to *stir*. And at first, these matters are precisely that: slow, timid, chaotic, and we don't yet understand if we would even recognize whether or not something was telling in what we found.

Sunday, Monday, Tuesday, Wednesday, Thursday, Friday and Saturday.

This old Biblical round of seven. Even just saying this much causes inhalations of breath, a recognition that, not only have we spotted something about these matters, we have been spotted by something that knew us before we knew it. It becomes a bit more understandable why, if this is perceived as a threat, we might try to close such things down and prevent them from ever happening again. Here, in the comfort (etymologically linked to common strength or fortitude) of our class, we are left in peace and thankful for the leisure, time and opportunity that such thinking requires. Not all of my student-teachers are so blessed in their practicum placements, or will they necessarily be offered teaching positions in schools where such thinking is cultivated and condoned. This, too, is part of our hermeneutic conditionedness and a frequent topic in our classes.

The names that light day and night, a cluster of old Norse and German gods, and one old Roman name for one of the wanderers, one of the planets (itself from the Greek *planan*, "wanderer").

Moments of *aesthesis*, "brought up short and alerted to possible differences" (Gadamer, 1989, p. 268). "What?" "Really?" Plus, of course, a low-level anxiety as something heretofore seemingly fixed, finished and solid starts, just slightly, to *quicken*.

One brief text we read together more than once in this class is a passage from Clarissa Pinkola Estes' *Women Who Run with the Wolves* (1996, pp. 27–28). It reads like an allegory to the experiences we are undergoing in searching for the life in the often dull, dry bones we've inherited:

> The sole work of La Loba is the collecting of bones. She is known to collect and preserve especially that which is in danger of being lost to the world. Her specialty is said to be wolves.
>
> She creeps and crawls and sifts through the *montanas*...and *arroyos*...looking for wolf bones, and when she has assembled an entire skeleton, when the last bone is in place and the beautiful white sculpture of the creature is laid out before her, she sits by the fire and thinks about what song she will sing.
>
> And when she is sure, she stands over the *critura*, raises her arms and sings out. That is when the rib bones and leg bones of the wolf begin to flesh out and the creature becomes furred. La Loba sings some more, and more of the creature comes into being; its tail curls upward, shaggy and strong.
>
> And La Loba sings more and the wolf creature begins to breathe.
>
> And La Loba sings so deeply that the floor of the desert shakes, and as she sings, the wolf opens its eyes, leaps up, and runs away down the canyon.
>
> Somewhere in its running, whether by the speed of its running, or by splashing its way into the river, or by way of a ray of sunlight, or moonlight hitting it right in the side, the wolf is suddenly transformed into a laughing woman who runs free toward the horizon. (Estes, 1992, pp. 23–24)

My students had already expressed how this routine of calendar had become like dry bones, and we've started to collect more and more at first skeletal pieces until, as we start to sing over these bones, they begin to flesh out, to take on a life of their own, a life we are able to experience as a living world into which we are drawn.

And that last few lines about La Loba, that, by some happenstance of sunlight, moonlight, splashing or running, the wolf becomes the one who has been singing, now laughing. As happens so often in this class, once the dry bones get sung over properly, the life they take on proves to be the life in the midst of which I have already been living without quite knowing it.

This "doing calendar" business is not an arms-length object we're exploring, but—as paradoxical as it might seem—it is something of our own living we've been singing over. We, too, have quickened.

Breathe. This quickening is not a threat but a sign of life, and again, hermeneutics claims this experience as an immediate phenomenological reality, one that happens over and over again in classrooms dedicated to a pedagogy left in peace. It is not some sort of poetic trick (even though Hermes, along with the wolf's cousin, Coyote—see Jardine, Clifford, & Friesen, 2008a—were most certainly tricksters). It is experientially available, cultivatable, repeatable, and, over time, we can become experienced in such "singing."

This quickening is a sign, like a track that has been found that portends something as yet unseen, a clue to an always already everywhere world of living relations we didn't quite know we had.

Tracks. Latin: *vestigia*, like the root of the word "investigation."

So, the Sun, the Moon, Tiw, Odin, Thor, Frieia and Saturnus.

Day, Night, Law/War/Heroism, Wisdom/Magic/Poetry/Leadership, Thunder, Love/Beauty and Agriculture (but also slowness and melancholy).

"Every experience worthy of the name thwarts an expectation. Insight is more than the knowledge of this or that situation. It always involves an escape form something that had deceived us and held us captive" (Gadamer, 1989, p. 356). This captures another thread of the German term *Erfahrung*—it means suffering something in the sense of undergoing something, being affected by or subjected to something. The old familiar belief that these names of days were just names is shown to be deceptive and to have been holding us captive, and letting go of that familiarity and its cold comforts lends credence to the idea, explored by Gadamer (1989, p. 356), of "'learning through suffering' (*pathei mathos*)." The trick, of course, is to not retract from such learning as if it were a threat to myself. It is, rather, formative of my self, my becoming who I am (*Bildung*), and without it, I simply, as Wendell

Berry (1983, p. 92) put it, arrive at the world unprepared. *This* is what is involved in the hermeneutic version of the Enlightenment call "*Sapere Aude!*" Thinking for oneself about and in the midst of this convivial world in which we live must be won and re-won over the course of one's life. "This experience is always to be acquired, and from it no one can be exempt" (Gadamer, 1989, p. 356), and, as my student-teachers slowly learned, every time a new topic, a new curriculum mandate, a new routine, a new student, arrives, one must venture *all over again*.

Make no mistake, "understanding is an adventure and, like any adventure, it always involves some risk" (Gadamer, 1983, p. 141). (An "adventure is 'undergone,' like a test or a trial from which one emerges enriched and more mature"; Gadamer, 1989, p. 69—this is why, in schools, there is a great conversation to be had about having *good* tests). The thing that takes courage and resolve is to experience how venturing out into these surroundings is not a threat to my*self*. It *is* "myself" in its full countenance. What is put at risk is only that false sense of permanence and self-containment and that false security belief in the permanence and containability of the things we teach and learn.

So, perhaps, with "doing calendar," what has become routine is in reality a ritual, festive, weekly return, a whiling and recurring time, perhaps, to remember something that is easily forgotten. Instead of just being a way to memorize the days' names (like a curriculum requirement to be "covered"), perhaps this passage of names and days also can be taken up as a way to make these matters alive and *memorable*, even *memorial* (Jardine, 2006; see Jardine, Bastock, George, & Martin, 2008).

Our classroom conversations then began to roil. Students began experiencing that these threads were no longer simply a vast pile of anonymously amassed knowledge but rather sketches of a convivial life we were *already living*, around which we had already been convivially gathering, day after day, without quite knowing it.

"What about, every Monday, reading an old story about the moon?"

"The Hubble has new pictures. I saw them this morning on the news."

Already it seems like we memorially remember and invoke the night and its light, the Moon, every seven days. Nocturnalness is part of who we are in a myriad of ways (cascade—night-time animals, what the city does at night, darkness and light, and on and on).

> A new idea is never only a wind-fall, an apple to be eaten. It takes hold of us as much as we take hold of it. The hunch that breaks in pulls one into an identification with it. We feel gifted, inspired, upset, because the message is also a messenger that makes demands, calling us to quite a present position and fly out. (Hillman, 2005a, p. 99)

Monday on the calendar (from the Latin *calendarium*, "the account book") becomes an opportunity, an opening, into old and multifarious tales about the world, one seemingly being now told *to* us, faint whispers at first.

"Perhaps something about storms on Thursday?"

"We need to talk about that hail we had, and this climate change thing."

Or some old mythological tales of Odin and his Northern European wanderings? Perhaps any old tale of journeys, then, might befit something of Wednesday and its convivial undertow. Perhaps even Max's journey to and from *Where the Wild Things Are* (Sendak, 1988) might be worth reading here, read differently than we had perhaps first imagined, read as a distant kin to those journeys of Odysseus delved deeply into years and years ago with Grade Two students (Jardine, Clifford, & Friesen, 2008b). Wednesday—the day we celebrate journeys—might become *interesting* and its repeated return might become of *festive* celebration and returning and gathering:

> In each of these diverging stories all the others are reflected, all brush by us like folds of the same cloth. If, out of some perversity of history, only one version [A=A] of some mythical event has come down

to us, it is like a body without a shadow, and we must do our best to trace out that invisible shadow. (Calasso, 1993, pp. 147–148)

As we slowly worked our way, in our class, to trace out these invisible shadows, what slowly developed was

a polyphonic text, none of whose participants would have the final word in the form of a framing story or encompassing synthesis. It might just be the dialogue itself, or possibly a series of juxtaposed paratactic tellings of a shared circumstance, or perhaps only a sequence of separate tellings in search of a common theme, or even a contrapuntal interweaving of tellings, or of a theme and variations. (Tyler, 1986, p. 126)

Slowly, our own festive returning and reweaving of this once-routine and untelling list of names and days became an allegory for how these student-teachers might begin weaving their way through these tales in their own classrooms.

VIII

Then, in that university class and its interweaving and criss-crossing roil of days and names and stories, two sudden events.

One student mentioned French day-names, *Lundi*, Luna, and the old tales of madness, lunacy. Another feature of *aesthesis*: laughter, where the moon and Luna and lunacy suddenly reveal themselves as having always been enjoined and the insight hits home.

Another, German, Thursday, Thor's day, *Donnerstag*. "*Donner* is the word for thunder in German, like Thor and his hammer."

Another student called out, "Donner and Blitzen, yeah, thunder and lightning" and that *aesthesis* moment that James Hillman spoke about, the "uh" of halted breath that indicates the truth of such experiences, occurred in spots around the class.

One student, in hearing what was for him the long familiar, Christmassy names of Donner and Blitzen, and experiencing them breaking open right before his eyes, smiled, yet muttered, "Oh no." Something is going on, always, already, everywhere, "even there…in that ordinary place where every thing and every condition, each deed and thought is intimate and commonplace" (Heidegger, 1977b, p. 234). We are "always already affected" (Gadamer, 1989, p. 300). Spotted!

But there is always a sting, here in this "oh no." One might believe that we are just playing with possibilities, here, brainstorming, seeing opportunities everywhere. However,

opportunities are not plain, clean gifts; they trail dark and chaotic attachments to their unknown backgrounds, luring us further. One insight leads to another; one invention suggests another variation. More and more seems to press through the hole, and more and more we find ourselves drawn out into a chaos of possibilities. (Hillman, 2005a, p. 99)

We can easily get caught up in flightiness and, "before we have taken thought, we have been seduced into enterprises beyond our resources" (p. 99). Or, as Gadamer (1989, p. 106) describes, the onrushing *Spiel* of these matters can "outplay" us. This is why, after a long section on play as a clue to an ontological explanation of this eruptive, convivial ontology, Gadamer has a section in *Truth and Method* (1989, pp. 110–120) rather ominously called "Transformation into Structure and Total Mediation" It is easy to let these storming experiences simply unravel, overwhelm and exhaust us. Hermeneutics is not a chance for us, inquiring into these lives of ours, to simply become the flighty *puer*-spirit that runs off in all directions and in haste. In not repudiating childhood but embracing its vivifying potentialities, hermeneutics does not then want to be left "stand[ing] helpless before the child" (Arendt, 1969, p. 181) and simply overrun with enthusiasm, breathlessness, haste, difference, newness and flight. Key to hermeneutic work is the need, in the face of and in thanks to these flighty gifts, to compose ourselves in the middle of all this tumultuousness, to become experienced in these matters, not to be simply unravelled into an interdependent, co-arising world.

Herewith is named the great ambivalence of a pedagogy left in peace. It neither repudiates the flight of the new while sternly holding traditions closed against its arrival, nor the opposite:

> In education [we] assume responsibility for both the life and development of the child and for the continuance of the world. These two responsibilities do not by any means coincide; they may indeed come into conflict with each other. The responsibility for the development of the child turns in a certain sense against the world: the child requires special protection and care so that nothing destructive may happen to him from the world. But the world, too, needs protection to keep it from being overrun and destroyed by the onslaught of the new that burst upon it with each new generation. (Arendt, 1969, pp. 185–186)

> The old unilateral options of *gericentrism* (appealing to the authority of age, convention, tradition, nostalgia) and *pedocentrism* (child-centered pedagogy) only produce monstrous states of siege which are irresponsible to the matters at hand, that is, to the question of how life is mediated through relations between old and young. (Smith, 1999, p. 140)

Hermeneutics, therefore, requires "living in the belly of a paradox wherein a genuine life together is made possible only in the context of an ongoing conversation which never ends yet which must be sustained for life together to go on at all" (p. 138).

> Ambivalence, rather than being overcome…is a way in itself. *Ambivalence is an adequate reaction*…to these whole truths. Thus, going by way of ambivalence circumvents *coniunctio* efforts of the ego, because by bearing ambivalence one is in the *coniunctio* itself. This way works at wholeness not in halves but through wholeness from the start. The way is slower, action is hindered, and one fumbles foolishly in the half-light. The way finds echoes in many familiar phrases from Lao Tzu, but especially: "Soften the light, become one with the dusty world."(Hillman, 2005b, p. 41)

> The true locus of hermeneutics is this in-between. (Gadamer, 1989, p. 295)

IX

What kind of truth is there in such hermeneutic experiences, if they are so full of ambivalence, paradox, fumbling, hindrances and unfinishedness? It cannot be the sort of truth that pertains to knowledge that has amassed, where statements that are true of "X" are statements that properly correspond, within prescribed methodological and evidential limits, to objective states of affairs. In hermeneutics, we are no longer talking about statements matching up to objective states of affairs, but an experience of the breaking forth and opening up of the world in which we *already live* and in relation to which we are not the commanding, clarifying and demanding centre of that life. When we find that the names of the days of the week are cascading with possibilities, multiple, hidden lives and possible ventures, the truth of this finding does not precisely have an "object" to correspond to. We experience how what once seemed to be just amassed ("all this information is on the Internet, so why do we need to go over this?") is actually living threads that have long since been pulling on our lives and the lives of our teachers and students, shaping and defining us, beyond our wanting and doing. Opening up our ability to experience these ways of the world is opening ourselves up to its truth and ours. We have, it seems, been living a life which knows us without our quite knowing it.

That is why Martin Heidegger (1977a) reverts to a pre-Socratic term to describe this experience of truth: *aletheia*. This term has multiple connotations. It entails

- opening up and revealing what was concealed or closed

- enlivening that which seemed routine, deadened and lethal and

- remembering that which was forgotten (in the passage over the river Lethe, to the Greek under-world (see Jardine, 2006)

This is how the truth of convivial life is experienced (in contemporary Greek usage, *aletheia* is translated into English as "*really?*").

My knowledge of the convivial life of the world and my convivial life in it is never simply experienced as a given but rather as a task that I continually face, "a task that is never entirely finished" (Gadamer, 1989, p. 301). I experience myself, these university students and this small inheritance under consideration as "being situated within an event [an "opening," if you will] of tradition [all these names, these gods, these forgotten memories, these wild things, that old Odyssey and the jingling of reindeer, uncover, open and start to enliven those heretofore closed off and deadened routines, and all my hitherto concealed complicities and locatedness in such matters], a process of handing down" (p. 309). "Doing calendar" is thus a process of "handing down," and the truth to be had here is one of opening up what was closed, enlivening that which has become sedimented and dead, and struggling to remember what has been forgotten in this thing handed to us and handed down in schools. The terrible moral quandary here—the quandary about what the right thing to do might be—is that even the deadly and boring routine that many of those student-teachers experienced in their practicum placement is *itself* a "handing down." Either way, the truth to be had is *about this thing in the world, about those with whom I engage* in thinking about this thing, and, of course, it is *about me and the convivial life I've been living* beyond my wanting and doing.

Here is another feature of our hermeneutic conditionedness. A quick and cursory look around the hallways and classrooms of many schools quickly proves that there is nothing necessary or unavoidable about taking up the task of learning to experience the abundance of the world:

> The Gadamerian dystopia is not unlike others. In his version, to be glib, little requires human application, so little cultivates it. Long alienated from abiding in inquiry as a form of life and way of being, a restless humanity defers to models, systems, operations, procedures, the ready-made strategic plan, and first and last to reified concepts, long impervious to deconstruction. (Ross, 2004)

The nature, culture, language, history and institutional encoding of this type of "levelling down" (Heidegger, 1962, p. 165) inherent in everyday life, and how to learn to live out from under its shadow, is part of the difficult and treacherous venture of becoming a teacher. The flatness and self-enclosedness of things is thus a product not simply of a sort of war consciousness bent on threat and doubting demands, but is also in the very nature of convivial life itself. This convivial life can fall into a zone of deep shadow with equal ease under the numbness of familiarity and routine. Ironically, leaving things thus numbed gets identified with leaving things in peace, and disturbing the peace on behalf of our convivial life becomes experienced as a threat

X

"*Understanding proves to be an event*" (Gadamer, 1989, p. 308), a moment of the fluttering open of the meticulous co-arisings that repose around any thing. A second small event in our university class discussion demonstrates anew what Gadamer called this "fecundity of the individual case" (1989, p. 38) and its centrality to the cultivation of our convivial experience of the world.

The previous week, one student had mentioned that two newly arrived Afghani children, brother and sister, had joined their Grade 2 class. Both knew a bit of English, but their first language was Pashto. Suddenly, now that our discussion had cracked the dull surface of the routine, "doing calendar" became disorientingly alive. It was no longer especially warrantable to simply say that these two new children would pose special problems in learning the names of the days of the week. These new arrivals were not a *problem*.

The living knowledge of days and their names is not just held by "us," nor is it held anonymously online. It is convivially held, in lives, in places, in languages, in traditions, as a living topic in the world. It, so to speak, faces us and addresses us while, at the same time, also faces elsewhere and speaks in languages and tones that are beyond us. And this occurs such that this thus-far presumed "us" rebounds back, such that not only calendar, but "us" started to break open as if from a center, witness, not just witnessing, known, not just knowing. This is its life and ours and theirs and now ours anew as this "us" shifts, and brushes by us again, folds of the same cloth, these children, here, asking after the names of days in English, asking parents for Pashto names and their origins, helping open anew the now-very-strange Northern Europeanness of our ongoing discussions.

"What *are* the days of the week called in Afghanistan?"

Silence.

No one in our university class knew, but everyone experienced, in different ways, how the world itself unravelled and unrolled ahead in great, almost unbearably rich abundance. We settled down a bit (one mild version of "transformation into structure" out of the cascading *Spiel* of things are those moments in a class when we gather together and gather up what we've done, what we've found) and talked, too briefly, about how the arrival of these two new students in the Grade 2 class potentially made what was originally the dull routine of "doing calendar" even *more* convivially alive than it would have been without their arrival. If we begin exploring these threads, they do not just add themselves to knowledge already amassed. What we find will, inevitably, rattle through what we've come to already know and experience, reopening, re-enlivening, remembering (both in the sense of the cultivation of memory and in the sense of adding new members to this "we," new folds to this cloth, this weave, this text). Knowledge convivially held in the life world is, *of ontological necessity*, vulnerable to being taken up anew in the midst of the ongoing exigencies of everyday life. This vulnerability is in its nature, and securing it against such vulnerability changes its nature.

The wonderful and difficult pedagogical news here is that the more we come to know about this matter and therefore about these worldly selves that we seem to have lost track of, the *greater* is that sense of being drawn. As happens in becoming familiar with learning to love a work of art, so, too, with these old names of days: "[The world] compels over and over, and the better one knows it, the *more* compelling it is. This is not a matter of mastering an area of study" (Gadamer, 2007, p. 115).

XI

Why did he tell us to practice and find out for ourselves? Some people really worry about this. "If the Buddha really knew," they say, "he would have told us. Why should he keep anything hidden?" This sort of thinking is wrong. We can't see the truth in that way. We must practice, we must cultivate, in order to see. (Chah, 2005, p. 111)

"Why don't you just tell us?" This is a common and understandable complaint. If the knowledge in question is already amassed on the Internet, why do we need to have these discussions? Can't I just have my class look it up if they are interested?

Gadamer (2007) says that hermeneutics is, in the end, a practical philosophy that must needs be practiced. These students' complaints are always *almost* correct. There *is* something hidden from view. However, the demand to be just "told" has a hand in *keeping it hidden*. The error is in believing that someone "has" what is hidden and amassed somewhere and could just tell it if they wanted to. This hidden thing *is* available, but I, for myself, must cultivate my ability to invite, experience, articulate, remember and care for it appearance, as must these students asking to be just told. This is a form of knowledge, but it is knowledge only cultivated and gained through *practice*. Each of these students-teachers, now having opened up a bit about "doing calendar," must, each in their own ways, find out how they might make their way with these openings and opportunities in their classrooms and in their and their students' lives, and they know that their students, each year, even each turn of days, will have something to say about how this unfolds and remains practicable. Their knowledge of these convivial threads of the world must thus be "ke[pt] open for the future" (Gadamer, 1989, p. 340) where the prospect of setting right anew, with new students, and new circumstances, will always be at hand.

This is why learning to teach matters such as calendar cannot involve teachers simply "downloading" everything they have found onto their students. But neither can students be simply "left to their own devices" (Arendt, 1969, p. 196). You cannot practice this knowledge by yourself and alone and only within the confines of the devices you have already mastered, because this *is not how this knowledge is held in the world.* Conversing, debating, investigating, reading, exploring, studying, composing, changing your mind, illustrating, performing, demonstrating what you know and giving a public account of that knowledge, letting others read back to you what they understand your understanding to be—these are not just effective pedagogical techniques, means or vehicles for "getting across" amassed knowledge that could have just been *told.* These are not *means* but are rather *constitutive conditions of the life of this knowledge.* They are *how* this knowledge lives and is held and is cultivated in the world, and practice in these practices is becoming knowledgeable, becoming "educated." If my student-teachers want their future students to understand how this knowledge actually lives in the world and what must be engaged for such living to be cared for, they must invite their own students into the living practicability of these days and their names, and this is a one-way street. Thus, practical knowledge "demands of the person learning it the same indissoluble relationship to practice that it does of the one teaching it" (Gadamer, 2007, p. 232).

Over time, becoming more experienced in such pursuits makes you more able and willing to let this process unfold anew and more able to feel less threatened by such ventures and the transformations, small and large, that they ask of us. One learns, slowly, and left in peace, to trust, more and more, how we might "entrust ourselves to what we are investigating to guide us safely in the quest" (Gadamer, 1989, p. 378). The more I practice experiencing the world this way, the more practiced I become. And the more practiced I become, the more experienced I become in being able to experience the world this way:

> The truth of [hermeneutic] experience always implies an orientation to new experience. "Being experienced" does not consist in the fact that someone already knows everything and knows better than anyone else. Rather, the experienced person proves to be, on the contrary, someone who…because of the many experiences he has had and the knowledge he has drawn from them, is particularly well equipped to have new experiences and to learn from them. Experience has its proper fulfillment not in definitive [amassed] knowledge but in the openness to experience that is made possible by experience itself. (Gadamer, 1989, p. 355)

It was, after all, *because of* our opening up of calendar to Norse gods and reindeer that the absent names of days in Afghanistan hit so hard and true to the life of these matters. Our expanding experiences not only made the object under consideration more compelling the more we experienced. It made us more able to experience the compelling, reinvigorating, setting-right-anew truth (*aletheia*) of this new arrival. Unpracticed, the arrival of these new children would have been simply one more thing to fit into an already established routine.

New knowledge is thus created in becoming experienced, but this new knowledge does not amass but rather, so to speak, always accrues to *someone.* It is always *someone* who is becoming experienced, and no one can become experienced on someone else's behalf. This is in the nature of our convivial knowledge of the convivial world, that it is a knowledge we have learned to live with, and we are not replaceable with each other in this learning. As such, each of us has an irreplaceable part in this convivial whole. To re-cite, "each and every thing becomes the center of all things. This is the absolute uniqueness of things, their reality" (Nishitani, 1982, p. 146). Or, differently put, if those Afghani children were *not* in that student-teacher's classroom, if that speculation about their language and its names for days did not arise, *everything* would shift. Each of us thus takes on an *irreplaceable role* in the community of conversation that ongoingly constitutes this knowledge and its cultivation. For this type of knowledge, "just tell me" is inadequate.

Thus, even though this hidden thread of our convivial life *is* available, it is never fully available, all out in the open and once and for all. This hints at another feature regarding what kind of truth hermeneutics cultivates:

> Truth has in itself an inner tension and ambiguity. Being contains something like a hostility to its own presentations. The existing thing does not simply offer us a recognizable and familiar surface contour; it also has an inner depth of self-sufficiency that Heidegger calls "standing-in-itself." The complete un-hiddenness of all beings, their total objectification (by means of a representation that conceives things in their perfect state) would negate this standing-in-itself of beings and lead to a total leveling of them. A complete objectification of this kind would no longer represent beings that stand in their own being. Rather, it would represent nothing more than our opportunity for using beings, and what would be manifest would be the will that seizes upon and dominates things. [In becoming experienced] we experience an absolute opposition to this will-to-control, not in the sense of a rigid resistance to the presumption of our will, which is bent on utilizing things, but in the sense of the superior and intrusive power of a being reposing in itself. (Gadamer, 1977, pp. 226–227)

Becoming experienced in some topic and practiced in its ways, therefore, has a strange effect, requiring a strange formulation: "beings hold themselves back by coming forward into the openness" (Gadamer, 1977, p. 227). It is not only that the more experienced I become, the more compelling does that topic become. The more experienced I become, the more I experience how my experience is incommensurate with the living reality of the thing. Even this small elementary school topic of calendar—the more I explore it, the more it starts to "stand there," "reposing in itself" over and above my wanting and doing. The more experienced I become, the more able I become to leave this reposing thing in peace in my understanding and experience of it. To become educated, then, means to learn to let things stand *there*, not here under the shadow of my wanting and doing.

Practice helps cultivate a sense of the abundant array of possibilities that are housed there, in the thing under consideration, and to experience them *as* possibilities that surround and house our lives, always already and everywhere. This is "not merely mastery of…expertise, whose task is set by an outside authority or by the purpose to be served by what is being produced" (Gadamer, 2007, p. 232). Neither is it "a question of a mere subjective variety of conceptions, but of the [topic's] own possibilities of being that emerge as the [topic] explicates itself, as it were, in the variety of *its* aspects" (Gadamer, 1989, p. 118, emphasis added). Thus, part of what we are becoming experienced in is the knowledge that new students will arrive, and these old matters in which we've been living will be called to account in ways that are unforeseeable. We "must accept the fact that future generations will understand differently" (Gadamer, 1989, p. 340), not because of our failure to gain command over these things, but because we succeed in understanding that the things under consideration stand there beyond any attempts to stop them from being "set right anew" (Arendt, 1969, p. 192) by the interdependent conditionedness and occasionality of the convivial world.

There is thus something deeply temporal in hermeneutic work, and we can catch a quick glimpse of how profound was Martin Heidegger's linking up of *Being and Time*. "Understanding and interpretation are not constructions based on principles, but the furthering of an event that goes far back" (Gadamer, 1989, p. xxiv). Things do not *exist* as objects that simply are what they are. Things *are*, in their lived, convivial reality, inherited from the past that has already shaped us, and, at the same time "open for [a] future" (Gadamer, 1989, p. 340) that has yet to arrive and that will reshape what we have understood that shaping to have been. Even that which seems over and done with will turn out to be different than it was. (After all, who would have imagined that speaking in particular of the arrival of Afghani children would have the portent it has come to have? This is as much beyond our wanting and doing as is what might come of this in the future.) The full reality of things is thus always experienced as "standing in a horizon of…still undecided future possibilities" (Gadamer, 1989, p. 112). This is why David G. Smith's (2006) explorations of "frozen futurism" are so important to the prospect of hermeneutic pedagogy left in peace, as is a consideration of the developmentally sequenced futurism of developmental theory in education.

Knowledge of such matters, then, always involves getting in on the always already, everywhere ongoing conversation, "the conversation that we ourselves *are*" (Gadamer, 1989, p. 378). Such conversations "keep the object, in all its possibilities, fluid" (p. 330) as per their convivial life. As such, the economic, political, linguistic, institutional, cultural and other forces that set up regimes aimed at excluding voices, closing off possibilities and shutting down such conversations are the perennial target of hermeneutic critique and hermeneutic labor.

XII

An aesthetic response to particulars would radically slow us down. To notice each event would limit our appetite for events, and this very slowing down of consumption would affect inflations, hyper-growth, the manic defenses and expansionism of civilization. Perhaps events speed up in proportion to their not being appreciated; perhaps events grow to cataclysmic size and intensity in proportion to their not being noticed. (Hillman, 2006, p. 41)

We are…active participants in the communality of our experience of the world. Discussion bears fruit. The participants part from one another as changed beings. The individual perspectives with which they entered upon the discussion have been transformed, and so they have been transformed themselves. This, then, is a kind of progress—not the progress proper to research but rather a progress that always must be renewed in the effort of our living. (Gadamer, 2007, p. 244)

There is a pedagogy here, and it is, in its own way, hard work to maintain ourselves in this spot. I've had the luck and great fortune to spend time in dozens of classrooms with dozens of teachers and hundreds of students who understand things about these matters and their living practice, even in the shadows of troubled schools and troubled students. This way of teaching can, in small ways, begin to ameliorate suffering, and heal something of lost relations.

This spot of being left in peace so that things might break forth in all their relations and where we might then become educated and experienced in these ways of the world—this is not a spot of quietude and laxity, and it is also a bit of a rare gift, fragile, fleeting, finite. It is much easier to lose than it is to win, and is often embattled, given the embattlements that have shaped modern schooling.

This pedagogy left in peace bespeaks a type of knowledge and a type of truth about our existence, that we and the things of this living world are always becoming what they we, and we are never finished, and this is not a problem that needs fixing or one that the promise of an ever-accelerating amassing of knowledge might ever outrun:

One has to ask oneself whether the dynamic law of human life can be conceived adequately in terms of progress, of a continual advance from the unknown into the known, and whether the course of human culture is actually a linear progression from mythology to enlightenment. One should entertain a completely different notion: whether the movement of human existence does not issue in a relentless inner tension between illumination and concealment. Might it not just be a prejudice of modern times that the notion of progress that is in fact constitutive for the spirit of scientific research should be transferable to the whole of human living and human culture? One has to ask whether progress, as it is at home in the special field of scientific research, is at all consonant with the conditions of human existence in general. Is the notion of an ever-mounting and self-perfecting enlightenment [a notion that finds its ideal in the self-containedness of the "I am" and its objective correlate, A=A] finally ambiguous? (Gadamer, 1983, pp. 104–105)

References

Arendt, H. (1969). *Between past and future: Eight exercises in political thought*. New York: Penguin.

Arthos, J. (2000). "To be alive when something happens": Retrieving Dilthey's *Erlebnis. Janus Head, 3*(1). Retrieved August 30, 2010, from http://www.janushead.org/3–1/jarthos.cfm

Berry, W. (1983). *Standing by words*. San Francisco: North Point Press.

Bordo, S. (1987). *The flight to objectivity*. Albany: State University of New York Press.

Calasso, R. (1993). *The marriage of Cadmus and Harmony*. New York: Alfred Knopf.

Caputo, J. (1987). *Radical hermeneutics: Repetition deconstruction and the hermeneutic project*. Bloomington: Indiana University Press.

Chah, A. (2005). *Food for the heart*. Somerville, MA: Wisdom Publications.

Derrida, J., & Ferraris, M. (2001). *A taste for the secret*. Cambridge, England: Polity Press.

Descartes, R. (1955). Discourse on method. In *Descartes Selections*. New York: Charles Scribner. (Original work published circa 1637)

Estes, C. P. (1996). *Women who run with the wolves*. New York: Random House.

Friesen, S. (2010, October). Uncomfortable bedfellows: Discipline-based inquiry and standardized examinations. *Teacher Librarian: The Journal for School Library Professionals*. Retrieved January 29, 2011, from http://www.encyclopedia.com/Teacher+Librarian/publications.aspx?pageNumber=1

Gadamer, H. G. (1977). *Philosophical hermeneutics*. Berkeley: University of California Press.

Gadamer, H. G. (1983). *Reason in the age of science*. Cambridge, MA: MIT Press.

Gadamer, H. G. (1989). *Truth and method* (J. Weinsheimer, Trans.). New York: Continuum.

Gadamer, H. G. (1994). *Heidegger's ways*. Boston: MIT Press.

Gadamer, H. G. (2001). *Gadamer in conversation: Reflections and commentary* (R. Palmer, Ed. & Trans.). New Haven, CT: Yale University Press.

Gadamer, H. G. (2007). *The Gadamer reader: A bouquet of later writings* (R. Palmer, Ed. & Trans.) Evanston, IL: Northwestern University Press.

Gadamer, H. G., & Derrida, J. (1989). *Dialogue and deconstruction: The Gadamer-Derrida encounter*. Albany: State University of New York Press.

Gray, J. (2001). *False dawn: The delusions of global capitalism*. New York: New Press.

Heidegger, M. (1962). *Being and time*. New York: Harper & Row.

Heidegger, M. (1977a). The essence of truth. In *Basic writings* (pp. 113–142). New York: Harper & Row.

Heidegger, M. (1977b). Letter on humanism. In *Basic writings* (pp. 189–242). New York: Harper & Row.

Hillman, J. (2005a). Notes on opportunism. In *Senex and puer* (pp. 96–112). Putnam, CT: Spring.

Hillman, J. (2005b). Senex and puer: An aspect of the historical and psychological present. In *Senex and puer* (pp. 30–70). Putnam, CT: Spring.

Hillman, J. (2006). Anima mundi: Returning the soul to the world. In *City and soul* (pp. 27–49). Putnam, CT: Spring.

Huntington, S. (2003). *The clash of civilizations and the remaking of world order*. New York: Simon & Schuster.

Husserl, E. (1970). *The crisis of European science and transcendental phenomenology*. Evanston, IL: Northwestern University Press.

Illich, I. (1992). *In the mirror of the past: Addresses and lectures, 1978–1990*. New York: Marion Boyars.

Jardine, D. (2005). *Piaget and education: A primer*. New York: Peter Lang.

Jardine, D. (2006). Youth need images for their imaginations and for the formation of their memories. *Journal of Curriculum Theorizing, 22*(4), 3–12.

Jardine, D. (2008a). "'I Am' has sent me": Arguments with myself and others on the subject of certain suspected allegories regarding democracy and education. In J. Wallin (Ed.), *Democratizing educational experience: Envisioning, embodying, enacting* (pp. 110–129). Troy, NY: Educator's International Press.

Jardine, D. (2008b). The surroundings. In D. Jardine, P. Clifford, & S. Friesen (Eds.), *Back to the basics of teaching and learning: Thinking the world together* (2nd ed., pp. 159–164). New York: Routledge.

Jardine, D., Bastock, M., George, J., & Martin, J. (2008). Cleaving with affection: On grain elevators and the cultivation of memory. In D. Jardine, P. Clifford, & S. Friesen (Eds.), *Back to the basics of teaching and learning: Thinking the world together* (2nd ed., pp. 31–58). New York: Routledge.

Jardine, D., Clifford, P., & Friesen, S. (Eds.). (2006*). Curriculum in abundance*. Mahwah, NJ: Lawrence Erlbaum.

Jardine, D., Clifford, P., & Friesen, S. (2008a). *Back to the basics of teaching and learning: Thinking the world together* (2nd ed.). New York: Routledge.

Jardine, D., Clifford, P., & Friesen, S. (2008b). "Whatever happens to him happens to us": Reading Coyote reading the world. In D. Jardine, P. Clifford, & S. Friesen (Eds.), *Back to the basics of teaching and learning: Thinking the world together* (2nd ed., pp. 67–78). New York: Routledge.

Jardine, D., Clifford, P., & Friesen, S. (2008b). Scenes from Calypso's cave: On globalisation and the pedagogical prospects of the gift. In D. Jardine, P. Clifford, & S. Friesen (Eds.), *Back to the basics of teaching and learning: Thinking the world together* (2nd ed., pp. 211–222). New York: Routledge.

Kant, I. (1983). What is enlightenment? In *Perpetual peace and other essays.* Indianapolis: Hackett. (Original work published 1794)

Nishitani, K. (1982). *Religion and nothingness.* Berkeley: University of California Press.

Norris-Clarke, W. (1976). Analogy and the meaningfulness of language about God: A reply to Kai Nielsen. *The Thomist, 40,* 176–198.

Palmer, R. (2007). Introduction to "Aesthetics and hermeneutics." In H. G. Gadamer, *The Gadamer reader: A bouquet of later writings* (R. Palmer, Ed. & Trans. pp. 124–131) Evanston, IL: Northwestern University Press.

Piaget, J. (1965). *Insights and illusions of philosophy.* New York: Meridian Books.

Ross, S. M. (2004). Gadamer's late thinking on *Verweilen. Minerva—An Internet Journal of Philosophy, 8.* Retrieved July 19, 2010, from http://www.ul.ie/~philos/vol8/gadamer.html

Sendak, M. (1988). *Where the wild things are.* New York: Harper & Row.

Smith, D. G. (1999). *Pedagon: Interdisciplinary essays on pedagogy and culture.* New York: Peter Lang.

Smith, D. G. (2006). *Trying to teach in a season of great untruth: Globalization, empire and the crises of pedagogy.* Rotterdam: Sense.

Tyler, S. (1986). Post-modern ethnography: From document of the occult to occult documentation. In J. Clifford & G. Marcus (Eds.), *Writing culture: The poetics and politics of ethnography* (pp. 122–140). Berkeley: University of California Press.

Wallace, B. (1987). *The stubborn particulars of grace.* Toronto: McClelland & Stewart.

Wittgenstein, L. (1968). *Philosophical investigations.* Cambridge, England: Blackwell.

Wood, E. M. (2006). Democracy as ideology of empire. In Colin Mooers, (Ed.). *The new imperialists* (pp. 9–24). Oxford, England: One World Press.

CHAPTER ELEVEN

Circulating Critical Research: Reflections on Performance and Moving Inquiry into Action

Madeline Fox and Michelle Fine

In times of economic, educational and racial "crisis," as the inequality gap widens and youth of color are targeted by social policies that further erode their opportunities, we are interested in the design, analysis and activist possibilities of participatory youth studies. Thus, we start at the end, at a performance of Polling for Justice, a participatory action research project surveying youth experiences of education, criminal justice and health care across communities, sexualities, genders, race/ethnicity and class in New York City, in order to theorize how critical research can circulate through the academy, communities, youth organizing and social policy—and maybe even theatre.

The Polling for Justice (PFJ) research performance opens with a lone bespectacled academic-looking person standing on stage in a white lab coat and fumbling through a sheaf of papers, mumbling:

> Hello. My name is Dr. Researchy, and I am going to be presenting a paper to you on "The Urban Teen" and a theory I developed that is a framework for looking at one of the major problems that growing urban U.S. city centers have been faced with—namely the adolescent…

Played by PFJ artistic director Una Osato, the character is designed to represent traditional positivist academic research where older White men visually represent the privileged status of expert. The Dr. Rebert Researchy character reads his paper on "The Urban Teen" in a slow, monotonous ramble. Before long, the audience hears the voices of the Polling for Justice researchers discussing Dr. Researchy's talk from offstage.

> "This is boring!"
> "What is he saying?"
> "I think he just said something about the 'urban teen'."
> "Ohhh he's talking about you!"
> "No I think he's talking about you!"
> "I got no idea what he's talking about, all I know is this is boring."

"No one understands him but himself!"

"You know what, I'm going to go up there and say something."

One by one, Polling for Justice youth researchers walk up on stage, interrupting Dr. Researchy by taking the microphone and insisting that he sit down and listen to the results of their youth research on youth experiences in New York City. In the last moment, as Dr. Researchy is being escorted off stage, one of the youth researchers, Darius Francis, admires Dr. R's lab coat and takes it for his own, wearing it for the rest of the performance.

The depiction of Dr. Researchy was meant to critique and provoke. As a caricature of the disembodied and "objective" researcher who studies *on* but not *with* youth, he pushes audiences to rethink their assumptions about where expertise lives, troubling notions of objectivity, validity and the celebrated distance of academic research. In their initially disruptive presence, the PFJ researcher-performers raised equally compelling questions about critical research, participation, social representations of youth and social justice. By modeling talking back and speaking out from their seats, they encouraged other audience members to do more than watch; to engage actively in the production.

We offer this chapter to introduce the notion of "circuits" into the grammar of critical research, inviting a sharp turn away from the individualism that saturates most U.S.-based social inquiry—whether quantitative or qualitative in design. Instead, here, we want to argue that critical inquiry take seriously the circuits of dispossession, privilege and possibility that run between us, across zip codes and dangerous power lines, through youth bodies, connecting, in this case, youth researchers/actors and audiences of privilege.

While our participatory action research approach (Torre et al., 2008; Tuck et al., 2008) derives from social scientists and practitioners including Orlando Fals-Borda, Paulo Freire, and Ignacio Martin-Baro, as performative researchers we align ourselves, as well, with Augusto Boal's recognition that there are no spectators, only spect-*actors*, linked in the social drama of witnessing and responsibility. We introduce circuits as foundational to our theoretical perspective on *circuits of dispossession, privilege and possibility*; to participatory methods and analytic "camps," and to our thinking about how critical inquiry travels into popular culture, social movements and policy.

Theorizing Circuits of Dispossession in Critical Youth Studies

Political theorist David Harvey writes on neoliberalism and dispossession: "Accumulation by dispossession is about dispossessing somebody of their assets or their rights…we're talking about the taking away of universal rights and the privatization of them so it [becomes] your particular responsibility rather than the responsibility of the State (Harvey, 2004, p. 2). In the United States, public resources, opportunities, dignity and therefore aspirations are being redistributed by public policies, from poor communities to elites. Youth of color, those living in poverty, and youth who are immigrants are increasingly denied access to or detached from public access to high-quality education and health care as their families and housing are destabilized. Shamefully, at the same time the state has invested heavily in their criminalization and surveillance.

In 2009 Fine and Ruglis migrated Harvey's theoretical work into critical youth studies to understand how neoliberal policies activate what we call "circuits of dispossession," in the lives of low-income youth of color, such that they are increasingly *detached* from public institutions of development such as education and health care, and *attached* to public institutions of containment such as criminal justice and the military. In the original article Fine and Ruglis (2009) document, for instance, how the simple condition of being a high school drop-out/push-out cascades into a flood of negative outcomes in education and economics, of course, but also health outcomes, parenting practices, voting and community participation and criminal justice involvement. Fine and Ruglis document that these outcomes are dramatically worse for drop-outs/push-outs who are Black or Latino than those who are White or Asian.

Just as dispossession *accumulates* within communities and across sectors, it is also the case that dispossession is unevenly distributed across communities. The loss of resources, human rights, dignity, legitimacy and opportunities in one community corresponds with their respective accumulation in another. As the *inequality gap* widens across communities, social outcomes worsen—for all of us. Thus we should be interested in understanding and undermining circuits of dispossession and privilege for purposes of progressive solidarity, and perhaps even for self-interest.

British epidemiologists Richard Wilkinson and Kate Pickett published *The Spirit Level: Why Greater Equality Makes Societies Stronger* (2009), in which they argue that severely unequal societies produce high rates of "'social pain": adverse outcomes including school drop-out, teen pregnancy, mental health problems, lack of social trust, high mortality rates, violence and crime, low social participation. Their volume challenges the belief that the extent of poverty in a community predicts negative outcomes. They assert instead that the size of the *inequality gap* defines the material and psychological contours of the chasm between the wealthiest and the most impoverished, enabling various forms of social suffering to saturate a community, appearing natural. In societies with large gaps, one finds rampant state and socially reproduced disregard, dehumanization, policy neglect and abuse. As you might guess, the inequality gap of the United States ranks among the highest in their international comparisons.

Moving these notions of cross-sector dispossession and cross-community dispossession into critical youth studies, Maddy Fox and Michelle Fine, collaborating with the Urban Youth Collaborative of the Annenberg Institute for School Reform and other colleagues, developed Polling for Justice (see M. Fox et al., 2010), a multigenerational, participatory action research project designed to document youth *experiences of dispossession* and *sites of youth resistance* in New York City.[1] PFJ surveyed more than 1,000 NYC youth about their experiences in schools, with police and health care (see Fine, Stoudt, Fox, & Santos, 2010) toward four ends:

1. document the *geography and demography of dispossession and privilege* by detailing empirically where and for whom social policies, institutions and practices enable and constrict opportunities for youth development across the boroughs of New York City;

2. track the *cross-sector consequences of dispossession* by investigating how dispossession in one sector (e.g., not earning a high school diploma) adversely affects outcomes in other sectors (e.g., economic, health and criminal justice outcomes);

3. chronicle the ways in which youth and adult allies *mobilize to resist,* negotiate and challenge collectively these policies and practices;

4. design activist *scholarship to "be of use"* in varied organizing campaigns for youth justice and human rights policy struggles.

And then, most recently, given the radical assault on public education, the hyper reliance on school closings and charter openings, we added a fifth goal:

5. to examine the extent to which *school closings and charter openings map onto zones of dispossession*; that is, to assess the extent to which high drop-out/discharge rates are associated with heavy police presence/surveillance/criminalization of youth (a link that the youth researchers emphasized and insisted that we study), and then to consider the extent to which these are communities declared educational disasters by the DOE, where schools are being closed and selective admissions/charter schools opened.

As U.S. public policy floats resources and opportunities upward toward a gentrified community of young people viewed as "entitled" to public support, social suffering anchors the aspirations and mobility of poor youth. New York City may be a caricature of these global dynamics. In our research, presented briefly below, we were interested in theorizing and documenting how the retreat of the state from social welfare, mobilized since the Reagan years, has swollen the stress load on poor and working-class youth while disabling the very relationships and institutions that might provide support for youth in crisis. We were interested, further, in the capillaries that could carry critical, participatory research from the halls of the CUNY Graduate Center into theatre, theory building, youth organizing, community life and social policy circles.

Design, Methods and Analysis Camps: Circuits of Collaboration

Polling for Justice is a large-scale, participatory action research project designed by a research collective of youth and adults, focused on youth experiences of (in)justice in education, criminal justice, and health. An interdisciplinary collaboration among faculty and students at the City University of New York, a committed group of youth co-researchers, Brown University's Annenberg Institute for School Reform and the Urban Youth Collaborative,[2] our primary methodological instrument was a (rather lengthy) text-based and Internet-based survey co-constructed by youth and adults. With participation at the heart of theory, methods, crafting questions and analyzing the data, we gathered data from more than 1,000 New York City youth.

In the early spring of 2008, PFJ embarked on designing a citywide survey. Noting the fraught political, social and educational context for youth in the city, we were interested in amassing a public archive/database of youth knowledge and experiences to speak back to neoliberal forces aimed at privatizing and/or cutting publicly funded resources. Designed with colleagues from inside and outside the academy, with young people, and with advocates from the field of public health, we structured the work through circuits of collaboration across research, advocacy and organizing.

The PFJ researchers set out to study, theoretically and empirically, what we call *circuits of dispossession* (Fine & Ruglis, 2009) and *pools of youth resistance* in New York City, the ways in which social policies, institutions and practices systematically deny youth of color key human rights across sectors (education, criminal justice and health care) and the ways in which youth mobilize to resist, negotiate and challenge collectively these very forms of dispossession. We sought to investigate how urban youth, living with rapid gentrification, intense police surveillance in communities of color, privatization of schooling under the guise of choice, the deportation of massive numbers of immigrants, shrinkage of the supportive public sphere and expansion of the "disciplining" public sphere, experience, respond to and organize against the profoundly uneven opportunities for development across the five boroughs of New York City in three sectors: education, health care and criminal justice. PFJ was explicitly designed to gather and funnel social science evidence into organizing campaigns for youth justice—violence against girls and women, police harassment, college access, high-stakes testing, and access to comprehensive sexuality education, to name just a few.

In 2008, at our first gathering, more than 40 youth arrived, recruited from activist organizations, public schools, detention centers, LGBTQ youth groups, foster care, undocumented youth seeking college and elite students from private schools, joined by educators, representatives of the NYC department of adolescent health, immigrant family organizers, lawyers, youth workers, psychologists, planned parenthood researchers, geographers, psychology and education doctoral students, in the basement of the Graduate Center of CUNY.

We posed a single, simple challenge to the group: We would like to collectively design a large-scale, citywide research project, creating a youth survey of standardized and homegrown items and conducting a series of focus groups, to document youth experiences across various public sectors of the city. We explained that the youth and adults were recruited because of their distinct experience, knowledge and expertise, and the young people and adults formed groups to pool their knowledge about prisons and their impact on youth, about foster care, immigration and deportation, homeless shelters, peer relationships, access to health education, worries about feeling safe, and concern for communities. Once groups were formed, jackets and hats came off and the groups began their work. We created a graffiti wall where youth could jot down the questions they would want to ask of other NYC teens.

We organized groups across certain experiences of urban youth: In one corner was a young man whose father was in prison, a girl worried her mother would be deported and a ninth grader expressed concerned about gentrification; they designed questions about the real homeland security. In another corner, youth were reviewing standardized health items, such as the Youth Behavior Risk Survey (YRBS) and the National Longitudinal Study of Adolescent Health (AddHealth) about sexuality, reproduction, health and nutrition. Angry about these surveillance systems asking questions that are "none of their business" and equally concerned with "risky" health behaviors without accounting for questions and issues of access, resources, opportunity (educational or otherwise), and cultural differences, we worked to understand why it would be important to track the relation of unsafe sex practices with type, quality and access to comprehensive sexuality education (versus abstinence only, or none at all), or violence in a relationship, or dropping out of school. But these workgroups also helped to stimulate critical youthful discussions on the meaning of "health"; societal fears of and judgments about adolescence; cultural influences on health; reified and racist perceptions of "urban" youth and youth of color; and about how health behaviors cannot be divorced from opportunity structures and the social, economic and political contexts into which one is embedded.

Down the hall, yet another group was talking about where they felt safe. At home? On the streets? In school? And a fourth group discussed youth experience with the criminal justice system. Together, in a participatory approach to survey construction, this group created a long checklist of contacts with police. What grew out of this was the most politically mobilized set of questions contained within the survey. In fact, nearly all of the criminal justice survey questions were developed by the youth. It became overwhelmingly evident that existing measures of youth experiences with policing in New York City failed to capture their realities.

Our work was designed as a contact zone (Torre, 2005) among youth from varied communities and ethnicities; between young people and adults; advocates, educators, practitioners and researchers from education, criminal justice and public health. Within our research team, questions of privilege, power and oppression were interrogated collaboratively; youth experiences led the inquiry and adult skills surrounded and supported; expertise was democratized and the "right to research" assumed fundamental (Appadurai, 2004). The process wasn't always smooth, but we tried to create spaces in our youth research camps where diverse forms of experience, analysis, theory and affect could be held, and explored delicately.

Within the Public Science Project at the Graduate Center, CUNY (Torre, Fine, Stoudt, & Fox, in press; Torre & Fine, 2010), research camps have been crafted as a third space/process for building the democratic capacity of a research collective where questions of difference, power and solidarity can be engaged. We begin our first sessions with exercises designed to strip away misconceptions about what constitutes scientific inquiry and who can engage in social research, democratizing notions of knowledge and expertise. We design scavenger hunts to reveal the distinct insights that differently situated researchers import. For instance, we are always amazed (and yet, by now, never surprised) that it is often the least *formally educated* members of our collectives (e.g., students in special education classes) who most astutely read between the lines of dominant storylines. We develop exercises and activities in the traditions of critical pedagogy and popular education to extract and honor multiple perspectives—not just one designated right answer. Acknowledging many forms of intelligence is sometimes resisted by students who have been "at the top" of their schools, or privileged, or professionals who believe it is their job to teach the youth what they do not know. We spend much time helping young people explore themselves as intersectional; defined at once by culture, neighborhood, gender, class, adolescence, interest in books, music, politics, sexuality, gender, language, humor, how people treat them, how they resist and how they embody their worlds.

We read psychological theory, critical race theory and methods, newspaper articles and listen to music to "hear" how youth are represented, and to search for voices of dissent, challenge and resistance; we "take" standardized scales and try out new survey questions; we learn to conduct interviews and role play focus groups; we watch films and create questions; we spend time writing, discussing issues on the streets, in their schools, homes, meeting other youth researchers from other regions; building research skills, designing the survey, piloting items, collecting and analyzing qualitative and quantitative data; presenting findings across New York City and at professional meetings.

In PFJ, we launched "seminars" for youth researchers and doctoral students where everyone took a set of questions to investigate the growing PFJ data. The collective was trained to approach their questions inductively using the philosophy and techniques of Tukey's (1977) exploratory data analysis (Stoudt, 2010). And all participating researchers—both youth and adult—took on the responsibility to "train" the next generation of youth researchers on future projects that grow out of the Public Science Project at the Graduate Center of CUNY.

Over 18 months, PFJ organized a series of multigenerational research camps focused, at the beginning, on building research expertise, sharing readings on the issues, histories of injustice and political struggles of resistance, refining our research questions, specifying the design and sample, exploring intersectional analyses of qualitative and quantitative data and generating provocative ideas for products, actions, scholarly papers, testimony, white papers and performances.

Analyzing/Embodying the Circuits—Bodies of Data Analysis

By the time we closed the survey in August 2009 we were swimming in data. We organized the data to examine what we called *cumulative dispossession*, trying to understand the extent to which youth who have been pushed out/dropped out of schools, for instance, and also have no health insurance, have had negative encounters with police and disrupted home lives were more likely to report depression, risky sexual engagements, involvement with violence and lower levels of psychological well-being. The youth researchers were adamant that PFJ *not* simply report racial "disparity" data, for they knew too well how such data were used to smear their communities, racial groups and individuals who were victims, but discursively turned into perpetrators of injustice through victim-blaming analyses. We were, instead, interested, as a collective in how policies of dispossession affect the lives, aspirations and care that different groups of youth engage as they navigate lives in communities made treacherous by these reckless social policies. And indeed, for every indicator we studied, those youth who scored as "highly dispossessed" by educational, housing/family, criminal justice and health care policy reported much higher rates of negative outcomes (for detailed findings see Fine, Stoudt, Fox, & Santos, 2010).

We also arrayed our survey material so as to create citywide maps to display the dramatically uneven geographic implementation of policies for youth development and policies for youth containment. With an analytic eye on class, gender, race/ethnicity, sexuality, immigration status, disability status and neighbor, we reviewed the geography of police harassment.

Bronx	Manhattan	Queens	Brooklyn
LGBTQ = 87.5% Straight=53.8% 33.7% pt. diff	LGBTQ = 52.4% Straight=35.0% 17.4% pt. diff	LGBTQ = 31.6% Straight=44.7% 13.1% pt. diff	LGBTQ = 69% Straight=50.7% 18.3% pt. diff

Negative Police Contact

Once we developed a preliminary analysis of the quantitative mapping of youth experiences of cumulative and community dispossession, we launched a set of data-driven focus groups in the neighborhoods where we found "hot spots" of dispossession (e.g., high rates of school push-out; high rates of criminalization of youth of color; high rates of surveillance on LGBT youth). In these focus groups, young people were asked to interpret, for and with us, the distributions and circuits of injustice we had documented. Conducting focus groups with youth who sit at the intersections of our statistical findings, we hear that young people remain buoyant through a sense of solidarity, critical understandings of unjust arrangements to stay positive, and through actively imagining a different tomorrow.

In one focus group with youth who identify as lesbian, gay, bisexual, queer, questioning and/or transgender, as they pored over findings about negative youth interactions with police, they discussed their anger in response to experiences like getting ticketed on the subway for putting their feet on a seat, for sitting in a playground after dark, or getting harassed for wearing the wrong clothes ("gay wear") in the wrong neighborhood.

They explained that outrage at these conditions is paired with an understanding of limited potential for appeal, and therefore, they find ways to dissipate their anger and move forward with their lives. As one focus group participant put it,

> It's like an everyday life in the city. It's like cops are mean, we just have to deal with because it's really like, there's really not much I can do with arguing with a cop. So it's like move on and keep on going, and it's every day. So it gets to the point where you no longer, it's not as shocking to us anymore. It just goes away after a while, you know, you walk it off, you watch TV, take a shower, and then it's like, okay, just another day in New York City.

The focus group participants offered up their critique of current realities and their vision for the kind of world they wish exists, a world rich with supports, access and resources for all young people (Brewster, Billies, & Hyacinthe, 2010).

The PFJ analyses provided evidence of circuitries in the form of cumulative dispossession of youth of color in low-income communities and then across communities: low-income young people of color from poor communities and LGBQ youth have the lowest rates of graduation, the highest rates of negative interactions with police, the most experiences of violence and the most alarming reports of depressive symptoms (Fine, Stoudt, Fox, & Santos, 2010). As PFJ youth researcher Jaquana Pearson always makes sure we emphasize, our data shows how young people are resisting oppression, redefining reality, aspiring to greatness and insisting on change. We also see evidence of the positive impact meaningful relationships with adults and participation in youth organizations can have in young peoples' lives.

Circuits of Analysis

From our participatory stance, in PFJ, we pencil a distinction between methods for *data collection* and methods for *analysis*. Participatory action research projects make use of both qualitative and quantitative methods. When participatory projects use quantitative methods, the *collaboration* that is inherent in a PAR approach adds new dimensions to analysis. The diverse nature of our research teams means that we must take multiple perspectives into account in relation to the interpretation of quantitative data, and this can sometimes pose challenges for finding approaches to collaboratively analyze quantitative data. In our case, when faced with a largely quantitative data set as a multigenerational research team, we were pushed to develop innovative methods for analysis—critical methodologies that include using qualitative (inductive, artistic, consciously subjective) methods to understanding our "bodies" of data.

As a research team, we spent time developing mathematical and statistical skills to be able to understand percentages and interpret cross-tabulation tables. It was one thing to intellectually understand what *87.5%* means; however, it was another thing to make sense of *87.5% of LGBQ youth living in the*

Bronx report negative experiences with police. We decided that we would use embodied approaches to developing analyses of our largely quantitative data. In the beginning of July 2009, our research team retreated to a college campus for five days to steep in the data and learn an improvisational theatre method that emphasizes audience participation called Playback Theatre (H. Fox, 2007; J. Fox, 1994; Salas, 2007).

Circuits of Affect Within and Across Bodies

We turned to embodied methodologies in part because we needed an approach to quantitative data analysis that made room for multiple ways of knowing. However, we also used embodied methodologies because we wanted to find ways to communicate our findings that made explicit that the justice work and responsibility for action is held collectively in the bodies of both audience *and* performer, reader *and* researcher, adult *and* youth. Through drama and art, the PFJ researchers performed our findings on circuits of dispossession in a way that moved the work into the audience meaningfully—not as youth ventriloquy, but as intimate communication of the material and engagement with the audience.

We used drama and other embodied methods to make meaning from the survey data within our research collective. Our research meetings began with personal updates and physical, playful warm-ups that brought whimsy (creativity) into our research space. Without minimizing the seriousness of our roles as knowledge producers, we played games to establish a dynamic where everyone was invited and urged to contribute—to play (Boal, 1997). In fact, the more we all contributed, the more the "game" succeeded. We found there was power in play—our approach encouraged collaboration and creativity that opened up new insights about our data. Maxine Greene writes on the powerful potential of imagination and the arts to pry open fresh awareness of what's possible (1995). Through the warm-up process we were reminded that our data needed our brainpower, yes, but also our life experiences, and the knowledge stored deep in the muscles of our bellies, arms, calves and shoulders. The ritual reestablished our research space as collaborative and shared, and developed our capacity for thinking critically together, as an ensemble.

In order to dive into the survey data, we started in front of a large projection screen running statistical analysis in real time, *Stats-in-Action* (Stoudt, 2010). In order to make sense of the data, we moved the data off the screen and put the numbers "on their feet," creating scenes and human images of the data. We found that when we put the numbers in our bodies, through sculptures or scenes, we made room for differences in understanding and experience to come into our research collective.

An illustration: The survey data showed that level of mother's education was a powerful indicator of survey respondents' school experiences, mental health, and involvement with violence and police. For instance, of the 1,110 people who took the survey, more than half of those who had dropped out also had a mother who dropped out of high school.

When we looked at the table, we could understand the data intellectually as powerful evidence of cross-generational fallout of inadequate access to education. When we moved this data *to its feet* the analysis became more complex and delicate. As we worked data over months and through images (digital photos), personal stories, scenes, and human sculptures, we came to understand the impact of the level of a mother's education from multiple perspectives.

Several members of the research collective could identify intimately with this finding, and as we theorized from the data, our personal experiences kept us accountable to ourselves, the survey respondents, our communities, our mothers, and our social justice goals. Embodied methodologies were elastic enough for us to be able to make sense of the survey data, reconciled with what we knew from our diverse personal experiences. Through art, we found a means to uncover and express various kinds of knowledge—including affective ways of knowing. The embodied methodologies made room for pain and shame, for anger, for frustration, making visible circuitries of affect orbiting the data. As a result, our group developed a critical analysis of educational betrayal that moved blame from the individual to the structural.

Finding creative ways to dramatize the data during analysis was especially effective for creating a highly collaborative space, and for developing complex, layered analyses of the survey data. In Polling for Justice, we conceptualized the shift from the intimate backstage of our research space to the public stage of research dissemination as a moment of action and an opportunity to explore together with audiences *what is* and *what is possible* (Gallagher, 2007; Greene, 1995; Salverson & Schutzman, 2006).

Circuits of Representations and Responsibility—The Performance Lab

Ignacio Martín Baró conceptualized public opinion polls as *social mirrors* designed to provide a scientific reflection of lived realities that might speak to power and disrupt injustice (1994; Torre et al., in press). In PFJ, in line with our commitment to do social research of use (Fine & Barreras, 2001), we turned to performance methodologies that might interrupt hegemonic (mostly negative) representations of adolescence and adult complacency. We imagined our performance spaces as *labs* where we played with and dismantled the wall that can separate audience from performer-researcher. We thought of performances as opportunities for the PFJ researchers to hold up a "social-mirror-in-the-round," making visible the link between youth, adults and structural inequalities.

We took this turn to drama and performance allied with social scientists who insist on doing research with social relevance and impact, and the particular community of scholars and social scientists who incorporate the arts into their research process and products. In our case, we self-consciously followed in the footsteps of the performance work of W. E. B. Du Bois.[3]

Although this line of Du Boisian work is little known, as a social scientist, Du Bois used pageantry, performance, and circus theatre in order to explore alternative possibilities about African American history and reality. He conceived of art, the stage, drama and theatre as a vehicle through which to educate, inspire and unite Black audiences (Horne & Young, 2001). Through theatre, Du Bois was able to share histories, and historical figures, to audiences without reliance on literacy. Committed to theatre with Black people, for Black people, he used the stage to insert productive stories of African Americans into the public discourse and imagination (Krasner, 2001).

Humbly following in this tradition, the Polling for Justice project turned to dramatic performances of our research project as a way to disseminate our research and engage with audiences. In Polling for Justice, our turn to art and performance grows out of a similar commitment to social justice,[4] and we build not only on the Du Boisian legacy and other social science research entwined with the arts (Gallagher, 2007) but also the work of community art projects that make social justice claims. The discipline of community-based art has much overlap with participatory action research, as illustrated by Jan Cohen-Cruz: "Community-based art is a field in which artists, collaborating with people whose lives directly inform the subject matter, express collective meaning" (2005, p. 1). In line with these commitments, we took seriously the *performance* of our data, as well as the *process* of encountering and analyzing the data through embodied methods as well.

We turned to performing the PFJ data in order to incite engagement from the audience but wary of arousing a simply empathic response. Megan Boler (1999) cautions that empathic readings permit the reader to go under the false assumption that it is possible to fully imagine others, and allow for a passive consumption of the subject's experience/emotions without also having to examine the reader's social responsibilities. She calls instead for an active empathy, or a "testimonial reading," where the responsibility for action lies with the reader. In PFJ, as a group of mostly African American and Latina young people, we were especially concerned that we not encourage our predominantly White, adult, middle-class audiences to want to save or rescue poor Black and Brown youth. We used playful, nuanced, powerful embodiments of our data as one way to guard against portraying youth of color as suffering and as victims. We worked to avoid a performance setting where rows of comfortable audience members reenacted the watching of other's pain as onlookers. We understood bystanders, witnesses, and non-victims, though seemingly unaffected, as actually being in potentially powerful, liminal roles (Fine, 2002). Our hope was to facilitate our audiences to notice, that is, to incite a recognition that their contribution towards collective responsibility could be to do a careful interrogation of their own story/future actions and recognize the cross-circuits of dispossession, privilege and responsibility coursing through the performance space. We wanted to make visible the power lines and the braiding of our collective circuits (Salverson & Schutzman, 2006).

The PFJ performances were conceived as an extension of the ethic of participation across the inequality gap. Audiences included teachers, parents, school administrators, young people, social scientists, community members, police, Department of Education officials, and policy makers. In order to activate the participation of audience members, the performances had three phases. The researchers started with a presentation of the PFJ data in embodied, visual, storied ways that employed metaphor, humor, maps, graphs, and numbers. In the second phase audience members were invited to respond and react to the data using Playback Theatre improvisation (J. Fox, 1994; Salas, 2007) to transform the audience members' affective responses into theatre on the spot. Finally, in the third phase, the PFJ researchers invited audience members to contribute their own expertise and experience in generating knowledge and visions for action in light of the PFJ data.

Provoking a Politic of Solidarity

According to Augusto Boal's theoretical frame, we are all actors. In Boal's theatre form, Theater of the Oppressed, no audience member simply watches; there are no spectators, only spect-*actors* (Boal, 1997). Theatre of the Oppressed dramas are designed to simultaneously be productive for transforming real issues of social injustice, and as an allegory for the kind of democratic, participatory politic possible in the world outside the performance space. In PFJ we too did not want our audiences to remain passive. We wanted audience members to grasp the analyses we presented on youth social psychological experience of circuits of policy dispossession, and we wanted audience members to recognize their own roles in the arrangements that produced the conditions we performed. Towards the end of the PFJ performances, once the audience had seen embodied interpretations of the survey data, we broke the fourth wall of the performance space, turned up the house lights, and explained that it was time for the audience members to take on a more active role in the performance lab. We passed a microphone around and heard audience members' affective responses to hearing the data: "That was powerful, I feel shocked by some of the data."; "Amazed at how many police are in the NYC school system."; "I feel frustrated and lost. How do I keep going as an educator?"; "I feel inspired by seeing young people full of knowledge and critique." After each response, the PFJ researcher-performers would turn the responses into theatre on the spot in the form of a human sculpture that could simultaneously hold multiple interpretations.

The purpose of the Playback Theatre was to make visible some of the circuitry of emotion swirling around statistical representations of life for young people in New York City. The human sculptures opened fissures in the divide that usually exists between performer and audience, researcher and reader, and youth and adult. These openings made space for more meaningful collaborations to germinate and grow.

In the PFJ performances, audiences had to make sense of the paradox between the data on dispossession and negative experiences they were hearing, and the sophisticated work of the youth researchers presenting/performing the research. Through a small scene, or a physical sculpture, the researcher-performers could quickly communicate multiple and complex perspectives. The ultimate goal of the PFJ performances was to provoke a sense of solidarity between audience, researchers, youth, and adults. In the presentations of our data, as in our research camps, we made strides to create spaces that allowed for interaction, and exposed (explicitly and implicitly) the circuitry that connects us all. With performance, we stretched the web of participation to include the outer circle, the audience, as those who bear witness, in the hopes that we would engage. In this way, our research itself was an intervention in the institutional and policy-based production of adolescent experiences of injustice. Through PFJ performances the audience could identify with youth of color in new ways, across power, suggesting a shift in collective identity, and perhaps making political engagement more likely.

At the very end of the PFJ performance, Dr. Researchy is brought back on stage. He has been watching, thinking, and he has had an awakening. He says,

> Well I was just thinking that we should really ask teens what they think the questions we should ask are and find out their ideas on the best solutions to some of these problems. I mean, you all are the ones living it each day, and together we can think about we can do next…

The PFJ researcher-performers, glad Dr. Researchy finally "gets it," invite him into the research collective. But their final move is to turn questions of "what next" back to the audience; to re-place responsibility collectively.

Thus, in the final scene of the PFJ performance, the youth researchers explained that there was no ending to the show. Instead we insisted the audience take responsibility for imagining what should happen next. Audience members popcorned suggestions for future research, policy change, and organized community responses:

> I'd like to see some opportunity for other young people to do research like this with allied adults and for it to go viral worldwide, standing up together to change policy.

> Let's show the data to police departments and police officers and figure out how to change the policies and realities.

The performances were not designed to be solutions. Instead, they were meant to expose, provoke and motivate people to contend with their own/our own collusion in the inequality gap, worsened by policies that privilege those already privileged. Theatre allowed us to collectively hold the complexity, particulars, the broad analysis, the contradictions and the dream—all at the same time. With policing data, we could know the numbers, the discrimination, and still communicate the need for protection, or share our aspirations to be a police officer in what could be a stable career. With education or economics, we could critique capitalism or privatization, but still explain why we advocate for our younger brothers and sisters to get into the new charter school on the block with better resources.

As an art form, our performances were at once an encounter and a metaphor—the performances slowed down time somewhat to allow for a close examination of particular realities, and through art we invited audiences and performers to experiment with what is and expand what is possible. Outside the performance space, PFJ data circulated in more concrete ways. The research findings traveled into public hearings, policy reports, community speak-outs and academic papers on education, safety reforms, and social critique. In every arena, the aim was to maintain the live-wire connection between the findings, the researchers, and audience. The PFJ data made evident how the impact of certain policies ripple out in young people's lives along circuits of dispossession, and our approach to disseminating the data made sure that audiences of the research felt their own location in that roughly circular arrangement we call a revolution.

Notes

1.   Polling for Justice was made possible thanks to the Surdna Foundation, Overbrook Foundation, Hazen Foundation, Glass Foundation, Schott Foundation, Urban Youth Collaborative, and the Public Science Project and the Youth Studies Research Fund at the CUNY Graduate Center.

2. Polling for Justice research collective includes Niara Calliste, Michelle Fine, Madeline Fox, Darius Francis, Candace Greene, Jaquana Pearson, Una Osato, Dominique Ramsey, Maybelline Santos, Brett Stoudt, Paige Taylor, Jose Torres, Isabel Vieira, and Jessica Wise.

3. In November 1913, *The Crisis* magazine published a detailed description (nearly a script) of a pageant of African American history written by W. E. B Du Bois. The pageant was performed as a celebration of the Emancipation Proclamation, was entitled *The People of Peoples and Their Gifts to Men* (Du Bois, 1913, p. 339), and was produced by over 300 and performed by over 1,000 people (Du Bois, 1913; Horne & Young, 2001).

   The sketch of *The People of Peoples and Their Gifts to Men* begins with four heralds yelling, "Hear ye! Hear ye! Men of all the Americas, and listen to the tale of the eldest and strongest of the races of mankind, whose faces be Black. Hear ye, hear ye, of the gifts of Black men to this world, the Iron Gift, the Gift of Faith, the Pain of Humility and the Sorrow of Pain, the Gift of Freedom and Laughter, and the undying Gift of Hope. Men of the world, keep silence and hear ye this!" (Du Bois, 1913, p. 139). The pageant continues, telling the history of the successes and strengths of African people. Through dramatic effect, Du Bois and colleagues told audiences about early African technologies, of ancient civilizations in Egypt, of old roots of modern religions, of survival, of pain, and of "Struggle Toward Freedom" (Du Bois, 1913, p. 340). This pageant, later called *The Star of Ethiopia*, was "a great human festival" with a cast of 1,000 African Americans using procession, story and extravagant costumes (Du Bois, 1915).

4. Du Bois was explicitly uninterested in art for art's sake; he was interested in art as propaganda (Krasner, 2001). He turned to performance and art in order to take action with scholarship and reach masses of people.

References

Appadurai, A. (2004). Capacity to aspire: Culture and the terms of recognition. In R. Vijayendra & M. Walton (Eds.), *Culture and public action* (pp. 59–84). Stanford, CA: Stanford University Press.

Brewster, K., Billies, M., & Hyacinthe, Z. (2010). Presentation: LGBTQ youth experiences with police in neighborhoods, subways, and to and from school. Syracuse University Queering Education Research Institute (QuERI) Roundtable on LGBTQ Issues in Education. New York, NY.

Boal, A. (1997). *Games for actors and non-actors*. London, England: Routledge.

Boler, M. (1999). *Feeling power: Emotions and education*. New York, NY: Routledge.

Cohen-Cruz, J. (2005). *Local acts: Community-based performance in the United States*. New Brunswick, NJ: Rutgers University Press.

Du Bois, W. E. B. (1913, November). *The Crisis, 6*, 339–345.

Du Bois, W. E. B. (1915, December). Star of Ethiopia. *The Crisis, 11*.

Fine, M. (2002). 2001 Carolyn Sherif Award address: The presence of an absence. *Psychology of Women Quarterly, 26*, 9–24.

Fine, M., & Barreras, R. (2001). To be of use. *Analyses of Social Issues and Public Policy, 1*, 175–182.

Fine, M., & Ruglis., J. (2009). Circuits and consequences of dispossession: The racialized realignment of the public sphere for U.S. youth. *Transforming Anthropology, 17*(1), 20–33.

Fine, M., Stoudt, B. G., Fox, M., & Santos, M. (2010). The uneven distribution of social suffering: Documenting the social health consequences of neo-liberal social policy on marginalized youth. *European Health Psychologist, 12* (September), 30–35.

Fox, H. (2007). Playback theatre: Inciting dialogue and building community through personal story. *The Drama Review, 51*(4), 89–105.

Fox, J. (1994). *Acts of service: Spontaneity, commitment, tradition in the nonscripted theatre*. New Paltz, NY: Tusitala.

Fox, M., Mediratta, K., Ruglis, J., Stoudt, B., Shah, S., & Fine, M. (2010). Critical youth engagement: Participatory action research and organizing. In L. Sherrod, J. Torney-Puta, & C. Flanagan (Eds.), *Handbook of research and policy on civic engagement with youth* (pp. 621–649). Hoboken, NJ: Wiley.

Gallagher, K. (2007). *The theatre of urban: Youth and schooling in dangerous times*. Toronto, ON, Canada: University of Toronto Press.

Greene, M. (1995). *Releasing the imagination: Essays on education, the arts, and social change*. San Francisco, CA: Jossey-Bass.

Harvey, D. (2004). Conversations with history: A geographer's perspective on the new American imperialism [Webcast transcript]. Berkeley: University of California Institute of International Studies. Retrieved May 10, 2007, from http://globetrotter.berkeley.edu/people4/Harvey/harvey-con0.html

Horne, G., & Young, M. (2001). *W. E. B. Du Bois: An encyclopedia*. Westport, CT: Greenwood Press.

Krasner, D. (2001). "The pageant is the thing": Black nationalism and *The Star of Ethiopia*. In J. Mason & E. Gainor (Eds.), *Performing America: Cultural nationalism in American theater* (pp. 106–122). Ann Arbor: University of Michigan Press.

Martín-Baró, I. (1994). *Writings for a liberation psychology*. Cambridge, MA: Harvard University Press.

Salas, J. (2007). *Improvising real life: Personal story in playback theatre*. New York, NY: Tusitala.

Salverson, J., & Schutzman, M. (2006). Witnessing subjects: A fool's help. In J. Cohen-Cruz (Ed.), *A Boal companion: Dialogues on theatre and cultural politics* (pp. 146–157). New York, NY: Routledge.

Stoudt, B. (2010, June). *Testing circuits of dispossession: An exploratory look*. Presentation to Pathways to Resilience II: The social ecology of resilience, The Resilience Research Centre, Halifax, NS, Canada.

Torre, M. (2005). The alchemy of integrated spaces: Youth participation in research collectives of difference. In L. Weis & M. Fine (Eds.), *Beyond silenced voices* (pp. 251–266). Albany: State University of New York Press.

Torre, M., & Fine, M. (2010). A wrinkle in time: Tracing a legacy of public science through community self-surveys and participatory action research. *Journal of Social Issues, 67,* 106–121. doi:10.1111/j.1540–4560.2010.01686.x

Torre, M., Fine, M., Alexander, N., Billups, A., Blanding, Y., Genao, E.,...Urdang, K. (2008). Participatory action research in the contact zone. In J. Cammarota & M. Fine (Eds.), *Revolutionizing education: Youth participatory action research in motion* (pp. 23–44). New York, NY: Routledge.

Torre, M., Fine, M., Stoudt, B., & Fox, M. (in press). Critical participatory action research as public science. In P. Camic & H. Cooper (Eds.), *Handbook of research methods in psychology.* Washington, DC: American Psychology Association.

Tuck, E., Allen, J., Bacha, M., Morales, A., Quinter, S., Thompson, J., & Tuck, M. (2008). PAR praxes for now and future change: The collective of researchers on educational disappointment and desire. In J. Cammarota & M. Fine (Eds.), *Revolutionizing education: Youth participatory action research in motion* (pp. 49–83). New York, NY: Routledge.

Tukey, J. W. (1977). *Exploratory data analysis.* Reading, MA: Addison-Wesley.

Wilkinson, R., & Pickett, K. (2009). *The spirit level: Why greater equality makes societies stronger.* New York, NY: Bloomsbury Press.

CHAPTER TWELVE

The Critical Aesthetic: Living a Critical Ethnography of the Everyday

Andrew Hickey

I want you to get up right now, sit up, go to your windows, open them and stick your head out and yell, "I'm as mad as hell and I'm not going to take this anymore!" Things have got to change. But first, you've gotta get mad!…You've got to say, "I'm as mad as hell, and I'm not going to take this anymore!" Then we'll figure out what to do about the depression and the inflation and the oil crisis. But first get up out of your chairs, open the window, stick your head out, and yell, and say it:
  [screaming at the top of his lungs] "I'M AS MAD AS HELL, AND I'M NOT GOING TO TAKE THIS ANYMORE!"
—Howard Beale (Peter Finch), in *Network*, 1976

Visions from Hell

This is an age when words don't count for much. Promises can be overturned in an instant and the old certainties and guarantees that came with one's word are gone.

Large-scale language games confront at every turn. Sentiments are blurred and grand pronouncements hold nothing more than fleeting platitude. Towering proclamations hung actually or virtually from billboards, television screens and the web tell of what must be done to maintain a sense of self and social status. Representatives of governments, bureaucrats and public officials weigh up prospects for reelection against things said and done at the expense of *real* action. Faceless "public relations" representatives, now operating under the far less beguiling terms "customer satisfaction spokesperson", "brand manager" or "marketing communications consultant", ensure that the public face of the brands they are employed to protect stay positively in mind, regardless of the social, environmental and economic damage they yield. Modern-day oracles, masquerading as celebrities, provide reference points to those vain or obsessed enough to *believe*, according to how en vogue or passé (either end of the spectrum provides lessons) these products of pop culture happen to be at any given time of the day. Advice, as style tips or cautionary tales, disseminates in the form of the "latest finding", "breakthrough" or "exclusive" from "experts" who, in areas as diverse as health, psychology, entertainment and sport, are called upon in talk shows, magazine exposés, or that other great simulacrum of information, the infomercial, to provide seemingly obligation-free pointers on how to live, ensure or retrieve a happy life.[1]

This should be a vision of hell. But instead, we accept as part of a "rapidly privatised and individualised, fast globalising world" (Bauman, 2001, p. 15) that this is just the way it is; happy to exist around the edges, between the predominant imagery, the ordinary person decreasingly has any ability to shape. This of course isn't to say that we have consciously *given up*, but that the mechanisms for speaking in the public spaces of the global world have changed. It is a site in which demonstrations of power form behind the scenes in the politico-corporatised economy. A site in which the basic premise of being-as-citizen isn't enough to ensure that one given opinion is as valid as another; a site in which the expectation that we might all engage and have the ability to speak falls under increasing contestation. Our late-capitalist, neoliberal, global, post-modern world isn't utopian; far from it. It doesn't afford opportunity to equally get involved but requires cunning and the "right" connections to the "right" networks. These channels connect those with the "right" *stuff*—the right social and cultural capital, familial ties and political collegiality (often in conjunction with those age-old, and perennially significant, demarcations of the right gender, sexuality, age, and ethnicity):

> The members of the tiny capitalist class at the top of the hierarchy have an influence on economy and society far beyond their numbers. They make investment decisions that open or close employment opportunities for millions of others. They contribute money to political parties, and they often own media enterprises that allow them influence over the thinking of other classes. (Gilbert, 1998, p. 286)

It is these same people[2] who ensure that the logic of the world is maintained according to specific desires and privilege. As David Harvey (2005) notes:

> If the preferred policy of the ruling elites is *après moi le déluge*, then the deluge largely engulfs the powerless and the unsuspecting while elites have well-prepared arks in which they can, at least for a time, survive quite well. (p. 153)

Such expressions of privilege by association have long been in existence (and have, perhaps, also been recognised), but now articulate unflinchingly and unashamedly in the public spaces we share. The rest of us meanwhile carry on doing our best on a path that isn't of our own construction, but one that we are expected to work collectively at repairing when things go wrong.[3] Joseph Stiglitz (2008) notes that

> We had become accustomed to the hypocrisy. The banks reject any suggestion they should face regulation, rebuff any move towards anti-trust measures—yet when trouble strikes, all of a sudden they demand state intervention: they must be bailed out; they are too big, too important to be allowed to fail. (para. 2)

The mechanisms by which these associations of privilege (those networks of mutual support inaccessible to those inhabiting spaces outside of the nexus of privilege) operate are fundamental to how the world is configured and framed at this point in history. This is not a social dynamic designed to cater for all, but is one that is concomitantly accepted as "normal". Whilst lament that this "normal" is far from acceptable to the majority of the world's populations rarely finds mainstream voice, it is via the continued and systematic marginalisation of those who find themselves at the wrong end of the scale of privilege that manifestations of privilege (such as personal wealth, power, and the ability to mobilise one's agency to the detriment of others) are maintained.[4] These individualist and competitive logics, played out on a field that is never even, simply cannot be justified in light of the social, economic and ecological state the globe is in. But still we carry on living as we do.[5]

It is time to be angry and incensed by the way things are. The shaping of public discourses through the mediation of specific experiences, pre-framed identity locations and "market-friendly" discursive formations must be critiqued and challenged. With indignation at the plight of those of us who rest precariously on the edge of social, economic and ecological predicaments daily (that is, the bulk of populations throughout the world who exist under economic and social regimes that allow for such things as global financial crises, wars against terror and large-scale environmental destruction), something more must be argued for. It is not enough to be delivered empty rhetoric whilst being implicated in situations for which there is little opportunity for genuine engagement and response. What is needed is a way to write back; a mechanism through which challenges might be issued to the discursive formations and operations of power that masquerade as "normal".

Prospects

In this chapter I will chart a vision for activating a "critical ethnography of the everyday" in the hope that such a methodology—as a personal aesthetic—might reinvigorate democratic participation in the public arena. Such an argument carries a dual purpose; firstly, the reclamation of senses of Self via agentic social action, and secondly, a writing-back to culture to balance the way public dialogue might be mediated.

A number of assumptions are implied within such an approach. The vision I alluded to above, in the opening to this chapter, suggests that the world as it currently stands in this age of global capitalism, neoliberalist ideology and individualised habits of consumption has fundamentally gone wrong at some point. Our globe cannot continue to sustain us. Our social networks are breaking down at the same time the largest corporations post continually increasing profit margins. We find ourselves embroiled in faraway battles that we argue are about democracy whilst our own civil liberties are cynically scrutinised and reduced. *The first assumption that I make at the outset of this chapter is that the globe is in a state of crisis: socially, economically and ecologically.*

This is a concern for culture. Culture as that thing that binds us together operates from a necessarily symbolic basis in that it exists outside of each of us, but is core to our being. It is culture that provides the symbolic logic by which we understand how things *are* and how things come to *be*. While we might see expressions of culture presented in physical "artifacts"—all of those products of culture, from simple gossip between friends to what the design of a specific type of building suggests about its creators—it is to what these artifacts refer that is important. With this, I take Anthony Cohen's (2004) ideas on the formation of culture being accorded a "boundary" logic. As humans, we are deeply symbolic and understand the abstracted connections between signifier and referent to the point that codes of logic related to the very act of living, being, representing oneself and understanding one's "situation" in the world are encoded in the format of our culture. For Cohen (2004), and for this chapter at the very least, the "boundary" exists as that point of symbolic exchange that refers to

> an entity, a reality, invested with all the sentiment attached to kinship, friendship, neighbouring, rivalry, familiarity, jealousy, as they inform the social processes of everyday life…[it] is more than oratorical abstraction: it *hinges crucially on consciousness.* (p. 13, emphasis added)

I would add that in this global-economic age, with its vast divisions in the distribution of wealth and differential opportunities for the expression of agency in the politico-economic complex, the manifestation of culture exists according to more than "kinship, friendship, neighbouring, rivalry, familiarity, jealousy" alone; the manner in which "everyday" life is framed in our global world is affected by the material conditions within which we operate. As such, the effects of globalised capitalism and those competition-oriented social relationships that determine how we live and go about our daily business must also be considered. *This is the second assumption drawn upon in this chapter: the social order of the world is derived from conditions that globalised capitalism determines.*

Within such a cultural system, in which individuals with varying levels of agency and personal "will" compete for the ability to alter and form cultural logics in their image, the act of *speaking* falls under contestation. We have long understood, and accepted, that some possess the ability to speak (and be heard) more than others. But whilst we don't think twice when a politician, professional, publicly recognised "expert" or celebrity speaks on a topic seen as relevant to their knowledge and sensibilities, we aren't so quick to recognise that "grey" messages distributed in less formalised pronouncements through television programmes, advertisements, contrived-to-look-natural poses of models in magazines, video game storylines simulating actual battles fought in faraway places, amongst multiple other instances, are presented according to harder-to-spot, shadier manipulations of cultural logics that aren't necessarily interested in the collective good. These are the sorts of "grey" messages that constitute the "public pedagogies" of our contemporary world (Sandlin, Schultz & Burdick, 2010; Giroux, 1999, 2004).

It also follows that we have perhaps lost sense of the ability with which we might accept or reject ideas thrust onto the public. In a typically Foucauldian sense, we can "cut off the king's head" (1977) and reject claims as a public if we so desire. The trick, of course, is in knowing when and why one should accept or reject an idea. Such a dynamic requires a critically engaged public to recognise when things might well be "on the nose" and to be cognisant of what is and what might be to the extent of imagining possibilities outside of the limits of the boundary; to hope for something beyond what our cultural logics currently prescribe. As per the hopes that public intellectuals of the likes of Paulo Freire (1985a, 1985b, 2000), John Dewey (1997, 2008), Herbert Marcuse (1991) and more recently Henry Giroux (1988, 2004, 2005, 2008, 2009) held for a participatory "democracy", the public with which democracy grows must be both aware of itself, as well as cognisant of the power relationships at play in the cultural dynamic. This is a concern for what is possible; what might be imagined beyond what currently is. *This is the third assumption for this chapter: if a genuinely democratic public sphere is sought, then opportunity for a genuinely democratic dialogue affirmed through a critically cognisant and responsive public must be available through "formal" cultural channels, or through illicit demonstrations of resistance when those formal channels fail.*

Of course, cognisance as a citizen requires both a sense of self (as *being-in-the-world*) combined with a sense of social purpose and visioning for what *must* be in the interests of all. This is an ethical-moral concern for viewing the world as an organism and the Self as a component of the cultural dynamic that both situates and provides epistemological grounding for what is possible. Knowing Self is a necessary first step, but understanding how one is being positioned according to those facets of privilege or marginalisation experienced (in terms of the social locatedness born into and lived) must also be gained. Only from this can an awareness be encountered of how positionality is arranged and maintained, and what limits this places on who we each *might* become. *This is the fourth assumption drawn on in this chapter: we are, through acts of agency and ascription, identifiable according to positionality and situatedness within the cultural dynamic, and that this is mediated by the logics of the cultural system in which we are placed.*

I suggest that from these assumptions a prescription for seeing the world, our identity, ways of living and ways of behaving socially as mediated and "normalised" might be deployed. As connected to the conditions within which we are expected to function as individuals, these assumptions offer an approach for configuring understandings of the world that might be mobilised for an active and critical citizenship that doesn't allow itself to "get fooled again".[6]

The Aesthetics of Being Critical

What is at stake here is the development of a critical aesthetic as a *way-of-life*. Such an "aesthetic" isn't interested in "beauty" and "form", but draws on both the application Kant suggested as being that "which treats the conditions of sensuous perception" (1990, p. 66) combined with a critical impetus to *name, understand and reclaim*. Within this approach, an intent to critically understand and read the world according to the experience of the material condition of that world is suggested. Such a *critical* aesthetic understands that the social contexts we inhabit are crafted according to specific desires and that these must be interrogated and critiqued if hope for genuine democratic participation in the formation and operation of our world is to occur. The critical aesthetic operates as a "mood" or disposition through which the citizen-as-critic might negotiate the manufacturings of culture, and then, most importantly, be in a position to write back. Such an aesthetic, therefore, operates as a way-of-being via a way-of-experiencing the world that isn't "tried on" but operates as a level of consciousness about the world and its meanings. This is a critical consciousness that doesn't accept that the world *must* be the way it is and seeks both agency and resistance in localised, personalised ways at all times; this is critique *on-the-spot*, in the everyday locales of personal experience, ready for deployment in an instant. These are little criticalities that claim back an agency to name and appropriate, and that happen in the ordinary situations of our daily experiences (working those everyday aspects of social interaction is important and mustn't be forgotten).

As the site "closest in" (de Beauvoir, 1949), it is via the Self that culture manifests, and in accordance to the Self that situated practices and knowledges find activation. As an articulation of culture, the Self operates as the site upon which cultural expectations are mobilised, and hence must also be the site upon which these operations are opened for critique and interrogation. Through such an approach to living, the citizen-as-critic deploys a critical aesthetic as a disposition through which readings and negotiations of the manufacturings of culture might be made, as they are experienced. It is also through this disposition that an activation for something more might be realized: a "writing-back" activated through the critical assessment of what is and what might be for culture.

In this regard, the critical aesthetic suggested here celebrates an anarchist logic of individual determination through democratic dialogue about the structure and nature of culture. If indeed a split could be argued, it isn't a purely intellectual endeavour but also involves a soul—a deep care and emotionality for the world and each other. The critical aesthetic asks what is in the interests of all, via democratic engagement in the decision making of culture, with its central purpose resting in the reclamation of an agency with which the citizen-as-critic might play a part in naming and appropriating cultural meanings. There is a realisation at the core of the critical aesthetic that suggests that we *can* détourné and aren't automatically destined to be held captive by totalising ideas and ideals that work through a sort of cultural imperialism. But equally, the critical aesthetic must strive for and expect participatory, democratic social contexts in which a respect for agency works both ways: from speaker-listener, listener-speaker. The point, of course, is to uncover an aesthetic that allows individuals to "create for their lives the meanings they will" (Bauman in Denzin & Lincoln, 2005, p. 1085).

Effectively, the critical aesthetic has an expectation for a shared, collective response to how things are done, and does not simply secede power to those wishing to shape, name and configure the world by force (through such mechanisms as the law, or through property ownership, or access to certain types of economic acuity, the "right" identity characteristics and connections etc.). Those existing cultural logics mediated through laws, values, mores, hierarchies and politics that govern our behaviour are not enough, and represent the structural elements of a culture that has allowed the perpetuation of the very power dynamics that a critical aesthetic, through an empowered citizenry, seeks to unsettle. What is required is a critical citizenry that might collectively work at shaping what *should* be in the interests of all and that disregards the existing lay of the land. This requires a new and radicalised method by which the world might be viewed and understood.

Methodological Foundations

Autoethnography and Critical Ethnography, as they have come to be understood in the academy (Austin & Hickey, 2008; Hickey & Austin, 2007a; Madison, 2005; Saukko, 2005; Ellis, 2004; Ellis & Bochner, 1996), form a foundation upon which the critical aesthetic might be deployed. As a *dynamic* ethnography, the critical aesthetic draws a concern for the locatedness of the Self as a social being via autoethnographic exposé and the deployment of a critical viewpoint derived from the concerns of critical ethnography. The concerns of these "new" ethnographies, as Goodall (2000) would identify them, fit neatly with the purposes of the critical aesthetic in that they provide a foundation for a criticality that is both self-conscious and "located" in the material realities of the citizen-as-critic. Such an approach "combines hermeneutic focus on lived realities, a (post)structuralist critical analysis of discourses that mediate our experiences and realities, and a contextualist/realist investigation of historical, social and political structures of power" (Saukko, 2005, p. 343).

It also goes some way to meeting the demands of the later "moments" of qualitative research identified by Denzin and Lincoln (2005), in which concerns for

> messy, uncertain, multivoiced texts, cultural criticism, and new experimental works will become more common, as will more reflexive forms of fieldwork, analysis, and intertextual representation. (p. 26)

The little criticalities that develop from the readings of the world undertaken by the citizen-as-critic add a multivocality to the cultural dynamic and seek localised responses to (now) global concerns. The point of engagement with the field, production of analysis and writing back to culture are all situated within the experience of the citizen-as-critic, according to how those experiences of *being* are situated at that point in space and time.

What is in operation here is an ethnographic bricolage of sorts. With the concerns for "being there"—in amongst the cultural dynamic—a feature of traditional ethnography, the combination of the sense of Self provided by autoethnography and the critical imperative of critical ethnography, an approach keenly centered on reading and being-in-the-world develops. This is the core concern of the critical aesthetic—the consciousness by the citizen-as-critic of the locatedness they hold and the manufactured nature of social positionality that casts individuals and situations in prescribed ways according to race, ethnicity, class, gender, sexuality and those innumerable other ways of dissecting and "fixing" identity. What is needed here is a method as dynamic and ready to deploy as those social situations the citizen-as-critic encounters. There is no time to craft and select a methodology to fit as the encounter occurs. The critical aesthetic requires immediacy and an ability for the critical dissection and appraisal of the logics of power and representation that occur right here, right now. The critical aesthetic must function as an always-ready tool-kit of ethnographic skills, focused on reading the world as it happens and is experienced.

Another realisation for the citizen-as-critic must be that of their own partiality—defined according to the interplay of their locatedness in the cultural dynamic and the social "naming" of that positionality. In recognising the reflexive turn of contemporary, qualitative research, Steinberg (2006) notes:

> …bricoleurs attempt to widen their perspectives through methodological diversity. In no way, however do they claim that as the result of the multiperspective bricolage they have gained "the grand view"— from their poststructuralist perspective they understand that all inquiry is limited and incomplete. (p. 120)

A necessary reflexivity exists within the critical aesthetic of the critic-as-citizen. As a methodologist who deploys "…strategies when the need arises in fluid research situations" (Kincheloe, 2008, p. 4), the imperative for the realisation of partiality, in conjunction with the understanding that this partiality is as valid as that of any other citizen-as-critic, is a central element of the critical aesthetic.

The purposes of such a critical aesthetic shouldn't come as a surprise. By de-centering the ethnographic project away from the academy to skirmishes undertaken "on the street" by the citizen-as-critic in confrontation with a global political, economic and communication complex, the intent is to "help create and imagine a free democratic society" (Denzin & Lincoln, 2005, p. x) that looks beyond what *is* by identifying and opening for scrutiny existing relationships of power, discursive formations and prescriptions for being as they are encountered daily. Such an approach concerns itself with working towards something better—"rage is not enough" as Olesen notes (2000, p. 215). Something more—something better—must be willed into creation. With this, I borrow Denzin and Lincoln's (2005) concern:

> How do we move the current generation of critical, interpretative thought and inquiry beyond rage to progressive political action, to theory and method that connects politics, pedagogy and ethics into action *in the world?* (p. x, emphasis added)

The response provided here: de-centre the work of the critical ethnographer away from the academy with its protocols for undertaking and reporting on formally constituted "research", and open access to the tools of the critical ethnographer for the citizen-as-critic to meet the ends of "on-the-spot" little ethnographies that respond directly to concerns realised locally, by those people living with them. These ideas aren't new; the likes of Freire (1985a, 1985b, 2000, 2006), Dewey (1997, 2008) and more recently Giroux (1988, 2008, 2009) have argued for localised democratic involvement for some time, and in general this branch of individual-oriented activism has assumed the title "active citizenship". But what is different here is the formation of a distinct method for engaging as a citizen-as-critic that moves away from the academy and sees the site of activism not only in "social problems" but in the entire logic of culture and the everyday realities of people's lives as they are lived locally. This is an activism that seeks its impetus from the awareness and cognisance of a *critically* active citizenship.

Epistemologies: Thinking and Being

All research, whether willing to admit it or not, carries the hopes and desires, imperatives and motivations of the researcher as an embodied and socially located being. These epistemological conditions within which research is conducted must be acknowledged up front and honestly if any legitimacy for the findings of that research can be claimed. This carries a necessarily moral-ethical focus point in terms of what it is the ethnographer is looking to uncover or selecting to see (because we as human beings always frame our view in certain ways):

> The ethnographer works within a "hybrid" reality. Experience, discourse, and self-understandings collide with larger cultural assumptions concerning race, ethnicity, nationality, gender, class, and age. A certain identity is never possible; the ethnographer must always ask not "*Who* I am?" but "*When, where, how* am I?" (Denzin & Lincoln, 2005, p. xvi)

I would add to this that the concerns of *how* "I" am might also extend to "*How* are *we?*" Any ethnography is a necessarily social undertaking, and, in terms of a critical aesthetic, concerns how collectives of individuals might come together as communities, groups, enclaves and so on, to name their own experience.

To this end, I would suggest that there exists a core ethic central to the critical aesthetic. Such an ethic stands as a valuable reference point for the deployment of the "method" of the critical aesthetic and is vital for the design of its mobilisation and purpose (as with any critically ethnographic pursuit). There is no "Truth", but there are "truths" realised by individuals in localised settings. There is no essential "Human Spirit", but there are ways-of-knowing and ways-of-being that maintain shared elements in localised arenas. There is no single motivation for which we as humans should seek to build our world, but there are desires and hopes that mark the experience of being, according to the locations in which these are held. Naturally, it follows that there can never be one account of what a people "are" or "do", and to this end the critical aesthetic is always an unfinished project and prone to new readings, changed conditions and shifts in relationships. What is brought into consciousness by the critical aesthetic is the realisation that human experience and the locations in which we enact our relationships are fluid, dynamic and changing. It follows that any critical ethnographic endeavour that seeks to work from such a basis, will necessarily also be temporary and relevant to the moment of its creation only. This is an ongoing project.

Building on these principles, the following epistemological "commandments" form a foundation for the realisation of a critical aesthetic. In naming a fluid, and ever-changing world for themselves, the citizen-as-critic might:

- Show incredulity towards "meta-narratives" that claim an all-encompassing logic, claim to "Truth" or totalising system of operation.

- Express indignation towards social contexts that marginalise people through both organised, formal systemic and less formal, "everyday" social processes.

- Commit to the betterment of the experience of all peoples according to localised action by "the people".

- Resist as intolerable any convention, practice, set of assumptions or "common sense" that marginalises according to identity characteristics, including such aspects of identity as race, ethnicity, gender, sexuality, class, age, ability and belief.

- Show concern for the way that both the built and natural environments within which we live and depend for our survival can be transformed and overrun in ways that aren't in the interests of all (particularly those who inhabit these spaces).

- Show incredulity towards the meta-narratives of advertising and marketing that deploy hyper-real imagery and symbolism to cast a simulacrum of a reality that will never be realised.

- Actively critique representations of human experience and diversity that are mediated and distributed socially according to ulterior motive and vested interest.

- Seek to engage and understand difference rather than confront and dominate.

- Express hope for something better, and work towards the development of an entirely democratic and participatory society as if this were an expectation to be met.

- Never concede that the way it *is*, is the way it *should* be, but select battles carefully and with cognisance of the health and well-being of the Self in arguing for something more.

This approach does not attempt to be an impartialised Truth-claim or rarefied and unquestioned moral purpose in and of itself. It is an ethic, but one that recognises that as human beings we are capable of making decisions and go about constructing the world in our own image. It also recognises that current distributions of power are anything but equitable and result in selected individuals maintaining an agency more capable of shaping the world than that of others. What these epistemological foundations provide for the critical aesthetic is a basis from which the understanding of the realities of the world, as they currently stand for each of us, might be opened for scrutiny and critique. From this a dialogue that engages a cognisant and critically empowered citizenry in the naming and shaping of the world might be realised. This isn't an ethic of powerful leaders, unquestioned policy or pre-ordained process, but a call for an engaged and critical citizenry that is capable of determining collectively what is best for itself.

Pragmatics: Employing a Critical Aesthetic

Ethnography, as traditionally interested in the cultural goings-on of people, situates the site of study very much in the *real*, material locations in which people go about their lives. But rather than merely "reporting" on what those goings-on are, ethnography also shapes the way culture is understood through a direct representational imperative—the ethnography, via the evidence selections, research foci, epistemological bent, institutional demands, and so on faced by the ethnographer, "writes" the culture (Jameson, 1990). Denzin and Lincoln (2005) similarly suggest that

> qualitative research is a situated activity that locates the observer in the world. It consists of a set of interpretive, material practices that make the world visible. These practices transform the world. They turn the world into a series of representations... (p. 3)

The critical aesthetic suggested here seeks to de-centre the interpretive gaze by engaging multiple "little" ethnographies generated by citizens-as-critics. Such ethnographies would be on-the-spot skirmishes performed as the reading of the cultural landscape is made. Concerns for methodological precision aren't paramount here, but the ability to "read", situate the Self and engage a response to the cultural landscape is a key imperative for the critical aesthetic. This approach to ethnography seeks to *localise* the ethnographic experience and open for critique those findings made by the critically cognisant citizen-as-critic in a participatory and democratic dialogue.

The attendant criticality that critical ethnography adds to this happens to also coincide with the ideas of those who believe that real social activism must happen where people are and where culture "happens". As a method interested in the "cultural practices, praxis, social texts [and] subjectivities" (Denzin & Lincoln, 2005, p. 24) of the everyday, critical ethnography fits the bill nicely as a method that might go beyond being something that is deployed from the tool-box of skills the contemporary academic methodologist might draw on, to being the basis of the way of life of the citizen-as-critic.

Such an approach

> is concerned with moral discourse, with the development of sacred textualities.... [It] asks that the social sciences and the humanities become sites for critical conversations about democracy, race, gender, class, nation-states, globalisation, freedom and community. (Denzin & Lincoln, 2005, p. 3)

Every aspect of culture, "its logic, its arrangements, its explicit and implicit rules" (Miles & Huberman, 1994, p. 6) is target for analysis and critique, and is liabel to be drawn into the set of evidence utilised to make the analysis of culture from the perspective of the citizen-as-critic.

Such methodological positioning requires the maintenance of an approach to "fieldwork" and "data collection" that sees data as being potentially everywhere, and as potentially anything. Everything from the way that space is designed and structured to how individuals go about their everyday activities, to the formation of discourses in advertising, to the composition and form of a piece of graffiti constitutes the "experience" of the field for the citizen-as-critic, and adds contextually to understandings of its boundary. The point is to consciously go looking for the *ordinary* and *everyday* aspects of culture that might normally have been passed by without notice. The critical aesthetic in this regard requires cognisance and recognition of all aspects of the cultural dynamic and the part that even the most seemingly inconsequential cultural artifact plays in making sense.

To this end, while culture may well be ordinary, to paraphrase Raymond Williams (1958), I would add that it is also *everywhere*. It is from this basis that being *in* the field requires recognition of the "total" cultural experience. It is a "total" experience, as the citizen-as-critic never really leaves the field (even if geographically removed, those cultural logics linger on in the learned behaviours of the critic as a culturally grounded individual). The cultural milieu doesn't commence or end necessarily anywhere. But it is within this fluid conceptual location, and not simply the geographic space of a culture alone, that the citizen-as-critic must decipher through selection, analysis and interpretation what *is* culture. These key bits of evidence, extracted from culture as significant by the citizen-as-critic, point to what is and form the locus of a critical reading of what might be. It is from expressions of culture considered as significant that the critical aesthetic can be drawn on to explicate and identify the way things are (as seen by the citizen-as-critic) and then move to offer a view of how things *could* be.

Three bases mark the method of the critical aesthetic conceptualised here:

• Getting one's Self "right"

• Experiencing culture

• Writing back

The first is concerned with how things might be understood and how the experience of being-in-the-world might be mobilised according to the critical aesthetic. This is the concern of coming-to-be as critic from the epistemological vantage point of knowing Self. The second involves the core methodological processes of going out to find *evidence* from culture; this is fieldwork in the strict, academic sense of ethnography. Thirdly, finding avenues in which to write back and develop a dialogue forms the final basis of the critical aesthetic. This last stage intends to have the critical ethnographic pursuit of the second stage actively and meaningfully deployed. This is about giving purpose to the knowledge generated out of the critical ethnographic act, and is interested in mobilising what might be understood after the critical gaze is cast.

Getting One's Self "Right"

"Being" incorporates two fundamental elements: first, that will-to-power of agentic choice and determination and, secondly, the assumption of who one *must be* according to the boundary logic of culture. This is a fluid interplay between the cognisant Self and an ascribing culture, with the understanding of one's Self predicated upon that Self being always situated *in* culture (we can never escape our cultural contexts). As such, coming to terms with how one is positioned socially is the first great step in deploying a critical aesthetic.

Autoethnography opens possibilities for the development of a critical reflexivity wherein senses of Self might come to be understood in terms of the social processes that mediate lived experience and the material realities individuals encounter. It is on this basis that autoethnography offers opportunity for the enactment of a genuinely *critical* aesthetic by means of exploring the Self as a social construct. Within such a critique, possibilities for exposing the mediating role that culture plays in the construction of identities, behaviours and practices become apparent and open a way for deep critique and change.

Of the many purposes to which autoethnographic approaches have and might be put, the view of autoethnography promoted by Holman Jones (2005) is one that offers possibilities for the critical aesthetic. Holman Jones views autoethnography, the personal text, as a critical intervention in social, political and cultural life", one that can "move writers and readers, subjects and objects, tellers and listeners into this space of dialogue, debate and change" (2005, pp. 763–764). Similarly, Ellis sees autoethnography as "research, writing, story and method that connect the autobiographical and personal to the cultural, social, and political" (2004, p. xix). This is a view shared by Spry with her suggestion that autoethnography functions as "a self-narrative that critiques the situatedness of self with others in social contexts" (2001, p. 710), while Neumann adds that autoethnographic "texts democratize the representational sphere of culture by locating the particular experiences of individuals in a tension with dominant expressions of discursive power" (1996, p. 189). This is furthered by Reinelt's assertion that autoethnography operates as "a radical democratic politics—a politics committed to creating space for dialogue and debate that instigates and shapes social change" (1998, p. 285).

Autoethnographies, as personal texts that take account of social, political and cultural experience, present as a mechanism through which a continuum of *conscientisation* (Freire, 2000) might develop, and in which critical interrogations of Self might be mobilised to gain a consciousness of Self. This is an always incomplete process and requires constant renewal and engagement (just as the entire approach to the critical aesthetic requires perpetual deployment in the constantly changing world we inhabit), but it is through autoethnography that a sense of Self as socially constructed/culturally crafted might be gained and recognised.

A couple of things are required processually for this element of the critical aesthetic:

• Firstly, get over yourself, and accept that the epistemological location inhabited by your Self isn't the only epistemological location available, and that, crucially, other individuals will encounter positionings that will differ from that of you. Don't be tempted to run your own imperial adventure by assuming the world to operate under the conditions from which you alone view/believe/enact. There are ways of knowing and ways of being that differ to yours, with the first step of the process of knowing oneself being the acceptance that you are uniquely individual and hence carry the epistemological positioning of an individual. It follows that any such views of the world developed by you will hence speak truth to you; but cognisance that other *truths* also exist must be recognised.

• Start to look around and begin charting your identity, the bases of your beliefs and the pragmatics of your practices against those expected of you. What is expected of who you are? How do these expectations of who you are *supposed to be* mediate your behaviours and those like you? What does it mean to be male-female, black-white, privileged-underprivileged, abled-disabled, young-old as you experience these things and as the cultural logic prescribes these locations? What did it mean to be spoken to or looked at in a certain way, treated in a particular manner or dismissed or engaged according to who you are and the location you hold in the social strata? This is the act of realising Self in context of culture, and sifting through the mediations of those identity locations you inhabit. This should also be an act of historicisation—seeing Self as a temporal being that is not only shaped and formed by culture now, but has been from the moment of birth.

• Begin questioning the nature of those identity locations you inhabit and the manner with which these are mediated. What evidentiary bases provide you with a sense of who you are, as they are presented in the normalised, "everyday" locales of culture? Where do you see your culturally mediated Self represented in culture and how might you enact an agency that allows space to move and *be* outside of the mediated prescriptions set forth? This is an act of actively seeking out those artifacts of culture that prescribe and frame identity locations to open these for critique and dismantling.

The autoethnographic process articulated here holds as its principle concern the "getting right of one's Self" through the realisation that identity locations are mediated. It is important to note here that "there is no pretense that one is on a mission to reconstruct the *Truth* of a life lived" (Austin, 2005, p. 21, emphasis added), but that

the intention is to open up the [Self] for interrogation in the present so as to contribute to a greater self-awareness and self-understanding. How I am today is in part the result of how I have acted, believed, rejected, derided, ignored and embraced certain views of the world, and in this, my worldviews haven't been the sole creations of myself, but the outcomes of interactions between myself and the array of social forces that have acted upon me. (Austin, 2005, p. 21)

It is from such a basis that encountering culture head-on is made possible.

Experiencing Culture

Get out, look around and notice things.[7] Look for those things that were once passed by as just being there, as ordinary.[8] Look for the "little" mediations of gender, race, class, ability, age that filter through those unnoticed artifacts of culture, just as you would the stark, grand expressions. Actively engage in "moments of bafflement" (Spivak, 1990, p. 137) and problematise the everyday in order to consider it anew; as a site as worthy of investigation as those less-familiar or out-of-the-ordinary pronouncements of culture that capture your attention. Look beyond the symptoms of things gone wrong—things problematic—and get to the core of the cultural logic that mediates and makes sense of the artifact under investigation. Exert a criticality that isn't content to repair the cracks whilst ignoring underlying fissures, and seek understandings that go to the heart of the matter—culture itself. But in doing so, identify "evidence" in the cultural artifacts that fill our world and stand as signifiers of the logics that power our collective understandings. Remember that culture is everywhere, and that it is through its artifacts that it comes to *mean*. This is the stage of the critical aesthetic in which the citizen-as-critic gains an understanding of what is happening and how it happens in the world by deliberately seeking exposure to it.

Methodologically, Seidel's (1998) model of analysis, in which a tripartite arrangement of *Noticing*, *Collecting* and *Thinking About Interesting Things* constitutes the basis of a fieldwork, is an analytic strategy that applies neatly to the critical aesthetic. Albeit a methodological approach to ethnography and qualitative data analysis deployed in the academy, the significance of Seidel's (1998) approach as it applies to the critical aesthetic lay in its recognition of the cyclical nature of the analytic process and the continual reference it makes to the cultural contexts from which evidence is yielded. There isn't a necessary or linear flow through each stage, as Seidel (1998) notes when suggesting that

> when you are thinking about things you also start noticing new things in the data. You then collect and think about these new things. In principle the process is an infinite spiral. (p. 2)

There is an iterative nature in Seidel's model that works precisely with the concerns of the critical aesthetic. Just as culture is never fixed and constant, nor should any analytical process deployed with the intention of understanding culture be locked into a processual framework. There must be an interplay and an inbuilt ability to revisit, reframe and reconsider evidence in light of shifts and changes (both in culture and on the researcher citizen-as-critic).

In terms of deploying the analytic process, *Noticing* constitutes "going out into the world and noticing interesting things" (p. 3). This is a core aspect of the "fieldwork" element of the critical aesthetic, and is activated according to being-in-the-world as a critically conscious, Self-aware citizen-as-critic. The things being noticed might variously relate to what *happens* in culture and how this comes to situate the Self and those around; the determination of what should be noticed and signified as "interesting" phenomena will rest with the citizen-as-critic. As a cognisant and critically conscious being, those aspects of culture that matter and impact on the citizen-as-critic will present in culture and be the focus of the critical aesthetic at that moment. By noticing certain aspects of culture, the citizen-as-critic is holding that aspect as worthy of attention and as something that matters (if only to the experience of the world by the citizen-as-critic as an individual alone).

Collecting, for Seidel (1998), is about actually "collecting" evidence from culture. It is this act of collecting, whether it be through the physical act of accumulating artifacts of culture, or the storing in the memory of things encountered whilst noticing, that the evidentiary base is formed. In line with Seidel's suggestions that this process is cyclical, with each stage interconnected with the other, collecting becomes a process of "mining" areas/situations/events/artifacts/behaviours/patterns noticed until a *saturation* becomes evident. It may well occur, however, that prior to a theme being saturated to the point that the citizen-as-critic can learn nothing more from it, related areas emerge, in which the "noticing" of new sub-themes leads to the subsequent "collection" and "thinking" about these evidence sources in new ways.[9]

Thinking About Interesting Things must be an ongoing part of the critical aesthetic, and does not stop after the citizen-as-critic "goes home". Thinking is where the interpretative lens is applied to the evidence gathered whilst collecting, and where a conceptualisation of how things "are" forms in the mind of the citizen-as-critic. "*What am I looking at, and what does this mean*" is the motivating question at this point in the process.

Overall, Seidel's model provides a useful framework from which the deployment of the critical aesthetic might happen. In continually connecting to culture, the Self-conscious citizen-as-critic might mobilise a method for viewing and noticing the operations of culture from a critical standpoint, and most significantly, have space and an evidentiary set of experiences from which to write back.

Writing Back

Armed with a Self-conscious and evidence-rich reading of the world, the citizen-as-critic must now mobilise a response that expresses the interests of all and meets the needs of those "commandments" detailed above. It isn't enough to simply "know" how culture operates and be outraged at how things are; the citizen-as-critic must assume a responsibility for setting things right. It is not enough to be able to deconstruct a text or decode a film, or read the artifice within a television programme, or know why a particular billboard sign is sexist, or why the use of a certain word carries racial legacies, and then go home and keep doing what you did the way you did it the day before. It is far more important than that. If we are indeed to have a genuinely democratic and participatory social order, we need to move beyond being *only* aware of how that social order is constructed and functions, and *apply* a criticality by mobilising *change*. This might be uncomfortable—it might mean coming to terms with one's own privilege and the marginalisation exerted passively over others through simply being who you are. Other times it might seem impossible, as if the entire weight of "the system" is pitted against your race, ethnicity, class, gender or sexuality and the efforts you make to balance the score.

This stage of the critical aesthetic requires the consciousness of Self and awareness of being-in-the-world undertaken in the autoethnographic stage, linked with what was uncovered in the act of experiencing culture, to prompt insight, indignation and humility at what confronts us as individuals. It also requires the awareness that even the most localised, ordinary and everyday interactions can be transformative, and that the will to do *something* must exist as a fundamental and necessary part of the critical aesthetic.

Demonstrations of exactly the sort of ethic suggested here might include the stark, large-scale demonstrations of resistance and change expressed in revolutionary activism, but equally include more localised pronouncements such as Talen's (2003) critique and action against the monopolising of public space by various "corporate" giants, Lee's (2010) online mobilisation of unionists internationally to speak out against marginalisation of workers, Hagan's (see Hickey, Austin, & Hagan, 2007) challenge to a local council and sports club over the display of racist language in a public sporting oval, Nolan's (see Hickey & Austin, 2007b) responses as an activist teacher and scientist to a specific "action group" interested in contriving public opinion during a local government referendum. Even closer in, simply engaging and challenging discriminatory banter in conversations, speaking out in public forums when things aren't right and exposing things for what they are matters. *Doing something* is an imperative with which the citizen-as-critic must engage the critical aesthetic. For transformation to occur, imagining the way things could be and seeking to enact these visions is fundamental.

Conclusions

All the critical aesthetic asks is for each of us to simply *be*, but, in doing this, to *be critically* and begin expecting more from culture. The manner with which culture is produced and mediated needs to be reframed to include each of us. As Giroux (2004) reminds us, "profound transformations have taken place in the public space" (p. 498), with the public spaces we inhabit functioning as both active hosts of artifacts of public pedagogical production that frame ways of knowing and ways of being according to specific interests. This is the production of the boundary of culture, but in our late-capitalist, neoliberalised, global world, the reassertion of our own interpretative agency as individuals must occur. As citizens we negotiate our public spaces whilst being bombarded with information flows, each drawing their own discursive formations and identity-forming practices. We absorb the flows and interact as individuals contextualised by our cultural environments. But it is how we come to see these things and how we connect what is promised by culture to what *is* that matters. Our experience must not be voyeuristic alone; it must be active and critical. It must seek out the logic of power plays and contested meaning. It must look for manufacturings of identity. In short, if any intent for democratic participation in the formation of our culture is to occur, we must engage as individuals our own critical aesthetic and begin reading the world critically whilst also casting back our views, ideals and opinions. To do anything else is to largely accept the way things are.

The critical aesthetic is a methodological approach that asks for critical ethnographic concern to be liberated from the academy; to do more than reside in journal articles and books. It also asks for a critical citizenry to deploy the tools of the academician and methodologist to *read* the social landscapes we inhabit in localised, individualised ways. But at core, its purpose is clear. It hopes to dismantle uncontested expressions of power via acts of critique and resistance. It seeks the formation of a participatory social landscape that people might actively be a part of, instead of simply witnessing and accepting unwittingly those machinations a selected few might mobilise in their own interests.

Notes

1. In these forums, knowledge as *knowing* becomes a casualty. Knowledge is now entertainment, or more precisely, the ability to gain access to those channels of entertainment that maintain cultural logics and present as guides for being. We exist between images of what we expect and desire, with "the word" now relegated to the back seat, unable to mean in our visually frenetic world as it may have once.

2. Referred to variously as the "super-rich" (Beeghley, 2004), the "superclass" (Rothkopf, 2008), the "nomenklatura" (Voslensky, 1984), the "over-class" and the "top-out-of-sight class" (Fussell, 1992).

3. No other "event" like the Global Financial Crisis provides a more fitting example of the insidiousness of socialised responsibility when things go wrong. Those "elites" who were happy to take what they could from the global economy when the going was good quickly pressured for government assistance when unfettered capitalism turned out to be not such a good idea. Naturally, some economists will note that government intervention was necessary to soften the blow of the downturn, but it still remains that this sort of capitalism was allowed to get to the point of catastrophe that it did.

4. A simple, but stark, statistic that has to some extent entered the public consciousness, and is generally agreed to be unconscionable but still accepted as "the way it is", relates to the United Nations finding that the wealthiest 10% of the world's population account for 85% of the world's wealth (Davies, Sandström, Shorrocks, & Wolff, 2008). Why are we not outraged to the point of action on this? Possibly because we know, deep down, that our own prosperity in the West hinges on this sort of inequity.

5. As David Harvey cogently points out, "how is it then, that the 'rest of us' have so easily acquiesced in this state of affairs?" (2005, p. 38).

6. To borrow very loosely from the title of The Who's seminal track, "Won't Get Fooled Again".

7. This does not automatically suggest that the citizen-as-critic must "get out" according to the geographic locatedness they hold. Getting out equally refers to leaving the realm of those deeply held assumptions and perspectives of the world that the autoethnographic stage of the critical aesthetic hopes to encounter and open for interrogation. Nor does it suggest that culture only happens "outside"; just as much impetus for the critical aesthetic should be given in those quieter moments, excavating those spaces closest in.

8. By means of this "re-experiencing of the ordinary" (Shor, 1987, p. 93) and an intentional critical excavation of ordinary social practices, a conceptual space to consider the constructedness and imperatives of power that are bound up in everyday practices emerges.

9. Sorting becomes a component of this point of Seidel's process. How should multiple sources of evidence be considered and organised? Seidel notes that at this point, your goals are 1) to make some type of sense out of each "collection" of evidentiary sources; 2) look for patterns and relationships both within a collection, and also across collections; and 3) to make general discoveries about the phenomena you are researching (1998, p. 5). The continual linking back to culture of assumptions drawn and interpretations made must be credenced by the citizen-as-critic if the interpretations made are to have any weight in the attempt to understand the way things are in culture.

References

Austin, J. (2005). Investigating the self: Autoethnography and identity work. In J. Austin (Ed.), *Culture and identity*. Frenchs Forest, NSW, Australia: Pearson Education Australia.

Austin, J., & Hickey, A. (2008). Critical pedagogical practice through cultural studies. *International Journal of the Humanities, 6*(1), 133–140.

Bauman, Z. (2001). *Community: Seeking safety in an insecure world*. Cambridge, England: Polity.

Beeghley, L. (2004). *The structure of social stratification in the United States*. Boston, MA: Allyn and Bacon.

Cohen, A. (2004). *The symbolic construction of community*. London, England: Routledge.

Davies, J. B., Sandström, S., Shorrocks, A., & Wolff, E. N. (2008). *The world distribution of household wealth* (UN-WIDER Discussion Paper 2008/03). Retrieved April 10, 2010, from http://www.wider.unu.edu/publications/working-papers/discussion-papers/2008/en_GB/dp2008–03/

De Beauvoir, S. (1949). *The second sex*. London, England: Vintage.

Denzin, N. K., & Lincoln, Y. S. (Eds.). (2005). *The Sage handbook of qualitative research* (3rd ed.). Thousand Oaks, CA: Sage.

Dewey, J. (1997). *Democracy and education: An introduction to the philosophy of education*. New York, NY: Free Press.

Dewey, J. (2008). *The school and society*. Dehli, India: Aakar Books.

Ellis, C. (2004). *The ethnographic I: A methodological novel about teaching and doing autoethnography*. Walnut Creek, CA: Alta Mira.

Ellis, C., & Bochner, A., (Eds.). (1996). *Composing ethnography: Alternative forms of ethnographic writing*. Walnut Creek, CA: Alta Mira.

Foucault, M. (1977). *Power/knowledge: Selected interviews and other writings 1972–1977*. New York, NY: Pantheon.

Freire, P. (1985a). *The politics of education: Culture, power and liberation*. London, England: Macmillan.

Freire, P. (1985b). *The politics of education: Culture, power, and liberation*. South Hadley, MA: Bergin & Garvey.

Freire, P. (2000). *Pedagogy of the oppressed*. New York, NY: Continuum.

Freire, P. (2006). *Teachers as cultural workers: Letters to those who dare to teach* (2nd ed.). Boulder, CO: Westview.

Fussell, P. (1992). *Class: A guide through the American status system*. New York, NY: Touchstone.

Gilbert, D. (1998). *The American class structure*. New York, NY: Wadsworth.

Giroux, H. (1988). *Schooling and the struggle for public life*. New York, NY: Routledge.

Giroux, H. (1999). *The mouse that roared: Disney and the end of innocence*. New York, NY: Rowman & Littlefield.

Giroux, H. (2004). Public pedagogy and the politics of neo-liberalism: making the political more pedagogical. *Policy Futures in Education, 2*(3/4), 494–503.

Giroux, H. (2005). *Border crossings: Cultural workers and the politics of education* (2nd ed.). New York, NY: Routledge.

Giroux, H. (2008). *Against the terror of neoliberalism: Politics beyond the age of greed*. Boulder, CO: Paradigm.

Giroux, H. (2009). *Youth in a suspect society: Democracy or disposability?* New York, NY: Palgrave-Macmillan.

Goodall, H. L. (2000). *Writing the new ethnography*. Walnut Creek, CA: Alta Mira.

Harvey, D. (2005). *A brief history of neoliberalism*. Oxford, England: OUP.

Hickey, A., & Austin, J. (2007a). Pedagogies of self: Conscientising the personal to the social. *International Journal of Pedagogies and Learning, 3*(1), 21–29.

Hickey, A., & Austin, J. (2007b). Engaging community resource issues: The Toowoomba water futures debate. In J. Austin & A. Hickey (Eds.), *Education for healthy communities: Possibilities through SOSE and HPE*. Frenchs Forest, NSW, Australia: Pearson Education Australia.

Hickey, A., Austin, J., & Hagan, S. (2007). Standing up to racism: The "nigger brown" stand. In J. Austin & A. Hickey (Eds.), *Education for healthy communities: Possibilities through SOSE and HPE*. Frenchs Forest, NSW, Australia: Pearson Education Australia.

Holman Jones, S. (2005). Autoethnography: Making the personal political. In N. K. Denzin & Y. S. Lincoln (Eds.), *The Sage handbook of qualitative research* (pp. 763–791). Thousand Oaks, CA: Sage.

Jameson, F (1990). *Signatures of the visible*. New York, NY: Routledge.

Kant, I. (1990). *Critique of pure reason*. Amherst, NY: Prometheus.

Kincheloe, J. L. (2008). Critical pedagogy and the knowledge wars of the twenty-first century. *International Journal of Critical Pedagogy, 1*(1), 1–22.

Lee, E. (2010). About LabourStart. Retrieved April 20, 2010, from http://www.labourstart.org/

Madison, D. S. (2005). *Critical ethnography: Method, ethics and performance*. Thousand Oaks, CA: Sage.

Marcuse, H. (1991). *One dimensional man*. Boston, MA: Beacon Press.

Miles, M. B., & Huberman, A. M. (1994). *Qualitative data analysis: An expanded sourcebook* (2nd ed.). Thousand Oaks, CA: Sage.

Neumann, M. (1996). Collecting ourselves at the end of the century. In C. Ellis & A. Bochner (Eds.), *Composing ethnography: Alternative forms of ethnographic writing* (pp. 172–198). Walnut Creek, CA: Alta Mira.

Olesen, V. L. (2000). Feminisms and qualitative research at and into the new millennium. In N. K. Denzin & Y. S. Lincoln (Eds.), *Handbook of qualitative research* (2nd ed., pp. 215–255). Thousand Oaks, CA: Sage.

Reinelt, J. (1998). Notes for a radical democratic theatre: Productive crisis and the challenge of indeterminancy. In J. Colleran & J. S. Spencer (Eds.), *Staging resistance: Essays on political theatre*. Ann Arbor: University of Michigan Press.

Rothkopf, D. (2008). *Superclass: The global power elite and the world they are making.* New York, NY: Farrar, Straus and Giroux.

Sandlin, J., Schultz, B., & Burdick, J. (Eds.). (2010). *The handbook of public pedagogy.* New York, NY: Routledge.

Saukko, P. (2005). Methodologies for cultural studies: An integrative approach. In N. K. Denzin & Y. S. Lincoln (Eds.), *The Sage handbook of qualitative research* (3rd ed., pp. 343–356). Thousand Oaks, CA: Sage.

Seidel, J. (1998). *Qualitative data analysis.* Retrieved May 5, 2010, from ftp://ftp.qualisresearch.com/pub/qda.pdf

Shor, I. (1987). *Critical teaching and everyday life.* Chicago, IL: University of Chicago Press.

Spivak, G. C. (1990). *The post-colonial critic: Interviews, strategies, dialogues.* New York, NY: Routledge.

Spry, T. (2001). Performing autoethnography: An embodied methodological practice. *Qualitative Inquiry, 7*(6), 706–732.

Steinberg, S. R. (2006). Critical cultural studies research: Bricolage in action. In K. Tobin & J. Kincheloe (Eds.), *Doing educational research: A handbook*. Rotterdam, The Netherlands: Sense.

Stiglitz, J. (2008, September 16). The fruit of hypocrisy: Dishonesty in the finance sector dragged us here, and Washington looks ill-equipped to guide us out. *The Guardian.*

Talen, B. (2003). *What should I do if Reverend Billy is in my store?* New York, NY: New Press.

The Who (1971). Won't get fooled again. On *Who's Next* [CD]. London, England: Polydor.

Voslensky, M. (1984). *Nomenklatura: The Soviet ruling class.* London, England: Doubleday.

Williams, R. (1958). *Culture and society.* London, England: Chatto & Windus.

CHAPTER THIRTEEN

Critical Cultural Studies Research: Bricolage in Action

Shirley R. Steinberg

I n the contemporary information environment of the twenty-first century—so aptly named hyper-reality by Jean Baudrillard—knowledge takes on a different shape and quality. What appears to be commonsense dissipates slowly into the ether, as electronic media refract the world in ways that benefit the purveyors of power. We have never seen anything like this before, a new world—new forms of social regulation, new forms of disinformation, and new modes of hegemony and ideology. In such a cyber/mediated jungle new modes of research are absolutely necessary. This chapter proposes a form of critical cultural studies research that explores what I refer to as cultural pedagogy. Cultural pedagogy is the educational dimension of hyperreality, as learning migrates into new socio-cultural and political spaces. In these pages, I will focus my attention on my research with film, specifically on *doing educational research* with a bricolage of methods leading to tentative interpretations.

Cultural Studies

Observing that the study of culture can be fragmented between the disciplines, those who advocate cultural studies look at an interdisciplinary approach, that which transcends any one field. Additionally, a critical cultural studies does not commit a qualitative evaluation of culture by a definition of "high" or "low" culture, and culture may be the most ambiguous and complex term to define in the domain of the social sciences and humanities. Arthur Asa Berger (1995) estimates that anthropologists alone have offered more than one hundred definitions of culture. At the risk of great reductionism, I use the term in this chapter to signify behavior patterns socially acquired and transmitted by the use of social symbols such as language, art, science, morals, values, belief systems, politics, and many more. Educators are directly implicated in the analysis of culture (or should be) in that culture is transmitted by processes of teaching and learning, whether formally (schools) or informally (by wider social processes, e.g., popular culture). This pedagogical dynamic within all culture is a central concern of this chapter.

Indeed, culture is inseparable from the human ability to be acculturated, to learn, to employ language and symbols.

Culture, in this chapter, involves specifically its deployment in connection with the arts. This is where we move into the social territory traditionally referred to as elite or high culture, and popular culture. Individuals who attend symphonies, read the "great books," enjoy the ballet, are steeped in elite culture—or, as it is often phrased, "are cultured." Referring to "low" culture, many scholars assert that the artifacts that grew within a local or regional movement are indeed low. Fitting neither into a category of low or high culture is mass culture. Cultural theorists do not agree on any one definition for each type of culture. However, Dwight MacDonald summarizes the difference between the three, and the propensity of all types of culture to become political:

> Folk art grew from below. It was a spontaneous, autochthonous expression of the people, shaped by themselves, pretty much without the benefit of High Culture, to suit their own needs. Mass Culture is imposed from above. It is fabricated by technicians hired by businessmen; its audiences are passive consumers, their participation limited to the choice between buying and not buying.... Folk Art was the people's own institution, their private little garden walled off from the great formal park of their master's High Culture. But Mass Culture breaks down the wall, integrating the masses into a debased form of High Culture and thus becoming an instrument of political domination. (MacDonald, 1957, p. 60)

Within critical cultural studies it is maintained that the boundary between elite/high culture and popular/low culture is blurring. Such occurrence holds important ramifications for those interested in pedagogy (Berger, 1995). The study of culture, for the purposes of this chapter, is not to delineate the "level" or "type" of culture invoked by popular films, but to discuss the pedagogical, sociological, and political themes within the films. Consequently, a debate as to the "quality" of popular culture or its place in the light of elite culture will not be undertaken. I will use the term popular culture to define that which is readily available to the American public as a form of enjoyment and consumption.

Popular culture defies easy definition. It can be defined as the culture of ordinary people—TV shows, movies, records, radio, foods, fashions, magazines, and other artifacts that figure in our everyday lives (Berger, 1995). Often analysts maintain that such artifacts are mass-mediated and consumed by large numbers of individuals on a continuing basis. Such phenomena are often viewed condescendingly by academicians as unworthy of scholarly analysis. As addressed in this chapter, the aesthetic dynamics of popular culture are not the focus; rather the social, political, and pedagogical messages contained in popular culture and their effects are viewed as some of the most important influences in the contemporary era. In this context the study of popular culture is connected with the sociology of everyday life and the interaction and interconnection of this micro-domain with macro-socio-political and structural forces. Thus, the popular domain—as ambiguous and ever-shifting as it may be—takes on unprecedented importance in the electronically saturated contemporary era.

Cultural Studies and Pedagogy

Cultural studies and pedagogy involves education and acculturation that takes place at a variety of cultural locations including but not limited to formal educational institutions. Cultural studies scholars extend our notion of cultural pedagogy, focusing their attention on the complex interactions of power, knowledge, identity, and politics. Issues of cultural pedagogy that arise in this context include:

1. the complex relationship between power and knowledge.

2. the ways knowledge is produced, accepted, and rejected.

3. what individuals claim to know and the process by which they come to know it.

4. the nature of cultural/political authority and its relation to the dialectic of empowerment and domination.

5. the way individuals receive dominant representations and encodings of the world—are they assimilated, internalized, resisted, or transformed?

6. the manner in which individuals negotiate their relationship with the "official story," the legitimate canon.

7. the means by which the official and legitimated narrative positions students and citizens to make sense of their personal experience.

8. the process by which pleasure is derived from engagement with the dominant culture—an investment that produces meaning and formulates affect.

9. the methods by which cultural differences along lines of race, class, gender, national origin, religion, and geographical place are encoded in consciousness and processed by individuals.

10. the ways scientific rationality shapes consciousness in schools and the culture at large.

It is with the above issues in mind that I create my bricolage.

The attempt to delineate a universal research method for the study of the cultural curriculum and cultural pedagogy is a futile quest. The critical research of cultural studies and cultural pedagogy can make no guarantee about what questions will be important in different contexts; thus, no one method should be promoted over others—at the same time, none can be eliminated without examination. Ethnography, textual analysis, semiotics, deconstruction, critical hermeneutics, interviews, psychoanalysis, content analysis, survey research, and phenomenology simply initiate a list of research methods an educational scholar might bring to the table. Such an eclectic view of research has been labeled *bricolage* by several scholars. A term attributed to Claude Lévi-Strauss (1966), bricolage (use of a tool box) involves taking research strategies from a variety of scholarly disciplines and traditions as they are needed in the unfolding context of the research situation. Such an action is pragmatic and strategic, demanding self-consciousness and awareness of context from the researcher. The *bricoleur,* the researcher who employs bricolage, must be able to orchestrate a plethora of diverse tasks including interviewing and observing, to historiographical analysis, to self-monitoring and intrapersonal understanding.

The text produced by this research process of bricolage should be a complex collage, as it weaves together the scholar's images, insights, and interpretations of the relationship between the popular cultural text, critical questions of justice, the social context that produced it, and its effect on youth and the cultural curriculum (Kincheloe & Berry, 2004). Using theoretical and conceptual frames drawn from critical theory, poststructuralism, postmodern epistemologies, feminism, psychoanalysis, hermeneutics, recovery theory and other traditions, bricolage interprets, critiques, and deconstructs the text in question. Because scientific research has traditionally offered only a partial vision of the reality it seeks to explore, pedagogical bricoleurs attempt to widen their perspectives through methodological diversity. In no way, however, do they claim that as the result of the multiperspective bricolage they have gained "the grand view"—from their poststructuralist perspective they understand that all inquiry is limited and incomplete. Humble in this knowledge, the bricoleur attempts to gain expanded insight via historical contextualization, multiple theoretical groundings, and a diversity of knowledge by collecting and interpreting methodologies (Kincheloe, 2005).

Theoretical bricolage compensates for the blindness of relying on one model of reading a cultural text. Bricolage does not draw upon diverse theoretical/methodological traditions simply for the sake of diversity. Rather, it uses the different approaches to inform and critique each other. A critical theoretical analysis of popular culture, for example, that is informed by psychoanalysis will be different than one that relies only on the sociological dimension of the text under analysis. Such an interpretive process subverts the tendency of knowledge producers to slip into the position that their interpretation is the "right one" (Kincheloe, 2005). As we study the pedagogy of film, we are able to position it not only in historical, socio-political, and economic context, but in relation to other films on a particular topic, with similar themes, or identified with a particular genre—for example, the films of John Hughes concerning middle-class male misbehavior. Expanding our ways of seeing with diverse perspectives, we begin to grasp the ideological dimensions of films that often fall through the cracks. A more specific focus on how particular methodologies may be used in this popular cultural/film context may be in order.

Critical Ethnography

Critical ethnography is an example of a critical research methodology that can be used within the bricolage. Ethnography is often described as the most basic form of social research: the analysis of events as they evolve in their natural setting. While ethnographers disagree about the relative importance of each purpose, ethnography attempts to gain knowledge about a cultural setting, to identify patterns of social interaction, and to develop holistic interpretations of societies and social institutions. Thus, typical educational ethnographies attempt to understand the nature of schools and other educational agencies in these ways, seeking to appreciate the social processes that move educational events. Ethnography attempts to make explicit the social processes one takes for granted as a culture member. The culture could be as broad as the study of an ethnic culture or as narrow as the middle-class white male culture of misbehavior. The critical ethnographer of education seeks to describe the concrete experiences of everyday school/educational life and the social patterns, the deep structures that support it (Hammersley & Atkinson, 1983). In a bricolage, ethnography can be used in a variety of ways to gain insight into film. The most traditional involves audience studies where ethnographers observe and interview film audiences. John Fiske (1993) began his book *Power Plays, Power Works* using such a methodology, as he observed and interviewed a group of homeless men in a shelter as they watched the movie *Die Hard*. What was the nature of the interrelationship between the viewers and the text? What did the men's responses to the film tell us about their self-images? What did the men's responses tell us about film viewing in general and its ideological effects? Fiske's effort to answer these questions—to interpret his data—constitutes much of the content of the book.

In addition to such "audiencing" ethnographies, scholars can use ethnographic methods to explore the characters and cultures portrayed within the film and their relation to social dynamics outside the texts. Gaining knowledge about the "film culture" provides insight into the ideological orientations of film makers and entertainment corporations. Through the identification of patterns of cultural expression and social interaction, researchers can begin to specify the ideological dynamics at work. As socio-political processes are exposed, hidden agendas and tacit assumptions can be highlighted so as to provide new appreciations of the power of film to both reflect and shape culture. Poststructuralist forms of ethnography have focused on the discontinuities, contradictions, and inconsistencies of cultural expression and human action. As opposed to more modernist forms of ethnography, poststructuralist methods refuse to reconcile the asymmetries once and for all. The poststructuralist dimension of ethnography highlights the tendency of classical ethnography to privilege a dominant narrative and a unitary, privileged vantage point. In the effort to connect knower and known, the poststructuralist ethnographer proposes a dialogue between researcher and researched that attempts to smash traditional hierarchical relations between them (Atkinson & Hammersley, 1994).

In this critical process the modernist notion of ethnography as an instrument of enlightenment and civilization of the "native" *objects* of study is overthrown. Poststructuralist ethnographies are texts to be argued over, texts whose meaning is never "natural" but are constructed by circumstance and inscribed by context (Aronowitz, 1993). Thus, a film never stands alone as an object of study in poststructuralist ethnography. Seen as a living part of culture and history, the film takes on new meaning and circumstances, and contexts change. How different the movie *The Green Berets* (1968) looked to the young audience that viewed it in the late 1960s and early 1970s than it does to young people viewing it in the post-Gulf War 1990s. More young people of the present era may positively resonate with the ideological intentions of the film makers than did young, anti-war viewers of the era in which it was produced. Circumstance and context must always be accounted for in critical poststructuralist ethnography. In this context poststructuralist ethnography informs and is informed by feminist and minority researchers concerned with the status quo of apologetics of film and traditional ethnography itself.

Content Analysis

Traditionally a content analysis could be considered methodical and quantitative in nature. The important issue about literally analyzing text is to allow the text to open and present themes for the researcher. Following is a method I have used with success in first, analyzing text, and second, in letting the textual analysis speak to me and suggest the themes that can be included. The content analysis then becomes an authentic interpretive analysis that precludes preliminary hypotheses, and instead waits to allow the data to speak for themselves in muli-layered ways. The analysis especially lends itself to research in film, written text, visual text (comics, photography, etc.). It then becomes ready for the critical hermeneutic interpretation which is my tentative research goal.

In addition to such ethnographic analysis, critical educational scholars use other methods of studying the social dynamics and effects of film. Douglas Kellner (1995) performs content analyses of film reviews and criticisms, in the process gaining new vantage points on the ways that film texts become embedded in popular discourses. This "mode of reception" study was promoted by the Frankfurt School critical theorist Walter Benjamin (Kellner, 1995). Appropriating Benjamin's methodology, literary critics and theorists developed literary reception research that continues to contribute innovative ways of exploring textual effects. Distributed throughout Aaron Gresson's analysis of *Forrest Gump* is the discussion of the film by various critics and the news media. Beginning with the traditional "thumbs up" or "thumbs down" types of articles and moving to more esoteric and scholarly discussion, Gresson is able to trace themes relating back to his original suggestion of the recovery of whiteness and maleness in film (Gresson, 1996). In this context, various research methodologies can be added to the bricolage, in the process providing ever more nuanced forms of insight into popular cultural texts.

Semiotics plays an invaluable role in the methodological pantheon with its focus on codes and signs that contribute to individuals' attempts to derive meaning from their surroundings. Educational researchers can use semiotic methods to gain insights into the social dynamics moving classroom events. Classrooms are full of codes calling out for semiotic analysis. Not only are classrooms saturated with codes and signs, but they are characterized by rituals and conventions that are rarely questioned. The ways teachers, students, and administrators dress; pupils' language when speaking to teachers as compared to conversations with classmates; graffiti in a middle school restroom; systems of rules of behavior; the uses of bells and the intercom in schools; memos sent to parents; and the nature of the local community's conversation about school athletics are only a few of the topics an educational semiotician could study.

Observation Methods

Contrary to notions that qualitative research dealing with popular culture is vacuous and without rigor, I submit my methodology in the spirit of academic scholarship and, indeed, a poststructuralist, feminist, pedagogical research in which I am not seeking answers, but seeking questions, questions and more questions in which to make sense of the world of youth and of education. In their *Handbook of*

Qualitative Research, Norm Denzin and Yvonna Lincoln (2005) discuss their union of poststructural/postmodernist cultural research (Denzin) and constructivist/pedagogical research (Lincoln). They contend that traditional research stops short of boundary crossing within interpretation. Observing that "over the past two decades, a quiet methodological revolution has been taking place in the social sciences" (1994, p. ix) Denzin and Lincoln define this revolution as the "blurring" of the boundaries within disciplinary research. As I discuss my methods and objectives in my research, keep in mind that I want to make "noise" in this so-called "quiet" revolution. In fact, I question whether or not it has ever been quiet. Certainly there have been attempts to silence the noise caused by radical qualitative research—silence in the denial of the politicization of the research of pedagogy; however, my qualitative predecessors have worked long and hard in the legitimization of the discipline. The word *rigor* seems to rear its ugly head at methodological junctures. I assert here that my research is indeed rigorous, challenging, and constantly changing. Unlike a statistical formula, an organized hypothesis, and a proven theorem, I am not beginning with any assumptions other than the one that popular culture must be studied. My thoughts about my subjects and my expectations in my observations changed each time I analyzed and recorded (for lack of a better word) *data.* It was within this discovery and rediscovery that I found rigor and challenge. It is within this context that I present my *literal method of interpretation.* I assert that rigorous scripting, recording, and viewing/re-viewing (or consuming/re-consuming) is essential for critical hermeneutical research, and it is this process I delineate here.

The postmodern condition has also re-determined and re-defined the actual research methods and practices that we use. No longer, as in earlier cultural research, do we view a film at the theater, go to the typewriter and write a response and review. We have the tools of hyperreality: through portability, films are readily available in VHS, DVD, and iMovie. Consequently, we are able to view, then script, interpret, re-interpret, then problematize our interpretations as we attempt to make meaning from the text. Unlike viewer/historians of the past, we are able to re-visit an event, a text, and look for the tacit assumptions that reside within each signifier, floating signifier, code, and ideology presented within the film.

Materials and Process

In order to be able to re-visit and re-view text, I found it essential to have access to videotapes of the films I wished to discuss. Wherever possible, I have avoided even alluding to films still in the theater as I feel they are available for a shallow interpretation at best (unless, of course, one owns his or her own theater). Along with the video tapes, I needed a video recorder, television, and a good remote control. Other "equipment" I needed was an unlimited amount of colored pencils, ruled notebooks, and a pen. However, on review of these methods, I feel that the use of a laptop computer while viewing could have or would have enhanced and possibly quickened the recording method.

In the manner of traditional ethnography, I used scripting as my form of recording. I wrote constantly through each film, usually filling up my notebooks after two films. I wrote quickly and intuitively. I cannot delineate *what* to record. I can only describe that I recorded *everything* that made me think; consequently I relied on my own pedagogical intuition in my records. The use of the remote was essential in being able to rewind and record exact dialogue or to view a scene closely. In some films, I recorded no dialogue, only impressions of the scenery or music or cinematography. In most films I did record dialogue, discerning it as the salient data that would eventually be entered into my hermeneutical interpretations and discussions.

Each film took many hours to watch and re-watch. When I felt comfortable that I had scripted enough to begin my transcriptions, I transcribed the notebooks into word-processed form. Using phrases, I typed my entries going down each page as I had originally written them. After completing the transcription of all of the films, I read through the entire set of data. As I examined this completed set of scripting, themes and motifs started to emerge. As they began to repeat themselves, I wrote down my impressions of their emergence, *named* them as separate entities. After my first reading of the data, I used the colored pencils to code each theme/motif that I wanted to pursue. Underlining each item with a different color, macro-themes began to emerge, as the micro-themes seemed coalesced under the auspices of larger themes. Analyzing all the pages of scripting, I discovered additional themes each time. In many instances there would be three or four different colors under a certain situation or dialogue indicating an overlap among the themes.

A note: Not to appear a "Luddite," I want to clarify that I chose to use both video and DVD in my work. I feel organically connected to the materials in this way, as an audience participant. This is my quirk. However, those with the technical abilities and equipment will find this method quite easy to do digitally using iMovie and competent software.

Both visually and intuitively, I began the task of arranging micro-themes and placing them within the macro-themes. Given the thematic crossover, it was important to not essentialize any situation or dialogue and limit it to only one "category." I kept in mind that through my choice of bricolage, I was not adhering to one method of interpretation; consequently it was important to record and underline each micro-theme every time it emerged in all macro-categories.

Viewing and Naming Films

As this is a chapter discussing critical pedagogical research methods, I chose not to use traditional methods of film theory and criticism. I will delineate three terms that I used within my bricolage. As a bricoleur, I cut and pasted what I felt was significant and examined the multiple meanings that emerged. Traditional film criticism,like any form of sociological research, has categories and philosophies attached to methods of interpretation of audiences and of text. And, as in traditional research, this criticism essentializes and closes itself off to the boundary crossing to which Denzin and Lincoln have chosen to blur. By taking each interpretative method and applying it to a film bricolage, I was able to use film criticism and theory to my advantage in my critical hermeneutical readings.

Traditional film criticism "reads" film in many ways. The most compelling methods and classifications involve concepts such as 1) *auteurism* 2) *montage* and 3) *genre*. Each term has value in critical hermeneutics; however, using them in a unilateral deconstruction would limit interpretation to a dogmatic ideological framework established by the original researcher.

Auteurism

As the name suggests, auteurism refers to the authorship of the text. As in a Derridian deconstruction, the text becomes the only artifact examined, and unlike a Derridian deconstruction, the text in relationship to the author/creator is the essential interpretation. The entire act of meaning making in auteurism is restricted to who the author is, his or her positionality, and tacit and overt agendas in regard to the text. While I would be unable to discount the inclusion of auteurism in interpreting film text, in no way would I be comfortable limiting the interpretation to this narrow theory. In the case of the writer/director John Hughes—on whose films I rely heavily in my research—I cannot discount the fact that he is a white, middle-class male, and a baby boomer from Chicago. Further discovery of his own background and education *can* inform me about him and "where he comes from." However, to allow auteurism to define the purpose of his films, for example: Ferris Bueller *is* John Hughes, or Hughes's plotlines revolve around his own personal agenda for humiliating adults, would direct and possibly limit my interpretation(s). Robin Wood (1995) insists that limiting film theory to auteurism adds to the propensity of inconclusive, inaccurate research that insists "on its own particular polarization" (p. 59).

Montage

Like auteurism, montage relies on one lens through which to view a text. Unlike auteurism, montage examines the intent of the editor in the analysis of the "essential creative act" of film making (Wood,

1995). While auteur theory exclusively read the act of the author as the textual interpretation, montage theory introduces the notion that the cutting-room floor becomes the site for the decisive interpretative act. Once again, one cannot ignore the possible intent of the film editor and/or cinematographer, however, to limit interpretation to montage at the expense of any other aspect of film criticism and theory would once again limit the thickness of the interpretation.

Genre

In the traditional literary manner, the concept of genre is used to define and classify texts into manageable categories which immediately allow the interpreter to draw conclusions and make expected observations. For instance, when we refer to the Western as a genre, it is easy to imagine horses, Indians, pioneers, and a white cowboy on a majestic horse. Within genre theory we are able to find familiar Western themes of patriarchy, white supremacy, and colonialism without much effort. If we refer to *film noir*, we easily picture the frames of shadowy figures, a femme fatale and a Bogartesque antihero engaged in questionable activities. Once again, a prevailing theme of patriarchy emerges without question. Consider the 1950s sci-fi genre—a white, middle- to upper-middle-class scientist who goes against the odds to defeat an alien invader—back to patriarchy, colonialism, and so forth. Exclusive reliance on genre theory determines in advance which themes will be analyzed and which will not—again the possibility of new interpretations is truncated. Categorizing texts aids us in the ability to place films on the shelf, to place books in the library and to choose different genres in which to research. However, the discussion of genre should be used only to name, in a general sense, the macro-category of film that the researcher chooses to interpret. The catch is that the genre must be determined and defined by each researcher in the context of his or her own research. Consequently, what I view as a Western may indeed be viewed as a political satire to one researcher and a classic to another.

With the use of auteurism, montage, and genre, I have combined the qualitative method of bricolage using critical ethnography, semiotics, feminist theory, and critical hermeneutics to interpret my research.

Feminist Research

Another important aspect of the bricolage involves feminist research with its subversion of the principle of neutral, hierarchical, and estranged interaction between researcher and researched (Clough, 1992). It is important that no one body of feminist theory exists. Three forms of feminist analysis have dominated the feminist critique:

1. liberal feminism has focused on gender stereotyping and bias. While such analyses have provided valuable insights, liberal feminism in general has failed to engage issues of power. As a result, the position has been hard pressed to make sense of social reality with its subtle interactions of power, ideology, and culture—an interaction that needs to be analyzed in the larger effort to understand both the oppression of women and male privilege (Rosneau, 1992);

2. radical feminism has maintained that the subjugation of women is the most important form of oppression in that it is grounded in specific biological differences between men and women. In radical feminism concerns with race and class are more rejected than ignored, as radical feminists maintain the irrelevance of such categories in the study of women's oppression;

3. the form of feminist theory privileged in my research is critical poststructuralist feminism. This articulation of feminism asserts that feminism is the quintessential postmodern discourse. As feminists focus on and affirm that which is absent and/or peripheral in modernist ways of seeing, they ground the poststructuralist critique in lived reality, in the material world (Kipnis,

1992). As critical poststructuralist feminists challenge modernist patriarchal exclusions, they analyze the connections between an unjust class structure and the oppression of women (Ros- neau, 1992). Often, they contend, male domination of women is concretized on the terrain of class—e.g., the feminization of poverty and the growth in the number of women who are homeless over the last fifteen years (Kincheloe & Steinberg, 1997).

In this poststructuralist feminist context, research can no longer be seen as a cold, rational process. Feminist research injects feeling, empathy, and the body into the act of inquiry, blurring the distinc- tion between knower and known, viewer and viewed—looking at truth as a *process* of construction in which knowers and viewers play an active role, and embedding passion into the bricolage. Research- ers in this context see themselves as passionate scholars who connect themselves emotionally to what they are seeking to know and understand. Modernist researchers often weeded out the self, denying their intuitions and inner voices, in the process producing restricted and object-like interpretations of socio-educational events. Using the traditional definitions, these object-like interpretations were certain and scientific; feminist self-grounded inquiries were inferior, merely impressionistic, and journalistic (Reinharz, 1992). Rejecting the authority of the certainty of science, feminist researchers charged that the so-called objectivity of modernist science was nothing more than a signifier for the denial of social and ethical responsibility, ideological passivity, and the acceptance of privileged socio-political position of the researcher. Thus, feminist theorists argued that modernist pseudo-objectivity demands the sepa- ration of thought and feeling, the devaluation of any perspective maintained with emotional convic- tion. Feeling is designated as an inferior form of human consciousness—those who rely on thought or logic operating within this framework can justify their repression of those associated with emotion or feeling. Feminist theorists have pointed out that the thought-feeling hierarchy is one of the structures historically used by men to oppress women (Walby, 1990). In intimate heterosexual relationships, if a man is able to present his position in an argument as the rational viewpoint and the woman's position as an emotional perspective, then he has won the argument—his is the voice worth hearing.

Drawing from feminist researchers, critical poststructuralists have learned that inquiry should be informed by our "humanness," that we can use the human as a research instrument. From this perspec- tive inquiry begins with researchers drawing upon their own experience. Such an educational researcher is a human being studying other human beings focusing on their inner world of experience. Utiliz- ing his or her own empathetic understandings, the observer can watch educational phenomena from within—that is, the observer can know directly, he or she can watch and experience. In the process the private is made public. Not only do we get closer to the private experience of students, teachers, and administrators and the effect of these experiences on the public domain, but we also gain access to the private experience of the researcher and the effect of that experience on the public description the researcher presents of the phenomena observed (Reinharz, 1992). Thus not only do we learn about the educational world that surrounds us, but we gain new insights into the private world within us—the world of our constructed subjectivity. By revealing what can be learned from the every-day, the mun- dane, feminist scholars have opened a whole new area of inquiry and insight. They have uncovered the existence of silences and absences where traditional scholars had seen only "what was there." When the feminist critique is deployed within the methodological diversity of the bricolage, new forms of insight into educational and social affairs as well as the cultural curriculum emerge.

Connecting to Social Theory

In examining social dynamics of media/popular culture via the research methodologies of ethnography and semiotics and the political and epistemological concerns of poststructuralist feminism, an effort is made to connect research to the domain of social theory. Indeed, theory is very important in the bri- colage of critical poststructuralist research. Theory involves the conceptual matrix analysts use to make sense of the world. Theory, whether it is held consciously or unconsciously, works as a filter through which researchers approach information, designate facts, identify problems, and devise solutions to their problems. Different theoretical frameworks, therefore, privilege different ways of seeing the world in general or the domain of popular culture in particular (Kincheloe, 2001). The theory behind a critical poststructuralist way of seeing recognizes these theoretical dynamics, especially the potential tyranny that accompanies theoretical speculation. The problem that has undermined the traditional critical project of understanding and changing the inequality plaguing modernist societies has involved the production of a theory that was too totalizing (all-encompassing) and rigid to grasp the *complexity* described here. Critical poststructuralist theory is committed to a theoretical stance that guarantees the individual or community the capacity to make meaning and to act independently. Any theory accept-able to critical poststructuralists, thus, must take into account local divergence. This is not to adopt a position that insists researchers allow phenomena to speak for themselves. Theory in this context is a resource that can be used to generate a dialogue with a phenomenon; it is always contingent and it never whispers the answers to the researcher in advance (Grossberg, 1995). Theory does not travel well from one context to another. Indeed theory's usefulness is always mitigated by context.

Such a locally sensitive theoretical position allows bricolage research a space from which to view movies and popular cultural phenomena that maintains an oppositional but not a totalizing and deter-ministic interpretive strategy (Smith, 1989). Such a strategy searches for manifestations of domination and resistance in popular texts in light of larger questions of democracy (Kellner, 1995). Drawing upon the theoretical work of the Frankfurt School of Critical Theory, the concept of immanent critique helps us understand this oppositional dynamic. Critical theory, according to Max Horkheimer, attempts to expose and assess the breach between reality and ideas or "what is" and "what could be." Within capitalist society, Horkheimer maintained, there is an inherent contradiction between the bourgeois order's words and deeds. The more the power bloc speaks of justice, equality, and freedom, the more it fails under its own standards. Immanent critique, therefore, attempts to evaluate cultural production "from within," on the basis of the standards of its producers. In this way it hopes to avoid the accusa-tion that its concepts inflict superfluous criteria of evaluation on those it investigates. Employing such a theoretical critique, critical theorists hope to generate a new understanding of the cultural phenom-enon in question—an understanding that is able to articulate both the contradictions and possibilities contained with it (Held, 1980).

Critical Hermeneutics and the Process of Interpretation

I ground my research in the hermeneutical tradition and its concern with both the process of un-derstanding the meaning of various texts and the production of strategies for textual interpretation. Traditionally concerned with the interpretation of religious texts and canonical scriptures within their social and historical context, hermeneutics, after the scientific revolution of the European Enlighten-ment, emerged as the tradition that challenged the increasingly powerful shibboleths of the empirical scientific tradition. One of the central assertions of hermeneutics is that research and analysis of any variety involves an awareness of one's own consciousness and the values residing tacitly within it. Such values and the predispositions they support, hermeneuts maintained, unconsciously shape the nature of any project of inquiry. Such profound arguments, unfortunately, exerted little influence on their scientific contemporaries, as they held fast to their science of verification, the notion of objectivity, and the absurdity of the need for self-analysis on the part of the researcher (Kincheloe, 2005).

Central to the hermeneutic method is an appreciation of the complexity and ambiguity of human life in general and the pedagogical process in particular. Hermeneutics attempts to return lived experi-ence and meaning making to their original difficulty. In this context, words and images are relegated to the realm of the living with all the possibility for change such a state implies. Words and images to the hermeneutical analyst are not dead and static but alive and dynamic. Such a reality, of course, complicates the process of interpretation but concurrently provides a far more textured picture of human experience. The Greek root of hermeneutics, *hermeneuenin,* refers to the messenger god Hermes. Such an etymology well fits hermeneutics' ambiguous inscription, as Hermes was often a trickster in his official role of translator of divine messages to human beings. Interpretation is never simple and straight-forward—humans in the Greek myths learned this lesson frequently at the hands of their deceptive messenger. This lesson is not lost in twentieth-century hermeneutics, as analysts focus their attention on the sediments of meaning and the variety of intentions that surround social, political, and educational artifacts. Transcending the scientific empirical need for final proof and certainty, hermeneuts celebrate the irony of interpretation in the ambiguous lived world. Framing the methods of such interpretation as both analytic and intuitive, hermeneutics pushes the boundaries of human understanding in a manner more consonant with the contradictory nature of the world around us.

The Nature of Hermeneutic Interpretation

Hermeneutics insists that in social/educational science there is only interpretation, no matter how vociferously empirical scientists may argue that the facts speak for themselves. The hermeneutic act of interpretation involves in its most elemental articulation making sense of what has been observed in a way that communicates understanding. Not only is human science merely an act of interpretation, but hermeneutics contends that perception itself is an act of interpretation. Thus, the quest for understanding is a fundamental feature of human existence, as encounter with the unfamiliar always demands the attempt to make meaning, to make sense—but such is also the case with the familiar. Indeed, as in the study of commonly known popular movies, we come to find that sometimes the familiar may be seen as the most strange. Thus, it should not be surprising that even the so-called objective writings of qualitative research are interpretations, not value-free descriptions (Denzin, 1994).

Learning from the hermeneutic tradition and the postmodern critique, critical researchers have begun to re-examine textual claims to authority. No pristine interpretation exists—indeed, no methodology, social or educational theory, or discursive form can claim a privileged position that enables the production of authoritative knowledge. Researchers must always speak/write about the world in terms of something else in the world. As creatures of the world, we are oriented to it in a way that prevents us from grounding our theories and perspectives outside of it. Thus, whether we like it or not we are all destined as interpreters to analyze from within its boundaries and blinders. Within these limitations, however, the interpretations emerging from the hermeneutic process can still move us to new levels of understanding, appreciations that allow us to "live our way" into an experience described to us. Despite the impediments of context, hermeneutical researchers can transcend the inadequacies of thin descriptions of decontextualized facts and produce thick descriptions of social/pedagogical texts characterized by the context of its production, the intentions of its producers, and the meanings mobilized in the process of its construction. The production of such thick descriptions/interpretations follows no step-by-step blueprint or mechanical formula. As with any art form, hermeneutical analysis can be learned only in the Deweyan sense—by doing it. Researchers in this context practice the art by grappling with the text to be understood, telling its story in relation to its contextual dynamics and other texts first to themselves and then to a public audience (Kincheloe, 2005).

Thoughts about Hermeneutical Methods of Interpretation

These concerns with the nature of hermeneutical interpretation come under the category of philosophical hermeneutics. Working in this domain, scholars attempt to think through and clarify the conditions under which interpretation and understanding take place. The following analysis moves more in the direction of normative hermeneutics in that it raises questions about the purposes and procedures of interpretation. In its critical theory-driven cultural studies context, the purpose of hermeneutical analysis employed in this research is to provide understanding of particular cultural and educational phenomena of contemporary American life. Drawing upon the Frankfurt School's goal of theorizing the driving forces of the present moment, critical hermeneutics is used to develop a form of cultural criticism that sets the stage for a future politics/pedagogy of emancipation. Hermeneutical researchers operating with these objectives build bridges between reader and text, text and its producer, historical context and present, and one particular social circumstance and another. Accomplishing such interpretive tasks is a difficult endeavor, and scholars interested in normative hermeneutics push aspiring hermeneuts to trace the bridge-building process employed by successful interpreters of culture and pedagogy (Kincheloe 2005).

Grounded by this hermeneutical bridge-building, critical social analysts in a hermeneutical circle (a process of analysis where interpreters seek the historical and social dynamics that shape textual interpretation) engage in the back-and-forth of studying parts in relation to the whole and the whole in relation to parts. No final interpretation is sought in this context, as the activity of the circle proceeds with no need for closure (Kincheloe, 2005). This movement of whole to parts is combined with an analytical flow between abstract and concrete. Such dynamics often tie interpretation to the interplay of larger social forces (the general) to the everyday lives of individuals (the particular). A critical hermeneutics brings the concrete, the parts, the particular into focus, but in a manner that grounds it (them) contextually in a larger understanding of the social forces, the whole, the abstract (the general) that grounds it (them). Focus on the parts is the dynamic that brings the particular into focus, sharpening our understanding of the individual in light of the social and psychological forces that shape him or her. The parts and the unique places they occupy ground hermeneutical ways of seeing by providing the contextualization of the particular—a perspective often erased in modernist science's search for abstract generalizations (Kincheloe, 2005).

The give-and-take of the hermeneutical circle induces analysts to review existing conceptual matrixes in light of new understandings. Here preconceptions are reconsidered and reconceptualized so as to provide a new way of exploring a particular text. Making use of an author's insights hermeneutically does not mean replicating his or her response to the original question. In the hermeneutical process the author's answer is valuable only if it catalyzes the production of a new question for our consideration in the effort to make sense of a particular textual phenomenon (Gallagher, 1992). In this context participants in the hermeneutical circle must be wary of critical techniques of textual defamiliarization that have become cliched. For example, feminist criticisms of Barbie's figure and its construction of the image of ideal woman became such conventions in popular cultural analysis that other readings of Barbie were suppressed (Steinberg, 2004). Critical hermeneutical analysts in this and many other cases have to introduce new forms of analysis to the hermeneutical circle—to defamiliarize conventional defamiliarizations—in order to achieve deeper levels of understanding (Berger, 1995).

Within the hermeneutical circle we many develop new metaphors to shape our analysis in ways that break us out of familiar modes. For example, thinking of movies as mass-mediated dreams may help us reconceptualize the interpretive act as a psychoanalytic form of dream study. In this way, educational scholars could examine psychoanalytical work in the analysis of dream symbolization for insights into their studies of the pedagogy of popular culture and the meanings it helps individuals make via its visual images and narratives. As researchers apply these new metaphors in the hermeneutic circle, they must be aware of the implicit metaphors analysts continuously bring to the interpretive process (Berger, 1995). Such metaphors are shaped by the socio-historical era, the culture, and the linguistic context in which the interpreter operates. Such awareness is an important feature that must be introduced into the give-and-take of the hermeneutical circle. As John Dewey wrote almost a century ago, individuals adopt the values and perspectives of their social groups in a manner that such factors come to shape their views of the world. Indeed, the values and perspectives of the group help determine what is deemed important and what is not, what is granted attention and what is ignored. Hermeneutical analysts are aware of such interpretational dynamics and make sure they are included in the search for understanding (Berger, 1995).

Situating Interpretation

Researchers who fail to take Dewey's point into account operate at the mercy of unexamined assumptions. Since all interpretation is historically and culturally situated, it befalls the lot of hermeneutical analysts to study the ways both interpreters (often the analysts themselves) and the object of interpretation are constructed by their time and place. In this context the importance of social theory emerges. In this research critical social theory is injected into the hermeneutic circle to facilitate an understanding of the hidden structures and tacit cultural dynamics that insidiously inscribe social meanings and values (Kellner, 1995). This social and historical situating of interpreter and text is an extremely complex enterprise that demands a nuanced analysis of the impact of hegemonic and ideological forces that connect the micro-dynamics of everyday life with the macro-dynamics of structures of white supremacy, patriarchy, and class elitism. The central hermeneutic aspect of this work will involve the interaction between the cultural curriculum and these situating socio-historical structures.

When these aspects of the interpretation process are taken into account, analysts begin to understand Hans-Georg Gadamer's contention that social frames of reference influence researchers' questions which, in turn, shape the nature of interpretation itself. In light of this situating process the modernist notion that a social text has one valid interpretation evaporates into thin air. Researchers, whether they admit it or not, always have a point of view, a disciplinary orientation, a social or political group with which they identify (Kincheloe, 2005). Thus, the point, critical hermeneuts argue, is not for researchers to shed all worldly affiliations but to identify them and understand their impact on the ways they approach social and educational phenomena. Gadamer labels these world affiliations of researchers their "horizons" and deems the hermeneutic act of interpretation the "fusion of horizons." When researchers engage in the fusion of horizons they enter the tradition of the text. Here they study the conditions of its production and the circle of previous interpretations. In this manner they begin to uncover the ways the text has attempted to represent truth (Berger, 1995).

In the critical hermeneutical tradition these analyses of the ways interpretation is situated are considered central to the critical project. Researchers, like all human beings, critical analysts argue, make history and live their lives within structures of meaning they have not necessarily chosen for themselves. Understanding this, critical hermeneuts realize that a central aspect of their cultural pedagogical analysis involves dissecting the ways people connect their everyday experiences to the cultural representations of such experiences. Such work involves the unraveling of the ideological codings embedded in these cultural representations. This unraveling is complicated by the taken-for-grantedness of the meanings promoted in these representations and the typically undetected ways these meanings are circulated into everyday life (Denzin, 1992). The better the analyst, the better he or she can expose these meanings in the domain of the "what-goes-without-saying"—in this research those features of the media curriculum that are not addressed, that don't elicit comment.

At this historical juncture—the postmodern condition or hyperreality, as it has been labeled—electronic modes of communication become extremely important to the production of meanings and representations that culturally situate human beings in general and textual interpretations in particular. In many ways it can be argued that the postmodern condition produces a second-hand culture, filtered and pre-formed in the marketplace and constantly communicated via popular cultural and mass media. Critical analysts understand that the pedagogical effects of such a *media*ted culture can range from the political/ideological to the cognitive/epistemological. For example, the situating effects of print media tend to promote a form of linearity that encourages rationality, continuity, and uniformity. On the other hand, electronic media promote a non-linear immediacy that may encourage more emotional responses that lead individuals in very different directions. Thus, the situating influence and pedagogical impact of electronic media of the postmodern condition must be assessed by those who study the pedagogical process and, most importantly in this context, the research process itself (Kincheloe, 2005).

Critical Hermeneutics

Understanding the forces that situate interpretation, critical hermeneutics is suspicious of any model of interpretation that claims to reveal the final truth, the essence of a text or any form of experience. Critical hermeneutics is more comfortable with interpretive approaches that assume that the meaning of human experience can never be fully disclosed—neither to the researcher nor even to the human that experienced it. Since language is always slippery with its meanings ever "in process," critical hermeneuts understand that interpretations will never be linguistically unproblematic, will never be direct representations, critical hermeneutics seeks to understand how textual practices such as scientific research and classical theory work to maintain existing power relations and to support extant power structures (Denzin, 1992). This research draws, of course, on the latter model of interpretation with its treatment of the personal as political. Critical hermeneutics grounds a critical pedagogy that attempts to connect the everyday troubles individuals face to public issues of power, justice, and democracy. Typically, within the realm of the cultural curriculum critical hermeneutics has deconstructed popular cultural texts that promote demeaning stereotypes of the disempowered (Denzin, 1992). In this research, critical hermeneutics will be deployed differently in relation to popular cultural texts, as it examines popular movies that reinforce an ideology of privilege and entitlement for empowered members of the society—in this case, white, middle-upper-class males.

In its ability to render the personal political, critical hermeneutics provides a methodology for arousing a critical consciousness through the analysis of the generative themes of the present era. Such generative themes form the basis of the cultural curriculum of popular culture (Peters & Lankshear, 1994). Within the academy there is still resistance to the idea that movies, TV, and popular music are intricately involved in the most important political, economic, and cultural battles of the contemporary epoch. Critical hermeneutics recognizes this centrality of popular culture in the postmodern condition and seeks to uncover the ways it impedes and advances the struggle for a democratic society (Kincheloe, 2005). Appreciating the material effects of media culture, critical hermeneutics trace the ways movies position audiences politically in ways that not only shape their political beliefs but also formulate their identities. In this context, Paulo Freire's contribution to the development of a critical hermeneutics is especially valuable. Understanding that the generative themes of a culture are central features in a critical social analysis, Freire assumes that the interpretive process is both an ontological and an epistemological act. It is ontological on the level that our vocation as humans, the foundation of our being, is grounded on the hermeneutical task of interpreting the world so we can become more fully human. It is epistemological in the sense that critical hermeneutics offers us a method for investigating the conditions of our existence and the generative themes that shape it. In this context we gain the prowess to both live with a purpose and operate with the ability to perform evaluative acts in naming the culture around us. In the postmodern condition the pedagogical effects of popular culture have often been left unnamed, allowing our exploration of the shaping of our own humanness to go unexplored in this strange new social context. Critical hermeneutics address this vacuum (Kincheloe, 2005).

Critical hermeneutics names the world as a part of a larger effort to evaluate it and make it better. Knowing this, it is easy to understand why critical hermeneutics focuses on domination and its negation, emancipation. Domination limits self-direction and democratic community building while emancipation enables it. Domination, legitimated as it is by ideology, is decoded by critical hermeneuts who help individuals discover the ways they have been entangled in the ideological process. The exposé and critique of ideology is one of critical hermeneutics' main objectives in its effort to make the world better. As long as the various purveyors of ideology obstruct our vision, our effort to live in democratic communities will be thwarted (Gallagher, 1992). Power wielders with race, class, and gender privilege have access to the resources that allow them to promote ideologies and representations in ways indi-viduals without such privilege cannot. Resources such as entertainment and communication industries are used to shape consciousness and construct subjectivity (Kincheloe, 2005).

Critical Hermeneutics, The Production of Subjectivity and Cultural Pedagogy

Those who operate outside the critical tradition often fail to understand that the critical hermeneutical concern with popular culture in the postmodern condition is not a matter of aesthetics but an issue of socio-political impact. In light of the focus of this research on the cultural curriculum and cultural pedagogy, a key aspect of this socio-political impact involves the socialization of youth. Those same outsiders sometimes look down their noses at the popular texts chosen for interpretation in the critical context, arguing that a cultural production such as *Fast Times at Ridgemont High,* for example, doesn't deserve the attention critical scholarship might devote to it. Critical hermeneuts maintain that all popular culture that is consumed and makes an impact on an audience is worthy of study regardless of the aesthetic judgments elite cultural scholars might offer (Berger, 1995). In the case of a movie like *Fast Times at Ridgemont High,* it is important to critical analysts because it is both inscribed with profound cultural meanings, and so many people have watched it. In its interest in oppression and emancipation, self-direction, personal freedom, and democratic community building, critical hermeneutics knows that popular texts such as movies shape the production of subjectivity; it also understands that such a process can be understood only with an appreciation of the socio-historical and political context that supports it (Ellis & Flaherty, 1992).

Norm Denzin (1992) is extremely helpful in developing this articulation of critical hermeneutics, drawing on the sociological genius of C. Wright Mills and his "sociological imagination." A key interest of this tradition, which Denzin carries into the contemporary era, involves unearthing the connections among material existence, communications processes, cultural patterns, and the formation of human consciousness. This articulation of a critical hermeneutics has much to learn from Denzin and Mills and their concern with subjectivity/consciousness, their understanding that cultural productions of various types hold compelling consequences for humans. Denzin is obsessed with the way individuals make sense of their everyday lives in particular cultural contexts by constructing stories (narratives) that, in turn, help define their identities. Employing a careful reading of Denzin, a critical hermeneut can gain insight into how cultural texts help create a human subject. How, Denzin wants to know, do individuals connect their lived experiences to the cultural representations of these same experiences (Denzin, 1992)?

Following this line of thought, a critical hermeneutics concerned with the pedagogical issue of identity formation seeks cultural experiences that induce crises of consciousness when an individual's identity is profoundly challenged. Such moments are extremely important to any pedagogy, for it is in such instants of urgency that dramatic transformations occur (Denzin, 1992). In this research it is argued that such moments are not uncommon in individual interactions with popular texts and that the results of such experiences can be either oppressive or liberatory in nature. Indeed, some peda-gogical experiences may be characterized as rational processes, but they almost always involve a strong emotional component. Too often in mainstream research this emotional dynamic has been to some degree neglected by logocentric social science (Ellis & Flaherty, 1992). A critical hermeneutics aware of such cultural pedagogical dynamics will empower individuals to make sense of their popular cultural experiences and provide them with specific tools of social interpretation. Such abilities will allow them to avoid the manipulative ideologies of popular cultural texts in an emancipatory manner that helps them consciously construct their own identities. Critical social and educational analysis demands such abilities in its efforts to provide transformative insights into the many meanings produced and deployed in the media-saturated postmodern landscape (Kellner, 1995).

Conclusion

This chapter describes the way that cultural studies can be used with a bricolaged approach; combining critical research methods in order to critically interpret film, in this case, for a cultural pedagogical reading. As one who self-defines herself as abstract random, with a strange penchant for organization, I believe that cultural studies is best read through an approach that does not limit itself to one research method.

References

Aronowitz, S. (1993). *Roll over Beethoven: The return of cultural strife*. Hanover, NH: Wesleyan University Press.

Atkinson, P., & Hammersley, M. (1994). Ethnography and participant observation. In N. Denzin & Y. Lincoln (Eds.), *Handbook of qualitative research*. (pp. 83–97). Thousand Oaks, CA: Sage.

Berger, A. (1995). *Cultural criticism: A primer of key concepts*. Thousand Oaks, CA: Sage.

Clough, P. (1992). *The end(s) of ethnography: From realism to social criticism*. Newbury Park, CA: Sage.

Collins, J. (1990). *Architectures of excess: Cultural life in the information age*. New York: Routledge.

Denzin, N. (1992). *Symbolic interactionism and cultural studies: The politics of interpretation*. Cambridge, MA: Blackwell.

Denzin, N. (1994). The art and politics of interpretation. In N. Denzin & Y. Lincoln (Eds.), *Handbook of qualitative research* (pp. 500–515). Thousand Oaks, CA: Sage.

Denzin, N., & Lincoln, Y. (2005). The *Sage handbook of qualitative research* (3rd ed.). Thousand Oaks, CA: Sage.

Ellis, C., & Flaherty, M. (1992). An agenda for the interpretation of lived experience. In C. Ellis & M. Flaherty (Eds.), *Investigating subjectivity: Research on lived experience* (pp. 1–16). Newbury Park, CA: Sage.

Fiske, J. (1993). *Power plays, power works*. New York: Verso.

Gallagher, S. (1992). *Hermeneutics and education*. Albany: State University of New York Press.

Gresson, A. (1996, Spring). Postmodern America and the multicultural crisis: Reading *Forrest Gump* as the call back to whiteness. *Taboo: The Journal of Culture and Education*, 11–34.

Grossberg, L. (1995, Spring). What's in a name (one more time)? *Taboo: The Journal of Culture and Education*, 1–37.

Hammersley, M., & Atkinson, P. (1983). *Ethnography: Principles in practice*. New York: Tavistock Publications.

Held, D. (1980). *Introduction to critical theory*. Berkeley: University of California Press.

Kellner, D. (1995). *Media culture: Cultural studies, identity and politics between the modern and the postmodern*. New York: Routledge.

Kincheloe, J. (2001). Describing the bricolage: Conceptualizing a new rigour in qualitative research. *Qualitative Inquiry, 7*, 679–692.

Kincheloe, J. (2005). On to the next level: Continuing the conceptualization of the bricolage. *Qualitative Inquiry, 11*, 323–350.

Kincheloe, J., & Berry, K. (2004). *Rigour and complexity in educational research: Conceptualizing the bricolage*. London: Open University Press.

Kincheloe, J., & Steinberg, S. (1997). *Changing multiculturalism*. London: Open University Press.

Kipnis, L. (1992). Feminism: The political conscience of postmodernism. In A. Ross (Ed.), *Universal abandon? The politics of postmodernism*. (pp. 149–166). Minneapolis: University of Minnesota Press.

Lévi-Strauss, C. (1966). *The savage mind*. Chicago: University of Chicago Press.

MacDonald, D. (1957). A theory of mass culture. In B. Rosenberg & D. White (Eds.), *Mass culture* (pp. 59–73). Glencoe, IL: Free Press.

Peters, M., & Lankshear, C. (1994). Education and hermeneutics: A Freirean interpretation. In P. McLaren & C. Lankshear (Eds.), *Politics of liberation: Paths from Freire* (pp. 173–192). New York: Routledge.

Reinharz, S. (1992). *Feminist methods in social research*. New York: Oxford University Press.

Rosneau, P. (1992). *Postmodernism and the social sciences: Insights, inroads, and intrusion*. Princeton: Princeton University Press.

Smith, P. (1989). Pedagogy and the popular-cultural-commodity text. In H. Giroux & R. Simon (Eds.), *Popular culture: Schooling and everyday life* (pp. 31–46). Granby, MA: Bergin and Garvey.

Steinberg, S. (2004, 1997). The bitch who has everything. In S. Steinberg & J. Kincheloe (Eds.), *Kinderculture: The corporate construction of childhood* (pp. 207–218). Boulder, CO: Westview Press.

Walby, S. (1990, July/August). *Theorizing patriarchy*. Utne Reader, 64, 63–66.

Wood, R. (1995). Ideology, genre, auteur. In B. Grant (Ed.), *Film genre reader II* (pp. 59–73). Austin: University of Texas Press.

Filmography

Die Hard, 1988. John McTiernan, Director.

Fast Times at Ridgemont High, 1982. Amy Heckerling, Director.

Forrest Gump, 1994. Robert Zemeckis, Director.

Ferris Bueller's Day Off, 1986. John Hughes, Director.

The Green Berets, 1968. Ray Kellogg and John Wayne, Directors.

PART THREE
On the Political

Maintaining a Vibrant Synergy among Theory, Qualitative Research, and Social Activism in This Ever-Changing Age of Globalization

Pepi Leistyna

In order to bring about social change, cultural activists have access to a rich theoretical and empirical history of different ways of thinking about the relations between intellectual and political practice. In fact, armed with a deep understanding of the synergy that exists among theory, qualitative research, and activism—a firm grasp of the multidirectional relationships within which each component influences and strengthens the other—people and organizations have long worked to secure human, economic, and political rights.

At its foundation, the dialectical relationship among theory, qualitative research, and activism is relatively simple. As theory—through interpretation and explanation—begs empirical and practical questions and illuminates research findings and activist efforts, research not only puts theory to the test and provides the potential for its expansion, but it can also offer activists tangible models to critically appropriate from in order to address the specificities of their current predicaments. Meanwhile, activism can simultaneously push theory forward into uncharted territory and expand the horizons of empirical analysis. All of this ongoing interaction helps us better make sense of and act upon the world in far more informed, efficient, and effective ways.

Making use of this synergy is of particular importance in this age of globalization—largely driven by changes in global economics and interactive technologies—where social agency is taking on new forms. While many members of the global justice movement have been making effective use of existing theory and qualitative research to inform their strategic maneuvers, their actions are simultaneously bringing into focus new questions for analysis and exploration. Before elaborating on these movements and their theoretical and empirical appropriations and implications, it is helpful to briefly point out some of the intellectual traditions that have come to inform most radical, contemporary, cultural activism.

The Role of Theory in Qualitative Research and Activism

Theory embodies existing ways in which people have interpreted, analyzed, and made generalizations about *why* the world works the way that it does. It is the *why* and *how* of what has been happening around us and not simply a focus on *what* is occurring and how to effectively respond. There are vast traditions of such reflection and analysis that provide conceptual tools to help recognize, engage, and critique (so as to transform) any existing undemocratic social practices and institutional structures that produce and sustain inequalities and oppressive social identities and relations.

While the following examples of critical social theory represent areas of thought that are internally diverse, frequently the result of different theoretical appropriations, and part and parcel of ongoing debates, there are nonetheless important analytic insights about the role of culture in political action that are woven through these various understandings that have informed social agency directed at the democratization of society. While providing a definitive list of such theoretical (and in the following section empirical) insights is obviously beyond the scope of this chapter, some key examples are useful in illustrating the importance and influence of theory, and pointing to its ever-evolving nature as it is confronted by new ideas, emerging research, and real world struggles.

Since the early 1930s, activists have critically appropriated from the Frankfurt School and its many influential thinkers, including Max Horkheimer, Theodor Adorno, and Herbert Marcuse, who conducted an extensive ideological critique in order to understand the uses and abuses of power so as to be able to transform them. Such scholars pioneered the systematic analysis of mass-mediated culture and communications and worked to reveal how the "culture industry" co-opts society and reinforces capitalist social relations—part of what became better known as *critical theory*. The word *critical* implied a break from the limits of positivism, pragmatism, phenomenology, historicism, existentialism, and scientific socialism. It also drew on Karl Marx's earlier call for philosophers to *change* the world rather than simply interpret it.

Interdisciplinary in its approach to understanding domination and the interconnections among economics, politics, psychology, technology, and culture, many intellectuals associated with the Frankfurt School explored how the irrationalism and alienation embedded in capitalism and Western civilization work to defuse and disarm any possibility for revolution. Many of these analyses of authoritarianism and the irrational behavior that permeated the industrialized society in which these intellectuals were living were largely influenced by the critical philosophy of Immanuel Kant (especially his ideas on reflection, how to explore the conditions that produce a particular phenomenon, and moral autonomy), G. W. F. Hegel's dialectical method of negation and contradiction, Marx's analysis of the role of ideology in reinforcing the capitalist system, Sigmund Freud's work in psychoanalysis, and Max Weber's critique of rationalism and bureaucratic domination in capitalist societies. While relying on tools of the Enlightenment for empirical exploration, many of these critical theorists nonetheless fought the notion of a single, centered, and essentialized route to human rights and emancipation, insisting that the search and imposition of ultimate rationality and order has historically perpetuated theoretical orthodoxies and relations of domination. For decades, critical theory has provided researchers and activists with profound insights about the structures and formative powers of society and culture, and how to access the liberatory possibilities of knowledge and revolutionary agency. As a consequence, the complex, interdisciplinary, and diverse perspectives of critical theorists continue to this day to inform social thought, research, and action.

The study of culture, domination, and liberatory practices has also been greatly advanced by anti-colonial, anti-racist thinkers and activists of the 1950s and 60s such as C. L. R. James, Frantz Fanon, Amilcar Cabral, Aimé Césaire, and Albert Memmi. These revolutionaries, also influenced by Marxist, neo-Marxist, and psychoanalytic theories, were fighting (and continue to fight through the work of such theorists as Edward Said, Gayatri Spivak, and Homi Bhabha) against a long history of global colonialism and white supremacy. They understood that economics and politics are important forces in maintaining unequal relations of power in society, but they also recognized the power of culture and the central role of ideology in working to control the psyche of people and public opinion, and consequently in maintaining systems of oppression. For these activists, all cultural terrain is worth fighting over. If it weren't, then colonizers and fascists alike wouldn't immediately go after schools, media, and other public spheres that produce and disseminate knowledge. These revolutionaries have provided theoretical frameworks for confronting the ideologies, authority, and social relations that have driven the oppressive legacy of colonialism, imperialism, and white supremacy, and they have inspired critical educational practices and liberation movements around the world for decades.

Since the 1960s, poststructuralists have also been interested in understanding the power/knowledge configuration. By no means a monolithic group, many of these theorists, notably Roland Barthes, Michel Foucault, Pierre Bourdieu, Jacques Lacan, and Jacques Derrida, have argued that consciousness, identity, meaning, and cognitive development are social constructions—the central idea being that systems of communication informed by particular values and beliefs play a significant role in shaping human faculties, sensibilities, and subjectivities.

Much more flexible than the Marxist interpretation of ideology and the hitherto structuralist theorists who were in search of universal processes and mechanisms that could systematically explain meaning and human behavior, poststructuralists have been engaged in an exploration of how knowledge is constructed within specific social conditions and relations of power. Of particular importance to Foucault was *discourse*, which refers to the way reality is perceived through and shaped by historically and socially constructed ways of making sense—that is, languages, systems of meaning, and practices that order and sustain particular forms of social existence. As oppressive discourses and discursive formations are understood as social constructions rather than inevitabilities, they can therefore be deconstructed through human action and reconstructed into more democratic and liberatory structures and practices.

Poststructuralism, and its linguistic, cognitive, and cultural turn toward language, affect, consciousness, and systems of meaning, would theoretically pave the way for the emergence of postmodernism in the late 1970s. While by no means a monolithic entity, postmodernists, also influenced by phenomenology, structuralism, and existentialism, and the work of Friedrich Nietzsche, Martin Heidegger, and Ludwig Wittgenstein, have great disdain for positivism, instrumental reason, and any other paradigm that subsumes every aspect of social reality into one totalizing theory—that is, to *grand* or *master narratives*. Universals in the form of absolute truth, certainty, and objectivity are cast aside in the name of heterogeneity, contingency, intersubjectivity, and indeterminacy. Because of their invaluable contributions to social theory, especially around issues of identity and difference, poststructuralism and postmodernism have been readily appropriated from, expanded upon, and used to inform a wide range of political movements including feminism, anti-racist/multiculturalism, and queer rights.

Primarily occupied with how meaning is produced, circulated, legitimated, and consumed in society, and how relations of power affect this complex and multidirectional process, much of cultural studies has also had major political implications. In fact, its roots in the Centre for Contemporary Cultural Studies at the University of Birmingham, founded in England in 1964 by Richard Hoggart, were directly connected to political projects. The primary figures in this movement (e.g., Raymond Williams and Stuart Hall) understood theory as being strategic, performative, and directed towards solving important pressing economic, social, and political problems.

Institutionally, cultural studies began to find its place in the world in the 1970s, and it is now widely used to theorize how culture and representation shape our lived experiences and sense of political agency. The work of Antonio Gramsci in the 1920s and early 30s has had a major impact on the trajectory of cultural studies as it relates to political projects.

Like Karl Marx and Vladimir Lenin, Gramsci worked to explain why the oppressed were not revolutionary. This resulted in the reinvention of the ancient Greek concept *hegemony*, which he used as a point of analysis to examine how the imposition of particular ideologies and forms of authority results in the reproduction of social and institutional practices through which dominant groups maintain not only their positions of privilege and control, but also the consensual support of other members of society, even those most exploited. Shifting away from Marx's focus on economics, Gramsci looked instead at cultural relations and their effects on politics. He was interested in how, along with state coercion, the forces of civil society such as the family, houses of faith, educational institutions, and so on, often worked in the interests of the ruling classes. Gramsci's theory was far more open than the Marxist concept of *false consciousness*: he understood that hegemony was full of contradictions, and he recognized people as being able to resist domination in their everyday lives.

Over the years, advocates of cultural studies have appropriated, battled over, and expanded upon some of the theoretical ideas of humanism, formalism, Marxism, structuralism, poststructuralism, semiotics, deconstructionism, new historicism, interpretivism, hermeneutics, constructivism, critical theory, psychoanalysis, postmodernism, ethnomethodology, and feminism, among others (Alasuutari, 1995). This transdisciplinary practice has also influenced a vast range of fields including ethnic, critical race, and queer studies, globalization, communication, and media studies, postcolonial, indigenous, and diaspora studies, sociology, psychology, and cultural anthropology (Frow & Morris, 2000).

As the educational arm of critical social theory, critical pedagogy, which emerged in the early stages of decolonization, has been used to help understand and respond to oppressive social practices, especially those that manifest in educational institutions. The Brazilian adult educator Paulo Freire (1921–1997) is the most widely recognized and influential theorist and practitioner of critical pedagogy. He is perhaps best known for his literacy work in the decolonization process in a number of countries in Latin America, Africa, and Asia, and for his first of many books, *Pedagogy of the Oppressed*, a theoretical guide to revolution published in 1970.

In addition to the phenomenology of Hegel and Edmund Husserl (1859–1938), the sociological and psychoanalytic work of Erich Fromm (1900–1980), and the neo-Marxist ideas of Antonio Gramsci (1891–1937), Louis Althusser (1918–1990), and Georg Lukács (1885–1971), Freire was also drawn to the existentialism of Jean-Paul Sartre (1905–1980), and the ideas of human revolution of Rosa Luxemburg (1870–1919) and Che Guevara (1928–1967). Furthermore, he was motivated by progressive Christian intellectuals, in particular, Jacques Maritain (1882–1973) and his views on knowledge analysis and critical realism, liberal Christian humanism, and the defense of natural rights. Spiritually grounded, Freire also maintained a symbiotic relationship with Liberation Theology, which emerged in the 1960s out of the economic, political, and military turmoil in Latin America. Its proponents have taken a political stance against the exploitation and tyranny of market forces and other oppressive practices, thus making a profound link between Christianity and socialism.

Arguing that education is an inherently political act where values and beliefs are transmitted, or at best struggled over, critical pedagogy encourages, as a fundamental part of the learning process, examination of the exploitation of labor and the concomitant class divisions and conflicts that reveal different economic, political, and cultural interests in society. In its more mature form it also addresses how oppression affects people of all walks of life who fall outside of mainstream norms of identity and "acceptable" behavior. In order for people to be active "subjects" of history rather than passive "objects" to be acted upon, manipulated, and controlled, critical pedagogues argue that literacy needs to work in a way that helps them read the economic, social, and political realities that shape their lives in order to develop the necessary critical consciousness, to name, understand, and transform them. Research of this sort has to begin with where people are and critical pedagogy thus uses generative themes and codes—that is, areas of interest and objects from peoples' actual lives—to begin the political process of making meaning and enabling people to become transformative agents, rather than victims or mere reproducers of existing ideologies.

All of the aforementioned theoretical efforts to understand the important role of culture in any struggle for social control have enhanced and been enhanced by qualitative empirical studies that are attuned to the dire need for radical social change.

The Role of Action and Social Movement Research in Activism

The trouble is that once you see it, you can't unsee it. And once you've seen it, keeping quiet, saying nothing, becomes as political an act as speaking out. There's no innocence. Either way, you're accountable.—Arundhati Roy[1]

Qualitative research that is oriented towards the study of culture has always had theoretical and political implications, regardless of its ostensible goal. Progressive researchers that have concerned themselves with issues of power, social injustice, and how people work to transform society have developed explicit political dimensions as part of their exploratory studies (Denzin & Lincoln, 2000; Gitlin, 1994; McGuigan, 1997; Rosaldo, 1989). These empirically guided projects of change exemplify what Raymond Williams referred to throughout his work as "knowable communities" by showcasing groups actually engaged in cultural and political reflection and struggle. However, it is important to note here that while the idea of knowable communities, as it pertains to political movements, is both appealing and useful, neither Williams nor this chapter aspire to essentialize geographies and identities by assuming that there are biologically determined or culturally fixed thoughts and practices at play that are easily identifiable, readily accessible, and necessarily indicative of what other groups are experiencing and how they are responding.

In fact, progressive qualitative researchers' biggest milestone has been to break free from the clutches of positivism that have stifled the empirical world for centuries. Abstracted from concerns for history, ideology, relations of power, and the political implications of research, the ultimate goal of the positivist tradition is to "discover" the universal laws that reveal the essence of nature and human behavior. Associated with Enlightenment thinkers and modernism—Francis Bacon, John Locke, René Descartes, Isaac Newton, and Auguste Comte—positivism is a defense of a scientific basis for the study of the world in its entirety in which knowledge and reason are seen as neutral and universal rather than social constructions that reflect particular ideologies and interests.

This research paradigm came under heavy criticism from such scholars as Willard Van Orman Quine, Karl Popper, Thomas Samuel Kuhn, Paul Feyerabend, Imre Lakatos, and Jean-François Lyotard. Anti-positivists (who differentiate between the natural and the social sciences), post-positivists, and postmodernists have helped guide and expand progressive and radical theory and research oriented towards the study of culture and the transformation of society, especially action-based and social movement research.

Action-based research has always had a qualitative political and transformative agenda explicitly woven into its theoretical and empirical fabric. Fleeing Nazi Germany, social psychologist Kurt Lewin came to the United States and in 1946 coined the term *action research* (AR) to describe his new way of conducting research that attempts to use theory and the production of knowledge in action to address systemic social problems. Lewin, who is often recognized for his famous words "Nothing is as practical as a good theory", and "The best way to understand something is to try to change it", created a model of research that consists of three basic stages: breaking down existing structures—*unfreezing*, transforming them—*changing*, and subsequently putting them back together as a fixed functioning system—*freezing* (Greenwood & Levin, 1998). AR is thus substantively different from applied research in that praxis is not seen as a distinct separation between theory and practice, given that knowledge is constructed and evaluated in the midst of action as the two dialectically feed off of each other in the process.

The philosophical influences on the early development of the various strains of action research are many. Some camps have taken from John Dewey who, influenced by William James's radical empiricism and pragmatism, elaborated on the important links among experience, reflection, knowledge production, and personal growth.[2] Because interpretation, meaning-making, accessing the "Other's" experience, and understanding what shapes human consciousness, have all played such an important role in action research, so have the influences of humanistic psychology, interpretivism, hermeneutics, and phenomenology—and thus the work of Edmund Husserl, Maurice Merleau-Ponty, Martin Heidegger, Hans-Georg Gadamer, and Paul Ricoeur.

While attempting to abide by the laws of objectivity, Lewin challenged the traditional researcher/ subject binarism by making the researcher an active participant in the localized action rather than a passive observer. Advocates of this new model embraced the idea of doing research *with* others rather than *on* them, and thus speaking *with* rather than *to* what are now often referred to as "clients", "stakeholders", or "co-inquirers". As a result, identifying pertinent issues and making decisions about how to proceed are done collaboratively, although the researcher and the clients in the early efforts maintained separate roles in the problem-solving process. In their exchange, the client was able to solve the problem while the researcher, who provided the empirical tools, was able to expand on existing theoretical and empirical knowledge.

Validity issues were called into question as researchers within this new paradigm were caught in the contradiction of remaining objective while joining in the action. In the 1960s, AR lost some of its momentum, in part because it was being associated with the radical movements of the time, but mostly because it was eclipsed by traditional experimental, quantitative approaches that were faithful to the myths of positivism and thus institutionally supported and funded.

Resurfacing in the 1980s, and moving away from the confines of the positivist grip of objectivity, validity, and generalizability, advocates of action research were inspired by the work of Gramsci, critical theory, postcolonial theory, critical pedagogy, poststructuralism, cultural studies, systems thinking, and structuration, postmodern, constructivist, and feminist theory (Reason & Bradbury, 2004). Making the linguistic, cognitive, and cultural turn, many advocates of action research felt that traditional empirical constraints were not applicable to the social sciences. Recognizing research and knowledge production as inherently political acts, it was widely understood that the goal of AR isn't to be able to generalize about human experience (Pilotta et al., 2001). Instead, making use of any and all methodological approaches—even creating new ones to address the specific set of conditions—these researchers focused on how a particular group and its individual members come to know something within the actual struggle to transform it. Validity was now being based on the changes that were achieved as a result of the project.

AR's embrace of participation also matured as practitioners expanded the paradigm's collaborative and dialogical dimensions. Rather than framing collaboration as a short-term intervention where the researcher is rewarded with new theoretical ideas and the clients get their change, AR now placed greater emphasis on co-generative learning and theorizing, and making sure that clients are strategically apprenticed into conducting research (Atweh, Kemmis, & Weeks, 1998; Bray, Lee, Smith, & Yorks, 2000; Brown & Jones, 2001; Fals Borda, 2004; Jason, Keys, Suarez-Balcazar, Taylor, & Davis, 2002). In this way, they are better equipped to bring about continuous change on their own, long after the departure of the initial support group.

Action research has inspired many other qualitative empirical practices that are also concerned with personal and social change, among them practitioner research, action inquiry, teacher-as-researcher, experimental learning, action science, community development, new paradigm research, appreciative inquiry, empowerment-based research, action learning, collaborative inquiry, community-based action research, and participatory action research. While there is a great deal of ideological and practical variation within and among these action-based models, many of them have the same progressive intent: to create the self-empowering conditions within which people can conduct their own research, create democratic organizational structures and decision-making processes, and work towards generative learning and personal and social transformation through praxis.

Action-based researchers have learned much from each other and have consequently expanded their theoretical and empirical horizons. They have also been influenced by what's referred to as *new ethnography*—research that is clearly directed towards social change. Lois Weis and Michelle Fine (2004) capture this radical spirit:

> Our commitment to revealing sites for possibility derives not only from a theoretical desire to re-view "what is" and "what could be", but also from an ethical belief that critical researchers have an obligation not simply to dislodge the dominant discourse, but to help readers and audiences imagine where the spaces for resistance, agency, and possibility lie. (p. xxi)

Unlike the early examples of AR, more contemporary practices have placed even greater importance on reflexivity (deep self-analysis of all those involved in the project), and on people's existential realities, lived experiences, discursive practices, emotions, and cultural sensibilities, and how these elements can contribute to community development and ongoing community action (Kemmis & Wilkinson, 1998; Stringer, 1999). Recognizing the existence of multiple realities, identities, and voices, action-based researchers continue to work to create spaces within which subaltern voices can emerge under their own volition.

But these qualitative researchers are often caught in the complex tension of trying to simultaneously be "truer to people's lived experiences (new ethnography) and critically analyze problematic social discourses that seep into those experiences (poststructuralism)" (Saukko, 2003, p. 89). In fact, a recurring problem with identity politics of this sort is that experience is often left at the level of description; that is, narratives are welcomed at the expense of theoretical analysis (Scott, 1992). Such an atheoretical posture gives the erroneous perception that subject position—the place that a person occupies within a set of social relationships shaped by such factors as social class, gender, race, religion, and sexual orientation—is inherently linked to critical consciousness. In other words, when a person shares the pains of social injustice, this narration, in and of itself, is thought to necessarily bring about the intra- and interpersonal political understanding of such oppressive acts. Peter McLaren (1995) warns of this pitfall:

> Either a person's physical proximity to the oppressed or their own location as an oppressed person is supposed to offer a special authority from which to speak…. Here the political is often reduced only to the personal where theory is dismissed in favor of one's own personal and cultural identity—abstracted from the ideological and discursive complexity of their formation. (p. 125)

Countering this tendency to conflate location and consciousness, activists are encouraged to nurture the kinds of critical, inclusive dialogue that work to explain/theorize why everyone involved and affected thinks a particular experience has occurred so as to be able to act in solidarity to change any and all unjust material, political, and symbolic conditions.

Within this new era of globalization, action-based research also encourages participants to look beyond the micro-politics of the system under immediate examination, and when possible connect their efforts to larger struggles for social justice. In fact, all theoretical and qualitative empirical camps oriented towards democratic social change, such as social movement research, are being radically challenged by globalization and its discontents.

As David Meyer and Sidney Tarrow (1998) note, social movements "are best defined as collective challenges to existing arrangements of power and distribution by people with common purposes and solidarity, in sustained interaction with elites, opponents, and authorities" (p. 4). It's thus not surprising that social movement research, like the other theoretical and empirical models discussed, also has enormous political potential.

Concerned with the power of movements and their impact on people, public discourse, policy, institutions, and governments, social movement research has looked at the ways in which activists understand and make use of the cracks of agency made possible by shifting economic, political, and cultural relations, and how organizations and networks develop, mobilize, and change (Diani & McAdam, 2003; Freeman & Johnson, 1999; Guidry, Kennedy, & Zald, 2000; Khagram, Riker, & Sikkink, 2002; Klandermans, Hanspeter, & Tarrow, 1988; Tilly, 2004).

It was during the turmoil of the 1960s that theoretical and empirical interest in social movements in Europe and the United States found new life. The early studies focused on how public grievances lead to collective action, but this initial phase was quickly followed by the *resource mobilization* paradigm that has been preoccupied with the kinds of resources that movements have available to them and how they are put to use. Researchers also developed an interest in *mobilizing structures*—the organizational bodies and techniques used to enable people to take action—as well as the impact that existing organizations and networks have on new movement progress.

At the same time, many researchers began examining the political opportunities available to activists within particular historical and geopolitical conditions, giving rise to *political process theory*. This focus on how national institutionalized politics, and the opportunities and constraints therein, affect collective action has produced new research methods, including protest analysis (Klandermans & Staggenborg, 2002).

Appropriating from this empirical past, the *new social movement* theorists emerging out of Europe added a comparative dimension to the study of political conditions, possibilities, and actions. Researchers have since been intrigued by international differences in the organizational structures and strategies that activists design and implement, and the interplay between these structures and society's dominant political forces and institutions (Keck & Sikkink, 1998; McAdam, McCarthy, & Zald, 1996; Smith, Chatfield, & Pagnucco, 1997).

These structural approaches to understanding the politics of change would eventually be challenged and complemented by research and analysis concerned with how emotions, consciousness, and identity affect social movements. Influenced by the work of Gramsci, Habermas, E. P. Thompson (1924–1993), Erving Goffman (1922–1982), Clifford Geertz (1926–), and the poststructuralists—as well as by the emergence of identity politics in the 1960s—a number of social movement researchers made the linguistic, cognitive, and cultural turn towards the dialectical relations among language, meaning, identity, structure, and change (Klandermans & Staggenborg, 2002; Melucci, 1996; Tarrow, 1998).

A significant part of this shift in focus has been on *framing processes*—the ways in which groups self-represent, explain and legitimate their causes and concerns, develop solidarity, and mobilize. Researchers have also looked at whether or not these collective action frames resonate publicly, and at the representational conflicts that are generated by the competition among movement members, as well as by the counter-messages put forth by government forces, the media, and other opponents.[3]

Benefiting from its embrace of methodological pluralism, social movement research has extended its reach beyond the halls of sociology and into political science, psychology, history, anthropology, cultural studies, and international relations (Klandermans & Staggenborg, 2002). "Students of social movements have conducted quantitative and qualitative studies, surveys, and in-depth interviews, archival studies and participant observation, single-case studies and complex comparative designs, mathematical simulations, protest event analyses, ecological studies of multiorganizational fields and life-history interviews, discourse analysis, and studies of narratives" (Klandermans & Staggenborg, 2002, p. xii). However, much of this theoretical and empirical work, even the comparative studies, has been limited by its preoccupation with examples of movements within nation-states. Like all analytical frameworks, it too is now being radically challenged by globalization and transnational global justice movements.

Qualitative Research, Theory, and the Global Justice Movement

> Globalization falls outside the established academic disciplines, as a sign of the emergence of a new kind of social phenomenon.... —Fredric Jameson[4]

Without a doubt, we've entered a new era of global social and economic relations that are not only changing how we think about economics, but also politics and culture and the complex interrelationships among these forces. While this transformation should not be confused with one of those *post* trends where supposedly there's a clearly definable gap between what was and what is, the global economy—a product of the last 500 years of invention and imperialist expansion (Chomsky, 1993)—has entered a new phase made possible by innovative technologies, transnational institutions, and the logic of neoliberalism.

As capitalism has been undergoing radical change, the new political order of globalization simultaneously emerging differs in many respects from previous forms of imperialism (Bauman, 1998; Castells, 1996; Hardt & Negri, 2000; Harvey, 2001; Lash & Urry, 1987). Obsessed with privatization, deregulation, and restructuring, elite private powers have been successful in using the state to protect corporate interests and dismantle many of the rights and protections achieved internationally by grassroots activists, organized labor, and social democracies.

Since the birth of the nation-state, progressive and radical activists have challenged governments and private power in an effort to ensure that the interests of the people and different cultures are recognized and realized. However, what has dramatically changed over the years has been the power of the private sector. These days—with 51 of the planet's 100 largest economies being corporations—new global justice movements are vehemently working against the hegemony of corporate rule (Danaher & Mark, 2003). Many contemporary activists are eyeing and responding to the undemocratic governing bodies that have achieved supranational power—institutions like the International Monetary Fund, the World Bank, and the World Trade Organization (Hall & Biersteker, 2002; Wilkinson & Hughes, 2002).

> Globalization has been accompanied, some would say driven, by a thickening web of multilateral agreements, global and regional institutions and regimes, transgovernmental policy networks and summits. This evolving global governance complex regulates and intervenes in virtually all aspects of global affairs. It is far from being a nascent world government, but it is much more than a system of limited intergovernmental cooperation. (Held & McGrew, 2004, p. xi)

Needless to say, globalization is by no means a monolithic entity, and there is a radical difference between the top-down economic versions whose proponents are looking to ensure access to cheap labor and raw materials in order to maximize their profits, and what is being referred to as "globalization from below"—transnational networking to democratize global technologies, environmental resources, and media, information, and financial systems (Brecher, Costello, & Smith, 2000).

As a response to the injustices produced by neoliberal and neoconservative versions of globalization (Harvey, 2003; Kim, Millen, Irwin, & Gershman, 2000), vast multi-interest coalitions have sprung up that include human rights, environmental, faith, indigenous, student, and consumer groups, along with trade unionists, feminists, anti-sweatshop activists, anarchists, and anti-war protestors. These networks are demonstrating how a critical and inclusive public can effectively wage war against abusive states and international actors and institutions. Confronting oppression from economic, political, technological, and cultural fronts, this transnational collective action is helping people understand and fight to transform how these forces currently organize societies.

Contemporary cultural activists and social movements are compelled to adjust to shifting power relations that are the result of globalization, especially when it comes to their organizational frameworks, collective identities, and actions (della Porta & Tarrow, 2005). However, while these activists are crossing into uncharted territory, many of their theoretical orientations and organizational styles and strategies are by no means new.

Activists have inherited an immense legacy of radical thought, research, and action (Alinsky, 1971; Bobo, Kendall, & Max, 2001; Duncombe, 2002; Fox & Starn, 1997; Freeman & Johnson, 1999; Klandermans, Hanspeter, & Tarrow, 1988; Piven & Cloward, 1977; Tilly, 2004; Wieringa, 1997). An indispensable part of praxis is to make use of existing theory and research in order to study historically significant events and the actors and organizations therein that have worked towards economic and social justice; to name a few: the Abolitionists, the First and Second Internationals, the Cuban, Mexican, and Russian Revolutions, anarcho-syndicalism, experiments in social democracy, first- and second-wave feminism, and anti-colonial, civil rights, indigenous, and anti-war movements. There is also much to learn from the histories of trade union revivals, labor and environmental coalitions, anti-nuclear protests, and the global networks that have developed in the fight against AIDS. The intent of exploring the history of activism is not to generate nostalgia in these conservative times, nor does it offer up a recipe book to be followed to the last grain of salt; rather, it is a way to inspire the critical appropriation and reinvention of revolution as these struggles offer theoretical, empirical, and practical springboards for contemporary efforts.

Take for example the sociohistorical underpinnings of the 1999 "Battle for Seattle". Largely coordinated by the Direct Action Network (DAN), this multi-interest decentralized manifestation was the product of years of political reinvention (Kauffman, 2002). Seattle protestors found strength in the history of the peace movement, the civil rights activism of the 1950s and 60s, anti-nuclear and environmental movements beginning in the early 1970s, the actions against U.S. intervention in Central America in the 1980s, and decades of anti-colonial, feminist, queer, and anti-racist theory, research, and activism.

Many of the techniques and strategies used in Seattle, such as affinity groups, spokescouncils, consensus building and the use of non-violence, also have historical roots. Affinity groups—small protest units that choose targets and tactics—are derived from the Iberian Anarchist Federation in Spain, who used this underground organizing structure in the 1930s during the Spanish Civil War. It was later reinvented by chapters of Students for a Democratic Society (SDS) and other civil rights and anti-war activist groups in the late 1960s and early 1970s (Kauffman, 2002). Spokescouncil meetings have descended from the early Soviets of the Russian Revolution. Internationally, the "No Nukes" protestors of the 1970s critically appropriated this format so that representatives of affinity groups could meet, dialogue, and develop action plans. The idea of consensus decision-making was handed down by the Quakers and enhanced by feminist movements that have also valued voice, inclusion, and dialogue. Non-violent civil disobedience was inspired by Mahatma Gandhi's struggle to liberate India from British colonial rule, and later by the civil rights movement in the United States under the guidance of Martin Luther King, Jr.

The forces that made Seattle possible were also influenced by the anti-Vietnam war movement in the early 1970s that implemented small and decentralized operational strategies as opposed to many of the massive and unwieldy organizational structures of the 1960s.

In addition, many protestors in Seattle benefited from the work of the organization ACT UP, a radical coalition of activists that got its start in the late 1980s in the fight against AIDS. Its members were tired of typical party politics, the divisiveness of identity politics, and the general ineffectiveness of endless lectures at fixed protest sites. "Through innovative use of civil-rights-era nonviolent civil disobedience, guerrilla theatre, sophisticated media work, and direct action, ACT UP helped transform the world of activism" (Shepard & Hayduk, 2002, p. 1). Pushing the boundaries of protest, and borrowing aspects of the carnivalesque approach to politics that have been around since the Middle Ages

(Bakhtin, 1984), contemporary activists have made effective use of technology, street theater, puppets, block parties, art, music, and dance.[5]

Many of the activists fighting for economic and social justice in Seattle also learned about coalition building from the anti-IMF agitation of the mid-1970s, efforts to bring down the apartheid government in South Africa, battles against the North American Free Trade Agreement (NAFTA), the Zapatista revolution, the WTO protests in 1995, the shutdown of the Multilateral Agreement on Investments of 1998, and the anti-World Economic Forum (WEF) demonstration in Davos that same year.

While benefiting enormously from the invaluable lessons of history, contemporary global justice movements have also made important contributions to working for social change—contributions that are challenging existing theoretical and empirical models.

> Now that the great utopias of the nineteenth century have revealed all their perversion, it is urgent to create the conditions for collective effort to reconstruct a universe of realist ideals, capable of mobilizing people's will without mystifying their consciousness.—Pierre Bourdieu[6]

Contemporary global justice movements have critically appropriated a great deal from the Left, reinventing its possibilities while abandoning many of its dysfunctional qualities (Chong, 1991; Duncombe, 2002; Epstein, 2002; Fox & Starn, 1997; Freeman & Johnson, 1999; Tilly, 2004). Over the years, many activists have become disenchanted with the totalitarian structure of the old-guard articulation of communism, as well as its exploitation of labor within the new global economy. Progressive and radical activists have also been losing faith in organized labor because of the unequal relations of power maintained by the bureaucracies of these organizations, and their frequent capitulation to neoliberal policies. In addition, they have found little to no inspiration in the unpleasant realities of the majority of postcolonial governments. Fed up with the dogma, undemocratic structures, and intolerance to difference of these leftist movements and the slow death of social democracies at the hands of capital over the last 30 years, global justice activists have ushered in new kinds of organizing, protest, cooperation, consciousness-raising, and coalition-building—that is, a new kind of politics (Bennett, 2005; Danaher & Mark, 2003; Diani & McAdam, 2003; Guidry et al., 2000; Khagram et al., 2002; Leistyna, 2005; Mertes, 2004; della Porta & Tarrow, 2005; Shepard & Hayduk, 2002; Welton & Wolf, 2001).

Contemporary global justice movements have been effective in transcending the inhibiting walls that have been erected between what is referred to as "real" versus "cultural" politics. Many activists are cognizant of the fact that neoliberal and neoconservative versions of globalization not only consist of a structural reality built on political and economic processes and relationships, they also rely on symbolic systems to shape the kinds of meaning, identity, desire, and subjectivity that can work to ensure the maintenance of their imperial logic and practice. Influenced by many of the early critical and anti-colonial theorists, researchers, and revolutionaries, as well as by the radical activists of the civil rights era, this new generation of activists knows that imperialists have always relied on the relationship between knowledge and power to control people. They recognize how material conditions, politics, and culture are interlaced and how subordination, resistance, and opposition take place in both the physical and symbolic realm. Consequently, these new activists not only take seriously the fact that culture is a pedagogical force that shapes our sense of political agency and mediates the relations between everyday struggles and structures of power, but this time around, as will be discussed later, they are harnessing its potential in far more sophisticated and productive ways. In other words, many activists in these new movements are not only thinking about culture politically, but they are also thinking about politics culturally, with an understanding that culture and politics coexist in a symbiotic relationship in which effective political mobilization can create new cultural spaces, and such transformative political movements emerge out of progressive cultural shifts.

Regardless of their stance in the on-going debate over the power of the state—whether it has sovereignty or its power has been eclipsed by supranational organizations—virtually all factions of the global justice movement believe that national governments are often deeply implicated in perpetuating economic and social injustices, either because incumbent politicians are ideologically in line with neoliberalism, or they have been strong-armed by supranational powers. Many progressive and radical activists believe that the institutions within existing states severely limit what civil societies are able to accomplish and have thus lost faith in representative democratic structures and left-wing parties that have not offered support for their most recent responses to social and economic injustice. Instead, when it comes to participation in public life, far beyond simply voting for candidates to represent them (who usually don't come from the same social class and experience), or merely volunteering to join civil society organizations, they strive for active involvement and communicative autonomy. As Simone Chambers (2002) explains, "Communicative autonomy refers to the freedom of actors in a society to shape, criticize, and reproduce essential norms, meanings, values, and identities through communicative (as opposed to coercive) interaction" (p. 93).

She argues that voting-centric democratic theory is being replaced by talk-centric models of participation, and points to ways of moving beyond the idea of an all-inclusive vote, and away from the corrupting influences of economic and political party interests, to a democratized public sphere that creates the conditions within which all people, even those that have been historically excluded from the political process, can express themselves and work to shape the future. "Addressing public opinion directly, the activists seem to attempt (with some success) to create public spaces that are autonomous from the political parties, but also from the commercial logic of the mass media" (della Porta & Tarrow, 2005, p. 14). In addition, as Lance Bennett (2005) notes, instead of solely relying on existing governments, they strive to develop "new kinds of political relationships involving non-national mechanisms of political accountability and community, from standards monitoring and certification regimes, to demands for direct popular inclusion in supranational decision processes" (p. 214).

What makes the global justice movement different from the non-governmental organizations (NGOs) and international non-governmental organizations (INGOs) that have been at the forefront of global civil society for decades is that these more traditional organizations are often less radical in their theories and strategies and focus much of their energy on working with existing governments and institutions for policy reforms. Many members of the global justice movement, on the other hand, often distrust established institutions and nation-states and generally prefer to transform, rather than merely reform, the system. And, any neoliberal use of global civil society, which is generally understood by capitalists as a charity, non-profit, voluntary "third sector" that is responsible for replacing the welfare state, is viewed with contempt. Many advocates of the global justice movement, who are trying to democratize globalization rather than pave the way for neoliberalism, often criticize NGO/INGOs for merely tinkering with the machine, or for actually reinforcing the institutions of oppression that they claim to be challenging.

Recognizing that globalization is a crisis in representative democracy, global justice activists have been experimenting with novel approaches for bringing together multiple identities, issues, and alliances—doing so, in part, to balance the demands of political unity and cultural diversity. The goal has been to search out new forms of democratic and revolutionary identification, to recognize differences and commonalities within struggles for economic and social justice, and to work through dialogue and action to sustain what has become a "movement of many movements" (Klein, 2004, p. 220).

Rather than solely focus on class issues and economics, or on the interests of the nation-state, many global justice activists have created multi-interest coalitions, and their politics are concerned with any and all forms of exploitation and oppression, wherever they may occur. This democratizing project includes, but is not limited to, a battle against the social class structures and agenda of capitalism, racism, sexism, heterosexism, discrimination against persons with disabilities, and ethnocentrism. As such, they are working to move beyond the false binarism that has been constructed between "real" and "identity" politics. Their goal is to work towards group recognition and self-representation (allowing theoretical flexibility as such identities shift and have internal diversity), and movement interrelationships that can actually realize the redistribution of resources and the guarantee of public access and democratic rights.

Benefiting from empirical studies focused on their work (while also providing data for researchers and conducting ethnographies of their own), these activists are strategizing and building larger collective responses that have both local and global dimensions. At this historical juncture in which no society is entirely isolated, the global justice movement's innovative efforts illustrate some of the ways that it is possible to work simultaneously through a politics of location (i.e., area-specific conditions, traditions, and economic interests) and a politics of global unity. "If globalization is an amorphous phenomenon, 'glocalism'—political activism based on the insight that every local action has a global component—has been a coherent response" (Shepard & Hayduk, 2002, p. 5).

Many of these coalitions are appropriating the best of what modern and postmodern theory have to offer, finding ways of creating unity without denying specificity, and becoming politically flexible without collapsing into a pluralism of indifference. Such solidarity, as opposed to isolated localized efforts, may present the only way of combating transnational corporations that no longer need to negotiate with local labor organizations for living wages and realistic environmental protections or with area-specific human rights groups—they just go elsewhere, leaving trade restrictions, unemployment, poverty, and political chaos in their path.

These more sophisticated attempts at coalition building, developing cross-border solidarity, and influencing the means of cultural production and distribution have been made possible, in large part, by the radical changes that have taken place in the world of technology.

> In every revolution there is the paradoxical presence of circulation.—Paul Virilio[7]

Within the current stage of global techno-capitalism, corporate media are some of the most influential and powerful forces not only shaping what and how we see, but also who gets access to information. However, this corporate-driven, neoliberal revolution is being challenged by an uprising whose diverse members also clearly understand that the circulation of information is pivotal in generating collective identity and mobilizing people to act against the tyranny of market forces and other oppressive institutions, policies, and practices.

In this postmodern phase of human interaction, the circulation of information has reached unprecedented levels, made possible by advanced global communication technologies that contribute greatly, on the one hand, to the corporate model of globalization. As Mark Poster (1990) reminds us, "Cheap, reliable, durable communication is a necessity of empire" (p. 7). But, on the other hand, cyber-democracy has also been realized through more progressive and radical uses of these innovative media and the relatively autonomous zones for political activity that they offer. This cultural force has given rise to new forms of civic engagement and social capital, relations and movements. As Manuel Castells (1996) notes about this network society, "Interactive computer networks are growing exponentially, creating new forms and channels of communication, shaping life and being shaped by life at the same time" (p. 2).

While media have always played a pivotal role in activist efforts—with the advent of printing, newspapers, telephones, radio, TV, film, and so on—the power of cultural production and circulation has taken on new life with digital, multimedia, and wireless technologies, and especially with the Internet (Anderson, 2002; Bell & Kennedy, 2000; Davis, 1999; Hill, 1998; Kamark & Nye, 1999; Rash, 1997; Wilhelm, 2000). The ideas that inspire social protest now have vast geographical reach, with far greater efficiency in diffusion and influence than ever before. As Martha McCaughey and Michael Ayers (2003) observe about the Internet: "It is more immediate than a newspaper, more interactive than

TV…. It is not only instant and trans-spatial but multilateral, including many participants and connecting many different activist groups" (p. 5). Combining traditional methods of cultural activism with new interactive modes and technopolitics has not only helped individuals and organizations mobilize, but the art of organizing is undergoing radical changes as a result.

This new wireless, multimedia palette includes notebook computers, PDA (personal digital assistant) devices, cell phones (with digital cameras built in), text messaging, pagers, global GPS positioning systems, and digital camcorders. Along with the aforementioned tools, and often in connection to them, the Internet has ushered in a revolution in cultural activism. Unlike the activists of yesteryear who accomplished so much with so little, the new hybrid "smart mobs" (Rheingold, 2003) have access to email, podcasts, computer-faxes, listservs, hyperlinks, chat rooms, and downloadable street instructions. These and other cyber-tools are all used for educating the public on pertinent issues, building and mobilizing communities, coordinating events locally, nationally, and internationally, and influencing policy initiatives both locally and globally. They can also be used to transcend the language divide with software that instantly translates messages.

It is widely recognized that activists can now *be* the media. New affordable technologies and the Internet have made possible independent media sites such as Alternet, Indymedia, Truthout, and Common Dreams. Making effective use of webcasting, such news outlets offer access to Internet radio and video feeds, information and photo archives, and frequently updated news reports. There is an abundance of hyper-organization websites that keep the public up to date on current events, that support real-life mobilization, and that connect activists to other like-minded organizations through hyper-links. And, there is an endless stream of electronic information that is readily available through e-journals, blogs, online zines, and info-pages.

These innovative technologies have also made possible the reinvention of many traditional methods of activism into electronic civil disobedience in the form of online petitions, boycotts, blockades, sit-ins, hacktivism, and other kinds of cyberprotest (Jordan & Taylor, 2004).[8] What's particularly powerful about virtual agency is that people can participate from anywhere.

Perhaps the most revolutionary contribution these technologies have made is that they've radically advanced social networking. The Internet allows people, with relative facility, to cross geographical, political, and professional boundaries (Harcourt, 1999). As cyberculture helps groups transcend traditional borders, develop cross-interest coalitions, and forge collaborative knowledge, it simultaneously opens the door to more inclusive and effective political struggle. As Richard Kahn and Douglas Kellner (2005) note:

> Thus, while new mobile technology provides yet another impetus towards experimental identity construction and identity politics, such networking also links diverse communities like labor, feminist, ecological, peace, and various anti-capitalist groups, providing the basis for a new politics of alliance and solidarity to overcome the limitations of postmodern identity politics. (p. 224)

In the early 1990s, the Zapatistas in Chiapas Mexico provided an invaluable model of using media in this postmodern age in order to connect to a global audience and to cross traditional borders and forge an online transnational movement. Playing a critical role in contemporary acts of mass mobilization, the Internet has also made possible the largest coordinated international demonstration in history—the post-Iraq invasion, anti-war protest.

New Questions and Directions for Theory, Qualitative Research, and Activism

Given its appropriations from the past, and its ever-increasing push forward, the global justice movement presents a number of challenges that demand reflection, qualitative research, and innovative practical responses.

As progressive and radical transnational movements have learned much from the Left's successes and failures, there is a real effort to avoid the dangers of sectarianism, as dogma of any type inevitably leads to an extremely limited sense of community, solidarity, and agency. Instead, global justice activists are searching out new forms of democratic and revolutionary identification where a plurality of perspectives based on difference, antagonisms, and dissent are experienced as productive rather than disruptive and unacceptable. While this tactic is virtuous in any participatory democracy, it raises some red flags when it comes to social agency. Given its embrace of diversity and open exchange, the global justice movement will need to reconcile at some point the disparity that exists among its constituents in order to continue to maintain cooperative relationships among groups that have a contentious past. As Michael Hardt (2004) recalls:

> This is one of the characteristics of the Seattle events that we have had the most trouble understanding: groups which we thought in objective contradiction to one another—environmentalists and trade unions, church groups and anarchists—were suddenly able to work together, in the context of the network of the multitude. (p. 236)

While this short-term resistance movement represents a healthy democratic sphere, and challenges our understanding of how political antagonists operate, it nonetheless points to the problem of when push comes to shove in realizing specific demands, far beyond the ambiguities of mass protest, long-term co-existence is surely far more difficult to maintain and merits serious qualitative empirical investigation.

The idea of practical politics compels the individuals and groups of the global justice movement to define their action plan and terms. Identifying adversaries, articulating a clear collective agenda, teasing out contradictions in political thought and practice, and drawing new political frontiers presupposes defining the concepts of political "Left" and "Right", progressive thought and social agency, as well as hegemonic and anti-hegemonic sociocultural practices. The global justice movement is forced to risk fragmentation by carving out a more specific set of ideological parameters through which it operates, beyond the World Social Forum's Charter. The goal of achieving unity in diversity while also maintaining an activist stance requires that we work through what need not be a contradiction between a Gramscian vision of civil society and war of position intended to use cultural and political practices on multiple fronts to lead to revolutionary change rather than just mere representation, while creating and protecting a Habermasian public sphere that can burgeon within a liberal democracy to serve as a venue for the free exchange of ideas—an exchange through which mobilization can germinate. The possibilities of this open interaction/intervention dialectic also calls for extensive empirical work.

The diverse groups that make up the global justice movement are usually geographically separated and often rely solely on technologies in order to communicate and network. They also are working within the realities of flexible citizenship—a product of the cultural logics of transnationality (Ong, 1999). While this phenomenon of cross-border coalition building leads to a more globalized framing of issues and identity, the struggle to maintain a coherent political front and action plan is made that much more difficult as "different parts of advocacy networks need to appeal to belief systems, life worlds, and stories, myths, and folk tales in many different countries and cultures. This is even more problematic when networks link activists from highly industrialized and less developed countries" (Meyer & Tarrow, 1998, p. 224). As such, global justice activists will need to continuously overcome cultural, linguistic, material, and ideological differences—differences in political orientation—and continue to achieve substantive change of the likes of environmental treaties, the World Commission on Dams, protection of indigenous rights, international agreements on standards, and the defeat of the Multilateral Agreement on Investment. Research in how this has been and continues to be achieved is sorely needed given that the West is already guilty of "premature formulation of universal civic values before there had been sufficient intercultural discourse to establish an authentic consensus about such values, particularly in relation to individual rights versus group rights" (Boulding, 1997, p. ix).

This issue of inclusion and opt-in membership also points to the problem of political capacity and direction. Creating the self-empowering conditions within which the subaltern can speak—a critical feature of any participatory democracy—does not mean that their participation comes with ideological guarantees. Empowered communities could in fact result in the rule of an oppressive majority. There is an extensive history of cases where feminist movements, working-class struggles, Gay and Lesbian groups, anti-racist efforts, and anti-globalization movements have experienced discriminatory and conservative tendencies; and where some struggles for national sovereignty have turned fascist, mass revolutions have become totalitarian, or social democracies have capitulated to capitalist demands. Within the complex set of social relations that make up global governance, global justice networks need to pay close attention to and document the very real risks of the emergence of reactionary movements and the risks of general co-optation. There is a good deal of research that is insightful in providing historical examples of how this has happened.

If "equality" is really one of the ultimate goals of a participatory democracy, and this call is not limited to the liberal notion of "equal opportunity" within existing economic relations, then social class has to be eliminated altogether, and with it capitalism as class is a structural inevitability of its logic. Ellen Meiksins Wood (1995) reminds us that unlike a world that can strive to provide social justice for and harmony among racial, ethnic, religious, sexual, and gender differences, it's impossible to imagine "class differences without exploitation and domination" (p. 258). Is the global justice movement working to define and implement a new socialist agenda, and if so, what shapes will it take? Different social, economic, and political commitments will also require different tactics in how anti-capitalist, anti-statist groups strategically work with the NGO/INGOs who are aligned with national governments and working towards a "more humane" form of capitalism (Gautney, 2005). In fact, while interacting with existing political parties, structures, and institutions, progressives and radicals will have to reconcile the contradiction of building a new world order with some old world tools.

Activists are also confronted with three contradicting options that have serious implications for the future of social agency: working towards a democratized world government that bypasses the oppressive nature of nation-states; looking to maintain national borders and develop the kinds of sovereignty that ensure protection from the colonizing forces of capital; or searching for alternative, non-national, horizontal networks with a local focus and global voice.[9] Commitments to different governing structures will certainly change the movement and thus need to be theorized through, observed and investigated in great detail, and challenged by researchers/activists.[10]

While cyberactivism is theoretically, empirically, and practically interdisciplinary, there is a great deal of theoretical and empirical work that also needs to be done in this area in order to combine these forces and make possible greater economic, political, and cultural change. One way to maximize its effectiveness would be to establish a network of scholars and activists that could combine forces in producing more effective online activism (McCaughey & Ayers, 2003). In addition, using quantitative and qualitative methodologies, researchers need to look into the pros and cons of working relationships that exist between offline and online activists. And, while collective identity development has been explored by social movement research, it would be enormously beneficial to research the kinds of community commitment that actually emerge from cyberspace.

Theorists, researchers, and activists concerned with cyberdemocracy also need to continue to focus on the vast poststructural work that addresses the role of language and framing in shaping consciousness and collective identity (Lakoff, 2004; Melucci, 1996). They need to explore in far greater depth the dialogical and dialectical relationship between changes in communication patterns and changes in activists. If Poster (1990) is correct in arguing that "changes in the configuration or wrapping of language alters the way the subject processes signs into meanings, that sensitive point of cultural production. The shift from oral and print wrapped language to electronically wrapped language thus reconfigures the subject's relation to the world" (p. 11), then we desperately need to examine the effects of electronically mediated communication on activists.

Technological advances have already given rise to new kinds of research, such as interface analysis, which studies the interface as a medium of cultural production that generates particular kinds of interaction (McCaughey & Ayers, 2003). Within the Internet's realm of symbolic exchange, it is important to look at what ideological and tactical effects the organizers of these cyber-bases have had on real-life activists.

Theorists, researchers, and activists also need to pay more attention to online movements of the political Right, and how they (of course recognizing this category as diverse and complex) have used cyberspace to promote their causes and build their constituencies.

We should also pay close attention to how the race to commercialize the Net is impacting politics—both real and virtual. As part of this effort, a great deal more investigation is necessary into the corporate and government bodies currently trying to colonize cyberspace. This is a particularly urgent mission in a post-9/11 world where the threat of "terrorism" is being used as the pretext for curbing online rights, privacy, and access to information. There is much to learn from the victories that have been won by groups who are fighting against this repression—groups such as the Electronic Frontier Foundation (EFF), the Center for Democracy and Technology (CDT), and Computer Professionals for Social Responsibility.

While some theorists see the Internet as working within a Habermasian public sphere—as a communication medium that is decentered and nonhierarchical (Salter, 2003)—a key issue that needs to be confronted pertains to the realities of the digital divide. We need to work to link *all* groups, both locally and globally, as computer technologies, software, and technological literacy are so unequally distributed, especially in poor communities and between the North and the South.

As this chapter has worked to point out, for those of us who wish to visualize and realize change in a world that is rapidly spinning out of control, it's critical that we continue to make effective use of the synergy that exists among theory, qualitative research, and activism. In order to assist people and organizations in securing human, economic, and political rights in this age of globalization, we need to continue to critically appropriate from the past, actively theorize the present, and forge new frameworks of analysis, new research methods, and creative and courageous actions that, when realized and mobilized with others around us—whether that be with our neighbors next door or the ones 6,000 miles away—allow us to work together towards short- and long-term strategies directed at radical but achievable democratic change.

A crucial part of this democratizing project is to realize, as the global justice movement has, that theory needs to be flexible. While understanding the ways in which existing theories explain social reality is enormously important, *theorizing* is the ability to actively engage bodies of knowledge and human practices for the logics and sociohistorical conditions that inform them so that they can be reworked. It encourages individuals to evaluate, based on their own experiences, expertise and insight, the strengths and weaknesses of any conceptual and practical movement, and recontextualize and reinvent its possibilities for one's own predicaments, while extending, when possible, its geographical reach (Leistyna, 2005).

It is important to re-emphasize that while engaged in the exploratory and creative process that theorizing offers, one's own subject position should always be held in a critical light, not only for the purposes of continued self-actualization, but also, as action-based research has long pointed out, so that the ethical stances that are taken on an issue allow a person to speak to particular problems and in solidarity *with* others rather than *for* people from different backgrounds. In this way, theory does not have a monopoly on understanding, rather it reveals much about how we relate to the world and the assumptions that guide our political actions. As Cornelius Castoriadis (1987) argues:

More than in any other area, here the idea of pure theory is an incoherent fiction. There exists no place, no point of view outside of history and society, or "logically prior" to them, where one could be placed in order to construct the theory of them.... (p. 3)

As an integral part of any political project, theorizing presents a constant challenge to imagine and materialize alternative political spaces and identities and more just and equitable economic, social, and cultural relations. It makes possible consciousness raising, coalition building, resistance, activism, and structural change.

Likewise, qualitative research—all empirical work for that matter—has to maintain methodological flexibility in order for it to provide a lifeline to theory and "knowable communities" engaged in cultural and political reflection and struggle. Advocates of such exploratory processes need to learn from action research's model of doing research *with* others rather than *on* them, and thus speaking *with* rather than *to* people engaged in eradicating injustice. Making use of any and all methodological approaches—even creating new ones to address a specific set of conditions—researchers can help create the self-empowering conditions within which people can conduct their own studies, forge democratic organizational structures and decision-making processes, and work towards generative learning, social networking, and personal and social transformation through praxis.

Notes

1. Arundhati Roy (2001, p. 7).
2. They have also been influenced by classical theories of participation and cooperation e.g., the ideas of Jean-Jacques Rousseau, Robert Owen, and John Stuart Mill.
3. While coming from the field of cognitive linguistics, George Lakoff (2004), who has worked in the area of political leadership, reminds his readers, in his more recent analysis of frames, that neoliberals and neo-cons have been successful because they have put an enormous amount of capital and energy into developing think tanks, spokespeople, and media outlets that have effectively used language to dominate politics in the U.S. He argues that reframing is social change.
4. Fredric Jameson (1999, p. xi).
5. Instead of continuing the binarism between artistic expression and social responsibility, radical street activists have learned much from the Brazilian Theater of the Oppressed of Augusto Boal, as well as from the Butoh dancers of Japan, Bread and Puppet Theater, and the San Francisco Mime Troupe (Starr, 2001).
6. Pierre Bourdieu (1998, p. 9).
7. Paul Virilio (1977, p. 3).
8. In addition to informing and mobilizing groups, the Internet has also expanded the terrain of culture jamming with laser-projected messaging, the creation of subversive websites (such as those generated by the Yes Men), and Google bombs that expose and ridicule abusive individuals and corporations. The Electronic Disturbance Theater embodies this new electronic ethos. Its members, who have combined theory and politics with performance art, and computerized resistance with mass decentered electronic direct action, have, for example, developed a webjamming tool called Flood-Net to flood and block corporate and supranational organization websites. It's important to note here that there's a long history of electronic hacking that has been critically appropriated by this new generation of hacktivists (Jordan & Taylor, 2004). Hacktivism—a combination of grassroots political protest and computer hacking—has assumed the earlier waves' electronic populist and anti-corporate values, and has become a powerful force in the globalization debate.
9. For example, "Indigenous forms of organization continue to provide a radical challenge to modern political organization—in particular the nation-state—and offer possibilities that need to be considered seriously in any speculation over place-based democratic alternatives to the abstractions of both national and transnational political identities" (Prazniak & Dirlik, 2001, p. 9). The current experiments with democracy in Argentina—with neighborhood and citywide delegate assemblies—are not relying on the maintenance of the nation-state.
10. As the idea of civil society has always presupposed a politically defined territory, many theorists are concerned about how global civil society can function without such a geopolitical focus—that is, without a global state (Colás, 2002). Some activists have simply retheorized civil society as a free-standing entity that does not need a fixed governing apparatus to grieve and work for change, relying instead on autonomous social movements and the mass mobilization of people. Another response to this dilemma is that there are indeed international governing bodies and doctrine in existence, and others that are emerging on a regular basis that can support activist efforts or be challenged, e.g., the United Nations, the European Union, the establishment of laws protecting international human rights, the development of an international criminal court, and global treaties (Kaldor, 2003). At the same time, as mentioned earlier, there are forces of the likes of the G-8, the World Bank, the IMF, and the WTO that do resemble independent global governance—albeit mostly through private authority—that is often beyond the power and influence of the state.

References

Alasuutari, P. (1995). *Researching culture: Qualitative method and cultural studies.* London, England: Sage.

Alinsky, S. (1971). *Rules for radicals: A pragmatic primer for realistic radicals.* New York, NY: Vintage.

Anderson, D. M. (Ed.). (2002). *The civic web: Online politics and democratic values.* Boulder, CO: Rowman & Littlefield.

Atweh, B., Kemmis, S., & Weeks, P. (Eds.). (1998). *Action research in practice: Partnerships for social justice education.* New York, NY: Routledge.

Bakhtin, M. (1984). *Rabelais and his world.* Bloomington: Indiana University Press.

Bauman, Z. (1998). *Globalization: The human consequences.* New York, NY: Columbia University Press.

Bell, D., & Kennedy, B. M. (Eds.). (2000). *The cybercultures reader.* New York, NY: Routledge.

Bennett, L. W. (2005). Social movements beyond borders: Understanding two eras of transnational activism. In D. della Porta & S. Tarrow (Eds.), *Transnational protest and global activism: People, passions, and power* (pp. 203–226). Boulder, CO: Rowman & Littlefield.

Bobo, K., Kendall, J., & Max, S. (2001). *Organizing for social change: Midwest Academy manual for activists.* Washington, DC: Seven Locks Press.

Boulding, E. (1997). Foreword. In J. Smith, C. Chatfield, & R. Pagnucco (Eds.), *Transnational social movements and global politics: Solidarity beyond the state* (pp. ix–xi). Syracuse, NY: Syracuse University Press.

Bourdieu, P. (1998). *Acts of resistance: Against the tyranny of the market.* New York, NY: New Press.

Bray, J. N., Lee, J., Smith, L. L., & Yorks, L. (2000). *Collaborative inquiry in practice: Action, reflection, and making meaning.* London, England: Sage.

Brecher, J., Costello, T., & Smith, B. (2000). *Globalization from below: The power of solidarity.* Cambridge, MA: South End Press.

Brown, T., & Jones, L. (2001). *Action research and postmodernism: Congruence and critique.* Buckingham, England: Open University Press.

Castells, M. (1996). *The rise of the network society.* Oxford, England: Blackwell.

Castoriadis, C. (1987). *The imaginary institution of society.* Cambridge, MA: MIT Press.

Chambers, S. (2002). A critical theory of civil society. In S. Chambers & W. Kymlicka (Eds.), *Alternative conceptions of civil society* (pp. 90–110). Princeton, NJ: Princeton University Press.

Chomsky, N. (1993). *Year 501: The conquest continues.* Boston, MA: South End Press.

Chong, D. (1991). *Collective action and the civil rights movement.* Chicago, IL: University of Chicago Press.

Colás, A. (2002). *International civil society.* Oxford, England: Polity.

Danaher, K., & Mark, J. (2003). *Insurrection: Citizen challenges to corporate power.* New York, NY: Routledge.

Davis, R. (1999). *The web of politics: The Internet's impact on the American political system.* Oxford, England: Oxford University Press.

Della Porta, D., & Tarrow, S. (Eds.). (2005). *Transnational protest and global activism: People, passions, and power.* Boulder, CO: Rowman & Littlefield.

Denzin, N. K., & Lincoln, Y. S. (Eds.). (2000). *Handbook of qualitative research* (2nd ed.). London, England: Sage.

Diani, M., & McAdam, D. (Eds.). (2003). *Social movements and networks: Relational approaches to collective action.* Oxford, England: Oxford University Press.

Duncombe, S. (Ed.). (2002). *Cultural resistance reader.* London, England: Verso.

Epstein, B. (2002). The politics of prefigurative community: The non-violent direct action movement. In S. Duncombe (Ed.), *Cultural resistance reader* (pp. 333–346). London, England: Verso.

Fals Borda, O. (2004). Participatory (action) research in social theory: Origins and challenges. In P. Reason & H. Bradbury (Eds.), *Handbook of action research: Participative inquiry and practice* (pp. 27–37). London, England: Sage.

Fox, R., & Starn, O. (Eds.). (1997). *Between resistance and revolution: Cultural politics and social protest.* New Brunswick, NJ: Rutgers University Press.

Freeman, J., & Johnson, V. (Eds.). (1999). *Waves of protest: Social movements since the sixties.* Boulder, CO: Rowman & Littlefield.

Frow, J., & Morris, M. (2000). Cultural studies. In N. K. Denzin & Y. S. Lincoln (Eds.), *Handbook of qualitative research* (2nd ed., pp. 315–346). London, England: Sage.

Gautney, H. (2005). The World Social Forum: From protest to politics. *Situations: Project of the radical imagination, 1*(1), 75–86.

Gitlin, A. (Ed.). (1994). *Power and method: Political activism and educational research.* New York, NY: Routledge.

Greenwood, D. J., & Levin, M. (1998). *Introduction to action research: Social research for social change.* Thousand Oaks, CA: Sage.

Guidry, J. A., Kennedy, M. D., & Zald, M. N. (Eds.). (2000). *Globalizations and social movements: Culture, power, and the transnational public sphere.* Ann Arbor: University of Michigan Press.

Hall, R. B., & Biersteker, T. J. (Eds.). (2002). *The emergence of private authority in global governance.* Cambridge, England: Cambridge University Press.

Harcourt, W. (Ed.). (1999). *Women@Internet: Creating new cultures in cyberspace.* London, England: Zed Books.

Hardt, M. (2004). Today's Bandung? In T. Mertes (Ed.), *A movement of movements: Is another world really possible?* (pp. 230–236). London, England: Verso.

Hardt, M., & Negri, A. (2000). *Empire*. Cambridge, MA: Harvard University Press.

Harvey, D. (2001). *Spaces of capital: Towards a critical geography*. New York, NY: Routledge.

Harvey, D. (2003). *The new imperialism*. Oxford, England: Oxford University Press.

Held, D., & McGrew, A. (Eds.). (2004). *Governing globalization: Power, authority and global governance*. Oxford, England: Polity.

Hill, K. A. (1998). *Cyber politics*. Boulder, CO: Rowman & Littlefield.

Jameson, F. (1999). Preface. In F. Jameson & M. Miyoshi (Eds.), *The cultures of globalization* (pp. xi–xvii). Durham, NC: Duke University Press.

Jason, L. A., Keys, C. B., Suarez-Balcazar, Y., Taylor, R. R., & Davis, M. I. (2002). *Participatory community research: Theories and methods in action*. Washington, DC: American Psychological Association.

Jordan, T., & Taylor, P. A. (2004). *Hacktivism and cyberwars: Rebels with a cause?* New York, NY: Routledge.

Kahn, R., & Kellner, D. (2005). Internet subcultures and political activism. In P. Leistyna (Ed.), *Cultural studies: From theory to action* (pp. 217–230). Oxford, England: Blackwell.

Kaldor, M. (2003). *Global civil society: An answer to war*. Oxford, England: Polity.

Kamark, E., & Nye, J. (1999). *Democracy.com?: Governance in a networked world*. Hollis, NH: Hollis.

Kauffman, L. A. (2002). A short history of radical renewal. In B. Shepard & R. Hayduk (Eds.), *From Act Up to the WTO: Urban protest and community building in the era of globalization* (pp. 35–40). London, England: Verso.

Keck, M. E., & Sikkink, K. (1998). *Activists beyond borders: Advocacy networks in international politics*. Ithaca, NY: Cornell University Press.

Kemmis, S., & Wilkinson, M. (1998). Participatory action research and the study of practice. In B. Atweh, S. Kemmis, & P. Weeks (Eds.), *Action research in practice: Partnerships for social justice education* (pp. 21–36). New York, NY: Routledge.

Khagram, S., Riker, J. V., & Sikkink, K. (Eds.). (2002). *Restructuring world politics: Transnational social movements, networks, and norms*. Minneapolis: University of Minnesota Press.

Kim, J. Y., Millen, J. V., Irwin, A., & Gershman, J. (Eds.). (2000). *Dying for growth: Global inequality and the health of the poor*. Monroe, ME: Common Courage Press.

Klandermans, B., Hanspeter, K., & Tarrow, S. (Eds.). (1988). *From structure to action: Comparing social movement participation*. Greenwich, CT: JAI Press.

Klandermans, B., & Staggenborg, S. (Eds.). (2002). *Methods of social movement research*. Minneapolis: University of Minnesota Press.

Klein, N. (2004). Reclaiming the commons. In T. Mertes (Ed.), *A movement of movements: Is another world really possible?* (pp. 219–229). London, England: Verso.

Lakoff, G. (2004). *Don't think of an elephant!: Know your values and frame the debate*. White River Junction, VT: Chelsea Green.

Lash, S., & Urry, J. (1987). *The end of organized capitalism*. Madison: University of Wisconsin Press.

Leistyna, P. (Ed.). (2005). *Cultural studies: From theory to action*. Oxford, England: Blackwell.

McAdam, D., McCarthy, J. D., & Zald, M. N. (Eds.). (1996). *Comparative perspectives on social movements: Political opportunities, mobilizing structures, and cultural framings*. Cambridge, England: Cambridge University Press.

McCaughey, M., & Ayers, M. D. (Eds.). (2003). *Cyberactivism: Online activism in theory and practice*. New York, NY: Routledge.

McGuigan, J. (Ed.). (1997). *Cultural methodologies*. London, England: Sage.

McLaren, P. (1995). *Critical pedagogy and predatory culture: Oppositional politics in a postmodern era*. New York, NY: Routledge.

Meiksins Wood, E. (1995). *Democracy against capitalism: Renewing historical materialism*. Cambridge, England: Cambridge University Press.

Melucci, A. (1996). *Challenging codes: Collective action in the information age*. Cambridge, England: Cambridge University Press.

Mertes, T. (Ed.). (2004). *A movement of movements: Is another world really possible?* London, England: Verso.

Meyer, D. S., & Tarrow, S. (Eds.). (1998). *The social movement society: Contentious politics for a new century*. Boulder, CO: Rowman & Littlefield.

Ong, A. (1999). *Flexible citizenship: The cultural logics of transnationality*. Durham, NC: Duke University Press.

Pilotta, J. J., McCaughan, J. A., Jasko, S., Murphy, J., Jones, T., Wilson, L.,... Endress, K. (2001). *Communication and social action research*. Cresskill, NJ: Hampton Press.

Piven, F. F., & Cloward, R. A. (1977). *Poor people's movements: Why they succeed, how they fail*. New York, NY: Vintage.

Poster, M. (1990). *The mode of information: Poststructuralism and social context*. Chicago, IL: University of Chicago Press.

Prazniak, R., & Dirlik, A. (2001). Introduction: Cultural identity and the politics of place. In R. Prazniak & A. Dirlik (Eds.), *Places and politics in an age of globalization* (pp. 3–13). Boulder, CO: Rowman & Littlefield.

Rash, W. (1997). *Politics on the net: Wiring the political process*. New York, NY: Freeman.

Reason, P., & Bradbury, H. (2004). *Handbook of action research: Participative inquiry and practice*. London, England: Sage.

Rheingold, H. (2003). *Smart mobs: The next social revolution*. New York, NY: Basic Books.

Rosaldo, R. (1989). *Culture and truth: The remaking of social analysis*. Boston, MA: Beacon Press.

Roy, A. (2001). *Power politics*. Cambridge, MA: South End Press.

Salter, L. (2003). Democracy, new social movements, and the Internet: A Habermasian analysis. In M. McCaughey & M. D. Ayers (Eds.), *Cyberactivism: Online activism in theory and practice* (pp. 117–144). New York, NY: Routledge.

Saukko, P. (2003). *Doing research in cultural studies: An introduction to classical and new methodological approaches.* London, England: Sage.

Scott, J. (1992). Experience. In J. Butler & J. Scott (Eds.), *Feminists theorize the political* (pp. 22–40). New York, NY: Routledge.

Shepard, B., & Hayduk, R. (Eds.). (2002). *From Act Up to the WTO: Urban protest and community building in the era of globalization.* London, England: Verso.

Smith, J., Chatfield, C., & Pagnucco, R. (Eds.). (1997). *Transnational social movements and global politics: Solidarity beyond the state.* Syracuse, NY: Syracuse University Press.

Starr, A. (2001). Art and revolution: Revitalizing political protest. In N. Welton & L. Wolf (Eds.), *Global uprising: Confronting the tyrannies of the 21st century.* Gabriola Island, BC, Canada: New Society.

Stringer, E. T. (1999). *Action research.* London, England: Sage.

Tarrow, S. (1998). *Power in movement: Social movements are contentious politics.* Cambridge, England: Cambridge University Press.

Tilly, C. (2004). *Social movements, 1768–2004.* Boulder, CO: Paradigm.

Virilio, P. (1977). *Speed and politics.* New York, NY: Semiotext(e).

Weis, L., & Fine, M. (2004). *Working method: Research and social justice.* New York, NY: Routledge.

Welton, N., & Wolf, L. (Eds.). (2001). *Global uprising: Confronting the tyrannies of the 21st century.* Gabriola Island, BC, Canada: New Society.

Wieringa, S. (Ed.). (1997). *Subversive women: Women's movements in Africa, Asia, Latin America and the Caribbean.* London, England: Zed Books.

Wilhelm, A. (2000). *Democracy in a digital age: Challenge to political life in cyberspace.* New York, NY: Routledge.

Wilkinson, R., & Hughes, S. (Eds.). (2002). *Global governance: Critical perspectives.* London, England: Routledge.

CHAPTER FIFTEEN

Enlightening the Stranger Within: (Re)viewing Critical Research from/on/in the Centre

Jon Austin

Sometimes I say, why do empirical work at all? What does it mean to use other people's lives as data?
— Patti Lather, 2007

Researching the social world is always a troubling and frequently a morally tortuous process, and for many decades, the question of the veracity of social research has been exposed as a major one of confidence for those who would see a contribution to social betterment as the fundamental purpose behind inquiring into social problems. The literature that traverses this terrain of uncertainty is voluminous, and it is not the place of this chapter to engage in anything akin to even a summary excursion through it. Suffice to say, questions of purpose, method and methodology, epistemological integrity, representational appropriateness, technical accuracy and trustworthiness and the like have all figured at various points as major areas of concern, scrutiny and development of critical qualitative research.

There are three sources of inspiration or relevance to my conceptualization of my research work in what I am wont to believe resides in the area of critical praxis/practice: Norm Denzin and Yvonna Lincoln's (2005) characterization of the development of qualitative research as moving through a number of moments; Patti Lather's recent work on various paradigms of interpretivist research; and Brian Fay's examination of the foundations of a critical social science. While evincing a number of contiguities and commonalities, each of these contains important, almost unique, points of relevance for the consideration of what constitutes a critical qualitative research approach. In this section, I undertake very brief discussions of these views of critical social research in order to set up a base for presenting and interrogating one particular strand of research work with which I have been engaged for well over a decade-and-a-half: explorations of the White Self. It is not my intention to engage in any sort of detailed description or discussion of these works or ideas as a whole, but to bring to the front the parts of each that have resonated with my own engagement with a critical social praxis.

221

This first section, then, turns its scrutiny to the question of what might be the essential features of a critical engagement with knowing, of a schematic response to the question of what a contribution to a critical social science might require. In this, I work the boundaries of Brian Fay's (1987) schema of a critical social science to throw up evaluative criteria for determining the genuine criticality of my White Self project. Thinking here in terms of both evaluation and criteria is not, hopefully, to succumb to the demands of what Strathern has called a worldwide audit culture (2000). It is, instead, a move to deploy such a schema as a provocation to a considered critique of particular research work from the perspectives of its success or failure in being critical enough. It is, as Lather says, a way of "negotiating what it means to (re)think critique and practice in such 'dark enough' (MacLure, 2004) times" (Lather 2007, p. 3).

A Few Moments with Norm Denzin (and Yvonna Lincoln)

Norm Denzin has been a passionate and articulate advocate of the importance of social betterment as the function of research, particularly qualitative inquiry, for many years. With Yvonna Lincoln, he has vigorously analyzed the development of qualitative inquiry over what currently amounts to nine particular "moments". This work has become something of an organizing and identity marker—a rallying point almost—for those looking to embrace research as a form of emancipatory activity. In essence, qualitative research can be seen to have moved through a number of stages, crises or moments. Such stages are not necessarily carved out by any identifiable school of thought or methodological movement as such, but arise because of the challenges and forces extant in particular socio-political contexts. The moments coalesce around and are circumscribed by "the appearances of new sensibilities, times when qualitative researchers become aware of issues they had not imagined before" (Denzin & Lincoln, 2005a, p. 1116).

While analyzing the emergence of these moments from a largely chronological approach, Denzin and Lincoln emphasize the fact that none of these moments are ever not in the process of being and becoming. The moments circulate at all times, with the current moment—the methodologically contested present—perhaps best evincing the whirlpool effect of this methodological swirling. This is the new age "where messy, uncertain, multivoiced texts, cultural criticism, and new experimental works will become more common, as will more reflexive forms of fieldwork, analysis and intertextual representation" (2005b, p. 26), and yet while new ways of engaging the world and coming to know and understand those aspects of the lives of people that have previously been largely untouched or unsought by researchers now present to us, the legacies and practices of previous/other moments of research remain in many ways as unthinking invisible indicators of what constitutes "research".

We currently face what Denzin and Lincoln have identified as the ninth moment: the "fractured future" in which "methodologists will line up on two opposing sides of a great divide" (2005a, p. 1123). One of these sides is that of the seemingly ascendant, scientifically based research movement based upon the standards of proof, objectivity, generalizability and explanatory/control power that fall from a biomedical research paradigm. This is the so-called "gold standard", epitomized by quantitative experimental-design approaches. On the other side assemble those who would see research having transformative rather than control potential and purpose. These are proponents and practitioners of a whole new range of qualitative social research, who draw on and from feminist, poststructuralist, indigenous, queer, critical and related traditions and methodologies. The fractured future is where critical social research finds both its moment of truth and its nemesis in the struggle over what constitutes science and scientific ways of knowing and doing.

In his more recent work, Denzin has redoubled his efforts in exhorting, almost pleading with, members of the moral community that qualitative researchers inhabit to look to the opportunities open to them—the privileges granted to them *qua* researchers—to work for an "interpretive social science that is simultaneously autoethnographic, vulnerable, performative and critical" (2009, p. 240).

Research within this moral community "is rooted in a concept of care, of shared governance, of neighborliness, of love, kindness and the moral good" (2009, p. 292). In a manner consistent with the very basics of critical social science and research as described by Fay (see below), Denzin's expectations of those works that emanate from the endeavors of socially oriented researchers is that they should "generate social criticism and lead to resistance, empowerment, and social action, to positive change in the social world" (2009, p. 292).

From Denzin's individual and collaborative work, I can find a very comfortable space for the location of my views about, hopes for and ways of going about inquiry into the sorts of things that seem(ed) to me to be important, crucial to the social betterment aim that rested within the transformative intentions of critical social research. I could identify with the emancipatory quest of that work being done within the eighth moment, and I cheered the emergence of the possibilities attendant upon the emergence of the ninth.

Getting Lost with Patti Lather

Continuing the intellectual bowerbird/bricoleur *modus operandi* a little further, my view of what a critical qualitative research project should be has recently been strongly influenced by a series of powerful statements and questions from Patti Lather in her book *Getting Lost: Feminist Efforts Toward a Double(d) Science* (2007). In this work, Lather draws upon the experience of working with and then writing about (Lather & Smithies, 1997) a group of women diagnosed with AIDS as a provocation to consider many aspects of what it means to research and report critically. Lather celebrates a methodology of getting lost—"the ruins of methodology, the end of transcendent claims and grand narratives: methodology under erasure…the loss of absolute knowledge" (2007, pp. 2, 3)—that contributes to a less comfortable social science. Ethnography—as a dominant form of and a virtual codeword for qualitative inquiry these days—becomes "a space surprised by difference into the practices of notknowing" (p. 7) and the ethnographer/researcher's maturity and confidence in their craft would see him or her embracing the thought that "'getting lost' might both produce different knowledge and produce knowledge differently" (p. 13).

Lather's ideas in *Getting Lost* have unsettled my own degree of comfort with what I had considered to be one of my more satisfying pieces of critical ethnographic work: my doctoral project on white racial identity. What particularly triggered the intellectual uneasiness and methodological squirming on my part were Lather's thoughts about her whole motivation for involvement with the women of her study. She asks two awkward questions of herself that read like they were aimed at possibly any qualitative researcher but certainly resonated squarely with me:

What work do we want inquiry to do? (p. 39)

What does it mean to use other people's lives as data? (p. 52)

These are central concerns for the critical qualitative researcher, questions that go to the heart of the project and, more importantly, to the heart of the researcher. Let me explore just a couple of points about each of these questions a little further here, in order to establish a base for my reconsideration of my own performance (in a Denzian sense) of being a critical qualitative researcher later in this chapter. In this, I cannot do justice to the deep and poetic timbre of Lather's own words, but am looking to highlight some lessons, caveats and "moments of bafflement" (Spivak, 1990, p. 55) that presented themselves to me as I read—increasingly uncomfortably—her dissection and exposure of herself/Self *qua* researcher and as person.

Lather wrestles with her motives for participating in the *Troubling the Angels* project and in the process engages the (frequently unquestioned) purpose of critical qualitative research. As I will return to later in this section when considering the ideas of Brian Fay, critical social inquiry, research, theory—in fact, critical *anything*—has as its teleological purpose the emancipation of those affected by oppression, disadvantage and marginalization. This end often goes both unchallenged and unproblematized by those who decide or need to work for social betterment. Lather, however, explores the problematic question, What does it mean to be emancipatory? Of her own work with women dying of HIV/AIDS, she asks:

> I mean, who is going to get emancipated here? They've got AIDS and they brought me into the project to get their stories out to help other women. I mean where is the emancipatory intention, where is the direction of the intention, for whom is this emancipatory and in what way? (2007, p. 50)

This questioning of the presumed purpose and outcome of engaging in self-proclaimed critical activity bites twice as hard in Lather's case when she then teams this question with the one that, with delicious double meaning, asks: "What does it mean to use other people's lives as data?... Why do I want them to be data, rather than my teachers?" (2007, p. 52). In the case of *Troubling the Angels*, Lather is almost literally using the lives—and deaths—of her participants as data in ways that she struggles to reconcile with an emancipatory purpose or intention. How can her work be emancipatory for these women, many of whom will presumably have died by the time her project work is more than a year or two old? How does one determine the worth of social inquiry from an emancipatory perspective unless one can see a connection to those for whom emancipation is likely to occur? This presents to me as a very sobering and disruptive thought: for all my work, which I felt was surely contributing to making the world a better place for those connected in some way to the thrust of my activity—typically in the area of race and ethnicity—did I have any real idea for whom this work might be emancipatory and how such liberation might actually occur?

Further, in looking at the representational work involved in the reporting on social research, Lather opens the topic of how genuinely the words and images of the researcher—however well intentioned— might ever not constitute violence to those whose lives are being represented. She lays bare the often unspoken guilt that attaches to any research work: the uneasiness with the fact that no matter how democratically, authentically or empathetically the researcher might go about her or his work, "you can't get away from manipulating the data. It's what we do!" (2007, p. 29). This leads her to another crucial point about social research, even of the critical, emancipatory-oriented kind: "How can writing the other not be an act of continuing colonization?" (2007, p. 13). In looking to overcome oppression and disadvantage, we are driven to engage in our own form of making the victim in our preferred image of them. This, clearly, requires that the researcher be aware of her or his own motives, positionality and politics—that there be a personal reconciliation of motive and action, that at the very least the colonization engaged in is more defensible than that being disrupted through the research work.

In response to the question of her greatest fear in her reconsidered view of the work she had been engaged in, Lather answers with what should be a prompt to any researcher to hesitate and think: "[My greatest fear in all of this is] that I will kill them with my high theory, that I will eat away their stories" (2007, p. 51).

Revisiting the Beginning: Fay's Critical Social Science

I now want to return to one of the texts I began with as I commenced my doctoral research, Brian Fay's *Critical Social Science* (1987). There were, of course, many others that had opened my eyes and mind to the need for exposé-type research, that had fed my interest in critical work. Some of these were philosophical calls-to-arms: George Counts' *Dare the School Build a New Social Order* (1932), Henry Giroux's *Teachers as Intellectuals* (1988), Richard Dyer's *White* (1997) and Edward Said's *Orientalism* (1978). Others were more methodological: Denzin (1995, 1997), Studs Terkel's oral histories, everything I could find by Harry Wolcott, and Jipson and Paley's wonderful book *Daredevil Research* (1996). But the single most influential book about research I read at this time was Fay's. It still provides me with a provocation to consider the features of my research work that might at times run the risk of descending into overly self-centered concerns, largely because of the way in which Fay articulates what social science research might need to aim for, work at being and demonstrate in order to satisfy the tag of "critical".

Fay's ideas reside squarely within the boundaries of "orthodox" critical theory, and he seeks in *Critical Social Science* to explore the foundations of a social science that might emanate with integrity from that same theoretical space and resonate with the same emancipatory aims. Essentially, he sees life for most people in the world as having been mediated by false consciousness—"they unwittingly fashion their lives in necessarily self-defeating ways" (p. 15)—and that until an explanatory power (a science) arises that can demonstrate the falsity of the dominant views of social relationships, forms of community organization and the like that combine to forge the conditions under which such oppressive and alienating forms of living arise and thrive, humans will continue to be less than themselves. Such a science could only emerge from a coalescence of what Fay calls the "tripartite process of enlightenment, empowerment, and emancipation" (p. 29). It is within this process that research or inquiry into the nature of the social, its problems and their causes assumes such a significance—as the enlightenment part of the trio—but this is by no means sufficient. To be genuinely critical, such inquiry needs to then contribute to the development of a theory of social estrangement *and* to antidotes to that estrangement (the empowerment project). Finally, with knowledge or understanding of what has led to a less-than-satisfying life, coupled with a vision of and hope for desired alternatives, a critical social science would then expose avenues for the journey from the former to the latter (the emancipatory finale).

In summary, Fay sees a critical social research agenda contributing to the deepening of a critical social science, one that "can legitimately hope not only to explain a social order but to do so in such a way that this order is overthrown" (p. 31). The theories emerging from such forms of social inquiry must be seen to be three things: scientific, critical and practical.

> These theories would be scientific in the sense of providing comprehensive explanations of wide areas of human life in terms of a few basic principles, explanations subject to public, empirical evidence. They would be critical in the sense of offering a sustained negative evaluation of the social order at hand. And they would be practical in the sense of stimulating members of a society to alter their lives by fostering in them the sort of self-knowledge and understanding of their social conditions which can serve as the basis for such an alteration. (p. 23)

Through the workings of such a critical social science "it is possible for human beings…to become enlightened as to their condition and, on the basis of this enlightenment, to create a new form of life in which their genuine interests are satisfied. This is not an easy process because it involves shedding illusions that are central to our very identity" (Fay, 1987, p. 12).

Fay's ideas have found similarly passionate fellow travelers over the past couple of decades, Joe Kincheloe being one: "My hope is that [these ideas] will serve as a grain of abrasive sand which induces [people] to name their discontent, to act on such an articulation. To embrace hope in this era of cynicism is a revolutionary act. But as long as we can formulate visions, possibility persists" (Kincheloe, 2003, p. 2). This is the essence of critical qualitative research.

Taking a seminal thought from each of these inspirational sources leaves me with something of an epistemological and ontological GPS for locating my work as a researcher, but also provokes something of a confessional as I look with (hopefully) less naïve eyes through these thoughts at the research I've undertaken in the past. These unsettling points are:

From Norm Denzin: Critical social research occurs in a moral community that is rooted in a concept of care, of shared governance, of neighborliness, of love, kindness and the moral good.

From Patti Lather: What does it mean to use other people's lives as data?

From Brian Fay: A critical social science is one that will simultaneously explain, criticize and empower its audience to overthrow the social world.

How closely had my work met the expectations and the deep moral questions that reside within these statements? In what ways might these function as guides or at least signposts to a more worthwhile form of engagement with the social world in the future?

The Project

For reasons that I'm still not entirely sure of, my personal/professional trajectory has seen me move intellectually and politically more deeply into the area of race and anti-racist work over a period of almost a quarter of a century in teacher education. Always harboring an affinity with the critical pedagogical community, race and ethnicity as axes of identity appeared to throw up opportunities for the type of disruptive educative work that seemed to me to form the curriculum of the critical educator. This is perhaps the type of work Lather had in mind when she described her motives and intentions as "wanting to trouble the straight-ahead story" (2007, p. 27).

By the mid-1990s, I had become convinced of the importance of looking at racism and, more importantly, anti-racist practice from the point of view of the beneficiaries—whites—rather than necessarily and always from the point of experience of the victims—non-whites. While the characteristics of whiteness—its invisibility yet universality, its conferral of unearned privilege on its wearers, its less-than-subtle yet sledgehammer-like shaping of measures of excellence in its own form are today relatively unremarkable for their novelty, at that time the idea of studying something called whiteness was somewhat more strange. But, this was where my personal path into and with critical educative work had led me.

One of the projects I set up revolved around the question of how whites come to recognize and understand themselves as racialized people. This was my doctoral project, and it was concluded and submitted for the award of PhD in the year 2000. It remains unpublished because I've not ever really returned to it to prepare it for anything other than display purposes on bookshelves: my own, those of my supervisors and the faculty research office. It had also remained lodged in the comfort zone of my professional environment; it was completed, was examined and commented on extremely favorably by the examiners, won a research award and is trotted out occasionally when new doctoral students ask to read it. I think I've presented one seminar from the project, although I have presented and published other items connected to the topic. I want to return to that project in this chapter and look at it again with a view to thinking about what it means to engage in critical research. This is the type of research that is imagined by the three authors introduced in the early part of this chapter. It has the *conscientização* imperative that underpinned Freire's work. Through a reconsideration of what it meant to research within and about the white centre, this project may well present a second expression of considerably greater value to me some decade and a half after its inception than it did the first time around.

My hope for that project at the time was that by coming to understand and, more importantly, perhaps provide the catalyst for the participants to come to self-understanding, I might be able to contribute to a group of intending teachers enacting pedagogies that could lessen the racially located effects of an unthinking whiteness in the classroom. This, to me, was a way to contribute to the development of a critical racial consciousness (again, Freire's [1974] idea of *conscientização*).

I saw the project of disrupting the settled and ubiquitous nature of whiteness as a very long-term one, with the doctoral thesis merely one report on this ongoing project. I wrote about the question of leaving the research field, typically the mark of the conclusion of a project, at the time:

> I don't leave the field—I continue to live within it and to work on my understandings of it. I consider this ongoing flow of growth to constitute an enlightened unwhitened experience and understanding of the everyday. As with many examples of qualitative research, the project upon which this report is based is far from complete. Perhaps this report should be considered as but one of a number of articulations of thoughts about and insights into racialised identities and social betterment. (Austin, 2001 pp. 69–70, emphasis added)

In brief, I worked with 13 volunteer teacher education students, all of whom identified at the commencement of the project as white (not all did at the time their involvement concluded, however). Over the course of 18 months, these participants—all women—and I engaged in a process of trying to retrieve experiences of theirs that had led them to see themselves as being raced, of having a racialized aspect to their identity. In the report that constituted my doctoral thesis, I chose to foreground one of these participants, Teresa, and used her part of the project as the basis around which I worked the other participants' experiences and reflections on those experiences. In keeping with the ethics committee requirement at the time that I mask the identity of participants as much as possible, Teresa is not the participant's real name, and I also replaced the names of places she referred to in her account of her racialized experiences so as to further protect her anonymity. This is one of many aspects of this project that currently causes me some concern, and to which I return later in this chapter.

In the course of the project, I utilized forms of data gathering that seemed to provide me with the most effective means of exposing the biographies, thoughts, analyses and conjectures of the participants. The methodology was one rooted in ethnography, and the methods employed included learning conversations, visual (photographic) research and elicitation, reflective journals, auto/biography and documentary analysis. I used children's poems (Guyanese poet John Agard's "Happy Birthday, Dilroy", 1983, was particularly important), personal reflections and life history, critical incidents, popular cultural artifacts and more. At the time, data and evidence that would allow me to work the *verstehen* rather than the discovery furrows of research were what I was concerned to uncover, to extract. It was the effectiveness and legitimacy of these techniques for strip-mining the data field that probably focused my attention as much as anything else, and apart from the concern to "protect" my participants from being identified and outed, the general well-being of the human beings involved didn't really figure at all. This presents as a second area of unease for me as I return to this work.

The doctoral report about this project allowed me the space and the privilege to draw conclusions and make recommendations for further research. As I suspect is the case for all doctoral candidates at this point in their dissertation writing and researchers at the report writing stage, it was here that I was able to, in effect, make a claim to have uncovered something of significance, something whose visible existence would now trigger other work along the lines that I had at least in part marked out. My conclusions and recommendations were serious ones for me at the time. Without going into detail, I was able to draw conclusions about the ways in which the participants conceptualized whiteness:

From the experience of having spoken at length with the participants about their senses of racial identity, I have categorised their views of whiteness as follows:

1. Whiteness as a transitory element in identity;
2. Whiteness as fashionable or as an expediency;
3. Whiteness as a cosmetic identity feature; and
4. Whiteness as a safe haven. (Austin 2001, pp. 206 ff.)

I was able to (almost) generalize about the features of the ways in which thinking and talking about whiteness in the then Australian context:

> It is apparent that white identity presents and is experienced as fluid, uncertain and extremely variegated and yet crossing all of the stories of the participants were a number of features which, for want of a more appropriate term, I have called themes of whiteness. By this, I mean certain commonalities in thinking about, being aware of and utilising white racial identities. In talking with and listening to the participants, there seem to be four such themes:
>
> 1. A continuum of white racial self-consciousness
> 2. Ebbs and flows in the acknowledgment and application of whiteness
> 3. A strategic filtering of whiteness in various teaching contexts and
> 4. A growing robustness in acknowledging whiteness in the Australian context. (Austin 2001, pp. 209 ff.)

With regard to a reformulation of teacher education, I concluded that:

> 1. There is a need to articulate the racial dimensions of everyday life, curriculum and pedagogy, especially from the perspective of whiteness.
> 2. Notions of difference and how it is constructed should be central to the teacher education process and a vital plank in teacher education pedagogy.
> 3. Dialogic forms of engagement, particularly with regard to identity, are essential.
> 4. White pre-service teachers need to spend time in situations where they are and come to recognise themselves as minority group members. (Austin 2001, pp. 221–222)

These are/were statements of authority: I had done the research, I had worked out what the participants were thinking, saying and suggesting, and I had been able to distil the forms of meaning from their life experiences that they, presumably, had been unable to do for and by themselves. This presents as a third area of considerable concern for me, a decade and more on.

In looking at the third aspect of a critical social science—socially transformative action—how does my performance since this time shape up in terms of having worked towards these imperatives? My study had intended to capture the types of experiences racially aware white pre-service teachers had that had led them, at least in part, to this point of self-awareness, such that the experiences and approaches seemingly necessary for development of a white racial awareness might become part of the teacher education curriculum. For all but the fourth of these recommendations, I believe I can say I have been able to move from the theory to the practice of a racially consciousness-raising focus in the parts of the teacher education programs in which I work (see, for example, Austin & Hickey, 2007, 2009).

What I need to turn to are the three areas of discomfort/discomfit that have presented themselves to me in reconsidering what it means to engage in critical social research. The first of these forms around Patti Lather's question of what it means to use other people's lives as data.

Teresa, the main character in my report, had been very open with me about her life as a child in an Australian military family and about her recollections of growing up in a family she saw at the time of the project as racist. There was a small shopping centre close to where Teresa's family lived when she was preschool aged. This became a place of racialized space, a location of dangerous territory for Teresa as she grew up. For (white) children in this neighborhood, the cake shop was an attractive place. Not only did the operators sell cakes, bread, buns and other types of bakery goods typical of the time, it was also the nearest source of lollies. It was here that the constructions of Self and Other already put in place from the conceptions of Home as raced space were further reinforced:

> Teresa: We had a cake shop where you bought lollies, you'd have all the Aboriginals sitting in the middle of the shopping centre drunk because the pub was part of the shopping centre. (Conversation T1, text unit 37). I think I was so little that usually with Mum, she'd just grab my hand and take me home. We'd

all go down to the cake shop, but if I was there too long, they'd come down and get me. (Conversation T1, text unit 43–45)

Teresa: We weren't allowed down to the shops after 2 o'clock in the afternoon. We had a cake shop which sold lollies and things like that and we weren't allowed down there because after 2 o'clock they'd all come out of the pub and sit in the outside area and our families weren't allowed down there.

Jon: Because of the possibility of danger for you?

Teresa: Yep.

Jon: Physical danger or cultural danger?

Teresa: I think a bit of both. (Conversation T3, text units 33–40)

In the course of our conversations, Teresa had described her family life—culturally and politically—and had wondered how it was that she had managed to escape the racist environment (as she saw it) relatively untouched. In these descriptions and recollections, she had made a number of comments about her mother and her brothers, comments she confirmed she was happy to have included in the data and evidentiary set of the project at the time and in any reporting from it. She had talked about her mother's relatively recent diagnosis with terminal cancer, of her extended family travelling from around the world to visit her mother, and of what this experience had meant for her own personal ethnic and cultural awareness, particularly of her Irishness:

Teresa: My mum was diagnosed with terminal cancer this year.

Jon: This year? Since we talked last?

Teresa: Yeah. We knew there was something wrong at Christmas time and anyway so she went through chemo[therapy]—a very religious family, [and I'm] a little bit on the outer with them since I found out the news, but like last week we found out she was in remission but the chemo's knocked her about so badly anyway and it was just amazing to see that it wasn't just the direct family, it was the extended family coming in—that's why everybody's over from Ireland—because, like, we just converged in Brisbane and it was amazing. You do get to know your family then, like your direct family more. (Conversation T2, text units 252–259)

She related episodes from her life where her mother's views on the racially Other were of great concern and embarrassment to Teresa. By way of example:

And like even the other day on the phone she [Teresa's mother] turned around, and it's just a saying, she said—we had something happen in my family, I rang up my mother and said 'I've got a secret, they've told me, but I think you should know, and she said 'there's always a nigger in the firewood' and I said 'now I'm pretty offended and I'm not going to talk to you' and she said 'I didn't mean to say that' [laughs]. (Conversation T3, text units 70–71)

Teresa had previously told me of the ways in which her mother and, less visibly in her recollections, her father had described indigenous Australian parts of towns in which her family lived when Teresa was a child. These places were "Coon County" where "the aboriginals got a new housing estate and they used to rip out the walls and burn them" (Conversation T1, text unit 36); places where her mother had embedded the dangers of encountering "all the aboriginals sitting in the middle of the shopping centre drunk" (Conversation T1, text unit 37); where the family wisdom had it that indigenous Australians "were all 'Oh, filthy, filthy, filthy'" (Conversation T3, text unit 12). To her amazement, Teresa had been able to escape the racist mindset that a reflection on her childhood environment might have suggested she was destined to sustain.

The type of research I had been engaged in here clearly exposes the researcher to what Lather called "the anxiety of voyeurism" (2007, p. 44). I was privy to all sorts of stories from everyday life, the sorts of stories that are perhaps more typically forgiven and forgotten within the familial context but which are drawn out for the purposes of participating in a research project. These are the sorts of stories that researchers encourage participants to recall and retell—the cake shop story was retold at least three different times, each one with more detail and apparent clarity—where the researcher almost becomes a story junkie. I recall the anticipation with which I waited for each conversation with the participants in this project because of the stories I hoped they would bring out for me to use. What *does* it mean to use other people's lives as data, indeed!

When I think about this now, the voyeuristic aspect of social research is apparent, and from a critical perspective, one might argue that such is the price for the possible contribution to a greater, common good. But I return to Lather's questioning of her own role in the women with HIV/AIDS project: in Teresa's case, for whom was/is this emancipatory?

My experience with Teresa took another turn 10 years after our first engagement. In early 2008, I had a chance conversation with someone who knew of Teresa's employment as a teacher upon her graduation, and I was able to find a contact phone number for her. She had been employed for a time as a classroom teacher with the state education department and was at the time a visiting advisory teacher with expertise in the behavioral management field—and she was working about an hour's drive away from the university I was attached to. We arranged to meet to catch up and to look at what she saw in and of the project a decade down the track. I was curious to know what effect her participation in the project had had on her subsequent professional practice—had the project had the type of consciousness-raising impact that I had argued it should/would?

In preparation for the reunion I emailed Teresa the chapter from my dissertation that focused almost exclusively on her. She had read this at the time I was preparing for submission, but I had wanted her to refresh her memory of her role in my thesis. The following extract from our pre-meeting email communication conveys a response to the work that she had already read and approved for use a decade earlier that clearly alerted me to the likelihood that Teresa had more recent reservations about the stories and their analysis:

> On 27/2/08 2:14 PM, "XXXXX Teresa" <email address deleted > wrote:>
> Hi Jon,
> >
> > Before replying I read the extract, a little confronting I must say,
> > and I will probably read it again as I have time to process and gather my thoughts.
> >
> > I think at this stage I would probably like to come in uncensored,
> > flying blind, which would probably allow for more honest and less
> > contrived answers. As I age I have become more watchful of what I
> > say, soo…Not knowing may elicit more truths
> >
> > Though as the time nears I may desparately [sic] email you with—give me the questions so I can practice the answers!
> >
> > Anyway I will probably have questions for you too to dismiss my fears.
> >
> > Catch up with you at Rusty's
> >
> > Regards,
> > Teresa

We arranged to meet at a point roughly equidistant from both of our workplaces. This was Rusty's, a truck stop on the very busy Warrego Highway between Brisbane and Toowoomba. We sat at a typical truck stop café table—aluminum and formica table, plastic garden-style chairs, plastic tablecloth—amongst the remnants of that morning's truckie breakfasts. (The two other patrons in the café at the time Teresa and I began talking were clearly bemused at the sight of two very non-truckie-looking people, one holding a digital audio recorder, a pile of papers and a laptop computer bag, using this spot as an office.)

Our first conversation in the research project had occurred on 20 October 1998, and here on 28 February 2008 we were revisiting that experience and exchange. This meeting was to be the pebble in the shoe that led me to rethink exactly what it meant to engage in (critical social) research. One of the first things I noticed was that Teresa had printed out, added cardboard covers and had bound two copies of the chapter I had sent her. In these she had highlighted sections and points that she wanted to talk about. Some were questions about the meaning of language I had used that she hadn't wanted to ask earlier, but with the confidence of several years of professional experience behind her now felt comfortable doing so. Some of her points were about the accuracy of some of the language she had used in our conversations that I had claimed as verbatim ("I can't imagine I ever spoke like that—it's so embarrassing").

But the most significant point of her review of the document pertained to her mother. She asked if there was any possibility of the records of the project and the dissertation being revised to remove the comments she had made about her mother as holding racist attitudes. Since we had last met, her mother had succumbed to the cancer Teresa had referred to in our early conversations. Now she didn't want to have one of her few publicly recorded views of her mother to be that she was a naïve racist. She felt embarrassed, uneasy and less than a proper daughter for having made those comments a decade earlier. Even more, she had approved their use; she had agreed then that they captured a certain aspect of her life but now felt her memory of her mother deserved a different image. I had used her mother's life as data and now I was being asked to surrender that use, to erase it.

I explained that I couldn't alter the hard copy of the dissertation, but that the electronic copy housed in my credentialing university's library archives might admit of change. The dilemma then arises that the changed dissertation would no longer be that which was examined and accepted for the PhD conferred. While history is amenable to all sorts of retrospective alterations and erasures, are doctoral theses? I offered to see what I could do to effect the type of changes she would like to see made. Thus far, the dissertation remains unchanged, but not untroubling.

Have I eaten away Teresa's and her mother's stories in the pursuit of theoretical understanding, as Lather wonders of her work? What had been and perhaps continues to be the effect and the cost to me and them of using their lives as data? Are the costs acceptable in the pursuit of a greater good?

As a researcher and a member of the moral community Denzin describes, did I have an obligation to excise aspects of the accounts given to me by the participants in my study that I might reasonably have foreseen to be troublesome for them down the track? Having secured their agreement and approval to use these accounts at the time, what is the extent of my obligation to the well-being of these participants once life paths have had a chance to be trodden in particular directions? As a consumer/user of parts of these lives, how might I ensure the sustainability of those lives? To whose vulnerability is Denzin referring when he talks of a vulnerable ethnography? How does one, as a researcher intent on making people's lives better, enact an ethic of care and kindness? As a critical social researcher, what does it mean to be neighborly? Has my work here been conscientizing, awareness-raising? Has it met Fay's expectations of enlightenment and empowerment? Does the project hold an obvious answer to Lather's question of for whom it has been emancipatory?

I can review my actions and my decisions in this project and wonder about missed opportunities and paths to kindness and care that might not have been trodden. Apart from personal soul-searching and guilt-purging, do such considerations make any difference to those who have opened their lives to me? Probably not, although I will send Teresa a copy of this piece to let her know that a couple of years now since our most recent encounter, her concerns about how her mother might have been presented by the project have unsettled my satisfaction with the work and led me to a deeper understanding of what it means to work as a (critical) researcher.

But the most significant effect of this return and review will, I suspect, be on the work I do in the future and hopefully on the work of others with whom I engage—doctoral students, research collaborators, and reviewing bodies. I take three main thoughts of my own to these yet-to-emerge locations of social research.

First, there is a need to avoid harm and distress in and through our work. While ethics committees have expectations that researchers will minimize the likelihood of harm to the participants in their studies, the type of harm I'm thinking of here goes beyond those concerns of IRBs and similar organizations to the heart (almost literally) of what it means to exercise membership of a moral community of researchers. I don't think the greater good is a sufficient reason to warrant accepting distress on the part of a small(er) number of participants. Foresight should perhaps become a crucial part of research training. As much as learning to code, categorize, (re)present and review, researchers need to learn to foresee the consequences of their work, and to continue to do this over much longer time frames than the typical project might envisage.

Second, there is a need to ensure that the humanity of our work remains at the forefront of our minds. As researchers, we must remain vigilant to the encroachment of a data mentality upon the fact that we are working with human lives. People are not data, but there is a tendency to throw away the chaff of humanity in the search for the kernels of data that will expose something for us to analyze. The challenge for all critical social researchers is to honor the commitment and connection to the social betterment of people, individually and in communities, in ways that buoy the human even if at the expense of the inquisitory.

Third, researchers should engage in considered reviews of their research every so often. Those researchers who are academics are probably involved annually or so in reviews of our teaching: how well it has been done, what those involved in it with us—students, fellow teachers, and the like—think about it, how successful it has been as compared with certain criteria. We are asked to account for less-than-positive evaluations of our teaching, less frequently congratulated for "above average" ratings. Why should we not also engage in deep reflection on the quality of our research with similar seriousness?

Typically, a research project is considered complete and thereby finished once the reports, the reconciliation of budgets and the storage of project documents and data are effected. But what might be the contribution to a critical research community if researchers were to consider the consequences of their work in terms of individual projects, or even more powerfully, by a consideration of the compendiums of their projects against such expectations as those held by Denzin, Lather and Fay?

In my project on white racial/ethnic identities, how well did I meet Fay's action imperative? All pre-service teachers at my current university now engage this crucial aspect of identity and the politics that flow from it in a core course. This seems to me to be a reasonable outcome of the research, particularly when I see evidence of a glimmer of *conscientização* in the discussions, the written and visual assessment items and, more importantly, in the incorporation of such awareness into some of the in-schools activities these pre-service teachers undertake.

Has it been emancipatory for anyone? This I'm unsure of. The participants in the original study certainly spoke of being far more ethically and racially conscious as a result of engaging in the work. Two who commenced the project identifying as white certainly didn't at the conclusion—one as a result of feeling confident in bringing her Chinese matrilineal heritage to the foreground more than she had in the past, the other who uncovered a Torres Strait Islander aspect to her family lineage that she had suspected but kept hidden until her involvement in the project. As personally and individually "liberating" for each of these participants as the project might have been, I'd like to think the broader social transformation imperative of this project will have found some of its traction in the work the participants have done in their classrooms as teachers over the past decade. Here, their awareness of the particularity of white ethnicity, of its invisible but certainly not intangible or insignificant privilege, and the consequences for Others might mean their professional practices have assumed a form different to what might have been the case had they not been involved. I'm unsure, of course, and would need to locate these participants and talk again with them. Perhaps this is a necessary step for any critical social researcher to build into their work: a determination to reconnect and re-engage with their participants to construct a feel for the worth of their time spent.

How well did I deal with or minimize using the lives of the people with whom I worked as data? Did I "eat away their stories" in the pursuit of insight, understanding, and theory? With hindsight, I probably did. Teresa's return to those aspects of her life that she later wished to recant, or at least recast, is an indication of the vulnerability critical qualitative research often engenders in those who agree to open their experiences to the gaze of the researcher. That I am now cognizant of the importance of extending and ensuring more genuine care and concern to participants beyond the typical IRB or ethics committee expectations is one thing. The challenge, though, is to look to how this might become as integral a part of my research plans and design as anything else. How might I go about altering the electronic version of the dissertation to give effect to one of my major participant's concern that her mother's life not remain brushed by her daughter's characterization of it as racist?

Critical qualitative research requires that we open ourselves to stories from the lives of others, and in return we researcher/activists (implicitly, at least) promise to use those stories to contribute to social betterment. It is essential that the idea of the greater good not swamp the well-being of those individuals who prompt, provoke and push us to this work through their lives of suffering, marginalization, disadvantage and sadness. When we look to the heart of qualitative research, we need of necessity to look to the heart of the researcher. We can't imagine that we are doing good whilst perpetrating the opposite on those we work with. Goodness of heart is not a frequently identified characteristic of "acceptable" research projects: perhaps that's a genuine challenge for the IRBs and ethics committees to grapple with when determining the beneficence of a research proposal.

There is an enlightening component to reflecting on our work as critical researchers that, if my own experience is anything to go by, strengthens a resolve to recast our work as something we do with rather than on or even for others. My experience also tells me that we can't afford to overlook the importance of theories and philosophies in our development as researchers. Critical qualitative research is much more than a collection of epistemologically consistent techniques or strategies. It is a moral activity. My debt to the three theorists whose work has unsettled me here should be obvious, but there are so many others from whom I've taken inspiration, affront, confusion and at times outright annoyance.

All of this has stimulated deeper levels of connection to the task and purpose of using my own life as data as I work more heavily into autoethnographic forms of research. In a certain sense, the point of turning the gaze back onto the invisible centre of whiteness that had driven my earlier research work now appears in a slightly different but equally discomfiting form as my gaze as researcher turns more and more back onto myself. Perhaps in another 10 years, Teresa and I will have something quite different to talk about!

References

Agard, J. (1983). *I din do nuttin and other poems*. London, England: Methuen Children's Books.

Austin, J. (2001). *Becoming racially aware: Explorations of identity and whiteness with pre-service teachers* (Unpublished doctoral thesis). University of Southern Queensland, Toowoomba, QLD, Australia.

Austin, J., & Hickey, A. (2007). Autoethnography and teacher development. *International Journal of Interdisciplinary Social Science, 2*(2), 369–378.

Austin, J., & Hickey, A. (2009). Repatriating race: Exorcising ethno-exclusion. *International Journal of Interdisciplinary Social Science, 4*(7), 223–233.

Bodone, F. (Ed.). (2005). *What difference does research make and for whom?* New York, NY: Peter Lang.

Britzman, D. (1995). The question of belief: Writing poststructural ethnography. *Qualitative Studies in Education, 8*(3), 233–242.

Counts, G. (1932). *Dare the school build a new social order?* Carbondale and Edwardsville: Southern Illinois University Press.

Denzin, N. K. (1995) The experiential text and the limits of visual understanding. *Educational Theory, 45,* 7–18.

Denzin, N. K. (1997). *Interpretive ethnography: Ethnographic practices for the 21st century.* Thousand Oaks, CA: Sage.

Denzin, N. K. (2009). *Qualitative inquiry under fire: Towards a new paradigm dialogue.* Walnut Creek, CA: Left Coast Press.

Denzin, N. K., & Lincoln, Y. S. (Eds.). (2005). *The Sage handbook of qualitative research* (3rd ed.). Thousand Oaks, CA: Sage.

Denzin, N. K., & Lincoln, Y. S. (2005a). Epilogue: The eighth and ninth moments—Qualitative research in/and the fractured future. In N. K. Denzin & Y. S. Lincoln (Eds.), *The Sage handbook of qualitative research* (3rd ed., pp. 1115–1126). Thousand Oaks, CA: Sage.

Denzin, N. K., & Lincoln, Y. S. (2005b). Introduction: The discipline and practice of qualitative research. In N. K. Denzin & Y. S. Lincoln (Eds.), *The Sage handbook of qualitative research* (3rd ed., pp. 1–32). Thousand Oaks, CA: Sage.

Dyer, R. (1997). *White.* London, England: Routledge.

Fay, B. (1987). *Critical social science: Liberation and its limits.* Cambridge, England: Polity.

Freire, P. (1974). *Pedagogy of the oppressed* (M. B. Ramos, Trans.). New York, NY: Seabury.

Giroux, H. (1988). *Teachers as intellectuals: Toward a critical pedagogy of learning.* Westport, CT: Bergin & Garvey.

Jipson, J., & Paley, N. (1996). *Daredevil research: Recreating analytic practice.* New York, NY: Peter Lang.

Kincheloe, J. (2003). *Teachers as researchers: Qualitative inquiry as a path to empowerment* (2nd ed.). London, England: Routledge.

Lather, P. (2007). *Getting lost: Feminist efforts toward a double(d) science.* Albany, NY: SUNY Press.

Lather, P., & Smithies, C. (1997). *Troubling the angels: Women living with HIV/AIDS.* Boulder, CO: Westview/HarperCollins.

Said, E. (1978). *Orientalism.* London, England: Routledge & Kegan Paul.

Spivak, G. C. (1990). *The post-colonial critic: Interviews, strategies, dialogues.* London, England: Routledge.

Strathern, M. (2000). *Audit cultures: Anthropological studies in accountability, ethics and the academy.* London, England: Routledge.

CHAPTER SIXTEEN

Avoiding the Missionary (Dis)position: Research Relations and (Re)presentation

Mairi McDermott and Athena Madan

The purpose of this chapter is to discuss particular historical conditions in qualitative social research. Working with a Critical Qualitative Research (CQR) framework, we seek to challenge normative truth claims in research as posited through social, symbolic, and linguistic constructions. Despite genuine intentions, dominant social science research has the potential to reify the colonial encounter through a rhetoric of "mission to civilise," particularly in relation to ethnography, where the research subject can become objectified in the quest for objectivity and objective naming in research. An initial inquiry thus focuses on the symbolic power in and of research and asks where this power may be oppressive and where it may be productive.

As authors, we share many fields; for example, we met and work together in the academy. We also bring many divergent relations and positions in the social world. We will examine these positionalities, grounded in a Bourdieusian analysis of power relations. Locating respective fields, dispositions, and habitus, while examining how space is inhabited and how we each position ourselves in relation to "others", we ask: How can the researcher be seen as an ethnographic subject herself to offset the colonial relationship?

By providing these two differential (dis)positions as the subject of study, our end focus is on the potential to rupture dominant narratives, and dominant research paradigms. We ask, how do these locations / (dis)positions come to organize the process(es) of enquiry? What are the politics of the particular locations in relation to the research she can conduct? What, too, are the politics in play around researchers' differential (dis)positions in relation to collaboration? And what are the conditions made possible in the continual re-thinking in and through critical qualitative research?

Anti-racist Framework as CQR

As we have spent time coming to know the anti-racist framework, we have recognized it as one of many forms CQR can take. Within our respective research engagements, we have found it necessary

235

to be critical in looking at the merits and faults of the structures, groups, and individuals in society at large and within particular communities, to better address social inequities. This includes detailing relationships with scholarly analysis; acknowledging that the current structures are themselves ill and need intervention; using CQR as a tool to transform how societal inequalities are shaped; and finally, recognizing that this work is extremely urgent.

Kincheloe and McLaren (2008) emphasise three relevant points relating to the research process: "(a) there are many critical theories, not just one; (b) the critical tradition is always changing and evolving; and (c) critical theory attempts to avoid too much specificity, as there is room for disagreement among critical theorists" (p. 403). As a form of critical qualitative research, or rather as a discursive framework to guide our research, anti-racism, as described by Dei (2000),

> is a critical discourse of race and racism in society that challenges the continuance of racializing social groups for differential and unequal treatment. Anti-racism explicitly names the issues of race and social difference as issues of power and equity, rather than as matters of cultural and ethnic variety. (p. 27)

Both anti-racism and critical qualitative research methods are helpful frames of research for the transformation of oppressive power relations, through their questioning of the positionalities of dominant ideology (see Nkrumah, 1970/2004). Kincheloe and McLaren (2008) additionally advocate "inquiry that…attempt[s] to confront the injustice in a particular society or public sphere within the society" for research to "thus [become] a transformative endeavor unembarrassed by the label 'political' and unafraid to consummate a relationship with emancipatory consciousness" (p. 406). To undertake research without considering the scope of these underpinnings risks becoming ideologically imperialistic, perpetuating systems of hierarchy, control, and "civilizing" missionary relationships.

Bourdieu and CQR

The concept of habitus (Bourdieu, 1977) is a tool we have found helpful in interrogating our own locations and politics, "spheres", and embodied dispositions that guide our inquiries. Bourdieu describes habitus thus (1977):

> The structures constitutive of a particular type of environment (e.g. the material conditions of existence characteristic of a class condition) produce *habitus*, systems of durable, transposable *dispositions*, structured structures predisposed to function as structuring structures, that is, as principles of the generation and structuring of practices and representations which can be objectively "regulated" and "regular" without in any way being the product of obedience to rules.… (p. 72)

As Reay (2004) summarizes: "Habitus is a way of looking at data which renders the 'taken-for-granted' problematic" (p. 437). The use of habitus as a tool of analysis has the potential to mitigate the imperial relations found in traditional research, and better understand contexts of the field influencing behaviour, responses, and certain life outcomes.

In the Spirit of Habitus: Mairi

Celebration: Food, Drink, and Music

Food, Body, Knowledge: I was born and raised in New York, as were both of my parents and all of my grandparents; however I have vivid memories of referring to the Irish or the Italian side of my family. The maternal side of my family is historically southern Italian, and food plays a large role in family life. Food is the centerpiece of every get-together, and the place most occupied by family and guests alike was the kitchen, regardless of whether food is being served or consumed, although it typically is. The kitchen was—and still is—the place where we reminisce, where the children learn about where we come from, where we play cards and tell jokes, and where we laugh and cry and hug one another.

The kitchen is often chaotic, but there is a certain calmness in the loud uproars of laughter or bantering. One story that is still told to this day by my 90-year-old grandfather is about when he first married my grandmother. In the traditional southern Italian families where both my grandfather and my grandmother were raised, the women cleared and cleaned the dishes after each meal while the men ate fruit and nuts and played pinnacle. One day my grandfather walked away from the men playing cards and went into the kitchen. He proceeded to tell the women that since they had been on their feet all day he would help with the dishes. Hearing this story when I was younger intrigued me—I knew it was a powerful story, but I could not identify the particular flavor. I was used to my father being the cook in the family; even though he was raised in an Irish family where food was intended simply for consuming, he taught himself to cook gourmet meals while my mother worked towards her PhD. These moments, in shaping my habitus, were moments of rupture to the assumed norms surrounding family and expected gender roles.

Along with these personal attachments to food in my life, food also represents knowledge and rote "facts". Food and knowledge are both necessary, but not enough. While I was being fed knowledge at school, I began to feel indigestion from the same food prepared with Western/Eurocentric "facts" as the ingredients. I came to feel like I needed something to wash the food down with.

Water, Mind, Wisdom: I grew up on Long Island, a 10-minute walk from Long Island Sound. Frequently when I felt frustrated and needed time to think and explore my own mind, body, and soul (and not simply the material that was fed to me in school), the sound of the water immediately calmed me down, the feeling of the sand under my feet put me at peace, and the smell of the salty air took me to another place. The vastness of the ocean allowed my imagination to wander; I was able to take myself beyond my frustrations. It was at the water's edge that I reflected on the ever-mounting pile of food, and I learned to wash out my system to make room for something beyond the mono-theorizing as experienced in school.

For me, water represents my unlearning of the dominant paradigms, for water is constantly reprocessing, blending, smoothing, and rejecting. With water we can clear the dirt off our bodies and out of our minds (and I do not mean to suggest that what remains is pristine). In reflecting on these images, I must also acknowledge that for much of my life, as a White body, I have been floating comfortably on top of the water, gliding easily over the rapids in a solidly built canoe, and it was not until I looked into the frothy water and saw my distorted face that I jumped out of the canoe and began my attempt to swim against the current. As a safety feature, when I was placed in that canoe, a life jacket was strapped to my body, so I must recognize that my journey in disrupting oppressive relations in society will be less dangerous than others who have been swimming upstream for their whole lives. I desired, initially, to take my life jacket off and share it with others who were in the water with me; however, how many could I "help" with one life jacket? I soon found that while I can be an ally to the oppressed, I must acknowledge my complicities in the system of oppression, and by simply placing myself in the rapids I do not have the right to appropriate the experiences of "others". In other words, I feel that while I may be able to share my life jacket with a few people, I must also keep my attention on working to disrupt the flow of the current. I still have a lot of unlearning to do, and the longer I stay in the water (which currently takes the form of a PhD program), the clearer my role becomes.

Music, Soul, Understanding: The food (knowledge) that I had consumed was converted into energy and muscles, but in pushing against the currents, I needed to find a rhythm to be able to last. Music has always played a significant role in my life, (as with food and water). I grew up with my father playing traditional Irish music around the house and I found listening to music takes me to another place. I remember getting my first job at the age of 13—I would hand out menus for a restaurant that my father frequently played music at, and when I got paid, I would walk to the music store downtown and pick up as much music as I could afford. I would spend the walk home opening the CD cases and reading the liner notes, anxiously waiting to put the new music on as soon as I got home.

In the spirit of enquiry: After teaching high school English Language Arts for four years, I was driven to learn more about the overall structures of education, and have since spent a lot of time focusing on the neoliberal agenda. Neoliberalism is not only impacting and influencing multiple aspects of society at the same time, but it does so in a variety of ways, across time, across institutions, and across geographical spaces; yet there is a discourse of standards and sameness in neoliberalism, particularly as it relates to education. My overall questions have been: How did the current conditions of education, using contradictory notions of markets and standards, come to be normalised? What are the tensions of creating universal standards and requiring the individual to take responsibility to meet those standards? What are the implications of utilizing an anti-racist framework to push back against neoliberalism, and what conditions are made possible for the future of education and society? How can the dichotomy between dominant and non-dominant be broken to rebuild a community that recognizes difference, but does not hierarchize difference? In other words, what would a space that is co-constructed by multiple ways of knowing look like?

While engaging this line of enquiry, I must continually confront myself with the following considerations: How does my body, as a White female, affect the interactions with the research participants and data? What are the everyday enactments of Whiteness that I participate in and perpetuate? How can I hold myself accountable for these moments and reconcile the contradictory positions of challenging the neoliberal agenda while working within it (for further discussion, see Fine, 1994; and Dei, 1999, 2005)? How does situating my body as a site of knowledge affect my habitus? Conversely, how does my habitus affect my understanding of the body as a site of knowledge? Finally, how can I avoid the risk of re-centering my voice in the construction of race narratives (see Howard, 2006)?

In the Spirit of Habitus: Athena

Inheritance

Eyes: My gaze meets the world as a brown bilingual (French/English) woman with mixed heritage: Filipino and Punjabi Hindu, first-generation born in Canada/Canadian-born, but who has lived outside of Canada for more years than in. Here is where I first see the world.

Stomach: I absorb the post-cyclical impact of Spanish, Japanese, American, and dictatorial control in the Philippines; the intergenerational impact of displacement from the 1947 Partition of India and its "colonial blueprint" (Shamsuddin, 2009); the residual tensions from colonial clashes of England and France in Québec; and an assimilationist model of immigration to North America in the 1960s. Here is where I first feel struggle and tension.

Brain: There is a certain amount of autobiographical truth to my choices of study. And as I have studied to learn the "meanings" of those truths, I have solidified my ground.

Feet: So I am not without reference in understanding my location. But, at times, I still lack a foundation whereupon to spring my climb.

Mouth: For no single voice has spoken, yet, to my particular collective.

Skin: And here is where the world first meets me. If I were to dissociate myself from my skin perhaps I would have a peer.

Teeth: They are the colour of bone and the x-ray of beauty and genetically constructed for vegetables. Which supposedly means I will live longer and healthier but also that I am predisposed to a certain passivity.

Blood: The only space where I am dominant is in my blood: I am type O-, which is universal donor. But interestingly, I don't weigh enough to exercise this claim.

Hands: So what will I contribute? What can I help build?

Spine: And how tall will I stand as I stake my claim?

In the spirit of enquiry: I am interested in mental health programming for war-affected populations—historical, socio-cultural, and racial assumptions within the clinical treatment frame, and relevant social and geopolitical determinants of mental health. I am also interested in merging collectivist ways of learning when it "comes to" reconstructing nations/remembrance and reconciliation.

Inevitably when I tell people my intended scope of study I am asked why I chose this particular area. I generally hesitate before answering—I've realised over time how my answers are never quite the same.

Sometimes I start with practical reasons: It's marketable. I see it as a trend—not only because war-affected populations are increasingly becoming more global, but because "trauma" will probably always be funded, at least as a crisis response (resources unfortunately are not allocated for preventative actions). And art, one of my skill sets, also works really well to rehabilitate/assimilate/assess trauma.

Sometimes I share more personal reasons. Part of me feels like I just "fell into" it, being in particular places at particular times: jobs were available, and nobody had yet filled "war trauma as it affects communities" as a specialty. Another part of me feels that as I get older, and as I interrogate my habitus/embodied dispositions, I realise that *chacun à son histoire*:[1] mine includes the intergenerational impact of Partition; "home" (on an army compound) in the Philippines; my parents' careful construction of a multi-faith, multi-cultural home as we grew up in überconservative 1970s Alberta; the dissolution of family ties from India following my father's death; attending high school on two continents, worlds apart; or my work in France for a time, which evolved into doing relief work for Algerian refugees.

But I don't think I've *ever* said that I've been consistently critical of issues of power and politic as they play out in life, and how they affect us. That's largely why I've remained working with people who are "vulnerable" (or, at least, vulnerable in this culture). I've never said such, but I have wished to say: My parents came to Canada and the U.S. with hopes ahead of their time. I am their generation, motivated to help create a world worthy of their dreams.

So I am interested in the possibilities and limitations in applying anti-racist principles (Joseph, 2009; Kafele, 2004; McKenzie, 2003; Short, 2005; Wahab, 2005) to PTSD treatment for war trauma induced from *la guerre Rwandaise*;[2] namely, in acknowledging the cultural, historical, political, and racial assumptions relevant to the experiences of a "survivor of" war. I am preoccupied—not only as a researcher and practitioner, but also as a woman (of colour)—with the negotiation of relationships, relating, and reconciliation in post-conflict societies. In both clinical contexts and the contexts of everyday life and living, I seek to raise points interrogating the following: How is the therapeutic encounter—given its affiliation with phrmaceuticals and Eurocentric, "enlightenment" thought, especially in the contexts of postcolonial genocide—apolitical? Is it not simply a new "mission to civilize"? How can (psycho)education reconcile or transform disconnect: disconnect between continents, between communion, between communities? And how can the potential to inflict further psychological/psychic damage in these contexts be monitored and prevented accordingly?

Sharing Doxa

Though both of us entered the academy at the same year, and though we each carried with us various experiences and different questions, we discovered a similarity in our approach to respective topic areas of study and choices of framework to inform our enquiries. Interestingly, in preparing separate papers, we both found that we had also turned to spirituality and healing as guiding features in both life and in research. Critical qualitative research asks that we recognize and put on the table our own biases and assumptions (Kincheloe & McLaren, 2008, p. 406); that we not only identify societal injustices, but also work in tandem to transform the situation and circumstances that surround the injustice. In both of these instances we must be able to recognise and deconstruct the individual and societal assumptions before we can work with them. As Kincheloe & McLaren (2008) continue, "Critical theorists become detectives of new theoretical insights, perpetually searching for new and interconnected ways of understanding power and oppression and the ways they shape everyday life and human experience" (p. 407).

In Bourdieu's earlier work, he questioned the formation of shared societal and community assumptions using the notion of doxa, and in this work he considers the stability of the "norms" of society. "The mutual reinforcement between field and habitus strengthens the prevailing power of the doxa, which guides the appropriate "feel" for the game of those involved in the field," writes Deer (2008, p. 121). She continues: "The conceptualisation of doxa as unquestioned 'shared beliefs' constitutive of a field, underpins the related notion of symbolic power" (p. 121). In this sense, *doxa* takes the form of symbolic power which is mediated by various forms of accumulated capitals (such as cultural, economic, and social capital). Explicit physical force is replaced by implicit social habits, mechanisms, differentiations, and assumptions; the "natural" strength and legitimacy of which reside in the misrecognition of the arbitrary nature of their socio-historical emergence and reproduction. "Symbolic power is embedded in recognised institutions as well as institutionalised social relations (education, religion, art) which have the power to establish categories and allocate differential values in the market of symbolic goods, legitimising themselves further in the process" (Deer, 2008 p. 121).

Deer (2008) also tells us:

> For Bourdieu, any common-sense reflection on established rules is necessarily mediated—and therefore restricted—by day-to-day experiences, by taken for granted practice, in short by *what is*; as such it is stifled by the lack of means to express and therefore question what is implicit and taken for granted. (p. 123, emphasis in original)

Traditionally, research has further reified the unquestionability of the "natural state of things".

The Emperor's Clothes:
Avoiding Colonial Encounters/Ideological Imperialism in Research

The potential within social science research to reify the colonial encounter can be seen in a number of ways. Research is "legitimised" through funding (and fundability), organizational propriety or ownership of the research, and status of titles (such as Ph.D. or P.I.) of the individual researcher. Additionally, human "subject bodies" are dissected according to the singular experience/phenomenon under research; this risks considerations of human subject as "capital" more than as "humans", with immediate benefit limited to the researcher and his/her field of research, along with insufficient reflexivity of relationships within the research process, from the inception through to dissemination, of research questions and findings. This kind of research relationship holds an inherent, unyielding power paradigm: the Dr.-scientist-researcher traditionally defines the parameters of the research engagement through the identification of "the problem", asking questions for the import of information, and deciding how to ultimately shape the analysis (and subsequent presentation) of the data. It is not necessary to consider various power differentials—such as social standing, economic capital, race, gender, allocation of funding, and factors contributing to actual lived experience—in traditional research methods' frames.

But the individuals (or groups) involved in the research relationship hold varying power relations—amongst themselves as participants, amongst their respective institutions, and amongst their relative positions and relations to other power structures in society. As such, in a traditional research relationship, power is used in an oppressive manner. Kincheloe and McLaren tell us that, "A consensus seems to be emerging among criticalists that power is a basic constituent of human existence that works to shape the oppressive and productive nature of the human tradition" (2008, p. 411), and that, once located on the hierarchy of knowledge, there is little upward mobility: "lower" bodies must always "remain unrefined" (Ahmad, 1984/2004, p. 62). Even in a multi-ideological society, one ideology becomes dominant, or as a "ruling group...defining the morality" of all groups (Nkumrah, 1970/2004, p. 65). Consequences to this tension contribute to oppression, social control and coercion, and disruption of unity and cohesion. While these tensions can be kept at bay by contextualising and questioning the position of the dominant, controlling ideology, it is not often "easy" to include such spaces of dialogue.

An Experience as a Researcher in the Academy: Athena

Some time ago, I acted as a research assistant on a project promoting histories of migrant children ("stories of our journeys") in schools. I was the newest of three team members, brought into the project as it embarked on its second year. This experience has shaped my thoughts on the necessity to mitigate the potential of "researcher" as coloniser; I have since reflected that the dynamics at play in this instance are a prime example of colonial habitus in present-day research.

During our first team meeting, I discovered that the principal methodology of collecting data from the children emphasized the use of art. My master's thesis and clinical work were on the use and the processes of creativity, specifically in children and with art, in psychotherapy. I recognized that the particular arts tools proposed in the project were not designed to facilitate *therapeutic* outcome; however, I did feel that personal feelings, impressions, and reflections could not be separated from the proposed kinds of work (see also Bell, 2003; and Dillard, 2008).

The first activity involved the children taking photos in groups at school. One week's visit consisted of equipping children with cameras to take photos at will of their favourite activities and spaces in and around the school. For the next week's visit, we printed and returned the photos to the groups, with the end goal for the children to create collages.

During the collage creation activity, many of the groups had taken more photos than could fit on the actual paper for the collage. So the children discussed amongst themselves—a process that was at times accompanied with much animation—in choosing "the most important ones" to share. The rest of the class time was spent creating and presenting the collages. Following their respective presentations, our team hung the collages up in the hallway.

Collectively, the collages captured a spirit of both formal and informal "congregating" that seemed active, free, open, and fun. There were photos of people, photos of spaces, and photos of transition or movement between those spaces. Of the inside of school, we saw photos of classrooms, locker and hallway decorations, classroom pets, and friends playing dress-up in the "lost and found". Of the outside, we saw photos of the playground, people playing soccer, the soccer ball, running shoes, people eating, and someone's apparently highly desirable lunch.

Our team leader looked at one of the collages. The group had chosen to display one particular photo showing all of their names, written on an Agency envelope. It was the only group to have done so, and it was featured in the very centre of the collage.

The research team leader expressed some discomfort with the photo displaying names, saying it contained "identifying information" associated with the Agency. While the children were in the next room, unavailable to consult with about their choice, the research team leader promptly reached up to the collage and removed the "offending" photo.

I remember a visceral reaction to that act of revision. My body physically protested—my stomach felt sick with intrusion and my spine forced both my head and my feet some steps back; it was as though the collage had come under attack, or had been irreversibly contaminated, somehow. I remember sputtering out a series of phrases: that the children selected that photo for a reason; it was obviously an important photo to them, having been featured in the centre of their collage; there was other identifying information on all of the collages, such as faces (including people from other classrooms), car license plates, and names on other students' "history-writing" books. Removing the photo was altering their work, without their agency. I expressed my thoughts that "even if" the photo did need to be removed, that the children should be the ones to do so, with explanation and a selected replacement photo beforehand. The team leader listened silently to my protests, with eyes still focussed on the collage; when I was finished stammering, she said quietly, "I understand your point of view, but according to the methodology and its ethics, there is no other way."

The children came out a few minutes later, ready and armed with soccer balls to head out for recess. The team leader stopped the group of boys: "We decided we didn't want names," she said. "So we had to remove your photo." The boys looked at the collage. I wondered what they were thinking, considering all (perhaps even my own) possible projections: How had the photo been taken off—they had taken such careful consideration in crafting the collage and attaching the photo just so? Why had it been taken off—what had they done? What was so "wrong" with their names, or identifying that the collage "belonged" to them, that necessitated such direct and central (and symbolically violent; see, for example, Bourdieu, 1977) correction?

It felt like the longest pause ever in the most awkward of worlds. In that moment I felt ashamed for having "belonged to" this particular methodology. I further wasn't convinced that we were interpreting "ethics" in similar ways—more thought was needed towards the implications of who the ethics were designed "to protect". And though I had no personal "problem" with the members of the team, it would be dishonest to say that my relationship of trust with them was unaffected. Within this kind of frame there was little room for personal agency to intersect with the research process, to co-construct any knowledge, or even share any particular claim with the P.I. I chose to fill the silence with what voice I had, asking the children: "Would you like to choose another photo?"

Anti-racism and Autoethnography:
Personal Phallus-ease According to Mairi

In using Bourdieu's tools, it is helpful to remember that he intended them to be viewed as a process, as relational and influenced by each other, not as stagnant and deterministic. There is room for change, but first we must identify the necessary change. In the field of education neoliberalism has a hegemonic location which configures the current conditions of the conventional classroom. With this understanding, how does one change the field or the rules of the game? Who is more or less inclined to do so? How do I, as someone who embodies many identities that are given dominance in the society where I reside, avoid "[reproducing] power by playing to power," as Michelle Fine (1994, p. 80) warns?

While I must recognize that my voice is accorded more weight and legitimacy in the academy, there is an epistemic saliency of marginalized voices in anti-oppression work (Dei, 1999, 2005). In making this statement, though, I must caution that we avoid a re-hierachizing who has the right to narrate for whom and about what. When I expressed the difficulties I had transitioning into a new academic program, where I felt that everyone knew each other and the "appropriate" discourse to use, a colleague told me that there were conversations around who I was and whether I was truly an ally. I spent the first semester, relatively unknowingly, being scrutinized by my colleagues.

I do not think that the scrutinizing of my dominant body will stop while we remain in this tumultuous and yet obfuscatory White supremacist culture, nor do I think it should, as I feel a visceral reaction to those who masquerade as anti-racist workers because it has been appropriated and positioned as a hot topic. Without those challenges, both overt and subtle, and without that scrutiny, I may have risked avoiding my own complicities in the system of oppression. In this, I recognize my complicity in the current conditions by needing those who are always already othered to hold me accountable, to push me to understand the urgent need for dominant bodies, as allies, to come to mark and name these spaces they occupy with privilege. I also recognize my complicity that even in this moment when I am acknowledging the work done in the scrutinizing of my body and my position, I am relying on my location as privileged by allowing "the other" to be responsible for marking my complicities.

I have been misguided in the work that I have done and as a result I have perpetuated the current social structures. While teaching, I felt passionate that a person should not be judged based on the color of their skin or their gender, (dis)ability, and sexuality. I frequently heard students say that I was "Black" in an effort to identify with me, as they simultaneously suggested that they felt I could identify with them. I would remind the students that I was White, but that did not mean that I could not understand them. What I was unable to see at that time was that every day, by walking in my skin, I am implicated in White supremacist culture, and that there is no way of shedding my skin. I also missed the opportunity to engage with the students about why they felt drawn to labelling me as Black and what that says about social relations in society or the social construction of race (Omi & Winant, 1993). I did not need to ask those questions because I could move comfortably (while ignorantly) through various fields: my physical being as well as my habitus is supported by the dominant structures.

Anti-racism and Autoethnography: Personal Phallus-ease According to Athena

I shared a private practise once. As mild-to-moderate mental health conditions are not funded by public health (services are not free), we solicited and found success recruiting clientele from one particularly wealthy suburb near downtown. While the money averaged the higher end of the sliding pay scale, I soon found myself at a loss in the face of a particular ensemble set of complaints. They came to be so particularly reflective of a certain privilege that I started calling it the "But I have nothing to wear in Paris" trend. I tried to reposition my reactions, as I am "supposed to be", as the therapist, unconditionally "neutral"; but I could not reframe or reconsider my feelings that those particular sessions were among the most indifferent time I'd ever spent or money I'd ever made.

I also remember last year, a friend and I went to an awards ceremony for local businesses that was held the same night as a Diwali party. We decided to go to both events, in succession. I wore a black-and-gold sari; my friend wore a black-and-white tux. I also wore some bangles, dangly gold earrings, and a bindi.

One of the awards presented at the ceremony was for a woman who had recently opened her own yoga studio, called "Yoga by Rachel" or something evidently non-Indian. I found myself consciously struggling, as I often do, to keep my dislike and my suspicion of "white people who do/commodify yoga" (when as a child doing yoga in the contexts of morning meditation at home, all the white people thought we were "weird") at bay. I looked at her; she was long, lean, and lithe. I was happy, though, that her business had seen such a success. She seemed in addition quite young.

By coincidence, I later found myself standing behind her in the coat check line as we were leaving. "Congratulations on your success," I said. She turned around, and smiling, said, "Why thank you." Her eyes registered the bodily length of my sari as she continued, "So tell me. You should come to the studio sometime. Have you ever tried yoga?"

I was a bit flustered and didn't know how to respond: It wasn't as if yoga *started* as a pair of Lulu Lemon™ pants, or as a branded 2-ply polyurethane mat, or ever even *associated*, really, with someone named Rachel. It was in that moment that my dislike of "white people doing yoga" concretized—and still largely remains with me.

I relate these experiences to share (acknowledge) that I, too, have my own resistances and emotionalities to unlearn. So I am also, perhaps however conversely, part of this reconciliation process.

Echoing the admonitions of Bourdieu:

> Of course, by definition, scientific questioning excludes the intention of exerting any type of symbolic violence.… Yet it remains the case in these matters [of scientific questioning] that one cannot trust simply to one's own good faith, and this is true because all kinds of distortions are embedded in the very structure of the research relationship. (1999, p. 608)

In Conclusion/Thoughts to Conclude By (For Now)

It is important to recognize that while there may be similarities in the effects of different forms of oppression, unless we ground our work in the specifics of who we are (our own habitus, spirituality, and subjectivities) in relation to the social structures we are observing—and sometimes also partaking in—we are not giving heed to the particularities or reflexivities of the lived realities of oppression. Van Ausdale and Feagin (1996) suggest that the "interconnected nature...of thinking and behaviour...are fully apparent only when interactions are viewed over time and in context" (p. 790). It's true that to ignore cultural and ethnic referents wherein colonial relationships were constructed (see Duncan, 2002; McKenzie, 2003; van Dijk, 1993) only serves to perpetuate further (colonial) injury at hand.

"In our quest to enlist participants, we may unknowingly use tactics that [they] experience as subtle forms of coercion," writes Tilley (1998, p. 324). The researcher, directing and controlling their particular research agenda, also ultimately manipulates (who) what is told and (who) what is (in)visible. "In becoming self-conscious...researchers can see a history of qualitative research that has been deeply colonial, surveilling, and exotic" (Fine, 1994, p. 75). Dillard (2008) suggests that "there can be no doubt that...a real and important topic in the research process invites us to reconsider deeply our positionalities in the research endeavor, to take into account new possibilities in our work, to remember intuition, and to pay special attention to what indigenous cultures can offer in terms of concrete ways to read/re-read our current situations in the world" (pp. 277–278). (Re)presentation may be a "right" in the academy, but it also carries with it a responsibility to recognize the potential for further colonial exploit. It has been valuable for us to consider: Whose needs are being served in the research agenda? Whose understanding/frame of reference are we listening with, as we "talk about" problems and tensions? To ignore these in encounters, whose sense of humanity is being given privilege, or access? Research can encompass deeper, more systemic, and ingrained long-term implications at play. That is worth taking some time to deliberate.

Notes

1. "Each one has their own story" (trans.), or demonstrated adversities (French).
2. "The Rwandan war" (trans.), believed to be the parent of the Congolese war.

References

Ahmad, J. (2004). Diagnosing an illness. In P. Duara (Ed.), *Decolonization: Perspectives from now and then* (pp. 56–63). New York, NY: Routledge. (Reprinted from *Occidentosis: A plague from the west*, pp. 27–35, 1984, Berkeley, CA: Mizan Press)

Bell, L. A. (2003). Telling tales: What stories can teach us about racism. *Race, Ethnicity, and Education, 6*(1), 3–28.

Bourdieu, P. (1977). Structures and the habitus. In *Outline of a theory of practice* (pp. 72–95). London, England: Cambridge University Press.

Bourdieu, P. (1999). Understanding. In P. Bourdieu et al. (Eds.), *The weight of the world* (pp. 607–627). Stanford, CA: Stanford University Press.

Deer, C. (2008). Doxa. In M. Grenfell (Ed.), *Pierre Bourdieu: Key concepts* (pp. 119–130). Stocksfield, England: Acumen.

Dei, G. J. S. (1999). Knowledge and politics of social change: The implications of anti-racism. *British Journal of Sociology of Education, 20*(3), 395–409.

Dei, G. J. S. (2000). Towards an anti-racism discursive framework. In G. J. S. Dei & A. Calliste (Eds), *Power, knowledge and anti-rasicm education*. Nova Scotia: Fernwood Publishing.

Dei, G. J. S. (2005). Critical issues in anti-racist research metholodology: An introduction. In G. J. S. Dei & G. Johal (Eds.), *Critical issues in anti-racist research methodology* (pp. 1–28). New York, NY: Peter Lang.

Dillard, C. (2008). When the ground is black, the ground is fertile: Exploring endarkened feminist epistemology and healing methodologies of the spirit. In N. Denzin, Y. Lincoln, & L.T. Smith (Eds.), *Handbook of critical and indigenous methodologies* (pp. 277–292). Los Angeles, CA: Sage.

Duncan, G. A. (2002). Critical race theory and method: Rendering race in urban ethnographic research. *Qualitative Inquiry, 8*(1), 85–104.

Fine, M. (1994). Working the hyphens: Reinventing self and other in qualitative research. In N. K. Denzin & Y. S. Lincoln (Eds.), *Handbook of qualitative research* (pp. 70–82). Thousand Oaks, CA: Sage.

Howard, P. S. S. (2006). On silence and accountability: A critical anticolonial investigation of the antiracism classroom. In G. J. S. Dei & A. Kempf (Eds.), *Anticolonialsim and education: The politics of resistance* (pp. 43–62). Rotterdam, The Netherlands: Sense.

Joseph, C. (2009). Postcoloniality and ethnography: Negotiating gender, ethnicity and power. *Race, Ethnicity, and Education, 12*(1), 11–25.

Kafele, K. (2004, October). *Racial discrimination and mental health: Racialized and aboriginal communities.* Published paper from the Race Policy Dialogue Conference, Toronto, ON, Canada. Retrieved June 15, 2010, from http://www.ohrc. on.ca/en/issues/racism/racepolicydialogue/kk?page=kk.html#fnB3

Kinclehloe, J., & McLaren, P. (2008). Rethinking critical theory and qualitative research. In N. K. Denzin & Y. S. Lincoln (Eds.), *The landscape of qualitative research* (pp. 433–488). Thousand Oaks, CA: Sage.

McKenzie, K. (2003). Racism and health. *British Medical Journal, 326*(7380), 65–66.

Nkrumah, K. (2004). Society and ideology. In P. Duara (Ed.), *Decolonization: Perspectives from now and then* (pp. 64–77). New York, NY: Routledge. (Reprinted from *Consciencism: Philosophy and ideology for decolonization*, 56–77, 1970, New York, NY: Monthly Review Press)

Omi, W., & Winant, H. (1993). On the theoretical concept of race. In C. McCarthy & W. Crinchlow (Eds.), *Race, identity, and representation in education* (pp. 3–10). New York, NY: Routledge.

Reay, D. (2004). It's all becoming a habitus: Beyond the habitual use of habitus in educational research. *British Journal of Sociology of Education, 25*(4), 431–444.

Shamsuddin, A. K. (2009, February 25). Bureaucracy in Bangladesh [Letter to the editor]. *The Bangladesh Observer,* p. 5.

Short, D. (2005). Reconciliation and the problem of internal colonialism. *Journal of Intercultural Studies, 26*(3), 267–282.

Tilley, S. A. (1998). Conducting respectful research: A critique of practice. *Canadian Journal of Education / Revue Canadienne de l'éducation*, 23(3), 316–328.

Van Ausdale, D., & Feagin, J. R. (1996). Using racial and ethnic concepts: The critical case of very young children. *American Social Review, 61*(5), 779–793.

Van Dijk, T. A. (1993). Analyzing racism through discourse analysis : Some methodological reflections. In J. H. Stanfield & R. M. Dennis (Eds.), *Race and ethnicity in research methods* (pp. 53–74). Thousand Oaks, CA: Sage.

Wahab, A. (2005). Consuming narratives: Questioning authority and the politics of representation in social science research. In G. J. S. Dei & G. S. Johal (Eds.), *Critical issues in anti-racist research methodologies* (pp. 29–52). New York, NY: Peter Lang.

CHAPTER SEVENTEEN

Who Will Be Heard?
Qualitative Research and Legal Decisions about Facilitated Communication

Missy Morton

Introduction

In this chapter I look at two court cases that considered the admissibility of out-of-court statements or direct testimony made by people using facilitated communication (part of a larger examination of six cases; Morton, 2006a, 2006b). Both cases reported in this study were, directly or indirectly, resulting from reports of allegations of abuse. *Matter of M.Z. et al.* dealt explicitly with the admissibility of testimony made by a ten-year-old girl using facilitated communication, in which she alleged sexual abuse by a family member. *Hahn v. Linn County* was about the refusal of a county to pay an agency for provision of facilitated communication. One of the reasons presented for not paying for, or providing, facilitated communication was fear of false allegations of abuse. The county had the previous experience of a former local police chief accused of abusing his son, and this case had been dismissed.

At first glance, the cases appear quite unalike. *Matter of M.Z.* was a 1992 preliminary hearing in a family court case. The defense attorney had requested a *Frye* hearing, arguing that the technique of facilitated communication was a *novel scientific technique*. The issue was not about whether the particular child, *M.Z.,* could communicate. The issue was whether or not anybody could reliably communicate using facilitated communication. *Hahn v. Linn County* was a disability discrimination case heard in a U.S. District Court in 2002. The judge in that case decided the pivotal issue was whether or not the plaintiff, Mr. Douglas Hahn, could communicate using facilitated communication.

Legal decisions convey much more than the narrow application of precedent. Minow (1990) and Austin (1994) both suggest that decisions and analyses can be read for their expression of the worldviews that shape those analyses. They both present detailed analyses of cases, drawing out the worldviews expressed in those cases. Minow (1990) ultimately argues for a *social-relations* approach to legal analysis. Denno (1997) similarly makes the case for a more contextualized approach to considerations of competence.

246

In the rest of this chapter I describe Minow's framework for approaches to legal analysis. I then present the arguments and decisions in the two cases. The next part applies Minow's framework to the decisions, and also identifies ways of thinking about science and about disability that make these analyses possible (i.e., the larger worldviews that underpin the attorneys' arguments and the judges' decisions). I suggest that Minow's social-relations approach to legal analysis offers a way to counter the dominant empiricist discourses of disability research in the legal setting. I conclude the chapter with some suggestions about how the courts might embrace Minow's social-relations approach in more obvious ways.

The Framework for Analysis

A product of legal analysis, according to Minow (1990) and to King and Piper (1995), is the reduction of complex issues to fit into simplified, pre-existing categories for analysis and comparison. On one level, law can present itself as a neutral process, the simple application of precedent. Yet, Minow (1990) argues, the choice of appropriate pre-existing categories, precedent, is always contestable.

> In the United States, litigation is based on the adversary system. This system is founded on the belief that the most effective way to arrive at just results in litigation is for each side of a controversy to present the evidence that is most favorable to its position and to let a *neutral* judge or jury sift through the conflicting evidence and decide where the truth lies. In other words, the truth emerges from a clash of legal adversaries in the *controlled environment* of a courtroom. (Myers, 1992, p. 2, my emphases)

The attorneys have the task of selecting the relevant traits or aspects of a case, in order to identify the relevant case law or precedent that will allow evidence "that is most favorable" to their client's position. They must successfully and aggressively make the argument that the precedent they have distinguished best fits the issues at hand. With Minow (1990), Stubbs (1993) argues that judges have and exercise choice in their application of precedent, "delimiting the scope of statutes and distinguishing and rejecting authorities" (Stubbs, 1993, p. 464). As Minow puts it, "The judge then selects the winning side" (1990, p. 2). Once the relevant precedent is chosen, the outcomes are often reasonably predictable: the judge chooses the winning argument, "accepting the consequences assigned to particular legal categories" (Minow, 1990, p. 1).

Minow's (1990) description of three approaches to legal analysis provides a useful framework for interrogating the two decisions. The abnormal-persons approach "treats classifications on the basis of mental incompetence as natural and immutable" (p. 105). Of particular interest is the person's competence. This idea is important to this study because one of the attorneys' strategies is to present their witnesses as competent, and to undermine the competence of the witnesses from the other side. Defense attorneys sought to present potential disabled witnesses as inherently incompetent. This strategy can be seen as located within a wider understanding of those with autism or of Down syndrome as invariably incompetent. According to Minow (1990), the act of denoting difference is a key component of the abnormal-persons approach to legal analysis.

> Naming another seems natural and obvious when other professionals, social practices, and communal attitudes reinforce that view—and yet these sources of confirmation may merely show how widespread and deep are the prejudice and mistaken views about the "different" person. (Minow, 1990, p. 111)

The rights-analysis approach "addresses errors in classification and invokes the rights of individuals to be free from such errors by governmental officials" (p. 105). At first glance, the rights-analysis approach represents an advance on the abnormal-persons approach, mainly because it challenges the traditional attributions of difference, as those attributions have "mistakenly" denied access to rights on the basis of, for example, race, gender, sexuality or religion. Within a rights-analysis approach there are, however, still some attributions of differences that "correctly" deem some individuals to be incompetent. This approach relies on an understanding of progress in disability and special education research being a matter of better diagnosis, intervention and rehabilitation. Minow argues that the perception of an advance is illusory.

> Indeed, an examination of contemporary legal theory shows that both the traditional theories justifying rights and the major contending theories replicate the distinction between normal and abnormal persons, thus perpetuating the assumptions that trap us in the difference dilemma. (pp. 144–145)

For Minow, the dilemma of difference is an issue that the courts have yet to address:

> When does treating people differently emphasize their differences and stigmatize and hinder them on that basis? And when does treating people the same become insensitive to their difference and likely to stigmatize or hinder them on that basis? (p. 20)

According to Minow, we would expect that the rights-analysis approach would ultimately individualize the approach to be taken, and that it would ultimately replicate (reinvoke) the discourses of difference. For example, rather than revise fundamental assumptions that it is possible to tell a lot about a person's cognitive abilities by their group membership (race, gender and so on), we just learn to revise our assessments of particular groups of people.

The social-relations approach is an emerging view that "focuses on how classifications reveal relationships of power between those who label and those who are labeled" (Minow, 1990, p. 105). Minow suggests that this approach is starting to be adopted because of more recent awareness that mistakes have been made in how people have assigned these categories of difference, and the implications of those differences. The social-relations approach adopts a critical stance towards the assumptions that problems of difference lie within the individual, rather than in the relationships between individuals and society. This is familiar ground to social constructionists. Finally, the social-relations approach calls into question both the hidden nature of the power of the labelers, and the institutional arrangements that preserve that power.

Minow (1990) described an important set of strategies that could contribute to legal treatment of people with disabilities:

> For legal analysis, relational approaches may best be articulated as imperatives to engage an observer—a judge, a legislator, or a citizen—in the problems of difference: *Notice* the mutual dependence of people. *Investigate* the constructions of difference in the light of the norms and patterns of interpretation and institutional relationships, which make some traits matter. *Question* the relationship between the observer and the observed in order to situate judgments in the perspective of the actual judge. *Seek out* and *consider* competing perspectives, especially those of people defined as the problem. *Locate* theory within context; *criticize* practice in the light of theoretical commitments; and *challenge* abstract theories in light of their practical affects. *Connect* the parts and the whole of a situation; *see* how the frame of analysis influences what is *assumed* to be given. (p. 213)

The Decisions

The descriptions of the two court cases that follow draw on material that is already in the public domain, maintaining the level of confidentiality that is present in the published legal decisions or media reports of the cases. Each description will begin with a brief background of the circumstances leading to the hearing. I then outline the decision, setting out how the judges communicate their accounts of what was relevant. I describe the judges' presentations of, and responses to, the arguments made by the attorneys.

Matter of M.Z. et al. (September 16, 1992)

This decision by Judge Minna Buck concerns a preliminary hearing on the admissibility of facilitated communication. Prior to this hearing, Micah was 10 and went to a special school. She was in a class with five other children who were also 10 years old with disabilities. Her teacher was using facilitated communication with Micah, who could speak, albeit with some difficulty. The teacher was also using facilitated communication with two other students in the class. On returning to school in the spring semester, Micah's school reported to the CPS Hotline that Micah had made an allegation of sexual abuse against her father. While CPS was investigating the allegation, there was a family court order made restricting contact. Micah and her younger brother were removed from the family home and placed in foster care pending the outcome of the hearing.

This preliminary hearing, a *Frye* hearing, was held at the request of the defense attorney. The case of *Frye v. U.S.* was decided in 1923. The Supreme Court was asked to decide whether or not evidence obtained by polygraph (lie detector) should be admissible. The Supreme Court ruled that such evidence was not admissible. The standard that was applied concerns the general acceptance of a scientific technique or theory within the relevant field or scientific community. Since the 1923 decision, *Frye* hearings have been held on the admissibility of expert scientific testimony as related to DNA testing, hypnosis as an aid to recall for victims or witnesses, and the use of validation interviews to determine the presence or absence of child sexual abuse syndrome or rape trauma syndrome as corroborating evidence. Etlinger (1995) notes that the *Frye* standard of general acceptance requires more than demonstrating that the "underlying theory and research technique are scientifically valid" (p. 1268). According to Etlinger, a dilemma that courts face when using the *Frye* standard is that "the basis for acceptance in the relevant scientific community is, ironically, not necessarily measured by scientific reliability or validity. Consensus in the scientific community does not necessarily represent empirical verification" (p. 1269).

In a section titled "The Nature of the Evidence," Judge Buck begins her decision with a brief synopsis of facilitated communication. Judge Buck's description is prefaced with "as described to the court" and "according to its practitioners" (p. 565). This background section concludes with a description of Micah: "the individual whose 'facilitated communication' is at issue in this hearing is one of the subject children, a 10–year-old partially verbal child afflicted with Down's syndrome" (p. 565).

Considering the Arguments

Her first decision was that the *Frye* standard was applicable. This section of the decision covers the scope of the *Frye* hearing. Judge Buck sets out four issues. First, she considers the applicability of the *Frye* test. Judge Buck determined that *Frye* was appropriate, even in considering "soft sciences" but "with an emphasis on the reliability of the evidence" (p. 566). She then poses and answers four "threshold questions": "What must be accepted, who must accept it, how extensive must such acceptance be, and what evidence is acceptable to reflect the extent of acceptance?" (p. 566).

In answering her first question, Judge Buck places facilitated communication in the category of a new forensic technique:

> New "forensic technique…may involve either the new application of a well-established theory or the application of a new theory. In the latter case, the theory can be validated only empirically or inferentially, not deductively.… In terms of the *Frye* test, if the technique is generally accepted, then the theory must be valid although not fully understood or explainable." (*Matter of M.Z.*, p. 566)

In other words, the underlying theory of the technique must be accepted as valid.

Judge Buck then asks, "Who are the experts whose opinion on facilitated communication must be considered?" (p. 567). She noted that who is considered an expert depended on which theory of etiology was adopted, acknowledging that there was more than one theory. The third finding of the court was that

> under any theory, the experts whose opinion on facilitated communication would be relevant would include psychologists, psychiatrists, speech and language pathologists, special education practitioners,

and neuro-scientists (i.e., neurologists, researchers and clinicians in this field). Also included would be other clinicians or educators with experience and training in evaluating data for purposes of diagnosis, treatment or research (e.g., physicians who have diagnosed or treated patients with the aid of facilitated communication). (p. 567)

Judge Buck then went on to explicitly exclude from the list of experts parents who have used, or observed the use of, facilitated communication with their children.

Turning to the issue of how much acceptance was required, Judge Buck found that this was a matter of discretion for the court. She noted that "*expert testimony, scientific literature and court precedents*" (p. 567, emphasis added) were useful for establishing the degree of acceptance. Scientific literature was admissible if it "appeared in a peer-review journal in a relevant field and/or were published by acknowledged experts in the field" (p. 567).

The prosecutor argued that Rule 402 of the *Federal Rules of Evidence* should apply, rather than *Frye*. Rule 402 states, "All relevant evidence is admissible, except as otherwise provided [by rule or statute]" (as cited in *Re M.Z.*, p. 571). Judge Buck rejected this argument on the grounds that *Frye* was still the prevailing rule in New York at the time of the hearing. The remainder of the decision then addresses the expert testimony, the scientific literature, and court precedents.

Only the prosecutor called expert witnesses. The summary of the testimony quotes the opinion of a psychiatrist, Dr. K., about the possible underlying theory for facilitated communication.

Facilitated communication is a means to overcome speech impairments in the case of individuals suffering from autism, by allowing them to bypass impaired limbic function of the brain; in the case of other disabilities, it overcomes "dispraxia" [*sic*]—a condition described as an inability to make the appropriate physical or neurological response to a verbal command even though the latter is understood. Dr. K. acknowledged, however, that she was not aware of any studies as to either of these theories as they related to facilitated communication, and that they involved premises about the nature of both autism and Down's syndrome which differed from the current prevailing view as to the etiology of those conditions. (p. 573)

Judge Buck made six points in her summations of the expert witness testimony:

1. Each of these experts testified, in effect, that there was no prescribed method of training facilitators. (p. 574)

2. Nor are there any requirements imposed by law or practice to certify the skill level of facilitators. (p. 574)

3. Each of the experts acknowledged concern about the possibility of manipulation by the facilitator. (p. 575)

4. None of these experts were able to refer to any empirical studies concerning the validity of the communications or the degree to which they were subject to suggestion or interpretation. (p. 575)

5. There was no research design they were aware of which might produce any empirical data. (p. 575)

6. Each of these witnesses did acknowledge their awareness of others, particularly those considered expert in the fields of autism, who either disagreed with the assumptions on which facilitated communication is based and/or called for more research to test the reliability of the technique. (p. 575)

The expert testimony put forward by the prosecutor was characterized as insufficient to make the argument.

Near the end of her decision, Judge Buck commented:

> It should be pointed out that these findings do not constitute any judgment on the utility or reliability of facilitated communication.... Nor do they imply any criticism or demeaning of the motives and conduct of those who have been studying and promoting facilitated communication. (p. 579)

However she is very critical, and dismissive of, the published research. Having noted earlier that scientific literature is permitted as evidence if published by an acknowledged expert and/or appearing in a peer-reviewed journal, she decided that the article by Biklen (1990) in the *Harvard Educational Review* would not be allowed as evidence:

> The petitioners here also offered the article by Dr. Biklen referred to above. That article, identified on this record as having appeared in the *Harvard Education* [sic] *Review* of August 1990, had been discussed on direct and cross-examination of each of the expert witnesses in the instant case. It apparently contained a summary of Dr. Biklen's work to date regarding facilitated communication, as well as discussion of his experience with facilitated communication or something similar in another program in Australia, and a discussion of some of the issues raised by his findings. (pp. 577–578)

She added, as an apparent aside, "(It should be noted that Dr. K. had previously testified that the *Harvard Education* [sic] *Review* was not a peer-review journal)" (p. 578, parentheses in original). There is, however, no description or explanation of the process of peer review for any journals, so it is not clear how the *HER* process of peer review is less rigorous than any other process. Finally, she summarized her comments about the published research by stating "Petitioner has presented no scholarly literature about facilitated communication" (p. 578). Because Dr. Biklen had not appeared as an expert witness, Judge Buck ruled "he was not called to establish a foundation for the purpose of receiving the article into evidence and, over respondents' hearsay objection, the court declined to receive the article in evidence" (p. 578).

The prosecution put forward the results of two earlier hearings. The first was a due process hearing from a Tennessee Administrative Law Judge (*Matter of L. v. Public Schools*, Dept. of Educ. 90–47, June 27, 1991). The summary of this case includes a description of the research reported in the *Harvard Educational Review.* The judge ruled that L. be placed in a school in Missouri that would look at using facilitated communication

> at the School District's expense in order to "evaluate more fully L's communication abilities, identify the best teaching modalities...and to provide a highly controlled environment in order to obtain an accurate assessment of L's potential." The order was to remain in effect for six months, with the implication that it would thereafter be reviewed. No information was provided in the instant proceeding about further proceedings or findings in the Tennessee case. (p. 577)

The decision makes no further reference to *Matter of L. v. Public Schools,* and it appears that Judge Buck considers it to have no bearing on the *Matter of M.Z.*

The second case the prosecutor put forth was one that Judge Buck had herself previously considered:

> Petitioner here also requested the court to take notice of its own rulings (N-72/3-90 and N-37/8-91, June 20, 1991) in *Matter of Barbara M. and Kenneth M.,* an unrelated article 10 proceeding in which a witness was allowed to testify as to statements made by a child outside the courtroom using facilitated communication. (p. 577)

The judge distinguished *Matter of Barbara M. and Kenneth M.* from the present case on the grounds that the prior case was dispositional only and was concerned only with the credibility of another witness (i.e., did not involve fact-finding regarding the truth of the communication).

Judge Buck decided that the petitioners had not presented sufficient evidence to meet the *Frye* standard. She concluded:

> The foregoing findings are limited to a determination that, in the case of the use of facilitated communication as described here, there has not been sufficient proof of its general acceptance or reliability to permit its use in a fact-finding proceeding under article 10 of the Family Court Act. (p. 579)

This decision ignored the published research about facilitated communication (e.g., IDRP, 1989; Biklen, 1990; Biklen et al., 1991). The *Matter of M.Z.* does not consider how the court might have used its discretion to find means of determining how someone might be able to use facilitated communication. The *Matter of M.Z.* similarly precludes Micah, the individual child, from demonstrating whether or not *she* could use facilitated communication without undue influence.

Hahn v. Linn County (February 2, 2001 and March 11, 2002)

Douglas Hahn, through and with his two sisters and co-guardians Barbara Axline and Judith Barta, claimed that Discovery Living and Linn County were denying him access to services. *Hahn v. Linn County* (2001) was a motion by the defendants, Linn County and Discovery Living, for summary judgment in a disability discrimination case in which the "[d]efendants raise the following novel question: Whether the defendants' refusal to provide facilitated communication, an alternative form of communication, to an autistic individual violates both federal and state disability discrimination laws" (p. 1040). The motion for summary judgment was dismissed, and the substantive issue taken up in the 2002 case. Chief Judge Mark Bennett, writing for the U.S. District Court for the Northern District of Iowa, described *Hahn v. Linn County* (2002) as a "disability discrimination case of first impression" (p. 1052).

Doug Hahn had lived away from home since he was 12, when he moved to Woodward Hospital State Hospital-School in Iowa. He lived there for 30 years. In 1987 he moved into a group home run by Discovery Living, a non-profit organization contracted by Linn County. There is always at least one Discovery Living staff member to supervise Doug and his two housemates. Five days a week, from 9:00 to 2:30, Doug goes to Options, which is a sheltered workshop, that also contracts with Linn County. At Options he assembles boxes and latches.

The use of facilitated communication in Linn County-funded programs was short lived. In August 1993, staff at Options and at Discovery Living began using facilitated communication with people at the workshop and at home. Karen Kray, a program manager at Options, learned how to facilitate from a speech-language therapist at a nearby high school. Karen Kray introduced facilitated communication to staff and a number of clients, including Doug Hahn. But by October of that year, Linn County had stopped funding the use of facilitated communication in any of the services it contracted, including both Options and Discovery Living.

Linn County cited two reasons for ceasing funding-facilitated communication. First, the county said there was a lack of research to validate facilitated communication. Second, the county was concerned about "surfacing concerns over allegations of sexual abuse by means of facilitated communication" (*Hahn v. Linn County,* 2002, p. 1057). While not mentioned in the court decision, the local media was also reporting the story of a 1993 allegation of sexual abuse made using facilitated communication. In 1993, in an unrelated case, a former local Cedar Rapids police commander was accused by his disabled son of sexual abuse. The son, who was living in Colorado at the time, had used facilitated communication to make the allegation (Kutter, 1999, 2001).

Linn County spent about a year trying to develop and implement a policy that would allow it to continue to use facilitated communication with clients. It required that Doug Hahn undertake a literacy test. The county also tried to develop a research protocol. In the end, it never resumed funding the use of facilitated communication in its services. Doug Hahn's sister, Judith Barta, continued to use facilitated communication with him, both when he visited his sisters at their homes, and when they visited him at his home. The decision notes,

> …neither Linn County nor Discovery Living has banned the use of FC in their facilities; the defendants merely refuse to fund FC. Thus, Ms. Barta is free to facilitate with Mr. Hahn at both Discovery Living and Options, but neither defendant will fund facilitation with the use of its staff. (p. 1058)

It was this refusal by Linn County to fund facilitated communication in its services that was at the core of the complaint by Doug Hahn and his sisters.

The plaintiffs, Doug Hahn, Barbara Axline and Judith Barta, thus argued that the defendants, Linn County and Discovery Living, were discriminating against Doug Hahn. Specifically, by refusing to fund and provide facilitated communication, the defendants were "in violation of Section 504 of the *Rehabilitation Act*, the Titles II and III of the *Americans with Disabilities Act* of 1990 (ADA), and the *Iowa Civil Rights Act* (ICRA)" (p. 1051).

Considering the Arguments

Judge Bennett's first ruling was that "the court must first determine whether Mr. Hahn communicates through facilitated communication because any failure on the part of the plaintiffs to carry their burden of proof on this point renders unnecessary reaching the other issues" (p. 1058). Unlike the *Matter of M.Z.*, proponents in *Hahn v. Linn County* argued that the ADA provided guidance to the court. A further similarity is that both courts found that it was necessary to first make a determination about facilitated communication. Where the *Matter of M.Z.* used the *Frye* standard to consider the general acceptance of facilitated communication, *Hahn v. Linn County* considered the specific reliability of Doug Hahn's use of facilitated communication.

Both parties called expert witnesses to testify about the reliability and general acceptance of facilitated communication. Judge Bennett described this issue as "moot" because the "pivotal issue" was Doug Hahn's communication (p. 1060). The plaintiffs also wanted their expert witnesses, Dr. Biklen and Dr. Kleiwer, to testify about the effectiveness of facilitated communication for Doug Hahn in particular, and the defense objected to this testimony, citing *Daubert* (1993).

The guidelines provided by *Daubert* are that the

> district court must "ensure that an expert's testimony both rests on a reliable foundation and is relevant to the task at hand."… That is so because, absent some indicia of reliability and relevance to the case before the trier of fact, the testimony cannot "assist" the factfinder, as required by Rule 702. (p. 1060)

In their turn, *Federal Rules of Evidence* Rule 702 stipulates that

> If scientific, technical, or other specialized knowledge will assist the trier of fact to understand the evidence or to determine a fact in issue, a witness qualified as an expert by knowledge, skill, experience, training, or education, may testify thereto in the form of an opinion or otherwise, if (1) the testimony is based upon sufficient facts or data, (2) the testimony is the product of reliable principles and methods, and (3) the witness has applied the principles and methods reliably to the facts of the case. (p. 1060)

Ultimately, the court decided that it did not need to decide the applicability of either *Daubert* or *Federal Rules of Evidence* 702, because the court found "that Mr. Hahn's facilitators, and not Mr. Hahn, author the facilitated communications" (p. 1064).

Judge Bennett invited Judith Barta to demonstrate facilitated communication to the court, either with Doug Hahn or anyone else. All parties agreed, and Doug Hahn and Judith Barta met with the judge in his chambers. The decision documents the judge's interpretation of what he saw:

> During this in-court demonstration, Mr. Hahn did not look at the keyboard despite Ms. Barta's prompts. Yet, his responses to Ms. Barta's typed questions were glaringly absent of the kind of typos one would expect when typing without looking at the keyboard and without a "home row" of keys. The plaintiffs' experts agree that an individual must look at the keyboard before there can be any question that the output is authentic. During the demonstration, Mr. Hahn never looked at the keyboard, while Ms. Barta's eyes never strayed from the keyboard. In addition, from the demonstration, it was clear that Ms. Barta was guiding Mr. Hahn's finger and not merely providing resistance. Her hand was directly under Mr. Hahn's hand and essentially placed Mr. Hahn's finger on the key to be typed. In combination, Mr. Hahn's failure to look at the keyboard and Ms. Barta's direction of Mr. Hahn's finger, compel this court to conclude that the output generated by Mr. Hahn was not genuine, i.e., was not Mr. Hahn's. (p. 1062)

Judge Bennett noted that his decision was limited to the issue of whether Doug Hahn could communicate using facilitation. Given that this was not proven in court, he ruled that Discovery Living and Linn County were not required to "fund an ineffective means of communication" (p. 1064). The decision also clearly stated that this finding was limited *only* to Doug Hahn, as "another Options or Discovery Living consumer might be one of the few individuals who is able to communicate his or her own thoughts through facilitated communication" (p. 1064). Nevertheless, because the court determined that facilitated communication was not effective for Doug Hahn, the defendants were not in violation of the Rehabilitation Act, ADA or the Iowa Civil Rights Act.

Discussion and Conclusion

An important debate in these cases was what would count as research into facilitated communication, and who would be considered to have the necessary expertise to be able to comment on facilitated communication in particular, and disability in general. This debate emerged from the strategic maneuvrings of the attorneys to frame the issues in particular ways. In framing the debates, the attorneys were able to invoke discourses of disability and of research that were easily recognized by their audiences of judges and other attorneys, who were also writers of legal analyses. The written decisions then place "on the record" the arguments and the outcomes of these debates. The published decisions add to the canon of "what is known" about facilitated communication, about disability and how it should be studied.

The predominant approach has been the abnormal-persons approach to legal analysis. This approach both depends upon and supports an expert or medical discourse of disability. When a rights-analysis approach was used, the rights of the "abnormal" purported victims were pitted against are the "normal" accused, which invariably led to a collapse in the abnormal-persons approach to analysis. The social-relations approach to legal analysis seems to offer the most cogent challenge to the normal science approach that both underpins and is supported by the abnormal-persons approach to legal analysis.

In the cases described in this chapter, the judges (and attorneys) writing about the applicability of *Frye* or *Daubert* were not explicit that they were also writing about themselves (and juries) and their ability to "tell" if someone was communicating, their ability to understand and apply disability research to the person before them. They were not yet self-consciously writing about their relationships with the people who were used as experts to support the work of the courts, and their relationships with those they did not recognize as experts. They were not yet deliberately writing about their relationships with those they presumed to be like them, and about those they presumed to be different from themselves.

While it is beyond the scope of this chapter to dictate the proper form of legal analysis, I want to suggest some questions that judges might consider as they determine the procedures that will be followed in *their* courts, the precedents that *they* will apply, *their* frameworks and perspectives that will shape *their* analyses and decisions. Judges would need to answer these questions for themselves, for the other participants in a specific case, and for the wider audiences who read the decisions and use these decisions to then guide their practices.

- What do I think we can achieve by setting up the interactions in this setting in this way?

- Whose voice is heard, whose argument is privileged by setting up the interactions in this way? What are the costs, and to whom?

- When a particular line of argument, or a particular piece of evidence, is compelling, why is it compelling? What are (my) assumptions, experiences and/or beliefs that make this compelling?

- What is it about a particular witness that makes her or him more or less convincing? What are (my) assumptions, experiences and/or beliefs that make this person more or less convincing? What are the shared experiences, values and understandings that I might assume we have? What are our differences that I might be assuming? What significance do I give to these assumed similarities and differences?

I do not mean to suggest that there will not be tensions as these questions are addressed. For example, people who are accused will want to feel that their perspective and their situation is well represented, that due process is followed. There will be a need to establish the competence and credibility of all witnesses, including ensuring that an individual using facilitated communication is in fact able to do so in the court setting. The challenge for judges will be to ensure that those they have seen as most different to themselves are not required to reach different, and more restrictive, standards than those who already enjoy privileged positions in the legal setting. The challenge for judges will be to ensure that those they have seen as least like themselves are no longer the people most likely to be silenced.

References

Americans with Disabilities Act of 1990 (ADA), Pub L. No. 101–336, §2, 104 Stat. 327 (1991).

Austin, G. (1994). *Children: Stories the law tells*. Wellington, New Zealand: Victoria University Press.

Biklen, D. (1990). Communication unbound: Autism and praxis. *Harvard Educational Review, 60,* 291–314.

Biklen, D., Morton, M. W., Saha, S. N., Duncan, J., Gold, D., Hardardottir, M.,…Rao, S. (1991). I AMN NOT A UTIS-TIVC OH THJE TYP ("I am not autistic on the typewriter"). *Disability, Handicap and Society, 6*(3), 161–180.

Daubert v. Merrell Dow Pharmaceuticals Inc., 113 S.Ct 2786 (1993).

Denno, D. W. (1997). Sexuality, rape and mental retardation. *University of Illinois Law Review, 1997*(2), 315–434.

Etlinger, L. (1995). Social science research in domestic violence law: A proposal to focus on evidentiary use. *Albany Law Review, 58,* 1259–1306.

Frye v. United States, 293 F 1013 (1923).

Hahn v. Linn County, IA #C99–19, 130 F.Supp. 2d 1036, (2001) U.S. Dist. LEXIS 1419, 11 Am. Disabilities Cas. (BNA) 177.

Hahn v. Linn County, IA #C99–19–MWB, 191 F.Supp. 2d 1051; (2002) U.S. Dist. LEXIS 4249; 13 Am. Disabilities Cas. (BNA) 1869.

Intellectual Disability Review Panel (IDRP). (1989). *Report to the Director General on the reliability and validity of assisted communication.* Melbourne: Department of Community Services, Victoria.

King, M., & Piper, C. (1995). *How the law thinks about children* (2nd ed.). London: Arena.

Kutter, E. (1999, February 5). Lawsuit challenges Linn's ban on "facilitated communication." *The Gazette (Cedar Rapids-Iowa City),* p. B3.

Kutter, E. (2001, May 7). Expression going on trial: Facilitated communication case begins today in C.R. *The Gazette (Cedar Rapids-Iowa City),* p. A1.

Matter of L. v. Public Schools, Tenn. Dept. of Educ. (90-47, June 27, 1991).

Matter of M.Z. et al., 590 N.Y.S. 2d 390 (NY Family Court, Onondaga County, Sept. 16, 1992, Buck, J.).

Minow, M. (1990). *Making all the difference: Inclusion, exclusion and American law*. Ithaca, NY: Cornell University Press.

Morton, M. (2006a). *Silenced in the court: Facilitated communication and the meanings of disability and disability research in the legal setting.* (Unpublished PhD dissertation). Syracuse University, Syracuse, NY.

Morton, M. (2006b). Regulating bodies: The discursive production of disability research in the legal setting. *Disability Studies Quarterly, 26*(1). Retrieved March 13, 2006, from http://www.dsq-sds.org/_articles_html/2006/winter/morton.asp

Myers, J. E. B. (1992). *Legal issues in child abuse and neglect*. Newbury Park, CA: Sage.

Stubbs, M. (1993). Feminism and legal positivism. In D. Kelly Weisberg (Ed.), *Feminist legal theory: Foundations* (pp. 454–475). Philadelphia: Temple University Press.

CHAPTER EIGHTEEN

Governing Young Children's Learning through Educational Reform: A Poststructural Analysis of Discourses of Best Practice, Standards, and Quality

Marianne N. Bloch and Ko Eun Kim

Introduction

In the majority of western industrialized countries, early care and education policies have been an important topic for over three centuries. Very recent international agency reports such as OECD's (2006) *Starting Strong*, which focuses on "early childhood education and care" (or ECEC), and UNESCO's (2006) report *Strong Foundations* in "early childhood care and education" (or ECCE) in countries around the world, illustrate the diverse ways in which policy analyses have begun to focus new attention on issues related to the education and care of young children. Moreover, the differences in emphases in the texts illustrate the ways in which discursive language illustrates priorities, current ways of reasoning about what is important to policy analysts, and social inclusions and exclusions. The discursive titles and use of different terms in their texts highlight the importance of policy discussions around young children (e.g., *Strong Foundations* vs. *Starting Strong*), but also the continuing debates (should it be "early child care and education" or "early childhood education and care"?).

While the above examples help us to look directly at the notion of discursive language and reasoning systems, many other questions are embedded in the policy documents, with little interrogation. For example: When the reports recommend or refer to the need for higher-quality care, we can ask, what is "quality care?" (see Dahlberg, Moss, & Pence, 2007); Who do the reports imply should be cared for and who should be educated, and at what age/stage, or grade? Who should "care" and "educate" "other people's children"? (Delpit, 1995); Should health care be included in a society's or nation's policy priorities in relation to early education and child care?; What is meant by "school" in school-based early childhood programs? (what is included/excluded from this term?); and also, How should we provide a socially just opportunity for *all* young children *and their families* to succeed (learn, thrive, achieve) as we consider policy in the USA, as well as elsewhere? Finally, what do we/others mean by "socially just?"

While not all of these questions will be examined here, our purpose is to focus on a textual analysis of five U.S. states' early learning standards that can begin to illustrate the importance of critical qualitative research as a way to open up to new ways to interrogate reasoning systems, current naturalized ways of acting, and important aspects that are excluded from our reasoning by the texts we have available to us. We use a Foucauldian discourse analysis of cultural ways of reasoning to illustrate some of the answers to the above questions, and remaining places where meanings and practices, as well as their material effects, are obscured. At the end of the paper, we return to the importance of critical qualitative research in policy analysis. Where is the place for critical critique in today's "evidence based," "gold standard" educational research and policy world? (Bloch, 2004; Popkewitz, 2004).

Theoretical and Methodological Framings

We draw on several aspects of Michel Foucault's theoretical toolbox (1977, 1980, 1991) in our analyses, especially his concepts of governmentality and power/knowledge, which we discuss briefly below. In addition, we describe notions of the rhizome from Gilles Deleuze and Felix Guattari's writings (1988) that also inform our theoretical and methodological work.

We use the notion of governmentality (Foucault, 1991) and the rhizome (Deleuze & Guattari, 1988) to focus on how language/discourses combine to form the way we think and act, policing action, forming ways of reasoning that privilege some senses of words as normal/natural while demoting others to "abnormality" (Bloch, Kennedy, Lightfoot, & Weyenberg, 2006). The notion of policing comes from Donzelot's (1979) focus on "policing of families," where policies represent approaches to produce people, knowledge, and action. In the use of both terms, *governmentality* and *policing*, we use the sense of knowledge as productive rather than simply repressive (thou shalt not) and knowledge in relation to power (knowledge/power). Knowledge is productive in that it relates to the sense we make of objects, as well as groups, locations, and people; knowledge relates to power in that certain knowledge takes on a sense of a "regime of truth" (Foucault, 1980) or legitimacy, while other knowledge, ways of thinking appear to be unnatural, even unthinkable, or considered "illegitimate."

According to Jennifer Gore (1998), in *Discipline and Punish*, Foucault illustrated several examples of techniques of power relevant to prisons that she argues could be extended to an examination of schools.

> Using the exemplar of the Panopticon, with its normalizing surveillance, Foucault describes disciplinary power as circulating rather than being possessed, productive and not necessarily repressive, existing in action, functioning at the level of the body, often operating through "technologies of the self."…There is general agreement that Foucault provided a careful elaboration of specific techniques of power in penal institutions—techniques of surveillance, normalization, individualization, and so on. (Gore, 1998, p. 233)

Gore then extends Foucault's analysis to school pedagogical practices by focusing on eight "techniques of power": 1) surveillance, 2) normalization, 3) exclusion, 4) classification, 5) distribution, 6) individualization, 7) totalization, and 8) regulation. While we believe that there are more technologies at play, drawing on Foucault's analyses of "technologies of the self" (1988) and "biopower" (1998), we believe Gore's eight techniques of power are helpful in framing our state-by-state analysis of early learning standards.

Finally, the notion of *rhizomatic thinking* used by Deleuze and Guattari (1988) allows us to move from a rooted tree concept where things are static and unchangeable to a metaphor or concept of a rhizomatic plant that can move in different, unpredictable directions. We can think of the roots of a tree locked into the ground, or an iris that spreads its roots near the surface, moving in multiple unexpected ways as a way to conceptualize this idea. Drawing on the analysis of "standards" in Bloch et al. (2006), we can (again) illustrate how the rhizome can also be useful in an analysis of early learning standards (or reform texts related to standards and indicators of quality more generally).

Rhizomatic space incorporates three overlapping, complex, but distinct spaces. The first space is "striation" or "bounded space." This space denotes the linear, unitary, and progressive reasoning through which the object/subject of knowledge is constituted. In the case of early childhood studies, discourses on this level include the normative discourses of development and of universalizing "neutral" or "objective" concepts of the "good" child, the "good" parent or teacher, and of "best practices" in education. Another space referred to by Deleuze and Guattari as "*lines of flight*," is an undefined, abstract realm, where understandings and possibilities are so numerous that they cease to take on normative meaning (pp. 88–89). Lines of flight open up conceptual space and meanings attached to childhood and the possibility for new ways of "becoming" with a multiplicity of pathways that are not predefined or predetermined.... (Rhizomatic spaces are situated) in an area between these spaces. This is the *"rhizomatic" space*, where it is possible to approach lines of flight and to question the boundaries produced in *striated space*. This is a space where we can reexamine our commonplace understandings and accepted truths without being so abstract or open that our analysis has no connection and no meaning. (Bloch et al., 2006, pp. 4–5)

The poststructural theoretical traditions we draw on emphasize how the ways in which we form our "sense" of logic and practice are based on a circulation of governing discourses that travel from place to place, and are culturally and historically contingent (see Popkewitz & Bloch, 2001; Bloch, 2003; Bloch et al., 2006). These theoretical stances focus on "standards" as a form of regulated, normalized, and surveyed space where the child and pedagogy are constructed within bounded, knowable, rational, and, drawing on Deleuze and Guattari's notions discussed above, "striated spaces." Thus, rather than having a universal set of standards, or a universal sense of what every child needs, and how every child develops, these theoretical frameworks combine to allow us to interrogate how we come to reason as we do about the child, childhood, policies and pedagogical practices of a particular moment. They allow us to ask how we come to know who and what the normal child, teacher, and program should or could be like at a given time/place or space. These theoretical traditions (and others) ask us to interrogate reform texts as they form our reason of what is natural and, apparently, neutral and good as expressed within policy. From these perspectives, we examine discourses of "best practices," "standards," and indicators of "quality" as these appear in our current case study of specifically selected texts from five states' policies on early learning standards and quality indicators in the USA.

In our discourse analysis, we can open up these discursive texts to scrutiny; for example, when and why do they appear at certain times/places and in certain conceptual spaces? What meaning do they have at specific times and places—if we assume history is not linear but filled with ruptures, contingencies, rather than linearity and progress. What do the cultural reasoning systems embedded in texts include as well as exclude? In particular, who and what reasoning is excluded in the name of social inclusion (Popkewitz & Lindblad, 2000)?

For our analysis, we ask what is meant by high quality standards or best practices *IF* many are excluded by the curriculum, the programs, or the opportunities offered? Do the ideas inserted into curriculum standards for "good quality" privilege some ways of being, some ideas of "normal" and "good" or "best," while excluding other ideas and practices from possibility?

Discourse Analysis. While there is much more that could be discussed, we now turn toward the critical discourse analysis of texts done (to date) for this project. As suggested, we draw on work by Gore (1998), Popkewitz and Brennan (1998), Popkewitz (1998) and Bloch (2003) as ways to frame critical policy discourse analysis, but especially focus on what is included and excluded in textual statements. In addition, Foucault directs our attention to the

"rules of [discursive] formation" in the study of discourses or discursive practice. We must grasp the statement in the exact specificity of its occurrence; determine its conditions of existence, fix at least its limits, establish its correlations with other statements that may be connected with it, and show what other forms of statement it excludes.... We must show why it could not be other than it was, in what respect it is exclusive of any other, how it assumes, in the midst of others and in relation to them, a place that no other could occupy. (Foucault, 1972, p. 28)

Finally, in this analysis, there is no pretense that we will represent a new truth, new better "standards" for consideration; rather we want to open up new spaces for discussion and recognize that there are spaces for rhizomatic possibilities—a becoming rather than a closing down through the notions of striated spaces and in the concept of the rooted tree (Deleuze & Guattari, 1988). We can open up to ways in which current discussions continue to exclude in the name of social inclusion, and begin again to imagine differently and "otherwise."

A Case Study of Five States in the USA and Reforms Related to Early Learning Standards, and Indicators of "Quality"

What are the cultural reasoning systems embedded within some of the national cross-state analyses and a sample of different states' decisions about their early care and education systems? This chapter uses as a theoretical/methodological example the educational discourses embedded in reform reports within five states to discuss the contested policy and pedagogical orientations that are "travelling" in the USA today. Based on these reform reports, as well as a macro-political analysis of discourses about what constitutes "quality" and for whom, it focuses on both educational policy texts and the ways in which "policing" of children from low-income, often "urban," backgrounds appears within these texts. We argue that the "urban" or the low-income child and his family who are "under the poverty line" in the USA are often conceived of as "different" and in need of intervention.

Although only illustrative of how policy makers, teachers, or parents believe or act, this chapter focuses on these early 21st-century policy reports on early learning standards as examples of the standards movement in the USA in the late 20th and early 21st centuries, and cultural systems of reasoning about "best practice," standards for "high quality," and "best" curricular/pedagogical practices. We examine the "cultural reasoning systems that include as well as exclude certain groups and concepts from appearing to be normal"; we examine how standards for early learning normalize, regulate, categorize, and individualize children and their families and teachers. We examine how the "standard" child, program, and teacher (and parent) should be acting, and assessed for normality, or for "quality."

Textual Sources. From national sources, we drew especially from state-by-state comparisons done by the National Center for Children in Poverty (NCCP; www.nccp.org) and the National Institute for Early Education Research (NIEER; see www.nieer.org).[1] We also drew from state profiles available at the Pre-K Now website (www.prek-now.org). At the state level, we drew on state websites for early learning standards and "quality rating and improvement systems" (QRIS). As necessary, these will be cited below.

In the chapter, we provide a glimpse of what some states are saying they are doing in their policy texts, and what some of the language within policy texts implies is important, truth, taken to be natural or normal. Again, we do not pretend to be "telling the truth," but only to allude to different representations of truths that may be part of the cultural reasoning systems that are guiding policy documents.[2]

Early Child Care and Education. Before discussing criteria for selection of states and texts, in the next section we briefly discuss the reasoning behind our use of the term "early child care and education system" as a starting point for analysis.

Using cross-national policy reports as a starting place, the first point of interrogation was how are national and state policy texts organized by institution, funding, alliances, and what do they speak about in relation to all children's care and education in the USA? While some reports from the early 2000s called for a national system of early care and education in the USA, as many of the "industrialized" (read this as richer) European countries appear to have (see Lubeck, 2001), few of the reports from the above-named USA-based organizations focused on a particularly integrated approach to their state-by-state analysis.

The National Institute for Early Education Research (NIEER)'s report on the *State of Preschool* is one example that we draw on heavily, as it provides significant data for this project. Despite the resources provided, the charts and texts clearly focused on the development of state-by-state prekindergarten (pre-K, for 3- and/or 4-year-olds) programs, policies, quality, access criteria, funding averages/child, etc. Despite the data presented, the report very clearly states that funding by state for child-care programs as well as other sources of funding that might go to *subsidized* (read as low-income or lower-income "working class" parents) child-care systems (e.g., Office of Child Care's Child Care and Development Fund or CCDF dollars, Temporary Assistance for Needy Families or TANF funding) could not be included in the report, nor was there a way to estimate the number of children in organized family or group child care that was not also counted as a state pre-K program (or Head Start full-day program, presumably, though not stated directly).

The language of inclusion/exclusion is very apparent in the NIEER report's criteria for what qualifies as a state preschool program as shown below:

> The initiative serves children of preschool age, usually 3 and/or 4. Although initiatives in some states serve broader age ranges, programs that serve *only* infants and toddlers are excluded…. *State-funded preschool education initiatives must be distinct from the state's system for subsidized child care….* Although some of these child care funds (CCDF dollars, TANF funds) may be used for high-quality, educational, center-based programs for 3- and 4-year-olds *that closely resemble programs supported by state-funded preschool education initiatives*, it is nearly impossible to determine what proportion of the child care funds are spent this way. (NIEER, 2008, p. 21, italics added for emphasis)

Similarly, the report emphasizes statistics in states that provide *at least* access to *half-day* care in public pre-K programs, though state priorities that focus on full-day programs are mentioned in the state-by-state profiles in the 2008 NIEER report.

There is little discussion of state choices to augment half-day programs (2.5 hours, four to five days per week) in most state profiles other than to highlight the increasing (or decreasing) numbers of children who can access such programs. Discussion of cultural reasoning systems that exclude a priority for or recognition of the large need for full-day programs for young children from infancy onward in the USA privileges the growth of a certain type of "early education" over full-day child care needed by many American families (see Polakow, 2007; Fuller, 2007):

> Access to state pre-K, or any other publicly funded pre-K program, is of significant value to children and the nation only if those programs are *educationally effective*…. By itself, cheap child care with low standards may reach more families, but it is bad policy, and may even harm child development. Quality pre-K can work together with child care to help parents and children now in ways that will increase future prosperity. (NIEER, 2009, p. 9)

In the text above, there is a clear demarcation between publicly funded state pre-K programs and child care programs. These pre-K programs are distinguished in multiple places from *child care*, especially when *cheap* and of *low standards*. The case for standardized, expensive, publicly funded, high quality, educationally effective programs that will be of value to children and the nation proclaims what is "best," and excludes from reasoning that cheaper private child care with lower standards could be good or supported. Thus, while different international agency reports focus on the right of children and their families to full- and/or half-day child care that is *educational* (OECD, 2006; UNESCO, 2006), the NIEER reports (2008, 2009) maintain a separation between what is education and what is care. Also, although other research suggests that the majority of low-income children in the USA use family, kith and kin, and child-care services considered of *low to mediocre quality* (Cannella, 2003; Fuller, 2007; Polakow, 2007), most research also suggests families have, at times, a forced "choice" of child care because of need for full-day care to receive TANF funds, proximity and cost, access to openings in community settings, or cultural and linguistic relevancy for their children (Polakow, 2007; or Fuller, 2007).

In yet another example of the maintenance of a "fragmented" or historically segregated "system" of early care and education in the USA, the National Center for Children in Poverty (NCCP) at Columbia University focused its state-by-state profile report, *State Early Childhood Policies* (2007), entirely on full-day child-care programs responsive to the special needs of infants and toddlers (group care, not family care, we believe), and, especially, on provisions for low-income families and the needs of working parents. (The NCCP report includes both quality child care and state prekindergarten programs, although its primary focus is child-care programs, and it is critical that many state prekindergarten programs are provided as part-day and part-year options.)

While this focus is more than helpful when trying to patch together a portrait of the "child-care system" in the USA, it is partial, and again excludes the possibility of compiling state-by-state access or funding for early care and early education programs for children aged 5 and under in the USA. While some US Census Bureau population reports attempt to portray all types of provision of child care and early education in the USA (e.g., *Current Population Reports* such as http://www.census.gov/prod/2010pubs/p70–121.pdf, retrieved July 23, 2011, or other similar citations from NCCP.org), their more comprehensive focus is directed at population description, often without prescriptions on quality, funding, or assessment. Therefore, the picture of reasoning embodied in these various reports retains a fragmented and exclusionary system of reasoning that breaks populations into have and have-not age groups (nothing for 0–3s in the pre-K program, prioritization of half-day education for all, or subsidized child care for those "in poverty" or lower working class).

One could assume that the two- to three-hundred-year history of different types of early care and education opportunities in the USA is simply being continued through the different emphases in the various reports (see Bloch, 1987). However, another way to interrogate the ways these reports present themselves textually is to reinforce the privileging of some forms of care/education over others, for some types of children over others. When one combines these discursively formed ways of reasoning with the growth of poverty in urban areas throughout the USA, and the continued harsh regulatory rules for low-wage work for women/men who receive Temporary Assistance for Needy Families (TANF) funds under the welfare-to-work reforms implemented in 1996 (see Cannella, 2003; Polakow, 2007), we can again ask this question: Why is half-day public preschool for low-income and/or at-risk families privileged over a more systematic push for quality full-day child care, or options for this, across the states? As the next section begins to look at selective state policies related to provision, funding, and quality, especially related to early learning standards (ELS), we continue to look at these issues.

State-by-State Portraits: Descriptive and Discursively Presented. In selecting states for our early analyses, we examined multiple reports done by foundations (National Institute for Early Education Research, [NIEER], National Center for Children in Poverty, [NCCP]). Some of the states were originally selected because of proximity and accessibility for research (Wisconsin, Illinois), and/or because of our knowledge about state programs (Massachusetts, Wisconsin, Illinois, California, and New York). Some were also selected based on the criterion that the states cover a large population of children (e.g., New York, California). All states mentioned were selected for the first stage of research (and included in this chapter) because they were, at least, in the top 10 ranking of providers of public pre-K, Head Start, or special early education for 3- and/or 4-year-old children (according to the NIEER 2008 report on pre-K). We also looked at poverty levels and other demographic indicators, discussed in greater detail below, within each state from the 2008 NCCP report on United States early childhood profiles by state (NCCP, 2009a).

The choices of particular states also reflect individual state descriptions in terms of the aim to provide access to early care and education for many children from diverse family backgrounds, and/or that were also represented in the NIEER report as having different models of accessibility as well as "high-quality" programs, represented by the adoption of quality rating and improvement systems (QRIS) and state early learning standards.

States examined most fully for this paper were California, Illinois, Massachusetts, Wisconsin, and New York.[3] This calls into question the "depth"-versus-"breadth" component of qualitative research, and the use of critical qualitative and quantitative indicators as ways to select which texts to examine in research, and from which sources. In this analysis, we used "statistical" and "populational" reasoning as represented in reports and other texts as representations of "truth" for selecting which states to examine. Given that this chapter is illustrative of dilemmas in critical qualitative research, the selection of states based upon reports we then examine discursively, and on reports of data that not only change in a dynamic way, but assume a certain reasoning about "populational" categories, should also be problematized (see Hacking, 1986, 1991).

State-by-State Analyses: Statistical and Populational Indicators in Qualitative Research. Demographic indicators as well as the percentage of children enrolled in pre-K programs, as suggested above, were used as some of the ways states were selected. In particular, from the NCCP report (2009a) and the NIEER 2010 report, we examined characteristics or percentages of adults and children in poverty, demographics suggesting state diversity, high numbers of children in programs, and large number of single parents with young children in the state. Data on the proportion of children in programs for the five states selected for this illustrative analysis are presented below:

State	Rank among states		covered(%)	
	3 yr olds	4 yr olds	3 yr olds	4 yr olds
Calif.	#6	#23	17.9%	31.4% (13.4%)*
N.Y.	#24	#8	14.8%	59.4% (22.6%)*
Mass.	#14	#28	13.6%	25.9% (8.8%)*
Wi.	#20	#6	13.4%	62.5% (26.1%)*
Ill.	#1	#14	28.5%	44.5% (24.8%)*

Table 1. Rank and % among states in access to programs for 3–4 year olds. Source: *The State of Preschool 2010* (NIEER, 2010), Table 1, p. 6 and Table 4, p. 14; *total % of 3- and 4-year-olds enrolled in pre-K programs only by state, Table 2, p. 12 (combined program % not provided in report).

Below we draw from the National Center for Children in Poverty 2009 report (NCCP, 2009b) on demographic descriptions of the states we selected for this first portrait. They provide data focused on families and children "in poverty" (below the federal poverty level, which was $22,050 for a family of four in 2009), and in "low-income" families (defined in the USA as 200% of the federal poverty level). The data provides a different, albeit incomplete, lens on the contexts of the states we looked at above in Table 1.

State-by-state analyses related to America's children (defined as under 6) suggest the following brief portraits of the states we examined:

- *California: 1,466,426 young children lived in low-income families in 2009* (46% of all young children), while 22% were categorized as "poor," and approximately 46% of young children in low-income families lived with single parents. In terms of ethnicity (using report categories and terms), 24%, 60%, 62%, and 24% respectively of all white, black, Hispanic, and Asian children were from low-income and/or poor families. Sixty-one percent of young children of immigrant parents lived in low-income and poor families.

- *New York:* Forty-one percent of young children (593,942) lived in low-income families in 2009. Nineteen percent of all young children were categorized as low income and 22% as poor (41% total); 52% of children who were low-income or poor lived with single parents. Twenty-eight percent, 55%, 60%, and 39% of all white, black, Hispanic, and Asian children were from low-income and poor families. Fifty-six percent of young children of immigrant parents were categorized as low income.

- *Massachusetts:* 134,703 young children lived in low-income families; 15% of children were classified as low income while another 14% were classified as poor (29% of all young children under 6 total); 59% of all low-income children lived in single-parent homes. Nineteen percent, 54%, 64%, and 20% of white, black, Hispanic, and Asian children were from low-income or poor families. Forty-four percent of children from immigrant families were low income.

- *Wisconsin:* 169,839 young children were from low-income families in 2009; 21% of all young children were classified as low income, and another 20% were classified as poor (totalling 41% low income/poverty among young children under 6). Fifty-seven percent of the low-income/poor children lived in single-parent family homes. Thirty-one percent, 81%, 70%, and 75% of white, black, Hispanic, and American Indian children were considered low-income or poor. Seventy percent of young children of immigrant parents lived in low-income families.

- *Illinois:* 447,262 young children classified as low income or poor; 22% of all young children were considered to be low income while 21% were considered poor (43% of all children under 6). Fifty-five percent of low-income/poor children lived in single-parent families. Twenty-seven percent, 73%, 64%, and 21% of all white, black, Hispanic, and Asian children were considered low income or poor in the state. Sixty-two percent of young children of immigrant parents lived in low-income families.

While the demographics of each state are incompletely presented here, they do indicate (as do many other states in the country) that a large proportion of children are considered low income or poor in each of the states. Given that early child care and education programs often focus on low-income and at-risk children as a starting point for providing funds and program access, even when aiming for universal access eventually, these statistics suggest why so few states (and none in the group we have examined most closely) have achieved universal public access for even half-day programs for 4-year-olds. In addition, the high percentages of children living in single-parent homes, and the high potential percentage of children whose first language is not English, is also represented in the brief state profiles above.

We can see that inequality of income distribution, differential opportunities for employment, but also considerable data pointing to the need for full-day programs for working single parents (also in the NCCP report) indicate that early care and education may be out of reach and/or necessary for the large number of children in working poor families. (Discursively the words care and education could be combined, e.g., "educare" is one alternative starting to be used internationally, and in certain programs in the USA. Other alternative language is simply "child care systems," which include education/ child care—half day, full day—as a taken-for-granted way of thinking about children and family needs; OECD, 2006.)

Cross-national policies related to early care and education in many countries, including the USA, increasingly focus on a notion of "universal" access; the Pre-K Now policies promoted by different non-profit organizations in the USA present universal accessibility as a way to encourage early education programs, at least at age 4 years, and garner political support for funding programs for more targeted groups of young children (those from low-income backgrounds, whose primary or first language is not English, and those identified with disabilities[4]). Despite the discursive language, and probable needs, there are significant differences in state priorities.

Historical and Cultural Reasoning Systems Behind/Alongside Apparent Priorities and Decisions for Policies Related to Young Children. Within the five states we examined most closely, we could see that the states of California, New York, and Wisconsin all have recent policies to move toward universal access. The states' histories, however, vary somewhat. Before discussing the historical/cultural reasoning systems, a brief "description" of how the states vary may be important to present below.

California had initiatives toward provision of publicly subsidized or free preschool/child care since at least 1965 when it began offering the California State Preschool Program, and it was the state that developed the most comprehensive full-day child-care policies under the Lanham Act during World War II. That long history of serving preschoolers may be behind the move to include 3- as well as 4-year-olds in state-funded programs, as well as to highlight funding of half-day as well as full-day programs (see NIEER, 2008, p. 38, for a brief description).

New York's Universal Prekindergarten (UPK) program began in 1998 with an aim to serve all of the 4-year-olds in the state; however, it also had an early foundation with a Targeted Prekindergarten Program (TPK) beginning in 1966. Despite that history and the aim for universal access, many were not served in the various programs. Because of the large population to be served, and the large network of Head Start, preschool, and child-care programs already in existence, the New York State policies for Universal Pre-Kindergarten (UPK) were immediately organized around a collaborative community model, with at least 10% of funding to be distributed to community programs, rather than public schools. Indeed more than half of UPK funding was given to existing community-based programs in 2007–08, while public school programs have also expanded around the state despite more recent economic difficulties. In New York, prekindergarten programs, by policy, can be half-day or full-day. In 2006, the New York State Board of Regents recommended that the UPK and TPK be combined to maximize coordination of funding and collaborations for children's access to programs.

Wisconsin, the state which began voluntary kindergarten for 4-year-olds in the mid-19th century (see Bloch, Seward, & Seidlinger, 1989), currently focuses on funding universal half-day programs for all 4-year-olds. These can be combined with full-day programs, but funding is targeted toward a 2.5 hour/five day a week program for as many 4-year-olds as possible (note some programs are four half-days per week with the fifth focused on teacher-parent collaborations). A "collaborative" state program ("Collaborating Partners," http://www.collaboratingpartners.com/) focuses on combining funds and administration of programs across different state departments (Department of Workforce Development, Department of Health and Human Services, Department of Public Instruction), with a focus on a collaborative community-based model with local control, and emphasis on funding through state-administered Department of Public Instruction and federal Department of Education monies.

Massachusetts and Illinois, in contrast to the other states, have both aimed at universal provision of preschool/child care for all 3- and 4-year-olds. Both, however, have begun to move toward universal access through *targeting* lower-income children and "at risk" children in their early efforts to move toward universal access. In addition, whereas Massachusetts focused (according to interviews and report records) on 3- and 4-year-olds in full or part-day programs, including family child care, Illinois focused on a targeted program for *all* 3- and 4-year-olds, with funding aimed at a half-day program, five days per week—beginning with low income children and children identified as "at risk," and moving from these populations toward "Preschool for All."

While the descriptions above are important, the focus of this chapter is on a critical analysis of the governing discourses and cultural reasoning systems that include as well as exclude possibilities for thinking and action for different people and groups. We also interrogate how discourses that embed certain reasoning over other ways of thinking and acting normalizes certain types of policy over other ways of thinking or making up policy and action. The variations described briefly above then become very interesting. Briefly, they relate to decisions about which children need what type of education and care, as well as which families should be targeted for intervention, help, or extra support and/or funding. First, few of the programs attend to preventive health insurance (aside from Head Start), though Illinois, for example, did build preventative health check-ups, as well as parent/family participation into their models for the new Preschool for All program. As the NCCP reports on early education opportunities and policies suggest strongly, when thinking about families from poorer backgrounds especially, a combined early childhood investment in family economic security, health, and infant-toddler as well as preschool (3–4-year-old) programs would, they believe, be "best policy." Despite the high numbers of children 'in poverty' in each state, only Illinois had explicitly directed attention toward health. Second, as one other example, while several states allowed for inclusion of half-day and full-day programs in their state programs, most focused on half-day programs, access to something over access for more children vs. access to programs that will serve family needs. Third, though many perceive preschool as encompassing 3–4-year-olds (and younger children as well), the larger focus on 4-year-olds in some states' programs helps us to see these new initiatives as a *readiness for school*-type of program rather than more comprehensive early education programs; while this is no surprise, it reminds us that neither child care, nor language development, nor early stimulation (birth to three) programs garnered support across the states in the same way that *preschool readiness and school achievement* did. Though these are only three points to be raised immediately, these and other points will be returned to later in this discussion.

Quality Rating Scales versus Early Learning Standards: State-by-State Analyses. Moving now to state funding for quality programming, early learning standards, and the movement toward quality rating and improvement systems (QRIS) in most of the states in the United States, we can begin to address other texts that discursively frame the reasoning about what teachers and programs should be doing, and what children's experiences (learning/developmental or otherwise) *should* be like.

Thus, to begin this discussion, it is important to talk about the development of early learning standards, as these have emerged during and after the No Child Left Behind Act of 2001, as well as the Good Start Grow Smart Initiative (2002) aimed at pushing standards and assessments into the federally funded Head Start programs. While many have examined the development of these early learning standards, as well as the quality rating scales being developed within each state to improve program quality (especially in child care programs; e.g., Scott-Little, Kagan, & Frelow, 2003; Scott-Little, Lesko, Martella, and Milburn, 2007), little research has focused precisely on debates related to play, literacy, and development, in the ways these ideas or experiences and priorities are discursively framed within notions of quality: what counts, what and who should be prioritized, what is included while excluding certain things from "reason."

Reasoning Behind Universal Preschool Policies: Discourses of Human Capital Formation. In the majority of reports, there are texts that speak to the evidence that "early childhood education" (particularly educationally effective pre-K programs) works to help children become successful students with benefits such as "closing the persistent academic achievement gap between low-income children and their more well-to-do peers...reduced retention rates in school, lower dropout rates, decreased need for special education, and decreased juvenile crime rates" (Stone, 2006, p. 3).

References to numerous studies and reports (e.g., Chicago Longitudinal Study, The Carolina Abecedarian Project, The High/Scope Perry Preschool Project) in most documents enhance the argument that even a half day of preschool education for both low-income and middle-income children will be "cost-beneficial" for society by constructing children as future "Responsible Adults" and emphasizing "pre-kindergarten as a sound public investment strategy that yields impressive fiscal returns, reduces spending on crime and remedial and special education, generates increased tax revenues, and improves short- and long-term outcomes for children, families, and communities" (Wat, 2007)

This "human capital" perspective pushes state policies toward the money that will be saved if we invest in early preschool education, even one year at age 4, for all of a state's children, but especially those of low-income and at-risk status. The human capital perspective is well known and a potent argument for preschool and early education as shown in the title of a Pew Foundation advertisement, published in *Roll Call*, February 3, 2009: "The best economic recovery plan builds our nation's human capital, starting with the youngest Americans" (Pew Center on the States, 2010, p. 7).

The human capital perspective, and the longitudinal studies that are continually referenced, frame young children as "potential future criminals" unless they have at least one year of decent-quality learning prior to kindergarten, and positions states toward "education"—half-day programs if they cannot afford more, and targeted programs that are "educationally effective" for "the child and the nation" (NIEER, 2009, p. 9). It draws on economic, neoliberal, free choice, and global capitalist market imaginaries of the child that circulate throughout the documents, as well as internationally as global discourses about the fabrication of a future productive citizen for the nation. While the discourses are about universal access and opportunity, the texts focus on studies of "costs and benefits," largely related to low-income children and their families. Whose children are envisioned in the call for "universality?"

Another example is illustrated in pre-K advocacy groups' emphasis toward the "shift from a focus on child care as a support for working parents toward a more complete recognition that quality early learning is a powerful strategy to strengthen education and close the achievement gap" (Illinois Early Learning Council, 2006, p. i). In relation to other countries' "publicly funded child care systems approaches" that include attention to full-day working families as well as family child care and education within the notion of "care," these governing discourses within USA-based policy texts, with some exceptions, frame "education" as superior to as well as significantly different from "child care," and focus attention, as we've done for nearly two centuries, toward half-day preschool programming that is both developmentally appropriate and provides "learning." As Sonya Michel (1999) and others have argued, these notions pit children's rights against mothers'/family interests, and reflect the long-term liberal welfare state philosophies that aim to target, especially, "different" children and their families, and raise them to "standard quality."

Early Learning Standards. The standards movement in the USA in the past two decades, particularly since No Child Left Behind was started as a reform in 2002, includes as well as excludes in the reasoning about the "urban child and his/her family." The quest for a universal standard that fits all has been part of the project of modernity where universal notions of child development as well as learning have often been held as ideals. No Child Left Behind, followed by Good Start Grow Smart in Head Start programs, focused on universal standards that were oriented toward all, but with a focus on "difference," "otherness," and fixing deficiencies from the home and community of the children who were deemed unready for school, or at risk of failure in school.

While many states have extended this particular logic to state-by-state early learning standards, aligned with assessments for teachers, families, and, particularly, children, NO states that we reviewed maintained a comparison by Dr. Wade Horn, in an early Head Start National Training Meeting of organizational management that compared many teachers and many children to individuals who can be "standardized and regulated like cars, pharmaceutics, home building, or nursing homes…" (2003, cited in Bloch, Keintz, & Kim, 2005). Nonetheless, since 2002/2003, every state in the country has taken on the mantra of standards for early learning, most often aligned with somewhat developmentally appropriate and alternative forms of assessment systems. It is important, despite this, to see the logic of universal standards that fit all, while also targeting some for remediation more than others. From research and policy reports from No Child Left Behind as well as the assessments done, and compliance mechanisms, and regulatory systems put into Head Start over the past decade, we know indeed that standards *can* and have led to a narrowing of the curriculum toward what is to be taught, how and what pedagogical aims and values are to be considered, and which are to be assessed and are prioritized.

Quality Rating and Improvement Systems. Though the notion of quality has great appeal in an era where most child-care programs are found sadly lacking in "quality," and constructed mediocre to poor (Fuller, 2007; Polakow, 2007), the discourse of quality related to that of standards emerges from a market mentality that considers children, parents, and schools as a marker of quality "products" and business practices. Parents are both consumers and clients to be pleased, while schools become metaphors for businesses that must be efficiently producing high-quality and competitive as well as universally recognizable and assessable products. The neoliberal discourses of quality, the market, consumer, choice, and commodification and surveillance of its products (in the current example, young children) is rarely interrogated by the American early childhood community. Yet others (e.g., Dahlberg, Moss, & Pence, 1999/2007; Burman, 1994/2007; Cannella, 1997) have found that the notion of "quality" has become synonymous with other discourses that have also come under attack: developmentally appropriate practices (or DAP), the use of the Early Childhood Environment Rating Scale-Revised (ECRS) (Harms, Clifford, & Cryer, 1998) as the primary tool for measuring "quality" in many state QRIS rating scale reforms, and with a privileging of programs that have sufficient resources to become accredited by the National Association for the Education of Young Children (NAEYC), or other similar federal and state/municipality governing and certification "of quality" units.

Yet the notions of DAP have been critiqued as favoring programs and practices available to middle-class white children, based on norms of development that largely evolved from research exclusively with middle-class ("non-urban"/non-white) children and their families (see Bloch, 1991; Lubeck, 1998; Kessler & Swadener, 1992, and others). These indicators of quality reinforce the notion of the "developing child," innocent, dependent, and uniformly developing from immature to maturity; they correspond with economic development conceptions of the immature savage who can be made to be "civilized" and assimilated to the majority/dominant culture. While our arguments are briefly described here, our analysis here of five sample states, and arguments that occur in national reports and policy statements across the nation interrogate the state-by-state (virtually every state in the USA) movement in the past decade toward drawing on NAEYC accreditation as the highest-quality rating indicator, or indicators like those. "Other" cultural systems of belief related to good programs, different funds of knowledge that might be privileged, and the diversity or variety of ways to communicate, socialize, and learn that we've seen, in cross-cultural research in the USA and beyond, privilege a variety of ways to perform/learn/and be successful, at least outside "schools." Thus the NAEYC standards and other assessments, such as the ECRS scale, that are used so frequently to differentiate programs "of quality" from those "not of quality" also reinforce certain ways of thinking and behaving that privilege some knowledge, behavior, language, and families/children over others. The outcome is new forms of governance, surveillance, regulation, and classification that lead to intervention to fix "difference" or perceived deficiencies to help children and families become normal. There may be other ways to think about these issues.

Early Learning Standards Across the Different States. While the NAEYC and ECRS environmental assessment tools still privilege the "whole" child who is developing, they also now include emphases on curriculum content such as early literacy, science, math, art, music, physical activities, and socio-emotional development. The state-by-state *early learning standards*, within the reports we examined, and the policy texts of the states we focused on, *also* focus on the discourse of the *whole child*, an historically important term used in early education curriculum across most of the 20th century. As Barbara Bowman, President Emeritus of the Erikson Institute in Chicago, Illinois, indicates below, the whole child and the developing child are still priorities in many states' standards and assessment philosophy, as is the linkage with learning we see in this paragraph:

> Standards are an essential first step for designing effective preschool curricula since they represent an agreed upon *agenda for teaching and learning*. The Illinois Early Learning Standards are excellent because they recognize the interconnectedness of emotional, social, cognitive, and physical development and learning—*the whole child*. Like all good standards, they should be used as the base for reflective teachers as they create learning experiences that build on what children already know *and capture their interest in learning*. (Illinois State Board of Education, 2002, pp. 3–4) (italics added)

Programs are to be developmentally appropriate, and follow guidelines that are consistent with a focus on fostering developmental skills, attitudes, and dispositions of young children across the above domains (academic, physical, socio-emotional); program assessments categorize programs as good, mediocre, or bad. Pedagogical and curricular choices are surveyed and regulated as normal and categorized in terms of the degree of alignment with these curricular content and developmental areas, and whether they are "appropriately" assessing young children according to predetermined standards and the "quality rating indicators" measuring children's and program's ability to meet standards.

Play vs. Academic/Cognitive or Literacy/Math/Science. At the center of many debates is a false hierarchy, division, and privileging of subject matter content (developmentally appropriately conveyed) over traditional "activities/projects" focusing on children's play, experiential learning, socio-emotional development (peers and adults), and fine/gross motor development. Central to the discussions over the past decade or since the 1980s has been a more perennial question: What is appropriate for young children to *learn*? Should "play" remain at the center of a curriculum for young children, ages 3, 4, and older, as some fear that play replaces valuable and necessary *learning time*? From the inception of recent reforms such as the No Child Left Behind reforms in the USA, focused on elementary, middle, and secondary schools, the debates about what constitutes *learning* and *best practice* or *high quality* have augmented significantly. Children considered "at risk" for failure (Swadener & Lubeck, 1995), their families, and their teachers and schools have been the focus of a particular question: What is the most successful educational intervention for those children most likely to be at risk for failure in public schools? The answer perhaps all too often is reading, math, and science curricula adapted for preschool ages (Bloch, Keintz, & Kim, 2005; Fuller, 2007; Polakow, 2007). Drawing on the discourse of research-based evidence, evidence-based outcomes, high expectations for "all," and a privileging of cognitive/literacy/math/science over play, art, music, even motoric activities as *educational*, and necessary for school achievement at higher grade levels, these different ways of reasoning have led many state policy groups to highlight *education, learning, and readiness for school content* within a language that appears to support "developmentally appropriate," "play-based," "socio-emotional," and other common indicators of "quality" early childhood curriculum. A push for high standards in early literacy, math, and science for preschoolers—pushed into reforms for Head Start as well as public school preschool programs—and scientific research suggest too little attention has been focused on these important cognitive and academic areas.

Play, long held as a primary way for children to learn, as well as the arts, has remained important in most curricula focused on "best practices" (e.g., DAP, Creative Curriculum, High Scope, the Project Approach), but is often seen as a way to facilitate early learning. Indeed, in most "quality rating" scales and performance-based assessments (ECRS, CLASS), there is continued support of play and "responsive teacher-child interactions" during curriculum activities. Nonetheless, the state standards also pressure teachers and parents, as well as children, to think of literacy, numeracy, and scientific activities as "superior" uses of time.

To illustrate the concept of "academic push-down," we draw on Scott-Little et al.'s (2003) state-by-state comparison of early learning standards in which they classified state early learning standards either as "primarily developmental" (i.e., heavy emphasis on children's developmental behavior and growth) or "primarily academic" (i.e., heavy emphasis on academic content or knowledge). In their analysis of states' early learning standards, Massachusetts and New York are categorized as primarily academic while California and Illinois as primarily developmental. Wisconsin's early learning standards were in process at that time, thus it was not included in this classification, but we would call it "developmental" after our own review.

Whether each early learning standard is classified either as developmental or academic, all five states' early learning standards reviewed in our current case study include play as an important part of the curriculum. For example, Massachusetts' early learning standard, *Guidelines for Preschool Learning Experiences* (Massachusetts Department of Education, 2003), is categorized as being primarily academic according to Scott-Little et al.'s study. The guidelines are organized around the academic contents: English language arts, mathematics, science, technology/engineering, history and social science, health education, and arts. However, interestingly, Massachusetts emphasizes learning through play (a developmental perspective) as much as *Wisconsin Model Early Learning Standards* (Wisconsin Model Early Learning Standards Steering Committee, 2003) and *Illinois Early Learning Standards* (Illinois State Board of Education, 2002) embrace play.

> *Guidelines for Preschool Learning Experiences* structures learning through play and meaningful activities in a developmental sequence. The mark of a superior teacher is the ability to select materials and interact with children in ways that help them learn through their own play and these planned activities.…These guidelines are not intended to be implemented through direct instruction but rather through developmentally appropriate play experiences in the typical daily preschool setting. (Massachusetts Department of Education, 2003, pp. 4–5)

In the case of New York's *Preschool Planning Guide* (University of the State of New York, 1998), the importance of play in children's growth and development is highlighted as follows: "Play is active learning.… Play is a critical part of the growth and development of young children. Children are learning when they explore, discover, investigate, role play, and use tools and materials in creative ways. Play is closely linked to cognitive, social, emotional, and physical development"(p. 9).

Play for play itself is characterized as a process that leads toward learning. But the standards suggest it can be used as a context for teaching other key skills, attitudes, and dispositions such as a context for learning literacy, language, mathematics, science, and socio-emotional skills of interacting appropriately with peers as well as adults. In many of the standards, play is mentioned briefly and *often* as a context for other learning.

In some of the reports and assessments, play is a *lower* step of learning and development that, if done correctly, can lead toward *higher* learning in other areas (play as lowest indicator of learning; early literacy as higher indicator of learning).

Most early learning standards imply that there are many different types (or levels) of play, following the notions of developmental stages of play (e.g., child-initiated play, children's play in the environment that is provided by teachers' purposeful and intentional plan, teacher-initiated play, and eventually playful instruction or lesson). Some developmental domains (such as early literacy) require more teacher-initiated play type of learning. It seems that there are more and less advanced levels of playing that enable children to acquire certain skills better than others. This, then, of course, reinforces notions of normalization of play and other activities as well as a hierarchical categorization and classification system for rating "best play" only in relation to "best learning" in terms of academic/literacy/

numeracy/scientific skill learning that is most highly valued. In the sample strategies for adults in the *Wisconsin Model Early Learning Standards* (2003), we can frequently see this phrase "play the game." For example, in the sub-domain of early literacy,

> *Play the game*, Cross the Bridge. Say to the child, "I am the lion that guards the bridge; you may not cross the bridge until you tell me what animal you are." The child says, "Tiger." "What is the first sound in tiger?" the lion asks. The child says "/t/." "You may cross the bridge," says the lion.... *Play the game*, I am hungry what can I eat? Someone models, saying, "I am hungry for a gr-ape" and the child says, "Grape." (p. 61)

Here, the more advanced play type is considered the one with intention and purpose. Play should be carefully planned and prepared by teachers and other adults. So how is play conceptualized or reasoned about in the early 21st-century concepts of "quality" programs for preschool? It is no longer "free play," a recognition that many have made (e.g., Cannella, 1997), but it is also rated, ranked, and policed as well as classified as inferior/superior in relation to other skills learned.

Furthermore, *New York Early Literacy Guidance: Prekindergarten–Grade 3* (University of the State of New York, n.d.) implies that some literacy competencies require explicit teaching. In other words, there are certain developmental areas or academic competencies that cannot be addressed by play itself. Play itself is not enough for teaching higher levels of developmental or academic competencies. For example, sample instructional activities in word recognition including phonics guide us to

> teach the alphabetic principle explicitly by pointing to a letter, saying its sound, and having children repeat the sound; introduce letter-sound correspondences beginning with single letters in the initial position of one syllable words; teach that letters represent sounds, and a sequence of letters in printed words represents a sequence of sounds in spoken words; trace words, letter by letter, saying each sound as the letter is traced. (p. 25)

Discursive analyses of texts retain long-term notions of "standards" for "all" (or particularly some, such as the urban, to-be-fixed, remediated child), so long as many programs are particularly targeting low-income, high-risk children explicitly or implicitly in their program policy documents and actions. While there are clear directives to try to maintain, whenever possible, children's first, primary language, the standards focus large proportions of their document discussion on how to inject literacy, math, and science into curricular practices. Particularly, development of children's English-language skills are considered as critical to all other curriculum areas and "a major goal of preschool programs" (Massachusetts Department of Education, 2003, p. 9; University of the State of New York, 1998, n.d.). Learning English appears to be hierarchically privileged over first-language maintenance simply by the extent of curriculum topics included, and the emphasis on English-language learning in what is often short, half-day programs, often taught in public school venues, by certified teachers who are most often not bilingual or fluent speakers of many children's first or primary language.

Given the early childhood workforce, it would seem that programs that could approach multi-language, multiple literacy learning in classrooms, recognizing some of the diverse types of ways of communicating and literacy/math/science knowledge already within children's environments, could be a more privileged focus than the "standard" way to help the whole child learn everything—as divided and hierarchically privileged/less privileged curriculum for *other peoples' children* (Delpit, 1995).

As states use human capital theory to make sure the "at risk" child has appropriate opportunities to learn prior to kindergarten, to enhance achievement in school, we have to ask again, are there things that are missing from the logic of these practices, or *the practice of this logic* (Bourdieu, 1990)? Should children be readied for the school curriculum through enhanced curricular input and a standards approach in 3–4-year-old programs across the nation, or should the schools be made more ready for a diverse group of children, with diverse and rich sets of competencies, cultural knowledge systems, and

skills? Should we make sure, as Lisa Delpit (1995) suggests, that schools and teachers teach in culturally relevant and sensitive ways, but also teach the codes and languages of power (e.g., learning early
literacy skills prior to kindergarten in Head Start and other programs for better success in school,
learning to control "impulses" so they can be calmer in kindergarten and first grade, learning English
and maintaining their primary language)? Or, are our schools and teachers more prepared to teach according to standards that pressure them to teach literacy, math, and social skills that are less culturally
responsive and sensitive to children's ways of behaving and knowledge as they enter preschool? These
are unresolved issues, but the notion of targeting "difference," and making these little people "normal"
at an earlier age in relation to a standardized childhood and child that is expected to be ready for the
standardized school, still seems to us after reviewing five states and their standards to be embedded in
many policies and texts.

Closings and Rhizomatic Openings

Using the notion of the rhizome from Deleuze and Guattari (1988) allows us to think of the child as
multiple, diverse, unpredictable, a thinking child (not at risk or abnormal and in need of surveillance,
classification, and regulation), with competencies that are beneath the surface but that can emerge in
unpredictable ways. Using the notion of the rhizome rather than the tree (like striated standards locked
in place—with little flexibility once assessments and alignment with schools are taken into account) allows us to imagine the child not as normally developing or normally learning according to a competency or skill/performance check list, but as an emerging, becoming social being who is unpredictable and
filled with possibilities. This individual, in his/her diverse social spaces and relations, should allow us to
resist categorization and premature classification, or the risk of being part of a vision of "standardized
childhood" (Fuller, 2007.) As we continue our linear progress toward quality indicators in the USA,
across states, as well as standards and assessments for young children, we need to continue to interrogate
what children know/families know/communities know, and how their diverse perspectives and knowledge systems, as well as economic/social needs, might also be brought into our learning communities.

If the National Center for Children in Poverty (NCCP) is correct, we must not only think of the
whole child perspective (which they recommend), but rather be concerned with "state early childhood
policies" that have as their goal "improving the odds" (Stebbins & Knitzer, 2007). We need to recognize the vast income inequalities, as well as the regulatory and surveillance mechanisms on families and
teachers in the poorest areas, states in our nation, and take care of our communities, including families and their children. This would mean a recognition of many aspects of learning and development,
including health, nutrition, and, largely, opportunities within states for subsidizing full-day programs
that match the needs of families, and a harsh regulatory governance system that treats many families as
"at risk," abnormal, and in need of categorization and intervention themselves. Many of our nation's
poorest children and their families, we suggest, are in the gaze of those who are insisting on more "standardized childhoods," more "education" of a certain sort with little attention to an ethics or politics of
care. Based on our brief analysis, we believe the focus on half-day programs that are *educational, readiness, and closing-the-achievement-gap-oriented are too narrowly focused* ; within a broader vision of early
education and child care, we could envision policies that offer a half day of public subsidies in full-day
school or child-care-based programs that are more comprehensively envisioned for *all* families and also
filled with educational opportunities for *all* children and their families and communities. With an eye
toward rhizomatic possibilities, a broader vision toward supporting families (child care, health support, economic support) while providing a rich multi-lingual/multi-cultural preschool curriculum that
assumes all families and children are competent, rich, and knowledgeable, could be privileged over a
curriculum that is more deficiency-oriented. These ideas seem obvious, but they are once again escaping the attention of many states in their policy developments and reforms. States that value "all" young
children and their families will build policies that support the "whole family," not only the child; they

will recognize the resilience, strength, and cultural knowledge built into the ways we learn in different communities, and our need to respect languages and cultural knowledge systems within our programs. We saw very little attention to these issues in the early learning standards, which build on NAEYC, or the ECRS or other rating systems or scales that are supposed to represent "highest quality."

In these ways, we wonder which normal child and normal family is the vision of perfection in our standards. Are the standards and policies for public pre-K, or state standards and their assessments by quality rating indicator systems "bad?" Not as bad as some have feared. Are they repeating exclusions we have already seen and critiqued? Yes, most of the states (and this was a selection of states within the USA with somewhat progressive histories) whose policies we examined are doing so—and there is little indication that other states that could have been included in this analysis are doing things differently, unless they are placing more focus on academics in their standards. While diverse ideas are beginning to be entertained in other countries and regions of the world, the *new* directions of reforms in the USA seem very old indeed (for example, see Bloch, 1987.) Thus while critiques have taken place already, we can ask "is there still a place for new criticism? Is there any reason for continuing critique?" But the place for critique is often in a corner, a margin, and not in the mainstream; and we look to bell hooks (1996), who claims there is no other place to be than in the margin, and that continuing critique remains essential.

From the Margin—Critical Qualitative Research

This case study has tried to illustrate various dilemmas in the "doing" of critical qualitative research through certain poststructural frameworks. We have focused our attention on Foucauldian and Deleuze and Guattari's approaches toward discourse analysis, and on a way of examining the "reasoning of the present," given our focus on recent state standards. As we are nested within a context of globally circulating discourses that promulgates the "good" of standards, testing, evidence, and the neoliberal discourses of quality and human capitalism in/within education and schooling, we suggest the place for critical reflection, critical interrogation of current discourses is ever more necessary; while "in the margin," would these critiques be possible from some metaphorical "center?" As a chapter in this handbook, we raise more questions than we answer in our illustrative analysis, but this, too, seems to be a good place for a handbook chapter to be, and to end—with new and continuing questions to enter into a rhizomatic space—the lines of flight we imagine, and in many ways, *desire*.

Notes

This is a paper first presented as part of a symposium entitled *Revisiting Ecological Contexts of Urban Children's Play: Implications for Learning Literacy and Development*, presented at the American Education Research Association, Denver, CO, May 3, 2010.

1. We drew on *The State of Preschool 2008* report, which focuses on the 2007–2008 school year in this study, though the most recent 2009 NIEER report has just been published.
2. By not examining further what is "happening on the ground" in the discursively "lived experience" of teachers, children, programs, or in the intentions of policy actors, we need to qualify what we are doing in this case study (see Scott, 1991, for the way in which we would hope to analyze interviews in the future). We are trying to use current state standards and other documents to illustrate how what appears as simple empirical documents, presentations of statistics, and other neutral language and texts can guide belief, action, and conduct as though "truth," and taken for granted. In our analyses, we try to open up these same documents for interrogation, and to new questions. We are not providing a comprehensive study at all levels, but aim to illustrate the importance of poststructural discourse analysis for critical policy studies and research.
3. Additional states that could be included in this analysis in the future, based upon criteria of child population, diversity of the state, population considered "in poverty," single parents in the state, or funding for programs include Arkansas, New Jersey, Oklahoma, Georgia, Florida, Texas, Vermont, Nebraska, and West Virginia. These states were all part of the initial group considered for this analysis.
4. While each population category could be analyzed separately for the discourses that have led to the category, and for social inclusions/exclusions in the discourses that surround the category, we can point them out as classificatory/surveillance/and exclusionary categories here at least, with separate and important historical reasoning systems.

References

Bloch, M. N. (1987). Becoming scientific and professional: An historical perspective on the aims and effects of early education. In T. S. Popkewitz (Ed.), *The formation of the school subjects* (pp. 25–62). London, England: Falmer Press.

Bloch, M. N. (1991). Critical science and the history of child development's influence on early education research. *Early Education and Development, 2,* 95–108.

Bloch, M. N. (2003). Global/local analyses of the construction of "family-child welfare." In M. N. Bloch, K. Holmlund, I. Moqvist, & T. S. Popkewitz (Eds.), *Governing children, family, and education: Restructuring the welfare state* (pp. 195–230). New York, NY: Palgrave.

Bloch, M. N. (2004). A discourse that disciplines, governs, and regulates: The National Research Council's report on scientific research in education. *Qualitative Inquiry, 10*(1), 96–110.

Bloch, M. N., Keintz, C., & Kim, K. (2005, April). *Head Start: Quality programs, teachers, parents, and children—No Child Left Behind, Start Smart, Start Strong; In search of a system of childcare for the USA that will reach for the stars.* Paper presented at the meeting of the American Educational Research Association, Denver, CO.

Bloch, M. N., Kennedy, D., Lightfoot, T., & Weyenberg, D. (Eds.). (2006). *The child in the world/The world in the child.* New York, NY: Palgrave Macmillan.

Bloch, M. N., Seward, D., & Seidlinger, P. (1989). What history tells us about public schools for 4-year-olds. Special Issue: Public Schooling at 4? (R. M. Clifford & S. Lubeck, Guest Eds.). *Theory into Practice, 28,* 11–18.

Bourdieu, P. (1990). *The logic of practice.* Stanford, CA: Stanford University Press.

Burman, E. (2007). *Deconstructing developmental psychology.* London, England: Routledge. (Original work published 1994)

Cannella, G. (1997). *Deconstructing early childhood education: Social justice and revolution.* New York, NY: Peter Lang.

Cannella, G. (2003). Child welfare in the United States: The construction of gendered, oppositional discourse(s). In M. N. Bloch, K. Holmlund, I. Moqvist, & T. S. Popkewitz (Eds.), *Governing children, families and education: Restructuring the welfare state* (pp. 173–193). New York, NY: Palgrave.

Dahlberg, G., Moss, P., & Pence, A. (2007). *Beyond quality in early childhood education and care: Postmodern perspectives.* Abingdon, England: Routledge. (Original work published 1999)

Deleuze, G., & Guattari, F. (1988). *A thousand plateaus: Capitalism and schizophrenia* (B. Massumi, Trans.). London, England: Athlone.

Delpit, L. (1995). *Other people's children: Cultural conflict in the classroom.* New York, NY: New Press.

Donzelot, J. (1979). *The policing of families* New York, NY: Pantheon.

Foucault, M. (1972). *The archaeology of knowledge and the discourse of language.* New York, NY: Pantheon Books.

Foucault, M. (1977). *Discipline and punish.* New York, NY: Vintage Books.

Foucault, M. (1980). *Power/knowledge: Selected interviews and other writings 1972–1977* (C. Gordon, Ed.). Brighton, England: Harvester.

Foucault, M. (1988). Technologies of the self. In L. H. Martin, H. Gutman, & P. H. Hutton (Eds.), *Technologies of the self* (pp. 16–49). Amherst: University of Massachusetts Press.

Foucault, M. (1991). Governmentality. In G. Burchell, C. Gordon, & P. Miller (Eds.), *The Foucault effect: Studies in governmentality* (pp. 87–104). Hemel Hempstead, England: Harvester Wheatsheaf.

Foucault, M. (1998). *The history of sexuality: Vol. 1. The will to knowledge.* London, England: Penguin.

Fuller, B. (2007). *Standardized childhood: The political and cultural struggle over early education.* Stanford, CA: Stanford University Press.

Gore, J. (1998). Disciplining bodies: On the continuity of power relations in pedagogy. In T. S. Popkewitz & M. Brennan (Eds.), *Foucault's challenge: Discourse, knowledge and power in education* (pp. 231–254). New York, NY: Teachers College Press.

Hacking, I. (1986). Making up people. In T. C. Heller, M. Sosna, & D. E. Wellberg (Eds.), *Reconstructing individualism: Autonomy, individuality, and the self in western thought* (pp. 222–236). Stanford, CA: Stanford University Press.

Hacking, I. (1991). How should we do the history of statistics? In G. Burchell, C. Gordon, & P. Miller (Eds.), *The Foucault effect: Studies in governmentality* (pp. 181–196). Hemel Hempstead, England: Harvester Wheatsheaf.

Harms, T., Clifford, R.M., & Cryer, D. (1998). *Early Childhood. Environment Rating Scale.* New York: Teachers College Press.

hooks, b. (1996). Choosing the margin as a space of radical openness. In A. Garry & M. Pearsall (Eds.), *Women, knowledge, and reality: Explorations in feminist philosophy* (2nd ed., pp. 48–56). New York, NY: Routledge.

Illinois Early Learning Council. (2006). *Preschool for all: High-quality early education for all of Illinois' children.* Chicago, IL.

Illinois State Board of Education. (2002). *Illinois early learning standards.* Springfield, IL: Division of Early Childhood Education. Retrieved on April 2, 2010, from http://www.illinoisearlylearning.org/standards/ielstandards-mar02.pdf

Kessler, S., & Swadener, B. (Eds.). (1992). *Reconceptualizing the early childhood curriculum: Beginning the dialogue.* New York, NY: Teachers College Press.

Lubeck, S. (1998). Is developmentally appropriate practice for everyone? *Childhood Education, 74*(5), 283–292.

Lubeck, S. (2001). Early childhood education and care in cross-national perspective. *Phi Delta Kappan, 83*(3), 213–216.

Massachusetts Department of Education. (2003). *Guidelines for preschool learning experiences.* Malden, MA. Retrieved on April 2, 2010, from http://www.doe.mass.edu/els/guidelines.pdf

Michel, S. (1999). Children's interests/mothers' rights: The shaping of America's child care policy. New Haven, Conn.: Yale University Press.

National Center for Children in Poverty (NCCP). (2007). State early childhood policies. New York, NY: Author. Retrieved on April 14, 2010, from http://www.nccp.org/publications/pub_725.html

National Center for Children in Poverty (NCCP). (2009a). United States early childhood profile. New York, NY. Retrieved on November 16, 2010, from http://www.nccp.org/profiles/pdf/profile_early_childhood_all.pdf

National Center for Children in Poverty (NCCP). (2009b). Demographic profiles. Retrieved on April 15, 2009, from http://www.nccp.org/profiles/demographics.html

National Institute for Early Education Research (NIEER). (2008). *The state of preschool 2008*. New Brunswick, NJ. Retrieved on April 14, 2010, from http://nieer.org/yearbook2008/pdf/yearbook.pdf

National Institute for Early Education Research (NIEER). (2009). *The state of preschool 2009*. New Brunswick, NJ. Retrieved on November 20, 2010, from http://www.scstatehouse.gov/citizensinterestpage/K12FundingSelectCommittee/October-192010Meeting/4_NIE%204K%20Rankings.pdf

National Institute for Early Education Research (NIEER). (2010). *The state of preschool 2010*. New Brunswick, NJ. Retrieved on November 20, 2010, from http://nieer.org/yearbook/pdf/yearbook.pdf

Organization for Economic Co-operation and Development (OECD). (2006). *Starting strong II: Early childhood education and care*. Paris, France: OECD.

Pew Center on the States. (2010). The right policy at the right time: The Pew pre-kindergarten campaign. Retrieved on November 15, 2010, from http://www.preknow.org/documents/2010_RightPolicy.pdf

Polakow, V. (2007). *Who cares for our children? The child care crisis in the other America*. New York, NY: Teachers College Press.

Popkewitz, T. (1998). *Struggling for the soul: The politics of schooling and the construction of the teacher*. New York, NY: Teachers College Press.

Popkewitz, T. S. (2004). Is the National Research Council Committee's report on SBR scientific?: On trusting the manifesto. *Qualitative Inquiry, 10*, 62–78.

Popkewitz, T. S., & Bloch, M. N. (2001). Administering freedom: A history of the present rescuing the parent to rescue the child for society. In K. Hultqvist & G. Dahlberg (Eds.), *Governing the child in the new millennium* (pp. 85–118). London, England: Routledge.

Popkewitz, T. S., & Brennan, M. (1998). Restructuring of social and political theory in education: Foucault and a social epistemology of school practices. In T. S. Popkewitz & M. Brennan (Eds.), *Foucault's challenge, discourse, knowledge and power in education* (pp. 3–38). New York, NY: Teachers College Press.

Popkewitz, T., & Lindblad, S. (2000). Educational governance and social inclusion and exclusion: Some conceptual difficulties and problematics in policy and research. *Discourse: Studies in the Cultural Politics of Education, 21*, 5–44.

Scott, J. (1991). The evidence of experience. *Critical Inquiry, 17*, 773–795.

Scott-Little, C., Kagan, S. L., & Frelow, V. S. (2003). Creating the conditions for success with early learning standards: Results from a national study of state-level standards for children's learning prior to kindergarten. *Early Childhood Research and Practice, 5*(2). Retrieved on April 14, 2010, from http://ecrp.uiuc.edu/v5n2/little.html

Scott-Little, C., Lesko, J., Martella, J., & Milburn, P. (2007). Early learning standards: Results from a national survey to document trends in state-level policies and practices. *Early Childhood Research and Practice, 9*(1). Retrieved on April 14, 2010, from http://ecrp. uiuc. edu/v9n1/little. html

Stebbins, H., & Knitzer, J. (2007). *State early childhood policies: Highlights from the Improving the Odds for Young Children project*. New York, NY: National Center for Children in Poverty.

Stone, D. (2006). *Funding the future: States' approaches to pre-K finance*. Washington, DC: Pre-K Now.

Swadener, B., & Lubeck, S. (Eds.). (1995). *Children and families "at promise": Deconstructing the discourse of risk*. Albany: State University of New York Press.

United Nations Educational, Scientific and Cultural Organization (UNESCO). (2006). *Strong foundations: Early childhood care and education* (EFA Global Monitoring Report). Paris, France.

University of the State of New York. (1998). *Preschool planning guide: Building a foundation for development of language and literacy in the early years*. Albany, NY: State Education Department.

University of the State of New York. (n.d.). *New York early literacy guidance: Prekindergarten–Grade 3*. Albany, NY: State Education Department.

Wat, A. (2007). *Dollars and sense: A review of economic analyses of pre-K*. Washington, DC: Pre-K Now. Retrieved on November 11, 2010, from http://www.preknow.org/documents/DollarsandSense_May2007.pdf

Wisconsin Model Early Standards Steering Committee. (2003). *Wisconsin model early learning standards*. Madison, WI: Department of Public Instruction.

CHAPTER NINETEEN

Asking Critical Questions of Philanthropy and Its Impact on U.S. Educational Policy: Tracking the Money in School Reform

Kathleen deMarrais

If you scratch a theory, you will find a biography. (Duster quoted in Torres, 1998, p. 1)

To introduce his book *Education, Power, and Personal Biography: Dialogues with Critical Educators*, Carlos Torres (1998) begins with the above quote sociologist Troy Duster liked to use in teaching his classes. In my own teaching of qualitative research courses, as we're exploring the students' research interests, I modify the statement slightly to remind them that if you scratch a research project, you will find a biography. Of course, this interweaving of biography and research is evident in my own work as well. Having grown up in the 1950s and 1960s in a struggling working-class family on the wrong side of town, I became painfully aware early of inequities of social class, gender, and due to the racist attitudes evident in my family and community at that time, race. In my doctoral program, I found a theoretical home as I was introduced to the new sociologists of education and critical theorists in education such as Henry Giroux and Peter McLaren. My dissertation (Bennett, 1990) was a critical ethnography that examined ability-grouped reading instruction in an urban Appalachian first grade classroom. The theoretical framework in that study informed my first book (with Margaret LeCompte), *The Way Schools Work: A Sociological Analysis of Education*. Now, after many years in the academe, teaching social foundations of education and qualitative research methods, I find I continue to ask research questions from critical and feminist perspectives. My most recent set of research projects has tracked the funding of philanthropists that have shaped the landscape of educational policies and practices in the U.S. (deMarrais, 2006). This chapter builds on my earlier study of neo-conservative philanthropic funding as reported in "'The Haves and the Have Mores': Fueling a Conservative Ideological War on Public Education" (deMarrais, 2006), but is focused specifically on philanthropic contributions aimed at in-centing whole school reform, charter schools, and alternative teacher education programs to improve educational outcomes for students. While not limited to neo-conservative philanthropists, the study demonstrates the interconnected web of philanthropists and their selected initiatives across ideological lines. Incorporated into this account is a discussion of the methodological challenges of this work.

A Brief History of Philanthropy in U.S. Education

Since the turn of the 20th century, philanthropists have had as their mission the reform of the field of teacher education and P-12 education. Much of this work began as piecemeal efforts to build institutional capacity both in public P-12 schools and universities, so funding was given to existing institutions to seed reform efforts and bring about change in both the quantity and quality of new teachers. However, while they realized successes, philanthropists recognized the complexities of reforming existing educational institutions and turned their attention to agencies outside traditional institutions to re-engineer the field through building models of school reform focused on demonstrated student achievement. In addition, philanthropically funded research and policy advocacy organizations have influenced state and federal policy initiatives as well as funding in education, including teacher education. Colleges and universities that have traditionally prepared teachers, currently experiencing budget shortfalls as well as feeling the pressure from more nimble, well-funded organizations, compete for funding from both private and public sources to support their efforts to respond to public critique of teacher preparation.

For over a century, philanthropists in the United States have been committed to the improvement of elementary, secondary, and higher education. An early example is that of Grace Dodge's support of the founding of Teachers College in 1887 to train teachers in pedagogy. National philanthropies such as the Carnegie, Ford, and Rockefeller Foundations trace support for educational improvement, including teacher effectiveness, from the early years of the 20th century. These philanthropists tended to work within existing colleges and universities and K-12 schools. In the late 1990s, when longstanding philanthropies such as the Carnegie, Ford, and Rockefeller Foundations reduced their support in the K-12 arena, a group of "new philanthropists" (Hess, 2005; Colvin, 2005) or "venture philanthropists" (Scott, 2009) turned their attention to educational reform with significant contributions targeted for the improvement of K-12 schools through school reform efforts and the improvement of teacher effectiveness.[1] This shift in philanthropic funding was dramatic. In 1998 more traditional philanthropies like the Annenberg Foundation, the Lilly Endowment, the David and Lucille Packard Foundation, and the W.K. Kellogg Foundation were at the top of the list of giving in elementary and secondary education with focus areas in curricular reform, professional development for teachers, and community participation. Hess (2005) reported these top four foundations accounted for 30% of giving to K-12 education by the top 50 donors. At that time, the Walton Family Foundation (Walmart) was 26th on the list and the Gates Foundation was not on the list at all.

In his assessment of the intent of the new venture philanthropists, Colvin (2005) argued they "share the belief that public education has not done well by immigrants or poor students" and that they are "less likely than were donors in the past to think that the solution to that problem lies solely or even primarily in spending more money or even in making the allocation of resources more equitable, which has been a common thread in work that many better-established foundations have pursued" (p. 36). The top three philanthropists, the "billionaire boys club", as Ravitch (2010) refers to them, are the Bill and Melinda Gates Foundation, the Walton Family Foundation, and the Broad Foundation. The Gates Foundation and the Walton Family Foundation, in that order, topped the list of education funders in 2002. Other well-known corporate executives that have contributed large sums to educational funding include Jim Barksdale (Netscape CEO), Eli Broad (KB Home and SunAmerica), Michael Dell (Dell Computers founder), Michael Milken (financier), and Donald Fisher (GAP Clothing CEO). Colvin (2005) theorized that these new philanthropists tend to

---

1   For an analysis of the shift to venture philanthropy, see Saltman (2010, 2011).

believe that schools, in addition to securing adequate financial resources, need to embrace accountability and to overhaul basic functions. Many are personally involved in overseeing the grants they give and they insist on results from educators and schools. They believe good leadership, effective management, compensation based on performance, competition, the targeting of resources, and accountability for results can all pay dividends for education as well as for foundations. They tend to set ambitious goals for their own work and to be aggressive in pursuit of their agendas. That, too, is something of a departure for philanthropists, who have tended to stay in the background and let their grantees set their own goals while they bask in the spotlight. (p. 37)

Kramer (2009) articulated the differences between conventional, venture, and catalytic philanthropy,[2] distinguishing these latter two where venture philanthropy's focus is on increasing organizational effectiveness and capacity building of non-profits while catalytic philanthropy is aimed at motivating change through a campaign that has measureable impact and uses all possible donor tools and resources. In this latter, the funders, rather than the non-profits, take responsibility for success. Gates, Walton, and Broad incorporate aspects of both venture and catalytic philanthropy.

Steiner-Khamsi (2008) found that the new philanthropies such as The Soros Foundation Network and Gates Foundation, unlike more traditional foundations designed to outlive their founders, are organizations with a limited lifespan. She reported that the Soros Foundation Open Society Institute "places a great emphasis on carefully planning, from the onset, 'spin-off' and exit strategies for every major new program it launches" (p. 12). These philanthropies "scale up their impact differently…and prioritize institutionalization over any other sustainability strategy" (p. 12). Barry Munitz, president and CEO of J. Paul Getty Trust, described the new philanthropists as "high net worth, first generation folks…[who] approach their gift-giving the way they approached their investing—due diligence, measures of accountability, a lot of involvement, each with an agenda. It's very different from spending money on the system and standing back and letting it work" (quoted by Colvin, 2005, p. 37).

Created in 2000, the Bill and Melinda Gates Foundation, largest and perhaps best known of the new philanthropies, ranked first in the top 10,000 U.S. foundations by assets, with a 2008 income of $3,318,318,073 and assets of $29,889,702,125. Its 2009 assets were $33,912,321,000; its 2010 total assets were $37,430,151,000. The purpose of the foundation was to improve health and reduce extreme poverty in the developing world and to improve high school education in the United States. With a personal net worth Forbes estimates to be about $46 billion, Gates vowed to give away 95% of this within his lifetime (Colvin, 2005). In 2004, 58% or $1.3 billion of the foundation's funding for that year was allocated for education (Hill, 2006). By 2008, Gates had already spent $2 billion in efforts to improve high schools and to increase graduation rates and announced a shift in their funding strategy to "undertaking a more sweeping approach to grantmaking that appears aimed at reshaping some core elements of the US education system" (Robelen, 2008, p. 1). The foundation's current agenda is focused on standards for college readiness, improving teacher quality, and fostering innovations to assist struggling students. Gates American Diploma Project, a Gates-funded initiative of Achieve, Inc.,Washington, DC, had the support of 33 states in 2008 that pledged to adopt college-ready standards and tests (Robelen, 2008). With this brief introduction to the shift in philanthropic funding to education in the 21st century, I turn next to the critical qualitative methods used in this study.

Asking Critical Research Questions of Philanthropy: A Methodological Rabbit Warren

My attention over the past two years was increasingly drawn to philanthropists such as Gates, Walton, and Broad through my involvement with a research group funded by the Ford Foundation focused on philanthropic funding in teacher quality. That study, *Critical Contributions: Philanthropic Investment in*

---

2 For purposes of simplicity, I will use the more common term, venture philanthropy, to refer to these philanthropists throughout the chapter.

Teachers and Teaching (Suggs & deMarrais, 2011),[3] reviewed the philanthropic funding to teacher quality and effectiveness over the several past decades through the use of scholarly literature, current educational journalism, and financial data from MetaSoft System's FoundationSearch America, an online database, to identify key funders, types of projects funded, grantors, grantees, and levels of funding to support projects and programs that invested in teachers and teaching. While that study was not framed as critical qualitative research, as one of the authors of that work, I saw connections to my earlier critical research focused on neo-conservative philanthropists as well as ways to extend that previous work across a broader spectrum of philanthropists. Using a critical lens to examine philanthropic funding in this first decade of the 21st century, the interconnectedness of philanthropists, their focused political agendas, and their impact on current educational policy became evident. For this current study, I framed the work using the following critical questions:

1. What are the ideologies of leading philanthropists in school reform?
2. How have these philanthropists focused funding into specific initiatives and to specific "educational entrepreneurs" over time?
3. What are the connections across philanthropically funded initiatives?
4. What structures were created to facilitate and promote this work?
5. How has the "rock star" quality of leading philanthropists shaped evaluation processes for their initiatives?
6. How have the philanthropies influenced current education policy and federal funding?

Like my earlier work on the neo-conservative philanthropists, I found the doing of this online research much like getting lost in a rabbit warren. Rabbits, as you may be aware, live in a series of interconnected underground tunnels or burrows; a group of these burrows is called a warren. One burrow leads to another, then another, and another. The rabbits may well know where they are going from one point to another but perhaps not. The rabbit warren serves as interesting metaphor for this type of online research that relies heavily on online data sources, including the websites of philanthropic organizations and educational non-profits, and websites that track this funding, where one project leads to another, one philanthropist leads to another, one board members leads to another, and so on. As I examined web pages of individual philanthropies, charter school networks, teacher and leader professional development sites, and venture capitalist non-profits, I found at first glance each appears to operate independently of others, but gradually the connective tissue becomes evident through the board of directors memberships, similar initiatives, and common language. As I immersed myself in this philanthropic rabbit warren of online sources, I might begin in one place and end up finding an unexpected trail to another connection. There was no telling where I might end up, usually surprised to find myself in a new, unexpected turn with the realization that most likely there is no end. Hence, it is necessary to attempt to construct boundaries to such a study or it will never be finished. For this chapter I have paused momentarily, placing a boundary around the creation of a structure that illustrates connections across philanthropically funded non-profits and the educational entrepreneurs spearheading those efforts. I provide examples here for each aspect of the structure, but do not promise an exhaustive analysis of each of the components within the larger structure. My research agenda continues with forthcoming pieces specifically on charter management organizations and Teach for America.

For the financial aspects of this study, I again used Metasoft System's FoundationSearch, an online subscription database that compiles information reported by non-profit philanthropic organizations on their IRS 990s. The data provided in this chapter draws from all available data in FoundationSearch between 1999 and 2011. While the data in this system is extremely useful, the challenges and limita-

---

3 My work here is a sharp departure from that 2011 report and reflects my own work and perspectives. It does not reflect the views of the Ford Foundation or any of the other authors or participants in the study.

tions of using the system must be understood. The database is limited to the publicly available IRS 990 forms submitted by the 501c3 non-profit organizations to the federal government. In addition, since federal tax laws allow two years for non-profit organizations to file their IRS 990 forms, data provided for 2010–2011 is partial data. FoundationSearch is searchable by grantors, grantees, location of both, type of foundation, category or area of impact, and by key words assigned by FoundationSearch based on the abstract submitted by the foundation. Throughout the chapter I provide the key words that were used to generate any financial data reported.

A Philanthropically Funded Structure of Educational Reform

As I wove my way through the rabbit warren of philanthropists and their funded initiatives, I began to discern a number of categories of initiatives that were connected to one another either though their purposes or individuals involved across efforts. I offer here a structure, largely outside traditional educational P-12 and higher education institutions, that reflects philanthropic efforts to create educational reform as models for larger scale practices as well as national policies. Figure 1 illustrates the key components of this structure. The structure has emerged over time as philanthropists have focused their funding on specific initiatives, often identifying educational entrepreneurs, who can more nimbly accomplish the goals of the philanthropists. In this next section, I begin with the notion of educational entrepreneurs, describe the work of the NewSchools Fund in supporting these educational entrepreneurs as they created non-profit charter management organizations (CMOs), alternative teacher and leadership preparation programs, and other educational management organizations (EMOs).

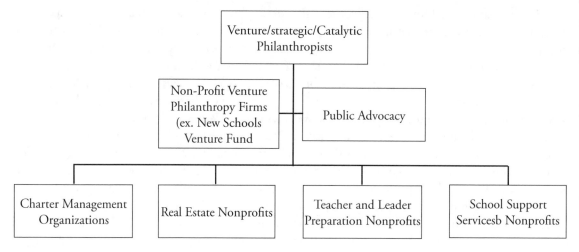

Figure 1. Philanthropic Funding for Educational Reform

Since the late 1990s, the new philanthropists increasingly sought to change the landscape of education by identifying and supporting the work of "educational entrepreneurs" working outside traditional institutions in non-profit organizations. The NewSchoolsVenture Fund defines education entrepreneurs as "visionary thinkers who create brand new for-profit or nonprofit organizations that seek to have a large-scale impact on the entire public school system and in so doing, redefine our sense of what is possible in public education" (http://www.newschools.org/about/publications/education-entrepreneurs).The next sections provide examples of philanthropically funded educational entrepreneurs who established charter management organizations as well as alternative teacher and leadership education programs.

As the philanthropists turned to whole school reform for the creation of newly designed model schools to address the achievement gap and high school graduation rates for students in high poverty communities, they supported projects for different models of schools in an attempt to learn what works best, especially in poor, urban communities. Many of the model schools were small schools with personalized instruction. Teacher training, professional development, and mentoring were seen as significant aspects of the new schools to promote teacher effectiveness, and hence, higher student achievement.

The Bill and Melinda Gates Foundation, a leading funder of school reform since the late 1990s, articulated clear, ambitious goals: to improve the national graduation rate to at least 80% from 65%, while increasing the likelihood that all high school graduates are college-ready (Colvin, 2005, p. 34). Under the leadership of Tom Vander Ark, former Seattle-area school superintendent, the Gates K-12 strategy was developed with a focus on high school reform through the creation of small, innovative schools. Hill (2006) noted:

> Vander Ark hoped to change K-12 education by helping individuals with great ideas. These individuals would create schools so good that the whole public education would be forced to imitate them…which mirrors Microsoft's operating style: identify an unmet need and invest in multiple approaches until the best one emerges. (p. 47)

Early funding went toward progressive efforts within school districts. In 2002, the Gates Foundation broadened its efforts beyond school districts to alternative methods including charter schools and early college high schools. Colvin (2005) reported:

> Since 2002, the Gates Foundation has allocated more than $1.2 billion toward creating about 820 new high schools and breaking down about 750 large, comprehensive high schools into smaller, more focused, more intimate academies that aim to send far more students off to college prepared to succeed. The foundation is also the lead partner in a $125 million experiment in "early college" high schools which are designed to enable 9th graders to get their high school diplomas as well as two years of college credit, all within four or five years. To increase the impact of its initiatives, the Gates Foundation has involved 13 other foundations and is working with more than one hundred intermediary organizations in two hundred cities located in almost every state. (p. 34)

As part of its model school effort, the Bill and Melinda Gates Foundation provided substantial support to the Coalition of Essential Schools (CES), a signature school reform project funded by multiple philanthropists. Between 1998 and 2010, the Gates Foundation provided $28,624,882 of the total $35,182,984 invested in this organization, all supporting innovative small high schools primarily in Seattle, Washington, and Bay Area, California. Theodore Sizer founded CES, an organization devoted to the creation of new practices within existing schools, following publication of his *Horace's Compromise* (1984), a critique of high schooling in the U.S. "CES practice is exemplified by small, personalized learning communities where teachers and students know each other well in a climate of trust, decency and high expectations for all. Modeling democratic practices with a strong commitment to equity" (http://www.essentialschools.org/pub/ces_docs/about/about.html).

In addition to the above described model, non-charter schools, philanthropists funded a number of initiatives for the creation of new charter schools and academies, primarily in poor, urban communities that could develop models of teaching and learning not constrained by existing bureaucratic policies and could demonstrate school reform efforts to solve persistent problems of poor achievement, low graduation rates, and limited access to college in these communities. In 1991 Minnesota's enactment of the first charter school law in the U.S. provided a model for other states to enact similar legislation, with 41 states now recording charter school policies on their books.[4] Charter schools are "publicly funded elementary or secondary schools that have been freed from some of the rules, regulations, and statutes

---

4   See http://nces.ed.gov/programs/statereform/tab4_3.asp for charter school legislation by state.

that apply to other public schools, in exchange for some type of accountability for producing certain results, which are set forth in each charter school's charter" (http://www.nea.org/home/16332.htm).

A 2009 study, *Multiple Choice: Charter School Performance in Sixteen States*, was funded by charter school advocates including the Joyce Foundation and conducted by Stanford's Center for Research on Educational Outcomes (CREDO). The study described the scope and variation of the charter school movement in the U.S.:

> As of 2009, more than 4700 charter schools enroll over 1.4 million children in 40 states and the District of Columbia. The ranks of charters grow by hundreds each year. Even so, more than 365,000 names linger on charter school wait lists. After more than fifteen years, there is no doubt that both supply and demand in the charter sector are strong. In some ways, however, charter schools are just beginning to come into their own. Charter schools have become a rallying cry for education reformers across the country with every expectation that they continue to figure prominently in national educational strategy in the months and years to come. And yet, this study reveals in unmistakable terms that, in the aggregate, charter students are not faring as well as their TPS [traditional public schools] counterparts. Further, tremendous variation in academic quality among charters is the norm, not the exception. The problem of quality is the most pressing issue that charters and their supporters face. (CREDO, 2008, p. 6)

As the charter school movement grew, significant philanthropic efforts identified and supported educational entrepreneurs to create non-profit charter management organizations (CMOs), each with a vision for effective teaching and student achievement. Smith, Farrell, Wohlstetter, and Nayfack (2009) defined charter management organizations as:

> nonprofit organizations that manage a network of charter schools to differentiate them from for-profit education management organizations. The CMOs we studied shared three additional characteristics: First, each CMO had a common, identifiable mission or instructional design across its schools. Second, every CMO had a home office or management team that provides significant, ongoing administrative support to its schools. (p. 3)

In their 2009 study Smith et al. examined 25 of the existing CMOs and found that "nearly two thirds of these organizations were established between six and ten years ago, with two in operation for more than ten years" (p. 3). Of these CMOs, 18 had between two and 10 campuses, five had between 11 and 30 campuses, and two had more than 30 campuses. The 25 CMOs reported having schools in 26 of the 41 states with charter school laws.

These new entities created networks of public charter schools, typically in urban areas, although some now have networks of schools across the U.S. (e.g. Knowledge Is Power Program, KIPP) and tend to focus on a central mission. The CMOs develop an identity that guides each of its network schools. For example, the Mastery Charter Schools website captures the beliefs expressed by many if not all of the charter management school organizations that developed between 1994 and today: "We believe that educational inequity is the most pressing social problem facing our country—the civil rights issue of our day" (www.masterycharter.org/masteryModel.html). The CMOs manage all aspects of the school including its budget, staffing for leaders and teachers, buildings, and support services (e.g. food services, curriculum and assessment programs). Like the non-charter model schools, the CMOs report a focus on the development of highly effective teachers through teacher professional development, mentoring programs, annual summer summits for professional development, and consistent teacher evaluation based on student achievement data. There are currently approximately 39 charter management organizations. They rely on both public and private donations to support the schools in their networks.

Using the key words "charter" and "schools" in FoundationSearch reveals that between 1998 and 2011, a total of $410,850,939 in philanthropic funding was donated in 6,422 grants for the support of charter schools. The majority of these grants went directly to support charter school organizations;

others went to organizations advocating for charter schools such as the Massachusetts, New Jersey, and New York Charter School Associations. Only 59 of the charter school grants were over $1 million. The majority of the grants, 5,301 (83%) were between $100,001 and $999,999. There were 542 from the Walton Family Foundation, totaling $72,560,739, which provided "general support" for charter schools in 24 states and the District of Columbia. The Bill and Melinda Gates Foundation contributed 22 grants totaling $15,984,384.[5] The Broad Foundation, third of the "big three of education," as Ravitch (2010) refers to them, contributed 6 grants totaling $5,683,000. NewSchools contributed 12 grants for a total $4,643,437. Some donors focus on a geographic area or specific city for their giving. For example, between 2000 and 2009, Robin Hood Foundation was a significant contributor to the following charter schools in New York: Bronx Preparatory Charter School, Harlem Day Charter School, KIPP, and New York City Charter School Center with support of $10,940,950. An example of a family-based foundation, the William E. Schrafft & Bertha E. Schrafft Charitable Trust focused its grant activity supporting 11 charter schools in Boston with 43 smaller grants totaling $790,600. Table 1 illustrates the top recipients of grants to charter management organizations from 1998 to 2011. These 14 charter school organizations were given nearly 27% of the total funding provided to charters during this time period.

Recipient Name	Location	# of Grants	Total Grants Received
Chicago International Charter School	Bucktown, IL; Chicago, IL	54	$13,721,469
Bronx Preparatory Charter School	Bronx, NY; New York, NY	95	$12,950,375
New York City Charter School Center	New York, NY	4	$9,200,300
Friendship Public Charter School	Washington, D.C.	26	$8,484,205
Perspectives Charter School	Chicago, IL; South Chicago, IL	125	$8,347,995
William Penn Charter School	Philadelphia, PA; Austin, TX; Williamsburg, VA	225	$8,285,582
Knowledge Is Power Program (KIPP)	Los Angeles, Oakland, & San Francisco, CA; Washington, D.C.; Chicago, IL; Gary, IN; Lynn, MA; Camden, NJ; Bronx, Brooklyn, Buffalo, & New York, NY; Oklahoma City, OK; Philadelphia, PA; Houston, TX	167	$7,415,677
Harlem Day Charter School	New York, NY	97	$7,377,866
Neighborhood House Charter School	Atlanta, GA; Boston, MA; Dorchester, MA	211	$7,195,976
Newark Charter School	Newark, DE; Newark, NJ	15	$6,883,275
Roxbury Preparatory Charter	Boston, MA; Roxbury, MA	161	$5,984,086
Young Women's Leadership Charter School	Chicago, IL; New York, NY	157	$5,458,626
North Lawndale Preparatory Charter	Chicago, IL	157	$4,927,888
Mastery Charter School	Philadelphia, PA	45	$4,627,755
Total			$110, 861, 075

Table. 1. Top 14 Charter management organization recipients with total grants greater than $4.5 million (FoundationSearch, 1998–2011)[6]

5   While the Bill and Melinda Gates and Broad Foundations funding seems relatively low here for charter schools, their contributions tend to be for broader categories of education funding and intermediaries such as NewSchools Venture Fund, so do not show up in a search limited to charter schools.

6   These totals do not include funds allocated specifically for building school facilities.

In addition to those described above, the Michael and Susan Dell Foundation invested heavily in charter schools' management organizations with $3.65 million in grants to the California Charter Schools Association program, $4 million to Green Dot Public Schools, $2.5 million to Aspire Public Schools, and $7.1 million to the YES Prep program in Houston between 2005 and 2011. I have identified but a few of the many other national, regional, and community philanthropists that have contributed to this growth of charter schools in the U.S. In addition to direct support by individual philanthropic foundations, charter management organizations have been heavily supported by non-profit organizations such as the NewSchools Fund. I turn next to the work of this organization.

The Role of the NewSchools Venture Fund in Creation of Charter Management Organizations

In addition to the individual philanthropic foundations such as those noted above, an intermediary non-profit organization funded by many of the same philanthropists, the NewSchools[7] Venture Fund, invests "almost exclusively in CMOs. As Kim Smith, co-founder and former CEO of New Schools Fund, argued, 'It doesn't make sense to reinvent the wheel every time a new charter school opens'" (Smith et al., 2009, p. 2). The following section details the extensive role the NewSchools Venture Fund has played in the growth of these CMOs. The NewSchools website describes the organization as "a nonprofit venture philanthropy firm working to transform public education for low-income children" (www.newschools.org).

In 1998, "social entrepreneur" Kim Smith collaborated with venture capitalists John Doerr and Brook Byers to found the NewSchools Venture Fund, an intermediary non-profit venture capital organization whose mission is "to transform public education through powerful ideas and passionate entrepreneurs so that all children—especially those in underserved communities—have the opportunity to succeed" (www.newschools.org.). Philanthropists (The Annie E. Casey Foundation, The Broad Foundation, CityBridge Foundation, Doris and Donald Fisher Fund, Bill and Melinda Gates Foundation—gift of $22 million, The Goldman Sachs Foundation, The William and Flora Hewlett Foundation, The James Irvine Foundation, HARRISmyCFO Foundation, Noyce Foundation, Perkins Malo Hunter Foundation, Robertson Foundation, The Walton Family Foundation) as well as the Aspen Institute and the U.S. Department of Education funded the NewSchools Venture Fund. Using the FoundationSearch key words "New Schools Fund" and "New Schools Venture Fund"reveals that from 1998 to 2011, 88 grants totaling $98,818,152 were given to support the work of this organization. Of those grants, 31 were given by the Bill and Melinda Gates Foundation ($64,057,390), seven by the Annie E. Casey Foundation ($1,150,000), 14 by the Broad Foundation ($11,901,000), three by the Walton Family Foundation ($8,224,395), four by venture capitalist John Doerr's Benificus Foundation ($7,569,067), and the remaining grants by various foundations. The NewSchools Fund's approach, as stated on its website, is worth quoting at length to demonstrate its philosophy, investment practices, and commitment to establishing connected networks of initiatives with the ultimate goal of transforming public education:

> NewSchools Venture Fund believes that *all* children are entitled to a high-quality public education and that the best way to reach this goal is to transform our current systems of public schools into performance-driven organizations that focus on student achievement. We believe that education entrepreneurs can spark this broader transformation in the public school system.
>
> As a nonprofit venture philanthropy firm, we raise capital from both individual and institutional investors; we then use those funds to support promising education entrepreneurs, help them grow their orga-

---

7 For an analysis of the NewSchools Venture Fund, see Horn, J., & Libby, K. (2011). The giving business: Venture philanthropy and the NewSchools Venture Fund. In P. E. Kovacs (Ed.), *The Gates Foundation and the future of U.S. "public" schools*. New York, NY: Routledge.

nizations to scale, and connect their work with public school systems particularly within targeted urban areas. We analyze the national education landscape and the ecosystem for this type of dramatic change in each of our key urban areas to determine how education entrepreneurs are poised to make a difference.

Once potential ventures are identified, our team engages in a rigorous investment process that includes due diligence on the organization, its management team, its model, product, and results, as well as the market it seeks to address. When we invest in an organization, we serve as active partners by taking a seat on the board of directors and by providing ongoing management assistance to the leadership team as the venture grows to scale.

In order to maximize the impact of our ventures, NewSchools also connects the work of these entrepreneurs with one another and with the broader field through events and publications. Ultimately, our goal is to empower the entrepreneurs we support to transform public education so that *all* children have the opportunity to attend a high-quality public school. (http://www.newschools.org/work)

The following brief examination of the growth and focus of the NewSchools Fund illustrates its history of funding innovation and reform since its inception. The first NewSchools Venture Fund (1998–2002) supported nine entrepreneurial non-profit and for-profit efforts to support organizations that "started systems of public charter schools, while others focused on preparing and supporting teachers and leaders, developing research-based curricula, or providing school performance information that parents and community members need to make effective decisions about education"(http://www. newschools.org/work).

The second NewSchools Venture Fund (2002–2006), totaling nearly $50 million, supported the creation of the first non-profit charter management organizations to design and operate integrated networks of public charter schools. According to the fund's website, this second fund supported "more than two dozen CMOs that manage over 100 schools serving tens of thousands of students" as well as organizations to provide support services such as facilities development, academic support, and administrative services.

Between 2006 and 2010, the NewSchools Venture Fund of $75 million focused on the development of alternative approaches to public education in key cities: New York City, Chicago, Los Angeles, Washington, DC, Oakland, and New Orleans. The fund supported "new and expanding CMOs and invested in tools and services designed to improve instruction through the rigorous use of performance data, and expanded alternative pathways into teaching" (http://www.newschools.org/investment/history).

Between 1998 and 2010, NewSchools Venture Fund awarded 58 grants totaling $30,368,540 to venture projects that included (1) school organizations in urban centers (California, New York, Washington, DC, Chicago, Illinois, Philadelphia, PA, Boston and Framingham, MA, New Orleans); (2) human capital providers to recruit, train, support, and provide professional development to teachers and leaders (New Leaders for New Schools, Teach for America, New Teacher Center, The New Teacher Project, and TeachScape); (3) school support organizations that develop school facilities (Civic Builders, Pacific Charter School Development), provide food services (Revolution Foods), support data-based teaching strategies (Acelero Learning, The Achievement Network; and (4) academic tools organizations (Carnegie Learning, Success for All, Great Schools).

The current fourth fund, the NewSchools Innovation Fund, is designed to close the achievement gap for underserved students through the following investments:

• *People*: educator training providers that increase the pipeline of teacher and leader talent and define their performance—and the performance of those they train—in terms of impact on student achievement;

- *Tools*: technology-enabled products, platforms, and services that help educators improve instruction, enable customized student learning, or otherwise maximize student achievement;

- *Schools*, including:
  — School Turnarounds: organizations that take over and turn around chronically failing schools; and
  — Charter Management Organizations (CMOs): organizations that create scalable, sustainable school systems. (http://www.newschools.org/work/investment-strategy)

NewSchools staff provides financial, operational, and education support for its ventures, typically sits on boards of directors for its charter school management organizations, and creates opportunities for the CMOs to meet together to share effective strategies. Using funds primarily from venture philanthropists, NewSchools Fund has served as a primary organization for the development and expansion of a national network of charter management organizations in the U.S. since its inception in 1998.

Philanthropic Investment in Non-Profit Teacher and Leadership Preparation Programs

Other educational entrepreneurs established non-profit organizations for teacher and leadership preparation. Perhaps the best-known example is Teach for America. In 1990, with $2.5 million in start-up funding, Wendy Kopp, a Princeton graduate, launched Teach for America, a program whose mission is "to build the movement to eliminate educational inequity by enlisting our nation's most promising future leaders in the effort." TFA recruits high-quality college graduates from all disciplinary backgrounds to commit to teach in urban and rural low-income communities for two years. In 2011, the TFA website summarized the current impact of its members:

> Since 1990, nearly 33,000 leaders have joined Teach for America to help move us closer to that vision. As corps members and alumni, they have reached more than 3 million students across 43 urban and rural communities, founded dozens of high-performing schools, boldly led school districts and charter management organizations, and helped pass groundbreaking education legislation. In the 2011–12 school year, more than 9,300 corps members will teach 600,000 students while nearly 24,000 alumni will continue to deepen their impact as educational leaders and advocates.(http://www.teachforamerica.org/our-organization)

As indicated, many of the TFA's members work in the CMO school networks described above. Two TFA alumni, Dave Levin and Mike Feinberg, founded the Knowledge Is Power Program (KIPP) and Chris Barbic founded YES Prep Public Schools. Both of these CMOs are among the largest recipients of philanthropic funding. Michelle Rhee is the founder of The New Teacher Project, former Chancellor of the District of Columbia Public Schools system, and founder of StudentsFirst, a non-profit, political advocacy organization whose mission is "to defend the interests of children in public education and pursue transformative reform, so that America has the best educational system in the world" (www.studentsfirst.org). The organization's current efforts are focused on fighting teacher layoffs based on seniority. Another former TFA member, Kaya Henderson, is DC's current Chancellor. Alec Ross, a member of President Obama's campaign and contributor to his technology and innovation plan, is now Senior Adviser for Innovation for Secretary of State Hillary Clinton.

Using FoundationSearch data, between 2000 and 2011, the total funding given to Teach for American by philanthropic organizations totaled $267,165,222 in 4,155 grants. Of those, 53 grants were over $1 million. Many of the grants were given in general support or general operating support, totaling over $93 million. The following table summarizes the 25 most significant funders during the time period:

SIGNIFICANT FUNDER	GRANTEE LOCATION	TOTAL FUNDING
ROBERTSON FOUNDATION	New Orleans, LA	$20,140,000.00
FIDELITY INVESTMENTS CHARITABLE GIFT FUND	New Orleans, LA	$10,000,000.00
THE MICHAEL AND SUSAN DELL FOUNDATION	New York	$9,580,000.00
BROAD FOUNDATION	New York	$8,050,000.00
C. D. SPANGLER FOUNDATION INC	New Orleans, LA	$5,500,000.00
JOHN S. AND JAMES L. KNIGHT FOUNDATION	New York	$4,800,000.00
STARR FOUNDATION	New York	$4,700,000.00
WALTON FAMILY FOUNDATION INC	New York, Arkansas	$3,546,382.00
AMGEN FOUNDATION INC		$3,000,000.00
CARNEGIE CORPORATION OF NEW YORK	New York	$3,000,000.00
LEHMAN BROTHERS FOUNDATION	New York	$3,000,000.00
THE GOIZUETA FOUNDATION	New York	$2,850,827.00
ROBERT K. STEEL FAMILY FOUNDATION	New York	$2,000,000.00
LENFEST FOUNDATION INC	New York	$1,700,000.00
HELIOS EDUCATION FOUNDATION	Phoenix, AZ	$1,500,000.00
LINCY FOUNDATION	Las Vegas	$1,075,500.00
JOEL E. SMILOW CHARITABLE TRUST	New York	$1,015,674.00
THE SKOLL FUND	New York	$1,015,000.00
SCHWAB CHARITABLE FUND	New York	$1,010,250.00
BILL AND MELINDA GATES FOUNDATION	New York	$1,000,000.00
COMMUNITY FOUNDATION OF MIDDLE TENNESSEE INC	New York	$1,000,000.00
D AND DF FOUNDATION	New York	$1,000,000.00
MEDTRONIC FOUNDATION	New York	$1,000,000.00
SAN FRANCISCO FOUNDATION	New York	$1,000,000.00
THE CARROLL AND MILTON PETRIE FOUNDATION INC	New York	$1,000,000.00
TOTAL		$93,483,633.00

Table 2: 2000 - 2011 Teach for America Top Funders

Teach for America's website lists donors at funding levels of $50 million and above (Sue and Steve Mandel and The Walton Family Foundation), $25 million to $49,999,999 (Laura and John Arnold Foundation, The Eli and Edythe Broad Foundation, Doris and Donald Fisher Fund, and Robertson Foundation), $10 million to $24,999,999 (Anonymous, Michael and Susan Dell Foundation, Martha and Bruce Karsh, The Lenfest Foundation, Rainwater Charitable Foundation, and Arthur and Toni Rembe Rock), and $1 million to $9,999,999 (100 donors listed here including Bill and Melinda Gates, NewSchools Venture Fund, and others, both traditional and venture philanthropies; http://

www.teachforamerica.org/get-involved/donors). According to Susan Ohanian (2011), the significant contribution by Sue and Steve Mandel, whose fortune was earned as founders of the hedge fund Lone Pine Capital, was part of Broad's effort to establish a $100 million endowment for Teach for America. The TFA website features a list of "National Growth Investors" who "committed to support significant growth by investing in our 2006–2013 growth campaigns." Those listed for $10 million are The Eli and Edythe Broad Foundation, Michael and Susan Dell Foundation, Doris and Donald Fisher Fund, Martha and Bruce Karsh, Steve and Sue Mandel, Rainwater Charitable Funds, Robertson Foundation, and The Walton Family Foundation. Those listed for $5 million to $9,999,999 are Marsha and James McCormick and Arthur and Toni Rembe Rock. Many more investors and supporters are listed for other years and for lesser amounts of support. In fall 2010, Teach for America listed its public funding as including Americorps, U.S. Department of Education, Mississippi Department of Education, New York Department of Education, Texas Education Agency, the Office of the State Superintendent, District of Columbia, and the National Aeronautics and Space Administration.

The New Teachers Project (NTP), a non-profit founded by former TFA member Michelle Rhee, was designed to provide quality teachers for urban classrooms by training mid-career professionals. The project, initiated in 1997, was funded in part, typically 30%, by the following philanthropies: Bill and Melinda Gates Foundation, the Arnold Family Foundation, the Joyce Foundation, the Carnegie Corporation of New York, and the Charles and Helen Schwab Foundation. NTP has a goal to address teacher shortages and teacher quality in the U.S.; its mission is "to end the injustice of educational inequality by providing excellent teachers to the students who need them most and by advancing policies and practices that ensure effective teaching in every classroom" (http://www.tntp.org/aboutus/our_business_model.html). It offers four primary initiatives including a teaching fellows program, staffing initiatives, training and certification, and policy and research. The organization works with school systems to recruit, hire, and support teachers for urban and high-poverty schools. For example, following Hurricane Katrina, the NTP worked with school personnel in New Orleans to establish Teach NOLA to recruit high-quality teachers for the city's schools.

Related to efforts to improve teacher effectiveness, philanthropic foundations have supported programs for leadership effectiveness with the premise that good leadership in schools will enhance and improve the effectiveness of teachers and, thus, student achievement. New Leaders for New Schools (NLNS) (http://www.nlns.org/) is an organization that relies on philanthropic foundations for 71% of its funding, with its key donors ($2 million and above), The Bill and Melinda Gates Foundation, The Broad Foundation, Carnegie Corporation of New York, The Hyde Family Foundations, Michael and Susan Dell Foundation, The Noyce Foundation, and The Pearson Foundation. The non-profit organization, founded in 2000 by five "social entrepreneurs" (business and education graduate students), has as its mission to "ensure high academic achievement for every student by attracting and preparing outstanding leaders and supporting the performance of the urban public schools they lead at scale." The vision of NLNS is "One day every student will graduate from high school ready for success in college, careers and citizenship…in at least 10 U.S. cities by 2020." The organization works with districts in the Bay Area, Charlotte, Chicago, Greater New Orleans, Maryland, Memphis, Milwaukee, New York City, Newark, and Washington, DC. A second model of school leadership is the Academy for Urban School Leadership (AUSL) funded by billionaires Michael and Susan Dell.

Venture Philanthropy's Impact on Educational Policy

While not able to engage in political advocacy, non-profit philanthropies are able to support organizations whose mission is one of advocacy. As was mentioned briefly above, philanthropists contributing to charter schools provided funding to support organizations like the state charter school associations created to advocate for educational policy and practice based on the charter school models. In another example using these data, between 2003 and 2007 the Bill and Melinda Gates Foundation provided five grants totaling $747,638 to the right-leaning Thomas B. Fordham Foundation. The stated purposes of these funds was to "inform public debate and advance academic achievement in Ohio Charter Schools by convening charter school leaders, producing research, and disseminating information on charter school issues" and "strengthen Ohio's charter school program by recruiting, training, and supporting quality sponsors for existing and future charter schools." Through these means philanthropists like the Bill and Melinda Gates Foundation have been highly successful at using their extensive wealth to change state and federal policies through advocacy agencies.

In a 2008 interview study of 19 senior staff members of primarily nationally focused foundations, Ferris, Hentschke, and Harmssen (2008) examined their decisions to engage in K-12 education policy. They investigated the policy domain and whether their involvement was at the national, state, or district level. Much of the education policy work is done at the state and district levels, with much effort directed at district-level school reform. Researchers found the primary influence for policy involvement was the foundation leadership, with the organization's vision guiding overall policy direction. A second motive was the philanthropic environment and the extent to which the foundations could fund the development of models for others to learn from. All those interviewed identified the problem of low student achievement and sought solutions for that issue. The study identified the following five policy areas on which these foundations focused: (1) child and family services including early education and parenting education; (2) professional development for certified staff and administrators primarily as in-service rather than pre-service education; (3) curriculum and instruction emphasizing specific content areas, categories of students (e.g., ESOL) and student performance (e.g., standards-based instruction and data-based decision making); (4) school management and governance including school and district management, leadership training, and effective organizational conditions; and (5) school choice including public and private school vouchers, charter schools, home schooling and more broadly enhancing school options. The researchers found that professional development and school governance and management were the most often cited areas for policy, but argued:

> foundations as a whole tend to be focused on direct approaches to changing educator behavior in a subset of schools, presuming or hoping these efforts will pay off in improved practices first, then in improved levels of student achievement, then in changes in policy that will institutionalize these improved practices. (p. 729)

Ferris et al. (2008) found these foundations emphasized professional development and school governance as leading improved student outcomes through policy change with 13 of the 19 foundations involved in policy primarily at the early stages of *problem identification* and *agenda setting* rather than the later stages of policy adoption, implementation, and evaluation. The most common way for foundations to become involved with policy was in the funding of demonstration projects and new models, with research and development next. Ten of the foundations reported funding advocacy groups; nine supported work to create policy networks. The majority of the foundations partnered primarily at the local level with community groups, schools, and other foundations with only eight partnering with school reform advocacy organizations. In their interviews with foundation staff, researchers found a focus on developing models in partnership with schools and communities for improving student achievement; "however, given the wide range of activities and models funded within the study underscores the fact that the foundations, as a group, do not have a single answer to the question of how to improve student achievement" (Ferris et al., 2008, pp. 725–726).

Hess (2005) argued that the fame of "business superstars" like Bill Gates, Michael Dell, and Michael Milken command the attention of major media and public officials, and consequently help to frame the public debate about educational issues. For example, realizing its potential impact on policy, in 2002–2003, the Gates Foundation reorganized its staff into teams for research, policy, and advocacy with Vander Ark recruiting resident staff members in the six states the foundation primarily works—Washington, California, Illinois, New York, Ohio, and North Carolina. At this same time, the foundation shifted from predominately grants to progressive reforms and balanced those with grants for new charter schools, research on choice-related approaches such as charter schools, accountability and performance-based funding of education, and school finance reform (Hill, 2006). According to Hill, in 2006, one-third of the Gates Foundation funding went to charter schools and choice initiatives. Clearly, with this level of funding in targeted areas, the Gates Foundation has engaged in the problem-identification and agenda-setting stages of policy development, but with the high level of media attention on philanthropists such as Gates, there is significant impact on educational policy at all levels.

One specific example of the influence of philanthropic funding on educational policy is the federally funded Teacher Incentive Program modeled after the success of The Milken Family Foundation's Teacher Advancement Program (TAP). This program "annually provides funding for school districts and states to develop and implement innovative ways to provide financial incentives for *teachers and principals* who raise student achievement and close the achievement gap in some of America's highest-need schools" (http://www.tapsystem.org/policyresearch/policyresearch.taf?page=legislation). This program was initiated in 2006 with $99 million in funding. An additional $200 million was added to the program through the American Recovery and Reinvestment Act (ARRA). The impact of the TAP program was evidenced in the most recent federal education funding initiative, President Obama and Education Secretary Arne Duncan's $4.35 billion Race to the Top competition for states to support innovation and school reform. This competition addressed reform in the following four areas: (1) adopting internationally benchmarked standards and assessments that prepare students for success in college and the workplace; (2) recruiting, developing, retaining, and rewarding effective teachers and principals; (3) building data systems that measure student success and inform teachers and principals how they can improve their practices; and (4) turning around lowest-performing schools (http://www2.ed.gov/news/pressreleases/2009/07/07242009.html).

To illustrate a further connection between philanthropies and federal policy initiatives, in 2009 at the NewSchools Venture Fund Summit, Secretary of Education Arne Duncan appointed Joanne S. Weiss, a NewSchools Venture Fund partner and chief operating officer, to lead the Race to the Top effort. In addition to her role at NewSchools, Weiss serves on the boards of New Leaders for New Schools and Teachscape, an educational management non-profit. State applications for Race to the Top funding were scored on specific criteria worth a total of 500 points including the following, all reflecting goals and funding initiatives of key venture philanthropists: (1) raising achievement and closing gaps; (2) developing common standards from the Common Core State Standards Initiative, a project funded in part with support from The Bill and Melinda Gates Foundation; (3) ensuring successful conditions for the creation of high-performing charter schools and other innovative schools; and, (4) implementing a statewide longitudinal data system. Ravitch (2010) argued:

> Together these foundations [Gates, Dell, Robertson, and Broad] wield immense economic and political power. During the 2008 campaign the Gates and Broad foundations jointly contributed $60 million to launch a project to make education reform a national campaign issue, while advocating for national standards, a longer school day, and merit pay. (p. 217)

She reminded us that after his election and appointment as Secretary of Education, Arne Duncan appointed a former program officer of the Gates Foundation, James H. Shelton II, to oversee the $650 million Invest in What Works and Innovation Fund (Ravitch, 2010, p. 218). Interestingly, Shelton was a partner in the NewSchools Venture Fund.

While individual philanthropists can do much to shape educational policy, in collaboration with one another they are highly effective. I turn next to the growing trend toward leveraging change through focused, collaborative giving.

Leveraging Impact Through Philanthropic Collaboration

Traditional philanthropists tended to work alone. Venture and catalytic philanthropists are interested in launching campaigns to solve what they perceive to be pressing social problems, an approach that, as Kramer reminds us, "achieves measurable impacts" and "uses all possible tools and donor resources" (Kramer, 2009). With a desire to mobilize change more quickly, there is increasing willingness to collaborate with other foundations as well as with community groups and institutions. The Gates Foundation works in partnership with other foundations from varying neo-conservative and neo-liberal ideological perspectives. It contributed $11 million to a San Diego traditional curriculum-centered reform in partnership with the Broad and William and Flora Hewlett Foundations, which work to support the existing system. Gates also collaborated with those foundations, whose funding is focused on charter school and choice options such as the Walton, Pisces, and Bradley Foundations. Hill (2006) provided these examples of collaboration, arguing that the foundation moved from "utopian to pragmatic, from progressive to agnostic, and from person-focused to system-focused" (p. 50).

The umbrella organization for the nation's most conservative philanthropists, the Philanthropy Roundtable, has published *Achieving Teacher and Principal Excellence: A Guidebook for Donors* (Rotherham, 2008). Rotherham, the guidebook's author, proposes "ten big ideas in need of support," one of which is the focus on "a single, proof-point location" (p. 111). As an example of this idea, he described what he considered to be one of the largest and most impressive collaborations to date, the $17.5 million Fisher, Gates, and Broad joint project over three years to "support special programs run by organizations like Teach for America, New Leaders for New Schools, and the New Teacher Project" (2008, p. 111). This guide explicitly calls for philanthropists to "work with others. Wherever possible, develop strategies to leverage funding through collaboration with other grantmakers. When making risky or politically contentious investments, collaboration can also help mitigate exposure to negative publicity" (p. 108).

Conclusions

This chapter has focused on the work of the venture philanthropists committed to transforming public education as well as federal and state educational policy. Unlike their predecessors who tended to focus on specific projects, typically within existing schools and colleges, these funders have succeeded well in creating an expansive network of heavily funded charter management organizations, non-profit, tax-exempt organizations for teacher and leader preparation, and assorted non-profit real estate and school support services to provide curriculum, instruction, assessment, and even food services. The shift from traditional to venture philanthropy has moved the wealthiest among us to positions of education leadership and policy in the United States. No longer do philanthropic foundations take the role of supporting and encouraging change while their grantees take the lead in how these changes might be accomplished. The new philanthropists believe in a free marketplace of schools that reflect a corporate model where teacher effectiveness is determined by student achievement as measured in standardized tests and is rewarded by pay for performance schemes. Personally involved in their projects and expecting quick results, they have focused their funding largely outside traditional educational institutions, believing that these institutions are not nimble enough to create the kind of educational transformation they want. Using a multi-pronged approach, these billionaire philanthropists have been highly successful in establishing a network of interconnected non-profit organizations where charter management organizations are the central entities around which other non-profits—often funded by the same group of philanthropists—for teacher preparation (e.g., Teach for America, The New Teachers Project, New Teachers Center) and leader preparation (e.g., New Leaders for New Schools, Urban Teacher Residency Program, Academy for Urban Leadership), supply the workforce or "human capital" for these charter schools. Non-profit real estate ventures, like the Pacific Charter School Development organizations (funded by Gates, Broad, NewSchools Venture Fund, Walton, and Wingart to the tune of $17,885,500 from 2000 to 2008) and Civic Builders develop the school properties, then lease them to the charters. Non-profit educational services like the Big Picture Company, Success for All, Carnegie Learning, and Teachscape provide curricular and assessment tools, professional development for teachers, and even food services such as Revolution Foods, for the charter schools. These non-profits are media and marketing savvy, creating identities for themselves that communicate to the public their high levels of quality and effectiveness as compared to traditional public schools. However, these charter schools and teacher preparation programs have had mixed results when held up to rigorous scrutiny by the research community. For example, the 2009 Stanford CREDO study, "the first national assessment of charter school impacts" (p. 1), found:

> 17 percent provide superior education opportunities for their students. Nearly half of the charter schools nationwide have results that are no different from the local school options and over a third, 37 percent, deliver learning results that are significantly worse than their students would have realized had they remained in traditional public schools. (p. 1)

In addition to creating this expansive network of charter management organizations and supporting service non-profits, venture philanthropists have been highly successful in political advocacy resulting, as described above, in federally funded initiatives such as Race to the Top, which uses the reform elements of the philanthropists as its scoring criteria to determine who gets funded. As Sarah Mosle (2011) noted in her review of Steven Brill's *Class Warfare*, the coordinated efforts of the philanthropists and their impact on educational policies discourages models of reform outside this philanthropic agenda. She argued:

> The problem isn't just that the hard evidence, looked at dispassionately, doesn't always support reformers' claims. It's that the insurgents are in danger of becoming the very thing they once (rightly) rose up against: subject to groupthink, reluctant to hear opposing views or to work with anyone perceived to be on the other side. (p. 3)

The nation's wealthiest philanthropists have successfully created a national reform movement based on their visions for schooling, not only through their funding initiatives, but through marketing and media events such as the film *Waiting for Superman*, a film largely funded by Bill Gates and fellow philanthropist Warren Buffett, and supported and promoted by NewSchools Venture Fund (www.waitingforsuperman.org). This film promotes a romanticized view of the charter school reform movement while demonizing traditional public school organizations, teachers' unions, and uninspired teachers. Perhaps it is because of media attention like this over the past few years that scholars have recently turned their attention to the work of these philanthropists (cf., Hill & Kumar, 2009; Kovacs, 2011; Ravitch, 2010; Saltman, 2010). In 2005, Hess called for increased scholarly scrutiny of the efforts of the wealthy foundations. Citing examples of the Walton and Gates Foundations, which are donating 80% of their education funding to choice-based reform efforts, Hess argued (2005) that a handful of foundations have "a huge role in advocacy and reform efforts" (p. 133) and urged scholars, journalists, and practitioners to monitor the role donors play in these policy areas with "unsentimental scrutiny" (p. 134). His analysis of 2005 newspaper articles on five leading foundations revealed there were 13 positive stories for every critical assessment. Hess argued his point was to "stir a more skeptical, sophisticated, and engaged discussion about the hows, whys, and wherefores of K-12 philanthropy.... Open, honest, and skeptical discussion is the linchpin in the democratic compact governing philanthropic attempts to reform public institutions" (Hess, 2005, p. 137). While focused more on international work, Steiner-Khamsi (2008), too, argued for more scholarly study of the work of philanthropy in education. She argued, based on a review of academic journals in international and comparative education as well as journals focused on NGO research, new donors have not yet become an object of professional interest and academic curiosity.

So why should we examine the work of the philanthropists so closely? Is it a surprise that those with money and, hence, power, set the educational agenda? While not surprising, only when one looks deeply into the funding efforts of individual foundations, as well as the interconnections among the foundations and their non-profits, does the reach of this labyrinth of influence become clear. On the surface, each organization appears to be a singular entity, but it is just one within a network of similarly focused efforts that have had significant impact on the educational landscape of the 21st century.

I offer here a concluding thought as well as a challenge to venture philanthropists. With the exception of their focus on test-based accountability measures, anti-union efforts, and teacher pay for performance schemes, the promotional materials of philanthropically funded urban charter management organizations identified in this chapter describe school practices progressive educators have argued for years will improve educational achievement for all students. These reforms include the establishment of small community schools, clean, inviting physical environments, healthy meals, personalized instruction with high expectations for teachers and students, engaging relevant, learner-centered activities, mentoring, collaboration, and support for teachers, particularly during pre-service and induction years, and family/community involvement in schooling. Over the past decade venture philanthropists have been brilliantly successful in creating a national reform movement reflective of their views, focusing public attention on low-performing schools and blaming ineffective teachers, teachers unions, and heavy urban bureaucracies, thus ignoring an economic system that creates a persistent underclass in America's urban and rural communities. Ironically, they have also been successful at poignantly demonstrating how their version of school reform requires large infusions of money if real change is to occur in the nation's lowest-performing schools, much more funding than is available through the inequitable funding formulas currently in place for urban schools. Despite the arguments of charter school advocates who argue that on average they receive less per pupil than traditional public schools in the same district, as has been demonstrated here, well-funded charter management organizations benefit from millions in philanthropic support.

Herein lies my challenge to philanthropists. What we know to date about how charter management organizations and their network schools work is largely through reports of test scores, graduation rates, college admittance rates, and media events suggesting that superman lives in these schools. I argue here for a higher level of philanthropic transparency and accountability. There are few critical qualitative studies that document the daily lives of students, teachers, and administrators in these schools.[8]Since venture philanthropists pride themselves as being learning organizations (one need only to look at their websites for this claim), I challenge them to open their schoolhouse doors to critical qualitative examination guided by the following research questions: What level of funding does it really take to transform urban schools into high-performing learning communities for all children? How specifically are public, as well as philanthropic, funds used in the charter management organizations? Who benefits from these funds and how? What are the per-pupil expenditures in urban charter schools as compared to traditional public schools in those neighborhoods? Beyond test scores, what evidence demonstrates that students in these charters are gaining the critical thinking and analysis skills needed for college and beyond? What happens to students who do not succeed in these environments? What are the long-term results of these reform efforts on the local community? How do these connections privilege some reform efforts and not others? What are the connections between the philanthropists, venture philanthropy firms, non-profit organizations, and those in power in Washington, DC? More in-depth qualitative case studies and longitudinal research within specific public charters would enable contextually rich examinations of how these large charter management organizations work within specific communities over time and how interconnections among the philanthropists, educational entrepreneurs, and political players at the state and federal levels enact educational policy favorable to venture philanthropists and their non-profits. Whether or not we are invited into these schools, there is

---

8   Jessica Shiller's (2011) study is a good example of a critical ethnographic study in one school in New York City.

much work for critical qualitative researchers in making clear to educators and the general public how the wealthiest philanthropists have shaped U.S. public education and policy. I invite researchers to join me in the rabbit warrens of critical philanthropic inquiry.

Acknowledgments

I would like to thank Grace Thornton, College of Education, University of Georgia, for her thorough assistance with the FoundationSearch database. Many thanks to Todd Stephenson and Lauren Moret, graduate assistants in the Department of Lifelong Education, Administration, and Policy, University of Georgia, for their excellent support in the completion of this chapter.

At the time of this writing, Harlem Day Charter School, founded in 2001, was closed by the State University of New York due to a record of "low test scores and poor performance." In June 2011, the SUNY system approved Democracy Prep Public Schools' takeover of the school, which will reopen with the name Harlem Prep Charter School (http://insideschools.org/elementary/browse/school/1287).

References

Bennett, K. (1990). Doing school in an urban Appalachian first grade. In C. Sleeter (Ed.), *Empowerment through multicultural education*. New York: SUNY.

Center for Research on Education Outcomes (CREDO). (2009). *Multiple choice: Charter school performance in 16 states*. Stanford, CA: Author.

Colvin, R. L. (2005). The new philanthropists: Can their millions enhance learning? *Education Next, 5*(4), 34–41.

deMarrais, K. (2006). "The haves and the have mores:" Fueling a conservative ideological war on public education. *Educational Studies, 39*(3), 204–242.

Ferris, J. M., Hentschke, G. C., & Harmssen, H. J. (2008). Philanthropic strategies for school reform: An analysis of foundation choices. *Educational Policy, 22*(5), 705–730.

Hess, F. M. (2005). Inside the gift horse's mouth: Philanthropy and school reform. *Phi Delta Kappan, 87*(2), 131–137.

Hill, D., & Kumar, R. (Eds.). (2009). Global neoliberalism and education and its consequences. New York, NY: Routledge.

Hill, P. T. (2006). A foundation goes to school: Bill and Melinda Gates shift from computers in libraries to reform in high schools. *Education Next, 6*(1), 44–51.

Kovacs, P. (2011). *The Gates Foundation and the future of US public schools*. New York, NY: Routledge.

Kramer, M. R. (2009). Catalytic philanthropy. *Stanford Social Innovative Review*, Fall, 30–35.

Mosle, S. (2011, August 18). Steven Brill's report card on school reform. *New York Times Book Review*, p. 3.

Ohanian, S. (2011) Outrages: Comment on "Donors urged school ouster". Retrieved from http://susanohanian.org/show_atrocities.php?id=9736

Ravitch, D. (2010). *The death and life of the great American school system: How testing and choice are undermining education*. New York, NY: Basic Books.

Robelen, E. W. (2008). Strategy retooled at Gates. *Education Week, 28*(13), 1.

Rotherham, A. J. (2008). *Achieving teacher and principal excellence: A guidebook for donors*. Washington, DC: Philanthropy Roundtable.

Saltman, K. J. (2010). *The gift of education: Public education and venture philanthropy*. New York, NY: Palgrave Macmillan.

Saltman, K. J. (2011). From Carnegie to Gates: The Bill and Melinda Gates Foundation and the venture philanthropy agenda for public education. In P. E. Kovacs (Ed.), *The Gates Foundation and the future of U.S. "public" schools*. New York, NY: Routledge, 1–20.

Scott, J. (2009). The politics of venture philanthropy in charter school policy and advocacy. *Educational Policy, 23*(1), 106–136.

Shiller, J. (2011). Marketing new schools for a new century: An examination of neoliberal school reform in New York City. In P. Kovacs, *The Gates foundation and the future of US public schools*. New York, NY: Routledge, 53–79.

Smith, J., Farrell, C., Wohlstetter, P., & Nayfack, M. (2009). *Mapping the landscape of charter management organizations: Issues to consider in supporting replication*. Washington, D.C.: National Resource Center on Charter School Finance & Governance.

Steiner-Khamsi, G. (2008). Donor logic in the era of Gates, Buffett, and Soros. *Current Issues in Comparative Education, 10*(1/2), 10–15.

Suggs, C., & deMarrais, K. (with Watkins, K., Horne, A., Swett, K., & Kronley, R.). (2011). *Critical contributions: Philanthropic investment in teachers and teaching*. Athens: University of Georgia and Kronley Associates. Retrieved from http://kronley.com/criticalcontributions.php

Torres, C. A. (1998). *Education, power, and personal biography: Dialogues with critical educators*. New York, NY: Routledge.

PART FOUR
On the Marginalized

CHAPTER TWENTY

Writing Diasporic Indigeneity Through Critical Research and Social Method

George J. Sefa Dei and Marlon Simmons

There are ongoing contestations on what it means to speak about Diasporic Indigeneity. This paper will offer a research methodological approach to the study of Diasporic Indigeneity. The learning objective is to explore some methodological challenges and examine the possibilities and limitations of locating the self as method. The discussion is oriented towards an anti-colonial approach to dialogue with questions of Indigeneity. Our goal is to know and understand embodied Indigenous epistemes as experienced through the socio-cultural field of the Diaspora. The site of interest is the Indigene as it resides within the different spatio-temporal geographies of the Diaspora. Among the questions we ask are: Does the Diasporic context render African Indigeneity (im)possible or non-existent? What does studying such Indigeneity mean and require by way of research? In the discussion we search for ways to make meaning of the ontological primacy immanent within Indigenousness, that is, to disentangle the liminal discursive that informs the everyday Diasporic life. With disentangling the everyday Diasporic liminal, the aim is to make sense of local cognitive interpretations of our social environment as experienced through Indigenous cultural ways of knowing.

Our chapter does not presume to offer some strict methodological guidelines to be followed in studying the self as an Indigenous identity in a Diasporic context. What we are interested in is to raise some key issues of the Diasporic Indigeneity when it becomes a site for methodological investigation in critical social research. As a method/vantage point we begin with the experiential self, local stories/dialogue. We broach self-reflexivity through the text of writing and the oral to voice subversive pedagogies. We write through the flux of Indigeneity, through personal geo-histories, through cultural memory to reclaim identities, and to help with understanding our social experiences. We are guided through our Diasporic subjectivities. We situate Indigenous knowledge as counter-hegemonic and anti-colonial. At the same time we are not preoccupied with formulating fixed meanings of Indigenousness or drumming up step-by-step methods to approach Diasporic Indigeneity. We write through local subjectivities, through historic specific locations, to identify and sift deeply embedded codifications of race that inform the myriad communicative exchanges of the Diaspora. Indigenous epistemologies allow us to interpret these colonially imbued moments where different Diasporic bodies come to negotiate with the particular historic-cultural tapestry of Euromodernity. With Indigeneity as method, we query the socio-cultural practices that come to co-determine identities, dispositions and desires, of what it means to be human within the different geographies of the Diaspora. We will not attempt to historically trace the Diaspora; instead we are interested in the experience of the Diasporic identity as it comes to be historically shaped through the social conjunctures of the many cultural formations of Indigeneity.

We engage this chapter from particular vantage points of our Indigeneity and how this location shapes our thinking on critical social research method. As Dei (2011) has repeatedly noted, there is a particular intellectual politics of researching and understanding the Indigenous experience as a form of knowing. It is argued that despite contestations to "what is Indigenous", there is an Indigeneity to be claimed for those whose relations to particular histories, cultures, places and identities also symbolize particular ways of knowing. The self is an important methodological feature in critical research. Writing through the personal subject(ive) location is important in terms of what brings the self to the particular time/place/space, insofar as the contextualization of writer/self as a methodological and discursive feature of the conversation helps the reader to understand the perspective from which one is conducting her or his discussion/analysis. Research is also about representation. We know also that representation is not only about subject identities and identifications. The politics of representing one's self and her or his ideas should lead to fundamental issues of economic, material and structural changes in existing human conditions. This is a complex responsibility for critical social research in terms of how we come to understand our world and also change or transform our social conditions. Any exercise of locating the self through Diasporic Indigeneity is meaningful if it seeks to challenge or even change existing power relations. We must note that bodies matter in social research not simply in terms of identities and the politics of such identities, but also in terms of methodological cautions. Today there is an infatuation about complexities of difference, which cannot obscure the saliency of the Indigenous identity in a colonial and colonizing world. We cannot discuss our identities, subjectivities and their subsequent representations in fragments and stripped of their complexities and specificities.

A critical social research/researcher can and must understand what Indigenousness says, think or desire. Critical research must challenge and decenter so-called "enlightenment rationality". The search for humanness through research can only be effective if we start locating ourselves and noting the methodological implications. A researcher seeing her/his own location in the world is about relation(ship)s with difference within the socio-cultural environment. This is the human side of doing research work. Consequently, researching Diasporic Indigeneity means a researcher must be willing to acknowledge, and come to terms with the struggle to conceptualize the Indigenous self in terms of how one is positioned, imagined, and comes to be known in the context of the Diaspora. In the methodological sequence/foray, critical social research will entail/require an explicit recognition of and commitment to cogitate the multiple constructions of social, political, cultural and ideological representations of power.

Locating Indigeneity

Concerning the contentious site of Diasporic Indigeneity, we conceptualize Diasporic Indigeneity through a particular geo-time/space in which the body of the Diaspora becomes constituted by way of the governing form of localized knowledge. As argued elsewhere, "Indigenousness" may be seen as a knowledge consciousness arising locally and in association with the long-term occupancy of a place (Dei, 2000, p. 72; see also Smith, 1999; Semali & Kincheloe, 1999; Kincheloe & Steinberg, 2008; Dei, 2008). With long-term dwelling or "occupancy of a place", we view Diasporic Indigeneity as embedded through a particular geography of time and place. The task for Diasporic Indigeneity, as Ladson-Billings (2000) argues, is coming to recover the Diasporic self through "ontological alterity". With *ontological alterity*, we are thinking of the ways in which the Diasporic self, through experiencing the governing contemporary epoch, comes to know, recover, disentangle and understand, by way of having historical lineage to a particular geography through time and space, knowledge immanent to the said local body of the Diasporic self. Diasporic Indigeneity then is not fixed, not easily pinned down, but Diasporic Indigeneity forms itself through the flux of the episteme. Diasporic Indigeneity is transformative. Diasporic Indigeneity is about interconnectedness. Diasporic Indigeneity is about intimate relations with the cultural reservoir of self. Diasporic self as method cohabits-coexists with participants, with the researched, and the researcher. Diasporic self as method moves beyond the rigid systems of inquiry that historic social science research calls for. Diasporic self as method is subjective, political and laden with passion and emotions.

Historically, with the claim to know and understand the lived experiences of different peoples, social science research as embedded though positivist epistemologies installed the objective voice as the self. The self in a sense ought to be posited as being distinct from the ontological, as being distinct from primacy, as external to Diasporic embodiment. Yet as the ontological self comes to be constituted discursively *from*, *with*, *through* and *out* of the Diaspora, the Diasporic subject comes to know the self through interpolating procedures, as organized through colonial customs, expressions, attitudes and experiences. What is important for this discussion, though, is to extricate the particular immanent relationship with the ontological self and the Diasporic subject, to understand how these moments come to be constituted through Indigeneity. We position the Indigene as spatio-temporally located through epistemological geographies, as ontologically constituted through historic specificities. We call for a *hermeneutic of the self* (see Ricoeur, 1994; Gallagher, 1992) as imbued through anti-colonial epistemes, whereby the Diasporic body becomes cognizant of the ontological self through the Indigene, that is, through innate ways of knowing, through intuition, through the indwelling of the spirit (Moustakas, 1990). At the same time the ontological self, being aware of how these same said experiential moments, comes to be discursively organized and inscribed onto the Diasporic body. In a sense, then, with the *hermeneutic of the self*, one of the challenges we are faced with is extricating the way in which the Indigene come to be epistemologically constituted, while at the same time concealing the Indigenous self. Yet the Indigenous self *always already* articulates itself spatiotemporally through different geographies, such as the land, spirituality, language, local narratives, folklore, proverbs, oral histories and ancestral relations, to name some.

Difference as engendered through Diasporic Indigeneity forms a particular relationship with the self, materializing at times as oneness with the localized body of the Diaspora, or for some, materializing at times as a colonial encounter, as foreign, as alien to the Diasporic self. It is important to note that difference, in and of itself as immanent to Indigeneity, does not readily appear as some protean formation within the Diasporic self. Difference is already embodied, for within the colonial schema that governs the human condition therein lies the property of manicheism, that of alienation (Fanon, 1967). What then does it mean for the Diasporic subject to come to know and understand the experiential self through alienation? In that, alienation gives us the de-agentize self. Alienation articulates itself through epistemological disembodiment whereby the Diasporic self dialogues, engages, understands the Indigene as abject, in a sense the Diasporic self becomes *overdetermined from without* (Fanon, 1967, p. 116). The Indigene in a sense becomes constituted through an ontology of difference, that of an oppositional ontology to hegemonic ways of knowing. Ultimately, dialoguing with the Indigene involves a particular spatio-temporal relationship in which historic specific geographies of memory come into embodiment. The Indigene concerns fluidity, concerns flux, yet at the same time Indigeneity constitutes itself through temporal permanence, through a changing fixity of the corporeal. Concerning the corporeal, we must think of the materiality of identity, we must think about the ways in which language comes to be embodied and the implications of the socio-cultural; how power and privilege come to be ascribed to a particular self whereby the self becomes preconditioned through the idealized language constituting the imperial self. We are wary of the relationship between the Indigenous self and the Imperial self; how these moments become constitutive, immanent and internalized by the said Diasporic body. As Fanon (1967) notes, we seek to extricate the colonial self as embedded within the Indigene. Vital to this task is the process of decolonization. Decolonization is about praxis, and Smith (1999) also reminds us decolonization is about healing, transformation, recovery, development, survival and self-determination.

Within the myriad configurations of Euromodernity, explicating the Indigenous experience as lived through the Diaspora is quite a complex process. For example, how we come to know the Indigene through the governance of uncertainty presents the Diasporic self with particular questions, such as: Where does knowledge reside? What counts as knowledge? How do we come to know and understand knowledge? Part of writing Diasporic Indigeneity means the Diasporic self ought to be cognizant at any given time of surroundings, everyday social interactions. One of the challenges here for the Indigene is teasing out the way, or making sense of how, the self comes to know a particular moment, or understanding how a particular experience is speaking to or resonating with the body. Be it the Diasporic self having an innate sense, or being intuitive, or if we want to talk about spirituality, we have this trust in the self, this firm belief of knowing or of framing a particular time of space as meaningful, as of telling us something, as of speaking back to us. But how does the Diasporic self come into the material conditions of time and space? How does the Diasporic self pedagogically recognize the material conditions of that experiential moment which is incommensurable (van Manen, 1997)? How does the Diasporic self reconcile with not being able, in a sum tangible way, to determine/interpret as an assured given some quantified value of one's lived experience?

Indeed, given the constellation of Diasporic Indigeneity and the ensuing interwovenness within the contemporary epoch of globalization, the Diasporic experience ought not be *bracketed* to some irreducible protean moment. Writing through Diasporic Indigeneity is countervailing to the dominant historical tropes of social science research. Diasporic Indigeneity challenges the dissemination of value-free, neutral-objective forms of knowledge and works to shift the governing edict of what it means to engage in critical social science research. Writing through the Indigene is always already a site of contestation for research and knowledge production. Indigeneity as method is about embodied knowledge, in that Indigeneity as method is about writing/thinking through Diasporic ways of knowing one's reality. With Diasporic Indigeneity, the self, the body, personal memory and experiences congeal to form the contentious relationship of researcher/researched. Diasporic Indigeneity as method means engaging the Diasporic self through voice, subjectivity and local politics that move beyond historical positivist social science research methods.

Writing and Researching the "Diasporized Identity"

The term "Diasporized identity" is used to gesture to the dynamism, transitional and fluidity of identities, and more importantly, to the claim that presence in the Diaspora itself shapes and informs the very identities we claim for ourselves. How bodies are read in a Diasporic context is relevant in this assertion. At this juncture we reiterate a critical question: What are the ways in which Diasporic Indigeneity experiences race and simultaneously attend to the tacit ways in which the Diasporic self come to identify and understand the racialization process? That is, to attend the ways in which the Diasporic self senses race beyond its phenotypical configurations, to be able to retrieve deeply embedded codifications of race in any given space, to be cognizant about the terms in which race comes to be embodied, be it absent or present. We must ask then, how do spaces come to be codified, named, organized, represented and acknowledged? In that, spaces are not encoded without a body. Be it past, present or future, spaces come to be encoded through an embodied historical materialism. What we are concerned with here is, how then do these embodied historic material conditions come to exist and inform the everyday lived experiences of the Diasporic self? How does the Diasporic self, be it through innate/intuition, come into such political/critical interpretive strategies to engage the ensuing public sphere? So against the particulars and universals of race, the myriad binary coordinates of the human experience, existentially existing through historic-specific constellations of race, how does the Diasporic self know and under-stand when the particular space, interaction, communicative exchanges come to be nuanced through colonial meanings of race and simultaneously engender a particular performative action onto the self that culminates in desire as a way of knowing, as a way of making meaning, as a way of understand-ing the self? What then is this materiality of desire, this materiality of longing for a particular type of humanism as colonially configured through the classifications of Euromodernity?

It is worth noting that we are thinking of desire/longing immanent to the Diasporic self in the con-text of Western geographies. The challenge here for the Indigene is not only to interpret these incom-mensurable moments of desire immanent to the experience of the Diasporic self, but also to interpolate these incommensurable moments into some textualized medium from which critical social science research can draw. Such is the challenge for social science research when the Indigene is not readily ac-cessible, from let us say, primarily textual documents, cultural artifacts, memoirs, photographs, video texts, or when the Indigene is not retrieved through the formal communicative exchange of interviews. One of the struggles for the researcher(s) is to have to present or to write from these spatio-temporal moments deeply tucked away within the Diaspora, so concerning the lived experience of the Diasporic self, past and present alike; personal memory of the *before*, *then* and *now* forms the material provisions for the Indigene. We locate these memorable pedagogical moments as vantage/starting points from which to critically interpret the lived social environment of the Diasporic self. We speak through these local socio-cultural histories, that is, think through these histories, these personal lived moments as a raw resource, as a reservoir for the Indigene. With this approach, we seek to understand how different Diasporic bodies come to be equipped with or strategically maneuver through the cosmopolitanism of Euromodernity by way of negotiating within their tapestry of selected cultural attitudes, choice of expressions, ways of knowing, speech patterns, the how-to-act moments, the everyday variables that the "Othered" body comes to know and understand (Hall, 2005, 2007a, 2007b; Giddens, 1991; Trifonas, 2005; Appadurai, 1996; Anderson, 1991; Foster, 2007).

Today we know social thought/theory is not constructed in some pure, pristine, utopian context. Social thought is very much filled with the presupposed, or has been filled with/through previous experiences. We are all bringing to our present-day communicative moments experience/knowledge from the *before*. Humanism as we have experienced today involves different socializing processes. To say to be human is to be social, then, is a bit of an understatement. One quality of the human that we are working through throughout this chapter is this concept of the spiritual self/the authentic self/ the archetype self. How does one come to recognize this being of a spiritual self? In a sense it is about coming to know and understand a particular self as being distinct from the everyday discursive practice. Historical readings of social science research have recognized the spiritual self as a contentious site. If we are attempting to have an honest conversation concerning the different humanisms we experience, we have to speak about the limits and possibilities concerning the existential subject as being formed through multiple socio-cultural conditions, to think about the Diaspora through the different loci of the self as embodied through *ontological lineage/ontological primacy*, to have to work with this concept of the *primordial*, and historical traces of Indigenous memory (Fanon, 1967; Sekyi-Otu, 1996; Senghor, 2001; Dei, in press; Gordon, 1995). How do these moments become dependent on the particular body being the dominant body or the racialized/minoritized body? And also how do these bodies indepen-dently become codependent on particular variants of, let us say, the land, the ocean and the time and space of the transatlantic?

We have to speak about, and as Marcuse (1991) mentions, when the deepest level of intuition and our innate ways of knowing are always already preconditioned through the dominant epistemes of Euromodernity and, as Chomsky and Foucault (2006) have discussed, the relationship between in-nate ways of knowing as being codetermined through the social environment. Many who have written before have said writing is not neutral, innocent or apolitical, that all bodies of writing are political, having an invested interest with consequences and implications (Denzin & Lincoln, 2000; Smith, 1999; Guba & Lincoln, 1994; Dei, 2005; Gubrium & Holstein, 2000; Ladson-Billings, 2000; Clifford, 1986; Okolie, 2005) At the same time, we join other scholars working for equity and social justice in being compelled to push back against writing as a form of scientism (Habermas, 1971); that is, knowledge becoming legitimized through particular procedures of standardized inquiry. We are well aware that historically the trope of positivism has saturated the social sciences and educational research philosophies, that writing denotes objectivity.

Presently, conventional educational philosophies continue to organize contemporary classroom curricula, continue to inscribe the everyday socializing processes for youth as they play out in the context of schooling and education (Marcuse, 2009a, 2009b; McLaren & Farahmandpur, 2005; Apple, 1995: Giroux, 2001; Bourdieu & Passeron, 2000). With the Diasporic body becoming more and more implicated with the complicity of capitalist West, and as the benevolent humanitarianism of the neo-liberal agenda is mouthed, we ought to think of the ways in which these partitioned spaces, these legitimized boundaries of the Western state come to be accepted within the public sphere through particular pieces of writing, from journalism to the academic text, from electronic public images to recognizing the different ways in which citizenship comes to organize the everyday social space.

The Question of Research and Method

How then and what are the ways in which the public/social space of the Diasporic self comes to be constituted? What are the colonial variants involved? And how does the Diasporic self come to recognize and know the colonial variant in relation to, let us say, schooling and education, governance and state formation, development and imperialism, to citizenry and identity formation, to the quality of the human condition? As such Diasporic Indigeneity draws from the historic-personal, from the self, from personal narratives, from local histories, to autobiographical stories to counter the immanent imperial self. Needless to say the lived experiences of Diasporic Indigeneity are subjective moments through which the Diasporic body comes to know/understand the Diasporic self through the complex lived experience of race/racism. Diasporic Indigeneity is about a history of embodied knowledge. We are mindful of the way these knowledges come to congeal through a series of colonial histories and of them having centered and continued to shape and inform the Diasporic self. So again, in more ways than one, we are writing to not necessarily undo these moments, but more to find ways to unlearn these colonial imbued ways of knowing and understanding the everyday lived social of the Diaspora. This speaks to the lifelong journey of decolonization. Coming to better know and better understand the colonial logic is part of the decolonization process, part of the never-ending journey of coming to always have the need to make some sense of this experience of race. Yet, some have asked, decolonization for whom?

Decolonization is about dialoguing with the present, past, future alike; decolonization is about being reflexive through the experiential self and, as Smith (1999) says, lending to healing and transformation. Decolonization is about thinking through personal memory to a politics of action. Decolonization ought to be for all; hence we write self-reflexively as a strategic method to decolonize. Writing Diasporic Indigeneity is about transforming the Indigenous self by way of decolonizing; it is about writing Indigenous experiences into text, to claim agency through writing; it is about claiming epistemological authority.

Noting Diasporic Indigeneity involves some complexities. Research, in and of itself, has historically been revealed as a colonial nomenclature. Yet as the Diaspora becomes driven from and through the experience of race, the Diasporic self becomes constituted through a myriad of complex classifications as discursively entangled through the humanism of Euromodernity. Diasporic self is always already embedded within the governing imprint of colonial modernity as interwoven through the complexities of gender, ableism, race, religion and sexuality; that is, the self comes to be performed and desired through the congeries of gender, race, heterosexuality and masculinist ableism. We are asking: Is the colonial ableist gendered self the archetype of race? What then are the implications for critical qualitative research when writing Diasporic Indigeneity through the experience of the Indigenous self? And what are the ways in which the Indigenous self comes to know, understand and dialogue with the historical, colonial, ableist self? How might we understand the ontological ableized self through Indigeneity and the colonial encounter? By way of an anti-colonial interpretive framework, how might we understand the Indigenous self through the Diaspora and as emerging through the human conditions of colonial modernity? We have a passion for social change, social justice and equity. Our hearts particularly relate with peoples who have been oppressed because of color, peoples who have been oppressed because of this thing called race; our politics draw from people who have violently been determined as sub/less than human because of the determinants of race, gender, class, disability and religion.

Writing Diasporic Indigeneity is to deliberately move away from such tropes of positivism as *fieldwork*, *empiricism*, *sample size*, and *data*. Instead we posit these moments as being experiential, whereby the Diasporic self has embodied agency to impute limits and open up possibilities for the Indigene. These limits, in and of themselves, are constituted through the lived experiences of the Diaspora, which are also contingent on local histories and socio-cultural orientations. To write Diasporic Indigeneity means having a dialogue with these experiential moments; to write Diasporic Indigeneity means thinking through what, for the purpose of this study, we are locating here as artifacts. It means coming to pin down, to disentangle temporal moments as being artifactual; it means thinking through the materiality of race to come to know and understand the Diasporic self. In a sense, then, the Diasporic self forms the governing artifact for the Indigene. It becomes the question of how the self recognizes race through various objects, through different bodies, through different moments in time, through different places. It becomes about the ways in which the self comes to interpret a given experience through colonial codifications of race. It is about the coming to make tangible, to make material sense of these spatial moments in a way that comes to archive the self as a governing artifactual trope through the experiential contexts of race as immanent to histories of colonial time and space.

Diasporic Indigeneity is historically specific to the self, in that the Indigene is augured in and through the lived experiences, personal narratives, personal memory of the self. One of the challenges for the self, then, is retrieving/recalling Indigeneity, the coming to know, understand, to make sense of these local inscribed moments; how these experiential moments of the Diaspora come to be represented in a tangible way. Writing Diasporic Indigeneity through the self is about being present through transparency, through being accountable and responsible. Writing Indigeneity through the self is about being present in a way that gives from within the human: it is about self-reflexivity, it is about transformation—transformation in a particular way, which starts from within the self. Writing Diasporic Indigeneity means thinking through colonial geographies, those spaces we come to problematically know as *Third World*; those spaces where embedded are histories of enslavement, militarized violence, colonial pillage; those spaces where embedded are histories of destruction as being willed through Euromodernity. Writing Indigeneity is about making sense of particular geographies of impoverishment—that form of impoverishment that has been historically ontologized, whereby local peoples with colonizing histories have come to know and accept it as some said birthright.

We approach the Indigenous self as if the self were a pastiche, being mindful that the human experience collectively works in and out of tandem, that the human experience is relational, not independent of bodies—that we are existing with each other, not in some formula-like, straight-line method, seeking some pristine utopia of harmony. Instead we acknowledge the myriad intersections, the interwovenness of how the self comes to socialize, how the self recognizes the interplay of difference embedded in the human experience, the ensuing entanglements, the different power arrangements as they come to be classified through race, ethnicity, culture, ableism, sexuality, gender and class. We are cognizant of not positioning these classificatory arrangements in some said hierarchal order. But at the same time we are saying, for the purpose of writing Diasporic Indigeneity, that given the specific histories embedded in colonialism, race takes up the central location to critically engage the lived experiences of the self in order to understand the circumscribed social context of the Diaspora. Hence, we work critically to engage the different intersections of race, and in particular, locate race as a material artifact, as a vantage point to come to dialogue with these intersectional entanglements of the human experience. We work with embodied ways of knowing—those knowledges formed through the experiences of being racialised-minorotised/oppressed—to converse with the different practices which come to shape and form the Diasporic self; to come to identify the limitations and possibilities concerning the politics of the different geo self within the Western metropolis.

Too often, these embodied ways of knowing from racialised-minoritised bodies are discarded, or swept to the side, determined as not having a contributing value towards the meaningful production of knowledge. But who gets to decide what is meaningful, and what exactly is this thing called knowledge? In many ways writing Diasporic Indigeneity is about writing back to these historically institutionalized, augured constructs of what, in a sense, defines knowledge. In doing so, and through the Diasporic self, we are committed to the processes of decolonization and the importance of finding anti-colonial ways of knowing, keeping in mind that central to anti-colonial knowledging is coming to know through the embodied experience of racialized-minoritized bodies. Writing Indigeneity involves interpreting and speaking from personal memory in order to understand the experience of self within the governing social context; it involves telling one's story. Writing Diasporic Indigeneity ought to engage with a critical, integrative, anti-colonial discursive framework; writing Indigeneity ought to be imbued ethically and morally. Writing through the Diasporic self is about personal inventory to hold the said self accountable and responsible. It is about coming to know and understand the colonial that governs the everyday local space. The caution here is that these ethical and moral principles might be, in some tacit way, colonially informed.

One of the questions emerging from the foregoing discussion is that, given the different ethno-cultural bodies, ethno-cultural bodies that come to know and understand differently, how do we come to make sense of some governing ethical and moral principle on society, and whose principle are we talking about? Writing Diasporic Indigeneity must consider the different ethno-cultural communal ways of knowing, the many historic specificities of colonialism and the manner in which these ethical and moral principles come to be formed in and through these historic, specific colonial epistemologies. Writing Indigeneity through the Diasporic self must consider the necessity to speak and write from the everyday localized voice. To return to the matter of ethical and moral principles and coming to understand the Diasporic self differently through Indigeneity, through ethno-cultural bodies, the question of essentializing is important; that is, to strategically essentialize or not to (Gunaratnam, 2003; Dei, 2005; Razack, 1998; Bulmer & Solomos, 2004). Much has been written on "strategic essentialism"; by strategic essentialism, we are thinking about the limits and possibilities of reading particular bodies through fixed discursive scripts as contextualized through colonial geographies of time and space. We are thinking about the social conditions of existence, the relationship concerning the historic material restrictions of modernity, and the way in which power and privilege come to determine the location and simultaneously dislocate particular bodies. How often does the Indigenous self come into a particular body or a particular space and quietly assign colonial values to these interactive moments? In that, the Indigenous self knows how to act, or address the conversation, be it colonially imbued through innate ways of knowing or understanding through intuition.

It is important that we counter those colonial narratives that come to reduce racialized bodies; hence part and parcel of this process of naming the materiality of day-to-day colonial artifacts is acknowledging those binary encoded meanings, which cryptically script the different geographies of race, keeping in mind the limitations, possibilities, consequences and implications of approaching this human experience through these textualized frames. Hence, to write Indigeneity is to consider race/ethnicity/culture. Writing the Indigenous self implicitly means working with and against essentialism; it is to wittingly dialogue with colonial narratives as if it were some spatial *Truth* system. Writing from, with and through the Indigenous self is not without risks and perils. One has to think about questions concerning privacy; one has to ponder how much of the Indigenous self to reveal, how much of one's emotions and feelings ought to be expressed in the writing, what stories to tell, what stories not to tell, what histories, what memories to include. Writing Diasporic Indigeneity means dialoguing with one's feelings; it means writing from places embedded with emotions; it means working with memories of pain, memories of rage, memories of violence; it means dialoguing through honesty; it means acknowledging power and privilege; it means recognizing the need to open up spaces for racialized bodies; it means all bodies being committed to social justice, to social change, be it the privilege, the dominant or the oppressed. Writing Diasporic Indigeneity also means writing from a particular place where rage resides; writing Indigeneity means writing, speaking through rage, through spiritual injury, through loss, through suffering. Yet for the Indigenous self to speak about suffering and violence in the context of ethics and morals to some extent becomes silencing. The experience of rage is alive for all bodies that have experienced oppression and cannot be discounted (see also hooks, 1995).

To reiterate, conceptualizing Diasporic Indigeneity through the Indigenous self and coming to do anti-colonial theorizing are not distinct moments (Fanon, 1963; Memmi, 1991; Césaire, 1972; James, 1989; Dei, 2000; Dei & Kempf, 2006; Dei & Asgharzadeh, 2001). We understand these approaches as being part and parcel of each other, as being constitutive of the lived struggle and political practices of the Diaspora. If Diasporic Indigeneity concerns itself with thinking through the lived experience of the Indigenous self in order to make meaning of one's governing social reality—and if the central question is, how does the Indigenous self make meaning of the Diaspora?—then we ought to think of these moments, these approaches as not disjointed, compartmentalized or fragmented, but existing constitutively. Yet writing Diasporic Indigeneity involves coming to know and coming to disentangle the politics of the Indigenous self; it involves the politics of the researcher. If we are talking about how the Indigenous self experiences race/racism, then we must engage in dialogue with the theoretical framework of the anti-colonial. Yet the anti-colonial framework is not partial, neutral or without a politics.

Every methodological framework is embedded with its politics. The concerns, though, are more about the consequences, the implications for taking up such a methodological position within academe, and the ways in which these theoretical frameworks accord methodological currency to the researcher. We also need to remind ourselves of the way knowledge comes to reside within publication houses, to remember what is deemed knowledge and how this knowledge comes to be positioned/classified hierarchically. We also need to think about how Indigenous ways of knowing, this human experience as revealed through publications and research, come to be treated as abject by particular archives of knowledge, or particular publishing houses. So be it the body of the dominant, or the body of the racialised-minoritized, one has to engage with these ethical and moral questions. For example, what does it mean for the dominant self to have to have to write about the experience of race? What does it mean to engage qualitative research through thinking about society in terms of race, Diaspora, nation-state, modernity, identity and culture? What does it mean to write from and through these locations where, in a sense, the Indigenous self has to write back; where, in a sense, the Indigenous self is writing from a different and simultaneously from the same place? What is at stake and what are the challenges? These are some of the questions posed through the anti-colonial framework. If we are embodying this classification of researcher, then as researcher we must question how we come to know and make sense of our experiences of race/racism; we must be cognizant of the underlying assumptions of coming to know and understand these interactive moments that concern race. We know that historically with the modernist project, social science research was everything but ethical or moral—in fact being ethical, being moral meant conclusively producing a particular type of subject, a particular type of human. Writing Diasporic Indigenity is about coming to know and understand the humanism of the particular, lived Indigenous self. It is about understanding the relationship of freedoms and unfreedoms, the liberal and illiberal tensions, which come to entangle and envelop what it means to be human through the web of local histories.

Conclusion

In concluding, we assert that, ultimately, writing Diasporic Indigeneity affirms the Indigenous self; writing Diasporic Indigeneity affirms local ways of understanding the said experience through personal memory/histories, through different geographies as contextualized through time, place, space and bodies alike. It is about being reflexive on the *before, now, then* to come to locate particular moments, exchanges, objects, artifacts through the Indigene. In fact, it is like a continued reified process, having to think through local events, local experiences, to search through time and space in order to retrieve and at the same time transform these intangible moments to some tangible good. There is no guarantee here that those moments selected are some pure, absolute, ideal moments that become the right fit. Such is the challenge in doing qualitative research through the Indigenous self, that human relations are not some rigid, finite variable ready to be plugged into some homogenous equation that, in only a matter of time, some eager expert body will rush to solve. We all know that human relations are filled with incommensurable moments, some of which are love, joy, sorrow, the unknowing, pain, pleasure, emotions, the sensual, the erotic and, let us say, spirituality. The challenge for critical social science research is coming to know and understand these incommensurable moments of the Indigene under the historical colonial nomenclature of research.

References

Anderson, B. (1991). *Imagined communities: Reflections on the origin and spread of nationalism.* London, England: Verso.

Appadurai, A. (1996). *Modernity at large: Cultural dimensions of globalization.* Minneapolis: University of Minnesota Press.

Apple, M. (1995). *Education and power.* New York, NY: Routledge.

Bourdieu, P., & Passeron J.-C. (2000). *Reproduction in education, society and culture.* Thousand Oaks, CA: Sage.

Bulmer, M., & Solomos, J. (Eds.). (2004). Introduction: Researching race and racism. In *Researching Race and Racism* (pp. 1–15). London, England: Routledge.

Césaire, A. (1972). *Discourse on colonialism.* New York, NY: Monthly Review Press.

Chomsky, N., & Foucault, M. (2006). *The Chomsky-Foucault debate: On human nature.* New York, NY: New Press.

Clifford, J. (1986). Introduction: partial truths. In J. Clifford & G. J. Marcus (Eds.), *Writing culture: The poetics and politics of ethnography* (pp. 1–26). Berkeley: University of California Press.

Dei, G. J. S. (2000). The role of indigenous knowledges in the academy. *International Journal of Inclusive Education, 4*(2), 39–56.

Dei, G. J. S. (2005). Critical issues in anti-racist research methodologies: An introduction. In G. J. S. Dei & G. S. Johal (Eds.), *Critical issues in anti-racist research methodologies* (pp. 1–28). New York, NY: Peter Lang.

Dei, G. J. S. (2008). Indigenous knowledge studies and the next generation: Pedagogical possibilities for anti-colonial education. *Australian Journal of Indigenous Education, 37* (Suppl. 2008), 5–13.

Dei, G. J. S. (Ed.). (2011). *Indigenous philosophies and critical education.* New York, NY: Peter Lang.

Dei, G. J. S. (in press). *Racial politics and the question of black unity: Theorizing Africa beyond its boundaries.* Toronto, ON, Canada: University of Toronto Press.

Dei, G. J. S., & Asgharzadeh, A. (2001). The power of social theory: Towards an anti-colonial discursive framework. *Journal of Educational Thought, 353,* 297–323.

Dei, G. J. S., & Kempf, A. (Eds.). (2006). *Anti-colonialism and education: The politics of resistance.* Rotterdam, The Netherlands: Sense.

Denzin, N. K., & Lincoln, Y. S. (2000). Introduction: The discipline and practice of qualitative research. In N. K. Denzin & Y. S. Lincoln (Eds.), *Handbook of qualitative research* (2nd ed., pp. 1–28). Thousand Oaks, CA: Sage.

Fanon, F. (1963). *The wretched of the earth.* New York, NY: Grove Press.

Fanon, F. (1967). *Black skin, white masks.* New York, NY: Grove Press.

Foster, C. (2007). *Blackness and modernity: The colour of humanity and the quest for freedom.* Montreal, QC, Canada: McGill-Queen's University Press.

Gallagher, S. (1992). *Hermeneutics and education.* Albany: State University of New York Press.

Giddens, A. (1991). *Modernity and self-identity: Self and society in the late modern age.* Stanford, CA: Stanford University Press.

Giroux, A. H. (2001). *Theory and resistance in education: Towards a pedagogy for the opposition.* Westport, CT: Bergin & Garvey.

Gordon, R. L. (1995). *Fanon and the crisis of European man: An essay on philosophy and the human sciences.* New York, NY: Routledge.

Guba, E.g., & Lincoln, Y. S. (1994). Competing paradigms in qualitative research. In N. K. Denzin & Y. S. Lincoln (Eds.), *Handbook of qualitative research* (pp. 105–117). Thousand Oaks, CA: Sage.

Gubrium, J. F., & Holstein, J. A. (2000). Analyzing interpretive practice. In N. K. Denzin & Y. S. Lincoln (Eds.), *Handbook of qualitative research* (pp. 487–508). Thousand Oaks, CA: Sage.

Gunaratnam, Y. (2003). *Researching race and ethnicity: Methods, knowledge and power*. London, England: Sage.

Habermas, J. (1971). *Knowledge and human interests*. Boston, MA: Beacon Press.

Hall, S. (2005). New ethnicities. In D. Morley & K. Chen (Eds.), *Stuart Hall: Critical dialogues in cultural studies* (pp. 441–449). New York, NY: Routledge.

Hall, S. (2007a). The global, the local, and the return of ethnicity. In S. Hall, D. Held, D. Hubert, & K. Thompson (Eds.), *Modernity: An introduction to modern societies* (pp. 623–629). Oxford, England: Blackwell.

Hall, S. (2007b). Fundamentalism, diaspora and hybridity. In S. Hall, D. Held, D. Hubert, & K. Thompson (Eds.), *Modernity: An introduction to modern societies* (pp. 629–632). Oxford, England: Blackwell.

hooks, b. (1995). *Killing rage: Ending racism*. New York, NY: Henry Holt.

James, C. L. R. (1989). *The Black Jacobins: Toussaint L'Ouverture and the San Domingo Revolution*. New York, NY: Vintage Books.

Kincheloe, J., & Steinberg, S. (2008). Indigenous knowledges in education: Complexities, dangers and profound benefits. In N. K. Denzin, Y. S. Lincoln, & L. T. Smith (Eds.), *Handbook of critical and indigenous methodologies* (pp. 135–156). Los Angeles, CA: Sage.

Ladson-Billings, G. (2000). Racialized discourses and ethnic epistemologies. In N. K. Denzin & Y. S. Lincoln, *Handbook of qualitative research* (2nd. ed., pp. 257–277). Thousand Oaks, CA: Sage.

Marcuse, H. (1991). *One dimensional man: Studies in the ideology of advanced industrial society*. Boston, MA: Beacon Press.

Marcuse, H. (2009a) Lecture on education, Brooklyn College, 1968. In D. Kellner, T. Lewis, C. Pierce, & K. Daniel Cho (Eds.), *Marcuse's challenge to education* (pp. 33–38). New York, NY: Rowman & Littlefield.

Marcuse, H. (2009b). Lecture on higher education and politics, Berkeley, 1975. In D. Kellner, T. Lewis, C. Pierce, & K. Daniel Cho (Eds.), *Marcuse's challenge to education* (pp. 39–43). New York, NY: Rowman & Littlefield.

McLaren, P., & Farahmandpur, R. (2005). *Teaching against global capitalism and the New Imperialism*. New York, NY: Rowman & Littlefield.

Memmi, A. (1991). *The colonizer and the colonized* (Introduction by J.-P. Sartre). Boston, MA: Beacon Press.

Moustakas, C. (1990). *Heuristic research: Design, methodology, and applications*. Newbury Park, CA: Sage.

Okolie, A. (2005). Towards an anti-racist research framework. In G. J. S Dei & G. S. Johal (Eds.), *Critical issues in anti-racist research methodologies* (pp. 241–268). New York, NY: Peter Lang.

Razack, S. (1998). *Looking white people in the eye: Gender, race and culture in courtrooms and classrooms*. Toronto, ON, Canada: University of Toronto Press.

Ricoeur, P. (1994). *Oneself as another*. Chicago, IL: University of Chicago Press.

Sekyi-Otu, A. (1996). *Fanon's dialectic of experience*. Cambridge, MA: Harvard University Press.

Semali, M. L., & Kincheloe, L. J. (1999). Introduction: What is indigenous knowledge and why should we study it? In M. L. Semali & L. J. Kincheloe (Eds.), *What is indigenous knowledge?: Voices from the academy* (pp. 3–57). New York, NY: Falmer Press.

Senghor, L. (2001). Negritude and modernity or negritude as a humanism for the twentieth century. In R. Bernasconi (Ed.), *Race* (pp. 143–166). Malden, MA: Blackwell.

Smith, L. T. (1999). *Decolonizing methodologies: Research and indigenous peoples*. London, England: Zed Books.

Trifonas, P. P. (2005). Communities of difference: A preface to a knowledge of ourselves as another. In P. P. Trifonas (Ed.), *Communities of difference: Culture, language, technology* (pp. xiii–xix). New York, NY: Palgrave Macmillan.

Van Manen, M. (1997). *Researching lived experience: Human science for an action sensitive pedagogy*. London, ON: Althouse Press.

CHAPTER TWENTY-ONE

Choosing Agency in the Midst of Vulnerability: Using Critical Disability Theory to Examine a Disaster Narrative

Elizabeth McAdams Ducy, Laura M. Stough, and M. Carolyn Clark

Critical Disability Theory examines the ways in which individuals with disabilities have historically, socially, and politically been marginalized and disenfranchised in society, and challenges traditionally held assumptions and presumptions. Critical Disability theorists see the status of individuals with disabilities as embedded in the political structure of societies, which can lead to "dis-citizenship," and that the struggle for equality by individuals with disabilities is an issue of power (Devlin & Pothier, 2006). Disability in this view can be seen as socially constructed in societies that privilege the "normal" over the "abnormal." Recent literature on disability was heavily influenced by the civil rights movement of the 1960s, and the field continues to be dominated by discussions of policy matters (Gleeson, 1997). This orientation has made disability theories compatible with critical research in that it holds injustice and inequality towards individuals with disabilities as central concerns.

Our work in critical disability studies is concerned with the role of disability in disasters, with both how disasters impact individuals with disabilities and how societal factors predispose individuals with disabilities to disaster risk. As such, our work aligns most closely with the social vulnerability perspective of disaster, which was primarily developed by researchers from the field of sociology (see Cutter, Boruff, & Shirley, 2003; Peacock & Ragsdale, 1997; Philips & Morrow, 2007). While disasters are usually perceived as random events, the social vulnerability perspective argues that some groups are placed disproportionately at risk to disaster due to a combination of societal, economic, and political factors (Cutter et al., 2003; Fothergill & Peek, 2004). The social vulnerability perspective thus argues that societies collectively determine who lives in disaster-prone areas and who subsequently will have limited defenses against disasters (Hewitt, 1997). From this perspective, disasters not only affect some groups differentially, but expose pre-existing inequalities leading to disproportionate damage, loss of property, or even death (Wisner et al., 2004). Children, the elderly, women, racial minorities, the poor, persons with physical or mental disabilities, and immigrants have been identified as especially vulnerable to the harmful impacts of disaster (Cutter et al., 2003). For example, the cheap prices of land in flood plain areas make it more likely that people living in poverty rent or buy residences in these areas. When flooding occurs, those that are poor are more likely to be affected by the disaster, while those of more affluent means living in less affected areas nearby are less likely to experience personal or material harm. Researchers using a social vulnerability perspective not only are interested in the effects of disaster on marginalized populations but also examine the social factors that mitigate the effects of disaster on these groups. As a result, vulnerability to disasters is not seen as situated within individuals; rather it is presented as the result of choices that societies make about what populations have access to protection from disasters and their aftermath.

Research on disasters and individuals with disabilities has been limited, and most of this work consists of studies and commentaries that were completed post-Katrina. Hurricane Katrina was one of the most destructive storms in United States history in terms of strength, damage, and loss of life (Blake, Rappaport, & Landsea, 2007). At the time Hurricane Katina made landfall, it was estimated that 23 percent of the population in New Orleans were individuals with disabilities (National Council on Disability, 2006). This reflects a higher incidence of disability than the reported 19 percent of the population for the United States (U.S. Census Bureau, 2008). The increased vulnerability of people with disabilities was documented by reports of individuals with disabilities who faced life-threatening situations. For example, many people with physical disabilities were found to be unable to evacuate during Hurricane Katrina due to inaccessible transportation (National Council on Disability, 2006). Other studies (see White, Fox, Rooney, & Cahill, 2007; White, B., 2006) found that systems of emergency notification, for example television and radio broadcasts, were inaccessible to many individuals and that emergency management organizations were unprepared for the needs of people with disabilities. As a whole, the literature in disaster and disaster recovery suggests that individuals with disabilities are disproportionately affected by disaster (Fox, White, Rooney, & Rowland, 2007; Hemingway & Priestley, 2006; McGuire, Ford, & Okoro, 2007; Peek & Stough, 2010).

The purpose of these studies has been to illustrate the unequal impact that disasters have on individuals with disabilities, primarily those with physical disabilities. This emphasis has been, in part, a response to the previously described negative outcomes following Hurricane Katrina, and a push for social and legislative safeguards against the reoccurrence of such events. However, the activist stance simultaneously has inadvertently portrayed people with disabilities as victims in that they are portrayed as being more vulnerable to disaster, as encountering more societal discrimination, and as experiencing more negative outcomes. In our own work we have also highlighted discrepancies in the supports and services made available to individuals with disabilities during disasters. As a result, these reports do not provide examples of people with disabilities taking action; rather they are stories of how individuals with disabilities have been acted upon. The inadvertent message that may be construed from this work is that people with disabilities have less agency and are always highly dependent on others when disasters occur.

Long-term Recovery Study

In 2005, the second author began studying the recovery of individuals with disabilities following Hurricane Katrina, and was later joined by the first and, for the purposes of this project, the third author. Some of this research consisted of evaluating the services that people with disabilities were receiving post-disaster, some included interviews or surveys of disaster case managers, some used focus groups or interviews with people with disabilities. Much of what was learned was gathered from governmental white papers, disability advocacy groups, and from press reports.

Our stance in conducting the research described in this manuscript admittedly aligned with that of the predominant discourse in which researchers highlight the disadvantages and difficulties that people with disabilities encountered in response to the storm. As part of this study, we conducted in-depth, face-to-face interviews with individuals with disabilities who had been living in southern Louisiana during the storm and who had relocated to Texas. We were interested in the changes that had taken place in their lives and their current long-term recovery status. The interview questions addressed issues pertaining to their daily functioning, such as their income, employment, leisure activities, place of residence, and medical needs both before and after the storm. These interviews generated significant information on the changes in the participants' daily functioning after the storm and difficulties encountered in their long-term recovery. The interviews also provided an opportunity for many of the participants to share their narratives on their experience with Hurricane Katrina. It was in this context that we met Mark, an African American male with a mild intellectual disability. His narrative challenged us to rethink our assumptions about how those with disabilities deal with natural disasters. In this chapter we examine one story in his narrative that was especially salient because it shaped his sense of identity and gave us insight into how the disabled can claim agency in the midst of disaster.

Mark's Introduction and Story: "Drowning Excerpt"

Mark was 47 years old at the time Hurricane Katrina hit. He was part of a close-knit family, he was living at his brother George's apartment, and he had constant interaction with his other two brothers and four sisters who lived in the New Orleans area. One of his sisters was diabetic, and Mark visited her daily to assist her with any needed tasks. Mark worked full time at the New Orleans Superdome. His work duties included setting up for sporting events, and he often put in long hours. Despite the hard work, Mark enjoyed the job and felt that he was making good money. Mark did not have a lot of free time because of his work commitments, but in his time off he shot pool or visited with friends and family. He was also a lead singer in a New Orleans church choir. Mark did not have his own transportation and would usually walk, catch a ride with someone, or take the bus to get around town. Mark did not finish high school but did receive his GED from a local education center. He spoke English, as well as some Creole.

Mark relocated to San Antonio, Texas, after the storm and was living with his brother George in a large apartment complex. His remaining six siblings all relocated to different cities. The geographical separation meant that Mark no longer communicated daily with his siblings. In the new city, Mark spent his time walking around, talking to neighbors, or watching television. Mark did not have steady employment and completed odd jobs to get income. He also received initial financial assistance from FEMA and partial assistance from employees of the apartment complex. Mark did not have any involvement with church activities in San Antonio. After the storm, Mark developed knee problems and walked with a limp. His life in Texas was radically different from his life in New Orleans.

During his interview, Mark told a dramatic story about his experience as the flooding of the city began to reach dangerous levels.

> So anyway, when we came downstairs it was flooded downstairs inside the apartment building, right. That is where my oldest brother stay at. Okay, so we out there and you don't, you forget where your bearings at, you know what I am saying, and the next thing I know my other older brother, not Freddie, but George, dipped off, so I had go out there and jump out there and get him, oh man, and bring him back; the water was over our head. And my younger brother, all he was doin was stood back and the water was up to his neck. And he was just hollerin "Get him, get him!" and I said, "I got him, I got him." And both of us went under water and some kind of way, man, both of us came out of the water, and I brought him back, back to where he can stand level where the water was level up to his chest. Man, that was weird. My brother was crying, he had me crying, everybody was crying. There was all kinds of things happening, man.

Mark told this story in response to a question about where he was living in New Orleans. His response, which varied from what we sought to elicit with our research question, alerted us that this chosen narrative was pivotal in Mark's lived experience with Hurricane Katrina. Mark revisited this event two additional times during the interview, with each narrative recounting made in response to a fixed question. In telling his varied narrative, Mark was determined to claim an identity that differed from what we had anticipated. Narrative is a fundamental mode of meaning-making, one that is distinctly human; Fisher (1984) goes so far as to characterize human beings as *homo narrans*. Telling stories is how we make sense of our experience. It is in times of chaos and uncertainty that the importance of narrative is most evident, as Riessman (2008) notes: "Telling stories about difficult times in our lives creates order and contains emotions, allowing a search for meaning and enabling connection with others" (p. 10). Mark clearly creates meaning through his story of saving his brother from drowning. From our perspective as researchers, it offered us a point of entry into his experience and the meaning he gives to it.

The purpose of our chapter is to critically examine the experience of one man against the backdrop of the social vulnerability of individuals with disabilities following Hurricane Katrina. We analyze Mark's story in depth to provide a detailed understanding of how one man with a disability responded to the dangers and challenges of a natural disaster and to understand how that experience impacted him and shaped his identity. Riessman (2008) underscores the power of narrative in this regard by referencing Jerome Bruner: "Individuals, he argues, *become* the autobiographical narratives by which they tell about their lives" (p. 10).

Method

Any story contains both what is said (content) and how it is said (structure), and these elements provide two ways to analyze a narrative. We chose both a thematic approach and a structural approach to analyze Mark's interview. A thematic approach was selected in order to examine the themes present throughout Mark's interview, which was appropriate as it enabled us to understand his experience as a whole. To understand the story Mark told about saving his brother from drowning, we used a structural approach; this approach enabled us to see how he constructed his identity as a hero.

To analyze the entire interview we used holistic content analysis, an approach developed by Lieblich, Tuval-Mashiach, and Zilber (1998). This method involves several steps. First we read the interview multiple times in order to discern overarching patterns in the content. Then we wrote our global impression of the interview and further developed our sense of the whole narrative. With that in mind, we then identified specific themes that we considered salient; these could be marked by the amount of space taken up by a theme, repetition of certain thoughts or ideas, and the amount of detail given to a particular event. We also looked for omissions, the absence of a topic that would be expected to be included. Once themes were identified, we reread the transcript for each theme, noting things like when it appeared and disappeared, the context surrounding the elaboration of that theme, and how the speaker evaluated or made sense of the theme. This provided a nuanced understanding of the content of the interview.

To analyze the details of the story of how Mark rescued his brother from the flood waters, which was embedded within the interview, we used a structural approach developed by Gee (1991) and adapted by Riessman (2008). Gee's method is built on the assumption that speech is poetic in structure; in using it, the researcher must first listen closely to the audio recording of the interview and attend to how the respondent speaks. Things like pitch, intonation, rate of speech, hesitations, emphases, and other linguistic markers are carefully noted so that speech units can be revealed. Gee identifies various levels of units, including lines, stanzas, strophes, and parts, but for analytic purposes the stanzas are particularly important:

> A stanza is a group of lines about a single topic, each stanza captures a single "vignette." Each stanza is a particular "take" on a character, action, event, claim or piece of information; each involves a shift of focal participants, focal events, or a change in the time or framing of events from the proceeding stanza. (Gee, 1991, p. 23)

In our analysis of Mark's story, after noting the various linguistic markers present, we retranscribed that portion of the interview to uncover its inner structure. In that process we saw that the story had six stanzas, and we titled each one in order to highlight the topic or main idea of the stanza. We also visually noted what words or phrases were said with emphasis, and we arranged the text on the page in a way that made repetition and parallel structure more obvious. The order in which the words were spoken remains unchanged; what Gee's method reveals is the internal structure of the telling. Riessman (2008) explains this with a musical analogy: "Gee slows down the [informant's] stream of talk to examine how each part fits into the whole, and what each topic shift contributes to the overall effect" (p. 94). We used Gee's structural analysis on Mark's story of rescuing his brother from the flood waters because it was a story he chose to tell three different times during the interview. The version we chose for analysis was the version he told first as it was the most detailed account of the event, and it served to lay claim to his identity as a hero, thus shaping the character of the interview as a whole.

Findings

We present our findings in two parts: those derived through thematic analysis and those uncovered through structural analysis.

Thematic Analysis

In using the holistic content approach of Lieblich et al. (1998), we first developed a global impression of the interview. Mark's narrative was one of a man who continued to struggle with recovery from an extreme catastrophe. His life post-Hurricane Katrina contrasted sharply with his life before the storm. He was forced to confront profoundly challenging situations that resulted in major dislocations, such as from his home and from most of his close-knit family. Despite the challenges discussed in the interview, Mark communicated a strong voice of power when recalling a heroic act in the midst of extreme chaos.

There were three predominant themes that emerged from Mark's interview and were present throughout his narrative. The themes were identified as disruption, the unknown, and chaos.

Disruption. A theme of disruption is not necessarily surprising given the context of a natural disaster. In Mark's narrative, however, disruption permeated different aspects of his life and was present three years after the storm. The theme of disruption was evident in his relationship with his family, his mental functioning, and his source of income. The passage below demonstrated how the disruption often stretched across different areas of his life. Mark commented,

> ....It all depends. When you have a really depressed stage you going to stay in at least like a semi-depressed stage 'cause everyone trying to talk to you, call you on the phone, which I have no more right now. And um, just wondering how your family doing, but you can't reach them, you can't reach out and touch them. Might can talk every couple of weeks or something. They might call a neighbor or they might even call the office upfront.

The passage revealed Mark's disruption within his family. Before Hurricane Katrina made landfall, Mark had close interaction with all of his brothers and sisters and saw four of them daily. Mark's relationship with his siblings was one filled with reciprocated support. Mark's brother allowed Mark to stay at their apartment while Mark assisted his sister with her daily chores. The effects of Hurricane Katrina caused Mark's close-knit family to be ripped apart initially at the evacuation phase of the disaster. Mark, when asked about the evacuation, explained: "They was trying to make sure everyone was together. All the family wasn't together. We worried about who, what, where, man, 'cause at the time, like I was saying, we didn't know where our sisters was." Even three years after the storm the family remained dispersed. Mark said, "We just split all over the place" and "Now everybody just spread all over." At the time of the interview Mark was living with two of his brothers but had little contact with another brother and four sisters. The difficulty in communication was increased, as Mark did not have his own phone and communication with most of his siblings had to be through another source, such as a neighbor or the apartment office. Mark addressed his human need for face-to-face contact when he said, "you can't reach out and touch them." The shift from daily face-to-face interaction to infrequent phone conversations was especially difficult, for him as Mark lost daily supports and the opportunity for him to be a source of support to his family.

The theme of disruption also surfaced when Mark talked about his mental functioning. He talked about being in a "depressed and semi-depressed stage" at the time of the storm. Mark made reference to the drowning experience as being one of the causes for his disrupted state of mental functioning. He said, "After my brothers almost drown that just messed up my head, you know what I am saying?" There were other comments throughout the narrative that hinted at his compromised mental state, such as when he commented, "I can't even think straight, and "…I don't know…distraught from all that…." Mark communicated that he was depressed and having difficulty thinking clearly after the storm. If his depressed mood was indeed the result of the disaster, it placed Mark within the shared narrative of other disaster survivors that developed psychological changes such as depression or post-traumatic stress disorder. Mark's network of support was decreased when his family contact was disrupted, and this could have been detrimental in his ability to seek treatment for his self-disclosed depression.

Mark also experienced disruption of employment after the storm. Mark expressed early in the interview that he enjoyed his full-time job at the Superdome. He displayed pride when talking about his duties and relationships with co-workers. However, Mark was not employed at the time of the interview. He explained his sources of income post-disaster:

> Well, you know FEMA was taking care of us. Every once in a while I might get a job with this man that do drywall or something, you know, to make a little money. And also the people here help me out 'cause they know my situation, the people up at the front office.

This disruption in employment caused Mark to go from being financially independent to relying on odd jobs and infrequent financial support from other sources. Mark reflected on the change of his income and expressed dissatisfaction with the situation when he commented: "That was good money and I miss it." The loss of employment and steady income contributed to Mark's dependence on others outside his family.

Mark reinforced the theme of disruption across different areas of his life when he reflected on the state of his life at the time of the interview. At the end of his narrative, he commented, "Things are just bad." This statement on his situation three years after the storm was in stark contrast to his attitudes expressed about his life before the storm.

The Unknown. The theme of the unknown first appeared in Mark's description of his brother almost drowning. Mark was exposed to unknown elements before he was able to successfully save his brother. He recalled, "You had to get underneath the water, dark water, you couldn't see nothing." His description similarly dragged us as readers beneath the murky, churning water with him, and for a brief moment we were unsure if we would surface with him. The unknown was again referenced during the description of the rescue when he said, "…some kind of way man, we came out of the water." Mark was not able to pinpoint exactly how he was able to pull his brother out from underneath the dark water, which left his source of strength in that defining moment unknown.

Mark's description of the evacuation also contained tones of the unknown. The evacuation caused separation from his family, and Mark was not aware of where all of his family members were being taken. He recalled,

Okay, let's see. Um, I got to think on this 'cause it's a trip. Okay, some people gone to Houston…it all depends on what car you in. Some was going here, some was going there, and some was coming to San Antonio. So it just so happens that we was on a military plane and our plane just so happened to come to San Antonio.

Mark did not have any control of the evacuation situation or of his final destination. Mark hinted at the unsteadiness of the situation when he first said, "…it's a trip." This statement was interpreted as him not solely referring to a trip in the sense of going somewhere but instead as an out-of-the-ordinary experience that had an unknown destination.

The theme of the unknown also appeared in Mark's life at the time of the interview and affected his long-term recovery. Mark's daily routine before the storm was established and included stopping at his sister's house before he went to work. Mark had clear expectations at his job, and he completed similar tasks daily. Mark acknowledged the predictably of his employment when he said, "I always stayed on the same job that had the same routine." He was also able to rely on his nearby family for support. After the storm, Mark described a situation that did not contain daily and structured routines, as well as one that lacked clear supports. The loss of steady employment, the sporadic income and decrease in family support led to Mark having days that were unpredictable and had no clear purpose. Mark, when asked about his daily routine after the storm, said, "I wander around a little bit and figure out what the world is going to do sometimes." Individuals with intellectual disabilities often benefit from predictable daily routines, and it can be stressful to the individual when these routines are disrupted. The uncertainty of Mark's day could have contributed to his self-disclosed depression.

Mark's specific use of language at times contributed further to the theme of the unknown. He used the words "go out there" or "out there" when he described the situation when his brother was being overwhelmed by the flood waters. His use of imprecise or vague language makes it impossible for the reader to visualize the chaotic scene, which, in turn, renders the scene more unknowable. Mark referred to Hurricane Katrina a number of times as a "thing" rather than a hurricane or storm. We interpreted this as meaning that Mark perceived the storm as an unidentifiable massive destructive force that was unknown.

Chaos. The theme of chaos emerged as Mark described his experience with the immediate aftermath of Hurricane Katrina. Many individuals watched the chaotic scene unfold in New Orleans on television from the safety of their living rooms. Mark was forced to witness the disorder firsthand. He described the first time he saw the chaotic scene:

Next thing we know we wake up and my brother says, "Man, come look at this!" and I [Mark] said "Come look at what?" "The water!" [his brother responds]… like 'cause he was still on the second floor and the water is like almost up to the window to the second floor. I [Mark] say, "Whoa, they got people floating out here in little things." Oh man, that when you see people going into the Winn Dixie super-markets, looting and all that kind of stuff.

Their frightening exposure to chaos continued during the evacuation phase. Mark described the chaotic scene:

When they came to the apartment building downstairs at the ground floor in a little boat, but first they tried to get us by helicopter, getting people out of the window. Oh man, we was waving our white sheets and everything.…They took us in a boat and we were riding over the cars, cars were underneath the water and then the boat would hit it.

Mark further described how the evacuation continued with him having to ride in a military truck, bus, helicopter, plane, and finally another bus that took him to his final destination. His retelling of his experience swept us into the narrative drama of the situation, and we began to get some sense of the overall turmoil that the residents of New Orleans experienced.

The thematic analysis gives us an overall sense of what Mark experienced during and after Hurricane Katrina. Our structural analysis of his narrative gives us different insights.

Structural Analysis

We chose to use Gee's (1991) structural approach to analyze a key story within Mark's interview that presents how he acted decisively in the midst of chaos. Our purpose here is to explore how this incident shaped his identity. What follows is the story as it appeared when we applied Gee's approach.

Stanza 1:   Location
01   When we came downstairs
02   it was *flooded*   downstairs
03   inside the apartment building
04   right.
05   That is where
06   my oldest brother stay at.

Stanza 2:   Lost at Sea
07   Okay so we   *out there*
08   and   you don't,
09   you forget
10   *where your bearings at,*
11   you know what I am saying,

Stanza 3:   The Call to Heroism
12   The next thing *I* know
13   my other older brother,
14   not Freddie, but George,
15   dipped off
16   so *I* had to go *out there*
17   and jump *out there*
18   and get *him*.
19   Oh man,
20   and bring *him* back,

Stanza 4:   It's Up to Me
21   the water was over our head.
22   And my younger brother
23   *all he* was doin was stood back
24   and the water was up to his neck.
25   And *he was just*
26   hollerin "Get him, get him!"
27   and *I* said   "*I* got him, *I* got him."

Stanza 5:   I Brought Him Back
28   And *both of us* went under water
29   and some kind of way,

30	man,
31	*both of* us came out of the water
32	and *I brought him back*,
33	back to where
34	*he* can stand level
35	where the water was level
36	up to his chest.

Stanza 6:   Emotional Release

37	Man, that was weird.
38	My brother was cryin,
39	he had me cryin,
40	everybody was cryin,
41	There was *all kinds* of things
42	happening man.

In Stanza 1, Mark sets up the scene of the narrative by paying particular attention to location. He included the physical location as well as the location of characters. His focus is on the rising water and the threat it presents. Not only is it flooded downstairs, it is his older brother's apartment that is filled with water, which makes the flooding a very personal, very imminent threat. The second stanza connects to the category of the unknown as evidenced in his choice of language. What is no longer known is where exactly he is—Mark has lost his bearings, and "out there" is a very frightening place. The third stanza signals the beginning of the dramatic event, with Mark's older brother being engulfed by the murky flood waters. We again are connected back to the unknown and the threatening flood waters because of Mark's choice of the words "out there" and bringing his brother back from "there." The third stanza is when we first see Mark's identification of himself as a hero. He is the person that *had* to go get his brother; there was no one else who could do it. In Stanza 4, Mark emphasizes the increasing danger when he notes that the water was already over his head and, by inference, over his brother George's head. Significantly the water is not over the head of his younger brother, who stands back and hollers for Mark to rescue George. The contrast between Mark's actions and the inaction of his younger brother further defines Mark's identity as a hero. Stanza 5 describes the dramatic rescue, but without giving much detail on how exactly Mark saves his brother George; Mark himself is unsure how he did it ("some kind of way"), but he is unequivocal in claiming responsibility for the act ("*I brought him back*"). Mark clearly makes the claim that he is the hero in this story. In the final stanza, Mark shifts to the emotion of the event by describing how everyone, including himself, cried. Their tears also consist of water, but these emotional waters signal relief that Mark was able to rescue George from the threatening waters of the flood. While "there was all kinds of things happening," the most important thing that happened in this narrative was Mark's heroic rescue of his brother.

Discussion

Mark was an individual multiply classified as intellectually disabled, a racial minority, of low income, a resident of an area prone to natural disasters, and without a car—all factors identified by researchers as contributing to physical and social vulnerability in disaster. Our thematic analysis revealed that Mark was indeed negatively affected by Hurricane Katrina. He was exposed to chaotic experiences that individuals with better evacuation resources did not have to confront. Post-disaster, Mark had difficulty gaining employment, establishing new social contacts, and accessing disaster-related supports—all of which influenced his recovery from the storm. Mark became reliant on others for financial assistance in contrast to before the storm when he had been the prideful source of his own income. The challenges

Mark experienced aligned with the dominant disaster narrative of individuals with disabilities as vulnerable in disaster and in need of others to act on their behalf.

However, Mark directly challenged the view of individuals with disabilities as socially vulnerable and changed the focus of the interview when he asserted his identity as a hero. No matter the interview question he was asked, Mark insisted on telling the near-drowning story in three different narratives, underscoring the importance that this heroic identity had for him. Narrative provides an arena for individuals to perform identities to their audience. Riessman (2008) remarked on the function of identity performance in narrative: "We are forever composing impressions of ourselves, protecting a definition of who we are, and making claims about ourselves and the world we test out and negotiate with others" (p. 106). We interpreted Mark's strong identity performance as serving two purposes: Mark used his identity portrayal to communicate his role in the natural disaster to the researcher as well as to lay claims on his current overwhelming circumstance in recovery.

Mark's performance as a hero demonstrated his agency in the disaster: He was the one in his family that acted during the near-drowning. Devlin and Pothier (2006) stress that individuals with disabilities often demonstrate agency:

> For every moment and instance of "power over" there are moments of "power to"….persons with disabilities have engaged in empowering strategies—at the level of the self; in the family; at school; at work; in local, national, and international politics; in the social realm; and in the cultural realm. (p. 13)

Mark's narrative provides an example of "power to" in the realm of disaster. His presented identity as an active, powerful agent shaped a counter-narrative that conflicted with the dominant narrative of individuals with disabilities as "acted upon" during disaster. The power to act came from within Mark and contrasts sharply with previous work that presents the disaster vulnerability of individuals with disabilities as determined by external societal factors. Mark's narrative is one of immediate action. He rescued his brother from the flood waters as opposed to passive reliance on the emergency management system—which failed to meet the needs of many other individuals with disabilities in Hurricane Katrina. The repetition of his heroic story establishes Mark as someone with agency, and with a hero identity that suggests he will conquer his current challenges.

An important distinction must be made between our chosen label of Mark's performed identity as a hero and the concept of the "super crip." Critical disability scholars and members of the disability community have adapted the term "super crip" in reference to individuals with disabilities that have accomplished tremendous feats or have achieved extreme advancements in their professions, such as Helen Keller or Christopher Reeve (Smart, 2009). The concept of the "super crip" reflects societal tendencies to praise such heroic acts and can lead to an expectation that all individuals with disabilities should overcome their disability. We caution that this narrative of the "hero" is not meant to reinforce the stereotype of a "super crip" but instead reflects Mark's chosen narrative as an act of agency. Mark's story is not significant because he took extraordinary measures, rather it is significant because he narrates a heroic identity that directly challenges the narrative of individuals with disabilities in disasters as helpless victims. Mark's counter-narrative also challenged us as researchers who ascribe to the social vulnerability perspective to rethink our own assumptions about the role of individuals with disabilities during disaster.

Conclusion

Mark found a powerful voice, generated from his own heroic narrative, despite the inferior status typically assigned by society to individuals with disabilities. His decision to portray himself with agency assisted him in processing his experience of Hurricane Katrina. Mark was a disaster survivor who was able to identify his own role in disaster as important. In Mark's narrative we discover an individual who chose an identity of agency instead of one of vulnerability.

References

Blake, E., Rappaport, E., & Landsea, C. (2007). *The deadliest, costliest, and most intense United States tropical cyclones from 1851 to 2006 (and other frequently requested hurricane facts)*. Retrieved from National Weather Service, National Hurricane Center: http://www.nhc.noaa.gov/pdf/NWS-TPC-5.pdf

Cutter, S. L., Boruff, B. J., & Shirley, W. L. (2003). Social vulnerability to environmental hazards. *Social Science Quarterly, 84,* 242–261.

Devlin, R., & Pothier, D. (2006). Introduction: Toward a critical theory of dis-citizenship. In R. Devlin & D. Pothier (Eds.), *Critical disability theory: Essays in philosophy, politics and law* (pp. 1– 22). Vancouver, BC, Canada: UBC Press.

Fisher, W. R. (1984). Narration as a human communication paradigm: The case of public moral argument. *Communication Monograms, 51*(1), 1–22. doi:10.1080/03637758409390180

Fothergill, A., & Peek, L. (2004). Poverty and disasters in the United States: A review of the sociological literature. *Natural Hazards, 32,* 89–110. doi:0.1023/B:NHAZ.0000026792.7681.d9

Fox, M. H., White, G. W., Rooney, C., & Rowland, J. L.(2007). Disaster preparedness and response for persons with mobility impairments. *Journal of Disability Policy Studies, 17*(4), 196–205. doi:10.1177/10442073070170040201

Gee, J. P. (1991). A linguistic approach to narrative. *Journal of Narrative and Life History, 1*(1), 15–39.

Gleeson, B. J. (1997). Disability studies: A historical materialist view. *Disability & Society, 12*(2), 179–202. doi:10.1080/09687599727326

Hemingway, L., & Priestley, M. (2006). Natural hazards, human vulnerability, and disabling societies: A disaster for disabled people? *The Review of Disability Studies, 2*(3), 57–67.

Hewitt, K. (1997). *Regions of risk: A geographical introduction to disasters*. Boston, MA: Addison Wesley Longman.

Lieblich, A., Tuval-Mashiach, R., & Zilber, T. (1998). *Narrative research: Reading, analysis, and interpretation*. Thousand Oaks, CA: Sage.

McGuire, L., Ford, E., & Okoro, C. (2007). Natural disasters and older US adults with disabilities: Implications for evacuation. *Disasters, 31*(1), 49–56. doi:0.1111/j.1467–7717.2007.00339

National Council on Disability (NOD). (2006). *The impact of Hurricanes Katrina and Rita on people with disabilities: A look back and remaining challenges*. Washington, DC: Author.

O'Keefe, P., Westgate, K., & Wisner, B. (1976). Taking the naturalness out of natural disasters. *Nature, 260,* 566–567. doi:10.1038/260566a0

Peacock, W. G., and Ragsdale, A. K. (1997). Social systems, ecological networks and disasters. In W. G. Peacock, B. H. Morrow & J. Gladwin (Eds.), *Hurricane Andrew: Ethnicity, gender and the sociology of disasters.* (pp.20–35) New York: Routledge.

Peek, L., & Stough, L. M. (2010). Children with disabilities in the context of disaster: A social vulnerability perspective. *Child Development, 81*(4), 1260–1270.

Phillips, B. D., & Morrow, B. H. (2007). Social science research needs: Focus on vulnerable populations, forecasting, and warnings. *Natural Hazards Review, 8*(3), 61–68. doi:2048/10.1061/1527–69888:3

Riessman, C. K. (2008). *Narrative methods for the human sciences*. Thousand Oaks, CA: Sage.

Smart, J. (2009). *Disability, society, and the individual*. Austin, TX: Pro-Ed.

U.S. Census Bureau. (2008). Current population reports: Americans with disabilities: 2005. Retrieved from http://www.census.gov/prod/2008pubs/p70–117.pdf

White, B. (2006). Disaster relief for deaf persons: Lessons from Hurricanes Katrina and Rita. *The Review of Disability Studies, 2*(3), 49–56.

White, G. W., Fox, M. H., Rooney, C., & Cahill, A. (2007). *Assessing the impact of Hurricane Katrina on persons with disabilities*. Retrieved from University of Kansas, Research and Training Center on Independent Living website: http://www.rtcil.org/products/NIDRR_FinalKatrinaReport.pdf

Wisner, B., Blaikie, P., Cannon, T., & Davis, I. (2004). *At risk: Natural hazards, people's vulnerability, and disasters* (2nd ed.). New York, NY: Routledge.

CHAPTER TWENTY-TWO

Excluded Narratives, Anti-racism and Historical Representation: Methodological Implications

Timothy J. Stanley

This chapter discusses the use of anti-racism as a methodology. Although I focus on historical methodology and draw on a particular narrative of the 1922–23 students' strike in Victoria, British Columbia, to illustrate my point, my argument is broadly applicable to qualitative research methodologies as well as to other approaches in the humanities and social sciences more generally. Similarly, although my argument applies to racisms, the social relations they construct and the relations of knowledge they engender, I believe that much of my analysis can also be broadly applied to studies of other social phenomena.

In 1922–23 the Chinese Canadian community of Victoria, British Columbia, organized a year-long students' strike or boycott of the provincially controlled school system in response to the local school board's attempted segregation of all students racialized as Chinese (Ashworth, 1979; Lai, 1987; Stanley, 1990). As a historian, I am interested in constructing a narrative that explains the history of the strike (Stanley, 2011). I understand narrative here in a sense that is familiar to historians. History as formal discipline, at least in the dominant European tradition, is less concerned with what happened in the past than it is with explaining why it happened (Carr, 1961). Although today most historians accept that events have complex causes, most also see their own narratives as establishing these causal relations (e.g., Gaffield, 2006). The difference is nicely summarized by the literary critic Hayden White. In his critique of history, White points out that historical narratives establish, implicitly or explicitly, sets of causal relationships through emplotment. Borrowing E.M. Forster's (1927) famous example, "'The king died and then the queen died' is a story. 'The king died and then the queen died of grief' is a plot" (as cited in Vellemen, 2003, p. 2), White asks whether the historical plot is in the real past as lived by human beings or in the mind of the historian (White, 1987; also, White, 1980, 1998). While today few scholars would readily accept the structuralist argument that White advanced, literary theorists, philosophers of history and historians themselves, from a variety of epistemological positions, have argued back and forth over whether historians' narratives are in any way approximations of a reality external to their texts, and whether this approximation, if it exists in the first place, can ever be established (e.g., Ankersmit, 2001; Ankersmit & Kellner, 1995; Evans, 2000; Jenkins, 2009; Martin, 2004; Mohanty, 1997). However, most historians would probably agree with Martin Bunzl (1997) that history only makes sense as a genre if it seeks to approximate a real past, even if that real past is ultimately unknowable in any objectively verifiable sense. Historians trained in European approaches to the discipline would further argue that all historical arguments are not equal, that some better make use of and explain the available historical evidence than others. As such the narratives constructed by historians are always contingent, based on the sources and understandings available at the time they were written. Thus, I seek to construct a "small narrative," one that accounts for a particular group of people's historical experiences and the available evidence, rather than a "grand narrative" (Megill, 1995) that constructs a metahistory of a reified subject like "the nation," "the people" or "the race" allegedly for all time and all places. While it is important to note that other traditions of historical research, such as the 2000-year-old tradition of Chinese historiography, do not share the same interest in constructing coherent narratives as those operating in the European tradition (e.g., Hardy, 1995), since it is the dominant tradition in the part of the world that I inhabit, my argument focuses on the European tradition. Following Edward W. Said (1994), I would also argue that, like it or not, this is the dominant tradition with which we need to come to terms if we are to construct contrapuntal post-colonial approaches. Anti-racism can help to construct such approaches.

At one level, anti-racism is anything that opposes or mitigates a particular instance of racism (Bonnett, 2000); at another, it is a diverse body of theory and practice (see, for example, Essed & Goldberg, 2002) that is as old as racisms themselves. From the admittedly vast literature on anti-racism, I glean three basic perspectives (Stanley, 2011). I elaborate on these in the following sections.

Racisms Exist in the Plural

The first perspective is that racism is not a singular phenomenon, but something that exists in the plural. Thus, there are racisms, each with its own history and consequences. For example, anti-Semitism in Canada is a different racism from anti-African or anti-Asian racisms. Racisms in the plural have no essential or inevitable form, but are highly changeable in specific contexts, i.e., they vary in form and intensity with time and place. Because there are different racisms, it is possible for a particular racisms to be at play in a specific time and place and in the next moment another racism to be at play (Goldberg, 1993, Chapter 5). One racism can exist in conjunction or even in opposition to another. Methodologically, the idea that racisms exist in the plural points to four key issues. First and foremost, it suggests that in building an understanding of a particular racism, everything depends on context. Indeed, historians argue that this is the case with everything else that is human. In effect, this means that particular racisms have no essential form. Although a particular racism may have a specific configuration in one time and place, there is no reason to assume that it will automatically have this configuration in another time and place. Rather, its configuration is a matter to be investigated. Second, a particular racism can articulate (as in the sense of give voice or form to) another racism and can articulate with (in the sense of being consistent with) another racism. Thus, for example, in a particular time and place it is possible for anti-Semitism and anti-Asian racisms to come together. I borrow the concept of articulation from Stuart Hall (1980 and 1986). The advantage of this concept is that it allows for relationships between cultural or knowledge systems and social systems without falling into predetermined positions. Third, the plurality of racisms and their articulations suggests that there are no essential connections between particular racisms and other social phenomena, and especially those of gender, class, sexuality, ability/disability, ethnicity. Different phenomena get enacted in and through each other in specific ways according to time and place (Dei, 1996; Alexander & Mohanty, 1997). For example, if at a particular time and place white supremacy both articulates and articulates with patriarchy (Leonardo, 2004), it is this articulation that needs exploration and explanation. To assume that it is the essential quality of

men of European origins for all times and places is to fail to ask questions about things that might become matters of life and death. We have seen this historically. For example, the assumption that there
is a necessary connection between Nazism and German nationalism fails to recognize the international
nature of the Nazi movement (Marrus, 1987). Fourth, if a stable pattern exists over time, such as an association between a particular historical system of patriarchy and a particular racism, the idea that there
are racisms in the plural calls attention to the ongoing acts of power, whether social, cultural, economic
or political, that maintain this particular pattern.

Conditions for Racisms

The second perspective that I glean from the literature on anti-racism is that there are racist conditions. Following especially Robert Miles (1989) and David Theo Goldberg (1993), I argue that all
historic racisms meet three different conditions :they involve racializations, they organize exclusions
along racialized lines and the resulting racialized exclusions have significant negative consequences for
the racialized and excluded. Each of these conditions is a necessary but insufficient condition for racism. The claim being made here is both conceptual and empirical. Conceptually, I am not proposing
a definition that seeks to specify the usages of the term "racism" and its cognates, but rather one that,
as Miles (1989) suggests, defends the usage of the term as a category for analysis, differentiates it from
other social phenomena and prevents it from degenerating into a mere term for political abuse. Empirically, it suggests ways of analyzing and grouping together phenomena as diverse as the Holocaust, the
Rwandan Genocide, the colonization of the Americas, why there are restaurants that sell "Canadian
and Chinese food" and why some children in grade 3 do not get invited to certain of their classmates'
birthday parties. I will now look at each of these conditions by turn.

Racialization is the social process of making "race" (Fanon, 1967; see also Barzun, 1938; Arendt,
1944; Montagu, 1964; Allen, 1994; Frankenberg, 1993; Gilroy, 2000; Lewis, 2003). Racialization
is fundamentally what Miles (1989, Chapter 3) calls a signifying practice, one in which a particular
aspect of real or imagined human difference is selected to mark one group in relation to another, i.e.,
is signified in essentialized and inescapable ways. Historically a number of factors have contributed to
racialization including geographic and institutional segregation, apparent skin color, cultural, religious
or linguistic differences, people's height in the Rwandan case. As a representational or meaning-making
process, racialization involves the representation of real or imagined human cultural or phenotypical
difference in essentialized terms (Miles, 1989, pp. 74–75). Racialization only allows that someone is
either an "X" or a "Y". It does not allow for anyone to be both an X and a Y. Racialization is always
relational as one group is racialized in relation to another.

Recognizing racialization as a representational process (Hall, 1997) rather than as an artifact of
some preexisting essentialized difference—i.e., as language that makes "race" rather than "race" making
language—calls attention to the performances of texts, linguistic and otherwise. It leads to a more active reading of historical sources, readings that recognize that their representations of difference do not
so much reflect preexisting natural differences on the ground, but actively create or recreate knowledge
of difference. This approach can also be used for contemporary sources, for example, for reading interview transcripts, and I would argue for other processes of social categorization as well. One implication
of reading racializations as active processes of reinscribing difference is that it suggests that such reinscription is only necessary because like all other representations, the original significations of difference
have slipped and hence need to be re-marked. This leads to questions about what is going on outside the
particular text under consideration, encourages us to ask about whether there are other texts that can be
investigated as well and points to texts as artifacts of social processes that contest meanings.

Racializations alone do not make racisms. They enter into racisms when people organize racializations into exclusions. Thus, the organization of exclusions is the second condition for racisms. Racialized exclusions take different forms. They can be social, economic, political or territorial. They can

involve exclusions from certain social or institutional positions, or they can be symbolic, for example, exclusions from having one's meanings seriously engaged. They can be exclusions from life itself. Racialized exclusions of one sort often act in and through racialized exclusion of other sorts as well as in conjunction with the exclusions of gender, social class, sexuality, ability/disability, or age, but racialized exclusions are always purposive. They are not only the result of bad intentions, but are matter of fact. Someone is either excluded or not (Goldberg, 1993, p. 98). Racialized exclusions are things that one human being or group of human beings has done to another. Thus they are organized, even if the original circumstance of this organization has become silent or forgotten. Finally, if someone is being excluded, someone else is being included. In speaking of racialized exclusions as an organization, following Goldberg (1993), I depart from Miles (1989), who sees racism as merely an ideology. However, I borrow the concept of organization from Hannah Arendt, who spoke of the Nazi program as being organized into "a texture of life" that made its propaganda unquestionable: "as real and untouchable an element in [people's] lives as the rules of arithmetic" (Arendt, 1979, p. 363).

This condition urges the historian to see racialized social relations as dynamic enactments rather than as stable artifacts of prearranged sets of relations, i.e., as ongoing processes of inclusion and exclusion, their creation and recreation. It also calls attention to a rather old-fashioned question in social investigations: Who are the actors? Who is doing what to whom and how? As with other social patterns it also leads to the question of how the particular enactment is part of, or reinforces, a larger pattern. We can also consider the articulations of racialized exclusions, one organization of racialized exclusion in relation to another, or we can consider the articulations of one kind of exclusion with another. For example, exclusions from particular institutions often are closely related to symbolic exclusions, to people not having their meanings taken seriously. The logics of racism get built into cultural landscapes and social geographies. Perhaps most importantly, racialized exclusions point to the operations of power. In the normal processes of human interaction, racialized meanings and racialized organization should slip as people enter into them and remake them for their own purposes, as is the case with other meanings and efforts at organizing the world (Hall, 1997). However, many forms of racialized exclusion appear to be relatively stable over time as is, for example, the case with racisms directed at African Americans or Canadian First Nations, Inuit and Métis peoples. Something or someone must intervene to reimpose meanings and forms of organization that would otherwise slip and eventually disappear. The methodological challenge is to identify these things, individuals or groups. It also urges attention to the role of government and of state formation in racisms (Omi & Winant, 1986; Goldberg, 2002; also Curtis, 1988).

Racialization and exclusion alone do not make racisms. Historically many groups subject to racism have found it necessary to come together separately from their oppressors to organize resistance or survival. While these are racialized exclusion, they are for anti-racist purposes, and it would do violence to the concept of racism to call such actions in and of themselves racist (although over time they might become such). Thus the third condition is that racisms must have significant negative consequences for the excluded (Miles, 1989, esp. p. 134; Goldberg, 1993, Chapter 5). Amongst other things this means that to determine whether a racism is present, the consequences of the racialized exclusion on the excluded themselves must be considered. This in turn requires that the meanings and self-representations of those who are racialized and excluded must be brought into knowledge and engaged. Indeed, failing to do so reenacts the very racialized exclusions upon which the racism is based.

This third condition has enormous consequences for historians of racisms and indeed for other scholars. Amongst other things it means that we cannot understand a racism if we do not seek out and bring into our knowledge the self-representations of the excluded. At the most mundane level, scholarship needs to move beyond what my PhD co-supervisor, the late Vincent D'Oyley, used to call "the sample of convenience" if we really want to understand the human condition. Most research in the humanities and social sciences focuses on people who are most like the researcher. In Canadian historical research, this means that most research is conducted on groups who leave behind historical records in the national official languages, English or French. This is despite the fact that today Canada is built on territory in which approximately 50 languages were spoken for thousands of years before English and French, and in which today 20% of the population speaks languages other than English or French. At a larger level, racist systems survive because the relations of power at work ensure that the meanings created by the excluded do not need to be engaged by those the racism empowers. The challenge is to remake these relations of power so that the meanings of the excluded are engaged. Here, critical scholarship has an important role to play in ensuring that excluded meanings are brought into wider knowledge and taken seriously.

Anti-racisms

The third overall perspective that I have gleaned from my reading and experience in anti-racism is that the above analysis of racisms also shapes anti-racisms (Stanley, 2011, p 14). Just as there are racisms in the plural, there are anti-racisms in the plural. If racisms take no essential form, the same is the case with anti-racisms. It is possible for someone to be anti-racist with respect to one racism and at the same time racist with respect to another. Even the most committed racists can have their anti-racist moments. Anti-racisms can also be addressed around some or all of the specific conditions for racism identified earlier. Thus anti-racisms can either separately or in combination challenge racializations, can foster inclusions across racialized lines, or can seek to mitigate the negative effects of racist exclusions. Like racisms, anti-racisms are specific to time and place. An anti-racist strategy that is effective in one time and place may not be in another.

This view of anti-racisms also has important methodological consequences. It means that racisms and anti-racisms go hand in hand, that as an oppressive system, racist practices are continually being challenged, resisted, accommodated or circumvented. It suggests that racisms are dynamic systems in which particular measures are continually being disrupted or falling into disuse at the same time that new measures are being created or are being put into place. It also suggests that when a particular racialized exclusion is being reasserted, it is likely because it had begun to slip. Indeed, if it had not slipped, there would be no need for its reinscription. Most importantly it suggests that the racialized and excluded continually affirm their humanness in the face of its denial. Historians know that the historical records and experiences of the most powerful are those that are the most likely to survive. In North America, this means that the records of older men of European origins who speak English, own significant property and are politically active, are preserved much more so than those of any other group. But if we recognize that enactments of power are continually being contested, even if we do not have access to the sources of the excluded, we should still be able to see this contest in the dominant records. In effect, we need to read our sources for what Bakhtin (1984) calls "hidden dialogicality," as if we are recreating a conversation in which we have overheard only one of the speakers, "for each present, uttered word responds and reacts with its every fiber to the invisible speaker, points to something outside itself, beyond its own limits, to the unspoken words on another person" (as cited in Wertsch, 2002, p. 91).

An Example

With these perspectives in mind, I would now like to turn my attention to a specific example. On September 20, 1922, two weeks after the students' strike began, Victoria's *The Daily Colonist* newspaper published a letter to the editor by one "H. Hastings" under the heading "Segregation Question" (Hastings, 1922b). The letter-writer first explains why he is writing. "Knowing the Oriental mind, as I believe I do," he had hitherto confined himself "to taking up the Oriental question only when... it may affect our international relations." He further notes that as the students' strike was "merely" a local matter, and that "there are enough well-educated Chinese in our midst who should fight their own battles," he originally had no intention of commenting, but had changed his mind since "a number of 'white' [original quotation marks] friends" had asked him "to explain the actual situation, which seems rather confusing to them." He had accordingly decided to write in order "to try and put the situation impartially and clearly." He then proceeds to explain the strike as the result of two different phenomena coming together. He notes that until 1919, "there had been no trouble of any sort" with Chinese students, since the majority were "mainly the children of Canadian born Chinese (in some cases, second and third generation Canadian born)"; however, since that time there had been a significant migration of children from South China because of the dangers of kidnapping and brigandage there. It seems their parents were already in Canada, thus their families were assumed to be rich. This had produced an "influx" into the schools and a larger number of older boys (ages 13–16) who did not speak any English and who "have necessitated a good deal of the attention of the teachers, to the neglect of the other children." The other factor that contributed to the situation was the "strong anti-Oriental campaign" of the province's attorney-general and of "certain trade interests." The result was that the school board decided to segregate all racialized Chinese pupils, including the locally born who spoke English. That those whom Hastings called "the Chinese" were convinced that the board was pursuing a racial policy is explained by the fact that when segregation was carried out, a number of children called out of their classes objected that they were Japanese and not Chinese: "Immediately they were allowed to go back to school, so that the Chinese children were very plainly shown that of all races on this earth, they, and they alone, are considered not good enough to mix with the 'white' [original quotation marks] children." Hastings concluded, "The Chinese are correct in their attitude" and warned, "The Canadian 'white' [original quotation marks] may be the lions and the Orientals the lambs, but take care that you do not, by studied insults, rouse the one thousand million 'lambs' who inhabit Asia to regrow their horns."

A traditional historical analysis would seek to understand this text and its biases. All historical sources are biased in the sense that they are recorded from a particular point of view. The challenge is to recreate that point of view so as to read through the source back to the reality articulated by the source. This in turn requires interpreting the particular source and its contents in context, i.e., in light of what else was going on at the time and place. In practice this means in light of what else we know or can discover about the time and place (e.g., Davidson & Lytle, 1992). A text's biases can only be understood if we understand its provenance. Where did it come from? What were the conditions that produced it? Why was it written? What were the motives of its author? Why was it reproduced?

On the question of provenance, the document itself helps. Hastings states his reasons for writing at the beginning of the letter. It would appear from this that Hastings considers himself an expert on "the Oriental question," that he was not himself Chinese (he consistently refers to "the Chinese" as a group separate from himself) and that at least some people racialized as white may also see him as an expert on the matter. In effect, he positions himself as an expert knower, a kind of cultural interpreter of the Chinese to "whites," a term that he himself places in scare quotes. How it is that he is an expert, whether his claim to expertise was considered credible at the time and whether I as historian looking back almost a century later should believe him, are all questions that need to be investigated to see whether and how this particular text could contribute to an explanation for the students' strike. My other knowledge of the times, i.e., what I know of its context, helps with some of these questions. I know this context primarily through the work of other historians, each of whom has explored a different aspect of it: British Columbia as colonized territory (Harris, 1997, 2002; Perry, 2001), the prevalence of racist discourse (Ward, 1978; Roy, 1989, 2003), the histories of the Chinese themselves (Lee, 1967; Con, Con, Johnson, Wickberg, & Willmott, 1982; Chong, 1994). For example, my reading of Paul Rutherford's (1982) study of 19th-century newspapers in Canada allows me to extrapolate that newspapers were mass circulation publications, often highly partisan, but that they also tended to publish every letter they received. Much like small-town newspapers today, they ensured their market by making sure that all of the community's members felt that the paper was their bulletin board. But in the end I answer these questions of provenance and bias through the process of external and internal criticism, by examining the document itself and by then comparing it to other documents.

Examining other documents around the strike, I quickly find that this letter is the beginning of a series of letters and formal analyses of the strike written by Harry Hastings and published in Victoria's English-language newspapers (e.g., Hastings, 1922a). Indeed, although he claims to be impartial in this first letter, he quickly becomes not only a partisan of the cause of the so-called Chinese, but the leading critic of the school board in the Victoria papers (e.g., Hastings, 1923). The local commercial directory lists him as an importer/exporter and as a Chinese-English interpreter (e.g., Wrigley Directories Limited, 1925). Thus, his self-appointed claim to expert cultural knowledge appears to have some credibility. Eventually, I will read the two interviews with him in the 1924 Survey of Race Relations and discover that Hastings was living with his sister and her husband (Hastings, 1924a, 1924b). I also find that he was born in Taiwan of missionary parents, that his father was English and his mother Chinese. The Survey interviews suggest that people in Victoria saw him as having an Oxbridge education, while in fact he had attended a British-style boarding school in Hong Kong. The Survey erroneously refers to him as having school-aged children (1924a), while in fact his death notice shows that he was unmarried and had no children, and the children in his household were his sister's ("Harry Hastings Obituary," 1967). His mixed race status seems to account for his pretence to neutrality, while his background and life experience underlay his claim to expert knowledge of "the Oriental mind."

What happens when we reread all of this through an anti-racist lens? Taking seriously the third perspective advanced above, the idea that there are anti-racisms in the plural, that they have no essential form, and can address some or all of the conditions for racism, we can ask whether the letter was an anti-racist intervention and if so of what sort. Is this part of its provenance? The fact that he ended up playing such a prominent role in the strike suggests that it was. However, examining his statement in light of the three conditions for racisms (and hence for anti-racisms) begins to point to the ways in which anti-Chinese racism had been organized into the political, cultural and social landscape of British Columbia.

Hastings appears to be trying to mitigate the consequences of racism by bringing into circulation within the English-language public sphere knowledge of "the Chinese" that he has and that others do not. Since he was literate in Chinese, along with one or two Christian missionaries, he would have been one of the few non-Chinese residents of Victoria who had direct access to what was being written about the students' strike and other matters in the Chinese-language newspapers. From a methodological perspective, he is pointing the present-day historian to the existence of excluded knowledges. Once we begin asking about these excluded knowledges, we find that there are significant Chinese-language sources available, including a daily Chinese-language newspaper published in Vancouver, British Columbia, *The Chinese Times*, and archival sources of Victoria's Chinese Consolidated Benevolent Association (CCBA), and of leading merchants in Vancouver and Victoria (e.g., Yip Family and Yip Sang Papers of the City of Vancouver Archive). These sources have also been addressed in the secondary literature (e.g., Lai, 1987). Taking seriously Chinese-language sources also radically changes the understandings of context that have framed so much scholarship on racism in Canada. It points to the transnational nature of phenomena previously seen only within a narrow nationalist context (e.g, Huang, 2009).

There are at least two ways in which Hastings' letter articulates a social organization that racializes and excludes people from China and their locally born descendants living in British Columbia. First, he points to the migration of a significant number of teenaged boys from South China in recent years. This voices the patriarchal nature of Chinese society in the Pearl River delta from which people in British Columbia came, as well as the patriarchal nature of the migrant community in Canada (Stockard, 1989; Chong, 1994). Although Hastings refers to the "parents" being in Canada, not just the fathers, apparently the concern for the safety of children who might be kidnapped extended only to boys and not girls. More importantly for my purposes, it points to the gendered and racist nature of Chinese exclusion in Canada. The immigration head tax on Chinese workers and their families had privileged the migration of men and was designed to ensure that other family members remained in China. At the same time, the merchant economy valued the migration of a second wife (Adilman, 1984). The result was that the violence of the Canadian state system forced the family relations of the Chinese diaspora in Canada to be transnational and to remain so for all of the 19th and most of the 20th centuries. For example, the profound gender imbalances it engendered in Canada's Chinese communities only disappeared in the 1980s (Li, 1998).

Hastings' letter also points to another aspect of the organization of Chinese exclusion. He explains that some of his "white" friends are confused by the strike. We quickly find that before Hastings' letter, self-identified Chinese had published a series of letters explaining the strike and their motivations in Victoria's English-language papers (Joe, 1922; Lowe, 1922; Wen, 1922; Won, 1922). These would appear to be the "well-educated Chinese in our midst who should fight their own battles" to whom Hastings refers in his own letter. Yet, it would appear that their statements were unintelligible to "whites"—this despite the fact that they were writing in English, which was in many cases the letter writers' first and only language. What the writers were saying was that the only possible explanation for the school board's actions was "race prejudice" and that segregation would prevent them from properly learning English and integrating into "Canadian" ways (see esp. Joe, 1922). This articulates with one of the defining characteristics of the context of the times, a context that is rarely addressed in the secondary literature, that is, the dominance of an absolute racialized and racist binary between "Canadians" and "Chinese," and indeed between the former and other groups of Asian and African origins. In the face of this binary, for people racialized as Chinese to call for their integration into the equally racialized category of Canadian was simply unintelligible to most people on the "Canadian" side of the binary. If this is true, it also helps to explain the actions of the school trustees who also accepted this binary. Their logic becomes self-contained in a series of mutually supported propositions: "Chinese-speaking students need special instruction in English and hence need special schools"; "All Chinese were aliens, fundamentally different from Canadians, and hence needed to be segregated"; "Since the Chinese were alien whatever they said made no sense and they were only upset because they misunderstood the board's educationally sound motives." And indeed, this remains the school board's position throughout the strike (e.g., Victoria School Board, 1922).

Seen in this light, Hastings is making a brave intervention because he is directly challenging the received racialized binary of Canadian and Chinese, a challenge that his own life circumstances also articulate. He introduces a new category that troubles racialized binaries, what he calls the "Canadian born Chinese," and hence addresses the first condition for racisms and anti-racism, that of challenging racializations. In fact this tiny group of people, no more than a few hundred, had come to call themselves "Chinese Canadians" in a direct challenge to their exclusion and in articulating the reality of their lives, which was across and in-between racializing binaries. Indeed, as I argue, these Chinese Canadians were the main activists behind the students' strike, an insight that I acknowledge comes first from Harry Hastings (Stanley, 2011).

Thus, from an anti-racist perspective it is possible to develop a much richer reading of Hastings' letter, a reading that acknowledges it as an act of contest that was challenging racialized binaries at the same time as it was articulating with a racist social and political organization, while also trying to engage the meanings of those who are racialized and excluded. However, turning to the first perspective on anti-racism that I noted, the idea that racisms exist in the plural and hence can come together in specific ways, it also reenacts another very significant racialized exclusion that has enormous consequences for the racialized and excluded. Hastings' letter, the technology of dissemination it uses, the language in which it is written, the categories and actors it takes for granted—school boards, students, migrants from China, "whites," "Canadian born Chinese"—are all artifacts of the dominant racism of early 20th-century British Columbia, and indeed of Canada more generally up to the present day. This is the exclusion of Aboriginal peoples, First Nations, Inuit and Métis, something that was the result of a deliberate project of marginalization, apartheid and ethnic cleansing (see Harris, 1997, 2002). The entire exchange, indeed the entire discussion in English and in Chinese of the students' strike, makes no reference to the fundamental fact that it is taking place on a territory that within living memory had been that of the Songhees people; indeed, their reservation had been ethnically cleansed from Victoria's inner harbour only 11 years before the students' strike. Once this is taken seriously, we very rapidly find that the anti-Chinese racism involved in school segregation was built into the colonizing project that created the Canadian state system, a project that ensured the local dominance of those of European origins, and especially of men, by trying to effect the genocide of First Nations and the exclusion of Asians. Indeed, the British Columbia legislature often enacted Chinese and First Nations exclusions together in the same legislation, as was the case with its third act, which took the right to vote away from all Chinese and all First Nations men. (This became law in 1874; see An Act to Make Better Provision for the Qualification and Registration of Voters, 1875). At the time, First Nations and Chinese were conservatively estimated to be close to 90% of the male population (Galois & Harris, 1994). Men from China were often the majority population in certain districts and may have been the majority of non-First Nations men at the time. Thus the supremacy of men racialized as white was built into the state system at its inception (Stanley, 2011). Once this is grasped it is easy to find other evidence asserting it, evidence that is in easily accessible public records. For example, John A. Macdonald, the first Prime Minister of Canada, justified the disenfranchisement of those racialized as Chinese on the grounds that Canada should be "an Aryan nation." His comments are recorded in the official debates of the House of Commons, copies of which are available in any public or university library in Canada (Canada, 1885).

Conclusion

Anti-racism as historical methodology promises a richer reading of sources, a better understanding of context, and leads to better and more interesting questions and lines of inquiry. It should be able to play a similar role for contemporary methodologies, especially for qualitative studies including ethnographies, interviews and critical discourse analysis. It also encourages self-reflectivity on our own implications in the very phenomena that we study. For example, scholars often struggle to collect and analyze interviews and understandably get caught up in the details of their work, recruiting participants and transcribing and analyzing the interviews. It is easy to forget to ask about the provenance of the interviews, the cultural and social processes that lead to their creation and the narratives and meanings that they can easily and unintentionally exclude. Anti-racism might assist us in thinking through some of these engagements, in getting to the sample of inconvenience. The mere fact that we recognize the existence of excluded narratives allows us to ask about our own research, to recognize that our knowledge is always limited, always contingent, always partial. This alone promises more textured and nuanced understandings and can lead to better and more fruitful questions.

More importantly, in contrast to other approaches that do not ask the kinds of critical questions that it does, anti-racism offers a better picture of reality, and is more alive to the complex social dynamics that continually reproduce and circulate certain people's meanings while excluding the meanings of most of the people in the world. Like other critical methodologies, it highlights the role of scholarship in addressing the issues of our times. The white supremacist nature of Canadian state formation in its origin and consequences is not hidden deep within the bowels of a restricted archive. It is evident in widely available and increasingly digitized sources as well as in everyday life. Yet, in the dominant mythologies of Canada as the nation of multicultural tolerance, the kinder and gentler America, the white supremacist nature of Canadian state formation is almost never signified either in public discourse or in scholarship. Instead it is celebrated. The white supremacists, the masterminds of genocide, the architects of apartheid become the heroes of the national past, while the racialization and exclusion of

Aboriginal people and people of colour continues (Stanley, 2009). This urges critical intervention in our scholarship as in our lives.

References

An Act to Make Better Provision for the Qualification and Registration of Voters. (1875). *Statutes of the Province of British Columbia.* Victoria, BC: Richard Wolfenden, Government Printer, p. 18.

Adilman, T. (1984). A preliminary sketch of Chinese women and work in British Columbia 1858–1950. In B. K. Latham & R. J. Pezdro (Eds.), *Not just pin money: Selected essays on the history of women's work in British Columbia* (pp. 53–78). Victoria, BC: Camosun College.

Alexander, M. J., & Mohanty, C. T. (1997). *Feminist genealogies, colonial legacies, democratic futures.* New York, NY: Routledge.

Allen, T. (1994). *The invention of the white race* (Vol. 1 & 2). London, England: Verso.

Ankersmit, F. R. (2001). *Historical representation.* Stanford, CA: Stanford University Press.

Ankersmit, F. R., & Kellner, H. (Eds.). (1995). *A new philosophy of history.* Chicago, IL: University of Chicago Press.

Arendt, H. (1944). Race-thinking before racism. *Review of Politics, 6,* 36–73.

Arendt, H. (1979). *The origins of totalitarianism* (New ed. with added prefaces). San Diego, CA: Harvest/HBJ.

Ashworth, M. (1979). *The forces which shaped them: A history of the education of minority group children in British Columbia.* Vancouver, BC: New Star Books.

Barzun, J. (1938). *Race: A study in modern superstition.* London, England: Methuen.

Bonnett, A. (2000). *Anti-racism.* London, England: Routledge.

Bunzl, M. (1997). *Real history: Reflections on historical practice.* London, England: Routledge.

Canada. House of Commons. (1885, May 4). *Debates,* 17, 1582.

Carr, E. H. (1961). *What is history?* London, England: Macmillan.

Chong, D. (1994). *The concubine's children: Portrait of a family divided.* Toronto, ON: Penguin.

Con, H., Con, R. J., Johnson, G., Wickberg, E., & Willmott, W. E. (1982). *From China to Canada: A history of the Chinese communities of Canada* (Edgar Wickberg, Ed.). Toronto, ON: McClelland & Stewart.

Curtis, B. (1988).*Building the educational state: Canada West, 1836–1871.* London, ON: Althouse Press.

Davidson, J. W., & Lytle, M. H. (1992).*After the fact: The art of historical detection* (3rd ed.). New York, NY: McGraw-Hill.

Dei, G. J. S. (1996). *Anti-racism education: Theory and practice.* Halifax, NS: Fernwood.

Essed, P., & Goldberg, D. T. (2002). *Race critical theories: Text and context.* Oxford, England: Blackwell.

Evans, R. J. (2000). *In defence of history* (new ed.). London, England: Granta Books.

Fanon, F. (1967).*Black skin, white masks.* New York, NY: Grove Press.

Frankenberg, R. (1993). *White women, race matters: The social construction of whiteness.* Minneapolis: University of Minnesota Press.

Gaffield, C. (2006). The blossoming of Canadian historical research: Implications for educational policy and change. In R. Sandwell (Ed.), *To the past: History education, public memory and citizenship in Canada* (pp. 88–102). Toronto, ON: University of Toronto Press.

Galois, R., & Harris, R. C. (1994). Recalibrating society: The population geography of British Columbia. *Canadian Geographer, 38*(1), 37–53.

Gilroy, P. (2000). *Against race: Imagining political culture beyond the color line.* Cambridge, MA: Harvard University Press.

Goldberg, D. T. (1993). *Racist culture: Philosophy and the politics of meaning.* Cambridge, MA: Blackwell.

Goldberg, D. T. (2002). *The racial state.* Oxford, England: Blackwell.

Hall, S. (1980). Race, articulation and societies structured in dominance. In UNESCO (Ed.), *Sociological theories: Race and colonialism* (pp. 305–345). Paris, France: United Nations Educational, Scientific and Cultural Organization.

Hall, S. (1986). The problem of ideology: Marxism without guarantees. *Journal of Communication Inquiry, 10*(2), 28–44.

Hall, S. (1997). The work of representation. In S. Hall (Ed.), *Representation: Cultural representations and signifying practices* (pp. 13–74). London, England: Sage.

Hardy, G. (1995). Can an ancient Chinese historian contribute to modern Western theory? The multiple narratives of Ssu-Ma Chien.*History and Theory, 33*(1), 20–39.

Harris, R. C. (1997). *The resettlement of British Columbia: Essays on colonialism and geographical change.* Vancouver: University of British Columbia Press.

Harris, R. C. (2002). *Making native space: Colonialism, resistance, and reserves in British Columbia.* Vancouver: University of British Columbia Press.

Harry Hastings obituary. (1967, February 8). *The Daily Colonist* (Victoria), p. 20.

Hastings, H. (1922a, October 8). Analysis of the Chinese segregation question in Victoria. *The Daily Colonist* (Victoria), p. 14.

Hasting, H. (1922b, September 20). Segregation question [Letter to the editor]. *The Daily Colonist* (Victoria), p. 4.

Hastings, H. (1923, February 1). Chinese segregation [Letter to the editor]. *The Daily Colonist* (Victoria), p. 13.

Hastings, H. (1924a, May 26 & 30). Tea with Harry Hastings, the half breed Chinese intellectual of Victoria. Interview with W. Raushenbush. Survey of Race Relations, Major Documents, Box 24, file 31. Hoover Institution Archives, Stanford University, Palo Alto, CA.

Hastings, H. (1924b, May 26 & 30). Interview Mr. Harry Hastings regarding the school strike and other matters. Survey of Race Relations, Major Documents, Box 24, file 32. Hoover Institution Archives, Stanford University, Palo Alto, CA.

Huang, B. (2009). Teaching Chineseness in the trans-Pacific society: Overseas Chinese education in Canada and the United States, 1900–1919 (Unpublished PhD dissertation). Princeton University, Princeton, NJ. Retrieved from UMI Microforms, 3364537.

Jenkins, K. (2009). *At the limits of history: Essays on theory and practice.* London, England: Routledge.

Joe, Kwong [Hope, Joe or Low Kwong Joe] (1922, September 10). Chinese in schools [Letter to the editor]. *The Daily Colonist* (Victoria), p. 4.

Lai, D. C. (1987). The issue of discrimination in education in Victoria, 1901–1923. *Canadian Ethnic Studies, 19*(3), 47–67.

Lee, D. T. H. (Lee T'ung-hai). [Li Donghai]. (1967). *Jianada Huaqiaoshi* [A history of the overseas Chinese in Canada]. Taibei, Taiwan: Zhonghua Da Dian BianyingHui.

Leonardo, Z. (2004). The color of supremacy: Beyond the discourse of white privilege. *Educational Philosophy and Theory, 36*(2), 137–152.

Lewis, A. (2003). *Race in the schoolyard: Negotiating the color line in classrooms and communities.* New Brunswick, NJ: Rutgers University Press.

Li, P. S. (1998). *The Chinese in Canada.* Toronto, ON: Oxford University Press.

Lowe, C. C. (1922, September 14). Segregation [Letter to the editor]. *Victoria Daily Times*, p. 4.

Marrus, M. R. (1987). *The Holocaust in history.* Toronto, ON: Lester & Orpen Dennys.

Martin, G. (2004). *Past futures: The impossible necessity of history.* Toronto, ON: University of Toronto Press.

Megill, A. (1995). "Grand narrative" and the discipline of history. In F. Ankersmit & H. Kellner (Eds.), *A new philosophy of history* (pp. 151–173). Chicago, IL: University of Chicago Press.

Miles, R. (1989). *Key Ideas Series: Racism.* London, England: Routledge.

Mohanty, S. P. (1997). *Literary theory and the claims of history: Postmodernism, objectivity, multicultural politics.* Ithaca, NY: Cornell University Press.

Montagu, A. (Ed.). (1964). *The concept of race.* New York: Free Press of Glencoe.

Omi, M., & Winant, H. (1986). *Racial formation in the United States from the 1960s to the 1980s.* New York, NY: Routledge.

Perry, A. (2001). *On the edge of empire: Gender, race, and the making of British Columbia, 1849–1871.* Toronto, ON: University of Toronto Press.

Roy, P. E. (1989). *A white man's province: British Columbia politicians and Chinese and Japanese immigrants, 1858–1914.* Vancouver: University of British Columbia Press.

Roy, P. E. (2003). *The Oriental question: Consolidating a white man's province, 1914–41.* Vancouver: University of British Columbia Press.

Rutherford, P. (1982). *A Victorian authority: The Daily Press in late nineteenth-century Canada.* Toronto, ON: University of Toronto Press.

Said, E. W. (1994). *Culture and imperialism.* New York, NY: Vintage Books.

Stanley, T. J. (1990). White supremacy, Chinese schooling and school segregation in Victoria: The case of the 1922–1923 Chinese students' strike. *Historical Studies in Education, 2*(2), 287–305.

Stanley, T. J. (2009). The banality of colonialism: Encountering artifacts of genocide and white supremacy in Vancouver today. In S. R. Steinberg (Ed.), *Diversity and multiculturalism: A reader* (pp. 143–159). New York, NY: Peter Lang.

Stanley, T. J. (2011). *Contesting white supremacy: School segregation, anti-racism and the making of Chinese Canadians.* Vancouver: University of British Columbia Press.

Stockard, J. E. (1989). *Daughters of the Canton delta: Marriage patterns and economic strategies in South China, 1860–1930.* Stanford, CA: Stanford University Press.

Velleman, J. D. (2003). Narrative explanation. *The Philosophical Review, 112*(1), 1–25.

Victoria School Board. (1922, October 21). Segregation plan to aid efficiency in public schools. *Victoria Daily Times*, p. 24.

Ward, W. P. (1978). *White Canada forever: Popular attitudes and public policy toward Orientals in British Columbia.* Montreal, QC: McGill-Queen's University Press.

Wen, Q. Y. (1922). Chinese in schools [Letter to the editor]. *The Daily Colonist* (Victoria), p. 4.

Wertsch, J. V. (2002). *Voices of collective remembering.* Cambridge, England: Cambridge University Press.

White, H. (1980). The value of narrativity in the representation of reality. *Critical Inquiry, 7*(1), 5–27.

White, H. (1987). *The content of the form: Narrative discourse and historical representation.* Baltimore, MD: Johns Hopkins University Press.

White, H. (1998). The historical text as literary artifact. In B. Fay, P. Pomper, & R. T. Vann (Eds.), *History and theory: Contemporary readings* (pp. 15–33). Malden, MA: Blackwell.

Won, G. (1922, September 10). School problem [Letter to the editor]. *The Daily Colonist* (Victoria), p. 4.

Wrigley Directories Limited. (1925). *Wrigley-Henderson Amalgamated British Columbia directory, 1924–25.* Vancouver, BC: Author.

CHAPTER TWENTY-THREE

Researching the Discursive Function of Silence: A Reconsideration of the Normative Communication Patterns in the Talk of Children with Autism Labels

Jessica Nina Lester

Since the 1940s, with the construction and popularization of autism as a diagnostic category (Asperger, 1944/1991; Kanner, 1943/1985), the extensive research on autism has focused on identifying, describing, and treating children who exhibit what Kanner originally called "fascinating peculiarities" (p. 217). Autism has often been positioned within a discourse of disease and deficit, with metaphors of "medical intervention" and "cure" frequently evoked in research communities and popular media outlets (Broderick & Ne'eman, 2008, p. 469). In light of these deficit and medical models of representation, the majority of research within the field of autism has focused on identifying the (presumed) core deficits, etiology, and effective treatments for what has come to be named a spectrum of autistic disorders (Glynne-Owen, 2010). As medical and scientific literatures have represented autism as a biological fact to be understood primarily through the lens of positivistic methodologies and the "assumptions of the natural sciences," the social conditions and everyday practices that make possible the naming, representing, treating, and performing of autism have been often overlooked (Nadesan, 2005, p. 2).

Further, with a predominant focus on etic representations of autism, little research has aimed to understand autism from an emic perspective. Qualitative inquiry in a field as highly medicalized as autism is inherently challenging, in that "most of the language of the field assumes a shared, normative perspective" (Biklen et al., 2005, p. 14). There is a small yet growing corpus of qualitative studies focused on the life stories of individuals with autism labels (e.g., Ashby, 2010; Ashby & Causton-Theoharis, 2009), the everyday practices of "high-functioning children with autism and Asperger syndrome" (Ochs, Kremer-Sadlik, Sirota, & Solmon, 2004, p. 147) and identity construction of individuals with autism labels (Bagatell, 2007). Although some conversation analysis studies exist, examining the organization of the talk of individuals with autism labels (Stribling, Rae, & Dickerson, 2007; Wootton, 1999), little research has applied discursive approaches to understanding dis/ability as situated and locally produced (O'Reilly, 2005; Rapley, Kiernan, & Antaki, 1998).[1] Much of the discursive research has presumed that autism, as a *real*, ahistorical entity, organizes discourses versus discourse itself organizing the very meanings attached to autism.

Drawing from a larger discourse analysis study (Lester, 2011), in this chapter I focus on findings drawn from the analysis of therapy sessions of children with autism labels and their therapists, fieldnotes, and parent and therapist interviews. I highlight one particular finding—the way in which the parents, therapists, and children worked to reframe communication patterns often constructed as "abnormal" by outsiders, particularly as related to longer-than-expected silences. With this study positioned at the intersection of dis/ability studies, critical notions of human learning and development, and discourse studies, I considered how children with autism labels and their parents and therapists managed, contested, resisted, and made relevant "problematic" moments with and/or "concerning behaviors" of children in the context of a therapy center, focusing my analysis on naturally occurring waiting-room conversations, occupational, speech-pathology, and physical therapy sessions, and hallway conversations. Moving away from an etic perspective, I took up discourse theory and analysis, situating this work within a discursive psychology framework (Edwards & Potter, 1993) that was informed by poststructural understandings of discourse (Derrida, 1981; Foucault, 1971), certain aspects of conversation analysis (Sacks, 1992), and a social relational model of dis/ability (Thomas, 2004). I invite the reader to engage with and question the findings, seeking to produce knowledge that is layered (Bochner, 2009) and imbued with multiple and competing perspectives (Noblit & Engels, 1999).

Positionality and Theoretical Commitments

I begin by situating this research in relation to my positionality, recognizing that I am always negotiating, constructing, and reconstructing my multiple, intersecting social locations (Fine, 1994). I challenge objective and realists' notions of research, and in such challenging, locate the positionality of the researcher and the practice of reflexivity as critical to the research process (Skeggs, 2002). I bring to this work my history as a friend and former teacher of individuals with autism labels and assume, like postcritical ethnographers Noblit, Flores, and Murillo (2004), that I "exist within a critical discourse that in part makes" me "responsible for the world" I am producing when I describe, interpret, and critique social phenomena of interest (p. 24). Thus, throughout the research process, I turn back on myself, acknowledging the personal and political dimensions of my positionality and the intersectionality of my own identities.

I view social life as constructed in contexts of power (Noblit et al., 2004), e.g., one individual is labeled while the other does the labeling, and acknowledge the non-neutral and political nature of language, viewing dis/ability as being (1) a social construct; (2) political; and (3) made relevant through discourse. I take up critical notions of dis/ability and "normative" human development, orienting to such a critical stance as one which compels me to deny "easy, dichotomous explanations" as I aim to make "contradictions transparent" (Wodak, 1999, p. 186). Throughout this work, I positioned my understanding of dis/ability within a social relational model of dis/ability (Thomas, 2004), in which dis/ability is conceptualized as relevant only when socially imposed restrictions of activity are experienced by people labeled dis/abled. In this way, a distinction is made between dis/ability and bodily realities or impairment effects. With dis/ability only coming into play when there is a restriction placed on one's activities, Thomas suggested "that it is entirely possible to acknowledge that impairments and chronic illness [may] directly cause *some* restrictions of activity—but such non-socially imposed restrictions of activity do not constitute 'disability'" (p. 581).

Methodological Commitments and Method

While I relied upon a discursive psychology framework, attending closely to the discursive features made relevant within the local and situated talk of the participants (Edwards & Potter, 1993), I also worked to position each claim in relation to the broader discourses and socio-political context. The study took place at The Green Room (pseudonym), a therapeutic clinic in the Midwest region of the United States. Being sensitive to the power inherent in naming others, I invited all of the parents, therapists, and children to select their own pseudonyms. I report here on the analysis of 70 hours of the naturally occurring data—the audio-recorded therapy sessions and waiting room conversations of the 12 participating children with autism labels, seven therapists (three speech, two occupational, and one physical therapist, as well as one teacher), and 17 parents. I also draw upon 14 parent interviews and seven therapist interviews, as well as my fieldnotes from approximately 330 hours of observations. Drawing upon the traditions of discourse analysis (Edwards & Potter, 1993), I carried out the following six phases of data analysis: (1) intensive listening; (2) transcription; (3) repeated reading and listening; (4) selection, identification, organization, and further analysis of patterns across the discourse segments (i.e., episodes or segments of talk) related to the various discursive features and/or broader discourses and institutionalized practices; (5) generation of explanations/interpretations; and (6) reflexive and transparent sharing of findings.

Throughout my analysis of the data, I broadly defined the notion of a "pattern" or "recurring" discursive event. I sought to identify common ways in which the doing of therapy was managed in and through the discursive practices of the participants. Yet, even while identifying commonalities, I presumed that each pattern was variable; each interactive moment was locally situated and not without contradiction (whether I noted it or not). Furthermore, one of the ways that discourse analysts produce trustworthiness with the reader is by illustrating the steps involved in the analysis of a given excerpt of the data. Thus, in lieu of simply telling the reader about a given interpretation and pointing to an excerpt that illustrates my point, in the next section I walk the reader through my decision-making process while also making transparent the way I analyzed the selected excerpt and came to particular interpretations (Wood & Kroger, 2000).

Defining and Redefining Communication: Re-knowing Silences in Talk

While I ultimately settled on the research question noted above, coming to this decision was difficult. Early in the analysis process, I realized that I needed to narrow my analysis, as there were many striking and telling discursive features across the data. To inform this decision, I returned to my evolving research questions and also began to ask the following questions: (1) Who has the power to decide what I choose to analyze most closely? (2) Who has the power to determine the results I share first? and (3) Who has the power to name the research questions that are worth asking (Kvale, 1995)? I recognized that I, as researcher, would ultimately determine the questions I brought to the data and chose to explore and share with others. Yet, I desired to make my decisions as transparent and open to public critique as possible (Flyvberg, 2001). Thus, I began to share my interpretations of the data with the participating parents and therapists, explicitly inviting them to tell me what I was perhaps failing to make sense of and to evaluate the interpretations I proffered.

After engaging in a discussion around alternative interpretations of the talk and the practical implications of the findings, the participating therapists suggested that I more closely explore "wait time" (i.e., silences and pauses between each turn) in the interactions between the therapists and children. During one meeting with the participating therapists in which I shared my unfolding interpretations, Megan stated:

> So have you looked at turn-taking like with wait time stuff? Like the pauses? Because I think a lot of the children we work with have patterns that are dispreferred; so what often happens is people fill the space after "How are you?" with a million questions. Like it totally makes people uncomfortable when people don't answer a question.

Her response led me to return to the therapy session data and more closely attend to turn-taking organization, considering what the pauses and silences were *doing* across the data.

I was particularly intrigued by this additional analytic focus; previous research has often suggested that pauses, non-responses, or silence often signal a problem within the conversation itself (Pomerantz, 1984). Such research has pointed to a preferred pattern that speakers often take up: one speaker speaks at a time, with little or no gap between turns. An unexpectedly long pause may be oriented to as a reluctance to participate or signal that a speaker has disengaged from the conversation itself (Sacks, Schegloff, & Jefferson, 1974). Jefferson (1989) noted that in Anglo and Dutch conversations, the length of comfortable silence, not without variation, was around a one-second interval (0.9-1.2 seconds). When longer silences were not oriented to as problematic, they were typically associated with non-conversational activities, such as writing down a phone number (Goodwin, 1981).

While Jefferson's (1989) extensive work around conversational practices has provided much empirical evidence regarding how silences and gaps are often managed in talk, there is also a significant body of ethnographic and sociolinguistic work that has attended to the varied meanings of silences and conversational gaps across geographic spaces, family units, and cultures. Tannen (1984) described the conversational style of New York Jewish culture as privileging simultaneous talk, with silences or lengthy pauses often signaling a lack of involvement in the interaction. On the other hand, Mushin and Gardner (2009) conducted a conversation analysis focused on silences in talk recorded in Australian Aboriginal communities. They reported that "comfortable silence" was much longer than Jefferson's (1989) one-second interval "rule," with even 13-second silences not being correlated with interactional problems (p. 2049). Comfortable silence, then, varies across space and place.

Within the broader body of literature around autism, conversational pauses, silences, and/or non-responsiveness are often coupled with evidence of a pathology or communicative deficit; a defining and commonly agreed-upon characteristic of autism is poor orientation to speech. In fact, the very assessments utilized to determine whether a child "has" a communication disorder often privilege immediate responses to questions and requests, with pauses and/or silences of more than one to two seconds being viewed as problematic (Newcomer & Hammill, 1977). Without exhibiting an immediate response, the individual with an autism label may be quickly presumed to be intellectually disabled and incapable of participating with other social actors. The autobiographical accounts of adults with autism labels have highlighted how people with autism labels are aware and troubled that others, most often those without autism labels, underestimate their competence and view them as inept due to a delayed or lack of verbal response (Rentenbach, 2009).

I was thus intrigued and somewhat surprised by how the participants oriented to longer than expected pauses as nothing unusual, in that these silences did not align with the aforementioned norms. I wondered if the ways in which the therapists oriented to silences pointed to the institutionality and particularity of the therapy talk. Returning to the data, I noted that silences, even up to 60 seconds, were not usually treated as problematic, particularly by the therapists. Instead, when a participating child did not respond to a parent's or therapist's request and/or question, the therapists simply waited, reworded/rephrased the question, or offered other modalities by which the child might respond (e.g., communication device, writing, or signing).

I begin with an excerpt (see Appendix A for transcription symbols) drawn from a parent interview in which Amelia responded to my first interview question, "What things might you want someone who has just met your child to know about him?" In her response, Amelia made relevant the need to "be patient" and wait for her son, The Emperor (pseudonym selected by the child), to respond after posing a question.

Excerpt One

1   *Amelia*: Um wow that's a good question um (4) eh (1) y- I guess i-i-it's to be patient
2   [with him↑ I think
3   *Jessica*: hm

4   *Amelia*: a] lot of people ask him questions and then (1) it takes him it will take The
5   Emperor a good thirty seconds sometimes to think of the answer but it's in↑ there=
6   *Jessica*: =Mm hm=
7   *Amelia*: =I mean he knows what you're saying to him and he knows the answer to
8   what you're asking him↑=
9   *Jessica*: =Mm hm (1)
10   *Amelia*: sometimes it comes out and sometimes it doesn't so most of it is patience
11   most of it is you know (1) don't expect even though he looks like he should
12   react↑=
13   *Jessica*: =Mm hm=
14   *Amelia*: like everybody else's kid (1) he's not gunna react [like
15   *Jessica*: mm hm]
16   *Amelia*: everybody else's kid um (2) but he's (.) he's smart I mean he knows (1) he
17   knows what's going on he knows (2) everything anybody else's child that age knows
18   he [just can't
19   *Jessica*: Mm hm]
20   *Amelia*: just can't get it out so

In the above excerpt, Amelia initially acknowledged my question, paused, said "eh," and then paused again (line 1). She then said, "y- I guess i-i-it's," followed by "to be patient." I was struck by the way in which Amelia's initial pauses and repairs ("y- I guess i-i-it's") delayed the progressivity or forward action of the interaction. Behaviors and/or conversational features that stall the forward action of talk often signal some kind of trouble and/or that a delicate matter is being made relevant (Lerner, 1996).

As such, in my analysis of this excerpt, I closely attended to what followed Amelia's delay and oriented to the statement, "to be patient," as likely being of interactional import, making relevant what she *really* wanted others to know about her son. In lieu of offering a description of her son (which she did much later in the interview), Amelia began by emphasizing what others should do in response to The Emperor. She then moved to justify why being patient with The Emperor was indeed necessary, with 30-second silences constructed as a typical occurrence (line 5). By establishing that 30 seconds of silence is not unusual for The Emperor, Amelia pointed to the normative communication pattern of responding immediately after being asked a question or being given a command. Furthermore, by adding, "but it's in↑ there," Amelia attended to the societal presumption that long pauses or non-responsiveness is typically indicative of cognitive impairment. Thus, even though 30-second delays were common for her son, The Emperor was constructed as competent.

Like the parents of other participating children who communicated more nonverbally than verbally, Amelia presumed that silence or a lack of response was not equivalent to not understanding what someone was saying. Indeed, as Lewiecki-Wilson (2003) noted, historically, a verbal response of some kind has often been connected to one's very "humanness" (p. 157). Conversation analysts have argued that people often draw moral conclusions based on the absence of a response (Drew & Toerien, 2011). Thus, I suggest it is fair to presume that there is much at stake for Amelia. If, for example, she constructed a 30-second communication delay as pathological and indicative of a cognitive disorder, her son might have been positioned as a dis/abled body with little to no capacity to actively participate in the world around him. Yet, by constructing The Emperor as capable, even though he might take 30 seconds to respond to another speaker, Amelia left open the possibility that The Emperor is competent, "like everybody else's kid."

While Amelia constructed her son as competent, she did not evade his communicative differences, stating, "sometimes it comes out and sometimes it doesn't." Yet, Amelia did not orient to this *reality*, or what Thomas (2004) might call The Emperor's primary impairment effect, as a static entity, for in the end "most of it is patience." Her move to reemphasize "patience" brought to the fore the idea that the *real* issue was not that her son was incapable, but that other speakers did not know how to interact with him or were simply impatient. She furthered this idea stating, "you know (1) don't expect even though he looks like he should react," also pointing to the idea of a look or body of normality. Perhaps, then, for Amelia, the construction of The Emperor as dis/abled occurred when his body was oriented to by others as *hearably* dis/abled; that is, when he failed to respond to another speaker, the speaker took note of this response and "read" his performance as incompetent. While Amelia constructed The Emperor's impairment as *invisible*, as "he looks like he should react" when spoken to, he failed to pass as an abled speaker. The Emperor, though, was *hearably* anomalous to the degree that his communication patterns challenged the normative standards of communication, which Amelia highlighted in her talk. Over and over again, with different phrases, Amelia made a case for her son's competence, moving from state- ments such as, "but it's in↑ there" to "he knows what you're saying to him" to "he's smart."

In offering a different "read" on The Emperor's silence, Amelia contrasted his reaction to that of other children, presumably children using normative communicative patterns (lines 14–17). While she acknowledged that The Emperor did not communicatively react like other children, she resisted the idea that he knew less than "anybody else's child that age." In comparing him to other children, Amelia indeed normalized his communication style and positioned him as being not that dissimilar from others. Even still, Amelia made relevant the presumably recognizable issue: "he just can't get it out." Her use of the word "just" possibly functioned to minimize The Emperor's difficulty in getting "it out," reestablishing the *real* problematic issue as being how others orient to and interact with her son. Impairment effects, as Thomas (2004) noted, often lead to exclusion, to barriers to doing and being. Nevertheless, exclusionary communication practices could be conceivably avoided by orienting to non- normative communication patterns, such as 30-second delays, as nothing more than "just" signaling the need for "patience."

As I continued to work across the therapy data, focusing primarily on how silence, as a discursive resource, played out in the context of The Green Room, I collected those instances in which silences or delayed responses were oriented to as relevant by the participants. Excerpt Two illustrates the way in which many of the parents and therapists often oriented to and worked through silence linked to initial greetings, often occurring in the waiting room of The Green Room. This particular interchange oc- curred about one minute after Amelia and The Emperor arrived at The Green Room. Both Amelia and The Emperor were sitting in the waiting room, waiting for The Emperor to have a speech-pathology session with Jennifer, one of his therapists.

The excerpt begins just after Jennifer has walked out of the main office into the waiting room area.

Excerpt Two

1   *Jennifer*: I think I'm ready↑ (Jennifer kneels down, positioning herself in front of
2   The Emperor. She reaches her hand out to The Emperor.)=
3   *The Emperor*: =(Places his hand in Jennifer's hand)=
4   *Jennifer*: =(Gazes at The Emperor and moves his left hand to her right cheek,
5   holding his hand throughout the interchange.)(3)
6   *The Emperor*: (Gazes directly at Jennifer, making eye contact with her)=
7   *Jennifer*: =Hi The Emperor (5)
8   *Amelia*: Hello (Gazes directly at The Emperor) (1)
9   *The Emperor*: (Gazes at Amelia and then makes eye contact with Jennifer)=
10   *Jennifer*: =Hi The Emperor (4) hi (2) can you [tell me hi↑
11   *Amelia*: °the lights are on°] the lights are on but nobody's home=
12   *The Emperor*: =(Looks out the front door of The Green Room) duh duh duh=
13   *Jennifer*: =(Laughs) boo=

14   *The Emperor*: =(Looks at Jennifer)=
15   *Amelia*: =who is this↑ (points to Jennifer) (4) The Emperor=
16   *Jennifer*: =(Laughs)=
17   *Amelia*: =Say hello (2) who is that (points to Jennifer) (2) who is it↑=
18   *Jennifer*: =Am I George↑(1)
19   *Amelia*: Who is this↑ (2)
20   *The Emperor*: Halfie (1)
21   *Amelia*: who is [that
22   *Jennifer*: look] (Pats The Emperor's hand on her right cheek)
23   *The Emperor*: (Gazes directly at Jennifer, making eye contact with her)=
24   *Jennifer*: =Hi The Emperor↑ (3)
25   *The Emperor*: Hi Jennifer (.)
26   *Amelia*: [oof
27   *Jennifer*: (Laughs)]=
28   *Amelia*: =Made me break a sweat there↑=
29   *Jennifer*: =(Laughs) we got there right↑

Jennifer began by announcing her presence and that she was ready to begin the therapy session (line 1). She then moved to kneel down in front of The Emperor, extended her hand toward his hand, as he extended his hand toward her (lines 1–4). She then held his hand near her cheek (line 5). Throughout this initial, nonverbal interaction, Jennifer maintained her gaze on The Emperor. This initial, primarily nonverbal interaction was a common interactional sequence across the data, particularly during the initial waiting-room greetings. This sequence pointed to the institutionality of the therapy talk, highlighting the ways in which conversational sequences, such as an initial waiting-room greeting, were performed in particular ways with a recognizable shape or sequence (Drew & Toerien, 2011).

In the above excerpt, after a three-second pause, The Emperor gazed at Jennifer (line 4), which she immediately responded to with, "Hi The Emperor." Note that the therapist did not fill the silence with requests or verbal commands, which is often what occurs in conversations filled with silences of this length (Pomerantz, 1984). Furthermore, Jennifer's response to The Emperor's gaze made relevant the action-oriented nature of his gaze. His gaze was attended to and responded to, making evident the interactional importance of gazing at another speaker. With lack of eye contact often associated with a diagnosis of autism and addressed by requesting that children look and then rewarding their look with some kind of item of interest, I was particularly interested in how the participating therapists might take up and make relevant eye contact. In the above excerpt, mutual gaze or eye contact was coupled with a greeting, pointing to the ways in which this nonverbal discursive resource (eye contact) was privileged and made relevant. Not surprisingly, then, Jennifer responded to The Emperor's gaze with a greeting two additional times in this excerpt (lines 9–10 and lines 23–24), with a multitude of additional instances of similar sequences noted across the data set.

As I considered what eye gaze *did* in therapy talk, I made sense of this interactional resource in local and situated ways, presuming that its function was particular and not necessarily generalizable to other therapeutic contexts. I kept in mind that while many cultures privilege mutual gaze between children and adults, there are indeed wide variations across contexts. Some caregivers encourage eye gaze patterns in interactions, with early socialization around eye gaze often being linked to cultural values (Keller, 2003). More specifically, at The Green Room, privileging eye contact was something that the therapists considered in relationship to a given family's cultural preference. For instance, Michelle, a participating therapist, reported during her interview that she had recently worked with a child whose family "did not view eye contact as a polite" interactional resource; thus, she worked to communicate with the child in other nonverbal and verbal ways.

Nevertheless, in the excerpt above, Jennifer oriented to The Emperor's eye gaze with a greeting, pointing to the way in which eye gaze was institutionally coupled with official greetings. Typically, when greeted, a preferred or expected response is for a speaker to reply with a return greeting, generally with promptness (Sacks, 1992). However, in this case, The Emperor did not return Jennifer's verbal greeting. When a dispreferred response occurs, such as a non-response to a greeting, the response is often oriented to as problematic and accounted for in subsequent conversational turns (Pomerantz, 1984). If, for instance, a greeting is not returned, the greeting may be repeated by the first speaker, implying that the first speaker assumed that the second speaker failed to hear or understand the greeting. Another possibility is that the speaker who stated the first greeting might simply walk away and assume that the second speaker is incapable of responding or does not desire to respond. Yet, in the excerpt above, Jennifer waited, holding The Emperor's hand on her face and gazing at him (line 7). While Jennifer made no move to fill the silence, after five seconds Amelia quietly voiced a "hello" (line 8), possibly making relevant her own discomfort with his non-responsiveness. After The Emperor gazed at Amelia, he immediately returned his gaze to Jennifer (line 9). Jennifer responded (again) to The Emperor's gaze with "Hello," further making relevant the situated, cultural norm linking eye contact to a greeting.

After another pause, Jennifer requested that The Emperor "tell" her "hi." Her request was interrupted by Amelia, who stated, "the lights are on…but nobody's home." This statement perhaps marked Amelia's discomfort and concern with her son's non-responsiveness. Following this statement, Amelia both directly and indirectly requested for The Emperor to respond. She began by simply asking "who is this," stating his name with added emphasis (line 15). Then, she directly requested that he "say hello" and repeatedly asked "who" his therapist was (line 15, line 17, and line 21). Her repeated questions and direct requests made relevant the import (at least for Amelia) of The Emperor (1) responding to a greeting with a greeting and (2) greeting his therapist by name.

Jennifer, on the other hand, laughed (line 13 and line 16) and said "boo." Laughter, as an action-oriented resource, has been shown to function as a way to add levity when reporting troubles or making complaints (Edwards, 2005), to deal with delicate matters (Haakana, 2001), to mitigate disagreement in meetings (Osvaldsson, 2004), or to manage dispreferred responses in television talk (Stokoe, 2008). In the above excerpt, I interpreted laughter as functioning to both manage The Emperor's dispreferred response and deal with the delicate matter of what most would name The Emperor's primary impairment effect, his minimal or delayed verbal response. Nonetheless, after 17 turns (from the initial "hello" on line 7), The Emperor responded with "Hi Jennifer" (line 25). Following this, Amelia uttered "oof" and stated, "made me break a sweat." The use of the "oof" and the idiomatic expression, "made me break a sweat," made visible the troubling and delicate work of dealing with silences and dispreferred responses. Jennifer, on the other hand, laughed again and responded to Amelia with "we got there." Jennifer's response perhaps worked to mitigate Amelia's hearable concern, with Jennifer taking up her institutional role as a therapist and ever-so-subtly challenging Amelia's concern about her son's non-normative way of greeting others.

All of the parents of those children described as taking longer than normatively expected to respond emphasized the importance of waiting for a response or assisting their child in the use of alternative means of communicating. Across the data set, the therapists, in particular, oriented to communication as extending far beyond the use of words, phrases, and sentences, and reworked, in their practice, all that gets named normative communication.

Concluding Thoughts: Transgressing the Normative

As I made sense of the data, I began to view the therapeutic talk itself as functioning to transgress normative ways of communicating and behaving, with transgression being that which involves pushing the limits or boundaries imposed by others that operate to establish what is deemed ordered or disordered, abled or dis/abled, or autistic or non-autistic. Yet, as Foucault (1977) noted, while these boundaries themselves may never be fully transcended, challenging them is possible. According to Allan (1999), transgressive acts allow "individuals to peer over the edge of their limits, but also confirms the impossibility of removing them" (p. 48).

The very positioning of the participating children as competent, regardless of their communication style and what might otherwise be named their impairment effects (Thomas, 2004), left open the possibility for the participants, particularly the children, to subvert norms and perform something other than an incompetent, dis/abled subject. For instance, when a child was allowed to perform something other than *threatening*, *troubled* and *inept*, what had been named threatening or abnormal (e.g., "waving fist" or using alternative modes of communication) was reframed and reoriented to as explainable, albeit often misinterpreted by outsiders. It follows then that the everyday work of the participating therapists was not simply about teaching or even training the child to respond to questions more quickly or behave more "appropriately." Instead, perhaps the discursive practices of the participants functioned to construct what Lewiecki-Wilson (2003) called "mediated rhetoricity" or a "language used for the benefit" of the person with a communicative difference (p. 161). According to Lewiecki-Wilson, this "mediated rhetoricity" requires "attention" to the individual's "embodied nonverbal performances and gestures," as their friends, family, and advocates work to "carefully and ethically co-construct narratives and arguments from" their perspective (p. 161). The included excerpts and interpretations highlight the ways in which the participants' discursive practices challenge the "perceived wisdom of those at society's center," providing "a context to understand and transform established belief systems" (Solorzano & Yosso, 2002, p. 156).

It was the examination of the process of doing therapy, the daily interactions between the children and therapists, that moved me and challenged my own presuppositions about communication and appropriate versus inappropriate actions. When I shared my unfolding interpretations of the way in which silences were taken up (or not) across the data with the participants, Megan, one of the therapists, responded with the following:

> I guess, when you think about it, so much about The Emperor is about people being uncomfortable with that pause or wait time or him not looking at them. It's not just about inclusion or just including The Emperor. I think the community sort of needs to include themselves in this. Or I think there just must be a better word for that, but they need to become active participants. I think, you know, like people in the community, I guess including teachers, but even beyond that, you know, instead of just looking and keep going that they would try to initiate some sort of conversation.

Megan's response pointed to the inadequacy of inclusion as simply being about including The Emperor in society, shifting the focus on how the surrounding environment and its social actors might change themselves. Instead of saying, "the community needs to include the child," she stated, "the community sort of needs to include themselves in this." Rather than suggesting that the child should be the first to change, to adapt, or to be fixed, Megan oriented to the community as needing to adjust their interactions in response to the child. This evolving understanding was captured in the following research journal entry:

> July 21, 2010
> Today, this fieldwork has been a place of feeling deeply, feeling that I am responsible for all that I have stood witness to, at least in some small way. The participants have told me, taught me, shown me so much. One thing that keeps standing out for me is the *future*. "Who will be here for our child? Who will see what we see?" the parents ask me, often, usually through tears. What will the future hold for the child I observed today? Will those around him learn to be okay with the way in which he communicates? Can we learn to orient to silence as something other than problematic? Can we learn to engage in interactions that don't require or demand preferred, immediate responses? What would happen if we did? What would the future look like?

Now, I wonder and ask: what is my next step, not simply as a researcher, but as a friend and teacher of individuals with autism labels, and as a community member committed to finding comfortable and effective ways to increase participation with each other across social and communicative differences?

I recognize that meanings, even the meaning of silence and what comes to count as normative communication, are never given or guaranteed, but rather negotiated. At some level, then, the discourses that we come to take up and deploy as truth concern and involve all of us. The current ways of orienting to and constructing notions of normal, abnormal, abled, or disabled "reflect a series of choices made at different times between different possible worlds" (Skinner, 1998, p. 117). At each moment in history, we have opportunities to generate and offer new possibilities for discursively constructing and positioning one another (Weedon, 1987). "Equipped with a broader sense of possibility, we can stand back from the intellectual commitments we have inherited and ask ourselves in a new spirit of enquiry what we should" (Skinner, 1998, p. 117) and can do in our everyday interactions, particularly with individuals "whose physical, mental, cognitive and sensory abilities…fall outside of the scope of what is currently defined as socially acceptable" (Rauscher & McClintock, 1996, p. 198). Through a commitment to questioning taken-for-granted discourses, we can create moments of solidarity and perhaps even ruptures in the dominant discourses that work to pathologize, exclude, and stereotype.

Note

1. I separate "dis" from "ability" to emphasize the presumption of ability and competence that I take up when working with and for individuals with dis/ability labels.

Appendix A

The transcription conventions utilized were developed by Jefferson (2004) and adapted for use within the context of this research study.

↑	Upward arrows represent marked rise in pitch.
↓	Downward arrows represent a downward shift in pitch.
=	Equal signs at the end of a speaker's utterance and at the start of the next utterance represent the absence of a discernable gap.
Cu-	Cut-off word or sound
e	Underlining represents a sound or word(s) uttered with added emphasis.
° °	Text encased in degree symbols is quieter than surrounding speech, with double degree signs indicating whispered speech.
(laugh)	Descriptions of what can be observed and/or heard are in parentheses.
[ ]	Extended square brackets mark overlap between utterances.
(7)	Numbers in parentheses indicate pauses timed to the nearest second. A period with no number following (.) indicates a pause which is hearable, yet too short to measure.

References

Allan, J. (1999). *Actively seeking inclusion: Pupils with special needs in mainstream schools.* Philadelphia: Falmer Press.

Ashby, C. E. (2010). The trouble with normal: The struggle for meaningful access for middle school students with developmental disability lab. *Disability & Society, 23*(3), 345–358.

Ashby, C. E., & Causton-Theoharis, J. N. (2009).Disqualified in the human race: A close reading of the autobiographies of individuals identified as autistic. *International Journal of Inclusive Education, 13*(5), 501–516.

Asperger, H. (1991). "Autistic psychopathy" in childhood. In U. Frith (Ed. & Trans.), *Autism and Asperger syndrome* (pp. 21–37). Cambridge: Cambridge University Press. (Original work published 1944)

Bagatell, N. (2007). Orchestrating voices: Autism, identity and the power of discourse. *Disability & Society, 22*(4), 413–426.

Biklen, D., Attfield, R., Bissonnette, L., Blackman, L., Burke, J., Frugone, A.,…Rubin, S. (2005). *Autism and the myth of the person alone.* New York: New York University Press.

Bochner, A. (2009). Warm ideas and chilling consequences. *International Review of Qualitative Research, 2*(3), 357–370.

Broderick, A. A., & Ne'eman, A. (2008). Autism as metaphor: Narrative and counter narrative. *International Journal of Inclusive Education, 12*(5–6), 459–476.

Derrida, J. (1981). *Positions*. Chicago: University of Chicago Press.

Drew, P., & Toerien, M. (2011). *An introduction to the methods of conversation analysis* [Short course on conversation analysis]. University of York, York, England.

Edwards, D. (2005). Moaning, whinging and laughing: The subjective side of complaints. *Discourse Studies, 7*(1), 5–29.

Edwards, D., & Potter, J. (1993). Language and causation: A discursive action model of description and attribution. *Psychological Review, 100*(1), 23–41.

Fine, M. (1994). Working the hyphens: Reinventing self and other in qualitative research. In N. Denzin & Y. Lincoln (Eds.), *Handbook of qualitative research* (pp. 70–82). London: Sage.

Flyvberg, B. (2001). *Making social science matter: Why social inquiry fails and how it can succeed again*. Cambridge: Cambridge University Press.

Foucault, M. (1971). Orders of discourse. *Social Science Information, 10*(2), 7–30.

Foucault, M. (1977). A preface to transgression. In D. F. Bouchard (Ed.), *Language, counter-memory, practice: Selected essays and interviews by Michael Foucault* (pp. 29–52). Oxford: Basil Blackwell.

Glynne-Owen, R. (2010). Early intervention and autism: The impact of positivism and the call for change. *International Journal of Children's Rights, 18,* 405–416.

Goodwin, C. (1981). *Conversational organization*. New York: Academic Press.

Haakana, M. (2001). Laughter as a patient's resource: Dealing with delicate aspects of medical interaction. *Text, 21*(1–2), 187–219.

Jefferson, G. (1989). Preliminary notes on a possible metric which provides for a standard maximum silence of approximately one second in conversation. In P. Bull & R. Derek (Eds.), *Conversation: An interdisciplinary approach* (pp. 166–196). Clevedon, England: Multilingual Matters.

Jefferson, G. (2004). Glossary of transcript symbols with an introduction. In G. H. Lerner (Ed.), *Conversation analysis: Studies from the First Generation* (pp. 13–31). Amsterdam: John Benjamins.

Kanner, L. (1943/1985). Autistic disturbances of affective contact. In A. M. Donnellan (Ed.), *Classic readings in autism* (pp. 11–50). New York: Teachers College Press.

Keller, H. (2003). Socialization for competence: Cultural models of infancy. *Human Development, 46,* 288–311.

Kvale, S. (1995). The social construction of validity. *Qualitative Inquiry, 1*(1), 19–40.

Lerner, G. H. (1996). On the semi-permeable character of grammatical units in conversation: Conditional entry into the turn space of another speaker. In E. Ochs, E. A. Schegloff, & S. Thompson (Eds.), *Interaction and grammar* (pp. 238–276). Cambridge: Cambridge University Press.

Lester, J. (2011). The *discursive construction of autism: Contingent meanings of autism and therapeutic talk* (Unpublished doctoral dissertation). University of Tennessee, Knoxville.

Lewiecki-Wilson, C. (2003). Rethinking rhetoric through mental disabilities. *Rhetoric Review, 22*(2), 156–167.

Mushin, I., & Gardner, R. (2009). Silence is talk: Conversational silence in Australian Aboriginal talk-in-interaction. *Journal of Pragmatics, 41,* 2033–2052.

Nadesan, M. H. (2005). *Constructing autism: Unraveling the "truth" and understanding the social*. New York: Routledge.

Newcomer, P. L., & Hammill, D. D. (1977). *The test of language development*. Austin, TX: Empire Press.

Noblit, G., & Engels, J. D. (1999). The holistic injunction: An ideal and a moral imperative for qualitative research. In G. W. Noblit (Ed.), *Particularities: Collected essays on ethnography and education* (pp. 53–60). New York: Peter Lang.

Noblit, G. W., Flores, S. Y., & Murillo, E.g. (Eds.). (2004). *Postcritical ethnography: Reinscribing critique*. Cresskill, NJ: Hampton Press.

Ochs, E., Kremer-Sadlik, T., Sirota, K. G., & Solmon, O. (2004). Autism and the social world: An anthropological perspective. *Discourse Studies, 6*(2), 147–183.

O'Reilly, M. (2005). "What seems to be the problem?": A myriad of terms for mental health and behavioral concerns. *Disability Studies Quarterly, 25*(4), 1–18.

Osvaldsson, K. (2004). On laughter and disagreement in multiparty assessment talk. *Text, 24*(4), 517–545.

Pomerantz, A. (1984). Agreeing and disagreeing with assessment: Some features of preferred/dispreferred turn shapes. In J. M. Atkinson & J. Heritage (Eds.), *Structure of social action: Studies in conversation analysis* (pp. 57–101). Cambridge: Cambridge University Press.

Rapley, M., Kiernan, P., & Antaki, C. (1998). Invisible to themselves or negotiating identity? The interactional management of "being intellectually disabled." *Disability & Society, 13*(5), 807–827.

Rauscher, I., & McClintock, J. (1996). Ableism curriculum design. In M. Adams, L. S. Bell, & P. Griffen (Eds.), *Teaching for diversity and social justice* (pp. 198–231). New York: Routledge.

Rentenbach, B. (2009). *Synergy*. Bloomington, IN: AuthorHouse.

Sacks, H. (1992). *Lectures on conversation*. Oxford: Blackwell.

Sacks, H., Schegloff, E. A., & Jefferson, G. (1974). A simplest systematics for the organization of turn-taking for conversation. *Language, 50*(4), 696–735.

Skeggs, B. (2002). Techniques for telling the reflexive self. In T. May (Ed.), *Qualitative research in action* (pp. 349–374). London: Sage.

Skinner, Q. (1998). *Liberty before liberalism*. Cambridge: Cambridge University Press.

Solorzano, D. G., & Yosso, T. M. (2002). A critical race counterstory of race, racism, and affirmative action. *Equity & Excellence in Education, 35*(2), 155–168.

Stokoe, E. (2008). Dispreferred actions and other interactional breaches as devices for occasioning audience laughter in television "sitcoms." *Social Semiotics, 3*(18), 289–307.

Stribling, P., Rae, J., & Dickerson, P. (2007). Two forms of spoken repetition in a girl with autism. *International Journal of Language & Communication Disorders, 42*(4), 427–444.

Tannen, D. (1984). *Conversational style: Analysing talk among friends.* Norwood, NJ: Ablex.

Thomas, C. (2004). How is disability understood? An examination of sociological approaches. *Disability & Society, 19*(6), 569–583.

Weedon, C. (1987). *Feminist practice and poststructuralist theory.* Oxford: Blackwell.

Wodak, R. (1999). Critical discourse analysis at the end of the 20th century. *Research on Language and Social Interaction, 32*(1–2), 185–193.

Wood, L. A., & Kroger, R. O. (2000). *Doing discourse analysis: Methods for studying action in talk and text.* Thousand Oaks, CA: Sage.

Wootton, A. J. (1999). An investigation of delayed echoing in a child with autism. *First Language, 19,* 359–381.

Indigenous Knowledges in Education: Complexities, Dangers, and Profound Benefits

Joe L. Kincheloe and Shirley R. Steinberg

Since the time that I (Joe Kincheloe) published *What Is Indigenous Knowledge? Voices From the Academy* (Semali & Kincheloe, 1999), 1 have had an opportunity to speak to a variety of audiences about the topic around North America and the world. Of course, many individuals from diverse backgrounds are profoundly informed about the topic and have provided me with a wide variety of insights to my efforts to better understand and engage the issue of indigenous knowledge in the academy. At the same time, numerous individuals engaged in research and education—especially from dominant cultural backgrounds—continue to dismiss the importance of indigenous knowledge in academic work and pedagogy. In the last half of the first decade of the 21st century, in an era of expanding U.S. empire replete with mutating forms of political, economic, military, educational, and epistemological colonialism, indigenous knowledge comes to be viewed by the agents of empire as a threat to Euro/Americentrism and/or as a commodity to be exploited.

This chapter explores the educational and epistemological value of indigenous knowledge in the larger effort to expand a form of critical multilogicality—an effort to act educationally and politically on the calls for diversity and justice that have echoed through the halls of academia over the past several decades. Such an effort seeks an intercultural/interracial effort to question the hegemonic and oppressive aspects of Western education and to work for justice and self-direction for indigenous peoples around the world. In this critical multilogical context, the purpose of indigenous knowledge does not involve "saving" indigenous people but helping construct conditions that allow for indigenous self-sufficiency while learning from the vast storehouse of indigenous knowledges that provide compelling insights into all domains of human endeavor.

By the term indigenous knowledge, we are referring to a multidimensional body of understandings that have—especially since the beginnings of the European scientific revolution of the 17th and 18th centuries—been viewed by Euroculture as inferior and primitive. For the vast numbers of indigenous peoples from North America, South America, Australia, New Zealand, Africa, Asia, Oceania, and parts of Europe, indigenous knowledge is a lived-world form of reason that informs and sustains people who make their homes in a local area. In such a context, such peoples have produced knowledges, episte-mologies, ontologies, and cosmologies that construct ways of being and seeing in relationship to their physical surroundings. Such knowledges involve insights into plant and animal life, cultural dynamics, and historical information used to provide acumen in dealing with the challenges of contemporary existence.

Our use of this definition of indigenous knowledge accounts for the many complexities that sur-round the term and the issues it raises. We are aware of our privileged positionalities as Western scholars analyzing cultural, political, and epistemological dynamics as power inscribed as indigeneity and indig-enous knowledge. In this complex context, we are aware that many problematize the term indigenous itself, as it appears to conflate numerous, separate groups of people whose histories and cultures may be profoundly divergent. Obviously, in this chapter, it is not our intent to essentialize or conflate di-verse indigenous groups. It is important also to note that our definition of indigeneity and indigenous knowledge always takes into account the colonial/power dimensions of the political/epistemological relationship between the indigenous cosmos and the Western world. A critical dimension of the study of indigenous knowledge involves the insight indigenous peoples bring to the study of epistemology and research as colonized peoples (Dei & Kempf, 2006; Mutua & Swadener, 2004; G. H: Smith, 2000; L. T. Smith, 1999). In this context, the standpoint of colonized peoples on a geopolitics built on hierarchies, hegemony, and privilege is an invaluable resource in the larger effort to transform an unjust world.

The Unique Power of Indigenous Knowledge: Transformational Possibilities

We believe in the transformative power of indigenous knowledge, the ways that such knowledge can be used to foster empowerment and justice in a variety of cultural contexts. A key aspect of this transfor-mative power involves the exploration of human consciousness, the nature of its production, and the process of its engagement with cultural difference. As Paulo Freire and Antonio Faundez (1989) argue, indigenous knowledge is a rich social resource for any justice-related attempt to bring about social change. In this context, indigenous ways of knowing become a central resource for the work of academ-ics, whether they are professors in the universities, teachers in elementary and secondary schools, social workers, media analysts, and so on. Intellectuals, Freire and Faundez conclude, should "soak themselves in this knowledge...assimilate the feelings, the sensitivity" (p. 46) of epistemologies that move in ways unimagined by most Western academic impulses.

We find it pedagogically tragic that various indigenous knowledges of how action affects reality in particular locales have been dismissed from academic curricula. Such ways of knowing and acting could contribute so much to the educational experiences of all students, but because of the rules of evidence and the dominant epistemologies of Western knowledge production, such understandings are deemed irrelevant by the academic gatekeepers. Our intention is to challenge the academy and its "normal science" with the questions indigenous knowledges raise about the nature of our existence, our consciousness, our knowledge production, and the "globalized," imperial future that faces all peoples of the planet at this historical juncture.

Some indigenous educators and philosophers put it succinctly: We want to use indigenous knowl-edge to counter Western science's destruction of the Earth. Indigenous knowledge can facilitate this ambitious 21st-century project because of its tendency to focus on relationships of human beings to both one another and to their ecosystem. Such an emphasis on relationships has been notoriously ab-sent in the knowledge produced in Western science over the past four centuries (Dei, 1994; Keith & Keith, 1993; Simonelli, 1994).

The stakes are high, as scholars the world over attempt to bring indigenous knowledge to the academy. Linking it to an educational reform that is part of a larger sociopolitical struggle, advocates for indigenous knowledge delineate the inseparability of academic reform, the reconceptualization of science, and struggles for justice and environmental protection. Ann Parrish (1999) maintains, for example, that an understanding of agricultural knowledge may be necessary to any successful contemporary effort to feed the world. The work that has taken place in the field of Native American and First Nations (Canadian) studies over the past couple of decades grants other advocates of indigenous knowledge a lesson in how such academic operations can be directly linked to political action. Indigenous/Aboriginal scholars use their indigenous analyses to inform a variety of Native American legal and political organizations, including the Indian Law Resource Center, the National Indian Youth Council, the World Council of Indigenous Peoples, and the United Nations Working Group on Indigenous Populations, to mention only a few.

In indigenous studies, such as the Native American academic programs, emerging new political awarenesses have been expressed in terms of the existence of a global Fourth World indigeneity. Proponents of such a view claim that Fourth World peoples share the commonality of domination and are constituted by indigenous groups as diverse as the native peoples of the Americas, the Innuit and Sammis of the Arctic north, the Maori of New Zealand, the Koori of Australia, the Karens and Katchins of Burma, the Kurds of Persia, the Bedouins of the African/Middle Eastern desert, many African tribal peoples, and even the Basques and Gaels of contemporary Europe. In this context, it is important to avoid the essentialist tendency to lump together all indigenous cultures as one, yet at the same time maintain an understanding of the nearly worldwide oppression of indigenous peoples and the destruction of indigenous languages and knowledges. We will address this complex dynamic throughout this chapter, pointing to the constant need for awareness of the ambiguous theme in all academic and political work involving indigenous peoples and their knowledges (Hess, 1995; Jaimes, 1987).

As complex as the question of indigeneity may be, we believe that the best interests of indigenous and nonindigenous peoples are served by the study of indigenous knowledges and epistemologies. An appreciation of indigenous epistemology, for example, provides Western peoples with another view of knowledge production in diverse cultural sites. Such a perspective holds transformative possibilities, as people from dominant cultures come to understand the overtly cultural processes by which information is legitimated and delimited. An awareness of the ways epistemological "truth production" operates in the lived world may shake the Western scientific faith in the Cartesian-Newtonian epistemological foundation as well as the certainty and ethnocentrism that often accompany it. Indeed, in such a metaepistemological context, Westerners of diverse belief structures and vocational backgrounds may experience a fundamental transformation of both outlook and identity, resulting in a much more reflective and progressive consciousness. Such a consciousness would encounter the possibility that the de/legitimation of knowledge is more a sociopolitical process than an exercise of a universal form of disinterested abstract reason.

In this context, the Western analyst confronts the need to reassess the criteria for judging knowledge claims in light of the problems inherent in calling upon a transcultural, universal faculty of reason. Questioning and even rejecting absolute and transcendent Western reason does not mean that we are mired forever in a hell of relativism. One of the concepts Western analysts have learned in their encounters with non-Western knowledge systems is that Western certainty cannot survive, that the confrontation with difference out of necessity demands some degree of epistemological contingency. Universality cannot escape unscathed in its encounter with sociocultural, epistemological particularity, just as Newtonian physics could not survive the Einsteinian understanding of the power of different frames of reference. In these antifoundational (a rejection of a transcultural referent for truth such as the Western scientific method) dynamics, the hell of relativism is avoided by an understanding of culturally specific discursive practices.

For example, the indigenous knowledge produced by the Chagga people in Tanzania can be both true and just in relation to the discursive practices of the Chagga culture (Mosha, 2000). The Chagga criteria for truth make no claim for universality and would not feign to determine truth claims for various other cultural groups around the world. Thus, Chagga truth as a contingent, local epistemology would not claim power via its ability to negate or validate knowledge produced in non-Chagga cultures. Such an epistemological issue holds profound social and political implications, for it helps determine the power relations between diverse cultural groups. Culture A certainly gains an element of domination over Cultures B and C, if it can represent its knowledge as transcendent truth and Culture B and C's knowledge as a "superstition." This is, of course, an example of the epistemological colonialism referenced above.

In this reconceptualized, antifoundational epistemological context, analysts must consider the process of knowledge production and truth claims in relation to the historical setting, cultural situatedness, and moral needs of the reality they confront. Such understandings do not negate our ability to act as political agents, but they do force us to consider our pedagogical actions in a more tentative and culturally informed manner. In this new reconfigured context, we no longer possess the privilege of simply turning to the authority of "civilization" for validation of the "unqualified methods of truth production." Such a position removes some simplistic certainty but at the same time provides great possibility for Western and indigenous people to enter into a profound transformative negotiation around the complexity of these issues and concepts—a negotiation that demands no final, end-of-history resolution.

Indigenous Knowledge in Critical Multilogical Contexts: The Benefits to Individuals from Dominant Euro/Americentric Cultures

Our point here is on one level quite simple—humans need to encounter multiple perspectives in all dimensions of their lives. This concept of multilogicality is central to our understanding of indigenous knowledges. I (Joe Kincheloe) have expanded these notions in my extension of Denzin and Lincoln's (2000) description of the research bricolage. A complex science is grounded on this multilogicality. One of the reasons we use the term *complex* is that the more we understand about the world, the more complex it appears to be. In this recognition of complexity, we begin to see multiple causations and the possibility of differing vantage points from which to view a phenomenon. It is extremely important to note that the context from which one observes an entity shapes what he or she sees—the concept of standpoint epistemology delineated by Sandra Harding (1998) and many other feminist theorists. Here the assumptions or the system of meaning-making the observer consciously or unconsciously employs shape the observation.

This assertion is not some esoteric, academic point—it shapes social analysis, political perspectives, knowledge production, and action in the world. Acting upon this understanding, we understand that scholarly observations hold more within them to be analyzed than first impressions sometimes reveal. In this sense, different frames of reference produce multiple interpretations and multiple realities. The mundane, the everyday, the social, cultural, and psychological dimensions of human life are multiplex and continuously unfolding—while this is taking place, human interpretation is simultaneously constructing and reconstructing the meaning of what we observe. A multilogical epistemology and ontology promotes a spatial distancing from reality that allows an observer diverse frames of reference.

The distancing may range from the extremely distant, like astronauts looking at the Earth from the moon, to the extremely close, like Georgia O'Keeffe viewing a flower. At the same time, a multilogical scholar values the intimacy of an emotional connectedness that allows empathetic passion to draw knower and known together. In the multiplex, complex, and critical view of reality, Western linearity often gives way to simultaneity, as texts become a kaleidoscope of images filled with signs, symbols, and signifiers to be decoded and interpreted. William Carlos Williams illustrated an understanding of such complexity in the early 20th century as he depicted multiple, simultaneous images and frames of reference in his poetry. Williams attempted to poetically interpret Marcel Duchamp's "Nude Descending a Staircase," with its simultaneous, overlapping representations serving as a model for what postformalists call a cubist cognition.

Teachers and scholars informed by this critical multilogicality understand these concepts. Such educators and researchers work to extend their students' cognitive abilities, as they create situations where students come to view the world and disciplinary knowledge from as many frames of reference as possible. In a sense, the single photograph of Cartesian thinking is replaced by the multiple angles of the holographic photograph. Energized by this cubist cognition, educators come to understand that the models of teaching they have been taught, the definitions of inquiry with which they have been supplied, the angle from which they have been instructed to view intelligence, and the modes of learning that shape what they perceive to be sophisticated thinking all reflect a particular vantage point in the web of reality. They seek more than one perspective—they seek multilogical insights. Of course, in such a context, one can discern the value of indigenous knowledges to such pedagogues.

Like reality itself, schools and classrooms are complex matrices of interactions, codes, and signifiers in which both students and teachers are interlaced. Just as a complex and critical pedagogy asserts that there is no single, privileged way to see the world, there is no one way of representing the world artistically, no one way of teaching science, no one way of writing history. Once teachers escape the entrapment of the positivist guardians of Western tradition and their monocultural, one-truth way of seeing, they come to value and thus pursue new frames of reference in regard to their students, classrooms, and workplaces. In this cognitivist cubist spirit, critical multilogical teachers begin to look at lessons from the perspectives of individuals from different race, class, gender, and sexual orientations. They study the perspectives their indigenous, African American, Latino, White, poor, and wealthy students bring to their classrooms. They are dedicated to the search for new perspectives.

Drawing on this critical multilogicality in this pedagogical pursuit, these educators, like liberation theologians in Latin America, make no apology for seeking the viewpoints, insights, and sensitivities of the marginalized. The way to see from a perspective differing from that of the positivist guardians involves exploring an institution such as Western education from the vantage point of those who have been marginalized by it. In such a process, subjugated and indigenous knowledges once again emerge allowing teachers to gain the cognitive power of empathy—a power that enables them to take pictures of reality from different vantage points. The intersection of these diverse vantage points allows for a form of analysis that moves beyond the isolated, decontextualized, and fragmented analysis of positivist reductionism.

Cognitively empowered by these multiplex perspectives, complexity-sensitive, multilogical educators seek a multicultural dialogue between Eastern cultures and Western cultures, a conversation between the relatively wealthy Northern cultures and the impoverished Southern cultures, and an intracultural interchange among a variety of subcultures. In this way, forms of knowing, representing, and making meaning that have been excluded by the positivist West move us to new vantage points and unexplored planetary perspectives. Understandings derived from the perspective of the excluded or the "culturally different" allow for an appreciation of the nature of justice, the invisibility of the process of oppression, the power of difference, and the insight to be gained from a recognition of divergent cultural uses of long-hidden knowledges that highlight both our social construction as individuals and the limitations of monocultural ways of meaning-making.

Taking advantage of these complex ways of seeing, a whole new world is opened to educators and scholars. As cognitive cubists, teachers, students, psychologists, and cultural analysts all come to understand that there are always multiple perspectives; no conversation is over, no discipline totally complete. The domain of art and aesthetics helps us appreciate this concept, as it exposes new dimensions of meaning, new forms of logic unrecognized by the sleepwalking dominant culture. As a cognitive wake-up call, art can challenge what Herbert Marcuse (1955), in *Eros and Civilization,* called "the prevailing principle of reason" (p. 185). In this context, we come to realize that art and other aesthetic productions provide an alternate epistemology, a way of knowing that moves beyond declarative forms of knowledge. Here we see clearly the power of multilogicality and the bricolage: educational psychologists gain new insights into the traditional concerns of their academic domain by looking outside the frameworks of one discipline. It could be quantum physics, it could be history, or, as in this case, it could be art and aesthetics.

The Study of Indigenous Knowledge for Social Change: Making Sure the Interests of Indigenous People Are Served

The transformation of Western consciousness via its encounter with multilogicality vis-à-vis indigenous knowledges takes on much of its importance in relation to a more humble and empathetic Western perspective toward indigenous peoples and their understandings of the world. Such a new perspective will manifest itself in a greater awareness of neocolonialism and other Western social practices that harm indigenous peoples. It will be the responsibility of social and political activists all over the world to translate these awarenesses into concrete political actions that benefit indigenous people. While in no way advocating that Western peoples speak and act for indigenous peoples, it is important for indigenous peoples to have informed allies outside their local communities. Such allies can play an important role in helping indigenous peoples deal with the cultural, psychological, and environmental devastation of traditional colonialism and neocolonialism.

In the Republic of Congo (formerly Zaire), for example, before the advent of Western colonialism, local peoples lived in what has been described as a "cereal civilization." In this agricultural society, individuals sowed grain in a land that could easily support good harvests. When the European colonists arrived, however, they destroyed the land to the point that it could no longer sustain the cereal way of life (Freire & Faundez, 1989). With their land and their civilization in shambles, what were the indigenous peoples to do? In this case and many others, Westerners cannot simply say, "Let the Congolese tribesmen reclaim and redeploy their indigenous agricultural and social practices and solve their problems in their own way." Traditional knowledge has been lost and worldviews have been shattered. Questions of cultural renewal and indigenous knowledge are not as easy as some represent them to be. In these (yet again) complex circumstances, we examine the ways the indigenous knowledge studies advocated here can facilitate indigenous people's struggle against the ravages of colonialism, especially its neocolonialist articulation in the domains of the political, economic, and pedagogical. Scholars conversant with the transformative dynamics of the multilogical epistemological insights emerging from the critical confrontation with indigenous ways of seeing will be far less likely to formulate, for example, anthropological studies of indigeneity in traditional unreflective ways. One of the criteria for anthropological studies in a reconceptualized Western social science would involve the relevance and benefits of the work for the indigenous group studied. In this reconceived anthropology, research methodologies could be adjusted to account for the interests of indigenous subjects.

An important aspect of such a transformed social science would involve the pedagogical task of affirming indigenous perspectives, in the process reversing the disaffirmations of the traditional Western, social scientific project. Operating in this manner, social scientists could make use of a variety of previously excluded local knowledges (Sponsel, 1992). Such knowledges could be deployed to rethink the meaning of development in numerous locales where various marginalized peoples reside. Using such knowledges, indigenous peoples—with the help of outside political allies to facilitate their fight against further neocolonial encroachments—could move closer to the possibility of solving their problems in their own ways. The possibility of some magical return to an uncontaminated precolonial past, however, does not exist. Thus, the use of indigenous knowledge as the basis of local problem-solving strategies will always have to deal with the reality of colonization, not to mention the effects of the economic globalization that will continue to challenge indigenous peoples. Resistance to such powerful neocolonial movements will need all the transformative knowledges and political allies it can get.

The Road of Good Intentions: Western Scholars and Their Efforts to Help Indigenous Peoples

Western scholars and cultural workers concerned with the plight of indigenous peoples and their knowledges are faced with a set of dilemmas. Not only must they avoid essentialism and its accompanying romanticization of the indigene, but they must also sidestep the traps that transform their attempts at facilitation into further marginalization. Walking the well-intentioned road to hell, Western scholars dedicated to the best interests of indigenous peoples often unwittingly participate in the Western hegemonic process. The question, "How can the agency, the self-direction of indigenous peoples be enhanced?" must constantly be asked by Western allies. What is the difference between a celebration of indigenous knowledge and an appropriation? Too often, Western allies, for example, do not simply want to work with indigenous peoples—they want to transform their identities and become indigenous persons themselves. As a teacher and researcher on the Rosebud Sioux Reservation in South Dakota, I (Joe) watched this "wannabe" phenomenon play out on numerous occasions. As White allies worked out their identity crises in the indigenous cultural context, they appropriated not only the cultural styles of the Sioux but many times claimed their "oppression capital"—the "status" of marginality among proponents of social justice. Ironically, the counterhegemonic label of an "FBI" (full-blooded Indian) was a clever double-consciousness description that not only pointed to federal interference but to the non-Indian Whites who attempted to claim Indian status. This phenomenon plays itself out continually within the wigger tradition as non-Blacks appropriate the discourse, dress, and cultural manner of African Americans, even going so far as to claim the disenfranchisement of Blacks.

Such a vampirism sucked the blood of indigenous suffering out of the veins of the Native Americans/Canadians, in the process contributing little to the larger cause of social justice. The only struggle in which many of these vampires engaged was a personal quest for a new identity. Sioux leaders recognized this tendency and in our conversations referred to it as "playing Indian." Such an activity was viewed by tribal members with contempt and condescension. The Sioux, like other indigenous peoples, understood the dangers of Western "help." In this context, the following question must be asked: Is the study of indigenous peoples and their knowledges in itself a process of Europeanization? In some ways, of course, it is, as Western intellectuals conceptualize indigenous knowledge in contexts far removed from its production. In other ways, however, Western intellectuals have little choice; if they are to operate as agents of justice, they must understand the dynamics at work in the world of indigenous people. To refuse to operate out of fear of Europeanization reflects a view of indigenous culture as an authentic, uncontaminated artifact that must be hermetically preserved regardless of the needs of living indigenous people (Ashcroft, Griffiths, & Tiffin, 1995; Howard, 1995).

The process of Europeanization, with its colonialist perspectives toward indigenous knowledge, continues to operate despite both insightful and misguided attempts to thwart it. In this context, ethnocentric Western science claims a value for indigenous ways of seeing as an "ethnoscience." Western scientists maintain that much can be learned from a number of ethnosciences, including ethnobotany, ethnopharmacology, ethnomedicine, ethnocosmology, and ethnoastronomy. The concept discursively situates indigenous knowledge systems as ways of knowing that are culturally grounded, simultaneously representing Western science as "not culturally grounded" or transcultural and universal. Thus, in the process of ascribing worth to indigenous knowledge, such analysis implicitly relegates it to a lower order of knowledge production. Also, to speak of indigenous knowledge systems in Western terms such as botany, pharmacology, medicine, and so on is to inadvertently fragment knowledge systems in ways that subvert the holism of indigenous ways of understanding the world (Hess, 1995).

In this Western gaze, indigenous knowledge is tacitly decontextualized, severed of the cultural connections that grant it meaning to its indigenous producers, archived and classified in Western databases, and eventually used in scientific projects that may operate against the interests of indigenous peoples. All of this takes place in the name of Western scientific concessions to the importance of the information generated by local peoples. Arun Agrawal (1995) labels this archival project as *ex situ* conservation—a process that removes it from people's lives. Such indigenous knowledge is always changing in relation to the changing needs of its producers; ex situ conservation destroys the dynamic quality of such information. Despite their overt valorization of indigenous knowledge, these Western scientific archivists refuse to accept the worthiness or "raw" indigenous knowledge—upon collection, Western scientists insist on testing its validity via Western scientific testing. As Marcel Viergever (1999) maintains, this archival project and the scientific validation that accompanies it illustrate the Western disregard of the need to protect and perpetuate the cultural systems that produce dynamic indigenous knowledge. In this context, the Western proclamations of valorization ring hollow.

The Burden of Essentialism in the Study of Indigenous Knowledge

We continue to struggle with the problems inherent in the study of indigenous knowledge. How do we deal with the understandable tendency within indigenous studies to lapse into essentialism? Before answering that question, a brief discussion of essentialism is in order. Essentialism is a complex concept that is commonly understood as the belief that a set of unchanging properties (essences) delineates the construction of a particular category—for example, indigenous people, African Americans, White people, women, and so on. Addressing the problem of essentialism is a complex but necessary step in the study of indigenous knowledge. While there is no problem examining indigenous people/knowledge *as a discrete category*, we must always be careful to avoid racial or ethnic designations that fail to discern the differences between people included in a specific category. Cultural anthropology in its traditional effort to name and categorize indigeneity has produced a notion of essentialist authenticity that is now difficult to question.

In an indigenous context, this essentialist authenticity involves a semiotic of the prehistoric. Such a signification inscribes indigeneity as a historical artifact far removed from contemporary life. Activities or identities thus that fall outside of this narrow backward-looking classification are deemed unauthentic, impure, or phony. Indigenous knowledge in this essentialist configuration is caught in the prehistoric, stationary, and unchanging web that is ever separate from nonindigenous information. Indigeneity in this context becomes romanticized to the point of helpless innocence. Paulo Freire and Antonio Faundez (1989) warn us that our appreciation of indigenous peoples and their knowledges must avoid the tendency for romanticization. When advocates for indigenous peoples buy into such romanticization, they often attempt to censor "alien" presences and restore the indigene to a pure precolonial cosmos. Such a return is impossible, as all cultures (especially colonized ones) are perpetually in a state of change. The Aborigines of Australia, for example, were profoundly influenced by Indonesian peoples and vice versa. The premise that indigenous peoples were isolated from the rest of the world until European conquest and colonization is a myth that must be buried along with other manifestations of essentialist purity (Agrawal, 1995; Ashcroft et al., 1995; Goldie, 1995; Hall, 1995; Mudrooroo, 1995; Pieterse & Parekh, 1995).

Without such a burial, indigenous cultures are discouraged from shifting and adapting, and indigenous knowledges are viewed simply as sacred relics fixed in a decontextualized netherland. Any study of indigenous knowledge in the academy must allow for its evolution and ever-changing relationship to Eurocentric scientific and educational practice. The essentialized approach undermines this relational dynamic, as it encodes indigeneity as freedom/nature and European culture as culture/reason—here, no room for dialogue exists. Our examination of indigenous knowledge attempts to enlarge the space for such dialogue, denying the assertion of many analysts that European and indigenous ways of seeing are totally antithetical to one another. These cultural and epistemological issues are complex, and our concern is to avoid essentialist solutions by invoking simplistic binary oppositions between indigeneity and colonialism. Once the binary opposition is embraced, we have to choose one and dismiss the other—not only indigeneity and colonialism but also local knowledge or academic knowledge. In this dichotomous mode, either everything academic is of no worth or, from the other way of seeing, everything indigenous is primitive.

The either-or approach leaves little room for dialogue, little space to operate. Counteressentialist views of indigenous knowledge understand the circulation of culture, the reality of "contamination." In a more complex, anticolonialist anthropology, for example, cultures are no longer seen as self-contained social organisms but as interrelated networks of localities. In such an anthropology, the cultural position of the observer helps construct the description of such cultural dynamics. The focus of the ethnographies produced in this context moves away from finite cultural systems operating in equilibrium to networks shaped and reshaped by boundary transgressions. If the emphasis is on transgressions, then no one is culturally pure. Western knowledge, for example, reaches indigenous peoples in a variety of ways from mass communications to developmental projects. In this increasingly globalized world, transnational population movements, refugee diasporas, and multinational capital infusions disrupt traditional cultural systems.

Another aspect of the essentialist demarcations concerning indigeneity involves the assertion of a fixed and stable indigenous identity. In our multilogical understanding of indigenous knowledge, we maintain that all identities are historically constructed, always in process, constantly dealing with intersections involving categories of status, religion, race, class, and gender. Such a position is conceptually unsettling, we admit, with its denial of the possibility of some final freedom from the cultural ambiguities that shape consciousness and subjectivity. If all of this were not enough, we question the essentialist assertion that there is a natural category of "indigenous persons." Indeed, there is great diversity within the label *indigenous people*. The indigenous cultural experience is not the same for everybody; indigenous knowledge is not a monolithic epistemological concept. In this context, the uncomfortable problem of cultural hybridity emerges. We will discuss this dynamic in more detail later, but suffice it to say here, many advocates of indigenous knowledge resent the use of the term *hybridity* and find it inappropriate in indigenous studies.

Concerned with the use of indigenous knowledge in education, we use our counteressentialist understandings to argue that there is no unitary indigenous curriculum to be factually delivered to students in various locations. Not everyone who identifies with a particular indigenous culture produces knowledge the same way, nor do different indigenous cultures produce the same knowledges. Even after delineating counteressentialist arguments, however, we still believe that the study of indigenous knowledge is valuable and that there may be some common threads running through many indigenous knowledge systems. A central feature of our work with indigenous knowledge in the academy involves exploring the political and curricular implications of the ways many indigenous cultures (a) relate to their habitat in ways that are harmonious, (b) have been conquered by a colonialist nation-state, and (c) provide a perspective on human experience that differs from Western empirical science (Apffel-Marglin, 1995; Appiah, 1995; Dei, 1994; Hall, 1995; Hess, 1995; Jaimes, 1987).

These features tell us that indigenous knowledge deserves analysis on a global level with particular attention directed to the epistemological patterns that emerge in a variety of cultural contexts. Such studies, we believe, are often so powerful that new understandings of the world appear and reinterpretations of "the way things are" materialize. Similarities between African, Native American/Canadian, Chinese, and even feminist views of the relationship between self and world provide us with fascinating new ways of making sense of realities and compelling topics for intercultural conversations (Kloppenberg, 1991). Our counteressentialist imperatives must always be understood within the framework of our valuing the diverse perspectives of indigenous peoples and our understanding of the continuing marginalization of their cultures and their perspectives. Indigenous studies may be problematic and complex, but educators will be well served to examine its provocative themes in light of the Western Enlightenment project, Euro/American colonialism, and its epistemological and pedagogical expressions.

Having made this antiessentialist argument, it is still important to note that within indigenous communities, the concept of essentialism is sometimes employed in ways significantly different than in the anti/postcolonial critical discourses of transgressive academics around the globe. Finding themselves in disempowered positions where they have to worry about basic human rights and survival, many indigenous peoples have claimed essential cultural characteristics for not only strategic purposes but also in relation to spiritual dynamics involved with one's genealogical connection to the Earth and its animate and (in Western ontologies) inanimate entities. Here the importance of geographical place in the construction of indigeneity is manifested in ways the land, flora and fauna, natural resources, and numerous other dynamics are integrated into indigenous identity. No discussion of essentialism vis-à-vis indigeneity should fail to account for these unique dimensions of indigenous life (G. H. Smith, 2000; L. T. Smith, 1999).

Insurrections: Indigenous Knowledge as a Subjugated Knowledge

While operating at a far more subtle and sanitized manner in the contemporary era, epistemological tyranny still functions in the academy to undermine efforts to include other ways of knowing and knowledge production in the curriculum—it subverts mulilogicality. The power issues here are naked and visible to all who want to look through the epistemological glory hole: The power struggle involves who is allowed to proclaim truth and to establish the procedures by which truth is to be established; it also involves who holds the power to determine what knowledge is of most worth and should be included in academic curricula. In this context, the notion of indigenous knowledge as a "subjugated knowledge" emerges to describe its marginalized relationship to Western epistemological and curricular power. The use of the term subjugated knowledge asserts the centrality of power in any study of indigenous knowledge and any effort to include it in the academy. Despite all the debates about what constitutes indigenous knowledge and separates it from scientific knowledge, one constant emerges: All indigenous knowledge is subjugated by Western science and its episteme (its rules for determining truth).

Regardless of what area in the world it is found in, indigenous knowledge has been produced by peoples facing diseases brought by European cultures, attempts at genocide, cultural assimilation, land appropriation, required emigration, and education as a colonial tool. Because of such oppressive processes, indigenous knowledge has, not surprisingly, often been hidden from history. It is our desire to become researchers of such repressed knowledges, to search out what Western and Western-influenced academics have previously neglected, to recover materials that may often work to change our consciousness in profound ways. When Western epistemologies are viewed in light of indigenous perspectives, Western ways of seeing, Western education cannot remain the same. Analyzing these power dynamics surrounding indigenous knowledge, Gelsa Knijnik (1999) warns of their complexity and the need for the student of indigenous knowledge to explore the many ways power operates in the interactions of indigeneity, science, and epistemology.

In the reconceptualized academic curriculum that we imagine, indigenous/subjugated knowledge is not passed along as a new canon but becomes a living body of knowledge open to multiple interpretations. Viewed in its relationship to the traditional curriculum, subjugated knowledge is employed as a constellation of concepts that challenge the invisible cultural assumptions embedded in all aspects of schooling and knowledge production. Such subjugated knowledge contests dominant cultural views of reality, as it informs individuals from the White, middle/upper-middle-class mainstream that there are different ways of viewing the world. Indeed, individuals from such backgrounds begin to realize that their textbooks and curriculum have discarded data produced by indigenous peoples. The White dominant cultural power blocs that dominate contemporary Western societies reject the need to listen to marginalized people and take their knowledge seriously. Western/American power wielders are not good at listening to information that does not seem to contribute to hegemony, their ability to win the consent of the subjugated to their governance. Knowledge that emerges from and serves the purposes of the subjugated is often erased by dominant power wielders, as they make it appear dangerous and pathological to other citizens (Dion-Buffalo & Mohawk, 1993).

Many scholars, Graham Hingangaroa Smith (2000) in particular, have written about the labeling of indigenous peoples and indigenous knowledges. While is it vital that we understand the nature of oppression of indigenous peoples and the subjugation of their knowledges, it is also crucial that students of indigeneity and indigenous knowledge not see them only through the lens of subjugation. African American literary and aesthetic scholar Albert Murray (1996) agrees with Smith's point, maintaining that viewing an oppressed culture only in terms of its oppression unwittingly tends to reproduce and exacerbate the dynamics of disempowerment. Taking his cue from the African American blues aesthetic, Murray writes of the ability to acknowledge the pain of oppression at the same time we celebrate the genius of our cultural productions. Indigenous peoples with whom I have worked possess their own version of Murray's blues aesthetic.

In the years I (Joe Kincheloe) have worked with the peoples of the Rosebud Sioux Reservation in South Dakota, I have often observed the irreverent humor of tribal members making fun of the oppression they have faced. I find their ability to celebrate those dimensions of their culture that bring them great joy in the midst of tragedy to be profoundly informative to academics working in the area. Because of the gravitas surrounding the study of the oppression of indigenous peoples, the idea of celebration or laughter in a context where subjugation has occurred is viewed very negatively in many academic situations. Here is a space where we begin to understand the profound importance of Smith's and Murray's call to not simply view and name indigenous peoples as "the oppressed."

No doubt the dance connecting the celebration of the affirmative dimensions of indigenous cultures engaging in humor in the midst of pain, and fighting against mutating forms of colonial oppression is a delicate and nuanced art form—but it is one worth learning. In this complex space, we begin to understand the value of understanding and developing multiple ways of viewing the power and agency of indigenous peoples and the brilliant knowledges they produce. Those of us who do not come from indigenous backgrounds learn to listen quietly in such contexts, in the process learning much about the indigene, the tacit privileges that accrue from coming from the world of the colonizers and the cosmos in general.

Thus, critical multilogical educators devoted to the value of subjugated knowledges uncover those dangerous memories that are involved in reconstructing the process through which the consciousness of various groups and individuals has come to be constructed. Such awareness frees teachers, students, and other individuals to claim an identity apart from the one forced upon them. Indeed, identity is constructed when submerged memories are aroused—in other words, confrontation with dangerous memory changes our perceptions of the forces that shape us, which in turn moves us to redefine our worldviews, our ways of seeing. The oppressive forces that shape us have formed the identities of both the powerful and the exploited. Without an analysis of this process, we will never understand why students succeed or fail in school; we will be forever blind to the tacit ideological forces that construct student perceptions of school and the impact such perceptions have on their school experiences. Such blindness restricts our view of our own and other people's perceptions of their place in history, in the web of reality. When history is erased and decontextualized, teachers, students, and other citizens are rendered vulnerable to the myths employed to perpetuate social domination.

In this multilogical context informed by indigenous knowledge, historians and other educational researchers enter a new domain of understanding and practice. In this zone of critical multilogicality, such scholars, if they are operating in North America, work in solidarity with Asians, Africans, Latin Americans, indigenous peoples, and subcultures within their own societies. In their "interracialism" and "interculturalism" they understand that there is far more to history than the socially constructed notion that civilization began in ancient Greece, migrated to Europe, and reached its zenith in the contemporary United States. In histories and other scholarly work that emerge in various fields, this assumption exists in an influential and unchallenged state. Critical multilogical scholars informed by indigenous knowledge challenge this monological Eurocentrism and search for the ways it insidiously inscribes knowledge production. At this point, researchers look for various forms of subjugated indigenous knowledge both as a focus for historical research and for their epistemological and ontological insights. Not only do we learn about such knowledges and the cultures that produced them, but we also use their ways of seeing and being to challenge Western monological perspectives. Here critical multilogical researchers use indigenous perspectives to question reductionist notions of epistemological objectivity and superficially validated "facts" that have for centuries been used to oppress indigenous peoples and degrade the value of their knowledges.

Historiographical multilogicality (Villaverde, Kincheloe, & Helyar, 2006) is a break from the class elitist, White-centered, colonial, patriarchal histories that have dominated Western history for too long. While many successful efforts have been made to get beyond elite, White, male history and other forms of knowledge, critical historians sensitive to the value of indigenous knowledge want to go farther—they want to understand the colonial impulses that work to exclude important insights into the social, cultural, historical, political, philosophical, psychological, and educational domains provided by indigenous peoples. Learning from previously dishonored indigenous knowledges, African, Islamic, Asian, and Latin American philosophies of history, critical historians, for example, learn new ways of practicing their craft. Those peoples who have suffered under existing political economic and social arrangements are central to the project of critical historiography. Because those who have suffered the most may not have left written records—the bread and butter of traditional historiographical source material—critical historians employ oral history and other research methods that grant voice to indigenous peoples while learning from and validating indigenous insights lost to traditional history.

Linda Tuhiwai Smith (1999) provides valuable insights into these issues of subjugated knowledges vis-à-vis historiography and other research methods. A central dimension of self-determination for indigenous peoples, she contends, has entailed questions related to indigenous histories and an analysis of how otherized indigenous peoples have been represented in traditional Western historiography. Indigenous historiography informs a critical multilogical view of the past because all indigenous history is, as Smith argues, "a *re*writing and *re*righting [of] our position in history" (p. 28). As indigenous peoples tell their stories and rethink their histories, it is the duty of critical multilogical historians to listen carefully and respectfully. In this process, historians from around the world can become not only better allies in the indigenous struggle against colonial subjugation, for social justice, and for self-determination. In the process, they also become better historians. Smith makes her point in a compelling manner:

> It is not simply about giving an oral account or a genealogical naming of the land and the events which raged over it, but a very powerful need to give testimony to and restore a spirit, to bring back into existence a world fragmented and dying. The sense of history conveyed by these approaches is not the same thing as the discipline of history, and so our accounts collide, crash into each other. (p. 28)

Indigenous Knowledge and Academic Transformation

In light of these insights, the following is an outline of the educational benefits to be gained from an analysis of academic practices vis-à-vis indigenous/subjugated knowledges. Keeping in mind both old and new ways Western researchers have appropriated indigenous knowledges for their own enrichment, the promoters of the educational benefits of indigenous knowledges are ever aware of the possibility of exploitation. To avoid such exploitative appropriation of indigenous wisdom, critical researchers should adhere to a strict set of ethics devoted to the self-determination of indigenous peoples; an awareness of the complex, ever-evolving ways that colonialism oppresses them; the intercultural nature of all research and analysis of indigenous knowledge; and the dedication to use indigenous knowledge in ways that lead to political, epistemological, and ontological changes that support the expressed goals of the indigene. With these caveats in mind, the research and curricular use of such knowledges:

1. Promotes rethinking our purposes as educators. An understanding of indigenous ways of seeing as a subjugated knowledge alerts us to the fact that multilogicality exists—there are multiple perspectives of human and physical phenomena. With this understanding in mind, it becomes apparent that school and university curricula privilege particular views of the world. Those who hold Western views of the world and value them over all others are often deemed "intelligent" by positivist methods of measuring intellectual capabilities. According to mainstream Western educational psychology and cognitive science, the way of knowing ascribed to "rational man" constitutes the highest level of human thought. This rationality or logic is best exemplified in symbolic logic, mathematics, and scientific reasoning. With the birth of modernity (the Age of Reason) and its scientific method in the 17th and 18th centuries, scientific knowledge became the only game in the academic town. In this context, individuals can be represented in a dramatic new form—as abstracted entities standing outside the forces of history and culture. This abstract individualism eclipsed the Western understanding of how men and women are shaped by larger social forces that affect individuals from different social locations in different ways.

Western society was caught in a mode of perception that limited thinking to concepts that stay within White, Western, logocentric boundaries, far away from the "No Trespassing" signs of indigeneity. As academics begin to uncover these hidden values embedded in both prevailing definitions of intelligence and our scientific instruments that measure it, they embark on a journey into the excitement of a pedagogy that takes indigenous knowledges seriously. As they begin to search for forms of intelligence that fall outside traditional notions of abstract reasoning, they come to appreciate the multiple forms of intelligence that different individuals possess. In this context, academic analysts become detectives of intelligence, searching the world for valuable ways of making sense of the world. Operating this way, educational purpose cannot remain static, as academics explore the relationship between differing epistemologies and the knowledges they support. The purpose of schools no longer simply involves the transmission of validated Western information from teacher to student. Instead, a more compelling form of analysis is initiated with teachers engaging students in the interpretation of various knowledges and modes of knowledge production.

2. Focuses attention on the ways knowledge is produced and legitimated. As we have maintained throughout this chapter, the study of indigenous knowledges that we advocate is concerned with the process of knowledge production. Such an awareness is too often absent in Western education. In mainstream pedagogies, we are taught to believe that the knowledge we consider official and valid has been produced in a neutral, noble, and altruistic manner. Such a view dismisses the cultural and power-related dimensions of knowledge production. Knowledge of any form will always confront other knowledge forms. When this happens, a power struggle ensues; the decisions made in struggles between, for example, indigenous and Eurocentric views of colonialism exert dramatic but often unseen consequences in schools and the political domain. For example, the role of the academic as a neutral transmitter of prearranged facts is not understood as a politicized role accompanying knowledge production.

If schools are to become places that promote teacher and student empowerment, then the notion of what constitutes politicization will have to be reconceptualized. Battle with texts as a form of research,

Ira Shor and Paulo Freire (1987) exhort educators. Resist the demand of the official curriculum for deference to texts, they argue in line with their larger, critically grounded political vision. Can it be argued that capitulation to textual authority constitutes political neutrality?

In this indigenously informed curriculum, educators and their students come to appreciate the need to analyze what they know, how they come to know it, why they believe or reject it, and how they evaluate the credibility of the evidence. Starting at this point, they begin to understand the social construction of knowledge and truth. In school, for example, they recognize that the taken-for-granted knowledges that are taught do not find justification as universal truth. Instead, they appreciate the fact that the purveyors of such information have won a long series of historical and political struggles over whose knowledge and ways of producing knowledge are the best. Thus, educators are able to uncover the socially created hierarchies that travel incognito as truth. Though everyone knows their nature, these hierarchies mask their "shady" backgrounds of political conflict. As truth, they are employed as rationales for cultural dominance and unequal power relations.

3. Encourages the construction of just and inclusive academic spheres. Indigenous/subjugated knowledges are not seen here as mere curricular add-ons that provide diversity and spice to Western academic institutions. Curricular reforms based on our analysis of indigenous knowledge require that educators become hermeneuts (scholars and teachers who structure their work and teaching around an effort to help students and other individuals to make sense of the world around them) and epistemologists (scholars and teachers who seek to expose how accepted knowledge came to be validated). Such educators bring a new dimension to the academy, as they use subjugated knowledges to reconceptualize the practices of the academy, to uncover the etymology (origin) of its inclusions and exclusions, notions of superiority and inferiority, racism, and ethnocentrism. This historical dynamic is extremely important in the context of subjugated knowledge. Antonio Gramsci (1988) noted that philosophy cannot be understood apart from the history of philosophy, nor can culture and education be grasped outside the history of culture. Our conception of self, world, and education, therefore, can only become critical when we appreciate the historical nature of its formulation. We are never independent of the social and historical forces that surround us—we are all caught at a particular point in the web of reality. One of the most important aspects of subjugated knowledge is that it is a way of seeing that helps us to expose the fingerprints of power in existing academic knowledge. Subjugated knowledge, by its mere existence, proves to us that there are alternatives to knowledge produced within the boundaries of Western science.

4. Produces new levels of insight. Keeping in mind the dangers of essentialist readings of indigenous knowledge, we see such perspectives as subjugated knowledges that are local, life experience based, and non-Western science produced. Such knowledge is transmitted over time by individuals from a particular geographical or cultural locality. Indigenous ways of knowing help people to cope with their sociological and agricultural environments and are passed down from generation to generation. A curriculum that values subjugated knowledge in general realizes that indigenous knowledge is important not only for the culture that produced it but also for people from different cultures. Only now in the first decade of the 21st century are European peoples beginning to appreciate the value of indigenous knowledge about health, medicine, agriculture, philosophy, ecology, and education. Traditionally, these were the very types of knowledge European education tried to discredit and eradicate. Of course, unfortunately, the Western valuing of such knowledges emerges from a recognition of its monetary value in global markets.

A critical multilogical education sees a variety of purposes for the inclusion of indigenous knowledges in the school and university curriculum. Since indigenous knowledges do not correspond to Western notions of discrete bodies or practices of data, they must be approached with an understanding of their ambiguity and contextual embeddedness. Thus, any effort to understand or use such knowledges cannot be separated from the worldviews and epistemologies embraced by their producers. The confrontation with such non-Western ways of seeing moves the power of difference to a new level of utility, as it exposes the hidden worldviews and epistemologies of Westerners unaccustomed to viewing culture—their own and other cultural forms—at this level. In this context, the critical multicultural encounter with indigenous knowledge raises epistemological questions relating to the production and consumption of knowledge, the subtle connections between culture and what is defined as successful learning, the contestation of all forms of knowledge production, and the definition of education itself. An awareness of the intersection between subjugated ways of knowing and indigenous knowledge opens a conversation between the "north" and the "south," that is, between so-called developed and developing societies. Critical educators seek to use their awareness of this valuable intersection to produce new forms of global consciousness and intercultural solidarity.

5. Demands that educators at all academic levels become researchers. Contrary to the pronouncement of reactionary protectors of the Western academic status quo, a subjugated/indigenous knowledge-informed curriculum pushes education to achieve more rigor and higher pedagogical expectations. In the schools we envision, teachers and students understand multiple epistemologies, possess secondary and primary research skills, and can interpret the meaning of information from a variety of perspectives. In positivist Eurocentric education, teachers learned to say, "Give me the truth and I will pass it along to students in the most efficient manner possible." In the indigenously informed schools we advocate, teachers are encouraged to understand a variety of subjugated knowledges, to support themselves, to assert their freedom from Eurocentric all-knowing experts. Such teachers might say, "Please support me as I explore multiple ways of seeing and making sense of the world." In this context, such teachers are intimately familiar with the Western canon but refuse to accept without question its status as universal, as the only body of cultural knowledge worth knowing. Of course, in light of No Child Left Behind legislation with its standardized curriculum, ideological cleansing, and scripts for teachers, these calls take on a new urgency. Thus, as scholars of Western knowledge, non-Western knowledge, and subjugated and indigenous knowledges, such teachers are not content to operate in socioeducational frameworks often taken for granted. Such culturally and epistemologically informed educators seek to rethink and recontextualize questions that have been traditionally asked about schooling and knowledge production in general.

Diverse Constructions of the World: Indigeneity and Epistemology

On one level, the critical multilogical analysis of indigenous knowledge is an examination of how different peoples construct the world. Of course, such an epistemological study cannot be conducted in isolation, for any analysis of indigenous knowledge brings up profound political, cultural, pedagogical, and ethical questions that interact with and help shape the epistemological domain. This is why the questions—what is indigenous knowledge, and why should we study it?—do not lend themselves to easy and concise answers. With our concern with essentialism in mind, we attempt to answer these complex questions. When we focus on the first question—what is indigenous knowledge?—several descriptors quickly come to mind. We explore such characterizations from a meta-analytical perspective, maintaining throughout a tentativeness and contingency that comes from our appreciation of diversity within the category of indigeneity.

June George (1999) posits that *indigenous knowledge* is a term that can be used to designate knowledges produced in a specific social context and employed by laypeople in their everyday lives. It is typically not generated, she argues, by a set of prespecified procedures or rules and is orally passed down from one generation to the next. Mahia Maurial (1999) emphasizes this everyday use of indigenous knowledge, pointing out that it lives in indigenous people's cultures—not in archives or laboratories. While George's and Maurial's assertions are not meant to deny the cultural locality of Western scientific knowledge, they do induce us to provide a definition for who qualifies as an indigenous person. The World Council of Indigenous Peoples maintains that such individuals occupied lands prior to populations who now share or claim such territories and possess a distinct language and culture. With only a few exceptional cases, dominant ethnic groups control nation-states in which the indigene live. As a result, indigenous peoples are relatively excluded from power and occupy the lowest rungs of the social ladder. We understand that sociocultural interaction between dominant groups and the indigene is inexorably increasing, and any test of cultural purity for classification as indigenous is misguided and in opposition to the best interests of indigenous peoples.

Though the boundaries are blurring, indigenous peoples produce forms of knowledge that are inseparable from larger worldviews. Although similarities exist between indigenous and Western scientific knowledges—for example, their mutual status as locally produced ethnoknowledges—Consuelo Quiroz (1999) argues that modernist knowledges are situated in written texts, legal codes, and academic canons. Thus, a profound difference between the different knowledges involves mainstream societies' perception and qualitative evaluation of them as much as anything else. This concept of perception is becoming more and more important in the analysis and classification of different knowledge forms as indigenous studies matures as a field. All knowledges are related to specific contexts and peoples. The questions become, what context, and what peoples? Though locality is implicated in any form of knowledge production, the worldview of the cultures that inhabit different locales may be profoundly different.

With these dynamics in mind, it appears that Cartesian-Newtonian-Baconian epistemologies and many indigenous knowledge systems differ in the very way they define life—moving, thus, from the epistemological to the ontological realm. As we have maintained in our indigenously informed work in postformalism (Kincheloe & Steinberg, 1993; Kincheloe, Steinberg, & Hinchey, 1999), the characteristics that scientific modernism defined as basic to life are found both in what the Western scientific tradition has labeled "living" and "nonliving." Many indigenous peoples have traditionally seen all life on the planet as so multidimensionally entwined that they have not been so quick to distinguish the living from the nonliving. The positivist use of the term *environment,* for example, implies a separation between human and environment. At what point, it may be asked, do oxygen, water, and food become part of the human organism, and at what point are they separate? In this context, for example, the Andean peasants' and other indigenous people's belief that the rivers, mountains, land, soil, lakes, rocks, and animals are sentient may not be as preposterous as Westerners first perceived it.

From the indigenous Andean perspective, all these sentient entities nurture human beings, and it is our role as humans to nurture them. In this belief, the Andeans are expressing both an epistemological and ontological dynamic—a way of knowing and being that is *relational.* Indeed, the Western scientific epistemological concept of "knowing" may not fit the Andean context; the Andeans' connection with the world around them is not as much an expression of knowing as much as it is one of relating. Such relating is undoubtedly a spiritual process, as Andean peoples speak of their relations or kinship system as including human beings as well as animals, the elements and creations of nature, and deities of their "place." In Andean culture, these life forms relate to one another and work together to regenerate life. Thus, in Andean knowledge and many other indigenous knowledges, all aspects of the universe are interrelated; knowledge is in this context holistic, relational, and even spiritual. The rhetoric of conversation with the world is a more accurate descriptor of the process than the discourse of knowing in this context, for the Andeans do not conceptualize a knower and known. The point of the conversation is not the gaining of knowledge; it is to nurture and regenerate the world of which the individual is a part.

In such indigenous knowledge systems, the Eurocentric epistemology of studying, knowing (mastering), and then dominating the world seems frighteningly out of place, as it upsets the sacred kinship between humans and other creations of nature. From the perspective of many indigenous peoples, therefore, Cartesian-Newtonian-Baconian science is grounded on a violent epistemology that seeks to possess the Earth like a master owns a slave. In this context, the master seeks a certainty about the nature of his slave that allows complete control (Apffel-Marglin, 1995; Aronowitz, 1996; Dei, 1994). A less-than-certain knowledge is not good enough for the master and his goal of domination—for example, Sir Francis Bacon's attempt to "bind" nature and put it to work in service of human needs. The indigenous epistemologies referenced here are not uncomfortable with a lack of certainty about the social world and the world of nature, for many indigenous peoples have no need to solve all mysteries about the world they operate *with* and in.

The Power of Indigenous Knowledge to Reshape Western Science: Rigor in Multilogicality

The past 30 years have witnessed sharp criticisms of the Western scientific establishment by scholars engaged in cultural studies of science, sociologists of scientific knowledge, multiculturalists who uncover the gender and race inscriptions on the scientific method, and philosophers exposing science's bogus claims to objectivity. The purposes of such studies do not involve some effort to critique the truth-value of Western scientific knowledge, which is the correspondence of a scientific pronouncement to a reality existing in isolation to the knower. Rather, such critiques of science point out that Western science has created a self-validating frame of reference that provides authority to particular Western androcentric and culturally specific ways of seeing the world. Contemporary science studies apply the same forms of analysis to both physical and social sciences, asking in both domains how knowledge is produced and how do implicit worldviews shape the knowledge construction process.

Such questions, unfortunately, tend not to come from within the scientific establishment but from outsiders such as students of indigenous knowledge. From the voices and the knowledge of the indigene, Westerners may be induced to take a new look at positivism's decontextualized rationality and the harm it can cause in people's lives around the planet. Indigenous knowledge provides a provocative vantage point from which to view Eurocentric discourses, a starting place for a new conversation about the world and human beings' role in it. In some ways, the epistemological critique initiated by indigenous knowledge is more radical than other sociopolitical critiques of the West, for the indigenous critique questions the very foundations of Western ways of knowing and being (Aronowitz, 1996; Harding, 1996; Kloppenberg, 1991; Ross, 1996; L. T. Smith, 1999).

Thus, our intention here is to make the argument that a scholarly encounter with indigenous knowledge can enrich the ways we engage in research and conceptualize education while promoting the dignity, self-determination, and survival of indigenous people. It is, of course, extremely important to consider the types of questions we ask about the relationship between indigenous knowledges and these matters. As Marcel Viergever (1999) points out, what we know is contingent on the types of questions we ask and the manner in which we interpret the answers. Along with Viergever, we believe that familiarity with indigenous knowledge will help academics both see previously unseen problems and develop unique solutions to them,

Again, we simultaneously heed the warning that the emerging Western academic interest in indigenous knowledge may not be a positive movement if such knowledge is viewed as merely another resource to be exploited for the economic benefit of the West. Understanding this admonition, we frame indigenous knowledge not as a resource to be exploited but as a perspective that can help change the consciousness of Western academics and their students while enhancing the ability of such individuals to become valuable allies in the indigenous struggle for justice and self-determination. In the contemporary context where some Western academics are reassessing their science, their epistemology, their research methods, and their educational goals, the questions raised by indigenous knowledge hold a potential revolutionary effect. What a radical change this could initiate—Western researchers and educators learning from indigenous peoples in a respectful, nonexploitive manner.

The goal of such a learning process is to produce a transformative science, an approach to knowledge production that synthesizes ways of knowing expressed by the metonymies of hand, brain, and heart. Keeping in mind the omnipresent danger of the Western exploitation of indigenous knowledge, it may be possible to examine the relationship between Western science and indigenous ways of knowing in a manner that highlights their differences and complementarities. The purpose here is not simply to deconstruct Western methods of knowledge production or to engage Western scientists in a process of self-reflection. While deconstruction and self-reflection are important, we are more concerned with initiating a conversation resulting in a critique of Western science that leads to a reconceptualization of the Western scientific project and Western ways of being-in-the-world around issues of multiple ways of seeing, justice, power, and community. Our notion of an indigenously informed transformative science is not one that simply admits more peoples—"red and yellow, black and white"—into the country club of science but challenges the epistemological foundations of the ethnoknowledge known simply as science.

A transformative scientist understands that any science is a social construction, produced in a particular culture in a specific historical era—Sandra Harding (1998) turns positivism on itself, calling such a process a stronger form of objectivity (i.e., better science). Via a study of indigenous knowledge, Western scientists come to understand their work in unprecedented clarity. As they gain a critical distance from their scholarship, they also gain new insights into the culturally inscribed Eurocentrism of the academy and the politics of knowledge in general. Such informed scientists could begin to point out the similarities that connect indigenous perspectives with certain schools of feminism, agroecology, critical theory, and multilogical critiques. While obviously these perspectives are different and come from diverse contexts, there are points around issues of knowledge production where they all intersect. Important and strategic alliances can be constructed around these intersections. Operating in solidarity, individuals from these different backgrounds can ask new questions about what it means "to know," about the role of love and empathy in the epistemological process, and about the purposes of a critical multilogical education.

Transformative researchers do not see themselves as saviors. An offshoot of colonialism is the notion by the researcher (many times White, European) that the research or pedagogy he or she is introducing to the community is somehow a way to *benefit* his or her "subjects." Using Western tools of research and observation, the researcher acquires an elevated positionality within the venue of the research. I (Shirley) recall vividly situations on the Blood Reserve in Stand-Off, Alberta, in which the university researchers entered schools with the intent of enlightenment via the research they were pursuing. Instead of genuinely observing students in literacy classes and reading acquisition, the researchers attempted to implant reading curricula in what they already saw as a deficit-laden reading curriculum. By doing this, they made clear their expectation that what they introduced was superior. The cooperating teachers from the reserve felt compelled to make sure that the new reading curriculum *worked*. Interviews with the teachers were overwhelmingly positive about the introduced curriculum; there were no protestations or disagreements about the appropriateness of the new work. The experimental curriculum consisted of comic books depicting the literary "classics." Not only was the use of comic books pejorative in nature, but there was no connection to indigeneity or acknowledgment as to the definition of a classic as Western in origin. This example exhibits most of the research and pedagogy that is conducted on reserves and reservations in North America today. The residents are still the manifestation of the *White man's burden,* the same philosophy that was popularized by the Carlisle Indian School: *Kill the Indian, save the man.*

Multilogical Epistemologies:
Producing Dialogical Systems of Knowledge Production

Once individuals come to believe that Western science is not the only legitimate knowledge producer, then maybe a conversation can be opened about how different forms of research and knowledge production take issues of locality, cultural values, and social justice seriously. Our goal as educators and researchers operating in Western academia is to conceptualize an indigenously informed science that is dedicated to the social needs of communities and is driven by humane concerns rather than the economic needs of corporate managers, government, and the military. Much too often, Western science is a key player in the continuation of Euro-expansion projects that reify the status quo and further the interests of those in power. In this context, we are not attempting to produce a grand synthesis that eventuates in one final epistemological knowledge production system. Instead, we hope that we all can learn from difference, from the profound insights and the limitations of various ways of seeing the world and the humans who inhabit it.

Thus, different ways of seeing can coexist, many of them in what might be labeled confederations of solidarity, around a compact to encourage and engage in dialogue about the ethical, political, and pedagogical consequences of various forms of knowledge production. Caution is necessary here, for the types of dialogue that have taken place about these matters to date have too often been condescendingly Eurocentric. Indigenous knowledge producers have been positioned as exotic inferiors who must be introduced to the advanced world of Western science (Airhihenbuwa, 1995; Kloppenberg, 1991). With these ideas in mind, the term *hybridity* has been injected into the conversation about the dialogue between Western and indigenous knowledges. Such a term consciously references the effort to transcend essentialism with its understanding that cultural interaction is a historical inevitability. Frederique Apffel-Marglin (1995) is uncomfortable with the use of *hybridity* in this context, arguing that the concept renders the creative work and ingenuity of indigenous peoples invisible. Apffel-Marglin is writing in this case from the perspective of indigenous culture making use of Western knowledge; the point is still important to consider, even though in the context of this chapter we are focusing on the role of indigenous knowledge in the Western education and knowledge production.

How are different cultural perspectives incorporated into other ways of seeing and systems of knowledge production? Can the indigenous confrontation with the Western paradigm help bring about a deep modification of Western perspectives? As previously asserted, our essentialism detector tells us that no cultures exist in a pristine, uncontaminated state and that some form of cultural interaction is always taking place. Yet, how does such interaction relate to the concept of cultural continuity and regeneration in light of the reality of the perseverance of long-lasting distinctive cultural traditions? Western students of indigenous knowledge and advocates of incorporating such knowledge into the Western curriculum must address these issues in their scholarship and pedagogy to protect themselves from simplistic applications of indigeneity to the Western context. Again, the purpose here is not to produce "the end of epistemological history," a final articulation of the best way to produce knowledge. Sandra Harding (1996), writing about a transformed science, uses the term *borderlands epistemology* to signify the valuing of different understandings of the world that diverse cultures produce.

Harding's (1996) concept of borderlands epistemology works well for our concerns. Western scholars in this context would be able to draw upon different systems of knowledge and knowledge production given the various situations they encounter. In this framework, we would not seek the final representation of the world or some infallible mapping of social and physical reality—the grand resolution of epistemological debate. While social, psychological, pedagogical, and physical scholars would modify their sciences in light of indigenous understandings, they would not work to merely copy non-Western ways of seeing. This is the type of dialogue we seek in indigenously informed knowledge production and curriculum development in Western societies. Thus, scientific boundaries would be redrawn and opened to new negotiations. Such a process not only will provide Western analysts with new physical and social scientific insights but will also open their eyes to the political and cultural forces at work in all scientific labor. Informed in this manner, Western scientists traditionally chained to their decontextualized "laboratories" will peer outside to study the effects of their isolated inquiries on living people in naturalistic environments. Indeed, neglected questions of sustainability and local contexts will enter the vocabularies of analysts who previously dismissed such concepts from the purview of their protocols (Kloppenberg, 1991; Ross, 1996).

A Modest Proposal: Generating an Intercultural, Synergistic Dialogue

What we are proposing here is a synergistic dialogue that pedagogically works to create conditions where both intra- and intercultural knowledge traditions can inform one another. Mahia Maurial (1999) well understands this concept as she imagines a dialogical educational future. These encounters reduce the ugly expression of epistemological xenophobia and the essentialism it spawns—whatever its source. In Australia's Center for Aboriginal Studies, Jill Abdullah and Ernie Stringer (1999) report this synergistic dialogue is encouraged by the assumption of the intrinsic worth of various frames of reference. Different ways of seeing can illuminate problems in unique ways and should be understood in this manner—a central tenet of multilogicality.

Questions about the nature of indigenous knowledge and its academic uses are obviously complex but central to the future of education—a just, critical, practical, anticolonial, and transformative education in particular. No one said it would be easy—we know it won't. It is our hope that work such as ours and the other authors in this handbook will help educators and researchers from diverse backgrounds appreciate this complexity and give one another space and respect as they struggle to address the various issues raised here. An intercultural, synergistic, and unresolved conversation among a wide variety of players is central to our task. While open-ended, such a conversation would be marked by a recognition on the part of non-indigenous researchers of the ways that their cultural orientations and values (L. T. Smith, 1999) and the processes through which such dynamics inscribe their epistemologies, ontologies, and research methods can do great harm to indigenous peoples. All of these aspects of research involve power and its ability to construct oppressive structures and knowledges that produce/inflict human suffering.

References

Abdullah, J., & Stringer, E. (1999). Indigenous knowledge, indigenous learning, indigenous research. In L. Semali & J. Kincheloe (Eds.), *What is indigenous knowledge? Voices from the academy* (pp. 143–156). Bristol, PA: Falmer.

Agrawal, A. (1995). Indigenous and scientific knowledge: Some critical comments. *Indigenous Knowledge and Development Monitor, 3*(3), 3–6.

Airhihenbuwa, C. (1995). *Health and culture: Beyond the Western paradigm.* Thousand Oaks, CA: Sage.

Apffel-Marglin, F. (1995). Development or decolonialization in the Andes? *Interculture: International Journal of Intercultural and Transdisciplinary Research, 28*(1), 3–17.

Appiah, K. (1995). The postcolonial and the postmodern. In. B. Ashcroft, G. Griffiths, & H. Tiffin (Eds.), *The post-colonial studies reader* (pp. 119–124). New York: Routledge.

Aronowitz, S. (1996). The politics of science wars. In A. Ross (Ed.), *Science wars* (pp. 202–225). Durham, NC: Duke University Press.

Ashcroft, B., Griffiths, G., & Tiffin, H. (Eds.). (1995). *The post-colonial studies reader.* New York: Routledge.

Dei, G. (1994, March). *Creating reality and understanding: The relevance of indigenous African world views.* Paper presented to the Comparative and International Education Society, San Diego, California.

Dei, G., & Kempf, A. (2006). *Anti-colonialism and education: The politics of resistance.* Rotterdam: Sense Publishers.

Denzin, N. K., & Lincoln, Y. S. (2000). *The Sage handbook of qualitative research* (2nd ed.). Thousand Oaks, CA: Sage.

Dion-Buffalo, Y., & Mohawk, J. (1993). Thoughts from an autochthonous center: Postmodern and cultural studies. *Akweikon Journal, 9*(4), 16–21.

Freire, P., & Faundez, A. (1989). *Learning to question: A pedagogy of liberation.* New York: Continuum.

George, J. (1999). Indigenous knowledge as a component of the school curriculum. In L. Semali & J. Kincheloe (Eds.), *What is indigenous knowledge? Voices from the academy* (pp. 79–94). New York: Falmer.

Goldie, T. (1995). The representation of the indigene. In B. Ashcroft, G. Griffiths, & H. Tiffin (Eds.), *The post-colonial studies reader* (pp. 232–236). New York: Routledge.

Gramsci, A. (1988). *An Antonio Gramsci reader* (D. Sorgacs, Ed.). New York: Schocken Books.

Hall, S. (1995). New ethnicities. In B. Ashcroft, G. Griffiths, & H. Tiffin (Eds.), *The post-colonial studies reader* (pp. 223–227). New York: Routledge.

Harding, S. (1996). Science is "good to think with." In A. Ross (Ed.), *Science wars* (pp. 16–28). Durham, NC: Duke University Press.

Harding, S. (1998). *Is science multicultural? Postcolonialisms, feminisms, and epistemologies.* Bloomington: Indiana University Press.

Hess, D. (1995). *Science and technology in a multicultural world: The cultural politics of facts and artifacts.* New York: Columbia University Press.

Howard, G. (1995). Unraveling racism: Reflections on the role of nonindigenous people supporting indigenous education. *Australian Journal of Adult and Community Education, 35*(3), 229–237.

Jaimes, M. (1987). American Indian studies: Toward an indigenous model. *American Indian Culture and Research Journal, 11*(3), 1–16.

Keith, N., & Keith, N. (1993, November). *Education development and the rebuilding of urban community.* Paper presented at the Annual Conference of the Association for the Advancement of Research, Policy, and Development in the Third World, Cairo, Egypt.

Kincheloe, J., & Steinberg, S. (1993). A tentative description of post-formal thinking: The critical confrontation with cognitive theory. *Harvard Educational Review, 63,* 296–320.

Kincheloe, J., Steinberg, S., & Hinchey, P. (Eds.). (1999). *The postformal reader: Cognition and education.* New York: Falmer.

Kloppenberg, J. (1991). Social theory and the de/reconstruction of agricultural science: Local knowledge for an alternative agriculture. *Rural Sociology, 56,* 519–548.

Knijnik, G. (1999). Indigenous knowledge and ethnomathematics approach in the Brazilian landless people education. In L. Semali & J. Kincheloe (Eds.), *What is indigenous knowledge? Voices from the academy* (pp. 179–208). New York: Falmer.

Marcuse, H. (1955). *Eros and civilization.* Boston: Beacon.

Maurial, M. (1999). Indigenous knowledge and schooling: A continuum between conflict and dialogue. In L. Semali & J. Kincheloe (Eds.), *What is indigenous knowledge? Voices from the academy* (pp. 59–78). New York: Falmer.

Mosha, R. (2000). *The heartbeat of indigenous Africa: A study of the Chagga educational system.* New York: Garland.

Mudrooroo. (1995). White forms, Aboriginal content. In B. Ashcroft, G. Griffith, & H. Tiffin (Eds.), *The post-colonial studies reader* (pp. 228–231). New York, Routledge.

Murray, A. (1996). *The blue devils of Nada: A contemporary American approach to aesthetic statement.* New York: Vintage.

Mutua, K., & Swadener, B. (2004). *Decolonizing research in cross-cultural contexts: Critical personal narratives.* Albany, NY: SUNY Press.

Parrish, A. (1999). Agricultural extension education and the transfer of knowledge in an Egyptian oasis. In L. Semali & J. Kincheloe (Eds.), *What is indigenous knowledge? Voices from the academy* (pp. 269–284). New York: Falmer.

Pieterse, I., & Parekh, B. (1995). Shifting imaginaries: Decolonization, internal decolonization, and post-coloniality. In J. Pieterse & B. Parekh (Eds.), *The decolonialization of imagination: Culture, knowledge, and power* (pp. 1–15). Atlantic Highlands, NJ: Zed.

Quiroz, C. (1999). Local knowledge systems and vocational education in developing countries. In L. Semali & J. Kincheloe (Eds.), *What is indigenous knowledge? Voices from the academy* (pp. 305–316). New York: Falmer.

Ross, A. (1996). Introduction. In A. Ross (Ed.), *Science wars* (pp. 1–15). Durham, NC: Duke University Press.

Semali, L., & Kincheloe, J. (Eds.). (1999). *What is indigenous knowledge? Voices from the academy.* New York: Falmer.

Shor, I., & Freire, P. (1987). *A pedagogy for liberation: Dialogues on transforming education.* South Hadley, MA: Bergin & Garvey.

Simonelli, R. (1994). Traditional knowledge leads to a Ph.D. *Winds of Change, 9,* 43–48.

Smith, G. H. (2000). Protecting and respecting indigenous knowledge. In M. Battiste (Ed.), *Reclaiming indigenous voice and vision* (pp. 209–224). Vancouver: University of British Columbia Press.

Smith, L. T. (1999). *Decolonizing methodologies: Research and indigenous peoples.* New York: Zed.

Sponsel, L. (1992). Information asymmetry and the democratization of anthropology. *Human Organization, 51,* 299–301.

Viergever, M. (1999). Indigenous knowledge: An interpretation of views from indigenous peoples. In L. Semali & J. Kincheloe (Eds.), *What is indigenous knowledge? Voices from the academy* (pp. 333–360). New York: Falmer.

Villaverde, L., Kincheloe, J., & Helyar, F. (2006). Historical research in education. In K. Tobin & J. Kincheloe (Eds.), *Doing educational research* (pp. 311–46). Rotterdam: Sense Publishers.

PART FIVE

On Pedagogy and Teaching

Teachers as Critical Researchers: An Empowering Model for Urban Education

Ernest Morrell

The Challenge and Opportunity of Urban Teachers in New Century Schools

For those of us concerned with attaining high-quality and equitable education for students of color attending urban schools, we have to be disturbed by the teacher attrition that disproportionally impacts urban schools. Darling-Hammond (2000) estimates that nearly 30% of new teachers leave the profession within five years, with this number rising much higher in urban districts. Simply "enlarging" teacher preparation within existing college programs will not be adequate to meet the need. Educational researchers and teacher educators must pursue well-grounded, if sometimes novel, ways to train and mentor urban teachers. New approaches to teaching and teacher development are critical for these teachers to be effective and for their students to succeed in new century schools.

Urban teacher educators today are challenged to stress to pre-service teachers the importance of establishing meaningful relationships with students who come from different worlds. Additionally, pre-service and professional development programs need to offer teachers the experiences and tools to forge such relationships, and to help teachers see how successful practice is built upon the relationships. Accepting this challenge presents a tremendous opportunity for progressive social justice educators to reconfigure urban teacher training and professional development in ways that value and affirm the contributions and experiences of urban students and members of urban communities.

In my previous work (Morrell, 2004, 2008) I have argued that fostering academic and critical literacy development among urban youth through engagement in critical research projects can respond to the cultural and experiential mismatch between urban students and urban teachers in several important ways. Blending academic and critical literacy can transform relationships between teachers and students because it repositions urban youth culture as a site of (educationally valued) expertise. This critical and sociocultural approach to classroom instruction recasts the authority and knowledge-generating roles of the teachers and students that must now act as intellectuals who make sense of and frame responses to challenges facing urban students, their families, and their communities. Further, this is an interdependent activity, with neither teacher nor student able to accomplish it on his or her own. Finally, there is a potential to attract more urban teachers of color into the profession as these new forms of engagement enable those from the outside to develop new proficiencies and validate the experience of urban residents.

This new model of teaching, however, requires us to think differently about the role of teachers and the practice of critical pedagogy in urban classrooms. Specifically, I argue that a classroom space that privileges youth voice and critical research demands that teachers act as intellectuals and critical researchers alongside their students. Towards these ends, this chapter explores the possibilities for teacher transformation and academic literacy development when authentic dialogue and critical research projects involving teachers and students are placed at the core of teacher development and teacher training. This particular chapter presents data from a multi-year critical ethnography that follows a practicing teacher as he works with secondary students on critical research projects relating to urban school reform, youth voice, and civic engagement. Data, which were collected over a two-and-a-half-year period, include observations, videotapes of classroom interactions and presentations, informal conversations, interviews, reflections, and analyses of student work. This chapter will focus on the changing ways that the teacher views himself, his students, student work, teacher learning, and student knowledge as a result of his own changing participation over time in a youth-led research community of practice.

Rethinking Teacher Knowledge: Lessons from Sociocultural and Critical Theories

The National Commission on Teaching and America's Future (Darling-Hammond, 1997) correlates quality teacher preparation with quality teaching. Our challenge, as teacher educators and educational researchers, is to define quality teaching in the context of the heterogeneous, multicultural, multilinguistic urban schools of the twenty-first century. I begin with sociocultural and critical theories, which I feel are important to creating learning communities within teacher training and development programs that simultaneously reflect on theory and honor diverse perspectives.

Many teacher training and development programs espouse a Vygotskian perspective where learning is viewed as a series of social interactions between experts and novices within a Zone of Proximal Development (ZPD) that extends students beyond what they can do without assistance, but not beyond links to students' prior knowledge (Vygotsky, 1978). Central to the ZPD, however, is an understanding of and respect for the funds of knowledge (Moll, Amanti, Neff, & Gonzalez, 1992) or cultural wealth (Yosso, 2005) that students bring into the classroom. Therefore, it is incumbent upon these programs to help prospective and practicing teachers develop strategies and skills needed to acquire such understanding with their own students, particularly when these students have very different life experiences than their teachers (Meier, 1995).

Lave and Wenger's (1991) situated cognition theory builds upon and adds to Vygotsky's theories of learning. They contend that learning is a social process that occurs as members of communities of practice engage in authentic participation around a joint enterprise through mutual engagement while tapping into an increasingly expanding shared repertoire. When urban teachers and students can engage in full and authentic participation in classrooms where their varied backgrounds and expertise become part of the shared repertoire, both student and teacher maximize their learning.

Critical educational theorists (Apple, 1990; Freire & Macedo, 1987; Giroux, 1997; hooks, 1994) claim that true teacher learning and classroom transformations will not occur until teacher-students and student-teachers engage in critical and liberating dialogue where each group informs the other as both grow in consciousness and sensitivity. Freire (1970), for instance, is highly critical of the tendency of many teachers to employ a banking education, where students are treated as empty receptacles waiting for deposits of knowledge from their teachers. What he argues for, instead, is a problem-posing education that is built upon critical and liberating dialogue centered in the experiences of oppressed people.

Freire's assertions are especially relevant for urban teacher education. Although many programs employ the literature of Freire and other critical pedagogues in their courses, few actually feature such dialogue in their programs. I argue that academic and critical literacy requires this dialogue. Further, this authentic discourse must invite urban students to play a prominent role alongside teachers and teacher educators. Students who have engaged in critical research on urban issues and cultures and reflected upon sociological theory have a most unique vantage point that could prove enlightening to both teachers and teacher educators (Morrell & Collatos, 2002).

New Literacy theorists (Barton & Hamilton, 1998; Heath, 1983; Mahiri, 1998; Pattison, 1982) critique autonomous models of literacy (Goody & Watt, 1968) that seek out the cognitive consequences of literacy and offer alternative, "ideological" models that incorporate social and cultural contexts as well as the power relations implicit in literacy practices. New Literacy Studies offers more anthropological and cross-cultural frameworks to replace those of a previous era, in which psychological and culturally narrow approaches predominated. Research into popular cultures and vernacular literacies within modern settings has begun to show the richness and diversity of literacy practices and meanings despite the pressures for uniformity exerted by the nation state and the modern education systems. My own research (Morrell, 2004; Morrell & Duncan-Andrade, 2003) has built upon these theories, showing the possibilities of using students' knowledge of popular cultures to facilitate the development of academic literacies.

Urban educators in new century schools need to understand the social, historical, cultural, political, and economic contexts of contemporary urban schools if they are to become effective critical pedagogues themselves (Anyon, 1997; Apple, 1996; Bartolome, 1994; McLaren, 1989; Shor, 1992), who are able to capitalize on students' knowledge to promote the development of academic literacies. Because students have essential and unique knowledge of youth, urban, and popular cultures, educational researchers and critical teacher educators require their participation—in many respects a collegial participation—in order to develop the consciousness and awareness of practicing teachers. These teacher-researchers can, in turn, utilize the cultural literacies (Gutierrez, 2008; Lee, 1992; Mahiri, 1998), funds of knowledge, and community cultural wealth (Moll, 2000; Yosso, 2005) to engage urban students in critical research relating to urban, youth, and popular cultures as a way to facilitate the acquisition of traditional academic literacies.

Methodology: Towards a Critical Sociology of Teacher Development

Hegemony, one of the most important concepts in critical theory, explains the process by which power elites maintain control in capitalist societies without the use of explicit force (Gramsci, 1971). Instead of relying on coercive measures, hegemony allows for the maintenance of power through the domination of ideas. Gramsci and other social theorists have explored how social institutions such as schools, the media, and government function as sources of dominant knowledge construction. Generally ordinary citizens, the targets of hegemony, are relegated to the role of knowledge consumers within these institutions, and institutional practices and norms reify this passive relationship to knowledge and authority. Paulo Freire's banking education, for instance, explains how this process occurs in schools that serve the poor and working class. In response, critical theories of education have called for the empowerment of historically marginalized individuals through pedagogy, racial counter-narratives, media production, and research methodologies that privilege the voices, experiences, and ways of knowing that have been silenced, muted, or largely disregarded by regimes of power.

For the purposes of this chapter I will focus largely on the relationship between critical qualitative research, teacher empowerment, and educational justice. My first task, then, is to define my use of a term such as critical qualitative research. Critical theorists argue that historically marginalized groups can use research as a tool of counterhegemony (Carspecken, 1996; Kincheloe & McLaren, 1998). Inquiry that aspires to the name critical must involve or exist in solidarity with those who experience injustice, and it must be connected to an attempt to confront the injustice of a particular society or sphere within the society. Critical research plays an important role in providing information to those engaged in public pedagogy and political action to redress the injustices found in schools, the larger society, or even the very act of research itself.

Critical research scholars view urban schools as social institutions designed for social and cultural reproduction, but also as potential sites for resistance and transformation. With this latter idea in mind, I conducted a critical ethnography of a school community where teachers, students, and university partners co-constructed educational knowledge to use to advocate for change at the school site, and ultimately throughout the state of California. I am defining a critical ethnography of education as a form of critical qualitative research that studies the multiple cultures of a school community (Bogdan & Biklen, 2007; Carspecken, 1996; Denzin & Lincoln, 2003). Ethnographic techniques become the strategies that critical researchers use to collect data about schooling practices and their relation to the social order to ultimately undermine or transform that order (Carspecken, 1996). Employing a critical ethnography (Merriam, 1998) I draw from a two-and-a-half-year study that follows Mr. Genovese, a high school teacher. I examine the impact of forging critical research communities of practice on teacher development and teachers' ability to promote the development of academic literacies with their students.

Mr. Genovese, Pacific Beach High, and the Pacific Beach Project in Brief

Gary Genovese was a native of the major city near Pacific Beach, attended college in this same city, and had been teaching in the Pacific Beach district for five years before being approached by university researchers to participate in the Pacific Beach Project. During his tenure in the district, Mr. Genovese also coached the varsity baseball team and was involved in many campus activities. An avowed Catholic and alumnus of a Jesuit university, Mr. Genovese was firmly committed to the project of social justice and had excellent rapport with his students. It was for these reasons that he was selected as the lead teacher for the project. He was a gregarious, dramatic, and powerful personality in his classroom and in the school. His concern for the treatment of African American and Latino students at the campus led him into the work of the AVID program, which targets and provides services for underrepresented students of color in selected California schools. So, though he had no experience in critical research or familiarity with the critical social theory which would come to dominate his life, informing his research, practice, and outlook on the world, Mr. Genovese, at the time of his initial involvement, was a conscientious and politically minded teacher already entrenched in the silent race and class warfare that tore at the soul of Pacific Beach High school.

Nestled along southern California's Pacific coast, Pacific Beach, at the time of this research, was a comprehensive high school with an enrollment of 3,100 students. Hailed as a school with a population that closely reflects the demographics of the state of California, Pacific Beach had the following ethnic breakdown: 46.9% White, 32.6% Hispanic, 12.7% African American, and 6.9% Asian. Four hundred and fifteen of the students were listed as English Learners with the overwhelming majority of those being Spanish speakers (298). Sixty-seven point eight percent of the graduates were eligible for admission to the state's public universities as opposed to the 36.6% statewide average. A significant percentage (24.1%) of the students also qualified to receive free or reduced meals. Sixty-six percent of the teachers at Pacific Beach were White, 17% were Hispanic, 8% African American, and 6% Asian. The average SAT score for Pacific Beach High was 1048 compared to a state average of 1011 and a national average of 1016.

Although these numbers seem to reflect that Pacific Beach was a successful or at least above-average school by traditional criteria, there existed huge disparities in achievement between students according to ethnic and socioeconomic background. The disparities were so great that Pacific Beach High School was often referred to as two schools: one highly successful campus that services the affluent population (which was largely composed of White and Asian American students who were residents of the northern portion of the city), and another, less successful urban school that serviced the low-income (African American and Latino) students who lived either in the Rivera corridor, the poorest section of the city, or commuted on permit from south Los Angeles. Frustration with the seemingly intractable nature of the two-schools phenomenon led university researchers and school administrators to create the Pacific Beach Project.

Formed through collaboration between university faculty and Pacific Beach educators and administrators, the Pacific Beach Project (PBP) was designed to study and intervene in the pathways students of color follow through high school into higher education and the workplace. The project intended to engage a group of Latino and African American students who were just beginning high school in a five-year study of a) themselves and b) a diverse cohort of students who were just completing high school. In addition to developing a body of information on the pathways which high school students commonly follow, the project planned to create an alternative trajectory that would take underrepresented students through high school and into four-year universities. Alongside this work with students, the Pacific Beach Project planned to support the efforts of educators at Pacific Beach High School to develop more powerful and equitable models of learning which offer students clear pathways to successful futures. It thus sought to reshape students' lives, the work of one high school, and the understanding of the broader educational policy community.

Project investigators believed that such a study would alert students to the social inequality at the school while imparting the critical and academic skills needed to more effectively navigate Pacific Beach High school. With the assistance of Pacific Beach High teacher Mr. Genovese and the university research group, the ninth grade students (Cohort B) began to examine the evolving roles, responsibilities, and aspirations of the 12th grade students (Cohort A) as well as their own development during the initial months of high school.

The Pacific Beach Project Class was originally designed to provide Cohort B with new ways of understanding how to achieve success in school, new skills in writing and social science research, and new roles to play in school and beyond. Its aim was to make students more conscious of—and capable of asserting control over—their own trajectories by engaging them in a study of the trajectories of other young people.

Over the four years of the project, however, the project class was incorporated into the social studies class associated with that grade, with Mr. Genovese teaching the project class all four years. During their ninth grade year, the project students took their Humanities class together. During their 10th grade year, however, the students actually enrolled together for a double period of both World History and English. Scheduling problems prevented the students from having US History together in the 11th grade. Instead, the project class became an A period research seminar that met before school. For 12th grade, the students were once again able to enroll as a unit in the American Government/Economics course.

The summer research seminar component of the project provided students with internships as researchers with the project. These internships were designed to give the students a sense of ownership over the research project, promote important academic skills, and encourage them to take on significant new responsibilities. In addition to gathering information about university requirements that might be shared with classmates and younger students, the summer internships were also used to engage in research relating to the sociology of education and youth access to civic life, the media, public space, and a livable wage in urban Los Angeles.

Finally, a major portion of the project was committed to college access. Time from class was taken to study colleges and fill out the necessary forms for standardized tests, scholarships, and applications.

The project also took the students on several field trips to colleges around the state of California, giving students the opportunity to sit in classes and talk with university students, professors, and college counselors about the experience of attending a major university.

Data Collection and Analysis

A goal of this study is to determine the impact of these communities of practice on a broad range of factors that affect teachers' identities and careers, while helping teacher educators shape meaningful training, advanced degree and professional development programs for pre-service and practicing urban educators. To assist in answering some of the research questions, I generated the following sources of data:

- Videotapes of classes and research activities involving Genovese and his students

- Photographs taken by the researcher to document the learning community

- Class planning artifacts for the project classes and the summer seminar

- Student research artifacts (protocols, memos, field notes)

- Student work products (i.e., reports, PowerPoint slides and digital videos)

- Formal interviews with Mr. Genovese

- Informal conversations with Mr. Genovese held in person and over the Internet

- Informal electronic communication among other adult participants in the project

- Field notes written during participant observation

Data were primarily analyzed to document Mr. Genovese's changing modes of participation during the length of the ethnographic study, paying close attention to the activity settings, the modes of participation within the activity setting, the artifacts that were manipulated as a result of this participation, and the relationship between the activity and the process of becoming a critical researcher. The data analyzed for this chapter were culled from a much larger study that followed the learning trajectories of the students in Mr. Genovese's class (Morrell, 2004). From this larger data set, then, I extracted all items that were coded as involving Mr. Genovese and separated them chronologically according to school year or summer seminar. I then analyzed each piece of data, tracing it to a particular activity such as classroom teaching, participation in a research meeting, or conducting research, or preparation for a department meeting. This longitudinal and categorical analysis allowed me to examine changes over time in Mr. Genovese's participation in the community of practice, correlating these shifting modes of participation with activities, work products, and identity transformations related to critical research.

The following sections are divided both chronologically and developmentally, tracking Mr. Genovese's learning through his changing participation in the critical research-focused community of practice over the course of the study. The findings are grouped into four chronological sections: the 1998–1999 school year, the 1999–2000 school year, the summer seminar of 2000, and the 2000–2001 school year.

1998-1999: Learning Critical Research

Gary Genovese enrolled in a doctoral program at a major research university during the second year of the project. In his courses, he was exposed to critical social theory and the methods of research. He also formed relationships with the principal investigator of the project and advanced graduate students from the university who were also research associates with the project. As a legitimate peripheral participant, Mr. Genovese's activities during the initial year were mostly relegated to taking the university's doctoral courses and teaching the project courses at the high school. More experienced researchers in the project, either the principal investigator or research assistants, handled most of the data collection and project research design. Lave and Wenger (1991) identify legitimate peripheral participation as having access to all that membership entails in a community of practice without having all of the responsibilities of membership. This arrangement allowed Mr. Genovese an opportunity to learn via a form of participation—teaching—with which he was familiar and comfortable. My first visit to the project came on the final class meeting of the students' 10th grade year at Pacific Beach High School. I accompanied Dr. Dewey, the project's principal investigator, along with several other graduate students who came to conduct end-of-year interviews with the students. The experienced research team members took the lead in developing the interview protocols and conducting the interviews. Mr. Genovese was conducting the oral component of the class's final exam while small groups of students were being pulled out. This day was emblematic of my early experiences with Mr. Genovese and the project. Such experiences, coupled with his university coursework, allowed him to learn the tools and processes of critical research even as he continued to participate in the project in his role as a teacher.

My first opportunity to work with Mr. Genovese and the Pacific Beach Project occurred as we began the process of the planning and teaching of the 1999 summer seminar. During the period between the end of the school year and the start of the summer seminar in August, research members met periodically to plan. As a collaborative team, we designed the instruction based on a set of principals about learning and about youth empowerment that were derived from our forays into sociocultural learning theory, specifically the situated cognition theory of Jean Lave and Etienne Wenger, and the critical pedagogy scholarship of Paulo Freire. At the time we were just beginning to understand the very different type of research that we were undertaking as a team and that we were helping the youth to produce. In the spirit of the work of Jean Lave, we too were changing members in a changing community of practice. I will say, though, that by the middle of the summer of 1999, critical qualitative research emerged as the practice even though it had yet to be named as such. The first summer seminar was designed to provide a combination of large-group and small-group activities. The 20 students were to be divided into four smaller research groups, each led by a graduate student involved with the project. During that first summer both Mr. Genovese and I led student research teams. His focused on models of student resistance and mine focused on the possibilities of hip-hop pedagogy to engage youth in literacy and learning. Each research team leader was asked to create a plan of action based on an assigned topic to bring to the larger group for discussion. Dr. Dewey, the director of the university project and the most experienced researcher of the group, often played the role of mentor and coach in these meetings, making suggestions for readings, activities, and assignments though Mr. Genovese, and myself, and the other two team leaders were responsible for fleshing out the curriculum and running the seminar. Ultimately it was Mr. Genovese who took the lead in framing, at least initially, the structure and content of the seminar. This changing role as both teacher and graduate student researcher allowed for increased participation, as Mr. Genovese is now not only the teacher being studied, but also a peer of the graduate students and a student himself, who is learning about the world of academic research while also absorbing the larger responsibility for the seminar as it pertained to knowledge of the project of critical research.

The seminar, however, did mark a turning point that was facilitated by Mr. Genovese's emergence as a scholar-activist, but was also facilitated by changes in the composition of the research team. One of the senior graduate students was in the process of completing her dissertation and had accepted an academic position outside of the immediate geographic area. The second graduate student, who had played such a pivotal role in the development of the seminar, also in the process of completing her dissertation, declined to work in the seminar so that she could focus on her studies. Further, Dr. Dewey commuted from out of the area and could only participate in person for two days of the week. This left Mr. Genovese in charge of the day-to-day workings of a seminar that was dedicated to the teaching of research and placed him in the soon-to-be-familiar role of simultaneously learning and teaching critical research. As an advanced graduate student myself, my role became similar to the two students who were moving on from the project. Mr. Genovese and I would huddle before and after sessions, debriefing, strategizing, and seeking additional resources as it fit the students' interests and needs. Any serious problem or question could be directed toward Dr. Dewey on a Tuesday or Wednesday, his two days in town, or, on other days, through the *Charlie's Angels*-type response on the speakerphone. Via his evolving role in this new activity setting, Mr. Genovese's membership shifted from learning via transmission in graduate classrooms and research project meetings to a form of cognitive apprenticeship (Lee, 1992) that involved many of the same activities that professionally trained social scientists took on: teaching at the university and collecting and managing data relating to a large-scale research project.

1999–2000: Teaching Critical Research

Following the tremendous success of the 1999 summer research seminar, the project of critical qualitative research became a major portion of the Pacific Beach Project curriculum. Following the summer seminar. Mr. Genovese, myself, and other colleagues at the university decided to make critical research a central component of the project class, which was again being taught by Mr. Genovese. Though he continued to take courses at the university and receive mentoring from the advanced graduate students, Mr. Genovese's primary activity for the project consisted of teaching the project students about the nature of critical research. This provided an interesting dynamic, as Mr. Genovese was himself learning the fundamentals of research.

Both the fall and spring projects that year (the junior year for the project participants) involved the high school students conducting and presenting research related to their concerns and experiences of living and attending schools in Southern California. For example, for the fall semester final, the students were assigned to one of six cases. Each of the six cases involved personal experiences of the students or people they knew. Students actually wrote proposals for cases, and six were selected for the final. Examples of cases ranged from dealing with peers who were using drugs and engaged in self-defeating behavior to challenging a school system that did not provide equal access to its students of color. The case study groups had to collect data on their issue/problem, and they had to make a presentation where they talked about how they would draw upon their emergent critical perspectives to address the problem or issue.

Mr. Genovese played key roles in this process. First, through his own critical inquiry he was attuned to the students' growing concerns about how they could apply their developing critical instincts to the most pressing problems in their lives. As an experienced teacher he had enough confidence in his ability to take these concerns and create an assignment that would be useful and pedagogical at the same time. Second, even though the cases were generated from student proposals, Mr. Genovese helped to structure the cases in ways that would allow the students to be able to generate data and analysis. This is a key step in developing a critical-research-focused community of practice; more experienced practitioners have to be able to help novices to turn problems or issues into questions that can be explored critically and systematically. This is very similar to what Paulo Freire would call a problem-posing pedagogy. In the context of critical research, this pedagogy requires the teacher to have both knowledge of the participants and the processes of critical inquiry. During the mornings when student groups were preparing their cases, Mr. Genovese played the role of a research advisor, very similar to the interactions between doctoral students and their doctoral advisors. He would read over their plans and push them to be more focused in their data collection and analysis. For the final presentations he asked critical questions and offered constructive feedback to the students on how they could improve their research or how they could organize for action based upon the conclusions of their research.

Summer 2000: Practicing Critical Research

It may seem odd that I would separate teaching critical research from practicing critical research, it being difficult to teach research without actually doing the work. Certainly, as the work of the hip-hop and resistance groups attests, Mr. Genovese and the students were involved in critical research throughout the 1999–2000 academic school year. The summer of 2000, however, marked a fundamental shift in the community of practice and its use of critical research. This summer also marked a significant shift in Mr. Genovese's role as a teacher of critical research, but most importantly, this period marks a significant transformation for Mr. Genovese as a critical researcher himself.

All of the members of the Pacific Beach Project team were looking forward with great anticipation to the summer seminar of 2000. While 1999 had been a major triumph, it only provided us with more ideas and inspiration for how we wanted to restructure the seminar the following year. All year long, it seemed, was one big planning and brainstorming session for the "next summer." Somewhere around the time of the first semester final, a faculty member at the university institute we worked for suggested that we select the Democratic National Convention (DNC) as our site of research. That summer, the convention was headed to Los Angeles, and there was a great deal of national energy surrounding issues of equity, access, and social justice. The WTO protests in Seattle had galvanized the activist community, and many groups were planning to descend on the city. Marches were being planned, organizations such as indymedia.org and Pacifica Radio planned to be integrally involved in the coverage, and the American Civil Liberties Union (ACLU) and the city were locked in dispute over the erection of a 13-foot concrete barrier fence perimeter that was to separate the protesters and the public from the convention attendees.

In short it was the perfect location to host the second summer seminar. This summer also marked a shift in the participants and the notoriety of the seminar. Now funded in part by a university grant targeted at increasing college access for local students who had been historically underrepresented, the seminar would enroll half of its students from schools throughout the Greater Metropolitan area. The other half would come from the Pacific Beach Project. Through various networks with city schools, we recruited an applicant pool of students from high schools throughout the Greater Los Angeles area. We also reached out to teachers and local graduate students to work with the project. A local church agreed to host the students during the week of the convention so that we wouldn't have to travel back and forth from the university to downtown.

We also instituted several major changes to give the summer program more of a look of a precollege program. We created course readers that looked very much like ones used for university courses. In fact, the course now had a college number, Education 98, and a new location. Our seminar headquarters would now be located in one of the major lecture halls of the university law school. We made many other changes as well. We would now have two days a week where student groups would venture into the field, which meant the city of Los Angeles, and we would be spending a week downtown during the convention, based at the church in Pico Union, a neighborhood within walking distance from downtown. Finally, we invited numerous speakers to come in and talk to the students about the convention, about the intersections between politics and education, and about their role as researchers and documenters of the youth experience in education. Some of these speakers included Father Greg Boyle of Homeboy Industries, former State Senator and member of the Chicago Seven Tom Hayden, and future mayor of Los Angeles Antonio Villairagosa. I spend significant time here talking about the set-up of the seminar because Mr. Genovese was very much involved in all of these changes along with Dr. Dewey and myself. These changes represent our evolving conception of critical research (even the name of what we were doing became apparent during this time) and our changing role as critical researchers during this time. These changes were so important to our enterprise that even now, in 2010, the summer seminar looks more like it did in 2000 than 2000 looks like the summer of 1999!

An analysis of data from the summer 2000 research seminar reveals how Mr. Genovese became immersed as a researcher even as we were still involved in the seminar as teachers. My examination of electronic conversations and memos from Gary show his progress as a researcher. The following exchange occurs between Mr. Genovese and me during the second week of the summer seminar. By this time we are both heavily involved in the work of the seminar as program coordinators, but we are also both fairly certain that the project of critical research is going to be central to each of our dissertations. Mr. Genovese and I, through our AOL chat, are having a conversation about the first week of the seminar, our impressions, and our strategies for improving the experience for the students. One of our concerns is that some of the teachers we have hired do not share our understanding of critical research or more importantly what it means to engage high school students in the project of critical research. Mr. Genovese's comments as a teacher-researcher show his ownership over the practice as well as his command of the critical research process:

Genovese: Anyway, I am, too, cautiously optimistic…I think in the future that a discussion about apprenticeship models, building communities, and how we deal with young adults would be helpful in terms of the dynamics and products of the group.

Morrell: For the fellows.

Genovese: Maybe even a clearer framing of the research process for the fellows before the seminar begins, even breaking down the research process into everyday terms.

Morrell: That we did.

Morrell: We had 10 hours of meetings before the seminar.

Genovese: Research questions, what do we want to know, how are we going to find out, what methods? Analyzing our data, and what are the implications?

Morrell: And went over this step by step.

Genovese: I think we trusted them.

Morrell: I think the pressure has scared them into amnesia.

Genovese: Maybe it is about teaching.

Morrell: We went over questions, theories, teaching strategies, activities, the DNC…

Genovese: I don't know, maybe we could try to apprentice more, model…I don't know.

Genovese: I don't want to step on anyone's toes, but a research question absolutely must be pinned down, data should be collected and everything should be ready to go in terms of whom do I want to interview and observe next week and what do I want to ask them?

There is a lot happening in this brief exchange. What comes out is our anxiety about the people we pull into our community of practice, Gary Genovese's frustration, and my defense of our approach to incorporating the new teachers as legitimate peripheral participants. What I would like to focus on, though, is the extemporaneous use of the language of critical research that Mr. Genovese uses as he forms his critique. The teachers should be using an apprentice model to push the high school students, they should be able to work more collaboratively with the youth, yet they should be more helpful in drawing upon the interests and motivations of the youth while also having a more explicit role in the framing of the research question and research design. We had subtly begun to use this approach to our critical work with youth (and for the most part we still do), but here Gary names it. In his critique of what is not happening he names exactly what it is that we do when working with the youth to develop their research projects.

During this summer and the successive school year, Mr. Genovese's work changed from the project's larger questions of college access to the workings of capital within the PBP cohort. This second summer marked a pivotal turn in his relationship to the project and to his own research. Certainly his work as a teacher and as a researcher were important to the project; however, the work began to become fundamentally his own. It is also key that central to the research of Mr. Genovese was the research of his students in the seminar. Kincheloe and McLaren (1998) remind us that critical research is fundamentally about working with and on behalf of members of marginalized populations. Mr. Genovese's critical research necessarily had to involve the critical research of his students and the other urban teens participating in the seminar. As a graduate student, Mr. Genovese was also in the process of beginning his dissertation work, which ultimately became an award-winning study of the relationship between college access and apprenticing youth as "equity researchers."

2000-2001: Critical Researcher as Teacher Educator, Mentor, and Activist

Coming off the "high" from the summer seminar, where the students were able to put their research into action, we knew that the senior year of the PBP students would be special. There was no doubt that the project of critical research would guide the work in their class together, which in the senior year was a government/econ course. Mr. Genovese wanted to allow the students to tackle a myriad of local problems in the school and community while also making certain that the students utilized their growing expertise in critical research to both facilitate change in local schools as well as their own college access.

During his final year with the students in the project, Mr. Genovese's role with the project would again take a dramatic turn. Not only was he one of the primary researchers now, he also felt it his mission to communicate the preliminary findings of the project research to his colleagues at Pacific Beach High, to school site and district administrators, to pre-service teachers at local universities, and to fellow members of the research community. His primary activities still involved teaching, but the final year was consumed more with writing, presentations, and lecturing at the university. Mr. Genovese really carried the banner for the project as a researcher and activist in this final year. During that academic year, I taught graduate-level courses at the university for pre-service teachers interested in urban education. Both Mr. Genovese and I had begun to see ourselves as teacher educators by this time, and we got the idea that the students, as emergent scholars with first-hand experience of schools, should also be involved in the process of educating new teachers. With this idea Mr. Genovese worked with groups of students to create presentations that could be given to teachers enrolled in credential programs and he, along with the students, traveled to local universities to speak with pre-service teachers. In my own university teacher education classroom, these "visits" were so powerful that we actually wrote a few pieces about this project. Mr. Genovese and I wrote one piece; the second piece was written in collaboration with a few of the PBP students and was published in a peer-reviewed journal.

Mr. Genovese's role as a teacher educator not only pertained to his work at the university. As a veteran teacher with considerable leverage among his colleagues, Mr. Genovese took it upon himself to communicate the implications of our findings in the project for how pedagogical practices and policies might facilitate increased college access for students of color attending Pacific Beach High School. Towards these ends he began a series of conversations with his colleagues in the social studies department about the nature of the discipline, about instructional practices in social studies classes, and about increasing academic achievement for African American and Latino students enrolled in social studies courses. Mr. Genovese would frequently tell me about the challenges and small victories that this work yielded, and in my relationships with other members of the social studies department I could see that the Pacific Beach Project, and Mr. Genovese in particular, were having an impact on practices in the department. Mr. Genovese also wanted to impact the larger administration and bring attention to the success of the project (by this time it was known that there would be a 100% graduation rate and nearly 100% college-going rate) and to some of the barriers at the school that mitigate against college access. With this goal in mind he also reached out to teachers in other departments as well as the school and district administration.

Finally, Mr. Genovese took students to regional and national conferences to present their work, and he traveled to other schools to share with students and teachers the model of critical research that had been developed in the project. In April of 2001, for example, Mr. Genovese brought students to the annual meeting of the American Educational Research Association, which was being held in Seattle, Washington. The students presented on their emerging work as teen sociologists, and the graduate student researchers each presented on their own work related to the project. Following is a slide created by Mr. Genovese that speaks to his complex and comprehensive understanding of the Pacific Beach Project and how it functioned as a community of practice.

Pacific Beach Project: A Community of Practice

- Student Activism
- Cyber-Space
- PBP Activities Extended Space
- PBP High School Classroom Space
- University Summer Seminar Research Space
- PBP and Families Space
- PBP as Academic Space

The presentations in Seattle were a huge success and marked the end of the formal research of the students in the Pacific Beach Project. As predicted, the students did graduate and most enrolled in colleges and universities. Many took on roles as leaders and scholars on these campuses. Almost half of the students continued to work in the summer seminar as researchers and teacher assistants. In the summer of 2004 two former Pacific Beach students, now entering college seniors, co-taught one of the research groups and virtually led the seminar. In 2007 we held a panel of youth activists, and three of the five panelists were alumni of the Pacific Beach Project. Mr. Genovese soon became Dr. Genovese and took a role as a teacher educator at a local university where he continues to engage students, parents, and community members in the project of critical qualitative research. Only a few weeks ago we took another group of high school researchers to the American Educational Research Association conference, this time in Denver. Dr. Genovese, in the back of a large conference room, addressed the newest version of the critical scholars and told them, as he became emotional, that the "Project" students would be proud of the legacy and the tradition that they had established. I was grateful for the opportunity to acknowledge Mr. Genovese and the leadership and inspiration he provided to work that endures and continues to advocate for change as it also provides access to students at the high school, undergraduate, and graduate levels who want to become involved in the practice of critical research.

It is always important for ethnographers to theorize or at least acknowledge themselves as participants in the work that they conduct, especially in the context of a critical ethnography whose goal is not only to understand cultural practice, but to intervene when necessary and to understand the processes by which members of historically marginalized groups work in solidarity with others in the struggle for social, economic, and educational justice. Mr. Genovese's story is also my own story of growth and development as a critical researcher and a teacher of critical research. During my involvement, my own role changed from that of a graduate student research associate to a university professor and postdoctoral research fellow. I also became a co-director of the summer research seminars, which were expanded to include pre-service and practicing teachers from throughout the city, which I will describe in the next section. I am also aware that Mr. Genovese simultaneously served as a subject of my research and as a partner in a learning community. In other words, I learned a great deal about myself and the process of critical research through active work and the investigation of Mr. Genovese's learning of critical research.

Through this process, itself an example of critical qualitative research, I played the roles of a fellow graduate student and a student of critical pedagogy and critical research; I also played the roles of mentor, critical friend, and co-teacher. Norm Denzin (1997) comments that the writing of poststructural ethnography is often the writing of our own biographies. As I revisit this data from many years ago I have come to understand this study as an investigation into my own learning about critical qualitative research, its relationships, its processes, and its implications for pedagogy, for teacher development, and for social action. A major finding of the study, then, is that collaborative critical research between teachers and students inspires generativity and reciprocal relationships that allow us to learn as we teach and to teach as we learn in the true Freirian sprit of problem-posing pedagogy. Though this is a central tenet of a critical epistemology, it challenges to some extent our sociocultural framework that insufficiently theorizes the apprentice as teacher and the "master" or "expert" as student. Nonetheless, it is upon this very idea, and of the success with Mr. Genovese and the Pacific Beach Project, that we expanded the summer seminar to include spaces for prospective, pre-service, and practicing teachers interested in learning and teaching critical research.

A Summer Critical Research Seminar for Urban Teachers: One Possible Response

For the summer of 2001, our third seminar, we expanded our agenda to work with practicing urban teachers as well as urban students. The focal teachers were all participants in a program for recent alumni of the Teacher Education Program, which remained committed to teaching for social justice in urban schools. Some of the goals of the seminar were to understand how to help teachers to effectively apprentice their students to conduct critical research, to create a space where teachers could critically reflect upon their instruction and the relationship between social theory and their pedagogy, and to create a context where teachers can learn with and from students as they engage in critical research on issues of import to the students' cultures. Other goals were to begin an extensive research project with these teachers where we follow the impact of the summer seminars on their practice and pathways as teachers and to articulate the viability of the summer laboratory as a space for teachers and teacher educators to learn about how teachers learn.

The work of the successive decade of summer seminars (as of 2011 we are still going strong) has yielded important information about the process of learning and development as critical researchers. Practicing teachers have attested to the function of the research seminar as a form of professional development (Morrell, 2003). Former alumni of the Pacific Beach Project are now working in the seminar as mentors to the new cohorts of high school seniors, and I am involved in explorations of how the seminar works as a pipeline to provide significant experiences for undergraduates of color to learn about teaching for social justice and to accumulate various forms of capital needed to access graduate education and teacher certification.

Conclusion

Given the tremendous challenges that urban educators face on a daily basis, educational researcher-activists need to find ways to help teachers develop empowered identities where they see themselves as intellectuals and change agents. Our dozen years of critical qualitative research at UCLA has shown that teachers who have a positive identity of themselves as intellectuals are more likely to remain in the profession, in urban schools, and committed to social justice (Oakes, Lane, & Joseph, 2000). Through these new forms of engagement, teachers can also gain an understanding of how to employ ethnographic techniques to learn about students' cultures in ways that would help to meet students within the ZPD.

Hopefully this study and ones like it can help us in radically altering how we think about urban teacher education and working with practicing teachers to align with the tenets of sociocultural and critical theories. Specifically, we can use the findings of this study to develop classes and projects in the teacher credential and master's degree programs that allow teachers to engage in critical research of urban, youth, and popular cultures. The presentations, reports, papers, articles, and books that emerge from this study can then serve as guides to teacher education programs and school districts all over the nation as they struggle to find more effective ways to train and mentor urban educators. Many states are moving toward post-certification requirements for the maintenance of a teaching credential. Many of these requirements include the pursuit of a graduate degree. Countless teachers enroll in courses and programs that are meaningless or irrelevant to them, other than providing the needed units for advancement on the pay scale or for the renewal of certification. Countless others still enroll in courses that, although relevant and meaningful, remove these teachers from the very students and communities that they desire to engage. The work of this ethnography, of the Pacific Beach Project, and of the summer seminar that it spawned suggest that teacher education departments endeavor to create meaningful educational programs that allow teachers to pursue graduate degrees and advance professionally as they also participate as members of research-oriented communities of practice.

There are also implications for how we think about the project of critical qualitative research in colleges and departments of education. All graduate students should have opportunities to learn about critical qualitative research in their coursework, and there should be opportunities to more fully engage with local communities struggling for educational justice. Our research communities need to better honor this tradition by creating more spaces in our formal structures for the presentation and discussion of critical qualitative research methods and methodologies. We will not have the ultimate impact that we can upon policy, practice, and reform until we begin to legitimate and reflect upon the promises and challenges of critical qualitative research within our own academic communities of practice.

References

Anyon, J. (1997). *Ghetto schooling: A political economy of urban educational reform.* New York, NY: Teachers College Press.

Apple, M. W. (1990). *Ideology and curriculum.* New York, NY: Routledge.

Apple, M. W. (1996). *Cultural politics and education.* New York, NY: Teachers College Press.

Bartolome, L. I. (1994). Beyond the methods fetish: Toward a humanizing pedagogy. *Harvard Educational Review, 64,* 173–194.

Barton, D., & Hamilton, M. (1998). *Local literacies: reading and writing in one community.* New York, NY: Routledge.

Bogdan, R.C., & Biklen, S.K. (2007). *Qualitative research for education: An introduction to theories and methods* (5th ed.). Upper Saddle River, NJ: Pearson Education.

Carspecken, P. F. (1996). *Critical ethnography in educational research: A theoretical and practical guide.* New York: Routledge.

Darling-Hammond, L. (1997). *Doing what matters most: Investing in quality teaching.* New York: National Commission on Teaching and America's Future.

Darling-Hammond, L. (2000). *Solving the dilemmas of teacher supply, demand, and standards: How we can ensure a competent, caring, and qualified teacher for every child.* New York, NY: National Commission on Teaching and America's Future.

Denzin, N. (1997). *Interpretive ethnography: Ethnographic practices for the 21st century.* Thousand Oaks, CA: Sage.

Denzin, N. K., & Lincoln, Y. S. (2003). Introduction: The discipline and practice of qualitative research. In N. K. Denzin & Y. S. Lincoln (Eds.), *Strategies of qualitative inquiry* (2nd ed. pp. 1–45). Thousand Oaks, CA: Sage.

Freire, P. (1970). *Pedagogy of the oppressed.* New York, NY: Continuum.

Freire, P. (1997). *Teachers as cultural workers: Letters to those who dare teach.* Boulder, CO: Westview.

Freire, P., & Macedo, D. (1987). *Reading the word and the world.* Westport, CT: Bergin & Garvey.

Giroux, H. A. (1997). Border pedagogy and the age of postmodernism. In *Pedagogy and the politics of hope* (pp. 147–163). Boulder, CO: Westview.

Goody, J., & Watt, I. (1968). The consequences of literacy. In J. Goody (Ed.), *Literacy in traditional societies.* Cambridge, England: Cambridge University Press.

Gramsci, A. (1971). *Selections from the prison notebooks of Antonio Gramsci.* New York, NY: International Publishers.

Gutierrez, K. (2008). Developing a sociocritical literacy in the third space. *Reading Research Quarterly, 43*(2), 148–164.

Heath, S. B. (1983). *Ways with words: Language, life, & work in communities and classrooms.* Cambridge, England: Cambridge University Press.

hooks, b. (1994). *Teaching to transgress: Education as the practice of freedom.* New York, NY: Routledge.

Kincheloe, J. L., & McLaren, P. L. (1998). Rethinking critical theory and qualitative research. In N. K. Denzin & Y. S. Lincoln (Eds.), *The landscape of qualitative research: Theories and issues* (pp. 260–299). Thousand Oaks, CA: Sage Publications.

Lave, J., & Wenger, E. (1991). *Situated learning: Legitimate peripheral participation.* Cambridge, England: Cambridge University Press.

Lee, C. (1992). *Signifying as a scaffold for literary interpretation: The pedagogical implications of an African American discourse genre.* Urbana, IL: NCTE Press.

Mahiri, J. (1998). *Shooting for excellence: African American and youth culture in new century schools.* New York, NY: Teachers College Press.

McLaren, P. (1989). *Life in schools: An introduction to critical pedagogy in the foundations of education.* New York, NY: Longman.

Meier, D. (1995). *The power of their ideas: Lessons for America from a small school in Harlem.* Boston, MA: Beacon Press.

Merriam, S. B. (1998). *Qualitative research and case study applications in education.* San Francisco, CA: Jossey-Bass.

Moll, L. (2000). Inspired by Vygotsky: Ethnographic experiments in education. In C. Lee and P. Smagorinsky (Eds.), *Vygotskian perspectives on literacy research: Constructing meaning through collaborative inquiry* (pp. 256–268). New York, NY: Cambridge University Press.

Moll, L. C., Amanti, C., Neff, D., & Gonzalez, N. (1992). Funds of knowledge for teaching: Using a qualitative approach to connect homes and classrooms. *Theory into Practice, 31,* 132–141.

Morrell, E. (2003). Legitimate peripheral participation as professional development: Lessons from a summer research seminar. *Teacher Education Quarterly, 30* (2), 89–99.

Morrell, E. (2004). *Becoming critical researchers: Literacy and empowerment for urban youth.* New York, NY: Peter Lang.

Morrell, E. (2008). *Critical literacy and urban youth: Pedagogies of access, dissent, and liberation.* New York, NY: Routledge.

Morrell, E., & Collatos, A. (2002). Toward a critical teacher education pedagogy: Using student sociologists as teacher educators. *Social Justice, 29*(4), 60–70.

Morrell, E., & Duncan-Andrade, J. (2003). What youth do learn in school: Using hip-hop as a bridge to canonical poetry. In J. Mahiri (Ed.), *What they don't learn in school: Literacy in the lives of urban youth.* New York, NY: Peter Lang.

Oakes, J., Lane, S., & Joseph, R. (2000, April). *Who leaves? Who stays? And why?: Examining trajectories of development in an urban teacher education program.* Paper presented at the annual meeting of the American Educational Research Association, New Orleans, LA.

Pattison, R. (1982). *On literacy: The politics of the word from Homer to the age of rock.* New York, NY: Oxford University Press.

Shor, I. (1992). *Empowering education: Critical teaching for social change.* Chicago, IL: University of Chicago/AMS Press.

Solorzano, D. (1998). Critical race and gender microaggressions, & the experiences of Chicana and Chicano scholars. *International Journal of Qualitative Studies in Education, 11,* 121–136.

Vygotsky, L. (1978). *Mind in society: The development of higher psychological processes.* Cambridge, MA: Harvard University Press.

Yosso, T. J. (2005). Whose culture has capital? A critical race theory discussion of community cultural wealth. *Race, Ethnicity, & Education, 8*(1), 69–91.

CHAPTER TWENTY-SIX

Listening in the Liminal:
The In-between Spaces of Teaching Youth About Career and Adulthood

Amanda Benjamin

As the labor market becomes increasingly volatile, there is unprecedented fear that young people are unprepared to enter the workforce and that this lack of preparation will mean a delayed entry into adulthood (Aronson, 2008). There is often pressure on schools to institute formal programs to prepare young people for their future as workers. One of the results is that there is an increased focus on career education programs in secondary schools, and these programs are influencing the ways in which young people learn about conceptions of work and resultantly what it means to be successful adults in North American society (Bortolussi, 2006). Additionally, schools, teachers and curriculum are having an important impact on career choices as schools become a significant mechanism for influencing and informing students about career options (Gaskell, 1992; Walshaw, 2006). Not surprisingly, there is a need for critical scrutiny with respect to how young people are learning about work, and the different ways they are being prepared for future employment.

In the public consciousness, secondary schools are often thought of as places that keep adolescents off the streets and engaged in some kind of learning process (Kincheloe, 1995). Because the assumption is that career education is de facto "good," there is very little critical examination of the values informing such curricula and the influence on students. There is a need for what Fraser and Gordon (1997) call "critical scrutiny" in order to pay attention to common sense assumptions about career and adulthood.

This chapter describes a year-long study of a group of young people in Vancouver (British Columbia, Canada) who were learning about work and adulthood in the context of their career education classrooms. The study employed document analysis of the British Columbia Career and Personal Planning (CAPP) curriculum, interviews with teachers and students, and classroom observations of four classrooms in order to illuminate how work and adulthood were constituted in the curriculum. The purpose of this chapter is not just to present the empirical data, but to explore the usefulness of critical theories for analyzing these data. Going beyond data is important in uncovering how the workings of power, subjectivity, and issues of voice and oppression can be addressed through research. If the purpose of critical research is to attend to societal structures and institutions that oppress and exclude, with the aim to reduce inequitable power relations, the first step for researchers must be to move towards finding new ways to uncover the silences and in-between spaces in order to develop a more activist understanding of the role of researcher. In the case of this study, one of the major questions was to consider whose knowledge and values were informing students and the consequent meaning that students were making of what they were learning, with the aim to transform the common sense good of career education in schools.

The premise of the CAPP program was that if schools provided students with certain generic and specific skills, these students were more likely to find and retain careers and become successful members of an adult community (Heinz, 2001; Shanahan, 2000). This was a belief held by government education officials. However, one of the problems with the rapid development of career education in general is a lack of discussion about the content and pedagogy of such curricula. At the heart of this problem is the suggestion that unemployment and underemployment are rooted in individual deficits rather than in the economic structures of society (Hyslop-Margison & Welsh, 2003). However, examinations of schools as ideological constructions are not new (Apple, 1990), and the work of critical theorists urges researchers to consider that knowledge is integrally linked to power. The way this power influences social structures can greatly affect how ideology permeates society (Giroux & Robbins, 2006; Kincheloe & McLaren, 2000).

The following discussion will first situate critical theory and its relationship to research in schools and then attempt to unravel some of the dominant ideological assumptions held by these adolescents as they made sense of their career and educational aspirations as well as their conceptions of adulthood. In examining discourses of career and adulthood that were found in these schools and with the lens of critical theory, it becomes possible to listen to voices and ways of knowing that are traditionally silenced.

Critical Theory and Research on Conceptions of Career and Adulthood for Adolescents

Educational research has a rich history of looking at how schools, and the teachers and students who inhabit these spaces, can be studied in critical ways. Some theorists, like Patti Lather (1991) and Henry Giroux (1997), would even argue that research should challenge "relations of dominance" and that through research practice it becomes possible to look at education in ways that both challenge hegemonic structures and at the same time move towards new and emancipatory understandings of how schools can work. Critical approaches to educational research help to provide a framework with which to look at how power, hegemony, and reproduction shape society, and for this study that meant focusing on conceptions of career and adulthood for young people. Lather (2004) reminds us that we "need to put our critical theory to work in this moment of our now" (p. 22).

Understanding how to conduct research and from which perspective is perhaps one of the most difficult choices of any researcher. Critical theory is a helpful lens because it can provide a way to look at the relationship between institutions such as schools and the larger society. Giroux (1983) points out that school "functions as a system of representation that carries meanings and ideas that structure the unconscious of students" (p. 81). It is necessary to pay attention to the ways in which power intersects in these spaces. Furthermore, the ideas and culture of the dominant class permeate the formal and (informal) school curriculum (Apple, 1990; Giroux, 1983).

It is from this starting place that my research methods and analytical approach considers schools as ideological institutions and attempts to address and situate schools in the wider context of the political dimensions of curriculum. As Althusser (1971) reminds us, ideology is found in the material practices of daily life (Stanley, 1992). McLaren (1989) furthers this discussion by adding that ideology is "the production and representation of ideas, values, and beliefs and the manner in which they are expressed and lived out by both individuals and groups" (p. 184). From this perspective, ideology refers to the production of meaning in the way the world is viewed and can in turn provide a framework with which to begin to look at how power, hegemony and reproduction shape employment in our society (Gramsci, 1971).

The other key theoretical lens incorporated in this study was how discourse, both dominant and subordinate, is essential to researching career education in schools. In this instance, discourse is based on an understanding of how our social worlds are inscribed in and expressed through language (Bové, 1990). Creese, Leonard, Daniels, and Hay (2004) describe discourse as

> a means of talking and writing about and acting upon worlds, a means which both constructs and is constructed by a set of social practices within these worlds, and in doing so both reproduces and constructs afresh particular social-discursive practices, constrained or encouraged by macro movements in the overarching social formation. (p. 192)

Thus, discursive practices do not just produce a discourse but also embody meanings. If knowledge is socially constructed, culturally mediated and historically situated, then the dominant discourses assert what is thought of as knowledge and truth (Cherryholmes, 1988). Phillips and Jørgenson (2002) connect discourse to ideology and hegemony by pointing to how discursive practice can be seen as an aspect that contributes to reproduction of the order and discourse of which it is a part.

The language used by the participants of this study was how the embodied discourses became apparent. But as Kincheloe and McLaren (2000) point out, language is not a mirror of society. It is rather an unstable social practice which shifts depending on context. Language is infused with power and thus not neutral, nor is it able to objectively describe the real world. Language is "simply about the world, but serves to construct it" (Kincheloe & McLaren, 2000, p. 284). In looking at schools, the language of career and adulthood should be viewed within their social context with the aim to examine how discourses function ideologically.

Data Collection

The four schools[1] in the study were marked by a diverse population of students. Cedar Valley, located in a middle-class community, had an artistic focus. Elmwood, on the other hand, was perceived to be churning out university-bound students of relatively high socioeconomic status. There were also two B.C. Ministry of Education-designated inner-city schools: Pine Tree, a school that was often perceived as catering to students headed for the trades, and Oak Hill, a large school located in a lower socioeconomic area but that prided itself on producing university-bound students.

The two main data collection methods were participant observation and interviews. The observations spanned almost 12 months during the time when the majority of career education activities or CAPP classes were held. Interviews were carried out with 20 secondary students from Grades 10–12 who were all looking towards graduation, as well as with eight CAPP and guidance teachers. The questions for students explored understandings of jobs and careers and how CAPP students believed they were being prepared for entering the post-high school world, whereas the teacher interviews focused on their perceptions of the students and their approaches to teaching about careers. An important consideration was that if the schools in this study were supposed to be preparing students for entering the workforce, then in what ways did these discourses encourage particular kinds of labor market identities?

The research was designed as a modified case study that integrated ethnographic methods of participant observation and interviewing. Ethnographic methods help to describe the social constructedness of the world within a particular set of power relations and located in a broad social and political framework (Quantz, 1992). Simon and Dippo (1986) suggest that ethnographic methods can aid researchers in engaging in a process of knowledge construction and can implicate the researcher in moral questions about desirable forms of social relations and ways of living. At the same time, it is also important to recognize that there are multiple realities that cannot be unified in a single social understanding.

Because this research framework adopted an overtly critical approach, it called into question not only the data, but the researcher, the research design and the analysis of the data (Alvesson & Skölberg, 2000). In keeping with a critical approach, reflexivity was an important part of the process of data collection and analysis (MacBeth, 2001). This involved thinking and rethinking the research questions and considering how they changed throughout the process of conducting research. This process also required a continual examination of the beliefs held by the researcher, and the process of conducting research, and questioning preconceived notions of what it meant to have a career and to be an adult. Care was taken to consider how personal understandings and experiences affected the ways in which data was "heard" and interpreted.

Reflexivity can be used to legitimate and validate research practices and at the same time researchers still must focus on what Pillow calls "reflexivities of discomfort," and attend to "reflexivity that seeks to know while at the same time situates this knowing as tenuous" (Pillow, 2003, p. 188). Critical research, in essence, is characterized not merely by an acknowledgment that relations between researchers and informants are complicated and fuzzy but by an understanding that within the very spaces of ethnographic practice, the informants are multiple and never tangibly located. Further, critical ethnographers insist on viewing power, practice, and meaning as essentially indivisible contours of history and society (Fruehling & King, 2001).

The Teaching of Career and Adulthood

The concept of career, as taught in schools, is straightforward upon first glance; it is "going to work" or "being employed." Students must be prepared to become workers in our society. Thus, it is the role of schools to help students ready themselves for this work world. However, when we accept this instrumentalist understanding of schools as preparing workers, then we ignore the structural dimensions of schools. The result can be the belief that everyone ought to have a career throughout adulthood. The image of a generic worker becomes central when we think of career in these ways, as it presumes a generic employed adult worker is one who is white, middle-class, able bodied and heterosexual (Benjamin, 2006; Butterwick & Benjamin, 2006; Griffith, 1988). If we start to think about how we teach careers to this targeted worker, we must therefore wonder about the values and expectations afforded to adult roles. Accordingly, the ways in which schools teach career education has implications for understanding what it means to be a successful adult in society.

In the analysis, employment became a central concept in the understanding of how schools are preparing students for their adult lives. Career education programs are often based on the concept of work (Hoyt, 2001). Generally, adult members of society become contributing "citizens"[2] who add to the economic structure of society. The idea of a worker becomes a common-sense term that inspires images of an adult person who makes a living by performing a task for which they are paid. It is expected that adolescents need to start planning for the time in their lives when they will be required to choose the employment at which they will work for the rest of their lives and contribute back to society. In asking questions about whose values and interests are being served by career education curricula, it becomes necessary to look at these curricula in ways that examine theory and practice.

Two significant discourses emerged in this research, those of career and adulthood. Similar to the work of Nancy Lesko (2001), whose research describes a discourse of adolescence as being part of a dominant set of assumptions and ideas that affect and influence all adolescents' lives, my presupposition was that the discourses of career and adulthood had become part of a taken-for-granted set of assumptions in schools about the ways in which a "normal" life course is travelled. All adolescents are subject to the ideas and expectations of adulthood, and along with this expectation of adulthood is that of having a career—one of the main defining factors of adulthood. While there will be cultural differences in the ideas and expectations around both adulthood and career across Vancouver and in other Canadian cities, the majority of adolescents have some kind of idea that society has particular expectations around the meanings of both adulthood and career, even if the localities and particular moments may vary.

A Pedagogy of Sameness: Listening in the Liminal

Talking to young people often requires a process of listening to what they are saying as well as the silences—or what they are not saying. Several tensions become apparent throughout this study, one of the most significant being the ways in which discussion of social locations or understandings of gender or race were (and were not) spoken about. Silences in educational spaces, or what I am describing as liminal spaces, can often be rewarding as you read between the lines and interpret silences (Poland & Pederson, 1998). One of the major findings of this research was that while race, class and gender existed in the classrooms, they were talked about in very covert ways. The CAPP curriculum did not account for issues of gender or race, nor the difficulties faced by minority groups in a meritocratic society (Bascia & Young, 2001), nor did it address the ways in which conceptions of employment are thought of as individual deficits.

There was one teacher where these tensions became central to my understanding of the school. I focus particularly on Mr. Christie's classroom at Pinetree for this discussion, because I spent the most time in his classroom and thus had the greatest opportunity to view the ways in which issues of class, gender and race played out. Mr. Christie provided a salient example of the ways in which teaching practice reflected sameness on the surface, but on deeper examination revealed the raced, classed and gendered intricacies of a Vancouver classroom. Mr. Christie's language in the classroom and in the interview highlighted how he thought about his students as being differentiated. He believed that all of his students should and could get jobs. However, this meritocratic belief of equal footing was in stark contrast to the way he actually talked about his students and how he taught them in the classroom. For example, when discussing the ways in which students envisioned their futures, Mr. Christie said:

> That's just a guess. I think some kids see the university as being the be-all and the end-all, and I think it's partly the immigrant parent. And I think, it's a good worthy goal, but sometimes I think we're putting square pegs into round holes. Some of these kids would make excellent electricians, plumbers and they would have a great, happy life. Sometimes you're just not meant to be academic. Get a job and enjoy life.

In this comment the immigrant community was viewed as better suited to manual labour or trades. This contradicted his approach to teaching all students to do well and succeed at getting jobs. McCallum and Demie (2001) found that there was a correlation between ethnicity and social class and how well students perform at school, suggesting that those students from different ethnicities are at a disadvantage. The previous quotation also pointed to the ways in which employment hierarchies privileged some forms of employment over others. In this case the trades were represented as a lesser kind of choice more suited to minority students.

In my observations of Mr. Christie's classroom I noted how he focused specifically on the male students. Mr. Christie embodied a masculinist and racist ethic in many of the ways he spoke to and taught students. For example, during his CAPP "nugget" on appropriate clothing, he brought in suits to demonstrate how one might dress for specific occasions. He did not, however, bring any examples for the women in his class. This lesson was geared solely to the boys, with only brief discussion on what girls should wear. This suggested that, in Mr. Christie's view, a worker is male, although in a later lesson he did tell the girls to prepare for interviews by putting on makeup, wearing low heels, and doing their hair and nails. Girls were often the subject of sexist comments in this classroom, including comments about girls being pretty, or that that girls' roles were to help the boys figure things out. Thus one of the key spaces of liminality was that of gender. The "students" that Mr. Christie tended to talk about were male. This lack of distinction between students, while not surprising, was quite shocking in this particular classroom in which there was very overt privileging of male students and masculine adult identities

(Davies, 1997). Thus, while Mr. Christie claimed to be teaching the same skills to all of his students, in fact he was describing working identities that were decidedly masculine and presumably of value.

Another example of a key silence was the way in which cultural bias was evident in Mr. Christie's classroom. This was found during a lesson on how people select their jobs. Mr. Christie highlighted some of the main criteria, including interest, talent/skill/ability, benefits, social aspects, vacation and leisure time. Mr. Christie then asked the students what kinds of jobs they wanted. A young Asian female answered the question by pointing out that "my parents will tell me what I will do when I grow up," intimating that it was part of her culture. Mr. Christie laughed at this comment and then quickly moved on, not stopping to address the ways in which culture might affect how career choices are influenced by cultural background and gender. In another instance he felt it was important that his students knew it was possible to get scholarships to go to university, that "it wasn't just the Chinese students" who received awards. This example highlights some of the ways in which difference played out in the classroom.

While Mr. Christie did not take up the relationship between culture and gender in career choices, the students in his class seemed to have an understanding of the ways in which this social position would affect the kinds of choices they could make. This was another example of the importance of listening to liminal spaces for students in order to understand how they were making sense of career outside of the ideological representations given by the teacher's pedagogy.

Nava was a student in Mr. Christie's class, and he talked a great deal about how his cultural background had affected his choices in school.

> I like school because back in my country, Sri Lanka is where I came from, it is really hard to get an education and my dad, he actually got kicked out of school in Grade 10. Well for me I didn't want to go to school myself, but I talked to myself, it's my goal to go past my dad because that's what he wants out of me, right? Go past school…that's what my father wants, and that's why I take school seriously and that's why I want to go as far as I can.

Nava had a very keen understanding that his educational choices were related in significant ways to cultural and familial expectations. Familial expectations and how that might influence career planning were rarely part of the purposive conversation in this classroom.

Other students in Mr. Christie's class made specific references to the ways they felt their cultures were influencing their experiences of careers. Alexandra talked specifically about how she was expected to follow a prescribed route from high school to university based on parental cultural expectation. "I've decided that I'm going to go to UBC…I want to do a lot of traveling too. At first I wanted to take a year off, but I'm first generation Chinese Canadian, so my parents, we have a lot of cultural and language barriers." Alexandra was keenly aware of the ways in which culture affected the choices one could make at school. She spoke specifically about the automobile mechanics courses as being influenced by cultural groups. "I took auto mechanics last year and a whole bunch of them were there. And a lot of it's divided by ethnicity too. General ethnicity. Maybe more Spanish or Latino. And then we've got what we call the Hongers."[3] Alexandra's discussion of her experience of career education in school was informed by a central understanding of the ways in which race could divide what they were learning.

It is important to point out that while Mr. Christie's classroom style was masculinist, racist and sexist, the students very much embraced his pedagogy. Some of the students felt like Mr. Christie was talking to them in "real world" kinds of ways and that as a teacher he was in fact "cool." Perhaps what this highlights is that students' expectations of the real world include language that pushes the boundaries of racism and sexism (Lesko, 2001). While Mr. Christie was teaching students that they could succeed if they just worked hard, his expectations of students was influenced by his perceptions of their social class, culture and gender.

The tension found with respect to class, gender and race, focusing specifically on Mr. Christie's classroom, shows the ways in which silences emerged. Issues of race, class and gender were intertwined in the reproduction of career understandings for students. While these issues were never spoken about explicitly in the pedagogy, they were very present in the language and function of the classroom. This highlights the potential for career education to reproduce societal inequalities and how these practices ignore issues of gender and social class and assume equality of opportunity (Coombs, 1994). When social locations are ignored, career education continues to reproduce a discourse of career as generic and accessible to all students, blatantly ignoring the social stratification and systemic barriers that many students face as they enter the workforce.

The Liminal Spaces of Adulthood

The other important finding of this research centered around the discourses related to what it meant to be an adult. Career education curricula are often built with the aim to teach adolescents how to become adults and enter the workforce and to work in the best interest of the economy. What this means is that curricula can influence identity formation. One of the identities fostered by such curricula is that of a working adult. What it means to be an adult in our society is greatly influenced by institutions like schools and accordingly the school curriculum. What became clear after a critical examination of the data was that the adolescents in the study were using a more nuanced understanding of what it meant to be an adult and that there was an important discourse that highlighted the in-between or liminal spaces of not quite adolescent and not quite adult. Thus, important disruptions of common sense, and even acts of resistance, were apparent in the ways in which young people in the study started to conceive of what it would mean to become an adult. They were starting to conceive of adulthood as outside of traditional age/stage conceptions of the transition to adulthood. This shift to a relational understanding of adulthood was key, as we often silence or discount the ways in which young people conceive of their self and development.

One of the ways in which listening to the silences becomes important was in the spaces and the disjuncture between how teachers perceived students and how the young people saw themselves. One teacher expressed this concern when he said, "I think some of them already think they're adults." Wyn and White (1997) offer an explanation for the positioning of students by teachers as "underdeveloped" because of the values placed on certain individual characteristics that are often constructed in deficit ways. These assumptions about how students could not possibly be adults reflected a developmental orientation whereby youth was this unfixed place where identity was more malleable, and the transition to adulthood was marked by an identity that was stable and fixed (Wyn & White, 1997). Adults were supposed to know who they are, while youth were supposed to learn the aptitudes and behaviors that would allow them to enter the adult world. These phenomena of arresting adolescent development are highlighted very clearly by Lesko (2001) and White and Wyn (2008), who point to how youth are positioned in ways that construct them as deficient or unable to take on adult roles.

In contrast to the teacher, leaving childhood behind emerged as one of the significant ways that students described adulthood. For some students it was a difficult process, and one they might resist. For example, Nava from Pinetree said, "I know it's going to be harder. I can't slack off. I mean I can't do the things I did in high school." Nancy from Cedar Valley had a similar understanding of leaving childhood behind when she said, "almost the fun, the childhood stuff. Like that's all behind now." Karen from Elmwood thinks that adults have a particular kind of identity that was different from adolescents. She said of adults:

> They're more mature. I find they can be more strict, I guess. Because right now in high school we're a little just like carefree, whatever, like we can slack if we want to and just do whatever. And I find that adults have more of that drive to like, like it needs to get done kind of thing.

These students constructed adulthood as the time to get serious, where fun was on the backburner; letting go of all aspects of a childish identity. In order to be an adult, many of the students felt that they were going to have to leave childhood behind and start behaving as adults, and this shift was to be resisted. Georgia from Elmwood expressed this when he said, "I guess I'd rather be a kid my whole life than an adult, but that's not the way it goes, I have to be an adult." There seemed to be this ominous feeling for some students of having to leave the fun aspects of their personalities behind in order to enter this place that was adulthood.

One of the ways that students showed some resistance to traditional developmental constructions was in the persistence of the belief that individual context must be taken into consideration. Dim Sum[4] from Cedar Valley seemed to have grasped an understanding of adulthood that was contingent on the experiences of each person.

> Depends on every single person. It's for some people, it might be really, really early, they know like. But for some people they get to realize it later in their life and sometimes it takes like a dramatic incident to happen to them to realize that, so they can become aware of the things going wrong.

For Dim Sum, life events could change the stable course of development for people. This reflection was important because it suggested that no two highways were the same. Some of these students seemed to recognize that a stable concept of adulthood was starting to unravel in some ways. They were, in effect, turning adulthood on its head by suggesting that adults could be kids, kids could be adults, and even more importantly, each individual might have a different experience of adulthood.

For the students, maturity was part of the lexicon of terms that defined adulthood. While this concept had slightly different meanings for teachers and students, it seemed to mark a stage of adulthood that was resistant to the developmental model. As Kea from Pinetree pointed out, "I just think if you were to analyze an adult or a grown up I think things would come out like mature, responsible. I don't know, most of the good qualities that a lot of nice people have, you know what I mean, of generousness and so on." The notion of maturity reflected an understanding of adulthood as more fluid. Alex, also from Pinetree, highlighted this point. "I've been trying to tell myself not to associate age with maturity [laughs]. Because I've met a lot of immature older people [laughs], but an adult I think it entails a lot of responsibility, somebody who's really responsible." Alex points to the variability of the concept of maturity, allowing for those already supposed to be ascended to adulthood as not yet able to take on that role.

The concept of maturity can be problematic when applied in decontextualized ways. Maturity must be troubled as a universal concept for both boys and girls. As Lesko (1996) points out, maturity is often thought of differently for girls; girls are believed to mature at a younger age than boys. Maturity can also be a code for sexuality or promiscuity that constructs girls in negative ways. Maturity is also used to refer to girls who are thought to be more responsible, or the "good girl." In my study, one teacher described maturity as an aspect of adulthood that might be different for girls. "And yeah, the attitude, well some of the girls are adult in Grade 10, but the boys are still pretty juvenile." In this example, gender intersects with some of the behavioural aspects of development that were applied to students.

Blatterer (2010) argues that recent changes in the timing and nature of how a person traverses a life course requires an unprecedented redefinition of adulthood. While some scholars such as Arnett (2000) conceptualize emerging adulthood as a distinct developmental stage spanning ages 18–25, characterized by the exploration of prospective adult roles in areas such as work, love and worldviews, a more useful notion to capture the margins of adolescence and adulthood is Raby's concept of *liminal adulthood*. Raby (2010) explains that "modern understandings of growing up have conceptualized childhood through progressive movement towards the endpoint of adulthood, with youth as a liminal, in-between phase before such adult stability" (p. 69). Raby, along with Blatterer (2007), argues that with neoliberal shifts in the global economy there is an unprecedented marketing of youthfulness and, consequently, adulthood is now also coming to be defined by liminality. A strength of this approach is that it takes into account how the transition to adulthood is socially constructed and historically and culturally specific. Thus, the ages, stages and actions that young people use to describe adulthood can be understood to be mired in their social positions within society (Weedon, 1997; Wyn & White, 1997).

Conclusion

Career education classrooms offer a unique opportunity with which to look at how adolescents learn to become workers and adults in our society. Since most adults must have employment to live in modern society, it follows that schools should train adolescents for the role of worker and consequently prepare them for adulthood—or at least that is the assumption. This chapter argues that career education has become a taken-for-granted part of the school curriculum, and a critical examination of the discourses of career and adulthood can reveal voices and ways of knowing that are traditionally silenced. There were two important silences found in the data outlined here. While young people were talking about race, class and gender as it related to their career choices, there was no provision in the curriculum and teaching style with which to address their experiences. The other important silence was the ways in which young people resisted how adulthood was being constructed for them, and how they reflected a more relational (liminal) understanding of both adolescence and adulthood, outside curricular and pedagogical constructions of allowable identities.

Education is not an equal playing field, and through a critical analysis it is possible to disrupt some of the "common sense" assumptions of equality. In my research a critical approach helps me to question the ways in which discourses of career and adulthood are embedded in the everyday practices of the classroom and the career education curricula, or what Apple (2004) would call "fundamental interruption of common sense" (p. 14). Hyslop-Margison (2000) argues for the need to reveal the ideological connections between the dominant social forces of a curriculum like CAPP by reflecting on the ethical, ontological and social viewpoints apparent in the text. In schools, there is an important correspondence between the attitudes and dispositions that are taught in career education classrooms that are presumed to be useful for adult activities such as work (Bowles & Gintis, 1976).

Fraser and Gordon (1997) speak about "unspoken assumptions and connotations…[that] can powerfully influence the discourses they permeate—in part by constituting a body or doxa, or taken-for-granted common sense belief that escapes critical scrutiny" (p. 122). Career education appears to have entered into this common-sense realm. It is crucial to ask particular kinds of questions of career education curricula and to disrupt the *normalcy* of teaching students how to be future workers and adults. Dismantling the common sense *good* of career education is becoming ever more important, as career education curricula are represented as a "last stop" or in some cases the "last resort" for preparing students to enter the adult world (Kincheloe, 1995). This is not to say that all career education curricula are *bad* or even unnecessary; rather my intent is to question whose interests are served and how career education and its representations of adulthood can work in the best interests of today's students and tomorrow's adults.

CAPP as it was presented in Vancouver schools taught career and adulthood as though they were natural stages of adult development. While many of the students were buying into this developmental model, there were fissures in the discourse. The students in my study were starting to think about the process of adulthood in more relational ways. This work needs to be continued. Career education programs like CAPP can only be useful if they are flexible enough to keep up with changing perceptions of adulthood and the entrances and exits that are a necessary part of the life course. Career education curricula need to be responsive to changing ways in which youth are constructed by themselves and by society (Wyn & White, 2000). Teachers must start to challenge the perception of abnormality for any student who does not fit ages and stages or culturally insular and masculinized conceptions of adulthood. We need a more nuanced understanding of adulthood in career education classrooms.

Notes

1. The pseudonyms for these four schools are Cedar Valley, Elmwood, Pine Tree, and Oak Hill.
2. In this definition the concept of citizenship includes the idea of a contributing member of society (Scott & Lawson, 2002).
3. Hongers refers to new immigrants from Hong Kong, although it is sometimes used as derogatory comment.
4. Note that students chose their own pseudonyms.

References

Althusser, L. (1971). Ideology and the ideological state apparatuses (B. Brewster, Trans.). In L. Althusser (Ed.), *Lenin and philosophy, and other essays*. New York, NY: Monthly Review Press.

Alvesson, M., & Sköldberg, K. (2000). *Reflexive methodology: New vistas for qualitative research*. Thousand Oaks, CA: Sage.

Apple, M. (1990). *Ideology and curriculum* (2nd ed.). New York, NY: Routledge.

Apple, M. (2004). Creating difference: Neo-liberalism, neo-conservatism and the politics of educational reform. *Educational Policy, 18,* 12–44.

Arnett, J. J. (2000). Emerging adulthood: A theory of development from the late teens through the twenties. *American Psychologist, 55,* 469–480.

Aronson, P. (2008). The markers and meanings of growing up: Contemporary young women's transitions from adolescence to adulthood. *Gender and Society, 22*(1), 56–82.

Bascia, N., & Young, B. (2001). Women's careers beyond the classroom: Changing roles in a changing world. *Curriculum Inquiry, 31*(3), 271–302.

Benjamin, A. (2006). *Grown-ups have careers: Discourses of career and adulthood in four urban Vancouver high schools* (Unpublished doctoral thesis). The University of British Columbia, Vancouver, Canada.

Blatterer, H. (2007). *Coming of age in times of uncertainty*. New York, NY: Berghahn Books.

Blatterer, H. (2010). Contemporary adulthood and the devolving life course. In H. Blatterer & J. Glahn (Eds.), *Times of our lives: Making sense of growing up & growing old*. Oxford, England: Inter-Disciplinary Press.

Bortolussi, V. (2006). Seamlessly connecting high school to college to career. *Techniques: Connecting Education and Careers, 81*(3), 34–36.

Bové, P. (1990). Discourse. In F. Lentricchia & T. McLaughlin (Eds.), *Critical terms for literary study* (pp. 50–65). Chicago, IL: University of Chicago Press.

Bowles, S., & Gintis, H. (1976). *Schooling in capitalist America: Educational reform and the contradictions of economic life*. New York, NY: Basic Books.

Butterwick, S., & Benjamin, A. (2006). The road to employability through personal development: A critical analysis of the silences and ambiguities of the British Columbia (Canada) life skills curriculum. *International Journal of Lifelong Education, 25*(1), 75–86.

Cherryholmes, C. (1988). *Power and criticism: Poststructural investigations in education*. New York, NY: Teachers College Press.

Coombs, J. R. (1994). Equal access to education: The ideal and the issues. *Journal of Curriculum Studies, 26*(3), 281–295.

Creese, A., Leonard, D., Daniels, H., & Hay, V. (2004). Pedagogic discourses, learning and gender identification. *Language and Education, 18*(3), 191–206.

Davies, B. (1997). Constructing and deconstructing masculinities through critical literacy. *Gender & Education, 9,* 9–30.

Fraser, N., & Gordon, L. (1997). A genealogy of "dependency": Tracing a keyword of the U.S. welfare state. In N. Fraser (Ed.), *Justice interruptus: Critical reflections on the "postsocialist" condition* (pp. 121–149). New York, NY: Routledge.

Fruehling, C., & King, C. R. (2001). Unsettling engagements: On the ends of rapport in critical ethnography. *Qualitative Inquiry, 7*(4), 403–417.

Gaskell, J. (1992). School, work and gender. In J. Gaskell (Ed.), *Gender matters from school to work* (pp. 16–35). Milton Keynes, England: Open University Press.

Giroux, H. A. (1983). *Theory and resistance in education: A pedagogy for the opposition*. South Hadley, MA: Bergin & Garvey.

Giroux, H. A. (1997). *Pedagogy and the politics of hope: Theory, culture, and schooling; A critical reader*. Boulder, CO: Westview Press.

Giroux, H. A., & Robbins, C. G. (2006). *The Giroux reader*. Boulder, CO: Paradigm.

Gramsci, A. (1971). *Selections from the prison notebooks of Antonio Gramsci* (Q. Hoard & G. Smith, Trans.). New York, NY: International Publishers.

Griffith, A. (1988). Skilling for life/living for skill: The social construction of life skills in Ontario schools. *Journal of Educational Thought, 22*(2A), 198–208.

Heinz, W. R. (2001). Work and the life course: A cosmopolitan local perspective. In V. W. Marshall, W. R. Heinz, H. Kruger, & V. Anil (Eds.), *Restructuring work and the life course* (pp. 3–22). Toronto, ON, Canada: University of Toronto Press.

Hoyt, K. (2001). Career education and education reform: Time for a rebirth. *Phi Delta Kappan, 83*(4), 327–331.

Hyslop-Margison, E. (2000). The employability skills discourse: A conceptual analysis of the career and personal planning curriculum. *Journal of Educational Thought, 34*(1), 59–72.

Hyslop-Margison, E., & Welsh, B. (2003). Career education and labour market conditions: The skills gap myth. *Journal of Educational Thought, 37*(1), 5–21.

Kincheloe, J. (1995). *Toil and trouble: Good work, smart workers, and the integration of academic and vocational education*. New York, NY: Peter Lang.

Kincheloe, J., & McLaren, P. (2000). Rethinking critical theory and qualitative research. In N. Denzin & Y. Lincoln (Eds.), *Handbook of qualitative research* (2nd ed., pp. 279–313). Thousand Oaks, CA: Sage.

Lather, P. (1991). *Getting smart: Feminist research and pedagogy with/in the postmodern*. New York, NY: Routledge.

Lather, P. (2004). This is your father's paradigm: Government intrusion and the case of qualitative research in education. *Qualitative Inquiry, 10*(1), 15–34.

Lesko, N. (1996). Past, present, and future conceptions of adolescence. *Educational Theory, 46*(4), 453–473.

Lesko, N. (2001). *Act your age!: A cultural construction of adolescence*. New York, NY: Routledge Falmer.

MacBeth, D. (2001). On "reflexivity" in qualitative research: Two readings, and a third. *Qualitative Inquiry, 7*(1), 35–69.

McCallum, I., & Demie, F. (2001). Soial class, ethnicity and educational performance. *Educational Research, 43*(2), 147–159.

McLaren, P. (1989). *Life in schools: An introduction to critical pedagogy in the foundations of education* (2nd ed.). New York, NY: Longman.

Phillips, L., & Jørgenson, M. (2002). *Discourse analysis as theory and method*. London, England: Sage.

Pillow, W. S. (2003). Confessions, catharsis or cure? Rethinking the uses of reflexivity as methodological power in qualitative research. *Qualitative Studies in Education, 16*(2), 175–196.

Poland, B., & Pederson, A. (1998). Reading between the lines: Interpreting silences in qualitative research. *Qualitative Inquiry, 4*(2), 293–312.

Quantz, R. A. (1992). On critical ethnography (with some postmodern considerations). In M. D. LeCompte, W. L. Millroy, & J. Preissle (Eds.), *The handbook of qualitative research in education* (pp. 447–506). San Diego, CA: Academic Press.

Raby, R. (2010). Theorising liminal adulthood and its consequences for childhood, youth and adulthood. In H. Blatterer & J. Glahn (Eds.), *Times of our lives: Making sense of growing up & growing old*. Oxford, United Kingdom: Inter-Disciplinary Press.

Scott, D., & Lawson, H. (2002). *Citizenship education and the curriculum*. Westport, CT: Ablex.

Shanahan, M. J. (2000). Pathways to adulthood in changing societies: Variability and mechanisms in life course perspective. *Annual Review of Sociology, 26,* 667–692.

Simon, R., & Dippo, D. (1986). On critical ethnographic work. *Anthropology & Education Quarterly, 17,* 195–202.

Stanley, W. (1992). *Curriculum for utopia: Social reconstructionism and critical pedagogy in the postmodern era*. Albany: State University of New York Press.

Walshaw, M. (2006). Girls' workplace destinations in a changed social landscape: Girls and their mothers talk. *British Journal of Sociology of Education, 27*(5), 555–567.

Weedon, C. (1997). *Feminist practice and poststructuralist theory*. New York, NY: Blackwell.

White, R. D., & Wyn, J. (2008). *Youth and society: Exploring the social dynamics of youth experience* (2nd ed.). South Melbourne, VIC: Oxford University Press.

Wyn, J., & White, R. (1997). *Rethinking youth*. London, England: Sage.

Wyn, J., & White, R. (2000). Negotiating social change: The paradox of youth. *Youth & Society, 32*(2), 168–187.

CHAPTER TWENTY-SEVEN

Action Research for Critical Classroom and Community Change

Greg S. Goodman, Walter Ullrich, and Pedro Nava

Knowledge emerges through invention and re-invention, through the restless, impatient, continuing, hopeful inquiry [we] pursue in the world, with the world, and with each other.
—Paulo Freire, *Pedagogy of the Oppressed*, 1970

Living and teaching in the heart of agrarian California's culturally, ethnically, and linguistically diverse and majority poor Central Valley, we take seriously the teaching of Brazilian educator and philosopher Paulo Freire. Freire—who "theorized that education is properly a process of learning to 'read' the world, and from his perspective, education and social activism are one and the same thing" (Hinchey, 2008, p. 15)— inspired our pedagogy to go beyond the simple process of helping practicing teachers adapt to a school's status quo. Rather, we furnish teachers with the tools for a transformative praxis that resists the social press for conforming to the forces of cultural reproduction in a school's traditional process. Educating practicing teachers involves building upon, extending, and reconstructing their schooling experiences—particularly their past experiences as students and today as they study the practice and art of critical pedagogy.

Equity-oriented teacher educators must encourage individuals to design schooling to radiate a truly democratic way of life, to be consistent with the ideals of equity and justice, and to be continually informed by an action research that is, as John Dewey (Dewey, 1916, 1929, 1938) noted nearly a century ago, "educative"[1] (e.g., Cochran-Smith & Lytle, 2009; Kincheloe, 2010; Zeichner, 2009). This objective can be accomplished by addressing issues of cultural responsiveness between teachers and students; in doing so, the academic engagement, achievement, and productive social action increases in students and teachers alike. The action research that we employ is both critical and predominantly qualitative.

As equity-oriented teacher educators committed to a multicultural and social justice education, we have always been humbled by the "triple-consciousness" needed in this type of work. How do we simultaneously (1) model multicultural, social justice education (MSJE), (2) transform the perspectives of practicing teachers who have succeeded with many of their students in conventional school conditions, and (3) remain steadfast in our resolve that an emancipatory orientation to teaching and learning is developmentally appropriate and egalitarian (Ullrich, 2001)? One answer is that we need to continuously exemplify these beliefs through an action research-based pedagogy and praxis based upon the example of Paulo Freire. Freire's "conscientization" is the enduring example of awakening through the thoughtful and critical examination of one's experience while fighting for equitable outcomes for all students (May & Sleeter, 2010; Sleeter & Grant, 2009; Ullrich, 1992; Ullrich & Roessler, 1997). We hold such aims sacred and evident. However, support for MSJE is far from ubiquitous, and these purposeful and liberatory goals are fraught with obstacles.

As a result of the institutionalization of high-stakes testing as well as the stultifying effects of a standardized, standards-based education the past decade, our experiences in equity-oriented teacher education yield the following generalizations. First, MSJE informed by educative action research by practicing teachers is rare, even though they can be rigorously defended on academic, personal, and socially responsive developmental principles (Duncan-Andrade & Morrell, 2008; Dewey, 1904, 1916, 1938; Kliebard, 1995). Second, while MSJE curriculum clearly incorporates pupils' interests and capacities while simultaneously helping them to work against inequities and injustices that detract from so many young lives inside and outside of school, it is difficult even for those receptive to equity-oriented perspectives to defend such work on academic and developmental grounds. Third, since the passage of NCLB and the current Race to the Top legislation and the associated pressures of rigid, standards-based accountability systems in education at all levels, most of our graduate students show greater resistance towards becoming students of emancipatory teaching, let alone becoming a "transformative intellectual" (Aronowitz, 2000). In short, most of our beginning teachers are reluctant to simultaneously confront and redesign existing school conditions to be more consistent with democracy, equity, and justice—particularly during this era of high-stakes accountability for pupils and their teachers. To counter the hegemonic forces of mainstream educational politics, we needed to implement a strong action research process to support the structural changes a MSJE required.

Our purpose in this chapter is to present an integrated picture of critical qualitative research conducted by graduate students representing both an online, post-credential, Masters of Arts in Teaching (MAT) program and a doctoral student's investigations anchored in recent ethnographic work within California's Central Valley. Through these examples of action research, we hope to provide in-depth understandings upon which to base more insightful, equity-oriented teacher education. During the last decade, many universities (and school districts) have established MSJE teacher education (and professional development) programs to respond to the many challenges facing public education, particularly those associated with the demographic imperative (Zeichner, 2009) and culturally responsive teaching (Gay, 2010) outlined above. As these programs continue to gain momentum, critical questions become salient. On the one hand, there are few analyses of the classroom dynamics that emerge when diversity variables (e.g. race/ethnicity, gender, class, language, disability) are focal points in these programs or of the relationship of these dynamics to practicing teachers' understanding of equity-oriented teaching and learning. On the other, few studies actually examine what happens in public school classrooms as practicing teachers introduce MSJE informed by action research methods. Like others (e.g., Cochran-Smith & Lytle, 2009; Noffke & Somekh, 2009; Zeichner, 2009), we can provide evidence that when individuals—practicing teachers and their pupils—are provided opportunities to critically analyze and reflect on issues of diversity in school settings, their understanding of the importance of equity is enhanced, and concern for school as a site for social justice is encouraged.

Critical Qualitative Studies as Fuel for the Fight

Let us confess that our schools have never built a new social order, but have always in all times and in all lands been the instruments through which social forces were perpetuated. If our new curriculum revision is to do better, it must undertake an acceptance of the profound social and economic changes which are now taking place in the world. (Bond, 1935, p. 68)

This quotation illustrates a tradition seemingly disconnected from many common understandings of MSJE and educative action research. Yet for us and others (Noffke & Somekh, 2009), it raises issues that are at the core of equity-oriented teacher education and educative action research. First, it demands recognition of the essentially "conserving" function of schooling and highlights the need for educational responses to profound structural changes in society. Second, it comes out of a long-standing tradition of academic literature refuting the dominant narrative of educational history that claims education as a major vehicle for social advancement for subjugated peoples. Finally, it captures major questions that have haunted educators for years, namely to what extent and in what ways action research in educational work can play a role in building a "new social order" (Counts, 1932/78)—one in which economic and social justice are central aims (Noffke & Somekh, 2009).

As examples of critical qualitative research, we have selected five studies conducted within the classrooms of our MAT students and an ethnography from a representative Central Valley community. These examples reflect the real issues of oppressed, farm-working, and predominantly immigrant Spanish-speaking communities. All of these studies touch upon core issues of literacy and emancipatory education. In the first study, English teacher Raymundo Sanchez (all research-related place and person names are protected) exemplifies the calling of John Dewey to be "reflective." As Mr. Sanchez tests his own curriculum in the real world of practice, he is able to bring a dynamic, action research process into the unique world of his classroom. Mr. Sanchez describes his process as follows:

I have been teaching for four years in a low-income school situated in a small community located in central California. I teach an English Language Development (ELD) course. All of the students enrolled in my ELD course are considered Hispanic or Latino of Mexican descent. The majority of my ELD students have been living in the United States for no more than two years. Nearly 85% of the students receive reduced or free lunch. The majority of the students that attend the school are considered Hispanic or Latino. The school site has a total of 172 ELLs, and nearly 98% of the ELLs' primary language is Spanish.

In retrospect, identifying and implementing successful instructions for ELLs (English Language Learners) in the public education system challenged my pedagogical considerations. Prior to conducting my research, I superficially believed that my experiences of schooling as a bilingual were sufficient to fully understanding the context of my ELLs' English development. Furthermore, I ostensibly assumed that the difficulties my students encounter academically and socially were parallel to my lived experiences as a Filipino American as I struggled to acquire both my native and secondary languages. Based on my experiences during my primary and secondary schooling, I held on to the belief that acquiring and mastering basic skills was the prime objective to buffer the difficulties of reading, writing, and speaking in English.

As a novice ELD educator, I often questioned the efficiency of my teaching strategies when assisting ELLs to acquire a second language. Did I integrate a sufficient amount of textual materials that are conducive and appropriate to the process of my students' language acquisition? Did my students benefit from collaborative learning activities? Were the content and rigor of the homework assignments permissible to allow them to deem their learning significant? These lingering questions became my pedagogical concerns.

I vividly remember several of my ELLs' adamant questions after I assigned a lesson that required them to construct simple sentences based on the assigned weekly vocabulary words. At the time, the students were exercising their skills to incorporate basal vocabulary words into simple sentences. In spite of their progressive ability to convey the required skills to form simple sentences and despite their ability to identify rudimentary nouns, adjectives, and verbs in given sentences, my students' apprehensive reaction subsequent to assigning vocabulary homework furthered my concern. The students simply demanded reasons for their learning. In response, I justified their assignment from a context-centered point of view. I explained that the assignment was part of the process of learning how to hone their command of the English grammar. I also explained to them the amount of basic skills they needed to acquire in preparation for state-mandated exams such as the California High School Exit Exam (CAHSEE). In response, my students' unsatisfactory facial expressions rendered my defeated explanation.

My instructional practices ostensibly overlooked the underlying implications of their uncompromising demand for the significance of their learning. My concerns overlooked my students' apprehension. I should have recognized the possible questions implicated as a result of my students' request for the underlying objectives of the curriculum that goes beyond mastering basic skills. I should have also considered the following questions. How could my curriculum assist students to acknowledge the underlying importance of reading, writing, and speaking in English relative to their lived experiences? How will their second language assist them in other classes? More importantly, do my lessons provide ample opportunities for ELLs to truly deem applicable to their social and cultural contexts within and outside of the school community?

The purpose of conducting this qualitative research was to enhance my ELLs' English acquisition by utilizing their social and cultural identities and experiences. The central question (and sub-questions) for this phenomenological study are the following: In what specific and measurable ways can instruction that utilizes multimodal mediums (e.g., students utilize photography, artwork, and comic strips to convey understanding) for high school ELLs that have CELDT level 1 in an ELD class promote English vocabulary by connecting their social and cultural identities? In particular, what aspects of integrating comic strips into the instruction of figurative language (e.g., metaphor, simile, personification, and symbolism) do ELLs consider helpful or troublesome based on questionnaires and one-on-one interviews? How do ELLs view themselves adapting to life in the United States based on the analysis of their poem, artwork, and photography subsequent to lessons on simile, metaphor, personification, and symbolism.

This research helped me to determine specific and measurable ways that the use of multimodal mediums for ELLs considered to have a CELT level 1 could promote English vocabulary. The products of my students' multimodal poems demonstrated to me that multiple modes of conveying information to elicit students' understanding are an important integration to my instruction. Integrating the child-centered approach to teaching balanced the curriculum's overpowering focus on mastering basic reading, writing, and speaking skills. As a result of this research, I have learned some of my students' social outlook pertaining to the difficulties of field workers picking oranges. I have learned that some of my students do reflect on their inspiration and difficulties to bridge their cultural and social perspectives to that of their new homeland. I have learned some of my students' experiences of love expressed in their poetry. I have learned the pride my students have for their family member's occupation. Most importantly, I have learned that a context-centered approach to teaching alone is not sufficient to the experience and development of ELLs' secondary acquisition.

What Mr. Sanchez has described is the quintessence of Dewey's call for reflective practitioners (1933). Sanchez became motivated to change his standard, structured English instructional approach when he used the formative assessment of looking into his students' eyes and observed their blank stares. "The students simply demanded reasons for their learning." Being sensitive to the students, following Dewey, and being a thoughtful educator, Mr. Sanchez was able to conceive of a dynamic, culturally complex set of lessons. The example demonstrates the dual nature of action research: both the students and the teachers share in the process of learning.

*****

Eliza Cardoza has been teaching English language learners within California's Central Valley for many years. As a critical qualitative researcher, Ms. Cardoza exemplifies the work of the research bricoleur (Kincheloe, 2010). According to Kincheloe, the research bricoleur seeks a new "vantage point" from which to challenge the dominant discourse.

> The researchers are no longer merely obtaining information, but are entering a space of transformation where previously excluded perspectives (in this case the student's point of view) operate to change consciousness of both self and the world. Thus multicultural research in bricolage changes not only what one knows but also who one actually is. (Kincheloe, 2010, p. 42)

In Ms. Cardoza's work, the challenge is to ignite within her students a passion for learning despite the school's support of standards-based assessments and credit banking (Freire, 1970). As a feminist, Ms. Cardoza is also keenly aware of the essential role of feelings in the education of her students. "Feminist understandings are important to both men and women who are researchers, as they open doors to previously excluded knowledges" (Kincheloe, 2010, p. 31). Ms. Cardoza's research bricolage reflects the pedagogy of love (Freire, 1970).

As a social justice educator, I view my role to be a facilitator for my students. I want to validate that the feelings they may have from situations of discrimination or abuse *are* actually injustices in society, not just isolated feelings they're experiencing. I work in an agricultural town. This community's assets include a no-nonsense attitude where people take a direct approach about speaking their thoughts. The town rallies around community events and winning high school teams. Unfortunately, crime and gangs do play a part in the neighborhoods where most of my students reside. The town is quick to criticize, but this is mainly in the interests of wanting the best for their children and their futures.

Teachers share the feeling that their students all have great potential, and we are frustrated when we see students who do not see this same promise in themselves. Considering *potential*, I believe the ESL students I teach can be successful for several reasons. My students are immigrants, many of whom are non-citizens at this point. They came to the U.S. along with their parents' dreams. Usually children immigrate without having had a choice in the matter, and they hold either resentment or fear of new cultural experiences. Once they are given opportunities where they *can* be in control of something that affects their lives—their education—they often rise to the challenge. Challenges bring strength of character, and I always try to present challenges in a positive light. Many of my students also have to show determination—determination to find time to study while being responsible for younger siblings or determination to do well at school while working to add to their family's income. In this current school year, ninety-seven percent of my students are Hispanic, one is Punjabi, and another is Egyptian.

Through my studies of social justice and my experiences as an educator, my attention was especially drawn to the issue of high-stakes testing in my subject matter of English as a second language. Not only have I observed effects of these assessments on my students, but I also wondered about the effects of high-stakes testing on teachers. My researchable question is in what specific and measurable ways does high-stakes testing affect the teachers' role in secondary ESL classrooms? I conducted a phenomological research study. Initially, I read over twenty professional journal articles regarding prior studies on high-stakes testing ramifications on minority populations, teacher workload and burnout factors, high schools that have produced successful high-stakes test results with ESL students, and comparisons of types of achievement tests. Secondary ESL teachers and teachers working mainly with English language learners—not to be confused as the same—were then sent an on-line survey. The survey included open-ended questions, ranking questions, and multiple-choice responses. Topics which the participants considered were the pressure felt for accountability of high-stakes test results, teaching style, curricular issues, changes perceived over time, and awareness of different aspects of high-stakes testing, After receiving the completed survey responses, I first organized the data into two categories, teachers who had had significant amount of ESL experience and teachers who had little ESL experience, but who taught a high percentage of English language learners. Next, I analyzed the participants' responses for those indicating a negative or a positive effect of the high-stakes testing climate. Finally, I reviewed all my research findings to make sure ESL teachers' roles were specifically addressed, along with a discussion of how secondary ESL teachers face greater injustices. The compiled results indicated several benefits that have developed *due to* the challenges and demands of getting improved scores on high-stakes tests, although there are equal or greater negative ramifications on both ESL students' and teachers' motivational levels, as well as a blow to the level of respect given to the professionalism of teachers by administrators and politicians.

Throughout my research study, I have learned that injustice is apparent in situations where any of us are involved; it is not an inequity of "those other people." Although injustice is systemic and institutionalized, I found evidence of how groups of people—parents and educators in my study – have proactively taken the incentive to create more just alternatives for ESL education. These alternative schools, programs, and means of assessment also meet the political demands for improved student test results even more successfully than the methods for "improvement" strongly recommended for use in the majority of schools, districts, and states. This evidence of successful collaboration of stakeholders in students' education tells me not to lose my sense of optimism for my ESL students. I need to stay in the teaching profession because my students need an advocate who recognizes their daily growth and knows that they are valuable individuals for more reasons than merely the scores they produce on standardized tests.

Ms. Cardoza faces some daunting obstacles in her resistance to the school administration's almost exclusive attention to the state-mandated assessments. But her courage to resist is reinforced by the data she collects from her students. As Cardoza knows, "Once they (my students) are given opportunities where they *can* be in control of something that affects their lives—their education—they often rise to the challenge." Kincheloe (2010) would concur: "Indeed, bricoleurs refuse to be confined to one cultural way of seeing and making meaning" (p. 34). This is the true critical qualitative research methodology at work supporting a resistance to testing's domination of the instructional process.

*****

Juan Gomez is a third-grade teacher who has a clear passion for critical qualitative research. His extensive travel and foreign teaching experiences have given him a global vision of possibility. This is a CQR ready for action. As John Willinsky (2001) observed, "In the study of education, the action in action research is located in and around the classroom where teachers teach students, or better yet they educate each other" (p. 329). Mr. Gomez clearly loves this process of reciprocal learning.

I am a teacher who has struggled to find his way since I first began six years ago in Quito, Ecuador. While employment in Ecuador did not prepare me for the rigorous commitment of teaching and being obligated to standards and assessments, it did teach me about being the outsider in a classroom. This position required a certain openness to learn about the students' culture, families, and way of life, while learning the most successful ways for them to grasp the English language. This experience translated quite well to my current situation as I ensure that my students are not left to feel excluded. My students feel comfortable in *our* classroom. They know that I respect them and will keep them safe while doing my best to teach them the California third-grade standards.

As a social justice educator, it is my responsibility to familiarize my students with the world around them. Though my classroom lacks diversity, by introducing different literature and expanding on lessons with various cultures, my students can learn about the various cultures in our world. Being in such a small community also allows the students to recognize that coexistence requires compassion for others. Students need to understand as they grow up and leave their community that they will experience events and people that do not think or act like them. They will need to adapt and remember what they have been taught in regards to acceptance and caring for others.

The community I teach has many assets to include close-knit families, ambition for their young students and up-to-date technology at the student's disposal; most important is the hard work demonstrated daily. Most of our parents and adults go to work before the sun rises and come home after the sun goes down, sacrificing comfort for the needs of their children. In appreciation, these students want to make their families proud, striving to do their best. In each of the four years I have been a part of this working community, the school pride increases. This year we had the most family involvement on campus and in our school functions. The community is working hard to establish connections with the school for student success.

The students that I teach will be successful! They have a great attitude towards education requiring encouragement and nurturing. Many of the students in my class had a taste of success in second grade and they liked it, they now crave it, striving to achieve better scores with each lesson or assignment with success in mind. Students will also succeed because of my commitment to them. I want the best for them and I try to provide them with lifelong lessons that challenge, encourage, and promote personal growth. My students will succeed because I will guide them toward successful behaviors. I will teach them that mistakes and stumbles are acceptable if we will learn from those mistakes. At the end of our school year we'll be able to reflect on the mistakes that we learned from.

This study helped to identify the best program for students to comprehend English while allowing them to feel comfortable in the classroom. The programs being studied were an immersion program and mainstream English Program using SDAIE strategies. The identified issues included the studies of

English Learners' successes and weaknesses in order to best help the students. Since my school is comprised of mostly English language learners, I studied different ideas on how to best support my English language learners and how to help them adjust better to a classroom with proficient English language learning. We looked at the *Mainstream English Program Using SDAIE* strategies as it compares to *Structured English Immersion Program.*

In my research, I was responsible for obtaining data, interviewing participants, discerning data on teacher's observations from videos taken, and conducting the observations in my classroom. The data was collected from student class work, homework, teacher's observations, my observations and assessments. By collecting these data, I was able to gain a more accurate view of what the students' needs were and where they could be the most successful. The videotaped lessons allowed me to observe the various teaching strategies of my colleagues as well as my own use of the strategies, the similarities and differences, providing insight regarding whether or not the data correlated with the lessons that were taught. Observing the teachers that use an English program that implements SDAIE strategies (which is the majority of my school) and comparing the data to the teachers that implement an immersion program provided me the data validity needed to give this project the integrity needed. The use of teacher and student surveys and interviews provided me with the evidence that was used to determine how teachers felt in the environment and how they felt students responded, but more importantly I will have an indication of how students think, what is comfortable, and what provides a sense of accomplishment or frustration in the two different techniques of teaching.

The results indicate a greater improvement for the students in an English immersion program. The students stated that they felt more comfortable learning English with students with similar challenges. They felt that they could take more risks and didn't have to worry about mistakes being made. The data shows the success of immersion programs at our site and at other similar sites. Based on this success, I have learned that students want to learn English, but more importantly, they are more concerned about the non-judgmental atmosphere that the other students and teacher can provide. The students want to feel like they won't be punished or mocked for incorrect answers. Going forward in my career, this project has showed me that the students crave acknowledgment and freedom to explore their thoughts and ideas; I have the responsibility to provide this atmosphere.

By providing a natural approach and maintaining a "low anxiety situation" (Krashen, 2003), Mr. Gomez has synthesized the social justice multicultural education notions of valuing the experiences of the second language learner. Using action research, Gomez gleans an assessment yielding tremendous accountability in support of his thesis, that the non-judgmental atmosphere of English immersion is an effective tool for second language learning.

*****

Ms. Sharon Johnson is a second grade teacher, teaching in one of the most violent and economically challenged communities in California's East Bay. Because of the enormity of the community challenges, Ms. Johnson has chosen a participatory action research design to create a collaborative process among her classroom constituency (Hendricks, 2009). Her research included the use of Learning Centers based upon Gardner's multiple intelligences theory. This is an excellent example of participatory action research because it follows Hendricks' (2009) definition of being "emancipatory (the action researcher is able to explore practices within the limits of social structures), critical (the action researcher's goal is to challenge alienation, unproductive ways of working, and power struggles), and transformational (challenging both theory and practice)" (p. 10).

I chose to participate in the Kremen School of Human Development's Master of Arts in Teaching program because of its emphasis in multicultural and social justice education. The students at my school are approximately 70 percent African American, 25 percent Latino, and 5 percent Pacific Islander. Over 95 percent of students qualify for free or reduced lunch, a common marker for poverty. The city was recently recognized as the 9th most dangerous city in the United States. Furthermore, my school is situated in the Iron Triangle area of the city, an area of higher violence and poverty.

I have always held the belief that it is a teacher's duty to create an environment that is a safe haven for all students and conducive to learning. My role as a teacher at Richville College Prep K-5 Charter School carries with it some additional expectations. When teaching from a multicultural and social justice perspective I need to allow students to discover their own heritage, create lessons that embed standards within the context of social justice, and educate my students about how to create change. My future as a teacher will be a constant evolution of my practice to meet the needs of whoever my students may be. I have been working on identifying problems in my classroom and posing questions that get me thinking about how to reach the goal of social change. I have found this method of education to be a powerful force in moving our educational system to a better place.

I am proud to work in the Richville College Prep K-5 Charter School community because I am motivated by the excitement of many parents. Although parent participation is still lower than the school would like, it is on the rise. The enthusiasm of the parents that do participate is infectious, and it is clear that they want something different than their public schools can offer. The City of Richville, though, labeled negatively at the present time, is a city of rich history for the State of California and the United States military. The Kaiser Shipyards were the site of immense warship production during World War II. The never-before-seen speed at which the ships were built is often hailed as the reason for the United States gaining the upper hand against the Japanese during the war. Furthermore, it was women who were building these ships. Richville College Prep's permanent school site will be the renovated historic building that once housed the first state-run preschool, created to care for the children of these women. I would like for my students to learn as much as possible about the rich history of their city and work to begin changes that will restore its former reputation.

I believe the students I teach can be successful because they are so inquisitive. They are constantly asking questions and have a desire to know everything. Much of this may be due to their age, and I want to cultivate this thirst. I fear that if I do not cultivate this thirst now, it will be lost as they grow. I believe that allowing a child to question, explore, and investigate while young will keep these doors open throughout life.

The cultures of the students I serve are a mixture of African American and Latino with some Pacific Islander. The majority of Latino students and all of the Pacific Islanders are also English language learners. This poses additional challenges in the classroom as we do not yet have a school-wide ELD program and all of the ELD requirements must be met by the classroom teacher. This has pushed me to work heavily on vocabulary with the use of visual aids for all students, and I have seen the benefits of this work among English-language learners and native English-speakers.

My researchable question is: in what specific and measurable ways do Learning Centers improve mathematic concept attainment among English language learners, students performing below proficiency, and students of a low socio-economic status?

After obtaining parents' written permission, I identified and sorted my participants. Some students fell into more than one group. The participants are 23 second-grade students attending Richville College Prep K-5 Charter School that have been receiving academic intervention. Of the 44 second graders enrolled in the school, 23 have been identified as needed academic intervention based on school-wide benchmark assessments. Due to one student moving to a different school, complete data exists for 22 of the 23 students.

The subgroups studied included English language learners (6 students), students of low socio-economic households as determined by qualification for free or reduced lunch (21 students), and students still performing below levels of proficiency by the date of the most recent benchmark assessment (9 students).

I focused on designing Learning Centers that appeal to Multiple Intelligences and content chosen based on areas of need. The three instruments for this investigation are (1) the Multiple Intelligence assessment obtained from an online source, (2) a pre-test obtained from the Assessment Guide of the school's mathematics program, and (3) an identical post-test to be administered at the end of the study period.

The procedure for the Multiple Intelligence assessment was to read each yes or no question as students circle their responses. The procedure for the pre- and post-tests was to read each question out loud while projecting a copy of the test on the StarBoard. These assessments were read out loud so that they accurately assessed what was intended and were not influenced by the reading abilities of the students. Students filled in the bubble for their answer choice on their copy of the test. A piece of scratch paper was also be provided.

Results of the Multiple Intelligences survey indicate no students identified with Natural Intelligence, however there was a heavier concentration of students that identified with Linguistic, Logical-Mathematical, Musical, and Bodily-Kinesthetic Intelligences. Centers activities were designed to appeal to these four intelligences while also incorporating some activities that appeal to Spatial, Interpersonal, and Intrapersonal Intelligences.

When interpreting the results of the pre- and post-test by standard, I calculated that there were seven standards in which less that 60% of students chose the correct answer. Of the seven standards, I chose to focus on the four that I felt were most representative of their areas of need based on what I observe in the classroom. One question on the test that measured proficiency in measurement was not an accurate measure of their concept attainment. The question was poorly designed and results were not utilized when choosing content.

After implementation of the Learning Centers, the post-test was administered. There was a measured increase in the concept attainment for each of the focus concepts except those relating to counting and manipulating money. In addition, the average score of each of the subgroups increased. The greatest increase in performance was among English-language learners followed by students performing below proficiency, then students of low-income households. These results may suggest that incorporating Learning Centers, when planned based on student need and type of intelligences of the students, can significantly increase student achievement.

Since a classroom is by no means a static environment and good teachers are ever adjusting to meet the needs of the students, there are a few confounds to this study. First, at the same time that the study was being implemented, there was also heavy instruction in math vocabulary during the regular math period. This may attribute to the significant gains made by the English language learner subgroup. Also, there were a few content standards assessed that demonstrated a drop in proficiency. This may be due to the heavy focus on other standards resulting in students being "out of practice."

Overall, the results of the study to imply that Learning Centers can be beneficial to increasing the performance of students in a mathematics classroom. With proper planning and well-thought-out activity choices in addition to quality basic instruction, Learning Centers can be a beneficial teaching strategy. I will continue to use Learning Centers in my classroom in order to ensure that all students are receiving the support and style of instruction that they need to be successful.

Ms. Johnson's participatory action research is critical in its relevance to her daily practice within one of America's most challenging communities. Ms. Johnson needed to test a question specific to her unique situation, and her choice of building a community of learners within her second-grade classroom was both empowering and life-enhancing for her students (Mills, 2007). Rather than taking a standardized, cookbook approach to the problems of achievement, Ms. Johnson hit on the solution by carefully examining a unique and personally meaningful path using multiple intelligence theory. This study created an excitement for learning in her classroom.

*****

Danvi Tu is a dedicated teacher/researcher. Her teaching follows Sumara and Carson's (2001) conceptualization of action research as a lived practice. In their view, the teacher/researcher does more than simply apply research techniques within their classroom. "Rather, action research is a lived practice that requires that the researcher not only investigate the subject at hand but, as well, provide some account of the way in which the investigation both shapes and is shaped by the investigator" (Sumara & Carson, 2001, p. xiii). What Ms. Tu demonstrates to us is that these data are her life and her lived practice.

I am a teacher by definition, but a learner by choice. I am constantly observing, reflecting, and seeking to find opportunities to grow as a professional. From all of the different workshops and classes I attend, I take away so many fresh ideas. The tricky thing is being able to aggregate all the data and pulling out what I need to work with the students I have. Whenever I plan for a lesson, I am always thinking of my students first: What do they need to know? What will be interesting to them and make learning stick? How can they apply this to their lives?

As a social justice educator, this is my observation of my current role as a teacher: In teaching the primary grades, there has been little emphasis on writing besides what is expected of us from state standards. For example, in third grade, students are taught to write a descriptive paragraph, yet they are expected to write an essay in four different genres at the end of fourth grade for the state writing exam. Eight months is simply not enough time for students to learn all the skills necessary to tackle such a daunting task, especially considering 70% of my students are English language learners. Students need a lot more exposure to quality writing and time to practice writing in the primary grades. Many students come into my third-grade classroom unable to write a complete sentence. Some still struggle with spelling three-letter words. They are unmotivated to write and find story prompts boring and uninspiring. The challenge is finding ways to motivate these students to write profusely with creativity and accuracy. How can I structure my writing time to be meaningful? I need to be able to teach my students not only the mechanics of writing, but also the craft of it. How can I plan for the year ahead, so that by the time my students are in fourth grade, they are not completely overwhelmed by the state exam?

The community I work in has many assets. It is diverse and brings in different perspectives, ideas, and wonderful food. All parents want their children to be successful, and are willing to help out if given the opportunity. Families are working class, but they can contribute in other ways through chaperoning on field trips, volunteering in the classroom, or donating supplies. They can come into the classroom and share different cultural traditions and stories with the students.

I believe the students I teach can be successful because they are eager to learn and are pleased when they see how much they have accomplished. Some students are still struggling to sound out letters while others are on to chapter books. This has forced me to differentiate my teaching. In reading, we split up into groups of reading ability. For math, I also differentiate with the level of difficulty I give to students. By the end of the year, students will have made progress, whether it's a year's worth of growth or are working beyond grade level.

The language and culture of the students I serve is a mix of Spanish, Vietnamese, Chinese, and English. Many students have parents who came from another country, including Vietnam, Mexico, Philippines, and Cambodia. I enjoy teaching such a diverse group of students because we learn so much from each other. I enjoy hearing their stories and they enjoy hearing mine. It has also broadened my horizons by searching for books and other literature that will speak to my students, written by people who look like them.

My researchable question was: In what specific and measurable ways does the use of writer's workshop motivate English language learners to write creatively, use detail, and apply correct grammar skills to their writing? Sub-questions included: How can writer's workshop increase motivation for elementary school writers? Is it possible to integrate teaching the craft of writing with the mechanics of writing? What components should be added to aid English language learners? Can writer's workshop be combined with other writing programs such as Step Up to Writing? Will the workshop format translate to higher writing scores?

My qualitative research design is an inquiry on the use of writer's workshop inside a classroom and the effects it has on students' motivation to write. I gathered interviews, observations, and documents from my students. Specifically, I conducted an unstructured, open-ended interview with each of my students on their attitudes towards writing and took interview notes. I also gave them a survey on writing attitudes before the inquiry and at the end of the inquiry. I gathered field notes by conducting ongoing observations of my students while they were writing. Finally, I examined writing produced from my students throughout the inquiry to see their progress. To grade student writing, I used a rubric that scored students on having a story structure, details, conventions, and creativity.

I have learned that all students possess wonderful stories in their hearts. They are all capable of writing these stories if given the opportunity. They can be engaged to write even if they hated writing before. Implementing writer's workshop in my classroom has led to students writing for longer periods of time, writing longer pieces, and being reflective of their behavior and writing. I also learned that I was not able to bring all of my students' writing up to proficiency, but many factors came into play, including English learners. However, I still celebrate the small successes that all of my students were able to achieve. For example, I had one student who would only write one sentence at the beginning of the year. I knew he was capable of so much more, but refused to pick up his pencil to write. By the end of the inquiry, he had written an entire story with a beginning, middle, and end. He had many spelling mistakes and grammatical errors, but the success is in having him motivated enough to get his story out.

Overall, all of my students became better writers, both in their craft of writing and in mechanics. They were also more motivated to write and viewed writing in a positive light. Going forward in my career, I will continue to implement and refine writer's workshop in my classroom. I will integrate writing across all subject areas, especially in reading and science. Writer's workshop will be a constant part of my schedule, no matter what grade I teach, because all students can benefit from it.

Ms. Tu's work "shows the connections between researcher and subject of inquiry" (Sumara & Carson, 2001, p. xvi). In her own words, she iterates, "my research met Creswell's (2009) criteria because the inquiry took place in a natural setting, in the classroom where students normally learn, the researcher (myself) was a key instrument in collecting data, and multiple sources of data were used." In this case, the data are a living part of Ms. Tu's practice as a teacher. She stands up for her students and actively includes them in the writing process: an engagement that contagiously connects them to their learning and their teacher.

The Pedagogy of the Fields:
The Labor and Educational Histories of Migrant Farmworking Parents

My passion to become an educator is born from my experiences as the child of migrant farmworkers. I decided to conduct a study that examined how the life experiences of Mexican-origin, farmworking parents shape how they choose to engage in the schooling process of their children. I wanted to understand how farmworking parents, many who have little prior formal education, think about and support their child's education. The literature within the field of education over the past 20 years has demonstrated a *link* between parents being involved in the education of their children, and their children doing better in school, especially in the lower grades (Chavkin, 1989; Epstein, 1995; Henderson & Berla, 1997). While a growing and significant amount research has been conducted on understanding the educational involvement of Latino families, especially in urban areas (Auerbach, 2001; Ceja, 2004; Delgdo-Gaitan, 1991, 2001; Lawson, 2003; Lopez, 2001; Valdes, 1996), less research has focused on Mexican-origin migrant farmworkers families, a subgroup primarily located in rural areas. How do farmworking parents who often work so many hours manage to have a presence in the education of their children (Perez-Carreon, et al. (2005)? Answering this question and others led me to the community of *Trabajo*[2] to conduct my research study and investigate an understudied population within the field of education.

The city of *Trabajo* is a small, rural farmworking community located in Central California. The population of the city is almost entirely Latino, mostly of Mexican origin, with a high percentage of residents living in poverty. Furthermore, over half of the population of *Trabajo* is foreign born, with most in the community speaking a language other than English at home. The characteristics of this largely (im)migrant farmworking population is reflected in their low levels of educational attainment, as some estimates point to 20%[3] having completed high school—a total of one-fourth of the national average. The geographical isolation of *Trabajo* makes it increasingly difficult for its residents to have access to employment, education, health, and other public social resources that other communities often take for granted.

Trabajo has both an elementary and middle school, but does not yet have a high school. The students from *Trabajo* are bused to a nearby and more racially mixed community, which houses the high school for the district. The most recent demographics available for both of the schools at *Trabajo* show that the student populations mirror those of the community and are almost entirely Latino with a high percentage of Spanish-speaking English Learners. Both of *Trabajo's* schools have high rates of students who qualify for a free/reduced lunch, reflecting the high poverty levels of the community and the poverty wages that their farmworking parents earn. In terms of performance on statewide standardized tests, both of the schools have consistently received an API ranking of "1" for the last 10 years, the lowest score possible. At least by standardized measures utilized by the state of California, the two schools in the community are some of the lowest-performing schools in the state. In the following section, I detail a promising pedagogical approach towards creating the type of learning conditions that can potentially lead to stronger home, school, and community collaboration.

As a social justice educator, the work of Paulo Freire (2000) has been essential in helping me understand how education can either be used as a tool for oppression or for liberation. While Freire's work has commonly been utilized to examine the educational and political situation of urban schooling populations, hardly ever has his work been used in the context in which it originated—in rural communities and schools (McLaren & Giroux, 1990). Two of Paulo Freire's most useful pedagogical concepts are the notions of "banking" education and "problem-posing" education. For Freire, a banking education consists of teachers "filling" or creating deposits in the "blank slated minds" of their students. A banking education presumes that students from these communities and their culture have nothing of value to offer. Their prior "failure" to become "educated" is not a result of schools ill-serving these students and their families, but rather, their backwardness and inability to become civilized. Freire (2000) adds:

> The oppressed are regarded as the pathology of the healthy society, which must therefore adjust these "incompetent and lazy" folk to its own patterns by changing their mentality. These marginals need to be "integrated," "incorporated" into the healthy society that they have "forsaken." (p. 74)

Specific ways in which Freire's above explanation has been manifested have been through cultural deficit theories (Valencia & Solórzano, 1997; Valencia & Black, 2002), where the solution to "properly" educating these communities has been through the eradication of their culture, often seen as anti-intellectual. In the community of *Trabajo*, an educator espousing a "banking ideology" would be someone more interested in "changing the consciousness of the oppressed, not the situation[s] which oppress them" (p. 74). This ideology seeks to deny and silence the voices of these families and their struggles.

The solution to the banking system of education for Freire rests in a "dialogic education" (multidirectional) where the student and teacher both recognize that they are jointly responsible for educating one another. This pedagogical standpoint requires that the teacher be humble enough to have faith in his or her students' ability and capacity to become "critical co-investigators in dialogue with their teacher" (p. 81). According to Freire (2000),

> In problem-posing education, people develop their power to perceive critically *the way they exist* in the world *with which* and *which* they find themselves; they come to see the world not as a static reality, but as a reality in process, in transformation. (p. 83)

For youth and families residing in communities like *Trabajo*, an emancipatory, problem-posing education would allow their voices to be heard and require us to listen closely to understand what the causes of their continued poverty and social isolation are. An educator committed to a problem-posing education and deeply engaged in dialogue with the community would soon come to realize that the structure of farmwork is not just difficult and under-appreciated labor, but an intersection of multiple forms of oppression structured into their daily existence. For example, one might begin by posing questions like the following: Why do many (im)migrant farmworkers continue to live at or below poverty levels when their labor propels the state of California to a $36.2 billion agricultural output? Why then would a geographical region that produces so much wealth be identified in a recent study of human development indicators examining educational, health, and economic wellness as one of worst regions in the nation—worse off than even Appalachia? These types of questions would shift the discourse of parent involvement from "why didn't Juanito's parents come to the parent meeting?", to "Why do Juanito's parents work so much *yet* earn so little?" Problem posing in this way interrogates the political economy structure that allows these injustices to be created and perpetuated in the first place. These questions lead to complex answers which would challenge the dominant narrative about educational attainment, achievement, and inequality, held by many practicing educators. Unfortunately, in the current climate of NCLB and high-stakes testing, where students are often reduced to just a test score, these types of questions become harder and harder to ask—especially when the incentives structures are not aligned with this type of pedagogy and when most teachers are not prepared to teach or work closely with families in this critical manner.

This research study seeks to contribute to the professional educational literature that examines teaching, learning, and family-school relations and the social context of diverse communities of color. The researchable question informing this study is 1) How do the educational, migratory, and labor histories of Mexican (im)migrant farmworking families mediate their educational engagement? This study explores how the life histories of (im)migrant Mexican-origin farmworking families inform their engagement in their children's educational process. To answer this question, I utilized a qualitative methodological approach and case study design (Yin, 2003). This design allowed me to investigate the complex and rich life histories of farmworker parents in the context in which they occur. In exploring their life narratives, I examined the ways they support their children's educational endeavors and sought to understand what messages they are sending to their children about education. For me, parent engagement refers to more than school- or home-based forms of "involvement"; it also includes parents' "orientations to the world and how those orientations frame the things they do or choose not to do" (Calabrese-Barton et al., 2004, p. 3).

For the study, I began by conducting life history interviews with ten families, both mother and father, and specifically focused on their educational, labor, and migration histories. The principal selection criteria of families for this study was that they live in the community of *Trabajo*, work as farmworkers, and have at least one child attending the elementary or middle school. I would visit them at their homes and conduct interviews with them in Spanish, usually in the evening after a long day of work. The purpose of the oral history interviews was to gain an understanding of the socio-political factors that led these parents to migrate to Central California. What were the different life processes that brought them to the community of *Trabajo*? In other words, how have the families' perspectives on education been shaped by what they have experienced in their own educational process, their work experiences, moving from place to place, and now living in Central California?

The findings for this study revealed three significant themes. The first finding demonstrates that the parents' own prior educational experiences profoundly shaped their aspirations for their own children's educational trajectories. For example, all the parents were forced by finances to abandon their own educational pursuits in Mexico. Their own desires and goals for schooling were crushed, as their families' limited financial resources made it impossible for the majority to continue their schooling past the ninth grade. One parent indicated that her inability to continue her education in Mexico drove her to attend night school in the United States to show her daughters that if she was capable of obtaining her GED in the face of multiple obstacles, her daughters had no excuse not to succeed and reach their goals. She stated that conversations with her children are now about *what* university they will be attending, not *if* they will be attending.

The second significant finding pertains to the concept of *educación* and being of service to others. United Farmworkers of America (UFW) leader Cesar Chavez once stated, "The end of all education should surely be service to others." In that same spirit, several parents in the study shared that their own parents had instilled in them the value of service to others being a component of a good education, or *buena educación*. Part of having a *buena educación* goes beyond simply doing well academically in school; it also includes being "serviceable to others." This ethic was echoed by parents as they gave several examples of specific ways they ensured that they were responsive to the needs of others. A parent shared how her grandparents—by modeling multiple ways in which they helped and supported their neighbors—taught her that one should always think about others before thinking of one's self. She also gave the example of her father taking clothing and materials to less fortunate people in the U.S./Mexico border region when he would return to Mexico to visit his family. In a similar fashion, this parent would regularly volunteer at the local elementary school where both of her children attended to help some of the young students who needed additional academic support. The examples provided by these parents show that having a high-quality education should include a communal dimension that accounts for what one does for others as well.

The third and final set of findings pertains to the experiences that adolescents had when their parents took them to work alongside them in the agricultural fields of Central California. This "Pedagogy of the Fields" resulted in the children having direct experience with the type of labor exploitation their parents experience on a daily basis. One parent shared how he would take his son to work with him during his high school summer breaks so that he could have money to purchase his school clothing. In exposing his son to such a "life depriving" line of work, he hoped to teach him that a formal education was an escape from the poverty they lived in. Another parent indicated that she took her teenage daughter to work one day at an onion-packing house after the daughter began failing in her academics. Her goal was to show her daughter that if she did not want to do well in school, working in that type of job would require maximum sacrifice and effort. After her experience leaving their home at 4 a.m. that morning and returning at 10 p.m. that night, the daughter shortly thereafter began showing academic improvement in her classes. Finally, another parent indicated how she frequently tells her three young children who are not yet of working age how it would be heartbreaking to see them in the same "life depriving work" that she is forced to endure. These parents skillfully used their children's labor experiences working alongside them as a "generative theme" to discuss with them systems of oppression that control their lives and are "limiting-situations" (Freire, 2000). The new consciousness about labor exploitation that emerged from the children in the above examples allowed them to recognize and put into practice educational success as a "limit-act" that could allow them to escape a similar fate as their parents.

The findings from this study point to the importance of listening to and learning from the life stories of the parents whose children we teach. Engaging in these types of pedagogical exercises may not only serve as an important way of getting to know the families that work and live in the communities we teach, but also in them getting to know us more profoundly. If Mexican-origin, farmworking families possess the desire for their children to attain a higher education and support their efforts in doing so, how might we best build upon those assets? Also, how can structures be created in their communities that put into use the desire of many of these parents to be of service to others? While many of them are not materially rich, they possess a desire to see improvements in their community and are willing to participate to create greater opportunities for their children. Finally, how can educators create learning opportunities within the classroom which draw from the pedagogies of the fields? What can be learned about the structure of agricultural work directly from parents who are experts in what it means to be at the frontline of labor exploitation?

Do we have the will and the courage to include the voices of these parents in classroom spaces that are traditionally structured to deny their existence and contributions to the larger society? To answer these questions requires a problem-posing pedagogy in which teachers are willing to concede power to community members and acknowledge their expertise within the local, social, historical, and political context of the community.

Conclusions

Broadly conceived, education can be viewed as either domesticating or liberating (Freire, 1970; Macedo, 1994; Ladwig, 1999; Whitty, 1985). A domesticating education prepares students to acquiesce reflexively to the dictates of authority figures, uncritically consume information, and feel no compulsion to question or act. This might not be problematic if the world were harmonious and just. Because it is not, we have found post-colonial, critical, anti-racist, and feminist theories to provide essential insights into ways of achieving an education that frees students (and practicing teachers) from blind obedience, ignorant bliss, and complacent inaction. Post-colonial theorists, for example, draw attention to how dominant groups use research and knowledge to control those depersonalized as "others" (Smith, 1999). More precisely, defining "what counts as valued knowledge, skills, and traditions," as well as determining "who gets to ask," "what," and "to whom" afford great power to structure the world in a way that maintains power and privilege. Consequently, first-generation college students tend to go to schools that are less well-funded than many private and research-focused universities, and are structured around a "knowledge transmission" factory model rather than a "knowledge production" model (Aronowitz, 2000). This distinction means that students from historically underserved communities, such as our students and those in other CSUs (e.g., Sleeter, 2005) are likely to attend a university that is structured to enable them to consume knowledge produced by those from more affluent institutions.

Since the online MAT's inception in 2005, we have worked to disrupt the educational status quo or institutionalized domesticating system outlined above. By intentionally orienting this graduate program around knowledge production wherein practicing teachers work with knowledge frameworks and critically oriented, theoretical, and methodological traditions arising within historically oppressed communities, they create knowledge that is of, by, for, and about their community and its own empowerment. More specifically, we embraced the concept of transformative, emancipatory knowledge that "is based on different epistemological assumptions about the nature of knowledge, about the influence of human interests and values on knowledge construction, and about the purpose of knowledge" (Banks, 2006, p. 9). Transformative, emancipatory knowledge offers "an alternative narration of the arrangement of social space" (Gallegos, 1998, p. 236), and provides conceptual tools to address conditions that have historically been oppressed or excluded.

One such tool, our concept of social justice collaboration, involves our graduate students/practicing teachers using knowledge to enhance the collective condition. We use the term social justice from a Freirian perspective that focuses on transforming the school structures that perpetuate the unequal distribution of social power. Freire (1970) contends that changing the status quo involves naming injustices that oppress and then taking action with other people through dialogue and work. Naming injustice, particularly that in schooling, is critical, since so much of it is taken for granted or viewed as "common sense" (Kumashiro, 2004).

As alluded to earlier, teaching is inherently political and ethical because teachers have direct influence on the lives of others. As a social institution, education affords or denies access to resources that directly impact one's life changes. Because we see teaching as a process of engagement with knowledge that arises in part from lived experience, we value engaged pedagogy that facilitates honest, critical dialogues that allow consideration of significant issues among people who share experiences of oppression, as well as with those who do not. Understanding teaching as both a political and ethical act substantiates the need to prepare teachers who are able to act as committed transformative intellectuals (Giroux, 1983)—who have the confidence to use their knowledge, skills, and position to work toward positive change in classrooms, schools, and communities. The transformative intellectual must grasp the precondition of a collective process of liberation by participating in a community that values the need to change the social conditions of oppression inside and outside of school (Freire, 1970; hooks, 1994; Huiskamp, 2002). This is why many of our core program learning outcomes, described later and illustrated in the student mini-action research studies, reflect the knowledge, skills, and dispositions necessary to work as a change agent.

As traditionally structured, higher education does not support the vision sketched above. Structural conditions inside and outside post-secondary institutions privilege the academic success of students who are white, native English-speaking, and from affluent backgrounds. Beginning in 2005, we implemented a post-credential, Master of Arts in Teaching (MAT) program to support practicing teachers with complex lives and varying degrees of preparedness for academic rigor. Consequently, we have organized this chapter around three broad themes: a pluralistic academic community; student learning anchored in MSJE and educative action research; and support for student learning in an online environment.

Notes

1. While the critical pedagogies developed by educational scholars differ significantly, they do hold a number of common assumptions (Gitlin & Price, 1992; Leistyna, Woodrum, & Sherblom, 1996). The central purpose of these alternative pedagogies is to produce a political form of knowledge—a knowledge that makes problematic the relations among schools, the larger society, and the issues of power, domination, and liberation. Critical pedagogies also try to enable those traditionally silenced to play an active role in the learning process, consequently empowering the student in ways that reflect egalitarian and democratic ideals. Finally, critical pedagogies attempt to further consciousness and critical thinking where students delve into their own histories and meaning systems to learn about the structural and ideological forces that influence and restrict their lives (see, e.g., Apple, 1986; Apple & Beane, 2007; Camangian, 2008; Duncan-Andrade & Morrell, 2008; Giroux, 1983; Giroux & McLaren, 1986; McLaren, 1997).
2. The name of the community has been changed to protect the participants. Trabajo means "to labor" in Spanish.
3. This statistic refers to the population over the age of 25, a marker utilized by the U.S. Census.

References

Apple, M. W. (1986). *Teachers and texts: A political economy of class and gender relations in education*. London and Boston: Routledge and Kegan Paul.

Apple, M. W., & Beane, J. A. (Eds.). (2007). *Democratic schools* (2nd ed.). Alexandria, VA: Association for Supervision and Curriculum Development.

Aronowitz, S. (2000). *The knowledge factory: Dismantling the corporate university and creating true higher learning*. Boston: Beacon Press.

Auerbach, S. (2001). "Why do they give the good classes to some and not to others?" Latino parent narratives of struggle in a college access program. *Teachers College Record, 104*(7), 1369–1392.Banks, J. A. (2006). *Race, culture and education*. New York: Routledge.

Bond, H. M. (1935). The curriculum and the Negro child. *Journal of Negro Education, 4*(2), 159–168.

Camangian, P. (2008). Real talk: Transformative English teaching and urban youth. In W. Ayers, T. Quinn, & D. Stovall (Eds.), *Handbook of social justice in education*. Mahwah, NJ: Lawrence Erlbaum, Inc.

Calabrese-Barton, A., Drake, C., Perez, G., & St. Louis, K. (2004). Ecologies of parental engagement in urban education. *Educational Researcher, 33*(4), 3–12.

Carson, T. R., & Sumara, D. (2001). *Action research as living practice*. New York: Peter Lang.

Ceja, M. (2004). Chicana college aspirations and the role of parents: Developing educational resiliency. *The Journal of Hispanic Higher Education, 3*(4), 1–25.

Chavkin, N. F. (1989, Summer). Debunking the myth about minority parents. *Educational Horizons*, 119–123. In N. F. Chavkin (Ed.), *Families and schools in a pluralistic society*. Albany: State University of New York Press.

Cochran-Smith, M., & Lytle, S. L. (2009). *Inquiry as stance: Practitioner research for the next generation*. New York: Teachers College Press.

Counts, G. S. (1932/1978). *Dare the schools build a new social order?* Carbondale: Southern Illinois University Press. (Work originally published 1932)

Creswell, J. W. (2009). *Research design: Qualitative, quantitative, and mixed method approaches*. Thousand Oaks, CA: Sage.

Delgado-Gaitan, C. (1991). Involving parents in the schools: A process of empowerment. *American Journal of Education, 100*(1), 20–46.

Delgado-Gaitan, C. (2001). *The power of community: Mobilizing for family and schooling*. Denver, CO: Rowman and Littlefield.

Dewey, J. (1904). The relation of theory to practice in education. In J. Dewey, S. Brooks, & F. McMurry (Eds.), *The relation of theory to practice in the education of teachers* (Third Yearbook of the National Society for the Study of Education, Part 1, pp. 9–30). Bloomington, IL: Public School Publishing.

Dewey, J. (1916). *Democracy and education*. New York: Macmillan.

Dewey, J. (1929). *The quest for certainty: A study of the relation of knowledge and action*. NY: Minton, Balch & Company.

Dewey, J. (1933). *How we think: A restatement of the relation of reflective thinking to the educative process*. New York: D.C. Heath.

Dewey, J. (1938). *Experience and education*. New York: Macmillan.

Duncan-Andrade, J., and Morrell, E. (2008). *The art of critical pedagogy: The promises of moving from theory to practice in urban schools*. New York: Peter Lang.

Epstein, J. L. (1995). School/family/community partnerships: Caring for the children we share. *Phi Delta Kappan, 76*(9), 701–712.

Freire, P. (1970). *Pedagogy of the oppressed*. New York: Continuum.

Freire, P. (2000). *Pedagogy of freedom: Ethics, democracy, and civic courage*. Lanham, MD: Rowman & Littlefield.

Gallegos, B. (1998). Remembering the Alamo: Imperialism, memory, and postcolonial educational studies. *Educational Studies, 29*(3), 232–247.

Gay, G. (2010). *Culturally responsive teaching: Theory, research and practice* (2nd ed.). New York: Teachers College Press.

Giroux, H. (1983). *Theory and resistance in education: A pedagogy for the opposition.* South Hadley, MA: Bergin & Garvey.

Giroux, H., & McLaren, P. (1986). Teacher education and the politics of engagement: The case for democratic schooling. *Harvard Educational Review, 56*(3), 213–238.

Gitlin, A., & Price, K. (1992). Teacher empowerment and the development of voice. In C. Glickman (Ed.), *Supervision in transition.* Alexandria, VA: Association for Supervision and Curriculum Development.

Henderson, A. T., & Berla, N. (1997). *A new generation of evidence: The family is critical to student achievement.* Washington, DC: Center for Law in Education.

Hendricks, C. (2009). *Improving schools through action research: A comprehensive guide for educators.* Upper Saddle River, NJ: Pearson.

Hinchey, P. H. (2008). *Action research.* New York: Peter Lang.

hooks, b. (1994). *Teaching to transgress: Education as the practice of freedom.* London: Routledge.

Huiskamp, G. (2002). Negotiating communities of meaning in theory and practice: Rereading *Pedagogy of the oppressed* as direct dialogueic encounter. In J. J. Slater, S. M. Fain, & C. A. Rossatto (Eds.), *The Freirean legacy: Educating for social justice* (pp. 73–94). New York: Peter Lang.

Kincheloe, J. (2010). Beyond reductionism: Difference, criticality, and multilogicality in the bricolage and postformalism. In G. S. Goodman (Ed.), *Educational psychology reader: The art and science of how people learn.* New York: Peter Lang.

Kliebard, H. (1995). *The struggle for the American curriculum, 1893–1958* (2nd ed.). New York: Routledge.

Krashen, S. (2003). *Explorations in language acquisition and use.* Portsmouth, NH: Heinemann.

Kumashiro, K. K. (2004). *Against common sense: Teaching and learning toward social justice.* New York: RoutledgeFalmer.

Ladwig, J. A. (1996). *Academic distinctions: Theory and methodology in the sociology of school knowledge.* New York and London: Routledge.

Lawson, M. A. (2003). School-family relations in context. *Urban Education, 38,* 77–133.

Leistyna, P., Woodrum, A., & Sherblom, S. (Eds.). (1996). *Breaking free: The transformative power of pedagogy.* Cambridge, MA: President and Fellows of Harvard College.

Lopez, G. R. (2001). The value of hard work: Lessons on parent involvement from an (im)migrant household. *Harvard Educational Review, 71,* 416–437.

Macedo, D. (1994). *Literacies of power: What Americans are not allowed to know.* Boulder, CO: Westview.

May, S., & Sleeter, C. E. (2010). *Critical multiculturalism: Theory and praxis.* New York and London: Routledge.

McLaren, P. (1997). *Revolutionary multiculturalism: Pedagogies for dissent in the new millennium.* Boulder, CO: Westview Press.

McLaren, P., & Giroux, H. (1990). Critical pedagogy and rural education: A challenge from Poland. *Peabody Journal of Education, 67*(4), 154–165.

Mills, G. E. (2007). *Action research: A guide for the teacher researcher.* Upper Saddle River, NJ: Pearson.

Noffke, S. E. (1997). Professional, personal, and political dimensions of action research. *Review of Research in Education, 22,* 305–343.

Noffke, S., & Somekh, B. (2009). *The Sage handbook of educational action research.* London: Sage.

Pérez Carreon, G., Drake, C., & Calabrese-Barton, A. (2005). The importance of presence: Immigrant parents' school engagement experiences. *American Educational Research Journal, 42*(3), 465–498.

Schubert, W. H., & Lopez-Schubert, A. (1997). Sources of a theory for action research in the United States. In R. McTaggart (Ed.), *Participatory action research: International contexts and consequences* (pp. 203–223). Albany: State University of New York Press.

Sleeter, C. E. (2005). Working an academically rigorous, multicultural program. *Equity & Excellence in Education, 38,* 290–298.

Sleeter, C. E., & Grant, C. A. (2009). *Making choices for multicultural education: Five approaches to race, class, and gender* (6th ed.). Hoboken, NJ: John Wiley & Sons, Inc.

Smith, L. (1999). *Decolonizing methodologies: Research and indigenous peoples.* London: Zed Books.

Sumara, D., & Carson, T. R. (2001). Editor's introduction: Reconceptualizing action research as a living practice. In T. R. Carson & D. Sumara (Eds.), *Action research as a living practice* (pp. xiii–xxxii). New York: Peter Lang.

Ulrich, W. J. (1992). Preservice teachers reflect on the authority issue: A case study of a student teaching seminar. *Teaching and Teacher Education, 8*(4), 361–380.

Ullrich, W. J. (2001). Depth psychology, critical pedagogy, and initial teacher preparation. *Teaching Education, 10*(2), 17–33.

Ullrich, W. J., & Roessler, M. (1997). Curriculum that is multicultural and social reconstructionist. *Teaching Education, 9*(1). http://www.teachingeducation.com/vol9-1.ullrich.htmValdes, G. (1996). *Con respeto: Bridging distances between culturally diverse families and schools.* New York: Teachers College Press.

Valencia, R., & Black, M. (2002). "Mexican Americans don't value education!" The basis of the myth, mythmaking, and debunking." *Journal of Latinos and Education, 1*(2), 81–103.

Valencia, R., & Solórzano, D. G. (1997). Contemporary deficit thinking. In R. Valencia (Ed.), *The evolution of deficit thinking: Educational thought and practice* (pp. 160–210). London and Washington, DC: Falmer Press.

Wexler, P. (1987). *Social analysis of education.* New York and London: Routledge.

Whitty, G. (1985). *Sociology and school knowledge.* London: Methuen.

Willinsky, J. (2001). Accountability in action. In T. R. Carson & D. Sumara (Eds.), *Action research as a living practice*. New York: Peter Lang.

Yin, R. K. (2003). *Case study research: Design and methods*. London: Sage.

Zeichner, K. M. (2009). *Teacher education and the struggle for social justice*. New York: Routledge.

CHAPTER TWENTY-EIGHT

Technical Assistance as Inquiry: Using Activity Theory Methods to Engage Equity in Educational Practice Communities

Elizabeth B. Kozleski and Alfredo J. Artiles

The deepening and seemingly intractable inequitable educational opportunities, resource distributions, and outcomes documented for the last several generations in the US has renewed a sense of urgency in the research community to overcome the limitations of traditional work on educational change (Patton, 2011). Despite massive policy changes in recent years to address these challenges, key outcomes remain intractable. In the most recent data from the National Center on Educational Statistics (NCES), students categorized as Black, Hispanic, and Native American are more likely to struggle academically, drop out before graduation, be referred for disciplinary action, and be identified for special education services (Snyder & Dillow, 2010).

A growing critique of US educational gaps rests on the disproportionate poverty rate in minority communities and its concomitant influence on birth weight, nutrition, neighborhood environmental pollution, and family stress. Nevertheless, it is critical to note that an exclusive focus on poverty and its impact ignores many other critical factors, including historically grounded structural inequities and students' perspectives and experiences; to wit, "Adults often explain low achievement by saying, 'The children are poor.' Students tell us, 'Sure that matters. But what hurts us more is that you teach us less" (Haycock, 2001, p. 8). In addition, decades-long economic and educational policies havecontributed to this situation through the entitlement and enfranchisement of some American communities, while systemically excluding and marginalizing others (Anyon, 2005; Warikoo & Carter, 2009).

In spite of pockets of promising practice and new policies, investments in research and reform efforts have produced modest improvement in reading scores of eighth graders between 1998 and 2009on the National Assessment of Educational Progress (NAEP) in a few states, little or no improvement in another 16, with insufficient data in other states to understand trends (National Center for Education Statistics, xxxx). http://nces.ed.gov/nationsreportcard/naepdata/report.aspx, Other targets of national assessment have similar spotty outcomes overall and troubling trends for groups students by race and ethnicity, disability and language. One of the most heavily invested strategies of these reform efforts, technical assistance (TA), has the potential to influence, inform, and improve outcomes, but there is little theory or research to drive its implementation. Further, because of its focus on technical problem solving rather than on critical outcomes such as equity, access, and opportunities to learn, the outcomes of most technical assistance result in improvements to systems operations (what already exists) rather than improvements in how the system is organized to achieve equity in its outcomes.

In 2009 the US federal government invested more than $56 billion in discretionary federal programs of which approximately *one third* providedTA and professional development to states, local education agencies, and schools (US Department of Education, n.d.). Much of this assistance is framed in an expert/novice paradigm (Sawyer, 2005), in which the work of the TA experts is to (a) provide information; (b) assist local and state entities to use and apply the information to improve practice; and (c) where necessary to offer approaches to framing and developing policy that can drive adoption of new practice (Kozleski, 2004). For instance, the federal investment in 10 regional education labs that disseminate information throughout the 50 states and 10 territories was more than $70 million for fiscal year 2010 (U.S. Department of Education, n.d.). Another approximately $645 million was invested the same year in developing, validating, and scaling up educational programs through the Investing in Innovation program. These are but two of a myriad of programs at the federal level designed to support state education efforts that, according to the National Council of State Legislators (NCSL), constitute as much as a third of most state budgets (National Council of State Legislators, 2010).

TA models are aimed at changing policies and practices at different levels of the education system and are often combined with professional development efforts. TA has been defined as "the provision of quality content and/or process expertise via a responsive, continuous, and external system to assist clients and their organization to change or improve for the better" (Trohanis, 1982, p. 120). TA is often prized when it avoids critiquing the equity outcomes and focuses on improving operational aspects of education systems such as improved scientific rigor in assessment, identification, and intervention. This focus, we argue, deflects attention from equity as a core value of a public education system within a democracy, and therefore, the recipients of TA learn to view their work in terms of operational tasks while outcomes that benefit the most oppressed groups of students can become tangential to technical improvements to the system. TA, therefore, comprises content, outcome, and delivery mechanism dimensions (Trohanis, 1982). This approach to TA has been historically favored to initiate educational change. McInerney and Hamilton (2007) noted that two models have been commonly pursued. The first is a top-down approach to move policy and practice from the federal to the state to the local school district to schools and finally to classrooms. The second has been to pilot the development of a process for improvement in classrooms, expand it to schools, to school districts, and finally throughout states.

The top-down approach typically assumes that a practice or policy is designed to be adopted as originally designed without retrofitting or adapting the practice to local contexts. However, in many cases, complete adoption does not occur for a variety of reasons that include (a) insufficient access to resources, (b) lack of understanding of the fundamental principles of the practice, (c) a need to comply without sufficient knowledge and expertise to implement, and (d) a lack of technical assistance to solve emerging issues during the initial adoption phase. Bottom-up strategies also fail to sustain over time without strong policy at the local level to sustain new practice implementation across changes in superintendent leadership, as well as state and federal mandates (Kozleski & Smith, 2009). Thus, while leadership, context, policy development and implementation, and strong local expertise are important aspects of making substantive improvements in classroom and school practices, both top-down and bottom-up strategies have had limited impact (Fullan, 2008) in general and in particular on equity dimensions.

On the other hand, there are several important premises of TA work that have the potential to influence, inform, and improve educational outcomes, such as an ecological vision of everyday practice and human development, attention to local and state infrastructures, and personnel development design to scaffold change processes. Nevertheless, this is an under-developed/-used area of scholarship, since TA's location as the bridge between research/policy and practice makes it a potentially powerful resource for educational change. Thus, it is in our best interest to refine the way we theorize this practice and strengthen the links between these theoretical formulations and the methodological tools available to do such work. In this chapter we aim to transcend the limits of traditional approaches to change educational practice while we build on the strengths of previous work. We assume a cultural historical activity theory perspective to understand human practices in educational institutions (Engeström, 1999). We assume that human life is fundamentally rooted in participation in everyday activities, mediated by cultural artifacts, and oriented toward objects (Cole, 1996). Further, this approach provides a foundation for examining the moral and ethical outcomes of the ways that systems are organized and who benefits from their current configuration.

We propose an alternative perspective on the study and implementation of educational change for equity outcomes that addresses the limits of traditional work and contextualize our discussion in TA work that is concerned with educational equity for marginalized groups. In this chapter we suggest that TA is a critical opportunity to engage individuals and activity systems in changing the outcomes of their practice and, in doing so, shift their praxis in ways that can mediate future work. Because we locate this work within a methodology that is steeped in activity theory, we propose a methodology for TA that offers a rich context for ongoing research and inquiry as a critical feature for systems transformation. However, we propose using a different term to describe this approach; specifically, we suggest *transformative mediating structures* as the term that best captures the theoretical underpinnings of this approach. Some of this work offers a unit of analysis that links macro- with micro-level factors (Artiles & Dyson, 2005; Gallego et al., 2001). This emergent work also transcends fragmented views of individuals in which single markers of difference (e.g., race, social class, gender, etc.) constitute the focus of inquiry (Ladson-Billings & Tate, 1995). And, it moves beyond psychological notions of learning and development that cite knowledge development and change within individuals rather than the communities in which they experience, explore, and practice (Engeström, 1999). In subsequent sections, we explore the notion of TA as methodology and then propose a set of methods that comprise its practice.

Designing Transformative Mediating Structures for Educational Change

To understand what we mean by designing transformative mediating structures for educational change, we describe the activity arenas in which practice occurs, followed by examples of educational change experiences that offer a methodologically driven approach to designing, engaging, and improving outcomes as an approach to change. Embedded within this notion of *mediating structure* to promote change is the notion that this work is not only a *technical* act that is accomplished according to a set of scripted activities but that it is also a *situated* and *critically* examined methodology that explores the use of space and time in which mediated support is provided (Lektorksy, 2009). These three perspectives help to shape the strategies that are needed to move work forward (i.e., technical), create the contexts and structures that allow the cultural practice of schools to flourish (i.e., situated), and examine equity by understanding whose needs are being served and for what purposes (i.e., critical) (Van Manen, 1990).

The Critical Perspective: Improving Whose Education?

The redistribution of power and privilege within social systems like schooling is predicated on deep understanding of sociocultural and historical dynamics as well as psychological perspectives (Kozleski & Smith, 2009). In systems like education that have a long history across multiple cultures, many rituals, routines, and cycles of activity like knowledge production and use transcend national and historical boundaries (Cole, 2010). Social reproduction can be said to be part of the cultural work of systems, but systems like education have a dynamic of their own that is constantly negotiated and mediated through the introduction of disturbances and their mediation within the system (Gallego et al., 2001). For instance, an educational policy could constitute both a disturbance and a new tool that mediates and, in some way, changes the flow of practice within a community (Gutierrez & Voussoughi, 2010). In the 2004 federal reauthorization of the Individuals with Disabilities Education Act (2004), a new emphasis on prevention and response to intervention (RTI) in turn produced new state and local policy. Teachers were asked to redefine themselves as "interveners" who "progress monitor" their students' learning over time. These changes in policy were intended to transform the activity of teachers through reconstituting their identities from the outside and renegotiating how time is spent in classrooms and in teacher activity.

Much of federal and state educational policy is organized around trying to influence this kind of change (Kozleski, 2004). And once policy is created, TA teams funded by federal and state agencies set to work under the guise of translators, telling their audiences what is intended by the new policy and how to recognize it in practice. Very little work occurs within the TA arena to examine policy intent and its potential collateral damage to the development of professional expertise or the disenfranchisement of groups of students, families, and/or professionals. Instead, activity centers on understanding policy intent and unpacking its components to develop specific expertise in the translation of policy to practice. It is precisely this lack of uncritical translation that has made the TA providers experts in policy translation but has undercut their ability to help practitioners in schools, districts, and state education agencies make fundamental shifts in their praxis.

The Situated Perspective: How Do Time and Space Matter?

The perspective we advance offers an explanation for why attempts to change practice produce little effect in the object of their intent: student achievement gains. Rather than teachers and students together engaged in inquiry about their content learning processes, practitioners are busy adopting assigned practices and identities, obfuscating their roles as learning leaders in their classrooms, schools, and districts. Most policies deal with process and the measurement of output, without providing space for helping practitioners and students mediate their learning activities in pursuit of learning accomplishments.

The design of transformative mediating structures for educational change model suggests that smaller activity cycles influence how larger cycles operate and vice versa (Ferguson, Kozleski, & Smith, 2003). For example, teachers and students in classrooms negotiate the culture and practices of the classroom. Experienced classroom teachers talk about good and bad years based on the student composition of their classrooms and how the students themselves solidified as a community. Teachers who are able to negotiate their classroom cultures participate annually in transformational processes in which they learn about their students as their students learn about them and the schooling culture that they find themselves in. Over the year, negotiated rhythms help to soften potential conflicts and create spaces for connection and community to develop. Teachers experience the same kinds of patterns in their grade level teams and their academic homes. People within these activity arenas respond and interact, producing activity that accomplishes particular outcomes or goals (Engeström, 1999). Thus, systems may be said to be reciprocal and responsive to the people, practices, and policies that exist within these activity arenas (Klingner et al., 2005).

Educational systems engage these same processes. Smaller units like student/teacher interactions are influenced by curricula, classroom policies, and intentions, while curricular implementation, classroom policies, routines, and intentions are influenced by the kinds of teacher/student interactions that operate in any given context. Classrooms as activity arenas are influenced by and impact school organization and culture. Principals and other school leaders attempt to standardize practice following district and state mandates. They provide what could be described as TA by explaining what practices are valued, evaluating teacher performance based on those practices, and providing exemplars or discussions of what preferred practice might look like.

Schools are nested within districts, within states, and within federal mandates. Each of these levels is engaged in a reciprocal dance within level and between levels in which practice is described and assessed, all in pursuit of increased student performance. And, rather than one level being impacted only by its adjacent levels, each level is engaged in reciprocal interactions with all other levels. Boundaries are breached through boundary encounters such as classroom observations conducted as brief classroom walk-throughs performed by district administrators (Cobb & McClain, 2006), visits from other school teams, or site monitoring visits made in classrooms by state department representatives. Boundary objects like individualized educational plans (IEPs) or standardized test scores that are presumed to have the same meaning across boundaries are, in fact, objects that are constructed and interpreted in very different ways, making policy implementation complex and unpredictable (Cobb & McClain, 2006). Thus, policy and practice travel not in linear paths, as policy is often presumed to travel, but in non-linear networks that complicate the diffusion of innovation (Kozleski, 2004).

The Technical Perspective: Can You Tell Me How to Do It?

State and local educational leaders want to effect change in the classroom, where the outcomes of the educational system are measured. Accountability measures, structural and organizational changes, the adoption of curricula, and the physical arrangement of schools are designed to impact learning in classrooms. Ultimately, it is what teachers and their students do together that produces what counts as outcomes. Therefore, much of what passes as TA is designed to change or improve teacher practices. Yet, teachers' professional learning is a complex phenomenon. Sieveke-Pearson (2004) found that among a middle school team that received a week of intensive professional learning on embedding literacy skills in content areas, followed by a year of coaching and mentoring in their classrooms, content area teachers used only a few strategies to enhance their students' literacy skills. So, even when explicit embedded models of professional learning are employed to help teachers know how to use a set of teaching strategies, those strategies may not become part of a teacher's practice repertoire. In part, the commentary on critical and situated perspectives offers some insights into why this may occur, but it also may be that the concept that teaching is performance as opposed to a reciprocal mediation feeds into frequently encountered questions by teachers about "just tell me what to do."

As Artiles and Kozleski (2010) point out, understanding that students need to actively participate in learning changes the nature of teachers' roles and identities in learning. Moving away from what Sawyer (2005) calls "instructionism" requires understanding that learning occurs because of active engagement in meaning-making through engaging, resisting, and developing mental schemas about the way things work. The technical aspects of teaching become observing, listening, mediating, and supporting learning, informed by ongoing assessment and the calibration of learning tasks to scaffold continuing student progress.

Similarly, the design of transformative mediating structures for educational change does not entail telling teachers, principals, and other practitioners how to do something, but supporting their learning in how to refine their approaches to teaching in response to their students and the situated context in which they practice. In doing so, the methodology of transformative mediating structures becomes a set of inquiry cycles in which increasingly more finely tuned supports to practitioners produce deeper and more sustained learning in their students.

Designing Transformative Mediating Structures for Change: An Illustration

In this section we illustrate how transformative mediating structures can support learning at multiple levels of the education system including classroom and school-wide practices as well providing support to state education personnel who seek to lead and support policy development and change throughout local education agencies. We offer five interrelated methods to support systems learning through transformative mediating structures: (a) remediating understandings of the problem; (b) disrupting the view from above; (c) forging new spaces; (d) cycles of inquiry, reflection, and action; and (e) implementing and assessing change.

Background on the Exemplar: Changing the Racialization of Disability

We explore these five methods using examples from our own work in the field as principal investigators of the National Center for Culturally Responsive Educational Systems (NCCRESt). NCCRESt was a federally funded TA project designed to support local and state educational agencies as they learned to respond to the educational needs of students from a variety of cultural and linguistic backgrounds. The National Academy of Sciences' (NAS) report on *Minority Students in Special and Gifted Education* (2002) and the *20th Annual Report to Congress* provided evidence of the overrepresentation of minority students in special education. Of particular concern was (and is) the continued overrepresentation of students from African American and Native American backgrounds in particular disability categories. Both reports provided similar data on disproportionate over- or under-representation for Hispanics and for Asians and Pacific Islanders. The NAS report indicated a wide variation among states and notable inconsistencies within states. NCCRESt was designed to (1) increase the use of prevention and early intervention strategies; (2) improve the contexts for educational systems improvement; and (3) enhance the teaching and learning of practitioners and students alike. All three of these outcomes rested in large part on the center's ability to influence professional development agendas to embed cultural responsivity within the context of all teacher professional development agendas.

Remediating Understandings of the Problem: Tool Designs for Change

NCCRESt's responsibility was to engage the attention, learning, and subsequent action of all 50 states and the 10 U.S. territories. We began by designing tools that would mediate in new ways, that is, remediate personnel's understandings of the problem. We used available evidence on the problem to represent it in ways that would honor the complexity of educators' work at the intersections of policy, research, and practice (Engeström, 1999). We reasoned that by gathering, organizing, and engaging state and territory state department of education teams in examining their own data around disproportionality, traditional binary explanations of the problem that blame either students and their families or systems would be disrupted. Using GIS mapping technologies, we were able to create and sustain a data base, available on the web, so that educators, family members, students, and interested community members could learn about their state's status, compare their state to the progress of others, and move analyses from state-level data to local school districts patterns. These new tools also infused attention to time and space as they called attention to changes in the problem over time and the visual representations of the problem showed the changing topography of racial disproportionality across states and areas of cities.

We built these maps to engage the attention of state-level decision makers so that they could both understand the extent of the issue within their state and to begin to anticipate, predict, and explore the concept of disproportionality that was, at that time, relatively under the radar screen for many key education leaders. Once the Individuals with Disabilities Act of 2004 was passed and regulations were forthcoming, states began to respond to the requirements of the law. This meant that while the data were compelling, it was the policy that required compliance and monitoring that produced action. By anticipating the need for information, introducing the tools for understanding early and in new ways, and then linking the tools to responses for addressing compliance and monitoring, we were able to disrupt the traditional object of TA. And, in the development of other tools, we were able to disrupt and subsequently shift the nature of activity around disproportionality.

Rubric development for LEA monitoring and problem solving. IDEA 2004 required states to identify local education agencies (e.g., school districts or school systems) that had patterns of disproportionality. If the agency's pattern of disproportionality was the result of inappropriate identification of students from ethnic and racial minorities, the law required districtsto shift their state allocations of special education funds to general education in order to improve the quality of general education environments and supports. Because budgets at the local level are heavily invested in staff who, because of their funding sources,are required to work almost exclusively with identified special education students, shifting budgets from one category to another had profound implications for local staffing patterns. This provision in the law heightened local concern about the implementation of this aspect of the law. It also took control of local organizational patterns away from local decision makers. State department personnel who found instances of disproportionality could face the combined political wrath of school boards, educational leaders, and families who may want to maintain current practices. Therefore, the process used to determine the causes of disproportionality could send important messages about the nature of the relationship between the state and local districts. And the potential for power struggles also meant that districts and states might forget the primary intent of the law was to examine practices that may be leading to disproportionality in special education.

Our response was to design a tool that engaged local leaders and practitioners in an examination of their local policies, practices, and outcomes to help them link structural and practice decisions to the outcomes of interest. Four critical elements were embedded with the tool:(a) sanction of the process and the participants by the superintendent; (b) the use of artifact analysis to examine policy and policy implementation; (c) the use of rubrics to benchmark practice against evidence-based design; and (d) the participation of students and families in the process of analysis as well as professionals. Each element of the rubric was annotated to sections of the IDEA '04 law; each cell of the rubric described a level of performance that was distinct and described in some detail so that users could score their own performance with inter-rater reliability. The tool was embraced by state departments since it allowed local ownership over the process of analysis and preferred by local school districts over other external review processes because it gave the districts responsibility for understanding the impact of their own context in assessing their practice. In all, 30 out of 50 states adopted versions of this tool to examine findings of disproportionality at the local level.

Design of Practitioner Briefs. We created another mediating structure through the design and dissemination of booklets that had three components:(a) a problem space that reflected the everyday dilemmas that practitioners face that are related to how culture, power, and privilege are negotiated in districts, schools and classrooms; (b) an expansion of the historical and current understanding of issues and conundrums; and (c) some principles for examining and changing practice given the understanding. The design of these briefs was consistent across publications, not only to engage readers in the content of each brief but to offer a way of considering problem spaces and responses that expanded the local agency of the actors (in this case, practitioners). These briefs were downloadable on line as well as available in print.

Downloadable Leadership Academies. We also designed and created a set of downloadable professional learning materials that offered deeper experiences in learning and engaging in groups around topics that were similar to the practitioner briefs. Anyone—parent, student, teacher, principal, or other educational player—was able to access a printed manual that introduced a set of principles for learning in community, explained how learning in these academies was designed, and then described,PowerPoint slide by slide, activity by activity, a sequenced, layered set of learning activities, readings, and other materials for group-based professional learning. Each academy was comprised of three, three-hour learning events. All the materials needed to orchestrate such an activity were available on line.

Through the revisualization of data from local schools and districts, a rubric that guided self-examination of district-level practices, aligned professional readings developed specifically for this topic, and a set of group-learning activities, the project interrupted the most common interpretation of disproportionality: the process of identifying students for special education is flawed. This conventional wisdom was replaced with a more complex, nuanced understanding of how culture mediates the ways in which schooling environments sort and categorize students for a variety of purposes, some of which are not transparent to the individuals participating in the activities.

Disrupting the View from Above: Mediating New Objects in Educational Change

Throughout the history of TA at the state department level, the object of this work has relied on a view from above that often focuses attention and effort on the most vulnerable parts of systems that are perceived to have the fewest short-term political casualties. For instance, if state accountability systems produce results that show relatively poor student performance in some districts but not others, states have several options: (a) districts may be required to make changes in their policies, (b) state guidelines may be changed to lower thresholds for poor performance, (c) states may offer TA, or (d) they may require involvement in specific kinds of remedial activity. Selecting any one or a combination of these options, or creating others will be driven by what may yield changes in the data as well as the degree to which some kind of push back from the districts to the state may occur. This is in part due to limited resources, but also because state departments of education, as state bureaucracies, see human activities from a macro scale, based on the prevailing political view within the government regarding the state's regulatory and institutional missions. Our challenge, therefore, was to shift state department personnel's objects of activity from compliance to learning as the default. The new tools for understanding the problem, therefore, must afford opportunities to make connections between technical, situated, and critical factors that undergirded disproportionality. We did this by helping users to raise questions or advance theories about the problem that would require unveiling the ideological and semiotic underpinnings of education professionals' work at the local level. In other words, the tools were designed to encourage state department teams to reframe their object of activity from a view from above that was predominantly concerned with identifying disturbances and problems at the broadest level to linking a macro perspective with local practices, resources, and needs.

For example, the disability prevalence data represented the ways in which special education has conceptualized disability as deficiencies that exist within individuals. Nevertheless, risk and protective factors are nested within the cultural histories of communities, individuals' psychosocial development, and neighborhood ecologies, producing very different outcomes for children who grow up in *similar* but not the *same* circumstances (Anthony, 2008). To understand what the disproportionality data mean, SEA professionals needed to engage in interpretive processes to understand the meaning behind the numbers so that they could make sense of competing understandings of educational problems that are translated into inadequate explanations and solutions in dominant narratives of educational reform (Klingner et al., 2005). Conceptually, these explanations tend to be framed from a risk perspective; attention to assets, cultural resources, and protective processes is virtually nonexistent. As a result, state responses to the data on disproportionality have focused on psychological (i.e., give new skills to students) rather than socio-cultural solutions that offer the possibility of understanding the sociological, political, and cultural contexts that undergird disproportionality (e.g., limited opportunity to learn due to funding disparities, lower curricular quality, underprepared teaching force).

The tools designed to remediate understandings of the problem deliberately did not reveal the interactive dimension (and its attendant sets of assumptions) in which school cultural practices produced various placement patterns in special education at the local level. For instance, the southeastern part of the U.S. had a much higher probability of having states that over-identified their Black population with possessing intellectual disabilities, while the north, central, and northwestern states were more likely to identify Black students disproportionately in the special education category of emotional disturbance. Placement patterns at national, regional, state, and city levels allowed users to witness the metamorphosis of disproportionality across levels and shifted their analytic gaze from the view from above to local landscapes around a city. Hence, the new tools introduced disruptions in the staff's "common sense" and stimulated the creation of a new object that consistently raised questions about local practices to make sense of the problem.

Forging New Spaces for Praxis

The new tools presented evidence that afforded new objects of activity, and thus new understandings of the problem. However, the tools only embodied the *potential* for such outcomes. We still needed to create social spaces in which the tools would be used productively and where particular practices mediated people's engagements with the tools. In other words, our tools created new perceptual fields with visual representations that illustrate how spatial information along with discourse analysis offered the possibility of developing new knowledge (Paulston, 1997).

The design of two kinds of social spaces was instrumental in our work. First, we designed social spaces for labor-intensive meetings led by our staff with state Department of Education personnel. Second, we designed learning networks among states. These two strategies allowed us to infuse explicitly an introspective dimension through activities that promoted a "double move" (Hedegaard, 1998), in which participation structures compelled involved personnel to shift from personal/professional experiences to theoretical sense-making, based on a new vocabulary offered in these meetings. Simultaneously, the everyday experiences of the personnel offered a way into sense-making that was grounded in local state department problem spaces. These two processes constituted the double move in which both the TA staff and the government personnel engage in understanding the target problem. The TA staff created a platform for understanding while the government personnel brought their everyday conundrums into the space. For instance, a phone call from a mother requesting assistance because someone wants to label her son begins to be mediated by helping to identify the problem space (i.e., the object), as ways of engaging families and the schools that serve them. Shifting problematizing to engagement helps the participants begin to learn more about how they systematically categorize and organize their students in order to accomplish their own schooling tasks rather than how they organize their work to support their students. Central in this work is exposing the nature of assumptions about the roles that schools take on and their public purposes, as well as the identities that are conferred to those that hold the roles. Part of the TA work is to reveal through dialogue how these perceived identities as well as prescribed roles interact to afford certain kinds of responses to the phone while constraining others.

Another key assumption that informed our practices was that educators' professional learning is promoted through the use of data-driven and research-grounded content within the context of educators' practice-embedded activities (King, Artiles, & Kozleski, 2009). Thus, these social spaces were grounded in personnel's professional practices and evidence collected by the system in which they worked. Moreover, in response to a critique by Nutley, Walter, & Davis, (2003) of the use of research in policy and practice, we suggest that research methodologies need to transcend linear views of knowledge work in which researchers labor in specific contexts to produce knowledge that is transported into other settings. Instead, our approach provides action processes for the design, modeling, and development of research as practice. For this purpose, we followed cycles of inquiry, reflection, and action with state department teams.

Cycles of Inquiry, Reflection, and Action

We engaged state teams in activities that helped them to define the problem by looking at data through the geographic display of data across states. These geographic representations helped teams understand that issues arise in specific contexts and not in others. By locating data geographically, the nature of conversation changed from generalization to localization. It helped teams to examine context and pushed them closer to examining the critical features of power and privilege that played out in specific ways, depending on the local venue. This discussion helped to deepen the conversation, allowed the TA team to connect research to newly emerging topics and questions, and complicated the conversation so that the rush to solution was slowed and the need to understand was surfaced. This shift to understanding was key to being able to move to a critical feature of our joint inquiry. Rather than moving into brainstorming solutions, we asked participants to identify features of what good solutions might look like. This allowed us to pursue discussions around *good for whom* and *for what outcomes*. Of all our strategies for changing the trajectory of addressing seemingly intractable issues like disproportionality, this approach seemed to resonate most strongly across all states. Participants wanted to solve problems, so they stumbled as they stopped to consider what features of good solutions might entail. Once participants identified these, they were able to engage in identifying specific strategies to move forward, the need for further information, the identification of key leaders to advance the work, and a set of indicators to benchmark progress over time.

Implementing and Assessing Change: Complex Responses to Complex Problems

Connections between state teams were created when we solicited applications from every state to participate in a more intensive collaborative inquiry effort. Out of 15 applications, nine states were chosen to participate in a set of intensive meetings, frequent coaching calls, on-site technical assistance visits, more complete data collection, and work in interdisciplinary teams. Almost from the first hour that the teams assembled together for the first meeting, bonding across teams occurred. Teams wanted to know about each other's data, systems, political pressures, fiscal constraints, and models of understanding disproportionality. Our task was to help support their questioning, data gathering, and the ways in which they gauged the impact of their systems change efforts on equity outcomes (Nasir, Rosebery, Warren, & Lee, 2006). Further, teams learned to collect multiple kinds of data that helped them to understand what, why, when, how much, and how disproportionality seems to develop locally. Together, they began to develop feedback loops that traced their initial assumptions about what was needed locally, their efforts to implement, and the results of those efforts on changing patterns of performance locally.

Summary

As a methodology, the design and use of transformative mediating structures to engage networks of individuals in situating their practices in complex, refracted contexts, using data to visualize the flow and distribution of patterns of performance, and then focusing solution efforts on considering the critical features of solutions, helped teams to center their own work on learning through their practice. Inquiry as a way of doing the everyday work of state and local education systems transformed the nature of relationships within and across state and local teams. This is an under-theorized approach to scholarship that offers an important opportunity to reconceptualize the worlds of research and practice. By embedding our work in a cultural historical activity theory perspective (Engeström, 1999), we foreground the importance of the everyday activities that state education personnel conduct and the ways that these activities are mediated by the cultural artifacts of bureaucracies and the ways in which these activities and artifacts have unintended as well as intended outcomes (Cole, 1996). The importance of this theorized view of what TA is and how it can be a developmental learning process is critical to remediating how TA recipients and providers understand their roles and describe outcomes that reflect the dynamic environment of learning and schooling.

References

Anyon, J. (2005). *Radical possibilities: Public policy, urban education, and a new social movement.* New York, NY: Routledge.

Artiles, A. J., & Dyson, A. (2005). Inclusive education in the globalization age: The promise of comparative cultural historical analysis. In D. Mitchell (Ed.), *Contextualizing inclusive education* (pp. 37–62). London, England: Routledge.

Artiles, A. J.,& Kozleski, E. B. (2010). What counts as response and intervention in RTI? A sociocultural analysis. *Psicothema, 22,* 949–954.

Cobb, P., & McClain, K. (2006). The collective mediation of a high-stakes accountability program: Communities and networks of practice. *Mind, Culture, and Activity, 13,* 80–100.

Cole, M. (1996).*Cultural psychology: A once and future discipline.* Cambridge, MA: Harvard University Press.

Cole, M. (2010).What's culture got to do with it? Educational research as a necessarily interdisciplinary enterprise. *Educational Researcher, 39,* 461–470.

Engeström, Y. (1999). Expansive visibilization of work: An activity-theoretical perspective. *Computer Supported Cooperative Work, 8,* 63–99.

Ferguson, D. L., Kozleski, E. B., & Smith, A. (2003). Transformed, inclusive schools: A framework to guide fundamental change in urban schools. *Effective Education for Learners with Exceptionalities, 15,* 43–74.

Fullan, M. (2008). *Secrets of change: What the best leaders do to help their organizations survive and thrive.* San Francisco, CA: Jossey-Bass.

Gallego, M.A., Cole, M., & the Laboratory of Comparative Human Cognition (LCHC). (2001). Classroom cultures and cultures in the classroom. In V. Richardson (Ed.), *Handbook of research on teaching* (pp. 951–997). Washington, DC: American Educational Research Association.

Gutierrez, K. D., & Vossoughi, S. (2010). Lifting off the ground to return anew: Mediated praxis, transformative learning, and social design experiments. *Journal of Teacher Education, 61,* 100–117.

Haycock, K. (2001). Closing the achievement gap. *Educational Leadership, 58,* 6–11.

Hedegaard, M. (1998). Situated learning and cognition: Theoretical learning and cognition. *Mind, Culture, and Society, 5,* 114–126.

Individuals with Disabilities Education Act, 20 U.S.C. §1400 *et seq.* (2004).

King, K., Artiles, A. J., & Kozleski, E. B. (2009). *Professional learning for culturally responsive teaching (*NCCRESt Practitioner Brief Series). Tempe, AZ: NCCRESt

Klingner, J., Artiles, A., Kozleski, E. B., Utley, C., Zion, S., Tate, W., & Riley, D. (2005). Conceptual framework for addressing the disproportionate representation of culturally and linguistically diverse students in special education. *Educational Policy Analysis Archives, 13*(38). Retrieved September 9, 2005, from http://epaa.asu.edu/epaa/v13n38/

Kozleski, E. B. (2004). Technology transfer and the field of education: The research to practice conundrum. *Technology Transfer and Society, 2,* 176–194.

Kozleski, E. B., & Smith, A. (2009). The role of policy and systems change in creating equity for students with disabilities in urban schools. *Urban Education, 44,* 427–451.

Lektorsky, V. A. (2009). Mediation as a means of collective activity. In A. Sannino, H. Daniels, & K. D. Gutierrez (Eds.), *Learning and expanding with activity theory.* New York, NY: Cambridge University Press.

Ladson-Billings, G., & Tate, W. F. (1995). Toward a crucial race theory of education. *Teachers College Record, 97*(1), 47–68.

McInerney, M.,& Hamilton, J. (2007). Elementary and middle schools technical assistance center: An approach to support the effective implementation of scientifically based practices in special education. *Exceptional Children, 73,* 242–255.

Nasir, N. S., Rosebery, A. S., Warren, B., & Lee, C. D. (2006). Learning as a cultural process: Achieving equity through diversity. In R. K. Sawyer (Ed.), *The Cambridge handbook of the learning sciences* (pp. 489–504). New York, NY: Cambridge University Press.

National Center for Education Statistics. (2009). Retrieved January 16, 2011, from http://nces.ed.gov/nationsreportcard/naepdata/report.aspx

National Council of State Legislators. (2010). State legislators develop policy guidelines for federal role in education [Press release]. Retrieved November 12, 2010, from http://www.ncsl.org/default.aspx?tabid=19669

NCCRESt (2008). http://nccrest.eddata.net/maps/index.php?col=RACE_RRW& group=American%2520Indian%252FAlaskan%2520Native& f1=2006–2007& f3=HIGH+INCIDENCE+DISABILITIES+%28ED%2BLD%2BMR%29

Nutley, S., Walter, I., & Davies, H. (2003). From knowing to doing: A framework for understanding the evidence-into-practice agenda. *Evaluation, 9,* 125–148.

Paulston, R. G. (1997). Mapping visual culture in comparative education discourse. *Compare: A Journal of Comparative Education, 27,* 117–153.

Patton, M. Q. (2011). *Developmental evaluation: Applying complexity concepts to enhance innovation and use.* New York, NY: Guilford Press.

Sawyer, R. K. (2005). The new science of learning. In R. K. Sawyer (Ed.), *The Cambridge handbook of the learning sciences* (pp. 1–16). New York, NY: Cambridge University Press.

Sieveke-Pearson, S. J. (2004). Exploring relationships between professional development and student achievement (Doctoral dissertation). Retrieved from Dissertations and Theses database. (UMI No. 3138721).

Snyder, T., & Dillow, S. (2010). *Digest of educational statistics.* Washington, DC: National Center for Educational Statistics.

Trohanis, P. L. (1982). Technical assistance and the improvement of services to exceptional children. *Theory into Practice, 21,* 119–128.

US Department of Education. (n.d.). Overview: Budget history tables. Retrieved May 12, 2010, from http://www2.ed.gov/about/overview/budget/history/index.html

Van Manen, M. (1990). *Research lived experience: Human science for an action sensitive pedagogy.* Albany: State University of New York Press.

Warikoo, N., & Carter, P. (2009). Cultural explanations for racial and ethnic stratification in academic achievement: A call for a new and improved theory. *Review of Educational Research, 79,* 366–394.

CHAPTER TWENTY-NINE

Teaching in England: December 2010

Victoria Perselli

I n the action research project that I am currently undertaking on my practice as a teacher of educational research with students on doctoral and master's programmes, three conceptual tools have emerged which are useful towards the cyclical process of further thinking, reflection and action. They are *undecidablity*, *indeterminateness* and a *discourse of workload*. I will presently explain what these mean and how they have come to the fore, but firstly I will offer some contextualisation that I hope illustrates the interplay between the action research methodology and critical pedagogy and why this is particularly significant at this time.

A concern that is central to my daily work is *how to be in pedagogic relations* with my students, who are typically young and/or "mid-career" professionals from a diverse range of disciplinary backgrounds, the common denominator being that they are all have some form of educative role in their professional practice. My students include teachers and managers in schools, colleges or universities; teacher-practitioners in health settings such as radiography, physiotherapy, pharmacology, midwifery and nursing; also psychology, criminology, business and English language teaching. In their research projects students accordingly use a broad range of research methodologies and forms of representation; for example, action research (Reason & Bradbury, 2009), self-study (Struthers, 2010; Alderton, 2008), bricolage (Nah, 2011; in preparation; Kincheloe, 2004; Denzin & Lincoln, 2000, pp. 3–28), critical discourse analysis (Betzel, 2009; Fairclough, 1989), visual ethnography (Bedson, 2010; Pink, 2007; Dewdney et al., 1994). My greatest aspiration for my students is that they come to find deeper meaning and pleasure in their work through their master's and doctoral studies, and that they continue to research their practice following these accredited programmes. To this end, I am interested to understand what the various *lexicons* of our professional practices may be (Perselli, in press) and, significantly for this text, how we come to be more effectively engaged, emotionally and politically, in what it is we do.

This is a standpoint and value position regarding my role as a research supervisor and teacher that I have only arrived at through a long period of (postdoctoral) turmoil and struggle, and is by no means uncontestable or static. It does, however, provide something of a philosophical yardstick by which I can evaluate my work; for instance, in terms of how useful I am to my students towards the identification and realisation of their research projects, and to what extent they become active participants in research communities beyond those that are established as part of their studies. It also serves to alert me when things might be going wrong. My value position is relevant in this chapter not least because of its emphasis on diverse forms of knowledge and rationality (Oakley, 2000); that is to say, there is no innate contest in my mind between our physical, material presence in the world and the spaces of the head, heart and spirit. In practical terms this is manifest as the interplay between theory in the literature and theorising from practice, for example—as I hope my three conceptual tools will illustrate later.

Action research as an umbrella methodology not only accommodates both these forms of theory but also provides uncensored opportunities, methodologically speaking, for broad and deep readings of the world from sensory experience and the affective domain; a major challenge being—as so often happens in the context of formal accreditation, "generic" assessment criteria and so forth—how to represent this in words. To this end there is arguably nothing to prevent the researcher employing diverse media: performance or visual arts, the techniques of allegory or metaphor, or at least verbal references to artistic work in the public domain that may symbolically represent what straightforward description or "Cartesian" argumentation cannot (Perselli, 2005b, pp. 163–182; 2004, pp. 183–199). For these kinds of reasons, action research has possibilities that cohere with the other pluralisms that describe my values in relation to my practice specifically. (The "specifically" is important, since in saying this I do not wish to stake any particular claim regarding the so-called "paradigm wars" (Hammersley, 1992) or the larger debate about value and worth in educational research (Oancea, 2005, pp. 157–183; Pring, 2000), other than to restate the obvious—that action research, like any other method, can be done badly and it can be done well.)

From experience in the field it sometimes surprises me that even mainstream classroom teachers who are usually so adept in the fields of art and artistry get a bit stymied in their first (re)encounter with academia. Initial project ideas and draft texts vary immensely in style, content and texture—all my students are coming from such very different places and prior experiences—but rarely would they consider the visual or the concrete object as a starting point or stimulus for discussion without considerable encouragement in our classes. Yet criticality—another significant dimension of action research that aligns directly with being *in the political*—is something I would prefer to introduce informally at first, via illustrations from practice: anecdotes, photos, stories, policy documents, mission statements, items of news; in sum, concrete objects or "artefacts", and their significance for the contributor, around which questions can then be posed. These are both "objects that talk back to us" (Lather, in a personal communication, 2007) and symbols of our life world (*Lebenswelt*) that help to establish and maintain a sense of connection and fidelity to that life world. They are also means of generating different epistemologies of knowledge from those which come from verbal text or "traditional" academic writing.

I had an indelible experience of this during my own PhD research. I was working as a co-ordinator for special educational needs in a mainstream nursery and infant school (that is, children aged 2–7 years). My investigation was into the inclusion in the mainstream of children with learning disabilities such as autism and Down syndrome, as well as children with behavioural and learning difficulties. In preparation for the opening of a new school building, I had mounted a photographic display showing the daily activities of our pupils, their teachers, assistants and specialist teachers. I covered what I thought was a comprehensive range of places and people across the school, and I think I am right in saying that this was the first time photographic material had been used in quite this way. I was very satisfied with this work, which was in effect a visual representation of the action research. But on the night of the opening ceremony, as the guests were admiring my gorgeous pictures, an astute visitor said, "This is all very nice, Victoria, but why are there no men in your display?" This knocked me sideways because, two years into the project and following in-depth exploration of gender in the context of the children and their learning—including issues of "voice" and "representation"—I had omitted at any point to reflect on the significances, various, of being a predominantly female-populated staff. Neither had I considered how awkward I might feel about taking pictures of our two male colleagues (not atypically, the school keeper and the head teacher), or even requesting their permission to do so. Why was that exactly? Besides which and, more importantly, where were all the dads…?

The point here is methodological as well as epistemological, and in both instances concerned with *noticing*. That is, over-reliance on the spoken and written text sometimes prevents us from recognising something that may be in front of our very eyes. Secondly, that much of who we are and where we are coming from professionally is so deeply internalised that we ourselves cannot see it (the feminisation of infant education, for example). It necessitates the direct intervention of another critical or triangulatory commentator to enact the process which is routine procedure for ethnographers and anthropologists, of "making the familiar strange", in this case directly facilitated by the pictures.

I later reflected on the issue of noticing in a poem. Here I am contrasting that which appears to be perfect (but subtly off-balance) with that which is flawed, that releases us from this particular tyranny:

Cruelty
Once you had a vision of perfection,
of fame and fortune, brilliance and beauty,
and you thought
I could live there.
I could live there forever.
Then you saw something—
what was it exactly:
    a cracked cup
    a hurt paw
    a *wrong chromosome*?
What did you notice,
up there in the top left hand corner;
that made you retract—
    dissemble—
preferring your own imperfect poetry?
(Reproduced in Perselli, 2011)

The "cracked cup" is actually a reference to the character of Madame Merle in Henry James' *Portrait of a Lady*, someone who was magnificent but also corrupt; a symbol for James of "old" Europe in contrast with the wholesome ingenuousness of the New World, embodied by James' protagonist, Isabel Archer. The hurt paw, on the other hand, represents a simple vernacular statement: cruelty or neglect towards animals. Taken literally, both the cracked cup and the hurt paw are suggestive of minor and almost imperceptible violence "behind the scenes"; in the midst of otherwise "perfect" domesticity, perhaps? The wrong chromosome, in italics, represents quite another way of seeing; that of the scientist identifying something "abnormal" through the microscope. It symbolises, for example, the cruelty of nature in disability, a hand of cards shockingly dealt to some of the families in my study, above. But this is complicated, because that which is "flawed" in nature may also be essential to our humanity. Besides which, to love and to be among children with disabilities is often experienced as a gift and a revelation: that which is "perfect" in nature does not tell us anything practical about how to be in communion with difference.

The poem/riddle is doubly about noticing, since it involves two characters: one apparently making an observation of the other's sudden discomfort and subsequent rejection of the object of desire and a curiosity to know more. There is no dialogue; the questioner merely provides us with a picture of someone gazing into (a picture of) their own experience, followed by a question: "What did you notice, up there in the top left-hand corner?"

In this poem I was also harking back to W. H. Auden's *Musée des Beaux Arts*—a reflection on a painting, *The Fall of Icarus*, by Pieter Bruegel: "About suffering they were never wrong, The Old Masters", in which Auden evokes the casual ordinariness of suffering that is unwitnessed amid the preoccupations of everyday life. My poem intimates that where there is cruelty, there will be suffering: a hail to the power of observation and the special rationality of intuition—something teachers tend to have in spades, at least when our creative faculties are not overwhelmed with busywork and "stuff to do" ("waving or drowning"?). (See also Hannah Arendt (1994) on "the banality of evil".)

Nowadays what I get from this work is a moral maxim; something along the lines of "all that glitters is not gold", operating performatively as an antidote to unattainable desire, which in postmodernity is quite likely to take the form of "role models", "celebrity status", environmental damage or corrupt and inflated political power, as much as worldly goods or people who exhibit unearned authority. Which in turn is quite amusing: "what goes up must come down" if/when we persist in flying too close to the sun. Hence Icarus' ridiculous little legs sticking out of the sea in Bruegel's painting.

Methodologically, my poem serves to remind me that what we see in terms of surface features is never the whole story. There is always more; for which we—feminist methodologists like myself—have two old geezers, Freud and Marx, to thank, along with Bruegel, James, Auden, and so on and so on. The final line, "Preferring your own imperfect poetry" is a reiteration of beauty in imperfection and the liberatory feeling of "going your own way" (as a woman, not least); albeit rereading the poem today that strikes a rather lonely, modernist chord.

The point of observing the world is to change it, Marx said, and this is a central tenet of action research: change through intervention, which is truly the methodology of the common woman and man, yet which, like a good riddle, can be as simple or complex as you want it to be. (See McNamara, Hustler, Stronach, & Rodrigo, 2000, for a particularly sophisticated example of action research in application.) Artists, it could be argued, are not under the same obligation to make their meanings clear as are educational action researchers, but my point remains that *art as method* can be a powerful and penetrating tool for thinking, observation, action and representation: as a moral compass, a humorous aside, an expression of impasse or hopelessness, quitting, closure, passion or joy, *dissident scholarship*, a conundrum of practice expressed as a riddle.

Action research projects, unlike great or lesser works of art, are intrinsically flawed and messy and are concerned with the processes of articulating and working through this very messiness ("reflexivity"). They take place amongst the chaos and complexity of everyday life, which is perhaps why finding a focus and starting point for a new project can be so challenging. Until we "see" the necessity to query what is taken for granted, we are not yet thinking politically (that is, of the wider populace) or critically (of self, of systems). Change will be at the mundane level of a problem to fix via rather benign "craft knowledge", or as a technical rational solution to a perceived deficit, often expressed in terms of moral panics and policy hysteria (Stronach & MacLure, 1997, pp. 90, 150); the larger status quo, meanwhile, remaining comfortably undisturbed. Action research at this level has the tendency to be appropriated to instrumental means-ends objectives that make few intellectual demands of the practitioner, so very little can be learned from the exercise on the part of its audience. Furthermore, given that most research projects in professional practice are small scale, specific and non-generalisable in terms of their discrete *findings*, there is all the more reason to speak out in powerfully dialogic terms regarding the signifcance of the research question, if the work is to be valued for its wider relevance.

Yet the "mundane" is as good a place as any to begin. Concrete objects, a story, a picture, a joke; artefacts of professional practice such as policy documents, schoolwork, business plans, mission statements, evaluation feedback, can facilitate a range of questions and observations *in the dialogic*. Like my

PhD experience above, these will include the unexpected, left-field remark that enables the learner-researcher to begin to unpack, problematise and politicise aspects of the lived experience of the practice, not least because they will be coming from folk with very different perspectives from oneself.

A great benefit of the cohorts of students I work with is our collective and wide-ranging professional experience and cultural diversity, since it illustrates in lively and often contentious ways the issue that everyone will need to grapple with in devising their research project, which is education's *undecidability*, that is, its lack of easily discernable consequences. This has become a significant conceptual tool when thinking about my role as facilitator/supervisor/tutor in relation to what my students need to know in order to come to terms with what may be unfamiliar premises regarding research *in* (rather than on) education. Not least among these is the realisation of education's perennial vulnerability and permeability when mapped to the huge expectations held by society—often further manipulated by press and politicians—regarding what education can "deliver" (Bernstein, 1970); its *impact*, to use present-day policy-speak.

In the past the permeability of education's boundaries, in combination with its lack of traditions or disciplinary status (as compared with, say, medicine, history or law), can be illustrated—at least for the purposes of this chapter and using broad historical brush-strokes—via its general subservience, firstly to religion, then science (in the late 19th to early 20th century, psychometrics and the "medical model") and in the present era of mass communications and technological advance, political ideology. In postmodernity, ideology (I am using this in Marx's sense of "false ideas" about society; Allman, 2001; Small, 2005; Marx & Engels, 1976) is shot through the disciplinary/non-disciplinary field of education (Bilager, 2010); which is frequently referred to as a battleground, with its attendant masculinist metaphors of contestation, occupation and war. Therefore positioning oneself mid-field in this very unstable and interpenetrable territory for the first time—that is, being challenged to defend an opinion and hold a perspective—can be paradigmatically challenging for everyone, but especially so for folks schooled into methodological objectivity and neutrality.

Whilst I do love a good argument or fair fight, I also regret the "battleground" terminology and form of words. My temperament and gender incline me to think of education as a body (politic), with bones, blood, organs and tissues; involuntary muscles, leaky orifices and permeable membranes; free radicals, great ideas and sometimes uncontrollable emotions. When you cut us, sure enough, we bleed. The hurt factor in education should never be underestimated. However, I do not think this Mars/Venus, battleground/body duality particularly helpful just now. For me the urgent difficulty facing education is less about the usual antagonisms and inequalities (on which ideology flourishes) than about education and *commodification*—a specific form of ideology (Harvey, 2005, 2010a) towards which educators committed to critical pedagogy should constitute a unified objection.

I perceive undecidability to be a saving grace for education in this respect, inviting an ongoing dialogic of its value and worth, quality and usefulness. Education, on this view, refuses to stay put, whether as a metaphor or as a thing (Allman, 2001, pp. 37, 49). Attempts to objectify and quantify knowledge, whereby education—like the arts in fascist regimes—forms the conduit (body? territory?) to compliance and political docility, cannot possibly endure in a field where nobody really knows what success claims look like or what their measurement criteria may be. Rapid, serial oscillations among policy makers, politicians and educators wedded to the search for such positivistic ideals have created chaos for those of us who diligently attempt to follow through imposed projects founded on assumptions of quantifiable objectives and outcomes—but with no tangible sense of when these outcomes will arrive. Even where claims to attainment have been made in their own terms, such projects have produced other negative consequences. Generic, transferable skills for industry, unitary methodologies in the teaching of reading and "back to basics" curricula in mainstream schools—to mention three distinct preoccupations that have dominated education in the UK during my adult lifetime—have also been the attributed causes of boredom and disillusionment in learners and teachers, shallowness of understanding and an unhealthy, unfit population. The road to hell is paved with good intentions and doing the "right thing" may not always be the right thing to do.… Education's interpenetrability and its deeply imbricated relationship with larger society, together with—importantly for this text—our collective self-awareness and understanding of this as public intellectuals, ensures that the taming of education for the purposes of social manipulation (neoliberalisation, in this instance) will not work in the long run, any more than it has done in the past.

The implications here are manifold: everyone at some significant or sustained period of their life has experience of education, which means that everyone has an opinion to express or story to tell, especially those of us who are at the centre of this process in terms of our emotional, mental and physical labour (Colley, 2003). But centrality to the act of public education does not signify ultimate authority or supremacy either; left-field observations, above, are valued precisely because they come from outside our comfort zone and habitual way of thinking, and this is true also, I believe, for education writ large. The imbrication of education with society and the expectations to and fro, including significant present-day problematics such as accessibility, accountability and governance, suggest that education, like all other public bodies, must not be entirely self-regulating, any more than our understandings of self and others can be ahistorical or apolitical, our methodologies insular or narcissistic.

However, in the UK there now appears to be a distinct problem of balance, since education and larger society are so utterly dominated by business, in the form of neoliberal values and interests (Harvey, 2005), that the body/territory of education conveys only an enfeebled sense of self-regulation. What we have instead is the neutering of education through totalising systems and disciplinary forces: an "hegemony" in Marx's terms (Marx in Small, 2005, p: 181; Gramsci, 1971).

This can be simply illustrated in the current constitution of the British government, where approximately 60 non-elected captains of industry and chief executive officers (CEOs) are being appointed to Whitehall as non-executive directors of each department, headed up by Lord Browne of Madingley. Lord Browne is the former CEO of British Petroleum (BP). He resigned from that company in 2007 in "controversial circumstances" (Pickard, 2010; Rigby & Barker, 2010; Web, 2010). BP meanwhile has been responsible for a number of environmental disasters, notably in Alaska and most recently in the Gulf of Mexico, largely attributed to cost-cutting measures. Lord Browne now holds responsibility for advising government on the total financial reorganisation of higher education in England, via his "independent"—and by no means apolitical—inquiry: *Securing a Sustainable Future for Higher Education* (Browne, 2010). Unsurprisingly, bitter disputes of power and control have arisen around this policy move that will ensure continued *sufferance* for educators, learners and teachers for months to come. Expectations regarding education as a dynamic for change and continuity *in relations with* larger society surely requires that higher education be handled with insight, wisdom and astuteness regarding its future, yet it is difficult to see how Lord Browne qualifies for the task.

Until we (teachers, learners, educators) engage with wider debate of this kind it is hard to resist differentiating and internalising our experiences of education as serially insurmountable problems and difficulties; an ideology of education, in sum, for which we should feel somehow individually responsible and accountable. Our inherent ontological insecurity and the undecidability characteristic of our field, rather than being embraced as a creative space for questioning, "blue skies" dreaming and indeed robust power struggle, becomes a place of terror and intellectual paralysis (Davies, 2005). This is compounded by what I now propose as a *discourse of workload*—the second conceptual tool of my action research—that has arisen among practitioners in educative roles in recent times.

Discourse of workload (perceived and actual) is particularly dangerous in that it threatens to overwhelm the pedagogic, curricular and value-related concerns and interests that might otherwise constitute the heartland of practice. Unlike undecidability, which I have characterised as historical as well as contemporary, this discourse and its related, third conceptual tool, *indeterminateness* (of role boundaries, professional expectations, of life energy devoted to work), are a more localised modern/postmodern phenomenon, as I am operationalizing them here. They arise largely via legislative and quasi-legislative bodies, and are enforced through instruments of control such as the OFSTED system of inspection of teaching and the Research Assessment Exercise (latterly, Research Excellence Framework) in higher education. These instruments, alongside a battery of others, ensure that conscientious folk and those with sufficient physical and mental stamina are always kept busy; not just during measurable working hours, but also relentlessly and psychically, an invasion of personhood that can only be described as Foucauldian.

In terms of lived experience, *indeterminateness* and *discourse of workload* manifest primarily as lack of time: for reading, thinking, dialoguing; but also for the kinds of distantiation activities (Perselli, 2005a, pp. 22–33) that enable us to "see the wood for the trees": our criticality and sustained focus on a discrete problematic ("data gathering"), analysis and decision taking around aspects of pedagogy and curricula that we ourselves perceive as significant. I hasten to add that this is by no means experienced in the same way by all the folk around me, and in this chapter I have not sought to represent or differentiate the views of individuals in my action research, here there is only space to summarise. With regard to the argument put forward here, I can only observe that there are substantive differences of personal, economic and professional status within the various cohorts of students and colleagues with whom I work, whereby levels of material ("earned") freedom such as institutional trust and professional autonomy vary immensely (Frowe, 2005).

For all these reasons and very much against the odds, I think it vitally important that my students engage deeply with the literatures—albeit with a sensitised appreciation on my part of how difficult that may be for many of us, most of the time. Which therefore begs the question: which literatures? Here I have revised my thinking considerably in order to arrive at an economy of reading *theory* that has coherence with practitioner methodologies such as action research. I would hope from this that collectively we can gain a sense of the tradition and centrality of practitioner research and its interdependence with critical pedagogy that is not drowned out by the "white noise" of neoliberal forces in education. I am basing this conclusion on the observation I began with: not everyone finds it easy or perceives the relevance of speaking in the first person and articulating a problematic of practice until they feel ontologically comfortable in this modality, and until they come to understand that not to do so may be *unethical* within the paradigm of professional practice.

For a greater sense of ontological security and strength as learners and teachers, I think we should be reading about Marx—if not the man himself—and to this end there are a range of guides and secondary sources that fit the bill, some of which are referenced here. As accompaniment to this, *Pedagogy of the Oppressed* by Freire (1970), Donald Schön's *Reflective Practitioner* (1983) and the works of Lawrence Stenhouse are particularly fit for this purpose. Yet to impose these authors on my classes would be anti-Freirean and probably counterproductive. Instead what I intend to do—the intervention element of my action research— is to more proactively raise consciousness of their significance and relevance (not least to professionals suddenly recast as "learners") than I have done in the past; for example via the contextualising seminars that are provided as part of the induction process to our programmes and in our module guides. There is also an extensive repertoire of projects in professional practice now in the public domain, a few of which I have referenced above, that illustrate, simply or subtly, how theory in the literature emerges and meshes with the consciousness, value positions and activities of their protagonists: a cornucopia of good ideas and educative interventions.

Finally there is of course this piece of writing here, made available for deconstruction and critical appraisal by students of critical qualitative research. For which purpose I have attempted to articulate what I believe to be a significant methodological tradition and present-day political countermove to the commodification of education, from a personal, experiential perspective as a teacher of method and researcher of my practice. It is neither a panacea nor even a canon (Stronach & MacLure, 1997, pp. 150–152), and I am not confident that my operational conceptual tools and appeal to anti-hierarchical interaction with the social realm, through diverse epistemologies of knowledge, will have any impact on the faceless, creeping tendency of neoliberalism. It may be some time before this particular snake consumes its own tail. But in the meanwhile, when my children's children ask me "So what did you do in the war on intellectual terror, Big Mama?", I can at least demonstrate that I made a contribution.

References

Alderton, J. (2008). Exploring self-study to improve my practice as a mathematics teacher educator. *Studying Teacher Education, 4*(2), 95–104.

Allman, P. (2001). *Revolutionary social transformation: Democratic hopes, political possibilities and critical education.* Westport, CT: Bergin & Garvey.

Arendt, H. (1994). *Eichmann in Jerusalem: A report on the banality of evil.* New York: Penguin Books.

Bedson, H. (2010). *Where are they now? Using Facebook and photographs to discover the outcomes of ex-pupils from one specialist BESD setting.* Unpublished MA dissertation, Kingston University, Kingston upon Thames, England.

Bernstein, B. (1970). Education cannot compensate for society. *New Society,* Feb. 26, 1970: 344–347.

Betzel, A. (2009). *English language teaching: Ideology and deconstruction—A critique of ideologies and prevalent beliefs within the ELT profession.* (Unpublished MA dissertation), Kingston University, Kingston upon Thames, England.

Bilager, M. (2010). Education: Academic discipline or field of study? *Research Intelligence, 110,* 22–23.

Browne, J. (2010). *Securing a sustainable future for higher education: An independent review of higher education funding and student finance.* Retrieved from http://www.independent.gov.uk/browne-report

Colley, H. (2003). *Mentoring for social inclusion.* London, England: Routledge.

Davies, B. (2005). The (im)possibility of intellectual work in neoliberal times. *Discourse: Studies in the Cultural Politics of Education, 27*(1), 1–14.

Denzin, N., & Lincoln, Y. (2000). The discipline and practice of qualitative research. In N. Denzin & Y. Lincoln (Eds.), *Handbook of qualitative research* (2nd ed., pp. 3–28). Thousand Oaks, CA: Sage.

Dewdney, A. et al. (1994). *Down but not out: Young people, photography and images of homelessness.* Stoke on Trent, England: Trentham Books.

Fairclough, N. (1989). *Language and power.* Harlow, England: Longman.

Freire, P. (1970). *Pedagogy of the oppressed.* Harmondsworth, England: Penguin.

Frowe, I. (2005). Professional trust. *British Journal of Educational Studies, 53*(3), 34–53.

Gramsci, A. (1971). *Selections from the prison notebooks* (Q. Hoare & G. N. Smith, Ed. & Trans.) New York, NY: International Publishers.

Hammersley, M. (1992). The paradigm wars: Report from the front. *British Journal of Sociology of Education, 13,* 131–143.

Harvey, D. (2005). *A brief history of neoliberalism.* Oxford, England: OUP.

Harvey, D. (2010a). *The enigma of capital and the crises of capitalism.* London, England: Profile Books.

Harvey, D. (2010b). *A companion to Marx's capital.* London, England: Verso.

Kincheloe, J. (2004). *Rigour and complexity in educational research: Conceptualising the bricolage.* London, England: Open University Press.

Marx, K., & Engels, F. (1976). *The German ideology.* Moscow, Russia: Progress Publishers. (Original work published 1846)

McNamara, O., Hustler, D., Stronach, I., & Rodrigo, M. (2000). Room to manoeuvre: Mobilising the "active partner" in home-school relations. *British Educational Research Journal, 26*(4), 473–489.

Nah, G. (2011 in preparation). *Living the discourse of teaching and learning in higher education: The lived experience of participants of the Postgraduate Certificate in Learning and Teaching in the creative arts* (Unpublished doctoral thesis). Kingston University, Kingston upon Thames, England.

Oakley, A. (2000). *Experiments in knowing: Gender and method in the social sciences.* Cambridge, England: Polity Press.

Oancea, A. (2005). Criticisms of educational research: Key topics and levels of analysis. *British Educational Research Journal, 31*(2), 157–183.

Perselli, V. (2004). "A personal preview": or "Portraying my professional life in pictures": Image and performance as methodology for research in teaching and learning. In J. Satterthwaite, E. Atkinson, & W. Martin (Eds.), *Educational countercultures: Confrontations, images, vision* (pp. 183–199). Stoke on Trent, England: Trentham.

Perselli, V. (2005a). Heavy fuel: Memoire, autobiography and narrative. In C. Mitchell, K. O'Reilly-Scanlon, & S. Weber (Eds.), *Just who do we think we are? Methodologies for self-study in education* (pp. 22–33). Abingdon, England: Routledge Falmer.

Perselli, V. (2005b). The Silkscreen Vickies: Identity, images and icons (in the age of the Research Assessment Exercise). In J. Satterthwaite & E. Atkinson (Eds.), *Discourses of education in the age of the new imperialism* (pp. 163–182). Stoke on Trent, England: Trentham.

Perselli, V. (2011). *Painting the police station blue:* The almost impossible argument for poetry in the elite educational journals. *Power and Education, 3*(1), 64–80.

Perselli, V. (in press). A little night reading: Marx, assessment and the professional doctorate in education. In P. E. Jones (Ed.), *Marxism in education: Renewing the dialogue, pedagogy and culture.* London, England: Palgrave Macmillan.

Pickard, J. (2010, June 30). Lord Browne, former head of BP, to join coalition government. *Financial Times.*

Pink, S. (2007). *Doing visual ethnography: Images, media and representation in research* (2nd ed.). London, England: Sage.

Pring, R. (2000). Setting the scene: Criticisms of educational research. In *Philosophy of educational research* (pp. 1–7). London, England: Continuum.

Reason, P., & Bradbury, H. (2009). (Eds.). *The Sage handbook of action research*. London, England: Sage.

Rigby, E., & Barker, A. (2010, November 30). Browne lines up key business figures. *Financial Times*.

Schön, D. (1983). *The reflective practitioner: How professionals think in action*. London, England: Temple Smith.

Small, R. (2005). *Marx and education*. Aldershot: Ashgate.

Stronach, I. & MacLure, M. (1997). *Educational research undone: The postmodern embrace*. Buckingham, England: Open University Press.

Struthers, D. (2010). *Towards pedagogical partnership with teachers: Professional learning schools and the challenges for a schools partnership manager* (Unpubished EdD thesis). Roehampton University, London, England.

Web, T. (2010, June 30). Former oil chief admits to obsession and loneliness during his time at BP. *Guardian*.

CHAPTER THIRTY

A Critical Approach to the Teaching and Learning of Critical Social Science at the College Level

Claudia Sanchez and JoAnn Danelo Barbour

Critical Philosophical Groundings

The theoretical framing of critical social science occurs from the lineage of theorists or schools of thought from the critical and critical postmodern periods. Major theorists include Hegel and Marx, the Frankfurt School (Adorno & Horkheimer, 1947/1972), and Marcuse (1964), Habermas (1984, 1987), Gramsci (1971), and Bourdieu (1977, 1984). Relevant philosophical concepts important for critical social scientists to understand include the single unifier, Reason, dialectical (oppositional) thinking or contradictions, conflict, an historical perspective, emancipation, interdisciplinary thinking, the elimination of social injustice, and hegemony.

Hegel posited two concepts foundational to critical theory. The fundamental unifying principle that explains all reality is Reason, which is both a principle and a process; and change, the dialectic (conflict of opposites), is accomplished through conflict (Law, 2007). Accordingly, change occurs by the resolution of the conflict, and conflict is resolved through reason. Adding to both Hegelian concepts of the single unifier and the dialectic, Marx held that the single unifier was economics, based on the belief that one's being consists in labor, performed or framed within a division of labor based on class; additionally, the market dictates labor. Marxists generally focus on the dialectical clashes between the dominant and repressed classes in any given age. For critical educators, the dialectic on which university instructors should focus is the class system and power struggles perpetuated by the traditional teacher-student relationship.

Philosophers from the Frankfurt School, the three most important of whom were Adorno, Horkheimer, and Marcuse, attempted to adapt Marxism to the theoretical and political needs of post World War I Germany and the Russian Revolution. In political circles, propaganda replaced critical thinking, technology and science were being used as instruments of war, and rationality was used for control and domination. The Enlightenment, as a result, had become a tool of hegemony because reason was being used to strengthen systems rather than transform them. A group of critical theorists associated with the Institute for Social Research in Frankfurt, Germany, founded the Frankfurt School in 1923.

Critical theorists held that if there is only Reason as the unifier, then we repress or suppress the sensory, linguistic, and social interventions that connect knowing subjects to objects, persons, and nature. The task of philosophers, according to the Frankfurt School, is to identify and "critique" Enlightenment and instrumental reason and the obstacles that block the knowing. Critical theory developed more often as a cluster of themes rather than one definitive theory: inclusion of several disciplines of the social sciences, an historical perspective, dialectical contradictions, using formal rationality to deny power to classes of citizens, emancipation, and the elimination of social injustice. They held that humans create their history and society, which should be a society of free actors that go beyond the tension between, and abolish the opposition to, one's purposefulness, spontaneity, and rationality, and the results of one's labor. The use of oppositional thinking ought to help see anew ideas or processes taken for granted.

Because critical theorists believe that those in power often use formal rationality to deny power to those constrained by various forms of social, cultural, and political domination, scholars in various social sciences began to attend to race, class, and gender issues that include issues of power and action research. Critical theorists hope, therefore, that their work to explain the causes of oppression and totalitarianism, one result of capitalism and the capitalist mode of production, might result in practical efforts to eliminate oppression.

In his classic, *One-Dimensional Man*, Marcuse (1964) theorized that a revolt of the underclass and marginalized or disenfranchised would stimulate a broader social transformation. He held that to reach one's full potential, domination is unnecessary; one needs to be shown a better way. The task, therefore, is to identify and critique obstacles that block such better ways. An educator, thus, does not show the better way since to do so would be prescriptive. Marcuse held hope that the imagination could show politics the way (in education, for example, the creative teacher) and that society would not be filled with one-dimensional positivist thinkers.

Similar to earlier critical theorists, the central concerns of Habermas are modernity, rationality, autonomy, freedom, and human happiness, and how these concepts are connected as societies change. Habermas perceived work and labor as potentially freeing; that is, as the productive forces developed, the working class would create the possibility of a freer and more just society. Human creativity, according to Habermas, is two-fold: work or labor on one hand and social action on the other, and is limited by distortions of communication at the institutional and structural levels. Ending the distortions of communication would be the major route to overcoming creative limitations. The central problem of contemporary societies (university educators, for example) is to eliminate the barriers to and create conditions for what Habermas calls "communicative action."

Particularly significant for educators is Habermas' two-volume work *Theory of Communicative Action* (1984, 1987). His basic contention is that "it is through the action of communicating…that society actually operates and evolves…" (Habermas, 1984, p. 175). Habermas' focus is communication among people, interaction through communication, and the results of interactions as ways in which the social world operates. Four threads through his work include power (a key concept in his conception of communicative rationality), the notion of a meaningful concept of the *rationality* of actions, the problem of an appropriate *theory of action*, and a concept of *social order*. His social theory is multidisciplinary and intersects the individual and interaction, social institutions and structures, and forces of change and development in societies. Habermas links agency, the action, medium, and the structure within which agency operates, and combines these within an overall theory of historical change and evolution.

A criticism of Habermas' theory of communicative action is that it does not recognize or theorize relations of power and its effects on communication. Grappling with questions of authority and critical identity directs us to think about power discursively, that we "make connections between the workings of power in particular historical situations and the larger structures that organize social life, between who can speak and for what kind of world" (Hennessey, 1995, p. 148). The heart of Gramsci's theory is "the dialectical relationship between coercion and consent…precisely what is missing from Habermas' theory of society" (Ives, 2004a, p. 162) and the focus to which we now turn.

Critical Educational Groundings

Antonio Gramsci, a 1920s political activist in Italy's Socialist Party, was arrested and imprisoned by the Fascists, who accused him of various political offenses. In prison until his death in 1937, Gramsci wrote letters and his *Prison Notebooks*, wherein he developed many of the themes important to critical theorists—"the most important draft on the educational and political function of intellectuals" (Monasta, 1993, p. 597). According to Gramsci (1971), hegemony is a social condition, the process whereby the interests of a ruling group come to dominate by establishing the common sense; that is, those values, beliefs, and knowledges that implicitly guide the group. He associates hegemony with the complex web of power and influence (setting a direction) exerted by the most prevalent group(s) in civil society (Gramsci, 1971, pp. 12–13). Gramsci emphasizes that hegemony is forged out of social struggle and is identified with equilibrium, persuasion, consolidation, and consent as central to the struggle. "In a nutshell, Gramsci redefined hegemony to mean the formation and organization of consent" (Ives, 2004b, p. 2).

Gramsci recognized that social power is not simply a dialectic of domination versus subordination or resistance, but a more nuanced version of the interplay between domination and subordination or resistance. Hegemony from a civil perspective, with dominant groups throughout various societal systems, is maintained by "organic intellectuals," defined by Gramsci as the groups in a bureaucracy who have command or control functions, often have links to the old guard, and are the power groups in the civil society. They can be those at the highest level of society who would be the creators of the various sciences, philosophy, art, and at the lowest levels, administrators, military officers (Gramsci, 1971, pp. 12–13). Intellectuals, defined by the legitimizing role they play in society, function as intermediaries between the working class and the elite ruling culture and serve to legitimize that which the ruling class deems necessary, for example norms, values, important beliefs, policies, and so on. This legitimizing function is always, more or less consciously, that of the technical and political leadership of a group, either the dominant group or another tending towards a dominant position.

Dominant groups in democratic societies generally govern within an implicit theory of exchange, that is, with a good degree of consent from the people they rule. This consent is historically caused by the prestige and consequent confidence (reproduction and legitimizing powers) of those who maintain prominence in the dominant group. The ruler's power derives from the fact that the rule is seen as legitimate by the ruled, who have entered this unequal relationship on a voluntary basis. To Gramsci, the durability of hegemonic rule also manifests itself by allowing the consent of the weak to be contradictory and disjointed. Norms of social behavior, moral codes, ways of knowing, and so on, become such an accepted part of everyday life that they seem naturally to have always been the ways to navigate within the culture. For Gramsci,

> …culture does not simply emerge or exist; it is produced, brought into being, by intellectuals, who formalize and codify religious and social ideas and make them into a hegemonic ideology which they communicate to society at large, elaborating and reinforcing it continuously, transmitting it from generation to generation. (Worsley, 1997, p. 265)

The maintenance of the consent of the ruled and the maintenance of the ruling class occur because those in power are flexible enough to respond to new circumstances and the changing needs of those ruled as the rulers reposition the relationship between rulers and ruled (Jones, 2006). In other words, the ruling class keeps the ruled sufficiently happy while the rulers control the game and the way the game is played. Gramsci suggests that an effective hegemonic ideology perpetuated by the ruling class involves some sleight of hand, or language, wherein the subordinate group is kept mystified by an obfuscation of real meaning or intent. Causes of inequalities, for example, are obscured by finding scapegoats or by inventing links between situations or activities not truly causally connected, by blaming outside forces, by hiding conflicts of interest, by persuading people that the wealthy and the poor have common interests, and so on (Worsley, 1997). "For a hegemonic ideology to be truly successful, people have to *internalize* these ideas—*really* believe in them. A successful hegemonic ideology, then, penetrates the dominated class; it is a *cross-class* phenomenon" (Worsley, 1997, p. 265, italics in original). Bourdieu adds that the dominant class wields power, in part, through control of language and its meaning: "The constitutive power which is granted to ordinary language lies not in the language itself but in the group which authorizes it and invests it with authority" (1977, p. 21).

In sociology, Bourdieu's (1977) central construct is that practice consists of a continual production and reproduction of the combination of habitus or capital (agency—the means to exert power) and fields (structures, social arenas). In the field of education, then, those who possess the educational or cultural capital control the practice of schooling within the designed structural boundaries of schools and schooling. Bourdieu maintains that society's elite or upper class possess the agency to control the means of production and reproduction within a structure or system. These privileged social agents develop strategies adapted to the needs of the social spaces they inhabit. Individuals develop these dispositions in response to the objective conditions they encounter. In this way, the social structure is inculcated into the subjective experience of the participants of that social system. Gramsci connects language and culture through education when he argues that "every relationship of 'hegemony' is necessarily an educational relationship…" (1971, p. 350). It is to educational concerns that we now turn.

Critical Pedagogical and Curricular Considerations

In the following sections, we share some pedagogical and curricular considerations. Our discussion is guided by the assumption that pedagogy and its attending curriculum must be defined by the context, responding to conditions and problems that arise wherein education takes place.

> Rather than treating pedagogy as commodity, progressive educators need to engage their teaching as a theoretical resource that is both shaped by and responds to the very problems that arise in the in-between space/places/contexts that connect classrooms with the experiences of everyday life. (Giroux, 2001, p. 18)

Critical Social Science Pedagogical Considerations

"Critical pedagogy is a radical approach to education that seeks to transform oppressive structures in society using democratic and activist approaches to teaching and learning" (Braa & Callero, 2006, p. 357). As Shor (1992) points out, critical pedagogy is

> habits of thought, reading, writing, and speaking which go beneath surface meaning, first impressions, dominant myths, official pronouncements, traditional clichés, received wisdom, and mere opinions, to understand the deep meaning, root causes, social context, ideology, and personal consequences of any action, event, object, process, organization, experience, text, subject matter, policy, mass media, or discourse. (p. 129)

Giroux reminds us of the role that critical pedagogy plays in framing our study of social phenomena. In his words, critical pedagogy is "a referent for analyzing how knowledge, values, desire and social relations are constructed, taken up, and implicated in relations of power in the interaction among cultural texts, institutional forms, authorities, and audiences" (2001, p. 3). As such, "critical pedagogy is concerned about the articulation of knowledge to social effects and succeeds to the degree in which educators encourage critical reflection and moral and civic agency rather than simply mold it" (2001, p. 19). Our responsibility as educators is thus to "critically interrogate the fundamental link between knowledge and power, pedagogical practices and social consequences, and authority and civic responsibility" (2001, p. 22).

A discussion of critical pedagogy is paramount to gaining new insights on how to teach a critical social science course. We now propose some considerations relative to the art of teaching in a critical social science course. In this section, we discuss the *student*, the *teacher*, and the art of *teaching* in light of criteria guiding critical pedagogy (Ayers, Michie, & Rome, 2004; Bell & Russell, 2000; Braa & Callero, 2006; Degener, 2001; Freire, 1982, 1994; Giroux, 2001; Harding, London, & Safer, 2001; McLaren & Farahmandpur, 2001; and Shapiro, 2003). Much of the discussion is derived from Kincheloe's work on critical pedagogy (Kincheloe, 2000, 2005, 2008; Kincheloe & Steinberg, 1998).

The student. Students in a critical social science course drive the curriculum, become actively involved in their own education, and exercise their critical and reflective agency as they engage in critical analysis of the forces that shape the world (Kincheloe, 2008; Kincheloe & Steinberg, 1998). As a *critical agent of change*, the student in a critical social science course transforms his environment.

The teacher. The teacher of a critical social science course is a *critical facilitator* who infuses her courses with critical pedagogy. Critical teachers operate from the understanding that all education is inherently political, that dominant ideologies and culture dictate educational practices, that language is ideological and serves to construct norms within classrooms and society at large. This critical teacher approaches the art of teaching with an understanding of the political structure of schools, and the assumption that schooling and educational practices at all levels are invariably and inevitably politically contested spaces (Kincheloe, 2008). Indeed, classroom, curricular, and school structures are not neutral sites waiting to be shaped by educational professionals. They hold the values shaped by the ideologies and cultural assumptions of their historical contexts that are shaped in the same ways language and knowledge are constructed, by those who possess power (Kincheloe, 2008).

Critical teachers are aware that a *hidden curriculum* ensures educators socialize and behaviorally condition students to accept hierarchical structures of power (Apple, 1990) with structural enforcements that perpetuate dominant class interests (McLaren, 2003). For example, when the curriculum promotes the value of individualism as the basis of success and upward mobility, the reproduction of individualism over collaboration promotes a cultural ideology that serves to legitimate existing class dominance. The hidden curriculum omits certain forms of knowledge—including serious analyses of inequality, oppression, exploitation, imperialism, revolution, class struggle, and labor movements—that might raise critical questions about capitalism (Apple, 1990). In an authoritarian classroom, educators condition students to become passive, conformist, and obedient members of the school setting, then somewhat easily manipulated workers and passive, apathetic citizens (Shor, 1992).

The critical teacher is knowledgeable of her subject matter; critical pedagogy (the forces that shape the curriculum, the often conflicting purposes of education, the cultural experiences of students, diverse teaching styles); factors oppressing certain social and ethnic groups (racism, gender bias, class bias, cultural bias, heterosexism, and religious intolerance); and the ways in which culture and the media (TV, radio, popular music, movies, the Internet) operate to perpetuate the status quo (Kincheloe, 2008).

The teacher of a critical social science course is committed to exercising reflective agency by studying students in order to gain a better understanding of these students and the teaching context (Kincheloe, 2008). Following Freire's (1982) approach to teaching and learning, critical teachers and students engage in a constant dialogue that poses questions on the ways in which certain groups have been oppressed in particular contexts. Then, teachers guide students in framing these problems in a larger social, cultural, and political context and solving them (Kincheloe, 2008).

The relationships between students and teachers. Students and teachers in a critical social science course have roles different from their counterparts in traditional authoritarian courses. Gramsci holds that "the relationship between teacher and pupil is active and reciprocal so that every teacher is always a pupil and every pupil a teacher" (1971, p. 350); thus, from a critical perspective, the role of teacher "must shift from one of expert to one of collaborator" (Harding, London, & Safer, 2001, p. 506). "The most significant defining feature of critical pedagogy is its emphasis on the emancipatory potential of education" (Braa & Callero, 2006, p. 358).

Critical teachers admit that they are in a position of authority with respect to their students. However, critical teachers demonstrate that authority in their actions in support of students. In this sense,

> the authority of the critical teachers is dialectical; as teachers relinquish the authority of truth providers, they assume the mature authority of facilitators of student inquiry and problem posing. In relation to such teacher authority, students gain their freedom—they gain the ability to become self-directed human beings capable of producing their own knowledge. (Kincheloe, 2008, p. 17)

In a classroom that is grounded within a critical framework, instructors provide a democratic relational setting within a curriculum that encourages dialogue, deliberation, and the power of students to raise questions about that curriculum. "Such relations don't signal a retreat from teacher authority as much as they suggest using authority reflexively to provide the conditions for students to exercise intellectual rigor, theoretical competence, and informed judgments" (Giroux, 2001, p. 25).

The art of teaching. We view teaching as an art; that is, the conscious use of skill and creative imagination that promotes learning. We propose that the art of teaching, especially as it relates to a critical social science course, be inspired in and driven by critical pedagogy.

The foundation of critical pedagogy (Marcuse, 1964; Freire, 1982, 1994) is grounded on a vision of justice and equality. It is also grounded on a concern with human suffering; that is, human beings' enduring damage, loss, distress, pain, or death (Kincheloe, 2008). Unlike older inquiry traditions, critical social science "embodies an action-oriented commitment to the common welfare" (Greene, 1990, p. 241) by identifying and questioning structural conditions, the origin for these conditions, and the inequities or injustices these conditions endorse (Greene, 1990). In a critical social science course, the interdisciplinary and contextual nature of critical pedagogy would assist in discerning the ways in which particular groups of students and individuals in general are oppressed and get hurt. By embracing multiculturalism, a critical social science course would focus on the interaction of power and racism, sexism, class bias, and homophobia (Kincheloe, 2008). Further, critical pedagogy would inspire a critical social citizenship that would prompt course participants to action towards addressing inequitable practices that cause human suffering within their own socio-cultural contexts. The examination of factors interacting in inequalities, and course participants' actions towards change would be constantly contextualized, since the notion of context is paramount to critical pedagogy (Kincheloe, 2008).

In addition to examining the larger contexts in which students and teacher are immersed, a critical social science course includes dialogue, critique, and discussion as essential aspects of the learning process. Also, the course integrates constant critical reflection on one's own and others' beliefs, assumptions, and perspectives.

Critical Social Science Curricular Considerations

By curriculum considerations we mean elements pertaining to the specific course or set of courses devoted to the study of critical social science at the university level. We propose the construction of critical social science coursework that is infused with critical pedagogy (Kincheloe, 2008). As such, the construction of arguments, procedures, and language receive continual cross-examination and scrutiny, as the conditions of social regulation, unequal distribution, and power, which permeate social phenomena, are studied (Popkewitz, 1990). Inspired by Freire, critical pedagogy makes use of problem posing and generative themes to read the word and the world (Freire, 1982; Kincheloe, 2008). Freire's approach consisted of having students decode texts and connect the printed word to their understanding of their own contexts. This understanding was the result of a process whereby Freire generated themes from conversations with students and community members and then posed problems by generating questions in a reiterative fashion. The questions generated in this process were used to guide Freire's teaching. In his opinion, the problems that face teachers and students in their effort to live just and ethical lives should provide a framework for the curriculum (Kincheloe, 2008).

In addition to integrating problems faced by teachers and students, coursework infused with critical pedagogy openly and critically addresses the institutional constraints under which teaching takes place. The curriculum promotes an awareness of how issues of race, class, gender, and other social and structural inequalities affect the educational process and our opportunities for self-actualization and personal and collective self-determination.

The curriculum also integrates the study of the margins of society. In this sense, the critical social science coursework would consist of a curriculum at the margins; that is, a curriculum that studies the experiences and needs of individuals at the outside of what is considered *standard* or *normal* by the groups in power. Critical teachers and students are aware that by engaging in critical pedagogy, they become outsiders at the margins of the mainstream, and as a result are likely to also become marginalized.

Critical pedagogy promotes a focus on non-rational and relational ways of knowing and builds individual capacities that enable students to become critical agents who can link knowledge, responsibility, and democratic social transformation and understand the complex relationships between power and knowledge. The actual application of knowledge (praxis) is used to transform society. A critical social science course would equip students with a variety of tools to engage in *reflective agency*. We propose the term *reflective agency* in lieu of the term research, which often has a positivist connotation. The variety of tools for delving into inquiry has a basis in Kincheloe's (2008) multilogicality; that is, a critical pedagogy that integrates multiple perspectives and uses multiple methodological tools (for example, bricolage; Kincheloe, 2008).

Critical social science coursework integrates critical multiculturalism, which is concerned with factors that give rise to race, class, gender, sexual, religious, cultural, and ability-based inequalities (Kincheloe, 2008). Through a critical multicultural lens, teachers and students examine how power has operated through time to legitimate inequalities, and how power shapes self and knowledge (Kincheloe, 2008).

Finally, a critical social science curriculum acknowledges the struggles of emerging critical scholars. Emerging critical social scholars (critical and reflective agents of change) often feel overwhelmed by the challenges and struggles inherent to the new paradigm they begin to explore, both in terms of their need to get acquainted with a new purpose of inquiry and new methodological notions, and the realization that the nature of the new paradigm itself poses a threat to traditional ways of inquiry, which aim to silence and discredit critical social inquiry. As emerging critical and reflective agents of change delve into a new paradigm, we propose that their struggles be addressed in the curriculum. Some of the struggles we may need to address are the following:

Research: The why and the how. Emerging critical and reflective agents of change are faced with the need to anchor their endeavors in the humanistic purpose of research, which is the pursuit of justice, equality, and human rights (Denzin, 2009). No longer is the reason to do research of secondary importance in relation to issues associated with technique, faithfulness to methodological procedure, and orthodoxy in the selection of research methods. The question "Why do we do research?" has become as essential as the question "How do we do research?" Our new realization of the humanistic purpose of research liberates us, but also leaves us perplexed at first as we explore unknown territory, and as we gradually come back from this state, we become both fascinated and challenged to grow under and with a new paradigm.

Concrete social reform. The novel job of a critical and reflective agent of change is to bring social reform to a concrete level by committing to activism that promotes justice, equality, and human rights. The merit of critical social research lies in its power to transform the world. Emerging critical social research-ers will often struggle with establishing a clear link between their research endeavors and their potential to bring about concrete social reform (i.e., What line of research to pursue? What cause to embrace?). Secondly, this struggle also entails attempts to conceive of and actually arrive at this level of *concreteness* that social transformation necessitates (i.e., What does *concrete* social reform actually look like?).

New ethical questions. Under the new paradigm, new questions demand to be answered as we engage in and with our research efforts: Who initiates the research endeavor? Who carries it out? Who benefits from research being conducted? Further, who will own the research? and what difference will it make? (Denzin, 2009). Emerging critical and reflective agents of change face the continual need to examine and question (their own and others') research pursuits in light of critical theory.

Challenging old assumptions. Under the new paradigm that permeates a new role in research, critical and reflective agents of change are also faced with the need to resist the notion of methodological hierarchy, which was ingrained in them throughout their formal education. That is, they now need to refuse to accept the principles in traditional research that (a) quantitative methods are *the* means to doing valid research, and that (b) qualitative methods must be relegated to "a largely auxiliary role" in research (Denzin, 2009).

The role of double consciousness. Based on Du Bois' (1973) concept of double consciousness, emerging critical and reflective agents of change struggle to develop an understanding of themselves as subjugated individuals, as well as of the oppressing forces upon them, including the dominant ideological practices and discourses that shape our reality (Kincheloe, 2008). To arrive at this level of consciousness, one needs to make use of introspection as one searches for an awareness of self. Who am I and in what ways am I privileged as a human being, as a Westerner, as a researcher? Am I an indigenous individual…in relation to what/whom? (Denzin, 2009). In this new role, critical and reflective agents of change not only develop their own double consciousness, but also encourage this double consciousness among those with whom they come in contact as they engage in inquiry. In so doing, these reflective agents of change ought to remain conscious that exposure to oppression opens the eyes of the oppressed, but can also unleash a potential challenge that comes with the territory; that of distorting their own and others' self perceptions and interpersonal interactions (Kincheloe, 2008).

Methodological considerations. Another methodological issue critical and reflective agents of change face is the exciting possibility of both exploring and creating new research methods. However, this possi-bility is also a source of struggle. With respect to the integration of *bricolage* into research design, for instance, one would engage in interdisciplinearity as we look for "yet not imagined tools, fashioning them with not yet imagined connections" (Lincoln, 2001). In this case, the struggle of an emerg-ing critical and reflective agent of change consists of describing the nature of the relationship among *bricolage,* rigor, and multidisciplinearity. How to achieve systematic, disciplinary, rigorous, insightful analyses (Lincoln, 2001) via interdisciplinearity? Are multidisciplinary research teams the answer to this conundrum? If so, how are these teams formed and how would they operate?

Contributing to the institutionalization of critical social research. Finally, committing to critical social research also entails the struggle of advocating for its institutionalization in the midst of political and methodological challenges that permeate our reality. The issue of advocacy for the new paradigm's institutionalization is one that offers more questions than answers. How to advocate for institutionalization? What would be the framework for advocacy? How does the new paradigm defend itself against challenges posed by politics and traditional research methods? Moreover, on an individual level, what could be my contribution to the field? How can we help shape an Advocacy Agenda for critical social research? (Denzin, 2009).

In the middle of what many could call a curriculum immersed in a grim scenario filled with struggles for an emerging critical and reflective agent of change, Freire reminds us of the mutually complementing roles of *hope*, *struggle*, and *practice*: "Without a minimum of hope, we cannot so much as start the struggle. But without the struggle, hope, as an ontological need, dissipates, loses its bearings, and turns into hopelessness" (Freire, 1994, p. 3). Our responsibility as progressive educators (and reflective agents of change) is to "unveil opportunities for hope, no matter what the obstacles may be" (Freire, 1994, p. 3).

Considerations for the Design of Learning Activities

The concept of "practicing theory" is what "praxis meant to Freire and reflective action to Dewey, a close relationship between discourse and action, between symbolic analysis and concrete action, using language as a tool to enhance our understanding of experience—theorizing practice/practicing theory" (Shor, 1999, p. 12). In the following section, we offer some considerations for the design of learning activities in a critical social science course.

Critical social science courses as vehicles for transformation. When criticality is incorporated in course-work, courses can become vehicles for transformation by developing or cooperating with a grassroots community organization. A social theory course, for example, could begin with the identification of a salient local issue and use particular theories to achieve a more sophisticated understanding of the problems, discover solutions, and recommend strategies for change. Community organizing, therefore, becomes a viable critical topic in the sociology curriculum as the praxis for changing one's community (Braa & Callero, 2006). In the field of human resource development, instructors can develop activities within four critical dimensions of reform (Fenwick, 2004). An activity can have a political purpose to reform workplace organizations or development practices directed toward individuals and groups. Another activity can occur within workplaces that are contested terrains between worker and manager interests. A third and fourth dimension can include an activity involving inquiry into the history of conflict and power relations with the intent to reform, or research to expose and challenge existing organizational inequities and unfair practices, respectively.

Themes in a critical social science course. In agreement with critical pedagogy principles, we propose that the curriculum of a critical social science course be driven by the problems facing students and teachers in these courses. Some examples of themes that coursework could explore include:

- ways in which a world that is unjust by design shapes the classroom and the relations between teachers and students (Kincheloe, 2008);

- historical and contemporary aspects omitted in traditional curriculum (for example, the European colonization of Africa and the effects of the slave trade [Kincheloe, 2008]; the last 500 years of European colonialism, the anticolonial movements around the world beginning in the post-World War II era and their impact on the U.S. civil rights movement, the women's movement, the antiwar movement in Vietnam, Native American liberation struggles, the gay rights movement, and other emancipatory movements [Kincheloe, 2008]; multiple perspectives of the national and international community on the meaning of recent wars [Kincheloe, 2000]; and ecological disasters such as the 2010 oil spill in the Gulf of Mexico);

• ways in which cultural artifacts (cyberspace, TV, movies, video games, and music) perpetuate the status quo, and ways in which activists can draw upon these texts to contest power structures (Kincheloe, 2005);

• the journeys of critical pedagogists at the margins and their struggles;

• the ways in which schooling affects the lives of students from marginalized groups (e.g., poor, non-English as first language, gay, lesbian, and bisexual, physically challenged, nonathletic, non-white, overweight, shy, and short students); (Kincheloe, 2008);

• The struggles of university faculty conducting critical social research. When are faculty in a better position to delve into criticality as a scholarly pursuit, before or after tenure? Why?

Action-product research projects. An opportunity for critical social scientists in the field of education is to help schools with action research that includes opening critical space in the school community (Howes, 2001). The researcher creates a collaborative environment to support the action research needs of school staff, rather than bringing a research agenda to a particular school. Two challenges in the university classroom are how to make visible the desires and needs of students and teachers and how to articulate and shape experience, and to what ends. Lu and Horner pose the question, "How might teachers and students grasp what students want without the teacher prescribing what students 'really' want or should want?" (1998, p. 266). To critically and experientially involve adults in a graduate capstone project in education leadership, Barbour (2008) has students create a final product based on their needs and interests. Developed as "action product research," students use research *a priori*, that is, rather than conducting a traditional capstone research project, students use extant research to theoretically ground a project or product they design and build. Students do not conduct a formal research project, unless they choose to design and conduct a research project; rather, students are akin to artists who design an artwork and then build it or create that work of art. Students are encouraged to critically reflect on their needs and the needs of the schools in which they teach and then create a product that meets those needs, a product grounded in the research of others. Each component in the final product must be supported by research based in scholarly literature.

Paradoxical thinking. In the management classroom, authors Dehler, Welsh, and Lewis (1999) suggest using paradox as a pedagogical tool to develop students' capacities for *paradoxical thinking*. "'Working through paradox' in the management education classroom entails encouraging students to define and even exaggerate their polarized perceptions, thereby, tapping their natural tendency to stress contrast over connections" (p. 16). By designing contradictory situations, for example, participation and control, the authors wanted students to experience debating opposing perspectives and recognize the biases and limitations of their own sense-making processes.

Internal and external challenges. When creating lessons from the students' perspectives and in collaboration with the students, an instructor must be ready for challenges that are inevitable.

• Students' feelings of frustration as well as anger were reported by Wink (1997) in a graduate education course that implemented a learning activity in which her class experienced tracking and the feelings engendered by students who are tracked, whether in elementary school, high school, or college. How can teachers make discomfort a little more comfortable? Or is students' discomfort helpful in inspiring students to bring about change?

- In another study that used critical pedagogy to teach MBA students, Sinclair (2007) noted that students went so far as to question the legitimacy of the class as well as her expertise as the instructor.

- Factors external to a critical social science course will challenge a curriculum that contests current power structures. Critical teachers struggle to keep balance among three moving platforms: the policymakers' platform, the platform of the curriculum in place, and that of the new critical curriculum.

Conclusion

In this chapter, we made reference to foundational philosophy on which critical pedagogists have grounded their work. Through time, theorists have built from notions developed before them, and each iteration of new critical theorists in history has found a critical void and has tried to fill that void.

In light of critical theory, critical pedagogists have inspired the art of teaching. In the midst of a growing concern to understand how we teach at the university level, our field now needs rich scholarly literature with examples describing teaching and learning processes infused with criticality. When it comes to teaching and learning critical social science, what do we do? How we do it? In other words, how do critical educators actually walk the talk? In producing the literature we need, we might wish to rethink or reconceptualize the notion of scholarly publications, since these are usually associated with established work derived from completed research projects (in the positivist sense). Perhaps the study of criticality might necessitate that we become more accepting of and more comfortable with writing works in progress within inquiry project in progress as potential scholarly publications.

With this chapter, we hope to start the conversation on explicit ways to teach and learn critical social science, always with the grounding linked to critical theory. We challenge scholars to create and share inquiry projects that walk the reader through in-depth descriptions of lesson designs, relationships of teachers and students, critical course expectations, as well as the struggles, processes, and critical outcomes that come with the territory. Let us share with one another the ways in which we walk the pedagogical talk of critical theory.

References

Adorno, T. W., & Horkheimer, M. (1972). *Dialectic of enlightenment* (J. Cumming, Trans.). New York, NY: Herder and Herder. (Original work published 1947)

Apple, M. (1990). *Ideology and curriculum*. New York, NY: Routledge.

Ayers, W., Michie, G., & Rome, A. (2004). Embers of hope: In search of a meaningful critical pedagogy. *Teacher Education Quarterly, 31*(1), 123–130.

Barbour, J. D. (2008). Leadership and action "product" research. *Academic Exchange Quarterly, 12*(2), 176–182.

Bell, A. C., & Russell, C. L. (2000). Beyond human, beyond words: Anthropocentrism, critical pedagogy, and the poststructuralist turn. *Canadian Journal of Education/Revue canadienne de l'éducation, 25*(3), 188–203.

Bourdieu, P. (1977). *Outline of a theory of practice* (R. Nice, Trans.). Cambridge, England: Cambridge University Press.

Bourdieu, P. (1984). *Distinction: A social critique of the judgement of taste* (R. Nice, Trans.). Cambridge, MA: Harvard University Press.

Braa, D., & Callero, P. (2006). Critical pedagogy and classroom praxis. *Teaching Sociology, 34*(4), 357–369.

Degener, S. C. (2001). Making sense of critical pedagogy in adult literacy education. *Annual Review of Adult Learning and Literacy, 2,* 26–62.

Dehler, G. E., Welsh, M. A., & Lewis, M. W. (1999, July). Critical pedagogy in the "new paradigm": Raising complicated understanding in management learning. Paper presented at the Critical Management Studies Conference, Manchester, England. Retrieved from http://www.mngt.waikato.ac.nz/ejrot/cmsconference/1999/documents/Management%20education/emailversioncmcpaper.pdf

Denzin, N. (2009). *Qualitative inquiry under fire: Toward a new paradigm dialogue*. Walnut Creek, CA: Left Coast Press.

Du Bois, W. (1973). *The education of black people: Ten critiques, 1906–1960*. New York, NY: Monthly Review Press.

Fenwick, T. (2004). Toward a critical HRD in theory and practice. *Adult Education Quarterly, 54*(3), 193–209.

Freire, P. (1982). *Pedagogy of the oppressed.* New York, NY: Continuum.

Freire, P. (1994). *Pedagogy of hope.* New York, NY: Continuum.

Giroux, H. A. (2001). Pedagogy of the depressed: Beyond the new politics of cynicism. *College Literature, 28*(3), 1–32.

Gramsci, A. (1971). *Selections from the prison notebooks of Antonio Gramsci* (Q. Hoare & G. N. Smith, Trans.). New York, NY: International Publishers.

Greene, J. (1990). Three views on the nature and role of knowledge in social science. In E. Guba (Ed.), *The paradigm dialog* (pp. 227–245). Newbury Park, CA: Sage.

Habermas, J. (1984). *The theory of communicative action: Reason and the rationalization of society* (Vol. 1; T. McCarthy, Trans.). Boston, MA: Beacon Press.

Habermas, J. (1987). *The theory of communicative action: Vol. 2. Lifeworld and system; A critique of functionalist reason* (T. McCarthy, Trans.). Boston, MA: Beacon Press.

Harding, C. G., London, L. H., & Safer, L. A. (2001). Teaching other people's ideas to other people's children: Integrating messages from education, psychology, and critical pedagogy. *Urban Education, 36*(4), 505–517.

Hennessey, R. (1995). Subjects, knowledges,…and all the rest: Speaking for what? In J. Roof & R. Wiegman (Eds.), *Who can speak?: Authority and critical identity* (pp. 137–150). Urbana: University of Illinois Press.

Howes, A. (2001). School level action research: Creating critical space in school communities. *Improving Schools, 4*(2), 43–48.

Ives, P. (2004a). *Gramsci's politics of language: Engaging the Bakhtin circle and the Frankfurt school.* Toronto, ON, Canada: University of Toronto Press.

Ives, P. (2004b). *Language and hegemony in Gramsci.* Winnipeg, MB, Canada: Fernwood.

Jones, T. (2006). *Antonio Gramsci.* London, England: Routledge.

Kincheloe, J. (2000). Cultural studies and democratically aware teacher education: Post-fordism, civics, and the worker citizen. In D. Hursh & W. Ross (Eds.), *Democratic social education: social studies for social change* (pp. 97–120). New York, NY: Falmer Press.

Kincheloe, J. (Ed.). (2005). *Classroom teaching: An introduction.* New York, NY: Peter Lang.

Kincheloe, J. (2008). *Critical pedagogy* (2nd ed.). New York, NY: Peter Lang.

Kincheloe, J., & Steinberg, S. (1998). *Unauthorized methods: Strategies for critical teaching.* New York, NY: Routledge.

Law, S. (2007). *Philosophy.* London, England: Dorling Kindersley.

Lincoln, Y. (2001). An emerging new bricoleur: Promises and possibilities; A reaction to Joe Kincheloe's "Describing the bricoleur." *Qualitative Inquiry, 7*(6), 693–705.

Lu, M. Z., & Horner, B. (1998). The problematic of experience: Redefining critical work in ethnography and pedagogy. *College English, 60*(3), pp. 257–277.

Marcuse, H. (1964). *One-dimensional man.* Boston, MA: Beacon Press.

McLaren, P. (2003). *Life in schools: An introduction to critical pedagogy.* New York, NY: Pearson.

McLaren, P., & Farahmandpur, R. (2001). Teaching against globalization and the new imperialism: Toward a revolutionary pedagogy. *Journal of Teacher Education, 52*(2), 136–150.

Monasta, A. (1993). Antonio Gramsci. *Prospects: The Quarterly Review of Comparative Education, 23*(3/4), 597–612.

Popkewitz, T. S. (1990). Whose future? Whose past? Notes on critical theory and methodology. In E. Guba (Ed.), *The paradigm dialog* (pp. 46–66). Newbury Park, CA: Sage.

Shapiro, S. A. (2003). From andragogy to collaborative critical pedagogy: Learning for academic, personal, and social empowerment in a distance-learning Ph.D. program. *Journal of Transformative Education, 1*(2), 150–166.

Shor, I. (1992). *Empowering education: Critical teaching for social change.* Chicago, IL: University of Chicago Press.

Shor, I. (1999). What is critical literacy? *The Journal of Pedagogy, Pluralism & Practice, 4*(1). Retrieved September 16, 2010, from: http://www.lesley.edu/journals/jppp/4/index.html

Sinclair, A. (2007). Teaching leadership critically to MBAs: Experiences from heaven and hell. *Management Learning, 38*(4), 458–472.

Wink, J. (1997). *Critical pedagogy: Notes from the real world.* Boston, MA: Allyn & Bacon.

Worsley, P. (1997). *Knowledges: Culture, counterculture, subculture.* New York, NY: New Press.

CHAPTER THIRTY-ONE

One School's Approach to Enhancing Parental Well-being: A Collaborative Research Practitioner Model

Marcelle Cacciattolo, Joanne Richmond, and Denise Barr

I teach because I search, because I question, and because I submit myself to questioning. I research because I notice things, take cognizance of them. And in so doing I intervene. And intervening, I educate and educate myself. I do research so as to know what I do not know and to communicate and proclaim what I discover. (Freire, 2001, p. 35)

Freire's words echo the necessity of reflective inquiry in generating a more evolved sense of what one knows and where one is heading in the world. For teachers working in classrooms, being *reflexive* around those strategies that best assist parents to be actively involved in their children's schooling is the first step to overcoming barriers aligned with poor academic and social achievements.[1] For young people who regularly miss school, struggle with literacy and numeracy and encounter feelings of alienation and disengagement on a daily basis, having a parent's support can lead to a more positive outlook to learning (Greenwood & Hickman, 1991). This chapter reports on the evaluation of a parent program conducted by a primary school in the western suburbs of Melbourne.[2] At the time of the project the program was in its fourth year of operation and had at no stage been evaluated.

The evaluation team was made up of three classroom teachers, an assistant principal, a well-being co-ordinator, a university research colleague from Victoria University and two multicultural education aides (MEAs) who were also parents at the school. We met once every three weeks for 12 months to discuss and report back on stages leading up to the delivery of the parent program.[3]

In essence our research team sought to uncover answers to the following two questions:

• How does one parent program at Mondale Primary School impact on the construction of confident, well-informed, socially engaged parents?

• How does this parent program lead to stronger home-school and community relationships?

For the majority of the team of researchers this was also the first time many had participated in a project of this kind. Being given an opportunity to systematically document our perceptions of those structures that either thwarted or encouraged parent participation allowed for the free flowing of professional insights born out of a commitment to a socially just school vision. In documenting and articulating our beliefs, the team then set about a process of reflection that sought to challenge beliefs and practices that did not serve the best interest of students and their families at the school. Through engaging in a process of "critique" the team was able to articulate what it was that the school could be doing better. New awakenings of what effective parent programs could look and feel like soon emerged, which are included in the work that follows.

An additional outcome of our research team's participation was the emergence of a stronger insight into the role of collaborative practitioner research (CPR) in facilitating constructive change (Cherednichenko, Davies, Kruger, & O'Rourke, 2001). The nature of CPR ensures that the academic researcher did not dominate the collection and analysis of data collection. Too often schools are involved in joint projects with university colleagues where the research conducted is disconnected from the everyday lives of teachers (Ferrance, 2000, p. 13). Many academics "do their thing" and then conclude their work with a nice bunch of flowers and a box of chocolate that is circulated in staffrooms. This approach not only sucks dry the intellectual property of schools, but also dangerously positions academics as authority figures on how data findings *ought* to be translated into action. The writing that follows not only showcases the benefits of using a collaborative practitioner methodology but positions teachers, school personnel and parents as active agents in establishing transformative practices that lead to emancipatory learning.

Context of the School

Mondale Primary School[4] is made up of a school community that is culturally diverse and economically disadvantaged. Unemployment is high with approximately 85–90% of parents with Health Care Cards making them eligible for the Education Maintenance Allowance.[5] The population at the school is largely transient, which means that enrolments fluctuate significantly throughout a school year. On average the student population is between 270 and 280 students. Less than 25% of students continue their enrolment from Prep to Year 6 at the school. It is not uncommon to have at least 90 students in any given year who, as new arrivals or refugees, have only been in the country for a year.

Over the years the cultural background, too, has changed, and this has also impacted on the mobility of the school population as well as achievement levels. Many new arrivals and refugees are attracted to the area because of the large number of rental properties and the resources available to them such as the AMES Learning English outpost in Mondale. There is also a Western English Language School (WELS) outpost at the school, which operated four classrooms four days a week during 2008. The Western English Language School offers primary and secondary specialised language programs to new arrivals. WELS not only focuses on providing students with English-language skills needed to be able to succeed in mainstream schooling but also attempts to equip newly arrived students with cultural and social knowledge tied to Australian schooling. What this has meant is that there is an escalating diversity of cultural, religious and ethnic backgrounds represented at the school.

With over two-thirds of parents coming from refugee backgrounds, there are a range of challenges that are faced when new arrivals are confronted with Australian schooling. Some of these include little knowledge of the process of schooling, a lack of confidence in communicating with school personnel because of limited English-language skills, fear in dealing with perceived "authoritarian" structures and financial hardship as a result of being on social welfare. The Centre for Multicultural Youth Issues also makes note of the difficulties faced by new arrivals that are shared by the parents at this primary school.

Many parents or caregivers have patchy information about the Australian schooling system gleaned from friends, their children, information from the school, or from other members of the community. This information may be third hand and is not always comprehensive. While parents may understand some areas of the education system, there may be significant gaps, even around core issues such as uniforms, assessment, books, and so on. Often what is missing is an understanding of the bigger picture—the system as a whole and how individual school policies fit within this. (CMYI, 2006b, p. 10)

In light of these complexities outlined above and given the fact that Australia accepted a total of 13,700 refugees in its 2009–10 program, embedding effective, practical and sustainable parent programs in school curriculum is a necessity for all Australian schools (DIAC, 2009). For Mondale Primary School, the benefits of parent involvement in all matters to do with schooling impact greatly on the degree to which students feel engaged, connected and confident with their learning environment and their social development. These benefits are recorded in the data findings that are explored later on in this chapter. The next section of this discussion will draw attention to what the literature tells us about how parent involvement with their child's education can help to enhance their social and cultural capital.

What the Literature Has to Say

It is our contention that for parents, feeling deeply connected to a school begins when they are *welcomed* at the front gate. In the presence of school personnel who make it their business to involve parents in the establishment of school culture, there is likely to emerge a tightly knit community made of happy children (Epstein, Coates, Clark Salinas, Sanders, & Simon, 1997; Catsambis, 1998). Cohesive community ties are especially needed when addressing how best to support disenfranchised families who are marginalised by hegemonic ideals and eurocentric ways of seeing the world (MacLeod, 1987). It is not enough to adopt Ruby Payne's argument that middle-class rules need to be taken on by the least advantaged in order for them to succeed in schooling (2005). Rooted in this stance is a release clause for schools that shelters them from blame and responsibility when parents choose to disassociate themselves from their child's schooling. Institutions have a social and moral obligation to ensure that poverty stops at the school gate so that families who are economically, spiritually and culturally dislocated are not further penalised because they choose not to conform to ideals that set them up to fail (Darder, Baltodano, & Torres, 2009; Duncan-Andrade & Morrell, 2008). If it is that parents do not want to participate in school life, then it is imperative that schools find out the reasons why. Only then can respectful and practical strategies be established that give parents the option to become involved if they so wish. Establishing a whole-school approach that deals primarily with parent efficacy is an important strategic vision that needs to be in all school charters (Gonzalez-DeHass & Willems, 2003).

Durkheim's (1992) notion of "collective consciousness" is seeded in a whole-school approach that addresses the levels of complexities faced by families who are marginalised by school policies and ideals. Educational institutions that provide parents with opportunities to interact with school life in authentic and practical ways help to instil greater feelings of *belonging* and *connectedness.* For children, seeing their parents more connected to their school helps to create greater feelings of solidarity with teachers and school personnel. Such sentiments are supported by McConchie (2004), who makes note of the fact that parents and guardians who feel connected to schools are more likely to impact and contribute to their child's progress. For example, when it comes to fathers being involved in school matters, "adolescent perceptions of their father's involvement has been found to significantly influence students' positive attitudes towards school (and to be an important factor in school success)" (Fletcher & Silberberg, 2006, p. 28). Masters reiterates the importance of parental participation, asserting that successful schools are those that encourage parents to "take an active role in discussing, monitoring and supporting their children's learning and are involved in setting goals for the school and developing school policy" (2004, p. 24). We contend that the affirmative impact that parents and guardians can have on their children when they are involved in homework activities, school council, literacy and numeracy programs as well as community engagement forums is exceptionally powerful. When parents are given opportunities to help their children to succeed in schooling, there is a much greater likelihood that they will understand the positive influence they can have on shaping their child's future (Redding, Langdon, Myer, & Sheley, 2004).

Whilst parent programs vary from school to school and cater for a range of parent needs, having the right parent program is the result of schools knowing their parent community. Having an awareness of the literacy and numeracy skills of parents, understanding how a child's home life creates or hinders learning, being sensitive to the impact and toll that a refugee journey takes on all aspects of wellness are areas that can be supported through carefully crafted parent programs. If schools get it right, happier and more confident parents lead to happier and healthier school students. Such "knock-on" effects are well documented (Stone & Hughes, 2001). Yet despite this well-known fact, Decker and colleagues are perplexed as to why many schools fail to implement parent programs in their school curriculum. We see this when they state "given the widespread recognition that parent involvement in schools is important, that it is unequivocally related to improvements in children's achievement, and that improvement in children's achievement is urgently needed, it is paradoxical that most schools do not have comprehensive parent involvement programs" (Decker, Decker, Boo, Gregg, & Erickson, 2000, p. 37). Schools like Mondale PS that have a high intake of new arrivals and families living on the poverty line, need to maintain a commitment to facilitating parent awareness of processes and procedures that can enhance their livelihood.

For families who have endured the terrifying refugee journey, who struggle with daily life, who are unable to scrape together finances to pay for school camps, school uniforms or excursions, involvement in school activities can help to alleviate unwanted feelings of anxiety and stress. The Low Income Awareness Checklist, devised by Stafford and Stafford in 2004, highlights the role that schools can play in ensuring that support structures are in place to assist families in non-threatening ways. Schools that elect to utilise this tool when working with teams of teachers and school leaders can be mindful of those areas that they need to address in order to support parents in respectful ways (McInerney, 2004). Providing parents with access to secondhand books, offering art and craft lessons to families wanting to extend friendship circles, planning forum nights on themes tied to literacy and numeracy skill improvement can and does bring forth feelings of self-efficacy never before encountered due to their life circumstances prior to arrival in Australia. Current literature, such as CMYI's *Opening the School Gates: Engaging Culturally and Linguistically Diverse (CALD) Families in Schools* (2006a), identifies other actions and strategies that facilitate a greater likelihood of parent participation in educational experiences. Some of these actions include the establishment of parent networks, culturally sensitive functions and events for families and the inclusion of interpreters and multicultural education aides to bridge the gap between schools and parents (2006a, p.17).

Methodology Used by the Research Team

In order to gauge the kinds of sessions that parents wanted the school to deliver, we established a questionnaire. The MEAs at the school also contacted parents to ensure that they had received the questionnaire and also translated those aspects of the questionnaire that were unclear. Twenty parent responses were tabulated, which resulted in the following sessions being offered for the 2009 parent program:

Session Num-ber	Topic	Areas Covered	Facilitator
1	Children's Health	Bedwetting—shower/change underwear before school. Older children—what to do. Fever/Colds—identifying, what to do. Gastro—treatment / avoiding Chilblains—African Community Head lice—treatment Ringworms Role of school nurse (eyes) & refugee nurse (immunisation) Maintaining good health—wash hands, covering mouth, not coming to school ill. School injuries—broken bones, sprains, head injuries (concussion), eye injuries. General first aid Dental hygiene	School Nurse
2	Nutrition—lunch boxes	Food pyramid What makes a healthy lunch box? Make up a healthy lunch box (different choices) Discuss enough food to sustain energy throughout the day. Importance of breakfast, water Healthy snacks Portion size Food safety—food going off/storage e.g., fish, chicken, milk, yoghurt—recess foods.	Community Dietician
3	Routines and Managing Difficult Behaviour	Routines—TV/Comp/DS etc. Shower/changing underwear Sleep—regular bedtimes Quiet time before bed Responsibilities Morning routine Preparing for school Strategies for difficult behaviour: early childhood, mid childhood, teens. Consequences for misbehaviour Australian law regarding punishment Ask parents their strategies Where to go for help? Share cultural issues	School Psychologist
4	Child development: Helping your child at school	Language—Ed P–2—Early years of schooling, Chatterbox, literacy, numeracy, ways you can help at home. 3–6—education system differences, formalised learning—not ROTE, hands-on, inquiry, open-ended thinking curriculum, ways you can help at school Maths measurement money Critical literacy Footage of children in P–2 & 3–6 reading, inquiry, maths, Chatterbox.	Speech Pathologist

5	Centrelink (government agency that manages social welfare payments)	Single parents New mums Childcare benefits EMA Parenting payments Direct debit bill payments Form completion Carers allowance/payment Question time New job allowances New start Obligations Making appointments Services available i.e., interpreters etc.	Centrelink Official

Show bags and door prizes, which proved to be very popular, were attached to each of the parent sessions. They included the following items:

Session	Show bag Contents	Door Prize
1	Soap, facewasher, deodorant, Bandaids, no water hand wash, comb, hair ties, first aid booklet/fact sheet, sunscreen.	First aid kit x 2
2	Food pyramid—colour/laminate, recipes, healthy snacks—Uncle Toby's, pretzels, fruit, popcorn, lunch box, drink bottle	Shopping store gift voucher
3	Game ($2 shop card game, Connect 4), rewards/star chart, list of agencies for help, clock, websites (Brimbank Council, Westside Community Centre, Tin Shed), to-do list, parent magazines (McKillop, Melbourne's Child), free activities for families (Fed Square, Brimbank Council).	Movie tickets/voucher Picture story books Puzzle books
4	Cursive script Placemats Dictionary Calculator Pencils—grey leads Pencil case—coloured pencils, sharpeners, ruler. Dotted thirds books List of good websites—laminated Calendar—term dates 2010	Educational games
5	Brochures (ask Centrelink) List phone numbers of agencies Address/phone book ($2 shop) Pen Pocket diary Fridge magnet File for bills	Food hamper

Parent attendance at each of the sessions varied from week to week. Between 30 and 40 parents would attend each of the sessions of the five weeks with over 50 parents attending the Centrelink session. The Centrelink session therefore proved to be the most popular. Reasons for its popularity are outlined in the section below.

In addition to using a parent questionnaire, we also wrote cases about our feelings and perceptions tied to those factors that contribute to the construction of effective parent programs. The adoption of cases in the evaluation was based on the work of Judith Shulman (1991) and Marilyn Cochran-Smith (1991), whose work around case writing highlights the value of this research tool in drawing out contexts and feelings. We not only wrote cases but also maintained a journal. Both the cases and journal entries were examined through the use of a "threading" technique that allowed us to clarify key phrases or words. We discussed key phrases and words openly and then grouped them into subheadings that have formed the data themes below. It is also important to note that through engaging in a collaborative data theorising process, we were given an opportunity to develop understandings around practitioner-led research. The school teachers who made up our research team felt that they rarely took the opportunity to document their work in a systematic way. Through engaging in this kind of research, they agreed that this project had shown them the importance of developing reflective practices. In addition we all believed that our participation in the project had also allowed us to develop more meaningful relationships with school colleagues.

Facilitators involved in the parent sessions were involved in a focus group discussion. A focus group with three MEAs and eight parents was also conducted. It is worth noting, however, that feedback gained from parents was limited. This was largely due to the fact that while there were interpreters present at each of the sessions, parents and guardians had limited English. Secondly, for many parents, responding to questions about what they liked or disliked about the program was an action that was quite foreign to them; having a school ask their opinions on schooling matters was challenging from a cultural view in that quite often parents see schools as sites that provide knowledge rather than seek it. Yet, despite their limited responses, their attendance at each of the sessions was evidence of the program's success.

Data collected through the focus group sessions and the interviews were analyzed using a "thematic approach". Thomas and Harden (2008) note the effectiveness of using this kind of analysis in that it gives the researcher an opportunity to sift though the data "line by line" so as to generate overarching themes.

Data Themes Generated

Teacher/Well-being Co-ordinator/Assistant Principal Lens

As previously stated, our research team was made up of many members who had not been involved in previous research projects. Involvement in the research project provided all of us with an opportunity to strengthen and build professional relationships. For some of the teachers, involvement in the program provided them with their first opportunity to liaise with support staff, which included community agencies and services, school providers and support services. As a result they developed greater insight into their role in supporting families through accessing support services and the impact this knowledge has on improving student learning.

Our research team also commented on how participation in the project gave us an opportunity to work collegiately with each other. This was evidenced by a quote from Joanne's journal: "It was wonderful to see all the team members sharing in the discussion and proposing ideas and suggestions—building a sense of collegiality and teamwork." Another staff member noted in his case that "working collaboratively with other professionals has helped me develop a better understanding of good teaching and learning practices". Both practitioners highlight the importance of working with professional stakeholders in practical ways and see the benefits of this work in strengthening the depth of connectedness amongst colleagues on issues that are especially tied to social justice.

A strong focus of the parent program in this research project was around building social and cultural capital in the parents and enhancing relationships between the school (parents, teachers, students, multicultural education aides ([MEAs], school leaders and non-teaching staff) and the broader community. Through our involvement in the research project, we were able to build a depth understanding and awareness of the school's social justice vision. Mondale Primary School has a strong ethos for social justice and a commitment to building a sense of an equitable and just community. The parent program is a forum that empowers the participants in an informal setting. "Building cultural capital in Australia empowers all parties—especially the individuals who are the stake holders" (teacher journal entry).

Another key finding that emerges from the data was that participation in the parent program gave classroom teachers a greater insight and connection to the school community, helping to dispel teacher stereotypes and assumptions around low socioeconomics and cultural diversity. "It has been a great experience being a part of this program building a connection with the community and in particular the ladies in the group have given me a better insight into their lives. For this I feel privileged," wrote one of the teachers in a journal entry.

The parent program also empowered parents to better support their children both at school and at home. We observed changes that took place to children's learning as a result of parents becoming involved in the parent program. These changes included children

- having healthier lunches. One parent, Sarah, commented, "It gave us ideas to encourage our children to eat fruit and vegetables.";

- feeling more rested (bedtime routines were established for many of the children);

- reading more at home. In an interview after the literacy session, one parent stated: "I liked everything especially reading stories and asking questions." One teacher noted that "children in my class whose parents attended the parent program commented of changes within the household as a result of their parents having attended sessions. These changes included eating habits, bed times and engaging in homework activities" (journal entry). This reflection highlights the importance of embedding innovative curriculum projects like the parent program in schools in such a way that these strategies can lead to greater health and well-being for young learners and parental engagement.

An effective parent program requires a commitment to resourcing through timetabling allocations for the use of facilities and for staff to participate, including MEAs and teachers. We believe that the success of this program was directly related to the research grant, which enabled teachers to be released from their regular duties to participate in the program and research. This is evident in the commentary given by one teacher when he writes in his case, "If embedded action research is to be the future direction of education, consideration will have to be given to school structure to release people, give them time to research and not create a financial deficit in the school." Financial support to enable a program such as this to be realised cannot be diminished.

Parent/Guardian Lens

During the focus group, parents acknowledged the importance of being able to participate in the parent program and how such involvement made them more confident when engaging with school staff. They particularly enjoyed the opportunity to contribute to the content in each of the sessions. When we asked what do you want to learn today? James said, "How we can help our children to improve and understand. We need our children to improve." James further reaffirmed the importance of the parent program in giving him skills to better equip him as a parent to support his child at school: "I have enjoyed attending the parent program as I have learnt how to help my child with their reading and writing and homework. I am going to make sure we have some time as a family to all practise our reading and writing together." Another teacher involved in the project acknowledged the importance of being a part of the research project in that it enabled him to foster closer links with some of the parents in the school. He notes in his case, "One parent from the program felt confident enough to ask me to check on the progress and the help her child was receiving from his teacher. It did not matter that I was not his classroom teacher."

A Centrelink[6] information session in the project was extremely popular with over 50 parents attending. Overall parents/guardians valued having employees from Centrelink speak about mundane but challenging processes such as filling out forms to receive government financial assistance. What is also very important to note is that having Centrelink personnel present on school grounds was a very positive step, as it gave parents access to government services in a supportive rather than a punitive way. One area of discussion with the government official was the availability of English-language classes for the parents. Rebecca, one of the parents who attended the sessions, spoke of her experiences. She reflected on the 510 hours that AMES gives to new arrivals and asserted that it was not enough to help her literacy skills. "Five hundred and ten hours at AMES doesn't give enough English language to learn to read, write and speak and get a report," Rebecca said during the session. She was referring to having enough English-language skills to gain employment. One positive outcome of the session was that participants were informed of Job Services Australia, a service that provides 800 hours of further English classes.

In 2010 Rebecca has commenced her extended language classes. Her reflections support the findings that the parent/guardian program assisted many parents to not only develop greater insights into available services that are afforded to them through government agencies like Centrelink, but most importantly, parents felt "confident" to make further contact with Centrelink outside of the school grounds when considering issues they needed assistance with. In an interview Trang spoke about how she benefited from the Centrelink session: "The Centrelink staff confirmed what I knew and added more." She also noted that as a result of attending she was now aware of some of the payments that she was entitled to receive as a single parent from Centrelink, alongside the Youth Allowance, and what happens when her children turn 16. Prior to this, Trang was informed by her 15-year-old son as to how she needed to spend his Youth Allowance payments. At times this advice was incorrect and misleading

A strong theme to emerge from talking to parents and guardians during the focus group session was that they really appreciated the opportunity to further extend their knowledge base on a range of functional topics. Through attending sessions addressing healthy eating, literacy strategies in the home and managing difficult behaviour, parents and guardians felt more confident and better equipped to deal with a range of issues. One parent, for example, when interviewed about the parent program, exclaimed, "Ah yes. I learnt a lot. It is all about the children. Learning to help the children—so I can help them." Parents and guardians who feel more able to assist their children with schooling needs have a greater sense of self esteem and purpose. Truc said, "It [the parent program] helps me to help my children. Sometimes they tend to do things that they want. When they are doing well at school you feel happy, like you are being a good parent."

At the focus group session, the parents were willing to discuss their feelings about the program and what they had learnt. Laila commented, "I am happy with the sessions. I felt nothing was missing. I liked everything, especially about reading and asking questions." The data collected indicated that the families were all happy with the program and that they all learnt something. One of the teachers, in a journal entry, also reported a need to embed more ICT topics in the next parent sessions: "The group had never had a voice before and now it's time to think—all good. The parents wanted extra sessions on topics such as ICT."

The school's speech pathologist affirmed the need for families to speak to their children in their first language. He explained that children cannot distinguish between languages. Families need to have set times for speaking different languages. This approach is supported by research which notes the importance of maintaining your first language and transferring the skills to effectively communicate in other languages (Clarke, 2009). The point of this is that parents would not have had this opportunity to access this information had they not attended the parent program session.

The research findings indicated that the "show bags" or bags of freebies and giveaways were very popular and enthusiastically received by the participants. These show bags included support materials related to the particular focus session and were provided to all participants each week. The research funds were used to purchase the contents. The assistant principal spoke about the benefits of having the show bags in her journal entry: "The show bags were very popular and parents lined up weekly for their bag. We even had to keep bags for families who couldn't make the session. I saw the impact that these show bags had on the participants. They were very excited."

To ensure the engagement of individuals and to cater for the diverse learning needs of the parents/guardians, a variety of innovative teaching and learning approaches were used at each session. The healthy eating session, for example, provided participants with an experiential learning opportunity. The session involved a discussion followed by a workshop where group members were able to make healthy-eating lunch boxes. All ingredients were supplied to participants and members were able to take home their healthy lunch box. The lunch boxes consisted of a tuna and salad wrap, fruit juice and fresh fruit. This enabled families to show their children and other families members what a healthy lunch box looks like. "Making wraps was great. We learnt about grating vegetables," Mwjuma commented in an interview. Modelling healthy eating approaches was therefore another important theme to emerge from the evaluation of the parent program.

Through demonstrating to parents and guardians what a healthy lunch box looks and tastes like, there appeared to be greater understanding of the kinds of lunches that parents/guardians could prepare for their children in their homes. "The food table was very informative. All the fresh vegetables are good. I am going to try to make the wraps at home," said Sangeeta. Further, the experiential nature of this session for parents who have low literacy level skills meant that participants could visualise healthy school snacks as well as take pride in working with a nutritionist to make healthy school snacks during the session. The assistant principal noted the success of parental involvement in this session in her diary entry: "There was a very positive and happy atmosphere from everyone at today's session. I think the parents enjoyed the opportunity to mix and socialise with a common purpose."

One of the foci of the research project was to build and strengthen the school community's social capital (Putnam, 2000). Each week the parents were involved in formal learning experiences in areas of interest in the bid to broaden their understanding of the topics covered. We found that another positive aspect of the program was the ability for participants to develop friendship circles with other parents/guardians who attended. At the focus group the one parent, Lucia, said, "I liked coming to the parent program as I learnt how to help my children. It is good to have something to do when the children are at school. Often we just do the housework and don't have anyone to talk to." This was an important theme to evolve from the evaluation in that it highlighted how friendships can build cross-cultural links and foster acceptance and tolerance amongst people of diverse ethnic and cultural backgrounds. The parent program therefore celebrated participants having a greater knowledge of the school's cultural diversity, and the diversity of other parents and guardians connected to the school. At each session tea, coffee and sandwiches were organised for the participants as a courtesy but also as a way to build shared community time. Everyone was seated so that they could be involved in discussions. "It is apparent as you walk past the library and hear and see the community working together in this program to provide support for families and the opportunity to connect in such an open and inviting environment," wrote one of the teachers in a case writing entry.

In a diverse multicultural community there is a very valid need for multicultural education aides (MEA) to support the partnerships between the school, the families and the broader community. "MEAs are the voice of the people," asserted one teacher. Within the parent program, MEAs built links with the parents and they were often the initial point of contact with parents and guardians when it came to school matters. We see this when one EMA talks about her position at the school in the following way, "My role as an MEA at Mondale Primary School involves supporting parents in need and children from non English speaking backgrounds. Constant connection with families is maintained via telephone conversations and parent participation in parent programs, parent information sessions and

African women's groups organised within the school." What is evident from this evaluation project is the need to ensure that MEAs are involved in working with parents and guardians from the outset to alert them to the importance of the variety of school projects. What was also apparent from the data was the great respect that parents and guardians had for the MEAs employed at the school. This respect translated into trust and a willingness to be guided and mentored by the MEAs.

Hence the involvement of the MEAs, who are respected members of the school community, was instrumental in the success of the program as they were able to use their influence in the community. They were able to ensure regular attendance and inform the families of the importance of the program and the benefits they would receive from participation. The MEAs also assisted in surveying the families to determine the areas of interest for the program. Sarah commented at the focus session, "I knew about the parent program because Syama rang me. I am learning English and can't read the note. Sometimes my children will read it to me but they often forget." Such an insight made us aware of the importance of giving a voice to parents, as this helped to ensure a collaborative approach in the running of the program. In our reflections we feel that parental involvement in the choice of program sessions led to the regular attendance of parents and the overall success of the program.

The parents enjoyed the recognition and celebration of their achievement through participation in the program and were pleased to be presented with a certificate at the end of the last session. With enthusiasm and pride, the participants of the parent program received a certificate of participation during the final session. The parents/guardians proudly held their certificate for a group photograph. "The most poignant comment I heard throughout the parent program," reported one teacher, "was made by a parent at this table who said, 'This was the first certificate I have ever received in my life. As parents we should always be ready to learn'." By providing participants with a certificate that recognises and acknowledges their involvement in the program, parents and guardians are able to feel valued for their attendance and contribution to each of the sessions.

For many families, their first port of call to access information is the school. The assistant principal in a journal entry reinforced the finding that *the connection to the school becomes important to our families contributing to their social capital and understandings. The school and our MEAs are a resource for our families as they learn about life in Australia.* However, due to the cultural diversity of our community the school was unable to have MEAs for every language that is spoken by its community. As a result access to interpreters was limited and at times throughout the program did pose as a problem. Currently at Mondale Primary School there are 38 different languages spoken by the families, and the school's MEAs represent the larger cultural groups within the school. In order to ensure equity and participation in activities, external interpreters are used from the Department of Education and Early Childhood Development. This issue was indeed an area of concern that emerged from the evaluation. Ensuring that all parents/guardians feel included in the parent sessions was therefore a key aim for 2011. As to the logistics of making this happen, with limited interpreters it is questionable as to how this might take place. This is a further area of investigation that could be examined more closely in future projects.

Giving parents/guardians a voice as to the nature of the five-week session was a positive outcome of the parent session. In order to assess parent needs, an initial part of the program was to survey the parents and give them input into the program content. As part of this program, parents have expressed areas of interest for future sessions. Following the session with the psychologist, the parents were given the opportunity for group feedback. One of the teachers involved in the project noted the following in her journal when reflecting on parent needs: "They wanted to learn about bed time strategies, teenagers, study routines, morning routines, and afternoon/homework routines—in 2010 the school will organise a series of sessions with the school psychologist on these topics." Such insights demonstrated the importance of ensuring that parents and guardians are able to collaborate with school staff on the topics that they see as being most useful to enhancing their cultural and social capital.

Community Stakeholder Lens

Community stakeholders and school support staff facilitated sessions during the parent program. We liaised with all of the facilitators to ensure that each session met the needs of the participant as reflected in the pre-program survey. Following the parent program, all facilitators participated in focus groups to share their experiences.

Data collected indicated that a common thread for community stakeholders was the connection to the school and the parent community. "Parent programs can contribute to building a sense of community through engagement, a sense of belonging. It is not so much about the strategies that we teach the parents but the sense of belonging and being all here together," noted one of the facilitators. Participation in the parent program assists stakeholders to make connections with the school and the community. Staff from Centrelink highlighted that this was the first time they had spoken to members of the broader community in a school setting. Although government officials were unsure of what to expect, they enjoyed the session and were able to inform as well as answer participants' questions.

All facilitators in this research believed that the strength of the program was in its ability to establish links with the school and the community; opening up pathways for future work in the school was also noted as another positive outcome to emerge from the work. For example, the school psychologist who presented in one of the sessions asserted that "the partnerships with the school and the organisation have long term benefits for all key stakeholders." Often community agencies find it difficult to connect with their client base in the broader community. This is exacerbated by communication barriers including access to clients and interpreters. The parent program helps to connect all stakeholders. As one teacher notes, "My hope is that through this program the parents and community will be empowered to link themselves with agencies who are able to provide ongoing assistance as needed and develop the skills required to feel confident reaching beyond what they experienced through the program independently."

Facilitator reflections highlighted aspects of the program that may need to improve in the future, such as using more visuals and models to help with language barriers. For example, the dietician stated that "making the wraps and showing the healthy lunch boxes helped develop understandings related to the topic." She went on to say that "in further sessions I would use more visuals including food models." The facilitators reiterated the need for understanding key issues commonly faced by parent/guardian within an educational context.

The findings supported the need for collaboration between the school and the facilitators to ensure that the material presented at each session was relevant and met the needs of the parent/guardian community attending each session. We were alerted to the benefits of having the school community work together in collaborative and supporting ways. In the case of some of the organisations who presented, having direct contact with parents and guardians and listening to their stories provided facilitators with an opportunity to connect with parents/guardians in a different way. Understanding of the needs of their client base was enhanced and far richer. This is evident in the following response from the dietician, who noted that "participation in the parent program helped me to learn about different cultures and how to communicate with them."

During focus group sessions the facilitators were asked about the long-term benefits through their involvement in the parent program. Their responses identified a consistent theme: the involvement in the parent program gave them greater insight into the cultural and social needs of their client base. Involvement in the program has enabled community agencies to make links with the school and has resulted in future programs.

Parent Program—Conclusion

The evaluation into the parent program provided us with an opportunity to investigate innovative curriculum approaches to enhance student learning and well-being. From the case studies, journal entries, facilitator and parent feedback, the data collected gave us greater insight into those characteristics that make up an effective parent program.

The delivery model of the parent program included "hands-on" experiences with the use of visuals and models to help with language barriers. The facilitators reiterated the need for understanding key issues commonly faced by parent/guardian within an educational context. The interactive activities ensured that the program was inclusive and catered for the learning styles of the parents. For example, parent involvement in making wraps, language development via the use of a "feely bag" (a closed bag containing a variety of objects with different textures for language exploration), table discussions, role modelling, categorizing foods as per food pyramid, using real-life examples and viewing DVDs. Overall we found that a successful parent program is inclusive and includes experiential, audio and kinaesthetic activities as well as being embedded in a social justice framework.

The data gathered make note of the fact that the parent program was supportive of classroom curriculum through the incorporation of sessions related to nutrition, language development and helping your child at school. The session run by the physiologist that focused on student well-being helped to foster greater understanding of cultural and social expectations of discipline and classroom management. Laila, a parent, commented that she was "happy with the Australian system, children learn here compared to Africa. The difference is that [in Africa] there are 30–100 children in the class and teachers talk to those in the front. Here 15–20 children in the class with support. Groups with 5 children are a focus."

We argue that the parent program has opened a pathway for community services to develop a greater connection with parent and guardians as well as school colleagues.

Notes

1. The term parent is used to also represent guardian/s.
2. This project was funded by the Department of Education and Early Childhood Development.
3. The writers would like to acknowledge the work of Darren Thresher, Lis Surace, Syama Niout, Grace Elikana and Deborah Hirst, who also contributed to the evaluation process.
4. For confidentially purposes the name of the school has been changed.
5. Payment is around $230 for primary school students and $460 for secondary school students. To qualify for EMA, parents or guardians must be on a Centrelink allowance or pension. In essence, to be eligible parents or guardians must earn less than $35,000 annually.
6. Centrelink is a government department that provides individuals with advice on social welfare payments and services.

References

Catsambis, S. (1998). *Expanding knowledge of parental involvement in secondary education: Effects on high school academic success* (Report No. 27). Baltimore: Center for Research on the Education of Students Placed at Risk (CRESPAR).

Centre for Multicultural Youth Issues (CMI). (2006a). *Opening school gates: Engaging culturally and linguistically divers (CALD) families in schools.* Carlton, Australia: Author.

Centre for Multicultural Youth Issues (CMI). (2006b). *A three-way partnership? Exploring the experiences of CLD families in schools.* Carlton, Australia: Author.

Cherednichenko, B., Davies, A., Kruger, T., & O'Rourke, M. (2001, December). *Collaborative practices: From description to theory.* Refereed paper for Australian Association for Research in Education Conference, Fremantle, Western Australia.

Clarke, P. (2009). *Supporting children learning English as a second language in the early years (birth to six years)* (Discussion paper). Melbourne: Victorian Curriculum and Assessment Authority (VCAA).

Cochran-Smith, M. (1991). Reinventing student teaching. *Journal of Teacher Education, 42*(2), 104–118.

Darder, A., Baltodano, M. P., & Torres, R. D. (2009). Critical pedagogy: An introduction. In A. Darder, M. P. Baltodano, & R. D Torres (Eds.), *The critical pedagogy reader* (2nd ed.). New York: Routledge.

Decker, L. E., Decker, V. A., Boo, M. R., Gregg, G. A., & Erickson, J. (2000). *Engaging families and communities.* Fairfax, VA: National Community Education Association.

Department of Immigration and Citizenship (DIAC). (2009). *Fact sheet 60: Australia's refugee and humanitarian program.* Canberra: Author.

Duncan-Andrade, J., & Morrell, E. (2008). *The art of critical pedagogy: Possibilities for moving from theory to practice in urban schools.* New York: Peter Lang.

Durkheim, E. (1992). *The division of labour in society* (2nd ed.). Basingstoke, England: Macmillan.

Epstein, J. L., Coates, L., Clark Salinas, K., Sanders, M., & Simon, B. (1997). *School, family and community partnerships: Your handbook for action.* Thousand Oaks, CA: Corwin Press.

Ferrance, E. (2000). *Action research.* Providence, RI: Brown University.

Fletcher, R., & Silberberg, S. (2006). Involvement of fathers in primary school activities. *Australian Journal of Education, 50*(1), 29–39.

Freire, P. (2001). *Pedagogy of freedom: Ethics, democracy and civic courage.* Lanham, MD: Rowman & Littlefield.

Gonzalez-DeHass, A. R., & Willems, P. P. (2003). Examining the underutilization of parent involvement in schools. *School Community Journal, 13*(1), 85–99.

Greenwood, G. E., & Hickman, C. W. (1991). Research and practice in parent involvement: Implications for teacher education. *Elementary School Journal, 91*(3), 279–288.

MacLeod, J. (1987). *Ain't no makin' it: In a low-income neighbourhood.* Boulder, CO: Westview.

Masters, G. (2004). Beyond political rhetoric: The research on what makes a school good. *Online Opinion.* Retrieved from http://www.onlineopinion.com.au/view.asp?article=2100

McConchie, R. (2004). *Family-school partnerships issues paper.* Canberra: Australian Council of State School Organisations (ACSSO).

McInerney, P. (2004). *Making hope practical: School reform for social justice.* Flaxton, QLD: Post Pressed.

Payne, R. (2005). *A framework for understanding poverty* (Rev. 4th ed.). Highlands, TX: Aha! Process.

Putnam, R. (2000). *Bowling alone: The collapse and revival of American community.* New York: Simon & Schuster.

Redding, S., Langdon, J., Myer, J., & Sheley, P. (2004, April). *The effects of comprehensive parent engagement on student learning outcomes.* Paper presented at AERA conference, San Diego.

Schulman, J. (1991). Revealing the mysteries of teacher-written case: Opening the black box. *Journal of Teacher Education, 42*(4), 250–262.

Stafford, G., & Stafford, C. (2004). *Low income awareness checklist.* Brimbank, VIC, Australia: Brimbank Emergency Relief Network.

Stone, W., & Hughes, J. (2001, December). *Social capital: Linking family and community?* Paper presented at the Family Strengths Conference, University of Newcastle, NSW, Australia.

Thomas, J., & Harden, A. (2008). Methods for the thematic synthesis of qualitative research in systematic reviews. *BMC Medical Research Methodology, 8*(45), 8–45.

CHAPTER THIRTY-TWO

Democracy, Freedom, and the School Bell

Frances Helyar

Once upon a time it was possible for the researcher to describe the history of education as a straight narrative. That action led to this development, which led to that innovation and those consequences. Of course, history was never that simple; different historians produced widely varying accounts of the past and its relationship to the present. Today the researcher-as-bricoleur uses new and often multiple tools and methodologies to explore the same source materials, as well as some that have never been examined, in order to come to a deeper understanding of educational history. By weaving together a historiographical approach in which the researcher self-consciously examines not just the past, but also the way the past has been interpreted by others, combined with various other disciplinary approaches, the result is a richer tapestry of images, a broader narrative canvas, and a more complex conceptualization of education as it exists in the present—indeed, an affirmative presentism.

What follows on the next few pages is an example of this type of research. The initial impulse was to look at freedom, democracy, and educational history. But when this project began, the 2004 presidential election campaign was in full swing. The rhetoric swirled and the promises abounded. At the same time, I read William Reese's *Power and the Promise of School Reform: Grassroots Movements During the Progressive Era* (2002). The image that stayed with me was from that book's opening passage: a ship arrives in Toledo harbor carrying the new school bell. I began to think about that bell as a symbol, and to recognize that as such it was an image with rich and varied associations. Thus by using semiotics as a starting point I was able to embark on a study using multiple disciplines in a bricolage approach that combines historical research with the disciplinary knowledges of sociology, ethnography, political science, educational psychology, and more. The accompanying poems were written for oral presentation, to give a sense of the content of the text without resorting to a more traditional abstract.

Freedom is the expressed goal of democratic nations in 20th- and 21st-century political and social discourse. The terms freedom and democracy are intricately entwined; they appear repeatedly, for example, in the promotional material of the U.S. Republican Party (on average, the word democracy

455

shows up on over 30% of the pages in the Republican Party Platform [Republican National Committee, 2004], while freedom appears on about 75%). The U.S. Democratic Party mentions freedom and democracy in equal proportions (Democratic Party, 2004). Democracy as a search term generates 145 million hits on Google; freedom generates 415 million. The construct of each word in general Western discourse relies upon the notion that freedom and democracy are both homogeneous. In reality, however, the two concepts are equally complicated and multifaceted. Economic freedom is not necessarily the same as political freedom, and political freedom is not the same as social freedom. Democracy has gradations: "all the people" represented by government may exclude a significant portion of the population, whether by race, gender, class, sexuality, or other factors. Government practices may be overtly democratic, but populations are often willing to cede control in order to procure economic or other gains. Since the publication of Antonio Gramsci's work on hegemony, critical scholars understand that neither freedom nor democracy exist in any pure form.

The bell is an important symbol associated with freedom and, by extension, democracy in American folklore. Peter, Paul and Mary sang about the "Bell of Freedom" during the 1960s (Hays & Seeger, 1949). The Liberty Bell serves as an enduring example, as a result of its association with the American Revolution. "Let Freedom Ring" (Hirsch, 1997, p. 165) is one title by which E. D. Hirsch introduces the bell, including it in his list of vital knowledge for first graders. In educational history the bell appears regularly in accounts of schooling, both theoretical and narrative. William Reese opens his study of grassroots movements in education during the Progressive Era with the story of the arrival of a new school bell by boat to the city of Toledo. The scene is a celebratory one, but as Reese makes clear, the bell is not a symbol of freedom. It will ring out the hour to tell citizens when to begin and end their work and school days, imposing virtues valued by the elite upon public institutions (Reese, 2002). This tension between the ideal of freedom as symbolized by the bell and the actual function of the bell as a means of control mirrors the tension between the homogeneous notion of freedom and democracy, and the way freedom and democracy are actually experienced in the history of education.

The bell metaphor is an apt tool to dismantle the history of education in the twentieth century, and the course of education in the twenty-first. If the bell is a metaphor for freedom, and freedom is a hallmark of democracy, then a series of questions about school bells serves to frame an interrogation of developments in education over the last hundred years: What does the location of the bell signify? What does the lack of a bell signify? What does the shape of the bell signify? What does a broken bell signify, and what does the sound of the bell signify? Finally, who rings the school bell? By examining these questions using critical educational historiography, it is possible to approach an understanding of the complexity of developments in education, and indicate that this complexity continues into the 21st century.

These framing questions came late in the process of preparing this piece, which began with brainstorming about bells in general, and then bells in relation to education. During the brainstorming process the various directions of the research became clear. This is a semiotic study in which the bell is a symbol on many different levels. Thinking about church bells, the Liberty Bell, plantation bells, the handheld school bell, and the automated school bell led to thoughts of time and marking time, social control, Pavlov's dogs, wedding bells, John Donne, Hemingway, and even Mötley Crüe's "Smoking in the Boys' Room" (the last three of which I didn't use in the end). I investigated each to see how it related to developments in education. Cultural studies, poststructuralism, sociology, history, and psychology all came into play. Much later in the process when I felt I had explored the metaphor sufficiently, I organized the results loosely by three senses: sight, touch, and hearing.

What Does the Location of the Bell Signify?

High atop the school tower sits the ringing bell,
Where once it rang from steeples keeping us from hell.
Now it's not salvation but a better life through school
For it's through education that we learn the Golden Rule.

The growth of cities and the corresponding growth in the numbers of urban children was a major factor in the development of common schools in the U.S. How should these children be prepared for the future? How should they be controlled in the present? Parents no longer held sole responsibility for these tasks, nor did the church have as great an influence as in the past. In fact, cities

> placed added burdens on extant institutions, ranging from the insistence that they provide the social discipline essential to life amidst crowded conditions to the suggestion that they convey every manner of vital specialized knowledge. One result was that statements of educational purpose tended to broaden significantly. (Cremin, 1988, p. 7)

The school in an urban setting called for a bell, the sound of which was capable of being broadcast over a wide area. The Toledo school bell described by Reese (2002) had a place of honor alongside a brass town clock at the top of the tower of the new high school. Where in most communities the bell once stood atop a steeple calling worshippers to church, here education was usurping the role of religion as a locus of control in the community. In addition, schools assumed more responsibility within urban communities, to the extent that they became social centers and welfare agencies (Spring, 2005; Reese, 2002). Thus the location of the urban school bell atop a tower signifies a shift in the nature of society during the 20th century from religious to secular, so that one theologian

> maintained that the secular religion of Americans was not an implicit set of common values expressed diversely through the three great religious communities but rather a fourth religion standing alongside the three, with its own theological and educational apparatus centered in the public schools. (Cremin, 1988, pp. 61–62)

The shift was not a permanent one, however. The federal legislation No Child Left Behind includes provisions allowing faith-based organizations to become more involved in schools and schooling, presented under the aegis of local freedom. The U.S. Department of Education's website contains a section devoted to local freedom for schools, and it includes a page titled "No Child Left Behind and Faith Based Leaders." The page highlights a quote from George W. Bush saying, "The indispensable and transforming work of faith-based and other charitable service groups must be encouraged. Government cannot be replaced by charities, but it can and should welcome them as partners" (U.S. Department of Education, 2004). Thus in the 21st century, the effect of "compassionate conservatism" with its focus on faith-based initiatives is to place church bells alongside school bells.

This is an instance where the present day intruded upon a study of the past. My first impulse was to stop at the shift from religious to secular, but a reading of No Child Left Behind made that impossible. The reform document highlights the ebb and flow of educational developments and their complexity. The passage that follows and its description of automated school bell systems arises from my visits to schools in which I was surprised by the sound of the bells; they were unlike any sound I'd ever heard and somewhat startling. The world of school had definitely changed since I was a student. As a result of this ethnographic observation, I wanted to know who makes these bells and how they are marketed, and wondered whether or not the changes in the sound of the school bell resulted in a change in the effect of the school bell.

> Ain't no bell in this school, least not one we can see
> And yet it rings and rings and rings, alarming you and me.
> So classes start and classes end; it's Math and ABCs,
> And this will help us when we start our work in factories.

Throughout the 20th century, the school bell was central as a mechanism for controlling students. Cuban (1993) describes the way a 1926 handbook for a Washington, D.C. high school spells it out:

Students were told to go to their section (home-room) for opening exercises by 8:55 a.m. "In classrooms absolute quiet must prevail at this time," the handbook stated, because the students must have the "proper attitude" and "frame of mind necessary to start the day right." At 9:10 the bell rang to start the students' seven-period day—"six recitation periods" and lunch. Students had 4 minutes to move from one class to another. (pp. 107–108)

In contemporary schools the school bell is no longer visible. Instead it is hidden within the architecture of the school, and students experience it as a sound alone with a tone often more comparable to an alarm than to the tolling of a bell. Even this sound is changing in the 21st century as bell systems become increasingly computerized. One manufacturer promotes the benefits of its products by saying that administrators can "save thousands of dollars over out-of-date mechanical bell technology with low-cost standardized PC-based technologies" and "never be stuck with ordinary school bell sounds again" (AcroVista Software, n.d.). No matter the tone of the modern school bell, however, it always sounds with an impersonal efficiency, releasing "thousands of students into hallways six to 10 times a day for three to five minutes of chaos" (Rettig & Canaday, 1999, p. 14). Its function is automated so that only a technician can repair it. Moreover, particularly in the high school, the school bell rings not just to begin and end the school day but also to mark the beginning and end of each period, serving as an aural separation of discrete subject areas one from the other. In this way the 21st century school bell has a direct relation to the highly controlled organization of the 19th-century Lancasterian system of schools (Spring, 2005), the efficient and cost-effective platoon schools of the Gary Plan (Mirel, 1999), and the curriculum reforms of various eras that discourage integration of school subjects. The question becomes, by regimenting students' every move, are these schools democratic? If they keep children away from a life of crime and give them the tools they need to meet the demands of living in an adult world, the answer is yes. If they remove children's ability to think critically or to imagine a life outside of a regimented existence, the answer is no.

The complexity of educational research engulfs in a discussion of the "doing" of pedagogical research. For example, educational scholars find it difficult to speak definitively about the purpose of education; different interests define the purpose differently. Through a hermeneutic analysis I try to peel back the layers of meaning. The result is not a positivistic arbitration; I cannot determine which of the purposes of education is the "true" one. Indeed, I can only attempt to present a variety of perspectives. Of course, I have my own biases and preferences and they are ever present in my writing. The more aware I am of these dynamics, the more compelling, more informed by historical research my work will be.

What does the lack of a bell signify?

No school, no bell. Not fair? Oh well.

Among the recurring problems of education throughout the 20th and into the 21st century, particularly in the urban setting, are the insufficient number of school buildings, inadequate buildings, and in some cases, overcrowding in schools. Whether the goal of education is to challenge the status quo or strengthen the established order, such problems are major impediments. If there is no school building, there can be no school bell. The problem can take on racial and ethnic dimensions as it did in Boston in the mid 19th century where black schools were housed in African American church basements (Spring, 2005), or in Detroit in 1924 with the controversy emerging from the suspicion that school budgets were being spent on elaborate buildings in areas of high immigrant population (Mirel, 1999).

Even if there was a school building, the school may not have had a bell. Throughout the history of the American republic, the existence of inadequately funded and segregated schools calls into question the country's democratic identity. No bell of freedom rang in the antebellum American South where it was illegal to educate slaves, or in theCalifornia of 1872 where the school code excluded all but white children from admittance to public schools (Spring, 2005). The effect of such legal sanctions was that equal educational opportunity did not exist for every child. In a broad sense, schools became the battleground for conflicting ideas about social goals and norms, raising the question "how should the legitimate but often unclear and conflicting demands of liberty, equality and comity be resolved in and through programs of education?" (Cremin, 1988, p. 13).

> Our school is progressive, and so we have no bells,
> But if we did, you know that we would forge them by ourselves.

In a more literal sense, the lack of a school bell could also be a choice, turning away from traditional pedagogy to a progressive approach. Cuban describes the changes in a rural Michigan school in 1939 in which the newly progressive teacher cites the abandonment of the school bell as evidence of her conversion (Cuban, 1993). Even this transition, however, is complicated. The Michigan passage is followed by a long quote from John Dewey himself, expressing skepticism that much had changed in American schools. Helen Parkhurst took as fundamental principles of the Dalton School freedom and cooperation, and to that end, she refused to allow bells in the school (Semel, 1999b). But although the Dalton School may have started as a progressive school and Parkhurst may have espoused progressive principles in education, in the actual running of the school she was autocratic and controlling—qualities that eventually led to her downfall. Thus, her choice to abolish school bells and escape the tyranny of their regulation seems merely cosmetic and not reflective of a theory put into practice in a consistent way throughout the school. Just because Parkhurst called her school democratic did not make it so.

Although many progressive schools may have lacked a bell to signal the beginning and end of the day, it did not necessarily mean that bells were banned from the schools entirely. In fact, it was more likely that the bell would become an object of study. How does it work? What are its parts? What is it made of? When the children of the City and Country School needed an electric bell to call a Special Delivery postman to carry important messages, they installed it themselves (Semel, 1999a), illustrating the difference, in theory, between a progressive and a traditional system of education. While one of the goals of traditional education may have been to create citizens for a democratic society, the goal of the progressives was to create a democratic society within the school.

If the bricolage approach to research involves making connections between apparently disparate ideas, there is joy in the discovery that those connections are not tenuous at all. Once I undertook a semiotic study of the bell, I was surprised at how many interpretations of the symbol I could find, and how they helped to expand my understanding of developments in the history of education. The bell curve and the Liberty Bell are two that would seem to be obvious, but in examining them in the following short passages, I attempted to use starting points different from Herrnstein, Murray, and Hirsch.

What Does the Shape of the Bell Signify?

> The bell curve is a funny thing, you'd think it was unchangeable.
> Use hammer and a little heat, the bell curve's rearrangeable.

The shape of the school bell is the bell curve, and in the 1990s Herrnstein and Murray used this shape in order to explain the relationship between intelligence and class (and racial, though they denied it) structure. Intelligence is defined as a "general way to express a person's intellectual performance relative to a given population" and intelligence quotient is "a universally understood synonym for intelligence" (Herrnstein & Murray, 1994, p. 4). By stressing that IQ is the only way to measure intelligence and by thus reducing intelligence to a "single number capable of ranking all people on a linear scale of intrinsic and unalterable worth" (Gould, 1996, p. 20), Herrnstein and Murray reimposed a racist, elitist interpretation of intelligence that echoed Edward Thorndike's narrow assumptions favoring nature over nurture (Spring, 2005). They set up an "us" versus "them" scenario, in which "we" have plenty to fear:

The American family may be generally under siege…but it is at the bottom of the cognitive ability distribution that its defenses are most visibly crumbling (Herrnstein & Murray, 1994, p. 190)…[S]omething worth worrying about is happening to the cognitive capital of the country (p. 364)…The threat comes from an underclass that has been with American society for some years (p. 518)…Trying to eradicate inequality with artificially manufactured outcomes has led us to disaster. (p. 551)

Cloaked in a so-called scientific rationale, this educational determinism relies on the notion that the bell is made of a non-malleable substance. Herrnstein and Murray characterize their "facts" as irrefutable and unassailable, in spite of the origins of many in the literature of white supremacists (Kincheloe & Steinberg, 1997). But just as intelligence is not one fixed entity (Gardner, 1993; Gould, 1996; Kincheloe, 2004), the bell is malleable, both in reality and metaphorically; it can be shaped in any number of different ways.

What Does a Broken Bell Signify?

Ding dong, the Liberty Bell, the sound of freedom's ring.
The trouble is, a bell that's cracked is never going to ding.

There is obvious irony in the fact that the Liberty Bell endures as a symbol of American democracy. The inscription inside, "Proclaim liberty throughout the land unto all the inhabitants thereof" (Hirsch, Kett, & Trefil, 2002), speaks to an ideal that has yet to be met in America. Because it is cracked, the bell has not sounded since the mid 19th century. Democracy is flawed; freedom cannot ring because it has no voice. In the first edition of *What Your First Grader Needs to Know*, this irony is perfectly captured with the juxtaposition of a passage about the Liberty Bell, "a symbol of our country" (Hirsch, 1991, p. 131), with a passage titled "Freedom for All?" describing the denial of freedom for women and slaves by the men who signed the Declaration of Independence. The school as the provider of equal opportunity also has a cracked bell. Segregation, exclusion laws, language policies, and standardized testing are among the institutional means by which equal opportunity is denied.

When I began my original brainstorming about bells, ideas about their sound dominated, perhaps because as I wrote, I heard the hourly tolling of a church bell outside my window. Once I had imagined when and where different people heard bells in the past, and where people hear them today, I developed a list of questions that required historical research. By understanding the origins of bells and the changing nature of their use, I'm able to increase my understanding of their literal and metaphorical significance in education.

What Does the Sound of the Bell Signify?

The sound of the bell is many things:
Plantation, incarceration,
Emancipation, regulation
Domination,
Salvation.

The sound of a bell is replete with meanings. The ringing of a bell is a form of civic communication, and when not ringing from schools and churches, it often signals a warning. Fire and other alarms become an important part of public safety, inherently democratic because they serve to warn everyone who can hear them regardless of class, race, or other consideration. In pre-industrial times, the sound of the town crier's bell heralded important events and served to draw the community together. One of the most frequent functions of a bell is to indicate time, and its use grew concurrently with the introduction of clocks, signaling the shift from marking natural time (the rising and setting of the sun) to a preoccupation with the more specific marks of minutes and hours, as required in an industrial setting.

Where the Puritans originally believed that clocks marked God's time, eventually "aural time was used to announce not just God's time but increasingly to regulate the time of schools, markets and factories" (Smith, 1996, p. 1449). Public clocks served a valuable purpose in situations where industrialists, hoping to increase production, manipulated the factory clocks to lengthen the workday. The solution was a public clock marking the "true" time (Hensley, 1992). A worker could ignore the sound of the factory bell in favor of the public bell, erected for the public good.

Just as church bells peal to celebrate the conclusion of a wedding, the ring of the school bell at the end of the day can be cause for celebration for the student:

> Sitting here watching the clock tick away
> Tick-tock-tick-tock every day
> Waiting for the stupid little bell to ring
> So I can go home and do my thing… (Hynds, 1997, p. 29)

This function of marking time connects the school bell with the factory bell, and both serve a major function in controlling human capital (Reese, 2002). Embedded in the school and the factory are rewards for heeding the ringing of the bell and getting to class and to work on time. The closing bell in each setting brings a feeling of relief.

If a common culture existed, the bell would sound the same to everyone. But just as democracy and freedom have multiple dimensions, the sound of the school bell does not hold the same meaning for all who hear it. The sound has a particular set of associations for the prisoner whose day is regulated by the jailhouse bell. For the slaves or the sharecroppers who once rose and slept at the bidding of the plantation bell, that sound brought "thoughts of another day of unremitting and unrequited toil in the cotton fields" (Kester, 1969, p. 39). The school bell may have been the transformative sound of democracy, of equal access to education where before there was none, but it also may have been the sound of exclusion if it rang from a racially segregated or underfunded school. It may have been the sound of assimilation or deculturalization (Spring, 2005). The pealing of the bell echoes the celebratory sound of the original Liberty Bell, but when the bell rings in Puerto Rico or the former Mexican territories, it can also be symbolic of the imperialism of the colonizing power of America. The ringing of the bell may have become a secular call, but echoes of its earlier significance as a call to church remain, and in the 21st-century tower of education, the double peal of the school bell alongside the church bell has a different sound for different people. To the compassionate conservative and the fundamentalist Christian, the two bells ring in harmony; school and faith are inextricably linked. To the secular humanist, however, the combined sound is dissonant, disturbing, and in violation of the First Amendment to the United States Constitution.

> The elite does the ringing, the worker responds,
> And it's always been that way, I fear,
> But the ring of the Common School bell is a sound
> That everybody can hear.

Historically and in class terms, whether on the factory floor or in the dining room, the elite used the bell to summon the worker. In this sense, the bell of the common school was indeed democratic because it was used to supposedly eliminate distinctions between the rich and the poor. The workers and the elite may have had different notions of why schools were created in the first place, whether to provide equal opportunity for all or to prepare a compliant workforce (Spring, 2005). With the introduction of vocational education and the development of separate streams that separate the elite from the working class, however, the school became a site of further social and economic alienation of one group from another, and the school bell did not call all students to the same education.

The school bell rings, I salivate. No, that's the other bell, no wait,
I'm all confused, I'm in a state, I'm either hungry or I'm late.

The sound of a ringing of the bell is the sound of a stimulus-response experiment, and it suggests another significant development in education. Behaviorism, with its effect of excluding individuals from educational opportunities based on measured intelligence or scores on standardized tests, does not meet the critical definition of democratic. But couched as it was within the language of freeing every individual to match one's own intelligence with social needs (Spring, 2005), social efficiency practitioners such as Edward Thorndike could justify the use of behaviorism in a school setting, thus ushering in a century of scientific management of schools. If the ringing of the school bell made education available to a larger number of students, the resulting increased opportunity was indeed democratic. If the sound of the bell served to control the students and curtail their freedom of movement and freedom to choose their course of study, propelling them into predetermined careers from an early age, however, the bell is broken.

Research grounded on the bricolage often takes the researcher outside of her comfort zone. In my experience, the Securities and Exchange Commission's website was a mysterious place which became a rich source of information, particularly in the annual reports of publicly traded companies. It may take some effort to learn how to locate the data, but finding the information as presented in a corporation's own marketing materials is worth the effort. In this case it introduces a new perspective, which should be the goal of all educational research. Media reports also offer an alternative perspective on a given phenomenon.

Who Rings the School Bell?

Who rings this bell, I think I know. It's not as schools intended, though,
For business makes the clapper sound, and money jingles all around.

During an era of child labor, the ringing of coins drowned out the sound of the school bell. Sharecroppers' children in the late 19th century, for example, may have had access to education, but not necessarily the opportunity to participate because there was money to be made through their labor: "When the child can be spared from the labor in the field, the schoolhouse doors swing open; but when cotton beckons, the doors close in the face of thousands of youngsters who are an integral part of American life" (Kester, 1969, p. 46). In the 21st century the sound of the school bell is not just the call to the classroom; it is also the ringing of the cash register. Fast-food restaurants and computer software manufacturers insinuate themselves into the lives of students, while school administrations acquiesce. Thus in September 2005 McDonald's introduced its "Passport to Play" physical education curriculum, saying; "With the guide and materials we provide, approximately seven million children in grades 3–5 will learn about and play games from 15 countries around the world" (McDonald's Corp., n.d.). Those same seven million children become a captive audience for McDonald's promotions. Similarly, Microsoft captures the market for computer hardware and software with its School Agreement,

> ...a subscription licensing program specifically created to address the unique needs of primary and secondary schools and districts. With the simplicity of counting computers just once per year, School Agreement makes it easy for you to license all of your computers, whether in a single school or throughout the entire district. (Microsoft Corp., 2005b)

Notwithstanding the lawsuits charging market monopolization reported in Microsoft's 2005 Annual Report (Microsoft Corp., 2005a), by gaining exclusive access to schools the corporation ensures that a sizeable segment of its target consumers is familiar with its products from an early age. In an era in which school underfunding is the norm rather than the exception, profit and education thus are inextricably linked, whether promoted by the neoconservatives who encourage business involvement in government, including education, or by the neoliberals who espouse education as a means of increasing wealth (Spring, 2002).

The ring of the school bell, however, is replaced by the ring of the cash register in more ways than just these. For-profit schools and school management businesses proliferate in America, bringing to the forefront the conflict between competing notions of the purpose of education, articulated by David Labaree (1997) as a conflict between democratic equality, social efficiency, and social mobility goals. Christopher Whittle (the founder of Channel One, a technology that introduced commercial advertising along with packaged news shows to schools across the country), has as his main project Edison Schools, which has transformed over the years from a national network of for-profit schools to a public company (Whittle, 1997) and then to a privately held business managing public schools (Mezzacappa, 2005). The language Whittle uses to describe his project reflects a mélange of characterizations. If he sees Edison as "just the first colony in a new academic world," then he is a colonizer and American children are the colonized—replete with all the associated meanings of the term. If his schools "are simply its Model T's," then the education system is a factory, and the schools and children in them are simply widgets. Whittle may say that "parents he meets don't care if he makes a profit or not if he can help educate their children" (Baum, 2005). But make no mistake, Whittle himself certainly cares whether or not he makes money—otherwise he wouldn't be in business.

Whoever rings the school bell determines what definition of democracy prevails in education. Once that task fell to the schoolteacher. The bell would be a handheld model kept on the teacher's desk and rung by the teacher or an appointed bell ringer. As public education grew, control passed to headmasters, and then to school boards. The large ward-based systems, while responsive to and representative of the electorate, were also prone to misuse of political power (Reese, 2002). The smaller at-large boards focused the power in the hands of the elite, and as state departments of education shared the responsibility, the task of bell ringing fell to the so-called experts, to scientists, technocrats, and politicians. Today business leaders are just as likely as administrators or politicians to have their hands on the bell, but their grasp is not secured through democratic means, and the consequences lead to a fundamental change in the nature of education. Monica Pini (2001), in her examination of so-called educational management organizations (such as Edison), outlines the way such EMOs focus on parental and community involvement in for-profit schools, thus undermining public and social support for education. Pini explains,

> The logic of privatization says that anybody can sell educational services, as any other good. But education cannot be identified with any other industry, its nature is too rooted in the meaning of an authentic democracy to treat it as any business. That is why EMOs need and use such dramatic rhetoric....One can wonder if the ultimate political goal of this ideological and structural process is to stop the slow but constant trend to democratize the American educational system....Common people still have the opportunity to discuss social justice, wealth distribution, and educational policies in the public sphere, this is not the case in shareholders [*sic*] meetings. (pp. 39–40)

In spite of the rhetoric of the for-profit educators, the ring of a cash register can never be made to sound the same as a school bell.

Conclusion: Bells, Complexity, and Multilogicality

Freedom may be the stated goal of democratic nations, but both freedom and democracy are terms too complex to fit such a simplistic equation. As the school bell metaphor demonstrates, democracy has many layers, and what represents freedom to one sector of society may represent something entirely different to another. In education, each new policy, each new "ism," needs to be examined in order to determine what definition of democracy is implied. Who benefits and who loses as a result of that democracy needs to be examined as it applies to the definition. Only then can a socially just education system begin to develop, so that the sound of the school bell will indeed be a call with the same emancipatory message for all.

The process of doing historical research in education is complex and highly personal. The researcher brings to the task aptitudes and experiences that color his or her choices. Given the same topic, no two individuals choose to explore the same avenues, nor do they present their findings in identical ways. By using the bricolage and anticipating that the end result will not produce a definitive understanding of the topic, but a study that raises as many questions as it answers, it is possible to view research as a multilogical lifelong effort that continues well after each project is completed.

References

AcroVista Software. (n.d.) *BellCommander*. Retrieved October 10, 2005, from http://www. acrovista. com/

Baum, J. (2005, September). Chris Whittle, CEO, Edison Schools. *Education Update Online, 11*(12), 7. Retrieved October 28, 2005, from http://www.educationupdate.com/index.html

Cremin, L. A. (1988). *American education: The metropolitan experience (1976–1980)*. New York, NY: Harper & Row.

Cuban, L. (1993). *How teachers taught: Constancy and change in American classrooms 1880–1990* (2nd ed.). New York, NY: Teachers College Press.

Daniels, R. (2002). *Coming to America: A history of immigration and ethnicity in American life* (2nd ed.). New York, NY: Perennial.

Democratic Party (The). (2004). *Strong at home, respected in the world: The 2004 Democratic national platform for America*. Retrieved October 10, 2005, from http://www.democrats.org/

Gardner, H. (1993). *Frames of mind: The theory of multiple intelligences*. New York, NY: Basic Books.

Gould, S. J. (1996). *The mismeasure of man* (rev. ed.). New York, NY: W. W. Norton.

Hays, L., & Seeger, P. (1949). *If I had a hammer*. Lyrics retrieved October 10, 2005, from http://www.inlyrics.com/

Hensley, P. B. (1992, December). Time, work and social context in New England. *The New England Quarterly, 65,* 531–559.

Herrnstein, R. J., & Murray, C. (1994). *The bell curve: Intelligence and class structure in American life*. New York, NY: Free Press.

Hirsch, E. D., Jr. (Ed.). (1991). *What your first grader needs to know: Fundamentals of a good first grade education*. New York, NY: Doubleday.

Hirsch, E. D., Jr. (Ed.). (1997). *What your first grader needs to know: Fundamentals of a good first grade education* (rev. ed.). New York, NY: Doubleday.

Hirsch, E. D., Jr., Kett, J. F., & Trefil, J. (Eds.). (2002). *The new dictionary of cultural literacy* (3rd ed.). Boston: Houghton Mifflin. Retrieved October 10, 2005, from http://www. bartleby. com/

Hynds, S. (1997). *On the brink: Negotiating literature and life with adolescents*. New York, NY: Teachers College Press.

Kester, H. (1969). *Revolt among the sharecroppers*. New York, NY: Arno Press.

Kincheloe, J. (2004). *Critical pedagogy*. New York, NY: Peter Lang.

Kincheloe, J., & Steinberg, S. (1997). *Changing multiculturalism*. London, England: Open University Press.

Labaree, D. L. (1997). Public goods, private goods: The American struggle over educational goals. *American Educational Research Journal, 34*(1), 39–81.

McDonald's Corp. (n.d.) Good works: *Balanced, active lifestyles*. Retrieved October 17, 2005, from http://www.mcdonalds. com/

Mezzacappa, D. (2005, October 12). Edison schools can show gains over time, report says. *The Philadelphia Inquirer Online*. Retrieved October 29, 2005, from http://www.philly.com/mld/inquirer/living/education/12877813.htm

Microsoft Corp. (2005a) *Form 10–K: Microsoft Corporation annual report for fiscal year ending June 30, 2005*. Retrieved October 17, 2005, from http://www.sec.gov/index.htm

Microsoft Corp. (2005b). *Microsoft School Agreement*. Retrieved October 17, 2005, from http://www.microsoft.com/

Mirel, J. (1999). *The rise and fall of an urban school system: Detroit, 1907–81* (2nd ed.). Ann Arbor: University of Michigan Press.

Pini, M. E. (2001, April). *Moving public schools toward for-profit management: Privatizing the public sphere*. Paper presented at the meeting of the American Educational Research Association, Seattle, WA.

Reese, W. J. (2002). *Power and the promise of school reform: Grassroots movements during the Progressive Era*. New York, NY: Teachers College Press.

Republican National Committee. (2004). *2004 Republican party platform: A safer world and a more hopeful America*. Retrieved October 10, 2005, from http://www.gop.com/

Rettig, M., & Canaday, R. L. (1999). The effects of block scheduling. *The School Administrator, 56*(3), 14–16, 18–20.

Semel, S. F. (1999a). The City and Country School: A progressive paradigm. In S. F. Semel & A. R. Sadovnick (Eds.), *"Schools of tomorrow," schools of today* (pp. 121–140). New York, NY: Peter Lang.

Semel, S. F. (1999b). The Dalton School: The transformation of a progressive school. In S. F. Semel & A. R. Sadovnick (Eds.), *"Schools of tomorrow," schools of today* (pp. 171–212). New York, NY: Peter Lang.

Smith, M. M. (1996, December). Old south time in comparative perspective. *The American Historical Review, 101*(5), 1432–1469.

Spring, J. (2002). *Political agendas for education: From the religious right to the Green Party* (2nd ed.). Mahwah, NJ: Lawrence Erlbaum.

Spring, J. (2005). *The American school: 1642–2004* (6th ed.). New York, NY: McGraw-Hill.

United States Department of Education. (2004). *No child left behind and faith-based leaders.* Retrieved October 10, 2005, from http://www.ed.gov/

Whittle, C. (1997). Lessons learned. *The School Administrator, 54*(1), 6–9.

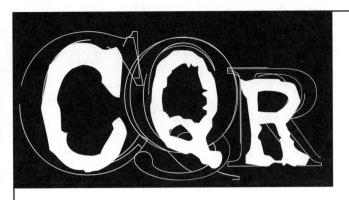

PART SIX

On Doing CQR

CHAPTER THIRTY-THREE

Towards a Rhizomatic Methodology: How Queer!

Mark Vicars

This chapter considers my experience of doing research as a gay man with other gay men in an original study: *Dissenting Fictions: A Study of the Formative Literacy Practices of Gay Men.* My thesis investigated the influence that childhood and adolescent reading practices had on identity formation, and I sought to map a relatively uncharted terrain of the socio-sexual contexts in which literacy behaviour is embedded. I struggled to discipline and disentangle my voice from the communities of practice in which I sought belonging, and in this chapter I consider how the rhizomatic nature of my positioning in the field as a man, as a friend, as a person aligned with a university doing a PhD, troubled the notion of a unified, authoritative stance from which to speak and write.

In this chapter I suggest how a rhizomatic methodology shifted the production of knowledge away from procedures guaranteeing uniformity, standardization and normalization into perspectival dispositions that rapidly erased and smoothed the surfaces between the researcher and the researched. In remapping together the textualities of our imagined and 'real' selves, we were ever mindful of the impossibility of finding spaces in texts and in 'everyday' lives for exploring and contesting the hegemony of regulatory heterogendered discourses. Working rhizomatically with our ways of being in and feelings of ourselves in the world became productive for our knowledge making and reinterpretation of our literacy practices "and [telling]ways of becoming subjects" (Masny & Cole, 2009, p. 8). The rhizome provided us with a smoothing space for a "continuous investment in reading the world, the word and self as texts" (Masny, 2006, p. 149). Adopting such astance made "it possible [for us] to see the world differently and so be able to act in different ways.... it [provided us] with the space to...be different" (Schratz & Walker, 1995, p. 125).

What, When, Where, How?

Without insider access, it would have proved difficult to find gay men in education that would have been willing and prepared to talk openly about their experiences (Squirrel, 1989). I contacted ex-colleagues and approached someone I had known for some time, who recruited friends and ex-lovers. The informants who took part in the group discussions eventually comprised three men who work in education and live in a major city in the north of England and two men who worked abroad. Due to their overseas location, my original design had to be modified, so over the stretch of one summer I had several meetings with these two informants and did one-to-one interviews. The group meetings began in September 2004; we met twice a month at the house of one of the men with the total number of sessions amounting to 16, each session lasting on average between four and five hours.

At the first meeting I solicited the men's opinions of conducting the interviews in a group setting, and we decided to pursue this arrangement as it was felt we might be able to cross-fertilise each other's stories with a collective commentary. We felt that the attraction of working within the context of a group was that we could discursively interrogate the wider contexts, social structures and social relations that have had an impact on our private and public lives. It was also felt that an open forum provided us with a space in which our identities could interact and "allow for the discovery of unanticipated issues" (Frith, 2000, p. 278).

As a preliminary interview technique, I drew guidance from the Biographic Narrative Interpretive Method (Chamberlayne, Bornat, & Wengraf, 2000), and asked the informants to tell me the story of their reading practices in relation to their life experiences. At the outset I didn't have any assumptions about the stories that would be told and the first session(s) got off to a clumsy start hampered by doubts of my efficacy as a novice researcher. I knew that I didn't want my presence in the interviews to be solely that of "researcher" and sought to work with the messiness and chaos that can happen in a different kind of communicative space. I hoped to "queer" the procedural rules that underpin fieldwork identities, construct social relations and govern the practice of the researcher's science. In being beside, I believed there might emerge the potential of dislocating and transforming relations within the field, as being "*beside* comprises a wide range of desiring, identifying, representing, repelling, paralleling, differentiating, rivalling, leaning, twisting, mimicking, withdrawing, attracting, aggressing, warping and other relations" (Sedgwick, 2004, p. 8).

> I was, at the outset, interested to work with chaos and uncertainty as a provocation to explore queer ways of "listening, reflection, interpretation, confrontation and discussion" (Dahlberg & Moss, 2005, p. 13)

Liminal…location, location, location

Russell and Kelly (2002) have noted how subjectivity in research information originates with both the researcher(s) and participant(s), each of whom brings individual experiences and pre-existing perspectives into the research event. However, within legitimising institutional discourses, "sexual identity is regarded as part of one's private life, and therefore, according to the prevailing norms of academic culture, not supposed to intrude into one's professional life" (Wafer, 1996, p. 262). Such a view has its origins in an ideological system that constructs and legitimises the terms and conditions of the sites of knowledge production. The tacit heteronormativity of 'everyday places' in which research gets done habitually reinforces the premise that sexuality should be absent or concealed in the research encounter. I soon came to realise that our way of being with each other was being cultivated by our willingness to participate in those habits of being through which we had become and are revealed as gay men, what Miller (1998) has termed the "open secret". Some of the men talked about how they made visible a queer identity through camp performance, and our conversation spiralled into how the use of campy language is often a way of acting visible within intricate relations with others. As a chosen manner of being in the world, we talked about the utility of using camp in terms of identity formation, self-definition as a means of affiliation and "as acts of activism that occur within 'everyday' places" (Moody & Haworth, 2009, p. 80) We referenced our encounters with camp and spoke of its utility as a form of fugitive knowledge (Hill, 1996) and a social semiotic through which dominant knowledge making systems can become queered, remanipulated and made improper.

In my attempt to make queer voice visible within the largely heteronormative framework of hegemonic educational discourse, I decided to represent our "improper" ways of being and speaking by utilising Polari inflected names to textualise positionality in the thesis.

Getting Stuck In

The discussions, held at the house of one of the informants, became increasingly "unpredictable affairs" and it would be fair to say that they didn't conform to my expectations of what I thought I would be doing when doing research. In our first encounter, we all brought flowers for the host, who in turn tried out his latest recipe book, and as we dined on a range of Mediterranean fare, we partook in scurrilous gossip and "dished the dirt" on each other's sexual antics. The ambience to our evenings was provided by our host's kitschy musical compilations and, after several gin and tonics, we could be heard singing along with Eartha Kitt, Doris Day, Barbra Streisand and a whole clutch of other such campy classics.

As the evening progressed, our collective conversation had not extended much beyond workplace bitching, sex encounters and boyfriend troubles, and the conversation spiralled off into 'lines of flight' of what Barton and Hamilton (1998) have called "ruling passions":

> When we went to interview people we wanted to find out about reading, writing and literacy practices. Unfortunately, it seemed the people we interviewed often wanted to talk about something else; each person has a ruling passion....We talked to them about literacy, it seemed, and they talked to us about their lives. (Barton & Hamilton, 1998, p. 83)

Boler (1999) has suggested how "Lines of flight suggest unpredictable directions for 'becoming' rather than 'being' (1997, p. 6), and we talked at some length about being positioned in relation to the straight cultural imaginary and how it produced varying degrees of anxiety about embodying a stigmatised identity. We spoke about how the prevailing narratives surrounding lesbian and gay subjects within the public order tend to normalise stories that habitually work to deposit sexual difference outside of accepted cultural and sexual boundaries, identities and communities. As we flowed in and out of each other's stories, we began to meander into intersubjective territories. Herda (1999) has noted how

> the creation of a text is a collaborative achievement and by virtue of people working together to uncover shared meanings there is opened in front of the text the possibility of a different and presumably a better world. This world is not validated by scientific criteria that measure neutrality, simplicity, or repeatability. (Herda, 1999, p. 2)

During the drive back home after that initial meeting, I was somewhat perplexed as to what had been going on and to what extent, if any, fieldwork had taken place. Admittedly, it had been a thoroughly enjoyable evening for all, and I felt that it had been successful in grounding our emerging relationships in a context of open, honest and trusting discussion. I had shared some of my own stories of disastrous blind dates and doomed sexual exploits, but I remained uncertain regarding the issue of what could be constituted as data. Playing back the recording of the evening a few days later, I struggled to find anything that I considered as being worthwhile. Could any of this be of any use?

Inauthentic Tales—Making a Dramatic Spectacle Out of Ourselves

Dramatis personae:

MOTHER—Flamboyant, all-singing and dancing host for the occasion
AUNTY—Mother's ex-lover, a butch(ish) top
INGENUE—Mother's protégé and work colleague

NOVICE RESEARCHER—Friend to Mother

Act One, Scene One

A dinner party. At the table are arranged four 30-something gay men. Tonight is the first time, as a group, they have met face to face. Two of the men are ex-lovers, two are current work colleagues and two are ex-flatmates from university. The conversation reveals their chosen occupations; all are teachers and as Mother, the slightly flamboyant host, clears away the dishes from the first course, refreshes drinks, changes the CD to yet another torch song compilation, he announces:

MOTHER: Enough, ENOUGH of work talk!

He embarks on a different course of conversation and as the talk shifts to "the dishing of dirt", the previously formal atmosphere is replaced by squeals of delight, a verbal applause at the revelation of the intimate. As more and more scurrilous gossip pours forth, appetites are whetted, another bottle of expensive imported red wine is opened and Mother embarks on exhaling the outrageous, each snippet punctuated with plumes and swirls of tobacco smoke.

MOTHER: M…… testicles are huge and my god can he fuck! All day Sunday in bed shagging, shagging and more shagging, my poor jemima! He just kept on going and going…

AUNTY: Well, I hope you remembered to douche. I did a guy in London last week and would you believe it, he had a tuft of toilet paper sticking out of his arse.

(Everybody laughs)

INGENUE: What did you do?

AUNTY: What did you think I did?

INGENUE: You mean you went ahead?

AUNTY: Listen and learn! His thighs were amazing, real rugby-player thighs…gorgeous! Wasn't going to pass up on those.

AUNTY: (To Novice Researcher) And what about you? I have been hearing some interesting stories about you.

MOTHER: He taught me all I know. When we first met I was a fresh-faced innocent…

NOVICE RESEARCHER: Err…well; I was thinking if you had all managed to get a look at the outline of the research that I e-mailed.

AUNTY: Oh we will get to that later, have something more to drink. Tell us about the bathhouses in Bangkok.

An hour later and after what could only be described as a confessional epic, the flow of conversation started to ebb…

INGENUE: Do you have any specific questions that you are going to ask us?

MOTHER: Where do you want me to start? I could about myself talk all night.

INGENUE: Well…I enjoyed reading Batman, Spiderman and Superman comics.

AUNTY: That's cos you're a closet Muscle Mary fan! All you were interested in was the pictures of rippling thighs and pecs. It was your formative wank fodder! Do we all remember the cartoon called He Man? He had unfeasibly large thighs, he was absolutely fantastic! I fucking love thighs! If you look at rugby players' thighs they are absolutely gorgeous. You know you couldn't possibly walk with the thighs of He Man. I love touching thighs…

INGENUE: Oh shut up about thighs. Can we talk about something else?

AUNTY: What about telly? I used to have a thing for the *Man from Atlantis*; he did this flagellic action that I found very, very erotic. I used to watch it loads and thought it absolutely fantastic! It turned me on in a way that I didn't know I could be turned on. I used to look forward to it on a Saturday evening and once it was finished I was upset 'cos I had to wait another week to see it again. I can't remember what the stories were about but I remember him going through the water. It must have been terrible special effects, but that action in the water turned me on, at the age of 8 or 9 that guy turned me on. It plugged me in to the whole idea that, you know, I might be gay.

MOTHER: Oh and *Thunderbirds*—what about that in terms of getting your rocks off, I mean in terms of cartoon characters. I thought Virgil was the better looking out of all of them in *Thunderbirds*

INGENUE: I must have been about eight or…me, my brother and his mates were on the school field, it was the only bit of grass we had nearby, and we came across a porn magazine, a straight porn magazine. My brother and the boys who lived next door started to tear it all up. There was this one bit where there was this man or woman and I wanted that bit. I only wanted the page with the boy bits…

Gossip has been acknowledged as important in establishing and maintaining social relations and norms within a group (Blum Kulka, 2000; Coates, 1998). Hodkinson (2005) in his work on using "insider re-search" in studying youth cultures has also noted how "an ability to share subcultural gossip, anecdotes and observations with respondents further enhanced initial rapport, as well as offering an invaluable and effective additional stimulus forconversation during the interviews themselves" (p. 139).

However, gossip is often constructed as an inauthentic discourse that merely repeats what is heard without critically examining the grounds or validity of the subject matter in question. Employing Roscoe's (1996) notion of "gay cultur-ing", a term that refers "to the negotiation and formulation of homosexual desire into cultural forms and social identities" (Roscoe, 1996, p. 201), enabled me to grasp the significance of the type of talk being traded in our interactions. Reflecting on the evening, I gradually realised how our gossiping acted as a type of dialogic interaction that helped to forge an emotional bond and build an interpersonal bridge that facilitated significant self-disclosure. Listening to accounts of how we stammered into knowing in relation to our sexuality, I realised that a "grid of intimacy" (Trow, 1981) had emerged that facilitated an almost seamless flow of stories. The absence of an asymmetry of power afforded another kind of space to develop. We shared the asking of questions, commented on each other's stories and supplemented each other's telling with fragments of knowledge that folded in our multiple identities into a spiral narrative as opposed to a logocentric sequence of events. The men and I worked together to uncover a collective understanding of the role that literacy had played in determining our preferred way of being within interactions with others and self. We talked about how books and movies became the main instruments of our confession. We discussed how we reconstructed texts for our own purposes and how we developed interpretive strategies that success-fully displaced what has been called the heterosexual imaginary (Ingraham, 1997), those heterosexual forms of meaning that make it almost impossible to consider being anything but straight. We spoke about elaborating on what a text had given to fashion new stories and as we unearthed the past in the present and we acknowledged our various attempts and struggles with identifying with "difference as the grounds for identity" (Britzman, 1995, p. 161).

Through the sharing of our life-world experiences, we were able to identify how our textual in-teractions had over time inculcated understandings of self as members of gendered, classed and sexual communities.

It's Not What You Do It's The Way That You Do It!

Individuals inherit a particular space within an interlocking set of social relationships; lacking that space, they are nobody, or at best a stranger or an outcast. (MacIntyre, 1981, p. 32)

Act One, Scene Two

Four weeks later. The men are seated on scatter cushions, Mother is finishing off lighting candles, pouring wine, rearranging cushions and making sure that the scattered bowls of olives and nuts are within easy reach.

NOVICE RESEARCHER: How do you feel about doing this as a group?

INGENUE: It's not a problem, it's not stopped me talking

MOTHER: I am happy to talk about myself. I am happy to talk in a gay context as well, in terms of my everyday life; I think I live in a very heterosexual world. A lot of my friends are straight and even though…I do have pockets of my friends who are gay, we don't normally talk about these issues. I mean, it's lovely that we can talk this way about being who we are.

INGENUE: Yeah! Even though we share lifts to work, we normally don't talk about this stuff.

MOTHER: This is just an extension of stuff that goes on in my head so for me I am trying to make it as sociable as possible. It's fun!

AUNTY: I find our evenings very interesting and at the moment it is even more so because at the moment I live with my parents. I moved back home recently as my father has been diagnosed with bowel cancer. I tend not to talk about my life with my parents 'cos even though they know that I am gay, it is not part of their life. I go down to London every two weeks to see my boyfriend and have a fantastic time and then I come back. I suppose I am living in a very heterosexual bubble so to do this…it's a bit like free therapy. I was saying jokingly to my boyfriend that it has been good for me as my therapist only ever made notes rather than recording my sessions. You know when you talk with people about things and they go "Oh yeah, I did that too"…you get a sense that you're not alone…and sometimes you just need reminding that gay people are everywhere. You know what I mean?

(To Novice Researcher)

I see you as a person who is actually in the group but you have to jump out sometimes. I suppose I see you as a subjective observer.

INGENUE: You are doing a PhD but this is not at all clinical or clear cut and you're not being unsympathetic. There is a friendship value to this so I don't feel defensive; I feel that you are…testing the waters.

MOTHER: Sweetie, you are being Mark. I actually think you are enjoying yourself, which is quite nice. I don't find you a threat whatsoever and…I am, it has to be said, thoroughly enjoying myself.

AUNTY: I think that you are getting a lot more than you anticipated. The brief that you gave us, whilst not narrow, I think has been exceeded…

MOTHER: I think the stories will come if you let us talk, that may mean endless eons of tape but I think the stories will come when we are talking. I have quite enjoyed hearing about our commonalities tonight. We have all lived through a common experience and thinking about it geographically, I mean (to Ingénue) you were in the Wirral, I was in Cheshire, (to Aunty) you were in Yorkshire and (to Novice Researcher) you were in Humberside. We were in one big line that spanned the breadth of England but we were all living through this same experience. I think that is interesting; maybe it's because we are gay that we recognise those things or maybe it is because we were all of a similar age at the same time.

Act One, Scene Three

The men are sat in Mother's front room. The remains of paella and sangria are strewn across the floor and as they stretch out, relax and make themselves even more comfortable they sink back into oversized armchairs, stretch out on sofas and start to make fun of the Novice Researcher's antiquated tape-recorder.

AUNTY: I've enjoyed tonight! It has been good to look back. I think that unless you live in a world of philosophical academia,which very few of us do, that there isn't time to reflect with a group of like-minded people about who we are. I think tonight has been very useful for me because I have been able to say what I am. In the discussions we have had tonight I have had to think more carefully while I have been talking and about what I have been saying. I think that through talking together I know myselfa little bit more than previously because in my head my mental voice tends to give out disjointed ideas, but by saying them they have become almost physical and I have been able to see what I think. Does that make sense?

MOTHER: I've enjoyed the commonalities. We have all had common experiences and since the last session I have thought about that quite a lot.

INGENUE: I would say that our commentaries on what each of us has had to say have made me think.

NOVICE RESEARCHER: How?

INGENUE: Oh…about stuff that happened in my past.

AUNTY: I don't feel it has hindered us doing it this way and that is the best you can get. At the outset I thought that you might have had a set agenda, that you had a list of research questions you wanted us to answer. What has happened from letting us talk is that things have come out and I guess that you will be able to pick from that what you need. I think it is important that this kind of research goes on because academia becomes stale without the human element. So often you get to read stuff that is supposed to be what is in people's minds, how they feel, but it reads like those doing that research haven't actually asked the people. It is the same in education with all that carry on and talk about psychology of education and the philosophy of children but as a teacher if you lose sight of that seven year old who comes in to your class in the morning with a snotty nose and a bloodied knee and…if you forget that child you might as well fucking light a match with your research because if it doesn't impact back on the people you are talking about. Don't kill the fucking rain forest to do it. I think of our conversations as being akin to free verse poetry. If you had started to restrict the stanzas of our speech by the way you formed the question then you are not going to get out of it what I think you want. Whereas when you let people talk within a loosely based frame, as we are doing, then I think we all get more out of doing this. Looking back I think the second group session was when we got started because in the first meeting you interrupted us with questions whereas…the second time we met youjust let us get on with it. While we had to go round the houses I think that you got a much more rounded and broader response, not just the "yes" and "no" answers and, while they have their place, you are not going to get full marks for "yes" and "no" answers. I think that we have got to continually refer to texts and my text is my experiences. Unless I am allowed to revisit quite a few of them there is no way I am going to bring out the one that I think is the best one. Revisiting my experiential texts is really a way about talking about my life in general.

MOTHER: I think I assumed that this would be quite easy because we have lots of things in common…but (To Aunty) I think your sexuality and personality as a gay man is very different to mine in respect of your experiences of growing up. I don't think that hinders, I think that in many ways it has helped.

INGENUE: I couldn't have talked to a straight man about some of the stuff I have talked to you guys about.

AUNTY: I don't think I would have signed up if I knew a straight guy was doing this.

MOTHER: I don't think it would have worked. I mean just listen to some of the stuff we have said and also it wouldn't have been any fun. This way we have not only told you about ourselves but we have had fun and camped it up. You couldn't do that with a straight guy, so, no it wouldn't have worked.

The way is which our stories came to be told productively yielded narratives of complexity, diversity and texture, and they did so by our being situated not only as confidants but additionally as co-generators, co-elaborators and co-interpreters of meaning. The men's willingness to reveal the intimate details of their lives had, I believe, much to do with becoming united in a common rhythm, in a different "dance of knowing" (Leck, 1994, p. 90). As each of us became witness to the processes of how as individuals we made sense of ourselves in the world, we drew upon shared frames of meaning to describe our experiences.

In the telling of their stories, the men often mixed styles; they were at times amusing, highly dramatic, sometimes sad, often ironic and camp. They refused to be constrained by convention and defied a model of operational logic. As we got lost in play and song, our discussions spiralled out of control, disturbing not only the techne of inquiry but also unsettled sedimented meanings, memories and desires. By evoking our histories together, we gave support, demonstrated care, and, in synergy, challenged interpretations. The stories we told of the self knitted together our individual orientations with the needs and structures of fear, passion, love, hate, sex and death of being and becoming. We came to understand how our queerly nuanced narratives could in themselves be read as texts that spoke of the micropractices of power relations (Foucault, 1986). As we recalled the names and places, the incidents and experiences of living we comprehended once more:

> The knowledge is indelible, but not too astonishing, to anyone with a reason to be attuned to the profligate way this culture has of denying and despoiling queer energies and lives....Everyone who survived has stories about how it was done. (Sedgwick, 1994, p. 1)

Through Thick and Thin

As a gay man doing research with other gay men I spent many months reconsidering what was happening through being together in a friendship group. I increasingly questioned taken-for-granted assumptions about what can constitute "knowledge." As we recalled the sensations elicited from texts past, as they flooded and coursed, transcending the separation between body and brain, we told of the risks that lurked in the most innocent of sentences and how we fell prey to the waiting page. We spoke of becoming hooked on the thrill of finding ourselves in text and of the shame we sometimes felt and how, with each turn of page, it grew stronger. As the words slipped from our mouths, there were many moments of doubt and uncertainty when reflecting on our ways of being. I stumbled and fell towards new horizons of understanding, reflexively thinking on the ways I behaved with the men involved negotiating the "Being Here" space of the field and the "Being There" space of the academy (Geertz, 1988, p. 148). However, being in-between is familiar territory, and I came to regard it as a productive location to connect, to make sense and write a way out of our experiences. In many ways, the field had induced intellectual and emotional uncertainties.

St. Pierre (1997) suggests that post-foundational research aims to produce different knowledge and to produce knowledge differently. I began to think about how the rhizomatic presence would come to contextualise the telling of the stories. I had entered the field with the belief that situatedness is not a hindrance to knowledge but rather its condition, and coming together as a group to explore our queer literacy practices, we found that we had shared many similar types of experiences. I used these and my knowledge of the men as the basis from which to start writing the stories of their lives (See Fig 1).

Performing the Page

Brah (1996) has noted, "if practice is productive of power then practice is also the means of challenging power" (p. 125) and a central concern in writing was to address the problem of trying to make queer voices visible within the largely heteronormative framework of hegemonic educational discourse. I wanted to erode the "proper" orthodoxies of representation and decided to play with style as a modality for representing the difference of how "being marginal and flowing in and out text is…a construction from…being QUEER" (Leck, 1994, p. 90).

Tyler (1986), writing about evocative postmodern ethnography, has commented that texts constructed from out of this paradigm consist of "fragments of discourse intended to evoke in the minds of both reader and writer an emergent fantasy of a possible world" (p. 125). Evocative narratives that engage a feeling as well as a thinking self are "at the boundaries of disciplinary practices" (Sparkes, 2000, p. 21) and by resisting telling a chronological story of my research, I felt better equipped to represent the non-linear relationships and the flow of voices of the field.

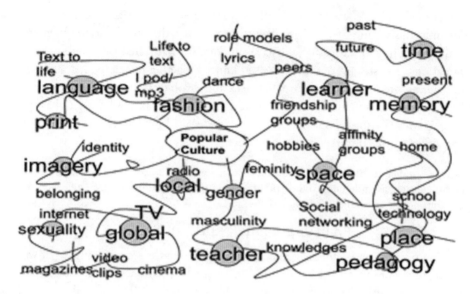

Figure 1: Rhizomatic readings

I attempted to write out of "*the enactment of hybridity,*" to construct a text of belonging that connected "simultaneously to the world of engaged scholarship and the world of everyday life" (Nayaran,
1993, p. 672). I did so to critically break with the notion of the researcher as having authority and
mastery over the research process and the written artefacts produced.

Plato (1974) spoke of how "we don't know the truth about the past but we can invent a fiction
as like it as maybe" (p. 138), and writing to resist the structural frameworks that legitimise a mode of
being and a method of telling, I offer the idea that the reconstructed life histories were/are socio-sexual
cultural scripts, materialised within a framework of evocative storytelling (Sparkes, 2004), constructed
on a canvas prepared by anthropological poetics (Brady, 2000) located within a temporal order of
chaotic and epiphanic research moments (Denzin & Lincoln, 2005). In my endeavour to queer disciplinary epistemologies I endeavoured to reconceptualise writing as a rhizomatic performative act. It has
been suggested that "writing has nothing to do with signifying. It has to do with surveying, mapping,
even realms that are yet to come" (Deleuze & Guattari, 1987, pp. 4–5), and the complexity and richness that is afforded by opening up new possibilities of understanding is made available by drawing on
multiple and overlapping histories. As we evoked the copious ways we have come to know the fabric of
our lives, we moved between and amongst socio-cultural identities constituted by relations of power,
and preoccupied with shifting the focus away from closure to opening up and trickily playing with the
ritualistic scripts of the privileged and the represented, our stories emerged as a blending of fact and
fiction, memory and amnesia, the referential and the textual, the historical and the rhetorical. At times,
I felt that I was journeying in foreign landscapes,

In troubling the methodological text, I have attempted to represent queer voices as necessary fictions that can parade the unspeakable and think the unthinkable. In moments of uncertainty and
fatigue in which Other voices urged:

> you must go on, I can't go on, you must go on, and I'll go on, you must say words, as long as there
> are any, until they find me, until they say me, strange pain, strange sin, you must go on, perhaps
> it's done already, perhaps they have said me already, perhaps they have carried me to the threshold
> of my story, before the door that opens on my story, that would surprise me, if it opens, it will be
> I, it will be the silence, where I am, I don't know, I'll never know, in the silence you don't know.
> (Beckett, 1997, p. 418)

Conclusion

Doing this with you, telling you about my life is difficult because it is putting me in a position to truth, and I feel that telling anyone about my life is the highest form of trust. It is about believing that one is not going to be betrayed. So when you say "Tell me about that", I think "Do I really want to?" However telling some people is a risk worth taking. Being gay is private, having a private life, except with you, we have a shared common experience and there are times when one has to recognise the context of the telling.

Ethnographic narratives that seek to construct knowledge from the complexity of the unknown must surely involve a questioning of the regimes of truth that naturalise knowledge production. In my research, I employed the rhizome to push the limits of ethnography and endeavoured to amplify how the formation of subjectivities and practices of self are discursively constituted along disorienting lines of flight in communities of practice and within queer relations of power. Halperin (1995) notes how

> Queer is by definition whatever is at odds with the normal, thelegitimate, the dominant. "Queer" then demarcates not a positivity but a positionality vis-à-vis the normative.… [Queer] describes a horizon of possibility whose precise extent and heterogeneous scope cannot in principle be delimited in advance. (Halperin, 1995, p. 62)

Reflecting on how my way of doing research questions emerged from my passions and preoccupations, I have subsequently come to understand that "research is not an innocent or distant academicexercise but an activity that has something at stake and that occurs in a set of political and social conditions" (Smith, 2001, p. 5). Becoming of and from the liminal situates a double knowledge, both of the centre and of the margins, and to queer within the field of educational practice and research, I have sought to speak this knowledge to "decenter centres and disrupt hierarchies" (Kamberelis, 2004, p. 167). By centring the queer I have endeavoured to trouble normalising expectations, practices and pedagogies within educational research and smooth the norms through which normativities are reiterated.

References

Barton D., & Hamilton, M. (1998). *Local literacies: Reading and writing in onecommunity*. London: Routledge.

Beckett, S. (1997). *Trilogy*. London: Kalder.

Blum Kulka, S. (2000). Gossipy events at family dinners: Negotiating sociability, presence and the moral order. In J. Coupland (Ed.), *Small talk*. London: Longman.

Boler, M. (1999). Feeling Power:Emotions and education. New York:Routledge.

Brady, I. (2000). Anthropological poetics. In N. K. Denzin & Y. S. Lincoln (Eds.), *The handbook of qualitative research* (2nd ed.). Thousand Oaks, CA: Sage.

Brah, A. (1996). *Cartographies of diaspora*. London: Routledge.

Britzman, D. P. (1995). Is there a queer pedagogy? Or stop reading straight. *Educational Theory, 45,* 151–165.

Chamberlayne, P., Bornat, J., & Wengraf, T. (Eds.). (2000). *The turn to biographical methods in social science: Comparative issues and examples.* New York: Routledge.

Coates, J. (1998). Gossip revisited: Language in all-female groups. In J. Coates (Ed.), *Language and gender: A reader.* Oxford: Basil Blackwell.

Dahlberg, G. & Moss, P. (2005). *Ethics and politics in early childhood education.* London & New York: RoutledgeFalmer.

Deleuze, G. & Guattari, F. (1987). *A thousand plateaus. Capitalism and schizophrenia.* London: Continuum.

Denzin, N. K., & Lincoln, Y. S. (2005). Introduction: The discipline and practice of qualitative research. In N. K. Denzin& Y. S. Lincoln (Eds.), *The handbook of qualitative research* (3rded.). Thousand Oaks, CA: Sage.

Foucault, M. (1986). *The history of sexuality* (R. Hurley, Trans.). New York: Random House.

Frith, H. (2000). Focusing on sex: Using focus groups in sex research. *Sexualities, 3*(3), 275–297.

Geertz, C. (1988). *Works and lives: The anthropologist as author.* Cambridge, England: Polity Press.

Halperin, D. (1995). *Saint Foucault: Towards a gay hagiography.* Oxford: Oxford University Press.

Herda, E. A. (1999). *Research conversations and narrative: A critical hermeneutic orientation in participatory inquiry.* Westport, CT: Praeger.

Hickey-Moody, A. & Haworth, R. (2009). Affective literacy. In D. Masny & D. Cole (Eds) Multiple literacies theory: A Deleuzian perspective. Rotterdam: Sense.

Hill, R. (1996). Learning to transgress: A socio-historical conspectus of the American gay life world as a site of struggle and resistanc e. *Studies in the Education of Adults, 28*(2), 253–279.

Hodkinson, P. (2005). Insider research in the study of youth cultures. *Journal of Youth Studies, 8*(2), 131–149.

Ingraham, C. (1997). The heterosexual imaginary: Feminist sociology and theories of gender. In R. Hennessy & C. Ingraham (Eds.), *Materialist feminism: A reader in class difference and women's lives.* New York: Routledge.

Kamberelis, G. (2004). The rhizome and the pack: Liminal literacy formations with political teeth. In K. Leander & M. Sheehy (Eds.), *Spatialising literacy research and practice.* New York: Peter Lang.

Kopleson, K. (2002). Dis/integrating the gay/queer binary: Reconstructed identity politics for a performative pedagogy. *College English, 65*(1), 17–35.

Leck, G. (1994). Queer relations with educational research. In A. Gitlin (Ed.), *Power and method: Political activism and educational research.* Routledge: New York.

MacIntyre, A. (1981). *After virtue: A study in moral theory.* Notre Dame, IN: University of Notre Dame Press.

Masny, D. (2006). Learning and Creative Processes: Apostructuralist perspective on language and multiple literacies. *International Journal of Learning, 12*(5) 149–155.

Masny, D. & Cole, D. (2009). Introduction To Multiple Literacies Theory: A Deleuzian Perspective. In D. Masny& D. Cole (Eds) *Multiple Literacies Theory: A Deleuzian Perspective.* Rotterdam:Sense.

Miller, J. (1998). Autobiography as queer curriculum practice. In W. Pinar (Ed.), *Queer theory in education.* London: Lawrence Erlbaum.

Nayaran, K. (1993). How native is a "native" anthropologist? *American Anthropologist, 95,* 671–686.

Plato. (1974). *The Republic* (D. Lee, Trans.). London: Penguin.

Rogers, C. R. (1962). The interpersonal relationship: The core of guidance. *Harvard Educational Review, 32,* 416–429.

Roscoe, W. (1996). Writing queer cultures: An impossible possibility? In E. Lewin& W. Leap (Eds.), *Out in the field: Reflections of lesbian and gay anthropologists.* Urbana: University of Illinois Press.

Russell, M. G., & Kelly, N. H. (2002). Research as interacting dialogic processes: Implications for reflexivity. *Forum:Qualitative Social Research, 3*(3). Retrieved January 16, 2005, from http://www. qualitative-research. net/fqs-texte/3–02/3–02rus-sellkelly-e. htm

Schratz, M., & Walker, R. (1995). *Research as social change.* London: Routledge.

Sedgwick, E. K. (1994). *Tendencies.* London: Routledge.

Sedgwick, E. K. (2004). *Touching feeling: Affect, pedagogy, performativity.* London: Duke University Press.

Smith, L. T. (2001). *Decolonizing methodologies: Research and indigenous peoples.* London: Zed Books.

Sparkes, A. C. (2000). Autoethnography and narratives of self: Reflections on criteria in action. *Sociology of Sport Journal, 17*(1), 21–43.

Sparkes, A. (2004). *Telling tale in sport and physical activity: A qualitative journey.* Leeds, England: Human Kinetics.

Squirrel, G. (1989). Teachers and issues of sexual orientation. *Gender and Education, 1*(1), 17–35.

St. Pierre, E. A. (1997). Methodology in the fold and the irruption of transgressive data. *Qualitative Studies in Education, 10*(2), 175–189.

Trow, G. W. S. (1981). *Within the context of no context.* Boston: Little, Brown.

Tyler, S. (1986). Postmodern ethnography: From document of the occult to occult document. In J. Clifford & G. Marcus (Eds.), *Writing culture: The poetics and politics of ethnography.* Berkeley: University of California Press.

Wafer, J. (1996). Out of the closet and into print: Sexual identity in the textual field. In E. Lewin& W. Leap (Eds.), *Out in the field: Reflections of lesbian and gay anthropologists.* Urbana: University of Illinois Press.

CHAPTER THIRTY-FOUR

In Search of Critical Knowledge: Tracing Inheritance in the Landscape of Incarceration

Carolina Muñoz Proto

When I was younger, people said, "You're going to end up like him"...I would like to end up like him, now. So now you could say all of that...because now you know he's doing the right thing. This is a positive time in his life. He's not in jail no more. So, hopefully, I can be like him now. (Rebuilding Communities life story interview with Sam, 19, African American)

Sam is the son of a formerly incarcerated father who, after completing a 12-year prison sentence, became a graduate student and a social service professional. Like most youth with formerly imprisoned parents, Sam cannot narrate his life without contending with two notions that frame public discourses about incarceration: inheritance and transformation. The Rebuilding Communities Project (RCP) is a multi-method, participatory study that traces the meanings of inheritance and transformation across individual lives, family dynamics and social discourse.[1] For 18 months, the RCP team carried out a case study of the College Initiative (CI), a post-prison college program located within the City University of New York that works to "rebuild lives, families and communities through higher education."[2] Since 2002 CI staff have supported nearly 500 men and women as they pursue a college or graduate education after prison. By offering services that are seldom available to this population, the CI opens an opportunity to learn about how former prisoners and their children fare in the presence of policies that increase their access to educational opportunities, resources and networks, thus capitalizing on a strengths-based model (Boudin & Zeller-Berkman, 2010). Deficit-based models, on the other hand, pay "an inordinate amount of attention to the assumed 'pathologies' of ghetto residents" (Wacquant, 1998, p. 348), emphasizing social exclusion, trauma, academic detainment, and risk of criminality (Foster & Hagan, 2007). Many studies about the injustice of mass incarceration imply that its causes and consequences live *within* individual prisoners, their families and their children. To avoid this trap, the RCP was based on Participatory Action Research (PAR), which denounces master narratives about what the world is and could be (Brydon-Miller, 2001; Fals-Borda & Rahman, 1991; Fine,

Roberts, Torre, & Upegui, 2001). PAR researchers distinguish between empirical-analytical knowledge—needed for survival, produced by positivist approaches and concerned with causality and determinism—and critical knowledge—rooted in social action and concerned with multiple relationships over determinism (Brydon-Miller, 2001; Fine, Roberts, Torre, & Upegui, 2001).

The search for critical knowledge led the RCP in a recursive journey through intimate stories of imprisonment and macro-level structures that sustain the violence of mass incarceration. In the spring of 2008, Professor Michelle Fine and CI founder Benay Rubenstein brought together trained researchers from the Public Science Project at the CUNY Graduate Center and an advisory board of CI staff, CI students, and teenaged children of CI students, to discuss the goals of the study. It was decided that the project would explore *how post-prison college contributes to rebuilding the lives, families and communities of formerly incarcerated adults.* Methodologically, the challenge was to (1) interrogate the meaning of post-prison college in the lives of students, their children, and communities; (2) go beyond evaluations that compare recidivism rates among CI students to that of the general population of former prisoners; and (3) produce knowledge that would have an impact on current debates about incarceration and education.

Tracing Inheritance

A First Approach: Self-education and Action

The RCP youth team brought together trained researchers, educators/filmmakers and New York City youth who have experienced the incarceration of a parent or close relative. We initially planned to carry out focus groups with children of CI students between ages 16 and 21 to explore how youth experience their parents' transition from prison to college. However, my co-researchers refused to make CI families look like isolated cases and quickly broadened our research question to the strengths and challenges in the lives of youth with incarcerated parents. This broadening vitalized the self-education and action aspects of the PAR process, during which we collaborated with educator and filmmaker Jeremy Robins on a video-documentary about the impact of parents' incarceration on New York City youth, titled Echoes of Incarceration.

As part of this work, we drew from various sources to develop memos with facts about incarceration like the following:

> According to the World Prison Population List (Walmsley, 2009) a fourth of the world's prisoners are in the United States (2.29 million). Based on a recent report by the Pew Center on the States (2008), incarceration and correctional control are raced, classed and gendered experiences. While one in 100 adults are incarcerated in the US, incarceration rates are higher for blacks and latina/os than for whites, and higher for males than for females: One in 15 black men are imprisoned as compared to one in 106 white males over 18; and one in 100 black women are incarcerated as compared to one in 355 for white women over 18. According to the Bureau of Justice Statistics (2000), incarceration has important consequences for the children of prisoners who in 1999 amounted to 2.1% of the 72.3 million minors in the country. According to the *From Prison to Home* conference report (2002), 7% of African American children have a parent inside compared to 2% of all children in the country. Over 43% of parents in federal facilities are held more than 500 miles away from their children.

These memos reaffirmed the team's goals, which were reflected in the following mission:

> We are a team of youth researchers and adult allies who are documenting the impact of incarceration and post-prison college on New York families. The goal of this project is to get a message across to young people who are experiencing the incarceration of their family members and friends. This project also hopes to educate the general public about what is going on in the country when it comes to incarceration and education. These goals are very important because the incarceration of young people's relatives is happening at high rates nation-wide. This affects young people's lives and must be changed.

Through self-education the youth research team came to a shared sense of urgency about mass incarceration as a form of collective punishment for underprivileged communities. Although the information had always been there, as facts in books and as individual intuitions and experiences, our shared learning allowed this knowledge to infuse and inspire the research. This process, which echoes Freire's notion of conscientization (1970/1990) inspired me to write about my position in the project:

> I've lived in the US for 7 years but I've been blind to mass incarceration until recently….At some point, I reached a critical level of information that makes one unable to forget this open wound….Racial and political surveillance, imprisonment, and mass punishment are not easy for me to accept because I grew up [during] Pinochet's dictatorship….Given my experiences in Chile, I would like to think that the reality of mass incarceration would be more obvious to me. This [tells me that], as a privileged visitor, one can live in the US for a long time, even years, without giving any thought to the one in one hundred people who live behind bars. [Also], having three friends and many acquaintances whose parents are/have been in prison does not make me immune to ignorance.

Over the months, our self-education work began to suggest that most studies and representations of youth with parents in prison highlight negative outcomes. The RCP, however, wanted to acknowledge the fact that CI students have wisdom to offer and that youth can take an active role in their lives as they take up useful advice from others. To this end we developed a written questionnaire asking CI students to provide an anonymous "statement of advice for a young person whose parents are or have been inside." Twenty-four CI students answered our questionnaire. Because the goal was to find new understandings of parental incarceration, we used a grounded theory approach (Charmaz, 2006) to look for emerging themes in the answers, first individually and then as a group. *Breaking the chains of despair* and *the strained parent-child relationship* emerged as important themes.

Regarding *breaking the chains of despair,* the statements of advice described three types of challenges that may cause young people to feel despair: (1) a fear that they might repeat their parents' mistakes; (2) a relative lack of guidance and protection compared to other youth; and (3) painful stereotypes and emotions. The statements also conveyed a strong sense of possibility in the form of concrete advice. CI students encouraged youth to focus on their positive goals ("Remain true and strong and do not give up on your dream regardless of how long it takes to materialize."), find positive role models ("Seek positive, strong and caring role models that will guide you through this disturbing time"), and reject the feeling of being doomed to repeat parents' mistakes ("Do not allow the stereotypes to take precedence"). Finally, CI students emphasized how education provides resources and opens horizons ("Education is very important. It shines some light and gives meaning to life"). In relation to the strained parent-child relationship, CI students highlighted: (1) the remoteness of prisons; and (2) the emotional distance, anger and pain felt when a parent is convicted. The advice told youth to take an active role in the parent-child relationship by communicating openly and often during incarceration and after release ("Communicate daily with them. Let them know how you feel and probe their feelings as well.") and providing support and encouragement ("Do not give up on them. Continue to support and love them with all your heart"). Similar themes emerged from interviews with siblings of the co-researchers during the making of the video documentary, as well as from three focus groups with a total of 20 youth, aged 16 to 21, from local community organizations. Focusing on their expertise, the focus group data took the form of life maps, stories about their communities, recommendations to policy makers and leaders and word maps about family and incarceration (see Table 1).

During the self-education and action phase, we learned that *both* the challenges of incarceration and the possibilities created by education are salient issues in the lives of youth with incarcerated parents (for a detailed discussion of the topic see Harris, Graham, & Carpenter, 2010). From this initial round of data collection we concluded that the incarceration and release of a parent can weaken young people's sense of hope and also take away emotional and material resources needed for a successful transition into adulthood. In addition, youth are often burdened by negative stereotypes but lack safe spaces where they can process their experiences. Finally, the parent-child relationship suffers from physical separation, feelings of anger, disappointment and sadness, and the disapproval of those who view parents as negative influences. From these challenges, however, youth can build a sense of determination towards their dreams, learn how to find positive role models, gain perspective about their own life choices, and find the motivation to grow in resources, purpose and pride through their own education. Although these findings are exploratory, they were a step towards more complex understandings of how inheritance and transformation relate to post-prison college.

Incarceration	Jail/Bars/Loneliness/No freedom/Abuse/Finding themselves/Lack of attention/Redemption/Goals/Justice
Family + incarceration	Hurt/Educated/Forgotten/Dysfunctional/Lost/Distance/Wanting better/Looking for love in the street/Motivation/Foster care/Single parent/ Hardship/Raising siblings/Hustle/Understanding/Secret/ Bad grades
Family	Love/Commitment/Patience/Fun/Loyalty/Caring/Trust/Fights/ Help/Home/Looking out/Being close-Being far/Respect/Reunion

Table 1. Word map about families and incarceration Example of a word map from focus group with 10 Latino/a, African American and South East Asian youth, ages16 to 21.

A Second Approach: Inheritance in Discourse

The self-education and action phases raised important questions about how to address race, class and power without perpetuating the notion that poor people of color are prisoners, and that prisoners are poor people of color. Reporting the challenges and achievements of our participants in a socio-cultural vacuum or through the lens of disparities research was not a satisfactory solution to this problem. It was vital to move beyond the redemption story that we were ready to gather, our participants ready to tell, and the world ready to hear. Otherwise, our well-intentioned research would portray at-risk youth whose lives can be saved through their parents' post-prison education. An important challenge was that our approach to the data gave us limited information about the power dynamics and discourses surrounding parental incarceration and post-prison college. Looking for clues, I began to re-read my notes in search of answers, and wrote the following:

> In the teams' discussions about youth with incarcerated parents [there is] a tension between a sense of hope that is infused with dreams of a college education, and the feeling of being doomed to a future of convictions ("They don't let me see my father cuz I might turn out like him"). Another tension is the relationship between shame ("I let people believe my foster mom's my real mom") and pride ("My friend tells everyone her father's inside and he's a Latin King")....So what is the "common sense" that surrounds incarceration?...What is really being inherited? Is it the role of "out of control"/"incorrigible"/"anti-social"/"super-predator"/"morally bankrupt" other?

Borrowing from Hole's (2007) work on narratives of deafness, I began to conceptualize the RCP and all other claims about prisoners and their children as part of the *discursive landscape of incarceration*. Hole argues that "surrounding any phenomenon there may be a variety of discourses...the set of meanings, metaphors, and representations, images, statements and so on that produce a particular understanding of an event, person, or experience...a different way of representing it to the world" (2007, p. 262). Within this framework, incarceration and inheritance are contested phenomena about which various discourses compete for legitimacy. In order to explore these meanings I decided to shift the unit of analysis away from the individual child-of-prisoner in order to ask the following questions: 1) *How do experts construct the intergenerational significance of incarceration through narratives of inheritance?* 2) *How do youth whose parents attend college after prison negotiate the intergenerational meaning of incarceration through their stories of post-prison college? What is at stake when youth speak of pride, shame, transformation and fate?*

To answer these questions I built a body of data from three purposive samples of experts who are differently positioned around the issue of incarceration. The first sample includes the expert sources that had informed our self-education and video work (Table 2), including five large-scale reports by research institutions and excerpts from the relevant chapters of nine criminal justice textbooks selected at random from the library catalogue of the John Jay College of Criminal Justice. These texts are worth examining because, as the voice of scientific objectivity, criminal justice experts affect the families of prisoners and the public opinion on parental incarceration through social policies and programs. The second sample includes song lyrics about incarceration by artists in the United States (Table 3). The sample stands in contrast to criminal justice textbooks in genre and in the social position of its authors, since hip hop, blues and jazz have historically been central to storytelling and self-representation by criminalized voices (Chang, 2005; Rose, 1994). Finally, the third sample includes the life stories of five young people—Charles, Sara, Jonathan, Marcus and Sam—who are 18 to 20 years of age and who, except for Charles, have seen their parents' transition from prison to college thanks to the CI. Their stories were co-constructed during audiotaped interviews using the Life Story Interview (McAdams, 1995), which invites interviewees to share their own analysis of the internal and external forces shaping their lives. Narrative research holds that "it is through the minutiae of daily life that human beings access the political ripples, and tidal waves, of their times" (Andrews, 2007, p. 2). Listening to these life stories in the context of other voices was a means to trace inheritance and learn about how the children of the "disposable" (Bauman, 2004) build lives of meaning (Hall & Fine, 2005) and thrive in double consciousness (Du Bois, 1903). This approach was inspired by the work of critical youth researchers whose work bypasses narratives of pathology (Brotherton & Barrios, 2004; Conquergood, 1992; Mendoza-Denton, 2008) by "bear[ing] witness to the ways in which young people are volunteered by their culture as a canvas for global economic, racial, cultural, gendered, and sexual conflicts" (Fine & Sirin, 2007, p. 34).

With these ideas in mind, I carried out a discourse analysis of the representations of what youth inherit from their parents at the material, symbolic, psychological, biological, legal and other levels. Using a code-book grounded on the data (Charmaz, 2006), I moved across the samples to understand contrasting representations as cultural tools (Vygotsky, 1978a, 1978b) used to celebrate or deny transformation. The analysis reveals parental incarceration and post-prison college as liminal spaces where determinism, hope, redemption and revision co-exist and also compete. The song lyrics represent inheritance in the context of raced and classed patterns of surveillance and conviction, highlighting the strengths of those who are criminalized and inscribing deficits on structural factors rather than on individuals and communities. In "Behind Enemy Lines," for instance, Dead Prez claim that Khadejah's father is incarcerated due to systematic race- and class-based repression of political leaders (see Table 4). Parental incarceration is represented as apart of oppressive structures in which the mass incarceration of poor black people is more a matter of fate than of personal choices:

> You know they got me trapped in this prison of seclusion / Happiness, living on tha streets is a delusion… Can barely walk tha city streets / Without a cop harassing me, searching me / Then asking my identity / Hands up, throw me up against tha wall. (From "Trapped," by Tupac, 1998)

In contrast, criminal justice experts weave inheritance into representations that highlight individual-level deficit in order to speak of the unjust causes and consequences of mass incarceration:

> The majority of female inmates are members of racial or ethnic minorities....*Only* four in ten report having had full-time employment at the time of the arrest, and *nearly* 30 percent were on welfare before incarceration, compared to just under 8 percent for male inmates....Health experts believe that [high] levels of abuse are related to the significant amount of drug and/or alcohol addiction that *plagues* the female prison population.... (Gaines & Miller, 2008, p. 342, italics added)

This focus on individual outcomes hides the fact that employment and self-reliance can be the exception rather than the norm among the urban poor whose jobs have been relocated to more profitable places (Bauman, 2004). The lyrics of prison songs, on the other hand, complicate the notion of inheritance; they reject intergenerational damage (see Cross, 2003), and locate the sources of disparity at the level of structural oppression. Consider the following lyrics by Tupac:

> When I was conceived, & came to be in this position / My momma was a panther loud / Single parent, but she proud / When she witness baby boy rip a crowd... / Will my child get to feel love / Or are we all just cursed to be street thugs / Cause being black hurts / And even worse if you speak first. (From "Letter to My Unborn Child, by Tupac, 1998)

Prison lyrics fracture narratives of urban primitivism about the urban poor (Conquergood, 1992) and portray children of prisoners who inherit a sense of pride from being part of a community that can be powerful and resilient despite oppressive circumstances—all indicators of an identity rooted in positive marginality (Hall & Fine, 2005; Unger, 2000). The lyrics also speak of loss but introduce another dimension to it: it is the state that has failed the children of prisoners and put them at risk, rather than their criminalized parents.

The contrasts and tensions that make up the discursive landscape of incarceration give us a sense of how much is at stake when Charles, Sara, Jonathan, Marcus and Sam speak of what they have inherited from their parents. It is with these insights in mind that I now turn to a more detailed discussion of the meaning of incarceration and post-prison college in the life stories of youth with formerly incarcerated parents.

Title	Author	Year
Criminal Justice: A Brief Introduction	Schmalleger	1999
American Criminal Justice: An Introduction	Bartollas & Jaeger	1988
Criminal Justice	Adler, Mueller & Laufer	2000
Criminal Justice in Action	Gaines & Miller	2008
Criminal Justice in America	Barlow	2000
Criminal Justice	Reid	2006
Introduction to Criminal Justice	Bohm & Haley	1997
Criminal Justice	Inciardi	1999
Crime and Justice: An Introduction	Abandinsky & Winfrey	1992
World Prison Population List	Walmsley	2009
One in 100: Behind Bars in America	Pew Center on the States	2008
Incarcerated Parents and Their Children	Bureau of Justice Statistics	2000
Bringing Families In	Christian et al.	2006
From Prison to Home	Department of Health and Human Services	2002

Table 2. Purposive sample of criminal justice textbooks and reports

Compilation Title	Label	Year
No More Prisons 2	Raptivism	2003
Tupac's Greatest Hits	Death Row Records	1998
In Prison: Afro-American Prison Music from blues to hip hop	Trikont	2006

Table 3. Purposive sample of song lyrics

Song Lyrics	
Pride	"Yo, little khadejah pops is locked…And she be dreamin bout his date of release…Her fathers a political prisoner, free fred / Son of a panther that the government shot dead /Back in 12-4-1969" *Dead Prez, "Behind Enemy Lines"*
Resilience	"Even as a crack fiend mama, / ya always was a black queen mama…ya always wuz committed, a poor single mother on welfare / tell me how ya did it" *Tupac, "Dear Mama"*

Textbooks and Reports	
Stigma	"Problems in school may be directly related to the alienation and stigma a child feel because a parent is incarcerated." *Christian et al., 2006*
Criminality	Inability of children to adopt productive coping mechanisms over time typically results in delinquency and adult criminal behavior." *From Prison to Home Conference: Background Paper, 2002*
Risk	"The children, families and former prisoners impacted by incarceration may represent a group more at-risk than any subculture in the country." *From Prison to Home Conference: Background Paper, 2002*

Life Stories	
Inspiration	"It was inspirational. I wanted to follow in [my father's] footsteps….That was why I really wanted to go to college." *Sam*
Resilience	"I remember Christmas…and this is a tough year but my mom had bought me a bunch of gifts. I remember her telling me my father couldn't be there, but he loves me, and he supports me." *Sam*
Pride	"I'm proud of him for staying clean, for getting back on his feet, helping other people." *Sara*

Table 4. Representations of inheritance

A third look at data: Listening to the ripples and the tidal waves

With the findings from the discourse analysis of inheritance, I went back to the life stories by Sam, Sara, Jonathan and Marcus and carried out a content analysis. Focusing on the impact of their parents' transition from prison to college and their involvement with the College Initiative, I searched once more for both strengths and challenges. In their stories, Sam, Sara, Jonathan and Marcus describe a new framework through which to tell their families' stories with pride, allowing them to speak of inspiration and guidance, solidarity and newfound stability. From them we learn that higher education makes CI students into legitimate mentors who inspire their children and provide guidance about life decisions, employment and educational opportunities ("And as far as the applying [to college]…my father told me what to do and where to go"). A parent's transition from prison to college or graduate school inspires youth to grow as individuals and motivates them to begin or complete their own college education:

> It was inspirational. I wanted to follow in [my father's] footsteps…He did 15 years in [prison]. He didn't even finish high school. You know, I finished high school, so I know if he could go, I could go. That was why I really wanted to go to college. You know, he's coming home, and going to college.…That's one of the major reasons I decided to go [to college]. *Sam*

In Sara's family "now we are all racing to see who finishes first since we all started around the same time." As parents and children attend college or graduate school around the same time, they are bonded by mutual support and healthy competition that brings them together despite living in different states or neighborhoods. Jonathan now sees "my aunt, my grandmother, cousins, uncles, everybody's all happy for [my father]. A lot of people come home and go back, so you know, everybody's happy for him. He's going to school, he's working."

This positive influence travels cities, households and generations, reinforcing the lives of young people who, like Sara and Sam, have excelled in high school and also opening new horizons for youth who face considerable challenges. Her father's example "gave [Sara's] sister the nudge to go back to school" at age 27 after becoming a mother at age 19 and finding herself overwhelmed by new responsibilities. Similarly, Jonathan's brother found in his father "a big incentive that he can [go to college], that 'if my father can do it…then I can also do it.'" This inspiration also travels outside the family, as the children of CI students become role models to their friends and schoolmates. Sam believes that "seeing me going to school and getting a degree will help [my friend] decide he wants to go back to school." Similarly, he sees himself as a role model for his 13-year-old half-brother, to whom he tells "Maybe one day you're going to want to go to college."

These experiences make post-prison college not only a source of inspiration but also an opportunity to tell a new story to teachers, friends and generations to come. This new story of achievement and transformation buffers the toxicity of negative stereotypes about parents as "ex-convicts" who are a weight on society, and youth as future criminals:

> Sam:…when I was younger, people said "you're going to end up like [your father],"…It wasn't a good feeling at all. I knew, at the time, I wasn't going to end up like that. It was a positive time in my life. And people telling me I'm going to end up like him. I just didn't know how to get to it.…
>
> Carolina: What do people say [now]? How does it feel?
>
> Sam: It feels good. I would like to end up like him, now. So now you could say all of that, whatever you want, because now you know he's doing the right thing. So you can't say you're going to end up like him no more, because he's moving forward. This is a positive time in his life. He's not in jail no more. So, hopefully, I can be like him now. I can receive my degree.

Jonathan, whose girlfriend was pregnant at the time of the interview, also finds himself with a new story to tell to his child: "Grandpa's life was kind of crazy, but it was very cool. It showed his inner strength. The strength of the mental." Through redemption narratives, youth can safely speak about the strengths that have always existed in their families and about the many possibilities that can open up during life after prison. This is clear in Sara's story:

> He used to be a paralegal before prison. He said now he wanted to become a counselor to help other people in his position. So he started the College Initiative process. I'm proud of him for staying clean, for getting back on his feet, helping other people….Having him back has been great because it shows there is hope, that there's life after jail. People say that there are no jobs, no love. But there is life after being incarcerated.

Their parents' experiences have taught the children of CI students about the value of educational opportunities and have made them aware of the need to overcome prejudice and to support formerly incarcerated individuals as they rebuild their lives and their communities through education. Jonathan believes that "[we] should have more programs for [college after prison] because it's pretty much a big advancement in civilization itself to [have been] in prison [and] know that you need to have your education."

Telling and living this new family story gives children of CI students a deep sense of pride in their parents' ability to give back to their communities. Jonathan and his siblings "are proud of [our father] for going to college." For Sam, silence about his father's incarceration has turned into pride:

> I feel more open to talking about [my father]…now he's home, doing the right thing. Working. Going to school. It feels great, because all this time he was in jail. So it's not like he came home and ended up right back in jail.

These accounts highlight the importance of including education as part of reentry policy. At the level of methodology, they also show how crucial it is to study the children of prisoners not only in their dispossession at the hands of defunded schools and a swollen prison system (Torre & Fine, 2005), but also in the face of opportunity. It is clear that Sara, Jonathan, Sam and Marcus would be telling different stories in the absence of the College Initiative program. Sara feels that if the father "wouldn't have went [to college], I wouldn't have had that talk with him. I wouldn't be going." Similarly, Jonathan believes that if his father had not become a student after prison this "probably would have led me to follow in his actions because that's what I would have seen him as doing." Sam, Jonathan and Sara base these answers on what they see in their communities:

> I know some people who haven't gone back to school and are back in jail or in a dead end job. It's hard for the children. One of my friends, he feels like his father doesn't care, doesn't love him, "because he couldn't make those changes for me." Another friend, he's working, and his mom is working too, and his dad is looking for a job, but it's hard without a degree. *Sara*

> Being from where I'm from, once [parents] come out pretty much within a reasonable amount of time go back [to prison]….So somebody going to school would be pretty abnormal. *Jonathan*

College, however, is not an antidote against dropping standards of living in the country. Parents who do go to college after prison must work hard to rebuild their lives and their communities. For Jonathan's father, being an MA student is challenging: "To be a parent, to go to school, to go to work, bills—everything is just hectic." For Sara, having her father back from prison and in school for a Master's degree "is hard…because he works a full-time and has a part-time job, and is a full-time student, so during the school year there isn't much communication." This suggests that successful post-prison programs must consider the needs of students' families. Only in this way can formerly incarcerated adults successfully meet their responsibilities and dreams as college students, parents and community members despite shrinking social services and rising costs of living. In the absence of affordable education, health, housing and well-paying jobs, lives become hectic and parents often drop out from school to address other pressing responsibilities.

Discussion

The positive intergenerational impact of higher education has been well documented among the families of non-traditional City University of New York students (Attewell & Levin, 2007). The life stories of children of College Initiative students suggest that such impact is also experienced among families of formerly incarcerated students, an important subcategory of non-traditional students. The life stories of the children of CI students teach us that higher education after prison can be a nutritious additive that protects youth at material, socio-psychological and also symbolic levels. The transformative power of higher education radiates from individual CI students and travels generations, households, neighborhoods and cities, touching the lives of their children, relatives and friends. This, in turn, nurtures the adult during and beyond reentry as in a virtuous cycle. Post-prison education interrupts intergenerational cycles of dispossession, disempowerment, social exclusion and despair as new resources and opportunities become available; stability, hope and trust grow among family members while the parent-child relationship finds new legitimacy.

Post-prison college helps fulfill the material and emotional needs identified in the self-education and action phases of the project. At the material level, educational achievement enables formerly incarcerated parents to obtain good employment and enter new social networks, thus breaking cycles of poverty and conviction and making new resources available to their children. At the socio-psychological and symbolic levels, youth experience their parents' educational achievements as a source of pride in their families and a new platform upon which to tell their stories. The transition from prison to college or graduate school gives parents new legitimacy as role models who can guide and inspire their children as they pursue a better education, employment and personal growth. The toxic effects of prejudice and stigma are buffered as children see their parents build meaningful lives after prison. However, it is not only individual youth who gain trust in their own ability to build meaningful and productive lives. Post-prison college also brings about new meanings to discourses of inheritance and reminds us, as a society, that ongoing positive transformation is possible for all.

Conclusion

Recursive and participatory methods are at the heart of the RC project and its study of post-prison college. At the policy level, the project queers the notion of inheritance by complicating deficit-based discourses about incarceration and post-prison college. At the methodological level, the project challenges the fantasy that research for critical purposes is a neat, linear endeavor.

Three lessons about critical knowledge are worth mentioning. First, participatory methods enabled us to document individual achievements and struggles without turning incarceration and reentry into issues that are relevant only to *them*—prisoners and their families. This, in large measure, is due to the fact that design of the RCP focuses on how adults, their families and their communities come to thrive and embody counter-narratives of inheritance of school-readiness, persistence and ongoing positive transformation in the presence of opportunity.

Second, collective self-education was a central aspect of this participatory approach. Conscientization carries the research towards critical knowledge and action because it reshapes the questions, methods, analyses and dissemination strategies. Self-education confirmed many intuitions and debunked others, empowered the members of the team, and inspired us to reframe the work at various points in order to avoid otherizing narratives of redemption. Changing ideas about what should be asked and from/of whom revealed parental incarceration and post-prison college as moving targets whose meanings cannot be understood solely through prison headcounts and surveys.

Finally, working between thematic and discourse analyses allowed the research to take on a more critical nature. This meant abandoning initial intentions to treat the experiences of youth and CI students as "data" to be inspected through criminal justice frameworks and instead using accounts by different kinds of experts (academics, musicians and youth) *both* as data and analytical frameworks. In this manner, we came to see inheritance as a place of struggle between strength and deficiency where youth with incarcerated parents negotiate between expert discourses and their lived experiences. Similarly, we recognized inheritance also as a place of struggle between otherizing and humanizing research recipes.

Tracing the methodological journey of the RC project offers some insights into the challenges of generating knowledge about normalized and invisible forms of dehumanization and inequality. These insights can help us unpack what we know about prisoners and their children, and also produce new knowledge towards more humanized ways of advocating for, serving, and accompanying them in their struggles. These reflections take individual and social transformation beyond the limited possibilities of redemption narratives; they highlight how emancipatory praxis and the constant process of becoming are defining aspects of the human experience.

Notes

1. The project, Rebuilding Urban Communities and Families through Higher Education: The Economic, Educational and Civic Impact of Post-Prison College on Adults and Their Children, was made possible by the generous funding of the Ford Foundation between January 2009 and January 2010.
2. The RCP youth team included B. J. Coleman, Carolina Muñoz Proto, Mayra Pacheco, Dominique Ramsey and Isabel Vieira, who were honored to collaborate with the College Initiative, the Polling for Justice Project, the Public Science Project of the CUNY Graduate Center, the Urban Youth Collaborative, Teen College Dreams, the Osborne Association, Exodus Transitional Communities, and the Center of Human Environments at the CUNY Graduate Center. The author and the RC youth team also thank Dr. Michelle Fine and Dr. Suzanne Ouellette for their valuable contribution to the development of this chapter.

References

Andrews, M. (2007). *Shaping history: Narratives of political change*. Cambridge: Cambridge University Press.

Attewell, P. A., & Levin, D. (2007). *Passing the torch: Does higher education for the disadvantaged pay off across generations*. New York, NY: Russell Sage Foundation.

Bauman, Z. (2004). *Wasted lives: Modernity and its outcasts*. Cambridge, MA: Blackwell.

Boudin, K., & Zeller-Berkman, S. (2010). Children of promise. In Y. R. Harris, J. A. Graham, & G. J. Carpenter (Eds.), *Children of incarcerated parents: Theoretical developmental and clinical issues* (pp. 73–102). New York, NY: Springer.

Brotherton, D., & Barrios, L. (2004). *The Almighty Latin King and Queen Nation: Street politics and the transformation of a New York City gang*. New York, NY: Columbia University Press.

Brydon-Miller, M. (2001). Participatory action research: Psychology and social change. In D. L. Tolman & M. Brydon-Miller (Eds.), *From subjects to subjectivities: A handbook of interpretive and participatory methods*. New York, NY: NYU Press.

Chang, J. (2005). *Can't stop, won't stop: A history of the hip-hop generation*. New York, NY: Picador.

Charmaz, K. (2006). *Constructing grounded theory: A practical guide through qualitative analysis*. Thousand Oaks, CA: Sage Publications.

Conquergood, D. (1992, April). On reppin' and rhetoric: Gang representations. Paper presented at the Philosophy and Rhetoric of Inquiry Seminar, University of Iowa, Iowa City.

Cross, W. E., Jr. (2003). Tracing the historical origins of youth delinquency & violence: Myths & realities about Black culture. *Journal of Social Issues, 59*(1), 67–82.

Du Bois, W. E. B. (1903). *The souls of black folk*. New York, NY: Dodd, Mead & Company.

Fals-Borda, O., & Rahman, M. A. (1991). *Action and knowledge: Breaking the monopoly with Participatory Action-Research*. New York, NY: The Apex Press.

Fine, M., Roberts, R. A., Torre, M. E., & Upegui, D. (2001). Participatory action research behind bars. *International Journal of Critical Psychology, 2*, 145–157.

Fine, M. & Sirin, S. R. (2007). Theorizing hyphenated lives: Researching marginalized youth in times of historical and political conflict. *Social and Personality Psychology Compass, 1*(1), 16–38.

Foster, H., & Hagan, J. (2007). Incarceration and intergenerational social exclusion. *Social Problems, 54*(4), 399–433.

Freire, P. (1990). *Pedagogy of the oppressed*. New York, NY: Continuum. (Original work published 1970)

Gaines, L. K. & Miller, R. L. (2008). *Criminal justice in action*. Belmont, CA: Wadsworth.

Hall, R., & Fine, M. (2005). The stories we tell: The lives and friendship of two older Black lesbians. *Psychology of Women Quarterly, 29*(2), 177–187.

Harris, Y. R., Graham, J. A., & Carpenter, G. J. (2010). *Children of incarcerated parents: Theoretical developmental and clinical issues.* New York, NY: Springer.

Hole, R. (2007). A poststructural analysis of three deaf women's life stories. *Narrative Inquiry, 17*(2), 259–278.

McAdams, D. P. (1995). The life story interview. Retrieved from http://www.sesp.northwestern.edu/foley/instruments/interview/

Mendoza-Denton, N. (2008). *Homegirls: Language and cultural practice among Latina youth gangs.* Malden, MA: Blackwell.

Rose, T. (1994). *Black noise: Rap music and black culture in contemporary America.* Hanover, NH: University Press of New England.

Torre, M. E., & Fine, M. (2005). Bar none: Extending affirmative action to higher education in prison. *Journal of Social Issues, 61*(3), 569–594.

Tupac. (1998a). Trapped. On *Tupac's Greatest Hits* (CD). Los Angeles, CA: Death Row Records.

Tupac. (1998b). Letter to my unborn child. On *Tupac's Greatest Hits* (CD). Los Angeles, CA: Death Row Records.

Vygotsky, L. S. (1978a). Tool and symbol in child development. In *Mind in Society* (pp. 19–30). Cambridge, MA: Harvard University Press.

Vygotsky, L. S. (1978b). Internalization of higher psychological functions. In *Mind in Society* (pp. 52–57). Cambridge, MA: Harvard University Press.

Unger, R. (2000). Outsiders inside: Positive marginality and social change. *Journal of Social Issues, 56,* 163–179.

Wacquant, L. (1998). Three pernicious premises in the study of the American ghetto. *International Journal of Urban and Regional Research, 22*(3), 507–510.

CHAPTER THIRTY-FIVE

Tradition, Authority, and the Doing of Research: Perspectives from the Middle East

Ramzi Nasser and Radhika Viruru

The ideas that we explore in this chapter come essentially from our experiences and our conversations about those experiences while teaching about and doing research in Qatar. We believe our experiences were certainly influenced by our somewhat complicated "expatriate" identities as non-Qataris, working in the Persian Gulf. As such we occupied positions that were neither "native" yet not quite "non-native" either. The first author is a native speaker of Arabic, and as such was able to participate, at least linguistically, in many of the conversations of our workplace, while the second author hails originally from India, and as such encountered many traditions and ideas that were familiar. As we engaged in our daily work as academics in Qatar, we continued, however, to encounter "fractures" in our discussions with our students that were extraordinarily interesting, yet difficult for us to understand. One example that stood out to both of us was that we both happened to mention to different classes, to different sets of students, that research had shown that over the years, the average height of human beings has gone up (O'Connor, 2010). We both encountered extraordinary resistance to this concept, with students arguing fervently that in fact the opposite was true. We both received emails from our students with pictures of what were meant to be human fossils from many centuries ago that proved, or so the students argued, that human beings long ago were in fact much taller than modern-day humans. Puzzled by this, we tried to investigate where this belief was coming from. Although we did not come to a conclusive answer, it appeared to be based on religious knowledge (some mentioned reading in a religious text about how the ancient prophets were extremely tall people and others mentioned family stories about visits to the graves of those prophets and how the size of their graves showed them to be indeed extremely tall). Students who were extremely receptive to many other ideas, and were eager to learn about what they often referred to as "modern" methods of teaching, learning and thinking about education, consistently refused to believe the "scientific" fact that over time, human beings have grown taller. We came to think of this as a representative example of the situation in present-day Qatar, which now ranks among the top 10 countries in the world in terms of spending on research, yet maintains a distinct set of traditions based on the religion of Islam. We found ourselves drawn to explore what form of co-existence would emerge between these two perspectives. The official discourses of the country seemed to be enthusiastically espousing scientific research as their next form of income-generating resource, as can be seen in the Request for Proposals for the latest cycle of national research funding in Qatar: "The NPRP will support basic and applied research, as both may lead to expertise in new sectors and to the creation of intellectual property as a powerful tool for economic development and wealth creation" (QNRF, 2010, p. 5).

However, living in Qatar one became aware of the many contradictions that existed within these discourses. For example, the country has invested millions of dollars in wireless and communication technologies, yet at many female-only social occasions cellular phones are prohibited and must be checked at the door, to guard against the possibility of taking pictures of unveiled women. Some women friends of the second author wished that they still made cellular phones without cameras. Qatar's unique situation, being as it is in the midst of negotiating two paradigms of what the future should look like while insisting that they must co-exist, raises many questions about the place of knowledge and ways of knowing. In this chapter we attempt to look at three of them: (1) why are the words research and scientific research being used interchangeably; (2) how does the indigenous knowledge that the state is often eager to enforce and police interact with current perspectives on knowing that have been actively sought out and brought to Qatar; and (3) what kind of role can critical qualitative research play in relation to the national agenda of reform? We will first present a brief introduction to the current situation in Qatar before engaging with these issues.

Introduction: Qatar's Modern Development

Qatar is one of the seven Gulf Cooperation Council (GCC) countries in the Persian Gulf and is approximately the size of the state of Delaware. It is also one of the richest countries in gas reserves in the world. In 2005, Qatar embarked on a national development program in education, science and community development. Qatar's vision focuses on four interconnected pillars: Human Development to sustain a prosperous society; Social Development, based on high moral standards, to play a significant role in global partnerships; Economic Development of a competitive and diversified economy; and Environmental Development to create harmony among economic growth, social development and environmental protection (Kelly et al., 2009). The vision was created to transform Qatar into an advanced economy, influenced by a Western human resource theory in which personal growth and development through intensive training and empowerment supplanted existing organizations. Modernity is thus characterized by bureaucratic structures, supervisory controls of regulations, situated monopolies and, profoundly, a hierarchical knowledge communicated by a downward flow of information (Grieves, 2005). Large national investments have been poured into infrastructure projects such as cultural and educational institutions and research centers, with the assumption that such investments could produce a modern technocratic and information-based society that could generate dividends.

Modernist projects from the West (which are now reinvigorated as globalization) have been adopted full-heartedly by Qatar in its pursuit to create a knowledge-based society. For example, Qatar's newest flagship projects have included the unveiling of a world-class educational biomedical research program, the first of its kind in the Middle East. Qatar has also established the Qatar Foundation, a national agency, with its primary function to fund and manage institutional development. Within the Qatar Foundation reside such prestigious institutions as Weill Cornell Medical School, Texas A&M School of Engineering and Cornell University (Rostron, 2009).

In 2007 a large number of Arab and Qatari "scientists" met at the Qatar Foundation's International Research in Science and Technology conference (QFIRST) and established a trans-national and national strategy for research priorities for the Arab world and Qatar in particular, namely the development of an institutional culture to promote research. The strategies envisioned were translated to micro-level institutional initiatives that encourage research projects aligned with national research priorities including (a) providing the necessary infrastructure and financial support for research, (b) establishing national research centers, (c) creating global networks with research scientists across the world, (d) identifying and developing strategic research partnerships within and outside Qatar, and (e) rewarding the achievement of recognized research performance. With such a vision and impetus and resources, Qatar is uniquely defining its development strategies in building a research base to sustain a knowledge-based society. The State of Qatar now invests 2.8% of its gross domestic product in research, placing it in the top 10 countries in the world that invest in research (www.qnrf.org).

Tremendous public investment has been felt in particular in fields such as the biomedical sciences, in support of research and development. For example, current projects include Hamad Medical Corporation (HMC) (a publicly funded medical service), the National Ministry of Health, Sidra Medical and Research Center (a private/public initiative for medical services and research and development), Qatar Science and Technology Park (an incubator for start-up enterprises, providing premises and services) and Weill Medical College of Cornell University. Based largely on British and American start-ups, these enterprises see researchers and academic faculty collaborating on different research priorities from inside and outside the nation. Qatar's impetus to improve and address some of the critical issues raised by the United Nations Development Programme's 2002 and 2003 Arab Human Development reports and the more recent Arab Knowledge Report (2009) has resulted in investment in human development projects and has set the road map of a modernist project in a quest to build a knowledge-based renaissance, seen as a prerequisite for any significant gains in human development.

Science as Commodity

The most authoritative statements about the place of research in Qatar come from the Qatar National Research Fund (QNRF), whose banner reads "Creating a knowledge based society" and which is the country's premier organization for research funding. They outline their vision as:

> Qatar Foundation envisions research as a catalyst for expanding and diversifying the country's economy; enhancing the education of its citizens and the training of its workforce; and fostering improvements in the health, well-being, environment, and security of its own people and those of the region. In striving toward this vision, Qatar will distinguish itself within the region and world as a cosmopolitan nation that embraces scholarly excellence, innovation, creativity, inclusiveness, and merit. (QNRF, n.d.)

As the fund invites research proposals, it outlines what it calls priority areas, listing eight areas of particular interest. These include industry and engineering, environment, computer science and information technology, health and life sciences, education, public policy and management, the arts and humanities and the social sciences (http://qnrf.org/fund_program/nprp/priority_lists/). Whereas detailed lists of priorities are outlined in the sections on engineering and technology in particular, the ones on education are quite brief and focus almost exclusively on the application of technology to education. The areas listed as priorities in education, social sciences and arts and humanities are listed below:

Education	Social Sciences	Arts and Humanities
E-learning	Regional history culture and law	Design
Open systems	Regional political science	Shari'ah
Distance learning	East/West understanding	Ethics of new technologies
Software	Behavior modification	
Methods and systems	Diet and exercise	
Virtual classrooms	Motivation	
	Conflict resolution	

As educational researchers we were intrigued by the invisible "keep out" sign that seemed to be posted for research in areas such as social justice, gender relationships and critical pedagogy. We were intrigued by the fact that although the goals of the research fund, as cited above, were to improve the lives of its people, the priority lists seemed, for the most part, non-human in their orientation. Much like the common living arrangement of "gated communities" prevalent in Qatar, it seemed as though research too was only allowed into some but not all gated communities (Glasze & Al Khayal, 2001). Thus it appears that although Qatar is taking aggressive steps to create a culture of research in the country, awarding over $113 million in funding in 2010 alone, the places and spaces where this research is allowed to be conducted are limited and, we would suggest, carefully controlled. An innovative way to improve mapping of existing natural gas resources is much more likely to be given priority than, for example, a study on how gender relations are impacted by online learning. By adopting science in isolation from the social world, which seems to be the focus of the national research initiatives, the image of science as a commodity is propagated: one that can easily be purchased and integrated into the landscape of the country, without significantly altering, or at least not immediately and visibly so, that landscape. What we would suggest, however, is that such a simplified approach does not take into account certain factors such as the complex interactions between the social and natural sciences. Collins (1985) has commented on the idea of the certainty of scientific constructions, suggesting that "there is an inverse relationship between the level of certainty attached to any particular scientific construction and proximity to its site of construction" (Lahsen, 2005, p. 895). Located as Qatar is, at a physical distance from the (recognized) sites of production of scientific knowledge, it seems as though governors of the research fund have subscribed to the social construction that science is "truth," without exploring many of the uncertainties that attend its production. It also represents an unquestioning acceptance of neoliberal views of science, that have resulted in what Lave, Mirowski, & Randalls (2010) have called "the narrowing of research agendas to focus on the needs of commercial actors" (p. 659). These authors contend that neoliberal emphasis on "the market as the central agent in human society" (p. 659) has resulted in a narrowing of research priorities, and heightened the need to produce knowledge that is easily translatable into wealth, where ideas essentially become commodities in the marketplace. Qatar's national policies towards research seem particularly well aligned with these ideas. By not including the social sciences as an important part of the research agenda (in the last cycle of funding approximately only 10% of the projects funded were in the social sciences) and in restricting research to natural sciences that do not (supposedly) intrude into the social world, the research that emerges is necessarily restricted and misses key issues such as the interaction between responsibility and technology (McCarthy & Kelty, 2010) and the role that ethnographic research can play in the processes of knowledge production (Beaulieu, 2010). Further, as Montgomery and Oliver (2009) have pointed out, research in science and technology has also raised many important questions about ethical issues, such as informed consent and social responsibility, that it does not have the tools to answer. Further, the processes of scientific "transfer" are fraught with complications (Hill, Loch, Straub, & El-Sheshai, 1998). Atiyya (1989) found, for example, that in neighboring Arab countries, the process of technology transfer was complicated by cultural issues. Similarly, issues of motivation and workplace culture have been found to impact this process (Al-Meer, 1990).

Disappearing Indigenous Knowledge

As science and research, words that are often used interchangeably in Qatari contexts, move at express train speed into Qatar's cultural landscape, a disconnect that we see unfolding is between the indigenous knowledges of the local people and the world of scientific knowledge and research. For the locals, the perception, as Atari (1996) suggests, is perhaps that if religion is not a source of generating knowledge, the knowledge may be opposing or irrelevant to religion. It places academics and others engaged in research, however, in spaces of conflict as mentors to our students. For example, in the first author's

Introduction to Education course, during a discussion with the students (there were 10 students in the class, all women, eight of whom were Qatari) about their philosophies of education, the instructor asked the students "whether their own personal values are changing" as a result of the class. A great majority of the students believed that their values were indeed changing; these students were also extremely religious and traditional (in the presence of the first author, who is male, they veiled themselves completely, so all he could ever see of them were their eyes). The instructor then probed the students further and asked whether they believed Islam was unified and unchanging. Most of the students commented that their belief in God (Allah) was absolute and unchanging. Later on in the semester, one of those students, who was also enrolled in a *tahfiz* school (specifically dedicated to the reading and study of the Koran), confided to the first author that she wished that in the *tahfiz* they would do more analysis than memorization. The propensity among the majority of our students was often to memorize rather than critically question or synthesize ideas, as reflected in the *tahfiz* methods of instruction. We see the student's situation as being reflective of this unique co-existence of the opposing perspectives of tradition and Western knowledge: when is questioning and analysis appropriate? Our experience as academics in the national university has also exposed us to the extent to which scientific knowledge has infiltrated through the university governance and policy, bringing a performance and standards-based orientation not only to program evaluation but to faculty performance as well. For instance, the general shift to measure faculty performance through a set of metrics has now been adopted at the university; this disadvantages many Qatari faculty who operate in the native language, due to the incommensurability of these metrics with indigenous forms of assessment. Furthermore, the national university has asked faculty to produce scholarship with relatively high impact factors. While many of the faculty write in Arabic and submit to Arabic journals, Arabic journals are not indexed and cannot be cited and the metrics are unobtainable. Policies that hinder indigenous faculty from writing in their own language pose a serious threat to the growth and maintenance of indigenous knowledge in Qatar.

Although we do not mean to set up the indigenous and the scientific as binaries that never intersect (the Arab world is known for its contributions to science; Qatar Foundation, 2009), there are various points of contention that we would like to explore. In particular we suggest that the creation of entities such as the Qatar National Research Fund and other such research-based institutions in Qatar, who speak an unabashed discourse of scientific progress, reflect the typology of Talcott Parsons' (Leys, 1996) notion of the social science as a science which has no people, no identities or psychologies. They reflect the influence of what Hanieh (2010) has called "khaleeji capitalism," referring to a set of ideas emerging from the oil-producing states in the Persian Gulf. Hanieh suggests that within the Persian Gulf, "a capitalist class—described as khaleeji-capital—is emerging around the accumulation-opportunities presented within the new regional space. The formation of khaleeji-capital represents the development of a class increasingly aligned with the interests of imperialism" (p. 35) and, we would suggest, in opposition to traditional Islamic values which have emphasized the importance of charity and collectivist identities.

In Qatar, as elsewhere in the Arab world, attempts to "modernize" have centered around the application of modern-day human resource theories, based on the notion of the human as known by science, rather than the human situated in religious and cultural contexts (Rostron, 2009). National authorities are committed to moving and invigorating development and applied research projects through a process in which the West transfers its expertise, i.e., knowledge, to the East. This, however, raises many profound questions about the new "reality" of the knowledge being generated and whom it may serve. Research often seems to be at the center of the knowledge schism between the scientific knowledge of the West and indigenous knowledge. Generally, drawn by our sensitivities, while we are critical of our own approaches and methods, we are also critical of the indigenous researchers' blind adoption of the scientific approach to research, particularly among our Qatari academic colleagues. Their adoption of Western models of social science—translation, measurement, validation and generalization—all seem to reside within a Western theoretical framework which has been unquestioningly generalized to the local context. For instance, the concept of achievement is very high on the list of priorities for educators and policy makers and spearheads education reform in Qatar. The stress on achievement, particularly of an individualistic nature, seems in direct conflict with the social and collective nature of Qatari society. As Ayish (1998) has said, "dignity, honor, paternalism, faith, worship, knowledge and community" are the characteristics most commonly used to describe traditional Arab societies. Singh and Pareek (1968) have suggested ways in which the concept of achievement can be adapted to local and indigenous contexts. Even if the measurement system remains the same, the construct could be extended and reconceptualized to fit diverse socio-cultural frames. Other concepts such as self-esteem or ingratiation that also hold particular importance in the Arab world, yet in different forms from those more commonly found in the West, are less likely to be integrated in the national research strategic vision for Qatar, due to the mismatch between those values and the neoliberal models of science being brought in from the West.

While as non-native researchers we believe that the indigenous inquirer/researcher has a significant role in the current "reform," specifically, the development of understanding and the generation of knowledge, we see little or non-existent involvement by the indigenous. Certainly there are reasons for this: secular understandings of society anchored within a positivist framework of progress and change often draw upon non-indigenous researchers to impart and tell about the indigenous as they are more likely to have training in Euro-American models of research. However, non-indigenous researchers often have few or no commonalities with the local knowledge or what may be considered as indigenous knowledge, as such knowledge is often authoritative and conflated in religious symbolism and tradition. As Rostron (2009) has commented, values that hold importance in Qatar include "tightness, collectivism and particularism, with a relatively vertical, passive, ascription-based outlook (Triandis, 2002, para. 18–24) and poly-chronic use of time" (p. 221) and as such can appear unintelligible to outsiders. Post-colonialists may raise cautions about this attempt to rely on the perspectives of outsiders and underline the significance of indigenous knowledge (Smith, 1999; Semali & Kincheloe, 1999) as a viable source of knowledge if it can formalized, although we recognize that all knowledge cannot be formalized. However, Western and Eurocentric models are seen as authoritative knowledge (as conceived by policy makers) and as such are necessary for the development of Qatari's scientific community. Therefore, on the one hand, there is the drive for progress and development through research; on the other hand, there is a sense of epistemological quandary. Religious and indigenous knowledge is conflated with tradition, and often operates as persuasive and uncritical, rarely negating or pushing the bounds of traditional knowledge and religious scriptures or challenging the modern. What appears to be lacking is an effort to stand out in the face of modernism, to profess and to guide or to alternate and show a sense of ownership of its development and change. As observers and researchers in social science practice, we are pulled into a dilemma as serving as the phantom of change within a secular-Western-looking prism.

One criticism that we highlight in particular is the manner in which research priorities are being defined, directing focus towards issues that are not recognized as issues within indigenous discourses. Examples of these would include discrimination, prejudice or even equality between genders; these are discourses or narratives about concepts that are "not there," nor has there been a movement among the indigenous people calling for their creation. One particular example of a Western notion is women's rights, as seen from a Western feminist perspective. The question arises whether it is called for in Qatar. We think not. From our own interactions with Qatari women, women in Qatari society have a special position where they are generally empowered in a "patriarchal society" to a "reversed matriarchal order" where there is a greater and implicit empowerment of women in the family as well as society. Women, in their rigorously controlled private domains, are supported in living their traditional roles in family and society, while concomitantly strengthening their role in the public world. The narrative and discourse which are shown aboveground for research studies, which are the only points that "research" can "see," thus can only provide limited glimpses into an alternative construction of what women's rights from an indigenous perspective might look like. The perceptions of Arab women as veiled, invisible and therefore powerless figures is belied by the facts that show that in almost all Arab countries, large numbers of women are seeking employment, and that in most countries, women have equal access to state-provided education and tend to outperform the males at most levels (Neal, Finlay, & Tansey, 2005). Many interpretations of Islam have also encouraged women to work, as long as it does not interfere with their family roles (Neal et al., 2005) and as Neal and his colleagues point out, this is "a traditional feature of life in the Arab world that corresponds closely with Hoschild's (1989) observations about American women's continued accountability to their "primary roles" of motherhood and house worker (p. 479).

The Role of Critical Qualitative Research in Current-Day Qatar

What role, then, can critical qualitative research play in a situation such as the one described above? There are, of course, many academics who are already attempting to engage in such research, although their efforts appear to be conducted in isolation, as there is no network that we are aware of that brings them together. The national university of Qatar, which has been in existence since 1973, has supported, even if in a limited way, the social sciences and social science research for many years now. Our experiences have brought us into contact with a variety of academics and other scholars, who all share similar concerns about the need for research that brings a sense of context to everything that is happening in Qatar. As postcolonial scholars who are also aware of what research has done, and what has been done in the name of research to indigenous peoples (Smith, 1999, 2005), we are more aware than ever that it behooves us all to tread extremely carefully. We are mindful, too, that neoliberal projects have often used social science research to further their own agendas (Apple, 2001) and are not unaware of the argument that perhaps research is better off outside organizations that push knowledge as a commodity. We do, however, believe that the methods and methodologies of critical qualitative research can provide valuable insights, particularly in such complex situations. As Smith (2005) has commented, on the doing of qualitative research in times of uncertainty, this kind of research can shed light on "the taken-for-granted understandings that are being applied to decisions being made under pressure" (p. 102).

Anderson, Adey, and Bevan (2010) make a salient case that the social and geographical places in which qualitative research is conducted add a vital dimension to our understanding of the process of knowledge production and the situated nature of that knowledge. Although qualitative research has traditionally insisted on the importance of context, the interactions between the social and geographical location, the researcher and the participants, has not heretofore been considered an important part of this way of knowing. These authors argue that the inclusion of place moves qualitative research from a dialogue between the researcher and participants, to what they refer to as a polylogue, or multi-pronged conversation. When we think specifically of Qatar, and the very recent impetus to make research a part of its national priorities, we are certainly reminded of the importance of place in the research process. No efforts have been spared in creating perhaps some of the most luxurious spaces for research in the world. One of the Qatar Foundation's recent projects includes the opening of the Qatar Science and Technology Park in March 2009, which describes itself as "a home for technology-based companies from around the world and an incubator for start-up enterprises…. Among our first proud members are EADS, ExxonMobil, GE, Microsoft, Shell and Total; bringing research and business together, while spurring the development of Qatar's knowledge economy" (http://www.qstp.org.qa/). The first phase of the QSTP alone cost 600 million dollars to build (http://www.qstp.org.qa/files/pdf/QSTPPressPack.pdf). The underlying idea seems to be that to "discover" the right kind of knowledge, one needs the right kind of facilities. However, if one uses the polylogical approach described above (Anderson, Adey, & Bevan, 2010), it is possible to ask questions such what relationship do luxury and knowledge have with one another? Such questions open up the door, too, to issues such as whose labor does it take to maintain this luxury?

Ackerly and True (2010) suggest that critical feminist research currently can build upon decades of feminist thought and research to engage with empirical research to engender dialogue with the following questions: the purpose of research (Why do humans engage in this activity?), conceptualization (How do language and theory influence the questions that we do want to answer?), epistemology (What does it mean to know? How do you know what you know?), and finally issues of power and its role in determining research questions. Referring back to the idea of time discussed above, we believe that it is still not too late for these questions to be asked as national priorities of research are determined. Given the abundant material resources available in Qatar, it appears to us as though it is through polyloguing with these questions that the current coexistence, which is rapidly being given the status of a binary, can be problematized and reshaped. As a former British protectorate itself, it appears as though Qatar has not sufficiently interrogated the relationship between science and colonialism (Cannella & Viruru, 2004) or considered some of the implications of neoliberal concepts of research. As Smith (2005) has pointed out, neoliberal redefinitions of knowledge as an instrument of wealth creation can result in invasive searches for "new" knowledge that lead inevitably into unexplored social spaces and spheres. The few remaining unexplored spaces in the world after colonization often belong to indigenous peoples. We believe, too, that it is essential that questions about conceptualization and epistemology be addressed. At one of the faculty meetings in the College of Education, a discussion arose as to whether undergraduate students should be asked to write a statement of philosophy as part of their professional preparation. Although this is not an unheard-of idea, several Arab faculty members were uncomfortable with the concept, believing that the students were simply too young and inexperienced to aspire to anything approaching a "philosophy," which is a word that is not used lightly in educational circles in the Arab world. In North American contexts, however, this is considered entirely appropriate: preservice teachers are expected to not only know what they believe about education but to possess the ability to articulate it in writing. As research from the West makes it way further and further into Qatar, whether in invited or uninvited areas, we believe that more and more such conflicts will arise, unless the nature of the endeavor is understood in its complexity.

References

Ackerley, B., & True, J. (2010). Back to the future: Feminist theory, activism, and doing feminist research in an age of globalization. *Women's Studies International Forum, 33,* 464–472.

Al-Meer, A. R. A. (1990). Organizational commitment: a comparison of Westerners, Asians and Saudis. *International Studies of Management and Organization, 19*(2), 74–84.

Anderson, J., Adey, P., & Bevan, P. (2010). Positioning place: Polylogic approaches to research methodology. *Qualitative Research, 10*(5), 589–604.

Apple, M. (2001). Markets, standards, teaching and teacher education. *Journal of Teacher Education, 52,* 182–196.

Atari, A (1996). Towards Islamization of the disciplines: Comparative education. *Muslim Education Quarterly, 14*(1), 1–42.

Atiyyah, H. (1989). Determinants of computer system effectiveness in Saudi Arabia. *International Studies of Management and Organization, 19*(2), 85–103.

Ayish, M. (1998). Communication research in the Arab world: New perspectives. *The Public, 5*(1), 33–57.

Beaulieu, A. (2010). From co-location to co-presence: Shifts in the use of ethnography for the study of knowledge. *Social Studies of Science, 20* (10), 1–18.

Cannella, G. S., & Viruru, R. (2004). *Childhood and postcolonization: Power, education and contemporary practice.* New York, NY: Routledge.

Collins, H. (1985). *Changing order: Replication and induction in scientific practice.* Chicago, IL: University of Chicago Press.

Glasze, G., & Al Khayal, A. (2001). Gated housing estates in the Arab world: Case studies in Lebanon and Riyadh, Saudi Arabia. *Environment and Planning: Planning and Design, 29,* 321–336.

Grieves, J. (2005). *Strategic human resource development.* London, England: Sage.

Hanieh, A. (2010). Khaleeji-capital: Class formation and regional integration in the Middle-East Gulf. *Historical Materialism, 18*(2), 35–76.

Hill, C. E., Loch, K. D., Straub, D., & El-Sheshai, K. (1998). A qualitative assessment of Arab culture and information technology transfer. *Journal of Global Information Management, 6*(3), 29–38.

Hoschild, A. R. (1989). *The second shift*. New York, NY: Avon Books.

Kelly, K., & Al-Maadadi, F. (2009). A qualitative study of home and school practices that support the English-language development of emergent bilingual children in Qatar. Paper presented at the second early childhood conference, Qatar University, Doha, Qatar. January 17–18, 2009.

Lahsen, M. (2005). Seductive simulations? Uncertainty distribution around climate models. *Social Studies of Science, 35*(6), 895–922.

Lave, R., Mirowski, P., & Randalls, S. (2010). Introduction: STS and neo-liberal science. *Social Studies of Science, 40*(5), 659–675.

Leys, C. (1996). *The rise and fall of development theory*. Bloomington: Indiana University Press.

McCarthy, E., & Kelty, C. (2010). Responsibility and nano-technology. *Social Studies of Science, 40*(3), 405–432.

Montgomery, K., & Oliver, A. L. (2009). Shifts in guidelines for ethical scientific conduct: How public and private organizations create and change norms of research integrity. *Social Studies of Science, 39*(1), 137–155.

Neal, M., Finlay, J., & Tansey, R. (2005). "My father knows the Minister": A comparative study of Arab women's attitudes towards leadership authority. *Gender in Management, 20*(7), 354–375.

O'Connor, A. (2010). *Never shower in a thunderstorm*. London, England: Macmillan.

Qatar Foundation. (2009). *Arab science: A journey of innovation*. Retrieved from http://www.grouporigin. com/clients/qatar-foundation/

Qatar National Research Fund (QNRF). (n.d.). Vision and mission. Retrieved from http://qnrf.org/about_qnrf/vision_mission/)

Qatar National Research Fund (QNRF). (2010). *National Priorities Research Program request for proposal*. Retrieved from http://www.qnrf.org/fund_program/nprp/download/4/nprp_4th_cycle_12102010.pdf

Rostron, M. (2009). Liberal arts education in Qatar: Intercultural perspectives. *Intercultural Education, 20*(3), 219–229.

Semali, L. M., & Kincheloe, J. L. (Eds.). (1999). *What is indigenous knowledge? Voices from the academy*. London, England: Falmer.

Singh, Y. P., & Pareek, U. (1968). A paradigm of sequential adoption. *Indian Educational Review, 3*(1), 89–114.

Smith, L. T. (1999). *Decolonizing methodologies: Research and indigenous people*. London, England: Zed Books.

Smith, L. T. (2005). On tricky ground: Researching the native in the age of uncertainty. In N. K. Denzin & Y. S. Lincoln (Eds.), *The Sage handbook of qualitative research* (3rd ed., pp. 85–108). Thousand Oaks, CA: Sage.

United Nations Development Programme. (2002). *Arab human development report: Creating opportunities for future generations*. New York, NY: Author. Retrieved from http://www. arab-hdr.org/publications/other/ahdr/ahdr2002e. pdf

United Nations Development Programme. (2003). *Arab human development report: Building a knowledge society*. New York, NY: Author. Retrieved from http://www. arab-hdr.org/publications/other/ahdr/ahdr2003e. pdf

United Nations Development Programme (UNDP). (2009). *Arab knowledge report*. Dubai, UAE: Mohammed bin Rashid Al Maktoum Foundation and UNDP. Retrieved from http://www. mbrfoundation.ae/English/Documents/AKR–2009–En/AKR–English. pdf

Psychiatric Survivors, Psychiatric Treatments, and Societal Prejudice: An Inquiry into the Experience of a Marginal Group

Michael O'Loughlin and Marilyn Charles

Genuine and thorough comprehension of Otherness is possible only if the self can somehow negate or at least severely bracket the values, assumptions, and ideology of his culture…this entails in practice the virtually impossible task of negating one's very being, precisely because one's culture is what formed that being. Moreover, the colonizer's invariable assumption about his moral superiority means that he will rarely question the validity of his own or his society's formation and that he will not be inclined to expand any energy in understanding the worthless alterity of the colonized. (JanMohamed, 1995, p. 18)

Leaving aside JanMohamed's incapacity to transcend gender bias in the above quote, his words offer a daunting challenge to anyone who aspires to engage in field research. Because culture inevitably constrains our views, if we are to truly be useful to those with less power, it is important to be mindful of these power dynamics and how they affect our data and findings. Since elite elements in the culture are more free to exercise the power to refuse the scrutiny of social science research, fieldwork tends to focus on studying down to less powerful groups. Studying down requires crossing the tracks, entering the arena of the Other to get the story. What if JanMohamed is correct that it is self-deluding to believe that we can divest ourselves of ourselves to enter the experience of an Other? Is qualitiative inquiry, then, an exercise in self-delusion?

The growing recognition that "getting the story" is a rather fraught enterprise can be seen as a result of the interpretive turn in anthropology that emerged as a result of the crisis in representation the field experienced in the 1980s. That crisis was precipitated, first, by Clifford and Marcus's (1986) *Writing Culture*, and then by the feminist critique of anthropology (embodied, for example, in Behar and Gordon's *Women Writing Culture*, 1995) that followed a decade later. Deborah Britzman noted, for example, that "the ground on which ethnography is built turns out to be a contested and fictive geography." She went on to state that "those who populate it—the identities of every participant, including the author and the reader—are in essence textualized identities…that, if carefully read, suggest just how slippery speaking, writing and reading subjectivity really is" (1995, p. 134).

The danger in this interpretive turn is that the positivist myth that we are "scribes of the real" (Britzman, 1995, p. 145) is then replaced by new solipsistic understandings of narrative that valorize personal experience at the expense of any understanding of the embeddedness of human activity in complex sociopolitical and sociohistorical contexts. There is, after all, no single story to be told. Instead, there are multiple tellings, each of which privileges certain aspects of the intersection of culture, power, and subjectivity in different ways. Our own insertion in privileged power relations as researchers, affluent people, and educated elites, laboring in the knowledge factory to achieve material and psychic rewards for ourselves and thereby to maintain or advance our own elite interests, puts us into a very troubled relation with subaltern Others whose lives we would presume to explicate. Whatever our conscious intentions, we are still driven by the cultural forces described by JanMohamed and, from our positions of privilege, have a privileged interest in getting a certain kind of story and telling it in a certain way.

The quote from JanMohamed invites us to question whether those of us who are members of this privileged elite—academic researchers endowed with the capacity to read and author texts like this book—can ever comprehend the experience of those whose Otherness we choose to describe. We have the descriptive tools to mine, extract, and interpret the experience of subaltern Others on our own terms and for our own purposes, but what does this process feel like for those put on display and subjected to our gaze? Fortunately, within Othered communities, there are some people who have acquired the master's tools, to use Audre Lorde's (1984) pointed phrase, and who can thereby talk back to us about the dangerous, self-interested gaze that we employ. Vine Deloria, Jr., is one such person.

In *Custer Died for Your Sins* (1988), Deloria describes how the scrutiny of anthropologists has been one of the greatest curses placed on American Indian peoples. Deloria speaks of the annual migration by anthropologists to reservations to produce "you were there" reports that purport to "tell it like it is." The problem, as Deloria notes, is that the anthropologist, embedded in an elite epistemology of social scientific inquiry, already knows what she or he will find:

> You may be curious as to why the anthropologist never carries a writing instrument. He never makes a mark because he ALREADY KNOWS what he is going to find. He need not record anything except his daily expenses for the audit, for the anthro found his answers in the books he read the winter before. No, the anthro is only on the reservation to VERIFY what he has suspected all along—Indians are a very quaint people who bear watching. (p. 80)

The time-honored literature review that sets up the fieldwork for many dissertation studies is a primary tool of socialization to a specific academic worldview such that it embodies many of the confirmation biases that Deloria describes. Even studies that are built around notions of grounded theory are vulnerable to being blinkered by the dogmas embedded in the macro-perspectives of disciplines such as ethnographic inquiry and educational research. Deloria speaks of how, following the conventions of academe, anthropologists begin their work having already developed a working concept of what it means to be Indian:

> The massive volume of useless knowledge produced by anthropologists attempting to capture real Indians in a network of theories has contributed substantially to the invisibility of Indian people today. After all, who can conceive of a food-gathering, berry-picking, semi-nomadic, fire-worshiping, high-plains-and-mountain-dwelling, horse-riding, canoe-toting, bead-using, pottery-making, ribbon-coveting, wickiup-sheltered people who began flourishing when Albert Frump mentioned them in 1803 in his great work on Indians entitled *Our Feathered Friends* as real?

> Not even Indians can relate themselves to this type of creature who, to anthropologists, is the "real" Indian. Indian people begin to feel that they are merely shadows of a mythical super-Indian. Many anthros spare no expense to reinforce this sense of inadequacy in order to further support their influence over Indian people. (pp. 81–82)

Deloria's concern about academics creating conceptual prisons within which whole groups of Indians are essentialized takes an even more sinister turn when the self-interest of the researchers is scrutinized. His views represent a cautionary tale regarding the hazards posed when professional esteem and status depends on one's ability to create a product as a result of one's interactions with individuals who have been designated "Other":

> Perhaps we should suspect the real motives of the academic community. They have the Indian field well defined and under control. Their concern is not the ultimate policy that will affect the Indian people, but merely the creation of new slogans and doctrines by which they can climb the university totem pole. Reduction of people to ciphers for purposes of observation appears to be inconsequential to the anthropologist when compared to the immediate benefits he can derive, the production of further prestige, and the chance to appear as the high priest of American society, orienting and manipulating to his heart's desire. (pp. 94–95)

Speech as Commodity: Annihilation Through Restorying

Even in a best-case scenario where an appropriately self-reflective and well-informed researcher works diligently to build ethical long-term relationships and collaborative knowledge-making with local participants, the process of getting the story is bedeviled with ethical complexity. We use the term *getting the story* intentionally because ultimately the researcher, even in the most enlightened or critical narrative paradigm, seeks to obtain some story to retell. In *Translated Woman*, Ruth Behar (1993) tells of the many problems she encountered in seeking to engage in collaborative ethnographic inquiry with Esperanza, an indigenous Mexican woman. As fieldwork approached, Behar experienced mounting anticipatory anxiety about inhabiting the role of ethnographer. However offensive it was to her ostensible good intentions, she was beset with images of herself as "inquisitor" and "extractor of confessions" (p. 3). She acknowledged that this feeling was exacerbated by her painful awareness of the class and race differences that demarcated her own privilege vis-à-vis the status of her "informant." Behar found Esperanza to be feisty and assertive, and she acknowledges both surprise and discomfort at Esperanza's skill in seeking to establish some symmetry in their relationship. This discomfort, however, seemed to evaporate once Behar was back within the confines of her university. At that point, Behar found herself leaving much of the Esperanza she had known on the cutting room floor. Any power Esperanza had to shape the narrative seemed to be liquidated as Behar, back in the ivory tower, wrote the book she needed to write:

> Unlike all the other listeners of Esperanza's story, it was up to me, as the researcher with access to the resources of bookmaking, to translate "from her spoken words into commodity." In my multiple roles as priest, interviewer, collector, transcriber, translator, analyst, academic, connoisseur, editor, and peddler of Esperanza's words on this side of the border, I had to cut, cut, and cut away at our talk to make it fit between the covers of a book, and even more important, to make it recognizable *as a story*, a certain kind of story, a life history. Although Esperanza in her own life is an immensely talented storyteller, the text of her life certainly did not come readymade.

> Calling a life history a text is, in one sense, already a colonization of the act of storytelling. (p. 12)

Behar is admirably honest about the "false document" she created through the process of restorying Esperanza's life according to the conventions of the story she, Behar, needed to tell in order to earn her place in the pantheon of successful academic writers: "As I undid necklaces of words and restrung them, as I dressed up hours of rambling talk in elegant sentences and paragraphs of prose, as I snipped at the flow of talk, stopping it sometimes for dramatic emphasis long before it had really stopped, I no longer knew where I stood on the border between fiction and nonfiction" (p. 16). What is most noteworthy here is that irrespective of what narrative strategy Behar chose, whether knowingly fictional or ostensibly veridical, she would end up in the same place: with a singular, partial account that had retrofitted Esperanza's words into a Western academic and literary frame that allowed Esperanza to be packaged for consumption by Western intelligentsia. The fact that Behar herself, like all academic inquirers, profited from this transaction only complicates the ethical conundrum. Thus, while Behar writes an elegant and compassionate meditation on herself and Esperanza, in the end she must rip out Esperanza's tongue, stamp on her words, silence her voice: "I fear I am somehow cutting out Esperanza's tongue. Yet when I am done cutting out her tongue I will patch together a new tongue for her…" (p. 19). In doing ethnography, therefore, we must ask, in Gayatri Spivak's (1988) famous phrase, whether we can ever allow the subaltern to speak.

The ethical conundrums of fieldwork come into sharp relief in Daphne Patai's (1987) exploration of the complexity of describing the life of a woman, Teresa, living in a poor community in Brazil. Patai ponders, for example, the meaning of the consent she had elicited from Teresa:

> Now as I sit down to write about Teresa other problems emerge. Did she imagine that I would describe her street and the poverty of her house? Did she have an inkling that the food she served me might become part of her story, that everything about the episode might in turn be served up to readers far away? How would she have felt about it if she had known? Would she have recognized herself in my sketch of her? Might she have noticed that I portrayed her weaknesses more than her strengths? And do these things matter? (pp. 6–7)

Patai also raises the thorny issues of relationship and intimacy. While fieldworkers pride themselves on building the kind of rapport needed to get the story, where is the line drawn between cynical exploitation and true human connection? Patai expresses discomfort at having created the illusion of intimacy and connection with Teresa, only to retreat to her academic sanctuary to write her version of Teresa's life. Her reflections again raise the issue of the commodification of speech and the ethical dilemmas posed by the self-interested restorying of the lives of subaltern research participants that even supposedly progressive research processes appear to demand: "Although our subjects agree to the interview and frequently seem to derive satisfaction from it, the fact remains that it is *we* who are using *them* for *our* books" (p. 21).

Patai concludes by raising an issue to which we will return below, namely the responsibility of researchers to return something of value to those who are the subject of fieldwork. Is Ruth Behar's purchase of a television for Esperanza adequate recompense for the contribution Esepranza has made to Behar's advancement in the academy and to the profits she may make from the sale of her book? From our privileged perch we might chide Behar for a gauche attempt at quid pro quo, but what if Esperanza's lifelong ambition has been to acquire a television, and what if this television not only increases her material status but, having been bestowed upon her by a high status *gringa*, also elevates her social standing in her own community? Aargh!

Research in a Zone of Social Abandonment: The Case of Psychiatric Disabilities

Psychiatric disability is an intensely contested site for fieldwork. Much of this has to do with the horrendous legacy of institutional psychiatry as a tool of oppression and control. In *Mad in America* (2003), Robert Whitaker recounts the appalling regimens of suffering, cruelty, and oppression to which psychiatrically disabled persons have been subjected in the name of subjugation and control. In the past these have included incarceration in penal institutions, physical abuse, lobotomies, Metrazol convulsive therapy, electric shock therapy, insulin shock therapy, and, most recently, treatment with cocktails of potentially dangerous antipsychotic medications (for further detail, see Andre, 2009; Bentall, 2009; Penney & Stastny, 2008; Read, Mosher, & Bentall, 2004; O'Loughlin, Newman, Charles, & Clemence, 2010; Saks, 2008; Watters, 2010; Whitaker, 2010). The deinstitutionalization begun in the 1960s of people objectified as "the mentally ill" has led, as Pete Earley (2006) reminds us in *Crazy*, not to the construction of the promised community-based mental health services, but rather to incarceration of a great many psychiatrically disabled persons in often draconian conditions in the penal system. Psychiatric "treatments," propelled by professional greed and an unscrupulous grab for profits by electric shock and psychosurgery device makers (cf. O'Loughlin, 2010a) and by pharmaceutical manufacturers ("Big Pharma"), have left many psychiatric survivors profoundly distrustful of the motives of mental health professionals. As one survivor noted recently on a listserv posting: "We must stop Psychiatry and Psychology, with its SELF obsession, from destroying SOULS, and CRUSHING the CREATIVE SPIRIT." The situation is further exacerbated by a long tradition of presuming that persons with schizophrenia or psychosis lack the capacity for sound judgment and that decisions about their treatment and welfare are best made by professionals. Nancy Scheper-Hughes (2003), referring to the annihilative processes of "total institutions" (cf. Goffman, 2007) such as schools, psychiatric facilities, geriatric facilities, and so on, does not hesitate to describe the regimens to which so many marginal people are subjected as "invisible genocide." Paradoxically, the very diagnostic tools that were intended to help provide better treatment now run the risk of dehumanizing those with severe problems by equating severe pathology with a lack of capacity for insight or decision making. This type of stance breaks down the human connections that research shows us are likely the most important element in producing positive outcomes, particularly for those designated psychotic (Charles, 2009).

Gaining entrée to psychiatric sites, building trust within communities of survivors, addressing issues of informed consent and gaining IRB approval for studies on psychiatrically disabled persons that federal regulations suggest are mentally incompetent, and figuring out how to build collaborative, counter-hegemonic, and participatory research structures (cf. Watkins & Shulman, 2008) in such circumstances is a formidable task. Nevertheless, this is the task we have set ourselves, as we will discuss below. There are precedents for this work, particularly in the field of medical anthropology. Researchers in that area (e.g., Biehl, 2005; Corin, 1998; Corin & Lauzon, 1992; Estroff, 1981, 2004; Good, Hyde, Pinto, & Good, 2008; Lally, 1989; Pandolfo, 2008) have avoided some of the egregious pitfalls of more naïve approaches to narrative inquiry by maintaining a commitment to social justice and liberatory research; by developing participatory and collaborative structures with participants; and by recognizing the importance of advocacy and intervention as a key role for researchers who are engaging in work with psychiatrically disabled persons to assist them in improving their lives rather than merely seeking to appropriate their stories. Medical anthropology has an advantage over the kind of ethnographic inquiry that Vine Deloria derides, in that the field is fundamentally oriented around understanding the nexus of social and institutional forces that produce subjectivity, rather than in explicating or fetishizing the personal narratives of individuals.

João Biehl's book *Vita: Life in a Zone of Social Abandonment* (2005) raises deep ethical questions about the complexity of engaging in research with persons who are socially marginalized and psychiatrically vulnerable. Biehl studied the life of "a young woman, named Catarina, increasingly paralyzed and said to be mad," living in Vita (in southern Brazil), in a garbage dump "where the unwanted, the mentally ill, the sick, and the homeless are left to die." Biehl's work vivifies in starkest form Spivak's (1988) question: "Can the subaltern speak?" His inquiry brings Catarina and her surroundings to life and raises deeply troubling questions about the capacity of societies to create what Nancy Scheper-Hughes (1992), referring to vulnerable children in Brazil, calls "garbage people" and "vermin people." Biehl's work is a triumph of advocacy and a compelling story of an odyssey into a netherworld of schizophrenia, abject poverty, addiction, infection, pharmacological control, exploitation, and bureaucratic amnesia. Nevertheless, despite its sophistication and the considered ethical and interventionist stance that Biehl brings to the work, it raises complex ethical questions and dilemmas, as we noted in a recent symposium (O'Loughlin, Balzafiore, et al., 2010):

Can the real voices of Catarina and her subaltern cohorts really be heard in this work? Is it possible to avoid voyeurism and self-interest in any work in which the powerful study down to the marginal? Is it possible to present artistically compelling photographs of suffering, as Torben Eskerod does in this work, without fetishizing suffering and gazing downward? How do we locate ourselves in this kind of anthropological inquiry? Is it ethically permissible to expose our research subjects, yet hide ourselves? Must we be only on the outside looking in? Is true collaboration possible when we may be the primary [or only?] beneficiaries of our inquiry? What if the conditions we see are appallingly unjust, must we still stay in our protected research bubble, or do we have responsibilities for ethical action and advocacy? Is co-inquiry feasible or a comfortable rationalization?

Beginning the ethnography with an interest in Catarina, a woman with apparent psychotic symptoms, Biehl refuses to be seduced by such symptoms and, as he widens the lens, he sees *social psychosis* as perhaps the greatest threat to Catarina and her peers:

> Catarina's human ruin is in fact symbiotic with several social processes: her migrant family's industrious adherence to new demands of progress and eventual fragmentation, the automatism of medical practices, the increasing pharmaceuticalization of affective breakdowns, and the difficult political truth of Vita as a death script. Adopting a working concept, I began to think of Catarina's condition as a social psychosis. By social psychosis I mean those materials, mechanisms, and relations through which the so-called normal and minimally efficient order of social formations—the idea of reality against which the patient appears psychotic—is effected and of which Catarina is a leftover. (p. 18)

Biehl's fine-grained study of subjectivity, perhaps most importantly, traces the discursive structuring of social experience through which society constructs subjectivities for certain people for certain purposes. One might ask, then, why would Brazilian society want to construct Catarina as mad? Why would a genetically inherited physical disorder become transmuted into a mental disorder? Why would a history of abandonment and domestic violence, similarly, become pathologized as the victim's madness? Why would a society permit pharmacology to function as a moral technology, and how are we to explain the apparent collusion between pharmaceutical companies, government bureaucrats, and the insistent demands of family members for medication for the afflicted one, in pathologizing individuals such as Catarina as sick and mad? Through widening the lens, Biehl exposes the disciplinary regimes underlying Catarina's construction as abject and, in this way, invites us to consider how the failure to examine such regimes allows them to flourish. Vita, a garbage dump filled with disposable people, as Biehl illustrates, is the ultimate logical outcome of a dehumanizing and totalitarian structure, the result of a process Biehl elegantly refers to as "the pharmaceuticalization of disarray."

Biehl takes an ethical position in describing his challenge as an ethnographer to do ethnography at the limit: "Nothing is simple as the abandoned engage those who listen to the limit" (p. 214). He emphasizes the need to resist closure and to view the inquiry as an opportunity for dialog: "The book brings forth the reality that hides behind this 'I,' coming to a final line in Vita. It also transmits the struggle to produce a dialogic form of knowledge that opens up a sense of anticipation in this most desolate environment" (p. 24). This opening up of dialogue leads Biehl to ask awkward questions, to challenge prevailing truth systems in Brazilian mental health, and ultimately to speak truth to power.

Biehl presents a theoretical grounding for his work that indicates his awareness of the complexity of "truth-seeking" and the inevitable tangle between the desire to know and the necessity for intervention. As Biehl notes, understanding the machinery of "social death" inevitably pulled him into a race against time to try to reclaim visibility, history, and benevolent medical attention for Catarina. He took her to see relatives more than once and yet on one occasion, despite her abject pleas, he refused to take her to visit her family:

> Catarina's overall condition was now worsening much more rapidly. It was very difficult to understand her, and her writing was truncated, with fewer verbs, and almost illegible, I feared. "At night I have this

burning anguish…to leave running," she told me. "It is quite horrible. It is my impossibility. I want to go to Novo Hamburgo…and I am not able to. Then I get this anguish. I roll in bed and think….Then I see that I am weeping." I offer to contact her brothers to arrange another visit. She said yes, but added, "They have no cell phone. It is not worthwhile to try to call them." She was afraid that they would say no. She asked me to put her in my car and take her there right away, but I replied that I could not. "They don't use the phone," she insisted. Enraged, she threw the notebook on the floor and wept. (p. 296)

Biehl used his influence to gain access to clinical trials and genetic research for Catarina, and he assisted her family in participating in genetic profiling to ascertain the heritability of the disease that both Catarina, her brothers, and their children carried. Catarina's family did not appreciate his efforts to try to reinscribe her in the family system, and their resistance caused Catarina considerable pain. We can ask in what ways Biehl, through his attempt to reunite the family, bears ethical responsibility for this pain and for the sequelae of Biehl's intrusions into the family life? For example, after one family member had established through the genetic testing program that he had the same incurable physical disease as Catarina, the young man's fiancée abandoned him. To what extent can Biehl's interventionist effort be rationalized in this case, and what is the price of such rationalization? How do we understand the complex consequences of our own interactions in this type of work; how do we figure out costs and benefits; and whose voice do we privilege in this process of weighing out consequences? Biehl witnessed many tragedies while visiting Vita, but he chose to adopt only Catarina as a subject of study. Inevitably, she became a recipient of privileged attention. What are the ethics of making such choices? We can ask too about the complex ethics involved in the photographic representations of people who not only do not have their identities disguised but are actually named in the book. Are they nameable only because they are nobodies?

The conundrum of the ethnographic gaze is evident, too, in the following:

> During the first day Torben [photographer] and I spent in Vita we came upon a middle-aged woman sitting on the ground; she crouched over a stream of urine, her genitals matted with dust. As we approached we could see that her head was full of small holes: worms burrowed in the wounds, and under her scalp…Torben could not bear to look. Momentarily paralyzed, he kept saying, "It is too much, It is too much." The reality of Vita had overwhelmed picture-taking too. This was a socially authorized dying, ordinary and unaccounted for, in which we participated by our gazing, both foreign and native, in our learned indifference and sense of what was intolerable. (p. 38)

Later, Biehl notes, "the photographer wants to focus on our learned indifference and provoke some ethical response" (p. 44). The difficulty, of course, is that Biehl cannot control the response of the viewer or reader. What if the camera gaze or the erudite description provokes voyeuristic curiosity, a fetishistic interest in poverty or deformity, or objectification leading to revulsion? And what does it mean for the subjects of such suffering to necessarily become objects of our attention, much as the abject are paraded on late-night television infomercials to drum up donations for sundry charities ministering in supposedly abject third-world countries to impoverished black children with vacant stares and outstretched hands? We raise these issues not to cast aspersions on Biehl's exceptionally fine, courageous, and ethically grounded ethnographic inquiry. Rather, these are dilemmas that are inherent in the attempt to examine the plight of the Other—dilemmas that cannot be eliminated but must, rather, be repeatedly recognized and negotiated with great care.

Imagining Psychiatric Research Otherwise

The inquiry being proposed here originated from collaboration between Marilyn Charles, Michael O'Loughlin, Jill Clemence, and Gail Newman in studying videotapes, transcripts, and patient records from the Follow-Along Study at Austen Riggs Center, a renowned psychiatric facility in Stockbridge, Massachusetts. Austen Riggs, with its proud history of respect for patients and for collaborative, psychodynamic work with patients and families, represents one of a few places in the U.S. where patients are afforded the opportunity to reflect on their psychic suffering while also being given opportunities to pursue meaningful life paths through introspection, relational exploration, and creative artistic exploration. The Follow-Along Study includes an archive of audiotaped and videotaped interviews with selected patients over a 10-year period. While these data have been a rich source of hypotheses and insights, they do not allow us to inquire further into the experiences of our subjects because the data were collected for other purposes and lack some of the elements that we feel are necessary to gain a fuller picture of patients' struggles. This lack has prompted us to seek to develop a more comprehensive inquiry into the contexts, precipitants, and course of schizophrenic and psychotic disorders.

There is little doubt that psychosis represents significant dis-ease for those who are designated psychotic. In fact, the disorder appears to induce sufficient discomfort in those who witness it, and in the psychiatric establishment that there is, as noted earlier, often a rush to medicate in order to mute the dissonant voices that psychosis represents. In addition to the quality-of-life issues this poses for patients designated psychotic, medication presents methodological difficulties for those who work therapeutically with psychotic persons. Are the confusions, the halting speech, the mutenesses, and the non-sequiturs in speech, symptoms of psychic disorder or are they merely manifestations of attempts to reach for meaning disrupted by chemical/pharmacological intrusion? Can we reach through the speech of psychotic persons to comprehend the signifiers that may reveal a quest for understanding? We have also come to increasingly appreciate the complicated effects of conventional psychiatric diagnosis and conventional psychiatric hospitalization on each patient's perception of self. We have seen individuals struggling to utilize offerings from mental health professionals in ways that at times enhance but at times obscure or obstruct self-understanding. These observations led us to wonder to what extent is each patient's subjectivity structured according to the discursive imperatives of "being a mental patient" or "being schizophrenic"?

Drawing on a strong European movement for patient rights, embodied in organizations such as the Hearing Voices Network (cf. Blackman, 2001), Gail Hornstein (2009) suggests that there is a compelling imperative to return to patient voices and to reconceptualize the experience of patients who express mental distress in terms of personal narratives of their suffering; narratives of potential traumatic antecedents; narratives of their life histories; narratives of their disappointments; and narratives of their own subjective experience as relational and emotional beings.

Our original study (cf. Charles, Clemence, Newman, & O'Loughlin, 2010; O'Loughlin, Newman, et al., 2010) grew out of our recognition that some of the patients in the Follow-Along Study were speaking at odds with the interview process. We noticed one woman, in particular, who seemed to be saying the same thing year after year, inviting us to inquire into her persistence. Was this perseveration a mark of her illness or did it mark, rather, a failure on the part of others to attend sufficiently to some important message she was attempting to impart? This question led us to pay close attention to the interplay between interviewer, interview style, and subject, so that we could note factors that seemed to inhibit speech or, alternatively, to invite the subject further into speech. We noted that a person who might seem dull and relatively lifeless in one moment could be pulled into speech and into greater vibrancy by a curious and respectful interviewer. Another subject might be pushed out of speech by too-close engagement by the interviewer. Empathic attunement and close attention to cues offered by the other seemed to be integral to obtaining information to which the interviewee seemed emotionally connected.

Important to our method was our ability to listen to audiotapes and watch videotapes together as a team. Not only did this engagement afford us the opportunity to discuss our experiences together, it also provided insight into difficulties afforded by transcription of tapes. We could see how easily, particularly for non-clinicians, a presumption of coherence could guide the transcription of the speech of interviewers, whereas a presumption of incoherence could guide the transcription of the speech of the patients/research subjects. This erasure of meaning was for us a profound demonstration of what can happen if we are insufficiently respectful of others. The current research attempts to remediate or at least offset the type of systematic erasure that can happen when professionals believe that we "know better" than the persons who entrust themselves to our care. We hope that by highlighting the voices of individuals suffering with psychotic illness we can invite more respectful collaborations between such individuals and those who would want to provide care.

Considerations in Developing the Proposed Inquiry

In brief, we have articulated the following goals for our inquiry based on extensive review of related studies:

- Inquiry into the subjectivity of persons diagnosed with schizophrenia or severe psychosis:

    ° our interest here is in the experience of "being schizophrenic" or "being psychotic" and to better understand how the psychotic elements of subjectivity coexist with parts of subjectivity that may be unaffected by psychosis.

- Inquiry into traumatic antecedents of schizophrenia and psychosis:

    ° our interest here is in exploring each participant's own life history and also the ancestral history of the participant's peoples of origin to understand potential stressors and traumas that may have contributed to breakdown.

- Inquiry into cultural variation in the expression of what Western medicine understands as schizophrenia and psychosis:

    ° our interest here is in understanding the epistemological beliefs and discursive understandings each participant brings to her or his understanding of the presenting difficulties and how this understanding is related to attitudes and beliefs about possible wellness.

- Inquiry into the experience of being diagnosed as psychiatrically disabled:

    ° our interest here is in understanding each participant's understanding of the phenomenology of being designated a psychiatric patient, and the ensuing constructions of mental disorder as biological, chemical, or socioculturally situated that the participant has developed as a result of their discursive positioning by institutional psychiatry.

- The dynamics of psychic suffering

    ° our interest here is in understanding the impasses and derailments that have caused the initial flight into psychosis, and the reasons why a particular participant is or is not managing to renegotiate (re)entry into a world of relationality, creativity, and possibility.

- The dynamics of family and community

    ° our interest here is in exploring the particular familial, community, and historical forces that may have contributed to a severance of social linkages or a loss of relational support that led to initial breakdown or that continue to obstruct recovery.

- Inquiry into social psychosis

    ° our interest here is in the nexus of social forces (hospitals, psychiatry, welfare services, social stigma, etc.) that contribute to the discursive construction of subjectivity in persons diagnosed as suffering from forms of schizophrenia or psychosis. Are these social forces capable of engendering healthfulness, as for instance Jaako Seikkula (Seikkula & Olson, 2003; Seikkula et al., 2003) claims for the Open Dialogue approach in Finland? Conversely, do the effects of social forces hold portents for the kind of social death so graphically described in Biehl's ethnographic study of Catarina and her peers?

A Methodology for Participatory, Respectful, Justice-Oriented Inquiry

Some aspects of the methodology already developed by others will carry over to the new study. For instance, the dynamic interview developed at Austen Riggs (Fowler & Perry, 2005; Perry, Fowler, & Semeniuk, 2005) offers a respectful method for engaging participants in psychoanalytically informed depth interviews. Protocols also exist for family history interviews, and the work of Davoine and Gaudillière (2005; O'Loughlin, 2010b, in press) and others offer useful directions for conceptualizing the historical and ancestral components of such an inquiry. Likewise, the work of Biehl, Corin, Estroff, Good et al., Scheper-Hughes and others, cited earlier, offer important precedents for studying the nexus of social forces that may not only produce schizophrenic and psychotic symptoms in individuals, but also construct the suffering individual's subjectivity in ways that may exacerbate the symptom or even annihilate the person completely.

Conceptually, therefore, the work is complex but possible. The issue of gaining informed consent from psychiatrically disabled persons and ensuring that they are fully briefed on the work may appear problematic from the outside, but we have sufficient confidence in the cognitive capacities of psychiatrically disabled persons to believe that they can be active participants in their own decision making. More challenging is to provide opportunities for co-construction of meaning and co-participation in the research project. We anticipate sharing information with participants, including seeking their active participation in the interpretation of their experiences and in the dissemination of findings. We are not naïve enough, however, to assume that the asymmetries built into our different educational, social, and wellness statuses will not have an impact on the quality and success of this collaboration. Therefore, to advance our goal of genuine collaboration and the advancement of social justice goals, we are proposing two ambitious extensions of the work.

First, we are hoping to develop an electronic archive of survivor testimony. This archive, similar to the Fortunoff Video Archive for Holocaust Testimonies (http://www.library.yale.edu/testimonies/) and Steven Spielberg's USC Shoah Foundation archive (http://college.usc.edu/vhi/) will provide a space in which participants can offer testimony to their experience in a collaborative space in which they will be the primary editors of their own experience. We view this as a valuable give-back to the psychiatric survivor community, and it will be part of an emerging trend of memorializing and honoring the struggles of psychiatric survivors (e.g., see Payne, 2009; Penney & Stastny, 2008).

Second, we are also optimistic that we can collaborate on developing a treatment modality where participants who join the project have an opportunity to engage in the kind of therapeutic healing that comes from the construction of democratic communities of support. Foremost in our minds is the underlying guiding principle that this work is about providing spaces for wellness, support, democratic participation, and individual and collective agency. We trust that enabling people to tell their stories and participate in their own wellness will be at least as important as motivators of this work as the production of academic knowledge. We recognize that both will be important in countering dominant discursive understandings of persons with schizophrenia or psychosis as crazy, with all of the attendant pejorative allusions such a term implies. We envision this research as an important attempt to conduct such research ethically in that we are attempting to construct a format that makes visible some of the potential pitfalls we have outlined above, such that they can be recognized and taken up as necessary by all participants. Implicit in this goal is the recognition that, at some level, we are all participant observers when we are studying culture and its effect on individuals.

References

Andre, L. (2009). *Doctors of deception: What they don't want you to know about shock treatment.* New Brunswick, NJ: Rutgers University Press.

Behar, R. (1993). *Translated woman.* Boston, MA: Beacon Press.

Behar, R., & Gordon, D. (Eds.). (1995). *Women writing culture.* Boston, MA: Beacon Press.

Bentall, R. (2009). *Doctoring the mind: Is our current treatment of mental illness really any good?* New York: New York University Press.

Biehl, J. (2005). *Vita: Life in a zone of social abandonment.* Berkeley: University of California Press.

Blackman, L. (2001). *Hearing voices: Embodiment and experience.* London, England: Free Association Books.

Britzman, D. (1995). Beyond innocent readings: Educational ethnography as a crisis of representation. In G. Noblit & W. Pink (Eds.), *Continuity and contradiction: The future of the sociology of education.* Cresskill, NJ: Hampton Press.

Charles, M. (2009). Psychosis and the social link: Fighting chronicity through human connections. *Bulletin of the Michigan Psychoanalytic Council, 5,* 33–44.

Charles, M., Clemence, J., Newman, G., & O'Loughlin, M. (2010). Listening to the dis-ease of psychosis: Preliminary reports from an interdisciplinary research study. In E. Degaiffier, A. Silver, M. Kelly, & J. Jarrardi (Eds.), *Title TBA.* Book proposal in preparation.

Clifford, M., & Marcus, G. (1986). *Writing culture: The poetics and politics of ethnography.* Berkeley: University of California Press.

Corin, E. (1998). The thickness of being: Intentional worlds, strategies of identity, and experience among schizophrenics. *Psychiatry, 61,* 133–145.

Corin, E., & Lauzon, G. (1992). From symptoms to phenomena: The articulation of experience in schizophrenia. *Journal of Phenomenological Psychology, 25,* 3–50.

Davoine, F., & Gaudillière, J. (2005). *History beyond trauma.* New York, NY: Other Press.

Deloria, V. (1988). *Custer died for your sins.* Norman: University of Oklahoma Press.

Earley, P. (2006). *Crazy: A father's search through America's mental health madness.* New York, NY: Berkley Books.

Estroff, S. (1981). *Making it crazy: An ethnography of psychiatric clients in an American community.* Berkeley: University of California Press.

Estroff, S. (2004). Subject/subjectivities in dispute: The poetics, politics, and performance of first-person narratives of people with schizophrenia. In J. Jenkins & R. Barrett (Eds.), *Schizophrenia, culture, subjectivity* (pp. 282–302). Cambridge, England: Cambridge University Press.

Fowler, J. C., & Perry, J. C. (2005). Clinical tasks of the dynamic interview. *Psychiatry, 68*(4), 316–336.

Goffman, E. (2007). *Asylums: Essays on the social situation of mental patients.* New York, NY: Aldine Transaction.

Good, M. J., Hyde, S., Pinto, S., & Good, B. (2008). *Postcolonial disorders: Ethnographic studies in subjectivity.* Berkeley: University of California Press.

Hornstein, G. (2009). *Agnes's jacket: A psychologist's search for the meaning of madness.* New York, NY: Rodale Books.

JanMohamed, A. (1995). The economy of Manichean allegory. In B. Ashcroft, G. Griffiths, & H. Tiffin (Eds.), *The postcolonial studies reader* (pp. 18–23). London, England: Routledge.

Lally, S. (1989). Does being in here mean there is something wrong with me? *Schizophrenia Bulletin, 15,* 253–265.

Lorde, A. (1984). The master's tools will never dismantle the master's house. In *Sister outsider: Essays and speeches.* Trumansburg, NY: Crossing Press.

O'Loughlin, M. (2010a). Shock me please, I'm crazy: Is Australia another victim of the delusions of psychiatry? *Arena Magazine, 104,* 23–26.

O'Loughlin, M. (2010b). Ghostly presences in children's lives: Toward a psychoanalysis of the social. In M. O'Loughlin & R. Johnson (Eds.), *Imagining children otherwise: Theoretical and critical perspectives on childhood subjectivity.* New York, NY: Peter Lang.

O'Loughlin, M. (in press). Trauma trails from Ireland's Great Hunger: A psychoanalytic inquiry. In B. Willock, R. Curtis, & L. Bohm (Eds.), *Loneliness and longings: Psychoanalytic perspectives on a crucial dimension of the human condition.* New York, NY: Routledge.

O'Loughlin, M., Balzafiore, D., Biehl, J., Castelhano, A., Charles, M., Indelicato, H., & Merchant, A. (2010, October). Ethical and social justice conundrums in doing research in zones of social abandonment: An exploration of João Biehl's *Vita.* Presented at the Association for the Psychoanalysis of Culture and Society Annual Conference, Rutgers University, New Brunswick, NJ.

O'Loughlin, M., Newman, G., Charles, M., & Clemence, J. (2010). Conceptual issues in analyzing the difficulty that is psychosis. In E. Degaiffier, A. Silver, M. Kelly, & J. Jarrardi (Eds), *Title TBA.* Book proposal in preparation.

Pandolfo, S. (2008). The knot of the soul: Postcolonial conundrums, madness and the imagination. In M. Good, S. Hyde, S. Pinto, & B. Good (Eds.), *Postcolonial disorders: Ethnographic studies in subjectivity.* Berkeley: University of California Press.

Patai, D. (1987). Ethical problems of personal narratives: Or who should eat the last piece of cake? *International Journal of Oral History, 8,* 5–27.

Payne, C. (2009). *Asylums: Inside the closed world of state mental hospitals.* Cambridge, MA: MIT Press.

Penney, D., & Stastny, P. (2008). *The lives they left behind: Suitcases from a state hospital attic.* New York, NY: Bellevue Literary Press.

Perry, J. C., Fowler, J. C., & Semeniuk, T. (2005). An investigation of tasks and techniques associated with dynamic interview adequacy. *Journal of Nervous and Mental Disorders, 193,* 136–139.

Read, J., Mosher, L., & Bentall, R. (2004). *Models of madness: Psychological, social and biological approaches to schizophrenia.* London, England: Routledge.

Saks, E. (2008). *The center cannot hold: My journey through madness.* New York, NY: Hyperion.

Scheper-Hughes, N. (1992). *Death without weeping: The violence of everyday life in Brazil.* Berkeley: University of California Press.

Scheper-Hughes, N. (2003). A genealogy of genocide. *Modern Psychoanalysis, 28,* 167–197.

Seikkula, J., & Olson, M. (2003). The open dialogue approach to acute psychosis. *Family Process, 43,* 403–418.

Seikkula, J., Alakare, B., Aaltonen, J., Holma, J., Rasinkangas, A., & Lehtinen, V. (2003). Open dialogue approach: Treatment principles and preliminary results of a two-year follow-up on first episode schizophrenia. *Ethical and Human Sciences and Services, 5,* 163–182.

Spivak, G. (1988). Can the subaltern speak? In C. Nelson & L. Grossberg (Eds.), *Marxism and the interpretation of culture* (pp. 217–313). London, England: Macmillan.

Watkins, M., & Shulman, H. (2008). *Toward psychologies of liberation.* New York, NY: Palgrave Macmillan.

Watters, E. (2010). *Crazy like us? The globalization of the American psyche.* New York, NY: Free Press.

Whitaker, R. (2003). *Mad in America.* New York, NY: Basic Books.

Whitaker, R. (2010). *Anatomy of an epidemic.* New York, NY: Crown.

CHAPTER THIRTY-SEVEN

Positive Education: The Use of Self-Study Research Methodology to Assess Its Place in Higher Education Settings

Jeanne Carroll, Marcelle Cacciattolo,
and Tarquam McKenna

This chapter had its genesis in the chance coming together of three colleagues who discovered they shared a common interest and commitment to the emerging theories of positive psychology. From this seed of personal and common interest grew our collaboration and the presently reported ongoing research project to explore the potential of positive psychology theories to alter our teaching and learning practices. This is a shared collaborative reflection and deliberates on the ongoing research process for Jeanne, Marcelle and Tarquam, who are the team of three university "teacher researchers", "teachers-as-researchers" or "researchers-as-teachers" in Melbourne, Australia. These three turns of phrase are deliberately presented here as interchangeable and will be shown to be central to the definition of our scholarly practice.

Our discussion is framed as an elaboration on self-study as a methodology and is intended to open up the next generation of questions for our research. We believe we are uncovering an important refinement in the understanding of the applicability of self-study methodology. This chapter is a reflection of how we have come to refine our individual and collective team experiences of the meanings of "self", the "other", "collegiality", "character", research that has now led us to reframe our teaching, researching and learning practices.

Introduction

It was agreed that a teaching and learning project would be conducted by three teacher educators (teachers-as-researchers), who were teaching three different units of academic study in the School of Education at Victoria University, Melbourne, Australia. We became a research team but we each had different key learning areas of teaching. Mathematics, Sociology of Education and the Arts are our separate "discipline" areas. We worked with the approaches from the literature on positive psychology, especially goal setting, mindfulness and character strengths, so these were integrated into the content of these units over a semester. As teachers-as-researchers we worked together in planning how the approaches would be introduced and implemented, we met together, and emailed each other to "discuss" the process of implementation during the semester. Throughout the project we kept journals of incidents and insights related to the teaching and learning. These activities constituted what we contend are the core data of the study.

From the outset of the research project, we framed our research as a traditional teaching "experiment". Then the idea emerged that we could choose a change of practice and evaluate its effect using self-study methodology. Approaches from the research literature on positive psychology field were trialled in two pre-service units and one postgraduate education unit taught by the teacher-researchers. We came to know our work as positive educational practice or "PEP". Our PEP approaches, focussing mainly on goal setting, mindfulness and character strengths, were included in addition to the typical content of the units, which were mathematics education, literacy education and postgraduate research methods. Even at this stage we had our eyes on two dimensions for the research. This can be seen in the first formulation of the research question:

> How could the use of positive psychology approaches assist teacher educators to develop a greater understanding of their teaching and learning practices?

The primary data consisted of minutes of the professional conversations between the three of us as a research team and a reference group of critical friends as advisors and participants. Meetings throughout the semester, the teacher-researchers' data sources—journal *entries* and *cases* reflecting on the process, *emails* between the teacher-researchers enabling ideas on the project to be clarified and discussed, *students' emails, written reflections* and *in-class discussions*—related to the use of positive psychology approaches in the units were all used by us. With this in mind the next section looks to what research tells us about the importance of embedding positive educational tools in our everyday lives.

Positive Educational Tools in Educational Contexts

Character Strengths

For a large part of this decade Park, Peterson, and Seligman (2006) have been developing a theory of character strengths and investigating how the use of character strengths can contribute to success and enhanced life satisfaction. They developed the VIA Survey of Character Strengths to determine which of 24 character strengths an individual draws upon and employs regularly in their lives. The VIA survey returns a person's top five strengths from a list of twenty-four strengths including creativity, curiosity, judgment, love of learning, perspective, bravery, industry, authenticity, zest, citizenship, fairness and leadership. Hundreds of thousands of people have undertaken the survey, enabling a huge range of data to be collected and analysed.

There is growing evidence that working with character strengths can assist young people to thrive rather than merely survive the trials of teaching and learning. Character-relevant assets like commitment to learning, positive values, social competence, and having a sense of purpose have been found to be associated with positive outcomes such as school success, leadership, helping others and delaying gratification. Particular strengths of character such as hope, kindness, social intelligence, self-control and perspective mitigated the effects of stress (Park, 2004). Park et al.'s (2006) research found the capacity to achieve goals is enhanced through the application of a person's top strengths in new contexts, as well as through the development of strengths that have previously been underutilised. Investigation of the relationship between academic achievement and character strengths for students in schools revealed that the character strengths of perseverance, fairness, gratitude, honesty, hope and perspective predicted end-of-year GPA (grade point averages) (Park & Peterson, 2009, p. 71).

Mindfulness

Another aspect of positive psychology explored in the PEP project context in the present research with pre-service and graduate teachers is mindfulness. For many years philosophical, religious and psychological traditions have recognised the benefits of enhanced consciousness. The benefits of being "present" or in the moment have attracted the attention of researchers in the area of positive psychology. A consequence arising from this diversity of attention is that the term "mindfulness" is now used to refer to a wide range of phenomena as diverse as the notion of mindfulness as a *state*, to mindfulness as a *trait* and mindfulness as an *independent variable* (Davidson, 2010).

Mindfulness is commonly taken to be the state of being aware of, or attentive to, what is happening in the present moment (Brown & Ryan, 2003). Kabat-Zinn (2003) stated, "Mindfulness has to do with particular qualities of attention and awareness that can be cultivated and developed through meditation" (p. 144). He cited a working definition of mindfulness as "the awareness that emerges through paying attention on purpose, in the present moment, and nonjudgmentally to the unfolding of experience moment by moment" (p. 144).

According to Langer (1993), much of education today encourages mindlessness. Rather than active involvement in their learning, engagement in a process of drawing distinctions and noticing novelty in the habituated and familiar and the familiar in the novel, students are often presented with facts, tightly packaged with little flexibility, to be mastered, encouraging mindlessness in their learning. The PEP project holds to the notion that education which encourages mindfulness should inspire students to examine the world around them, drawing their own conclusions, rather than imposing conclusions upon them or forcing them to premature conclusions.

The Teaching and Learning Project: Data Collection and Self-study Methodology

A range of data was collected during the teaching and learning project, and this data formed the basis of the team of teacher-researchers' reflective case writings on the project. Case writing employs a self-study methodology. This methodology is discussed below.

Self-study Methodology in Teacher Education Contexts

As the research on the teaching and learning PEP project was designed to enable us to critically inquire into our own teaching and learning practices, a self-study methodology was selected by us (Bullock, 2009; Kosnik, Beck, Freese, & Samaras, 2005; Berry, 2007). Our goals were to locate, systematically document and make public meaning-making experiences that inform our practice. The work of Donald Schon (1983) asserts that the need for reflection-in-practice epitomises and underpins self-study as a method of inquiry. Through reflection-in-action and reflection-on-action, the three teachers-as-researchers were able to locate a personal, professional and academic voice, thereby bringing clarity to our understandings of what effective teaching looks like. Reframing and interpreting new ways of examining the perplexities of what it means to be a collaborative and *reflexive* teacher and learner is always our work goal. This was and is at the heart of self-study as a research practice.

Self-study allows teachers, and allowed us, to construct and reconstruct critical incidents and moments so as to sort through how actions and behaviours influence self and other (Samaras, 2002). Hamilton, Smith, and Worthington (2008, p. 20) stated that "narrative inquirers are attuned to the feelings, desires, needs, aesthetic reactions, and moral dispositions of both self and other". This leads to greater social and emotional intelligence especially when there is a willingness to see the teaching and learning arena from different lenses. Whether it is through adopting a "Sociological Imagination" (Mills, 2000) or acquiring a state of "conscientização" (Freire, 1996), the self-study methodology allows us as the PEP practitioners to peel away those layers that can blur or tarnish judgment.

The term self-study is often referred to as a "paradox" amongst many academics in self-study circles (Loughran, 2007; Samaras & Freese, 2006; Kelchtermans, 2009). The title self-study presupposes an emphasis on individuals looking within themselves to find the answers they are searching for. However, as pointed out by Lassonde, Galman, and Kosnik (2009, p. 8), self-study involves, and involved this team of PEP researchers, working with others in a critical way so that theories and hunches can be tested, validated and shared. Having a set of critical friends who can be trusted to share personal insights about one's work is another key element of successful self-study practices. In sharing cases of practice through our conversations, journal entries or email exchanges with other colleagues and ourselves, there are opportunities to seek constructive feedback. Bass, Anderson-Patton and Allender articulated the value added when academics work with others to give advice and receive it:

> The self-study process—talking, writing, reflecting and articulating my teaching with others makes me more confident. I can be less defensive when I accept that others will see my teaching from their perspective. In doing so, they provide me with multiple ways of looking at what I do, but I must be able to retain agency, be who I want to be, and still hear them. (2002, p. 61)

For self-study practitioners, and us, receiving constructive feedback from each other as colleagues and responding proactively is central to the interpretative process of self-improvement; through working collegially and respectfully with others in a critical dialogue, the personal voice is able to traverse the pitfalls that tunnel vision brings and can be transformed into a four-lane highway. Engaging in scholarly work through reading current literature, adopting a disciplined approach to researching one's practice, listening to the narratives of each other and other teacher-educators and making public the work that is conducted is also essential to engaging in effective self-study practices (Shulman, 1999; LaBoskey, 2004). Self-study became the basis by which our shared meanings were constructed and, as noted earlier, was a methodology that built trust. Trust was shared as we attended to our collective and individual sense of insight around the application of PEP in action.

Cases

As three teachers-as-researchers, we prepared separate cases describing our individual experiences of introducing practices of positive psychology into our teaching. These data were used to inform the three cases[1] that are presented throughout the theoretical deliberation.

Jeanne's follows below:

Jeanne

My work is in the area of Mathematics Education in a Bachelor of Education for pre-service teachers training to work with primary students. As part of their preparation for teaching, students are required to pass a test based on the mathematics they will be teaching. Some students undertake an elective unit to help them with this. Many pre-service teachers enrolled in this unit have struggled with mathematics in their own schooling. Often their understanding is characterised by incomplete concepts and misunderstandings, a lack of connections between concepts and reliance on procedural rather than conceptual understanding. They frequently have negative attitudes towards mathematics and hold beliefs that they are not good at mathematics.

The elective unit was conducted over 12 evenings in semester 1, 2009. In session 1, after expressing their feelings about mathematics and examining their histories and the factors that led them to enrol in this class, I spoke with them about the need to leave the past in the past and to begin to view themselves as the teacher: as the person who takes responsibility not only for his/her own learning but also for the students they will teach.

The students undertook the VIA Survey of Character Strengths (Authentic Happiness website) following the second class and reported back on their results in the subsequent class. The most frequent strengths reported by the group were fairness, humour, kindness, gratitude and curiosity. Class discussion focussed firstly on the strengths they generally drew on for success in their lives. This revealed that while they were very happy with the ways they used strengths in other aspects of their lives, and were able to share instances of the successful use, they had not applied them to their mathematics learning. Initially, they found it difficult to see how their strengths might be applied in mathematics learning.

Discussion of the use of strengths in their work was revisited from time to time during the semester as we went about the work of constructing mathematics ideas. In the final class pre-service teachers were asked to reflect on how they had used their strengths. A number of students had perseverance in their top strengths. One used perseverance to understand the concepts and find strategies that worked for her. A student who identified "fairness, equity and justice" as a strength felt that he had been fairer on himself as a result of using this strength. This meant that he could give himself a fair go when working on questions. In giving advice to other students on developing their understanding of the mathematics, his advice of keeping at it, not giving up, as well as staying focussed when working on problem solving, reflected his strength of "industry and perseverance". Curiosity was important for one student in finding different strategies that lead to the discovery of simpler approaches and also helped in reading and researching useful approaches and new resources, resulting in greater knowledge.

One student in the group stood out for the way in which she harnessed her strengths during the semester. She was a final-year student who had been avoiding the fact that she needed to do the unit, work on her understanding, and pass the test. Her mathematical understanding was quite elementary and she was quite low in confidence about her ability to pass the test. I felt that she may need to do the unit more than once in order to develop her understandings. Following the class discussion on how kindness might be used, when other students had settled into their work, she explained to me that to add numbers she counted by ones on her fingers and for multiplication facts she "sang the song". While speaking she had tears in her eyes. We took up the discussion of kindness again, and talked about how she had been treating herself.

In the first session she was writing about her main concerns regarding the content of mathematics required for teaching in primary school. "Creating concrete understanding is my concern. As a student I missed key understanding, which prevented me to move forward with my understanding. I want to ensure I don't make the same mistakes."

When she took the VIA Survey of Character Strengths, her strengths were "kindness and generosity", "fairness, equity and justice", "humour and playfulness", "forgiveness and mercy", and "gratitude". When asked how she might use these strengths to achieve her goals in the unit, her initial response in the class discussion had been that she could not see how these strengths, which she viewed as being directed outward, could be of use to her in this situation. Her written response after considering the class discussion was to

> …be kinder to myself with Maths, treat myself for effort, any effort. I need to forgive myself for not being great at Maths, and move on to creating a fair opportunity for myself to improve.…Create a weekly timetable that is consistent, i.e. every Thursday so it just becomes a weekly job rather than allowing it to be put off and missed every week. Be grateful for the chance to improve and take it on. Accept that it's not a strength, laugh at it! Everyone can't be good at everything.

During the course of the semester this student worked very hard, dealing with her tears and frustrations but getting on with it. A peer acted as a tutor for her on some occasions. She persevered, continued to attend class, asked questions when she did not understand and dealt with her feelings that these might be "stupid questions" but asked anyway.

After session 3 she wrote, "I have been still very frustrated and grumpy with my Maths. I think I need to have a better/fun activity for afterwards". In the final week, reflecting on her use of strengths during the semester, she wrote, "I have been a lot kinder to myself, rewarding myself for even the little efforts. I am also being more fair on myself by giving myself more realistic expectations....Over the holidays I worked for a good 2 hours 3 times. Usually the holidays is the easiest time for me to get side tracked and not do any work". This student passed the test on her first attempt!

With only one semester to address issues in learning mathematics that had been built up by the pre-service teachers over a lifetime of schooling, I felt the time pressure, and while it had been my intention to work with the group on a range of positive psychology approaches, including mindfulness, the pressure of time meant that I did not investigate other aspects of positive psychology as fully as I would have liked to. The work on goals, reframing and character strengths provided a constructive environment for students to take back control of their learning and provided them with new strategies for making the learning process enjoyable, harnessing mental reserves and developing habits for persisting with their learning. An important aspect of this was moving the responsibility for their learning and the attribution for success from others to themselves.

This is an important issue for students in this unit, as typically at some time in their schooling, they have handed the control of their mathematics learning over to someone else. That is, they have attributed the responsibility and blame for failure in their mathematics learning to someone else, usually the teacher. This means that if someone else is to blame, then someone else is responsible for fixing it. There is often a feeling that "I will not be making much effort because I tried before and it did not work". The effectiveness of the character strengths in this context is that they allow the pre-service teachers to use personal resources that they already have proven work for them in other areas as well as providing the opportunity to use strengths that they may not have had significant use of previously. Very little effort is required other than the shift of mindset.

* * *

Cases like Jeanne's above are windows into the concerns and self-appraisals of ourselves as teachers-as-researchers. They were intended to open the examination of our "reflections-in-practice" as a means of establishing a state of "conscientização" (Freire, 1996), which would open us to the criticisms of the other.

Marcelle's case is noted below:

Marcelle

August 31st 2009, Marcelle Cacciattolo, Case of Practice: Topic Mindfulness

A few weeks ago, I gave out a handout on mindfulness to my first-year group of pre-service teachers. The hope was that they would use this handout as a prompt to think about how they could foster and nurture a spirit of mindfulness during their week block school placement. So I give out the handout with a reading attached by Thich Nhat Hanh (2008), a Buddhist monk whose name is enough to facilitate a state of meditative peacefulness within. I begin with a discussion around mindfulness and how it links to positive education and the importance of being mindful of our actions during episodes of confusion, anxiety and embarrassment. They collect the handout on their way out, and I feel pleased that I have managed to spend 15 minutes discussing this theme. I said I would speak about mindfulness to my project team and I have, so I can tick this job off the list of to-do things. I feel happy that I can report to my colleagues that I have fulfilled my end of the bargain and when my students report back to me about what they did, I will have something to present at our next positive education team meeting.

I have a whole day off from teaching because my first year tute group is on placement and I am happy, actually ecstatic. I am happy because I can use this time to catch up on all the outstanding work that is looming over me. On Thursday I can work on my SWIRL report, type up the B.Ed review minutes that I took a week before, plan for my Master of Education class and finish off all the other tasks that are piling up on my desk at home. There is then the gym, the weekend BBQ, cleaning my house, attending meetings upon meetings with schools, students and staff members and ensuring that

I have my brief prepared for the latest book that a group of colleagues want to write. Yes, the day off from teaching will do me just fine. I can even make time to prepare dinner for my husband, who has cooked for me every night for the past two weeks because I get home too tired to even speak. I might cook him some soup because it won't take a lot of time and while I am waiting for the soup to boil I can do my emails.

The art of mindfulness I think was a great 15 minutes spent with my students. They come back after their week block placement and tell me how they used the breathing techniques in the reading that I gave them to calm themselves down when they were feeling anxious.

"And you know what Marcelle I even spoke to my sister about the breathing techniques and told her that this can help us with our everyday lives when we are faced with problems that we do not know how to resolve."

"Marcelle," says another, "the mindfulness activity was great because I suffer from anxiety and the meditation exercise helped me stay calm and focused. This is really important if I want to be an effective teacher in the classroom"

"Yes," say I, "Yes Sam I know what you mean."

"Yes Sam," says the first-year lecturer, wife, lover, colleague, research assistant, secretary, cleaner, part-time cook, daughter, sister, friend, academic, writer, cousin, best friend and woman.

"Yes Sam," says the teacher who hasn't got a clue what mindfulness means.

* * *

These cases are the result of setting ourselves the task to "write a personal reflection on the meaningfulness of the project so far." What we wanted to see were our commonalities. What we found was the striking differences in our understanding of the task. At this point we needed a means of looking through the individual reflections to the processes of change at student, personal and institutional levels so that we could see what we were talking about in these three reflections. Somehow each authorial voice was incomplete in respect of the goal of the teaching "experiment", even though we had each noted positive changes that were a result of the broader project of assimilating the findings of positive psychology into our roles as academics. In other words we suspected there was a voice speaking behind the "conscious states" expressed in the three reflections. The concept of "voice" is tricky. When we use it we mean a perspective in a role as in authorial voice, dissenting voice, and even common voice. In particular we noted the limits of the three authorial voices in articulating a "conscientização". This phenomenon has been noted by Bakhtin (in Todorov, 1984) when he argued that no autobiography can be complete because the author is always outside the text as the writer of the text. It is this excess of meaning which interested us as a team.

Mindfulness

Jeanne's case describes how she, as a teacher, must be present in the classroom in the context of the past histories of her students. Evident in the case is Jeanne's determination to be with her students and work with the complexity of emotions, beliefs, values and goals they have brought to the classroom. From the perspective of the students, the broader focus of the classroom goes beyond the cognitive goals ahead of them as they focus on how the *whole person*—emotions, social, physical and cognitive—is present and how these aspects can be discussed.

In Marcelle's case there is a recounting of an experience of mindfulness that alerts the readers to a number of issues. Marcelle calls the authenticity of the teacher into question as she ticks the boxes and continues on her mindless way. It is her students and their authenticity in recounting the experiences in applying the mindfulness approaches that finally impacts upon her as the teacher-as-researcher. The case illustrates the complexity of the relationship cycle between teachers and students. The learning for both Marcelle and her students arises in their separate and collective interactions.

Tarquam's case refers to the toleration of ambiguity, flexibility, open-ended relationships, engagement and playful encounters. The student reflection speaks of appreciation, gratitude, hope, growth, beauty, creativity in relation to the learning environment: providing just the context Langer (2000) described as required for being mindful in learning. The students in this research unit are in the position of taking multiple perspectives on their learning rather than the narrow cognitive focus of more traditional classrooms. Here is Tarquam's case:

Tarquam

Academic Voice

(1) Relational Engagement. For me beginning in positive educational practice (PEP) is as much a way of being and belonging in the world as a set of theories. It requires a quality of engaged relationship which can be seen as somewhat different to the more didactic and transmissive space of the educator in the classroom. As a teacher in the School of Education I am consistently aware that I had deepened my understanding of positive psychology through a series of important and synchronistic encounters and in fact have lived many values of PEP for a long time. In 2001 I was recommended to read Seligman's book *The Optimistic Child* (2007) and then in a series of encounters with this information, I uncovered the signature strengths www sites and his work on optimism. I worked online to take a variety of tests to inform my own struggle with depression and used a variety of positive practices and mindfulness to drive my own inner life.

(2) Modelled Practice. The capacity of PEP to be experienced in a meaningful way required that the teacher-researchers also model the principles aligned with the work of positive psychology in our daily work. To this end the teacher-researchers in the PEP project noted various capacities that the team subscribe to and that inform their values, attitudes and beliefs around education. The modelling of practice is well documented in education but the particular "styles" of engagement that PEP requires are noted by the team and illustrate the relational aspect of the work in the teaching and learning space. Transmissive learning that is empathic, engaged and characteristically is emotionally accepting of a variety of responses, open-ended, warm-hearted and compassionate is noted in the work that was undertaken. Compassion in education is not unfamiliar, but the warmth and acceptance of the ambiguity of other ways of learning are accepted and modelled by the group throughout the research period. Between each other the teacher-researchers had moments of challenge and role-reversal and empathic encounters were characteristically light-hearted and at times humorous. The use of playfulness aligned with broadening and building (Fredrickson, 2001) and improvisation was also noted in the manner of encounter between the researchers.

(3) Application—Professional and Personal. As is illustrated above the personal attributes of valuing openness, being able to tolerate ambiguity and playful encounters drove a lot of the ways of being in the research. This is a characteristic of an open-ended relationship in terms of power and the style of engagement. All the group members adhere to notions of flexibility, careful encounter and respectful shared understanding of the work of teaching and learning. This is not unexpected, but that capacity to care for each other as we undertook the work together is unique. The goal of the research product was not more privileged than the process of being together in the group. Many times the personal application of empathic, interpersonally rich encounters was noted.

(4) Negative Critique. One characteristic of change in education is the rejection of the notions that are espoused as being "new" knowledge. PEP is not new, but many moments occurred in the academic community where heavy misrepresentation of "happiness" and its alignment with hedonistic styles of knowing seemed to deflate the value of the work being undertaken. Optimism, as is noted in the literature, is a natural characteristic but many colleagues took a moment to "belittle" the efficacy and capacity of positive psychology to have impact in the classroom. In some instances colleagues actually critiqued what "psyche" had to do with education, which in its strictest sense was, to their understand-

ing, "imparting" meaning. The move into PEP was at times seen as quasi-therapeutic and more the goal of a specialized school psychologist. Many times colleagues stated privately their interest, but it was clear that there were many times when colleagues were perceiving erroneously that this was a form of cult-like hedonistic engagement. The use of Seligman's notions of "meaningful, engaged and useful life" seemed to meet this clichéd critique.

(5) Postgraduate Voices. In the context of a research class for postgraduate students, around 20 graduate students undertook the work of signature strengths and worked online to complete the VIA strengths. All research students who commented incidentally and openly stated that they valued this way of knowing and that their strengths actually informed and impacted on research work they were formalizing. It was not at all unusual to align the strength work with the "question" they sought to answer in the class. Many colleagues, as mature-age students, valued VIA signature strengths and the importance of "passion" in defining a goal. Of note was one student who wrote an email to me stating:

> I undertook the VIA Signature Strengths questionnaire in 2008 for another subject and retook the questionnaire in 2009 in my research subject with you. The results had shifted… My sense of fairness and equity translates into a very democratic approach to my teaching—everyone has a fair go. I've cultivated an "attitude of gratitude" for some time now, which has helped me appreciate what I have, and I believe it's essential to have hope… I have experienced significant growth in my teaching—with my studies informing my work and with my workplace providing many opportunities for professional development. I'm a published poet and have recently had a publisher approach me regarding some of my latest work—very gratifying. The world needs appreciators—people who can see the beauty around them and in others, and who are not afraid to encourage and reward creative endeavours. Positive Psychology gives support and a much-needed boost to those of us who want to walk a different path to that of the well-worn cynicism and negativity that's all too prevalent.

* * *

The act of self-study implies mindfulness in the midst of the three PEP teacher-researchers' teamwork that perhaps is not always present in their classes. With the prospect of journaling and case writing, there is a heightened sensitivity to classroom dynamics evident in the cases that implies a focus in the moment of the teaching and a willingness to take multiple perspectives on the learning processes, even if, in the case of Marcelle, this response is delayed.

Relationships

The theme of relationships and its impact on self-esteem and well-being is central to establishing positivity within all educational arenas. The three cases that are presented by us attest to this and highlight the need for all teacher educators to create learning environments that give voice to meaningful moments. Opening up spaces for pre-service teachers to closely examine their character traits that either *hinder* or *support* their work with young learners *can only evolve in the presence of trusting relationships*. The same can be said for teacher educators—teacher educators need to set aside time with colleagues and pre-service teachers to reflect upon practices that allow for the emergence of opportunities that welcome criticality, inquiry, meta-cognition and self-awareness. We believe that higher thinking skills are more likely to emerge when teacher educators actively seek teaching and learning tools that lead to more sophisticated ways of knowing and acting in the world.

Trusting relationships between educators and pre-service teachers helped the team and the class to fuel the evolution of transformed mindsets steeped in agency and self-control. Jeanne's case highlights this point quite clearly. Through the use of the VIA Survey of Character Strengths, pre-service teachers were invited to reflect upon how they could use their own character strengths to improve their attitudes to mathematics. Whether this included pre-service teachers being kinder or fairer to themselves when grappling with mathematical concepts, or making a conscious effort to appreciate mathematical patterns, there prevailed a willingness to open oneself to thinking differently. In Jeanne's instance what may well be the most important thing in this case was the teacher educator's desire to create an opportunity for pre-service teachers to begin a conversation about their relationship with mathematics. Only in dissecting "negative" attitudes towards mathematics and preconceived notions of mathematical understanding could pre-service teachers then begin to modify their mindset in a positive way.

Awareness of one's relationship to content material was important for the team and what is being taught, as is evident in Marcelle's case above. Marcelle writes about feeling too constrained by the busyness of academic life to truly understand and connect with her work on mindfulness. What is apparent from Marcelle's writing is that a relationship with positive education theories and tools is not something that can be tacked on the end of a class. Rather, a personal and professional relationship with positive education is needed to be able to effectively model it to pre-service teachers. She holds that fostering and sustaining a relationship to a framework of teaching that utilises positive education techniques therefore requires time and careful planning. Indeed, Marcelle holds that positive education practices are very dependent on a conscious effort being made by educators to ensure that it is authentically integrated into course work.

Tarquam's case further illustrates this point when he reflects on the importance of embedding positive education in careful and respectful ways. In his postgraduate class Tarquam spoke about the need for teachers and students to be open to tolerating ambiguity in their discussion of character strength attributes. Being empathetic to the learning needs of others during group discussion was also central to his case. Bridging and bonding relationships through emotional and social intelligence leads to heightened relationships between peers, teachers and positive education practices. This bonding and bridging is central to the teamwork that we, as three researchers-as-teachers, came to value, and especially informs this discussion.

Comment on Commentaries

The team highlight the following themes in these commentaries that inform the development of a theoretical framework for elaborating the self-study methodology. Tarquam tags what we have taken as the core issue that has been identified in the chapter—the tension in explicating the relationship between character, selfhood and society in which the self is "performed". He also emphasises the sense of "playfulness" and "joy" that was essential as an enjoyment of each other, and most significantly, offers the distinction between deep and surface knowledge. Marcelle focuses on the need to experience trust as a mechanism, and she highlights the evolving and emergent nature of learning and introduced the notion of a "mindset", which has the potential to act as an analytic concept. She also directs us to think about the opening of self via the opening of spaces between people as "bridging and bonding". Jeanne addresses the complexity of the process that constitutes a constituency, emphasises "whole person", isolates the meaning of mindfulness as part of a creative process, and focuses attention on the space between people as the site of learning.

Central to our construction of the problem space is Jeanne's comment on Marcelle's case: "The learning of both arises in the interaction between the two". The notion of the *locus of learning being in the interaction* is precisely within the theorising about agency. When agency is spoken about without being coupled to an agent, what is being discussed is a mechanism that lies within and between the group. The locus of our learning is the quality of our interaction as the team of three researchers-as-teachers!

To go further we need to return to look for a deeper understanding of the founding of the group, namely positive psychology as PEP as a commitment to the relevance of character to the deeper learning for the whole person. The three teachers-as-researchers now have the challenge to provide a framework for articulating their shared experience of "thriving as learners" through belonging to the group. Developing a theoretical framework is a means of furthering the questioning, and we turn to that now.

Conclusion

As stated at the outset, this chapter is a point of reflection in an ongoing process of framing and reframing our team effort in collective understanding of ourselves and of our practices through the lens of us as "researchers-as-teachers" and "teachers-as-researchers". The marriage of research and teaching in self-study is lifelong for the three team members. The journey has opened out on a vista of optimism where the insights and work in positive psychology on character allow us to see both a methodological elaboration and a research program that points to a new and effective understanding of collegiality as an agency for changing teaching and learning practices. Though we began the journey thinking in terms of a teaching "experiment", our growing self-understanding prompted us to take up the research question in terms of our own intra-group interactions.

The next step is to return to our rich data set to deliberate on the quality of our interactions with the students and our peers and to see if we can operationalise the insights that the positive educational practice (PEP) project provided, perhaps to view how we provide ways for our teaching to enable students to "flourish" in their accessing and love of new knowledge (Seligman, 2011). It is our goal to develop further insight into how agency and character interact to map the deep effectiveness of practices for education, which is mindful, respectful and leads to flourishing, enthusiastic, positive changes in us as three researchers-as-teachers. Future inquiry will address especially what happens when our character strengths and mindful "selves" are further informed by an open interaction motivated by the three researchers' collective interests.

Note

1.   The language of the three cases is Australian English and is presented verbatim—at times as a flow of consciousness as emerging ideas. In some instances idiomatic Australian English is used and the reader is also advised that British English is used in writing in Australia.

References

Bass, L., Anderson-Patton, V., & Allender, J. (2002). Self-study as a way of teaching and learning. In J. Loughran & T. Russell (Eds.), *Improving teacher education practices through self-study.* London: RoutledgeFalmer.

Berry, A. (2007). *Tensions in teaching about teaching: Understanding practice as a teacher educator.* Dordrecht: Springer.

Brown, K. W., & Ryan, R. M. (2003). The benefits of being present: Mindfulness and its role in psychological well-being. *Journal of Personality and Social Psychology, 84*(4), 822–848.

Bullock, S. M. (2009). Learning to think like a teacher educator: Making the substantive and syntactic structures of teaching explicit through self-study. *Teachers and Teaching, 15*(2), 291–304.

Davidson, R. J. (2010). Empirical explorations of mindfulness: Conceptual and methodological conundrums. *Emotion, 10*(1), 8–11.

Fredrickson, B. L. (2001). The role of positive emotions in positive psychology: The broaden-and-build theory of positive emotions. *American Psychologist, 56,* 218–226.

Freire, P. (1996). *Pedagogy of the oppressed.* London: Penguin.

Hamilton, M., Smith, L., & Worthington, K. (2008). Fitting the methodology with the research: An exploration of narrative, self-study and auto-ethnography. *Studying Teaching Education, 4*(1), 17–28.

Kabat-Zinn, J. (2003). Mindfulness-based interventions in context: Past, present, and future. *Clinical Psychology: Science and Practice, 10*(2), 144–156.

Kelchtermans, G. (2009). Who I am and how I teach is the message: Self-understanding, vulnerability and reflection. *Teachers and Teaching, 15*(2), 257–272.

Kosnik, C., Beck, C., Freese, A., & Samaras, A. (2005). *Making a difference in teacher education through self-study: Studies of professional and program renewal.* Dordrecht : Springer.

LaBoskey, V. K. (2004). The methodology of self-study and its theoretical underpinnings. In J. J Loughran, M. L. Hamiliton, V. K. LaBoskey, & T. Russell (Eds.), *International handbook of self-study of teaching and teacher education practices* (pp. 817–870). Dordrecht: Kluwer.

Langer, E. J. (1993). A mindful education. *Educational Psychologist, 28*(1), 43–50.

Langer, E. J. (2000). Mindful learning. *Current Directions in Psychological Science, 9*(6), 220–223.

Lassonde, C. A., Galman, S., & Kosnik, C. (Eds.). (2009). *Self-study research methodologies for teacher educators.* Rotterdam: Sense.

Loughran, J. (2007). Researching teacher education practice: Responding to the challenges, demands and expectations of self-study. *Journal of Teacher Education, 58*(1), 12–20.

Mills, C. W. (2000). *The sociological imagination*. Oxford: Oxford University Press.

Park, N. (2004). Character strengths and positive youth development. *The Annals of the American Academy of Political and Social Science, 591,* 40–54.

Park, N., & Peterson, C. (2009). Strengths of character in schools. In R. Gilman, E. S. Huebner, & M. J. Furlong (Eds.), *Handbook of positive psychology in schools* (pp. 65–76). New York: Routledge.

Park, N., Peterson, C., & Seligman, M. E. P. (2006). Character strengths in fifty-four nations and the fifty US states. *The Journal of Positive Psychology, 1*(3), 118–129.

Samaras, A. P. (2002). *Self-study for teacher educators: Crafting a pedagogy for educational change*. New York: Peter Lang.

Samaras, A. P., & Freese, A. (2006). *Self-study of teaching practices*. New York: Peter Lang.

Schon, D. A. (1983). *The reflective practitioner: How professionals think in action*. New York: Basic Books.

Shulman, L. (1999). Taking learning seriously. *Change, 31*(4), 10–17.

Seligman, M. E. P. (2007). *The optimistic child*. Boston: Houghton Mifflin.

Seligman, M. E. P. (2011). *Flourish: A visionary new understanding of happiness and well-being*. New York: Free Press.

Thich Nhat Hanh (2008). The miracle of mindfulness. Sydney: Random House.

Todorov, T. (1984). *Mikhail Bakhtin: The dialogical principle*. Minneapolis: University of Minnesota Press.

CHAPTER THIRTY-EIGHT

Collective Narrative Analysis and the Understandings of Young People

Farhat Shahzad

Recent developments in the field of research methodologies have testified to the growing need of multiple methods in empirical research. Critical qualitative research (CQR) attempts to meet this demand by incorporating a variety of approaches to rethink purposes and methods of research. It provides researchers opportunities to deterritorialize the methodological space, as the heart of critical theory is ideological rather than methodological (Willis, 2007). It can integrate different epistemologies, critical research designs, multiple theoretical orientations, and methods with associated forms of data collection and analyses to facilitate critical and emancipatory purposes. This chapter draws a vivid picture of what it can mean to do CQR by walking readers through the different steps of a research on youth that is at the cutting edge of scholarship related to critical qualitative methods. This chapter also attempts to generate a space for talking about the role of collective narratives in experimental and innovative research methods. It is an emancipatory form of research that has the ability to empower youth and particularly marginalized youth, often silent in the public sphere, and to engage them in the rethinking of their positions and roles in the society (Kincheloe & McLaren, 2002).

A good deal of youth research has undertaken the important step of exploring and documenting the varied conditions of young people's lives (Asher, 2008; Saltzburg & Davis, 2010; Tolonen, 2009). However, in most of the cases it is a group that has been represented rather than allowed to represent itself. A power dynamics is always involved in dealing with young people in research projects, which allow experiences (often of marginalized and historically underexamined populations) to stand in for a more complex historicization of subjects and their lives (Scott, 1991). In addition, sometimes researchers' own relativistic moral positions as scholars and researchers blind them from digging deeper into the larger lived realities affecting youth (Prier & Beachum, 2008).

As a result, research projects about young people generally speak for them with both qualitative and quantitative approaches filtered through interpretations, framed by the research questions but rarely emancipatory (Rodriguez-Jiménez & Gifford, 2010). These challenges make doing research with young people especially demanding, and using innovative approaches all the more so. Taking an innovative approach itself is a challenge, but researchers who are concerned with the issues of youth must challenge themselves with how their work is relevant and relational to the contemporary everyday lived realities and understandings of youth (Prier & Beachum, 2008). I took an innovative methodological approach to gain an integrated and conceptual understanding of youth's lives as experienced, understood and described by themselves. It helped me to identify generic dimensions and processes that shape their lives more effectively.

I adopted an approach of collecting and analyzing collective narratives to explore what sort of larger cultural understandings Canadian youth share in the form of collective memories of "the War on Terror". I put the phrase *the War on Terror* in quotation marks to show its problematic nature. I used the term because it is commonly used in the public sphere. My focus was on how young people understand this term. Whether there is in fact such a war, what its activities involve and what their effects are in reality are matters that go beyond this research project. This war helped me to build a context for an exploration of young people's experiences, memories and understandings through critical qualitative methods. These methods offered a powerful way of creating a space for young people to speak for themselves. For researchers, whose lived experiences may be quite different from young people, collective narratives, if approached critically, can be the bridge that narrows the void and dissonance between them and young people as their participants. I took a critical approach to collective narratives in order to listen to the voices of Canadian youth, who gave social and political views about how hegemonic discourses of the larger society have affected their lives. In other words, I was interested in listening to their voices to explore the so-called war from the perspective of those who have grown up alongside it. All participants of this study were in their late childhood when the attacks on the World Trade Center and the Pentagon occurred on 9/11, 2001. Within less than a month, this young generation saw the beginning of a war against "the terrorists". The sample of my study was comprised of a heterogeneous group of Canadian youth that has witnessed a gradual development and even the consequences of this war. The so-called War on Terror is their Vietnam War or World War II, yet we know virtually nothing of how they understand it.

These young people construct collective memories to represent their understandings of the war in the form of collective narratives. Collective memory is constructed within social structures, institutions and collective norms. For example, the annual anniversary commemorations of September 11th, gatherings of the survivors and other people who did not directly experience the attacks, provide continued memory reinforcement with the roll call of the dead, bagpipes, recitations and floral offerings. These commemorations provide selected narratives of the war for those who did not experience it directly.

Young people's collective narratives of problematic episodes (e.g., the War on Terror) can challenge selected narratives and pose a threat to the dominant power structures in the society. As Beiner (2007) says, "Memory proves to be subversive so that, in the famous words of Milan Kundra, the struggle of man against power is the struggle of memory against forgetting" (p. 304). These collective narratives represent the struggle of memory against forgetting, and reflect the process of negotiation between Canadian youth, the disseminating vital mnemonic imaginaries and multiple narratives of the war available in their national and regional spaces. In order to build up a cause-and-effect relationship, they have selected some events for remembrance, eliminated others and then rearranged selected events to construct their narrative of the War on Terror.

This research found that an important phenomenon like the War on Terror is no longer necessarily centered around selected official narratives, but "decentered" and deconstructed by young people in a variety of ways. They are consuming multiple and contested narratives delivered through a variety of technologies. These technologies include television, personal websites (blogs), mobile phone communication, Google, YouTube, debates on myspace.com, or ohmynews (Volkmer, 2008). This complicated network of information technologies has enhanced the capacity of youth to devise new ways of thinking, framing problems and developing innovative languages to construct knowledge. Roman and Stanley (1997) remind us that "young people are not passive receivers of knowledge waiting to be acted upon by 'the right' or 'correct' interventions. Students are themselves active agents of cultural production" (p. 205). As active agents of cultural production, their voices and memories are difficult to manipulate, and even more difficult to control in the age of the Internet and global media.

I decided to adopt a methodology that can support young people to find their voices to represent who they are and who they are becoming. I collected young people's narratives around the same issue and then analyzed them for what they are saying about their collective understandings of the issue. It is important to discover how young people see the world around them and what sorts of collective narratives they have to share because their collective consciousness and understandings will shape the future. By critically examining and understanding young people's collective narratives, educators can gain insights about all types of youth issues and make meaningful connections with their students. Collective narratives can help teachers reduce many of the problems our youth face in schools and create a classroom "where students' personal experience intersects with academic knowledges" (Kincheloe, 2005, p. 4).

Why Collective Narratives?

My methodological choice was situated in Jocelyn Létourneau's (2006) argument that students' narratives reflect a historical collective memory. These students' narratives provided me with valuable insights into how Canadian youth construct collective memories in relation to the War on Terror. Reflecting critically on these narratives also helped me to understand how they structure the characters, main events and sequence of the events of the war to adopt a social position and perspective (Wertsch, 2002). The goal of this research methodology was "not to transmit a body of validated truths" about the war, but rather "engaging students in the knowledge production process" (Kincheloe, 2005, p. 3).

A narrative is an educative, interpretive and meaning-making tool, as Bruner (1996) claimed. He pointed to the fact that a narrative plays an important role in the construction and assimilation of knowledge, and identified humans as natural narrators. Furthermore, he argued that if education is to be effective, it has to help learners to use meaning-making and constructional tools so that they can interpret and adapt to the world. One such tool, he suggested, is narrative. Considerable work has demonstrated the importance of creating story-sharing opportunities for students (e.g., Engel, 1995; Niccolopoulou, 2007). Compelling arguments have been made for including narrative practices to understand youth in elementary, middle and high school settings (Daiute, 2000; Fine & Weis, 2003; Shultz, Buck, & Niesz, 2006; Weis & Fine, 2000). It has been suggested that teachers should offer students opportunities to experiment in their narratives with different approaches to situations, even if they are not culturally expected or accepted, in order to promote classrooms that empower students by giving voice to their experiences (Daiute, 2000; Fine & Weis, 2003; Weis & Fine, 2000). By using collective narratives teachers can also build up connections between their own stories and the stories of their students. They may feel, each in their own way, a terrain of tension within their own paradigms and practices—a terrain that might be explored if the teachers would be open to young people's collective narratives. An implication of this practice is that it is in times of tension (Dewey, 1938/1998; Vygotsky, 1978), or when we notice a "bump" in our planned or lived stories that we pause to rethink and sometimes deconstruct our views and practices (Clandinin & Connelly, 2000, p. 35). Another reason to use collective narratives as a tool in this research is that they

> can provide hints and clues about how to apply our basic mode of understanding to another person's reasons through empathetic re-enactment in situations where that seems to be *prima facie* difficult because of great cultural or social differences between interpreter and the person to be interpreted. (Stueber, 2008, pp. 34–35)

Through an analysis of collective narratives, I applied my mode of understanding to Canadian youth's reasons through empathetic re-enactment. By opening a window into the stories of young people, this methodology can be used to facilitate feelings of empowerment and experience of the connectedness of life in them, as "stories are linguistic expressions of this uniquely human experience of the connectedness of life" (Polkinghorne, 1995, p. 7). This methodology is suitable for any research project that deals with young people, as they are both imaginative and logical in their thinking, and narratives generally engage their attention and help in making new knowledge meaningful to them.

A Multi-Method Approach

Researchers' decisions about research methods generally depend upon their own paradigms, the specific context of the issues they want to study, the traditions of their own disciplines and, most importantly, the actual consequences of using them (Maxwell, 2005). The bottom line of my decision about research methods was the actual consequence of using them in my study. The actual consequence of this design was that it unearthed understandings originating from young people themselves. I value the intersubjectivity of my project, and the methodology values collaboration with the participants in a way that emphasizes the inability and undesirability of being a completely objective and innocent researcher. This form of emancipatory praxis aims to empower youth in positive trajectories of social actions and new possibilities.

I decided to get collective narratives of Canadian youth, instead of individual narratives, through a multi-method approach. Individual narratives might be idiosyncratic and in most of the cases can be non-contested, while collective ones are shared and hence cultural. They may be different in terms of their political content and conclusion. Most importantly, as compared to individual ones, collective narratives are multiple and contested (Boehm, 2006; Campbell, 2008; Connerton, 2008; Reese & Fivush, 2008). For example, sometimes narratives represented through monuments or museums become contested. They provoke controversies over whose curricular version of the past is represented or whose is absent. Mostly they convey different messages for different groups such as the representations of the Aboriginal Canadians in Canadian museums, which have been contested as newly empowered alternative voices have emerged (Paul, 2006; McLeod, 2007). In another example, Wertsch (2008) suggests that the real conflict between ethnic Russians and Estonians over the removal of the "Bronze Soldier" in April 2007 was due to two opposite readings of the monument. For Russians the statue was a monument of liberation, while for Estonians it was a statue of the "unknown rapist." A narrative of patriotism or national glory for one group can be a source of pain, grief and exploitation for another group because human beings construct collective narratives in the light of their multiple and contested memories. Collective memories of the War on Terror are contested just as the war as well as the term "terrorism" is. These narratives also reveal whether Canadian youth consider the phenomenon of terrorism a contested one or not, and where they stand in the space between terror and terrorism.

The field of collective memory has no agreed-upon set of methodologies (Wertsch, 2002). Critique and deconstruction of traditional concepts, models and methodologies go hand in hand with emerging alternative methodologies in this field. Some even complain about the non-paradigmatic, transdisciplinary, centerless qualities of the enterprise, qualities that seem to have persisted despite the exponential growth of work on collective memory (Olick, 2008). Nonetheless, this apparent weakness became the strength of my methodology because it allowed me to use an interactional approach in designing my research project. The research design resulted in an open and more flexible approach towards the epistemological and methodological issues in my research project. I negotiated these issues in my cross-disciplinary research project by using empirical evidence, multiple theoretical frameworks, and a multi-method approach for both data collection and data analysis. Many theorists argue in favor of cross-disciplinary research to solve paradigmatic issues in the field of collective memory (Olick, 2008; Radstone, 2008), and to design innovative ways of understanding representations of the past in order to study past, contemporary, and future collective memories. I found that there is a strategic room in memory studies for deterritorialization (Sutton, 2008, p. 23), and used a synthesis of multiple theoretical models from the field of collective memory studies (Halbwachs, 1980; Wertsch, 2002), nationalism studies (Anderson, 1983; Billig, 1995), and cultural representations (Hall, 1980, 1997, 2000, 2002; Said, 1985) to analyze narratives of collective memory.

Different scholars have used narratives as a means to study collective memory (Goldberg, Porat, & Schwarz, 2006; Létourneau, 2006; Penuel & Wertsch, 1998; Wertsch & O'Connor, 1994; Wertsch, 2002). For example, Wertsch and O'Connor (1994) conducted a qualitative study in which they asked college students to write narratives about the origins of the United States. In another project, Wertsch (2002) used narratives to understand the process of collective remembering in Russian society. His empirical research provided opportunities to trace the evaluation of different narrative templates over time. His methodology is also useful to understand the process by which collective memory is consumed and negotiated by a society. He used questionnaires and essays written in the form of narratives by high school students and adults to collect data. His participants were recruited through the "snowball" method. It was a comparative study between Soviet-educated and post-Soviet-educated Russians, and efforts were made to obtain participants from a range of class and educational backgrounds.

Létourneau (2004) also did a qualitative study and used textual analysis, though his sampling method was different from Wertsch's (2002). He used narratives of young students to understand their representations of the collective history of a mainly French-speaking Canadian province, Québec, and found that practically all students used a narrative that is at odds with the official narratives available in Québec. Their narratives were more influenced by cultural narratives situated in the historical experience of Québec as compared to the narratives available through the curriculum, history textbooks, or public school system. Létourneau (2004) used the "purposeful sampling" method to recruit his participants. In this qualitative study, he asked young people studying in high schools and a Québec university to write narratives about the history of their province in 45 minutes. The exercise took place in the classroom with their teacher present, but not providing input. All participants had a French-Canadian cultural background. Although the results of his research cannot be extended to all young people in Canada, his methodology can be. I borrowed my basic methodological approach from his inquiry.

I recruited my participants from large introductory first-year undergraduate Arts courses offered in a large urban university in Ontario. Two different courses were chosen in order to achieve possible variations in the participants, which offered comparisons between participants' narratives. The sampling strategy in this study was purposive (Patton, as cited in Maxwell, 2005, p. 88) and criterion based (Lecompte & Preissle, as cited in Maxwell, p. 88). My goal was to adequately capture the heterogeneity in the sample (Maxwell, 2005). The strategy provided a wide range of representations for the young populace that would not occur by utilizing a random sampling strategy (Creswell, 2007; Maxwell, 2005). Guba and Lincoln (1989) referred to this as "maximum variation sampling" (p. 178). Designed to reveal different facets of my participants' experiences and understandings, three methods were used to collect data: (1) in-depth interviews, (2) written narratives, and (3) demographic questionnaires. In order to get to know my participants as people, I asked each participant to fill out a demographic questionnaire before writing a narrative. These questionnaires provided me with information about his/her religion, ethnic background, location of high school, age, and gender. This questionnaire also gave me information about the language(s) spoken at their homes, and was an effective instrument of data collection that helped me to situate their voices in the context.

I collected my data in two different phases. In the first phase, I asked my participants to recall their memories, any information, feelings, and lived experiences related to "the War on Terror" and write down their narratives according to the following questions given in the questionnaire. These questions were designed to stimulate their memories and to generate narratives about the war:

1. Please write a short essay on: What has been the course of "the War on Terror" from its beginning until today, the way you see it, you remember it and you experience it?

2. How has "the War on Terror" affected you?

Question number one is a narrative prompt question, while the second is specifically designed to reveal how they construct the narratives. In narrative analytic terms it can be said that students were required to construct a narrative and then explicitly write down their experiences about the war. At the end of the exercise, I collected 103 narratives, but excluded four narratives because my study was focused only on young people (from 18–27 years old). Two narratives were not included because the participants were only 17 years old, and the other two were excluded because the participants were over 30, as indicated by their personal information in the demographic questionnaires.

In the second phase of my research project, I used follow-up interviews to collect additional information and to further expand my participants' narratives. My main intention was to obtain deeper insight into their narratives. Morgan (1997) believes it is an advantage to conduct individual interviews because it provides a way to gain more in-depth accounts of the participants' experiences as described in their narratives. I asked about the same events and characters that they mentioned in their narratives, rather than posing new questions that elicit only generalizations or abstract opinions (Weiss, 1994). The questions were developed in a way that directly and indirectly addressed my research questions. I conducted interviews in semi-structured format, with special attention given to ensuring homogeneous interview style and almost the same questions. An integration of the narratives, interview responses and demographic questionnaire information allowed for collective narrative analysis.

Collective Narrative Analysis

Studies of the War on Terrorism discourse have employed different units of analysis, such as membership categories (Leudar, Marsland, & Nekvapil, 2004), strategic speech acts (Lazar & Lazar, 2004), grammar (Butt, Lukin, & Matthiessen, 2004), discourse deixis and space (Chilton, 2004), informational accuracy and flow (Altheide, 2006; Kellner, 2005, 2007), and metaphors (Lakoff, 2004). Just as the multi-method approach was used to collect data, a multi-level approach was implemented to analyze data. I used a combination of socially informed critical discourse and textual analysis. I call this blended approach, which enabled me to use multiple lenses and a hybrid framework for data analysis, "collective narrative analysis".

As a result, my analysis was focused on both how and what things were said. Instead of simply looking at events and characters in the narrative of the war, the analytic lens was focused on how the stories about them were told (Riessman, 1993), how rhetorical styles were used to represent banal nationalism (Billig, 1995), and how the use of language was dialectically positioned in relation to larger socio-political concerns (Fairclough, 1992) about the War on Terror. Understandings gained from close attention to the language and narrative accounts were then deployed in exploring young people's collective understandings as represented by them. Critical discourse analysis (CDA) was used to analyze fragments of the language used by my participants to represent something and to relate discursive and socio-political aspects of the war with their lives. Among the scholars whose works have profoundly contributed to the development of CDA are van Dijk (1988, 1991, 1993, 1995, 1996, 1998, 2005, 2006), Wodak (2000), and Fairclough (1989, 1992, 1995, 1999). CDA provided me an analytical framework with vast and flexible boundaries because it is not a specific direction of analysis, nor does it depend on a unitary theoretical framework. In sum, it helped me to

- deconstruct narratives of my participants, expose dichotomies, examine silences, and attend disruption and contradiction (Czarniawska, 2004);

- link the micro-level use of language with macro-level socio-political concerns (Fairclough, 1992). Macro-level socio-political concerns depend on certain discourse strategies that typically influence young people's mental models. According to Van Dijk, one of these strategies is generalization. A concrete specific example that has made an impact on people's mental models is the manipulation of the U.S. and world opinion about terrorism after 9/11, in which very emotional and strongly opinionated mental models held by citizens about this event were generalized to more general, shared fears, attitudes and ideologies about terrorism and related issues (van Dijk, 2006, p. 370);

- study and analyze written and spoken texts to reveal the discursive sources of power, dominance, inequality and biases maintained and reproduced within specific social, political and historical contexts (van Dijk, 1998);

- create a research text that illuminates the experiences of not only Canadian youth in the context of the War on Terror, but also how the dominant discourses shape their relationships with each other and Canadian society itself. At the core of CDA is a detailed description, explanation and critique of the ways dominant discourse influences such socially shared knowledge, attitudes and ideologies (van Dijk, 1998, p. 258);

- analyze and make explicit mental representations articulated along us-versus-them dimension, " in which speakers of one group will generally tend to present themselves or their own group in positive terms, and other groups in negative terms" (van Dijk, 1998, p. 22).

I also employed textual analysis to understand how my participants construct collective memories of the war. This analytical framework was used to examine larger units of text devoted to participants' accounts of events and characters. The analysis itself may best be termed as "theoretically informed induction". That is, I approached the data with a theoretical framework in mind, and then attempted to pull out the larger patterns I saw in the texts.

The first phase of analytical process involved segregating 99 narratives into Muslim and non-Muslim, on the basis of knowledge obtained from their demographic questionnaires. The purpose was to analyze whether the War on Terror has affected Muslim youth differently as compared to non-Muslim youth. The next step involved a journey through the narratives as a reader without any prior themes or theory in my mind. In this phase of analysis, my data analysis involved readings for the following set of questions:

1. How do the participants of this study employ the narrative of "the War on Terror"?

   a. What do they identify as the start of "the War on Terror"?

   b. What events do they identify?

   c. What are the dominant characters in these narratives?

   d. Are there any differences or similarities in these narratives in relation to the events and characters of the narrative of "the War on Terror"?

Frequent presence of events or arguments was taken as an indication of what aspect of a situation the participants considered to be the most salient. In the third step, my data analysis involved readings for the following set of questions:

2. How do my participants understand "the War on Terror"?

   a. What is the nature of "the War on Terror" according to the participants of this study?

   b. What is the purpose of "the War on Terror" according to the participants of this study?

   c. What are the links between "the War on Terror" and the U.S. occupation of Iraq?

   d. What are the links between "the War on Terror" and the Canadian involvement in Afghanistan?

   e. What are the effects of this war on the lives of the participants of this study?

The data was the repository of information about how Canadian youth understand and construct their knowledge of the War on Terror. I analyzed whether these positions were the same, oppositional or were overlapping each other. I also looked at what type of knowledge their political positions allowed, and what they did not. I found that the war has personally affected the study's Canadian Muslim youth participants in ways that it has not the non-Muslim participants. I used theories from the fields of representations and narrative inquiry to situate my analysis in this step. In my next reading, the analysis involved readings for the following question:

3. How do my participants use a deixis of little words in their narratives?

I focused on the rhetorical style of my participants because narratives cannot be taken simply and interpreted solely for what has been said and told. Rather, they have to be *analyzed*, and the analysis of narratives has to work with what we have, the actual and the delivery/style of the wording (Bamberg, 2006). The analysis at this stage adhered to the rigor of detailed linguistic analysis by examining rhetorical styles of my participants in their narratives and transcripts of their interviews. Frequent use of a particular rhetorical style revealed a covert cultural and ideological message since "recurrent ways of talking…provide familiar and conventional representations of people and events, by filtering and crystallizing ideas, and by providing pre-fabricated means by which ideas can be easily conveyed and grasped" (Stubbs, 1996, p. 158). I analyzed the rhetorical style of my participants to understand how they positioned themselves and the characters of the war in the semiotic field. The cultural information and the discourse were inferred by examining the frequent use of deixis in a banal manner in the text. I analyzed how my participants use the deixis of small words like "we/us" or "they/them" to construct multiple imagined communities. I explored the implications of these deixis by drawing on theoretical concepts from the field of nationalism studies, and especially by considering the role of language in legitimizing certain type of knowledge while maintaining certain differences. Significantly, the hegemonic narrative, according to the participants of my study, is not the official Canadian government's narrative of the War on Terror. Rather they reject the image of Canada as a military nation in favor of that of a multicultural peaceful nation. In the last phase, I focused on the sources of information used by my participants, and what roles their personal context or background played in the selection of and access to these sources. The textual analysis involved readings for the following questions:

4. How do my participants construct collective memories of "the War on Terror"?

   a. How do technologies of memory enter into these narratives?

I relied heavily on theoretical concepts from the field of collective memory studies and found that the terrain of collective memory is like the topography. This topography has three main features: human agents, technologies of memory (Wertsch, 2002) and different social groups or communities. My participants construct collective memories through processes that involve a collectivity of significant "others", including parents and teachers, or what I call "interpretative communities". As this group of young people wrote their narratives, they remembered the instances and events in their lives related to the issue, they shared their thoughts, and during this process went back and forth in time. These young people may not necessarily tell stories, but excerpts from their stories. It was my task as a researcher to relate the events to each other in a way that created a holistic view. This aspect is important to the fit of this method, as the main purpose of this research was to listen and document young people's voices, understandings, and experiences as represented by them. During this collective narrative analysis, I continuously kept the following warning in my mind given by Atkinson and Delamont (2006) about the analysis of narratives:

> While the "voices" of otherwise muted groups may be charged with political significance, we cannot proceed as if they were guaranteed authenticity simply by virtue of narrators' social positions. The testimony of the powerless and the testimony of the powerful equally deserve close analytic attention. Moral commitment is not a substitute for social-scientific analysis. (p. 170)

I was conscious about this issue during my analysis and paid equal analytic attention to the voices of all participants. I repeatedly tried to take myself out of what my participants were saying and focus only on their representations. How I represented Canadian youth's understandings (expressed through interpretations) may sometimes differ (Clandinin & Connelly, 2000; Mishler, 1986; Riessman, 1993) from what they actually said. However, I do not view this risk as a threat to the validity of this critical qualitative research. First, valuing the interpretive openness allowed for competing explanations (Czarniawska, 2004); second, I strictly followed the procedure; and third, I have presented Canadian youth's voices as much as possible.

There are advantages as well as some disadvantages to this methodology. One disadvantage is that researchers can create their own meanings from their participants' representations. As a result, they may bring their own experiences into the readings. An advantage is that these narratives were less likely to be written for a person who was an outsider for the participants. These narratives were less shaped by who the writers think their audience is. Another advantage of this methodology is that it can be used to investigate and analyze young people's understandings of almost anything in their lives. An important aspect of collective narrative analysis is that it avoids essentialization of meanings. Collective understandings are always multiple and contested by different groups. There are always different patterns in collective narratives, and that collective construction need not be consistent or conceived as individual meanings writ large (Wertsch, 2002). Most importantly, this methodology can be used to explore how young people themselves understand the world. If we do not seek out and bring into knowledge our youth's understandings, then all emancipatory and educational projects will become meaningless.

Conclusion

This chapter illustrates an example of collecting narratives around the same issue and then analyzing them to discover the networks of young people's collective understandings. Although the results of this research cannot be extended to all young people, because they reflect one of the kinds of patterns that are available in Canadian youth, the methodology can be. Collective narrative analysis can be used to explore and analyze young people's understandings of almost anything related to their lives, such as the perception of math and math education among young people; the psychological world of young gay/lesbian/bisexual students; how young people connect the conceptual knowledge of physics to the procedural knowledge; how marginalized youth cope with social categorization and exclusion; to listen to the hyphenated-hybrid voices of immigrant youth and so on.

Representations of wars are primarily informed by the *big narratives* ("official narratives", Goldberg, Porat, & Schwarz, 2006; "grand narratives", Lyotard, 1984; Stanley, 2006). These narratives are circulated in the mainstream media or represented by politicians, often saturated with pre-approved, government-sanctioned images and political agendas. Scholars are skeptical about the political agendas behind the construction of these big narratives, and note that when it comes to collective memory, it is important to remember that a political narrative (e.g., that of triumph-over-alien-forces) always works as an underlying cultural tool behind the construction of narratives (Poole, 2008; Wertsch, 2002). Létourneau (2004) also talks about one of these political narratives that plays an important role in remaking of collective memory in young Québecois. He claims that collective memories of young Québecois are driven by a specific political agenda, that of the building of a new Québec nation. On a metaphorical level, though, these *small* narratives of young people are somewhat of an antidote formulation to a longstanding tradition of *big narratives*, and are used by them as a tool of empowerment. As majority of these young people are not buying into the representations of the War on Terror primarily informed by the *big narratives*. This methodology helped me to stimulate and start a dialogue about sensitive issues of wars, terrorism, and peace among young people, and facilitated them to take part in substantive discussions, dissent, arguments, questioning and critical thinking—the real stuff of all *emancipatory and educational projects.*

Narratives can be a potential tool of repression and misinformation as well as empowerment and enlightenment for young people, as they may reveal deep fears, perceived threats, and past grievances (Ross, 2001). These fears and grievances play an important role in the construction of young people's identities and their performances as students and humans. Collective narrative analysis can be used to expose and understand our youth's fears, perceived threats, and past grievances, as memory and identity are always implicated in narrative forms and content (Atkinson & Delamont, 2006). This methodology also allows researchers and teachers to "hang out in the epistemological bazaar listening to and picking up on articulations of subjugated knowledges" (Kincheloe, 2005, p. 127). Students' narratives' metaphors and images can represent a great deal about how they understand the contradictions and divisions of the social and political worlds, and how they relate them to inequitable power conditions. These understandings are prerequisites for emancipatory actions that lead to increased social justice and social transformation in the world.

References

Altheide, D. (2006). *Terrorism and the politics of fear.* Lanham, MD: Alta Mira Press.

Anderson, B. (1983). *Imagined communities.* London, England: Verso.

Asher, N. (2008). Listening to hyphenated Americans: Hybrid identities of youth from immigrant families. *Theory into Practice, 47*(1), 12–19.

Atkinson, P., & Delamont, S. (2006). Rescuing narrative from qualitative research. *Narrative Inquiry, 16*(1), 164–172.

Bamberg, M. (2006). Stories: Big or small. *Narrative Inquiry, 16*(1), 139–147.

Beiner, G. (2007). *Remembering the year of the French.* Madison: University of Wisconsin Press.

Billig, M. (1995). *Banal nationalism.* London, England: Sage.

Boehm, S. (2006). Privatizing public memory: The price of patriotic philanthropy and the post-9/11 politics of display. *American Quarterly, 58,* 1147–1166.

Bruner, J. (1996). *The culture of education.* Cambridge, MA: Harvard University Press.

Butt, D. G., Lukin, A., & Matthiessen, C. M. I. M. (2004). Grammar: The first covert operation of war. *Discourse & Society, 15*(2–3), 267–290.

Campbell, S. (2008). The second voice. *Memory Studies, 1*(1), 41–48.

Chilton, P. A. (2004). *Analyzing political discourse: Theory and practice.* London, England: Routledge.

Clandinin, D. J., & Connelly, F. M. (2000). *Narrative inquiry: Experience and story in qualitative research.* San Francisco, CA: Jossey-Bass.

Connerton, P. (2008). Seven types of forgetting. *Memory Studies, 1*(1), 59–71.

Creswell, J. W. (2007). *Qualitative inquiry and research design, choosing among five traditions.* Thousand Oaks, CA: Sage.

Czarniawska, B. (2004). *Nineties in social science research.* London, England: Sage.

Daiute, C. (2000). Narrative sites for youth's construction of social consciousness. In L. Weis & M. Fine (Eds.), *Construction sites: Excavating race, class, and gender among urban youth* (pp. 211–234). New York, NY: Teachers College Press.

Dewey, J. (1998). *Experience and education: The 60th anniversary edition.* West Lafayette, IN: Kappa Delta Pi. (Original work published 1938)

Engel, S. (1995). *The stories children tell: Making sense of the narratives of childhood.* New York, NY: Freeman & Company.

Fairclough, N. (1989). *Language and power.* London, England: Longman.

Fairclough, N. (1992). *Discourse and social change.* Cambridge, England: Polity Press.

Fairclough, N. (1995). *Critical discourse analysis: The critical study of language.* London, England: Longman.

Fairclough, N. (1999). A reply to Henry Widdowson's "Discourse analysis: a critical view". *Language and Literature, 5*(1), 49–56.

Fine, M., & Weis, L. (2003). *Silenced voices and extraordinary conversations: Reimagining schools.* New York, NY: Teachers College Press.

Goldberg, T., Porat, D., & Schwarz, B. B. (2006). "Here started the rift we see today": Student and textbook narratives between official and counter memory. *Narrative Inquiry, 16*(2), 319–347.

Guba, E.g., & Lincoln, Y. S. (1989). *Fourth generation evaluation.* Newbury Park, CA: Sage.

Halbwachs, M. (1980). *The collective memory.* Chicago, IL: University of Chicago Press.

Hall, S. (1980). Encoding/decoding. In S. Hall, D. Hobson, A. Lowe, & P. Willis (Eds.), *Culture, media, and language: Working papers in cultural studies 1972–1979* (pp. 128–138). London, England: Unwin Hyman.

Hall, S. (1997). The spectacle of the "other." In S. Hall (Ed.), *Representation: Cultural representations and signifying practices* (pp. 223–279). Thousand Oaks, CA: Sage.

Hall, S. (2000). The multi-cultural moment. In Barnor Hesse (Ed.), *Un/settled multiculturalism: Diasporas, entanglements, transruptions* (pp. 209–241). London, England: Zed Books.

Hall, S. (2002). Political belonging in a world of multiple identities. In S. Vertovec & R. Cohin (Eds.), *Conceiving cosmopolitanism* (pp. 25–32). Oxford, England: Oxford University Press.

Keller, S. L., Walton, M. D., & Nicolopoulou, A. (2006, March). *Narrative performance and the creation of local culture in two preschool classrooms.* Paper presented at the Annual Meeting of the Jean Piaget Society, Baltimore, MD.

Kellner, D. (2005). *Media spectacle and the crisis of democracy: Terrorism, war, and election battles.* Boulder, CO: Paradigm.

Kellner, D. (2007). Lying in politics: The case of George W. Bush and Iraq. *Cultural Studies & Critical Methodologies, 7*(2), 132–144.

Kincheloe, J. (2005). *Critical constructivism primer.* New York, NY: Peter Lang.

Kincheloe, J., & McLaren, P. (2002). Rethinking critical theory and qualitative research. In Y. Zou & E. T. Trueba (Eds.), *Ethnography and schools: Qualitative approaches to the study of education* (pp. 87–138). Lanham, MD: Rowman & Littlefield.

Lakoff, G. (2004). *Don't think of an elephant: Know your values and frame the debate.* White River Junction, VT: Chelsea Green.

Lazar, A., & Lazar, M. (2004). The discourse of the new world order: "Out-casting" the double face of threat. *Discourse & Society, 15*(2–3), 223–242.

Létourneau, J. (2004). *A history for the future: Rewriting memory and identity in Quebec.* Montreal, QC, Canada: McGill-Queens University Press.

Létourneau, J. (2006). Remembering our past: An examination of the historical memory of young Québecois. In R. Sandwell (Ed.), *To the past: History education, public memory, and citizenship in Canada* (pp. 70–87). Toronto, ON, Canada: University of Toronto Press.

Leudar, I., Marsland, V., & Nekvapil, J. (2004). On membership categorization: "Us", "them" and "doing violence" in political discourse. *Discourse & Society, 15*(2–3), 243–266.

Lyotard, J. F. (1984). *The post modern condition: A report on knowledge.* Minneapolis: University of Minnesota Press.

Maxwell, J. A. (2005). *Qualitative research design: An interactive approach* (2nd ed.). Thousand Oaks, CA: Sage.

McLeod, N. (2007). *Cree narrative memory.* Saskatoon, SK, Canada: Purich.

Mishler, E.g. (1986). *Research interviewing: Context and narrative.* Cambridge, MA: Harvard University Press.

Morgan, D. L. (1997). *Focus groups as qualitative research* (2nd ed.). Thousand Oaks, CA: Sage.

Nicolopoulou, A. (2007). From actors to agents to persons: The development of character representation in young children's narratives. *Child Development, 78*(2), 412–429.

Olick, K. O. (2008). Collective memory: A memoir and prospects. *Memory Studies, 1*(1), 23–29.

Paul, D. N. (2006). *We were not the savages: Collision between European and native American civilizations* (2nd ed.). Halifax, NS: Fernwood.

Penuel, W. R., & Wertsch, J. V. (1998). Historical representation as mediated action: Official history as a tool. *International Review of History Education, 2,* 23–39.

Polkinghorne, D. E. (1995). Narrative configuration in qualitative analysis. In J. A. Hatch & R. Wisniewski (Eds.), *Life history and narrative* (pp. 5–24). Washington, DC: Falmer.

Poole, R. (2008). Memory, history and the claims of the past. *Memory Studies, 1*(2), 149–166.

Prier, D., & Beachum, F. (2008). Conceptualizing a critical discourse around hip-hop culture and Black male youth in educational scholarship and research. *International Journal of Qualitative Studies in Education, 21*(5), 519–535.

Radstone, S. (2008). Memory studies: For and against. *Memory Studies, 1*(1), 31–39.

Reese, E., & Fivush, R. (2008). The development of collective remembering. *Memory, 16*(3), 201–212.

Riessman, C. (1993). *Narrative analysis* (1st ed.). Newbury Park, CA: Sage.

Rodriguez-Jiménez, A., & Gifford, S. M. (2010). Finding voices: Learning and insights from a participatory media project with recently arrived Afghan young men with refugee backgrounds. *Youth Studies Australia, 29*(2), 33–41.

Roman, L. G., & Stanley, T. (1997). Empires, émigrés and aliens: Young people's negotiations of official and popular racism in Canada. In L. G. Roman & L. Eyre (Eds.), *Dangerous territories* (pp. 205–231). New York, NY: Routledge.

Ross, M. H. (2001). The political psychology of competing narratives: September 11 and beyond. *Social Science Research Council.* Retrieved from http://www. Ssrc.org/sep11/essay/ross.htm

Said, E. (1985). *Covering Islam.* New York, NY: Pantheon Books.

Saltzburg, S., & Davis, T. S. (2010). Co-authoring gender-queer youth identities: Discursive telling and retelling. *Journal of Ethnic and Cultural Diversity in Social Work, 19*(2), 87–108.

Scott, J. W. (1991). The evidence of experience. *Critical Inquiry, 17,* 773–797.

Shultz, K., Buck, P., & Niesz, T. (2006). Authoring "race": Writing truth and fiction after school. *The Urban Review, 37,* 469–489.

Stanley, T. (2006). Whose public? Whose memory? Racisms, grand narratives and Canadian history. In R. Sandwell (Ed.), *To the past: History education, public memory, and citizenship in Canada* (pp. 32–49). Toronto, ON, Canada: University of Toronto Press.

Stubbs, M. (1996). *Text and corpus analysis: Computer-assisted studies of language and culture.* Oxford, England: Blackwell.

Stueber, K. R. (2008). Reasons, generalizations, empathy and narratives: The epistemic structure of action explanation. *History and Theory, 47*(1), 31–43.

Sutton, J. (2008). Between individual and collective memory: Coordination, interaction, distribution. *Social Research, 75*(1), 23–48.

Tolonen, T. (2009). Success, coping and social exclusion in transition of young Finns. *Journal of Youth Studies, 11*(2), 233–249.

Van Dijk, T. A. (1988). *News analysis: Case studies of international and national news in the press.* Hillsdale, NJ: Lawrence Erlbaum.

Van Dijk, T. A. (1991). *Racism and the press.* London, England: Routledge.

Van Dijk, T. A. (1993). *Elite discourse and racism.* London, England: Sage.

Van Dijk, T. A. (1995). Discourse analysis as ideology analysis. In C. Schaffner & A. L. Wenden (Eds.), *Language and peace* (pp. 17–33). Aldershot, England: Dartmouth.

Van Dijk, T. A. (1996). Discourse, opinions and ideologies. In C. Schaffner & H. Kelly-Holmes (Eds.), *Discourse and ideologies* (pp. 7–37). Clevedon, England: Multilingual Matters.

Van Dijk, T. A. (1998). Principles of critical discourse analysis. *Discourse and Society, 4*(2), 249–283.

Van Dijk, T. A. (2005). War rhetoric of a little ally: Political implications and Aznar's legitimatization of the war in Iraq. *Journal of Language and Politics, 4*(1), 65–91.

Van Dijk, T. A. (2006). Discourse and manipulation. *Discourse & Society, 17*(2), 359–383.

Volkmer, I. (2008). Conflict-related media events and cultures of proximity. *Media, War & Conflict, 1*(1), 90–98.

Vygotsky, L. S. (1978). *Mind in society: The development of higher psychological processes.* Cambridge, MA: Harvard University Press.

Weis, L., & Fine, M. (Eds.). (2000). *Construction sites: Excavating race, class, and gender among urban youth.* New York, NY: Teachers College Press.

Weiss, R. S. (1994). *Learning from strangers: The art and method of qualitative interviewing.* New York, NY: Free Press.

Wertsch, J. V. (2002). *Voices of collective remembering.* Cambridge, England: Cambridge University Press.

Wertsch, J. V. (2008). Collective memory and narrative templates. *Social Research, 75*(1), 133–156.

Wertsch, J. V., & O'Connor, K. (1994). Multi-voicedness in historical representation: American college students' accounts of the origins of the United States. *Journal of Narrative and Life History, 4*(4), 295–309.

Willis, J. W. (2007). *Foundations of qualitative research: Interpretive and critical approaches.* Thousand Oaks, CA: Sage.

Wodak, R. (2000, April). *Discourses of exclusion: A European comparative study.* Speech at the opening of the EU Observatorium, Hofburg, Vienna. Retrieved from http://www.tuwien.ac.at/diskurs/stellungnahmen/Wodak5.html

CHAPTER THIRTY-NINE

Exploring Possibilities for Critical Relational De/Colonising Methodologies in Early Childhood Education Contexts in Aotearoa

Jenny Ritchie and Cheryl Rau

The context for our work is that of early childhood education settings and pedagogies in Aotearoa (New Zealand). Despite enduring and managing the impacts of a colonisation process, during which the teaching and learning of Māori language and culture was discouraged, the indigenous Māori have strongly maintained that the government uphold the undertakings, for many years disregarded, of the 1840 Tiriti o Waitangi (Orange, 1987; Walker, 2004). This treaty enabled British governance in exchange for protection of Māori tino rangatiratanga (self-determination), whenua (lands) and taonga katoa (all things valued by Māori, including their language). In 1996 the early childhood sector in Aotearoa gained the first bicultural, bilingual education curriculum in this country, *Te Whāriki* (Ministry of Education, 1996). The bicultural nature of this document recognises the "first nation" status of the indigenous peoples, the Māori, as original inhabitants of these islands, and requires early childhood education settings to inclusively honour the Māori language and traditions, alongside that of the western dominant culture. Despite institutional-level commitments to honouring these "bicultural" expectations requiring delivery of the Māori language and cultural practices within early childhood settings, the predominately Pākehā (of European descent) educator workforce was not necessarily well equipped to do so (Ritchie, 2000, 2003).

Our research has been conducted in partnership with early childhood educators in childcare and kindergarten settings. Our first two research projects (Ritchie & Rau, 2006, 2008) focussed on identifying strategies for what we have come to term "Tiriti-based" pedagogies in early childhood. Tiriti-based early childhood care and education practices are grounded in a commitment to honouring taonga Māori (everything of value to Māori), and to ensuring that Māori retain their tino rangatiratanga (self-determination) in defining the nature and means for including these taonga within the early childhood education programme. Over the course of these studies we have come to a perspective that the ahua (ways of being), the spiritual presence and connectedness of educators, was more important than prescriptive kinds of teaching of language and cultural practices (Ritchie, 2010b). Māori and Pākehā (non-

Māori) teachers who chose to participate as co-researchers in our studies demonstrated commitment to the enactment of daily rituals that reflected tikanga Māori. This valuing of Māori knowledges and beliefs was evident, enabling Māori children and families to feel welcome, included and culturally safe (Ritchie & Rau, 2006). Interestingly, this sense of well-being and spiritual safety appeared to be shared by families of all ethnicities present in these early childhood centres (Ritchie & Rau, 2008). In our most recent study the focus on Māori understandings was applied more specifically within a kaupapa (focus) of caring for ourselves, others, and the environment (Duhn, Bachmann, & Harris, 2010; Ritchie, 2010a; Ritchie, Duhn, Rau, & Craw, 2010).

Ours is a hybrid methodology (Kaomea, 2004) which has evolved over the past six years of the three consecutive two-year studies (Rau & Ritchie, 2005). As Māori and Pākehā research co-director partners, we bring a shared commitment to incorporating Māori values and processes as foundational, whilst simultaneously integrating aspects of western narrative and ethnographic methodologies. Through our ongoing reflexive dialogue, we model a critical relationality respectful of the different positionings we hold in regard to historical, ancestral legacies (à Beckett & Proud, 2004). We begin this chapter by offering an explanation of kaupapa Māori elements that have underpinned the methodological processes within our projects, for which we have been fortunate to have received funding from the New Zealand Ministry of Education's Teaching and Learning Research Initiative (TLRI; Ritchie, et al., 2010; Ritchie & Rau, 2006, 2008). We then proceed to illustrate some ways in which our methodologies were enacted.

For Māori and many other peoples, storying is a traditional means of transferring knowledge across generations (King, 2005; Metge, 2010), and its value is now being recognised in its application as a tool in kaupapa Māori research methodologies (Lee, 2005). Our methodology has also been informed by western narrative approaches (Clandinin, 2007). All these applications recognise the inherent nature of storying as a means to understand and make sense of people's experiences. They operate in accordance with kaupapa Māori notions of relationality and collectivity, since "narrative inquiry is the study of people in relation studying the experience of people in relation" (Clandinin, Murphy, Huber, & Orr, 2010, p. 82). We further consider that our research methodologies have enabled the emergence of counterstories (Kaomea, 2009), which work as counter-colonial narratives (Ritchie & Rau, 2010), providing alternative readings that open spaces privileging of the voices of tamariki and whānau Māori (Māori children and families), and valuing of Māori ways of being, knowing and doing.

Critical Kaupapa Māori Underpinnings

Critical Māori research contexts require cognisance of both what is tika (right[1]) as well as of tikanga (ways of doing). Māori research protocols of kairangahau (researcher) enactment within a te ao Māori (Māori worldview) paradigm have been articulated by Linda Tuhiwai Mead/Smith (Mead, 1996; Smith, 1999, 2005). Respect is intrinsic to this paradigm. Although considered a "universal" principle of research ethics, the understandings pertaining to its enactment across different cultures is expressed through different meanings, rituals and social applications (Smith, 2005). Linda Smith has pointed out:

> From indigenous perspectives ethical codes of conduct serve partly the same purpose as the protocols which govern our relationships with each other and with the environment. The term "respect" is consistently used by indigenous peoples to underscore the significance of our relationships and humanity. Through respect the place of everyone and everything in the universe is kept in balance and harmony. Respect is a reciprocal, shared, constantly interchanging principle which is expressed through all aspects of social conduct. (Smith, 1999, p. 120)

In te ao Māori (the Māori world) respect is not only fundamental to the establishment and maintenance of relationships, but also integral to upholding the mana (maintaining the integrity) of both participants and researcher. Researchers need to work to sustain relationships and credibility through personal contact, making themselves and their purposes known, as in the expression "Kanohi kitea" (the seen face, that is present yourself to people face to face). Respect underlies further sayings, such as "Aroha ki te tangata" (respect for people) and "Kaua e takahia te mana o te tangata" (do not trample over the mana of people). Care, sensitivity and restraint are highlighted in "Titiro, whakarongo... kōrero" (look, listen...speak) and "Kia tūpato" (be cautious). An ethic of respect, in a Māori view, involves generosity and reciprocity, as expressed in "Manaaki ki te tangata" (share and host people, be generous) whilst valuing a disposition of humility, as in the exhortation "Kaua e mahaki" (don't flaunt your knowledge; Smith, 1999, p. 120).

"Aroha ki te tangata" (respect for people) is an integral principle of kaupapa Māori methodology, requiring kairangahau (researchers) to uphold the mana (prestige) of those involved and to adhere to tikanga (culturally correct values and practices). Integral to this paradigm is the capability and intention of the researchers to facilitate a research approach that will enrich, expand and shift collective understandings. To respect is to be open to new possibilities and to appreciate individuals and whānau as unique beings. The recent TLRI projects which we have led have been collaborative research journeys undertaken with educator co-researchers, these relationships involving mutual respect and trust evolving over time. "Aroha ki te tangata" prioritises relationships, deepening connectedness across place, space and time.

"Kanohi kitea" (the seen face), requires researcher presence, engagement which is "physically, ethically, morally and spiritually" tangible (Bishop, 1996, p. 216). It is a metaphorical concept involving kōrero (talking), debate and airing of issues within reciprocal relationships of mutual interest. Hui (gatherings) enable enactment of a respectful, considerate, patient and co-operative kaupapa (philosophy). With regard to research methodologies, Bishop (1996, 2005) considers hui to offer a process of collaborative meaning construction. Hui offer an inclusive approach whereby both researcher and participant are recognised as partners, providing the foundation for kanohi ki te kanohi (face-to-face) discussion within a whakawhanaungatanga (relationship building) context, giving expression to the voices of the research "whānau of interest" (Bishop, 2005, p. 121).

The guidance imparted in the saying, 'Titiro, whakarongo...kōrero' (look, listen...speak) reflects Māori ways of knowing, doing and being, in which whakamā (shyness), rangimārie (peacefulness), hūmārie (geniality) and silence are respected communication modes. The pause time allows not only for reflection, but for connection, empathy, intuition and wisdom to inform the eventual reply. Lisa Delpit has written evocatively of the struggle to attain a disposition of respectful openness toward the other:

> We do not really see through our eyes or hear through our ears, but through our beliefs. To put our beliefs on hold is to cease to exist as ourselves for a moment—and that is not easy. It is painful as well, because it means turning yourself inside out, giving up your own sense of who you are, and being willing to see yourself in the unflattering light of another's angry gaze. It is not easy, but it is the only way to learn what it might feel like to be someone else and the only way to start the dialogue. (Delpit, 1988, p. 297)

Māori belief systems are embedded in te reo Māori (the Māori language) and our communication codes, in which recognition of wairua (spirituality) is fundamental, and the whakatau of wairua (setting in place a sense of spiritual safety) is critical in rituals of encounter. Kaumātua (elders) are integral to Māori research, their kaitiakitanga (stewardship) invaluable. A kuia (female elder) and koroua (male elder) have supported our projects, raising our awareness of issues surrounding kupu Māori (Māori words) and hapū/iwi (sub-tribal and tribal) specificities, highlighting that one cannot homogenise or essentialise te ao Māori constructs.

Mason Durie (2002) has described how tikanga Māori reinforces our spiritual interconnectedness. Karakia (spiritual incantation), writes Durie, lifts the attention of listeners from mundane and terrestrial levels into higher spiritual planes, connecting people with the heavens, the winds, the stars, those long since departed deities, and the forces of nature. The effect is to elevate everyday mental preoccupations to a higher state of awareness, thereby promoting improved understanding based on higher levels of contextualization. By connecting planes of thinking and symbolism there is a psychological energy flow away from the centre, outwards to broader conceptual domains, a centrifugal force away from micro dimensions (an individual, a single issue) to macro levels (groups, broad encounters, spiritual influences). (M. Durie, 2002, p. 22)

The obligation of "Manaaki ki te tangata" (share and host people, be generous) is based on reciprocity. Manaaki is derived from the kupu (word) mana (power and prestige), a concept focused around nurturing and upholding the well-being of others. Associated qualities are aroha (love), hospitality, kindness, respect and a responsibility to uphold whakapapa (kinship and genealogical) obligations. Arohia Durie explains that a te ao Māori (Māori worldview) traditional paradigm prioritises the principle of "manaakitanga" (hospitality, generosity), with an emphasis on individuals being responsible to the collaborative upholding of mana for the benefit of all (A. Durie, 1997). The way in which we offer manaaki (or the absence of manaaki) can directly reflect upon whānau, hapū and iwi. Māori may feel uncomfortable if the quality of manaakitanga is perceived to be inadequate.

"Kia tūpato" (be cautious) is a reminder to researchers to be mindful of whakapapa (kinship and genealogy), whenua (land), tikanga (values) and kōrero (speech) when engaging in rangahau (research). If protocols are intact, mana tangata (people's prestige, authority and power) upheld, and respect for mana whenua (people of that land) enacted, then all should bode well for the research project. Adherence to the guideline, "Kaua e takahia te mana o te tangata" (do not trample over the mana of people) is imperative. Research rituals of engagement and collaboration must maintain protocols of respectful behaviour towards tangata (people). "Kaua e mahaki" (don't flaunt your knowledge) reminds kairangahau (researchers) that it is inappropriate to be whakahihi (arrogant). In a Māori world your individual capacity will be voiced by others, not yourself.

The methodological kaupapa (philosophy) underpinning the three TLRI projects, Whakawhanaungatanga (2004–5), Te Puawaitanga (2006–7) and Titiro Whakamua—Haere Whakamuri (2008–9) focused actively on working towards transformative shifts at the multiple levels of the tamaiti (child), whānau (extended family), early childhood centre, early childhood community, hapū, iwi and educator co-researchers. Research collaborations brought diversity of experiences and expressions of methodologies as shared in the following sections.

Upholding the Mana across Intersecting Sets of Relationships

The studies involved complex matrices of several layers of different sets of relationships, the intersections of these, and negotiations between and within these. As the research co-directors for each study,[2] we recruited a range of educator co-researchers, who in turn were charged with the key responsibility of working with the tamariki and whānau to gather data for the project(s). We were also supported in our studies by kaumātua, who attended the collective hui at the beginning and end of the studies, and were available for consultation and to support the educator co-researchers during the studies.

All these relationships require mindful attentiveness, openness, responsiveness, trust in order to uphold the mana of both individuals (researchers and tamariki/whānau participants) as well as the collective mana of the research project as a whole. Many of the co-researchers were teachers with whom we had already established relationships through previous associations. We were very aware that teachers are very busy, and are therefore necessarily careful about considering whether to become involved in research projects. The following quote is from Riana, a Māori kindergarten head teacher, in response to Cheryl's inquiry as to why she had been willing to participate in the Whakawhanaungatanga study:

I don't often become involved in research projects. I'm very particular about who I choose to research with and for. I've really got to believe in the kaupapa (philosophy) of the research and know that the input that I can have, coming from our centre is going to be put to really good use. I'm not just in there as the token Māori—quite often that's why we get offered to go into research projects...Probably one reason is because you and Jenny are both doing it. I think one of the other reasons is that I really believe in the kaupapa and I see huge gaps in terms of how our Māori tamariki and their whānau [are supported], but I have concerns about how *Te Whāriki* is actually delivered for the tamariki and for those whānau. [Riana, Whakawhanaungatanga]

Each of our studies began with an initial collective day-long hui for educators from all participating early childhood centres (around 10 in each study), during which research questions, methodological processes and ethical considerations were outlined and discussed. Educator co-researchers then proceeded to design and implement their own version of methodology for application within their own centre context, with support from the co-directors. As data gathering proceeded, a significant component of our methodology were regular "kanohi ki te kanohi" hui with co-directors. These opportunities for critical reflective feedback and dialogical discourse were viewed by Hawera Kindergarten teachers Judith and Joy as "kōrero which helped affirm. There was clarity there. The discussion highlighted what was relevant. I thought 'Wow! What's underneath is great!'" Collaborative hui were opportunities for kairangahau to peel back the layers and deepen lucidity.

For all the teachers who have worked with us over the three studies (Ritchie et al., 2010; Ritchie & Rau, 2006, 2008), their willingness to give of their precious time and energy was grounded in their personal philosophical commitment to the research kaupapa. It became evident over time that these educator co-researchers held a disposition of openness towards their engagement in a research process that inevitably involved a more intense degree of reflection on their work and their lives, evoking potentially discomforting realisations in negotiating the arising tensionality (Clandinin et al., 2010), and the concomitant impetus for change. It takes a certain courage to resist the inertia that can restrain our receptiveness to possibilities that may exist beyond our current habitual comfort zone, to engage in a lived process of becoming (Clandinin et al., 2006).

Educators were also mindful of the additional workload that their involvement as co-researchers would mean, sometimes requiring some gentle persuasion of colleagues by the team leader. At the final hui of the Puawaitanga study, Marion, a kindergarten head teacher, was frank about her leadership in a process for critique for her and her colleagues:

I have to say that I've probably "coerced" my team members into being part of this process and so like all of us we stepped onto the waka (canoe) at different points. And so as the team leader I felt responsible for ensuring that the team were comfortable in an area where perhaps they were a little bit uncomfortable. So the process has been a really gentle one and yet I'm, as the team leader, feeling really delighted in the team's progress and their acceptance and now their understanding, or their new insight as to what their practice looks like and why they do things a certain way. And why in the past we've talked about being a bicultural society and that we as teachers have a fundamental responsibility to delivering that understanding to our children and our families, but actually, how do we do that? And actually, who are we? And how do we fit in that? And if your background has been only Pākehā, middle-class Pākehā, then how does that all kind of mesh? [Marion, Te Puwaitanga]

There was evidence of a transformative process occurring in many of the early childhood centres as educators spent time in collaborative dialogue around their research data, which resulted in a strengthening of shared understandings. The Hawera Kindergarten team had reflected on their experiences of "becoming researchers". They reported that they had initially wondered: "Can we do this? We asked ourselves questions such as 'Would this mahi required of us as participants "fit" within an already busy work programme?', 'Did we have anything to contribute?', 'Are we "researchers"?'" They realised that "the opportunity to 'face ourselves in the mirror' had to be taken. We deserved to be reaffirmed about what we did well and to avail ourselves of experiences and people that would give us the 'positives' about aspects in our programme that had room for change and /or improvement." As the research journey progressed, they considered that their involvement had led to them "finding out more about ourselves, the impact of our practices and programme, on children and whānau." Joy, one of the Hawera teachers, considered that the team's collaboration during the course of the study had brought them closer together: "We feel like a unit rather than three individual people working on a project." At the end of the Puawaitanga study, the teachers from this kindergarten wrote that

> using narrative methodologies has absolutely enhanced our reflective understandings as we have travelled this special journey. Capturing the tamaiti (child) and whānau (family) "voice" is a challenge but so beautiful when we do! Sometimes we were so engrossed in conversations and in the experience that we "forgot" to record and document! As a team we would revisit these moments but even so they then became narratives of our "voice". Gathering data to actually capture the child's voice on the spot was difficult. We mostly discussed things with each other and used [a] voice recorder. Capturing the amazing journey we made as a team—our own understandings, experiences and expectations—will not be forgotten. We can only hope that we will always be able to practice and pursue the things we have come to treasure and value. (Hawera Kindergarten, Te Puawaitanga)

Tino Rangatiratanga: Self-determining Pathways

A valuing of evolved, deepened, respectful relationships with early childhood educators from diverse services grounded the research in a place of mutual trust and respect. Fluidic spaces of openness allowed kairangahau (co-researchers) to unravel methodological specificities. Tino rangatiratanga (self-determination, leadership) was integral to the research, kairangahau reviewing their contexts and determining their own approaches within the overall research kaupapa. Journeys which began with individuals connecting through collective visioning were to later become inexplicably linked through intangible threads of aroha (love, positive regard) and of wairua (spirituality). Reflecting on her perception of her involvement as an educator co-researcher, Adele from Richard Hudson Kindergarten stated that "there weren't really boundaries…the data seems very different, it's from our own angle, own whānau. It's not too prescribed."

Educator co-researchers employed a range of data-gathering strategies which included interviewing, videoing, note-taking, photographs of centre activities, and of children's art and narratives, and extended narratives of children's experiences. As co-directors travelled around the various centres, examples of work from other centres was shared and discussed. Photographs were particularly poignant as data, offering powerful visual narratives evocative of specificities of dimensions of place and representations of space. Photographic images were often positioned by the teachers centrally within their data, thus situating them as pivotal in our relational processes of narrative enquiry. In reflecting the "intentionality, the negotiated, and the recursive nature" (Bach, 2007, p. 283) of the meanings captured in these images, they came to represent much more than their ostensible presence as mere photographs of real work in centres.

We were mindful of the power of the research process and our role as leaders in shaping and privileging the meanings that eventually came to be presented as "knowledge" (Smith, 1999). Narrative methodologies are very powerful, since real stories from real settings have great resonance. They "do more than create examples—they create realities" (Pinnegar, 2007, p. 249). From initial "narrative moments" (Lincoln & Denzin, 2003, p. 240), interim raw texts of interviews, observations, photos and reflective co-theorising conversations, narratives were constructed incorporating shared, negotiated interpretations of meanings. Our methodology employed critical conversations, which we termed "co-theorising", as a means to deepen and challenge the meaning construction processes operating across the various layers and networks of those involved in the studies. These co-theorising conversations were conducted usually kanohi ki te kanohi (face to face), but also involved emailed responses to data. In both cases the intention was to open up spaces and positionings, enabling deeper narrative understandings (Otterstad, 2007). Educator co-researchers enjoyed sharing the data gathered from other centres, feeling resonances, showing respectful appreciation of others' efforts and demonstrating a sense of collectivity. They were also inspired to hear of other educators' endeavours and interpretations, subsequently applying ideas for Tiriti-based or sustainability practices that others had instigated.

During these co-theorising hui, teachers shared their understanding of the importance of families/whānau in providing the context that would enable them to understand the children's kōrero (speech). Many insights emerged from these cross-centre theorising discussions. In one example, Carolyn from Papamoa Kindergarten had recorded a conversation with children about a visit to a marae (village meeting place):

Teacher: Have you been to a marae?

Child: I have been to a marae. White dogs.

Teacher: What happened on the marae?

Child: The cat was going to bite me.

Teacher: Who did you go to the marae with?

Child: My mum. My aunty picked us up there.

Teacher: What did you do?

Child: Playing with L. He was laughing at me. He was naughty.

In discussing what appears to be a superficial exchange, educator co-researchers appreciated the contextual knowledge required to understand children's meanings, such as the sub-text of the value to children of hanging out at their marae, where they can play with their cousins. The teachers also realised that they could seek further understandings through following up children's comments by discussing these with their families. Carolyn explained that talking with families provides context for the children's experiences: "That's where with families, when they put it into context what [the children] are saying, like the 'white dog'…That was the way to extend it because actually that's what the child experienced but they might not be able to tell you.…" In a co-theorising discussion, Judith from Hawera Kindergarten commented in regard to the context implicit in the child's response:

When children talk about the marae: "We have kai [food], we play, there were dogs", because we as Māori know what those statements mean in context. It is most likely they have shared in a pōwhiri [greeting ceremony], karakia [prayers], waiata [songs], hongi [embrace], kissed lots of aunts, uncles, cousins and celebrated with kai. They will have also played with cousins, walked around the marae. It's also the innate learning that takes place—wairua [spirituality]. It's acceptance. There's trust in the people around them and they are not told what to do, they learn by being involved. It's ways of doing. The person that growled me would be the person that gave me kai. It gives a sense of whānau within whānau. It's an extension to the collective. They see they have a place there, they work it out—who is in the front, who is in the back [metaphor for those speaking in greeting, and those preparing food in the kitchen].

Judith was able to situate the children's kōrero in the wider context of her lived experience on marae, connecting their statements to the general experiences of tikanga (values), of kawa (protocols), and of whanaungatanga (relationships) enacted through everyday marae rituals. Knowing the significance of what happens for tamariki at the marae enables Judith to read Carolyn's conversation with the children with respect for the Māori ways of knowing, being and doing. She can read the narrative behind their narration.

Aroha ki te Tangata—Relationships with Whānau

Kairangahau, educator co-researchers, were positioned at the cutting edge of the research, the interface between co-directors, tamariki (children), whānau (families), early childhood centre and community. Their responsibilities involved maintaining the spark, the mauri (life force) of the research—they were in essence ahi kaa, guardians of the kaupapa. Co-directors and kairangahau envisioned reciprocal responsibilities, kairangahau the "faces seen and faces known" in their centres.

Educator co-researchers were conscious of the extra expectations they were placing upon parents/whānau of children attending their centre, since the research projects were framed around inclusion of a range of both Māori and Pākehā, parents' and children's voices, to be gathered by the teachers. As co-directors of the studies, we were reliant on the educator co-researchers to gather this data with care and integrity. The teachers worked diligently to firstly recruit families as research participants, and then take the time to record multiple interviews and narratives from these children and parents. They approached families to request their involvement with respect and intentionality. For example, at the outset of the Te Puawaitanga study, teachers from Hawera Kindergarten worked carefully through steps of informing their centre whānau/community. The team emphasised in their newsletters and wall displays for parents/whānau that their research approach would involve "building respectful relationships"; requesting the sharing of "child profile stories" with the project, encouraging parents to contribute their own stories through "parent/whānau voice" offerings; and ongoing "listening, responding, and sharing". This team of teacher/researchers intuitively enacted an awareness that "relationship is the heart of living alongside in narrative inquiry—indeed, relationships form the nexus of this kind of inquiry space" (Pinnegar, 2007, p. 247).

One of the key insights gained from the Te Puawaitanga project was the deepened understanding and empathy generated by the teachers when they made the time to sit and talk responsively with parents and other relatives of children in their centres. Carolyn, from Papamoa Kindergarten, had felt disappointed with the results of her attempts to "interview" children during the first phase of data gathering in the Te Puawaitanga study. On reflection, Carolyn decided to interview parents and children together for her second set of data:

> I went into the second set of data gathering with a sense of frustration so this time I interviewed the children and the parents together. The conversation was so much more valuable I found, and I found out a lot of things, like one family speak a lot of Māori together in the home. We've got a lot of families that don't go to their marae because it's quite far away. I thought that was kind of sad for those families because they were more isolated, I guess. I had much more fun and got more valuable information from this set of interviews as I saw the value of context being important. The parents being with the children during interviews added a whole new dimension to questioning and understanding how children had experienced and consolidated learning (ako). It was beautiful also seeing that family sharing of experiences, parents enjoyed it too, children revisiting and for me seeing that cultural connection. [Carolyn, Te Puawaitanga]

Through these interviews, Carolyn began to uncover the "multiple story lines shaping participants' lives" (Clandinin et al., 2006, p. 25), thereby gaining new insights into the dislocations that surround Māori parents' aspirations to support their children in accessing their identities as Māori. She later reflected on her process of gathering research data through interviews:

> This indeed has been a significant learning curve as in how to obtain information by interviewing. How do you find out how children respond to the bicultural programme by interviewing and questioning them? After a few attempts...I felt that to develop clearer understandings of a child you needed to know the context in which they were talking. This was okay with interviews that were about experiences at kindergarten, but what knowledge and understanding did children bring from home or transfer between home and kindergarten? It was about seeing a child's perspective of their life. Therefore by interviewing

both child and parent it gave a richer perspective and depth of understanding of their world. Question-ing became more relevant to their experiences and knowledge. [Carolyn, Te Puawaitanga]

In her quest for data-gathering methods that would deliver even richer sources of insight, Carolyn went on to experiment with video interviewing, which proved to be a useful process of making visible the taken-for-granted contextual factors.

Our next step was using the video. Once again how to capture the essence of children's perceptions with-out running the video for the whole session? We had a wonderful [Māori] parent interview that came out of asking for permission to film her child. She said: "What about me? I have things to say!!!!" I feel that by using the narrative form in the last set was much more useful and again contextual...Revisiting the videos we took of the children, we saw once again the integration [of Māori language and under-standings] throughout the programme. Children have these experiences every day.

Lourdes Diaz Soto (2005) considers that "narrative inquiry offers a contextualized experience de-veloped as a means of understanding events and processes across linguistic, cultural, visual, historical, and social boundaries" (p. 10). Carolyn's experimentation with different data-gathering strategies al-lowed her to move from a contrived interview format to an informal video record, which visibilised contextual factors such as temporal, spatial and personal dynamics, providing a backdrop for making sense of children's and parents' narratives and motivations (Clandinin & Connelly, 2000). Carolyn later reflected that

being part of the research also helps you to continue the journey. It highlighted specific needs, particular things became more apparent and encouraged us to look for solutions that reflected a more in-depth bicultural approach. It was about hearing and seeing the child's voice and their learning. It was about kōrero with whānau and developing closer relationships so that the wheels keep turning. The narrative methodology gives context and tells the whole story. It makes you reflect on your practice as often our day is busy and full.

Re-narrativisation as Restorative Practice

Re-narrativisation can be viewed as the process of generating narratives which restore a sense of connect-edness with histories, ancestors and identities that may have been ruptured by processes of colonisation, immigration and so forth. In this way, re-narrativisation can serve as a tool for projects of de/colonisa-tion (Otterstad, 2007). Russell Bishop considers kaupapa Māori counternarratives to be a powerful tool for the transformation of mainstream education settings, offering alternative pedagogies that reflect "the cultural sense-making processes of peoples previously marginalized by the dominance of colonial and neo-colonial educational relations of power" (Bishop, 2005, p. 457). The deep, extended narratives produced for these studies offered profound insights into the lives of children and their family contexts. In Aotearoa the form of early childhood assessment advocated by our Ministry of Education comprises narrative "learning stories" (Ministry of Education, 2004). Narrative assessment has potential for illu-minating similar depths of contextual insight into children and families' understandings.

Teachers from many of the early childhood centres reported gaining enhanced understandings of Māori parents' backgrounds and the translocation that had led these families to lose contact with their marae and other tribal connections. Joy of Hawera Kindergarten related her discussion with a child's mother regarding some research narratives she had been gathering about her child. This parent, who didn't know much about her own cultural background, had conveyed to Joy her appreciation of the op-portunity for gaining a sense of connecting at a deeper level with her cultural roots and of affirmation of her identity. Another scenario of intergenerational transformation is evident within the following excerpt from a narrative from Richard Hudson Kindergarten, which reports on a Māori child, Kiyana's, growing confidence in the use of te reo Māori (Māori language).

We believe that commitment and daily practice of integrating te reo and tikanga Māori (Māori language and culture) is very visible and supports our kaupapa—through Kiyana's keen response to new kupu (Māori words) when she is excited to transfer this to home. This is the [*Te Whāriki*] principle whānau tangata—family and community (Ministry of Education, 1996) in action. It also shows the tuakana–teina (older sibling-younger sibling) strategy, where she is the competent person sharing new info with others and helping them to this competency. We also celebrate the concept ako (learning/teaching), where the role of teaching and learning is reciprocal, Kiyana is the teacher with the new kupu. This further supports the information originally sent about the interview with Kiyana's parents (Warren and Kelly, 25th May) where Warren is feeling affirmed as a generation who missed the opportunity to live and learn his native tongue, his excitement and celebration of Kiyana's new learning is welcomed and implemented into their family context. We see him as proud and willing to learn alongside his daughter, who is actively participating in reo in the kindergarten context (Richard Hudson Kindergarten, Te Puawaitanga).

This narrative positions the child as a powerful resource within her whānau. Due to the historical policies which denied Māori access to education in their own language, and actively discouraged Māori parents from speaking Māori with their children, Warren does not speak his own language. However, his daughter Kiyana's enthusiasm for te reo, supported by her teachers, has contributed to re-establishing this family's links with their heritage. Research-inspired pedagogical practices such as these demonstrate the transformative power of de/colonising methodologies which, in drawing upon "collectivist, relational ways of being and acting" (Cannella & Manuelito, 2008, p. 56), offer "healing and empowerment", restoration of dignity and "pathways of self-determination" for those who have suffered the inter-generational impacts of colonisation (Kaomea, 2004, p. 43).

De/colonising and indigenous research and pedagogical practice is operative in contexts where there exist histories layered upon layer of pain and anguish, grief and loss. For this reason these methodologies need to be cognisant of the need for healing across multiple generations (O'Loughlin, 2009). We are hopeful that our research may contribute through its offering of counter-colonial narratives of pedagogical possibilities. We are deeply grateful to all the teachers, families and children who have contributed to this work.

Notes

1. These translations are offered as a support for clarity of meaning, with the proviso that they are necessarily only approximations of the depth of meaning imparted in te reo Māori (Māori language) expression. This privileging of the Māori terms recognises the particularity of their meanings as grounded in Māori epistemologies, and that these are not directly translatable into a single word in English.
2. In the third study, we were privileged to be able to share the co-direction with Janita Craw and Iris Duhn (Ritchie et al., 2010).

References

À Beckett, C., & Proud, D. (2004). Fall from grace? Reflecting on early childhood education while decolonizing intercultural friendships from kindergarten to university and prison. In K. Mutua & B. B. Swadener (Eds.), *Decolonizing research in cross-cultural contexts. Critical personal narratives* (pp. 147–158). Albany: State University of New York Press.

Bach, H. (2007). Composing a visual narrative inquiry. In D. J. Clandinin (Ed.), *Handbook of narrative inquiry: Mapping a methodology* (pp. 280–307). Thousand Oaks, CA: Sage.

Bishop, R. (1996). *Collaborative research stories: Whakawhanaungatanga*. Palmerston North, New Zealand: Dunmore.

Bishop, R. (2005). Freeing ourselves from neocolonial domination in research: A Kaupapa Māori approach to creating knowledge. In N. K. Denzin & Y. S. Lincoln (Eds.), *The Sage handbook of qualitative research* (3rd ed., pp. 109–164). Thousand Oaks, CA: Sage.

Bishop, R. (2008). Te Kotahitanga: Kaupapa Māori in mainstream classrooms. In N. K. Denzin, Y. S. Lincoln, & L. T. Smith (Eds.), *Handbook of critical and indigenous methodologies* (pp. 439–458). Los Angeles, CA: Sage.

Cannella, G. S., & Manuelito, K. D. (2008). Feminisms from unthought locations: Indigenous worldviews, marginalized feminisms, and revisioning an anticolonial social science. In N. K. Denzin, Y. S. Lincoln, & L. T. Smith (Eds.), *Handbook of critical and indigenous methodologies* (pp. 45–59). Los Angeles, CA: Sage.

Clandinin, D. J. (Ed.). (2007). *Handbook of narrative inquiry*. Thousand Oaks, CA: Sage.

Clandinin, D. J., & Connelly, F. M. (2000). *Narrative inquiry: Experience and story in qualitative research*. San Francisco, CA: Jossey-Bass.

Clandinin, D. J., Huber, J., Huber, M., Murphy, M. S., Orr, A. M., Pearce, M., et al. (2006). *Composing diverse identities: Narrative inquiries into the interwoven lives of children and teachers*. London, England: Routledge.

Clandinin, D. J., Murphy, M. S., Huber, J., & Orr, A. M. (2010). Negotiating narrative inquiries: Living in a tension-filled midst. *The Journal of Educational Research, 103,* 81–90.

Delpit, L. (1988). The silenced dialogue: Power and pedagogy in educating other people's children. *Harvard Educational Review, 58*(3), 280–298.

Duhn, I., Bachmann, M., & Harris, K. (2010). Becoming ecologically sustainable in early childhood education. *Early Childhood Folio, 14*(1), 2–7.

Durie, A. (1997). Te Aka Matua: Keeping a Māori identity. In P. Te Whāiti, M. McCarthy, & A. Durie (Eds.), *Mai i Rangiātea: Māori wellbeing and development* (pp. 142–162). Auckland, New Zealand: Auckland University Press with Bridget Williams Books.

Durie, M. (2002, November). *Is there a distinctive Maori psychology?* Paper presented at the National Maori Graduates of Psychology Symposium, Hamilton, New Zealand.

Kaomea, J. (2004). Dilemmas of an indigenous academic: A native Hawaiian story. In K. Mutua & B. B. Swadener (Eds.), *Decolonizing research in cross-cultural contexts: Critical personal narratives* (pp. 27–44). Albany: State University of New York Press.

Kaomea, J. (2009). Indigenous education for all? A metaphorical counterstory. *International Critical Childhood Policy Studies, 2*(1), 109–121.

King, T. (2005). *The truth about stories: A native narrative*. Minneapolis: University of Minnesota Press.

Lee, J. (2005, June). Māori cultural regeneration: Pūrākau as pedagogy. In *Indigenous (Māori). pedagogies: Towards community and cultural regeneration*. Symposium conducted at the Centre for Research in Lifelong Learning International Conference, Stirling Scotland.

Lincoln, Y. S., & Denzin, N. K. (Eds.). (2003). *Turning points in qualitative research. Tying knots in a handkerchief*. Walnut Creek, CA: Altamira.

Mead, L. T. T. R. (1996). *Ngā aho o te kākahu mātauranga: The multiple layers of struggle by Maori in education* (Unpublished D.Phil thesis). University of Auckland, Auckland, New Zealand.

Metge, J. (2010). Kōrero pūrākau: Time and the art of Māori storytelling. In *Tuamaka: The challenge of difference in Aotearoa New Zealand* (pp. 29–40). Auckland, New Zealand: Auckland University Press.

Ministry of Education. (1996). *Te Whāriki. He whāriki mātauranga mō ngā mokopuna o Aotearoa: Early childhood curriculum*. Wellington, New Zealand: Learning Media.

Ministry of Education. (2004). *Kei Tua o te Pae. Assessment for learning: Early Childhood Exemplars*. Wellington, New Zealand: Learning Media.

O'Loughlin, M. (2009). *The subject of childhood*. New York, NY: Peter Lang.

Orange, C. (1987). *The Treaty of Waitangi*. Wellington, New Zealand: Allen and Unwin/Port Nicholson Press.

Otterstad, A. M. (2007). Doing and unpacking de/colonising methodologies: Who is at risk? *Contemporary Issues in Early Childhood, 8*(2), 170–174.

Pinnegar, S. (2007). Starting with living stories. In D. J. Clandinin (Ed.), *Handbook of qualitative inquiry* (pp. 247–250). Thousand Oaks, CA: Sage.

Rau, C., & Ritchie, J. (2005). From the margins to the centre: Repositioning Māori at the centre of early childhood education in Aotearoa/New Zealand. *International Journal of Equity and Innovation in Early Childhood, 3*(1), 50–60.

Ritchie, J. (2000). Critical questions: Implementing a bicultural commitment in early childhood teacher education. *Australian Journal of Research in Early Childhood, 7*(1), 66–77.

Ritchie, J. (2003, January). *Whakawhanaungatanga: Dilemmas for mainstream New Zealand early childhood education of a commitment to bicultural pedagogy*. Paper presented at the 11th Reconceptualizing Early Childhood Conference, Tempe, Arizona. Retrieved from http://www.reconece.org/proceedings/ritchie_az2003.pdf

Ritchie, J. (2010a). Fostering communities. Ecological sustainability within early childhood education. *Early Education, 47* (Winter), 10–14.

Ritchie, J. (2010b). Mā wai he kapu tī?: Being, knowing, and doing *otherwise* in early childhood education in Aotearoa. In M. O'Loughlin & R. T. Johnson (Eds.), *Imagining children otherwise. Theoretical and critical perspectives on childhood subjectivity* (pp. 29–47). New York, NY: Peter Lang.

Ritchie, J., Duhn, I., Rau, C., & Craw, J. (2010). *Titiro Whakamuri, Hoki Whakamua: We are the future, the present and the past: caring for self, others and the environment in early years' teaching and learning; Final report for the Teaching and Learning Research Initiative*. Wellington: Teaching and Learning Research Initiative/New Zealand Centre for Educational Research.

Ritchie, J., & Rau, C. (2006). *Whakawhanaungatanga: Partnerships in bicultural development in early childhood education; Final report to the Teaching & Learning Research Initiative Project*. Wellington, New Zealand: Teaching Learning Research Institute/New Zealand Centre for Educational Research. Retrieved from http://www.tlri.org.nz/pdfs/9207_finalreport.pdf

Ritchie, J., & Rau, C. (2008). *Te Puawaitanga: Partnerships with tamariki and whānau in bicultural early childhood care and education; Final report to the Teaching Learning Research Initiative*. Wellington, New Zealand: Teaching Learning Research

Institute/New Zealand Centre for Educational Research. Retrieved from http://www.tlri.org.nz/pdfs/9238_finalreport. pdf

Ritchie, J., & Rau, C. (2010). Kia mau ki te wairuatanga: Counter-colonial narratives of early childhood education in Aotearoa. In G. S. Cannella & L. D. Soto (Eds.), *Childhoods: A handbook* (pp. 355–373). New York, NY: Peter Lang.

Smith, L. T. (1999). *Decolonizing methodologies: Research and indigenous peoples*. London, England: Zed Books.

Smith, L. T. (2005). On tricky ground: Researching the native in the age of uncertainty. In N. K. Denzin & Y. S. Lincoln (Eds.), *The Sage handbook of qualitative research* (3rd ed., pp. 85–107). Thousand Oaks, CA: Sage.

Walker, R. (2004). *Ka whawhai tonu matou: Struggle without end* (rev. ed.). Auckland, New Zealand: Penguin.

CHAPTER FORTY

Writing as Critical Literacy Engagement: Outliers and the Recursive Nature of Critical Qualitative Research

Jeff Park

This chapter considers the often recursive nature of critical qualitative research, and how the acknowledgement of social, cultural, political and power relationships in a research site often enhances the original research design and objectives. The chapter also re/conceptualizes the concept of *outliers* to reclaim their value in critical qualitative research.

Outliers

I have always believed that researchers have much to learn from the outliers in society—by exploring the edges, the margins, the borders, the verge, we have much to discover, especially at the limits of what we think we already know. Critical qualitative research provides us with a useful framework to acknowledge the value of outliers. Many traditional research models, including those in education, often ignore the outliers in order not to skew the research findings. Outliers are especially problematic in quantitative studies with their focus on numbers and statistics. The term *outlier*, common in quantitative research, is usually defined as "a score with an extreme value (very high or very low) in relation to the other scores in the distribution" (Aron & Aron, 2008, p. 38). Outliers are problematic because most statistical analyses rely on "checking for normal distribution" to find the median, or mean, a "fundamental building block for most other statistical techniques" (Aron & Aron, 2008, p. 420). Normality is one of the structural and epistemological constructs of quantitative analysis, and outliers, which are not normal, always cause problems. At times, outliers are discarded because they are considered design flaws of a study, or lead to skewness that can change 'normal distributions.'

At the very least, researchers are encouraged to explain, or 'explain away' outliers in light of the rest of the data. Yet we constantly need to remember that numbers are not meaning. Meaning is always contextual and in relationship. Because the term outlier in qualitative research is not as widely utilized, one of my purposes in this chapter is to de/construct its meaning, and to reclaim the term. In qualitative methodologies, participants, in many ways, become the data, or specifically in narrative and ethnographic methodologies evoke the data. My belief is that by focusing on outliers instead of ignoring them, researchers might find valuable and significant outcomes.

I work in a variety of research sites, mainly focusing on literacy issues, and I'm especially concerned with the act of writing. My longest research project, working with a writing group associated with a mental health organization, is one that I never intended to be a research project. Yet with this project I have learned the most about literacy, writing and especially how critical literacy can be explored through a methodology I would now label as critical qualitative research. It was through the recursive nature of critical qualitative research that I began to understand the value of outliers. The participants of the writing group are marginalized by society in a number of ways, and can be seen as social outliers. Instead of explaining them away, or minimizing their perspectives, or eliminating them from the research on writing and composition process theory, I decided to focus on them as a valuable source of new insights into the value of writing.

Research Site

Years ago, I volunteered to help set up and facilitate a writing group for mentally ill members of a local branch of the Canadian Mental Health Association (CMHA). Originally I thought I would volunteer for a few months, and then get back to focus on my 'real' work and writing projects. Eighteen years later, I'm still there—going every week to open up the building for whoever shows up that week wanting to write. And people show up every week no matter what the circumstances, no matter what the weather. I've had people appear even when it was 40 below, patiently waiting at the door, wanting to write as if their lives depended on it.

Several years later I decided to do my PhD and focus on the act of writing and writing process theory. At that time, I didn't have a clear focus or topic in mind; it took months for the apparent to become obvious. I eventually realized that the writing group was a unique site for studying the act, effects, and wonder of writing. The book *Writing at the Edge: Narrative and Writing Process Theory* (Park, 2005) came out of that experience. I interviewed several long-standing group members to create narratives that evoked their experiences of the writing group and the importance of writing in their lives. In doing so I explored a variety of qualitative research methodologies including narrative, ethnography, phenomenology, arts-based research and hermeneutics. Over the 18 years I've been involved with the group, I now realize I was involved in something bigger—a complex, interwoven world that defied easy solutions, easy answers.

The writing group is run as a drop-in activity, meaning that anyone from the mental health community can attend. Over the years, over a hundred participants have attended the sessions, all dealing with various mental illnesses. We meet once a week for an hour and a half, gathering around tables set together to form a circle. This simple physical act is extremely important to establish a pedagogical space for the participants. In that space, they are all acknowledged as individuals, and perhaps more importantly as writers whose words matter. We write on two or three topics each week, the act of writing being a dominant activity, rather than the critiquing of existing work, which is quite common at many writing groups. We write on any topic of interest to members of the group. Often I suggest topics, which can range from 'justice' to a free association on the color 'blue.' Participants are welcome to suggest topics, and in this way we deal with many of their concerns including health care, family, police, political issues and poverty. Many topics come out of our discussions and the experiences of their day-to-day lives. The process, similar to Freire's (Freire & Macedo, 1987) concept of *generative themes*, allows the writers to explore ideas that are extremely important to them.

Although this chapter focuses on research methodology, I think it is valuable to briefly discuss some of the participants and their exploration of emergent themes because of their importance in critical literacy concepts. Ken (all pseudonyms) wrote about poverty, and not being able to work his way from the oppressive weight of having nothing, to get anywhere in society. Albert wrote of racial, historical and political discrimination from the perspective of an aboriginal Cree man in a dominant white world, contained and controlled by the police, health workers, and the church and education systems. Caroline wrote of being invisible and dealing with dissociative identity disorder, trying to literally and figuratively "find herself." Warren attended the writing group for years, believing that he didn't exist. Warren had a psychotic episode involving a gun and was hospitalized for years, and in those years was severely abused, physically and mentally. When he was released from the ward, he lived as a recluse until Albert convinced him to attend the writers group, where he eventually wrote himself back into existence (Park, 2005).

We write for 15 minutes, and then read the result aloud. Their reading is always voluntary, but usually everyone wants to share. In fact, over the years, I have found that sharing of their words and ideas is one of the most central components of what occurs at the group. At the end of every session, I collect the writings and have them typed up. Every year a colleague and I compile the writing, edit the collection and self-publish a book, providing a copy for each member who attended that year. The year culminates with a book launch, with each participant reading from writing collected that year.

This simple structure of the writing group, and the process we engage in each week, is deceptive on many levels. Effectively facilitating the Writers' Group at CMHA involves understanding subjectivity and the complex relationships that result as a consequence of the process. What Kincheloe (2008) writes in regards to critical pedagogy is central to an understanding of what goes on at the CMHA Writers' Group:

> This theme of complexity is central to any critical pedagogy that works to avoid reductionism. Critical pedagogues who take complexity seriously challenge reductionistic, bipolar, true-or-false epistemologies. As critical teachers come to recognize the complexity of the lived world with its maze of uncontrollable variables, irrationality, non-linearity, and unpredictable interaction of wholes and parts, they begin to also see the interpretive dimension of reality. (p. 37)

Furthermore, understanding this complex social process is greatly facilitated by the recursive nature of critical qualitative research.

The Writing Group as Research Site

When I first considered the CMHA Writers' Group as a research site, I soon realized that the process was far more complex than I first thought. It was apparent to me from the years preceding the study that working with the Writers' Group involved creating meaningful relationships with the members, and therefore, subjectivity was brought to the forefront. The participants were not objectified, or 'studied' in a linear, positivist manner, and in doing so, trust became a central and significant factor. It is possible that we achieved this trust by focusing on the writing itself. For instance, when we wrote as a group I participated; when we read our work aloud, again, I participated. The group saw me as another member of the group. I will elaborate on the power and authority issues in a later section, but for now, it is important to see how we created a pedagogical space of trust through the simple act of participating in the act of writing together.

When I first began working with the Writers' Group, I alternated between being unemployed and teaching one or two first-year university English classes as a sessional lecturer, making very little money. It is possible that the members identified with me because of my economic situation, although it is probably more likely that they identified with me because I took them and their writing seriously. I remember once complaining about getting a speeding ticket. Albert looked up from his writing and said to me, "You're lucky." I looked at him with a surprised look. "How am I lucky?" I asked. "The ticket was over 100 dollars." Albert smiled. "At least you have a car that can go that fast." Eighteen years later, the writers still like to tease and make fun of me. I think that humor is one reason trust was established early on. It might also be because of the only real rules I have at Writers' Group—the writers can write about what they want, and they have to have fun.

Issues of Power and Authority

One needs to acknowledge the issue of power and authority in the group, with all its contradictions and complexities. The participants are largely marginalized and often excluded from the mainstream public—vocationally, economically, politically and socially. Many live in group homes with very little money or access to public forums. They are social outliers, often isolated from the rest of the population. At the Writers' Group they have voice.

As the facilitator, I am responsible for the creation of a safe pedagogical space, especially because of the vulnerability of some of the participants. In addition, the act of writing creates the space of a working writing community. Within that space the participants create very personal and expressive pieces often based on their own life experiences, as well as highly opinionated political, cultural and social commentaries. I do not limit their content or thematic foci, yet I always do my best to maintain a pedagogical space that is a safe container of respect for others and their writing.

Running the Writers' Group is often paradoxical, in that I'm both in control and not in control. I write and actively participate as an equal member, and hold the same responsibilities as the other members. I operate from a non-authoritarian position of power, encouraging all the writers to openly express their ideas and feelings. In this sense, I operate from a level of power that is perceived as being equal to the other writers. All participants are honored and respected as equals, and all have the right to voice their ideas. Yet at the same time I hold a non-judgmental, yet authoritative power that protects all members. I have the responsibility to create a sense of trust and confidence within the membership so that group members eventually protect themselves and each other within that space. In this sense, the pedagogical space contains trust and becomes a community to share ideas and thoughts, and to encourage without the threat of dominance. Constant vigilance is required, and I often use danger points constructively as teaching moments, rather than deny or avoid them. In this space, I am required to engage fully and listen deeply to others, while encouraging reciprocity at all times. It is always a balancing act, but in acknowledging issues of power and authority openly the group participants feel safe, and a pedagogical space of trust is created in the negotiation of the relationships.

Interview Process

Integrating issues of subjectivity, relationships and trust became central to the study. For instance, even something as 'simple' as the interview process didn't follow any of the singular qualitative methodologies for several reasons. I originally modeled the interview methodology on the work of Seidman (1998), who uses in-depth interviews from a phenomenological approach, trying to reach an understanding of the interviewee's point of view. The interviews were designed in a three-part framework. Each part of the interviewing process was approximately 90 minutes in length, though the time was always negotiable with the participants. The first interview tried to ground the context of the participant and create a miniature life story. The second interview looked at the experience of the Writers' Group, while the third interview focused on how the participant made sense of the act of writing, as well as the experience of belonging to a writing group. At all times I encouraged the participants to engage in an open discussion of why they found writing important in their lives, and to explore the social aspect of the Writers' Group. According to Seidman, people's experience and behavior become "meaningful and understandable when placed in the contexts of their lives and the lives or those around them" (1998, p. 11).

I found Seidman's interview structure valuable, although I had some concerns with his approach. In his interpretation of phenomenology, he assumes that it is possible to understand the "lived experience" of another being through observation, clear interview techniques and data analysis. Another assumption is that the respondent is constant over time and space. From my previous experience with the Writers' Group, I began to have doubts about Seidman's approach. In fact, I noticed that the participants were often far from being constant, especially those in extreme cycles in their mental health. Consequently, I have come to believe in the merit of the work of Holstein and Gubrium (1995, 1997) who focus on "active interviewing" that "brings meaning and its construction to the foreground" (Holstein & Gubrium, 1995, p. 73). Their work anticipates, in many ways, the complexity of voice in a research inquiry. They note that "the subject behind the respondent may change virtually from comment to comment" (1995, p. 74). Their work with active interviewing suggests that neither the subject nor the phenomenon is completely fixed. It might therefore be impossible to measure, or even to understand, a phenomenon or subject completely. Perhaps the best a researcher can accomplish is to create an agreed-upon meaning, acknowledging the subjectivity of a researcher, and the shifting subject behind a respondent, while looking at a phenomenon that also may change as it is being studied. This thought may best be referred to as the acknowledgment in the social sciences of Heisenberg's Uncertainty Principle. In this perspective, the research inquiry becomes a shifting dance of a phenomenon, participants and a researcher.

Using a combination of Seidman's phenomenological in-depth interviews, tempered with Holstein and Gubrium's active interviews, I gained a deep understanding of what writing and the writing group experience meant to the participants in my study. I recorded all the interviews and transcribed them. The participants read the transcripts to verify literal accuracy and contributed input into the final shape of their interviews. After consulting with the individuals involved, I retyped the clarified and corrected transcripts. The participants accepted the transcripts with few exceptions. When they did have concerns, their insights were perceptive and valuable. I began to work more and more with the participants in the creation of narratives to evoke their experiences at the writing group, and with the act of writing.

Further Recursions

The recursive nature of critical qualitative research became apparent very early in my study. A dominant focus of my research was to consider how the participants engaged in the act of writing, and how they developed their ideas in a writing process. In examining these aspects, I wanted to contextualize my findings in the vast research into writing process findings from the last few decades. This purpose was a valuable and extremely significant focus in my research into writing; however, because of my acknowledgement of subjectivity and the importance of relationship, other interests of the participants began to emerge. It became obvious that the social aspect of writing was far more important than I first anticipated. The writers wanted to talk and write about why writing was important to them, and why attending the Writers' Group was vital. Consequently, I began to look at *why* they wrote, as well as *how* they wrote.

Although one interpretation of this shift in focus could be a flaw or fault in the design of the research structure, one could also note that by valuing the subjectivity of the participants and their complex social relationships, I was able to broaden the research in a more contextualized manner. The importance of the community and the social aspects of the writing process became central to understanding what went on at the Writers' Group. And this understanding led inevitably to issues of power and subjectivity, and social tensions—cultural, social, political, ethnic, gender, medical and economic.

The recursive aspect of critical qualitative research helped me become more aware that the Writers' Group was an active, critical community of real, living literacy as envisioned by Paulo Freire. To many of the participants in the Writers' Group, writing was as important as anything in their lives.

The Value of Writing

All meaningful writing engages the self and others and the world in a complex, dialogical relationship—meaning is always contextual. The self constantly constructs itself and negotiates meaning with others in a series of social agreements. A writer, in creating a text, negotiates a meaningful relationship between a self and a culture, with text acting as the interface.

To the writers at CMHA, writing became a way of being, and served at least two purposes. Writing allowed them to express themselves fully, and "to push" feelings, thoughts, emotions, perceptions and perspectives outside of the turmoil within. Writing also allowed them, as Laurel Richardson (2001) noted with her own writing, "to gain a feeling of control over time and space" (p. 33). Writing was both freeing and empowering.

Richardson also notes that "writing was the method through which I constituted the world and reconstituted myself. Writing became my principal tool through which I learned about myself and the world" (p. 33). Writing fulfils a similar purpose for the participants of the writing group. Writing as seen from this perspective becomes an active agent of critical literacy—active, meaningful and liberating. Literacy in this sense becomes a driving force in the lives of the participants.

Narrative Constructions

Richardson (2000) suggests that writing itself can be a method of inquiry, and consequently I utilized writing as a dominant process in the research site because of the centrality of the act of writing to the study as well as to the participants of the CMHA Writers' Group. Richardson (2000) claims that writing is "a way of 'knowing'—a method of discovery and analysis. By writing in different ways, we discover new aspects of our topic and our relationship to it. Form and content are inseparable" (p. 923).

I decided to write narratives from my field notes and the interview transcripts of the participants of the writing group because narrative could both describe what occurred in the writing group, as well as evoke the experience.

Critical qualitative research in its acknowledgement of power relationships and the importance of the subjectivity of both researcher and research participants creates a sense of meditative reflection on the research that results in recursivity. For this project, I came to see writing as a far more dominant activity and methodology than I first anticipated. In the end, I used my own writing as a form of research inquiry, with narrative, or story, as the organizing methodology, weaving narrative knowing together with paradigmatic knowing (Bruner, 1986) to create a deeper sense of meaning. I was part of the study, both as an active participant of the Writers' Group, and as a researcher trying to gain an understanding into the nature of writing.

I looked at the writers in terms of an inter-textual story, rather than simply analyzing their writing and experiences from a paradigmatic, or logico-scientific, focus. Writing does not occur in isolation. As Perry (2000) has noted: "Writing knowledge, 'knowing how' to write, cannot be separated from the 'knowing what' and 'knowing that' of writing" (p. 206). Narrative inquiry provides a valuable framework for the examination of the value of personal writing because it "organizes human experiences into temporally meaningful episodes" and is "the primary form by which human experience is made meaningful" (Polkinghorne, 1988, p. 1).

I was committed to understand the experiences of the participants of the Writers' Group, and then evoke in the reader what occurs at the CMHA Writers' Group as accurately and with as much verisimilitude as possible, utilizing the voices of the participants as well as embedding my own subjectivity into the analysis of the phenomenon. Lincoln (1995) suggests that "attention to voice—to who speaks, for whom, to whom, for what purpose—effectively creates praxis, even when no praxis was intended" (p. 282). Voice, "as resistance against silence, as resistance to disengagement, as resistance to marginalization," is a necessary component of "passionate participation" (p. 282). Voice is central to interpretive work, and "the extent to which alternative voices are heard is a criterion by which we can judge the openness, engagement, and problematic nature of any text" (p. 283).

For this study, I used narrative to give voice to human outliers, the writing group participants who have been marginalized and often ignored by society. I wanted to evoke an understanding of their experiences with the act of writing, and with the social aspects of being a member of the writing group. Ellis (1997) also uses the concept of evocation in her research methodology, and is "less concerned with 'historical truth' and more involved with 'narrative truth'" (p. 128). Ellis will often "condense a number of scenes into evocative composites" instead of trying to create a "mirror representation of chronologically ordered events" (p. 128). In doing so, she would create a story "where the events and feelings cohered, and where readers could grasp the main points and feel some of what [she] felt" (p. 128). Because I am concerned with a reader's understanding of what occurs at the Writers' Group, the narratives I created are *evocative* rather than *representational*. These narratives do not try to mirror reality; they replicate lived experience. In my research and in the creation of my book (Park, 2005), the writing itself became the meaning-making site of the research inquiry, because "language does not 'reflect' social reality, but produces meaning, creates social reality" (Richardson, 2000, p. 928).

In this critical qualitative research project, I used writing as a research methodology and narrative to provide a framework to evoke the context and relationships of the participants essential to an understanding of the social phenomenon. As a researcher, I was within the phenomenon, not outside, looking in.

Conclusion

The CMHA Writers' Group is an example of Freire's concept of active critical literacy. Much of what I have learned, and continue to learn about the act of writing, writing process and the value of writing would not have come about if I had ignored issues of power—social, economic, culture, justice, health or political—or if I had discarded outliers by utilizing a different, more normalized research site. By taking a critical qualitative research stance that acknowledged issues of power, I focused on the edges, the margins and the borders to gain valuable insights into how and why people write. Instead of objectifying my research participants, I embraced their subjectivity and mine, and built a lasting relationship that allows me deeper insight into the research site. In reconceptualizing outliers, and focusing on their value and significance, rather than ignoring them or explaining them against a mean of normality, I engaged deeply with marginalized writers to explore the value of writing, and the importance of active critical literacy.

References

Aron, A., & Aron, E. (2008). *Statistics for the behavioral and social sciences: A brief course*. Upper Saddle River, NJ: Pearson Prentice Hall.

Bruner, J. S. (1986). *Actual minds, possible worlds*. Cambridge, MA: Harvard University Press.

Ellis, C. (1997). Evocative autoethnography: Writing emotionally about our lives. In W. Tierney & Y. Lincoln (Eds.), *Representation and the text: Re-framing the narrative voice* (pp. 115–139). Albany, NY: State University of New York Press.

Freire, P., & Macedo, D. (1987). *Literacy: Reading the word and reading the world*. Westport, CT: Bergin & Garvey.

Holstein, J. & Gubrium, J. (1995). *The active interview*. Thousand Oaks, CA: Sage Publications.

Holstein, J. & Gubrium, J. (1997). Active interviewing. In D. Silverman (Ed.), *Qualitative research: Theory, method and practice* (pp. 113–129). Thousand Oaks, CA: Sage Publications.

Kincheloe, J. (2008). *Critical pedagogy* (2nd ed.). New York, NY: Peter Lang.

Lincoln, Y. S. (1995). Emerging criteria for quality in qualitative and interpretive research. *Qualitative Inquiry, 1*(3), 275–289.

Park, J. (2005). *Writing at the edge: Narrative and writing process theory*. New York, NY: Peter Lang.

Perry, P. H. (2000). *A composition of consciousness: Roads of reflection from Freire and Elbow*. New York, NY: Peter Lang.

Polkinghorne, D. (1988). *Narrative knowing and the human sciences*. Albany, NY: State University of New York Press.

Richardson, L. (2000). Writing: A method of inquiry. In N. K. Denzin & Y. S. Lincoln (Eds.), *Handbook of qualitative research* (2nd ed., pp. 923–948). Thousand Oaks, CA: Sage.

Richardson, L. (2001). Getting personal: Writing stories. *International Journal of Qualitative Studies, 14*(1), 33–38.

Seidman, I. (1998). *Interviewing as qualitative research: A guide for researchers in education and the social sciences* (2nd ed.). New York: Teachers College Press.

CHAPTER FORTY-ONE

Foucauldian Scientificity: Qualitative Methodology-21

Patti Lather

The current debate offers important opportunities for reflecting on the definition and meaning of science, on the ways in which science is shaped by politics, on the limitations of political intervention into the practice of science, and of the conditions under which the meaning and definition of science are politically contested.... If the notion of randomized controlled trials as the gold standard for education research disappeared tomorrow, these issues would still be with us. (Walters and Lareau, 2009, p. 11)

This chapter addresses the increased calls for the usefulness of social research by putting to work Michel Foucault's concept of scientificity as a tool against the resurgent positivism at work in neo-liberal times. The chapter includes a sketch of a social science that stays close to the complexities of the social world in fostering understanding, reflection and action instead of a narrow translation of research into practice. It concludes with a discussion of qualitative research for the twenty-first century, what I am calling "methodology-21."[1]

Current talk about the relationship of research to educational policy is full of standards and accountability in neo-positivist terms. This is in spite of the genesis of a central strain of qualitative research in educational program evaluation with its links to policy (Patton, 1990; Guba and Lincoln, 1989; Rist, 2000). A challenge to the dominance of positivism in educational policy research is apparent on the part of applied cultural work and ethnography of policy as well as more general calls for qualitative policy analysis that can engage strategically with the uses of research for social policy toward the improvement of practice (Sutton and Levinson, 2001; Lather and Moss, 2005).

One potential tool in this push toward increasing attention to the uses of qualitative research in the policy arena is the concept of scientificity, a term I first encountered in my reading of Foucault. Quite distinct from the scientism (Sorell, 1991) with which it is usually equated, scientificity is a less familiar term for an old and difficult question regarding what makes a science a science. While the history of science makes it clear that the policy, economy and practice of science shift across historical times and places (Redner, 1987), a repositivization is at work in neoliberal times where refusing to concede science to scientism appears to be a central task of those invested in qualitative work.

In what follows, I probe the uses of a reinscribed scientificity in what might be termed the "rage for accountability" in educational research (Lather, 2005). Foucault's ideas concerning the thresholds of positivity, epistemologization, scientificity and formalization in the human sciences will be used to argue against the methodological reductionism in neoliberal policy discourse and how this affects the research, policy, practice nexus.

This Cloudy Distribution

My work?... There is beneath that which science knows of itself something that it does not know... I have tried to extricate... the unconscious of knowledge. (Foucault in Davidson, 1997, p. 7)

In *The Order of Things*, Foucault (1966/1970) advises that, rather than looking for a coherent definitional field, we attend to the overlapping, contradictory, and conflictual definitional forces that don't oversimplify our pursuit of a counter-science. Rather than the "physics envy" that characterizes the parade of behaviorism, cognitivism, structuralism, and neopositivism, he posits a social science that takes values and power seriously. Against the objectivist strands with their failure to successfully study human activity in a way modeled after the assumedly cumulative, predictive, and stable natural or "exact" sciences, Foucault locates the human sciences in the interstices of the mathematizable and the philosophical. "This cloudy distribution" (p. 347) is both their privilege and their precariousness.

As what Nietzsche terms the "unnatural sciences" (1887/1974, p. 301), they are opposed to the "great certainty" of the natural sciences. Across the sociological (Comte) and economic (Marx) models of earlier centuries, we arrive via the linguistic/interpretive turn (Freud) to a focus on the need for a "reflexive form of knowledge" where there is "always something still to be thought" (Foucault, 1966/1970, p. 372). The "primacy of representation" is "the very field upon which the human sciences occur" (pp. 362–363). "Unveil[ing] to consciousness the conditions of its forms and contents" (p. 364) is its task.

The human sciences do not answer to criteria of objectivity and systematicity, the formal criteria of a scientific form of knowledge, but they are within the positive domain of knowledge as much as any other part of the modern episteme. There is no internal deficiency here; they are not "stranded across the threshold of scientific forms" (Foucault, 1966/1970, p. 366). They are not "false" sciences; "they are not sciences at all" (p. 366). They assume the title in order to "receive the transference of models borrowed from the sciences" (p. 366).

Trying for some years now to understand what that sentence means, I found some help in a book on deconstruction and the remainders of phenomenology that uses Foucault to look at the human sciences. Working this section of *The Order of Things* very closely in relation to Husserl, the author, Tilottama Rajan (2002), unpacks Foucault to mean that the human sciences are necessarily situated between positivity and reflexiveness, "surreptitiously" de-mathematizing in ways that have an "entirely unconscious" deterritorializing effect on "the cartography of knowledge." Unable to achieve "the transcendence that Husserl sought through geometry," unable to be their own foundation, they "mimic the sciences, thus marking both themselves and the sciences with the negativity of being what they are not and not being what they are." This "doubling" sort of move situates the human sciences as "the unconscious of the sciences" (p. 194).

Such knowledges compose a "counter-science" (Foucault, 1966/1970, p. 379) that "unmakes" us as it "traverse[s], animate[s], and disturb[s] the whole constituted field of the human sciences... threatening the very thing that made it possible for man to be known" (p. 381). In short, by "counter-science,"

Foucault is referring to those knowledges that "'unmake' that very man who is creating and re-creating his positivity in the human sciences" (p. 379). Noting how his own work is tied to "that strange and quite problematic configuration of human sciences" (Foucault, 1998, p. 311), Foucault's interest is in "undoing and recomposing" the very ground he stands on. Here demarcation issues are refused, distinctions are seen as uncertain and "the play of immediacies" becomes the point of analysis (p. 306).

Foucault is most useful in seeing how the line between a narrowly defined scientism and a more capacious scientificity of disciplined inquiry remains very much at issue. In terms of the desirability of degrees of formalization, mathematized and not, generic procedures, and rigorous differentiations, there is virtually no agreement among scientists, philosophers and historians as to what constitutes science except, increasingly, the view that science is a cultural practice and practice of culture. What, then, is a Foucauldian take on scientificity?

Foucauldian Scientificity: Undoing Positivism

> For U.S. public and private foundations and university administrations, scientificity has meant "scientism," quantification, and neutralization of subjectivity. (Abend, 2006, p. 29)

Scientificity has long been at the heart of the demarcation debates. But one example is the "scientificity of psychoanalysis," the seemingly endless adjudications over the scientificity of Freud (Leupin, 1991). Also of note here would be the desperate quest across various fields for scientificity, from economists (Cullenberg, Amariglio and Fuccio, 2001) to the Institute of Educational Sciences and its determination to counter the "explosive growth of qualitative research studies" by funding only those studies that adhere to its "methodological orthodoxy" of experimental design (Bryant, 2004, p. 5). From Popperian falsifiability to Lakatosian research programs, from criteria of testability and prediction to more recent pronouncements on reliability and generalizability (National Research Council, 2002), scientificity is about the constitution of science as science. Although the recognition that science is evolving, social and historical is oftentimes spotty, even in philosophy of science where one might expect better, the criteria of scientificity are much debated.

Historically, scientificity in the social sciences has been based on measurability, the degree to which an area resembled inquiry in physics (Rorty, 2001). Two generations of post-Kuhnian work has "done its best to fuzz up the logicrhetoric and hard-soft distinctions" (ibid.). Although what Nancy Cartwright (1999) terms "scientific fundamentalists" still hold to the task of demarcation, focus has shifted to the general structure of scientificity with openness to specific disciplinarity. Here scientificity is continuously adapted to new contingencies. Isabelle Stengers (1997), for example, argues that scientificity is a productive constraint. Getting access to the singularity of scientific activity in the drive to address what makes a science a science, the pre-existent, neo-positivist criteria are but one form in "the criteria of scientificity that are currently on the market" (p. 81). Conditions of scientificity can be mutilating; they can construct object and question in a unilateral way, drawing on social power, eliminating a priori anything that does not appear to guarantee an objective approach (p. 146). Most importantly to Stengers, it is "trivial" to solve the problem of what science is by defining science "through its objectivity" (p. 81).

In mapping such territory, Foucault describes the thresholds of positivity, epistemologization, scientificity and formalization in his *Archaeology of Knowledge* (1972, p. 186). His interest is in how discourses that have the status of scientificity or pretensions to it function as an element of knowledge in presenting the formal criteria of a science (p. 184). What he does here is localize science in the framework of more general knowledge. He looks at how a science structures certain of its objects, systematizes parts of it, formalizes, underwrites strategies: here science finds its place where it functions among other practices; here is its ideological function. "Ideology is not exclusive of scientificity," Foucault writes (p. 186), and the role of ideology does not diminish as rigor increases and error is dissipated. For those who know their Althusser, this is quite another cup of tea than the science/ideology distinctions that formerly reigned in the Marxist claim to scientificity. To tackle the ideological functioning of a science is to take on the "system of formation of its objects, its types of enunciation, its concepts, its theoretical choices. It is to treat it as one practice among others" (p. 186). Foucault's question is "what is it for that science to be a science"? (p. 192) His answer is that to focus on demarcation criteria is to miss how "all the density of the disconnections, the dispersion of the ruptures, the shifts in their effects, the play of the interdependence are reduced to the monotonous act of an endlessly repeated foundation" (p. 188).

What Foucault helps us see is how the methodological reductionism that has radically flattened the methods into a single model is being displaced by a sort of situated scientificity that neither constricts "science" to one or two privileged models nor allows an anything-goes arbitrary concept of science. While a general attitude of and emphasis on rigor and objectivity are part of a plurality of models and types of scientificity suitable for the requirements of diverse fields, different but compatible models of scientificity are elaborated across disciplinary sites while working to avoid methodological fragmentation. Here the judgment criteria for scientificity enact an on-going crisis.[2] The question of what makes a science a science is about much more than the typical Popperian or even Kuhnian sorts of demarcation projects that have historically dominated in framing such questions.

In sum scientificity is an arena of struggle in broadening the definition of science. Given that the human sciences work with a vague concept of data, traditional notions of rigor are thwarted, especially epistemological definitions of objectivity. Socio-cultural context matters here, unavoidably. Focus shifts to the proper characterization of the object, not control of the subjectivity of the knower. A science defines its own scientificity by elaboration of the conditions that determine the objects of a science and data about them. These are methodologically built objects located between radical constructivism and objectivism, both found and made, always caught in flux, in-the-making. Here the "irreducible, irresolvable, and utterly necessary" interpretation that has historically been excluded from received understandings of science (Wilson, 1998, p. 79) is positioned as the generative undecidability that is constitutive of science itself. What are the implications of this for the research/policy/practice nexus?

The Uses of Foucault in Education Policy Analysis

Given renewed interest at the federal level in the relationship of educational research, policy and practice, what would it mean to put Foucault to work to foreground the complications and interrupt assumptions of a tidy, linear relationality? Suggestive here is *Making Social Science Matter* (2001) by Bent Flyvbjerg, a Danish urban developer, who argues for a move from a narrowly defined epistemic science to one that articulates a social science that integrates context-dependency with practical deliberation. Here considerations of power are brought to bear in delineating a knowledge adequate to our time. Rather than the objectivist strands of the social sciences, this is a social science that can contribute to society's practical rationality in clarifying where we are and where we want to be.

The social sciences become a sort of laboratory toward public philosophy, what Bourdieu terms "fieldwork in philosophy" (1990, p. 28, from J.L. Austin, quoted in Flyvbjerg, p. 167). Within such fieldwork, case studies assume prime importance as critical cases, strategically chosen, provide "far better access for policy intervention than the present social science of variables" (2001, p. 86). In such a laboratory, against a narrow scientism in policy analysis and program evaluation, Flyvbjerg's urgent questions become: Where are we going with democracy in this project? Who gains and who loses and by which mechanisms of power? Given this analysis, what should be done?

"Simultaneously sociological, political and philosophical" (Flyvbjerg, 2001, p. 64), this is a kind of science that does not divest experience of its rich ambiguity because it stays close to the complexities and contradictions of existence. Instead of emulating the natural or, in Edmund Husserl's (1954/1970) terms, "exact" science, the goal is getting people to no longer know what to do so that things might be done differently. This is the "yes" of the-setting-to-work mode of post-foundational theory that faces unanswerable questions, the necessary experience of the impossible, in an effort to foster understanding, reflection and action instead of a narrow translation of research into practice.

Suggestive in a different register is Peter Taubman's (2009) *Teaching by Numbers: Deconstructing the Discourse of Standards and Accountability*. Richly practice based, Taubman's book maps the transformation that has occurred across all levels of schooling over the last decade or so of neoliberalism. Taubman creates a theoretical assemblage, especially Foucault and Lacan, to help us think more deeply about a transformation that has left all but its architects, and even some of them, bewildered, adrift, at a loss.[3] Taubman's critique of the "inexorable and arbitrary" (p. x) nature of how the accountability movement comes to roost in teacher education via the National Council for the Accreditation of Teacher Education (NCATE) is a stunning example of what can happen when teacher educators get caught in the buzz saw of standards incorporated.[4] Sucked into this vortex and coming out "mad as hell" at the corporatization of education and our collusion in it, Taubman's intent is to "clear a space" (p. 201) where we might take stock of what is happening as opposed to providing answers. He is chillingly convincing that any answers are "too soon," vulnerable to appropriation into the same vortex. Particularly strong is his use of psychoanalytic theory to articulate the psychic vulnerabilities of teachers to such appropriation. Shamed on one side, glorified on the other, teachers (and teacher educators) are no match for the combined forces of the "education establishment" under conditions of neoliberalism, the weight of positivism and its reduction of education to the measurable, and the vacuum where "the learning sciences" in all of their thin certainty are turned to for answers.

Why are we so easily convinced that what happens in classrooms is best understood as objective, transparent, measurable, that mechanistic promises that all students can learn to the same standard make democratic sense, that the inner life of teachers is disposable in the quest for quality schools? How can Foucault and Lacan and a host of other theorists help us think in richer and more capacious, nuanced and complicated ways about the desires and fears of teaching and learning?

Taubman's perfect title helps us see that teaching by numbers reduces education just as painting by numbers reduces art. He presents the larger, deeper stage upon which neoliberal accountability movements are playing out and the high costs involved in how what gets normalized comes about via seemingly innocuous "standards" and "accountability" efforts. Perhaps it is his anchoring in his close relationship to helping to start and sustain a small high school since 2003. For sure it is his anger about the inanities of NCATE. How damaging the hegemony of the culture of accountability has become, a certain crushing: this is the story Taubman tells. He writes of "the night that has fallen on our field" (p. 13), the biggest shift in seventy-five years toward a "new educational order" (Taubman, 2007) and wonders what kids are learning from this impoverished view of educational reform, what person-making is going on here.

Taubman calls on some very basic Foucault: we are constituted by discourses that are under constant resignification; our agency is in reworking such spaces. Yet this "agency" is profoundly shaped by how neoliberalism works to convince us to be "both more governable and more able to service capital" in ways that mobilize "the discourse of inevitability" in order to "dismantle resistance itself" (Davies, 2006, p. 436). Produced by various discourses and practices, in turn producing ourselves in accommodation and resistance, how do we break the hold of the natural science imaginary and, in Foucault's terms (1982), "refuse what we are" in colluding in the reduction of qualitative research to an instrumentalism that meets the demands of audit culture? Flyvbjerg and Taubman provide us with exemplars that are empirical and "applied" in richly different ways. They provide grounding for the next section that turns to the question of the reinvention of qualitative work in audit culture to argue for a critical qualitative presence in fuzzying the lines between empirical research, politics, and the philosophical renewal of public deliberation.

The State of Qualitative Inquiry: Methodology-21

My interest is in empirical work that challenges the orthodoxies of what it means to do research of use in policy arenas. Such work is part of a critique unleashed against SRE and its efforts to impose "the science movement in education" (Baez and Boyles, 2009). Within this larger context, SRE becomes symptomatic, "a point of departure" (p. 13) for exploring what makes possible such "events," including their reception. Baez and Boyles position SRE as a "power play" (p. 29) in a sociology of professionalism, a legitimization strategy couched in "useful" terms that belie its policing, violent efforts to establish an authoritative voice, presently playing out in efforts to reshape doctoral education.[5] The "fevered pitch" around SRE is part of a long-running angst around education, fueled by federal intervention and the larger political forces that shape such heretofore unparalleled intrusion.

This critique has, in turn, created a backlash against education researchers who protest, especially, interestingly, postmodernists with their "purported arguments" (Phillips, 2009, p. 189), "who often still regard themselves as researchers" in spite of their critiques of "the traditional research enterprise" (p. 168). This comes from D.C. Phillips' contribution to *Education Research on Trial* (2009) that is scattered with admonishments of critics of the SRE such as: unruly, recalcitrant, querulous, "vituperative" (p. 167 & 187), and, tucked away in footnote 29 (p. 193), my favorite, "postmodernist contumely." I looked this up and found: "a reproach, haughty and contemptuous rudeness, insulting and humiliating abuse, scornful insolence." Contumely is right next to contuse: "to wound without breaking skin."

I leave it to the reader to make sense of what this says about those who so consider those who protest SRE. But one has to say, at the least, that such rhetoric bespeaks a situation where the "scientific culture wars" (O'Connor, 2007, p. 3) are far from over. The umbrage taken at the umbrage taken on the part of qualitative researchers who felt marginalized by calls for a "common language" and "unity of purpose" disallows the incommensurability at work in this struggle over science that has to be seen for what it is: power struggles over who gets to set the terms of debate and what it means to court interruption/ counter-narratives as a move toward better work all the way around. This is about difference, not sameness, and surely endorses the sort of "epistemic reflexivity" that Pam Moss (1996, 2005) has long called for. Qualitative and quantitative or positivist and interpretive/critical/post or "exact" and "conjectural," all would need to figure out how to work together in ways more and different than the descriptive/causal relation that SRE articulates.[6] This may include drawing on such resources as the 2004 NSF "Workshop on Scientific Foundations of Qualitative Research" and the 2009 NSF "Workshop on Interdisciplinary Standards for Systematic Qualitative Research" (Lamont and White, 2009) that focuses on the disciplines of sociology, political science, anthropology and law and related disciplines. It may as well include increasing moves into what I like to call "smart mixed methods."[7]

But it also requires that increasing efforts to "discipline" qualitative research be contested. In political science, for example, the widely cited efforts of King, Keohane and Verba (1994) to "help out" qualitative research by offering a "quantitative template" have been countered by Brady and Collier (2004) who call out this "quantitative imperialism" (p. 15). As a further example, the National Science Foundation's 2009 workshop on Qualitative Methods has evoked a letter of protest from the International Congress of Qualitative Inquiry regarding the focus on mainstream approaches that marginalizes the proliferation of kinds of qualitative research such as autoethnography, performance ethnography, and critical ethnography.[8]

That the resistance of qualitative researchers to relegation to "a separate table at the margins" goes on across fields is clear in Schwartz-Shea and Yanow's reading of methods textbooks in political science and policy studies (2002, p. 481). Uncannily similar to education in how "standards" are coming down, they especially draw attention to the weight of King, Keohane and Verba (1994) on fostering a "positivist qualitative research" (2002, p. 461) and the "disappearing" of qualitative research (p. 476). In reading the resistance of political science and policy studies to epistemological grounding, Schwartz-

Shea and Yanow posit that "[t]o make these silences 'speak' would focus attention on the problematic character of knowledge" (p. 479).

In the context of education, SRE aggravated the divisiveness by raising the stakes. The multiplicities and proliferations of ways of doing education research are in tension with both a resurgent positivism and calls for a set of principles to unite scientific practices (Lather, 2006). That the "science" or "validity" or even "usefulness" generated across qualitative positions is hardly recognizable as such by those from positions of "the received view of science" is no surprise.

The key is that what is being contested is not science or rigor or even evidence-based practice but, rather, orthodox views of such matters. What does it mean for one best-way thinking, especially as endorsed by governmental force, to continue to enact the management, containment, and marginalization of both qualitative research and, more importantly, research that might make a difference in improving our schools? How has the natural scientific imaginary been put into the service of government practices at great cost economically, politically and philosophically?

In terms of the war-zone nature of irreconcilable differences about the nature of knowledge formation and its uses, is a return to Gage's (1989) "détente" possible after this round of NCLB and SRE inflammation? Is there some more productive space than détente? The anxieties that follow the collapse of foundations, the reassertion of objective truth and value-neutral facts, the imposition of standards, the quite predictable push back on the part of those marginalized by such: the question is how we find a fruitful place to work in all of this, a place that fosters the capacity to negotiate across standard procedures from many paradigms to engage with the uncertainties of knowledge toward more nuanced thinking.

My interest is in the parameters of a science more accountable to complexity that might result in a less comfortable, less imperialist social science, a science capacious and democratic in its recognition of necessary contingency as the horizon of our intelligibility. In imagining a more complicated view of science that might become widely disseminated as part of a broad-based and fundamental questioning of foundations, if Wall Street expertise seems to have clay feet, can scientifically based practice be far behind? If climate scientists understand the enormous uncertainty of nonlinear systems within which decisions must be made and urge what they call "caustic honesty" about what we know and don't know (Revkin, 2009), can the Institute for Education Sciences (IES) continue to argue that its "strategic" success depends on its "yield" of "research proven interventions" of the one-size-fits-all model? (Whitehurst, 2008)

Out-going Director of the IES, Grover Whitehurst, in his November 2008 farewell report to Congress, situates qualitative research outside the bounds of science and, quite fascinatingly, finds "qualitative research grounded in post-modern philosophy and methodologically weak quantitative research" to be "the dominant forms of education research in the latter half of the 20th century" (p. 5). As Bettie St. Pierre (2009a) writes, "who knew" that postmodernism had achieved such, in Whitehurst's terms, "ascendance"? In the constantly changing landscape of education research, the application of technical methods and procedures will hardly suffice, IES not withstanding. After almost a decade of overblown rhetoric on how scientific rigor will heal our schools, how do we make productive use of being left to work within, against and across traditions that are all positioned within a crisis of authority and legitimation that go well beyond the academy? If, to use Bettie St. Pierre's (2009a) words, we stop trying so hard to be hard, can we change the terms of the debate we have both inherited and contributed to? How can we keep moving in order to produce and learn from ruptures, failures, breaks, refusals?

A Futuring for Qualitative Research: In spite of fears of a take-over by postmodernism, dominant ideas of qualitative research assume a modernist self, transparent methods, and reflexivity as a "solution" to whatever problems might arise. While the illusion of neat and tidy qualitative research has long been troubled, methodological examination tends to set up either/or dynamics in terms of "old school" and "new new" sorts of practices or, as evident in the 2009 NSF standards for "systematic" qualitative research, an either/or of "standardized" or "impressionistic" (Lamont and White, 2009).

Against this either/or dynamic, I offer a framework for doing qualitative research that works across layerings of 1.0, 2.0 and 3.0 methodologies. My interest is in what opens up in situating some practices as "positivist qualitative methods" (Schwartz-Shea and Yanow, 2002, p. 457) or "dominant postpositivist" (Mallozzi, 2009, p. 1043) or "conventional interpretive methodology" (St. Pierre, 2006, p. 239), or "plain old ethnography" (Erickson, 2009). What is possible in terms of a certain simultaneity in working both within and against established practices of what John Van Maanen, two decades ago, marked as "realist ethnography" (1988), toward the "always already" of that which begins to announce itself in terms of a futuring for qualitative research?

The 1.0, 2.0 and 3.0 "rubric" is dangerously linear and developmental, but it does focus on what is both gained and lost in movement, unlearnings, and resultant mournings. QUAL 1.0 grows out of Chicago School and anthropological roots; it precedes the linguistic turn and, hence, is relatively untroubled in its assumptions of transparency and interpretive authority. QUAL 2.0 gets messier (Marcus, 1994). Parallel to similar moves in feminist methodology (Fonow and Cook, 2005), focus in on an empowerment agenda, standpoint epistemologies, both troubled and not, a self-reflexive researcher in the driver's seat, invested in collaboration and co-participation within assumptions of necessary perspectivalism, and multiple realities. A sort of mediated multi-vocality emerges, something with which we are quite familiar: empowerment, voice, and reflexive collaboration.[9]

In computer speak, the shift to 2.0 entails a platform provided by 1.0 acknowledged as robust ground for innovation toward something more social, an evolution toward an "architecture of participation" that includes user modification, crowd-sourcing, accessing distributed knowledge, Second Life, where fiction becomes the real, remixing based on open access, the collective intelligence, citizen journalism and wisdom of crowds of Wikipedia and blogs where expertise is dispersed and (re)democratized. This is flexible, aggregative data sharing that features speed of use and learning from others as well as the leveling effects that make it difficult to tell the good from the bad. It involves open editing and review structure, swarms of feeds in a sort of "spidering"—cloud tags—1.0 without the anxiety of contamination—"higher cribbing," in the words of a piece on plagiarism in *Harper's Magazine* (Lethem, 2007).

For 3.0, Wikipedia is "locked" in terms of totally open access, displacing "scholar amateurs" or "trolls" as "a dictatorship of idiots" on the one hand, or introduction of "gentle expert oversight" on the other, with the use of real names accountability. What gets troubled is the romance of collective knowledge, the collapse of authority and the populism of a vanguard free and spontaneous theory of social change. There is renewed focus on content so that it is "capturable" for multiple purposings in "mash-ups" that combine various applications (and copyright trouble), a democratized user revolution of content creation and distribution toward the more immersive environment of "the cloud" or "live Mesh" that creates "the new personal internet" out of connecting devices and the "hive" of "mind share."[10] Here expertise will show itself in bottom-up forms of self-organization where multiple people co-write and co-edit in real time and legitimacy (non-authoritarian authority) comes from a very public vetting of greater accountability and questioning from all sides that creates an ease of entry into deeper levels of making meaning in negotiating the surfeit of information created by open content. Citton (2009), writing of Jacques Rancière's ideas of agency as a collective event, fleshes out such self-organization as "dynamics of general responsiveness, temporary guidance, coordinative framing, opening up of free spaces for individual explorations, exacerbation of singularity through common empowerment and reciprocal stimulation" (p. 134).

QUAL 3.0 moves further into the postmodern turn. What this might mean for methodology involves troubling questions about "giving voice," "identity politics," "dialogue," "telling and testifying," and "empowerment," all now encased in quotation marks indicating their loss of innocence (Fonow and Cook, 2005). Such issues are starter points for "fleshing out" the 3.0 move that questions heretofore taken for granted: validity, voice, data, empathy, authenticity, experience, interviewing, the field, reflexivity, clarity. As St. Pierre (2009b) points out, this is the work that was "stalled for years" when qualitative researchers were put on the defensive by SRE. What does it mean to pick this back up, to re-engage with "looking for trouble" (Childers, 2009), "weary of a decade of defending qualitative research and eager to get on with their work," to move beyond "a stale and overcoded qualitative inquiry" (St. Pierre, 2009b)?

What is to come in qualitative research is situated in negotiating kinds of practices that are on the edge of what is presently thinkable and doable. How do QUAL 1.0 and 2.0 provide platforms that make moving beyond them imaginable? What exemplars can we look to for guidance in such matters?

Conclusion

[W]e advocate the disruption of the hegemony of the positivist ideal of science. Meaning-focused methods of data access and analysis should be given a legitimate place…in ways that a Kuhnian analysis would predict—a politics of knowledge [is being] played out at the epistemological level. (Schwartz-Shea and Yanow, 2002, p. 481)

What I am urging is that qualitative research use this moment in the call for socially useful research to refuse the re-positivization and instrumentalist reductions of audit culture. To the extent we as a society agree to not trouble a scientificity that claims that objectivity is not political, empiricism is not interpretive, chance can be tamed via mathematization, and progress equals greater governmentality, we court not just a narrowed science but a narrowed future.

Foucault writes of the "absolute optimism" of "a thousand things to do" (1981/1991, p. 174) in our constant struggle against the very rules of reason and practice inscribed in the effects of power of the social sciences. To operate from a premise of the impossibility of satisfactory solutions means to not assume to resolve but, instead, to be prepared to meet the obduracy of the problems and obstacles as the very way toward producing different knowledge and producing knowledge differently. For those attentive to the demands of different contexts and different communities, my argument is that there is plenty of future for qualitative research that works within and against past practices and traditions in moving toward an engaged and engaging social science for policy.

Notes

1. My subtitle comes from the Maya Lin exhibition, *Systematic Landscapes*, Corcoran Gallery, Washington, DC, March 14–July 12, 2009. The title as well echoes Immanuel Wallerstein's 1999 edited collection, *The End of the World as We Know It: Social Science for the Twenty-first Century*.
2. For issues of validity in qualitative research in education, see Lincoln and Guba, 1985; Lincoln, 1995; Scheurich, 1996; Lather, 1993, 2001. Flyvbjerg, 2006, is especially useful in terms of validity in case studies.
3. Diane Ravitch, for example, has come to see the standards and accountability movement to which she has so contributed as "an end in itself… destroy[ing] not only the joy of learning, but learning itself " (2007, quoted in Taubman, 2009, p. 127).
4. For William Pinar's critique of NCATE, see *What Is Curriculum Theory?* (2004), chapter 9. Pinar concludes the section, "Betrayal by Professional Organizations," with "NCATE is no longer a credible organization for teacher education program review" and urges tenured senior faculty to take leadership in its repudiation.
5. I go on at some length about the implications of SRE for the training of educational researchers in Lather, 2006.
6. The difficulties are in evidence in Moss, Phillips, Erickson, Floden, Lather and Schneider, 2009.
7. Mixed methods, touted as a "paradigm whose time has come" (Johnson and Onwuegbuzie, 2004) are garnering increased attention from the side of qualitative research. See special issue of *Qualitative Research*, 6(1), 2006, and, for a smart review essay, Suri and Clarke, 2009. My beginning engagement with such issues is "Smart Mixed Methods?" co-authored with Daniel Newhart, presented at the Fifth International Congress of Qualitative Inquiry, University of Illinois at Urbana-Champaign, May 20–23, 2009, as part of a plenary, "Mixed Methods: Breakthrough or Muddle?" that included Joseph Maxwell, Frederick Erickson, Ken Howe and Harry Torrance.

8. (www. Icqi.org). See, also, the Consortium for Qualitative Research Methods, begun at Arizona State University and recently moved to the Maxwell School at Syracuse University, that promotes the teaching and use of qualitative research methods in the social sciences. According to Mihic et al., the Consortium demonstrates the "assimilating moves" at work in political science to take account of qualitative research (2005, p. 484). http://www.asu. edu/clas/polisci/cqrm.
9. For a critique of "voice," see Jackson and Mazzei, 2008.
10. From "After Bill: Briefing Microsoft after Gates." *The Economist*, June 28, 2008, 76–78.

References

Abend, Gabriel. (2006). "Styles of Sociological Thought: Sociologies, Epistemologies, and the Mexican and U.S. Quests for Truth." *Sociological Theory* 24(1): 1–41.

Baez, Benjamin and Boyles, Deron. (2009). *The Politics of Inquiry: Education Research and the "Culture of Science."* Albany, NY: State University of New York Press.

Brady, Henry and Collier, David, eds. (2004). *Rethinking Social Inquiry: Diverse Tools, Shared Standards.* Lanham, MD: Rowman and Littlefield.

Bryant, Miles. (2004). "Forcing Change in Educational Research." TEA/SIG, Division A, AERA 11(2): 5.

Cartwright, Nancy. (1999). *The Dappled World: A Study of the Boundaries of Science.* Cambridge: Cambridge University Press.

Childers, Sara. (2009, May). "What a (Feminist) Post-critical Policy Analysis of Urban Schooling Might Look Like." Paper presented at the Fifth Congress of Qualitative Inquiry, Urbana-Champaign, Illinois.

Citton, Yves. (2009) "Political Agency and the Ambivalence of the Sensible." In *Jacques Rancière: History, Politics, Aesthetics.* Edited by Gabriel Rockhill and Philip Watts. Durham, NC: Duke University Press, 120–39.

Cullenberg, Stephen, Amariglio, Jack and Fuccio, David, eds. (2001). *Postmodernism, Economics and Knowledge.* London: Routledge.

Davidson, Arnold. (1997). "Structures and Strategies of Discourse: Remarks toward a History of Foucault's Philosophy of Language." In *Foucault and His Interlocutors.* Edited by A. Davidson. Chicago: University of Chicago Press, 1–17.

Davies, Bronwyn. (2003). "Death to Critique and Dissent? The Policies and Practices of New Managerialism and of 'Evidence-based Practice.'" *Gender and Education 15*(1): 91–103

Davies, Bronwyn. (2006). "Subjectification: The Relevance of Butler's Analysis for Education." *British Journal of Sociology of Education 27*(4): 425–438

Erickson, Frederick. (2009). "Affirming Human Dignity in Qualitative Inquiry: Walking the Walk." Keynote address to the 5th International Congress of Qualitative Inquiry, University of Illinois, May 21.

Flyvbjerg, Bent. (2001). *Making Social Science Matter: Why Social Inquiry Fails and How It Can Succeed Again.* Cambridge: Cambridge University Press.

Flyvbjerg, Bent. (2006). "Five Misunderstandings about Case-study Research." *Qualitative Inquiry* 12(2): 219–45.

Fonow, Mary Margaret and Cook, Judith. (2005). "Feminist Methodology: New Applications in the Academy and Public Policy." *Signs* 30(4): 2211–36.

Foucault, Michel. (1966/1970). *The Order of Things: An Archaeology of the Human Sciences.* New York: Vintage Books.

Foucault, Michel. (1972). *The Archaeology of Knowledge and the Discourse on Language.* Translated by A.M. Sheridan. New York: Pantheon.

Foucault, Michel. (1981/1991). *Remarks on Marx: Conversations with Duccio Trombadori.* New York: Semiotext(e).

Foucault, Michel. (1998). "On the Archaeology of the Sciences: Response to the Epistemology Circle." In *Michel Foucault: Aesthetics, Method, and Epistemology*, Volume Two. Edited by James Faubion. New York: The Free Press, 297–333.

Gage, Nathaniel. (1989). "The Paradigm Wars and Their Aftermath: A 'Historical' Sketch of Research on Teaching Since 1989." *Educational Researcher* 18: 4–10.

Guba, Egon and Lincoln, Yvonna. (1989). *Fourth Generation Evaluation.* Newbury Park, CA: Sage.

Husserl, Edmund. (1954/1970). *The Crisis of European Sciences and Transcendental Phenomenology.* Evanston IL: Northwestern University Press.

Jackson, Alecia and Mazzei, Lisa, eds. (2008). *Voice in Qualitative Inquiry: Challenging Conventional, Interpretive and Critical Conceptions in Qualitative Research.* New York: Routledge

Johnson, R. and Onwuegbuzie, A. (2004). "Mixed Methods Research: A Paradigm Whose Time Has Come." *Educational Researcher 33*(14): 14–26.

King, Gary, Keohane, Robert and Verba, Sidney. (1994). *Designing Social Inquiry: Scientific Inference in Qualitative Research.* Princeton, NJ: Princeton University Press.

Lamont, Michele and White, Patricia. (2009). *Workshop on Interdisciplinary Standards for Systematic Qualitative Research: Cultural Anthropology, Law and Social Science, Political Science and Sociology Programs.* National Science Foundation Supported Workshop. Available on NSF website: www.nsf.gove/sbe/ses/soc/ISSQR_workshop_rpt.pdf.

Lather, Patti. (1993). "Fertile Obsession: Validity after Poststructuralism." *The Sociological Quarterly* 34(4): 673–93.

Lather, Patti. (2001). "Validity as an Incitement to Discourse: Qualitative Research and the Crisis of Legitimation." In *Handbook of Research on Teaching,* Fourth Edition. Edited by Virginia Richardson, Washington, DC: AERA, 241–250.

Lather, Patti. (2004). "Foucauldian 'Indiscipline' as a Sort of Policy Application." in *Dangerous Coagulations? The Uses of Foucault in the Study of Education.* Edited by Bernadette Baker and Katharina Heyning. New York: Peter Lang, 279–304

Lather, Patti. (2005, April). "Scientism and Scientificity in the Rage for Accountability." Paper presented at the annual conference of the American Educational Research Association, Montreal.

Lather, Patti. (2006). "Paradigm Proliferation as a Good Thing to Think with: Teaching Research in Education as a Wild Profusion." *Qualitative Studies in Education 10*(1): 35–58

Lather, Patti and Moss, Pam. (2005). "Introduction: Implications of the *Scientific Research in Education* Report for Qualitative Inquiry." *Teachers College Record 107*(1): 1–3.

Lethem, Jonathan. (2007, February). "The Ecstasy of Influence." *Harper's Magazine.* [Electronic version].

Leupin, Alexandre. (1991). "Introduction: Voids and Knots in Knowledge and Truth." In *Lacan & the Human Sciences.* Edited by A. Leupin. Lincoln: University of Nebraska Press, 1–23.

Lincoln, Yvonna. (1995). "Emerging Criteria for Quality in Qualitative and Interpretive Research." *Qualitative Inquiry 1*(3): 275–89.

Lincoln, Yvonna and Guba, Egon. (1985). *Naturalistic Inquiry.* Newbury Park, CA: Sage.

Mallozzi, Christine. (2009). "Voicing the Interview: A Researcher's Exploration on a Platform of Empathy." *Qualitative Inquiry 15*(6): 1042–60.

Marcus, George. (1994). "What Comes (Just) After the Post? The Case of Ethnography." In *The Handbook of Qualitative Research.* Edited by Norman Denzin and Yvonna Lincoln. Thousand Oaks, CA: Sage, 563–74.

Mihic, Sophia, Bugelmann, Stephen G. and Wingrove, Elizabeth Rose. (2005). "Making Sense in and of Political Science: Facts, Values, and 'Real' Numbers." in *The Politics of Method in the Human Sciences: Positivism and Its Epistemological Others.* Edited by George Stenmetz, Durham, NC: Duke University Press, 470–495.

Moss, Pamela. (1996). "Enlarging the Dialogue in Educational Measurement: Voices from Interpretive Research Traditions." *Educational Researcher,* January–February: 20–28, 43.

Moss, Pamela. (2005). "Towards Epistemic Reflexivity in Educational Research: A Response to *Scientific Research in Education.*" *Teachers College Record 107*(1): 19–29

Moss, Pamela, Phillips, D. C., Erickson, Frederick, Floden, Robert, Lather, Patti and Schneider, Barbara. (2009). "Learning from Our Differences: A Dialogue Across Perspectives on Quality in Educational Research." *Educational Researcher, 38*(7): 501–517.

National Research Council (NRC). (2002). *Scientific Research in Education.* Committee on Scientific Principles for Education Research. Edited by Richard Shavelson and Lisa Towne. Washington, DC: National Academy Press.

National Science Foundation. (2004). *Workshop on Scientific Foundations of Qualitative Research.* Available on NSF website.

Nietzsche, Friedrich. (1887/1974). *The Gay Science.* Translated by Walter Kaufmann. New York: Vintage.

O'Connor, Alice. (2007). *Social Science for What? Philanthropy and the Social Question in a World Turned Rightside Up.* Troy, NY: Russell Sage Foundation.

Patton, Michael. (1990). *Qualitative Evaluation and Research Methods.* (2nd ed.). Newbury Park, CA: Sage.

Phillips, D. C. (2009). "A Quixotic Quest? Philosophical Issues in Assessing the Quality of Education Research." In *Education Research on Trial: Policy Reform and teh Call for Scientific Rigor.* Edited by Pamela B. Walters, Annette Lareau, and Sheri H. Rannis. New York: Routledge, 163–195.

Pinar, William. (2004). *What is Curriculum Theory?* Mahwah, NJ: Lawrence Erlbaum Associates.

Rajan, Tilottama. (2002). *Deconstruction and the Remainders of Phenomenology: Sartre, Derrida, Foucault, Baudrillard.* Stanford, CA: Stanford University Press.

Revkin, Andrew. (2009, March 29). "Among Climate Scientists, a Dispute over 'Tipping Points'." *New York Times* A15.

Reducer, Harry. (1987). *The Ends of Science: An Essay on Scientific Authority.* Boulder and London: Westview Press.

Rist, Ray. (2000). "Influencing the Policy Process with Qualitative Research." In *Handbook of Qualitative Research.* Edited by Norman Denzin and Yvonna Lincoln. Thousand Oaks, CA: Sage, 1001–17.

Rorty, Richard. (2001). "History of Science: Studied Ambiguity." *Science,* V. 293, Issue 5539, Sept. 28.

Scheurich, James. (1996). "The Masks of Validity: A Deconstructive Investigation." *Qualitative Studies in Education 9*(1): 49–60.

Schwartz-Shea, Peregrine and Yanow, Dvora. (2002). "'Reading' 'Methods' 'Texts': How Research Methods Texts Construct Political Science." *Political Research Quarterly 55*(2): 457–486.

Sorell, Tom. (1991). *Scientism: Philosophy and the Infatuation with Science.* London: Routledge.

Stengers, Isabelle. (1997). *Power and Invention: Situating Science.* Minneapolis: University of Minnesota Press.

St. Pierre, Elizabeth. (2006). "Scientifically Based Research in Education: Epistemology and Ethics." *Adult Education Quarterly 56*(4): 239–66.

St. Pierre, Elizabeth. (2009a). "Feminists Keep on Deconstructing Science in Educational Research." Paper presented at the FEMMSS Conference, Columbia, South Carolina, March 19–21.

St. Pierre, Elizabeth. (2009b). "Post-qualitative Research: What Comes Next?" Session proposal for AERA, Denver, Colorado, April 20–May 4, 2010.

Suri, Harsh and Clarke, David. (2009). "Advancements in Research Synthesis Methods: From a Methodologically Inclusive Perspective." *Review of Educational Research 29*(1): 385–430.

Sutton, Margaret and Levinson, Bradley. (2001). *Policy as Practice: Toward a Comparative Sociocultural Analysis of Educational Policy*. Westport, CT: Ablex Pub.

Taubman, Peter. (2007). "The Tie That Binds: Learning and Teaching in the New Educational Order." *Journal of Curriculum and Pedagogy* 4(2): 150–60.

Taubman, Peter. (2009). *Teaching By Numbers: Deconstructing the Discourse of Standards and Accountability*. New York: Routledge.

Van Maanen, John. (1988). *Tales of the Field: On Writing Ethnography*. Chicago: University of Chicago Press.

Walters, Pamela Barnhouse and Lareau, Annette. (2009). "Introduction." In *Education Research on Trial: Policy Reform and the Call for Scientific Rigor*. Edited by Pamela Barnhouse Walters, Annette Lareau, and Sheri H. Ranis. New York: Routledge, 1–13.

Whitehurst, Grover. (2008). "Rigor and Relevance Redux: Director's Biennial Report to Congress." Washington, DC: IES.

Wilson, Elizabeth. (1998). *Neural Geographies: Feminism and the Microstructures of Cognition*. New York: Routledge.

About the Contributors

Artiles, Alfredo is Professor of Education and Society, Culture, & Equity in the School of Social Transformation at Arizona State University. He is Editor (with T. Wiley) of the *International Multilingual Research Journal*, and edits (with E. Kozleski) the book series *Disability, Culture, & Equity*. Artiles has been an advisor/consultant to organizations or projects such as Harvard's and UCLA's Civil Rights Project, the National Academy of Education, the Annenberg Institute for School Reform (Brown University), the Council for Exceptional Children, the American Association on Mental Retardation, the Southern Poverty Law Center, and the Joseph P. Kennedy Jr. Foundation. He was selected the 2009 Distinguished Alumnus by the University of Virginia's Curry School of Education Foundation.

Austin, Jon is an Associate Professor of Education at the University of Southern Queensland, Australia. Coming from an early childhood teaching background, he has been involved in teacher education for over 25 years, in particular in social education, education sociology and critical cultural studies. He is the editor and co-author of *Identity and Culture; Educating for Healthy Communities and (Re)Presenting Education*. Jon has conducted award-winning research and pedagogical work in schools through the Building Racial Harmony Project and has spent time as an invited visiting scholar at a number of universities in Australia, the People's Republic of China and Aotearoa, New Zealand. His recent work includes contributions to critical perspectives on migrant security, indigenous knowledge in the new national Australian curriculum, and, most importantly, a chapter in *Teaching Joe Kincheloe*. He also has a long-standing commitment to ensuring Neil Young's contribution to the pantheon of rock music is not underestimated.

Barr, Denise is a highly experienced educational leader who works in the area of student and family well being and eliminating educational disadvantages. She has spent her career in education working in Melbourne's Western Suburbs, which has helped her to gain an understanding of the importance of equity in education. Prior to becoming the Wellbeing Coordinator at St. Albans Primary School Barr was a highly experienced classroom teacher who was committed to providing quality learning experiences for the children in her classroom. Denise is currently working as the Assistant Principal at St. Albans and continues to support the wellbeing of students at the school.

Barbour, JoAnn Danelo is Professor of Leadership and Administration at Texas Woman's University. She is recent past Chief Editor of *Academic Exchange Quarterly Journal,* as well as its Feature Editor for the Leadership issue, she is currently on the Advisory Board of AEQ. The author of numerous presentations and several journal articles and book chapters on leadership or teaching leadership, she recently published a chapter titled "Critical policy/practice arenas predicting 21st century conflict" in the Handbook of Educational Leadership, 2nd Edition (2011). Recently, Barbour co-edited two volumes of ILA's *Building Leadership Bridges: Global Leadership: Portraits of the Past, Visions for the Future* (2009) and *Leadership for Transformation* (2011), and will edit the 2012 volume. Areas of inquiry include a multidisciplinary approach to studying and developing leaders through anthropology, biography, history, autoethnography, and philosophy examining topics such as artistry, creativity, culture, values, and language use.

Benjamin, Amanda is an Associate Professor of Adult Education in the Faculty of Education at the University of New Brunswick. Her publications and research interests include critical examinations of career education, transitions to adulthood, employability skills and how adolescents form aspirations and conceptions of what it means to be an adult.

Bloch, Marianne (Mimi) has been a professor in the Department of Curriculum and Instruction (as well as in the Department of Gender and Women's Studies) at the University of Wisconsin-Madison for thirty years; she is now professor emerita, having retired in 2011. She is one of the founding members of the Reconceptualizing Early Childhood Education (RECE) conference. Her research has focused on gender and child care policy, children's play, cultural histories of American early education/child care, and critical cultural studies of how "science" and evidence frame or govern children, teachers, and families. Her recent publications include, Bloch, Holmlund, Moqvist, and Popkewitz (Eds.), *Governing children, families, and education: Restructuring the welfare state* (2003), and Bloch, Kennedy, Lightfoot, and Weyenberg, *The child in the world/The world in the child* (2006). She is currently studying standards and teacher perspectives in a five State case study within the USA related to new publicly funded early childhood programs, and is co-editor of the new on-line open access *International Journal of Critical Childhood Studies.*

Cannella, Gaile S. A former classroom teacher in Tennessee, Cannella joined the faculty of the University of North Texas as the Velma E. Schmidt Endowed Chair in Early Childhood Studies, Critical Qualitative Research Methodologies in 2009. Cannella's graduate degrees are from Tennessee Technological University and the University of Georgia. She has served as a professor of education at Louisiana State University, Texas A&M University in College Station, and Arizona State University in Tempe. She has authored or edited several books, including: *Deconstructing Early Childhood Education: Social Justice and Revolution; Embracing Identities in Early Childhood Education: Diversity and Possibilities* (with Sue Greishaber)*; Kidworld: Childhood Studies, Global Perspectives, and Education,* (with Joe Kincheloe)*; Childhood and Postcolonization: Power, Education, and Contemporary Practice* (with Radhika Viruru), *and Childhoods: A Handbook* (with Lourdes Diaz Soto) as well as published articles in such journals as *Qualitative Inquiry* and *Critical Studies-Critical Methodologies.* Her current research projects are designed to support equity and increased opportunity for all young children, and especially for those who have faced increased conditions of oppression in contemporary neoliberalism. Additionally, she focuses on the development of critical qualitative research methods and the conceptualization of a critical social science across diverse fields/forms of knowledge.

Carroll, Jeanne is a Senior Lecturer at Victoria University. She has worked in teacher education and conducted research in mathematics education in universities and with teachers in schools, both in Australia and overseas. Her research addresses the enhancement of positive affect toward mathematics teaching and learning, and the development of connected mathematical and pedagogical understanding. She also has a special interest in the use of Mathematics in Architecture and is well known for her conference presentations integrating the two disciplines.

Carspecken, Phil Francis is Professor of Inquiry Methodology at Indiana University in Bloomington, Indiana. His work attempts to relate the philosophy of critical theory from the Frankfurt School and the Theory of Communicative Action of Jürgen Habermas in particular, to educational research. He is the author of *Critical Ethnography in Educational Research; A Theoretical and Practical Guide.* His most recent projects include an investigation into the limits of what can be known. At Indiana University, Carspecken has assisted in the development of the world's first graduate program in inquiry methodology. This program integrates both qualitative and quantitative methodology tracks of study within a single degree program. Carspecken has earned many awards for his teaching both at the University of Houston and Indiana University, where he has nurtured many generations of students.

Cacciattolo, Marcelle is a sociologist and a senior lecturer in the School of Education at Victoria University. She has taught across a wide range of education programs. Over the last decade her research has been cross-disciplinary involving health sciences and education-based research. She has been involved in research projects tied to young people and their wellbeing, refugee relocation, social justice and authentic teaching and learning pedagogies within tertiary settings. Cacciattolo is a senior researcher in Standpoint project and works closely with schools in the Western Region to examine how inclusive pedagogies can support children and families who are the least advantaged. She is the author of several research articles and book chapters and is the Chief Investigator of the Positive Education Project at Victoria University.

Charles, Marilyn is a staff psychologist at the Austen Riggs Center and a psychoanalyst in private practice in Stockbridge and Richmond, MA. She is also an Adjunct Professor of Clinical Psychology at Michigan State University, faculty at several psychoanalytic institutes, and a member of the editorial boards of numerous psychoanalytic journals. She is actively engaged in mentoring and promoting community involvement for those in the helping professions, and her research interests include creativity and psychosis. Marilyn has presented her work nationally and internationally, her books include: *Patterns: Building Blocks of Experience, Constructing Realities: Transformations Through Myth and Metaphor* and *Learning from Experience: a Guidebook for Clinicians. A sequel to Learning From Experience* is forthcoming.

Clark, Carolyn is an Associate Professor of Adult Development at Texas A&M University. She serves as Co-Editor of *the International Journal of Qualitative Studies in Education*. She conducts and teaches narrative analysis and life history approaches to qualitative analysis.

Carroll, Jeanne is Senior Lecturer at Victoria University. Her research addresses the enhancement of positive affect toward mathematics teaching and learning, and the development of connected mathematical and pedagogical understanding. Carroll was the principal investigator on the Positive Education in Practice Research Project which involved implementing a range of approaches designed to enhance pre-service teachers' performance in a range of pre-service and post-graduate units in the

School of Education at Victoria University. She has for many years convened the annual conference of the Mathematical Association of Victoria, one of the largest annual conferences in the Southern Hemisphere.

Dei, George J. Sefa is Professor of Sociology and Equity Studies, Ontario Institute for Studies in Education of the University of Toronto (OISE/UT). His teaching and research interests are in the areas of Anti-Racism, Minority Schooling, International Development, Indigenous Philosophies, and Anti-Colonial Thought. In 2000 he co-edited Indigenous *Knowledges in Global Contexts: Multiple Readings of Our World,* with Budd Hall and Dorothy Goldin Rosenberg. His most recent books include: *Teaching Africa: Towards a Transgressive Pedagogy; Fanon and Education: Thinking Through Pedagogical Possibilities,* (co-edited with Marlon Simmons); *Fanon and the Counterinsurgency of Education* (edited), *Learning to Succeed: The Challenges and Possibilities of Educational Achievement for All,* and *Indigenous Philosophies and Critical Education: A Reader.* In July 2007, he succeeded the occupant of the stool [Odikro] of Asokorekuma and was installed as a traditional chief in Ghana. His stool name is Nana Sefa Atweneboah I, the Adomakwaahene of the town of Asokore, near Koforidua in the New Juaben Traditional Area of Ghana.

deMarrais, Kathleen is Professor in the Department of Lifelong Education, Administration and Policy at the University of Georgia. From 1999-2004, she was the coordinator of the Qualitative Inquiry Program, and from 2004-2009 she served as Associate Dean for Academic Programs in the College of Education at UGA. She is a qualitative methodologist with interests in the ethics and politics of conducting qualitative research studies and in teaching qualitative research methodologies. Dr. deMarrais has a long history of teaching qualitative research methods courses as well as conducting qualitative evaluations and workshops in qualitative research methods. She has published numerous articles and book chapters, and numerous books including: *Foundations for research: Methods of Inquiry in Education and the Social Sciences* (with S. Lapan,); *Life at the Margins: Profiles of Diverse Adults* (with J. Merrifield, D. Hemphill & B. Bingman).

Ducy, Elizabeth McAdams is a doctoral student in Educational Psychology at Texas A&M University. Her research interests include disability and disaster, mental health of individuals with intellectual disabilities, and social supports for individuals with disabilities. She has a Masters in low incidence disabilities and taught children with disabilities for six years in the Houston area.

Easton-Brooks, Donald is an Associate Dean in the School of Education at Hamline University. He received his masters and Ph.D. from the University of Colorado at Denver. He research focuses on the impact of education policies, practice, and social factors on the achievement outcomes of African American students. While his research is based on advance quantitative analysis, his work is engaged by qualitative research on issues related to cultural relevancy in education.

Fine, Michelle is a Distinguished Professor of Psychology, Urban Education and Women's Studies at the Graduate Center of the City University of New York. Engaged with participatory and critical psychology, she is committed to social inquiry for social justice, in prisons, schools and communities. A student of Morton Deutsch, and therefore academic grandchild of Kurt Lewin, Fine is interested in the intersection of critical justice studies and social action. Recent publications include *Revolutionizing Education: Participatory action research in motion*, "Changing Minds: The impact of college in a maximum security prison for women" (with Kathy Boudin, Iris Bowen, Judith Clark, Donna Hylton, Migdalia Martinez, "Missy," Melissa Rivera, Rosemarie Roberts, Pam Smart, Maria Torre and Debora Upegu) and *Muslim American Youth: Studying Hyphenated Identities with Mixed Methods* (with Selcuk Sirin).

Fox, Madeline is a doctoral candidate in the Social-Personality Psychology program at the CUNY Graduate Center and director of the Polling for Justice project. Her participatory research focuses on youth experiences of every day criminalization, dignity, mutual implication and conditions for provoking political solidarity with adult audiences. She is co-editor of *Telling Stories to Change the World: Global Voices on the Power of Narrative to Build Community and Make Social Justice Claims.* Her work can be found in volumes such as *The Handbook of Research and Policy on Civic Engagement in Youth* and *Be The Change: Teacher, Activist, Global Citizen.*

Helyar, Frances is an Assistant Professor of Education at the Orillia, Ontario campus of Lakehead University. Her PhD is from McGill University in Montreal, and her areas of specialization are critical pedagogy and the social foundations of education, with a particular focus on the history of education in Canada and North America. She teaches courses in foundations, educational law and teaching in a non-school pedagogic site.

Goodman, Greg S. is an associate professor of education at Clarion University of Pennsylvania. His main research interests include teacher education, self-efficacy and education, and the value of alternative educational approaches. Dr. Goodman is the Executive Editor of Peter Lang Publishing's *Educational Psychology* series. He is the editor of *Educational Psychology: An Application of Critical Constructivism, The Educational Psychology Reader, Reducing Hate Crimes and Violence Among American Youths,* and *Alternatives in Education: Critical Pedagogy for Disaffected Youth.*

Hickey, Andrew is Senior Lecturer in Cultural Studies and Social Theory at the University of Southern Queensland, Australia. In conjunction with his research on public pedagogies and urban space, Andrew has led numerous projects exploring identity, community and race politics and has developed approaches in ethnographic and autoethnographic field practice. He is the author of *(Re)Presenting Education: Students, Teachers, Schools and the Public Imagination* (with Jon Austin), a sociology of schooling and popular cultural representations of education and *Cities of Signs: Learning the Logic of Urban Space,* an ethnographic study of urban space and public pedagogy.

Jardine, David is Professor of Education in the Faculty of Education at the University of Calgary. Recent work includes his new book, *Pedagogy Left in Peace* and a co-authored essay entitled "A Zone of Deep Shadow: Pedagogical and Familial Reflections on 'The Clash of Civilizations'," published in *Interchange: A Quarterly Review of Education.*

Kim, Ko Eun is a doctoral candidate in the Department of Curriculum and Instruction at the University of Wisconsin- Madison. Her research interests focus on the Early childhood education policy development and reform efforts as a discursive space for (trans)forming new subjectivities of young children and early childhood teachers.

Kincheloe, Joe L., (1950-2008) was the founder of The Paulo and Nita International Project for Critical Pedagogy and a Canada Research Chair. He was the author of over 50 books and hundreds of articles, producer of films on critical pedagogy, and advisor to hundreds of graduate students. Originally from the mountains of East Tennessee, his first teaching position was at Sinte Gleska on the Rosebud Lakota Reservation in South Dakota. After the publication of his first book, *Getting Beyond the Facts: Teaching Social Studies in the Late Twentieth Century,* he wrote *Teachers as Researchers: Qualitative Paths to Empowerment,* a book, which changed how qualitative research in education could be contextualized. He wrote books in critical pedagogy, vocational education, urban education, art and culture, cultural studies, his final books being *Knowledge and Critical Pedagogy: An Introduction* and co-editing *Christotainment: Selling Jesus Through Popular Culture* (with Shirley R. Steinberg). Kincheloe is considered the leader of the second generation of critical pedagogy theorists and remained devoted to the notion of a flexible and changing critical pedagogy throughout his life. He was an adamant qualitative researcher, and in the latter decade of the twentieth century conceptualized the research bricolage, which revolutionalized ways in which to perceive research as a philosophical and social theoretical construct. Known for his warmth and Southern charm, he was devoted to his family, rock n' roll music (he played in bands for over 40 years), the Democratic Party, and college football. As a critical theorist, he insisted on naming truths and naming names, and was a severe critic of the academic disasters created in faculties of education (eg, Penn State, Florida International University, Clemson University, Brooklyn College, and McGill University) and the horrendous inequities caused by NCATE, the US Department of Education, and standardized testing…indeed, after working for over 30 years, he realized that creating an equitable and empowering school of education could be almost impossible; however, he remained devoted to a critical pedagogy of hope.

Koro-Ljungberg, Mirka is an associate professor of qualitative research methodology at the University of Florida, in the School of human development and organizational studies in education. She received her doctorate from the University of Helsinki, Finland. Prior to joining the faculty at the University of Florida she was a visiting scholar at the University of Georgia. Her research interests focus on the conceptual aspects and empirical applications of qualitative, experimental methods, and participant driven methodologies.

Kozleski, Elizabeth B. is Professor of Culture, Society, and Education in ASU's School of Social Transformation. She holds the UNESCO Chair in Inclusive International Research. Her research includes examining and theorizing approaches to systems change in urban and large school systems, how identity, culture, ability and practice are negotiated in classrooms and schools, and how schools become conscious and purposeful sites for professional learning. Kozleski co-edits with Alfredo Artiles a books series on *Disability, Culture, and Equity*.

Lather, Patti is Professor in the School of Educational Policy and Leadership, has taught qualitative research, feminist methodology and gender and education at Ohio State University. She is the author of *Getting Smart: Feminist Research and Pedagogy With/in the Postmodern* (1991 Critics Choice Award), *Troubling the Angels: Women Living with HIV/AIDS*, co-authored with Chris Smithies (1998 CHOICE Outstanding Academic Title), and *Getting Lost: Feminist Efforts Toward a Double(d) Science* (2008 Critics Choice Award). Her recent book, *Engaging (Social) Science: Policy from the Side of the Messy*, is with Peter Lang. Lather has lectured widely in international and national contexts and held a number of distinguished visiting lectureships. Her work examines various (post)critical, feminist, and poststructural theories, most recently with a focus on the implications for qualitative inquiry of the call for scientifically-based research in education.

Leistyna, Pepi is Associate Professor of Applied Linguistics Graduate Studies at the University of Massachusetts Boston, where he coordinates the research program, teaches courses in cultural studies, media literacy, and language acquisition, and is the Director of the Center for World Languages and Cultures. He is a research fellow for the National Education Policy Center at the University of Colorado Boulder. His books include: *Breaking Free: The Transformative Power of Critical Pedagogy*; *Presence of Mind: Education and the Politics of Deception*; *Defining and Designing Multiculturalism*, and *Cultural Studies: From Theory to Action*. His forthcoming book is *Television and Working Class Identity: Intersecting Differences* and his documentary film is called *Class Dismissed: How TV Frames the Working Class* for which he received the Working-Class Studies Association's Studs Terkel Award for Media and Journalism. He is the co-editor of the Peter Lang Series, *Minding the Media*.

Lester, Jessica Nina's main research interests lie at the intersection of culture, psychological constructs (e.g., learning, motivation, emotions, etc.), and education, particularly as related to the education of marginalized and targeted youth. Situating much of her work in the learning sciences and disability studies in education, she takes an interdisciplinary approach. Lester primarily draws upon qualitative inquiry methods, particularly discursive and ethnographic approaches. She is the 2011 Recipient of the Extraordinary Professional Promise Chancellor's Award, University of Tennessee. The author of many papers, her newest article (with R. Gabriel) is: "Community performances and performative texts as tools for critical exploration" in *Power and Education*.

Lincoln, Yvonna S. is the Ruth Harrington Chair of Educational Leadership and Distinguished Professor of Higher Education at Texas A&M University, where she also serves as Program Chair for the higher education program area. She is the co-editor, with Norman K. Denzin, of the journal *Qualitative Inquiry*, and of the 1st, 2nd, 3rd and now 4th editions of the *Handbook of Qualitative Inquiry*, and the *Handbook of Critical and Indigenous Methodologies*. As well, she is the co-author, editor or co-editor of more than a half dozen other books and volumes, including *Effective Evaluation, Naturalistic Inquiry*, and *Fourth Generation Evaluation*, all with Egon Guba, and *Organization Theory and Inquiry*. She is the author or co-author of more than 100 chapters and journal articles on aspects of higher education or qualitative research methods and methodologies. Her research interests include development of qualitative methods and methodologies, the status and future of research libraries, and other issues in higher education. She currently writes an occasional column for the higher education blog, www.21stcenturyscholar.com, where she comments on the rapidly-evolving status of research universities in the U.S.

Madan, Athena is a doctoral student at the University of Toronto. She is a mental health practitioner and certified member of the Canadian Counselling & Psychotherapy Association. Her research interests include mental health equity, mental health education, the social aetiology of mental illness, and transcultural psychiatry.

McLaren, Peter is currently Professor at the University of Auckland. His most recent books include *Pedagogy and Praxis in the Age of Empoire, Teaching Against Global Capitalism and the New Imperialism* (with Ramin Farahmandpur), and *Critical Pedagogy: Where are we now?* (with Joe Kincheloe). He is well-known for his work in critical pedagogy and social justice.

McDermott, Mairi is a doctoral student at the University of Toronto in the department of Sociology and Equity Studies in the Ontario Institute for Studies in Education. She is also a New York State certified secondary English Language Arts teacher and is interested in researching student voice, literacy, and equity by way of the current neoliberal governance of schooling-and-education. Specifically, through an integrative anti-racist framework she is considering the ways in which racialized student subjectivities come to be desired, shaped, and performed in the context of schooling-and-education.

McKenna, Tarquam is an Associate Professor at Victoria University, Melbourne, Australia. Whilst he has been active as an Arts Psychotherapist for twenty years and edits the international *Australian and New Zealand Journal of Art Therapy* (ANZJAT) most of his life he has been a researcher-as-teacher in inclusive education and areas aligned with equity and well-being. Tarquam is past president and an honorary life member of ANZATA. He is also keenly interested in artful practice and research methods, which especially have applicability to Indigenous stories. The work in PEP project was combining the educational work he undertakes alongside his interest in art psychotherapies. He has been teaching in Thailand and Vietnam and he has published widely in the area of gender and sexuality. Along with

Marcelle Cacciattolo, Mark Vicars and Shirley Steinberg, he is a founding member of the Asia Critical Ensemble, which examines social justice and the legacies of Paulo Freire in particular, and how colonization has impacted on multiple lives around the world

Morton, Missy is Associate Professor of Education in the School of Educational Studies and Human Development in the College of Education, University of Canterbury, Christchurch, New Zealand. She coordinates the Masters program in the College of Education. She has taught qualitative research in education since 1994. Missy's research and teaching areas include Disability Studies in Education, social constructions of science and research in (special) education, and inclusive education.

Morrell, Ernest is the director of the Institute for Urban and Minority Education and Professor of English Education at Teacher's College. For over twenty years Morrell has worked with adolescents using popular culture to promote academic literacy development and civic engagement. Morrell's other interests include urban school reform, youth participatory action research, critical literacy education, youth media production, and urban teacher leadership. He is the author of *Becoming Critical Researchers: Literacy and Empowerment for Urban Youth*; *Critical Literacy and Urban Youth*; *Pedagogies of Access, Dissent, and Liberation*; *Linking Literacy and Popular Culture: Finding Connections for Lifelong Learning*, and *The Art of Critical Pedagogy: Possibilities for Moving from Theory to Practice in Urban Schools*. Formerly a high school English teacher and coach, Morrell worked with high school teens in Los Angeles for the past 12 years, directing the Council of Youth Research, a project that involves youth in researching issues in their communities and schools.

Nasser, Ramzi is currently the Director of the Center of Educational Development and Research and Associate Professor of Education at the Qatar University. He held various administrative, academic and research positions at Beirut University College, United Arab Emirates University, Emirates Center for Strategic Studies, University of Balamand (Lebanon), Bishops University (Canada) and Notre Dame University (Lebanon). He earned his Doctorate of Education from the University of Massachusetts at Lowell. His research work falls in the area of geriatric assessment, institutional research, misconceptions in mathematics, and psycho-social attribution.

Nava, Pedro E. is an advanced doctoral student at UCLA's Graduate School of Education in the Urban Schooling division. The focus of his research is urban and rural schooling inequality, critical pedagogy, family-school engagement, and undergraduate social justice based research. Mr. Nava has been published in *InterActions: UCLA Journal of Education and Information Studies*, in (Eds.) Hoosain & Salili's *Democracy and Multicultural Education*, and in *Teachers College Record* with Gilberto Q. Conchas. He is currently completing his dissertation, which examines how the life histories of migrant farmworking families shape their educational engagement practices in a small community in rural California.

O'Loughlin, Michael is Professor at Adelphi University in Long Island, New York, where he is on the faculty of Derner Institute of Advanced Psychological Studies and in the School of Education. He is a clinical and research supervisor in the Ph.D. program in Clinical Psychology, and he is a training analyst in the Postgraduate Programs in Psychoanalysis and Psychotherapy at Adelphi. He published *The Subject of Childhood* in 2009 and he edited *Imagining Children Otherwise: Theoretical and Critical Perspectives on Childhood Subjectivity* with Richard Johnson in 2010. He is co-editor with Glenys Lobban and Cora Smith of *Psychodynamic Psychotherapy in Contemporary South Africa: Theory, Practice, and Policy Perspectives*, and *Working With Children's Emotional Lives: Psychodynamic Perspectives on Children and Schools*. His interests include intergenerational and collective trauma, the social origins of psychosis and schizophrenia, and the emotional lives of children, particularly in indigenous communities.

Park, Jeff is an educator and writer, working in a number of genres including short fiction, poetry, and drama. He has published a book on writing theory and narrative entitled *Writing at the Edge*, and recently had three stories published in *Coming Attractions 09*. His book of poetry *The Cellophane Sky: Jazz Poems* has recently been published. He is now in the process of finishing a collection of short stories, and two new poetry manuscripts. He is currently at the University of Saskatchewan, where he teaches courses in writing, curriculum, and literacy, and is engaged in several research projects focusing on writing, literacy policy, and alternative literacies.

Perselli, Victoria is based at Kingston University UK, where she is currently Program Chair for the Joint Education Doctorate. Her research and teaching interests include curriculum design, equality and identity in higher education, critical leadership and research methodologies for professional practice. She has published in the areas of inclusive education, visual and performance arts, qualitative research methodologies, the self-study of teacher education practices, European 'high theory' and assessment in the context of doctoral research.

Proto, Carolina Muñoz is a doctoral student in the Social/Personality Psychology Program at the Graduate Center of the City University of New York. Her research lies at the intersection of psychology, participatory action-based research, and is influenced by the Latin American current of thought known as Universalist Humanism. Current projects explore individual and collective experiences with nonviolence activism and the criminalization of urban youth. Earlier projects explored cross-cultural mentoring relationships as sites for alliance building and peer-education towards multiculturalism and justice. She is affiliated to the Public Science Project at the CUNY Graduate Center and is a teaching fellow at the Hunter College Psychology Department, CUNY.

Rau, Cheryl is of Tainui, Kahungungu and Rangitane descent. Her educational and research focus has centered on Te Tiriti o Waitangi partnerships in Aotearoa, with Maori educators articulating strategies which nurture tamariki Maori potentiality across the early childhood community. From 2004 to 2008 she completed co-directing two research studies funded by the New Zealand government's Teaching and Learning Research Initiative, which centered on prioritizing Maori (indigenous to Aotearoa) ways of knowing, doing and being and transformative praxis within the sector. She has recently completed co-directing a further two-year TLRI project, which explored kaitiakitanga (ecological sustainability) utilizing an ethic of caring for self, others and the environment from both indigenous and western perspectives. During the past thirteen years she has been an early childhood educator and coordinator/director of Ngahihi professional learning programs, a Maori organization facilitating professional learning programs funded by the Ministry of Education. In 2009 she joined Te Tari Puna Ora o Aotearoa, The New Zealand Childcare Association as the Central Regional Manager.

Richmond, Joanne is the Principal of St Albans Primary School, located in Melbourne's Western Suburbs. The school community is socio economically disadvantaged and culturally diverse with a high number of refugee students. As an educator Joanne is committed to social justice and has a strong belief that all students can learn. Joanne's work as Assistant Principal was focused around supporting the social, emotional and academic wellbeing of all students. This included working closely with her colleague Denise Barr the school Wellbeing Coordinator to establish Programs such as a Breakfast Club, Active After School Communities, and Parent Programs to better support the needs of the school community.

Ritchie, Jenny is an Associate Professor in Early Childhood Teacher Education at Te Whare Wānanga o Wairaka - Unitec Institute of Technology, Auckland, New Zealand. Her teaching and research has focused on supporting early childhood educators and teacher educators to enhance their praxis in terms of enacting an awareness of cultural, environmental and social justice issues. She has recently led three consecutive two-year studies funded by the New Zealand Teaching and Learning Research Initiative, focusing on implementing early childhood pedagogies reflecting these commitments.

Sanchez, Claudia is Associate Professor of Bilingual Education and ESL at Texas Woman's University. Her research interests include mentorship in higher education, parental involvement, native language literacy through oral traditions, multiculturalism, and teacher training. As a grant writer, Sanchez has secured federal funding for TWU in the amount of over $4 million dollars since 2004. Sponsored by the U.S. Department of Education, these projects are partnerships with urban school districts in Texas and focus on teacher preparation in the areas of bilingual/ESL education, mathematics, and special education as well professional development for bilingual/ESL in-service teachers.

Schmidt, Renata is an assistant professor at Furman University in Greenville, SC. Nita teaches literacy methods courses, children's literature, and literacy assessment at the graduate and undergraduate level at Furman. Her research interests include the politics of literacy, critical topics in children's literature, and socio-political issues surrounding literacy teaching.

Shahzad, Farhat taught in Federal Urdu University of Science and Technologies, Karachi, Pakistan from 1993 to 2005. She teaches equity in education and educational foundations in the teacher education program at the Faculty of Education, the University of Ottawa. Her research focuses upon the "War on Terror," culture, society, education, national/ transnational identities, and collective memories. Her publications include "Forging the nation (2011)," and books on Pakistan Affairs.

Shields, Carolyn M. is the dean of the College of Education at Wayne State University. Her teaching is in the area of transformative leadership, deep democracy, equitable policy, social justice, and research methodology. Her research focuses on how educational leaders can create learning environments that are deeply democratic, socially just, inclusive of all students' lived experiences, and that prepare students for excellence and citizenship in our global society. These interests are reflected in her presentations and publications—over 100 articles, hundreds of conference and keynote presentations, and seven books—the most recent are *Transformative Leadership: A Reader* and *Courageous Leadership for Transforming Schools: Democratizing Practice*. She has received recognition for both her teaching and her career contributions to the field of educational leadership.

Simmons, Marlon is a doctoral candidate in the Department of Sociology and Equity Studies at the Ontario Institute for Studies in Education, University of Toronto. His current research interests include anti-colonial thought, issues of governance and self in the context of schooling, and educational reform. The foci of his thesis are about modernity and colonialism, with a particular attention to Diasporic experiences and the interplay in the context of the West. He recently co-edited *Fanon and Education: Thinking through Pedagogical Possibilities* (2010), with George. J. Sefa Dei, and *The Politics of Cultural Knowledge* (2011), with Njoki Wane and Arlo Kempf.

Somerville, Margaret is a Professor of Education (Learning and Development) at Monash University. She is a pioneer in place studies in Australia and in linking place to education through her research into enabling pedagogies of place. Her focus is on the critical power of place to open spaces for alternative gendered, classed and ethnic stories to emerge. This has led to her development of alternative methodologies and modes of representation in educational research, and to consider the ways that these can be relevant and engaging for diverse local communities. She is a co-editor of *Place Pedagogy Change* and co-author of *Change and Landscapes and Learning*.

Stanley, Timothy J. is professor of education foundations and antiracism education in the Faculty of Education, University of Ottawa. He publishes on antiracism and history. His most recent work, *Contesting White Supremacy: School Segregation, Anti-Racism* and the *Making of Chinese Canadians* (2011) explores the writing of antiracist history.

Steinberg, Shirley R. is the Director and Chair of The Werklund Foundation Centre for Youth Leadership in Education, and Professor of Youth Studies at the University of Calgary. Her most recent books include: *Kinderculture: The Corporate Construction of Childhood* (2011); *19 Urban Questions: Teaching in the City* (2010); *Christotainment: Selling Jesus Through Popular Culture* (with Joe Kincheloe) (2009); *Diversity and Multiculturalism: A Reader* (2009); *Media Literacy: A Reader* (with Donaldo Macedo) (2007); the award winning *Contemporary Youth Culture: An International Encyclopedia*; and *The Miseducation of the West: How Schools and Media Distort Our Understanding of the Islamic World* (with Joe Kincheloe) (2004). Originally a social/improvisational theatre creator, she has facilitate happenings and flashmobs globally. She is also the founding editor of *Taboo: The Journal of Culture and Education*, *The International Journal of Youth Studies*, and the Managing Editor of *The International Journal of Critical Pedagogy*. The co-founder of The Paulo and Nita Freire International Project for Critical Pedagogy, she is the organizer of The Critical Pedagogical Congress, she is committed to a global community of transformative educators and community workers engaged in radical love, social justice, and the situating of power within social and cultural contexts. Websites are http://wcmprod2.ucalgary.ca/werklundwide/ and freireproject.org

Stough, Laura is Associate Professor of Educational Psychology at Texas A&M University and Interdisciplinary Training Director at the Center for Disability and Development. She researches how disasters impact people with disabilities, and effective instruction of students with diverse abilities. She is interested in developing research methods for use with vulnerable populations and using grounded theory as an analytical tool.

Thomas, P.L. is Associate Professor of Education at Furman University, he taught high school English in rural South Carolina before moving to teacher education. He is currently a column editor for *English Journal* (National Council of Teachers of English) and series editor for *Critical Literacy Teaching Series: Challenging Authors and Genres* in which he authored the first volume—*Challenging Genres: Comics and Graphic Novels* (2010). Additional recent books include *Parental Choice: A Critical Reconsideration of Choice and the Debate about Choice* and *21st Century Literacy: If We Are Scripted, Are We Literate?* co-authored with Renita Schmidt. He maintains a blog addressing the role of poverty in education: http://livinglearninginpoverty.blogspot.com/. His teaching and scholarship focus on literacy and the impact of poverty on education, as well as confronting the political dynamics influencing public education in the U.S. His work can be followed at http://wrestlingwithwriting.blogspot.com/.

Tobin, Kenneth is Presidential Professor of Urban Education at the Graduate Center of the City University of New York. Prior to becoming a university science educator in Australia in 1974, Tobin taught high school physics, chemistry, biology general science, and mathematics for 10 years. He began a program of research in 1973 that continues to the present day—teaching and learning of science and learning to teach science. As well as research being undertaken in the Bronx of New York City, Tobin is involved in collaborative research in Brisbane, Australia; Sao Paulo, Brazil; and Kaohsiung, Taiwan. His current research involves multilevel studies of the relationships between emotions and physiological factors associated with the wellness of teachers and students. In his career Tobin has published many books, articles, and book chapters. With Barry Fraser and Campbell McRobbie, he is co-editor of the second edition of the *International Handbook of Research in Science Education* to be published in

2012. Tobin is the founding co-editor of *Cultural Studies of Science Education*. His most recent book is *Transforming urban education: Collaborating to produce success in science, mathematics and technology education*.

Ullrich, Walter J. is currently lead faculty and graduate program coordinator for the online Master of Arts in Teaching (MAT) at CSU Fresno. His scholarly interests integrate multicultural, social justice teacher education with action research in both school-based and virtual teaching/learning environments. Ullrich has also served as Regional Center Academic Director for CalStateTEACH/Fresno, a school-based, web-enhanced teacher preparation program and in middle level teacher education at St. Cloud State University, Minnesota.

Vicars, Mark is Senior Lecturer in Literacy in the School of Education at Victoria University, Melbourne, Australia. He has worked as a literacy educator within the compulsory and post-compulsory sectors, in Japan, Korea Thailand, Vietnam, Cambodia England and Australia. An overarching concern, in his work, is to understand ways in which individuals make use of language and literacy in identity work. He is particularly interested in intercultural literacy and Mark has recently been funded by DFAT/Australia-Thailand institute to work on developing participatory programs for English language and literacy teacher development in Thailand. In 2010, Mark was awarded the Australian Learning and Teaching Council Citation for Outstanding Contributions to Student Learning.

Viruru, Radhika is an Associate Clinical Professor in Early Childhood Education at Texas A&M University. Viruru's interests include postcolonial theory and its application to international early childhood education and qualitative research. She is the author of two books on childhood and postcolonial theory, Early Childhood Education: Postcolonial Perspectives from India and Childhood and Postcolonization: Power, Education and Contemporary Practice (co-author). She has recently been involved in multiple qualitative research and service projects connected to early childhood education and teacher professional development in Qatar.

Index

Aboriginal artists 76

action conditions 45-46, 59-60, 64-65

action research 19, 43-44, 153-156, 159, 161, 204-205, 217, 390-398, 404, 405, 420-426, 430, 438, 448

activism 6, 11, 44, 89, 112, 172, 174, 178, 200, 209, 212-217, 390, 436, 469

activist 2, 6, 10, 11, 153, 155, 156, 178, 200, 209, 212-214, 308, 370, 372, 374, 380, 431, 432

activity theory 408, 410, 417

address 195, 579

Adorno, Theodor 201, 429, 578

adulthood 92, 379, 380-387, 482

advocacy 3-11, 109, 156, 214, 267-277, 286-292, 308, 437, 504-505

aesthetics 134, 169, 196, 345-346
"the aesthetic" 139, 183, 196

agency 10, 11, 21, 25, 117, 119, 167-170, 173, 176, 179, 200-207, 210, 213-215, 241, 242, 246, 257, 261, 288, 301, 302, 307-309, 316, 317, 347, 351, 414, 430, 432, 433, 435, 446, 492, 509, 515, 520-522

Althusser, Louis 203, 380, 558

analyses 2, 4, 104, 105, 109, 117, 120-125, 158-162, 186, 189, 194, 201, 207, 227, 246, 247, 254, 257, 258, 260, 262, 263, 266, 271, 324, 343, 365, 391, 413, 433, 436, 488, 489, 524, 548

anthropology 16, 21, 26-27, 57, 203, 207, 346, 348-349, 500, 504, 560

anticolonial social science 88-89

anti-racism 236, 242-243, 318-326
framework 235, 238

Aristotle 35-36

art
    as enquiry 104, 129-131, 143, 191, 201, 204, 350, 429, 430
    exhibitions 78
    as public pedagogy 78, 80, 420,

Atwood, Margaret 102
    A Handmaid's Tale 102

audience 52-53, 78, 79, 100, 102, 107, 124, 153, 154, 160-163, 185-186, 188, 213, 226, 316, 423, 462, 532

audiencing 185

authenticity 6, 9, 10, 116-119, 348, 513, 518, 532, 563
    educative 10, 118
    tactical 10, 118-119

authority 17, 26, 27, 58, 60, 63, 93, 121, 145, 149, 184, 190, 192, 202, 203, 206, 228, 301, 344, 354, 357, 364, 366, 403, 423, 425, 430, 432-434, 442, 476, 539, 550, 551, 561, 562

autism 247, 250, 329-340, 421

autobiography 52, 53, 71, 518

awareness
    discursive 47, 61

Bacon, Sir Francis 204, 356, 357

Bakhtin, Mikhail 15, 210, 322, 518

Barthes, Roland 202

Baudrillard, Jean 15, 182

Being and Time (by Martin Heidegger) 149

beliefs 6, 11, 14, 34, 38, 39, 45, 47, 50, 52, 55-61, 64, 95, 138, 176, 195, 202, 203, 240, 255, 282, 380, 382, 391, 431, 434, 442, 508, 515, 518, 519, 537, 538

Bennett, Chief Judge Mark 252-254

Berger, Arthur Asa 182, 183, 193, 194, 196
Berry, Kathleen 16, 21, 184
"best practice" 257-273
Bhabha, Homi 201
bias 3, 5, 38, 39, 189, 323-324, 384, 433-434, 500
    confirmation 5
Biographic Narrative Interpretive Method 469
biography 67, 80, 227, 276
biopower 258
Birmingham (school) 202
Black feminism 39, 86, 107
Boal, Augusto 154, 160, 162
body
    discourses of the 67, 70, 73, 84-87, 117, 122-125, 144,
        189, 190, 237, 238, 241, 242, 258, 297-305, 319, 332,
        333, 334, 341, 350, 355, 368, 387, 424, 425, 475, 483,
        526
Bourdieu, Pierre 3, 7, 25, 26, 57, 58, 119, 202, 236, 240,
    242, 243, 271, 301, 429, 432, 558
Brandom, Robert 45
Breadwinner, The (by Deborah Ellis) 96
bricolage 14-32, 182-197
Britzman, Deborah 20, 472, 500-501
Bush, George W. 93-95, 457

Cabral, Amical 201
capitalism 17, 105-111, 163, 168, 201, 208, 211, 212, 215,
    273, 430, 433, 495
    hyper- 89, 105-106
Cartesian 130, 132, 133, 345, 421
    -Newtonian-Baconian epistemology 343, 345, 356
catalytic authenticity 10, 118
Chambers, Simone 211
Chinese Canadian community 318, 384
citation 99, 101
civilization 150, 185, 201, 344, 346, 352, 487
Civil Rights Act (1964) 37, 38, 253, 254
Cixous, Hélène 15, 73
class 4, 6, 8, 39, 40, 45-53, 51, 62, 65, 153, 158, 184, 185,
    188, 189, 190, 194, 195, 292, 368, 369, 516
classification 247, 258, 268, 270, 272, 304, 348, 356
closings 155, 272
coercive power 62
cogenerative dialogue (cogen) 116-120
collaboration 18, 97, 100-101, 156, 159, 160, 205, 235,
    290, 291, 293, 368, 374, 394, 401, 404, 433, 438, 452,
    505, 506, 509, 512, 527, 539, 541, 562
collective biography 67, 80
collective knowledge 34, 37-41, 562
collective memory 525-528, 532, 533
collective narratives 524-527, 532
collective reality 38
Collins, Patricia Hill 14, 39-40, 81, 105, 107
Collins, Randall 124, 494
colonization 9, 224, 320, 347-348, 437, 498, 502
comic books 91, 97, 358
communicative action 45, 48, 64, 430
communicatively coordinated action 46, 47
community 3, 8-10, 16, 18, 34, 37-40, 44, 60, 61, 69, 75,
    79, 80, 89, 94, 106, 107, 110, 112, 149, 154-156, 159,
    161-163, 174, 186, 191, 195, 196, 205, 206, 211, 214,
    215, 222, 223, 225, 226, 231, 232, 238, 240, 249, 262,

265, 267, 268, 276, 277, 284, 285, 289, 291-293, 316,
318, 323, 324, 337, 338, 358, 365-376, 380, 381, 383,
392-404, 408, 411, 413, 414, 435, 437, 438, 441-444,
447, 448, 450-453, 457, 460, 463, 481, 484, 488, 492,
496, 502-504, 508, 509, 519, 539, 543, 545, 549, 551,
552
complexity/complexities 106, 191, 341, 463
Comte, Auguste 204, 556
concept of knowledge 34
conditions of action 45, 59, 60, 62, 64
confirmation bias 5
conscientization 44, 488
consciousness 184, 190, 191, 196
    raising 43-45, 217
constructivism 36, 130, 187, 203, 558
contact zone 69-70, 78-80, 157
content analysis 27, 184, 186, 310, 486
context 6, 7, 16, 18, 19, 21-28, 33, 34, 39, 49, 50, 72, 83,
    85, 86, 87, 88, 89, 97, 101, 111, 112, 121, 122, 126, 132,
    135, 139, 145, 156, 176, 183-196, 214, 228, 230, 244,
    248, 270, 273, 296-304, 309-311, 319, 323-326, 330,
    334, 337, 341-359, 365, 371, 375-376, 379, 380-381,
    386, 392, 393, 397, 401-417, 421, 432-434, 452-453,
    469-470, 473, 477, 483, 496, 497, 514, 517, 518, 519,
    520, 525, 527, 528, 530, 531, 536, 538, 540-545, 551,
    554, 558, 560-561
contextualization 184, 193
contradictions 185, 191
conventionalism 36
convivial life of the world 146
co-researchers 116, 118, 156, 480, 481, 537, 538, 539, 540,
    541, 542, 543
corporatization of knowledge 110, 112
counter-hegemonic 296, 504
craft 91, 101, 171, 223, 352, 399, 423, 444
critical 182-197
    advocacy research 3, 5, 6
    aesthetic 169-179
    consciousness 195
    disability 307
    ethnography 26, 27, 43, 44, 45, 46, 58, 168, 171, 174,
        189, 276, 365, 367, 375, 560
    of the everyday 168
    feminism 3, 14,
    hermeneutics 182, 184, 188, 189, 193-196
    inquiry 4, 6, 97, 104, 112, 154, 371
    methodological theory 43-66
    multilogical education 354, 358
    literacy 95, 364, 366, 549, 553, 554
    ontology 23
    pedagogy 14, 17, 18, 19, 20, 28, 44, 94, 98, 106, 107,
        157, 195, 203, 205, 345, 365, 370, 376, 390, 420, 424,
        426, 432, 433, 434, 435, 437, 439, 494, 550
    perspectives 3, 5, 9, 89, 99-100, 104-108, 410, 434
    poverty theory 3
    publications 98, 99
    social research agenda 225
    social sciences 112
    social theory 46, 52, 194, 201, 203, 367, 369
    teacher research 19
    teachers 18, 19, 433, 434, 550
    theorist 186, 191

theory 2, 5, 14, 15, 16, 20, 28, 44, 45, 49, 64, 104, 184, 192, 201, 203, 205, 225, 236, 358, 366, 380, 429, 436, 439, 524,
    theory of society 64
    tradition 196
    youth studies 154, 155
criticality 14-16, 20, 23, 171, 174, 177, 178, 222, 421, 426, 437-439, 520
cultural
    activists 200, 208
    contestation 45
    hegemony 9, 17, 97, 182, 202, 203, 208, 342, 351, 366, 380, 381, 425, 429, 431, 432, 456, 468, 559, 563,
    pedagogy 182, 183, 184, 196
    production 191, 196
    structure 46, 58, 59
    structures 46, 53, 63
    studies 21, 182, 183, 184, 192, 197, 202, 203, 205, 207, 357
culture 8, 9, 11, 15, 16, 18, 20-27, 34, 38-41, 44-52, 55-58, 60, 62, 64, 65, 70, 76, 92, 98, 108, 117, 119, 120, 124, 126, 146, 150, 154, 158, 166, 168, 170-172, 174-179, 182-196, 201, 202, 204, 208, 210, 222, 239, 242, 243, 268, 302, 304, 332, 344, 346-351, 353-356, 358, 359, 364, 380, 384, 395, 399, 401, 411, 414, 415, 431-433, 443, 461, 469, 475, 483, 492-494, 500, 501, 509, 536, 545, 553, 554, 557, 559, 560, 563
Cummins, Jim 8-9
curriculum 184, 190, 194-196

Darling-Hammond, Linda 365
Darwin, Charles 72
data 185-187
data analysis 43, 65, 158, 160, 177, 331, 527, 529, 530, 551
Davidson, Donald 48, 50, 323, 514, 556,
decolonization 203, 299, 301, 303
deconstruction 6, 22, 72, 80, 146, 184, 188, 358, 426, 527, 556
decontextualized 192
deep mapping 75, 76, 80
Deleuze, Gilles 72, 258, 259, 260, 272-273
democracy 2, 6, 10, 112, 139, 168, 169, 174, 191, 195, 209, 211, 212, 214, 215, 391, 409, 455, 456, 460-464
Derrida, Jacques 15, 34, 130, 131, 202, 330
Descartes, Réné (*see also* Cartesian) 35, 133, 136, 204
Dewey, John 6, 44, 45, 169, 172, 193, 194, 204, 370-372, 390-393, 437, 459, 526
dialogue 7, 19, 24, 82, 84, 116-118, 144, 168-170, 173-176, 185, 187, 188, 191, 206, 209, 211, 241, 296, 302-304, 345, 349, 359, 360, 365, 366, 401, 404, 416, 423, 433, 434, 497, 498, 505, 515, 533, 537, 538, 540, 562
diasporic
    indigeneity 296-306
    self 297-306
dichotomies 116-117, 127, 529
difference 183
    centrality of 126
Dilthey, Wilhelm 52
disability and dis/ability 158, 246, 247, 248, 252, 254, 302, 307, 308, 309, 310, 316, 319, 321, 329-341, 391, 408, 413, 415, 422, 503
Discipline and Punish (by Michel Foucault) 258

discourse 4, 21, 27, 51, 68, 85, 93, 94, 99, 101, 102, 105, 108-112, 161, 172, 174, 189, 202, 206, 207, 215, 236, 238, 242, 254, 258, 259, 268, 269, 273, 308, 323, 326, 329, 330, 331, 347, 356, 366, 381, 382, 385, 387, 393, 401, 416, 420, 425, 426, 432, 437, 455, 456, 470, 472, 475, 479, 483, 486, 489, 495, 496, 529-531, 540, 556, 559
    analysis 4, 21, 85, 94, 207, 258, 259, 273, 326, 330, 331, 416, 420, 483, 486, 529
    of the body 67
    public 75, 76, 80
    of workload 420, 425, 426
discursive awareness 47, 61
discursive language 257, 265
disempower 9
dispositions 235, 236, 239, 269, 270, 297, 387, 404, 432, 468, 514
dispossession 154-163, 487, 488
distribution 61, 62, 65, 168, 206, 212, 258, 264, 404, 417, 434, 460, 463, 548, 556, 562
diversity 23, 25, 41, 82, 171, 173, 184, 185, 190, 211-214, 263, 268, 341, 349, 354, 355, 366, 391, 395, 424, 442, 448, 450, 451, 474, 514, 539
dominant culture 8, 9, 20, 22, 34, 40, 41, 98, 184, 268, 346, 536
domination 3, 7, 8, 9, 14, 22, 25, 83, 104, 105, 183, 184, 190, 191, 195, 201, 203, 215, 343, 344, 351, 357, 366, 395, 429-431
Du Bois, W.E.B. 37, 161, 436, 483
Duchamp, Marcel 345
durational space 85, 87
Durkheim, Emile 41, 124, 443

early childhood education 257-273, 445, 536-545
    and learning standards 257-273
ecological echo 136
educational policy 33, 260, 279, 288, 290, 291, 293, 368, 411, 555
    and reform 2, 277, 280, 343, 415, 559
educative authenticity 10, 118
efficacy 443, 444, 469, 519
Einstein, Albert 36, 127
    and general theory of relativity 36
Ellis, Deborah 96, 170, 175, 196, 554
Ellison, Ralph 97-98
emancipation 193, 195, 196
emotional 190, 194, 196
emotions 19, 67, 83, 97, 116, 117, 122-126, 161, 206, 207, 298, 304, 305, 310, 424, 481, 518, 553
empathy 190
empiricism 21, 25, 35, 36, 44, 127, 204, 302
    radical 104, 129, 130, 131, 143, 191, 201, 204, 350, 429-430
empowerment 3, 8, 11, 16, 18, 39, 101, 184, 205, 223, 225, 231, 342, 353, 366, 370, 404, 492, 496, 527, 533, 545
encoding 146
enlightenment 12, 150, 151, 185, 225, 231, 239, 297, 358, 533
Enlightenment, The 104, 129, 130, 131, 143, 191, 201, 204, 350, 429, 430
environment 104, 129, 130, 131, 143, 191, 201, 204, 350, 429, 430

epistemology 17, 21, 23, 24, 26, 33, 36, 44, 72, 80, 84, 86,
     130, 190, 194, 195, 342, 343, 344, 346, 350, 356, 357,
     359, 376, 498, 501
     of complexity 21
     of postmodern emergence 72
     pragmatic 36
equity 95, 112, 236, 281, 301, 302, 372, 374, 390, 391,
     392, 409, 410, 417, 451, 516, 520
Eros and Civilization (by Herbert Marcuse) 346
essence 195
essentialism 303, 304, 347-350, 350, 355, 359, 360
ethnography 21, 25-27, 185-190
     auto- 27, 170-172, 175-176, 242-244

ethnomethodology 203
     anti-racism as historical 236, 318-326
Euroculture 341
Euromodernity 297, 299-302
Europeanization 347
evaluation 182, 191
everyday
     critical ethnography of the 166-180
evidence-based research 108-110, 111
evolution
     theory of 48, 49, 80, 348, 397, 430, 520, 562
exclusion 4, 10, 82, 258, 261, 321, 322, 325, 326, 334, 460,
     461, 479, 488, 533
experience 7, 12, 18, 22, 25, 26, 33, 35, 36, 37, 38, 39, 52,
     56, 59, 65, 68, 73, 79, 88, 95, 98, 99, 116, 127, 130-150,
     156, 157, 160, 161, 162, 170, 171, 172, 173, 174, 175,
     176, 177, 179, 184, 190-192, 195, 205, 206, 211, 223,
     226-231, 233, 240, 241, 244, 246, 250, 251, 253, 297,
     299-305, 308-316, 322, 324, 343, 349, 354, 365, 367,
     369, 372-374, 384, 386, 391, 393-395, 403, 404, 410,
     411, 421, 423, 424-426, 432, 437, 438, 448, 458, 462,
     468, 473, 477, 480, 482, 488, 489, 495, 500, 501, 505,
     507, 508, 509, 514, 518, 521, 525-529, 537, 541, 542,
     544, 549-554, 558, 559, 563
     lived 189, 191, 196
experimental design 5, 11, 557
explicitization 45

Fairclough, Norman 4, 420, 529-530
fairness 6, 10, 513, 516, 520
fallibilism 36, 38
false consciousness 104, 203, 225
Fanon, Frantz 201, 298, 299, 300, 304, 320
Faundez, Antonio 19, 342, 346, 348,
feminism 3, 14, 22, 86, 184, 189, 190, 202, 203, 209, 358
     black 39, 86, 107
     critical 39, 67, 70, 73, 85, 86, 105, 107, 108, 109, 186,
          189, 190, 193, 205, 209, 213, 215, 222, 276, 344, 349,
          394, 403, 423, 496, 498, 500, 562
feminist research 189, 190
field 182
fieldwork 43, 65, 73, 171, 174, 175, 177, 222, 302, 337,
     469, 470, 500, 501, 502, 503, 558, 580
film 16, 178, 182, 185, 186, 187, 188, 189, 197, 212, 292,
     544
flow 193
flow experience 184, 190, 192, 195
foregrounding 52, 53

formalism 203
Foucauldian scientificity 554-563
Foucault, Michel 4, 15, 26, 169, 202, 258-260, 300, 330,
     336, 426, 475, 555, 556, 557, 558, 559, 563
     Discipline and Punish 258
     and eight techniques of power 258
framing processes 207
Frankfurt School of Critical Theory 191
Freire, Paulo 15-19, 23, 34, 39, 40, 41, 43, 44, 95, 101, 154,
     169, 172, 176, 195, 203, 226, 342, 346, 348, 354, 365,
     366, 370, 371, 390, 391, 394, 401, 403, 404, 426, 433-
     437, 441, 481, 514, 517, 549, 552, 554
Freud, Sigmund 73, 201, 423, 556, 557
Fromm, Erich 203

Gadamer, Hans-Georg 23, 129-151, 194, 205
Geertz, Clifford 207, 475
gender 16, 17, 20, 22, 38-40, 45, 53, 55, 65, 95, 105, 108,
     118, 124, 158, 167, 171-174, 177, 178, 184, 189, 195,
     206, 215, 237, 240, 242, 247, 248, 276, 301, 302, 319,
     321, 325, 345, 349, 357, 383-387, 391, 410, 421, 424,
     430, 433, 435, 456, 494, 500, 528, 552
     and bias 16, 17, 20, 22, 38, 39, 40, 45, 53, 55, 65, 95,
          105, 108, 118, 124, 158, 167, 171-174, 177, 178, 184,
          189, 195, 206, 215, 237, 240, 242, 247, 248, 276, 301,
          302, 319, 321, 325, 345, 349, 357, 383-387, 391, 410,
          421, 424, 430, 433, 435, 456, 494, 500, 528, 552
generative themes 16, 19, 195, 203, 435, 549
genre 185, 188, 189
geographical place 184
geographies 15, 22, 23, 25, 26, 27, 28, 70, 73, 76, 77, 80,
     83, 85, 86, 106, 189, 201, 237, 300, 301, 303, 341-359,
     442, 456, 492, 495, 496, 503, 508
getting lost 223, 279
Giddens, Anthony 57-59, 300
Giroux, Henry 14, 15, 20, 43, 99, 169, 172, 179, 224, 276,
     301, 365, 380, 401, 404, 432-434
globalization 57, 105, 200-216, 299, 347, 492
global justice movement 200-216
Goffman, Erving 39, 207, 504
Gore, Jennifer 258-259
governmentality 258, 563
Gramsci, Antonio 202, 203, 205, 207, 354, 366, 381, 425,
     429, 431, 432, 434, 456
Greene, Maxine 2, 4, 11, 160-161, 434
Gresson, Aaron D. 186
Gruenewald, David 68-70
Guattari, Felix 258-260, 272-273, 476
Guba, Egon 5-6, 10, 83, 118, 301, 528, 555
Guevara, Che 203

Habermas, Jürgen 15, 45, 48, 50, 52, 54, 65, 207, 301, 429,
     430, 431
habitus 236-238
Hall, Stuart 202, 208, 300, 319, 320, 321, 348, 349, 483,
     484, 528
hardened identity 132
Harding, Sandra 344, 357-359, 433, 434
hard sciences 33-37
Harvey, David 154, 167, 208, 424, 425
Hegel, Friedrich 15, 44, 201, 203, 429

hegemonic
  discourses 4, 5, 8, 9, 10, 11, 161, 194, 214, 242, 296, 298, 341, 347, 380, 391, 431, 432, 443, 470, 475, 504, 525, 531
hegemony 9, 17, 97, 182, 202, 203, 208, 342, 351, 366, 380, 381, 425, 429, 431, 432, 456, 468, 559, 563
Heidegger, Martin 132, 138, 144-149, 202, 205
hermeneutic conditionedness 130, 131, 141, 146
hermeneutical awareness 23,
hermeneutics 21, 23, 120, 129-133, 134, 136-139, 142, 144, 145, 147, 149, 184, 188, 189, 191, 192, 193, 195, 196, 203, 205, 549
  critical 182, 187, 194
hidden curriculum 45, 65, 433
high culture 183
historical analysis 323
historiography 21, 27, 319, 352, 456
history 3, 16, 20, 21, 26, 33, 34, 40, 41, 53, 59, 63, 71, 73, 74, 76, 79, 80, 95, 118, 124, 127, 143, 146, 161, 167, 186, 194, 200, 201, 203, 204, 207, 209, 210, 213, 215, 217, 227, 231, 241, 244, 259, 262, 265, 270, 285, 301, 308, 318, 319, 330, 338, 344, 345, 346, 350, 351, 352, 353, 354, 359, 380, 382, 392, 397, 402, 410, 415, 424, 430, 437, 439, 455, 456, 458, 459, 493, 502, 505, 506, 508, 509, 528, 556
HIV 224, 230
Hoggart, Richard 202
hooks, bell 273
Horton, Myles 16-17
Hughes, John 185, 188
human identity 44-56
humanism 203, 300-304
humor 102, 158, 162, 351, 550
Hussein, Saddam 95
Husserl, Edmund 136, 203, 205, 556, 558
hybridity 16, 70, 349, 359, 476
hyperreality 182, 187, 194

identity 44-64, 68, 72, 74, 88, 130-134, 163, 168-179, 183, 196, 222-232, 282, 296-317, 329, 343, 347, 349-351, 369, 377, 385-386, 430, 458, 468-470, 472, 483, 484, 533, 544, 550, 562
  claims 44-64, 68, 72, 74, 88, 130-134, 163-179, 183, 196, 202-215, 222-232, 282, 296, 297, 298, 299, 301, 304, 309-317, 329, 343, 347-351, 369, 377, 385, 386, 430, 458, 468-472, 483-484, 533, 544, 550, 562
  hardened 132
ideology 3, 4, 25, 26, 62, 63, 99, 101, 108, 168, 182, 187, 189, 195, 201, 202, 204, 236, 240, 241, 321, 380, 381, 401, 424, 425, 431, 432, 433, 500, 558
imagination 196
iMovie 188
imperialism 25, 170, 202, 208, 301, 433, 461, 495, 560
incarceration 2, 460, 479-489, 503, 504
inclusiveness 493
indeterminateness 420, 425, 426
Indian Relocation Act (1830) 41
indigeneity 342-360
indigenous
  identity 349, 350
  ways of seeing 349, 350
individualization 258

inequity 3, 4, 5, 6, 83, 112, 282, 286, 394
inferential network 5
inquiry 184, 190-191
interaction 183, 185, 189, 194
interdependent conditionedness 133, 149
interdisciplinary 21, 24, 156, 182, 201, 215, 417, 429, 434
International Monetary Fund (IMF) 208, 210
Internet 562
interpretation 4-6, 20, 24-27, 34, 74, 105, 120, 126, 127, 131, 138, 149, 159, 175, 185-196, 200, 202, 205, 248, 250, 254, 331, 344, 353, 415, 459, 469, 509, 551, 552, 558
interpretive
  gaze 174
  method 562
intuition 187
IQ 19, 459
Irigaray, Luce 15, 73

James, C. L. R. 144, 201, 204, 284, 288, 290, 304, 448
jazz 91-102, 483
justice 184, 191, 195

Kant, Immanuel 15, 52, 129-131, 169, 201
Katrina, Hurricane 288, 308-316
knowable communities 204, 217
knowledge 16-26, 33-47, 58, 61, 65, 69, 71, 74-89, 94-97, 106, 109-112, 117, 129-139, 142-150, 156, 157, 160, 162, 169, 175, 182, 183-185, 192, 201-205, 210, 213, 216, 223, 225, 237-242, 253, 258-259, 262, 268-273, 296-304, 318-326, 330, 341-366, 367, 370-371, 380, 381, 404, 409-410, 416, 421-435, 442, 447, 449, 450, 456-509, 516, 519, 521-522, 526-527, 530-533, 537-544, 553, 556-558, 561-563
  true 35, 38
Kristeva, Julia 15, 73,
Kuhn, Thomas Samuel 204, 557, 558, 563

Lacan, Jacques 16, 73, 202, 559
Lakatos, Imre 204, 557
language 182, 186, 195
  discursive 257, 265
Lave, Jean 365, 370, 494
laws of objectivity 205
leadership 44, 108, 278, 280, 281, 285, 286, 288, 289, 291, 375, 409, 431, 438, 513, 540, 541
Learning to Labor (by Paul Willis) 44, 45, 46, 58
legitimization 187
Lenin, V.I. 202
Lewin, Kurt 204, 205
LGBTQ 156, 158
liberation theology 17
life-history research 53
life stories 52, 53, 54, 329, 403, 483, 484, 486, 488
liminal 71, 162, 296, 383, 384, 385, 386, 387, 477, 483
Lincoln, Yvonna 5, 6, 9, 10, 16, 20, 21, 22, 25, 84, 89, 104, 108, 118, 170, 171, 172, 174, 187, 188, 204, 221, 222, 301, 344, 367, 420, 436, 476, 528, 541, 553, 555
linearity 82, 83, 98, 194, 259, 344, 550
literacy 16, 93, 161, 203, 266, 268-272, 358, 412, 441, 444, 448-450, 468, 513, 549, 552
  critical 95, 364, 366, 549, 553, 554
  technological 216

literal method of interpretation 187
lived experience 191, 196
Locke, John 204
low culture 183
Luxemburg, Rosa 203
Lyotard, Jean-François 204, 533

Macedo, Donaldo 18, 25, 365, 403, 549
macrosocial structures 25
Marcuse, Herbert 169, 201, 300-301, 346, 429, 430, 434
marginalized groups 23, 366, 376, 410, 438
Maritain, Jacques 203
Marshall, Chrissiejoy 5, 76
Marx, Karl, and Marxism 15, 17, 38, 44-45, 59, 201, 202, 203, 423-426, 429, 556, 558
Marxist 3, 17, 28, 85, 201, 202, 203, 558
    tradition 17
mass culture 183
Massumi, Brian 82-89
Mead, George Herbert 52, 54
meaning, systems of 202
media 15, 21, 27, 99, 107, 108, 112, 167, 182, 186, 190, 194, 195, 196, 202, 203, 207, 208, 209, 211, 212, 213, 248, 252, 289, 290, 292, 293, 329, 342, 366, 368, 421, 432, 433, 526, 533
Memmi, Albert 201, 304
memory, collective 527-532
meritocracy 6
Merleau-Ponty, Maurice 71, 205
meta-narrative 173
metaphors 193
methodology 185, 186, 192, 195
    eventhood of 87
    phenomenological 393, 551
    postmodern emergent 71-72
    rhizomatic 87, 258, 272-273, 468-477
Middle East 95, 491, 492
mindfulness 512-521
montage 188-189
movement(s) 183, 193
    global justice 200-217
    social 64, 206-208, 154

narrative 184, 185
    inquiry 504, 531, 537, 543, 544, 553
narratives 20, 21, 34, 35, 38-41, 52-54, 83, 84, 105, 120, 173, 193, 196, 202, 206, 207, 223, 235, 238, 298, 301-304, 309, 310, 316, 318, 319, 326, 337, 366, 402, 415, 470, 474-477, 479, 482-484, 487-489, 496, 504, 507, 515, 524-533, 537, 541, 543-545, 549, 552, 553, 554, 560
    master 20, 21, 34, 35, 38, 39, 40, 41, 52, 53, 54, 83, 84, 105, 120, 173, 193, 196, 202, 206, 207, 223, 235, 238, 298, 301-304, 309, 310, 316, 318, 319, 326, 337, 366, 402, 415, 470, 474, 475, 477, 479, 482, 483, 484, 487, 488, 489, 496, 504, 507, 515, 524, 525-529, 530-533, 537, 541, 543-545, 549, 552-554, 560
    collective 524-527, 532
network, inferential 5
Newton, Sir Isaac 33, 204
Nietzsche, Friedrich 72, 202, 556

Obama, Barack 95, 98, 286, 290

objectivity 190, 191
O'Keeffe, Georgia 344
ontological 195
ontology, critical 203
oppression 189, 190, 196
"other"
    generalized 54-56
    otherizing 488-489
overlap 188

pain, social 255
Parker, Charlie 97-98
pedagogical 182-197
    relations 184, 185, 192, 193, 195, 420
pedagogic relations 420,
pedagogy 182, 183, 184, 185, 187, 193, 196
    critical 420
    of sameness 420,
peer review 99, 251
performance 2, 53, 70, 72, 73, 74, 93, 108, 137, 153, 154, 161, 162, 163, 223, 228, 269, 272, 278, 284-293, 316, 334, 398, 400-417, 421, 459, 469, 493, 495, 560
perspectives
    critical (see also critical) 3, 5, 9, 89, 99-100, 104-108, 410, 434
    feminist (see also feminism) 86, 105, 276, 496
Peters, Frederick 195
phenomenological
    methodologies 393, 551
    reading 27
    tradition 184, 191-192, 194, 196
phenomenology 21, 23, 120, 138, 184, 201-203, 205, 508, 549, 551, 556
phenomenon 191, 193
philanthropy 277, 278, 284, 291, 292, 293
Piaget, Jean 130, 137, 140
place
    research 67-81
    story 67-81
Plato 35, 36, 476
play 7, 36, 55, 77, 87, 92, 139, 144, 158, 160, 169, 170, 190, 202, 204, 235, 236, 239, 241, 244, 258, 266, 269, 270, 271, 292, 301, 319, 322, 326, 330, 346, 347, 366, 368, 392, 394, 399, 431, 444, 456, 462, 475, 492, 494, 497, 533, 542, 557, 558, 560
Playback Theatre 160-162
police 47, 155, 156, 157, 158, 159, 160, 162, 163, 246, 252, 492, 549, 550
politicians 37, 38, 99, 109, 211, 394, 424, 463, 533
politics 182, 183, 193
Polling for Justice (PFJ) 153, 154, 155, 156, 161
Popper, Karl 204, 557, 558
Portrait of a Lady (by Henry James) 422
position 185, 189, 190, 191, 192, 195
positionality 169, 171, 188, 224, 330, 358, 470, 477
positivism and positivists 36, 44, 126, 201-205, 301-302, 357, 358, 555-561
    anti- 204
    post- 204
postmodern(ism) 14, 184, 187, 189, 192, 194, 195, 196, 202, 203, 560, 561
    emergent methodology 71

poststructuralism 14, 184, 187, 202, 205, 206,
poststructuralist 171, 184, 185, 186, 189, 190, 191, 222
  method 185
power 3-12, 15, 18-28, 34, 39, 41, 44-47, 50, 55, 56, 61-64, 68, 70, 80, 86-89, 91, 94, 97-101, 104-112, 122, 123, 129, 130, 133, 136, 149, 154, 157, 160-163, 167-169, 170-173, 175, 177, 179, 182, 183, 185, 189, 191, 195, 201, 202, 204, 206, 207, 208, 210, 211, 212, 222, 225, 235, 236, 239, 240, 242, 248, 258, 272, 290, 293, 297, 298, 302, 303, 304, 307, 310, 311, 316, 320-322, 330, 331, 342-346, 350, 351, 353-356, 358-360, 366, 379, 380-382, 396, 401, 403, 404, 410, 414, 417, 423, 425, 429-439, 461, 463, 472, 475-477, 482, 488, 498, 500-502, 505, 519, 524, 525, 530, 533, 539, 541, 544, 545, 548, 550-558, 560, 563
  coercive nature of 62
  of language 70
  relations 195
  socio-cultural forms of 62
practice
  transdisciplinary 273
pragmatic epistemology 36
pragmatism 36, 44, 45, 201, 205
praxis 27, 174, 204, 206, 209, 217, 221, 299, 390, 391, 410, 411, 435, 437, 489, 527, 553
privilege (see also white privilege, Western privilege) 3, 4, 6, 7, 11, 12, 23, 41, 105, 108, 154, 155, 157, 162, 163, 167, 169, 178, 185, 189, 191, 195, 196, 203, 226, 227, 233, 242, 243, 244, 258, 259, 268, 293, 298, 303, 304, 307, 332, 335, 342, 344, 353, 366, 404, 410, 414, 417, 501, 502, 506, 556
production, truth 343-344
proof 192
psychoanalysis 21, 73, 184, 185, 201, 203, 557
public
  discourse 99, 161, 207, 326
  pedagogy 78, 80, 367

Qatar 491-498
qualitative
  research 186, 192
  social research 52, 222, 235
quality rating 260-273
quantitative research 5, 28, 117, 548, 561
queer theory 3, 86, 105, 209, 222, 468-477
Quine, W. V. O. 204

race 3, 16-18, 20, 22, 38-40, 45, 53, 65, 95, 98, 105, 153, 158, 171-174, 177, 178, 184, 189, 195, 203, 206, 216, 224, 226, 236, 238, 240, 243, 247, 248, 276, 296, 299-304, 319, 320, 324, 325, 345, 349, 357, 367, 383-385, 387, 391, 408, 410, 430, 435, 456, 460, 482, 483, 502, 505
racialization 299, 320, 326
racism 4, 8, 10, 15, 17, 98, 105, 107, 211, 226, 236, 242, 243, 301, 304, 318-326, 354, 384, 433, 434
radical empiricism 104, 129, 130, 131, 143, 191, 201, 204, 350, 429, 430
radical thought 209
radio 183, 212, 213, 308, 433
rationality 184, 194
reading 184, 188, 196, 197

reality 2, 19, 20, 21, 24, 25, 33, 38, 44, 47, 72, 86-89, 92, 95, 102, 109, 131, 132, 134, 136, 138, 142, 143, 149, 150, 159, 161, 168, 172, 173, 184, 189, 191, 202, 210, 216, 299, 304, 319, 323, 325, 326, 333, 342, 344, 345, 347, 349-351, 354, 357, 359, 401, 429, 436, 437, 456, 460, 481, 495, 505, 506, 525, 550, 554
  collective 38
reason 3, 4, 22, 34, 40, 52, 61, 62, 104, 106, 110, 122, 139, 202, 204, 232, 241, 259, 266, 273, 319, 342, 343, 346, 348, 397, 423, 429, 430, 435, 475, 526, 540, 545, 550, 563
reconceptualized critical theory 14-15
reductionism 182, 345, 550, 556, 558
reference 194
reflective inquiry 441
regulation 111, 112, 167, 182, 258, 268, 272, 425, 434, 459, 460
relationships 20, 23, 24, 34, 44, 45, 49, 61, 89, 123, 130, 132, 156, 157, 159, 168, 169, 172, 173, 190, 200, 206, 210, 211, 214, 215, 225, 236, 239, 240, 244, 248, 254, 312, 318, 319, 342, 364, 370, 374, 376, 417, 434, 435, 439, 441, 447, 470, 472, 475, 480, 494, 502, 519, 520, 521, 530, 537, 538, 539, 541, 542, 543, 544, 548, 550, 551, 552, 553, 554
re-narrativisation 544
representation 27, 48, 52, 71, 72, 80, 85, 106, 149, 171, 202, 212, 214, 222, 297, 320, 329, 359, 380, 413, 420, 421, 422, 423, 475, 483, 500, 554, 556
repression 190
resistance 191, 195
resources 196
restorying 502-503
rhizomatic 87, 258, 259, 260, 272, 273, 468, 475, 476
  methodology 468-476
rigor 3, 7, 11, 18, 23, 24, 99, 100, 108, 186, 187, 355, 392, 404, 409, 434, 436, 531, 558, 561
role of theory 201-205

Said, Edward 7, 9, 201, 224, 528
sameness, pedagogy of 383
sample size 302
Sartre, Jean-Paul 203
scholarly writing 91, 99, 100, 101
scholars, indigenous 105
schools, urban 293, 364-377
science
  anticolonial social 88-89
  and dominance 136
scientificity 555-563
seeing, indigenous ways of 346-349, 353
self
  -consciousness 21, 133, 135, 138, 139, 184, 228
  diasporic 297-306
  -monitoring 184
  -narrative 52, 54, 175
  study 420, 512-515, 520, 521, 522
semiotic analysis 186
semiotician 186
semiotics 184, 186, 189, 190
sense 184, 186, 189, 191-193, 195, 196
Sewell Jr., William 119, 126-127
singular truth 104

Smith, Adam 83
Smith, Barbara 191
Smith, David 131, 132, 141, 145, 150,
social 182-196
    activism 44, 174, 390-404
    change 22, 40, 43, 44, 176, 200, 204, 205, 206, 210, 302,
        304, 342, 397, 562
    domination 3, 8, 351
    justice 10, 22, 83, 104, 106, 112, 154, 160, 161, 206,
        209, 210, 211, 215, 301, 302, 304, 347, 352, 359, 364,
        367, 372, 376, 377, 390-398, 401, 404, 447, 453, 463,
        494, 504, 509, 533
    media analysis 27
    movement research 204, 206, 207, 215
    movements 64, 154, 206, 207, 208
    pain 155
    phenomena 44, 84, 318, 319, 320, 330, 432, 434
    research 20, 24, 46, 52, 65, 157, 161, 185, 221, 222, 223,
        224, 225, 226, 228, 230, 232, 235, 296, 297, 436, 437,
        438, 555
    theory 21, 22, 26, 44, 46, 52, 59, 190, 194, 201, 202,
        203, 367, 369, 376, 430, 437
    thought 201, 300
    world 221, 223, 226, 235, 357, 430, 494, 555
socially just education 5, 464
space, durational 86-87
Spivak, Gayatri 82, 106, 177, 201, 223, 503, 504
stakeholders 7, 9, 120, 205, 394, 447, 452
standards 3-7, 18, 93, 97, 191, 211, 214, 222, 238, 255,
    257-263, 266-273, 278, 289, 290, 334, 391, 394, 395,
    397-399, 487, 492, 495, 555, 559, 560-562
Stephens, Rick 38, 39
stories, life 84-86, 483-488
story, place 68, 74, 76-81
storytelling 68, 73, 74, 75, 76, 79, 80, 100, 476, 483, 502
structuralism 57, 202, 203, 556
structuration 205
structure 190
stupidification 18
subjective claims 49, 50, 57
subjectivity 15, 24, 25, 48, 70, 86, 101, 109, 118, 133, 134,
    136, 190, 196, 210, 299, 349, 379, 469, 500, 501, 504,
    505, 507-509, 527, 550-554, 557, 558
subjugated knowledge 350, 353, 354
subjugation 189
surveillance 4, 130, 132, 154, 155, 156, 157, 159, 258, 268,
    272, 481, 483
symbolization 193
systems of meaning 202
systems thinking 205

tactical authenticity 10, 119
Taliban 96-97
teacher research 19
Teach for America 279, 285-291
teachers as researchers 18
technologies of the self 258
text 184-188, 192-195
    literary 186, 189
    narrative 184, 185
textbooks 9, 17, 61, 88, 95, 351, 483, 484, 528, 560

texts 19, 26, 91, 97, 99, 100, 171, 174-176, 185, 186, 189,
    191, 192, 195, 196, 222, 224, 257-261, 263, 266, 267,
    269, 271, 272, 300, 319, 320, 344, 353, 354, 356, 421,
    432, 435, 438, 468, 472, 474, 475, 483, 501, 530, 541
textual analysis 184, 186
Thayer-Bacon, Barbara 23, 86
Theatre of the Oppressed 162
thematic analysis 311, 314, 315
theology, liberation 17, 203
The Order of Things (by Michel Foucault) 556
theoretical framework 4, 11, 43, 64, 80, 121, 191, 276, 304,
    496, 521, 529, 530
theory 184, 188, 189-192, 194, 195
    activity 408, 410, 417
    of communicative action 45, 48, 430
    critical 2, 5, 14-16, 20, 28, 104, 184, 191, 192, 201,
        203, 205, 225, 236, 358, 366, 380, 429, 430, 436,
        439, 524
    critical methodological 43, 57
    critical poverty 3
    critical race 3, 158
    critical social 46, 52, 194, 201, 203, 367, 369
    of knowledge 44, 45
    of relativity 36
    of representation 72
    of systems 46
    reconceptualized critical 14, 15,
    sociocultural 116
thick description 23, 121, 192
thinking
    Cartesian 345
    rhizomatic 258
    systems 205
Thompson, E.P. 207
totalization 258,
tradition 4, 14-17, 20, 25, 27, 86, 97, 145, 146, 161, 191,
    192, 194, 196, 204, 236, 240, 318, 319, 345, 347, 356,
    375, 377, 392, 426, 495, 496, 504, 533
transcriptions 187
transdisciplinary practice 203
transformation 22, 70, 72, 84, 94, 95, 101, 131, 140, 147,
    178, 204, 206, 208, 217, 233, 236, 284, 291, 299, 301,
    302, 343, 346, 365, 367, 372, 393, 401, 410, 430, 435,
    436, 437, 479, 482, 483, 486, 488, 489, 533, 544, 559
transformative mediating structures 410, 411, 412, 417
transgression 20, 336
Troubling the Angels (by Patti Lather and Christine Smithies)
    223, 224
truth 4, 17, 27, 28, 35, 36, 38, 39, 41, 83, 84, 86, 94, 99,
    101, 102, 104, 107, 110, 129, 130, 132, 133, 134, 136,
    138, 140, 144-150, 176, 190, 194, 195, 202, 222, 235,
    238, 247, 252, 258, 260, 263, 338, 343-345, 350, 354,
    355, 357, 381, 434, 476, 477, 494, 505, 554, 561
    production 4, 17, 27, 28, 35, 36, 38, 39, 41, 83, 84, 86,
        94, 99, 101, 102, 104, 107, 110, 129, 130, 132, 133,
        134, 136, 138, 140, 144, 145, 146, 147, 148, 149, 150,
        176, 190, 194, 195, 202, 222, 235, 238, 247, 252, 258,
        260, 263, 338, 343, 344, 345, 350, 354, 355, 357, 381,
        434, 476, 477, 494, 505, 554, 561
TV 17, 159, 183, 195, 212, 213, 433, 438, 445

uniqueness 55, 138, 149

urban
  education 364, 374
  schools 374
  teacher education 374

validity 5, 10, 25, 26, 27, 48, 49, 50, 51, 52, 57, 59, 62, 68, 83, 100, 108, 110, 154, 205, 249, 250, 348, 396, 472, 500, 532, 561, 563,
  horizon 5, 10, 25, 26, 27, 48, 49, 50, 51, 52, 57, 59, 62, 68, 83, 100, 108, 110, 154, 205, 249, 250, 348, 396, 472, 500, 532, 561, 563
values 8, 11, 15, 19, 25, 26, 38-41, 47, 55, 58-60, 62, 65, 93, 104, 108, 110, 112, 170, 182, 191, 193, 194, 202, 203, 211, 214, 215, 240, 255, 268, 303, 335, 344, 353, 354, 359, 360, 379, 380, 382, 385, 404, 421, 425, 431, 432, 433, 457, 495, 496, 500, 513, 518, 519, 527, 537, 538, 539, 542, 556
variables 11, 33, 38, 40, 300, 391, 550, 558
vignettes 120-121
voice 11, 18, 40, 41, 53, 73, 98, 99, 101, 106, 109, 110, 121, 167, 190, 209, 215, 238, 242, 255, 296, 298, 299, 303, 311, 316, 319, 352, 365, 379, 422, 449, 450, 451, 460, 468, 470, 473, 483, 503, 506, 514, 515, 518, 520, 526, 541, 543, 544, 551, 552, 553, 560, 562, 563
Vygotsky, Lev 15, 365, 483, 526

War on Terror 525, 526, 527, 528, 529, 530, 531, 533
Washington, DC 37, 278, 281, 283, 285, 288, 290, 293, 375, 457

ways of knowing 22, 27, 84, 109, 128, 160, 176, 179, 222, 238, 296, 297, 298, 299, 300, 301, 303, 304, 342, 347, 350, 354, 355, 357, 358, 366, 380, 387, 431, 435, 492, 520, 538, 542
ways of seeing the world 191
Weber, Max 15, 201
Wenger, Etienne 365, 370
Western
  epistemology 23
  consciousness 346
  gaze 348
  geographies 300
Western tools of research 358
whiteness 105, 186, 226, 227, 228, 233
white privilege 3, 4, 6, 7, 11, 12, 23, 41, 105, 108, 154, 155, 157, 162, 163, 167, 169, 178, 185, 189, 191, 195, 196, 203, 226, 227, 233, 242-244, 258, 259, 268, 293, 298, 303, 304, 307, 332, 335, 342, 344, 353, 366, 404, 410, 414, 417, 501, 502, 506, 556
white supremacy 189, 194, 202, 319
Wikipedia 562, 580
Williams, Raymond 174, 202, 204
Williams, William Carlos 345
Woodson, Carter G. 37, 41
World Bank 208
World Trade Organization (WTO) 208, 210

youth researchers 154, 155, 158, 162, 163, 480, 483

Zone of Proximal Development (ZPD) 365, 377

critical qualitative research

Shirley R. Steinberg & Gaile S. Cannella, *General Editors*

The Critical Qualitative Research series examines societal structures that oppress and exclude so that transformative actions can be generated. This transformed research is activist in orientation. Because the perspective accepts the notion that nothing is apolitical, research projects themselves are critically examined for power orientations, even as they are used to address curricular, educational, or societal issues.

This methodological work challenges modernist orientations and universalist impositions, asking critical questions like: Who/what is heard? Who/what is silenced? Who is privileged? Who is disqualified? How are forms of inclusion and exclusion being created? How are power relations constructed and managed? How do different forms of privilege and oppression intersect to affect educational, societal, and life possibilities for various individuals and groups?

We are particularly interested in manuscripts that offer critical examinations of curriculum, policy, public communities, and the ways in which language, discourse practices, and power relations prevent more just transformations.

For additional information about this series or for the submission of manuscripts, please contact:
  Shirley R. Steinberg and Gaile S. Cannella
  msgramsci@aol.com | Gaile.Cannella@unt.edu

To order other books in this series, please contact our Customer Service Department:
  (800) 770-LANG (within the U.S.)
  (212) 647-7706 (outside the U.S.)
  (212) 647-7707 FAX

Or browse online by series:
  www.peterlang.com